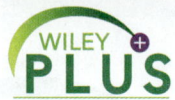

ALL THE HELP, RESOURCES, AND PERSONAL SUPPORT YOU AND YOUR STUDENTS NEED!

2-Minute Tutorials and all of the resources you & your students need to get started
www.wileyplus.com/firstday

Student support from an experienced student user Ask your local representative for details!

Collaborate with your colleagues, find a mentor, attend virtual and live events, and view resources
www.WhereFacultyConnect.com

Pre-loaded, ready-to-use assignments and presentations
www.wiley.com/college/quickstart

Technical Support 24/7 FAQs, online chat, and phone support
www.wileyplus.com/support

Your *WileyPLUS* Account Manager Training and implementation support
www.wileyplus.com/accountmanager

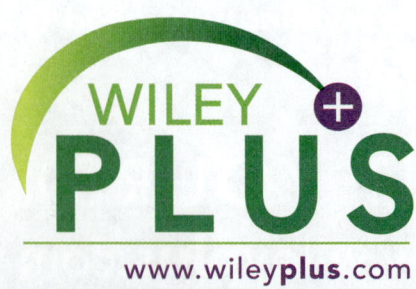

www.wiley**plus**.com

MAKE IT YOURS!

Management
Information
Systems
Moving Business Forward

Management
Information
Systems
Moving Business Forward

R. Kelly Rainer, Jr.
Hugh Watson

WILEY

John Wiley & Sons, Inc.

Vice President & Executive Publisher	Don Fowley
Executive Editor	Beth Lang Golub
Content Manager	Kevin Holm
Executive Marketing Manager	Christopher Ruel
Creative Director	Harry Nolan
Senior Designer	Maureen Eide
Senior Photo Editor	Lisa Gee
Editorial Assistant	Elizabeth Mills
Senior Content Editor	Wendy Ashenberg
Product Designers	Tom Kulesa/Jennifer Welter
Editorial Operations Manager	Melissa Edwards
Senior Production Editor	John Curley
Media Specialist	Lisa Sabatini
Content Assistant	Timothy Lindner
Production Management Services	Aptara®, Inc.
Cover Design	Howard Grossman
Cover Image	© Marina Strizhak/iStockphoto
Interior Design	Maureen Eide

This book was set in 10/12 Minion Pro by Aptara®, Inc., and printed and bound by Quad Graphics. The cover was printed by Quad Graphics.

This book is printed on acid free paper. ∞

Founded in 1807, John Wiley & Sons, Inc. has been a valued source of knowledge and understanding for more than 200 years, helping people around the world meet their needs and fulfill their aspirations. Our company is built on a foundation of principles that include responsibility to the communities we serve and where we live and work. In 2008, we launched a Corporate Citizenship Initiative, a global effort to address the environmental, social, economic, and ethical challenges we face in our business. Among the issues we are addressing are carbon impact, paper specifications and procurement, ethical conduct within our business and among our vendors, and community and charitable support. For more information, please visit our website: *www.wiley.com/go/citizenship*.

ISBN 978-0-470-88919-0 (Main Book)
ISBN 978-0-470-91765-7 (Binder-Ready Version)

Printed in the United States of America

10 9 8 7 6 5 4 3 2 1

Dear Student,

Why are you here? We're not asking you a philosophical question—that's a different course. We're asking, why are you about to spend an entire term learning about information systems? Why are you—an accounting major, or a marketing or management major—being required to study this topic? You may be asking "What's in IT for me?" The short answer is that "IT's About Business," and the longer answer is the goal of this book.

Information systems are making the world a very small place and are contributing to rapidly increasing global competition. As a result, organizations are constantly trying to find ways to gain a competitive advantage—by achieving operational excellence, developing new products and services, developing new business models, providing superb customer service, improving decision making, and so on. It should be obvious, then, that an introductory course in information systems is critically important for success in your chosen career.

Rapid advances in information systems mean that, as business students, change will be the only constant you will encounter in today's dynamic digital business environment. We wrote this book for business students of all majors who will soon become business professionals. We have three goals in mind:

1. to help you be immediately successful when you join your organization;

2. to help you understand the importance of information systems for individuals, organizations, and society as a whole; and

3. to enable you to become informed users of your organization's information systems.

To accomplish these goals, we have tried to provide the essential, relevant knowledge that you need to understand and effectively use information systems in your careers.

The way we propose to do this is to keep you *actively involved* in the material. Every section of the chapters has an activity that asks you to do something beyond just reading the textbook that will help you see why the content is useful for your future business career.

We hope you will enjoy this active approach and successfully complete the course with a richer understanding of what's in IT for you.

Kelly Rainer and Hugh Watson

Dear Instructor,

We are like you. All of us who teach the introductory course in information systems realize that it is difficult for students to understand the importance and relevance of the topics in the course. As a result, students often simply memorize the content just before the exam and then forget it as soon as the exam is over. We all want to engage students at a much deeper level. We know that the best way to accomplish this objective is through *hands-on active learning*, leading to *increased student engagement* in our course content.

Accordingly, active learning and student engagement are key principles of our new book. We recognize the need to actively involve students in problem solving, creative thinking, and capitalizing on opportunities. Every section of every chapter includes extensive hands-on exercises, activities, and mini cases, and end-of-chapter material includes exercises that require students to use software application tools. Through these activities, we enable students to actually do something with the concepts they learn, such as how to meet business goals using information systems, how to configure products, and how to use spreadsheets and databases to facilitate problem solving.

The preface on the next page further outlines the goals, features, and support material provided with our new text. We hope you will enjoy teaching with this approach!

Kelly Rainer and Hugh Watson

Preface

Chapter Organization

Each chapter contains the following elements:

- **Chapter Outline:** lists the major concepts covered in each chapter.
- **Learning Objectives**: provide an overview of the key elements that students should come away with after reading the chapter.
- **Chapter-Opening Case:** This is a short case that focuses on a small or start-up company that is using information systems to solve a business problem. Cases in introductory information systems textbooks typically involve very large organizations. In contrast, our chapter-opening cases demonstrate that small and start-up companies also have business problems that they address using information systems. Students will see that these firms usually have to be quite creative in creating and implementing IS solutions, because they do not have either MIS departments or large budgets. These cases also add an entrepreneurial flavor to each chapter for students who are planning to start their own businesses.
- **Ruby's Club Internship Case:**
  - At the start of each chapter is a "Ruby's Club Internship Scenario" that presents a problem at Ruby's Club, a downtown music venue that needs help with redesigning its online presence, overhauling its technological infrastructure, etc. Each chapter-opening scenario presents a problem that the student will be able to solve after reading that chapter.
  - Throughout the chapter are "Ruby's Club Questions" that help students focus on the content they will need to solve the problem. At the end of each chapter is a "Ruby's Club Internship Assignment" that puts students into the role of an IT decision-maker. Many assignments are in the form of a business letter that students must address to their internship managers and solve the problem. A supplementary chapter on business writing is available in WileyPLUS for students who need a review.
- **Student Activities:** This book uses a unique pedagogical structure designed to keep students actively engaged with the course material. Each chapter sub-section includes a Student Activity that immediately follows the reading material. Student activities include links to online videos and articles and other hands-on activities that require students to immediately apply what they've learned in that section. Via WileyPLUS, instructors can assign a section of text along with a student activity and gradeable quiz. Each Student Activity has the following elements:
  - > Objective (what students will gain from this activity)
  - > Chapter Connection (refers students to relevant material in the section)
  - > Prerequisites (what students should read before performing the activity)
  - > Activity (a hands-on activity that students are to carry out)
  - > Deliverables (various tasks for students to complete as they perform the activity)
  - > Quiz Questions (objective questions regarding the activity)
  - > Discussion Questions (discussion questions regarding the activity)

- **IT's About Business:** short cases that provide real-world applications, accompanied by questions that relate the case to concepts covered in the chapter. Icons relate these boxes to the specific functional areas.

- **Before You Go On:** End-of-section reviews that prompt students to pause and test their understanding of concepts before moving on to the next section.

- **Examples:** interspersed throughout the text, they highlight the use (and misuse) of information systems by real-world organizations and help illustrate the concepts discussed in the chapter.

- **What's in IT for Me?:** a unique end-of-chapter summary that demonstrates the relevance of the key chapter topics for different functional areas: accounting, finance, marketing, production/operations management, human resources management, and management information systems.

- **Summary:** keyed to the Learning Objectives listed at the beginning of the chapter, the summary enables students to review the major concepts covered in the chapter.

- **Discussion Questions, Problem-Solving Activities, and Team Assignments:** provide practice through active learning. These exercises are hands-on opportunities to apply the concepts discussed in the chapter.

- **Closing Cases:** Each chapter concludes with two cases that identify a business problem faced by an actual company, describe the IS solution applied to the problem, present the results of that solution, and summarize the key points that students can learn from the case. Each case is followed by discussion questions, so that students can further explore the concepts presented in the case.

- **Spreadsheet Activity:** Every chapter includes a hands-on spreadsheet project that students must solve using concepts they learned in the chapter in addition to practicing their Excel skills. Each activity includes deliverables, quiz questions, and discussion questions. These can be assigned within WileyPLUS for automatic grading. WileyPLUS includes lab material on Excel for students who need introductory coverage or review.

- **Database Activity:** Every chapter includes a hands-on database project that students must solve using concepts they learned in that chapter in addition to practicing their Access skills. Each activity includes deliverables, quiz questions, and discussion questions. These can be assigned within WileyPLUS for automatic grading. WileyPLUS includes lab material on Access for students who need introductory coverage or review.

- **Glossary:** a study tool that highlights the importance of the vocabulary within the chapters and facilitates studying.

Key Features

Student Engagement

As discussed in the note addressed to instructors at the beginning of this preface, one of the chief goals of this text to help engage students at a deeper level than memorizing vocabulary. We believe the best way to achieve this is through hands-on, active learning that will lead to increased student engagement in the course and its content.

Accordingly, every section of every chapter provides resources that actively involve students in problem solving, creative thinking, and capitalizing on opportunities. Every chapter includes extensive hands-on exercises, activities, and mini cases, including exercises that require students to solve business problems using Excel and Access.

Cross-Functional Approach

We emphasize the importance of information systems by calling attention in every chapter to how that chapter's topic relates to students in each business major. Icons guide students to relevant issues for their specific functional area—accounting (ACC), finance (FIN), marketing (MKT), operations management (OM), human resources management (HRM), and management information systems (MIS). Further, chapters conclude with a more detailed summary of how the key concepts in that chapter relate to each functional area (What's in IT for Me?').

Diversified and Unique Examples from Different Industries

Extensive use of vivid examples from large corporations, small businesses, and government and not-for-profit organizations helps to enliven the concepts by illustrating the capabilities of information systems, their cost and justification, and innovative ways that real corporations are using information systems in their operations. Small businesses have been included in recognition of the fact that many students will work in small to mid-sized companies—or start their own small business. Some may already be working at local businesses, and concepts they are learning in class can be readily applied or observed in their part-time jobs. Each chapter constantly highlights the integral connection between business and information systems. This connection is especially evident in the chapter-opening and closing cases, the 'IT's About Business' boxes, and the highlighted examples.

Successes and Failures

Like other textbooks, we present many examples of the successful implementation of information systems. However, we also provide numerous examples of IS failures, in the context of lessons that can be learned from such failures. Misuse of information systems can be very expensive, as we illustrate.

Global Focus

An understanding of global competition, partnerships, and trading is essential to success in the modern business environment. Therefore, we provide a broad selection of international cases and examples, highlighted by a global. We discuss the role of information systems in facilitating export and import, the management of international companies, and electronic trading around the globe. These global examples are highlighted with the global icon.

Innovation and Creativity

In today's rapidly changing business environment, creativity and innovation are necessary for a business to operate effectively and profitably. Throughout our book we demonstrate how information systems facilitate these processes.

Focus on Ethics

With corporate scandals appearing in the headlines almost daily, ethics and ethical questions have come to the forefront of business people's minds. In addition to devoting an entire chapter to ethics and privacy (Chapter 6), we have included examples and cases throughout the text that focus on business ethics. These examples are highlighted with the ethics icon.

Online Supplements

www.wiley.com/college/rainer

Our book also facilitates the teaching of an Introduction to Information Systems course by providing extensive support materials for instructors and students. Visit www.wiley.com/college/rainer to access the Student and Instructor Web sites.

Instructor's Manual

The *Instructor's Manual*, created by Dr. Ranida Harris at Indiana University Southeast and Dr. Judy Serwatka at Purdue University North Central, includes a chapter overview, teaching tips and strategies, answers to all end-of-chapter questions, supplemental mini cases with essay questions and answers, and experiential exercises that relate to particular topics.

Test Bank

The test bank, written by Dawna DeWire of Babson College is a comprehensive resource for test questions. Each chapter contains multiple-choice, true/false, short answer, essay questions. In addition, each chapter includes "Apply the Concept" questions that require more creative thought to answer. Further, each multiple-choice and true/false question is labeled to indicate its level of difficulty: easy, medium, or hard.

The test bank is available for use in Respondus' easy-to-use software. Respondus is a powerful tool for creating and managing exams that can be printed to paper or published directly to Blackboard, WebCT, Desire2Learn, eCollege, ANGEL, and other learning systems. For more information on Respondus and the Respondus Test Bank Network, please visit www.respondus.com.

PowerPoint Presentations

The Media-enriched *PowerPoint Presentations* created by Kelly Rainer consist of a series of slides for each chapter. The slides are designed around each chapter's content, incorporating key points from the chapter and chapter illustrations as appropriate. In addition, the slides include links to relevant Web sites, videos, and articles to enhance classroom discussion. They make extensive use of images and video clips.

Student PowerPoints

Posted on the Student Companion Site, these are stripped-down versions of the Instructor slides that students can use for note-taking.

Image Library

All textbook figures are available for download from the Web site. These figures can easily be added to PowerPoint presentations.

Wiley Information Systems Updates

(http://wileyinformationsystemsupdates.com)
Weekly updates, harvested from around the web by David Firth of University of Montana, provide you with the latest IT news and issues. These are posted every Monday morning throughout the year at http://wileyinformationsystemsupdates.com/ and include links to articles and videos as well as discussion questions to assign or use in class.

BusinessExtra Select

This feature allows instructors to package the text with lab manuals, cases, articles, and other real-world content from sources such as INSEAD, Ivey and Harvard Business School cases, *Fortune*, *The Economist*, and *The Wall Street Journal*. You can combine the book with the content you choose to create a fully customized textbook. For additional information, please visit www.wiley.com/college/bxs.

www.wileyplus.com

WileyPLUS

This online teaching and learning environment integrates the entire digital textbook with the most effective instructor and student resources to accommodate every learning style. With WileyPLUS:

- Students achieve concept mastery in a rich, structured environment that is available 24/7.
- Instructors personalize and manage their course more effectively with assessment, assignments, grade tracking, and more.

WileyPLUS can complement the textbook or replace the printed textbook altogether.

For Students

Different learning styles, different levels of proficiency, different levels of preparation—each of your students is unique. *WileyPLUS* empowers them to take advantage of their individual strengths.

- Integrated, multimedia resources—including audio and visual exhibits—provide multiple study paths to fit each student's learning preferences and encourage more active learning. Resources include:
    - > E-book
    - > Mini-lecture by author for each chapter section
    - > Student PowerPoints for note taking
    - > Video interviews with managers
    - > Lab Manual for Microsoft Office 2010
    - > How-to Animations for Microsoft Office 2010
- *WileyPLUS* also includes many opportunities for self-assessment. Students can take control of their own learning and practice until they master the material. Resources include:
    - > Automatically graded practice questions from the Test Bank,
    - > Pre- and post-lecture quizzes,
    - > Vocabulary flash cards and quizzes.

For Instructors

WileyPLUS empowers you with the tools and resources you need to make your teaching even more effective:

- You can customize your classroom presentation with a wealth of resources and functionality. You can even add your own materials to your WileyPLUS course. Resources include:
    - > Media-enriched PowerPoint presentations,
    - > Link to Weekly Updates
    - > Library of additional "IT's About Business" cases
- With *WileyPLUS* you can identify those students who are falling behind and intervene accordingly, without having to wait for them to come to office hours.
- *WileyPLUS* simplifies and automates such tasks as assessing student performance, creating assignments, scoring student work, keeping grades, and more.

Acknowledgments

Creating, developing, and producing a new text for the introduction to information technology course is a formidable undertaking. Along the way, we were fortunate to receive continuous evaluation, criticism, and direction from many colleagues who regularly teach this course.

We would like to acknowledge the contributions made by the following individuals who participated in focus groups, telesessions, surveys, chapter walkthroughs, classtests, and reviews:

Monica Adya	*Marquette University*
Lawrence Andrew	*Western Illinois University, Macomb*
Orakwue (Bay) Arinze	*Drexel*
Laura Atkins	*James Madison University*
Nick Ball	*Brigham Young University*
Nicholas Barnes	*Nicholls College*
Susan Barzottini	*Manchester CC*
Kristi Berg	*Minot State University*
David Bouchard	*Metropolitan State University*
Dave Bourgeois	*Biola University*
Mari Buche	*Michigan Tech University*

Richard Burkhard	*San Jose State University*
Ashley Bush	*Florida State University*
Donald Carpenter	*Mesa State College*
Teuta Cata	*Northern Kentucky University*
Wendy Ceccucci	*Quinnipiac University*
Susan Chinn	*University of Southern ME, Portland*
Richard Christensen	*Metropolitan State University*
Dmitriy Chulkov	*Indiana University Kokomo*
Phillip Coleman	*Western Kentucky University*
Emilio Collar	*Western CT State University*
Daniel Connolly	*University of Denver*
David Croasdell	*University of Nevada, Reno*
Reet Cronk	*Harding University*
Marcia Daley	*Clark, Atlanta*
Donald Danner	*San Francisco State University*
Roy DeJoie	*Purdue, West Lafayette*
Dawna Dewire	*Babson College*
Kevin Duffy	*Wright State*
Lauren Eder	*Rider University*
Ahmed Eshra	*St. John's University*
Jerry Flatto	*University of Indianapolis*
Jonathan Frankel	*University Massachusetts, Boston*
Judith Gebauer	*University of North Carolina, Wilmington*
Jennifer Gerow	*Virginia Military Institute*
Penelope (Sue) Greenberg	*Widener University*
Naveen Gudigantala	*University of Portland*
Saurabh Gupta	*University of North Florida*
Hyo-Joo Han	*Georgia Southern College*
John Hagle	*Texas State Technical College*
Peter Haried	*University of Wisconsin, LaCrosse*
Ranida Harris	*Indiana University Southeast*
Ranida Harris	*Indiana University Southeast*
Roslin Hauck	*Illinois State University*
Jun He	*University of Michigan, Dearborn*
Richard Herschel	*St. Joseph's University*
Bodgan Hoanca	*University of Alaska*
Mary Carole Hollingsworth	*Georgia Perimeter College, Clarkston Campus*
Terri Holly	*Indian River State College*
Derrick Huang	*Florida Atlantic University*
Maggie Hutchison	*Flagler College*
Mark Hwang	*Central Michigan University*
Lynn Isvik	*Upper Iowa University, Fayette*
Arpan Jani	*University of Wisconsin, River Falls*
Jonathan Jelen	*St. John's University*
Nenad Jukic	*Loyola University*
Stephen Klein	*Ramapo College*
Brian Kovar	*Kansas State University*
Subodha Kumar	*Texas A&M*
Diane Lending	*James Madison University*
Kevin Lertwachara	*Cal Poly San Luis Obispo*
Terry Letsche	*Wartburg College*
Victor Lipe	*Trident Tech*
Chuck Litecky	*Southern Illinois University, Carbondale*
Joan Lumpkin	*Wright State*
Nicole Lytle	*Cal State, San Bernardino*
George Mangalaraj	*Western Illinois University*
Michael Martel	*Ohio University*

Nancy Martin	*Southern Illinois University, Carbondale*
Richard McMahon	*University of Houston, Downtown*
Tony McRae	*Collin College*
Vishal Midha	*University of Texas, Pan American*
Esmail Mohebbi	*University West Florida*
Luvai Motiwalla	*University Mass Online*
Mahdi Nasereddin	*Penn State, Berks*
Sandra K. Newton	*Sonoma State University*
Ann O'Brien	*University of Wisconsin, Madison*
Sungjune Park	*University of North Carolina, Charlotte*
Yang Park	*Georgia Southwestern State University*
Alan Peace	*West Virginia University*
Jacqueline Pike	*Duquesne Univeristy*
Tony Pittarese	*East Tennessee State University*
Jennifer Pitts	*Columbus State University*
Richard Platt	*University of West Florida*
Larisa Preiser	*Cal Poly, Pomona*
Michelle Ramim	*Nova Southeastern University*
Alison Rampersad	*Lynn University*
Ralph Reilly	*University of Hartford*
Julio Rivera	*University of Alabama, Birmingham*
Thomas Roberts	*William Patterson University*
Cynthia Ruppel	*Nova Southeastern University*
Russell Sabadosa	*Manchester CC*
Tom Sandman	*Cal State, Sacramento*
Kala Seal	*Loyola Marymount*
Elaine Seeman	*East Carolina University*
Richard Segall	*Arkansas State University*
Lee Sellers	*EOU - Mt. Hood Metro Center*
Judy Ann Serwatka	*Purdue, North Central*
John Seydel	*Arkansas State University*
Jollean Sinclaire	*Arkansas State University*
Vivek Shah	*Texas State, San Marcos*
Mehrdad Sharbaf	*Loyola Marymount*
Suengjae Shin	*Mississippi State University, Meridian*
Jo Lynne Stalnaker	*University of Wyoming*
Nathan Stout	*University of Oklahoma*
Yi Sun	*Calif State University, San Marcos*
Winston Tellis	*Fairfield University*
Doug Francis Tuggle	*Chapman University*
Wendy Urban	*Temple University*
Darlene de Vida	*Lower Columbia College*
James Villars	*Metropolitan State University*
Padmal Vitharana	*Syracuse*
Haibo Wang	*Texas A&M International*
Hong Wang	*NC Carolina A&T State University*
June Wei	*University of West Florida*
Rosemary Wild	*Cal Poly San Luis Obispo*
Tom Wilder	*Cal State, Chico*
Marie Wright	*Western CT*
Yaquan Xu	*Virginia State University*
Bee Yew	*Fayetteville State University*
Grace Zhang	*Augusta State University*
Wei Zhang	*University of Massachusetts, Boston*
Zuopeng Zhang	*SUNY, Plattsburgh*
Fan Zhao	*Florida Gulf Coast University*
Robert Zwick	*Yeshiva University*

Special thanks to contributors Dawna Dewire, Joan Lumpkin, Kevin Lertwachara, Roy DeJoie, and Kala Seal for developing the Student Activities that appear in every chapter. Thanks also to Efrem Mallach for creating the database activities and to Brad Prince for creating the spreadsheet activities as well as developing all of the Ruby's Club material; to Dawna Dewire for writing test questions; and to Terri Holly, Penelope Greenberg, and Aditi Mukherjee for writing quiz questions. A particularly special thanks to Brad Prince for also helping out with scores of production details when we needed it most. We are grateful for the dedication and creativity of all these contributors in helping us craft this new text.

We would like thank the Wiley team: Beth Lang Golub, Executive Editor; Tom Kulesa, Product Designer; Wendy Ashenberg, Content Editor; Chris Ruel, Executive Marketing Manager; and Elizabeth Mills, Editorial Assistant. We also thank the Content Management team, including Kevin Holm, Content Manager; John Curley, Senior Production Editor; and Denise Showers of Aptara. And thanks to Harry Nolan, Art Director; and Lisa Gee, Photo Editor. We would also like to thank freelance editors John Haley of O'Donnell & Associates for managing all the many details of this new text and Robert Weiss for his skillful and thorough editing of the manuscript.

A NOTE ABOUT BROKEN URLs FOR STUDENTS AND FACULTY:

Please note that all URLs noted in the Student Activities in this book are "live" and accurate at the time of printing. However, due to the dynamic nature of the Internet, we know that some of these links will be broken by the time you read this book.

All URLs will be checked before the start of every term, and replacement URLs or new activities will be provided as necessary. These will be posted on the Student Companion Site for this textbook (*www.wiley.com/college/rainer*) under NEW URLs, organized by chapter.

If you find a broken URL . . .

- Please check the NEW URLs resource first.
- If there is no replacement, please alert the Publisher via email at RainerMail@wiley.com. We will post new material as soon as possible.

Thanks for your understanding and help with this, and if you have suggestions for other Student Activities or any comments about the book, please send us an email. We'd appreciate hearing from you!

—The Rainer Team at Wiley
RainerMail@wiley.com

Brief Contents

Contents

Management
Information
Systems

Moving Business Forward

1 | Introduction to Information Systems

LEARNING OBJECTIVES >>>

1. Begin the process of becoming an informed user of your organization's information systems.
2. Define the terms *data*, *information*, and *knowledge*, and give examples of each.
3. Define the terms information technology, information system, computer-based information system, and application.
4. Identify three ways in which you depend on information technology in your daily life.
5. Discuss three ways in which information technology can impact managers and three ways in which it can impact nonmanagerial workers.
6. List three positive and three negative societal effects of the increased use of information technology.

OPENING **CASE** > E-Mealz

Jane DeLaney grew up in a home where family meals around the table were the norm. She wanted the same for her family, but she found it very difficult due to everyone's busy schedules. She would go from one week of a somewhat organized meal plan to another week of sheer chaos. In 2003, Jane decided it was time to do something about the problem. She created a meal-planning service, called E-Mealz (www.E-Mealz.com), that she could both use herself and offer to other families.

How does E-Mealz work? Essentially, Jane and a few employees create a weekly meal plan for different-sized families. They then draw up a grocery list with prices from various grocery stores. Customers pay for the service—in April 2011, the cost was only $1.85 a week—and they receive their grocery list at the beginning of the week.

Jane needed to utilize information technology to enable her great idea to work. The E-Mealz Web site promotes her products and convinces customers to sign up for her service. If you visit her site, you will find that she also uses Twitter and Facebook to promote her product and to create a community of customers. Visitors can also submit their own recipes to be included in the system. Members can sign up for newsletters, and they can manage their accounts to determine which particular plan they will join. The Web site offers plans for couples and families, and it provides information about a host of nutritional needs, all of which is updated weekly. Although the tools that Jane uses are not complicated, she could not have transformed her dream into a reality without them.

When Jane DeLaney started E-Mealz, her objective was not to create a huge meal-planning service. Rather, her goal was simply to provide a way for families to spend time together, save money, and enjoy delicious meals. Since its inception, E-Mealz has been acclaimed for improving family meals while helping families to control their budget. Bloggers testify that they are able to shop more quickly and spend less money while feeling confident that they have purchased all the ingredients they will need for the week. Jane has successfully utilized technology to accomplish her goal of helping families spend time together, much as her family did when she was growing up.

Sources: Compiled from A. Caldwell, "E-Mealz.com—Meal Planning Resource Review," *Blissfully Domestic,* February 17, 2011; http://E-Mealz.com; http://maketimeforfamily.org; www.daveramsey.com/recommends/dave-recommends; accessed July 27, 2011.

Questions

1. Provide two examples of how Jane uses information technology to provide her service.

2. Provide two additional examples of how Jane might use information technology to improve her service. Be specific.

RUBY'S CLUB

Ruby's Club has recently closed for renovation. While it is closed, its two owners, Ruben and Lisa, have decided that this is a perfect time for them to reorganize, restructure, and reconsider the way they operate their business. They started this club in 2000 just after they graduated from college with their degree in business administration, and they have experienced much success as a result of their hard work.

>>> Information technology was not even taught when they were in college, so they have not used much (if any) technology in their club. While they are considering using IT as they restructure, they are not sure how much and in what ways they should pursue its use. To help them in this area, they have hired you as an IT intern to help answer many of their questions about technology. They have teamed up with your IT professor and designed questions to go along with the topics you will be learning in class.

This internship is designed to accomplish two things. First, it will give Ruben and Lisa the benefit of learning about information technology that was not taught when they were in school. Second, it will give you the benefit of applying the textbook knowledge you learn to the real world.

As this chapter states, your generation is considered *Homo conexus*. Your constant connectivity has to play a role in the restructuring of Ruby's Club. It is your job to help Ruben and Lisa understand exactly how this will look! As you read through the chapter, you will address discussion questions to help you (and Ruben and Lisa) see the impact of information systems on Ruby's Club.

INTRODUCTION

Before you proceed, it is important to define information technology and information systems. **Information technology (IT)** relates to any computer-based tool that people use to work with information and to support the information and information-processing needs of an organization. An **information system (IS)** collects, processes, stores, analyzes, and disseminates information for a specific purpose.

Information technology (IT) has far-reaching effects on us as individuals, on organizations, and on our planet. Although this book is largely devoted to the many ways in which IT has transformed modern organizations, you will also learn about the significant impacts of IT on individuals and societies, the global economy, and our physical environment. In addition, IT is making our world smaller, enabling more and more people to communicate, collaborate, and compete, thereby leveling the digital playing field.

When you graduate, you either will start your own business or you will go to work for an organization, whether it is public sector, private sector, for profit, or not for profit. Your organization will have to survive and compete in an environment that has been radically changed by information technology. This environment is global, massively interconnected, intensely competitive, 24/7/365, real-time, rapidly changing, and information intensive. To compete successfully, your organization must use IT effectively.

As the E-Mealz example illustrates, small business owners do not need to be experts in technology to be successful. The core competency of Jane's business is not technology. Rather, it is the service of saving time and money. However, she has effectively employed social media and available Internet-related tools to create a successful business.

As you read this chapter and this book, keep in mind that the information technologies you will learn about are important to businesses of all sizes. No matter what area of business you major in, what industry you work for, or the size of your company, you will benefit from learning about IT. Who knows? Maybe you will have a great idea and use the tools you learn about in this class to make your dream a reality much the way Jane DeLaney has!

The modern environment is not only intensely competitive for your organization, but for you as well. You must compete with human talent from around the world. Therefore, you will also have to make effective use of IT.

Accordingly, this chapter begins with a discussion of why you should become knowledgeable about IT. It also distinguishes among data, information, and knowledge, and it differentiates computer-based information systems from application programs. Finally, it considers the impacts of information systems on organizations and on society in general.

1.1 | Why Should I Study Information Systems?

You are the most connected generation in history. You have grown up online. You are, quite literally, never out of touch. You use more information technologies (in the form of digital devices) for more tasks, and are bombarded with more information, than any generation in history. The *MIT Technology Review* refers to you as *Homo conexus*. Information technologies are so deeply embedded in your life that your daily routines would be almost unrecognizable to a college student just 20 years ago.

Essentially, you are practicing continuous computing, where you are surrounded with a movable information network. Your network is created by constant cooperation between the digital devices you carry (for example, laptops, media players, and smart phones); the wireline and wireless networks that you access as you move about; and Web-based tools for finding information and communicating and collaborating with other people. Your network enables you to pull information about virtually anything from anywhere, at any time, and to push your own ideas back to the Web, from wherever you are, via a mobile device. Think of everything you do online, often with your phone: register for classes; take classes (and not just at your university); access class syllabi, information, PowerPoints, and lectures; research class papers and presentations; conduct banking; pay your bills; research, shop, and buy products from companies or other people; sell your "stuff"; search for, and apply for, jobs; make your travel reservations (hotel, airline, rental car); have your own blog and post your own podcasts and videocasts to it; have your own page on Facebook; make and upload videos to YouTube; take, edit, and print your own digital photographs; "burn" your own custom-music CDs and DVDs; use RSS feeds to create your personal electronic newspaper; text and tweet your friends and family throughout your day; and many other activities. (*Note:* If any of these terms are unfamiliar to you, do not worry. You will learn about everything mentioned here in detail later in this book.)

The Informed User—You!

So, the question is, Why should you learn about information systems (IS) and information technologies (IT)? After all, you can comfortably use a computer (or other electronic device) to perform many activities, you have been surfing the Web for years, and you feel confident that you can manage any IT application that your organization's MIS department installs. The answer lies in your becoming an **informed user**; that is, a person knowledgeable about information systems and information technology. There are several reasons why you should be an informed user.

In general, informed users tend to get more value from whatever technologies they use. You will enjoy many benefits from being an informed user of IT. First, you will benefit more from your organization's IT applications because you will understand what is "behind" those applications (see Figure 1.1). That is, what you see on your computer screen is brought to you by your MIS department operating "behind" your screen. Second, you will be in a position to enhance the quality of your organization's IT applications with your input. Third, even as a new graduate, you will quickly be in a position to recommend—and perhaps help select—the IT applications that your organization will use. Fourth, being an informed user will enable you to keep abreast of both new information technologies and rapid developments in existing technologies.

Remaining "on top of things" will help you to anticipate the impacts that "new and improved" technologies will have on your organization and to make recommendations on the adoption and use of these technologies. Finally, you will understand how IT can be used to improve your organization's performance and teamwork as well as your own productivity.

Students today are connected by many devices—almost all are wireless. (*Source:* Media Bakery)

USERS | MIS

Figure 1.1 IT skills open many doors because IT is so widely used. What do you think is this woman's job? (*Source:* © Slawomir Fajer/iStockphoto)

Managing the IS function within an organization is no longer the exclusive responsibility of the IS department. Rather, users now play key roles in every step of this process. Our overall objective in this book is for you to be able to immediately contribute to managing the IS function in your organization from your user's perspective. In short, we want to help you become a very informed user!

In addition, if you wish to become an entrepreneur, then being an informed user will help you use IT when you start your own business. "IT's About Business 1.1" illustrates how one couple uses IT to run their own multinational businesses from their home.

It's not just students. Today's professional must be able to use computing technologies to do their job. (*Source:* Howard Kingsnorth/The Image Bank/Getty Images, Inc.)

IT Offers Career Opportunities

Because information technology is vital to the operation of modern businesses, it offers many employment opportunities. The demand for traditional IT staff—programmers, business analysts, systems analysts, and designers—is substantial. In addition, many well-paid jobs exist in areas such as the Internet and electronic commerce (e-commerce), mobile commerce, network security, telecommunications, and multimedia design.

The information systems (IS) field includes the people in organizations who design and build information systems, the people who use those systems, and the people responsible for managing those systems. At the top of the list is the chief information officer (CIO).

The CIO is the executive who is in charge of the IS function. In most modern organizations, the CIO works with the chief executive officer (CEO), the chief financial officer (CFO), and

IT's ABOUT BUSINESS | 1.1

Build Your Own Multinational Company

Global outsourcing is no longer used only by big corporations. Increasingly, small businesses are finding it easier to farm out software development, accounting, support services, and design work to other countries than to perform these services themselves. Improved software, search engines, and new features are boosting the online services industry. Companies in this industry include Elance (www.elance.com), Guru (www.guru.com), Brickwork India (www.b2kcorp.com), and vWorker (www.vworker.com). As examples of added features, Guru has launched a system to avoid disputes over payments by allowing buyers put funds in escrow until the work is received. Meanwhile, Elance has developed software to track work in progress and to handle billing, payments, and tax records.

Take Randy and Nicola Wilburn, for example. Their house is the headquarters of a multinational company. The Wilburns operate real estate, consulting, design, and baby food enterprises out of their home. They accomplish these tasks by making effective use of outsourcing.

Professionals from around the world are at their service. For example, for $300 an Indian artist designed Nicola's letterhead as well as the logo of an infant peering over the words "Baby Fresh Organic Baby Foods." A London-based freelancer wrote promotional materials. Randy has hired "virtual assistants" in Jerusalem to transcribe voice mail, update his Web site, and design PowerPoint graphics. Retired brokers in Virginia and Michigan handle real estate paperwork.

The Wilburns began buying graphic designs through Elance in 2000. Today, remote help has enabled Randy to shift his emphasis within the changing economy. His real estate business has slowed in response to the housing crisis, so he spends more time advising nonprofit organizations across the United States on how to help homeowners avoid foreclosure. Virtual assistants handle routine correspondence and put together business materials while he travels, all for less than $10,000 per year.

Nicola decided to work from home after she had their second child. She now farms out design work to freelancers and is starting to sell organic baby food she cooks herself. She is setting up a Web site for that business and has offered $500 for the design work. Of the 20 bidders who responded via Elance, 18 were from outside the United States.

The couple employs two primary offshore vendors. One is GlobeTask (www.globetask.com), a Jerusalem-based outsourcing firm that employs graphic artists, Web designers, writers, and virtual assistants in Israel, India, and the United States. The company generally charges $8 per hour. The other vendor is Webgrity (www.webgrity.com), headquartered in Kolkata, India. For $125, Webgrity designed a logo for Randy's real estate business that he maintains would have cost as much as $,1000 in the United States.

Interestingly, the Wilburns employ representatives of a growing lifestyle trend, the digital nomads. In fact, the Wilburns are digital nomads as well. A digital nomad is someone who uses information technologies such as smart phones, wireless Internet access, and Web-based applications to work remotely—from home, a coffee shop, an Internet café, and similar locations. Digital nomads have location independence, and they frequently work as freelance writers, editors, photographers, affiliate marketers, Web designers, developers, graphic designers, and other types of knowledge workers.

Questions

1. Identify and evaluate the advantages and disadvantages of outsourcing work overseas.
2. Can anyone do what Randy and Nicola Wilburn are doing? Or, does their strategy require special qualifications or knowledge? Support your answer.
3. Explain how global outsourcing can affect people who are starting their own business. (Hint: Consider capital outlay, labor costs, IT infrastructure costs, and so on.)
4. Would you like to be a digital nomad? Why or why not? Be specific.

Sources: Compiled from B. Russell, "Ever Heard of a Digital Nomad?" www.brentonrussell.com, June 10, 2010; M. Elgan, "Is Digital Nomad Living Going Mainstream?" *Computerworld*, August 1, 2009; M. Rosenwald, "Digital Nomads Choose Their Tribes," *The Washington Post*, July 26, 2009; M. Elgan, "Recession Woes? Why Not Become a Digital Nomad," *Computerworld*, March 23, 2009; P. Engardio, "Mom-and-Pop Multinationals," *BusinessWeek*, July 14 and 21, 2008; T. Ferriss, *The 4-Hour Workweek: Escape 9-5,* *Live Anywhere and Join the New Rich*, 2007, Crown Publishing Group; B. McDermott, "Ahoy the Micro-Multinational," *Forbes*, September 14, 2007; S. Harris, "Rise of the Micro Giants," *San Jose Mercury News*, July 14, 2007; A. Campbell, "The Trend of the Micro-Multinationals," *Small Business Trends*, February 20, 2007; M. Copeland, "The Mighty Micro-Multinational," *Business 2.0 Magazine*, July 28, 2006; H. Varian, "Technology Levels the Business Playing Field," *The New York Times*, August 25, 2005.

other senior executives. Therefore, he or she actively participates in the organization's strategic planning process. In today's digital environment, the IS function has become increasingly important and strategic within organizations. As a result, although the majority of CIOs still rise from the IS department, a growing number are coming up through the ranks in the business units (e.g., marketing, finance, etc.). So, regardless of your college major, you could become the CIO of your organization one day. This is another reason to be an informed user of information systems!

Table 1.1 provides a list of IT jobs along with a description of each one. For further details about careers in IT, see www.computerworld.com/careertopics/careers and www.monster.com.

TABLE 1.1 Information Technology Jobs

Position	Job Description
Chief information officer	Highest-ranking IS manager; is responsible for all strategic planning in the organization
IS director	Manages all systems throughout the organization and day-to-day operations of the entire IS organization
Information center manager	Manages IS services such as help desks, hot lines, training, and consulting
Applications development manager	Coordinates and manages new systems development projects
Project manager	Manages a particular new systems development project
Systems manager	Manages a particular existing system
Operations manager	Supervises the day-to-day operations of the data and/or computer center
Programming manager	Coordinates all applications programming efforts
Systems analyst	Interfaces between users and programmers; determines information requirements and technical specifications for new applications
Business analyst	Focuses on designing solutions for business problems; interfaces closely with users to demonstrate how IT can be used innovatively
Systems programmer	Creates the computer code for developing new systems software or maintaining existing systems software
Applications programmer	Creates the computer code for developing new applications or maintaining existing applications
Emerging technologies manager	Forecasts technology trends and evaluates and experiments with new technologies

Network manager	Coordinates and manages the organization's voice and data networks
Database administrator	Manages the organization's databases and oversees the use of database-management software
Auditing or computer security manager	Oversees the ethical and legal use of information systems
Webmaster	Manages the organization's World Wide Web site
Web designer	Creates World Wide Web sites and pages

Career opportunities in IS are strong and are projected to remain strong over the next ten years. In fact, when *Money Magazine*'s Best Jobs in America (http://money.cnn.com/magazines/moneymag/bestjobs/2010) listed the "top jobs" in America in 2010, 10 of the top 30 jobs related directly to information technology. These jobs (with their ranks) are:

- Software architect (#1)
- Database administrator (#7)
- Information systems security administrator (#17)
- Software development director (#18)
- Information technology manager (#20)
- Telecommunications and networking manager (#21)
- Network operations manager (#24)
- Information technology business analyst (#26)
- Information technology consultant (#28)
- Software development engineer (#30)

Not only do IS careers offer strong job growth, but the pay is excellent as well. The Bureau of Labor Statistics, an agency within the U.S. Department of Labor that is responsible for tracking and analyzing trends relating to the labor market, notes that the median salary for "computer and information systems managers" is approximately $115,000.

Managing Information Resources

Managing information systems in modern organizations is a difficult, complex task. Several factors contribute to this complexity. First, information systems have enormous strategic value to organizations. Firms rely on them so heavily that, in some cases, when these systems are not working (even for a short time), the firm cannot function. (This situation is called "being hostage to information systems.") Second, information systems are very expensive to acquire, operate, and maintain.

A third factor contributing to the difficulty in managing information systems is the evolution of the MIS function within the organization. When businesses first began to use computers in the early 1950s, the MIS department "owned" the only computing resource in the organization: the mainframe. At that time, end users did not interact directly with the mainframe.

In contrast, in the modern organization, computers are located in all departments, and almost all employees use computers in their work. This situation, known as *end user computing*, has led to a partnership between the MIS department and the end users. The MIS department now acts as more of a consultant to end users, viewing them as customers. In fact, the main function of the MIS department is to use IT to solve end users' business problems.

As a result of these developments, the responsibility for managing information resources is now divided between the MIS department and the end users. This arrangement raises several important questions: Which resources are managed by whom? What is the role of the MIS department, its structure, and its place within the organization? What is the appropriate relationship between the MIS department and the end users? Regardless of who is doing what, it is essential that the MIS department and the end users work in close cooperation.

There is no standard set of choices for how to regulate and divide responsibility for developing and maintaining information resources between the MIS department and end users. Instead, that division depends on several factors: the size and nature of the organization, the amount and type of IT resources, the organization's attitudes toward computing, the attitudes of top management toward computing, the maturity level of the technology, the amount and nature of outsourced IT work, and even the countries in which the company operates. Generally speaking, the MIS department is responsible for corporate-level and shared resources, and the end users are responsible for departmental resources. Table 1.2 identifies both the traditional functions and various new, consultative functions of the MIS department.

So, where do the end users come in? Take a close look at Table 1.2. Under the traditional MIS functions, you will see two functions for which you provide vital input. Under the consultative MIS functions, you will see how the primary responsibility for each function is exercised, and how the MIS department acts as an advisor.

TABLE 1.2 The Changing Role of the Information Systems Department

Traditional Functions of the MIS Department

- Managing systems development and systems project management
  - As an end user, you will have critical input into the systems development process. You will learn about systems development in Chapter 14.

- Managing computer operations, including the computer center

- Staffing, training, and developing IS skills

- Providing technical services

- Infrastructure planning, development, and control
  - As an end user, you will provide critical input about the IS infrastructure needs of your department.

New (Consultative) Functions of the MIS Department

- Initiating and designing specific strategic information systems
  - As an end user, your information needs will often mandate the development of new strategic information systems. You will decide which strategic systems you need (because you know your business needs better than the MIS department), and you will provide input into developing these systems.

- Incorporating the Internet and electronic commerce into the business
  - As an end user, you will be primarily responsible for effectively using the Internet and electronic commerce in your business. You will work with the MIS department to accomplish this task.

- Managing system integration including the Internet, intranets, and extranets
  - As an end user, your business needs will determine how you want to use the Internet, your corporate intranets, and extranets to accomplish your goals. You will be primarily responsible for advising the MIS department on the most effective use of the Internet, your corporate intranets, and extranets.

- Educating the non-MIS managers about IT
  - Your department will be primarily responsible for advising the MIS department on how best to educate and train your employees about IT.

- Educating the MIS staff about the business
  - Communication between the MIS department and the business units is a two-way street. You will be responsible for educating the MIS staff on your business, its needs, and its goals.

- Partnering with business-unit executives
  - Essentially, you will be in a partnership with the MIS department. You will be responsible for seeing that this partnership is one "between equals" and ensuring its success.

- Managing outsourcing
  - Outsourcing is driven by business needs. Therefore, the outsourcing decision largely resides with the business units (i.e., with you). The MIS department, working closely with you, will advise you on technical issues such as communications bandwidth, security, and so on.

- Proactively using business and technical knowledge to seed innovative ideas about IT
  - Your business needs will often drive innovative ideas about how to effectively use information systems to accomplish your goals. The best way to bring these innovative uses of IS to life is to partner closely with your MIS department. Such close partnerships have amazing synergies!

- Creating business alliances with business partners
  - The needs of your business unit will drive these alliances, typically along your supply chain. Again, your MIS department will act as your advisor on various issues, including hardware and software compatibility, implementing extranets, communications, and security.

BEFORE *YOU GO ON . . .*

1. Rate yourself as an informed user. (Be honest; this is not a test!)
2. Explain the benefits of being an informed user of information systems.
3. Discuss the various career opportunities offered in the IT field.

RUBY'S CLUB QUESTIONS

1. Given that Ruby's customers are college-age *Homo conexus* users of technology, do you think it will be possible for the club to be successful moving into the future without a strong IT strategy?

2. If informed users provide more value to a company, can the same be said of informed customers?

Student Activity | 1.1

Objective: Computers and information systems have become a part of our everyday life not only in the workplace but also at home. This exercise will give you insight into some of the areas where information systems jobs are found.

Chapter Connection: This case relates to Chapter 1, Introduction to Information Systems, Section 1.1: "Why Should I Study Information Systems?"

Prerequisites: You should read Section 1 before doing this exercise to become familiar with the jobs and functions of information systems.

Activity:

In most business jobs you will interface with a computer information system to post transactions or find information easily. However, some jobs create, support, and manage these information systems on a daily basis.

Watch the following video:

www.youtube.com/watch?v=A9qBcdoEx00

Deliverables:

Prepare answers for the following questions:

1. What is involved in the job of an IT manager?
2. What is the schedule for an IT manager's work?
3. What training does an IT manager need?

Quiz Questions:

1. What is the benefit of being an informed IT user?

   (a) You are in a position to recommend solutions.
   (b) You can keep abreast with newer technology.
   (c) You can be a more productive employee.
   (d) All of the above.

2. What does a systems analyst do?

   (a) Interface between users and programmers
   (b) Coordinate all programming efforts
   (c) Writes computer code
   (d) Manages IS service

3. Which of the following is a career opportunity in IT?

   (a) Systems analyst
   (b) Web designer
   (c) Network security
   (d) All of the above

4. What makes managing information systems a difficult task?

   (a) They have strategic value to the organization.
   (b) The organization relies heavily on them.
   (c) They are very expensive to buy or create.
   (d) All of the above

5. What is true about the education of an IS manager?

   (a) An undergraduate degree is necessary.
   (b) Constant retraining is necessary.
   (c) An advanced degree is necessary.
   (d) A technical degree is necessary.

Discussion Questions:

Discuss some of the jobs available in the IT field. Do you know anyone who works directly in IT? What is the person's job title and functions? Does he or she like it?

1.2 | Overview of Computer-Based Information Systems

Organizations refer to their management information systems (MIS) functional area by several names, including the MIS Department, the Information Systems (IS) Department, the Information Technology Department, and the Information Services Department. Regardless of the name, however, this functional area deals with the planning for—and the development, management, and use of—information technology tools to help people perform all of the tasks related to information processing and management. IT relates to any computer-based tool that people use to work with information and to support the information and information-processing needs of an organization.

An IS collects, processes, stores, analyzes, and disseminates information for a specific purpose. It has been said that the purpose of IS is to get the right information to the right people at the right time in the right amount and in the right format. Because IS are intended to supply useful information, we need to differentiate between information and two closely related terms: *data* and *knowledge* (see Figure 1.2).

Data items refer to an elementary description of things, events, activities, and transactions that are recorded, classified, and stored but are not organized to convey any specific meaning. Data items can be numbers, letters, figures, sounds, and images. Examples of data items are a collection of numbers (e.g., 3.11, 2.96, 3.95, 1.99, 2.08) and characters (e.g., B, A, C, A, B, D, F, C).

Information refers to data that have been organized so that they have meaning and value to the recipient. For example, a grade point average (GPA) by itself is data, but a student's name coupled with his or her GPA is information. The recipient interprets the meaning and draws conclusions and implications from the information. Consider the examples of data provided in the preceding paragraph. Within the context of a university, the numbers could be GPAs, and the letters could be grades in an Introduction to MIS class.

Knowledge consists of data and/or information that have been organized and processed to convey understanding, experience, accumulated learning, and expertise as they

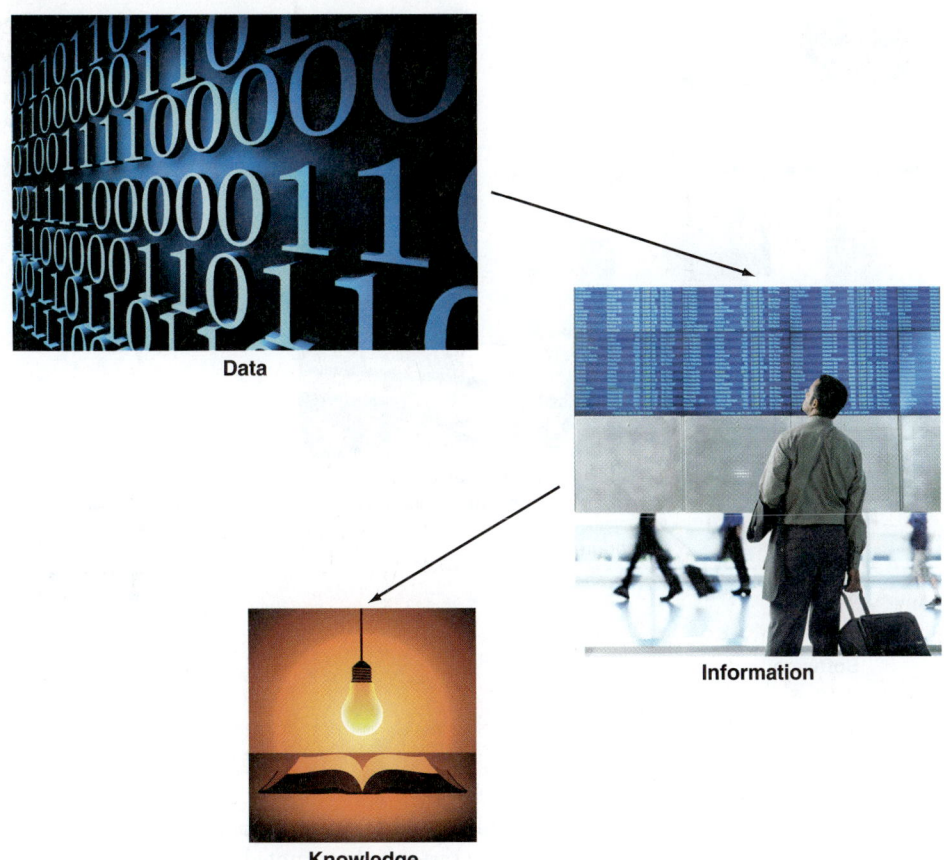

Data

Information

Knowledge

Figure 1.2 Binary Code, the foundation of information and knowledge, is the key to making complex decisions. (*Source:* © janaka Dharmasena-Fotolia.com; Exactostock/SuperStock; uttam gurjar/Shutterstock)

apply to a current business problem. For example, a company recruiting at your school has found over time that students with GPAs over 3.0 have experienced the greatest success in its management program. Based on this accumulated knowledge, that company may decide to interview only those students with GPAs over 3.0. Organizational knowledge, which reflects the experience and expertise of many people, has great value to all employees.

Consider this example:

Data	Information	Knowledge
[No context]	[University context]	
3.16	3.16 + John Jones = GPA	* Job prospects
2.92	2.92 + Sue Smith = GPA	*Graduate school prospects
1.39	1.39 + Kyle Owens = GPA	*Scholarship prospects
3.95	3.95 + Tom Elias = GPA	
[No context]	[Professional baseball pitcher context]	
3.16	3.16 + Ken Rice = ERA	
2.92	2.92 + Ed Dyas = ERA	*Keep pitcher, trade pitcher, or send pitcher to minor leagues
1.39	1.39 + Hugh Carr = ERA	*Salary/contract negotiations
3.95	3.95 + Nick Ford = ERA	

GPA = grade point average (higher is better)

ERA = earned run average (lower is better); ERA is the number of runs per nine innings accountable to a pitcher

You see that the same data items, with no context, can mean entirely different things in different contexts.

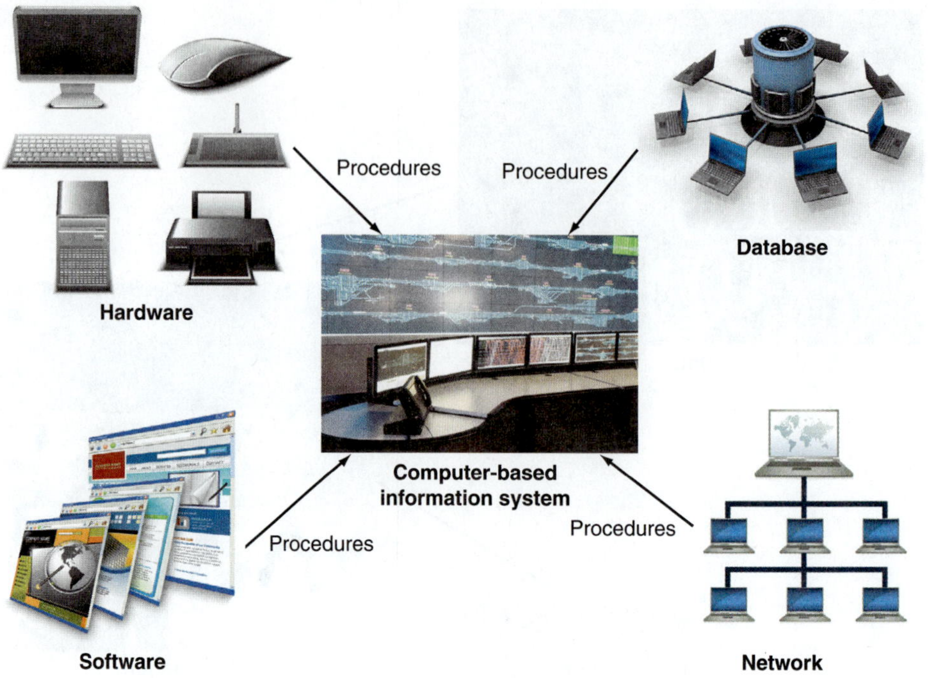

Figure 1.3 It takes technology (hardware, software, databases, and networks) with appropriate procedures to make a CBIS useful for people. (*Source:* Nasonov/Shutterstock; Angela Waye/Shutterstock; alexmillos/ Shutterstock; broukoid/ Shutterstock; zhu difeng/ Shutterstock)

Now that you have a clearer understanding of data, information, and knowledge, we shift our focus to computer-based information systems. As we noted, these systems process data into information and knowledge that you can use.

A **computer-based information system (CBIS)** is an information system that uses computer technology to perform some or all of its intended tasks. Although not all information systems are computerized, today most are. For this reason the term *information system* is typically used synonymously with *computer-based information system*. The following are the basic components of computer-based information systems. The first four are called **information technology (IT) components**. Figure 1.3 shows how these four components interact to form a CBIS.

- **Hardware** is a device such as a processor, monitor, keyboard, or printer. Together, these devices accept data and information, process them, and display them.
- **Software** is a program or collection of programs that enable the hardware to process data.
- A **database** is a collection of related files or tables containing data.
- A **network** is a connecting system (wireline or wireless) that permits different computers to share resources.
- **Procedures** are the set of instructions about how to combine hardware, software, databases, and networks in order to process information and generate the desired output.
- *Users* are those individuals who use the hardware and software, interface with it, or utilize its output.

Figure 1.4 shows how these components are integrated to form the wide variety of information systems in an organization. Starting at the bottom of the figure, you see that the IT components of hardware, software, networks (wireline and wireless), and databases form the **information technology (IT) platform**. IT personnel use these components to develop information systems, oversee security and risk, and manage data. These activities cumulatively are called **information technology (IT) services**. The IT components plus IT services comprise the organization's **information technology (IT)**

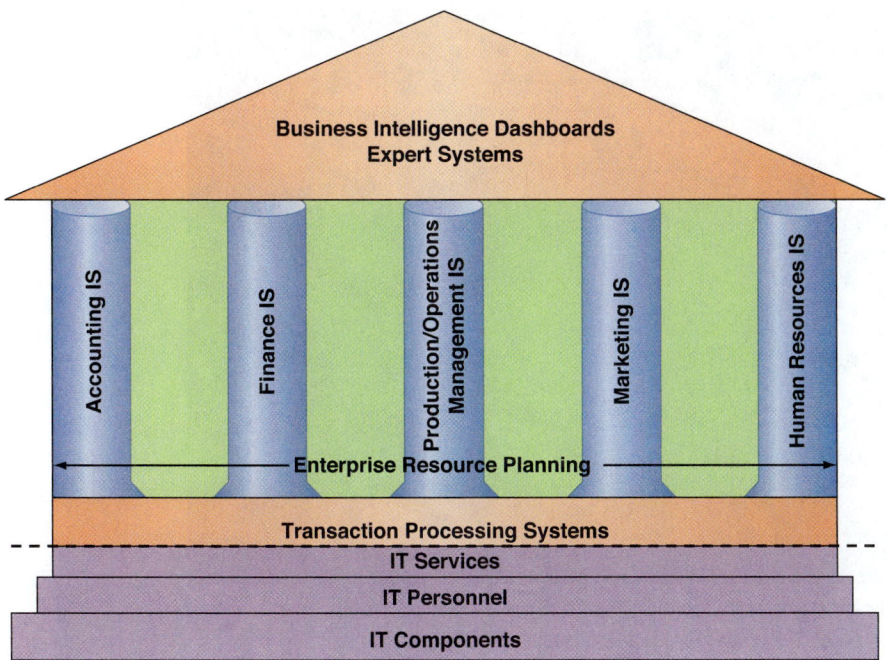

Figure 1.4 How IT components are integrated to form the wide variety of information systems within a single organization.

infrastructure. At the top of the pyramid are the various organizational information systems.

Computer-based information systems have many capabilities. Table 1.3 summarizes the most important ones.

Information systems perform these various tasks via a wide spectrum of applications. An **application (app)** is a computer program designed to support a specific task or business process. (A synonymous term is *application program*.) Each functional area or department within a business organization uses dozens of application programs. For instance, the human resources department sometimes uses one application for screening job applicants and another for monitoring employee turnover. The collection of application programs in a single department is usually referred to as a *departmental information system* (also known as a *functional area information system*). For example, the collection of application programs in the human resources area is called the *human resources information system* (*HRIS*). Collections of application programs—that is, departmental information systems—are used in other functional areas as well, such as accounting, finance, marketing, and production/operations. "IT's About Business 1.2" illustrates how electronic discovery software applications improve the efficiency and effectiveness of the legal discovery process.

TABLE 1.3 Major Capabilities of Information Systems

- Perform high-speed, high-volume, numerical computations
- Provide fast, accurate communication and collaboration within and among organizations
- Store huge amounts of information in an easy-to-access, yet small, space
- Allow quick and inexpensive access to vast amounts of information, worldwide
- Interpret vast amounts of data quickly and efficiently
- Automate both semiautomatic business processes and manual tasks

Applications can be downloaded to mobile device or computer.
(*Source:* © Cyberstock/Alamy Limited)

Electronic E-Discovery Software Replaces Lawyers

When the U.S. Justice Department sued CBS for antitrust violations in 1978, five television studios became involved. The cost to the studios was extremely high. As part of the discovery process—which involves providing documents relevant to a lawsuit—studio lawyers and paralegals examined 6 million documents at a cost of $2.2 million. Today, electronic discovery (e-discovery) software applications can analyze documents in a fraction of the time at a fraction of the cost. For example, in January 2011, Blackstone Discovery (www. blackstonediscovery.com) helped one company analyze 1.5 million documents for less than $100,000.

Some e-discovery applications go beyond just rapidly finding documents with relevant terms. They can extract relevant concepts, even in the absence of specific terms, and can deduce patterns of behavior that would have eluded lawyers examining millions of documents.

E-discovery software generally falls into two broad categories that can be described as "linguistic" and "sociological." The most basic linguistic software uses specific search words to find and sort relevant documents. More advanced applications filter documents through a large number of interrelated word and phrase definitions.

In contrast, sociological applications add inferential analysis, closely resembling human reasoning. For example, software from Cataphora (www.cataphora.com) analyzes documents for information pertaining to the activities and interactions of people—who did what and when, and who talked to whom. The software then manipulates this information to visualize chains of events. It identifies discussions that might have taken place across e-mail, instant messages, and telephone calls. The software then captures digital anomalies that white-collar criminals often create when they try to hide their activities. For example, the software finds "call me" moments—those incidents during which an employee decides to hide a particular action by having a private conversation. This process usually involves switching media, perhaps from an e-mail conversation to instant messaging, telephone, or even a face-to-face encounter.

The Cataphora software can also recognize the sentiment in an e-mail message—whether a person is positive or negative, or what Cataphora calls "loud talking"—unusual emphasis that might give hints that a document concerns a stressful situation. For example, a shift in an author's e-mail style from breezy to unusually formal can raise a red flag about illegal activity.

Another e-discovery company, Clearwell (www.clearwellsystems.com), has developed software that analyzes documents to find concepts rather than specific keywords. This process decreases the time required to locate relevant material in litigation. Clearwell's software uses language analysis and a visual way of representing general concepts found in documents. In 2010, for example, the DLA Piper law firm used Clearwell software to search through some 570,000 documents under a court-imposed deadline of one week. The software analyzed the documents in two days. The law firm required just one more day to identify more than 3,000 documents that were relevant to the discovery motion.

E-discovery software is doing an excellent job and, as a result, the discovery process is becoming increasingly automated, scientific, and objective. One lawyer used e-discovery software to reanalyze work his company's lawyers had performed in the 1980s and 1990s. He discovered that his human colleagues had been only 60 percent accurate.

Quantifying the impact of these software applications on employment is difficult. However, the founder of

Autonomy (www.autonomy.com), an e-discovery firm, is convinced that the U.S. legal sector will likely employ fewer people in the future. He estimates that the shift from manual document discovery to e-discovery will lead to a staff reduction because one lawyer can now do the work that once required hundreds of lawyers.

Questions

1. What are the advantages of e-discovery software? Provide specific examples.

2. What are the disadvantages of e-discovery software? Provide specific examples.

3. Based on this scenario, how do you think e-discovery software will affect the legal profession?

Sources: Compiled from B. Kerschberg, "E-Discovery and the Rise of Predictive Coding," *Forbes*, March 23, 2011; J. Markoff, "Armies of Expensive Lawyers, Replaced by Cheaper Software," *The New York Times*, March 4, 2011; K. Fogarty, "E-Discovery: How a Law Firm Slashes Time and Costs," *CIO*, February 15, 2011; B. Kerschberg, "Surviving e-Discovery with the Department of Justice's Antitrust Division," *Forbes*, February 14, 2011; M. Pratt, "E-Discovery Moves In-House," *Computerworld*, December 30, 2010; www.autonomy.com, www.blackwelldiscovery.com, www.cataphora.com, www.clearwellsystems.com, accessed July 27, 2011.

Types of Computer-Based Information Systems

Modern organizations employ many different types of information systems. Figure 1.4 illustrates the different types of information systems that function *within* a single organization, and Figure 1.5 shows the different types of information systems that function *among* multiple organizations. You will study transaction processing systems, management information systems, and enterprise resource planning systems in Chapter 11. You will learn about customer relationship management (CRM) systems in Chapter 12 and supply chain management (SCM) systems in Chapter 13.

In the next section you will learn about the numerous and diverse types of information systems employed by modern organizations. You will also read about the types of support these systems provide.

Breadth of Support of Information Systems. Certain information systems support parts of organizations, others support entire organizations, and still others support groups of organizations. This section addresses all of these systems.

Recall that each department or functional area within an organization has its own collection of application programs, or information systems. These **functional area information systems (FAIS)** are supporting pillars for the information systems located at the top of Figure 1.4: business intelligence systems and dashboards. As the name suggests, each FAIS supports a particular functional area within the organization. Examples are accounting IS, finance IS, production/operations management (POM) IS, marketing IS, and human resources IS.

Consider these examples of IT systems in the various functional areas of an organization. In *finance* and *accounting*, managers use IT systems to forecast revenues and business activity, to determine the best sources and uses of funds, and to perform audits to ensure that the organization is fundamentally sound and that all financial reports and documents are accurate.

Data from a coupon center will be connected to marketing and sales, but possibly inventory, accounting, and much more. (*Source:* © Sonda Dawes/The Image Works)

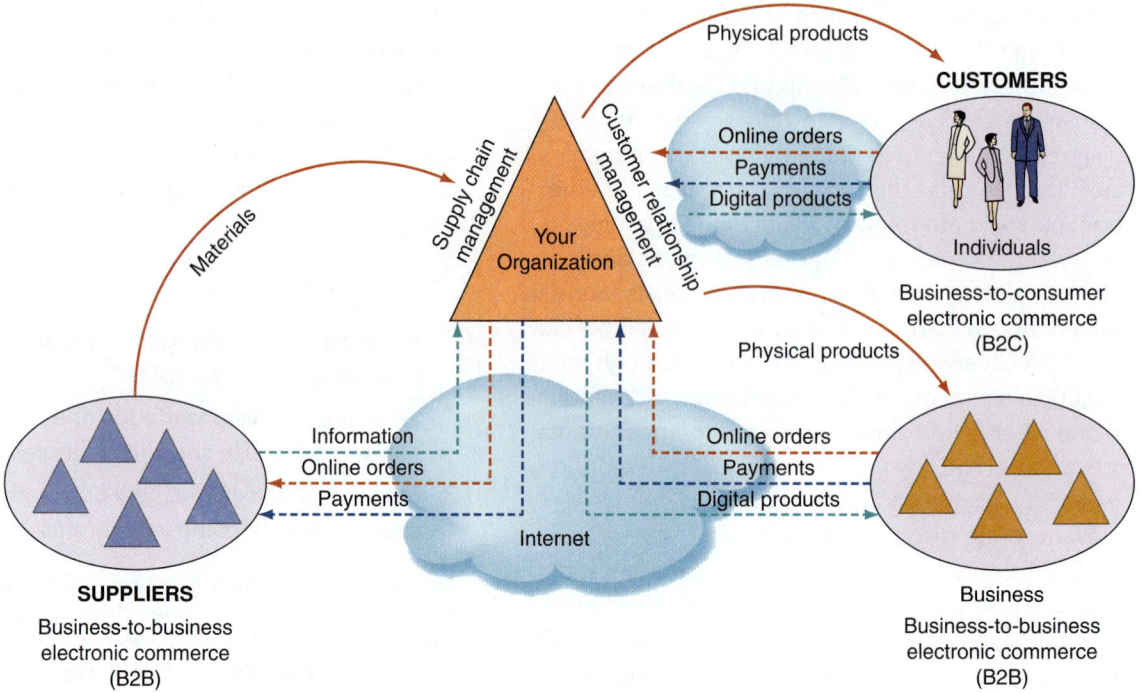

Figure 1.5 The different types of information systems that function among multiple organizations.

In *sales* and *marketing*, managers use information technology to perform the following functions:

- *Product analysis:* developing new goods and services
- *Site analysis:* determining the best location for production and distribution facilities
- *Promotion analysis:* identifying the best advertising channels
- *Price analysis:* setting product prices to obtain the highest total revenues

Marketing managers also use IT to manage their relationships with their customers.

In *manufacturing*, managers use IT to process customer orders, develop production schedules, control inventory levels, and monitor product quality. They also use IT to design and manufacture products. These processes are called computer-assisted design (CAD) and computer-assisted manufacturing (CAM).

Managers in *human resources* use IT to manage the recruiting process, analyze and screen job applicants, and hire new employees. They also employ IT to help employees manage their careers, to administer performance tests to employees, and to monitor employee productivity. Finally, they rely on IT to manage compensation and benefits packages.

Two information systems support the entire organization: enterprise resource planning systems and transaction processing systems. **Enterprise resource planning (ERP) systems** are designed to correct a lack of communication among the FAISs. As a result, Figure 1.4 shows ERP systems spanning the FAIS. ERP systems were an important innovation because the various FAISs were often developed as stand-alone systems and did not communicate effectively (if at all) with one another. ERP systems resolve this problem by tightly integrating the FAISs via a common database. In doing so, they enhance communications among the functional areas of an organization. For this reason, experts credit ERP systems with greatly increasing organizational productivity.

A **transaction processing system (TPS)** supports the monitoring, collection, storage, and processing of data from the organization's basic business transactions, each of which generates data. For example, when you are checking out of Walmart, each time the cashier swipes an item across the bar code reader, that is one transaction. Definitions of a transaction differ throughout an organization. In accounting, for example, a transaction is anything that changes a firm's chart of accounts. The information system definition of a transaction is broader: A transaction is anything that changes the firm's database. The chart of accounts is only part of the firm's database. Consider a scenario in which a student transfers from one section of an Introduction to MIS course to another section. This move would be a transaction in the university's information system, but not a transaction in the university's accounting department.

The TPS collects data continuously, typically in *real time*—that is, as soon as the data are generated—and provides the input data for the corporate databases. TPSs are considered critical to the success of any enterprise because they support core operations. Significantly, nearly all ERP systems are also TPSs, but not all TPSs are ERP systems. In fact, modern ERP systems incorporate many functions that have previously been handled by the organization's functional area information systems. You study both TPSs and ERP systems in detail in Chapter 11.

ERP systems and TPS function primarily within a single organization. Information systems that connect two or more organizations are referred to as **interorganizational information systems (IOSs)**. IOSs support many interorganizational operations, of which supply chain management is the best known. An organization's **supply chain** is the flow of materials, information, money, and services from suppliers of raw materials through factories and warehouses to the end customers.

Note that the supply chain in Figure 1.5 shows physical flows, information flows, and financial flows. Digitizable products are those that can be represented in electronic form, such as music and software. Information flows, financial flows, and digitizable products go through the Internet, whereas physical products are shipped. For example, when you order a computer from www.dell.com, your information goes to Dell via the Internet. When your transaction is completed (i.e., your credit card is approved and your order is processed), Dell ships your computer to you.

Electronic commerce systems are another type of interorganizational information system. An **electronic commerce (e-commerce) system** enable organizations to conduct transactions, called business-to-business (B2B) electronic commerce, and customers to conduct transactions with businesses, called business-to-consumer (B2C) electronic commerce. (*Note:* You will learn about other types of e-commerce systems in Chapter 9). E-commerce systems are typically Internet based. Figure 1.5 illustrates B2B and B2C electronic commerce.

Support for Organizational Employees. So far you have concentrated on information systems that support specific functional areas and operations. Now you will learn about information systems that typically support particular employees within the organization.

Clerical workers, who support managers at all levels of the organization, include bookkeepers, secretaries, electronic file clerks, and insurance claim processors. *Lower-level managers* handle the day-to-day operations of the organization, making routine decisions such as assigning tasks to employees and placing purchase orders. *Middle managers* make tactical decisions, which deal with activities such as short-term planning, organizing, and control.

Knowledge workers are professional employees, such as financial and marketing analysts, engineers, lawyers, and accountants. All knowledge workers are experts in a particular subject area. They create information and knowledge, which they integrate into the business. Knowledge workers act as advisors to middle managers and executives. Finally, *executives* make decisions that deal with situations that can significantly change the manner in which business is done. Examples of executive decisions are introducing a new product line, acquiring other businesses, and relocating operations to a foreign country.

Office automation systems (OASs) typically support the clerical staff, lower and middle managers, and knowledge workers. These employees use OASs to develop documents (word processing and desktop publishing software), schedule resources (electronic calendars), and communicate (e-mail, voice mail, videoconferencing, and groupware).

FAISs summarize data and prepare reports, primarily for middle managers, but sometimes for lower-level managers as well. Because these reports typically concern a specific functional area, report generators (RPGs) are an important type of functional area IS.

Business intelligence (BI) systems provide computer-based support for complex, nonroutine decisions, primarily for middle managers and knowledge workers. (They also support lower-level managers, but to a lesser extent.) These systems are typically used with a data warehouse, and they enable users to perform their own data analysis. You learn about BI systems in Chapter 5.

Expert systems (ESs) attempt to duplicate the work of human experts by applying reasoning capabilities, knowledge, and expertise within a specific domain. They have become valuable in many application areas, primarily but not exclusively areas involving decision making. For example, navigation systems use rules to select routes, but we do not typically think of these systems as expert systems. Significantly, expert systems can operate as standalone systems or be embedded in other applications. We examine ESs in greater detail in "Plug IT In 4."

Dashboards (also called **digital dashboards**) are a special form of IS that supports all managers of the organization. They provide rapid access to timely information and direct access to structured information in the form of reports. Dashboards that are tailored to the information needs of executives are called *executive dashboards*. Chapter 5 provides a thorough discussion of dashboards.

Table 1.4 provides an overview of the different types of information systems used by organizations.

TABLE 1.4 Types of Organizational Information Systems

Type of System	Function	Example
Functional area IS	Supports the activities within specific functional area	System for processing payroll
Transaction processing system	Processes transaction data from business events	Walmart checkout point-of-sale terminal
Enterprise resource planning system	Integrates all functional areas of the organization	Oracle, SAP
Office automation system	Supports daily work activities of individuals and groups	Microsoft Office
Management information system	Produces reports summarized from transaction data, usually in one functional area	Report on total sales for each customer
Decision support system	Provides access to data and analysis tools	"What-if" analysis of changes in budget
Expert system	Mimics human expert in a particular area and makes decisions	Credit card approval analysis
Executive dashboard	Presents structured, summarized information about aspects of business important to executives	Status of sales by product
Supply chain management system	Manages flows of products, services, and information among organizations	Walmart Retail Link system connecting suppliers to Walmart
Electronic commerce system	Enables transactions among organizations and between organizations and customers	www.dell.com

BEFORE *YOU GO ON . . .*

1. What is a computer-based information system?
2. Describe the components of computer-based information systems.
3. What is an application program?
4. Explain how information systems provide support for knowledge workers.
5. As we move up the organization's hierarchy from clerical workers to executives, how does the type of support provided by information systems change?

RUBY'S CLUB QUESTIONS

1. Given that Ruby's is a bar with a small food menu, what type of data do you think Ruben and Lisa should collect from a single transaction (an order for food)?

2. How can Ruby's use data from transactions over a month to help manage inventory?

3. If Ruben and Lisa have transactional data that are organized to create information regarding their customer base, what knowledge could be gained from this that would help them develop a marketing plan?

4. Ruben and Lisa have always spent hours going through paper receipts trying to determine past sales. They need these figures to know what quantities to purchase for the products they sell. Given that some of their products have a short shelf life (perishable foods), this needs to be very accurate. In what ways could the capabilities of information systems help them accomplish this task?

5. What type of procedures would Ruben and Lisa need to ensure that the people interacting with the information systems are doing so in an appropriate manner (i.e., correctly inputting data, not using customer data, etc.)?

Student Activity | 1.2

Objective: Computer-based information systems are used by employees in most businesses today. In this exercise we cover the functional groups in most companies and the various information systems that they would use.

Chapter Connection: This case relates to Chapter 1, Introduction to Information Systems, Section 1.2: "Overview of Computer-Based Information Systems."

Prerequisites: You should read Section 1.2 before doing this exercise to become familiar with the functional departments within most organization and the types of information systems.

Activity:

There are four major functional areas in most business: marketing, finance/accounting, manufacturing, and human resources. All of them use information systems, but often they are performing different activities relating to their job functions but using the same database.

Also, there are numerous types and levels of information systems. Many companies use transaction processing systems, management information systems, and decision support systems.

In this activity, we relate the functional groups with the specific type of information systems.

Deliverables:

1. Briefly define the major function of the following departments in most companies: marketing, finance/accounting, manufacturing, and human resources.

2. Define the basic function of the following types of information systems: transaction processing, management information, and decision support.

3. Based on the preceding definition, fill in the following chart with specific examples of each type of IS. For instance, marketing would *enter new orders* using transaction processing.

	Transaction Processing	Management Information	Decision Support
Marketing			
Accounting/Finance			
Manufacturing			
Human Resources			

Quiz Questions:

1. What department manages the financial needs of the company?
   - (a) Marketing
   - (b) Accounting
   - (c) Manufacturing
   - (d) Human resources

2. What department reviews the benefit packages for employees?
   - (a) Marketing
   - (b) Accounting
   - (c) Manufacturing
   - (d) Human resources

3. What information system tracks the day-to-day activity of a company?
   - (a) Transaction processing
   - (b) Management information
   - (c) Decision support
   - (d) Expert system

4. What information system conducts a what-if scenario to help determine the best alternative?
   - (a) Transaction processing
   - (b) Management information
   - (c) Decision support
   - (d) Expert system

Discussion Question:

How do the functions of the various departments within a company differ (i.e., marketing, human resources, etc.)? Discuss how the employees in each department within a company would use a computer-based information system with a database to do their jobs and interface with each other.

1.3 | How Does IT Impact Organizations?

Throughout this book you will encounter numerous examples of how IT affects various types of organizations. This section provides an overview of the impact of IT on modern organizations. As you read this section you will learn how each of these impacts will affect you as well.

IT Will Reduce the Number of Middle Managers

IT makes managers more productive, and it increases the number of employees who can report to a single manager. In these ways IT ultimately decreases the number of managers and experts. It is reasonable to assume, therefore, that in the coming years organizations will have fewer managerial levels and fewer staff and line managers. If this trend materializes, then promotional opportunities will decrease, making promotions much more competitive. Bottom line: Pay attention in school!

IT Will Change the Manager's Job

One of the most important tasks of managers is making decisions. One of the major consequences of IT has been to change the manner in which managers make many of their decisions. In this way IT ultimately has changed managers' jobs.

IT often provides managers with near real-time information, meaning that managers have less time to make decisions, making their jobs even more stressful. Fortunately, IT also provides many tools—for example, business intelligence applications such as dashboards, search engines, and intranets—to help managers handle the volumes of information they must deal with on an ongoing basis.

We have been focusing on managers in general in this section. Now, let's focus on you. Due to advances in IT, you will increasingly supervise employees and teams who are geographically dispersed. Employees can work from anywhere at any time, and teams can consist of employees who are literally dispersed throughout the world. Information technologies such as telepresence systems (discussed in Chapter 4) can help you manage these employees even though you do not often see them face to face. For these employees, electronic or "remote" supervision will become the norm. Remote supervision places greater emphasis on completed work and less emphasis on personal contacts and office politics. You will have to reassure your employees that they are valued members of the organization, thereby diminishing any feelings they might have of being isolated and "out of the loop."

Will IT Eliminate Jobs?

One of the major concerns of every employee, part time or full time, is job security. Relentless cost-cutting measures in modern organizations often lead to large-scale layoffs. Put simply, organizations are responding to today's highly competitive environment by doing more with less. Regardless of your position, then, you consistently will have to add value to your organization and to make certain that your superiors are aware of this value.

Many companies have responded to difficult economic times, increased global competition, demands for customization, and increased consumer sophistication by increasing their investments in IT. In fact, as computers continue to advance in terms of intelligence and capabilities, the competitive advantage of replacing people with machines is increasing rapidly. This process frequently leads to layoffs. At the same time, however, IT creates entirely new categories of jobs, such as electronic medical record keeping and nanotechnology.

IT Impacts Employees at Work

Many people have experienced a loss of identity because of computerization. They feel like "just another number" because computers reduce or eliminate the human element that was present in noncomputerized systems.

The Internet threatens to exert an even more isolating influence than computers and television. Encouraging people to work and shop from their living rooms could produce some unfortunate psychological effects, such as depression and loneliness.

IT Impacts Employees' Health and Safety. Although computers and information systems are generally regarded as agents of "progress," they can adversely affect individuals' health and safety. To illustrate this point, we consider two issues associated with IT: job stress and long-term use of the keyboard.

An increase in an employee's workload and/or responsibilities can trigger *job stress*. Although computerization has benefited organizations by increasing productivity, it has also created an ever-expanding workload for some employees. Some workers feel overwhelmed and have become increasingly anxious about their job performance. These feelings of stress and anxiety can actually diminish rather than improve workers' productivity while jeopardizing their physical and mental health. Management can help to alleviate these problems by providing training, redistributing the workload among workers, and hiring more workers.

On a more specific level, the long-term use of keyboards can lead to *repetitive strain injuries* such as backaches and muscle tension in the wrists and fingers. *Carpal tunnel syndrome* is a particularly painful form of repetitive strain injury that affects the wrists and hands.

Designers are aware of the potential problems associated with the prolonged use of computers. To address these problems, they continually attempt to design a better computing environment. The science of designing machines and work settings that minimize injury and illness is called **ergonomics**. The goal of ergonomics is to create an environment that is safe, well lit, and comfortable. Examples of ergonomically designed products

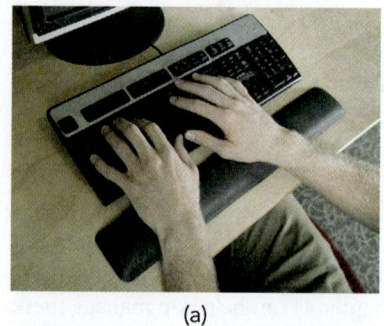
(a)

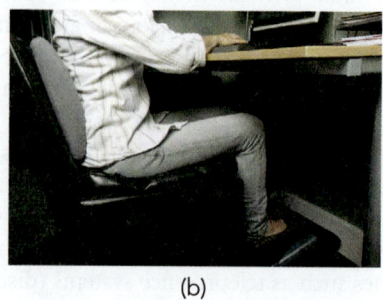
(b)

(c)

(d)

Figure 1.6 Ergonomic products protect computer users.
(a) Wrist support. (*Source:* Media Bakery)
(b) Back support. (*Source:* Media Bakery)
(c) Eye-protection filter (optically coated glass). (*Source:* Media Bakery)
(d) Adjustable foot rest. (*Source:* Media Bakery)

are antiglare screens that alleviate problems of fatigued or damaged eyesight and chairs that contour the human body to decrease backaches. Figure 1.6 displays some sample ergonomic products.

IT Provides Opportunities for People with Disabilities. Computers can create new employment opportunities for people with disabilities by integrating speech- and vision-recognition capabilities. For example, individuals who cannot type are able to use a voice-operated keyboard, and individuals who cannot travel can work at home.

Going further, adaptive equipment for computers permits people with disabilities to perform tasks they would not normally be able to do. You should note that the Web and graphical user interfaces (e.g., Microsoft Windows) can still make life difficult for people with impaired vision. Adding audible screen tips and voice interfaces to deal with this problem essentially restores functionality to the way it was before rich, graphical interfaces became standard.

Other devices help improve the quality of life for people with disabilities in more mundane, but useful, ways. Examples are a two-way writing telephone, a robotic page turner, a hair brusher, and a hospital-bedside video trip to the zoo or the museum. Several organizations specialize in IT designed for people with disabilities.

BEFORE *YOU GO ON . . .*

1. Why should employees in all functional areas become knowledgeable about IT?

2. Describe how IT might change the manager's job.

3. Discuss several ways in which IT impacts employees at work.

Student Activity | 1.3

Objective: This exercise is to help you understand why we study information systems and the impact they can have on the business organization.

Chapter Connection: This case relates to Chapter 1, Introduction to Information Systems, Section 1.3: "How Does IT Impact Organizations?"

Prerequisites: You should read Section 1.3 before doing this exercise to become familiar with the use of information systems.

Activity:

Chances are you own a personal computer that you use in some way every day. Think of five (5) activities that you use your computer for on a regular basis. Most likely many of these activities have to do with school and your classes. However, I would guess that you also use your computer to communicate with friends and family, to find out what movies are showing in theaters this weekend, or to check flights for travel on your next break. Most of us would miss our computers and the information systems we have available through them to help us with these tasks. They add "value" to our lives.

The same is true for most business organizations. They depend on computer information systems to complete their daily tasks and to add value to their organization.

Watch the following video on using a computer to your advantage:

www.youtube.com/watch?v=M56YKleMdNs&feature=related.

Deliverable:

Based on the video, list five (5) benefits mentioned for using information systems in a business. However, there are many other ways in which a business depends on information systems. Also name five (5) other benefits an information system can provide. Think of ways you have used information systems to interface with a business and the value you have found.

Quiz Questions:

1. Based on the video, which of the following would *not* be a benefit of a computer-based information system?
   (a) Global customer access
   (b) Decreased revenue
   (c) Reduced costs
   (d) Instant information

2. Based on the video, what is the biggest value of computer-based information systems in business?
   (a) Reduced costs
   (b) Instant distribution channel
   (c) Increased revenue
   (d) Current information

3. Information systems are important to:
   (a) Organizations
   (b) Society
   (c) People
   (d) All of the above

4. What are some ways in which computer information systems can help reduce costs?
   (a) Customer mailings
   (b) Letter writing
   (c) Administrative activities
   (d) All of the above

Discussion Question:

In our daily activities, we interact with many computer-based information systems. Think of places you have been in just the last week where an information system was being used to complete a transaction or activity. What would have been different had no computer system been available?

1.4 | Why Are Information Systems Important to Society?

This section explains in greater detail why IT is important to society as a whole. Other examples of the impacts of IT on society appear throughout the book.

IT Affects Our Quality of Life

IT has significant implications for our quality of life. The workplace can be expanded from the traditional 9-to-5 job at a central location to 24 hours a day at any location. IT can provide employees with flexibility that can significantly improve the quality of leisure time, even if it does not increase the total amount of leisure time.

From the opposite perspective, however, IT can also place employees on "constant call" where they are never truly away from the office, even when they are on vacation. In fact, a recent poll revealed that 80 percent of respondents took their laptop computers on their most recent vacations, and 100 percent took their cell phones. Going further, 80 percent did some work while vacationing, and almost all of them checked their e-mail.

Robot Revolution on the Way

Once restricted largely to science fiction movies, robots that can perform practical tasks are becoming more common. In fact, "cyberpooches," nursebots, and other mechanical beings may be our companions before we know it. Around the world, quasi-autonomous devices have become increasingly common on factory floors, in hospital corridors, and in farm fields. In our homes, iRobot (www.irobot.com) produces the Roomba to vacuum our floors, the Scooba to wash our floors, the Dirt Dog to sweep our garages, the Verro to clean our pools, and the Looj to clean our gutters.

Telepresence robots are a recent development in the field of robotics. The following example illustrates how organizations use these robots.

EXAMPLE

Telepresence robots have been humorously described as a cross between a Segway and Wall-E. These robots are designed to help companies save money on travel and on expensive teleconferencing technology. The robots enable people in remote offices or locations to have a rich communications experience without having to use a complicated videoconferencing system.

A telepresence robot has both a video camera and a video screen embedded in its "head." It also has wheels and can be moved around remotely by computer. It is designed to steer its way clear of obstacles or people.

The robots let a person maintain a consistent connection with co-workers, customers, or clients. The human user places the robot at a remote location and directs it to move around—for example, around a conference room during a meeting—while broadcasting what is going on to the human controlling it from afar. Interestingly, the robots actually break down barriers of awkwardness that people sometimes feel in person-to-person meetings.

Although this technology is rather expensive, some companies are buying multiple units to place in their remote locations. That way, someone running a meeting could obtain an easy and flexible view into what is being said—and what is being written on a whiteboard, for example—in each location, without having to spend hundreds of thousands of dollars on travel costs.

Business managers are using telepresence robots to walk factory floors. Healthcare organizations are employing them for home care. Storage companies are utilizing them for security. In the retail environment, a robot could wander the floor with a customer who asks it purchasing or support questions. The person controlling the robot could answer the questions, essentially making the robot a mechanical sales clerk.

Consider how Reimers Electra Steam uses a telepresence robot. One of the firm's electrical engineers, John Samuels, moved from the company's location in Virginia to the Dominican Republic. At first, he would attend meetings in Virginia through Skype. If he needed to see something on the shop floor, a colleague would carry around a laptop, pointing it to wherever Samuels instructed. Essentially, someone had to act as the remote virtual body for Samuels, and if

In an example of precision agriculture, Carnegie Mellon University in Pittsburgh has developed self-directing tractors that harvest hundreds of acres of crops around the clock in California. These "robot tractors" use global positioning systems (GPSs) combined with video image processing that identifies rows of uncut crops.

Many robotic devices are also being developed for military purposes. For example, the Pentagon is researching self-driving vehicles and beelike swarms of small surveillance robots, each of which would contribute a different view or angle of a combat zone. The Predator, an unmanned aerial vehicle (UAV), is being used in Iraq, Libya, Pakistan, and Afghanistan.

It probably will be a long time before we see robots making decisions by themselves, handling unfamiliar situations, and interacting with people. Nevertheless, robots are extremely helpful in various environments, particularly environments that are repetitive, harsh, or dangerous to humans.

Improvements in Healthcare

IT has brought about major improvements in healthcare delivery. Medical personnel use IT to make better and faster diagnoses and to monitor critically ill patients more accurately. IT also has streamlined the process of researching and developing new drugs. Expert systems now help doctors diagnose diseases, and machine vision is enhancing the work of radiologists. Surgeons use virtual reality to plan complex surgeries. They also have used a surgical robot to perform long-distance surgery by controlling the robot's movements. In addition, doctors discuss complex medical cases via videoconferencing, and new computer simulations recreate the sense of touch, allowing doctors-in-training to perform virtual procedures without risking harm to an actual patient.

Of the thousands of other applications related to healthcare, administrative systems are critically important. These systems range from detecting insurance fraud to creating nursing schedules to financial and marketing management.

The Internet contains vast amounts of useful medical information (see www.webmd.com, for example). In an interesting study, researchers at the Princess Alexandra Hospital in Brisbane, Australia, identified 26 difficult diagnostic cases published in the *New England Journal of Medicine*. They selected three to five search terms from each case and then conducted a Google search. The researchers selected and recorded the three diagnoses that Google ranked most prominently and that appeared to fit the symptoms and signs. They then compared these results with the correct diagnoses as published in the journal. They discovered that their Google searches had found the correct diagnosis in 15 of the 26 cases, a success rate of 57 percent. The researchers caution, however, against the dangers of self-diagnosis. They maintain that people should use the information gained from Google and medical Web sites such as WebMD only to participate in their healthcare by asking questions of their physician.

BEFORE *YOU GO ON . . .*

1. What are some of the quality-of-life improvements made possible by IT? Has IT had any negative effects on our quality of life?
2. Describe the robotic revolution, and consider its possible implications for humans.
3. Explain how IT has improved healthcare practices.

1. How might a well-designed IS impact Ruby's employees? Specifically, how might it impact Ruben and Lisa? What aspects of running a club would be easier on a computer than on paper?

2. Do you think the addition of an IS would create or eliminate jobs at Ruby's?

Student Activity 1.4

Objective: To explore ways in which computers and information systems have become a part of our everyday life not only in the work place but also in our personal lives.

Chapter Connection: This case relates to Chapter 1, Introduction to Information Systems, Section 1.4: "Why Are Information Systems Important to Society?"

Prerequisites: The student should read Section 1.4 before doing this exercise to become familiar with the influence information systems have had on society.

Activity:

One thing we all use information systems and the Internet for is to communicate with friends, family, and colleagues. Many use e-mail, Facebook, or other social networking sites to do this. However, what if you want to collaborate with others online? Google Docs provides an easy and free way to do this.

To do this exercise, you must first have a valid Gmail account. If you do not have a Gmail account, go to www.google.com, click "Gmail" at the top, and create a new account. Then click on the following link:

    docs.google.com

View samples of all that you can create using Google Docs.

Click ▶ Watch the videos to get an overview of how Google Docs works and its benefits.

Deliverable:

To really understand the benefits of Google Docs, you need to work in a group so you can share files. Select another classmate or two and create some documents together.

1. Create a document that has the following information:

    (a) The name of your university

    (b) The name, section, teacher, and meeting time of your class

    (c) The names of all teammates

    (d) A brief summary *written together* of some ways in which you feel you could use Google Docs in your classes. Have *each team member* add his or her own ideas and comments.

2. Create a presentation for the group with the following content:

    (a) An initial slide with the following:

        i. Class name, section, teacher, meeting time, and room

        ii. University name and location

    (b) A slide *for each member* of the team (created by each member) to include:

        i. Full name

        ii. Major and minor

        iii. Hometown

        iv. Some personal information, such as hobbies, children, jobs, and so on

        v. Student picture

Quiz Questions:

1. What can be created using Google Docs?

    (a) Resume
    (b) Monthly budget
    (c) Flowchart
    (d) All of the above

2. When using Google Docs, when are revisions saved?

    (a) When the session is complete
    (b) At the end of the day
    (c) Immediately
    (d) When you click "Save"

3. What can be included in a Google Docs presentation?
   (a) Images
   (b) Videos
   (c) Speaker notes
   (d) All of the above

4. What is used to collaborate with others in a "live" mode in Google Docs?
   (a) E-mail
   (b) Chat
   (c) Texting
   (d) All of the above

5. All documents created on Google Docs start out with what type of access?
   (a) Private
   (b) Public
   (c) Availability to anyone with link
   (d) All of the above

Discussion Questions:

Now that you have used Google Docs, discuss some of the benefits of its use. What are some ways in which you could use Google Docs on campus, at work, or at home?

What's in IT for ME?

 In a previous section of this chapter, we discussed how IT supports each of the functional areas of the organization. Here we examine the MIS function.

FOR THE MIS MAJOR

 The MIS function directly supports all other functional areas in an organization. That is, the MIS function is responsible for providing the information that each functional area needs in order to make decisions. The overall objective of MIS personnel is to help users improve performance and solve business problems using IT. To accomplish this objective, MIS personnel must understand both the information requirements and the technology associated with each functional area. Given their position, however, MIS personnel must think "business needs" first and "technology" second.

>>> SUMMARY

1. **Begin the process of becoming an informed user of your organization's information systems. The benefits of being an informed user of IT include the following:**

   > You will benefit more from your organization's IT applications because you will understand what is "behind" those applications.

   > You will be able to provide input into your organization's IT applications, thus improving the quality of those applications.

   > You will quickly be in a position to recommend, or participate in the selection of IT applications that your organization will use.

> You will be able to keep up with rapid developments in existing information technologies, as well as the introduction of new technologies.

> You will understand the potential impacts that "new and improved" technologies will have on your organization and, therefore, will be qualified to make recommendations concerning their adoption and use.

> You will play a key role in managing the information systems in your organization.

> You will be in a position to use IT if you decide to start your own business.

2. Define the terms *data*, *information*, and *knowledge*, and give examples of each.

> *Data* items refer to an elementary description of things, events, activities, and transactions that are recorded, classified, and stored but are not organized to convey any specific meaning. Examples of data items are a collection of numbers (e.g., 3.11, 2.96, 3.95, 1.99, 2.08) and characters (e.g., B, A, C, A, B, D, F, C).

> *Information* is data that have been organized so that they have meaning and value to the recipient. For example, a grade point average (GPA) by itself is data, but a student's name coupled with his or her GPA is information. In these examples, the numbers could be GPAs, and the letters could be grades in an Introduction to MIS class.

> *Knowledge* consists of data and/or information that have been organized and processed to convey understanding, experience, accumulated learning, and expertise as they apply to a current business problem. For example, a company recruiting at your school has found over time that students with GPAs over 3.0 have enjoyed the greatest success in its management program. Based on this accumulated knowledge, that company may decide to interview only those students with GPAs over 3.0.

3. Define the terms information technology, information system, computer-based information system, and application.

> *Information technology* (IT) relates to any computer-based tool that people use to work with information and to support the information and information-processing needs of an organization.

> An *information system* (IS) collects, processes, stores, analyzes, and disseminates information for a specific purpose. A *computer-based information system* (CBIS) is an information system that uses computer technology to perform some or all of its intended tasks. An *application* (or *app*) is a computer program designed to support a specific task or business process.

4. Identify several ways in which you depend on information technology in your daily life.

You are practicing continuous computing, where you are surrounded with a movable information network. Think of all you do online, often with your phone: register for classes; take classes, and not just classes from your university; access class syllabi, information, PowerPoints, and lectures; conduct banking; pay your bills; research, shop, and buy products from companies or other people; sell your "stuff"; search for, and apply for, jobs; have your own page on Facebook; text and tweet your friends and family throughout your day; and many other activities.

5. Discuss three ways in which information technology can impact managers and three ways in which it can impact nonmanagerial workers.

Potential IT impacts on managers:

> IT may reduce the number of middle managers.

> IT will provide managers with real-time or near real-time information, meaning that managers will have less time to make decisions.

> IT will increase the likelihood that managers will have to supervise geographically dispersed employees and teams.

Potential IT impacts on nonmanagerial workers:

> IT may eliminate jobs.

> IT may cause employees to experience a loss of identity.

> IT may cause job stress and physical problems, such as repetitive stress injury.

> List three positive and three negative societal effects of the increased use of information technology.

Positive societal effects:

> IT can provide opportunities for people with disabilities.

> IT can provide people with flexibility in their work (e.g., work from anywhere, anytime).

> Robots can take over mundane chores.

> IT can enable improvements in healthcare.

Negative societal effects:

> IT can cause health problems for individuals.

> IT can place employees on constant call.

> IT can potentially misinform patients about their health problems.

application (app) A computer program designed to support a specific task or business process.

business intelligence (BI) systems Provide computer-based support for complex, nonroutine decisions, primarily for middle managers and knowledge workers.

computer-based information system (CBIS) An information system that uses computer technology to perform some or all of its intended tasks.

dashboards (or **digital dashboards**) A special form of IS that supports all managers of the organization by providing rapid access to timely information and direct access to structured information in the form of reports.

data items Elementary descriptions of things, events, activities, and transactions that are recorded, classified, and stored but are not organized to convey any specific meaning.

database A collection of related files or tables containing data.

electronic commerce (e-commerce) system A type of interorganizational information system that enables organizations to conduct transactions, called business-to-business (B2B) electronic commerce, and customers to conduct transactions with businesses, called business-to-consumer (B2C) electronic commerce.

enterprise resource planning (ERP) systems ISs that correct a lack of communication among the FAISs by tightly integrating the functional area ISs via a common database.

ergonomics The science of adapting machines and work environments to people with the goal of creating an environment that is safe, well lit, and comfortable.

expert systems (ESs) Attempt to duplicate the work of human experts by applying reasoning capabilities, knowledge, and expertise within a specific domain.

functional area information systems (FAISs) ISs that support a particular functional area within the organization.

hardware A device such as a processor, monitor, keyboard, or printer. Together, these devices accept data and information, process them, and display them.

information Data that have been organized so that they have meaning and value to the recipient.

information system (IS) Collects, processes, stores, analyzes, and disseminates information for a specific purpose.

information technology (IT) Relates to any computer-based tool that people use to work with information and support the information and information-processing needs of an organization.

information technology (IT) components Hardware, software, databases, and networks.

information technology (IT) infrastructure IT components plus IT services.

information technology (IT) platform Formed by the IT components of hardware, software, networks (wireline and wireless), and databases.

information technology (IT) services IT personnel use IT components to perform these IT services: develop information systems, oversee security and risk, and manage data.

informed user A person knowledgeable about information systems and information technology.

interorganizational information systems (IOSs) Information systems that connect two or more organizations.

knowledge Data and/or information that have been organized and processed to convey understanding, experience, accumulated learning, and expertise as they apply to a current problem or activity.

knowledge workers Professional employees, such as financial and marketing analysts, engineers, lawyers, and accountants, who are experts in a particular subject area and create information and knowledge, which they integrate into the business.

network A connecting system (wireline or wireless) that permits different computers to share resources.

office automation systems (OASs) Typically support clerical staff, lower and middle managers, and knowledge workers to develop documents, schedule resources, and communicate.

procedures The set of instructions about how to combine the components of information technology in order to process information and generate the desired output.

software A program or collection of programs that enable the hardware to process data.

supply chain The flow of materials, information, money, and services from suppliers of raw materials through factories and warehouses to the end customers.

transaction processing system (TPS) Supports the monitoring, collection, storage, and processing of data from the organization's basic business transactions, each of which generates data.

>>> DISCUSSION QUESTIONS

1. Describe a business that you would like to start. Discuss how you would use global outsourcing to accomplish your goals.

2. Your university wants to recruit high-quality high school students from your state. Provide examples of (a) the data that your recruiters would gather in this process, (b) the information that your recruiters would process from these data, and (c) the types of knowledge that your recruiters would infer from this information.

3. Can the terms *data*, *information*, and *knowledge* have different meanings for different people? Support your answer with examples.

4. Information technology makes it possible to "never be out of touch." Discuss the pros and cons of always being available to your employers and clients (regardless of where you are or what you are doing).

5. Robots have the positive impact of being able to relieve humans from working in dangerous conditions. What are some negative impacts of robots in the workplace?

6. Is it possible to endanger yourself by accessing too much medical information on the Web? Why or why not? Support your answer.

7. Is the vast amount of medical information on the Web a good thing? Answer from the standpoint of a patient and from the standpoint of a physician.

8. Describe other potential impacts of IT on societies as a whole.

9. What are the major reasons why it is important for employees in all functional areas to become familiar with IT?

10. Refer to the study at Princess Alexandra Hospital (see "Improvements in Healthcare"). How do you feel about Google searches finding the correct diagnosis in 57 percent of the cases? Are you impressed with these results? Why or why not? What are the implications of this study for self-diagnosis?

>>> PROBLEM-SOLVING ACTIVITIES

1. Visit some Web sites that offer employment opportunities in IT. Prominent examples are www.dice.com, www.monster.com, www.collegerecruiter.com, www.careerbuilder.com, www.jobcentral.com, www.job.com, www.career.com, www.simplyhired.com, and www.truecareers.com. Compare the IT salaries to salaries offered to accountants, marketing personnel, financial personnel, operations personnel, and human resources personnel. For other information on IT salaries, check *Computerworld*'s annual salary survey.

2. Enter the Web site of UPS (www.ups.com).

   a. Find out what information is available to customers before they send a package.

   b. Find out about the "package tracking" system.

   c. Compute the cost of delivering a 10″ × 20″ × 15″ box, weighing 40 pounds, from your hometown to Long Beach, California (or to Lansing, Michigan, if you live in or near Long Beach). Compare the fastest delivery against the least cost.

3. Surf the Internet for information about the Department of Homeland Security (DHS). Examine the available information, and comment on the role of information technologies in the department.

4. Access www.irobot.com, and investigate the company's robots for education and research. Surf the Web for other companies that manufacture robots, and compare their products with those of iRobot.

>>> TEAM ASSIGNMENTS

1. a. Create an online group for studying IT or an aspect of IT that you are interested in. Each member of the group must establish a free Yahoo! e-mail account. Go to http://groups.yahoo.com.

   Step 1: Click on "Start Your Group."

   Step 2: Select a category that best describes your group (use Search Group Categories, or use the Browse Group Categories tool). Yahoo will force you to be very specific in categorizing your group. Continue until you see the button "Place My Group Here."

   Step 3: Name your group.

   Step 4: Enter your group e-mail address.

   Step 5: Describe your group.

   Step 6: Select your Yahoo! Profile and e-mail addresses for your group.

   Step 7: Customize your group and invite people to join.

   Step 8: Conduct a discussion online of at least two topics of interest to the group.

   Step 9: Find a similar group (use Yahoo's "Find a Group" and make a connection). Write a report for your instructor.

   b. Now, follow the same steps for Google Groups.

   c. Compare Yahoo Groups and Google Groups.

2. Review the *Wall Street Journal*, *Fortune*, *BusinessWeek*, and local newspapers for the last three months to find stories about the use of computer-based information systems in organizations. Each group will prepare a report describing five applications. The reports should emphasize the role of each application and its benefit to the organization. Present and discuss your work.

CLOSING **CASE 1** > Revolution!

<<<**THE PROBLEM**

In January 2011, the modern Arab world's first successful popular uprising, called the Jasmine Revolution (named for the national flower), erupted in Tunisia when a small-town policewoman slapped a fruit seller named Mohammed Bouazizi and ordered him to pack up his street cart. Bouazizi was a computer science graduate who was unable to find any work as a computer technician. As a result, he was forced to sell fruit to support his seven siblings. Bouazizi, like many young, educated Tunisians, was frustrated by the overall lack of opportunities. For him, the slap was the final straw. He went to the governor's office and demanded an appointment, threatening to set himself on fire in public if the governor refused to see him. Despite this dire warning, he was turned away. In response, on December 17, 2010, Bouazizi carried out his threat. When he died 18 days later, his story went viral, providing millions of angry young Tunisians with a martyr. Vast numbers of protestors took to the streets, sparking the Jasmine Revolution.

The Jasmine Revolution did not need any prominent leaders to rally the protesters or to organize the demonstrations. Instead, the revolution was fueled by a steady stream of anonymous text messages and Twitter and Facebook updates. Documents posted on WikiLeaks (see Chapter 6), in which U.S. diplomats had cataloged the corruption at the highest levels of the Tunisian government, deepened the popular rage. Mobile phone videos posted online documented the government's brutal response, including scenes of the police beating and shooting at protestors, leading to at least a hundred deaths. The protesters used the one weapon they understood much better than the government: the Internet. Young Tunisians—educated, multilingual, and wired—devised strategies to evade the government's crude firewalls. Protestors spent several hours each day on Facebook and other social networks. By rendering the state television and radio stations irrelevant, they were able to undermine the regime's propaganda for the first time in many years. Finally, on January 14, 2011, President Ben Ali was forced into exile.

Later that month another popular uprising broke out in a different Middle Eastern and Arab country: Egypt. In 2010, Khaled Saied, a young man from Alexandria with no history of political activism, had been beaten to death by the police. Protesters rallied around a Facebook page entitled "We Are All Khaled Saied." Mr. Saied's death became the focal point for Egyptians who had not been previously involved in the protest movement. Beginning on January 25, 2011, millions of protesters from a variety of backgrounds and religions demanded the overthrow of Egyptian President Hosni Mubarak, who had held office since 1981.

<<<**AN ATTEMPTED SOLUTION**

In an effort to silence the demonstrators and avoid the fate Tunisia's President Ben Ali, Mubarak "turned off the Internet." At 12:34 AM on January 28, Egypt's four primary Internet providers—Link Egypt, Vodafone/Raya, Telecom Egypt, and Etisalat Misr—all went "dark." That is, the four providers stopped transmitting all Internet traffic into and out of Egypt. The blackout appeared to be designed to disrupt the organization of the country's protest movement.

<<<**THE RESULTS**

"When countries block, we evolve," an activist with the group We Rebuild wrote in a Twitter message on January 28. We Rebuild and other activist groups scrambled to keep the country connected to the outside world, turning to landline telephones, fax machines, and even ham radio to keep information flowing in and out of Egypt.

The activists were successful. On February 2, Egypt's embattled leaders realized that the communications blockage was largely ineffective and indeed counterproductive. The shutdown proved to be more of a source of fresh anger than an impediment to the protest movement. Protesters had no trouble gathering larger and larger crowds, culminating with an estimated 250,000 people who assembled in central Cairo on January 29 to demand an end to Mubarak's rule. On February 11, following weeks of determined popular protest and pressures, Mubarak resigned from office.

The Jasmine Revolution and Egyptian Revolution helped to instigate major uprisings throughout the Middle East and North Africa. By April 2011, Algeria, Bahrain, Iran, Jordan, Libya, Morocco, and Yemen had all experienced major protests, and minor incidents had occurred in Iraq, Kuwait, Mauritania, Oman, Saudi Arabia, Somalia, Sudan, and Syria.

1. Describe how information technology enabled the Jasmine and Egyptian Revolutions.

2. Describe efforts by the Tunisian and Egyptian governments to quell the revolutions. In particular, describe the efforts that were directed at information technology.

3. Discuss how information technology contributed to higher oil prices and higher prices you pay for gasoline.

SOURCES: Compiled from J. Solomon and *C. Levinson," West to Isolate Gadhafi," Wall Street Journal*, February 26–27, 2011; "The Faces of Egypt's 'Revolution 2.0," *CNN.com*, February 21, 2011; "After Egypt, People Power Hits Like a Tsunami," *CNN.com*, February 15, 2011; "Egyptian President Steps Down Amidst Groundbreaking Digital Revolution," *CNN.com*, February 11, 2011; C. Levinson, M. Coker, and J. Solomon, "How Cairo, U.S. Were Blindsided by Revolution," *Wall Street Journal*, February 2, 2011; P. McNamara, "Egypt Lifts Blockade on Internet Service," *Network World*, February 2, 2011; V. Blue, "#Egypt Blocked in China: Is Internet Access a Human Right?" *ZDNet.com*, January 31, 2011; V. Walt, "Tunisia's Nervous Neighbors Watch the Jasmine Revolution," *Time*, January 31, 2011; N. Gohring and R. McMillan, "Without Internet, Egyptians Find New Ways to Get Online," *Computerworld*, January 28, 2011; J. Robertson, "The Day Part of the Internet Died: Egypt Goes Dark," *USA Today*, January 28, 2011; "Tunisia's Revolution Should Be Wake-Up Call to Middle East Autocrats," *Washington Post*, January 15, 2011.

CLOSING **CASE 2 >**

L'Oréal Retools Its Information Systems

THE PROBLEM >>> Headquartered in France, the L'Oréal Group (www.loreal.com) is the world's largest cosmetic and beauty products company. Concentrating on hair color, skin care, sun protection, makeup, perfumes, and hair care, the company is active in dermatology and pharmaceuticals. The company's philosophy is that everyone aspires to beauty, and its core mission is to help people around the world realize that aspiration.

L'Oréal employs more than 67,000 people in 130 countries, and it supports 23 global brands. The firm's products are manufactured in more than 40 factories located around the world. The company has a tremendous challenge to produce high-quality, consistent products globally. It must ensure that all of its products are created with uniform production processes and quality control.

By 2010 L'Oréal had come to realize that its current enterprise resource planning (ERP) system, based on software manufactured by SAP, could not support its goal of global product uniformity without consolidating its many different information systems located around the world. For example, L'Oréal had multiple versions of SAP running in different regions and countries. As a result, the company used to take between two and five years to upgrade to the latest version of SAP. L'Oréal also wanted to improve productivity, safety, and quality by standardizing the best-practice business processes throughout the firm.

THE SOLUTION >>> To accomplish its mission, L'Oréal re-engineered its entire manufacturing process to work more efficiently while still supporting the quality and integrity of its brands. The company integrated its SAP ERP system with Apriso's (www.apriso.com) FlexNet for operations management. FlexNet is a unified set of manufacturing software applications that coordinate a company's manufacturing operations within a plant, between plants, and across an entire supply chain. The integration of SAP and FlexNet resulted in a global, central IT system called the Integrated Solution for Industrial Systems (ISIS). ISIS consists of all the transactional applications, financial controls, and purchasing transactions integrated into the manufacturing operations on the plant floor. FlexNet and

ISIS support all factory processes—including production, quality assurance, and purchasing—while promoting L'Oréal's best practices.

ISIS runs in L'Oréal's central data center in Montpellier, France, where the master data for the business are stored. FlexNet runs on servers located in individual factories so that each factory can continue operations in case a problem arises in the central data center.

In its re-engineering process, L'Oréal implemented a single, global instance of SAP and FlexNet, so the last upgrade took only one weekend. By upgrading so quickly, the firm was able to update its systems without disrupting its factories. <<<**THE RESULTS**

The new software implementation also allows L'Oréal to bring factories online much more quickly. In the past, when L'Oréal acquired a factory, it took years to bring it online. In contrast, the new software enabled L'Oréal to integrate, in two months, an Yves St. Laurent factory that it had acquired, along with its quality assurance, safety, and efficiency practices.

Every one of L'Oréal's manufacturing facilities handles thousands of different recipes for L'Oréal cosmetic products. Every ingredient must be tested for quality, and every worker must follow each recipe exactly. This demanding level of complexity can lead to human error, which can threaten quality, slow the workflow, and create waste. The new software guides the operators through each recipe and automatically records the weight of each ingredient to ensure that the quantities are exactly correct. Once raw materials are tested for quality, they are given a label that the worker must scan before adding them to the recipe. This step ensures that all materials are tested. The labels also give forklift drivers directions as to which materials need to be taken to the packaging station. They also provide information on shelf life. Shop workers confirm that the new system is easy to use and has reduced confusion and stress.

By deploying a single, global instance of SAP and FlexNet, L'Oréal has increased its overall capacity, decreased its discrepancies in actual-versus-planned production, and reduced its wasted materials. As a result, the company is able to maintain lower, better-managed inventories at significant cost savings.

Questions

1. Describe several reasons why L'Oréal needed to reengineer its information systems.

2. Describe the benefits of L'Oréal's new information systems. Explain how the benefits you describe are related to L'Oréal's strategic goals, using specific examples to support your arguments.

SOURCES: Compiled from J. Playe, "L'Oréal's Manufacturing Makeover," *Baseline Magazine*, January 28, 2011; "Business Process Management in Manufacturing," *Aberdeen Research Report*, January 20, 2011; M. Littlefield, "Business Process Management in Manufacturing: Paving the Way for Effective Collaboration," *Aberdeen Research Report*, November 30, 2010; M. Johnson, "What's Happening with ERP Today," *CIO*, January 27, 2010; E. Lai, "Microsoft Brings BI to the Cloud," *Computerworld*, April 30, 2009; www.loreal.com, www.apriso.com, accessed March 1, 2011.

RUBY'S CLUB INTERNSHIP ASSIGNMENTS

Ruben and Lisa are seriously considering integrating technology into their club. However, they still need a little convincing because of their lack of experience with computers. Right now, they only have one old computer that is still running Windows XP. Just last year, they finally decided to have cable Internet installed so they could place product orders more quickly. Neither Ruben nor Lisa is on Facebook or Twitter.

For now, Ruben and Lisa need to know what types of IS are available and what they can do with them. With the information in this chapter regarding the different types and uses of ISs, write a business letter to Ruby's Club, detailing how the use of IS may help Ruben and Lisa manage their club on a day-to-day basis. Be sure to include information about the generation they serve and employ (*Homo conexus*) and how those people are already very connected and extremely comfortable with the use of computers and networks. Submit your letter to your instructor.

SPREADSHEET ACTIVITY

Objective: You need to understand the possible application of a spreadsheet as much as how to perform specific tasks. It is the endless application of skills that make spreadsheets so powerful. This activity will show you that this tool can be used for a variety of situations and purposes.

Chapter Connection: Data, information, and knowledge are the main focus of this chapter. Spreadsheets are just one of many tools (albeit the most widespread and easily accessible) that can be used to manage data, information, and knowledge.

Prerequisites: There are no prerequisites for this activity.

Activity: As the text introduces the concepts of *data*, *information*, and *knowledge*, this activity will introduce you to the vast possibilities of using spreadsheets to help manage and control data. Unmanaged data will never provide information or knowledge, and so it is imperative to understand not only how to use a spreadsheet but the possibilities of when to use it. Consider the following three examples, and then develop your own ideas about how spreadsheets can be used.

- *Individual:* Money is something everyone has to deal with. A spreadsheet is a great tool to help track and manage personal finances. Someone with a spreadsheet budget can quickly see where his or her money is being spent and make plans for where it will go in the future. With a little creativity and experience, one can quickly create a personal spreadsheet that will help track finances without purchasing a boxed program.

- *Organizations:* It is still the simple things that make a big difference. Companies still seek better ways to manage inventory, and often these systems incorporate a spreadsheet. Many supply chain management tools will export data into spreadsheets for analysis. Once in a spreadsheet, charts and graphs can be used to easily display how inventory is being handled.

- *Society:* Every 10 years, the U.S. government performs a census. Much of this information is available to the public. Much interesting information can be gained by placing these data in a spreadsheet. Charts and graphs can be used to analyze population changes, employment rates, demographic information, and trends over time. Spreadsheets can be used to tell a story with this information.

Having read these descriptions, describe to your professor three things about each example that a computer-based information system (in our case, a spreadsheet) would help. For example, you could say that a spreadsheet could help manage bills (individual), keep up with sales (organizations), and determine average salaries for a given area (society). Think of two examples for each case, describe them, and submit your work to your professor.

Deliverables: Students will write a paragraph demonstrating their own examples of the three areas already described in the activity. Follow up each application (individual, organizational, societal) with a description of the scenario that describes the business problem/need as well as the spreadsheet's answer.

Quiz Questions:

1. Spreadsheets are useful to individuals (as opposed to organizations or society at large) for which of the following reasons?

   (a) Tracking inventory

   (b) Budgeting

(c) Tracking population changes

(d) All of the above

2. True or False: Spreadsheets are best kept in the world of mathematics and not applied to business problems.

3. Data are collected and placed in a spreadsheet and organized to help generate which of the following?

   (a) Knowledge workers

   (b) Engineers

   (c) Information

   (d) Wisdom

4. True or False: Raw facts in a spreadsheet are considered to be information.

Discussion Questions:

1. For data to be turned into information, they often need to be cleaned, organized, calculated, and ultimately presented in some graphical format. Spreadsheets are excellent at all of these. Discuss three tools that help spreadsheets accomplish all of these goals.

2. Students have generated their own ideas for using spreadsheets. Be prepared to discuss your ideas with the class at large. Hopefully, you did not all come up with the same possibilities as other students, and this will help broaden their horizons even more.

Suggested Solution: There is no suggested solution. There is no end to the possible applications of spreadsheet tools. This is the major point of this exercise. It does not teach you anything in particular (although you may learn something); it simply opens your eyes to see that this tool will apply to you sometime. Hopefully it will make things more real to you as you work through the following exercises.

DATABASE ACTIVITY: INTRODUCTION TO THE DATABASE PROJECT

Objective

How to open and use an existing Access database, even if you've never done it before.

Chapter Connection

All aspects of modern information systems depend on shared databases. Being able to work with them is essential to any manager or knowledge worker of the twenty-first century. In this chapter, you saw how every department in a modern organization uses information systems. You saw how different departments use them differently: human resources staff in recruiting, marketing managers to select marketing channels, manufacturing coordinators to develop production schedules. Much of this information is not just for one part of the organization. Order information from sales, for example, goes to manufacturing (if you sell something, it must be produced), purchasing (materials come from suppliers), accounting (payments, adjustments to inven-

tory values), and more. Linking an organization through a shared database is a major benefit of today's systems.

These uses depend on data. You'll read more about that later in this book. However, it is never too early to start thinking about information systems in terms of the data they use. Computers can only work with the data they have. Having the right data is vital to any IS.

Prerequisites

None.

Activity:

1. Download the Ch 01 NeTrouble database from the Web site and double-click to open it.

2. Familiarize yourself with the parts of the Access window you see. The main ones are shown in Figure 1A.1. (It is from a different database, but the window has the same parts.)

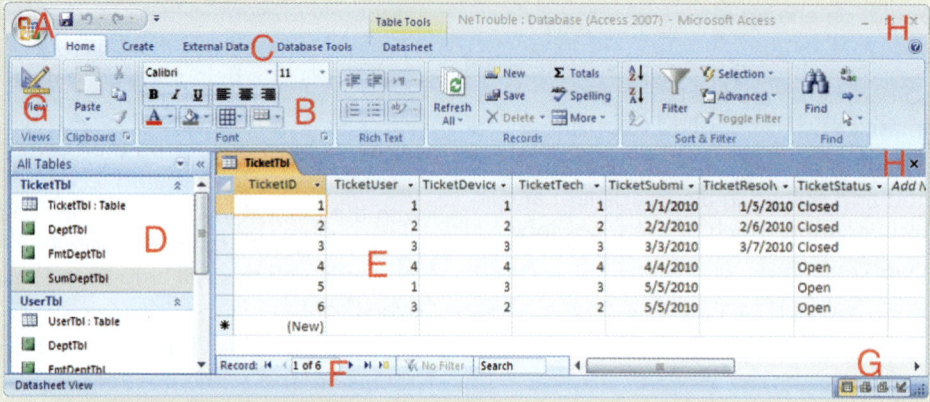

Figure 1A.1 Microsoft Access: Screen shot 1.

The ribbon, A, provides tools to manipulate your database. The tools depend on the object you are working with and are organized into groups accessed via tabs (B). The tabs vary with object type, but there will always be a Home tab at the left and a Create tab next to it.

The arrangement of the icons on the ribbon depends on how much space Access has to spread them out. Vary the width of your window to see how they rearrange as it becomes narrower. (On most displays it starts out wide enough for a full array, so making it wider will not change anything.) The sections stay the same, but some tools may lose their labels or disappear under an arrow indicating a pull-down menu when space is tight.

The File tab, letter C, controls the database as a file. You open, close, and save your work here. In Office 2007, this was done via the Office button. Prior releases used a File menu.

The navigation pane, D, lists the objects in the current database. You can choose which types of objects it lists via the pull-down menu that opens when you click the down arrow to the right of "All Tables." Each object type has its own icon. In the screen shot, the spreadsheets represent tables; the green booklets, reports.

Usage Hint: If you see just "Navigation Pane" vertically at the left of the window, click on that text or the » above to expand it. The « at the top of the navigation pane in the screen shot shrinks the pane. That leaves more space for other items.

The main part of the window, E, houses all open objects. The screen shot shows a data table. Each object has a tab with its name at the top. Clicking a tab brings that object to the front. You probably do not see any open tables in your database yet.

The navigation area, F, lets you move through individual records in a database. Here, it shows "1 in 6" corresponding to the highlighted first record of 6 in the table.

Most Access objects can be manipulated in several *views*. A table, for example, has one view (Datasheet

view) for reading and editing data, another (Design view) for designing the table itself. You can switch views by clicking the icon at the left of the ribbon (G), by pulling down the menu there, or via the icons at the lower right of the window (also G).

The Access window has two Close boxes (H). The one at the top right of the object area closes the object in front (here, the table TicketTbl). If other objects are open, one of them will now be in front. The Close box at the top right of the window closes the application and exits Access. (It prompts you to save unsaved work first.)

3. Open UserTbl (short for "User Table"). How many records are in it?

Usage Hint: Access can be set to open objects with a single or double click in the navigation pane. If you are using a personal copy, you can set this preference via Options under the File ribbon tab. Click Current Database, then Navigation Options.

4. Sort this table by date of birth: Click in the UserDOB column to select it, then click the top (A to Z) sorting icon in the Sort & Filter section under the ribbon. Who is the oldest user? How old is he or she?

5. Look at the UserDept (User Department) column of the User table. It does not have department names. Instead, it has numbers. The first user, Adam, is from Department 1.

6. Open DeptTbl (Department Table). What is the name of Department 1?

7. Open UserRpt (User Report). Adam is listed under that department. Access used his department number to connect his name in the user table with the department name in the department table. This is how relational databases link different types of data. How many users in the marketing department submitted network trouble tickets? After you find the answer, close the report.

8. Open UserFrm (User Form). You'll see information about the first user, Adam. In the navigation area

at the bottom of the window, F in the figure, click on the far right icon to insert a new record. Enter reasonable data. For the user's department, pick any department from the list to the right of the legend "Select department." What department did you pick? Note the User ID number of your new user. Click the New Record icon again to save your work.

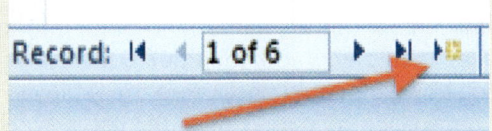

Figure 1A.2 Microsoft Access: Screen shot 2.

Usage Hint: Access saves new data in the database as soon as you exit a record. Changes to the design of the database, however, are saved only upon command.

9. Now open TicketTbl. Click in the "New" row of the table. Do not enter anything in the first column; it will be filled automatically with the next number. In the next column, TicketUser, enter the number of the user you just created. In the next two columns, TicketDevice and TicketTech, fill in any numbers that are already used in the existing rows of the table. In the next two, enter any dates you want. (If you click on the calendar icon that appears when you select either of those fields, you can use a built-in calendar to select dates.) In the last column, enter any data you want.

10. Open UserRpt again. How many users are in that department now?

Usage Hint: Reports are not automatically updated when data are changed. You have to close and reopen them.

Usage Hint: The reason you created a ticket for your new user is that this report shows only users who have submitted trouble tickets. It could have been designed to show all users, whether or not they submitted tickets, but it was not.

11. Open UserQry (User Query) to find all users born after a certain date. Key in 6/6/1986 (June 6, 1986) and confirm. How many users were born after that date?

Deliverables:

Submit answers to the eight questions posed in the preceding activity. Steps not listed have no questions.

In step 3: 1 question
In step 4: 2 questions
In step 6: 1 question
In step 7: 1 question
In step 8: 2 questions
In step 11: 1 question

Quiz Questions:

1. True or False? Access puts all the information about something of interest (such as an employee) into a single table.

2. Which of the following information items about a user is *not* given in UserTbl?
   (a) The user's name
   (b) The user's date of birth
   (c) The user's telephone number
   (d) The user's blood type

3. If you want to find out a user's age from UserTbl, which of the following is correct?
   (a) There is insufficient information here to determine it.
   (b) It can be found by subtracting the date of birth from today's date, dividing the difference in days by 365, and deleting any fractional remainder.
   (c) It can be found by subtracting the date of hire from today's date, dividing the difference in days by 365, and deleting any fractional remainder.
   (d) It can be found by asking the user or a member of his or her family.

4. The report you looked at in step 7 had all of the following elements, except:
   (a) An overall header at the top, to identify it
   (b) The number of trouble tickets submitted by each department, below the list of that department's employees
   (c) The number of trouble tickets submitted by each department, above the list of that department's employees
   (d) Detail rows with information about each user

Discussion Questions:

1. In step 9 of this activity, you entered a birth date cutoff for the query. User input like this, which determines what data a query returns, is called a *parameter*. Now, suppose you want to book a round-trip on an air travel reservation system. List three parameters you must enter into such a system before it can tell you about available flights.

2. The report you used in steps 7 and 8 of this activity included a summary field after each department. It was a simple summary: just a count of users in that department. Suppose this report also contained numeric data, such as user salaries. What other

types of department summaries could you have? What other summaries, other than the employee count, could you possibly create from this table as it exists here? (Be creative. Do not worry about whether or not it would make sense to create them. Just ask, Would it be possible?)

3. A university cafeteria checkout system reads the bar code on each item, looks it up in a table, and finds the product description and price. Using this information, it keeps track of the running total. At the end it calculates the total due and compares it to the student's account balance. If the balance is insufficient, it calls a supervisor. Otherwise, it subtracts the cost of the meal from the balance and prints an itemized receipt showing the remaining balance.

   (a) What tables does this database need? (One was mentioned in the description.)

   (b) Using paper and pencil or any other tools your instructor specifies, draw the tables as in TicketTbl in the Figure 1A.1. Show columns for all the data in them. Show a few sample rows. Also draw a sample itemized receipt as it might be printed for a student. For each different kind of data item on the receipt, say where it comes from: in the database or as the result of some other calculation.

4. The technician table (TechTbl) lists all the technicians, with their names and other information such as their pay grade (job title). Describe in words how you could find, using the tables in this database, the names of all the users whose problems a given technician worked with. Use the process you have described to find all the users Nancy helped.

2 | Organizational Strategy, Competitive Advantage, and Information Systems

LEARNING OBJECTIVES >>>

1. List and provide examples of the three types of business pressures, and describe one IT response to each one.

2. Identify the five competitive forces described by Porter, and explain how the Web impacts each one.

3. Describe the strategies that organizations typically adopt to counter the five competitive forces and achieve competitive advantage.

4. Define business–IT technology alignment, and describe the characteristics of effective alignment.

OPENING **CASE** > Before the Stores

Have you ever seen a commercial for something sold "As Seen on TV" and forgotten the phone number? Maybe you also heard about a Web site, tried to remember it, but just could not seem to get it right. Where would you start? How would you find that product that you wanted?

Amar Kahbuni has the answer to your problems. In 2008, as a sophomore in college, he founded a company called Before the Stores. His strategy was simple: Sell "As Seen on TV" products before they get into stores. However, rather than selling these products through commercials, Amar would capitalize on the commercials and sell them on the Web. He had sold items on the Web before, but to implement his new idea he would need a much more sophisticated order fulfillment system. And what college sophomore has time to develop this type of system?

Amar found his answer with the Amazon Web store. He used the Fulfillment by Amazon (FBA) service offered to Amazon's business customers. This service provides businesses with an easy method of listing products, inventories, and prices; taking orders; accepting payment; and, ultimately, scheduling deliveries.

In addition, Before the Stores would capitalize on two major markets: (1) the infomercials that often advertise these products and (2) Amazon's customer base. In fact, many people go to Amazon to try to find a product that they have heard about. Amar was going to make it easy for them to find his.

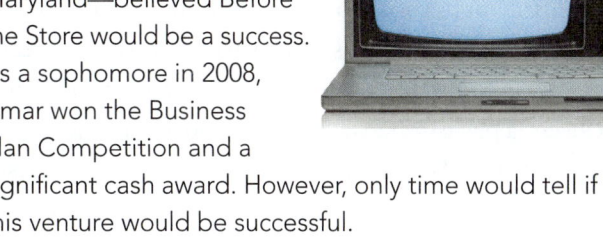

Fortunately for Amar, his school—Babson College in Maryland—believed Before the Store would be a success. As a sophomore in 2008, Amar won the Business Plan Competition and a significant cash award. However, only time would tell if this venture would be successful.

The results speak for themselves. Sales tripled from the third quarter of 2008 to the third quarter of 2009. Then, during the 2009 holiday season, sales increased 300 percent over the same period in 2008. By the fourth quarter of 2009, Amar was shipping more than 1,500 orders per week through FBA. Amar's business, Before the Stores, was a success.

Sources: Compiled from "Before the Stores Finds Success with Amazon Services," *Amazon Services Seller Success Story*, accessed March 22, 2011; "Incentive Targeting, Before the Stores LLC, Win Babson's 2008 Business Plan Competitions," *Babson College Press Release*, April 10, 2008.

Questions

1. Provide specific examples of the services that Fulfillment by Amazon provided for Amar.

2. Provide specific examples of the value that Amar provides his customers.

RUBY'S CLUB

Ruben and Lisa have a vision that their club will provide a relaxing, community atmosphere, with good drinks and good music. However, they operate in a very competitive business environment and feel market pressure to be everything to everyone, even though that is not what they want to be. They feel pressure from their customers to be more technologically advanced, even though they do not see any competitive advantage from it. They also feel a tremendous responsibility in response to legal and societal pressures to manage underage consumption of alcohol. However, they are not sure how to respond to these pressures while maintaining their desired atmosphere.

>>> Over the years, they have learned that they not only compete with other clubs and local restaurants, but the threat of substitute products or services includes theaters, athletic events, parties, and anything else college students choose to do for entertainment. To gain and maintain a solid customer base, they feel they really need this community feel to their club, like the TV show *Cheers*, a place "where everybody knows your name." To achieve this, they are not quite sure what mix of music, drinks, information, networks, data, advertisements, controls, policies, and procedures would position them where they want to be in the marketplace. Ruby's needs a solid strategy to accomplish Ruben and Lisa's vision.

INTRODUCTION

Information systems are critically important in helping organizations respond to business pressures and in supporting organizations' global strategy. As you study this chapter, you will see that any information system can be *strategic*, meaning that it can provide a competitive advantage—if it is used properly.

This chapter also demonstrates the incredible complexity of the information systems employed by a large, international company. As you see in this chapter's Closing Case 1, BP did an excellent job of revamping the information systems that support its business operations. However, the company seemed to neglect those information systems that support its drilling operations, which are clearly just as strategic as the firm's business information systems.

Competitive advantage is an advantage over competitors in some measure such as cost, quality, or speed; it leads to control of a market and to larger-than-average profits. Strategy and competitive advantage come in many forms. Amar Kahbuni found a niche where he could use existing electronic commerce (e-commerce) systems and advertising to create a competitive advantage. Capitalizing on Amazon's customer base and advertising from infomercials, he started a business that already had a market. He also enjoyed a distinct advantage over

stores that ultimately sell these items because he provided an easy way for customers to find the product as soon as they heard about it on TV. Basically, he got to the customers first. In addition, Amar had very little overhead because Amazon handled the e-commerce side of his operation. He did not have to purchase, design, set up, or secure costly information systems. He only had to sign up—not set up—to put his business in operation because Amazon provided the infrastructure for his business.

By the way, Amazon is always looking for unique business ideas. What could you do with an Amazon store?

Although there are many examples of companies that use technology in more expensive ways, Amar's example demonstrates that an entrepreneurial spirit and a solid understanding of what IT can do for you will provide competitive advantages to sophomores in college just as they do for Wall Street CIOs. As you study this chapter, think of the small businesses in your area that are doing interesting things with popular technologies. Do any of them use Twitter in an interesting way? Facebook? Amazon? PayPal? If not, can you think of any businesses that would benefit from using these technologies?

This chapter is important for you for several reasons. First, the business pressures addressed here will impact your organization, but they also will impact you. As a result, you must understand how information systems can help you, and eventually your organization, respond to these pressures.

In addition, acquiring competitive advantage is essential for your organization's survival. Many organizations achieve competitive advantage through the efforts of their employees. Therefore, becoming knowledgeable about strategy and how information systems impact strategy and competitive position will help you throughout your career.

This chapter encourages you to become familiar with your organization's strategy, mission, and goals and to understand its business problems and how it makes (or loses) money. It will help you understand how information technology contributes to organizational strategy. Further, it is likely that you will be a member of business–IT committees that decide (among many other things) whether to adopt new technologies and how to use existing technologies more effectively. After studying this chapter, you will be able to make immediate contributions in these committees when you join your organizations.

In this chapter, you will see how information systems enable organizations to respond to business pressures. Next, you will learn how information systems help organizations gain competitive advantages in the marketplace. You conclude the chapter by discussing business–IT alignment—in other words, how the IT function in an organization supports its strategy.

2.1 | Business Pressures, Organizational Responses, and IT Support

Modern organizations compete in a challenging environment. To remain competitive they must react rapidly to problems and opportunities that arise from extremely dynamic conditions. In this section you examine some of the major pressures confronting modern organizations and the strategies that organizations employ to respond to these pressures.

Business Pressures

The **business environment** is the combination of social, legal, economic, physical, and political factors in which businesses conduct their operations. Significant changes in any of these factors are likely to create business pressures on organizations. Organizations typically respond to these pressures with activities supported by IT. Figure 2.1 illustrates the

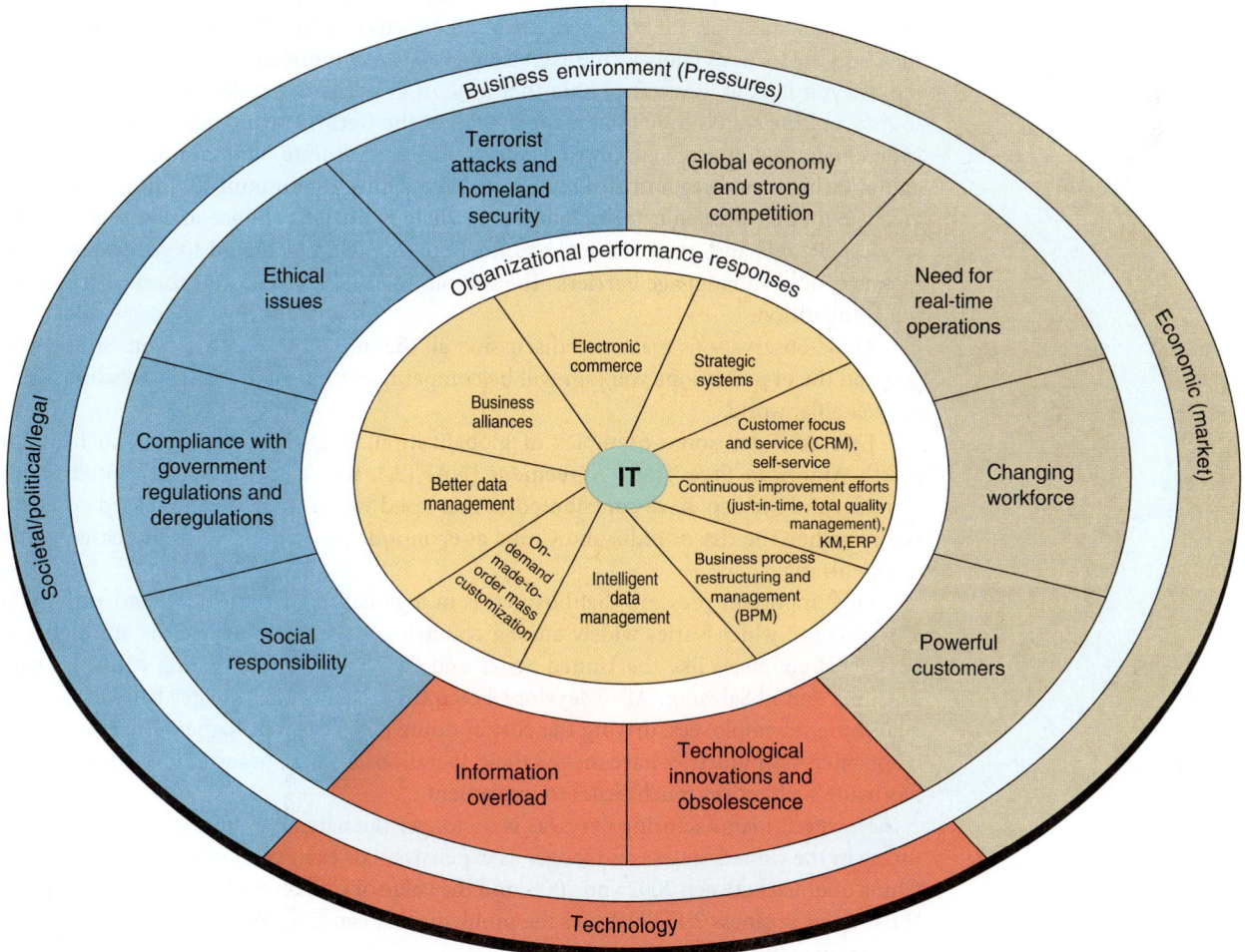

Figure 2.1 Business pressures, organizational performance and responses, and IT support.

relationships among business pressures, organizational performance and responses, and IT support. You will learn about three major types of business pressures: market, technology, and societal pressures.

Market Pressures. Market pressures are generated by the global economy, intense competition, the changing nature of the workforce, and powerful customers. Let's look more closely at each of these factors.

Globalization. **Globalization** is the integration and interdependence of economic, social, cultural, and ecological facets of life, made possible by rapid advances in information technology. In his book *The World Is Flat*, Pulitzer Prize–winning author Thomas Friedman argues that technology is leveling the global competitive playing field, thereby making it "flat."

Friedman identifies three eras of globalization. The first era, Globalization 1.0, lasted from 1492 to 1800. During this era, the force behind globalization was how much muscle, horsepower, wind power, or steam power a country could deploy.

The second era, Globalization 2.0, lasted from 1800 to 2000. In this era, the force behind globalization was the emergence of multinational companies—that is, companies that had their headquarters in one country but operated in several countries. In the first half of this era, globalization was driven by falling transportation costs, generated by the development of the steam engine and the railroads. In the second half, the driving force was falling telecommunications costs resulting from the telegraph, telephones, computers, satellites, fiberoptic cable, and the Internet and World Wide Web. The modern global economy began to evolve during this era.

Around the year 2000, the world entered Globalization 3.0. In this era globalization has been driven by the convergence of ten forces that Friedman calls "flatteners." Table 2.1 identifies these forces.

According to Friedman, each era has been characterized by a distinctive focus. The focus of Globalization 1.0 was on countries, the focus of Globalization 2.0 was on companies, and the focus of Globalization 3.0 is on groups and individuals.

As you look at Table 2.1, note that nine of Friedman's ten flatteners directly relate to information technology (all except the fall of the Berlin Wall). These flatteners enable individuals to connect, compute, communicate, collaborate, and compete everywhere and anywhere, anytime and all the time; to access limitless amounts of information, services, and entertainment; to exchange knowledge; and to produce and sell goods and services. People and organizations can now operate without regard to geography, time, distance, or even language barriers. The bottom line? Globalization is markedly increasing competition.

These observations make our discussion all the more important for you. Simply put, you and the organizations you join will be competing with people and organizations from all over a flat world.

Let's consider some examples of globalization. Regional agreements such as the North American Free Trade Agreement (NAFTA), which includes the United States, Canada, and Mexico, have contributed to increased world trade and increased competition. Further, the rise of India and China as economic powerhouses has increased global competition.

One important pressure that businesses in a global market must contend with is the cost of labor, which varies widely among countries. In general, labor costs are higher in developed countries like the United States and Japan than in developing countries such as China and El Salvador. Also, developed countries usually offer greater benefits, such as healthcare, to employees, driving the cost of doing business even higher. Therefore, many labor-intensive industries have moved their operations to countries with low labor costs. IT has made such moves much easier to implement.

However, manufacturing overseas is no longer the bargain it once was, and manufacturing in the United States is no longer as expensive. For example, manufacturing wages in China doubled between 2002 and 2008, and the value of China's currency has steadily risen. "IT's About Business 2.1" illustrates the problems that can arise when companies outsource their manufacturing processes overseas.

TABLE 2.1 Friedman's Ten Flatteners

- **Fall of the Berlin Wall on November 9, 1989**
  - Shifted the world toward free-market economies and away from centrally planned economies
  - Led to the emergence of the European Union and early thinking about the world as a single, global market

- **Netscape goes public on August 9, 1995**
  - Popularized the Internet and the World Wide Web

- **Development of work-flow software**
  - Enabled computer applications to work with one another without human intervention
  - Enabled faster, closer collaboration and coordination among employees, regardless of their location

- **Uploading**
  - Empowered all Internet users to create content and put it on the Web
  - Led the transition from a passive approach to content to an active, participatory, collaborative approach

- **Outsourcing**
  - Contracting with an outside company to perform a specific function that your company was doing itself and then integrating that work back into your operation (e.g., moving customer call centers to India)

- **Offshoring**
  - Relocating an entire operation, or certain tasks, to another country (e.g., moving an entire manufacturing operation to China)

- **Supply chaining**
  - Technological revolution that led to the creation of networks comprised of companies, their suppliers, and their customers, all of which could collaborate and share information for increased efficiency

- **Insourcing**
  - Delegating operations or jobs within a business to another company that specializes in those operations (e.g., Dell hires FedEx to "take over" Dell's logistics process)

- **Informing**
  - The ability to search for information, best illustrated by search engines

- **The Steroids** (computing, instant messaging and file sharing, wireless technologies, Voice-over-Internet Protocol (VoIP), videoconferencing, and computer graphics)
  - Technologies that amplify the other flatteners
  - Enable all forms of computing and collaboration to be digital, mobile, and personal

The Changing Nature of the Workforce. The workforce, particularly in developed countries, is becoming more diversified. Increasing numbers of women, single parents, minorities, and persons with disabilities are now employed in all types of positions. IT is easing the integration of these employees into the traditional workforce. IT is also enabling people to work from home, which can be a major benefit for parents with young children and for people confronted with mobility and/or transportation issues.

Powerful Customers. Consumer sophistication and expectations increase as customers become more knowledgeable about the products and services they acquire. Customers can use the Internet to find detailed information about products and services, to compare prices, and to purchase items at electronic auctions.

Organizations recognize the importance of customers and have increased their efforts to acquire and retain them. Modern firms strive to learn as much as possible about their customers to better anticipate and address their needs. This process, called *customer intimacy*,

Sleek Audio

The CEO of Sleek Audio (http://sleek-audio.com) was frustrated with a contract factory in Dongguan, China, that assembled the majority of his company's products. Not only did he have to travel to China every few months to troubleshoot quality flaws, but manufacturing problems in the factory threatened to bankrupt his company. In one case, Sleek Audio had to discard an entire shipment of 10,000 earphones because they were improperly welded, a mistake that cost the company millions of dollars. Further, delivery delays caused by the factory's lax approach to deadlines forced Sleek Audio to spend huge amounts of money air-freighting products to the United States. As a result, the company had far too much money tied up in inventory that took months to arrive after the prototypes were developed.

Sleek Audio decided to search for a manufacturing partner that possessed the necessary tools and expertise to produce their earphones. One was found in Dynamic Innovations (www.d-inno.com), located close to Sleek Audio's Palmetto, Florida, headquarters. One year later, Sleek Audio had a full-scale manufacturing operation that could be reached with a 15-minute car ride rather than a 24-hour flight. Each earphone costs roughly 50 percent more to produce in Florida than in China. Sleek Audio is happy to pay the premium, however, for the assurance that botched orders and shipping delays will not ruin the company. Based on enthusiastic customer response, Sleek Audio has projected 2011 to be its most profitable year ever.

When Sleek Audio was considering how the company could return manufacturing to the States with its higher labor costs, company executives realized that the only way to make the move feasible was to minimize the role of humans on the assembly line. This process meant redesigning products to take advantage of automated tools and robots.

Sleek Audio's earphones featured plastic side panels that the Chinese factory had to weld into place by hand. In the U.S. factory the company automated this process by replacing human labor with robots. Managers redesigned the entire product around a solid aluminum center into which robots fit the speaker. This new assembly process requires neither welding nor human hands. Moreover, as you saw in Chapter 1, robots are becoming more skilled and less expensive.

Questions

1. Which of Friedman's flatteners apply to Sleek Audio's decision to bring its manufacturing back to the United States? Support your answer.
2. Identify some potential negative implications of Sleek Audio's increasing reliance on robots in its manufacturing processes.

Sources: Compiled from "Bring Manufacturing Jobs Home!" *Deloitte Debates* (www.deloitte.com), 2011; R. Read, "In Reverse of Offshore Trend, Oregon Manufacturing Thrives When High-Tech, High-Quality Products Are Needed," *The Oregonian*, September 18, 2010; T. George, "U.S. Sourcing Firms Bid to Reverse Offshoring Trend," *Nearshore Americas*, April 8, 2010; B. Koerner, "Made in the USA," *Wired*, March, 2011; "Is Reverse Offshoring a Trend?" *Supply Chainer*, October 25, 2008; J. Aitoro, "Offshore Manufacturing: A Risky Proposition?" *CRN.com*, June 25, 2007; http://sleek-audio.com, accessed March 21, 2011.

is an important component of *customer relationship management* (CRM), an organizationwide effort toward maximizing the customer experience. You will learn about CRM in Chapter 12.

Technology Pressures. The second category of business pressures consists of those pressures related to technology. Two major technology-related pressures are technological innovation and information overload.

Technological Innovation and Obsolescence. New and improved technologies rapidly create or support substitutes for products, alternative service options, and superb quality. As a result, today's state-of-the-art products may be obsolete tomorrow. For

In-store comparison shopping is just one way customers are becoming more powerful. (*Source:* Studio Frank/Image Source Limited)

example, how fast are new versions of your smartphone being released? How quickly are electronic versions of books, magazines, and newspapers replacing traditional hard-copy versions? These changes force businesses to keep up with consumer demands.

Consider the Apple iPad (www.apple.com/ipad). Apple released the first iPad in April 2010 and sold 3 million of the devices in 80 days. Rather than taking time to enjoy its success, Apple made its iPad2 available for sale on March 11, 2011, only 11 months later.

Information Overload. The amount of information available on the Internet doubles approximately every year, and much of it is free. The Internet and other telecommunications networks are bringing a flood of information to managers. To make decisions effectively and efficiently, managers must be able to access, navigate, and utilize these vast stores

While this may be familiar, multitasking will become more complicated when your job depends on it. (*Source:* © Maria R.T. Deseo/PhotoEdit)

of data, information, and knowledge. Information technologies, such as search engines (discussed in Chapter 4) and data mining (discussed in Chapter 5), provide valuable support in these efforts.

Societal/Political/Legal Pressures. The third category of business pressures includes social responsibility, government regulation/deregulation, spending for social programs, spending to protect against terrorism, and ethics. This section will explain how all of these elements affect modern businesses.

Social Responsibility. Social issues that affect businesses and individuals range from the state of the physical environment, to company and individual philanthropy, to education. Some corporations and individuals are willing to spend time and/or money to address various social problems. These efforts are known as **organizational social responsibility** or **individual social responsibility**.

One critical social problem is the state of the physical environment. A growing IT initiative, called *green IT*, is addressing some of the most pressing environmental concerns. The following example illustrates how IT is instrumental in organizational efforts to "go green."

EXAMPLE

Companies Going Green Use Information Technology

Companies are "going green," and IT professionals are facing increasing pressures to help their companies accomplish their environmental goals. Organizations consider IT to be a natural choice to lead their sustainability efforts, because IT touches every area of an organization. In a series of interviews, several IT executives listed four areas where IT is particularly valuable.

Facilities design and management. Organizations are creating more sustainable work environments. Many organizations are pursuing Leadership in Energy and Environmental Design (LEED) certification from the U.S. Green Building Council, a nonprofit group that promotes the construction of environmentally friendly buildings. One impact of this development is that IT professionals are expected to help create green facilities. Consequently, IT personnel have to consider how their computing decisions impact sustainable design and, in turn, how the building's design impacts the IT infrastructure. Green design influences the type of IT devices used and the locations where IT clusters personal computers, people, and servers. IT must become familiar with the metering and monitoring systems used in green buildings and the requirements of buildings' computerized infrastructure.

Carbon management. As companies try to reduce their carbon footprints, they are turning to IT executives to develop the systems needed to calculate and track carbon throughout the organization and its supply chain, which can be global in scope. Therefore, IT employees need to become knowledgeable about embedded carbon and how to measure it in the company's products and processes.

Consider, for example, application development. IT managers will have to ask whether an application will require new hardware to test and run, or how much additional server space (and thus energy) it will require—and how these issues translate into carbon output.

International and U.S. state environmental laws. IT executives must deal with state laws and international regulations that impact everything from the IT products they buy, to how they dispose of them, to their company's carbon footprint. IT managers must understand environmental compliance issues so they can ask their vendors the right questions regarding specific state, national, and international environmental standards before buying, deploying, and disposing of equipment. In short, IT managers must have an equipment strategy from cradle to grave.

Energy management. IT executives must understand their entire organization's energy needs. They also need to establish a good relationship

---

with the suppliers of their company's electrical utilities, for several reasons. First, energy management systems are becoming increasingly sophisticated. To employ these systems effectively and make intelligent consumption decisions, IT personnel must familiarize themselves with the system's complex monitors and sensors. Second, more utilities are developing an expertise in creating energy-efficient IT departments. IT managers should tap that expertise to improve their own departments' energy performance. Third, utilities are offering incentives to commercial customers who take certain energy conservation steps, such as enabling computer power management across their networks and designing energy-efficient data centers. Finally, utilities are offering variable rate incentives depending on when companies use electricity and how much they use. These issues require IT systems that can regulate electricity use.

Sources: Compiled from J. Matthews, "For IT Managers, Going Green Can Save You Some Long Green," *Forbes*, March 31, 2011; A. Diana, "15 Green Tech Innovations," *InformationWeek*, January 5, 2011; A. Nguyen, "Hire Green IT Managers Now, Forrester Urges," *CIO*, November 23, 2010; M. Pratt, "How to Get Your Green IT Cred," *Computerworld*, September 2, 2010; C. Penttila, "Why—and How—Your Company Should Go Green," *InformationWeek*, January 30, 2009; www.usgbc.org, accessed March 15, 2011.

Continuing our discussion of social responsibility, social problems all over the world may be addressed through corporate and individual philanthropy. In some cases, questions arise as to what percentage of contributions actually goes to the intended causes and recipients and what percentage goes to the charity's overhead. Another problem that concerns contributors is that they often exert little influence over the selection of projects their contributions will support. As you see in "IT's About Business 2.2," the Internet can act as a facilitator of generosity.

IT's ABOUT BUSINESS | 2.2

The Internet Facilitates Generosity

The Internet can facilitate acts of generosity and true connection. Consider, for example, a Web site such as PatientsLikeMe (www.patientslikeme.com), or any of the thousands of message boards dedicated to infertility, cancer, and various other ailments. People use these sites and message boards to obtain information about life-and-death decisions based on volunteered information, while also receiving much-needed emotional support from strangers.

Sociologists contend that contributing to such communities helps people gain self-esteem by donating their time and experiences to people in need. People will most readily share information, followed by time, and then physical goods.

Many Web sites help concerned individuals provide goods and services to others. These hubs translate the peer-to-peer principles of sharing from the virtual world to the real world. For example, CouchSurfing (www.couchsurfing.org) has helped 2.3 million travelers find willing and free hosts throughout the world. What is the main reason that people allow strangers to sleep on their couch for free? The answer is that they give away something that has little marginal cost in exchange for the opportunity to meet people from all over the world.

Let's look at some additional examples of Web sites that enable generosity.

- GiftFlow (www.giftflow.org): GiftFlow is a virtual community where you can obtain things you need for free and find people who need the "stuff" you have to give away. GiftFlow connects community organizations, businesses, governments, and neighbors in a network of reciprocity, where they can share resources, meet one another's needs, and coordinate their efforts to build a better world.

- OurGoods (www.ourgoods.org): OurGoods enables creative people to help one another produce independent projects. More work is accomplished in networks of shared respect and shared resources than in competitive isolation.

- Sparked (www.sparked.com): Sparked is an online "microvolunteering" Web site where large and small organizations list opportunities for people looking to volunteer.

- Thredup (www.thredup.com): Thredup is a Web site where parents trade children's clothing and toys.

- Collaborative Consumption (www.collaborative consumption.com): This Web site is an online hub for discussions about the growing business of sharing, resale, reuse, and barter (with many links to Web sites engaged in these practices).

- Kiva (www.kiva.org): Kiva is a nonprofit enterprise that provides a link between lenders in developed countries and entrepreneurs in developing countries. Users pledge interest-free loans rather than tax-deductible donations. Kiva directs 100 percent of the loans to borrowers.

- DonorsChoose (www.donorschoose.org): DonorsChoose is an education-oriented Web site that functions entirely within the United States. Users make donations rather than loans. The Web site addresses the huge problem of underfunded public schools.

Questions

1. Discuss why people will give away their time and knowledge for free.

2. Describe the various ways in which the Internet can facilitate generosity.

Sources: Compiled from A. Kamenetz, "The Case for Generosity," *FastCompany*, March, 2011; N. Ferraro, "Lending and Philanthropy in the Internet Age," *InformationWeek*, February 2, 2008; www.giftflow.org, www.ourgoods.org, www.sparked.com, www.thredup.com, http://blog.p2pfoundation.net, www.collaborativeconsumption.com, www.kiva.org, www.donorschoose.org; accessed July 31, 2011.

Still another social problem that affects modern business is the digital divide. The **digital divide** refers to the wide gap between those who have access to information and communications technology and those who do not. This gap exists both within and among countries.

Many government and international organizations are trying to close the digital divide. As technologies develop and become less expensive, the speed at which the gap can be closed will accelerate.

A well-known project is the One Laptop per Child (OLPC) project (http://one.laptop.org). OLPC is a nonprofit association dedicated to research to develop a very inexpensive laptop—a technology that aims to revolutionize how the world can educate its children.

The first generation of inexpensive laptops appeared in 2007 with a price of $188, which was too high. The second generation of the laptop was scrapped because the price remained too high. The next generation of inexpensive laptops will be a touchscreen tablet computer for schoolchildren in the developing world that uses less power than a light bulb and is unbreakable, waterproof, and one-half the thickness of an iPhone. This computer will be a single sheet of plastic, and have a projected price of $75.

Compliance with Government Regulations. Another major source of business pressures is government regulations regarding health, safety, environmental protection, and equal opportunity. Businesses tend to view government regulations as expensive constraints on their activities. In general, government deregulation intensifies competition.

In the wake of 9/11 and numerous corporate scandals, the U.S. government passed many new laws, including the Sarbanes-Oxley Act, the USA PATRIOT Act, the Gramm-Leach-Bliley Act, and the Health Insurance Portability and Accountability Act (HIPAA). Organizations must be in compliance with the regulations contained in these statutes. The process of becoming and remaining compliant is expensive and time consuming. In almost all cases, organizations rely on IT support to provide the necessary controls and information for compliance.

Protection Against Terrorist Attacks. Since September 11, 2001, organizations have been under increased pressure to protect themselves against terrorist attacks. In addition, employees who are in the military reserves have been called up for active duty, creating personnel problems. Information technology can help protect businesses by providing security systems and possibly identifying patterns of behavior associated with terrorist activities, including cyberattacks (discussed in Chapter 7).

An example of protection against terrorism is the Department of Homeland Security's US-VISIT program. US-VISIT is a network of biometric-screening systems, such as fingerprint and ocular (eye) scanners, that ties into government databases and watch lists to check the identities of millions of people entering the United States. The system is now operational in more than 300 locations, including major international ports of entry by air, sea, and land.

Ethical Issues. Ethics relates to general standards of right and wrong. Information ethics relates specifically to standards of right and wrong in information-processing practices. Ethical issues are very important because, if handled poorly, they can damage an organization's image and destroy its employees' morale. The use of IT raises many ethical issues, ranging from monitoring e-mail to invading the privacy of millions of customers whose data are stored in private and public databases. (Chapter 6 covers ethical issues in detail.)

Clearly, then, the pressures on organizations are increasing, and organizations must be prepared to take responsive actions if they are to succeed. You will learn about these organizational responses in the next section.

Organizational Responses

Organizations are responding to the various pressures just discussed by implementing IT such as strategic systems, customer focus, make-to-order and mass customization, and e-business. This section explores each of these responses.

Strategic Systems. Strategic systems provide organizations with advantages that enable them to increase their market share and/or profits, to better negotiate with suppliers, and to prevent competitors from entering their markets. As an example, the IT department at Procter & Gamble (P&G; www.pg.com) developed a virtualized environment that the company uses for product design work, product placement research, and consumer feedback studies. P&G utilizes virtual reality models to test design ideas for the next breakthroughs in products such as diapers and cosmetics. Within these "cyberworlds," P&G can rapidly test product performance as well as consumer responses to various kinds of ingredient and packaging choices.

Customer Focus. Organizational attempts to provide superb customer service can make the difference between attracting and keeping customers and losing them to competitors. Numerous IT tools and business processes have been designed to keep customers happy. Consider Amazon, for example. When you visit Amazon's Web site anytime after your first visit, the site welcomes you back by name and presents you with information on books that you might like, based on your previous purchases. In another example, Dell guides you through the process of buying a computer by providing information and choices that help you make an informed buying decision.

Make-to-Order and Mass Customization. Make-to-order is a strategy of producing customized (made to individual specifications) products and services. The business problem is how to manufacture customized goods efficiently and at a reasonably low cost. Part of the solution is to change manufacturing processes from mass production to mass customization. In mass production, a company produces a large quantity of identical items. In **mass customization**, it also produces a large quantity of items, but it customizes them to fit the needs and preferences of individual customers. Mass customization is simply an attempt to perform make-to-order on a large scale. Bodymetrics (www.bodymetrics.com) is an excellent example of mass customization with men's and women's jeans.

Well-fitting jeans are notoriously difficult to find. To address this problem, Bodymetrics developed a "body scanner" that scans the customer's body, captures more than 150 measurements, and produces a digital replica of his or her size and shape. This scan is then used to provide three services: made-to-measure jeans, body-shape jeans, and online virtual try-on.

With made-to-measure jeans, the scan is used to create a pattern for the jeans, which are hand tailored to the exact lines and contours of the customer's body. The jeans are ready in three to six weeks, at which time the customer has a final fitting with a Bodymetrics tailor.

Based on its experience with made-to-measure jeans, Bodymetrics has identified three body shapes: straight, semi-curvy, and curvy. Body-shape jeans are specifically designed to fit these different body shapes. After customers are scanned, a Bodymetrics jeans expert helps them determine their body shapes. Customers can then instantly purchase jeans matching their body shapes off the rack in the store.

The online virtual try-on allows customers who have been scanned to try on jeans virtually on their own bodies without physically trying on jeans in a dressing room. The service creates an *avatar* (a three-dimensional graphical representation), which has an amazing resemblance to the customer. Then, the customer can pick various styles of jeans and "virtually see" what the jeans look like on her or his avatar.

Sources: Compiled from "The First Time I Had a Bodymetrics Scan," http://howfayeseesit. wordpress.com, March 23, 2011; L. Talbot, "Bodymetrics: What's Your Jean Shape?" http:// lisatalbot.blogspot.com, February 2, 2011; Asmita, "Custom-Fit Jeans with Bodymetrics," www. styleguru.com, January 18, 2007 (*Note:* StyleGuru is a promotional blog.); R. Young, "Turning Tailoring Over to a Computer," *International Herald Tribune*, January 15, 2007; www.bodymetrics. com, accessed March 1, 2011.

E-Business and E-Commerce. Doing business electronically is an essential strategy for companies that are competing in today's business environment. **Electronic commerce** (EC or e-commerce) describes the process of buying, selling, transferring, or exchanging products, services, or information via computer networks, including the Internet. **E-business** is a somewhat broader concept. In addition to the buying and selling of goods and services, e-business also refers to servicing customers, collaborating with business partners, and performing electronic transactions within an organization. (Chapter 9 focuses extensively on this topic. In addition, e-commerce applications appear throughout the book.)

You now have a general overview of the pressures that affect companies in today's business environment and the responses that organizations choose to manage these pressures. To plan for the most effective responses, companies formulate strategies. In the new digital economy, these strategies rely heavily on information technology, especially strategic information systems. You examine these topics in the next section.

BEFORE *YOU GO ON . . .*

1. What are the characteristics of the modern business environment?

2. Discuss some of the pressures that characterize the modern global business environment.

3. Identify some of the organizational responses to these pressures. Are any of these responses specific to a particular pressure? If so, which ones?

RUBY'S CLUB QUESTIONS

1. How could IT help Ruby's comply with legal requirements and social responsibilities surrounding the sale of alcohol?

2. Drinks and music never become obsolete, right? How could Ruby's lack of IT create the environment that makes them appear obsolete?

3. The sheer number of possibilities are creating "overload" for Ruben and Lisa before they even adopt any specific IT. How can technology be used to help them make a decision about the IT they choose to adopt?

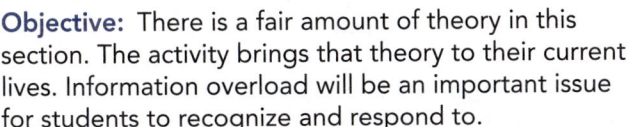

Student Activity | 2.1

Objective: There is a fair amount of theory in this section. The activity brings that theory to their current lives. Information overload will be an important issue for students to recognize and respond to.

Chapter Connection: This relates to the text discussion the role of IT in an organization.

Prerequisites: You should have read Section 2.1 before doing this activity.

Activity:

Review these three videos from IBM. These videos highlight how businesses are responding to the vast amounts of data that are available to them and that they have collected, as well as how information load is a personal issue.

Why Data Matters: Extracting Insights, Making Better Decisions

www.youtube.com/watch?v=sSSLYlURzmE

Why Data Matters: Context Reveals Answers

www.youtube.com/watch?v=ipxRA7ira4c&feature=channel

Why Data Matters: Age of Analytics

www.youtube.com/watch?v=EWL312zbEKg&feature=channel

Then review this video from CNN on *Digital Information Overload.*

http://video.search.yahoo.com/video/play?ei=UTF-8&fr=ie8&fr2=tab-web&p=information+overload&vid=219545994802&dt=1281640588&l=361&turl=http%3A%2F%2Fts3.mm.bing.net%2Fvideos%2Fthumbnail.aspx%3Fq%3D219545994802%26id%3Da335d270b50ef0234261a993620dcdf0%26bid%3DSKMMjnJGZuG9Wg%26bn%3DThumb%26index%3Dch1%26url%3Dhttp%253a%252f%252fwww.cnn.com%252fvideo%252f%253f%252fvideo%252fus%252f2010%252f08%252f12%252fnr.information.overload.cnn&rurl=http%3A%2F%2Fwww.cnn.com%2Fvideo%2F%3F%2Fvideo%2Fus%2F2010%2F08%2F12%2Fnr.information.overload.cnn&tit=Digital+information+overload&sigr=12a6egts3&newfp=1

Deliverables:

Consider and provide answers to the following questions:

1. Reflect on the amount of data that bombards you daily. How do you filter it? How much time do you use reacting to it?

2. How has technology changed the way you receive, store, share, and find data?

3. Think about a recent decision you made, such as which colleges to apply to. Consider all your sources for data (Web, print, friends/family, interviews, tours, surveys, rankings) and the elements of data you collected (cost, location, size, program of study, etc.). How did you organize the data? Filter them? Analyze them?

Quiz Questions:

1. Which of the following is classified as data?

   (a) Facebook posts
   (b) Book purchase
   (c) Your name
   (d) Surveillance video
   (e) All of the above

2. When making a business decision, you look at all the available data.
   (a) True.
   (b) You look at what you can find, piece by piece, until you reach the deadline by which the decision must be made.
   (c) You look at sources of data and prioritize your search based on the sources.
   (d) You set a time limit for accessing data and then use what you have and your instinct.

3. None of the above.

Discussion Questions:

1. The book and videos talk about information overload. Is there such a thing as too much information?

2. Is technology driving information, or is information driving technology?

3. How can technology help an information worker?

2.2 | Competitive Advantage and Strategic Information Systems

A *competitive strategy* is a statement that identifies a business's approach to compete, its goals, and the plans and policies that will be required to carry out those goals.[1] A strategy, in general, can apply to a desired outcome, such as gaining market share. A competitive strategy focuses on achieving a desired outcome when competitors want to prevent you from reaching your goal. Therefore, when you create a competitive strategy, you must plan your own moves, but you must also anticipate and counter your competitors' moves.

Through its competitive strategy, an organization seeks a competitive advantage in an industry. That is, it seeks to outperform its competitors in a critical measure such as cost, quality, and time-to-market. Competitive advantage helps a company function profitably with a market and generate larger-than-average profits.

Competitive advantage is increasingly important in today's business environment, as you will note throughout the book. In general, the *core business* of companies has remained the same. That is, information technologies simply offer tools that can enhance an organization's success through its traditional sources of competitive advantage, such as low cost, excellent customer service, and superior supply chain management. **Strategic information systems (SISs)** provide a competitive advantage by helping an organization to implement its strategic goals and to improve its performance and productivity. Any information system that helps an organization gain a competitive advantage or reduce a competitive disadvantage qualifies as a strategic information system.

Porter's Competitive Forces Model

The best-known framework for analyzing competitiveness is Michael Porter's **competitive forces model**.[2] Companies use Porter's model to develop strategies to increase their competitive edge. Porter's model also demonstrates how IT can make a company more competitive.

Porter's model identifies five major forces that can endanger or enhance a company's position in a given industry. Figure 2.2 highlights these forces. Although the Web has changed the nature of competition, it has not changed Porter's five fundamental forces. In fact, what makes these forces so valuable as analytical tools is that they have not changed for centuries. Every competitive organization, no matter how large or small, or what business it is in, is driven by these forces. This observation applies even to organizations that you might not consider competitive, such as local governments. Although local governments are not for-profit enterprises, they compete for businesses to locate in their districts, for funding from higher levels of government, for employees, and for many other things.

[1]Porter, M. E. (1985). *Competitive Advantage*. New York: Free Press.
[2]Ibid.

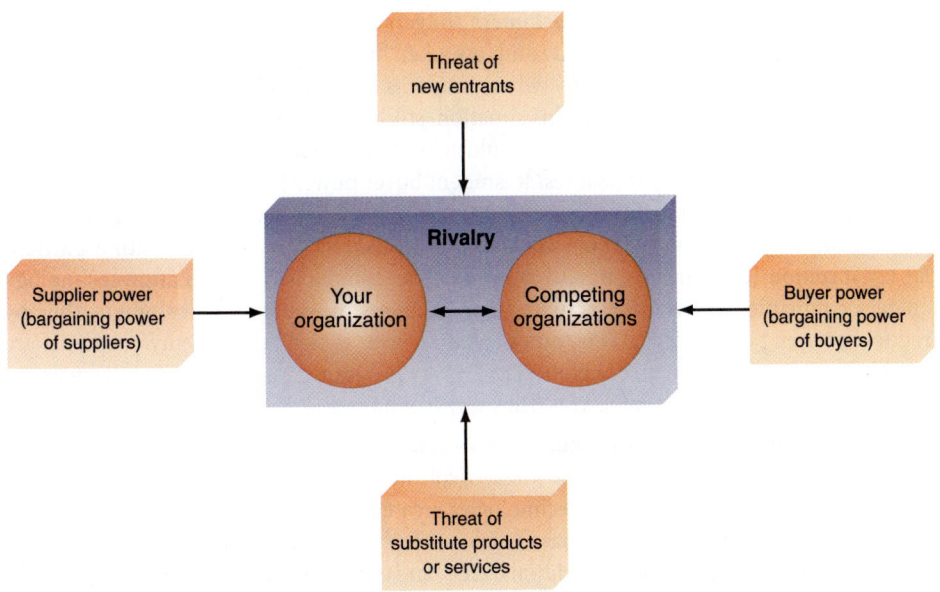

Figure 2.2 Porter's competitive forces model.

Significantly, Porter concludes that the *overall* impact of the Web is to increase competition, which generally diminishes a firm's profitability.[3] Let's examine Porter's five forces and the ways that the Web influences them.

1. *The threat of entry of new competitors.* The threat that new competitors will enter your market is high when entry is easy and low when there are significant barriers to entry. An **entry barrier** is a product or service feature that customers have learned to expect from organizations in a certain industry. A competing organization must offer this feature in order to survive in the marketplace. There are many types of entry barriers. Consider, for example, legal requirements such as admission to the bar to practice law or a license to serve liquor, where only a certain number of licenses are available.

Suppose you want to open a gasoline station. To compete in that industry, you would have to offer pay-at-the-pump service to your customers. Pay-at-the-pump is an IT-based barrier to entering this market because you must offer it for free. The first gas station that offered this service gained first-move advantage and established barriers to entry. This advantage did not last, however, because competitors quickly offered the same service and thus overcame the entry barrier.

For most firms, the Web *increases* the threat that new competitors will enter the market because it sharply reduces traditional barriers to entry, such as the need for a sales force or a physical storefront. Today, competitors frequently need only to set up a Web site. This threat of increased competition is particularly acute in industries that perform an *intermediation role*, which is a link between buyers and sellers (for example, stock brokers and travel agents), as well as in industries where the primary product or service is digital (for example, the music industry). In addition, the geographical reach of the Web enables distant competitors to compete more directly with an existing firm.

In some cases the Web increases barriers to entry. This scenario occurs primarily when customers have come to expect a non-trivial capability from their suppliers. For example, the first company to offer Web-based package tracking gained a competitive advantage from that service. Competitors were forced to follow.

2. *The bargaining power of suppliers.* Supplier power is high when buyers have few choices from whom to buy and low when buyers have many choices. Therefore, organizations would rather have more potential suppliers so they will be in a stronger position to negotiate price, quality, and delivery terms.

The Internet's impact on suppliers is mixed. On the one hand, it enables buyers to find alternative suppliers and to compare prices more easily, thereby reducing the supplier's bargaining power. On the other hand, as companies use the Internet to integrate their supply chains, participating suppliers prosper by locking in customers.

[3]Porter, M. E. (2001, March). "Strategy and the Internet," *Harvard Business Review*, pp. 62–78.

3. *The bargaining power of customers (buyers).* Buyer power is high when buyers have many choices from whom to buy and low when buyers have few choices. For example, in the past, there were few locations where students could purchase textbooks (typically, one or two campus bookstores). In this situation, students had low buyer power. Today, the Web provides students with access to a multitude of potential suppliers as well as detailed information about textbooks. As a result, student buyer power has increased dramatically.

In contrast, *loyalty programs* reduce buyer power. As their name suggests, loyalty programs reward customers based on the amount of business they conduct with a particular organization (e.g., airlines, hotels, and rental car companies). Information technology enables companies to track the activities and accounts of millions of customers, thereby reducing buyer power. That is, customers who receive "perks" from loyalty programs are less likely to do business with competitors. (Loyalty programs are associated with customer relationship management, which you will study in Chapter 12.)

4. *The threat of substitute products or services.* If there are many alternatives to an organization's products or services, then the threat of substitutes is high. If there are few alternatives, then the threat is low. Today, new technologies create substitute products very rapidly. For example, customers today can purchase wireless telephones instead of land-line telephones, Internet music services instead of traditional CDs, and ethanol instead of gasoline in cars.

Information-based industries experience the greatest threat from substitutes. Any industry in which digitized information can replace material goods (e.g., music, books, and software) must view the Internet as a threat because the Internet can convey this information efficiently and at low cost and high quality.

Even when there are many substitutes for their products, however, companies can create a competitive advantage by increasing switching costs. *Switching costs* are the costs, in money and time, of a decision to buy elsewhere. For example, contracts with smart phone providers typically include a substantial penalty for switching to another provider until the term of the contract expires (quite often, two years). This switching cost is monetary.

As another example, when you buy products from Amazon, the company develops a profile of your shopping habits and recommends products targeted to your preferences. If you switch to another online vendor, it will take time for that company to develop a profile of your wants and needs. In this case, the switching cost involves time rather than money.

5. *The rivalry among existing firms in the industry.* The threat from rivalry is high when there is intense competition among many firms in an industry. The threat is low when the competition is among fewer firms and is not as intense.

In the past, proprietary information systems—systems that belong exclusively to a single organization—have provided strategic advantage to firms in highly competitive industries. Today, however, the visibility of Internet applications on the Web makes proprietary systems more difficult to keep secret. In simple terms, when I see my competitor's new system online, I will rapidly match its features in order to remain competitive. The result is fewer differences among competitors, which leads to more intense competition in an industry.

To understand this concept, consider the highly competitive grocery industry, where Walmart, Kroger, Safeway, and other companies compete essentially on price. Some of these companies have IT-enabled loyalty programs in which customers receive discounts and the store gains valuable business intelligence on customers' buying preferences. Stores use this business intelligence in their marketing and promotional campaigns. (You will learn about business intelligence in Chapter 5.)

Grocery stores are also experimenting with wireless technologies such as radio-frequency identification (RFID, discussed in Chapter 10) to speed the checkout process, track customers through the store, and notify customers of discounts as they pass by certain products. Grocery companies also use IT to tightly integrate their supply chains for maximum efficiency and thus reduce prices for shoppers.

Competition also is being affected by the extremely low variable cost of digital products. That is, once a digital product has been developed, the cost of producing additional "units" approaches zero. Consider the music industry as an example. When artists record music, their songs are captured in digital format. Producing physical products, such as CDs or DVDs, with the songs on them for sale in music stores involves costs. The costs in a

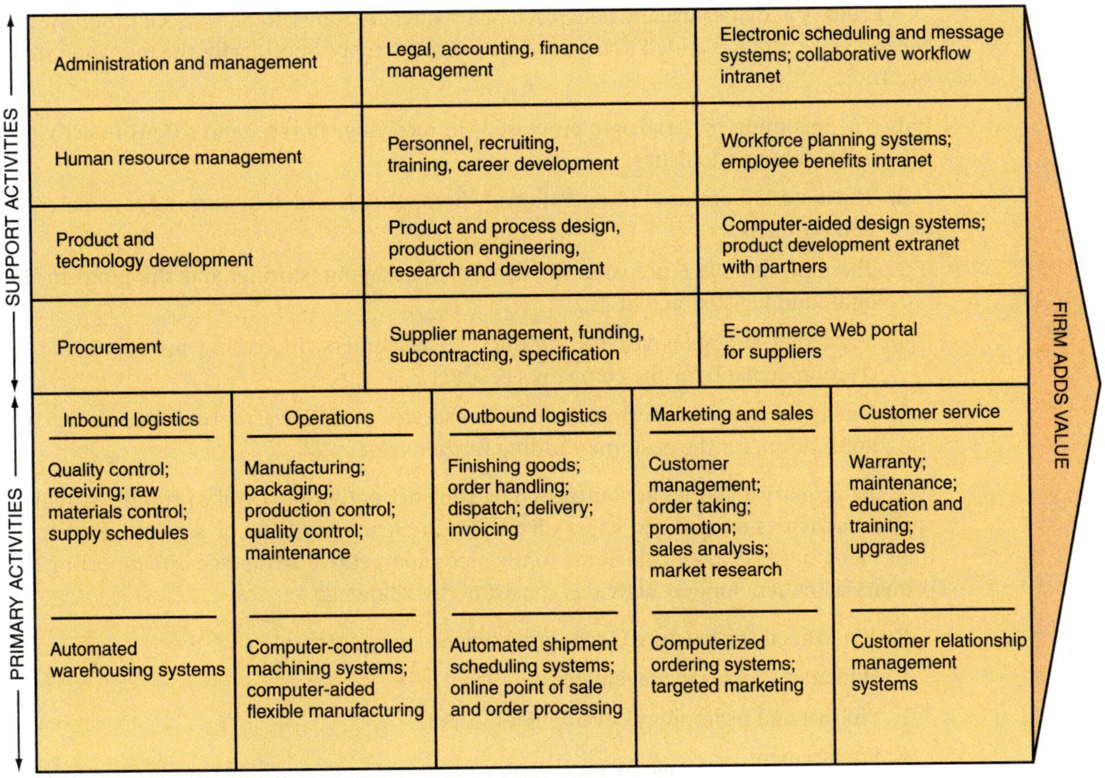

Administration and management	Legal, accounting, finance management	Electronic scheduling and message systems; collaborative workflow intranet
Human resource management	Personnel, recruiting, training, career development	Workforce planning systems; employee benefits intranet
Product and technology development	Product and process design, production engineering, research and development	Computer-aided design systems; product development extranet with partners
Procurement	Supplier management, funding, subcontracting, specification	E-commerce Web portal for suppliers

Inbound logistics	Operations	Outbound logistics	Marketing and sales	Customer service
Quality control; receiving; raw materials control; supply schedules	Manufacturing; packaging; production control; quality control; maintenance	Finishing goods; order handling; dispatch; delivery; invoicing	Customer management; order taking; promotion; sales analysis; market research	Warranty; maintenance; education and training; upgrades
Automated warehousing systems	Computer-controlled machining systems; computer-aided flexible manufacturing	Automated shipment scheduling systems; online point of sale and order processing	Computerized ordering systems; targeted marketing	Customer relationship management systems

SUPPORT ACTIVITIES — PRIMARY ACTIVITIES — FIRM ADDS VALUE

Figure 2.3 Porter's value chain model.

physical distribution channel are much higher than the costs involved in delivering the songs over the Internet in digital form.

In fact, in the future companies might give away some products for free. For example, some analysts predict that commissions for online stock trading will approach zero because investors can access the necessary information via the Internet to make their own decisions regarding buying and selling stocks. At that point, consumers will no longer need brokers to give them information that they can obtain themselves, virtually for free.

Porter's Value Chain Model

Organizations use the Porter competitive forces model to design general strategies. To identify specific activities in which they can use competitive strategies for greatest impact, they use Porter's **value chain model** (1985). The value chain model also identifies points where an organization can use information technology to achieve competitive advantage (see Figure 2.3).

According to Porter's value chain model, the activities conducted in any organization can be divided into two categories: primary activities and support activities. **Primary activities** relate to the production and distribution of the firm's products and services. These activities create value for which customers are willing to pay. Next, you are going to learn about the value chain of a manufacturing company. Keep in mind that other types of firms, such as transportation, health care, education, retail, and others, have different value chains. The key point is that every organization has a value chain: a sequence of activities through which the organization's inputs, whatever they are, are transformed into more valuable outputs, whatever they are.

In a manufacturing company, for example, primary activities involve purchasing materials, processing the materials into products, and delivering the products to customers. Companies typically perform five primary activities:

Inbound logistics (inputs)

Operations (manufacturing and testing)

Outbound logistics (storage and distribution)

Marketing and sales

Services

Primary activities usually take place in a sequence from 1 to 5. As work progresses in the sequence, value is added to the product in each activity. Specifically, the following steps occur:

1. The incoming materials are processed (in receiving, storage, and so on) in activities called inbound logistics.

2. The materials are used in operations, where value is added by turning raw materials into products.

3. These products are prepared for delivery (packaging, storing, and shipping) in the outbound logistics activities.

4. Marketing and sales sell the products to customers, increasing product value by creating demand for the company's products.

5. Finally, the company performs after-sales service, such as warranty service or upgrade notification, for the customer, adding further value.

The primary activities are buttressed by **support activities**. Unlike primary activities, support activities do not add value directly to the firm's products or services. Rather, as their name suggests, they contribute to the firm's competitive advantage by supporting the primary activities. Support activities consist of the following:

1. The firm's infrastructure (accounting, finance, management)

2. Human resources management

3. Product and technology development (R & D)

4. Procurement

Each support activity can be applied to any or all of the primary activities. In addition, the support activities can also support one another.

A firm's value chain is part of a larger stream of activities, which Porter calls a value system. A **value system**, or an *industry value chain*, includes the suppliers that provide the inputs necessary to the firm along with their value chains. After the firm creates products, these products pass through the value chains of distributors (which also have their own value chains), all the way to the customers. All parts of these chains are included in the value system. To achieve and sustain a competitive advantage, and to support that advantage with information technologies, a firm must understand every component of this value system.

Strategies for Competitive Advantage

Organizations continually try to develop strategies to counter the five competitive forces identified by Porter. You will learn about five of those strategies here. Before we go into specifics, however, it is important to note that an organization's choice of strategy involves trade-offs. For example, a firm that concentrates only on cost leadership might not have the resources available for research and development, leaving the firm unable to innovate. As another example, a company that invests in customer happiness (customer-orientation strategy) will experience increased costs.

Companies must select a strategy and then stay with it, because a confused strategy cannot succeed. This selection, in turn, decides how a company will utilize its information systems. A new information system that can improve customer service but will increase costs slightly will be welcomed at a high-end retailer such as Nordstrom but not at a discount store like Walmart. You learn about the most commonly used strategies in the following paragraphs. Figure 2.4 provides an overview of these strategies.

1. *Cost leadership strategy.* Produce products and/or services at the lowest cost in the industry. An example is Walmart's automatic inventory replenishment system, which enables Walmart to reduce inventory storage requirements. As a result, Walmart stores use floor space only to sell products, and not to store them, thereby reducing inventory costs.

2. *Differentiation strategy.* Offer products, services, or product features that are different from those of your competitor. Southwest Airlines, for example, has differentiated itself as a low-cost, short-haul, express airline. This has proved to be a winning strategy for

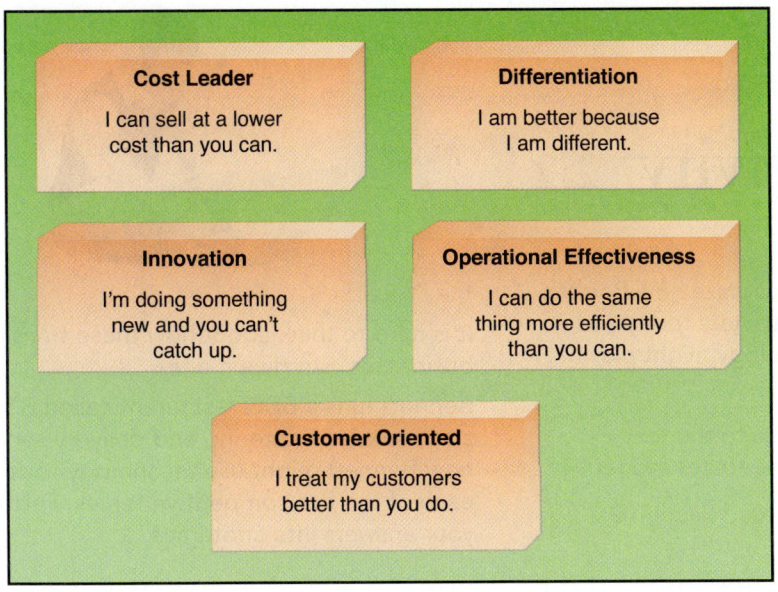

Figure 2.4 Strategies for Competitive Advantage.

competing in the highly competitive airline industry. Also, Dell has differentiated itself in the personal computer market through its mass-customization strategy.

3. Innovation strategy. Introduce new products and services, add new features to existing products and services, or develop new ways to produce them. A classic example is the introduction of automated teller machines (ATMs) by Citibank. The convenience and cost-cutting features of this innovation gave Citibank a huge advantage over its competitors. Like many innovative products, the ATM changed the nature of competition in the banking industry. Today an ATM is a competitive *necessity* for any bank.

4. Operational effectiveness strategy. Improve the manner in which internal **business processes** are executed so that a firm performs these activities better than its rivals. Such improvements increase quality, productivity, and employee and customer satisfaction while decreasing time to market.

5. Customer-orientation strategy. Concentrate on making customers happy. Web-based systems are particularly effective in this area because they can provide a personalized, one-to-one relationship with each customer.

BEFORE *YOU GO ON . . .*

1. What are strategic information systems?
2. According to Porter, what are the five forces that could endanger a firm's position in its industry or marketplaces?
3. Describe Porter's value chain model. Differentiate Porter's competitive forces model and his value chain model.
4. What strategies can companies use to gain competitive advantage?

RUBY'S CLUB QUESTIONS

1. In a college town, how strong is the threat of substitute entertainment?
2. Ruben and Lisa's vision for Ruby's is to create a relaxing, community atmosphere. Which strategy do you think best suits their desire? Cost Leader, Differentiator, Innovator, Operational Effectiveness, or Customer Orientation?
3. Which is more powerful for Ruby's: the bargaining power of suppliers or the bargaining power of customers?

Student Activity | 2.2

Objectives: Students should recognize how Porter's competitive forces play out in business today and begin to understand how technology might play a part.

Chapter Connection: This relates to the text discussion on Porter's competitive forces model.

Prerequisites: You should have read Section 2.2 before doing this activity.

Activity:

Customers must see a consistent difference between your product/service and those of your competitor. This difference needs to be obvious to your customers, and it must influence their purchasing decision. Porter's model lists five competitive forces that organizations need to consider: threat of entry of new competitors, bargaining power of suppliers, bargaining power of customers, threat of substitute products or services, and rivalry among existing firms in the industry. This textbook lists five strategies for competitive advantage: cost leadership, differentiation, innovation, operational effectiveness, and customer orientation.

Walmart is known for its low prices. It is difficult to compete against Walmart on price, so any new competitors need to provide some other competitive advantage to attract customers. Suppliers have no bargaining power—they either do it Walmart's way or lose the business. Walmart maintains its prices are already low so customers have no bargaining power. The notion of a substitute product does not really exist; a substitute store—maybe. But Walmart maintains that when compared to its competition's stores, its prices are still lower. The company uses technology to manage its inventory so that it gets just-in-time (JIT) shipments from its suppliers, thereby cutting costs since the inventory is sold almost immediately. Walmart uses technology to improve and enhance the operations in its stores, signaling when stock is low on shelves and speeding up checkout, to name just two examples. Walmart maintains a customer orientation in the stores with its culture to greet people as they walk into the store, and to do whatever is necessary to satisfy a customer. Its customer orientation is also evident on its retail Web site.

Deliverables:

It is hard to think about how these translate to smaller businesses. But give it a try.

Bennett runs a BBQ restaurant called B's BBQ, which also includes a catering and delivery service. Explain how Bennett might use technology to respond to each of the five competitive forces. Further develop your answers into strategies.

Quiz Questions:

1. B's BBQ decides to focus on the threat of substitution. Which of the following uses of technology will *not* minimize the threat of substitution?
   - (a) Online ordering
   - (b) Texting daily specials to B's BBQ customers
   - (c) Bar codes on the delivery bags that keep the order warm during delivery
   - (d) Customer's last order recall when a customer calls in an order
   - (e) Accepting online payments for catering orders

2. B's BBQ decides to allow catering customers to order online. Which of Porter's competitive forces is this attempting to minimize?
   - (a) Threat of entry of new competitors
   - (b) Bargaining power of buyers
   - (c) Threat of substitute products or services
   - (d) Bargaining power of suppliers
   - (e) Rivalry among existing firms

3. A new Mexican restaurant opens up around the corner from B's BBQ. Bennett realizes that he needs to do something to keep B's BBQ in his customers' minds when they are going out to eat. Which of the following uses of technology will minimize this rivalry?
   - (a) Update B's BBQ menu on the company's Web site with some new pictures of the inside
   - (b) Send a coupon to the customers that haven't been in for the last month
   - (c) Put a netbook on the counter so customers can sign up to receive weekly newsletters via e-mail
   - (d) B and C only
   - (e) All of the above

4. Which areas of the value chain should Bennett review in order to support an operational effectiveness strategy?

    (a) Procurement
    (b) Operations
    (c) Inbound logistics
    (d) Outbound logistics
    (e) All of the above

Discussion Questions:

1. After reviewing the competitive forces with the company's value chain, how does a company use the analysis of the results?
2. How does a company decide which strategy or strategies to use?

2.3 | Business–IT Alignment

The "holy grail" of organizations is business–IT alignment, or strategic alignment. **Business–IT alignment** (which we will call alignment) is the tight integration of the IT function with the strategy, mission, and goals of the organization. That is, the IT function directly supports the business objectives of the organization. There are six characteristics of excellent alignment:

- Organizations view IT as an engine of innovation that continually transforms the business, often creating new revenue streams.
- Organizations view their internal and external customers and their customer service function as supremely important.
- Organizations rotate business and IT professionals across departments and job functions.
- Organizations provide overarching goals that are completely clear to each IT and business employee.
- Organizations ensure that IT employees understand how the company makes (or loses) money.
- Organizations create a vibrant and inclusive company culture.

Unfortunately, many organizations fail to achieve this type of close alignment. In fact, according to a McKinsey & Company survey on IT strategy and spending, only 16 percent of the IT and business executives who participated agreed that their organization had adequate alignment between IT and the business.[4] Given the importance of alignment, why do so many organizations fail to implement this policy? The major reasons are these:

- Business managers and IT managers have different objectives.
- The business and IT departments are ignorant of each other's expertise.
- Communication is lacking.

Put simply, business executives know little about information technology, and IT executives understand the technology but do not understand the real needs of the business.

The good news is that some organizations "get it right." "IT's About Business 2.3" illustrates alignment at two companies: Progressive and Zappos. In fact, both companies maintain that business and IT are virtually indistinguishable in their strategy and operations.

[4]McKinsey & Company, "IT's Unmet Potential: McKinsey Global Survey Results," *McKinsey Quarterly,* www.mckinseyquarterly.com/ITs_unmet_potential_McKinsey_Global_Survey_Result_2277, accessed August 8, 2011.

Progressive

Progressive (www.progressive.com) markets itself as an insurance provider that offers choices to customers. Its mission is to make insurance easy to shop for, buy, and own. The insurer uses highly automated underwriting software, and it presents data to customers in an easily understandable way.

The company's exclusive IT-enabled online Name Your Price application allows customers to choose the price they would like to pay for insurance and then see the coverage they can buy for that price. After entering basic car and driver information, shoppers are offered a customized insurance package that includes the limits and deductibles that are available within that price range. Shoppers can also manipulate an online dial to change various options, and the application instantly responds with information about how such changes will affect the price. Progressive also allows customers to comparison-shop on its Web site, where they can find out what Allstate, State Farm, and other competitors charge for the same coverage.

To provide this transparency for its customers, Progressive developed software that allows the company to quickly extract pricing data filed with government regulators. The software allows Progressive managers to read a state regulatory filing, spot the key data, and determine a rating algorithm for competitors' rates.

Zappos

Zappos (www.zappos.com) is a major reseller of clothing, beauty aids, and accessories. The company's primary business platform is an enterprise data warehouse (discussed in Chapter 3) that essentially contains all of the company's data: Web site traffic, marketing data, merchandising analytics, and so on. This system handles the new business as Zappos expands its product and service offerings. For example, when Zappos expanded into selling luggage, it had to set up a special place at its distribution center to store the new items, because suitcases take up much more room than shoes. On the IT side, the company needed to reconfigure its data warehouse to reflect that change.

In another example, if a customer goes to zappos.com for a pair of red Clarks sandals in size 8, he or she can see all of the Clarks sandals available in stock. If the customer goes to www.clarks.com, he or she will be able to find all of the same information just as quickly. The reason for this is that a Zappos unit called Powered by Zappos built and runs the Clarks Web site. Launched in 2009, Powered by Zappos is a revenue-producing business application created by the Zappos IT department.

Questions

1. Consider the cases of Progressive and Zappos. What does it mean that the business strategy and information technology go hand in hand (that is, neither comes before the other)?

2. Provide specific examples of problems that could occur at Progressive and Zappos if the firms' business strategy and information technology are not aligned.

Sources: Compiled from M. Betts, "10 Megatrends Affecting Corporate IT Through 2020," *Computerworld*, March 7, 2011; C. Babcock, "Enterprise Architects' Role in Aligning IT with Business," *InformationWeek*, February 18, 2011; E. Sperling, "How CIOs See the World," *Forbes*, December 20, 2010; T. Wallgum, "Absolute Alignment: How One CIO Remains in Lock-Step with the Business," *CIO*, November 16, 2010; J. Scott, "Don't Just Build Business-IT Alignment, Map It," *CIO*, July 26, 2010; J. King, "Beyond Alignment," *Computerworld*, May 24, 2010; T. Wallgum, "CVS IT Chief on the Remedy for Business-IT Alignment," *CIO*, March 29, 2010; www.progressive.com, www.zappos.com, accessed March 19, 2011.

1. What is alignment?
2. Give examples of alignment regarding student systems at your university. (*Hint:* What are the "business" goals of your university with regard to student registration, fee payment, grade posting, etc.?)

RUBY'S CLUB Q U E S T I O N S

1. It seems like Ruby's is in a good position to create strategic IT alignment because the club can build its IT from the ground up to support its strategy. To gain alignment, do you think it is better to build from scratch or to have an existing system that is just being updated?
2. How do you think alignment could play a role in creating the desired atmosphere for Ruby's Club?

Student Activity | 2.3

Objective: This activity aims to bring some relevance to the material in this section. Students need to understand business strategy, the nature of alignment, and why IT has to be in alignment with the business strategy.

Chapter Connection: This activity deals with the concepts covered in Section 2.3, which is very short but at a very high level.

Prerequisites: You should have read Section 2.3 before doing this activity.

Activity:

Watch this video to gather some insights into how business and IT goals should be aligned: www.youtube.com/watch?v=jY1V7uBlTDM

Walmart has a very tight alignment between its business strategy and its IT strategy and we can see evidence of that as consumers. Do some online research on how Walmart uses technology.

Deliverables:

Provide answers to the following questions:

1. How has Walmart used IT to transform the business?

2. How does Walmart support customers and customer service?

Quiz Questions:

1. Walmart uses technology to:
   (a) Order inventory
   (b) Work with suppliers
   (c) Cut down transportation costs
   (d) Stay in touch with customers
   (e) All of the above

2. Alignment means:
   (a) Business decisions are made by IT.
   (b) IT sets its own goals and milestones.
   (c) The structure and goals of IT support the business strategy.
   (d) All the VPs are at the same level in the organization chart.
   (e) Managers all agree.

Discussion Questions:

1. How is technology aligned with the way you perform your job or

What's in **IT** for ME?

FOR ALL MAJORS

All of the functional areas of any organization are literally composed of a variety of business processes. Regardless of your major, you will be involved in a variety of business processes from your first day on the job. Some of these processes you will perform by yourself, some will involve only your group or department, and others will involve several (or all) of the organization's functional areas.

It is important for you to be able to visualize processes, understand the inputs and outputs of each process, and identify the "customer" of each process. These capabilities will enable you to make the organization's business processes more efficient and effective. This task generally involves incorporating information technology in the process. It is also important for you to appreciate how each process fits into your organization's strategy.

All functional areas in any organization must work together in an integrated fashion in order for the firm to respond adequately to business pressures. These responses typically require each functional area to utilize a variety of information systems. In today's competitive global marketplace, the timeliness and accuracy of these responses is even more critical.

Closely following this discussion, all functional areas must work together for the organization to gain competitive advantage in its marketplace. Again, the functional areas use a variety of strategic information systems to achieve this goal.

You have seen why companies must be concerned with strategic advantage. However, this chapter is particularly important for you for several reasons. First, the business pressures you have learned about impact your organization, but they also impact you as an individual. Thus, it is critical that you understand how information systems can help you, and eventually your organizations, respond to these pressures.

In addition, achieving competitive advantage is essential for your organization's survival. In many cases, you, your team, and all your colleagues will be responsible for creating a competitive advantage. Therefore, having general knowledge about strategy and about how information systems impact the organization's strategy and competitive position will help you in your career.

You also need a basic knowledge of your organization's strategy, mission, and goals, as well as its business problems and how it makes (or loses) money. You now know how to analyze your organization's strategy and value chain, as well as the strategies and value chains of your competitors. You also have acquired a general knowledge of how information technology contributes to organizational strategy. This knowledge will help you to do your job better, to be promoted more quickly, and to contribute significantly to the success of your organization.

>>> SUMMARY

1. List and provide examples of the three types of business pressures and describe one IT response to each.

> *Market pressures:* An example of a market pressure is powerful customers. Customer relationship management is an effective IT response that helps companies achieve customer intimacy.

> *Technology pressures:* An example of a technology pressure is information overload. Search engines and business intelligence applications enable managers to access, navigate, and utilize vast amounts of information.

> *Societal/political/legal pressures:* An example of a societal/political/legal pressure is social responsibility, such as

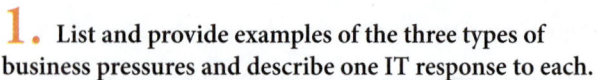

the state of the physical environment. Green IT is one response that is intended to improve the environment.

2. **Identify the five competitive forces described by Porter, and explain how the Web impacts each one.**

> *The threat of entry of new competitors:* For most firms, the Web increases the threat that new competitors will enter the market by reducing traditional barriers to entry. Frequently, competitors need only to set up a Web site to enter a market. The Web can also increase barriers to entry, as when customers come to expect a nontrivial capability from their suppliers.

> *The bargaining power of suppliers:* The Web enables buyers to find alternative suppliers and to compare prices more easily, thereby reducing suppliers' bargaining power. From a different perspective, as companies use the Web to integrate their supply chains, participating suppliers can lock in customers, thereby increasing suppliers' bargaining power.

> *The bargaining power of customers (buyers):* The Web provides customers with incredible amounts of choices for products, as well as information about those choices. As a result, the Web increases buyer power. However, companies can implement loyalty programs where they can use the Web to monitor the activities of millions of customers. Such programs reduce buyer power.

> *The threat of substitute products or services:* New technologies create substitute products very rapidly, and the Web makes information about these products available almost instantly. As a result, industries (particularly information-based industries) are in great danger from substitutes (e.g., music, books, newspapers, magazines, software). However, the Web also can enable a company to build in switching costs, which will result in costing customers time and/or money to switch from the company to a competitor.

> *The rivalry among existing firms in the industry:* In the past, proprietary information systems provided strategic advantage for firms in highly competitive industries. The visibility of Internet applications on the Web makes proprietary systems more difficult to keep secret. Therefore, the Web makes strategic advantage more short lived.

3. **Describe the strategies that organizations typically adopt to counter the five competitive forces in order to achieve competitive advantage.**

> *Cost leadership strategy:* Produce products and/or services at the lowest cost in the industry.

> *Differentiation strategy:* Offer different products, services, or product features.

> *Innovation strategy:* Introduce new products and services, put new features in existing products and services, or develop new ways to produce them.

> *Operational effectiveness strategy:* Improve the manner in which internal business processes are executed so that a firm performs similar activities better than its rivals.

> *Customer-orientation strategy:* Concentrate on making customers happy.

4. **Define alignment, and describe the characteristics of effective alignment.**

Alignment is the tight integration of the IT function with the strategy, mission, and goals of the organization. There are six characteristics of effective alignment:

> Organizations view IT as an engine of innovation that continually transforms the business.

> Organizations view customers and customer service as supremely important.

> Organizations rotate business and IT professionals across departments and job functions.

> Organizations provide clear, overarching goals for all employees.

> Organizations ensure that IT employees understand how the company makes (or loses) money.

> Organizations create a vibrant and inclusive company culture.

>>> CHAPTER GLOSSARY

business environment The combination of social, legal, economic, physical, and political factors in which businesses conduct their operations.

business–IT alignment The tight integration of the IT function with the strategy, mission, and goals of the organization.

business processes Related activities that produce a product or a service of value to the organization, its business partners, and/or its customers.

competitive advantage An advantage over competitors in some measure such as cost, quality, or speed; leads to control of a market and to larger-than-average profits.

competitive forces model A business framework devised by Michael Porter, that analyzes competitiveness by recognizing five major forces that could endanger a company's position.

digital divide The gap between those who have access to information and communications technology and those who do not.

e-business Buying and selling of goods and services as well as servicing customers, collaborating with business partners, and performing electronic transactions within an organization.

electronic commerce (EC or e-commerce) The process of buying, selling, transferring, or exchanging products, services, or information via computer networks, including the Internet.

entry barrier Product or service feature that customers expect from organizations in a certain industry; an organization trying to enter this market must provide this product or service at a minimum to be able to compete.

globalization The integration and interdependence of economic, social, cultural, and ecological facets of life, enabled by rapid advances in information technology.

individual social responsibility See **organizational social responsibility.**

make-to-order The strategy of producing customized products and services.

mass customization A production process in which items are produced in large quantities but are customized to fit the desires of each customer.

organizational social responsibility (also called **individual social responsibility**) Efforts by organizations to solve various social problems.

primary activities Business activities related to the production and distribution of the firm's products and services, thus creating value.

strategic information systems (SISs) Systems that help an organization gain a competitive advantage by supporting its strategic goals and/or increasing performance and productivity.

support activities Business activities that do not add value directly to a firm's product or service under consideration but support the primary activities that do add value.

value chain model Model that shows the primary activities that sequentially add value to the profit margin; also shows the support activities.

value system Includes the producers, suppliers, distributors, and buyers, all with their value chains.

>>> DISCUSSION QUESTIONS

1. Explain why IT is both a business pressure and an enabler of response activities that counter business pressures.

2. What does a flat world mean to you in your choice of a major? In your choice of a career? Will you have to be a lifelong learner? Why or why not?

3. What might the impact of a flat world be on your standard of living?

4. Is IT a strategic weapon or a survival tool? Discuss.

5. Why might it be difficult to justify a strategic information system?

6. Describe the five forces in Porter's competitive forces model, and explain how the Internet has affected each one.

7. Describe Porter's value chain model. What is the relationship between the competitive forces model and the value chain model?

8. Discuss the idea that an information system by itself can rarely provide a sustainable competitive advantage.

>>> PROBLEM-SOLVING ACTIVITIES

1. Surf the Internet for information about the Department of Homeland Security. Examine the available information, and comment on the role of information technologies in the department.

2. Experience customization by designing your own shoes at www.nike.com, your car at www.jaguar.com, your CD at www.easternrecording.com, your business card at www.iprint.com, and your diamond ring at www.bluenile.com. Summarize your experiences.

3. Access www.go4customer.com. What does this company do, and where is it located? Who are its customers? Which of Friedman's flatteners does this company fit? Provide examples of how a U.S. company would use its services.

4. Enter Walmart China (www.wal-martchina.com/english/index.htm). How does Walmart China differ from your local Walmart (consider products, prices, services, etc.)? Describe these differences.

5. Apply Porter's value chain model to Costco (www.costco.com). What is Costco's competitive strategy? Who are Costco's major competitors? Describe Costco's business model. Describe the tasks that Costco must accomplish for each primary value chain activity. How would Costco's information systems contribute to Costco's competitive strategy, given the nature of its business?

6. Apply Porter's value chain model to Dell (www.dell.com). What is Dell's competitive strategy? Who are Dell's major competitors? Describe Dell's business model. Describe the tasks that Dell must accomplish for each primary value chain activity. How would Dell's information systems contribute to Costco's competitive strategy, given the nature of its business?

7. The market for optical copiers is shrinking rapidly. It is expected that by 2010 as much as 90 percent of all duplicated documents will be done on computer printers. Can a company such as Xerox Corporation survive?

   a. Read about the problems and solutions of Xerox from 2000–2010 at www.fortune.com, www.findarticles.com, and www.google.com.

   b. Identify all the business pressures on Xerox.

   c. Find some of Xerox's response strategies (see www.xerox.com, www.yahoo.com, and www.google.com).

   d. Identify the role of IT as a contributor to the business technology pressures (e.g., obsolescence).

   e. Identify the role of IT as a facilitator of Xerox's critical response activities.

>>> TEAM ASSIGNMENTS

1. a. Create an online group for studying IT or a part of IT that interests you. Each member of the group must have a Yahoo e-mail account (free). Go to Yahoo! Groups (http://groups.yahoo.com) and at the bottom see a section titled "Create Your Own Group."

   Step 1: Click on "Start a Group Now."

   Step 2: Select a category that best describes your group (use the Search Group Categories, or use Browse Group Categories tool). You must find a category.

   Step 3: Describe the purposes of the group and give it a name.

   Step 4: Set up an e-mail address for sending messages to all group members.

   Step 5: Each member must join the group (select a "profile"); click on "Join this Group."

   Step 6: Go to the Word Verification Section; follow the instructions.

   Step 7: Finish by clicking "Continue."

   Step 8: Select a group moderator. Conduct a discussion online of at least two topics of interest to the group.

   Step 9: Arrange for messages from the members to reach the moderator at least once a week.

   Step 10: Find a similar group (use Yahoo's "Find a Group" and make a connection). Write a report for your instructor.

   b. Now follow the same steps for Google Groups.

   c. Compare Yahoo Groups and Google Groups.

2. Divide the class into teams. Each team will select a country government and visit its official Web site (e.g., United States, Australia, New Zealand, Singapore, Norway, Canada, the United Kingdom, the Netherlands, Denmark, Germany, and France). For example, the official Web portal for the U.S. government is www.usa.gov. Review and compare the services offered by each country. How does the United States stack up? Are you surprised at the number of services offered by countries through Web sites? Which country offers the most services? The least?

CLOSING **CASE 1 >** Double Trouble for BP

In 2008, CEO Tony Hayward of BP (www.bp.com) informed his top 500 managers that the giant oil company had become a serial underperformer. Among the audience was Dana Deasy, BP's chief information officer (CIO). Deasy understood that BP's IT group would have to do a much better job of supporting the CEO's goals: to restore revenue growth across the enormous (annual revenues of some $300 billion) company, to refocus the behavior of the company around high performance and accountability, and to reduce the complexity of the organization. The IT group had become bloated, passive, unfocused, and unconcerned with performance and accountability.

    Deasy wanted to eliminate $800 million in expenses from BP's overall IT budget of $3 billion, to cut in half the number of IT vendors, to evaluate BP's 4,200 IT employees, to reduce the 8,500 software applications in use at BP worldwide, and to transform the IT function from a cost center into a business-driven, strategic weapon. Confronted with a vast sprawl in people, budget, priorities, requirements, business objectives, and

<<<**BP'S FIRST PROBLEM**

suppliers, Deasy committed to a three-year overhaul of every facet of BP's IT operations.

THE SOLUTION TO BP'S FIRST PROBLEM>>>

Deasy made BP's IT employees his first priority. Significantly, only 55 percent of his IT personnel were actually BP employees. The rest consisted of some 1,900 contractors. Deasy cut 1,000 full-time contractor positions, reducing BP's reliance on outsiders. In addition, in his first 11 months as CIO, Deasy replaced 80 percent of the top IT leadership within the organization.

Deasy then hired IBM to conduct comprehensive assessments of the top 1,000 IT employees (excluding the remaining contractors). This assessment identified talent gaps as well as inherent strengths. The most pressing issues were the organizational location of the IT function, project and portfolio management, and vendor management.

In his next move, Deasy mandated that the CIO for each BP business unit work for the business unit leader while also reporting to Deasy in a matrix arrangement. Deasy made accountability the first priority for those CIOs—that is, their primary responsibility was to help the business units use IT effectively to drive new revenue and reduce costs.

Deasy then set out to reduce the number of IT vendors. Not only was BP currently contracting with more than 2,000 vendors, but the 20 largest vendors accounted for only 30 percent of IT spending. To make this arrangement more manageable, BP put 65 percent of its annual global IT spending—about $1.5 billion—up for rebid in one year. As a result of the bidding process, BP eliminated 1,200 IT vendors and saved the company $900 million over the next five years.

Deasy also aggressively reworked vendor relationships in the area of application development and maintenance. In this area, BP had been using some 50 vendors, most of whom refused to talk with one another for fear of losing their share of BP's business. BP rebid multiyear application development and maintenance contracts totaling about $2 billion and ended up with just 5 vendors. These vendors handle all of the work according to a standard operating model. Deasy predicts some $500 million in savings from this effort alone.

As one of SAP's largest customers, BP created a team focused on standardizing project delivery and management of SAP applications around the world. BP's goal was to deliver new SAP capabilities 50 percent faster and 40 percent cheaper than under the existing system.

THE RESULTS>>>

Deasy and his team accomplished their goals in two years instead of three. BP realized $800 million in IT savings, a 60 percent reduction in the number of vendors, a significant reduction in the number of applications, and an overhaul of the IT reporting structure in the business units.

However, the two major benefits may well have been these:

- The top-to-bottom changes in IT personnel, where long-time generalists were replaced with technology specialists or business-domain experts.
- The profound overhaul of the IT organization's culture, where Deasy changed the passive, inwardly focused, financially irresponsible, and unaccountable philosophy to a culture with a sense of purpose centered on business growth and success, excellence, and relentless improvement and innovation.

BP'S SECOND PROBLEM>>>

In April 2010, just as BP was beginning to profit from its IT innovations, the company's Deepwater Horizon oil well, located in the Gulf of Mexico, exploded, resulting in the largest marine oil spill in the history of the petroleum industry. The well took three months to cap, during which time oil continued to pour into the gulf.

The explosion was investigated by the Oil Spill Commission, an authority created by President Barack Obama. The key verdict of the commission was that BP's monitoring IT systems on the Deepwater Horizon oil platform had failed to provide automatic warning alerts. Instead, the system had relied on engineers who had to manually monitor and analyze complex data from the well for long periods of time. Because the engineers had to perform so many simultaneous functions over long work days, they needed much more support from BP's automated systems.

The commission further charged that BP had ignored the results of the OptiCem cement modeling software implemented by Halliburton, the cement contractor. OptiCem had indicated that more stabilizers were needed to support the underwater cement work. The commission also criticized Halliburton for failing to share data from tests on its cement mix with BP.

In addition to these problems, BP also failed to take advantage of social networking to open a clear line of communication with people living along the coast bordering the Gulf of Mexico and around the world. BP could have used social media sites such as Facebook, YouTube, and Twitter to report on the problem and explain what steps the company was taking to cap the spill and contain the damage.

Just a couple of decades ago, companies had time to devise strategies to deal with disasters. An excellent illustration is the Tylenol poisoning crisis of 1982, when seven Chicago residents died after they ingested Tylenol capsules laced with cyanide. Experts concluded that somebody had tampered with the capsules after they had been packaged and distributed. The drug's manufacturer, Johnson & Johnson, immediately shut down distribution and recalled all of the capsules that were on the market. Next, the company reintroduced Tylenol to the market packaged in a tamper-resistant pill container. This entire process, for which Johnson & Johnson received widespread acclaim, took several weeks. In contrast, in today's world of viral videos, bloggers, and social networks, companies cannot wait even a few days to generate a public response.

In addition to technological efforts to cap the spill, BP spared no expense on public relations. For example, it spent huge sums of money to buy Google ads, which routed people to BP's relatively inaccurate Web site. Reports from Reuters asserted that BP was buying Google ads "so its own Web site would rank higher or even at the top of the list of advertisements that appear with search results when Internet users search on terms such as *oil spill*, *volunteer*, and *claims*. The BP Web site contained press releases and photographs of people involved in the oil cleanup. Notably missing were any pictures of the oil spill itself, of oil-drenched wetlands, or of animals dying from the effects of the spill.

<<<THE SOLUTION (?) TO BP'S SECOND PROBLEM

It took three months, but BP was able to cap the spill. However, scientists said that the damage from the oil would continue for many years.

<<<THE RESULTS

At the end of 2010, the U.S. government launched a $21.1 billion lawsuit against BP and its drilling partners, alleging that they had "failed . . . to use the best available and safest drilling technology" to monitor pressure in the well. Other lawsuits are pending. Eventually, BP CEO Tony Hayward resigned his position on October 1, 2010.

Questions

1. Describe BP's first problem, which involved the firm's IT function. Discuss BP's solution to this problem.

2. Discuss BP's handling of its second problem: the well-head explosion.

3. Why did BP believe that its business information systems were of strategic importance to the firm (in the company's first problem), but that its drilling information systems were not of comparable strategic importance? Provide examples to support your answer.

Sources: Compiled from L. King, "BP Oil Spill IT Systems Lacked Key Alarms," *Computerworld*, January 6, 2011; S. Mufson, "BP, Transocean, Halliburton Blamed by Presidential Gulf Oil Spill Commission," *Washington Post*, January 5, 2011; D. Bates, "BP Accepts Blame for Gulf of Mexico Spill After Leaked Memo Reveals Engineer Misread Pressure Reading," *London Dailymail*, August 30, 2010; S. Gaudin, "BP, in Crisis Mode, Misses Social Networking Target," *Computerworld*, June 15, 2010; P. Gralla, "BP's Disaster Containment Plan—Throw Plenty of Money at Google," *Computerworld*, June 11, 2010; S. Power, R. Gold, and N. King, "Staffing Levels on Deepwater Horizon Are Questioned," *Wall Street Journal*, June 8, 2010; B. Evans, "BP's IT Transformation," *InformationWeek*, March 8, 2010; T. Kaplan, "The Tylenol Crisis: How Effective Public Relations Saved Johnson & Johnson," *New Jersey Bell Journal*, 1983; www.bp.com, accessed March 22, 2011.

CLOSING **CASE 2 >**

Two Financial Giants Merge

THE PROBLEM>>> On December 31, 2008, two giant financial institutions announced a merger, as Wells Fargo (www.wellsfargo.com) completed its $15 billion acquisition of Wachovia (www.wachovia.com). The combined company became the second-largest bank in the United States, with 2008 sales of $1.3 trillion, 300,000 employees, 10,400 branch and office locations, and 12,300 ATMs in North America. For the merger to be successful, the two companies had to merge their people and technology as well as their financial assets.

In particular, from an IT perspective, the merger required a major network integration to combine both banks' operations. When two giant financial firms merge, they have to consider more than just integrating their financial cultures. They have to consider their IT cultures as well. For example, what happens if one bank maintains a highly decentralized IT approach in which each individual business unit has its own IT policies, and the other bank has a centralized approach?

In addition, financial institutions use IT to strategically differentiate themselves from their competitors. As one financial consultant explained, "Banks have their brands, and those brands are delivered by their IT structure." Thus, Wells Fargo and Wachovia faced the added challenge of melding their distinctive identities into a new identity.

THE SOLUTION>>> The major initiative of the entire IT integration was to select and implement the best existing application in a business area, regardless of which bank already used that application. In this way the newly formed bank focused on business outcomes rather than technology. The overall goal of the transition team was customer retention—that is, customers were to experience no disruption in services during the merger process.

The transition team members realized that they were integrating disparate IT teams, where every team member had his or her individual preferences regarding the systems they were using. The challenge was to get all employees to focus on the overall goal, which was to evaluate which systems would best serve the new bank's customers.

The integration process was intricate because the two companies were using more than 4,000 IT systems in total. The transition team's strategy was to choose one business process (business processes are discussed in detail online in "Plug IT In 1"), select the most appropriate application for that process, and then made certain that all of the employees who were involved in that process knew how to use that application. Consider the mortgage lending and online banking business processes.

- The Wells Fargo mortgage lending application was superior in scalability, meaning that it could accommodate the increased processing needs generated by the merger. At the time of the merger, Wells Fargo was struggling to fill the demands created by the mortgage refinancing boom. In fact, the bank added 10,000 employees just to handle those orders. The Wells Fargo application was superior to the Wachovia application in handling that demand and conducting secure transactions, so the transition team used it.

- Wells Fargo's online banking applications were also found to be superior to Wachovia's. Wells Fargo's customers constantly commented on how easy these applications were to use and how intuitive the interface was.

To ensure that employees remained as productive as possible during the merger, Wells Fargo provided ongoing support for nearly all of the 4,000 applications the two pre-merger banks used. A group from the transition team oversaw the transition to new, best-of-breed applications.

At Wells Fargo, the focus is on providing a level of service that today's customers demand. The bank, with more than 48 million customers, has made mobility a key component of its business. For example, it now offers banking services through mobile channels: text banking, a mobile browser, and specialized smart phone applications. Nearly 25 percent of the customers who bank online also use mobile banking to check balances, make transfers, and pay bills. Further, customers who use text banking send about two dozen messages per month.

Also, Wells Fargo is combining physical and virtual tools. For instance, customers can have ATM receipts sent to their e-mail addresses rather than receiving paper.

The bottom line? In 2010, Wells Fargo posted a second-quarter profit of $2.5 billion, a third-quarter profit of $3.34 billion, and a fourth-quarter profit of $3.4 billion.

<<<THE RESULTS

Questions

1. Provide two specific examples of why it was so important for Wells Fargo and Wachovia to integrate their information systems so as to ensure the success of the merger.

2. Provide two specific examples of difficulties the companies experienced in integrating their information systems.

SOURCES: Compiled from S. Greengard, "Mobile Means Business," *Baseline Magazine*, January 28, 2011; K. Nash, "2011 State of the CIO," *CIO*, January 1, 2011; D. McCafferty, "Joining Two Financial Giants," *Baseline Magazine*, September 1, 2009; www.wellsfargo.com, www.wachovia.com, accessed February 15, 2011.

RUBY'S CLUB INTERNSHIP ASSIGNMENTS

Ruben and Lisa seriously need to understand their market. To help them, search the Web in your local area for bars, clubs, theaters, restaurants, and athletic events, then analyze the types of entertainment Ruby's Club will compete against. Rate each as to whether the strategy is cost leadership, differentiation, innovation, operational effectiveness, or customer orientation. Make notes about how each communicates with its customers. Does it use Facebook? Twitter? E-mail? Traditional mail?

Flyers on campus? How do they advertise themselves to their customers?

Finally, provide Ruben and Lisa (submit to your instructor) a competitive grid that outlines the competition and provide suggestions on how to accomplish Ruben and Lisa's vision (relaxing community atmosphere) by some combination of the above mentioned strategies. Be sure to discuss alignment in your submission.

SPREADSHEET ACTIVITY

Objective: Strategic information systems are designed to help create some type of competitive advantage. This activity teaches you that something as simple as sorting and filtering within a spreadsheet can be a form of a strategic information system in that it will help make strategic decisions.

Chapter Connection: Porter's five forces are demonstrated in this activity. The two most focused on are the bargaining power of customers and industry rivalry. These will be evaluated in the activity by working with multiple pages within one workbook. Each page will provide a different comparison that will provide new/different information.

Prerequisites: There are no prerequisites for this activity.

Activity: There are many factors that play a role in determining the final cost of a product. There are even more decisions that play into which options are chosen for a given product. Often, strategic information systems are used to help create competitive advantage. The recreational vehicle (RV) industry is no exception. Companies try to fit as many options into a camper as they can without dramatically increasing the weight, sacrificing the durability of the unit, or driving manufacturing costs so high that the price is uncompetitive. Industry innovations quickly become standard, customer desires change as gas prices go up and down, and businesses are left to sort everything out.

Go to www.screencast.com/t/JxuKQTOS and watch the video about sorting and filtering within spreadsheets. It will explain the process and how something this simple can be used to help make strategic decisions. Then download the file MIS–Chapter 2.xlsx from www.wiley.com/college/rainer. It includes a customer survey regarding RV options and customer preferences as well as a list of competitive offerings and prices.

Then sort and filter the information based on criteria given to you by your professor. By sorting and filtering, you are creating information from your data (the raw facts). You will then use this information to make strategic business decisions to help your RV company create a competitive advantage within the marketplace.

Deliverables: The final product will be a spreadsheet filtered to show rank of the organization among different criteria relative to their competition. Once you have filtered and ranked the data, you will make suggestions as to the best course of action that will provide the strongest possible competitive advantage for the company. This recommendation will come in the form of a business letter.

Quiz Questions:

1. True or False? Unsorted data are helpful to strategic decision makers.
2. When raw facts are organized, sorted, filtered, or otherwise processed, you have created:
   (a) Data
   (b) Information
   (c) Knowledge
   (d) Decisions
   (e) Competitive advantage
3. True or False? Spreadsheets, though somewhat rudimentary compared to the elaborate strategic information systems available, are still capable of supporting strategic decisions.
4. True or False? When data are filtered, they are erased from the spreadsheet.
5. True or False? When data are sorted, they are only sorted within their own column.

Discussion Questions:

1. Too often, information systems are viewed as complicated computer programs that are difficult to understand. However, spreadsheets can provide much of the needed functionality. At what point is it cost effective to purchase a more legitimate program than to use simple tools found within a spreadsheet?
2. Given the fact that information systems are there to support decisions, why do you think many opt for more expensive systems than the relatively easy-to-use spreadsheet?

DATABASE ACTIVITY: CREATING TABLES

Objective

In this activity, you will learn how to create Access tables from an existing design. The construction of any database begins with creating its data tables. If you can't create tables, you can't create a database. Even if you use a database that someone else has created, knowing where the tables come from will help you understand what you can do with it and why it sometimes behaves in ways that you might otherwise not expect.

The database has to be designed first, of course. You will do that in the Chapter 3 activity if your instructor assigns it. Here we've done the design for you, so you can "get your hands dirty" early in the course.

Chapter Connection

Competitive advantage and strategic information systems depend on high-quality data. The tables in a database determine what can be done with it. Understanding how its tables determine what a database can do will help you figure out what strategic systems your company can develop, or how its databases must change to support the systems it needs.

Prerequisites

None.

Activity:

1. In this activity, which you will find online, you will create a database of university departments and courses from scratch. You will create database tables, tell Access how they are related to each other, and enter data into them. You will use similar tables in future Access activities.

   The following database diagram (a type of diagram called an *entity-relationship diagram*, as you will learn in Chapter 3) describes part of the data for a university. Specifically, this part of the database will store data about four *entities*: departments, courses, students and grades.

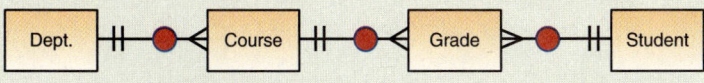

   The lines in the diagram tell us that:

   • Each department can have several courses, but might not have any.

• Each course belongs to exactly one department.

• Each course can have several students, but might not have any. (This would be a temporary situation when registration starts.)

• Each student in the course receives one grade.

• Each student can take several courses, but might not be registered for any (yet).

• Each course gives that student one grade.

This information is contained in four tables. You will create the two on the left of the ERD, the Department and Course tables. The first, the department table, will contain the same data that we see here on a spreadsheet:

	A	B	C	D
1	**Name**	**Prefix**	**Space**	**Created On**
2	English	ENL	2500	2/9/1894
3	History	HIS	3500	8/1/1892
4	Physics	PHY	4000	9/1/1892
5	Economics	ECO	2000	3/1/1926
6	Languages	LAN	2300	4/15/1918

2. To create the department table, start by launching Access. Click "Blank Database" at the upper left of the "Available Templates" section of its opening window. At the lower right, name this database Activity2.accdb (or as your instructor specifies). Then click "Create."

3. You will see the Datasheet view of the new table, with no data. You could start by entering column names and data in this view. If you do this, Access will make assumptions about your data. Its assumptions are usually correct, but they are wrong often enough to cause problems that are easier to avoid now than fix later. There are also things you cannot do in this view. So, switch to Design view by clicking the "Drafting Tools" icon at the top left corner.

Usage Hint: Most Access objects can be manipulated in three, four, or more views. The icon shows the view that Access designers thought you are most likely to want next. If you want a different view, you can click the triangle under the drafting tools icon to drop down a menu of icons, or click on one of the icons at the bottom right corner of the window, which shows all available views.

4. Before changing views, Access requires you to name your new table. Name it DeptTbl and click "OK." The ending "Tbl" identifies it as a table, distinguishing it from other things called "Dept" (such as, for example, a department list) that you might create later.

Usage Hint: Some people put the letters that identify the object type at the start of its name: TblDept, for example. That action groups objects of each type in an alphabetical list. Here, it is a matter of personal preference unless your instructor specifies otherwise. This project will put them at the end.

5. Access has already created the first field of your table, a unique identifier called "ID." It was not on the spreadsheet, but a true database needs it. The *AutoNumber* data type will assign a different number to every department, ensuring you will be able to tell them apart even if two have the same name. (This is why schools give students unique ID numbers.) In a database, such a unique identifier is called a *primary key.* Access indicates primary keys by keys to the left of their names. Change the name of this field from ID to DeptID, to avoid later confusion with primary keys of other tables.

6. Enter the name of the next column, DeptName, below DeptID. If you tab to the next field, you will see that Access automatically sets its data type to Text. Since department names are text strings, leave that alone. You can describe it in the third column if you want. (Your instructor may have requirements for this.)

Usage Hint: Both these names begin with "Dept." This helps us tell department names from student or instructor names outside the context of their tables.

7. The next row, which will become the next column of the table in Datasheet view, gives the three-letter prefix that applies to that department's courses. Call it DeptPrefix. It is of data type Text, too. In the Description column, enter "Three upper-case letters." This will help people who use the database know what to enter there.

8. The fourth column of the database table will say how many square feet of office space the department uses.

So, in the fourth row, enter the name DeptSpace. This time, click the down arrow at the right of its Data Type field to drop down a menu of data types. Select Number.

Usage Hint: You can also key in the word "Number." As soon as you enter "n" Access will complete the word, since no other data types start with that letter.

9. The fifth data column will say when the department was created. (This is needed because university tradition calls for departments to march into graduation ceremonies in order of creation, oldest first.) Call this field DeptCreated. Change its data type to Date/Time. In the Field Properties pane in the lower part of the window, click the blank area to the right of the word "Format." In the menu of date/time formats that drops down, select Medium Date.

At this point your table definition should look like this:

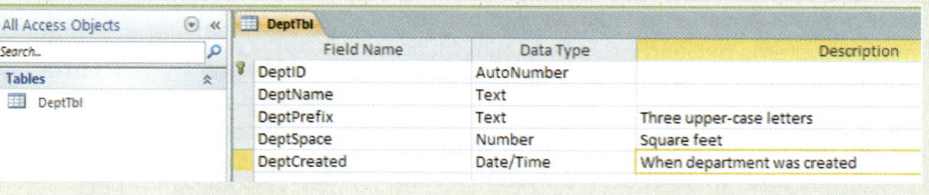

10. Now, click on the Datasheet icon at the top left of the window to return to Datasheet view and enter data. Access will prompt you to save the table. Answer "Yes." (Answering "No" would leave the table in Design view.)

Usage Hint: If you're defining a large data table, do not wait until it is all done to save your work. Click the File ribbon tab and choose Save, or click the diskette icon at the top left of the window, every few minutes.

11. In Datasheet view, click in the first row under DeptName to begin entering data for the first department. Enter the name "English," the prefix "ENG," an area of 2,500 square feet, and a creation date of September 2, 1894. Access automatically gave the first department a DeptID of 1. Your table should now look like this:

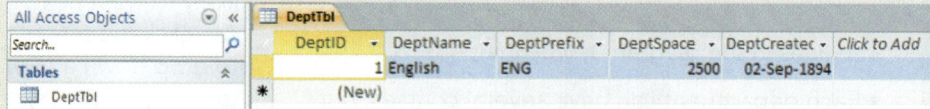

12. When you see this, you realize that the area should be formatted with a comma after the thousands digit. Select the DeptSpace column, or any data in it. Make the Fields ribbon tab active, and select Standard format from the Format pull-down menu in the Formatting section.

Usage Hint: Another way to do this is to click the Apply Comma Number Format icon (looks like a comma) in the Formatting section. That format also puts two decimal places after the integer part of the number. We do not want decimal places here, so click the Decrease Decimals icon (shows two zeroes with an arrow pointing to one zero) twice to get rid of them.

Usage Hint: A third option is to return to Design view, select DeptSpace, click in the Format row of the Field Properties panel, click the down arrow at the far right of that row to pull down the menu of formats, and select Standard format. Then return to Datasheet view. That is overkill for comma formatting, but you need to do it if the option you want is not in the ribbon.

13. Continue to add the remainder of the data shown in the preceding spreadsheet. If your instructor gives you different or additional requirements, follow them.

14. Now create the Course table, as shown in the following spreadsheet. Start by clicking the Create tab above the ribbon. In that ribbon click the leftmost icon, Table. Then continue as before, naming this table CourseTbl. Include a primary key, even though it is not shown in the spreadsheet. Be sure to give the CourseDept field data type Number, to match the Autonumber data type of the primary key in DeptTbl. Select data types for the other fields based on your understanding of their content. (A real database, rather than showing the instructor's name here, would have a link to a faculty table.)

15. The key characteristic of a database, that differentiates it from a file with information about one real-world entity, is that the tables in it are associated with each other. Look at the Course table. It does not show directly that the first course is taught by the English department. It does, however, contain the department key "1." That key identifies a row in the Department table. That row gives us the prefix ENG to create the complete identifier "ENG 307," the full name of the department ("English") if we need it, and anything else we want to know about the department.

Creating a column with department codes in the Courses table makes it possible for Access to connect the two tables. But what if we enter, say, 55 into a CourseDept field when we mean 5? Access will gladly accept the data, but later it will not be able to find a department to match it. That is because it does not know, yet, that these two fields are meant to match.

Now we have to tell it to make that connection. To do that, first close the tables, saving them if prompted. Then, click the Database Tools tab on the ribbon. On that ribbon click "Relationships," left of center. In the Show Tables dialogue box, shift-click the unselected table to select both of them, then click Add and close the box.

16. To tell Access about the connection, drag CourseDept in the Course table onto DeptID in the Department table. You will see a dialogue box with a check-box to "Enforce Referential Integrity." This means that Access will check that every CourseDept in the Course table matches an existing DeptID in the Department table: It will not let you assign a course to Department 55 unless Department 55 exists. Check this box and click Create.

If you carried out the previous steps correctly, you will see a line between these two data fields. It will have a "1" by DeptTbl and a ∞ (infinity) symbol by CourseTbl. This means the two are in a many-to-one relationship: a department can have many courses, but each course is in only one department. It should look like this:

	A	B	C	D	E	F	G
1	CrsDept	CrsNum	CrsTitle	CrsProf	CrsRoom	CrsDays	CrsStart
2	1	101	English Literature	Barker	McCosh 150	MWF	9:00
3	1	307	Chaucer	Robertson	Mahoney 301	MW	1:00
4	2	131	Asian History	Zhang	Healey 310	TR	1:00
5	2	225	World War II	Freedman	Healey 312	MWF	10:00
6	3	215	Quantum Mechanics	Wheeler	Palmer 242	MWF	11:00
7	4	101	Macroeconomics	Doody	Higgins 120	W	6:00
8	5	207	French Short Story	Malraux	Charlton 202	TR	11:30
9	5	321	Spanish Poetry	Garcia	Wexler 431	TR	8:30
10							

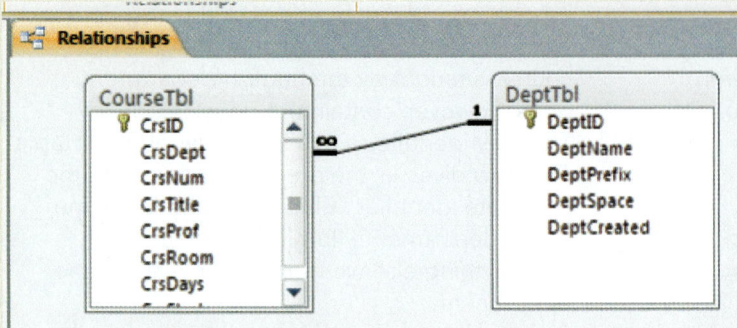

temporary file having the same name but extension .laccdb. This lock file prevents other programs from changing a database while it is in use. It goes away when you close the database. If you submit a database while it is open, it is easy to submit the lock file by mistake. The easiest way to avoid that error is to close the database first. If you send it while it is open, be sure you send the right file. A lock file will be of no use to your instructor.

If this did not happen, the most common reasons are these:

- **You got a line between the two, but there are no symbols at its ends.** You did not check "Enforce Referential Integrity." Double-click the line to edit it (or right-click and select Edit Relationship), check the box, and OK the change.

- **"The database engine could not lock table '[name]' because it is already in use by another person or process."** A table is still open. Cancel the request, bring the open table to the front by clicking its tab, close it (saving if asked), and repeat.

- **"Microsoft Office Access can't create this relationship and enforce referential integrity."** At least one CourseDept does not match a DeptID. Check that CourseDept is of data type Number and all values in that column are correct. If you used data from this activity, check your tables against the data here. If you used other data, such as your instructor's, check the tables against that data. If you used your own, confirm that all CourseDept values match DeptID values. Then repeat the process.

Deliverables:

Your database file with the two preceding tables, their data, and the relationship.

Usage Hint: Access 2010 can gives database files the file name extension .mdb (works with any recent Access release) or .accdb (works with Access 2007 and later). While it is open, Access 2010 creates a

Quiz Questions:

1. True or False? If a field has data type AutoNumber, it will never have the same value in two rows of the table.

2. Which of the following is *not* a valid Access data type?
   (a) Text
   (b) Date/Time
   (c) Color
   (d) Number

3. True or False? You must use the Description field in a table's Design view to describe what each field of the table is for.

4. True or False? To enter data into a table, you use Datasheet view.

Discussion Questions:

1. A primary key, such as DeptID in this activity, identifies a single row of a database table uniquely. It must meet two conditions: Every row of the table has to have one, and they must all be different. Would the three-letter prefix that a department uses for its courses be a suitable primary key? Why or why not?

2. Use Access online help and/or the search engine of your choice to learn the difference between Text and Memo data types. Explain, to a nontechnical reader, when to use each.

3. Suppose the English department changes its name to English Literature and its course prefix to ENL. The Department table is updated to reflect these changes. What changes must be made to the Course table in order to update all the course listings?

3 | Data and Knowledge Management

LEARNING OBJECTIVES >>>

1. List three common challenges in managing data, and describe one way each one can be addressed using data governance.

2. Name six problems minimized by using the database approach.

3. Demonstrate how to interpret relationships depicted in an entity-relationship diagram.

4. List one main advantage and one main disadvantage of relational databases.

5. Identify and explain the advantages of the four characteristics of data warehouses.

6. Demonstrate the use of a multidimensional model to store and analyze data.

7. List two main advantages of using knowledge management, and describe the steps in the knowledge management system cycle.

OPENING CASE > Crabby Bill's

Over 30 years ago Crabby Bill's began as a single restaurant. In those days, data management consisted of paper receipts in file cabinets. Over the years, Crabby Bill's grew to a chain of nine restaurants in the Tampa/St. Petersburg, Florida area. During that time, Crabby Bill's developed multiple databases to keep up with the different types of data used in the business (inventory, accounting, and so on). The problem is that these databases do not communicate with each other. This means that Luis Campuzano (chief financial and technical officer) has a very difficult time accessing and using the restaurants' data. He has to constantly copy and paste from one database to another to integrate the data in a spreadsheet where he can manipulate it to find useful information. These incompatible databases make planning and coordination between the multiple restaurants very difficult. Luis needed a solution to enable the multiple databases to share information quickly and seamlessly.

Luis turned to a database software product called FileMaker Pro (www.filemaker.com) and a third-party programmer for the solution he needed. First, Luis had to determine the relationships among the databases. Then, the programmer wrote the necessary computer code to allow the multiple databases to communicate. Once this process was finished, Luis used FileMaker Pro to query his databases and see his data in ways he had never seen before.

The integrated databases provide Luis with over 4 million table records to query. This data has allowed Luis to better plan, coordinate, and control the day-to-day operations of Crabby Bill's. He even wrote a seating program to better utilize their space based on the information he was able to find in his now integrated and accessible databases.

Sources: Compiled from www.crabbybills.com, www.filemaker.com, accessed May 22, 2011.

Questions

1. Why did Crabby Bill's develop multiple databases for its data? Are there any advantages in this approach? Support your answer.

2. What are the disadvantages of the multiple database approach (other than the disadvantages mentioned in this case)?

RUBY'S CLUB

Data collection has always been important to Ruben and Lisa. However, their form of data collection was to keep up with receipts from cover charges, drinks, food, etc. They mainly did this to create financial statements. Even with this, they aren't very accurate because many people pay with cash and no itemized receipt is printed. Therefore, often the best they can do is a general statement of costs and sales. They have no way to measure and track individual sales, customers, and products.

Ruben and Lisa have never been able to track sales to customers, weeknight, band (type of music playing), and so on. Even more important, they do not know very much about their customers. Why do they come? What do they like? What do they wish was better? What are the most popular drink items? How do people rate their overall experience? Which drink and food items are most popular and at what time of night? How can I best reach my customer base? Facebook? Twitter? E-mail?

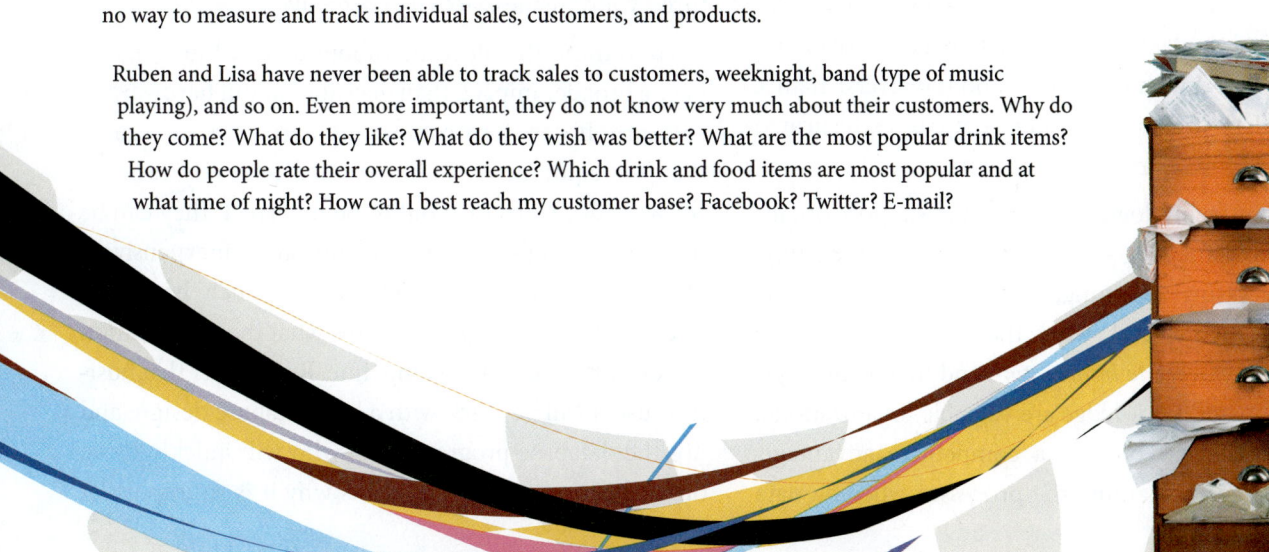

>>> The only way to answer these questions is to have data that can be analyzed to create information. The best way to capture the data in an organized format is to use a database.

INTRODUCTION

"Big Data" represents a very real problem that every business faces. This problem becomes even more pronounced when you consider the vast increases in the amount of data that organizations capture and store. The opening case describes the numerous problems caused by Big Data, the solutions that organizations are employing to manage these data, several good results, and a few poor results. The important idea to realize here is that Big Data will continue to get "bigger," and organizations will have to find ever-more creative solutions to manage it.

Between 2006 and 2010, the amount of digital information created, captured, and replicated each year added about 18 million times as much information as currently exists in all the books ever written. Images captured by billions of devices around the world, from digital cameras and camera phones to medical scanners and security cameras, comprise the largest component of this digital information.

We are accumulating data and information at a frenzied pace from such diverse sources as company documents, e-mails, Web pages, credit card swipes, phone messages, stock trades, memos, address books, and radiology scans. New sources of data and information include blogs, podcasts, videocasts (think of YouTube), digital video surveillance, and radio frequency identification (RFID) tags and other wireless sensors (discussed in Chapter 10). We are awash in data that we have to make sense of and manage. To deal with the growth and the diverse nature of digital data, organizations must employ sophisticated techniques for information management.

Information technologies and systems support organizations in managing—that is, acquiring, organizing, storing, accessing, analyzing, and interpreting—data. As you noted in Chapter 1, when these data are managed properly, they become *information* and then *knowledge*. Information and knowledge are valuable organizational resources that can provide a competitive advantage. This chapter will examine the processes whereby data are transformed first into information and then into knowledge.

Few business professionals are comfortable making or justifying business decisions that are not based on solid information. This is especially true today, when modern information systems make access to that information quick and easy. For example, we have technology that formats data in a way that managers and analysts can easily understand. Consequently, these professionals can access these data themselves and analyze them according to their needs, using a variety of tools. The result is useful information. Executives can then apply their experience to use this information to address a business problem, thereby producing knowledge. Knowledge management, enabled by information technology, captures and stores knowledge in forms that all organizational employees can access and apply, thereby creating the flexible, powerful "learning organization."

Clearly, data and knowledge management are vital to modern organizations. But, why should *you* learn about them? The reason is that you will have an important role in the development of database applications. The structure and content of your organization's **database**, a group of logically related files that stores data and the associations among them, depends on how users (you) look at your business activities. For example, when database developers in the firm's MIS group build a database, they use a tool called entity-relationship (ER) modeling. This tool creates a model of how users view a business activity. When you understand how to create and interpret an ER model, then you can evaluate whether the developers have captured your business activity correctly.

Keep in mind that decisions about data last longer, and have a broader impact, than decisions about hardware or software. If decisions concerning hardware are wrong, then the equipment can be replaced relatively easily. If software decisions turn out to be incorrect, they can be modified, though not always painlessly or inexpensively. Database decisions, in contrast, are much harder to undo. Database design constrains what the organization can do with its data for a long time. Remember that business users will be stuck with a bad database design, and not the database programmers, who will quickly move on to their next projects. This is why it is so important to get database designs right the first time—and you will be playing a key role in these designs.

Regarding relational databases, when you know how data are stored in tables, then you know what types of data you have available for analysis and decision making. Of course, your familiarity with data warehouses will serve the same purpose. Also, understanding relational databases will help you work with database developers in defining a new database or suggesting improvements to an existing one. It is one thing for you to say to a database developer, "I wish I could get this information from the database." It is quite another thing to say, "If you could add this column of data to Table A and this other column of data to Table B, then I could get this information from the database." Database developers enjoy responding to specific, knowledgeable requests from users!

In addition, you might want to create a small, personal database using a software product such as Microsoft Access. In that case, you will want to know at least the basics of the product.

After the data are stored in your organization's databases, they must be accessible to users in a form that helps users make decisions. Organizations accomplish this objective by developing data warehouses. You should become familiar with data warehouses because they are invaluable decision-making tools.

You will also make extensive use of your organization's knowledge base to perform your job. For example, when you are assigned a new project, you will likely research your firm's knowledge base to identify factors that contributed to the success of previous, similar projects.

You begin this chapter by examining the multiple problems involved in managing data and the database approach that organizations use to solve those problems. You will then see how database management systems enable organizations to access and use the data stored in the databases. Next, you study data warehouses and data marts and how you use them for decision making. You finish the chapter by taking a look at knowledge management.

3.1 | Managing Data

IT applications require data. Data should be of high quality, meaning that they should be accurate, complete, timely, consistent, accessible, relevant, and concise. Unfortunately, however, the process of acquiring, keeping, and managing data is becoming increasingly difficult.

The Difficulties of Managing Data

Because data are processed in several stages and often in several places, they are frequently subject to problems and difficulties. Managing data in organizations is difficult for many reasons.

First, the amount of data increases exponentially with time. Much historical data must be kept for a long time, and new data are added rapidly. For example, to support millions of customers, large retailers such as Walmart have to manage many terabytes of data.

In addition, data are also scattered throughout organizations and are collected by many individuals using various methods and devices. These data are frequently stored in numerous servers and locations and in different computing systems, databases, formats, and human and computer languages.

Another problem is that data come from multiple sources: internal sources (for example, corporate databases and company documents), personal sources (for example, personal thoughts, opinions, and experiences), and external sources (for example, commercial databases, government reports, and corporate Web sites). Data also come from the Web, in the form of clickstream data. **Clickstream data** are those data that visitors and customers produce when they visit a Web site and click on hyperlinks (described in Chapter 4). Clickstream data provide a trail of the users' activities in the Web site, including user behavior and browsing patterns.

Adding to these problems is the fact that new sources of data, such as blogs, podcasts, videocasts, and RFID tags and other wireless sensors, are constantly being developed. As you saw in the chapter-opening case, data degrades over time. For example, customers move to new addresses or change their names, companies go out of business or are bought, new products are developed, employees are hired or fired, companies expand into new countries, and so on.

Data are also subject to *data rot*. Data rot refers primarily to problems with the media on which the data are stored. Over time, temperature, humidity, and exposure to light can cause physical problems with storage media and thus make it difficult to access the data. The second aspect of data rot is that finding the machines needed to access the data can be difficult. For example, it is almost impossible today to find 8-track players. This means that a library of 8-track tapes has become relatively worthless, unless you have a functioning 8-track player or you convert the tapes to a modern medium such as CD.

Data security, quality, and integrity are critical, yet they are easily jeopardized. In addition, legal requirements relating to data differ among countries as well as industries, and they change frequently.

Another problem arises from the fact that, over time, organizations have developed information systems for specific business processes, such as transaction processing, supply chain management, customer relationship management, and other processes. Information systems that specifically support these processes impose unique requirements on data, which results in repetition and conflicts across an organization. For example, the marketing function might maintain information on customers, sales territories, and markets that duplicates data within the billing or customer service functions. This situation produces inconsistent data in the enterprise. Inconsistent data prevent a company from developing a unified view of core business information—data concerning customers, products, finances, and so on—across the organization and its information systems.

Two other factors complicate data management. First, federal regulations (for example, Sarbanes-Oxley) have made it a top priority for companies to better account for how information is being managed with their organizations. Sarbanes-Oxley requires that (1) public companies evaluate and disclose the effectiveness of their internal financial controls and (2) independent auditors for these companies agree to this disclosure. The law also holds CEOs and CFOs personally responsible for such disclosure. If their companies lack satisfactory data management policies and fraud or a security breach occurs, the company officers could be held personally responsible and face prosecution.

Second, companies are drowning in data, much of which is unstructured. As you have seen, the amount of data is increasing exponentially. To be profitable, companies must develop a strategy for managing these data effectively.

Because of these numerous problems, data are difficult to manage. As a result, organizations are turning to data governance.

Data Governance

Data governance is an approach to managing information across an entire organization. It involves a formal set of business processes and policies that are designed to ensure that data are handled in a certain, well-defined fashion. That is, the organization follows unambiguous rules for creating, collecting, handling, and protecting its information. The objective is to make information available, transparent, and useful for the people authorized to access it, from the moment it enters an organization, until it is outdated and deleted.

One strategy for implementing data governance is master data management. **Master data management** is a process that spans all organizational business processes and applications. It provides companies with the ability to store, maintain, exchange, and synchronize a consistent, accurate, and timely "single version of the truth" for the company's core master data.

Master data are a set of core data, such as customer, product, employee, vendor, geographic location, and so on, that span the enterprise information systems. It is important to distinguish between master data and transaction data. *Transaction data*, which are generated and captured by operational systems, describe the activities, or transactions, of the business. In contrast, master data are applied to multiple transactions and are used to categorize, aggregate, and evaluate the transaction data.

Let's look at an example of a transaction: You (Mary Jones) purchase one Samsung 42-inch plasma television, part number 1234, from Bill Roberts at Best Buy, for $2,000, on April 20, 2011. In this example, the master data are "product sold," "vendor," "salesperson," "store," "part number," "purchase price," and "date." When specific values are applied to the master data, then a transaction is represented. Therefore, transaction data would be, respectively, "42-inch plasma television," "Samsung," "Bill Roberts," "Circuit City," "1234," "$2,000," and "April 20, 2011."

An example of master data management is the city of Dallas, Texas, which implemented a plan for digitizing public and private records, such as paper documents, images, drawings, and video and audio content, that are maintained by the city. The master database can be accessed by any of the 38 government departments that have appropriate access. The city is integrating its financial and billing processes with its customer relationship management program. (You will learn about customer relationship management in Chapter 12.)

How will Dallas utilize this system? Imagine that the city experiences a water-main break. Before it implemented the system, repair crews had to search City Hall for records that were filed haphazardly. Once the workers found the hard-copy blueprints, they would take them to the site and, after going over them manually, would decide on a plan of action. In contrast, the new system delivers the blueprints wirelessly to the laptops of crews in the field, who can magnify or highlight areas of concern to generate a quick response. This process reduces the time it takes to respond to an emergency by several hours.

Along with data governance, organizations use the database approach to efficiently and effectively manage their data. You turn your attention to the database approach in the next section.

▶ BEFORE *YOU GO ON . . .*

1. What are some of the difficulties involved in managing data?

2. Define *data governance*, *master data*, and *transactional data*.

RUBY'S CLUB QUESTIONS

1. How many sources of information can you think of for Ruby's Club?

2. Even though Ruby's Club is not subject to Sarbanes-Oxley legal documentation requirements, can you think of any reasons why it would be a good idea for Ruben and Lisa to operate up to these standards?

Student Activity | 3.1

Objective: To give a sense of how much data and information is being created and digitized. This activity also discusses the challenges associated with the exponential growth of digitized information.

Chapter Connection: This activity relates to Section 3.1 and Learning Objective 1.

Prerequisites: You should read Section 3.1 prior to completing this activity.

Activity:

Watch the video "The Digital Universe Decade" at www.emc.com/collateral/demos/microsites/idc-digital-universe/iview.htm (video clip is under the "Digital Universe Decade" tab with an accompanying text transcript).

Deliverables:

Provide written answers to the discussion questions below.

Quiz Questions:

1. List at least three challenges in managing data.

2. Which of the following is an example of *unstructured data?*

(a) A student identification number
(b) A product bar code
(c) A driver's license number
(d) A video clip on the Internet
(e) A ZIP or postal code

3. Give an example of a government regulation that affects how companies manage their data.

Discussion Questions:

1. Describe the nature of data growth in the digital age. Where are the sources of these data?

2. What are the purposes of data governance? Why is it important for a company to institute data governance?

3.2 | The Database Approach

From the time of the first computer applications in business (mid-1950s) until the early 1970s, organizations managed their data in a *file management environment*. This environment evolved because organizations typically began automating one application at a time. These systems grew independently from one another, without overall planning. Each application required its own data, which were organized in a data file.

A data file is a collection of logically related records. Therefore, in a file management environment, each application has a specific data file related to it, containing all the data records needed by the application. Over time, organizations developed numerous applications, each with an associated, application-specific data file.

For example, you can relate to a situation where most of your information is in your university's central database, but a club to which you belong has its own files, the athletics department has separate files for student athletes, and your instructors may maintain grade data on their personal computers. It is easy for your name to be misspelled in one of these databases or files but not in others. If you move, your address might be updated correctly in one database or file but not in others.

Using databases eliminates many problems that arose from previous methods of storing and accessing data, such as file management systems. Databases are arranged so that one set of software programs—the database management system—provides all users with access to all the data. (You will study database management systems later in this chapter.) This system minimizes the following problems:

- *Data redundancy:* The same data are stored in many places.
- *Data isolation:* Applications cannot access data associated with other applications.
- *Data inconsistency:* Various copies of the data do not agree.

In addition, database systems maximize the following issues:

- *Data security:* Because data are "put in one place" in databases, there is a potential for losing a lot of data at once. Therefore, databases have extremely high security measures in place to deter mistakes and attacks. (You will learn about information security in Chapter 7.)
- *Data integrity:* Data meet certain constraints, such as no alphabetic characters in a Social Security number field.
- *Data independence:* Applications and data are independent of one another (that is, applications and data are not linked to each other, meaning that all applications are able to access the same data).

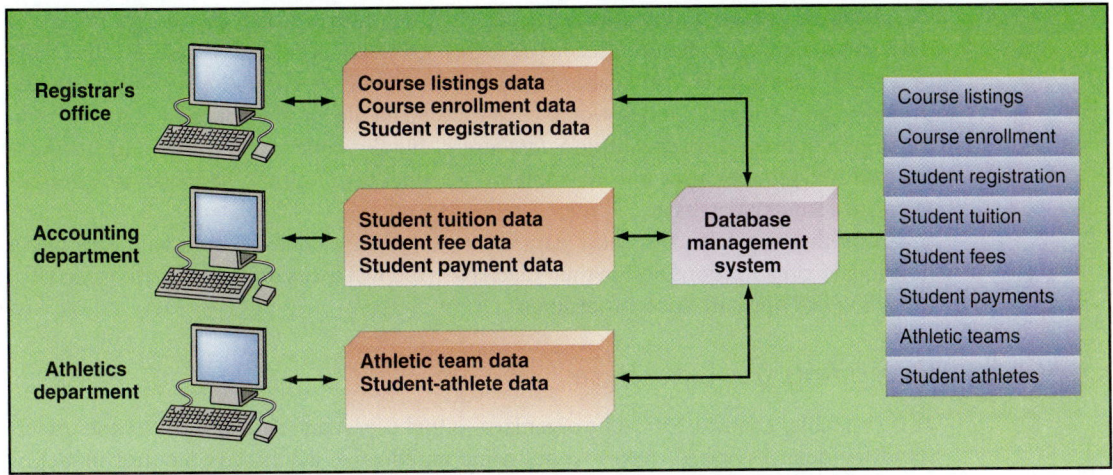

Figure 3.1 A database management system (DBMS) provides access to all data in the database.

Figure 3.1 illustrates a university database. Note that university applications from the registrar's office, the accounting department, and the athletics department access data through the database management system.

A database can contain vast amounts of data. To make these data more understandable and useful, they are arranged in a hierarchy. In the next section, you will become familiar with the data hierarchy. You will then see how databases are designed.

The Data Hierarchy

Data are organized in a hierarchy that begins with bits and proceeds all the way to databases (see Figure 3.2). A **bit** (*binary digit*) represents the smallest unit of data a computer can process. The term *binary* means that a bit can consist only of a 0 or a 1. A group of eight bits, called a **byte**, represents a single character. A byte can be a letter, a number, or a symbol. A logical grouping of characters into a word, a small group of words, or an identification number is called a **field**. For example, a student's name in a university's computer files would appear in the "name" field, and her or his Social Security number would appear in the "Social Security number" field. Fields can also contain data other than text and numbers. A field can contain an image, or any other type of multimedia. Examples are a motor vehicle department's licensing database containing a person's photograph; a field containing a voice sample to authorize access to a secure facility; and in the Apple iTunes Store, a song is a field in a record, with other fields giving the song's title, its price, and the album of which it is part.

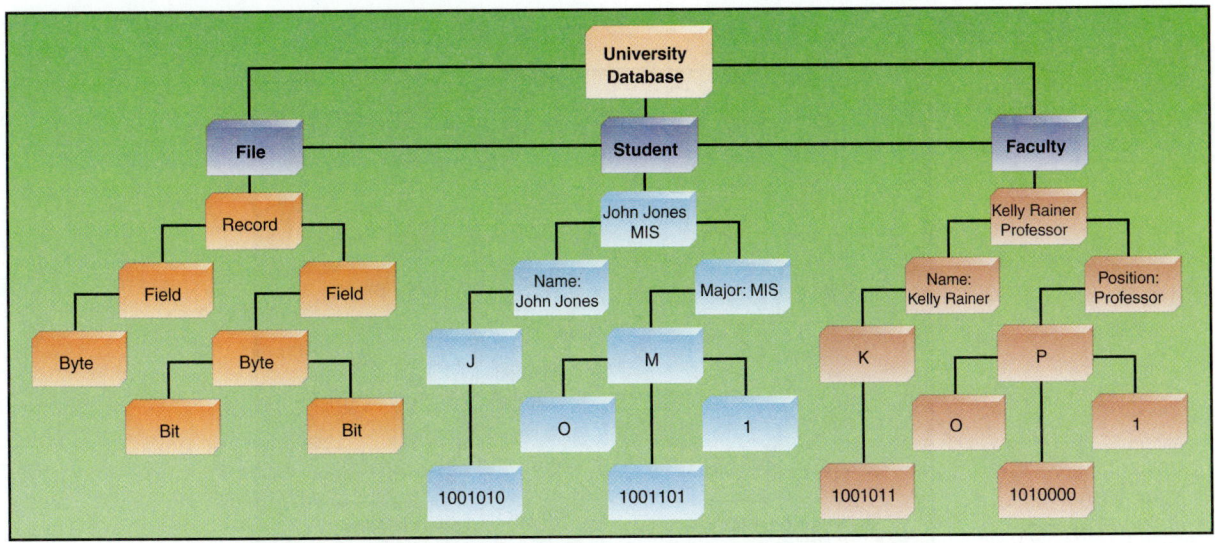

Figure 3.2 Hierarchy of data for a computer-based file.

A logical grouping of related fields, such as the student's name, the courses taken, the date, and the grade, comprise a record. A logical grouping of related records is called a **file** or a **table**. For example, the records from a particular course, consisting of course number, professor, and students' grades, would constitute a data file for that course. A logical grouping of related files would constitute a *database*. Using the same example, the student course file could be grouped with files on students' personal histories and financial backgrounds to create a student database.

Now that you have seen how data are arranged in a database, you will learn about how today's organizations design their databases. You will focus on entity-relationship (ER) modeling and normalization procedures.

Designing the Database

To be valuable, a database must be organized so that users can retrieve, analyze, and understand the data they need. A key to designing an effective database is the data model. A **data model** is a diagram that represents entities in the database and their relationships. An **entity** is a person, place, thing, or event—such as a customer, an employee, or a product—about which information is maintained. Entities can typically be identified in the user's work environment. A **record** generally describes an entity. An instance of an entity is a specific, unique representation of the entity. For example, an instance of the entity STUDENT would be a particular student.

Each characteristic or quality of a particular entity is called an *attribute*. For example, if our entities were a customer, an employee, and a product, entity attributes would include customer name, employee number, and product color.

Every record in a file must contain at least one field that uniquely identifies that record so that it can be retrieved, updated, and sorted. This identifier field is called the **primary key**. For example, a student record in a U.S. university would use a unique student number as its primary key. (*Note:* In the past, your Social Security number served as the primary key for your student record. However, for security reasons, this practice has been discontinued.) In some cases, locating a particular record requires the use of secondary keys. A **secondary key** is another field that has some identifying information but typically does not identify the file with complete accuracy. For example, the student's major might be a secondary key if a user wanted to find all students in a particular major field of study. It should not be the primary key, however, because many students can have the same major.

Entity-Relationship Modeling. Designers plan and create the database through the process of **entity-relationship modeling**, using an **entity-relationship (ER) diagram**. There are many approaches to ER diagramming. You will see one particular approach here, but there are others. The good news is that if you are familiar with one version of ER diagramming, then you will be able to easily adapt to any other type of ER diagramming.

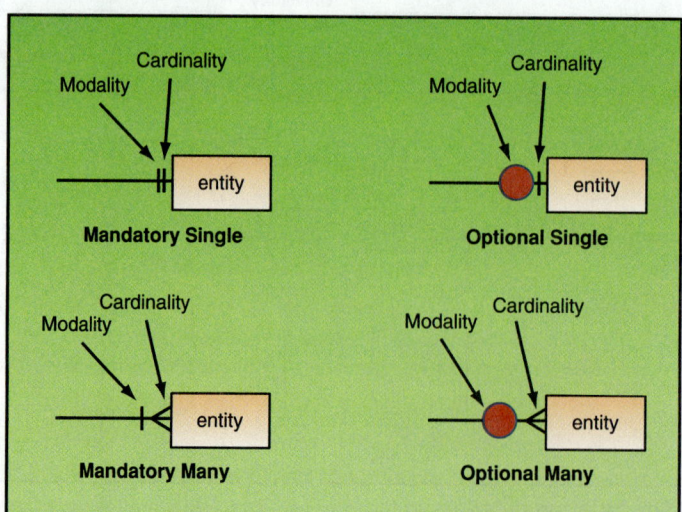

Figure 3.3 Relationships between entities reflecting business rules.

ER diagrams consist of entities, attributes, and relationships. Entities are pictured in boxes, and relationships are shown in diamonds. The attributes for each entity are listed, and the primary key is underlined.

Relationships illustrate an association between two entities. A relationship has a name that is a verb. Cardinality and modality are the indicators of the business rules in a relationship. *Cardinality* refers to the maximum number of times an instance of one entity can be associated with an instance in the related entity. *Modality* refers to the minimum number of times an instance of one entity can be associated with an instances in the related entity. Cardinality can be 1 or Many, and its symbol is placed on the outside of the relationship line, closest to the entity. Modality can be 1 or 0, and its symbol is placed on the inside of the relationship line, next to the cardinality symbol. Figure 3.3 shows the cardinality and modality symbols. Figure 3.4 shows an entity-relationship diagram.

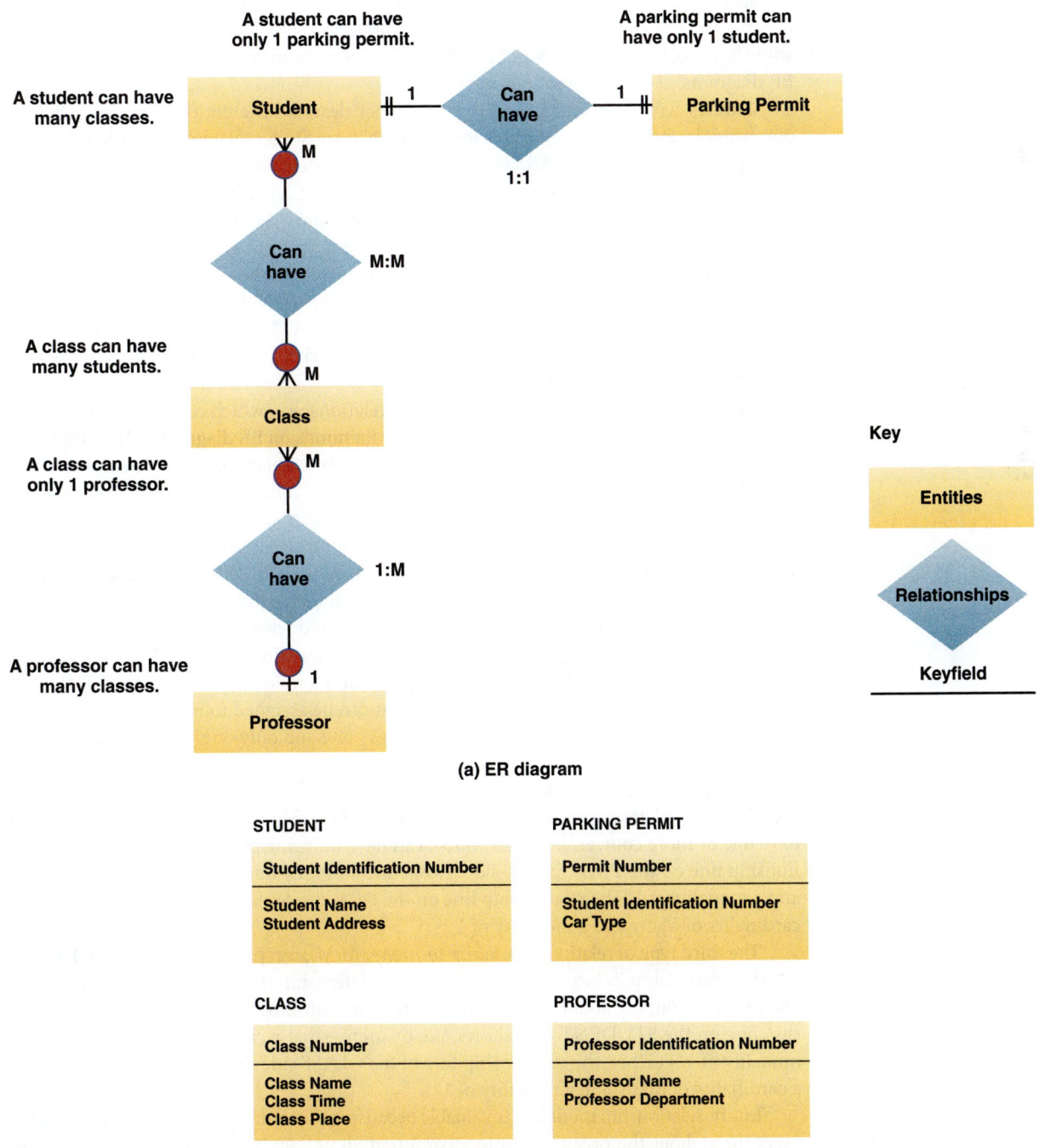

(a) ER diagram

(b) Entities, Attributes, and Identifiers

Figure 3.4 Entity-relationship diagram model.

As defined earlier, an *entity* is something that can be identified in the users' work environment. For example, consider student registration at a university. Students register for courses and register their cars for parking permits. In this example, STUDENT, PARKING PERMIT, CLASS, and PROFESSOR are entities, as shown in Figure 3.4.

Entities of a given type are grouped in **entity classes**. In our example, STUDENT, PARKING PERMIT, CLASS, and PROFESSOR are entity classes. An **instance** of an entity class is the representation of a particular entity. Therefore, a particular STUDENT (James Smythe, 145-89-7123) is an instance of the STUDENT entity class; a particular parking permit (91778) is an instance of the PARKING PERMIT entity class; a particular class (76890) is an instance of the CLASS entity class; and a particular professor (Margaret Wilson, 115-65-7632) is an instance of the PROFESSOR entity class.

Entity instances have **identifiers**, which are attributes that are unique to that entity instance. For example, STUDENT instances can be identified with StudentIdentification-Number; PARKING PERMIT instances can be identified with PermitNumber; CLASS instances can be identified with ClassNumber; and PROFESSOR instances can be identified with ProfessorIdentificationNumber. These identifiers (or primary keys) are underlined on ER diagrams, as in Part (b) of Figure 3.4.

Entities have **attributes**, or properties, that describe the entity's characteristics. In our example, examples of attributes for STUDENT are StudentName and StudentAddress. Examples of attributes for PARKING PERMIT are StudentIdentificationNumber and Car-Type. Examples of attributes for CLASS are ClassName, ClassTime, and ClassPlace. Examples of attributes for PROFESSOR are ProfessorName and ProfessorDepartment. (Note that each course at this university has one professor—no team teaching.)

Why is StudentIdentificationNumber an attribute of both the STUDENT and PARKING PERMIT entity classes? That is, why do we need the PARKING PERMIT entity class? If you consider all interlinked university systems, the PARKING PERMIT entity class is needed for other applications, such as fee payments, parking tickets, and external links to the state Department of Motor Vehicles.

Entities are associated with one another in relationships, which can include many entities. (Remember that relationships are noted by diamonds on ER diagrams.) The number of entities in a relationship is the degree of the relationship. Relationships between two items are called *binary relationships*. There are three types of binary relationships: one-to-one, one-to-many, and many-to-many.

In a *one-to-one (1:1)* relationship, a single-entity instance of one type is related to a single-entity instance of another type. Figure 3.4a shows STUDENT-PARKING PERMIT as a 1:1 relationship. The relationship means that a student can have a parking permit, but does not need to have to have one. (Clearly, if a student does not have a car, then he or she will not need a parking permit.) Note that the relationship line on the PARKING PERMIT side shows zero or one—that is, a cardinality of 1 and a modality of 0. On the STUDENT side of the relationship, only one parking permit can be assigned to one student. Note that the relationship line on the STUDENT side shows one and only one—that is, a cardinality of 1 and a modality of 1.

The second type of relationship, *one-to-many (1:M)*, is represented by the CLASS–PROFESSOR relationship in Figure 3.4(a). This relationship means that a professor can have one or more courses, but each course can have only one professor. Note that the relationship line on the PROFESSOR side shows one and only one—that is, a cardinality of 1 and a modality of 1. The relationship line on the CLASS side shows one or many—that is, a cardinality of Many and a modality of 1.

The third type of relationship, *many-to-many (M:M)*, is represented by the STUDENT–CLASS relationship in Figure 3.4(a). This M:M relationship means that a student can have one or more courses, and a course can have one or more students. Note that the relationship line on the STUDENT side shows one or more—that is, a cardinality of Many and a modality of 1. Further, the relationship line of the CLASS side shows one or more—that is, a cardinality of Many and a modality of 1.

Entity-relationship modeling is valuable because it allows database designers to talk with users throughout the organization to ensure that all entities and the relationships among them are represented. This process underscores the importance of taking all users into account when designing organizational databases. Notice that all entities and relationships in our example are labeled in terms that users can understand. Now that you understand how a database is designed, you can turn your attention to database management systems.

— BEFORE *YOU GO ON . . .*

1. What is a data model?
2. What is a primary key? A secondary key?
3. What is an entity? An attribute?

RUBY'S CLUB QUESTIONS

1. If the bartender, cover charge clerk, and chef all kept separate spreadsheets to keep up with customers, purchases, and payments, what type of data problems do you see they could have?

2. How could a networked database help to alleviate some of the problems in question 1?

Student Activity 3.2

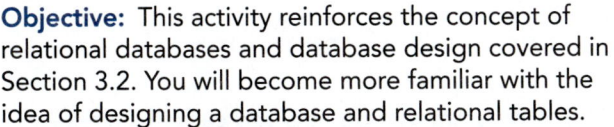

Objective: This activity reinforces the concept of relational databases and database design covered in Section 3.2. You will become more familiar with the idea of designing a database and relational tables.

Chapter Connection: This activity relates to Section 3.2 and Learning Objectives 2, 3, and 4 in this chapter.

Prerequisites: You should read Section 3.2 prior to completing this activity.

Activity:

Consider one of the following scenarios.

Scenario 1. Imagine yourself working as a coordinator of a company with several ongoing projects. As part of your job, you are supposed to keep track of its commercial projects, employees, and the employees' participation in each project. Usually, a project will have multiple team members, but some projects have not been assigned to any team member. For each project, the company must keep track of the project's title, description, location, estimated budget, and due date.

Each employee can be assigned to one or more projects. Some employees can also be on leave and will not be working on any particular assignment. Project leaders usually need to know the following information about their team members: name, address,

phone number, Social Security number, highest degree attained, and his/her expertise (for example, IS, accounting, marketing, and finance).

You have been asked by your manager to conceptually design a database that can help the company keep track of the information described in this scenario. To begin, you need to identify entity classes and their attributes and determine (or create) primary key attribute(s) for each entity class. In addition, you will need to identify foreign key attribute(s) and establish relationships among the entity classes you have identified.

Deliverables for Scenario 1:

(1) List the entity classes and their attributes, and (2) identify the primary key attribute(s) and the foreign key attribute(s).

Scenario 2. Imagine yourself working for a consultancy firm that helps small businesses design and implement their information technology infrastructures. One of your clients is a manufacturer of solar energy panels, Green Solar LLP, which wants to convert its handwritten order form (see following "Deliverables") into an electronic form that its sales representatives can use on handheld devices. The information entered in the electronic form will eventually be stored in a relational database at the company's main office.

Your manager has asked you to help this client design a relational database that will meet Green Solar's need. You will begin by identifying entity classes and their attributes as well as primary key attribute(s) for each entity class. You will also need to identify foreign key attribute(s) and establish relationships among the entity classes you identify. Draw an entity-relationship diagram to accompany your answer.

Deliverables for Scenario 2:

(1) List the entity classes and their attributes, and (2) underline the primary key attribute(s) (with solid lines) and the foreign key attribute(s) (with dotted lines).

Green Solar LLP

Date: _10/09/2011_____   Order No.:__158934_____

Client Name: _Sierra_Vista_Apartments_____   Client Account No.:_SVA001_____

Street Address: _283_Grand Avenue_____

City: _San Francisco_____   State/Province: _California_____

Postal Code: _92138_____   Telephone: _(784)_234-9004_____

Product ID	Description	Quantity	Unit Price	Extended Price
A231	Solar panel 250W	25	$718.75	$17,968.75
E006	Lighting controller	5	$108.00	$540.00
R984	Mounting rack—96 inch	7	$47.28	$330.96
. . .	. . . .	. . . .	. . . .	. . . .
			Grand Total:	$18,839.71

Note: Order Number and Product ID are foreign key attributes in the Order Details table. The two attributes combined make up the composite primary key for the Order Details table.

Note: The extended price and grand total can be calculated based on the attributes included in the preceding table.

Quiz Questions:

1. What is a database?
   (a) A computer file that contains important documents and free-form texts
   (b) The smallest unit of data a computer can process that consists only of a 0 or a 1
   (c) A logical grouping of characters into a word, a small group of words, or an identification number
   (d) A logical grouping of related files
   (e) A diagram that represents entities and their relationships

2. What is an entity?
   (a) A characteristic or quality of a particular person, place, or thing
   (b) A person, place, thing, or event about which information is maintained
   (c) A piece of information that uniquely identifies a person, place, or thing
   (d) A representation of binary information in a format that humans can understand
   (e) A diagram that depicts and captures a real-world scenario in a multimedia format

3. What is a primary key?
   (a) A binary value that forms a basic building block of a database file
   (b) A group of binary values that represents a single character
   (c) A specific, unique representation of a person, place, or thing
   (d) An attribute or a group of attributes that uniquely identifies a record in a database
   (e) A logical grouping of related records in a database

Discussion Questions:

1. What are the advantages in designing and implementing a database management system?

2. What are the purposes of designating primary and foreign key attributes in a database?

3.3 | Database Management Systems

A **database management system (DBMS)** is a set of programs that provide users with tools to add, delete, access, modify, and analyze data stored in one location. An organization can access the data by using query and reporting tools that are part of the DBMS or by using application programs specifically written to access the data. DBMSs also provide the mechanisms for maintaining the integrity of stored data, managing security and user access, and recovering information if the system fails. Because databases and DBMSs are essential to all areas of business, they must be carefully managed.

There are a number of different database architectures, but we focus on the relational database model because it is popular and easy to use. Other database models (for example, the hierarchical and network models) are the responsibility of the MIS function and are not used by organizational employees. Popular examples of relational databases are Microsoft Access and Oracle.

The Relational Database Model

Most business data—especially accounting and financial data—traditionally were organized into simple tables consisting of columns and rows. Tables allow people to compare information quickly by row or column. In addition, items are easy to retrieve by finding the point of intersection of a particular row and column.

The **relational database model** is based on the concept of two-dimensional tables. A relational database generally is not one big table—usually called a *flat file*—that contains all of the records and attributes. Such a design would entail far too much data redundancy. Instead, a relational database is usually designed with a number of related tables. Each of these tables contains records (listed in rows) and attributes (listed in columns).

These related tables can be joined when they contain common columns. The uniqueness of the primary key tells the DBMS which records are joined with others in related tables. This feature allows users great flexibility in the variety of queries they can make. Despite these features, however, this model has some disadvantages. Because large-scale databases can be composed of many interrelated tables, the overall design can be complex and therefore have slow search and access times.

Consider the relational database example about students shown in Figure 3.5. The table contains data about the entity called students. Attributes of the entity are student name,

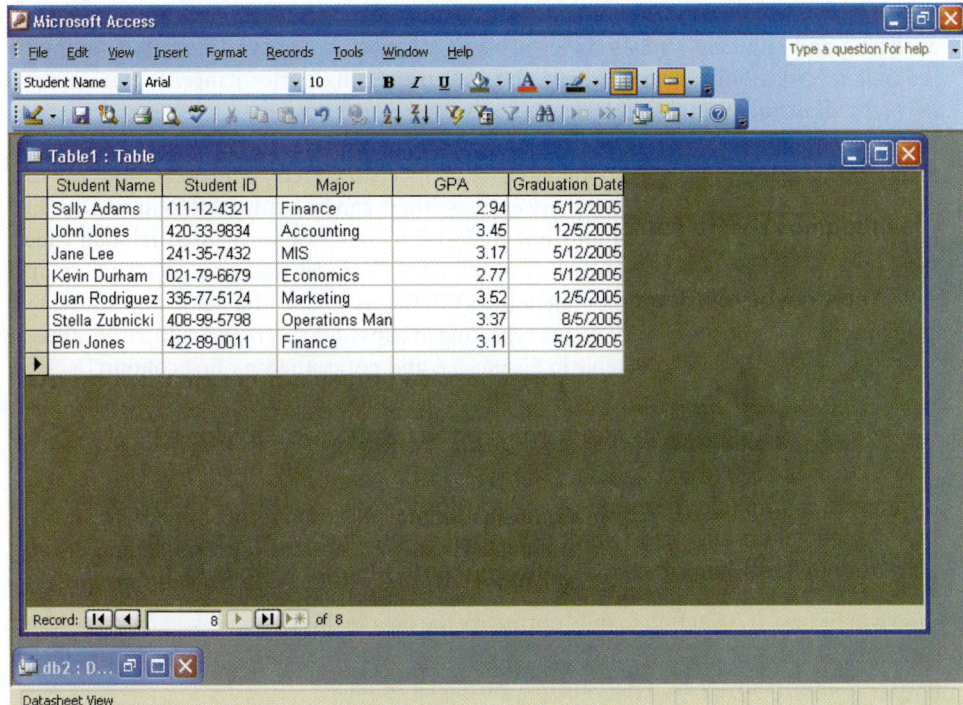

Student Name	Student ID	Major	GPA	Graduation Date
Sally Adams	111-12-4321	Finance	2.94	5/12/2005
John Jones	420-33-9834	Accounting	3.45	12/5/2005
Jane Lee	241-35-7432	MIS	3.17	5/12/2005
Kevin Durham	021-79-6679	Economics	2.77	5/12/2005
Juan Rodriguez	335-77-5124	Marketing	3.52	12/5/2005
Stella Zubnicki	408-99-5798	Operations Man	3.37	8/5/2005
Ben Jones	422-89-0011	Finance	3.11	5/12/2005

Figure 3.5 Example of a student database.

undergraduate major, grade point average, and graduation date. The rows are the records on Sally Adams, John Jones, Jane Lee, Kevin Durham, Juan Rodriguez, Stella Zubnicki, and Ben Jones. Of course, your university keeps much more data on you than our example shows. In fact, your university's student database probably keeps hundreds of attributes on each student.

Query Languages. Requesting information from a database is the most commonly performed operation. **Structured query language (SQL)** is the most popular query language used to request information. SQL allows people to perform complicated searches by using relatively simple statements or key words. Typical key words are SELECT (to specify a desired attribute), FROM (to specify the table to be used), and WHERE (to specify conditions to apply in the query).

To understand how SQL works, imagine that a university wants to know the names of students who will graduate cum laude (but not magna or summa cum laude) in May 2012. The university IS staff would query the student relational database with an SQL statement such as SELECT Student Name, FROM Student Database, WHERE Grade Point Average > 3.40 and Grade Point Average < 3.60. The SQL query would return: John Jones and Juan Rodriguez.

Another way to find information in a database is to use **query by example (QBE)**. In QBE, the user fills out a grid or template (also known as a *form*) to construct a sample or description of the data desired. Users can construct a query quickly and easily by using drag-and-drop features in a DBMS such as Microsoft Access. Conducting queries in this manner is simpler than keying in SQL commands.

Data Dictionary. When a relational model is created, the **data dictionary** defines the format necessary to enter the data into the database. The data dictionary provides information on each attribute, such as its name, whether it is a key or part of a key, the type of data expected (alphanumeric, numeric, dates, and so on), and valid values. Data dictionaries can also provide information on how often the attribute should be updated; why it is needed in the database; and which business functions, applications, forms, and reports use the attribute.

Data dictionaries provide many advantages to the organization. Because they provide names and standard definitions for all attributes, they reduce the chances that the same attribute will be used in different applications but with a different name. In addition, data dictionaries give organizations an inventory of their data resources, making it possible to manage that resource more effectively.

Normalization. To use a relational database management system effectively, the data must be analyzed to eliminate redundant data elements. **Normalization** is a method for analyzing and reducing a relational database to its most streamlined form for minimum redundancy, maximum data integrity, and best processing performance. When data are *normalized*, attributes in the table depend only on the primary key.

As an example of normalization, consider an automotive repair garage. This business takes orders from customers who want to have their cars repaired. In this example, ORDER, PART, SUPPLIER, and CUSTOMER are entities. There can be many PARTS in an ORDER, but each PART can come from only one SUPPLIER. In a nonnormalized relation called ORDER (see Figure 3.6), each ORDER would have to repeat the name, description, and price of each PART needed to complete the ORDER, as well as the name and address of each SUPPLIER. This relation contains repeating groups and describes multiple entities.

For example, consider the table in Figure 3.6 and notice the very first column (labeled Order). This column contains multiple entries for each order—four rows for Order 11, six rows for Order 12, and so on. These multiple rows for an order are called repeating groups. The table in Figure 3.6 also contains multiple entities: ORDER, PART, SUPPLIER, and CUSTOMER. When you normalize the data, you want to eliminate repeating groups and have normalized tables, each containing only one entity.

You might think that four entities would mean four normalized tables. (The ORDER, SUPPLIER, and CUSTOMER tables are shown in Figure 3.7(a), and the PART table is shown in Figure 3.7(b).) But, to fully normalize the data in this example, you must create an extra table, called ORDERED-PARTS. This table (see Figure 3.7[b]) contains the particular parts, and how many of each part are in a particular order.

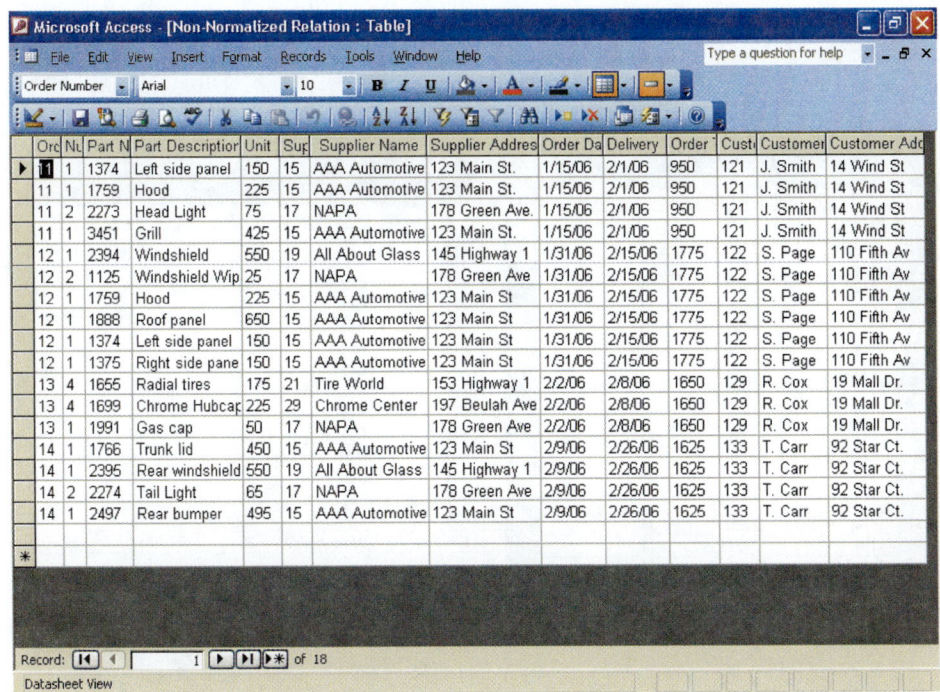

Figure 3.6 Nonnormalized relation.

The normalization process, illustrated in Figure 3.8, breaks down the relation, ORDER, into smaller relations: ORDER, SUPPLIER, and CUSTOMER (Figure 3.7[a]) and ORDERED PARTS and PART (Figure 3.7[b]). Each of these relations describes a single entity. This process is conceptually simpler, and it eliminates repeating groups. For example, consider an order at the automobile repair shop. The normalized relations can produce the order in the following manner (see Figure 3.8).

- The ORDER relation provides the Order Number (the primary key), Order Date, Delivery Date, Order Total, and Customer Number.

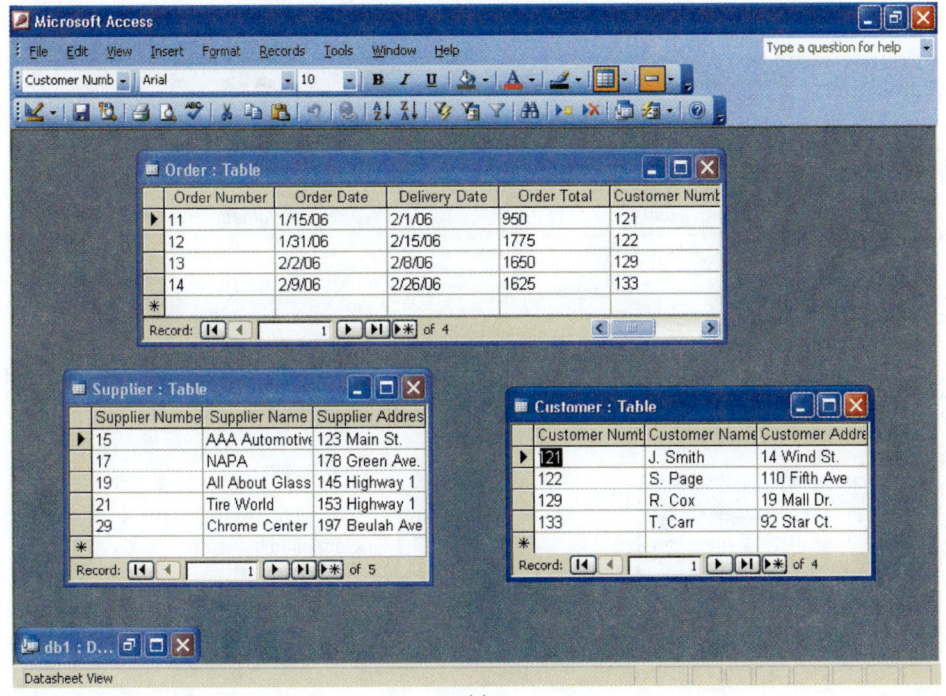

(a)

Figure 3.7 Smaller relationships broken down from the nonnormal relations. (a) Order, Supplier, Customer. (b) Ordered Parts, Part.

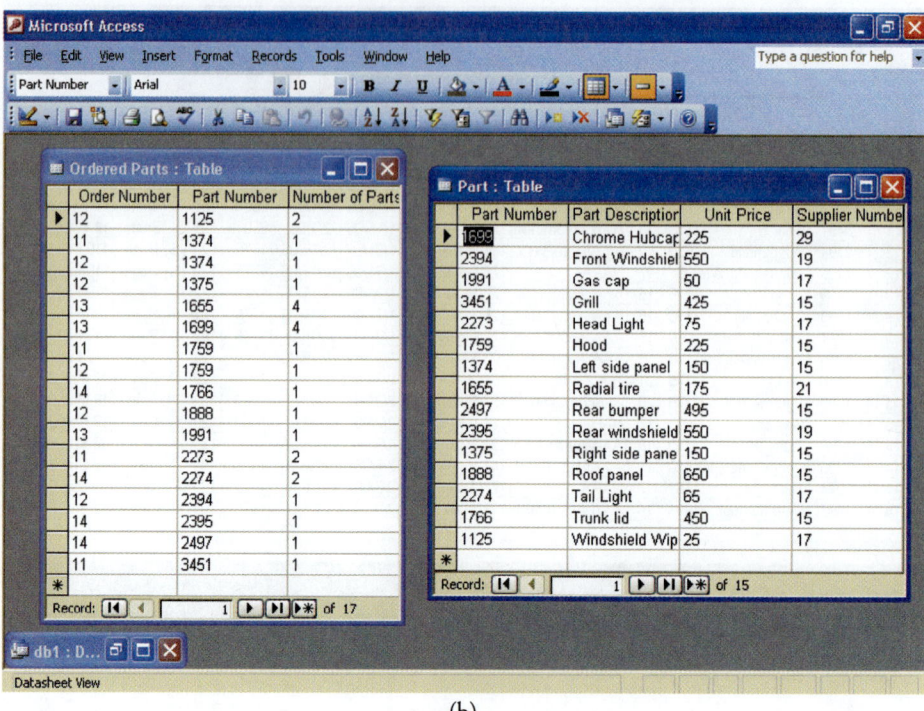

Figure 3.7 (continued)

(b)

- The primary key of the ORDER relation (Order Number) provides a link to the ORDERED PARTS relation (the link numbered 1 in Figure 3.8).

- The ORDERED PARTS relation supplies the Number of Parts information to ORDER.

- The primary key of the ORDERED PARTS relation is a composite key that consists of Order Number and Part Number. Therefore, the Part Number component of the primary key provides a link to the PART relation (the link numbered 2 in Figure 3.8).

- The PART relation supplies the Part Description, Unit Price, and Supplier Number to ORDER.

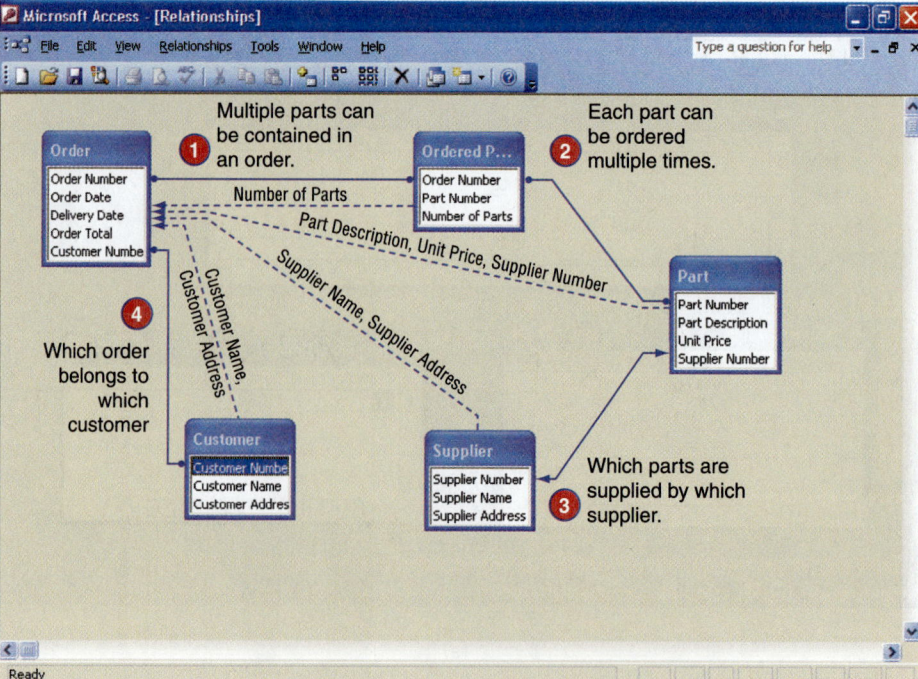

Figure 3.8 How normalized relations produce the order.

- The Supplier Number in the PART relation provides a link to the SUPPLIER relation (the link numbered 3 in Figure 3.8).
- The SUPPLIER relation provides the Supplier Name and Supplier Address to ORDER.
- The Customer Number in ORDER provides a link to the CUSTOMER relation (the link numbered 4 in Figure 3.8).
- The CUSTOMER relation supplies the Customer Name and Customer Address to ORDER.

Databases in Action

It is safe to say that almost all organizations have one or more databases. Further, there are numerous interesting database applications. However, not all databases turn out successfully. "IT's About Business 3.1" illustrates how the Mexican government mandated a nationwide database with poor results.

IT's ABOUT BUSINESS | 3.1

A Database for Cell Phone Owners in Mexico

To combat organized crime, in 2010 the Mexican government ordered the owners of every cell phone in the country to register their names, numbers, and addresses. The government planned to put all this information into a massive database.

The government's goals were laudable. With the end of cellular anonymity, authorities promised to combat the growing problem of virtual kidnapping, or phoning victims to claim—falsely—that a spouse or a child had just been kidnapped. In such crimes, the extortionists demand instant payment, by wire transfer or access to a bank account. The fake kidnapping calls are often accompanied by the muffled sound of someone whimpering in fear or pleading for help. Mexican prisons frequently serve as call centers for the extortionists, which operate in complicity with guards who provide phones and reportedly take a commission. In May 2010, in a raid on a state prison in Jalisco, authorities seized assault rifles, handguns, and 70 cell phones from inmates.

In a huge mass protest, even under threat of service interruption, millions of Mexicans are refusing to submit their personal data, because they simply do not trust their government. They assume that any personal information they give the government will flow into the hands of the very criminals that the new law seeks to foil.

As acts of protest, many Mexicans mocked the government, registering their mobile phones under the names of celebrities, prominent politicians, and law enforcement officials. In April 2010, 5,200 mobile phones were registered to President Felipe Calderón.

As the government tried to convince citizens to register their cell phones, the newspaper *El Universal* sent a reporter out to Tepito, the black market bazaar in Mexico City. There, he found that for $12,000 a person could buy the complete data set for every registered voter in Mexico—their names, addresses, dates of birth, driver's licenses, and social security numbers. The vendors in Tepito said that their best customers included organized crime and police agents.

According to the Mexican Federal Telecommunications Commission, a separate entity, 68 million cell phones were registered, but 17 million remain unlisted. Because so many Mexicans declined to give their personal information, and because the data they did submit could not be authenticated, the mobile-phone registry database is completely useless. Its future remains unknown.

Sources: Compiled from "Virtual Kidnapping—Be Careful," *hot-informations.blogspot.com*, December 11, 2010; W. Booth, "Wary Mexicans Shun Cellphone Database Meant to Bolster Security," *Washington Post*, May 14, 2010; M. Miller, "Mexico Tries to Tackle 'Virtual Kidnapping'," *CBS News*, April 26, 2010; M. Miller, "Mexico: A Phone Call, a Scream, and a Plea for Help," *Global Post*, April 23, 2010; M. Lacy, "Exploiting Real Fears with 'Virtual Kidnappings'," *New York Times*, April 29, 2008.

Questions

1. What types of problems characterized the cell phone database experience?

2. Why did the cell phone database exhibit these problems?

3. Would you classify the Mexican cell phone database a success? A failure? Partially successful? Why or why not? Support your answer.

Organizations implement databases to efficiently and effectively manage their data. However, because databases typically process data in real time (or near real time), it is not practical to allow users access to the databases. After all, the data will change while the user is looking at it! As a result, data warehouses have been developed that allow users to access data for decision making. You will learn about data warehouses in the next section.

BEFORE *YOU GO ON . . .*

1. What are the advantages and disadvantages of relational databases?
2. What are the benefits of data dictionaries?
3. Describe how structured query language works.

RUBY'S CLUB QUESTIONS

1. Given the type of information Ruben and Lisa want to find in their data, what advantages would they find in a relational database over multiple flat files (spreadsheets)?

2. What safety precautions could Ruben and Lisa implement for customers with a relational database? For example, a bartender may recognize that he has sold five shots to a particular customer and refuse further service more out of concern for the person's health. If that customer had purchased the shots from different bartenders, could this have occurred?

3. What are the implications of a serve/no serve decision (due to overindulgence) from the customer viewpoint and Ruby's Club?

Student Activity | 3.3

Objective: This activity reinforces the concept of relational database design and normalization covered in Section 3.3 (and Section 3.2). You will gain more experience in designing relational databases.

Chapter Connection: This activity relates to Sections 3.2 and 3.3 and Learning Objectives 3 and 4 in this chapter.

Prerequisites: You should read Sections 3.2 and 3.3 prior to completing this activity.

Activity:

Consider the following scenarios.

Scenario 1. A retail store decides to create a relational database to help keep track of its customers. The following is one of the tables included in this database.

Customer ID	First Name	Last Name	Income	Phones
1	John	Smith	$20,000	756-1111, 756-9111, 756-8400
2	Jane	Summers	$35,000	756-1000, 756-4567
3	Joe	Saunders	$30,000	756-6111
4	Jen	Smithson	$45,000	756-0094, 756-0924

Describe what potential problems might arise if the store continues to store its customer information in this table. What changes would you make to improve the design of this table?

Scenario 2. An office supply store creates a relational database to keep track of its sales transactions. The following is one of the tables included in the relational database the store employees have created.

Customer ID	First Name	Last Name	Customer Phone	Order Number	Order Date	Item Description	Quantity	Unit Price	Shipped
1	Kara	Liu	756-1111	0001	1/2/2010	Staplers	2	$18.99	Y
1	Kara	Liu	756-1111	0001	1/2/2010	Pens	20	$5.79	N
2	Kevin	Lawrence	756-1000	0002	1/3/2010	Staplers	5	$18.99	N
3	Kimberly	Long	756-6111	0003	1/5/2010	Pens	35	$5.79	Y

Describe what potential problems (if any) might arise if the store continues to store its sales information in this table. What changes would you make to improve the design of this table?

Deliverables:

Prepare written answers or, if your instructor prefers, create relational tables in MS Access as a solution to the assigned scenario.

Quiz Questions:

1. What is a database management system?
   - (a) A logical grouping of related computer files into one central folder
   - (b) A set of binary values that collectively represents a person, place, or thing with a unique identifier for each attribute
   - (c) A logical representation of entity classes and their attributes in a graphical format that nontechnical database users can understand
   - (d) A hierarchical grouping of binary files into a treelike structure
   - (e) A set of programs that provide users with tools to add, delete, access, modify, and analyze data stored in one location

2. What is normalization?
   - (a) When an electronic document defines the format necessary to enter the data into the database
   - (b) A method for analyzing and reducing a relational database to its most streamlined form
   - (c) A database procedure that involves extracting, transforming, and loading data
   - (d) An administrative policy that limits access to the most crucial data files within a company
   - (e) A set of logical steps to ensure the highest level of data security and privacy

Discussion Questions:

Instead of providing written answers, discuss the potential problems that might arise if the store continues to store its customer information in its current table. What changes would you make to improve the design of this table?

3.4 | Data Warehouses and Data Marts

Today, the most successful companies are those that can respond quickly and flexibly to market changes and opportunities. A key to this response is the effective and efficient use of data and information by analysts and managers. The problem is providing users with access to corporate data so that they can analyze it to make better decisions. Let's look at an example.

If the manager of a local bookstore wanted to know the profit margin on used books at her store, she could find out from her database, using SQL or QBE. However, if she needed to know the trend in the profit margins on used books over the last ten years, she would have a very difficult query to construct in SQL or QBE.

This example illustrates several reasons why organizations are building data warehouses and/or data marts. First, the bookstore's databases have the necessary information to answer the manager's query, but this information is not organized in a way that makes it easy for her to find what she needs. Second, the organization's databases are designed to process millions of transactions per day. Therefore, complicated queries might take a long time to answer and also might degrade the performance of the databases. Third, transactional databases are designed to be updated. This update process requires extra processing. Data warehouses and data marts are read-only, and the extra processing is eliminated because data already in the data warehouse are not updated. Fourth, transactional databases are designed to access a single record at a time. Data warehouses are designed to access large groups of related records.

As a result of these problems, companies are using a variety of tools with data warehouses and data marts to make it easier and faster for users to access, analyze, and query data. You will learn about these tools in Chapter 5: Business Intelligence.

Describing Data Warehouses and Data Marts

In general, data warehouses and data marts support business intelligence (BI) applications. As you will see in Chapter 5, business intelligence is a broad category of applications, technologies, and processes for gathering, storing, accessing, and analyzing data to help business users make better decisions. A **data warehouse** is a repository of historical data that are organized by subject to support decision makers in the organization.

Because data warehouses are so expensive, they are used primarily by large companies. A **data mart** is a low-cost, scaled-down version of a data warehouse that is designed for the end-user needs in a strategic business unit (SBU) or a department. Data marts can be implemented more quickly than data warehouses, often in less than 90 days. Further, they support local rather than central control by conferring power on the using group. Typically, groups that need a single or a few BI applications require only a data mart, rather than a data warehouse.

The basic characteristics of data warehouses and data marts include the following:

- *Organized by business dimension or subject.* Data are organized by subject (for example, by customer, vendor, product, price level, and region). This arrangement is different from transactional systems where data are organized by business process, such as order entry, inventory control, or accounts receivable.

- *Use online analytical processing.* Typically, organizational databases are oriented toward handling transactions. That is, databases use **online transaction processing (OLTP)**, where business transactions are processed online as soon as they occur. The objectives are speed and efficiency, which are critical to a successful Internet-based business operation. Data warehouses and data marts, which are not designed to support OLTP but to support decision makers, use online analytical processing. *Online analytical processing (OLAP)* involves the analysis of accumulated data by end users.

- *Integrated.* Data are collected from multiple systems and are integrated around subjects. For example, customer data may be extracted from internal (and external) systems and integrated around a customer identifier so that a comprehensive view of the customer is created.

- *Time variant.* Data warehouses and data marts maintain historical data (i.e., it includes time as a variable). Unlike transactional systems, where only recent data (such as for the last day, week, or month) are maintained, a warehouse or mart may store years of data. Historical data are needed to detect deviations, trends, and long-term relationships.

- *Nonvolatile.* Data warehouses and data marts are nonvolatile—no one can change or update the data. Nonvolatility means that the warehouse or mart reflects history, which is critical for trend analysis. Warehouses and marts are updated, but through IT-controlled load processes rather than by users.
- *Multidimensional.* Typically the data warehouse or mart uses a multidimensional data structure. Recall that relational databases store data in two-dimensional tables. In contrast, data warehouses and marts store data in more than two dimensions. For this reason, the data are said to be stored in a **multidimensional structure**. A common representation for this multidimensional structure is the *data cube*.

The data in data warehouses and marts are organized by *business dimensions*, which are the edges of the data cube and are subjects such as product, geographic area, and time period. If you look ahead briefly to Figure 3.11 for an example of a data cube, you see that the product dimension is comprised of nuts, screws, bolts, and washers; the geographic area dimension is comprised of east, west, and central; and the time period dimension is comprised of 2008, 2009, and 2010. Users can view and analyze data from the perspective of these business dimensions. This analysis is intuitive because the dimensions are in business terms, easily understood by users.

A Generic Data Warehouse Environment

The environment for data warehouses and marts includes the following:

- Source systems that provide data to the warehouse or mart
- Data integration technology and processes that are needed to prepare the data for use
- Different architectures for storing data in an organization's data warehouse or data marts
- Different tools and applications for the variety of users (you will learn about these tools and applications in Chapter 5)
- Metadata, data quality, and governance processes that are in place to ensure that the warehouse or mart meets its purposes

Figure 3.9 shows a generic data warehouse/data mart environment. Let's drill down into the component parts.

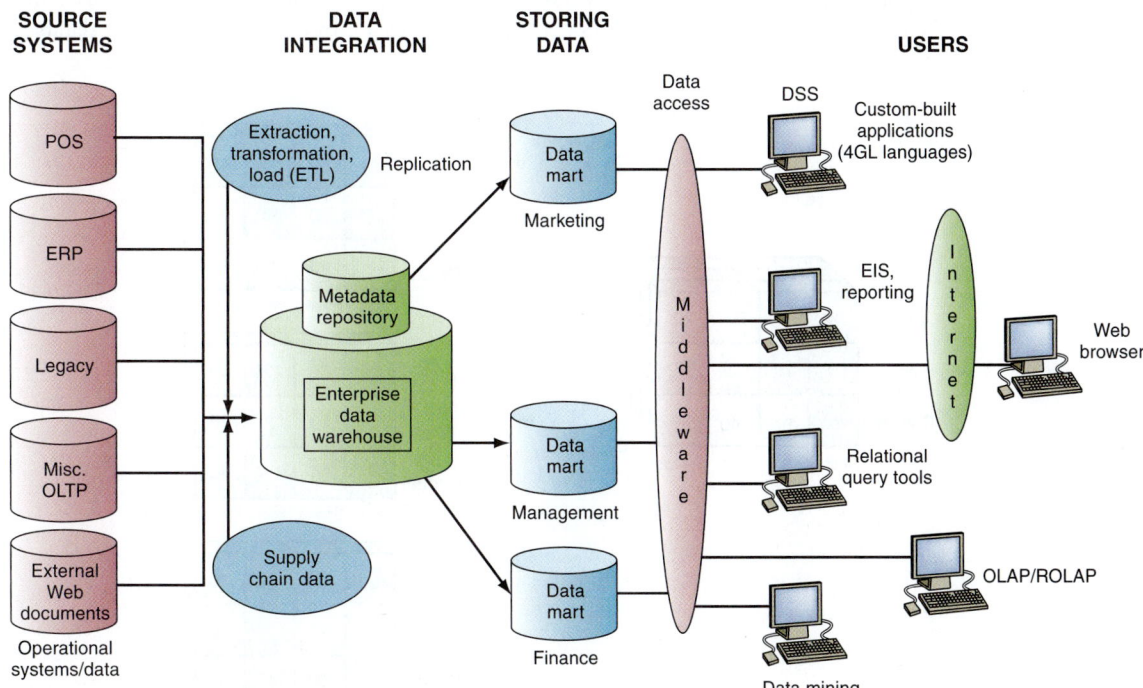

Figure 3.9 Data warehouse framework and views.

(a) 2009

Product	Region	Sales
Nuts	East	50
Nuts	West	60
Nuts	Central	100
Screws	East	40
Screws	West	70
Screws	Central	80
Bolts	East	90
Bolts	West	120
Bolts	Central	140
Washers	East	20
Washers	West	10
Washers	Central	30

(b) 2010

Product	Region	Sales
Nuts	East	60
Nuts	West	70
Nuts	Central	110
Screws	East	50
Screws	West	80
Screws	Central	90
Bolts	East	100
Bolts	West	130
Bolts	Central	150
Washers	East	30
Washers	West	20
Washers	Central	40

(c) 2011

Product	Region	Sales
Nuts	East	70
Nuts	West	80
Nuts	Central	120
Screws	East	60
Screws	West	90
Screws	Central	100
Bolts	East	110
Bolts	West	140
Bolts	Central	160
Washers	East	40
Washers	West	30
Washers	Central	50

Figure 3.10 Relational databases.

Source Systems. There is typically some "organizational pain" (i.e., business need) that motivates the development of BI capabilities in a firm. Working backward, this pain leads to information requirements, BI applications, and source system data requirements. The data requirements can require only a single source system, as in the case of a data mart, or hundreds of source systems, as in the case of an enterprisewide data warehouse.

A variety of source systems can be used. Possibilities include operational/transactional systems, enterprise resource planning (ERP) systems, Web site data, third-party data (e.g., customer demographic data), and more. The trend is to include more types of data (e.g., sensing data from RFID tags). These source systems often use different software packages (e.g., IBM, Oracle) and store data in different formats (e.g., relational, hierarchical).

A common source for the data in data warehouses is the company's operational databases, which can be relational databases. To differentiate between relational databases and multidimensional data warehouses and marts, suppose your company has four products—nuts, screws, bolts, and washers—that have been sold in three territories—East, West, and Central—for the previous three years—2008, 2009, and 2010. In a relational database, these sales data would look like Figures 3.10(a), (b), and (c). In a multidimensional database,

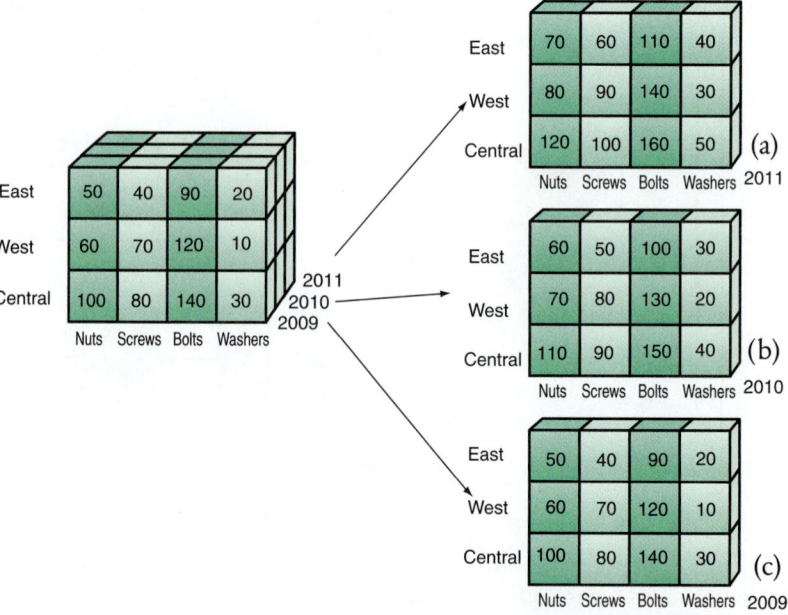

Figure 3.11 Data cube.

these data would be represented by a three-dimensional matrix (or data cube), as shown in Figure 3.10. You would say that this matrix represents sales *dimensioned by* products and regions and year. Notice that in Figure 3.10(a) you can see only sales for 2008. Therefore, sales for 2009 and 2010 are presented in Figures 3.10(b) and 3.10(c), respectively. Figures 3.12(a), (b), and (c) show the equivalence between these relational and multidimensional databases.

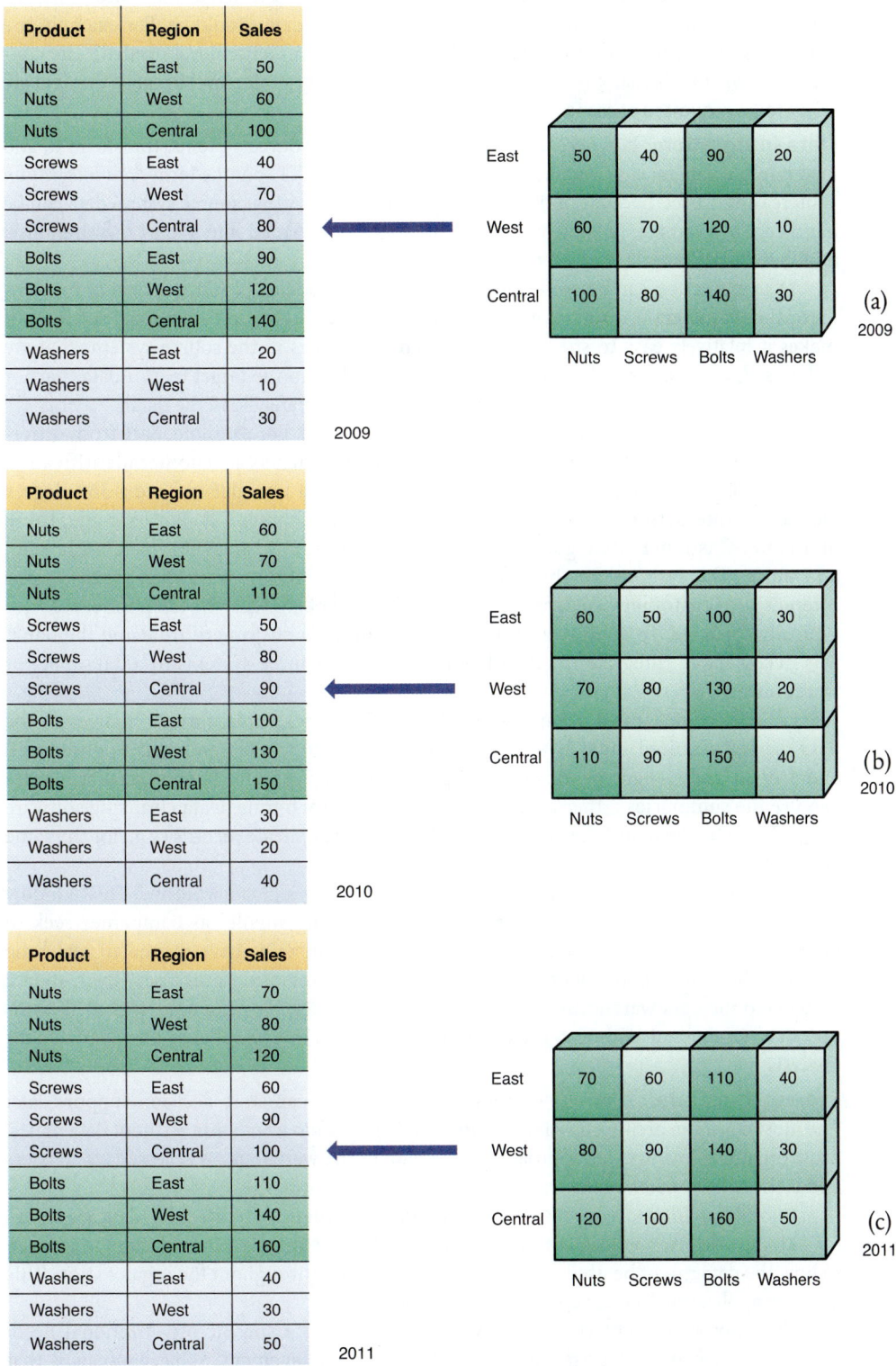

2009

Product	Region	Sales
Nuts	East	50
Nuts	West	60
Nuts	Central	100
Screws	East	40
Screws	West	70
Screws	Central	80
Bolts	East	90
Bolts	West	120
Bolts	Central	140
Washers	East	20
Washers	West	10
Washers	Central	30

2010

Product	Region	Sales
Nuts	East	60
Nuts	West	70
Nuts	Central	110
Screws	East	50
Screws	West	80
Screws	Central	90
Bolts	East	100
Bolts	West	130
Bolts	Central	150
Washers	East	30
Washers	West	20
Washers	Central	40

2011

Product	Region	Sales
Nuts	East	70
Nuts	West	80
Nuts	Central	120
Screws	East	60
Screws	West	90
Screws	Central	100
Bolts	East	110
Bolts	West	140
Bolts	Central	160
Washers	East	40
Washers	West	30
Washers	Central	50

Figure 3.12 Equivalence between relational and multidimensional databases.

Many source systems have been in use for years and contain "bad data" (e.g., missing or incorrect data) and are poorly documented. As a result, data profiling software should be used at the beginning of a data warehousing project to better understand the data. For example, data profiling software can provide statistics on missing data, identify possible primary and foreign keys, and reveal how derived values (e.g., column 3 = column 1 + column 2) are calculated. Subject area database specialists (e.g., marketing, human resources) can also help in understanding and accessing the data in source systems.

Other source systems issues must be addressed. Often there are multiple systems that contain some of the same data and the best system must be selected as the source. Organizations must also decide how granular (i.e., detailed) the data should be. For example, are daily sales figures needed or are data at the individual transaction level needed? The conventional wisdom is that it is best to store data at a highly granular level because the data are likely to be requested at some point.

Data Integration. It is necessary to extract data from source systems, transform it, and load it into a data mart or warehouse. This is often called ETL, but the term *data integration* is increasingly used because of the growing number of ways that source system data can be handled. For example, in some cases, data are extracted, loaded into a mart or warehouse, and then transformed (i.e., ELT rather than ETL).

Data extraction can be performed by handwritten code (e.g., SQL queries) or by commercial data integration software. Most companies ultimately use commercial software. It makes it relatively easy to specify the tables and attributes in the source systems that are to be used, map and schedule the movement of the data to the target (e.g., a data mart or warehouse), make the required transformations, and ultimately load the data.

The data are transformed to make them more useful. For example, data from different systems may be integrated around a common key, such as a customer identification number. This is the approach taken with customer data in order to have a 360-degree view of all interactions with customers (discussed in Chapter 12). For example, think of a bank. Customers may go to a branch, bank online, use an ATM, have a car loan, and more. The systems for these touchpoints (the numerous ways that organizations interact with customers, such as e-mail, the Web, direct contact, the telephone, etc.) are typically separate. To analyze and fully understand how customers are using the bank, it is necessary to integrate the data from the various source systems in a data mart or warehouse.

Other kinds of transformations are also made. For example, format changes to the data may be required, such as using *male* and *female* to denote gender, as opposed to 0 and 1 or M and F. Aggregations may be performed, say on sales figures, so that queries can use the summaries rather than recalculating them each time. Data cleansing software may be used to "clean up" the data, such as eliminating duplicate records (e.g., for the same customer).

Data are loaded into the warehouse or mart during a "load window." This window (i.e., the period of time for loading new data) is getting smaller as companies seek to have ever-fresher data in their warehouses. Many companies have moved to real-time data warehousing where data are moved (using data integration processes) from source systems to the data warehouse or mart almost immediately. For example, within 15 minutes of a purchase at Walmart, the details of the sale are in a warehouse and available for analysis.

Storing the Data. A variety of possible architectures can store decision support data. The most common architecture is *one central enterprise data warehouse*, without data marts. Most organizations use this approach, as the data in the warehouse is accessed by all users and is the *single version of the truth*.

Another architecture is *independent data marts*. With this architecture, data are stored for a single or a few applications, such as in marketing or finance. Limited thought is given to how the data might be used for other applications and throughout the organization. This is a very application-centric approach to storing data.

This approach is not very good. While it may meet a specific organizational need, it does not take an enterprisewide approach to data management. What happens is that independent data marts are created throughout the organization by various organizational units. Not only are the marts expensive to build and maintain, but they often contain inconsistent data. For example, they may have inconsistent data definitions (such as, What is a customer? Is one a potential or current customer?) or use different source systems (which may have different data for what should be the same, such as for a customer address). While independent data marts are an organizational reality, larger companies have increasingly moved to data warehouses.

Still another data warehouse architecture is the *hub and spoke*. With this architecture, data are stored in a central data warehouse with dependent data marts that source their data from the central repository. Because the dependent data marts get their data from the central repository, the data in the dependent data marts still comprise the *single version of the truth* for decision support purposes.

The dependent data marts store the data in a format appropriate for how the data will be used and for providing faster response times to queries and applications. As you have learned, users can view and analyze data from the perspective of business dimensions and measures. This analysis is intuitive because the dimensions are in business terms, easily understood by users.

Metadata. It is important to maintain data about the data (i.e., metadata) in the data warehouse. Both the IT personnel who operate and manage the data warehouse and the users who access the warehouse's data need metadata. IT personnel need information about data sources; database, table, and column names; refresh schedules; and data usage measures. Users' needs include data definitions; the report/query tools that are available; report distribution information; and help desk contact information.

Data Quality. The quality of the data in the warehouse must meet users' needs. If it does not, the data will not be trusted and ultimately will not be used. Most organizations find that the quality of the data in source systems is poor and must be improved before it can be used in the data warehouse. Some of the data can be improved through the use of data-cleansing software, but the better, long-term solution is to improve the quality at the source system level. This requires that the business owners of the data take responsibility for making the changes necessary to improve the quality of the data.

To illustrate a need to improve data quality, a large hotel chain wanted to conduct targeted marketing promotions using zip code data collected during the check-in process. When the zip code data were profiled, many of the zip codes were found to be 99999. Obviously, the clerks were not asking customers for their zip codes but needed to enter something to complete the registration process. A short-term solution was to conduct the marketing campaign using city and state data. The long-term solution was to get the clerks to enter the actual zip codes. The latter required the hotel managers to take the responsibility for getting their clerks to enter better data.

Governance. To ensure that BI is meeting organizational needs, it is necessary to have governance to plan and control BI activities. This requires that people, committees, and processes be in place. Companies that are effective in BI governance often have a senior level committee made up of vice presidents and directors who ensure that the business and BI strategies are in alignment; prioritize projects; and allocate resources. Then there is a middle management–level committee that oversees the various projects in the BI portfolio and sees that the projects are being completed effectively and efficiently. Lower-level operational committees perform tasks such as creating data definitions and identifying and solving data problems. All these committees require the collaboration and contributions of business and IT personnel.

Users. Once the data are in a data mart or warehouse, access is possible. This access begins the process of receiving business value from BI; everything else constitutes creating BI infrastructure.

Potential BI users are many, including IT developers; front line workers; analysts; information workers; managers and executives; and suppliers, customers, and regulators. Some of these users are *information producers* in that they primarily create information for others. IT developers and analysts typically are in this category. On the other hand, some users are *information consumers*, including managers and executives, because they consume information created by others.

Companies have reported hundreds of successful data-warehousing applications. For example, you can read client success stories and case studies at the Web sites of vendors such as NCR Corp. (www.ncr.com) and Oracle (www.oracle.com). For a more detailed discussion, visit the Data Warehouse Institute (http://tdwi.org). The benefits of data warehousing include the following:

- End users can access needed data quickly and easily via Web browsers because these data are located in one place.
- End users can conduct extensive analysis with data in ways that may not have been possible before.
- End users can obtain a consolidated view of organizational data.

These benefits can improve business knowledge, provide competitive advantage, enhance customer service and satisfaction, facilitate decision making, and streamline business processes. "IT's About Business 3.2" demonstrates the benefits of data warehousing at the Isle of Capri Casinos.

IT's ABOUT BUSINESS | 3.2

The Data Warehouse at the Isle of Capri Casinos

The Isle of Capri Casinos (www.isleofcapricasinos.com), one of the largest publicly traded gaming companies in the United States, operates casinos and associated entertainment and lodging facilities in the United States and overseas. Operating 15 casinos in six states across the United States, as well as a property in the Caribbean, Isle of Capri properties receive some 2 million visitors each year. The properties have a total of about 15,000 slot machines, 400 gaming tables, 3,100 hotel rooms, and three dozen restaurants.

The company bases its competitive strategy on guest relationships created and enhanced by an atmosphere that anticipates guests' needs and exceeds their expectations. Two things make this possible: a company culture focused on making every guest experience enjoyable and a data platform that enables in-depth understanding of the company's clientele.

The Isle of Capri has a difficult marketing challenge because of the geographical diversity of its properties and the diversity of its clientele in

Mississippi, Louisiana, Missouri, Iowa, Colorado, and Florida. The company needed to segment customers while maintaining and building an overall brand image. Historically, the firm managed its customer relationship management (CRM) efforts with a piecemeal direct mail program located in the casino management system housed at each property. This CRM approach did not allow for a complete view of the customer. For example, the company had difficulty with regular customers at one property who were not known at another property.

The Isle decided to implement a data warehouse to be able to have a "single view of the business" and a "single view of the customer." The goal was for the data warehouse to boost direct- and e-mail marketing campaigns.

The company began to implement a data warehouse in 2004, but then Hurricane Katrina hit the U.S. Gulf Coast in 2005. At that time, the Isle's headquarters were in Biloxi, Mississippi. The company shifted its focus to recovery efforts and relocation of its headquarters to St. Louis, Missouri. In 2006, the Isle turned its attention once again to implementing a data warehouse. The new system became operational in 2007.

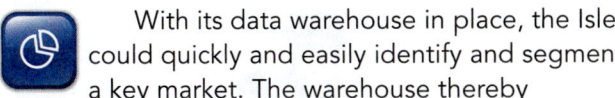

With its data warehouse in place, the Isle could quickly and easily identify and segment a key market. The warehouse thereby facilitated precisely targeted offers to successfully motivate people to visit the company's casinos and to be more profitable when they visited. For example, marketers segmented customers based on the frequency of their visits, which in turn became a factor in determining the number and value of offers. A company spokesperson noted that a player who visits four times a month needs a much less aggressive incentive package than one who comes only once a month.

The corporate marketing team now can obtain information and configure campaigns in one-half the time it used to require. Further, both the team and individual properties can more effectively track the results of campaigns and even know immediately when a customer redeems a coupon.

The gaming company then expanded the focus of its data warehousing effort. As a result, the casino moved from a system run by a few marketing analysts who generated reports to a system for multiple business users who may explore and make sense of the company's wealth of data.

The Isle has incorporated hotel and slot machine data and now labels guests by the number of days they stay at a hotel. With the new system, the company generates insights by experimenting with a series of segmentations—for example, "Who stayed at least two or three times?" "Who gamed and who didn't?" "How much did staying in a hotel affect a customer's gaming activity?"

The results of these experiments revealed a counterintuitive insight. Customers who live close to a casino and do not need to stay overnight game more when they stay in the hotel. Further, they play more than hotel guests who live farther away. The Isle developed marketing campaigns that successfully encourage local customers to stay overnight, including offers of a free night in a hotel.

The Isle then added slot machine data to the data warehouse. The short-term impact was an enhanced ability to determine where high-value players prefer machines to be located and to direct customers to new games based on past behavior. The company plans to closely track play activity on slots so it can deepen its knowledge of customers, more precisely target promotions, and adapt the floor in each casino to optimize revenue and profit.

Questions

1. Why was it necessary for the Isle of Capri Casinos to develop a data warehouse?
2. Describe the variety of benefits that the Isle realized from its data warehouse.

Sources: Compiled from L. Brockaw, "In Experiments We Trust: From Intuit to Harrah's Casinos," *Sloan Management Review*, March 3, 2011; "Data Warehouse Assessment Services Leads Ameristar Casinos to Select Teradata," *PR Newswire*, February 21, 2011; "Isle of Capri Casinos Makes a Sure Bet," *Teradata Magazine*, vol. 11, no. 1, 2011; "Harrah's Entertainment, Inc.," *IBM Case Studies*, November 2, 2010; www.isleofcapricasinos.com, www.teradata.com, accessed February 18, 2011.

Despite their many benefits, data warehouses do have problems. First, they can be very expensive to build and to maintain. Second, incorporating data from obsolete mainframe systems can be difficult and expensive. Finally, people in one department might be reluctant to share data with other departments.

BEFORE *YOU GO ON* . . .

1. Differentiate between data warehouses and data marts.
2. Describe the characteristics of a data warehouse.
3. What are three possible architectures for data warehouses and data marts in an organization?

Student Activity | 3.4

Objective: To understand the challenges of implementing a data warehouse in an organization and the potential benefits of data warehousing.

Chapter Connection: This activity relates to Section 3.4 and Learning Objective 5.

Prerequisites: You should read Section 3.4 prior to completing this activity.

Activity:

View the video "UNC Data Warehouse" at www.youtube.com/watch?v=3SemmiKGYEk.

Note: CPT (Current Procedural Terminology) codes are used to categorize medical procedures for billing purposes. ICD-9 (*International Classification of Diseases,* 9th revision) is used to classify illnesses and diseases on medical records.

Deliverables:

Prepare written answers to the following discussion questions.

Quiz Questions:

1. What is a data warehouse?
   (a) Documentation that defines the format of information to be entered into a database
   (b) A repository of information that defines how often a database should be updated and why the database is needed
   (c) A repository of data that are organized by business dimension or subject to support decision making
   (d) Documentation that provides general guidelines for data security and privacy policies
   (e) A repository of data that are grouped according to their level of security hierarchy

2. List three of the basic characteristics of data warehouses.
   (a) Day-to-day transaction data, integration of multimedia data, and a full security mechanism
   (b) Inclusion of only the most up-to-date data, organization by business departments, and full access provided to both external and internal business constituents
   (c) Access provided only to top management, multiple redundancies, and inclusion of external data sources
   (d) Integration of multiple data, inclusion of nonvolatile data, and multidimensional data
   (e) 100 percent accuracy, inclusion of real-time transaction data, and top-level security access

3. What are some of the potential benefits of implementing data warehouses?

Discussion Questions:

1. What were some of the challenges in implementing data warehouses at the University of North Carolina (UNC) Health System?
2. What were the benefits the UNC Health System gained from its data warehouse?

3.5 | Knowledge Management

As you have noted throughout this text, data and information are critically important organizational assets. Knowledge is a vital asset as well. Successful managers have always used intellectual assets and recognized their value. But these efforts were not systematic, and they did not ensure that knowledge was shared and dispersed in a way that benefited the overall organization. Moreover, industry analysts estimate that most of a company's knowledge assets are not housed in relational databases. Instead, they are dispersed in e-mail, word processing documents, spreadsheets, and presentations on individual computers. This arrangement makes it extremely difficult for companies to access and integrate this knowledge. The result frequently is less-effective decision making.

Concepts and Definitions

Knowledge management (KM) is a process that helps organizations manipulate important knowledge that is part of the organization's memory, usually in an unstructured format.

For an organization to be successful, knowledge, as a form of capital, must exist in a format that can be exchanged among persons. In addition, it must be able to grow.

Knowledge. In the information technology context, knowledge is distinct from data and information. As you learned in Chapter 1, data are a collection of facts, measurements, and statistics; information is organized or processed data that are timely and accurate. Knowledge is information that is *contextual*, *relevant*, and *useful*. Simply put, knowledge is *information in action*. **Intellectual capital** (or **intellectual assets**) is another term for knowledge.

To illustrate with an example, a bulletin listing all the courses offered by your university during one semester would be considered data. When you register, you process the data from the bulletin to create your schedule for the semester. Your schedule would be considered information. Awareness of your work schedule, your major, your desired social schedule, and characteristics of different faculty members could be construed as knowledge, because it can affect the way you build your schedule. You see that this awareness is contextual and relevant (to developing an optimal schedule of classes) as well as useful (it can lead to changes in your schedule). The implication is that knowledge has strong experiential and reflective elements that distinguish it from information in a given context. Unlike information, knowledge can be exercised to solve a problem.

Numerous theories and models classify different types of knowledge. Here you will focus on the distinction between explicit knowledge and tacit knowledge.

Explicit and Tacit Knowledge. **Explicit knowledge** deals with more objective, rational, and technical knowledge. In an organization, explicit knowledge consists of the policies, procedural guides, reports, products, strategies, goals, core competencies, and IT infrastructure of the enterprise. In other words, explicit knowledge is the knowledge that has been codified (documented) in a form that can be distributed to others or transformed into a process or a strategy. A description of how to process a job application that is documented in a firm's human resources policy manual is an example of explicit knowledge.

In contrast, **tacit knowledge** is the cumulative store of subjective or experiential learning. In an organization, tacit knowledge consists of an organization's experiences, insights, expertise, know-how, trade secrets, skill sets, understanding, and learning. It also includes the organizational culture, which reflects the past and present experiences of the organization's people and processes, as well as the organization's prevailing values. Tacit knowledge is generally imprecise and costly to transfer. It is also highly personal. Finally, because it is unstructured, it is difficult to formalize or codify, in contrast to explicit knowledge. A salesperson who has worked with particular customers over time and has come to know their needs quite well would possess extensive tacit knowledge. This knowledge is typically not recorded. In fact, it might be difficult for the salesperson to put into writing.

Knowledge Management Systems

The goal of knowledge management is to help an organization make the most effective use of the knowledge it has. Historically, management information systems have focused on capturing, storing, managing, and reporting explicit knowledge. Organizations now realize they need to integrate explicit and tacit knowledge in formal information systems. **Knowledge management systems (KMSs)** refer to the use of modern information technologies—the Internet, intranets, extranets, databases—to systematize, enhance, and expedite intrafirm and interfirm knowledge management. KMSs are intended to help an organization cope with turnover, rapid change, and downsizing by making the expertise of the organization's human capital widely accessible. "IT's About Business 3.3" describes a new type of knowledge management at Quora.

Organizations can realize many benefits with KMSs. Most importantly, they make **best practices**, the most effective and efficient ways of doing things, readily available to a wide range of employees. Enhanced access to best-practice knowledge improves overall organizational performance. For example, account managers can now make available their tacit knowledge about how best to handle large accounts. The organization can then use this knowledge to train new account managers. Other benefits include improved customer service, more efficient product development, and improved employee morale and retention.

At the same time, however, implementing effective KMSs presents some challenges. First, employees must be willing to share their personal tacit knowledge. To encourage

Building a Comprehensive Picture of the World

Two decades after the invention of the World Wide Web, vast areas of knowledge and experience are still not online, let alone searchable. "Ninety percent of the information people have is still in their heads and not on the Web," says one of Quora's co-founders. Quora's other co-founder calls it "experiential knowledge." Wikipedia (www.wikipedia.org) has amazing breadth and scope, but there is only so much that any encyclopedia, limited to verifiable facts about discrete nouns, can capture within the entirety of human knowledge. On the other end of the "knowledge" spectrum, Web sites such as Facebook and Twitter allow people to describe their lives and to make personal observations. However, on such networks it is difficult to separate the informed opinion from pure speculation.

The large gap between the two approaches— the objective (Wikipedia) and the subjective (social networks)—is the area that Quora (www.quora.com) hopes to occupy. For years, blogs have occupied this space, but their idiosyncratic style has left their insights largely difficult to search.

The co-founders were looking for areas of online behavior in which consumer demand was clear but existing solutions were lacking. They realized that a prime example was Web sites devoted to answering questions. A significant number of Internet searches are framed as questions.

For example, Yahoo! Answers, the Q&A Web site created by Yahoo! in 2005, attracts more than 50 million users in the United States each month. But few searches can be satisfied with Yahoo! Answers, where the questions are often silly, and the replies even worse. The replies tend to be guesswork offered by people with absolutely no knowledge of the subject.

On Quora's Web site, you can begin with the page—framed as a question—about getting started on Quora. Or you can begin by sifting through random questions that are displayed in the center of the screen. On top of the page is a large search bar. Using key words, you can find questions that others have already posed or choose topics to follow so that the Web site can begin serving up queries more suited to your interests. You can also start following people. That way, the questions they ask, answer, and follow will show up in your feed. You can also vote "up" answers that you think are helpful, and vote "down" those that are not. All of your activity shows up in your feed.

Real names are mandatory, so there is a heavy social cost to acting the fool. Quora does allow anonymous posts, though, which helps when asking about a personal health issue, for example, or responding about your own experience as a fellow sufferer.

Much of the conversation on the Internet takes place in short, timely bursts. Quora, by contrast, encourages answers that are thorough and in depth. In Quora's community, the most valued responses reflect your honest intelligence and wisdom.

It helps that users can vote an answer up or down, the better to push quality to the top and push down (if not off the page entirely) the frivolous and poorly conceived. Quora added a button that allows users to deem an answer "not helpful"—a signal to the Quora team or on of the site's hundred-plus volunteers that perhaps they should consider deleting it.

Unlike on Facebook, everything you write can be trimmed, corrected, or otherwise edited by one of the rigorous volunteers. Volunteers often send answers back to their authors marked up with suggested edits. Questions, too, can get extensively reworded.

Quora's goal is to capture as much of that subjective knowledge as possible. By creating an environment for members to post and answer questions, as well as rate the quality of others' answers, Quora is building a searchable repository of information while it also builds a community. Quora hopes to attract so many users that its subjective, experiential, inherent knowledge will construct a comprehensive picture of the world.

However, one major complaint has emerged, and it essentially boils down to declining quality. Both founders acknowledge that the average quality of answers on Quora has declined significantly. The site was flooded with so many new members at the start of 2011—a 500 percent increase in just one month—that at one point in mid-January 2011, half of Quora's users had been on the site for two weeks or less. Quora's "old hands" felt that the newcomers posed stupid questions.

Even worse, the newcomers pushed up other users' answers when those answers were off the point and not helpful.

Another problem is the large gaps in Quora knowledge areas, which would be expected as the Web site appeared only in 2009. For example, Quora has brilliant entries for high-tech startups but almost no entries for Hollywood.

At any rate, in mid-2011, approximately 200,000 people were visiting the site each month. Quora has not yet earned any revenue. But, if Quora can fulfill its vision—getting experts to engage in conversation and thus generate searchable and authoritative answers to many thousands of questions—then it may someday grab more page views than Wikipedia by filling in the gaps that no encyclopedia could ever address.

Questions

1. Compare and contrast Quora to an organization's knowledge management system. Could a Quora-type knowledge management system be used inside an organization? Why or why not? Support your answer.

2. Provide examples of how Quora can fill in the gaps in its knowledge gathering efforts.

Sources: Compiled from G. Rivlin, "Does Quora Really Have All the Answers?" *Wired*, April 26, 2011; M. Lowman, "The Mystery Behind Quora," *BostInnovation*, February 1, 2011; S. Goodson, "Why Is Quora Exploding?" *Forbes*, January 11, 2011; M. Siegler, "Quora Signups Exploded in Late December," *TechCrunch*, January 5, 2011; Q. Hardy, "What Does Quora Know?" *Forbes*, November 18, 2010; www.quora.com, accessed May 19, 2011.

this behavior, organizations must create a knowledge management culture that rewards employees who add their expertise to the knowledge base. Second, the knowledge base must be continually maintained and updated. New knowledge must be added, and old, outdated knowledge must be deleted. Finally, companies must be willing to invest in the resources needed to carry out these operations.

The Knowledge Management System Cycle

A functioning KMS follows a cycle that consists of six steps (see Figure 3.13). The reason the system is cyclical is that knowledge is dynamically refined over time. The knowledge in an effective KMS is never finalized because the environment changes over time and knowledge must be updated to reflect these changes. The cycle works as follows:

1. *Create knowledge.* Knowledge is created as people determine new ways of doing things or develop know-how. Sometimes external knowledge is brought in.

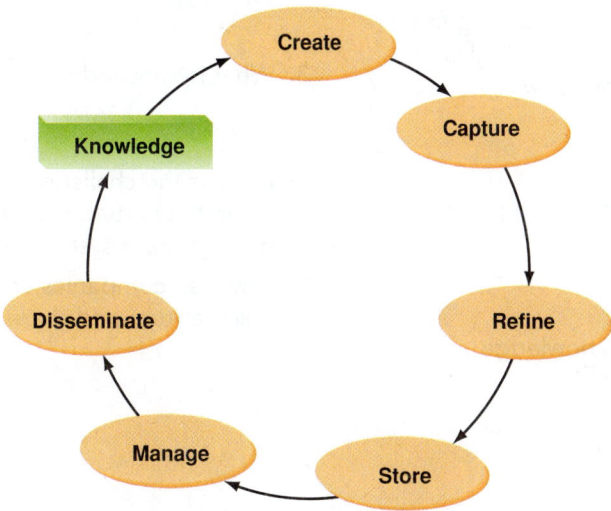

Figure 3.13 The knowledge management system cycle.

2. *Capture knowledge.* New knowledge must be identified as valuable and be represented in a reasonable way.

3. *Refine knowledge.* New knowledge must be placed in context so that it is actionable. This is where tacit qualities (human insights) must be captured along with explicit facts.

4. *Store knowledge.* Useful knowledge must then be stored in a reasonable format in a knowledge repository so that others in the organization can access it.

5. *Manage knowledge.* Like a library, the knowledge must be kept current. It must be reviewed regularly to verify that it is relevant and accurate.

6. *Disseminate knowledge.* Knowledge must be made available in a useful format to anyone in the organization who needs it, anywhere and anytime.

BEFORE *YOU GO ON . . .*

1. What is knowledge management?
2. What is the difference between tacit knowledge and explicit knowledge?
3. Describe the knowledge management system cycle.

Student Activity | 3.5

Objective: You will apply your knowledge from Section 3.5 and identify the importance and advantages of implementing knowledge management systems in an organization.

Chapter Connection: This activity relates to Section 3.5 and Learning Objective 5 in this chapter.

Prerequisites: You should read Section 3.5 prior to completing this activity.

Activity:

Watch the following two video clips.

1. Discover What You Know: www.youtube.com/watch?v=f_x78XLBBVM
2. "Lee Bryant–Knowledge Management" from HeadShift.com, an international consulting firm that helps its clients use social technologies to improve business performance: www.youtube.com/watch?v=LYq9jmVtQU8

Deliverables:

Prepare written answers to the following discussion questions.

Quiz Questions:

1. What are the six steps of the knowledge management system cycle?
   (a)
   (b)
   (c)
   (d)
   (e)
   (f)

2. What is tacit knowledge?
   (a) A type of knowledge that deals with objective, rational, and technical knowledge
   (b) A type of knowledge that can be easily codified or documented
   (c) A type of knowledge that is highly personal, imprecise, and difficult to transfer
   (d) A type of knowledge that includes the written policies and procedural guides of an organization
   (e) A type of knowledge that has been codified in a form that can be easily distributed to others

3. What is knowledge management?

Discussion Questions:

1. Discuss the challenges faced by companies when they attempt to implement a knowledge management system.

2. How can companies use Web 2.0 technologies to help capture and share knowledge?

What's in **IT** for ME?

FOR THE ACCOUNTING MAJOR

The accounting function is intimately concerned with keeping track of the transactions and internal controls of an organization. Modern databases enable accountants to perform these functions more effectively. Databases help accountants manage the flood of data in today's organizations so that they can keep their firms in compliance with the standards imposed by Sarbanes-Oxley.

Accountants also play a role in cost-justifying the creation of a knowledge base and then auditing its cost-effectiveness. In addition, if you work for a large CPA company that provides management services or sells knowledge, you will most likely use some of your company's best practices that are stored in a knowledge base.

FOR THE FINANCE MAJOR

Financial managers make extensive use of computerized databases that are external to the organization, such as CompuStat or Dow Jones, to obtain financial data on organizations in their industry. They can use these data to determine if their organization meets industry benchmarks in return on investment, cash management, and other financial ratios.

Financial managers, who produce the organization's financial status reports, are also closely involved with Sarbanes-Oxley. Databases help these managers comply with the law's standards.

FOR THE MARKETING MAJOR

Databases help marketing managers access data from the organization's marketing transactions, such as customer purchases, to plan targeted marketing campaigns and to evaluate the success of previous campaigns. Knowledge about customers can make the difference between success and failure. In many databases and knowledge bases, the vast majority of information and knowledge concerns customers, products, sales, and marketing. Marketing managers regularly use an organization's knowledge base, and they often participate in its creation.

FOR THE PRODUCTION/OPERATIONS MANAGEMENT MAJOR

Production/operations personnel access organizational data to determine optimum inventory levels for parts in a production process. Past production data enable production/operations management (POM) personnel to determine the optimum configuration for assembly lines. Firms also collect quality data that inform them not only about the quality of finished products but also about quality issues with incoming raw materials, production irregularities, shipping and logistics, and after-sale use and maintenance of the product.

Knowledge management is extremely important for running complex operations. The accumulated knowledge regarding scheduling, logistics, maintenance, and other functions is very valuable. Innovative ideas are necessary for improving operations and can be supported by knowledge management.

FOR THE
HUMAN RESOURCES MANAGEMENT MAJOR

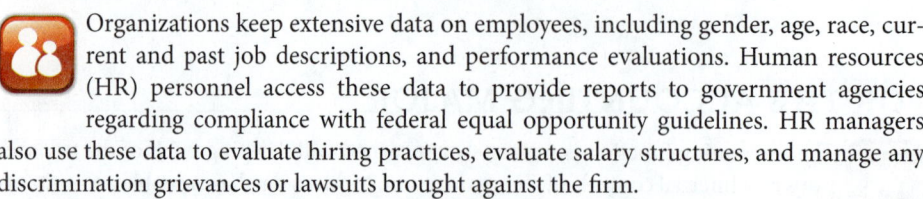

Organizations keep extensive data on employees, including gender, age, race, current and past job descriptions, and performance evaluations. Human resources (HR) personnel access these data to provide reports to government agencies regarding compliance with federal equal opportunity guidelines. HR managers also use these data to evaluate hiring practices, evaluate salary structures, and manage any discrimination grievances or lawsuits brought against the firm.

Databases help HR managers provide assistance to all employees as companies turn over more and more decisions about health care and retirement planning to the employees themselves. The employees can use the databases for help in selecting the optimal mix among these critical choices.

HR managers also need to use a knowledge base frequently to find out how past cases were handled. Consistency in how employees are treated not only is important, but it also protects the company against legal actions. Also, training for building, maintaining, and using the knowledge system sometimes is the responsibility of the HR department. Finally, the HR department might be responsible for compensating employees who contribute their knowledge to the knowledge base.

FOR THE MIS MAJOR

The MIS function manages the organization's data as well as the databases. MIS database administrators standardize data names by using the data dictionary. This process ensures that all users understand which data are in the database. Database personnel also help users access needed data and generate reports with query tools.

>>> SUMMARY

1. List three common challenges in managing data, and describe one way each one can be addressed using data governance.

Three common challenges in managing data are these:

> Data are scattered throughout organizations and are collected by many individuals using various methods and devices. These data are frequently stored in numerous servers and locations and in different computing systems, databases, formats, and human and computer languages.

> Data come from multiple sources.

> Information systems that support particular business processes impose unique requirements on data, which results in repetition and conflicts across an organization.

One strategy for implementing data governance is master data management. Master data management provides companies with the ability to store, maintain, exchange, and synchronize a consistent, accurate, and timely "single version of the truth" for the company's core master data. Master data management consistently manages data gathered from across an organization, consistently manages data from multiple sources, and consistently manages data across business processes in an organization.

2. **Name six problems minimized by using the database approach.**

The database approach minimizes the following problems: data redundancy, data isolation, data inconsistency, data security, data integrity, and data independence.

3. **Demonstrate how to interpret relationships depicted in an entity-relationship diagram.**

See Figure 3.4 and its accompanying explanation for a demonstration of interpreting relationships in an ER diagram.

4. **List one main advantage and one main disadvantage of relational databases.**

Relational databases allow people to compare information quickly by row or column. In addition, items are easy to retrieve by finding the point of intersection of a particular row and column. On the other hand, large-scale relational databases can be composed of many interrelated tables, making the overall design complex with slow search and access times.

5. **Identify and explain the advantages of the six characteristics of data warehouses.**

The basic characteristics of data warehouses and data marts include these:

> Data are organized by subject (for example, by customer, vendor, product, price level, and region). As a result, the analyses performed by users are intuitive because the dimensions are labeled in business terms.

> Data warehouses and data marts use online analytical processing (OLAP), which involves the analysis of

accumulated data by end users. OLAP allows users to "drive" their own data analyses and to examine data in unique ways to improve job performance.

> Data are collected from multiple systems and are integrated around subjects. For example, customer data may be extracted from internal (and external) systems and integrated around a customer identifier so that a comprehensive view of the customer is created.

> Data warehouses and data marts maintain historical data (that is, it includes time as a variable). A data warehouse or mart may store years of data. Historical data are needed to detect deviations, trends, and long-term relationships.

> Data warehouses and data marts are nonvolatile—no one can change or update the data. Nonvolatility means that the warehouse or mart reflects history, which is critical for trend analysis.

> Typically the data warehouse or mart uses a multidimensional data structure.

6. **Demonstrate the use of a multidimensional model to store and analyze data.**

See Figures 3.10(a), (b), and (c), 3.11, and 3.12(a), (b), and (c).

7. **List two main advantages of using knowledge management, and describe the steps in the knowledge management system cycle.**

Organizations can use knowledge management to develop best practices, to establish the most effective and efficient ways of doing things, and to make these practices readily available to a wide range of employees. Other benefits of knowledge management include improved customer service, more efficient product development, and improved employee morale and retention.

A functioning KMS follows a cycle that consists of six steps: create knowledge, capture knowledge, refine knowledge, store knowledge, manage knowledge, and disseminate knowledge.

>>> CHAPTER GLOSSARY

attribute Each characteristic or quality describing a particular entity.

best practices The most effective and efficient ways to do things.

bit A binary digit; that is, a 0 or a 1.

byte A group of eight bits that represents a single character.

clickstream data Data collected about user behavior and browsing patterns by monitoring users' activities when they visit a Web site.

data dictionary Collection of definitions of data elements; data characteristics that use the data elements; and the individuals, business functions, applications, and reports that use this data element.

data governance An approach to managing information across an entire organization.

data mart A low-cost, scaled-down version of a data warehouse that is designed for the end-user needs in a strategic business unit (SBU) or a department.

data model Definition of the way data in a DBMS are conceptually structured.

data warehouse A repository of historical data that are organized by subject to support decision makers in the organization.

database A group of logically related files that stores data and the associations among them.

database management system (DBMS) The software program (or group of programs) that provides access to a database.

entity A person, place, thing, or event about which information is maintained in a record.

entity classes Groupings of entities of a given type.

entity-relationship (ER) diagram Document that shows data entities and attributes and relationships among them.

entity-relationship (ER) modeling The process of designing a database by organizing data entities to be used and identifying the relationships among them.

explicit knowledge The more objective, rational, and technical types of knowledge.

field A grouping of logically related characters into a word, a small group of words, or a complete number.

file A grouping of logically related records.

identifiers Attributes that are unique to an entity instance.

instance A particular entity within an entity class.

intellectual capital (or **intellectual assets)** Other terms for knowledge.

knowledge management (KM) A process that helps organizations identify, select, organize, disseminate, transfer, and apply information and expertise that are part of the organization's memory and that typically reside within the organization in an unstructured manner.

knowledge management systems (KMSs) Information technologies used to systematize, enhance, and expedite intra- and inter-firm knowledge management.

master data A set of core data, such as customer, product, employee, vendor, geographic location, and so on, that spans an enterprise's information systems.

master data management A process that provides companies with the ability to store, maintain, exchange, and synchronize a consistent, accurate, and timely "single version of the truth" for the company's core master data.

multidimensional structure Storage of data in more than two dimensions; a common representation is the *data cube*.

normalization A method for analyzing and reducing a relational database to its most streamlined form for minimum redundancy, maximum data integrity, and best processing performance.

online transaction processing (OLTP) Processing of business transactions online as soon as they occur.

primary key The identifier field or attribute that uniquely identifies a record.

query by example (QBE) Database language that enables the user to fill out a grid (form) to construct a sample or description of the data wanted.

record A grouping of logically related fields.

relational database model Data model based on the simple concept of tables in order to capitalize on characteristics of rows and columns of data.

secondary key An identifier field or attribute that has some identifying information but typically does not identify the file with complete accuracy.

structured query language (SQL) Popular relational database language that enables users to perform complicated searches with relatively simple instructions.

table A grouping of logically related records.

tacit knowledge The cumulative store of subjective or experiential learning, which is highly personal and hard to formalize.

>>> DISCUSSION QUESTIONS

1. Explain the difficulties involved in managing data.

2. What are the problems associated with poor-quality data?

3. What is master data management? What does it have to do with high-quality data?

4. Explain why master data management is so important in companies that have multiple data sources.

5. Describe the advantages of relational databases.

6. Explain why it is important to capture and manage knowledge.

7. Compare and contrast tacit knowledge and explicit knowledge.

>>> PROBLEM-SOLVING ACTIVITIES

1. Access various employment Web sites (e.g., www.monster.com and www.dice.com) and find several job descriptions for a database administrator. Are the job descriptions similar? What are the salaries offered in these positions?

2. Access the Web sites of several real estate companies. Find the sites that take you through a step-by-step process for buying a home, that provide virtual reality tours of homes in your price range and location, that provide mortgage and interest rate calculators, and that offer financing for

your home. Do the sites require that you register to access their services? Can you request that an e-mail be sent to you when properties in which you might be interested become available?

3. It is possible to find many Web sites that provide demographic information. Access several of these sites and see what they offer. Do the sites differ in the types of demographic information they offer? If so, how? Do the sites require a fee for the information they offer? Would demographic information be useful to you if you wanted to start a new business? If so, how and why?

4. The Internet contains many Web sites that provide information on financial aid resources for students. Access several of these sites. Do you have to register to access the information? Can you apply for financial aid on the sites, or do you have to request paper applications that you must complete and return?

5. Draw an entity-relationship diagram for a small retail store. You wish to keep track of the product name, description, unit price, and number of items of that product sold to each customer. You also wish to record customer name, mailing address, and billing address.

You must track each transaction (sale) as to date, product purchased, unit price, number of units, tax, and total amount of the sale.

6. Draw the entity-relationship diagram for the following patient appointment system. The business rules of this system are the following:

A doctor can be scheduled for many appointments but might not have any scheduled at all. Each appointment is scheduled with exactly one doctor. A patient can schedule one or more appointments. One appointment is scheduled with exactly one patient. An appointment must generate exactly one bill, and a bill is generated by only one appointment. One payment is applied to exactly one bill, and one bill can be paid off over time by several payments. A bill can be outstanding, having nothing yet paid on it at all. One patient can make many payments, but a single payment is made by only one patient. Some patients are insured by an insurance company. If they are insured, they can only carry insurance with one insurance company. An insurance company can have many patients carry their policies. For patients who carry insurance, the insurance company will make payments, with each single payment made by exactly one insurance company.

>>> WEB ACTIVITIES

1. Access the Web sites of IBM (www.ibm.com), Sybase (www.sybase.com), and Oracle (www.oracle.com), and trace the capabilities of their latest data management products, including Web connections.

2. Enter the Web site of the Gartner Group (www.gartner.com). Examine the company's research studies

pertaining to data management. Prepare a report on the state of the art.

3. Calculate your personal digital footprint at www.emc.com/digital_universe/downloads/web/personal-ticker.htm.

>>> TEAM ASSIGNMENTS

1. Each team will select an online database to explore, such as AOL Music (http://music.aol.com), iGo (www.igo.com), or the Internet Movie Database (www.imdb.com). Explore these Web sites to see what information they provide for you. List the entities and the attributes that the Web sites must track in their databases. Diagram the relationship between the entities you have identified.

2. In groups, create a data model to include the following for a pet store:

- Customer data
- Product data

- Employee data
- Financial data
- Vendor data
- Sales data
- Inventory data
- Building data
- Other data (specify)

Create attributes (four or more) for each entity. Create relationships between the entities, name the relationships, and create an entity-relationship diagram for the pet store.

CLOSING **CASE 1** > Big Data

THE PROBLEM>>>

Organizations and individuals are facing an unimaginably vast amount of data that is growing ever more rapidly. In fact, the amount of digital data is increasing by a factor of 10 every five years. Consider these examples:

- Walmart processes more than 1 million customer transactions every hour, feeding its databases and data warehouses that are estimated to contain more than 2.5 petabytes of data.
- Facebook contains more than 40 billion photographs, totaling hundreds of terabytes of data.
- The job of the Large Hadron Collider at CERN, Europe's particle-physics laboratory near Geneva, Switzerland, is to take tiny particles of matter, accelerate them almost to the speed of light, smash them together, and then take pictures of the collisions. There are five collision detectors at the collider, with 150 million sensors, each snapping 40 million pictures per second. The collider generates 40 terabytes of data every second, much more data than can be stored or analyzed.

Scientists state that we are experiencing the "Industrial Revolution of Data," and have coined the term "Big Data" for the superabundance of data available today. Big Data makes it possible to do many things not previously possible: e.g., to spot business trends more rapidly and accurately, prevent disease, track crime, and many others.

On the other hand, Big Data is creating numerous problems. First, the amount of data exceeded the total amount of available storage space in 2007, and the gap continues to widen. Second, the quantity of data is growing faster than the ability of networks (particularly the Internet) to carry it. Third, ensuring the security of data and protecting privacy are becoming more difficult as the amount of data multiplies and data are shared more widely around the world. Fourth, the vast amount of data is making it increasingly inaccessible. Fifth, individuals are swamped with data, making decision making much more difficult. Finally, only 5 percent of the data is structured, meaning that it is in a standard format that can be read by computers.

IT SOLUTIONS>>>

The first step for many organizations was to integrate information silos into a database environment and then to develop data warehouses for decision making. After those efforts, organizations turned their attention to the business of information management—helping to make sense of their proliferating data. In recent years, Oracle, IBM, Microsoft, and SAP between them have spent more than $15 billion on buying software firms specializing in data management and business intelligence. (You will learn about business intelligence in Chapter 5.) In addition, IBM believes that business intelligence is a huge growth area. The IT giant invested $12 billion from 2006 through 2010, opening six business intelligence centers with 4,000 employees worldwide.

In addition, companies are turning to a new type of professional: data scientists. These experts combine the skills of software programmer, statistician, and storyteller/artist to extract valuable "nuggets of information" hidden in mountains of data.

THE RESULTS>>>

The way information is managed touches all areas of life. At the turn of the twentieth century, new flows of information through channels such as the telegraph and telephone supported mass production. Today, the availability of abundant data enables companies to cater to small niche markets (and even individual customers) anywhere in the world. For example, Best Buy (www.bestbuy.com), a retailer, found that 7 percent of its customers accounted for 43 percent of its sales, so it reorganized its stores to concentrate on those customers' needs.

Some industries have led the way in their ability to gather and exploit data. Consider these industry examples:

- Credit-card companies monitor every purchase and can accurately identify fraudulent ones, using rules derived by analyzing billions of transactions.
- Insurance companies are also effectively analyzing data to spot suspicious claims.

- Mobile-phone companies analyze subscribers' calling patterns to determine whether most of their frequent contacts are on a rival network. If that rival network is offering an attractive promotion that might cause that subscriber to defect, he or she can be offered an incentive to stay.
- Retailers effectively analyze customer transactions to tailor promotions.
- The oil industry examines seismic data before drilling new wells.

Unfortunately, despite years of effort, law-enforcement and intelligence agencies' databases are not particularly well integrated. In the healthcare industry, large-scale efforts to computerize health records have run into bureaucratic, technological, and ethical problems.

Success stories of effective data management in organizations abound. As just one example, take a look at Nestlé. Nestlé sells more than 100,000 products in 200 countries, using 550,000 suppliers, but the company was not using its huge buying power effectively because its databases had severe problems. Nestlé found that of its 9 million records of vendors, customers, and materials, about one-half were obsolete or duplicated, and about one-third of the remainder were inaccurate or incomplete. The company overhauled its databases, improving the quality of its data. For just one ingredient, vanilla, its American operation was able to use fewer suppliers and thereby save $30 million per year.

Questions

1. Is Big Data really the problem, or is it the use, control, and security of the data? Provide specific examples to support your answer.

2. What are the implications of having incorrect data points in your Big Data? What if customer information is incorrect or duplicated? How good are decisions made based on bad information derived from incorrect data?

SOURCES: Compiled from D. McCafferty, "The Big Data Conundrum," *CIO Insight*, November 9, 2010; D. Henschen, "What's at Stake in the Big Data Revolution?" *Information Week*, August 18, 2010; S. Nunziata, "Business Analytics: Turning IP into Opportunity," *CIO Insight*, August 17, 2010; D. Henschen, "The Big Data Era: How Data Strategy Will Change," *Information Week*, August 7, 2010; "Data, Data Everywhere," *The Economist*, February 25, 2010; D. Bollier, "The Promise and Peril of Big Data," *The Aspen Institute*, January 1, 2010; T. Davenport, J. Harris, and R. Morison, "Analytics at Work: Smarter Decisions, Better Results," *Harvard Business Press*, 2010; "Big Data—It's Not Just for Google Anymore," *AMD White Paper*, 2010; www.nestle.com, www.ibm.com, accessed February 19, 2011.

CLOSING **CASE 2** >

Company Strategy Thrives with Database Strategy

In the 1980s, data on commercial properties were scattered among guidebooks on sales and leasing activity, myriad public records, and real estate listings. What the commercial real estate industry needed was a compilation of all these different types of data. Such a compilation should enable real estate professionals and potential buyers and sellers to search much more efficiently and effectively for relevant information on commercial properties.

<<<THE PROBLEM

Andrew Florance, the founder of the CoStar Group (www.costar.com), began aggregating commercial real estate data in the Washington, D.C. area. His target audience was building owners, real estate agents, and banks. He developed databases that utilized software to reduce research time from hours to seconds. CoStar's core business is to gather and compile huge amounts of on-the-ground data on commercial buildings around the world.

Interestingly, CoStar faced pushback from the real estate community in the Washington area, and in every city where the company began operations. Simply put, the commercial

<<<THE SOLUTION

real estate brokers did not want the buying or selling process to be transparent. However, brokers soon learned that using the data could help them get better deals, and the service grew rapidly.

THE RESULTS>>> Over time, Florance's databases expanded to include details on properties in all 50 states, making his company the largest commercial real estate information firm in the United States. By subscribing to the service, the company's more than 80,000 clients can obtain such information as the vacancy rate in St. Louis, the demographics of a neighborhood in Atlanta that a retailer might be considering, and rental rates for small buildings in Scotland. CoStar also provides comprehensive information on revenues of buildings as well as asset values. This information did not exist prior to CoStar's execution of its database strategy.

CoStar's valuable data resource proved to be especially useful after the real estate market collapsed and owners were desperate to sell or refinance their commercial properties. CoStar experienced a surge in purchasing from big banks, the federal government, and institutional investors.

Recently, CoStar researchers have been involved in the green building movement. The company's team concluded that green properties—for example, buildings with lights that automatically shut off when people leave the room and with highly efficient heating and cooling systems—retain their value much more than conventional buildings.

Questions

1. Describe the problems in the commercial real estate market that led to Andrew Florance founding the CoStar Group.

2. Discuss the reasons why the established commercial real estate brokers felt that the CoStar Group was a competitive threat.

SOURCES: Compiled from D. Levitt, "Vornado Said to Pay $150 Million for Stake in 1 Park Avenue," *Bloomberg BusinessWeek*, February 25, 2011; C. Macke, "Commercial Real Estate Resurgence Needs Corporate Expansion to Continue," *Forbes*, January 4, 2011; F. Levy, "Real Estate Investing Is All the Rage Again—Should You Cash In?" *Forbes*, September 13, 2010; V. Haynes, "Data Strategy Propels CoStar Group," *Washington Post*, February 15, 2010; "CoStar #153 on the Best 200 Small Companies," *Forbes*, October 14, 2009; www.costar.com, accessed February 26, 2011.

RUBY'S CLUB INTERNSHIP ACTIVITY

It is important for those on the front end to determine the structure of their database. As you have learned in the chapter, this structure is called an entity relationship (ER) model and is shown by an ER diagram. For starters, Ruben and Lisa would like to collect customer name, drinks and/or food purchased by customer, sale amount, payment method, date and time of transaction, drinks sold by time, food sold by time, time from entrance or last purchase (that is, how long did it take the customer to buy a first drink), drink ingredients used, food ingredients used, band playing, and gender.

Ultimately Ruben and Lisa want a system to capture data on the way out the door for an "exit survey." It would be simple and only include a couple of items, but a quick rating of the overall experience by the user would be worth a lot for the planning process. Ruben and Lisa really feel these data items could be combined in various ways to give them very useful information. For now, they just need help getting the structure right. Take these items and create an appropriate ER diagram and submit it to Ruben and Lisa (your professor).

SPREADSHEET ACTIVITY

Objective: Normalization is taught in this chapter. Often, normalization begins when organizations are ready to transition from a large spreadsheet to a multidimensional database. This exercise will have you work your way through this transition.

Chapter Connection: *Primary key, secondary key,* and *attributes*: These terms are a bit abstract until you have to make these determinations yourself. The process of normalization is best when it is practiced. Spreadsheets provide the perfect opportunity.

Prerequisites: There are no prerequisites for this activity.

Activity: A local surgical group started keeping "digital records" as it called them. Basically the group kept a list of all its patients and the surgeries performed on any given day. Obviously the list grew long very rapidly. Then the group noticed a problem with its spreadsheet design. There was no way to reconcile that its repeat customers had been seen before. The spreadsheet treated each customer as a new entry and, therefore, a new patient. Furthermore, some patients changed addresses. In such cases, someone had to go back through the entire spreadsheet, find each instance of that patient, and change the address on all of them.

A database, no doubt, is more suited for this type of application. Normalization will prepare the group's document for conversion. Go to www.wiley.com/college/rainer, and download the spreadsheet for this exercise (MIS—Chapter 3.xlsx). Carefully choose your primary keys according to the definitions provided in this chapter. Take the single flat file sheet, and move the data into multiple sheets. Be sure to copy your primary keys onto each page so that the data can be reconciled.

Deliverable: The final product will be a normalized spreadsheet that is much easier to understand, update, and handle repeat customers/patients.

Quiz Questions:

1. Which of the following needs to appear on each page?
   (a) Secondary key
   (b) Primary key
   (c) 5 rows of information
   (d) Expressionary key

2. Once normalized and converted to a database, individual spreadsheet pages will become:
   (a) Tables
   (b) Rows
   (c) Columns
   (d) Database spreadsheets

3. Normalized spreadsheets will include:
   (a) Four tables per page
   (b) Three tables per page
   (c) Two tables per page
   (d) One table per page

Discussion Questions:

1. Even though this exercise is about normalization for a database, is it also helpful to have data normalized in a spreadsheet? Why or why not?

2. What are the differences in spreadsheets and databases when it comes to data manipulation?

DATABASE ACTIVITY: ENTITY-RELATIONSHIP DIAGRAMS (ERDs)

Objective

Just as every house begins with an architectural drawing, every database must begin with a data model. In this activity, you will develop the most common type of data model: an entity-relationship diagram (ERD).

Chapter Connection

Section 2 of this chapter introduces you to data modeling, specifically entity-relationship diagramming, as part of learning about database management. This activity applies those concepts.

Understanding the structure of a database is a good guide to developing one. It reduces the chances of errors that will be difficult to correct later on. In addition, professional database developers communicate with ERDs when they design a database for business needs. The ERD defines what the database will be. Knowing their language will improve your chances of getting a database that meets your needs.

Prerequisites

Read the following material before proceeding on to the activity. Reading this chapter also will put this activity in perspective.

ERD Styles

The ERD style that this book uses is one of many styles currently in use. The various styles are similar but differ in details. If you learn one, you will be able to understand an ERD in another, much as an English speaker from London can converse with someone from New York. Some differences among versions are:

- The name of an entity may be shown outside its box (usually just above it, as in part b of the figure in the book) or inside it (as in part a of the figure).
- The attributes of an entity may be shown in a separate box (as in the figure in the book), within its box, or in ovals surrounding the box and connected to it.
- An entity's primary key may be in bold type; starred; underlined; or, if the name of the entity is outside the box, in a separate part of the box (as in part b of the figure in the book).
- Foreign keys can be shown in italics or set off in any other way that is not the same as the one used for primary keys, not identified at all, or not shown at all. In this last case, the lines connecting entities convey the relationship information.
- Relationships can be described in diamonds on the lines (as in part a of the figure in the book), in text next to the lines, or not described in the ERD.

When relationships are described once, the direction of the description is not always clear. In the figure, does "Can have" between Class and Professor mean "a class can have a professor" or "a professor can have a class?" It does not say. That is why some diagramming methods describe each relationship twice: once for each direction.

- When a relationship has "one" at one end, there may be a short line across the relationship line (as in part a of the figure in the book) or no symbol at all. In that case, the information is conveyed by the absence of crows' feet.

ERD Symbols

An ERD shows the kind of relationship two entities have by symbols at the ends of the line that connects the entities. Each end of each line has two symbols.

The symbol all the way at the end of the line defines the maximum cardinality of the relationship: How many of that entity can there be? Rather than an exact count, the options are simply 1 or many, since that is all that matters in most database designs. A maximum of 1 is indicated by a short line across the line that connects the entities. A maximum of more than 1 is indicated by "crows' feet:" three lines spreading out like the toes on a bird's foot.

Farther away from that symbol is a symbol for minimum cardinality: What is the smallest valid number of this entity that there can be? Here, the choices are 0 (there does not have to be one) and 1 (there must be at least one). Zero is shown by a circle. You can think of it as representing the digit 0 or the first letter of the word *optional*. A short line across the line that connects the entities means a minimum of 1. This is the same symbol as is used to indicate a maximum of 1, but there is no possible confusion because they are in different places.

The four possible combinations of these two pairs of symbols, and their meanings, are as follows:

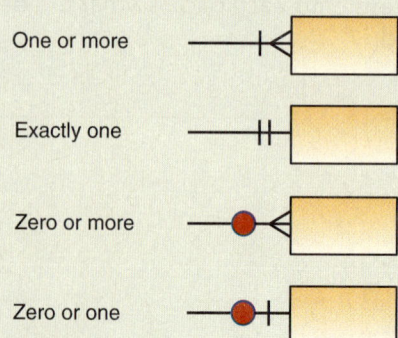

Suppose you have a database with information about students and their computers. Each computer belongs to exactly one student. A student, however, may have more than one computer—or may not have any. That one-to-many relationship would be shown this way:

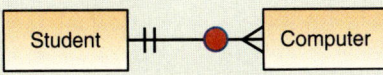

A relationship in which both entities have a maximum cardinality of one is called a one-to-one relationship. If one of the entities has a maximum cardinality of many, it is called a one-to-many (or many-to-one) relationship. If they both do, it is called a many-to-many relationship.

Associative Entities

Since foreign keys only work in one direction at a time, a many-to-many relationship requires a new table between the two entities. For example, consider a school database. There is a many-to-many relationship between students and courses: Each student can take more than one course, and each course can have more than one student. A database cannot show that directly. A row of the course table cannot have a foreign key for students, since there can be more than one. A row of the student table cannot have a foreign key for courses either, since there can also be more than one. The solution is to put a third entity between them. Each row in it reflects one student taking one course. Its ERD would look like this:

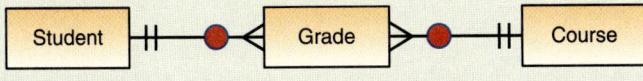

In this example, that entity also stores each student's grade in that course, and takes its name from this. The grade cannot be in the student tables, since students may earn different grades in different courses. It cannot be in the course table, since different students in the same course may earn different grades. It has to go in a table that describes that unique combination of student and course.

The circle symbols in this ERD fragment show that a student might not be in any courses and that a course might not have any students. This would be the situation before students register for courses. It also shows that, if there is a record in the Grade table, it goes with exactly one student, no more and no less, and with exactly one course, also no more and no less. Finally, it shows that a student may be in more than one course and that a course may have more than one student. Be sure you understand how the ERD shows these things.

Sales databases usually have a line item table that works this way. (The ORDERED PARTS table in Section 3.3 is an example of this.) Each order can be for many products. Each product can appear in many orders. Each row of this table is for one product in one order. In this case, the additional data in that entity comprise the quantity of the item in the order.

An entity that goes in the middle of a many-to-many relationship is called an *associative entity*. At a minimum, it contains two foreign keys: one for each connection. Often, as in these two examples, it also carries data. When an associative entity carries data, an ERD must show it. If it exists only to make the many-to-many relationship work and has no data of its own, some ER diagramming approaches show it but others do not.

An associative entity, like any other entity, needs a primary key. Neither foreign key is unique, so they will not work. Suppose Susan is registered for English 307. The foreign key that identifies Susan is not unique in the Grades table, since she has other courses. The one that identifies English 307 is not unique either, since other students also take it. However, Susan is only registered for it once, so the combination of Susan and English 307 is unique. Such a primary key, a unique combination of columns that are not unique individually, is called a *composite key*. To avoid dealing with composite keys, associative entities can be given separate primary keys such as sequence numbers. They do not mean anything, but they satisfy the requirement that every table must have a primary key.

Activity:

1. Read the following description of a business situation:

    A university needs a database to record student information. You know the following:

    • The database will store information on departments, courses, sections and students.
    • Each department can teach many courses.
    • Each course is taught by one department.
    • Each course can have many sections.
    • Each section belongs to one course.
    • Each section has many students.
    • Each student enrolls in many sections.

2. Draw an ERD for a database that will convey the information in the preceding description.

    • Show all relationships among entities. For each end of each relationship, use ERD symbols to show both the minimum cardinality (0 or 1; that is, can it be absent or must there be one?) and the maximum cardinality (1 or many). Use a short line across the relationship line to show a maximum cardinality of 1, as in the book.

- Show the primary key of each entity in a separate area at the top of the entity box.
- Show all the foreign keys in each entity. Underline them.
- Show at least three attributes of each entity, based on your understanding of the situation described. If you cannot think of three, show all you have.

Deliverable:

Your completed ER diagram.

Quiz Questions:

1. Which of the following is not a possible type of relationship between database entities as shown in an ERD?
   (a) 1 to 1
   (b) Many to many
   (c) 2 to 1
   (d) Many to 1

2. True or False? A many-to-1 relationship requires an associative entity.

3. An associative entity has a primary key and at least this many foreign keys:
   (a) 0
   (b) 1
   (c) 2
   (d) 3

4. The attributes of an entity are:
   (a) The data items that describe it in a database
   (b) The names it can be called by
   (c) The foreign keys in its database record
   (d) The date and time it was entered into the database, and the user ID of the person who entered it

Discussion Questions:

1. Why is it important for people who are not database specialists to be familiar with ER concepts and diagramming?

2. Where does an ERD show the attributes of an entity?

3. What ERD symbols indicate a many-to-one relationship?

4 | Telecommunications and Networking

LEARNING OBJECTIVES >>>

1. Define the term *computer network*, and compare and contrast the two major types of networks.

2. Describe the differences among the three types of wireline communications media, and discuss the main advantages and disadvantages of each type.

3. Differentiate between the Internet and the World Wide Web, and describe the most common methods for accessing the Internet.

4. Identify six major categories of network applications, provide an example of each one, and explain how that application supports business functions.

Mike Krahulik and Jerry Holkins were tired of the negative press surrounding video games, particularly the idea that all gamers were a little crazy. As gamers themselves, they knew that many gamers are good people. So, in 2003 they decided to start a nonprofit company called Child's Play Charity (www.childsplaycharity.org). Their intention was to inspire people to donate video games to children's hospitals so that children in long-term care could enjoy them. They just were not sure how best to communicate their idea to the public.

Mike and Jerry ultimately decided to utilize Internet-based technologies to get the word out. First, they used their for-profit business, Penny-Arcade (www.penny-arcade.com), to communicate with their customer base. Their plan included potential PayPal donations and an Amazon Wish List—created by the participating hospitals—where donors could simply purchase the requested items as a donation. The best part of this plan was that Mike and Jerry did not have to create any of these technologies. They simply employed existing information systems to connect with a very broad customer base.

Child's Play Charity has been wildly successful. In its first year, the program raised more than $250,000 in cash and game donations. By 2005, the total had more than doubled to $600,000, and in 2010 it exceeded $2.25 million. Donations since the beginning of the program have totaled almost $9 million. More important, many children in long-term hospital care are enjoying their favorite computer games!

Sources: Compiled from R. Wu, "Child's Play Charity—Gamers Give Back," *Intel Inside Scoop*, January 3, 2011; N. Nash, "Child's Play Gamers Charity Makes Giving Even More Fun," *Tech Republic*, November 24, 2010; www.childsplaycharity.org, www.penny-arcade.com, accessed May 11, 2011.

Questions

1. Explain why networks were essential for Mike and Jerry to grow their business.

2. Propose a charitable organization (or function) that you could set up at your university, and explain how you would use networks to make it a success.

RUBY'S CLUB

The network at Ruby's Club currently consists of a digital subscriber line (DSL) and a computer, which is not much of a local area network (LAN). The owners need to collect data from different customer contact points—for example, cover charge, food and/or drink purchases, exit questionnaires. Therefore, Ruben and Lisa will need multiple computers or devices connected to their network. Further, to create a community atmosphere, they want their customers to be connected wirelessly with all of their mobile devices so they never feel out of touch.

This process will require networking hardware. However, Ruben and Lisa know so little about establishing a network that the DSL was connected by their local telephone company. All they know is how to turn it on and the right phone number to call when they have a problem. Establishing and maintaining a LAN that connects employees and customers, while providing adequate security for all parties, will be quite an undertaking. However, Ruben and Lisa believe the benefits of establishing this network will far outweigh the costs.

>>> Because you are learning about telecom and networks, it will be very helpful for you to share this information with them with a recommendation on how to construct their network!

INTRODUCTION

You need to know three fundamental points about network computing. First, computers do not work in isolation in modern organizations. Rather, they constantly exchange data with one another. Second, this exchange of data—facilitated by telecommunications technologies—provides companies with a number of very significant advantages. Third, this exchange can take place over any distance and over networks of any size.

Without networks, the computer on your desk would be merely another productivity-enhancement tool, just as the typewriter once was. The power of networks, however, turns your computer into an amazingly effective tool for accessing information from thousands of sources, thereby making both you and your organization more productive. Regardless of the type of organization (profit/not-for-profit, large/small, global/local) or industry (manufacturing, financial services, health care), networks in general, and the Internet in particular, have transformed—and will continue to transform—the way we do business.

Networks support new ways of doing business, from marketing to supply chain management to customer service to human resources management. In particular, the Internet and private intranets—networks located within a single organization—have an enormous impact on our lives, both professionally and personally. In fact, for all organizations, having an Internet strategy is no longer just a source of competitive advantage. Rather, it is necessary for survival.

Computer networks are essential to modern organizations, for many reasons. First, networked computer systems enable organizations to be more flexible so they can adapt to rapidly changing business conditions. Second, networks enable companies to share hardware, computer applications, and data across the organization and among different organizations. Third, networks make it possible for geographically dispersed employees and work groups to share documents, ideas, and creative insights. This sharing encourages teamwork, innovation, and more efficient and effective interactions. In addition, networks are a critical link between businesses, their business partners, and their customers.

Clearly, networks are essential tools for modern businesses. But, why do *you* need to be familiar with networks? The simple fact is that if you operate your own business or work in a business, you cannot function without networks. You will need to communicate rapidly with your customers, business partners, suppliers, employees, and colleagues. Until about 1990, you would have used the postal service or telephone system with voice or fax capabilities for business communication. Today, however, the pace of business is much faster—almost real time. To keep up with this incredibly fast pace, you will need to use computers, e-mail, the Internet, cell phones, and mobile devices. Further, all of these technologies will be connected via networks to enable you to communicate, collaborate, and compete on a global scale.

Networking and the Internet are the foundation for commerce in the twenty-first century. Recall that one important objective of this book is to help you become an informed user of information systems. A knowledge of networking is an essential component of modern business literacy.

You begin this chapter by learning what a computer network is and identifying the various types of networks. You then study network fundamentals and follow by turning your attention to the basics of the Internet and the World Wide Web. You conclude the chapter by seeing the many network applications available to individuals and organizations—that is, what networks help you do.

4.1 | What Is a Computer Network?

A **computer network** is a system that connects computers and other devices (e.g., printers) via communications media so that data and information can be transmitted among them. Voice and data communication networks are continually becoming faster—that is, their bandwidth is increasing—and cheaper. **Bandwidth** refers to the transmission capacity of a network; it is stated in bits per second. **Broadband** refers to network transmission capacities ranging from approximately 1 million bits per second (megabits/sec) to as much as 20 megabits/sec with fiber-to-the-home (discussed later in this chapter). You are familiar with certain types of broadband connections, such as digital subscriber line (DSL) and cable to your homes and dorms. DSL and cable fall within the range of transmission capacity mentioned here and thus are defined as broadband connections.

The various types of computer networks range from small to worldwide. They include (from smallest to largest) personal area networks (PANs), local area networks (LANs), metropolitan area networks (MANs), wide area networks (WANs), and the Internet. PANs are short-range networks—typically a few meters—used for communication among devices close to one person. PANs can be wired or wireless. (You will learn about wireless PANs in Chapter 10). MANs are relatively large computer networks that cover a metropolitan area. MANs fall between LANs and WANs in size. WANs typically cover large geographic areas and can span the entire planet.

Local Area Networks

Regardless of their size, networks represent a compromise among three objectives: speed, distance, and cost. Organizations can generally have any two of the three. To cover long distances, organizations can have fast communication if they are willing to pay for it, or cheap communication if they are willing to accept slower speeds. A third possible combination of the three trade-offs is fast, cheap communication with distance limitations. This is the idea behind local area networks.

A **local area network (LAN)** connects two or more devices in a limited geographical region, usually within the same building, so that every device on the network can communicate with every other device. Most LANs today use Ethernet (discussed later in this chapter). Figure 4.1 illustrates an Ethernet LAN that consists of four computers, a server, and a printer, all of which connect via a shared cable. Every device in the LAN has a *network interface card* (NIC) that allows the device to physically connect to the LAN's communications medium. This medium is typically unshielded twisted-pair wire (UTP).

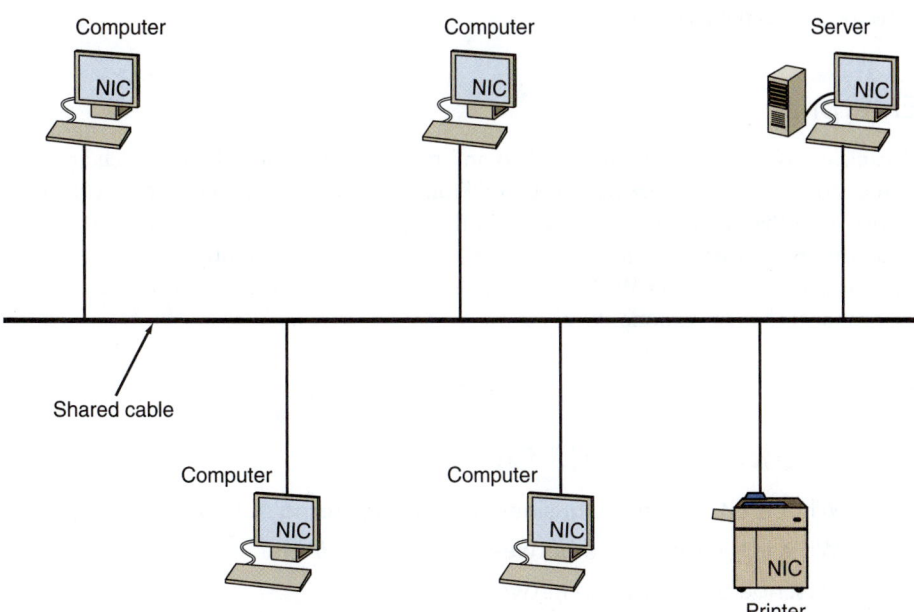

Figure 4.1 An Ethernet LAN.

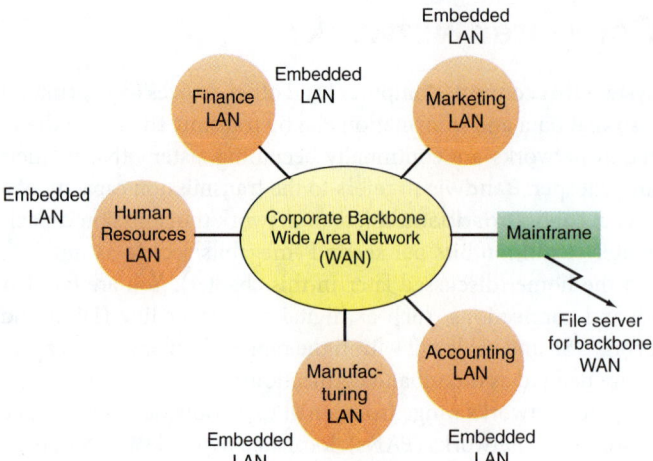

Figure 4.2 An enterprise network.

Although it is not required, many LANs have a **file server** or **network server**. The server typically contains various software and data for the network. It also houses the LAN's network operating system, which manages the server and routes and manages communications on the network.

Wide Area Networks

When businesses have to transmit and receive data beyond the confines of the LAN, they use wide area networks. Interestingly, the term *wide area network* did not even exist until local area networks appeared. Before that time, what we call a wide area network today was simply called a "network."

A **wide area network (WAN)** is a network that covers a large geographic area. WANs typically connect multiple LANs. WANs generally are provided by common carriers such as telephone companies and the international networks of global communications services providers. WANs have large capacity, and they typically combine multiple channels (for example, fiber optic cables, microwave, and satellite). The Internet is an example of a WAN.

WANs also contain routers. A **router** is a communications processor that routes messages from a LAN to the Internet, across several connected LANs, or across a wide area network such as the Internet.

Enterprise Networks

Organizations today have multiple LANs and may have multiple WANs, which are interconnected to form an **enterprise network**. Figure 4.2 displays a model of enterprise computing. Note that the enterprise network in the figure has a backbone network. Corporate **backbone networks** are high-speed central networks to which multiple smaller networks (such as LANs and smaller WANs) connect. The LANs are called *embedded LANs* because they connect to the backbone WAN.

BEFORE *YOU GO ON . . .*

1. What are the primary business reasons for using networks?
2. What is the difference between LANs and WANs?
3. Describe an enterprise network.

1. Which type of network would best suit the needs of Ruby's Club: a LAN, a MAN, or a WAN? Why?

2. What type of wired connections would you recommend to Ruben and Lisa for use within their club? Be sure to pick something that is widely used so it will be easy to find support.

Student Activity | 4.1

Objective: The objective of this exercise is to familiarize you with computer networks and some of the basic requirements for them to function.

Chapter Connection: This case relates to Chapter 4, Section 4.1—What is a Computer Network?

Prerequisites: You should read Section 4.1 before doing this exercise to become familiar with basic network components.

Activity:

Networks are the way in which workers at different locations share data and work together. However, for a network to function, various components are required. A list of four (4) locations of workers from the JLB TechWizards company follows. All must be able to connect to a database that is located at the headquarters in order to do their jobs or answer customer questions.

Deliverables:

From the following lists, indicate which components are needed to connect JLB TechWizards employees— so they can do their jobs and answer customer questions—to a database that is located at the company's headquarters. (You may need multiple components for each group.) If you are not familiar with any of the terms, review the text or do a Google.com search.

Components

1. *Network:* LAN, MAN, WAN
3. *Connection:* direct connection (in-house), dial-up, Internet
3. *Interface devices:* network interface card (Ethernet or wireless), server, routers, DSL/cable
4. *Channel:* twisted pair (UTP-Cat3 or 5), fiber, wireless (WAP, satellite, or tower)

JLB TechWizards

a. *Headquarters:* This international company manufactures and sells computer equipment and also services equipment it has sold. The company's headquarters are in Chicago, Illinois, and offices there include marketing, accounting, HR, and manufacturing. Each office has a number of PCs that connect with a main server in an IS. All offices are closely located and share data and printers.

b. *Offshore manufacturing:* A new manufacturing facility is opening in Hong Kong and needs to be connected 24/7 to company headquarters. There are 30 terminals at this plant. Inventory, orders, and schedules are shared during the workday at both locations.

c. *Sales force:* JLB TechWizards has about 15 technicians who service equipment sold within the United States. Each technician has a laptop that needs to connect off and on to the database (at headquarters) about 3 hours each day for checking inventory and entering repairs and orders. Technicians are constantly on the road to small, mountainous, rural cities and need to be able to check inventory whether in a hotel or at a customer site. Each evening technicians must log on for updates and to post daily activity. You may want to include multiple options so they can *always* connect!

d. *Employees from home:* JLB TechWizards has a number of employees that work from home part time on flextime. These employees need a fast, secure connection since some are dealing with financial data and the main computer and its databases at headquarters. They all live within 20 miles of their workplace.

4.2 | Network Fundamentals

In this section, you will learn the basics of how networks actually operate. You will then distinguish between analog and digital signals and explain how modems enable computer networks to "translate" among them. You follow by studying wireline communications media, which enable computers in a network to transmit and receive data. You conclude this section by looking at transmission technologies, network protocols, and types of network processing.

Analog and Digital Signals

Networks transmit information with two basic types of signals, analog and digital. **Analog signals** are continuous waves that transmit information by altering the characteristics of the waves. Analog signals have two parameters, *amplitude* and *frequency*. For example, all sounds—including the human voice—are analog, traveling to human ears in the form of waves. The higher the waves (or amplitude), the louder the sound; the more closely packed the waves, the higher the frequency or pitch. In contrast, **digital signals** are discrete pulses that are either on or off, representing a series of *bits* (0s and 1s). This quality allows digital signals to convey information in a binary form that can be interpreted by computers. Figure 4.3 illustrates both analog and digital signals.

The function of a **modem** is to convert digital signals to analog signals—a process called *modulation*—and analog signals to digital signals—a process called *demodulation*. (The name *modem* is a contraction of *mo*dulator-*dem*odulator.) Modems are used in pairs. The modem at the sending end converts a computer's digital information into analog signals for transmission over analog lines, such as telephone lines. At the receiving end, another modem converts the analog signal back into digital signals for the receiving computer. There are three types of modems: dial-up modems, cable modems, and DSL modems.

The U.S. public telephone system was originally designed as an analog network to carry voice signals or sounds in an analog wave format. In order for this type of circuit to carry digital information, that information must be converted into an analog wave pattern by a *dial-up modem*. Dial-up modems have transmission speeds of up to 56 kilobytes per second (Kbps).

Cable modems are modems that operate over coaxial cable—for example, cable TV. They offer broadband access to the Internet or corporate intranets. Cable modem speeds vary widely. Most providers offer bandwidth between 1 and 6 million bits per second (Mbps)

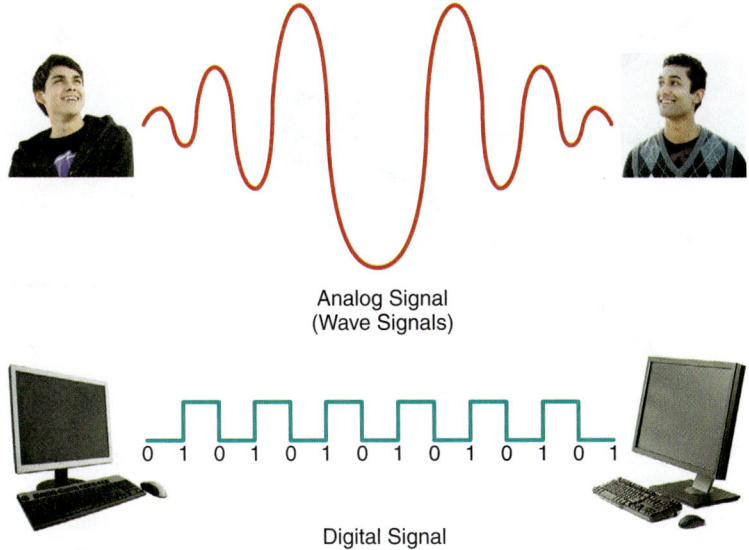

Analog Signal
(Wave Signals)

Digital Signal
(Stream of Bits)

0 1 0 1 0 1 0 1 0 1 0 1 0 1 0 1

Figure 4.3 Analog and digital signals. (*Sources:* Fancy/ Image Source; Media Bakery; © Zoonar/Dmitry Rukhle/Age Fotostock America, Inc.)

for downloads (from the Internet to a computer) and between 128 and 768 thousand bits per second (Kbps) for uploads. Cable modem services share bandwidth among subscribers in a locality. That is, the same cable line connects to many households. Therefore, when large numbers of neighbors access the Internet at the same time, cable speeds can decrease significantly during those times.

DSL (digital subscriber line, discussed later in this chapter) *modems* operate on the same lines as voice telephones and dial-up modems. DSL modems always maintain a connection, so an Internet connection is immediately available.

Communications Media and Channels

Communicating data from one location to another requires some form of pathway or medium. A **communications channel** is such a pathway and is comprised of two types of media: cable (twisted-pair wire, cable, or fiber-optic cable) and broadcast (microwave, satellite, radio, or infrared).

Cable media or **wireline media** use physical wires or cables to transmit data and information. Twisted-pair wire and coaxial cables are made of copper, and fiber-optic cable is made of glass. The alternative is communication over **broadcast media** or **wireless media**. The key to mobile communications in today's rapidly moving society is data transmissions over electromagnetic media—the "airwaves." In this section you will study the three wireline channels. Table 4.1 summarizes the advantages and disadvantages of each of these channels. You will become familiar with wireless media in Chapter 10.

TABLE 4.1 Advantages and Disadvantages of Wireline Communications Channels

Channel	Advantages	Disadvantages
Twisted-pair wire	Inexpensive Widely available Easy to work with	Slow (low bandwidth) Subject to interference Easily tapped (low security)
Coaxial cable	Higher bandwidth than twisted-pair Less susceptible to electromagnetic interference	Relatively expensive and inflexible Easily tapped (low to medium security) Somewhat difficult to work with
Fiber-optic cable	Very high bandwidth Relatively inexpensive Difficult to tap (good security)	Difficult to work with (difficult to splice)

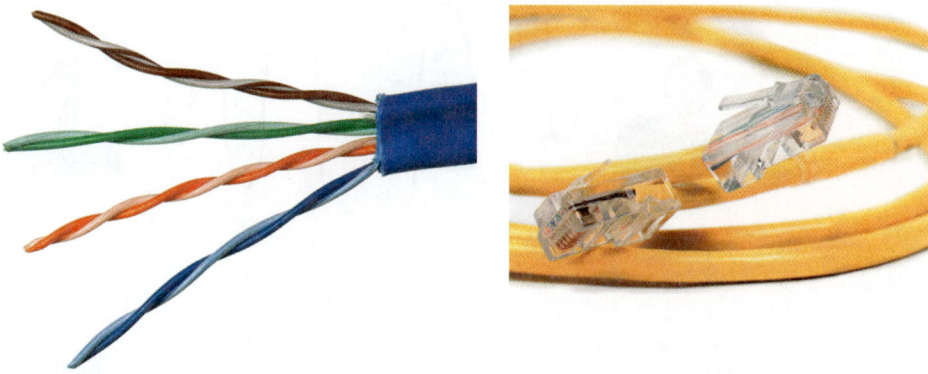

Figure 4.4 Two views of twisted-pair wire. (*Sources:* deepspacedave/Shutterstock; © Jack Kunnen-Fotolia.com)

Twisted-Pair Wire. Twisted-pair wire is the most prevalent form of communications wiring; it is used for almost all business telephone wiring. **Twisted-pair wire** consists of strands of copper wire twisted in pairs (see Figure 4.4). It is relatively inexpensive to purchase, widely available, and easy to work with. However, it also has some significant disadvantages. Specifically, it is relatively slow for transmitting data, it is subject to interference from other electrical sources, and it can be easily tapped by unintended receivers for gaining unauthorized access to data.

Coaxial Cable. **Coaxial cable** (Figure 4.5) consists of insulated copper wire. It is much less susceptible to electrical interference than is twisted-pair wire, and it can carry much more data. For these reasons, it is commonly used to carry high-speed data traffic as well as television signals (thus the term *cable TV*). However, coaxial cable is more expensive and more difficult to work with than twisted-pair wire. It is also somewhat inflexible.

Fiber Optics. **Fiber-optic cable** (Figure 4.6) consists of thousands of very thin filaments of glass fibers that transmit information via light pulses generated by lasers. The fiber-optic cable is surrounded by cladding, a coating that prevents the light from leaking out of the fiber.

Fiber-optic cables are significantly smaller and lighter than traditional cable media. They also can transmit far more data, and they provide greater security from interference and tapping. As of 2011, optical fiber had reached data transmission rates of more than 50 trillion bits (terabits) per second in laboratory experiments. Fiber-optic cable is typically used as the backbone for a network, whereas twisted-pair wire and coaxial cable connect the backbone to individual devices on the network.

Transmission Technologies

A number of telecommunications technologies enable users to transmit high-volume data quickly and accurately over any type of network. You explore these technologies in this section.

Figure 4.5 Two views of coaxial cable. (*Sources:* GIPhotoStock/ Photo Researchers; © airborne77-Fotolia.com)

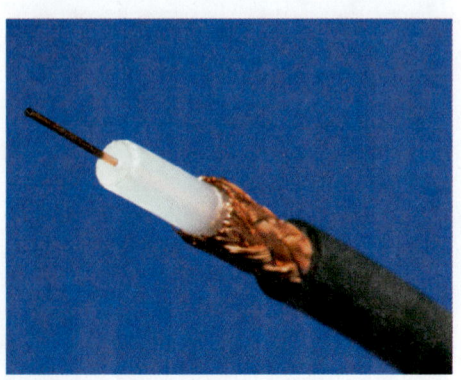

Cross-section view

How coaxial cable looks to us

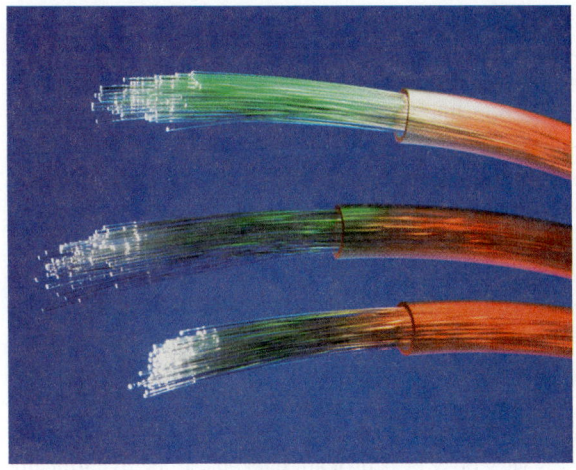

Cross-section view

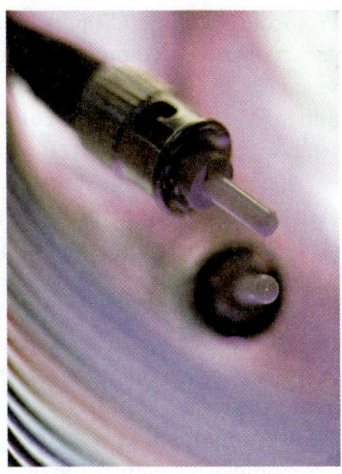

How fiber-optic cable looks to us

Figure 4.6 Two views of fiber-optic cable. (*Sources:* Phillip Hayson/Photo Researchers; Chris Knapton/Photo Researchers)

Digital Subscriber Line. A **digital subscriber line (DSL)** provides high-speed transmission of digital data from homes and businesses over an existing telephone line. Because the existing lines are analog and the transmission is digital, DSL systems must include modems. DSLs offer bandwidth from 128 Kbps to 3 Mbps. DSL service is typically available only within 18,000 feet of the provider's central office.

Asynchronous Transfer Mode. **Asynchronous transfer mode (ATM)** networks allow users to access almost unlimited bandwidth on demand. In addition, ATM provides support for data, video, and voice transmissions on a single communications line. Current ATM systems can transmit up to 2.5 gigabits (billions of bits) per second. On the downside, ATM requires fiber-optic cable and is therefore 21 percent more expensive than DSL.

Synchronous Optical Network. **Synchronous optical network (SONET)** is an interface standard designed to carry large volumes of traffic over relatively long distances using fiber-optic lines. SONET defines optical line rates, known as optical carrier (OC) signals. The base rate is 51.84 Mbps (OC-1), and higher rates are direct multiples of the base rate. For example, OC-3 runs at 155.52 Mbps, or 3 times the rate of OC-1.

T-Carrier System. The **T-carrier system** is a digital transmission system that defines circuits that operate at different rates, all of which are multiples of the basic 64 Kbps used to transport a single voice call. These circuits include T1 (1.544 Mbps, equivalent to 24 channels); T2 (6.312 Mbps, equivalent to 96 channels); T3 (44.736 Mbps, equivalent to 672 channels); and T4 (274.176 Mbps, equivalent to 4,032 channels).

Network Protocols

Computing devices that are connected to the network must access and share the network to transmit and receive data. These devices are often referred to as *nodes* of the network. They work together by adhering to a common set of rules and procedures—known as a **protocol**—that enable them to communicate with one another. The two major protocols are the Ethernet and TCP/IP.

Ethernet. A common LAN protocol is **Ethernet**. Most large corporations use 10-gigabit Ethernet, where the network provides data transmission speeds of 10 gigabits (10 billion bits) per second. However, 100-gigabit Ethernet is becoming the standard.

Transmission Control Protocol/Internet Protocol. The **Transmission Control Protocol/Internet Protocol (TCP/IP)** is the protocol of the Internet. TCP/IP uses a suite of protocols, the main ones being the Transmission Control Protocol (TCP) and the Internet

Protocol (IP). The TCP performs three basic functions: (1) It manages the movement of packets between computers by establishing a connection between the computers, (2) it sequences the transfer of packets, and (3) it acknowledges the packets that have been transmitted. The **Internet Protocol (IP)** is responsible for disassembling, delivering, and reassembling the data during transmission.

Before data are transmitted over the Internet, they are divided into small, fixed bundles of data called *packets*. The transmission technology that breaks up blocks of text into packets is called **packet switching**. Each packet carries the information that will help it reach its destination—the sender's IP address, the intended receiver's IP address, the number of packets in the message, and the number of the particular packet within the message. Each packet travels independently across the network and can be routed through different paths in the network. When the packets reach their destination, they are reassembled into the original message.

It is important to note that packet-switching networks are reliable and fault tolerant. For example, if a path in the network is very busy or is broken, packets can be dynamically ("on the fly") rerouted around that path. Also, if one or more packets does not get to the receiving computer, then only those packets need to be resent.

Why do organizations use packet switching? The main reason is to achieve reliable end-to-end message transmission over sometimes unreliable networks that may have transient (short-acting) or persistent (long-acting) faults.

The packets use the TCP/IP protocol to carry their data. TCP/IP functions in four layers (see Figure 4.7). The *application layer* enables client application programs to access the other layers, and it defines the protocols that applications use to exchange data. One of these application protocols is the **Hypertext Transfer Protocol (HTTP)**, which defines how messages are formulated and how they are interpreted by their receivers. The *transport layer* provides the application layer with communication and packet services. This layer includes TCP and other protocols. The *Internet layer* is responsible for addressing, routing, and packaging data packets. The IP is one of the protocols in this layer. Finally, the *network interface layer* places packets on, and receives them from, the network medium, which can be any networking technology.

Two computers using TCP/IP can communicate even if they use different hardware and software. Data sent from one computer to another proceed downward through all four layers, beginning with the sending computer's application layer and going through its network interface layer. After the data reach the receiving computer, they travel up the layers.

Email: Sending a Message via SMPT (Simple Mail Transfer Protocol)	Application	Email: Message received
Break Message into packets and determine order	Transport	Packets reordered and replaced (if lost)
Assign sending and receiving IP addresses and apply to each packet	Internet	Packets routed through internal network to desired IP address
Determine path across network/Internet to intended destination	Network Interface	Receipt of packets

Figure 4.7 The four layers of the TCP/IP. (*Source:* Dabroost/Shutterstock)

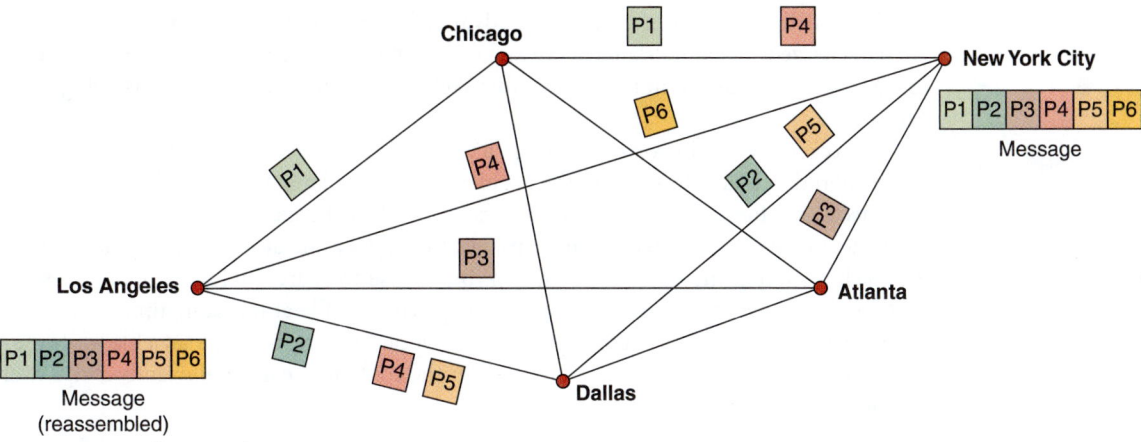

Figure 4.8 Packet switching.

TCP/IP enables users to send data across sometimes unreliable networks with the assurance that the data will arrive in uncorrupted form. TCP/IP is very popular with business organizations due to its reliability and the ease with which it can support intranets and related functions.

Let's look at an example of packet-switching across the Internet. Figure 4.8 illustrates a message being sent from New York City to Los Angeles over a packet-switching network. Note that the different colored packets travel by different routes to reach their destination in Los Angeles, where they are reassembled into the complete message.

Types of Network Processing

Organizations typically use multiple computer systems across the firm. **Distributed processing** divides processing work among two or more computers. This process enables computers in different locations to communicate with one another via telecommunications links. A common type of distributed processing is client/server processing. A special type of client/server processing is peer-to-peer processing.

Client/Server Computing. **Client/server computing** links two or more computers in an arrangement in which some machines, called **servers**, provide computing services for user PCs, called **clients**. Usually, an organization performs the bulk of its processing or application/data storage on suitably powerful servers that can be accessed by less powerful client machines. The client requests applications, data, or processing from the server, which acts on these requests by "serving" the desired commodity.

Client/server computing leads to the ideas of "fat" clients and "thin" clients. As discussed online in "Plug IT In 2," *fat clients* have large storage and processing power and therefore can run local programs (such as Microsoft Office), if the network is down. In contrast, *thin clients* may have no local storage and limited processing power. Thus, they must depend on the network to run applications. For this reason they are of little value when the network is not functioning.

Peer-to-Peer Processing. **Peer-to-peer (P2P) processing** is a type of client/server distributed processing where each computer acts as *both* a client and a server. Each computer can access (as assigned for security or integrity purposes) all files on all other computers.

There are three basic types of peer-to-peer processing. The first accesses unused CPU power among networked computers. A well-known application of this type is SETI@home (http://setiathome.ssl.berkeley.edu). These applications are from open-source projects and can be downloaded at no cost.

The second form of peer-to-peer is real-time, person-to-person collaboration, such as Microsoft SharePoint Workspace (http://office.microsoft.com/en-us/sharepoint-workspace). This product provides P2P collaborative applications that use buddy lists to establish a connection and allow real-time collaboration within the application.

The third peer-to-peer category is advanced search and file sharing. This category is characterized by natural-language searches of millions of peer systems. It enables users to discover other users, not just data and Web pages. One example of this category is BitTorrent.

BitTorrent (www.bittorrent.com) is an open-source, free, peer-to-peer file-sharing application that is able to simplify the problem of sharing large files by dividing them into tiny pieces, or "torrents." BitTorrent addresses two of the biggest problems of file sharing: (1) Downloading bogs down when many people access a file at once, and (2) some people leech, meaning they download content but refuse to share. BitTorrent eliminates the bottleneck by enabling all users to share little pieces of a file at the same time—a process called *swarming*. The program prevents leeching because users must upload a file while they download it. This means that the more popular the content, the more efficiently it zips over a network.

BEFORE *YOU GO ON . . .*

1. Compare and contrast the three wireline communications channels.
2. Describe the various technologies that enable users to send high-volume data over any network.
3. Describe the Ethernet and TCP/IP protocols.
4. Differentiate between client/server computing and peer-to-peer processing.

RUBY'S CLUB QUESTIONS

1. What networking model should work best for the employees of Ruby's Club? A client/server or peer-to-peer network? What aspects cause you to make this choice?

2. If the client/server method is chosen, do you think the data should be stored on the client or the server? Defend your view.

Student Activity | 4.2

Objective: Computer networks are the way in which most business workers receive and share information with customers, suppliers, and fellow employees. These networks work because they adhere to a common set of rules called a protocol. Two common protocols are Ethernet and TCP/IP. Ethernet is used more for a local area network within an office. TCP/IP is the protocol of the Internet. This exercise is aimed at helping you understand how TCP/IP and packet switching work and the benefits of their use.

Chapter Connection: This case relates to Chapter 4, Section 4.2: Network Fundamentals.

Prerequisites: To become familiar with the terminology of networking and the processes that occur, you should read Section 4.2 before doing this exercise.

Activity:

Chances are you have used the Internet for research, e-mail, or to share photos with friends. The Internet would not function without a network. In fact, it is probably the largest network since it allows us to communicate and share information all over the world. For all of us to be able to share files over this vast network, some standards are needed for the messages sent. The standard currently used is TCP/IP or Transmission Control Protocol/Internet Protocol.

Watch the following 2-part video:

Part 1—IS 300: Packet Switching and the Internet (I) (10 min.) (www.youtube.com/watch?v=u1l_aqDVgz0)

Part 2 IS 300: Packet Switching and the Internet (II) (3 min.) (www.youtube.com/watch?v=dYSld54dmEk)

Deliverables:

1. For TCP/IP to function, a number of components are involved. Based on the videos and your text, define the following components and their functions:

- Address
- Firewall
- Network interface
- Packet
- Paths of the packets
- Ports 80 and 25
- Proxy
- Router
- Web browser
- Web server

2. Draw a flowchart showing the steps a homework assignment sent via e-mail would take from your computer to your professors.

Quiz Questions:

1. The IP or Internet layer:
   (a) Prevents invalid packets from entering or leaving the network.
   (b) Adds a label to the packet.
   (c) Picks up the packet and places it on the network.
   (d) Controls where the packet goes by reading the address.

2. The network interface:
   (a) Prevents invalid packets from entering or leaving the network.
   (b) Adds a label to the packet.
   (c) Picks up the packet and places it on the network.
   (d) Controls where the packet goes by reading the address.

3. The firewall:
   (a) Prevents invalid packets from entering or leaving the network.
   (b) Adds a label to the packet.
   (c) Picks up the packet and places it on the network.
   (d) Controls where the packet goes by reading the address.

4. The router:
   (a) Prevents invalid packets from entering or leaving the network.
   (b) Adds a label to the packet.
   (c) Picks up the packet and places it on the network.
   (d) Controls where the packet goes by reading the address.

5. How does the packet travel from the source to its destination?
   (a) Via satellites
   (b) Via telephone lines
   (c) Via wireless connection
   (d) All of the above

Discussion Questions:

Discuss the steps your e-mail message would follow after you click "Send" from your computer and before your professor would receive it at her computer. Be specific as to what is involved at each phase.

4.3 | The Internet and the World Wide Web

The **Internet ("the Net")** is a global WAN that connects approximately 1 million organizational computer networks in more than 200 countries on all continents, including Antarctica, and features in the daily routine of almost 2 billion people. Participating computer systems include smart phones, PCs, LANs, databases, and mainframes.

The computers and organizational nodes on the Internet can be of different types and makes. They are connected to one another by data communications lines of different speeds. The primary network connections and telecommunications lines that link the nodes are referred to as the backbone. For the Internet, the backbone is a fiber-optic network that is operated primarily by large telecommunications companies.

As a network of networks, the Internet enables people to access data in other organizations and to communicate, collaborate, and exchange information seamlessly around the world, quickly and inexpensively. Thus, the Internet has become a necessity for modern businesses.

The Internet grew out of an experimental project of the Advanced Research Project Agency (ARPA) of the U.S. Department of Defense. The project began in 1969 as the *ARPAnet*. Its purpose was to test the feasibility of a WAN over which researchers, educators, military personnel, and government agencies could share data, exchange messages, and transfer files.

Today, Internet technologies are being used both within and among organizations. An **intranet** is a network that uses Internet protocols so that users can take advantage of familiar applications and work habits. Intranets support discovery (easy and inexpensive browsing and search), communication, and collaboration inside an organization. For the numerous uses of intranets, see www.intranetjournal.com.

In contrast, an **extranet** connects parts of the intranets of different organizations. In addition, it enables business partners to communicate securely over the Internet using virtual private networks (VPNs, explained in Chapter 7). Extranets offer limited accessibility to the intranets of participating companies, as well as necessary interorganizational communications. They are widely used in the areas of business-to-business (B2B) electronic commerce (see Chapter 9) and supply chain management (SCM; see Chapter 13).

No central agency manages the Internet. Instead, the cost of its operation is shared among hundreds of thousands of nodes. Thus, the cost for any one organization is small. Organizations must pay a small fee if they wish to register their names, and they need to have their own hardware and software to operate their internal networks. The organizations are obliged to move any data or information that enter their organizational network, regardless of the source, to their destination, at no charge to the senders. The senders, of course, pay the telephone bills for using either the backbone or regular telephone lines.

Accessing the Internet

The Internet may be accessed in several ways. From your place of work or your university, you can access the Internet via your organization's LAN. A campus or company backbone connects all of the various LANs and servers in the organization to the Internet. You can also log onto the Internet from your home or on the road, using either wireline or wireless connections.

Connecting via an Online Service. You can also access the Internet by opening an account with an Internet service provider. An **Internet service provider (ISP)** is a company that provides Internet connections for a fee. Large ISPs include America Online (www.aol.com), Juno (www.juno.com), Earthlink (www.earthlink.com), and NetZero (www.netzero.net). In addition, many telephone providers and cable companies sell Internet access, as do computer companies such as Microsoft. To use this service you need a modem and standard communication software. To find a local ISP, access www.thelist.com. There, you can search by your telephone area code for an ISP that services your area.

ISPs connect to one another through **network access points (NAPs)**. NAPs are exchange points for Internet traffic. They determine how traffic is routed. NAPs are key components of the Internet backbone. Figure 4.9 shows a schematic of the Internet. The white links at the top of the figure represent the Internet backbone; the brown dots where the white links meet are the NAPs.

Connecting via Other Means. There have been several attempts to make access to the Internet cheaper, faster, and easier. For example, terminals known as Internet kiosks have been located in such public places as libraries and airports (and even in convenience stores in some countries) for use by people who do not have their own computers. Accessing the Internet from smart phones and iPads is common, and fiber-to-the-home (FTTH) is growing rapidly. FTTH involves connecting fiber-optic cable directly to individual homes. This system initially was restricted to new residential developments, but it is rapidly spreading. Table 4.2 summarizes the various means that you can use to connect to the Internet.

Figure 4.9 Internet (backbone in white). (*Source:* © Mark Stay/iStockphoto)

Addresses on the Internet. Each computer on the Internet has an assigned address, called the **Internet Protocol (IP) address**, that distinguishes it from all other computers. The IP address consists of numbers, in four parts, separated by dots. For example, the IP address of one computer might be 135.62.128.91. You can access a Web site by typing this number in the address bar of your browser.

Currently, there are two IP addressing schemes. The first scheme, IPv4, is the most widely used. IP addresses using IPv4 consist of 32 bits, meaning that there are 2^{32} possibilities for IP addresses, or 4,294,967,295 distinct addresses. Note that the IP address in the preceding paragraph (135.62.128.91) is an IPv4 address. At the time that IPv4 was developed, there were not as many computers needing addresses as there are today. Therefore, a new IP addressing scheme has been developed, called IPv6.

IP addresses using IPv6 consist of 128 bits, meaning that there are 2^{128} possibilities for distinct IP addresses, which is an unimaginably large number. IPv6, which is replacing

TABLE 4.2 Internet Connection Methods

Service	Description
Dial-up	Still used in the U.S. where broadband is not available.
DSL	Broadband access via telephone companies.
Cable Modem	Access over your cable TV coaxial cable. Can have degraded performance if many of your neighbors are accessing the Internet at once.
Satellite	Access where cable and DSL are not available.
Wireless	Very convenient, and WiMAX will increase the use of broadband wireless.
Fiber to the Home (FTTH)	Expensive and usually only placed in new housing developments.

IPv4, will accommodate the rapidly increasing number of devices that need IP addresses, such as smart phones.

IP addresses must be unique so computers on the Internet know where to find one another. The Internet Corporation for Assigned Names (ICANN) (www.icann.org) coordinates these unique addresses throughout the world. Without that coordination we would not have one global Internet.

Because the numeric IP addresses are difficult to remember, most computers have names as well. ICANN accredits certain companies called *registrars* to register these names, which are derived from a system called the **domain name system (DNS). Domain names** consist of multiple parts, separated by dots, that are read from right to left. For example, consider the domain name *software.ibm.com*. The rightmost part of an Internet name is its *top-level domain (TLD)*. The letters *com* in software.ibm.com indicate that this is a commercial site. The following are popular U.S. TLDs:

com	commercial sites
edu	educational sites
mil	military government sites
gov	civilian government sites
org	organizations

To finish our domain name example, *ibm* is the name of the company (IBM), and *software* is the name of the particular machine (computer) within the company to which the message is being sent.

In other countries, the country name or designator is the TLD. For example, *de* stands for Germany, *it* for Italy, and *ru* for Russia. In essence, every country decides for itself whether to use TLDs. Moreover, those countries that use TLDs do not necessarily follow the U.S. system. For example, the United Kingdom uses *.co* where the U.S. uses *.com* and *.ac* (for academic) where the U.S. uses *.edu*. In contrast, many other non-U.S. Web sites use U.S. TLDs, especially *.com*.

The Future of the Internet

Consumer demand for content delivered over the Internet is increasing at 60 percent per year. In 2010, monthly traffic across the Internet totaled roughly 8 exabytes (1 exabyte is equivalent to 50,000 years of DVD-quality data). Many experts are now concerned that Internet users will experience brownouts due to three factors: (1) the increasing number of people who work online, (2) the soaring popularity of Web sites such as YouTube that require large amounts of bandwidth, and (3) the tremendous demand for high-definition television delivered over the Internet. These brownouts will lead to computers going offline for several minutes at a time. Researchers assert that if Internet bandwidth is not improved rapidly, then within a few years (see this chapter's "Closing Case 1") the Internet will be able to function only at a much reduced speed.

Even today, the Internet sometimes is too slow for data-intensive applications such as full-motion video files (movies) or large medical files (X-rays). In addition, the Internet is unreliable and is not secure. As a result, Internet2 has been developed by more than 200 U.S. universities collaborating with industry and government. **Internet2** develops and deploys advanced network applications such as remote medical diagnosis, digital libraries, distance education, online simulation, and virtual laboratories. Internet2 is designed to be fast, always on, everywhere, natural, intelligent, easy, and trusted. Internet2 is not a separate physical network from the Internet. For more detail, see www. internet2.edu.

The World Wide Web

Many people equate the Internet with the World Wide Web. However, they are not the same thing. The Internet functions as a transport mechanism, whereas the World Wide Web is an application that uses those transport functions. Other applications, such as e-mail, also run on the Internet.

The **World Wide Web (The Web, WWW, or W3)** is a system of universally accepted standards for storing, retrieving, formatting, and displaying information via a client/server architecture. The Web handles all types of digital information, including text, hypermedia, graphics, and sound. It uses graphical user interfaces (GUIs), so it is very easy to navigate.

Organizations that wish to offer information through the Web must establish a *home page*, which is a text and graphical screen display that usually welcomes the user and provides basic information on the organization that has established the page. In most cases, the home page will lead users to other pages. All the pages of a particular company or individual are collectively known as a **Web site**. Most Web pages provide a way to contact the organization or the individual. The person in charge of an organization's Web site is its *Webmaster*. (*Note: Webmaster* is a gender neutral title.)

To access a Web site, the user must specify a **uniform resource locator (URL)**, which points to the address of a specific resource on the Web. For instance, the URL for Microsoft is http://www.microsoft.com. Recall that HTTP stands for hypertext transport protocol. The remaining letters in this URL—www.microsoft.com—indicate the domain name that identifies the Web server that stores the Web site.

Users access the Web primarily through software applications called **browsers**. Browsers provide a graphical front end that enables users to point-and-click their way across the Web, a process called *surfing*. Web browsers became a means of universal access because they deliver the same interface on any operating system under which they run. As you see in "IT's About Business 4.1," companies are pouring resources into their browsers.

IT's ABOUT BUSINESS | 4.1

Browser Competition Heats Up

Companies are investing increasing amounts of resources in browsers, the programs for accessing content on the Web. The credit for this trend, which is good for consumers, goes to two parties. The first is Google, whose big plans for its Chrome (www.google.com/chrome) browser have forced Microsoft to pay fresh attention to its own browser, Internet Explorer (IE). Microsoft had all but stopped efforts to enhance IE after the company won the last browser war, defeating Netscape.

The European Union (EU) also played a role in this process. Starting in March 2010, the EU required companies that manufacture personal computers to offer customers who buy new computers in Europe more freedom to choose. Under this plan, part of an antitrust settlement with Microsoft, purchasers will be presented with a screen at startup that lists a dozen browsers in random order, all of which are free. Users can download any of these browsers and start roaming the Web.

Regardless of which browser users select, they should take into consideration, however, issues of security and privacy. Every company brags about its security features, but the term "secure browser" is questionable at best. Further, privacy is not much more dependable. All browsers offer "private" or "incognito" modes, but for the most part such settings only prevent people who might look at your computer from seeing the Web sites you have browsed. They do not stop those sites from keeping records of your visits.

Users should also keep in mind why companies give their browsers away for free. Chrome, for instance, is a key part of Google's strategy to make computer users comfortable with cloud computing (discussed in Plug IT In 3). The objective is to convince users to spend less money and time on programs they have to license from software companies (e.g., Microsoft) in favor of data and services such as Google Docs, which reside on servers and storage systems on the Internet. In this way, Chrome—which is available in versions for

Windows, Mac, and Linux—is designed to make users dependent on Google's own ad-driven services. But for Google's strategy to work, Chrome must be a good browser. In fact, Chrome is fast and takes up little space on users' hard drives.

Mac users should have no problem choosing a browser. Apple's own browser, Safari (www.apple.com/safari), is excellent, and it comes installed on every Mac. Microsoft adopted the same policy with IE, but the company was charged with antitrust violations. Presumably, Apple gets away with its policy because its market share is so much smaller. Safari is also available in a Windows version.

Another excellent browser is Mozilla Firefox (www.mozilla.com/en-US/firefox/fx/), a descendant of Netscape. Maintained by an open-source community, Firefox is the most commonly used browser behind Microsoft's IE. It is available for Windows, Macs, and Linux systems. Firefox benefits from a well-developed application base that includes thousands of add-ons for everything from speeding up YouTube downloads to StumbleUpon, which helps users discover and share Web sites that match their interests.

Opera (www.opera.com), created by the Norwegian company Opera Software, is also a good choice for a browser. Like Firefox, it is available in Windows, Mac, and Linux versions.

Finally, there is the market leader, Microsoft Internet Explorer. In mid-2011, Microsoft released IE 9 (www.microsoft.com/IE9), which contains many enhancements, including additional security features. Microsoft has promised that IE 9 will run faster than the previous version.

As of April 2011, usage statistics for the major browsers were as follows:

Microsoft IE	55.1 percent
Mozilla Firefox	21.6 percent
Google Chrome	11.9 percent
Apple Safari	7.2 percent
Opera	3.3 percent

Questions

1. Given that all browsers are free, what features do the major browser companies focus on to gain competitive advantage?

2. Which browser do you use? Why? Provide examples of why you use this particular browser.

Sources: Compiled from "Internet Browser Software Review," *TopTenReviews*, May 2011; R. Jaroslovsky, "Browser Wars: The Sequel," *Bloomberg BusinessWeek*, March 8, 2010.

BEFORE *YOU GO ON . . .*

1. Describe the various ways that you can connect to the Internet.
2. Identify the parts of an Internet address.
3. What are the functions of browsers?
4. Describe the difference between the Internet and the World Wide Web.

RUBY'S CLUB QUESTIONS

1. What is the difference between the Internet and an intranet? How can Ruby's use the strengths of each to better serve customers and make Ruben and Lisa's vision a reality?

2. Ruben and Lisa want to build a new Web site. Do you think they should host it locally or use a Web hosting service? What hardware and connectivity would they need to support a locally run Web site?

Student Activity | 4.3

Objective: The objective of this exercise is to familiarize you with the Internet and the World Wide Web. The Internet would not function without domain names and IP addresses. This exercise will help you learn how they are related.

Chapter Connection: This case relates to Chapter 4, Section 4.3: The Internet and the World Wide Web.

Prerequisites: You should read Section 4.3 before doing this exercise to increase your knowledge of the Internet and the World Wide Web.

Activity:

I'm sure you have accessed sites on the Internet many times by entering an address or a URL. We usually use an address that is easy to read and user friendly, such as www.google.com, so that we can remember it. However, what does the router use to connect to the actual server? Read the following information on how domain name servers work. You may even want to watch the video.

www.howstuffworks.com/dns.htm

For some additional details about domain names and IP addresses, refer to the following:

www.webopedia.com/TERM/D/domain_name.html

Deliverables:

Provide answers to the following questions:

1. What is the function of a domain name server?
2. What are three top-level domains?
3. What is the country code for Germany?

4. How many bits are in IPv4? Give an example of IPv4.
5. How many bits are in IPv6? Give an example of IPv6.

Quiz Questions:

1. What does *URL* stand for?
   - **(a)** Universal Resource Locator
   - **(b)** Uniform Resource Locator
   - **(c)** Unified Resource Location
   - **(d)** Universal Resource Location

2. What is the country code for China?
   - **(a)** .CH
   - **(b)** .CI
   - **(c)** .CN
   - **(d)** .CA

3. The function of the DNS is to:
   - **(a)** Translate domain names to IP addresses.
   - **(b)** Find valid domain names.
   - **(c)** Convert from IPv6 to IPv4.
   - **(d)** All of the above.

4. IPv6 is made up of how many bits?
   - **(a)** 32
   - **(b)** 64
   - **(c)** 128
   - **(d)** 256

Discussion Questions:

1. Discuss how the domain name that we enter to access a Web site is converted to an IP address.
2. How does IPv4 differ from IPv6? Why is the change being made?

4.4 | Network Applications

Now that you have a working knowledge of what networks are and how you can access them, the key question is, How do businesses use networks to improve their operations? This section addresses that question. Stated in general terms, networks support businesses and other organizations in all types of functions.

This section will explore numerous network applications, including discovery, communication, collaboration, e-learning and distance learning, virtual universities, and telecommuting. These applications, however, are merely a sampling of the many network applications currently available to users. Even if these applications formed an exhaustive list today, they would not do so tomorrow when something new will be developed. Further, placing network applications in categories is difficult because there will always be borderline cases. For example, the difference between chat rooms (in the communications category) and teleconference (in the collaboration category) is only one of degree.

Discovery

The Internet enables users to access or discover information located in databases all over the world. By browsing and searching data sources on the Web, users can apply the Internet's discovery capability to areas ranging from education to government services to entertainment to commerce. Although having access to all this information is a great benefit, it is critically important to realize that there is no quality assurance for information on the Web. The Web is truly democratic in that *anyone* can post information to it. Therefore, the fundamental rule about information on the Web is "User beware!"

In addition, the Web's major strength—the vast stores of information it contains—also presents a major challenge. The amount of information on the Web can be overwhelming, and it doubles approximately each year. As a result, navigating through the Web and gaining access to necessary information are becoming more and more difficult. To accomplish these tasks, people increasingly are using search engines, directories, and portals.

Search Engines and Metasearch Engines. A **search engine** is a computer program that searches for specific information by key words and then reports the results. A search engine maintains an index of billions of Web pages. It uses that index to find pages that match a set of user-specified keywords. Such indexes are created and updated by *webcrawlers*, which are computer programs that browse the Web and create a copy of all visited pages. Search engines then index these pages to provide fast searches.

In mid-2010, three search engines accounted for almost all searches in the United States: Google (www.google.com, 65.5 percent), Yahoo (www.yahoo.com, 16.8 percent), and Microsoft Network (now called Bing, www.msn.com, 11.8 percent In addition, there are an incredible number of other search engines that are quite useful, many of which perform very specific searches (see www.readwriteweb.com/archives/top_100_alternative_search_engines.php). The leading search engine in China is Baidu, with 64 percent of the Chinese market.

For an even more thorough search, you can use a metasearch engine. **Metasearch engines** search several engines at once and then integrate the findings to answer users' queries. Examples are Surf-wax (www.surfwax.com), Metacrawler (www.metacrawler.com), Mamma (www.mamma.com), KartOO (www.kartoo.com), and Dogpile (www.dogpile.com). Figure 4.10 illustrates the KartOO home page.

One interesting search engine, known as Qwiki, provides videos as your search results. "IT's About Business 4.2" explains how Qwiki works.

Publication of Material in Foreign Languages. Not only is there a huge amount of information on the Internet, but it is written in many different languages. How, then, do you

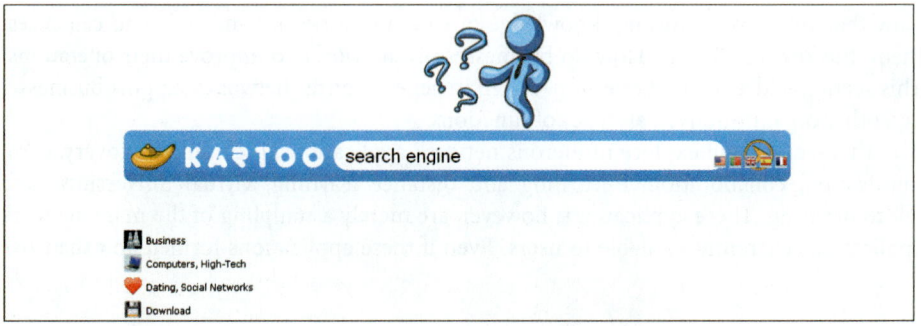

Figure 4.10 The KartOO home page (www.kartoo.com).

Informative Videos on the Fly

Enter "Buenos Aires" into the search bar on the Web site Qwiki (www.qwiki.com), and a video appears on your screen. It first zooms in on a map of the city as a voice describes its location. Then, information and graphics appear that illustrate the statistics on the city's population and density, and a series of photos and videos stream across the screen as the narrator discusses the city's main attractions.

Launched in January 2011, Qwiki offers videos on 3 million of the Internet's most popular topics. Pulling information from Wikipedia and other sources, Qwiki's algorithm compiles each video, including the information and graphics, in real time. In other words, Qwiki produces a search result in multimedia form. Research studies as well as anecdotal evidence indicate that presenting information in a multimedia format increases recall rates. Qwiki's goal is to turn information into an experience.

Search is not the only use envisioned for Qwiki's technology, however. A future goal is personalization. For example, the company is developing a custom alarm clock function that provides local weather and traffic reports and announces the user's daily schedule. In fact, thinking of Qwiki in terms of search may not be exactly correct. The company envisions itself as the creator of a new media format, a platform that will eventually be used for generating multimedia content from whatever source the user directs it to, be it an online profile or a restaurant review.

Questions

1. Describe the advantages of Qwiki over conventional search and metasearch engines.
2. Does Qwiki have a competitive advantage over conventional search and metasearch engines? Why or why not? Provide examples to support your answer.

Sources: Compiled from "Vision Quest," *Forbes Departures*, May 23, 2011; T. Geron, "Qwiki Launches iPad App with Location Focus," *Forbes*, April 20, 2011; A. Diana, "Qwiki Launches Multimedia Search Engine," *InformationWeek*, January 25, 2011; www.qwiki.com, accessed August 8, 2011.

---

access this information? The answer is that you use an *automatic translation* of Web pages. Such translation is available to and from all major languages, and its quality is improving with time. Some major translation products are Altavista (http://babelfish.altavista.com) and Google (www.google.com/language_tools) (see Figure 4.11), as well as products and services available at Trados (www.trados.com).

Should companies invest their time and resources to make their Web sites accessible in multiple languages? The answer is, absolutely. In fact, multilingual Web sites are now a competitive necessity because of the global nature of the business environment. Companies increasingly are looking outside their home markets to grow revenues and attract new customers. When companies are disseminating information around the world, getting that information correct is essential. It is not enough for companies to translate Web content. They must also localize that content and be sensitive to the needs of the people in local markets.

To reach 80 percent of the world's Internet users, a Web site needs to support a minimum of ten languages: English, Chinese, Spanish, Japanese, German, Korean, French, Italian, Russian, and Portuguese. At 20 cents and more per word, translation services are expensive. Companies supporting ten languages can spend $200,000 annually to localize information and another $50,000 to maintain the Web sites. Translation budgets for major

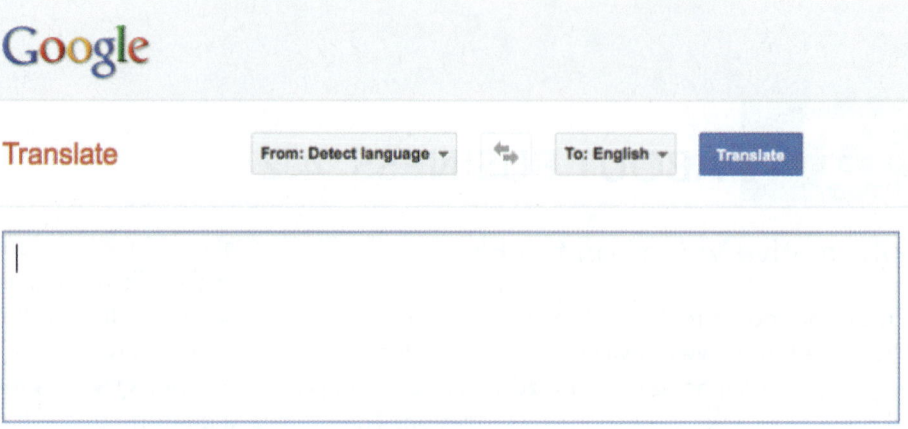

Figure 4.11 Google Translate.

multinational companies can run in the millions of dollars. Many large companies use Systran S.A. (www.systransoft.com) for high-quality machine translation services.

Portals. Most organizations and their managers encounter information overload. Information is scattered across numerous documents, e-mail messages, and databases at different locations and systems. Finding relevant and accurate information is often time consuming and may require users to access multiple systems.

One solution to this problem is to use portals. A **portal** is a Web-based, personalized gateway to information and knowledge that provides relevant information from different IT systems and the Internet using advanced search and indexing techniques. After reading the next section, you will be able to distinguish among four types of portals: commercial, affinity, corporate, and industrywide.

A **commercial (public) portal** is the most popular type of portal on the Internet. It is intended for broad and diverse audiences and offers fairly routine content, some of it in real time (for example, a stock ticker). Examples are Lycos (www.lycos.com) and Microsoft Network (www.msn.com).

In contrast, an **affinity portal** offers a single point of entry to an entire community of affiliated interests, such as a hobby group or a political party. Your university most likely has an affinity portal for its alumni. Figure 4.12 displays the affinity portal for the

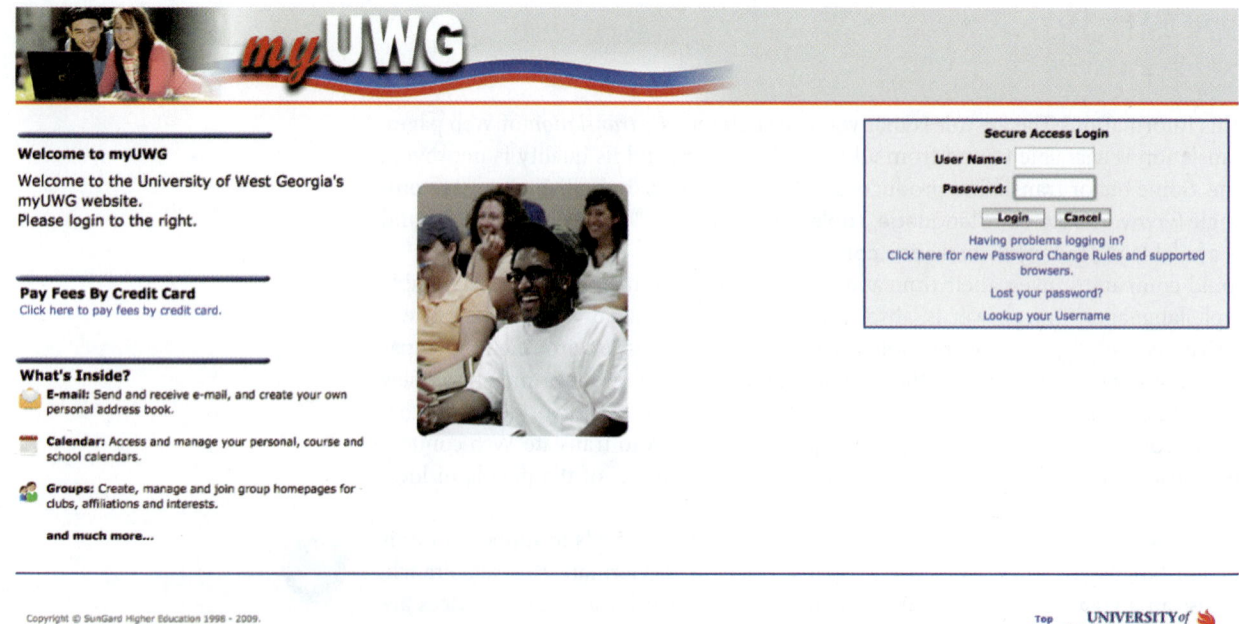

Figure 4.12 University of West Georgia affinity portal. (Courtesy of West Georgia University.)

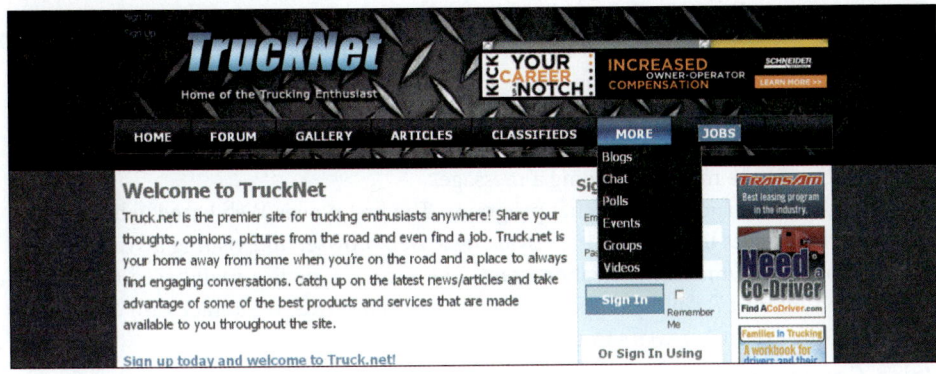

Figure 4.13 The TruckNet portal.

University of West Georgia. Other examples of affinity portals are www.techweb.com and www.zdnet.com.

As the name suggests, a **corporate portal** offers a personalized, single point of access through a Web browser to critical business information located inside and outside an organization. These portals are also known as *enterprise portals*, *information portals*, and *enterprise information portals*. In addition to making it easier to find needed information, corporate portals offer customers and employees self-service opportunities.

Whereas corporate portals are associated with a single company, an **industrywide portal** serves entire industries. An example is TruckNet (www.truck.net), a portal for the trucking industry and the trucking community, including professional drivers, owner/operators, and trucking companies (see Figure 4.13). TruckNet provides drivers with personalized Web-based e-mail, access to applications to leading trucking companies in the United States and Canada, and access to the Drivers Round Table, a forum where drivers can discuss issues of interest. The portal also provides a large database of trucking jobs and general information related to the trucking industry.

These four types of portals are differentiated by the audiences they serve. Another type, the mobile portal, is distinguished by its technology. A **mobile portal** is accessible from mobile devices, although any of the four portals just discussed can be accessed by mobile devices. Mobile devices are typically wireless, so you will study them in detail in Chapter 10.

Communication

The second major category of network applications is communication. There are many types of communication technologies, including e-mail, call centers, chat rooms, and voice. You learn about each one in this section. You will see another type of communication, blogging, in Chapter 8.

Electronic Mail. Electronic mail (e-mail) is the largest-volume application running over the Internet. Studies have found that almost all companies conduct business transactions via e-mail, and the vast majority confirm that e-mail is tied to their means of generating revenue. In fact, for many users, e-mail has all but replaced the telephone.

Web-Based Call Centers. Effective personalized customer contact is becoming an important aspect of Web-based customer support. Such service is provided through *Web-based call centers*, also known as *customer care centers*. For example, if you need to contact a software vendor for technical support, you will usually be communicating with the vendor's Web-based call center, using e-mail, a telephone conversation, or a simultaneous voice/Web session. Web-based call centers are sometimes located in foreign countries such as India. Such *offshoring* is an important issue for U.S. companies.

For several reasons, some U.S. companies are moving their call center operations back to the United States. First, they feel that they have less control of their overseas call center operations. They must depend on the vendor company, ensuring that it can uphold their standards, such as quality of service. Second, language difficulties can occur. Third, companies that manage sensitive information can run the risk of breaching customer confidentiality. Finally, the vendor company's call center representatives typically work with many companies. As a result, they may not deliver the same level of customer services that is required.

Electronic Chat Rooms. *Electronic chat* refers to an arrangement whereby participants exchange conversational messages in real time. A **chat room** is a virtual meeting place where many people (in fact, anyone) come to "gab." Chat programs allow you to send messages to people who are connected to the same channel of communication at the same time. Anyone can join in the conversation. Messages are displayed on your screen as they arrive, even if you are in the middle of typing a message.

There are two major types of chat programs. The first type is Web based, which allows you to send messages to Internet users by using a Web browser and visiting a Web chat site (for example, http://messenger.yahoo.com). The second type is e-mail based (text only) and is called *Internet Relay Chat (IRC)*. A business can use IRC to interact with customers, provide online experts' answers to questions, and so on.

Voice Communication. When people need to communicate with one another from a distance, they use the telephone more frequently than any other communication device. With the plain old telephone service (POTS), every call opened up a dedicated circuit for the duration of the call. A dedicated circuit connects you to the person with whom you are talking and is devoted only to your call. In contrast, as you saw earlier in this chapter, the Internet divides data into packets, which traverse the Internet in random order and are reassembled at their destination.

With **Internet telephony**, also known as **Voice-over Internet protocol** or **VoIP**, phone calls are treated as just another kind of data. That is, your analog voice signals are digitized, sectioned into packets, and then sent over the Internet. In the past, to utilize VoIP you needed a computer with a sound card and a microphone. Today, however, you do not need special phones or headsets for your computer.

VoIP can reduce your monthly phone bills. However, packet switching can cause garbled communications. For example, if the packets of a message arrive out of order, that is not a problem when you are sending an e-mail or transmitting a photo. Correctly reassembling the packets of a voice message, however, can garble the message. Fortunately, this is less of a problem than in the past, because VoIP software continues to improve, and typical communications links are much faster. So, although VoIP is not perfect, it is ready for prime time.

Skype (www.skype.com) provides several voice-over IP services for free: voice and video calls to users who also have Skype, instant messaging, short message service, voice mail, one-to-one and group chats, and conference calls with up to nine people (see Figure 4.14).

Figure 4.14 Skype 5.5 interface.

As of mid-2010, the most current version of Skype for Windows was version 5.5. Skype 5.5 offers full-screen, high-definition video calling, Skype Access (to access WiFi hotspots), call transfer to a Skype contact on a mobile or landline, improved quality of calls, and ease of use. In addition, it offers other functions for which users pay. For example, SkypeOut allows you to make calls to landline phones and mobile phones. SkypeIn provides a number that your friends can call from any phone and you pick up the call in Skype.

Vonage (www.vonage.com) also provides Voice-over IP services, but for a fee (approximately $25 per month). With Vonage you make and receive calls with your existing home phone through your broadband Internet connection. Your phone actually connects to Vonage instead of an actual phone company. The person whom you are calling does not need to have Vonage or even an Internet connection.

Unified Communications. In the past, organizational networks for wired and wireless data, voice communications, and videoconferencing operated independently, and the IT department managed each network separately. This arrangement increased costs and reduced productivity.

Unified communications (UC) simplifies and integrates all forms of communications—voice, voice mail, fax, chat, e-mail, instant messaging, short message service, presence (location) services, and videoconferencing—on a common hardware and software platform. *Presence services* enable users to know where their intended recipients are and if they are available, in real time.

UC unifies all forms of human and computer communications into a common user experience. For example, UC allows an individual to receive a voice mail message and then read it in his or her e-mail inbox. In another example, UC enables users to seamlessly collaborate with another person on a project, regardless of where the users are located. One user could quickly locate the other user by accessing an interactive directory, determine if that user were available, engage in a text messaging session, and then escalate the session to a voice call, or even a video call, all in real time.

Collaboration

The third major category of network applications is collaboration. An important feature of modern organizations is that people collaborate to perform work. **Collaboration** refers to efforts by two or more entities—that is, individuals, teams, groups, or organizations—who work together to accomplish certain tasks. The term **work group** refers specifically to two or more individuals who act together to perform some task.

Workflow is the movement of information as it flows through the sequence of steps that make up an organization's work procedures. Workflow management makes it possible to pass documents, information, and tasks from one participant to another in a way that is governed by the organization's rules or procedures. Workflow systems are tools for automating business processes.

If group members are in different locations, they constitute a **virtual group (team)**. Virtual groups conduct *virtual meetings*—that is, they "meet" electronically. **Virtual collaboration** (or *e-collaboration*) refers to the use of digital technologies that enable organizations or individuals to collaboratively plan, design, develop, manage, and research products, services, and innovative applications. Organizational employees frequently collaborate virtually with one another. In addition, organizations collaborate virtually with customers, suppliers, and other business partners to improve productivity and competitiveness.

One type of collaboration is *crowdsourcing*, which refers to outsourcing a task to an undefined, generally large group of people in the form of an open call. Let's look at some examples of crowdsourcing on college campuses.

- *Crowdsourcing help desks:* IT help desks are a necessary service on college campuses because students depend on their computers and Internet access to complete their school work and attend class online. At Indiana University at Bloomington, new IT help desks use crowdsourcing to alleviate the cost and pressure of having to answer so many calls. Students and professors post their IT problems on an online forum, where other students and amateur IT experts answer them.

- *Recruitment:* In 2010, Champlain College in Vermont instituted a Champlain For Reel program, inviting students to share via YouTube videos their experiences at the school and how they benefited from their time there. The YouTube channel serves to recruit prospective students and even updates alumni on campus and community events.

- *Scitable* (www.nature.com/scitable) combines social networking and academic collaboration. Through crowdsourcing, students, professors, and scientists discuss problems, find solutions, and swap resources and journals. It is a free site that lets each individual user turn to crowdsourcing for answers even while helping others.

- *The Great Sunflower Project:* Gretchen LeBuhn, an associate biology professor at San Francisco State University, needed help with her studies of honeybees, but she had limited grant money, so she contacted gardening groups around the country. Through this crowdsourcing strategy, LeBuhn ultimately created a network of more than 25,000 gardeners and schools to assist with her research She then sent these participants seeds for plants that attract bees. In return, the participants recorded honeybee visits and activity for her on her Web site.

Collaboration can be *synchronous*, meaning that all team members meet at the same time. Teams may also collaborate *asynchronously* when team members cannot meet at the same time. Virtual teams, whose members are located throughout the world, typically must collaborate asynchronously.

A variety of software products are available to support all types of collaboration. Among the most prominent are Microsoft SharePoint Workspace, Google Docs, IBM Lotus Quickr, and Jive. In general, these products provide online collaboration capabilities, workgroup e-mail, distributed databases, bulletin whiteboards, electronic text editing, document management, workflow capabilities, instant virtual meetings, application sharing, instant messaging, consensus building, voting, ranking, and various application development tools.

These products also provide varying degrees of content control. Wikis, Google Docs, Microsoft SharePoint Workspace, and Jive provide for shared content with *version management*, whereas Microsoft SharePoint Workspace and IBM Lotus Quickr offer *version control*. Products that provide version management track changes to documents and provide features to accommodate multiple people working on the same document at the same time. In contrast, version-control systems provide each team member with an account that includes a set of permissions. Shared documents are located in shared directories. Document directories are often set up so that users must check out documents before they can edit them. When one team member checks out a document, no other member can access it. Once the document has been checked in, it becomes available to other members.

In this section you review the major collaboration software products. You then shift your attention to two tools that support collaboration—electronic teleconferencing and videoconferencing.

Microsoft SharePoint. Microsoft's SharePoint product (www.microsoft.com/Sharepoint/default.mspx) provides shared content with version control. SharePoint supports document directories and has features that enable users to create and manage surveys, discussion forums, wikis, member blogs, member Web sites, and workflow. It also has a rigorous permissions structure, which allows organizations to control users' access based on their organizational role, team membership, interest, security level, or other criteria.

One company that has used SharePoint effectively is Continental Airlines. When new federal regulations regarding long runway delays went into effect, Continental responded by implementing a SharePoint system that puts various aspects of flight operations—aircraft status, pilots, crews, and customer care—on the same page. Using the system, the 135 general managers at the airline's domestic airports fill out a 16-page form online. The form includes the names and numbers of airport workers, from the airport authority to the person who drives the stairs to planes waiting on the runway. The general managers have to specify how they would manage delays of an hour, two hours, and two-and-one-half hours. The Sharepoint system includes a dashboard for Continental's centralized system operations center. People in the center can use the dashboard to find information about delays quickly and to communicate with pilots, crews, and dispatchers to decide what to do to mitigate any delays.

Google Docs. Google Docs (http://docs.google.com) is a free, Web-based word processor, spreadsheet, and presentation application. It enables users to create and edit documents online while collaborating with other users. In contrast to Microsoft SharePoint Workspace, Google Docs allows multiple users to open, share, and edit documents at the same time.

IBM Lotus Quickr. IBM's Lotus Quickr (www.ibm.com/lotus/quickr) product provides shared content with version control in the form of document directories with check-in and check-out features based on user privileges. Quickr provides online team spaces where members can share and collaborate by utilizing team calendars, discussion forums, blogs, wikis, and other collaboration tools for managing projects and other content.

Compagnie d'Enterprises (CFE), one of Belgium's largest construction companies, has put the collaboration tools of Quickr to good use. Construction projects require many parties to collaborate effectively. When these projects are conducted on a global scale and the parties are scattered throughout the world, the projects become incredibly complex. CFE needed to tap its best resources for its projects, regardless of where those resources were located. The company was using e-mail to share documents with suppliers and clients, but this process resulted in version-control errors and security vulnerabilities. To eliminate these problems, CFE deployed Quickr with its centralized document libraries and version control. The software reduced both the volume of large attachments sent through e-mail and the impact of those e-mails on the system. As a result, project teams were able to work more efficiently.

Jive. Jive's (www.jivesoftware.com) newest product, Clearspace, uses Web collaboration and communication tools such as forums, wikis, and blogs to allow people to share content with version management, via discussion rooms, calendars, and to-do lists. For example, Nike originally used Clearspace Community to run a technical support forum on Nike Plus (http://nikerunning.nike.com/nikeos/p/nikeplus/en_US), a Web site where runners track their miles and calories burned using a sensor in their shoes. The company soon noticed that runners were also using the forum to meet other athletes. In response, Nike expanded its forum to include a section where runners could meet and challenge one another to races. Since that time, 40 percent of visitors to the site who did not own the Nike Plus sensor ended up buying the product.

Electronic Teleconferencing. Teleconferencing is the use of electronic communication technology that enables two or more people at different locations to hold a simultaneous conference. There are several types of teleconferencing. The oldest and simplest is a telephone conference call, where several people talk to one another from multiple locations. The biggest disadvantage of conference calls is that they do not allow the participants to communicate face to face. In addition, participants in one location cannot see graphs, charts, and pictures at other locations.

To overcome these shortcomings, organizations are increasingly turning to video teleconferencing, or videoconferencing. In a **videoconference**, participants in one location can see participants, documents, and presentations at other locations. The latest version of videoconferencing, called *telepresence*, enables participants to seamlessly share data, voice, pictures, graphics, and animation by electronic means. Conferees can also transmit data along with voice and video, which allows them to work together on documents and to exchange computer files.

Several companies are offering high-end telepresence systems. For example, Hewlett-Packard's Halo system (www.hp.com), Cisco's TelePresence 3000 (www.cisco.com), and Polycom's HDX (www.polycom.com) use massive high-definition screens up to eight feet wide to show people sitting around conference tables (see Figure 4.15). Telepresence systems also have advanced audio capabilities that let everyone talk at once without canceling out any voices. Telepresence systems can cost up to $400,000 for a room, with network management fees ranging up to $18,000 per month. Financial and consulting firms are quickly adopting telepresence systems. For example, the Blackstone Group

Figure 4.15 Telepresence system. (*Source:* PRNews Foto/Polycom, Inc./NewsCom)

(www.blackstone.com), a private equity firm, has 40 telepresence rooms around the world, and Deloitte & Touche has 12.

Let's look at two other organizations that use telepresence systems.

The telepresence system of international law firm DLA Piper (www.dlapiper.com) saves the company approximately $1 million per year in travel costs and lost productivity. The firm realizes these savings by rescheduling half of its in-person board meetings as telepresence conferences and relying on at least two attorneys per week to use telepresence rather than travel. Making it possible for globally based attorneys to work closely together via telepresence helps drive home the reality that the firm has offices all over the world and therefore should have an international focus. This benefit of telepresence cannot be quantified in terms of dollars and cents.

The insurance giant MetLife (www.metlife.com) is using telepresence in three dedicated conference rooms in Chicago, New York, and New Jersey and is expanding the system to other offices nationally and internationally. MetLife has experienced a direct cost savings as well as better employee time efficiency. Further, telepresence is helping the company meet its "green initiative" goal of reducing its carbon emissions by 20 percent. Interestingly, one MetLife executive noted that when the company uses telepresence for meetings, employees who would not normally be asked to travel to headquarters now have the opportunity to make presentations and get valuable exposure to company executives.

E-Learning and Distance Learning

E-learning and distance learning are not the same thing, but they do overlap. **E-learning** refers to learning supported by the Web. It can take place inside classrooms as a support to conventional teaching, such as when students work on the Web during class. It also can take place in virtual classrooms, in which all coursework is done online and classes do not meet face-to-face. In these cases, e-learning is a part of distance learning. **Distance learning (DL)** refers to any learning situation in which teachers and students do not meet face-to-face.

Today, the Web provides a multimedia interactive environment for self-study. Web-enabled systems make knowledge accessible to those who need it, when they need it, anytime, anywhere. For this reason, e-learning and DL can be useful both for formal education and for corporate training. "IT's About Business 4.3" illustrates how high school students are using e-learning and distance learning to take advanced placement (AP) classes online.

Online AP Classes Are Big Business

A rapidly increasing number of high school students are taking advanced placement (AP) classes in an attempt to reduce college tuition costs and obtain an edge in the college admissions process. A record 2 million high school students took AP exams in May 2011, more than twice as many as in 2000. According to the College Board (www.collegeboard.org), the nonprofit organization that oversees AP courses and testing, approximately 90 percent of U.S. colleges and universities award college credit to high school students who pass the AP program's rigorous subject-matter tests.

However, AP courses can be expensive for high schools to offer because they often have fewer students than other classes, making it difficult to justify keeping them while teachers are being laid off and sports and arts programs that serve more students are being cut back. Adding to this expense, some schools also pay the $87 fee for a student to take an AP exam, and scholarships are available for some students who cannot afford the fees.

For all of these reasons, AP classes are under pressure in several states. In Michigan, for example, officials are predicting decreases in AP classes, where funding for 2012 may be cut by 10 percent. Some school districts in upstate New York are considering eliminating almost all AP courses. Budget problems in some Ohio and Maryland schools have generated talk of AP cutbacks.

For students in states and districts facing budget cuts, online AP courses are becoming an increasing popular option. Online courses require students to log on, and teachers are available by e-mail, phone, online discussions, and/or instant messaging. After completing an AP course, students take the AP exam in school like other students.

Online AP courses permit students to click on a current lesson, read materials, complete exercises or quizzes, and file assignments or exams online. Online whiteboards enable teachers to draw lecture notes or show solutions to problems. Students practice skills and problems through interactive quizzes or games, and they complete group projects on collaborative Web sites.

One potential drawback for students is that taking an AP course online requires advanced time-management skills. Another obstacle pertains specifically to science courses, particularly chemistry, that require students to perform laboratory experiments. Students can conduct some physics and biology lab exercises at home using lab kits and supplies. However, most online chemistry students have to travel to supervised labs to perform experiments, which frequently involve volatile chemicals.

Virtual AP courses are becoming available through online schools in 27 states. Students can also enroll directly in online AP classes for a fee through private companies that offer these classes directly. Examples of these companies are Advanced Academics (www.advancedacademics.com), Apex Learning (www.apexlearning.com), Aventa Learning (www.aventalearning.com), and the Florida Virtual School (www.flvs.net).

And the bottom line? The College Board claims there are no significant differences in average test scores between students from traditional AP courses and those taking online AP courses, meaning that both approaches appear to be equally effective.

Questions

1. Identify and discuss the disadvantages of taking online AP classes. Provide specific examples of disadvantages that are not mentioned in the case.

2. Apply your thoughts in question 1 to college education by discussing the advantages and disadvantages of taking college courses online. Extend your answer here to completing entire degree programs online.

3. After you answer questions 1 and 2, speculate on the future of online universities.

Sources: Compiled from S. Shellenbarger, "For AP Students, a New Classroom Is Online," *Wall Street Journal*, April 20, 2011; M. Horn, "More Interaction in Online Courses Isn't Always Better," *Forbes*, December 16, 2010; T. Walsh, "Higher Education in the Digital Age," *Forbes*, August 11, 2010; C. Christensen and

M. Horn, "Education As We Know It Is Finished Forever," *Forbes*, July 12, 2010; www.collegeboard.org, www.advancedacademics.com, www.apexlearning.com, www.aventalearning.com, www.flvs.net, accessed April 11, 2011.

There are many benefits to e-learning. For example, online materials can deliver very current content that is of high quality (created by content experts) and consistent (presented the same way every time). It also gives students the flexibility to learn at any place, at any time, and at their own pace. In corporate training centers that use e-learning, learning time generally is shorter, which means that more people can be trained within a given timeframe. This system reduces training costs as well as the expense of renting facility space.

Despite these benefits, e-learning has some drawbacks. For one, students must be computer literate. Also, they may miss the face-to-face interaction with instructors. In addition, accurately assessing students' work can be problematic because instructors really do not know who completed the assignments.

E-learning does not usually replace the classroom setting. Rather, it enhances it by taking advantage of new content and delivery technologies. Advanced e-learning support environments, such as Blackboard (www.blackboard.com), add value to traditional learning in higher education.

Virtual Universities

Virtual universities are online universities in which students take classes via the Internet at home or an off-site location. A large number of existing universities offer online education of some form. Some universities, such as the University of Phoenix (www.phoenix.edu), California Virtual Campus (www.cvc.edu), and the University of Maryland (www.umuc.edu/gen/virtuniv.shtml), offer thousands of courses and dozens of degrees to students worldwide, all online. Other universities offer limited online courses and degrees but use innovative teaching methods and multimedia support in the traditional classroom.

Telecommuting

Knowledge workers are being called the distributed workforce, or digital nomads. This group of highly prized workers is now able to work anywhere and anytime, a process called **telecommuting**. Distributed workers are those who have no permanent office at their companies, preferring to work at home offices, in airport lounges or client conference rooms, or on a high school stadium bleacher. The growth of the distributed workforce is driven by globalization, extremely long commutes to work, rising gasoline prices, ubiquitous broadband communications links (wireline and wireless), and powerful laptop computers and computing devices.

Telecommuting has a number of potential advantages for employees, employers, and society. For employees, the benefits include reduced stress and improved family life. In addition, telecommuting offers employment opportunities for housebound people such as single parents and persons with disabilities. Employer benefits include increased productivity, the ability to retain skilled employees, and the ability to attract employees who do not live within commuting distance.

However, telecommuting also has some potential disadvantages. For employees, the major disadvantages are increased feelings of isolation, possible loss of fringe benefits, lower pay (in some cases), no workplace visibility, the potential for slower promotions, and lack of socialization. In addition, telecommuting employees often have difficulties "training" their families to understand that they are at work even though they are physically at home.

Families have to understand that they should not disturb the telecommuter for anything that they would not have disturbed him or her about in a "real" office. The major disadvantages to employers are difficulties in supervising work and potential data security problems.

BEFORE YOU GO ON . . .

1. Discuss the network applications that you studied in this section and the tools and technologies that support each one.
2. Identify the business conditions that have made videoconferencing more important.
3. Differentiate between e-learning and distance learning.
4. Describe virtual universities.
5. What is telecommuting? Do you think you would like to telecommute? Why or why not?

RUBY'S CLUB QUESTIONS

1. How can Ruby's Club capitalize on network tools such as e-mail, chat, or instant messaging?
2. What type of work flow projects could help streamline the operations for Ruby's Club?

Student Activity | 4.4

Objective: The objective of this exercise is to familiarize you with applications that require a network in order to function.

Chapter Connection: This case relates to Chapter 4, Section 4.4: Network Applications.

Prerequisites: You should read Chapter 4 before doing this exercise to become familiar with various network applications.

Activity:

Many of us use Microsoft Office for our word processing, presentations, and spreadsheets. However, there are alternatives. One of these is Google Docs. One advantage of Google Docs is you can easily share your work with others online and even work together on the same project using the same files. Plus, it is free.

To use Google Docs you will need a Gmail account, so if you currently do not have one, go www.google.com,

click "Gmail," and create an account. Now you are ready to go!

Go to http://docs.google.com/. View the videos to learn all that you can do with Google Docs.

Deliverables:

Do the following activities using Google Docs and submit the results to your instructor via sharing or an e-mail link.

1. Create a new form using Google Docs to gather information from fellow students about Google Docs.
   (a) Include a multiple-choice question, a checkbox question, and a list question.
      i. Ask questions such as, How can Google Docs be used? Have you used it? How often? and so on.
   (b) E-mail the form to at least two other students plus your instructor for them to complete.
   (c) View the results of their entries.

2. Create a New Presentation. If you can, *share* it with fellow classmate(s) so both can edit it, all the better. Have one slide for each student in your group. On your slides, include the following:

(a) Your name(s)
(b) Your picture(s)
(c) A bulleted list of what you like about Google Docs
(d) A table with the schedule(s) of your classes

3. Share your presentation with your instructor.

Quiz Questions:

1. What is a benefit of Google Docs?

(a) Upload your files
(b) Access anywhere
(c) Share your work
(d) All of the above

2. What of the following can you *not* do on Google Docs?

(a) Forms
(b) Presentations
(c) Database
(d) Drawings

3. When creating a Google Form, the results are compiled in a:

(a) Presentation
(b) Database
(c) Spreadsheet
(d) All of the above

4. If you are doing a group paper for class, which of the tools would you select?

(a) Form
(b) Document
(c) Presentation
(d) Text

5. How many people can work on a spreadsheet at the same time?

(a) 2
(b) 1
(c) 10
(d) 50

Discussion Questions:

Discuss some of the benefits of using Google Docs. What are some of the included functions, and what does each allow you to do?

What's in IT for ME?

FOR THE ACCOUNTING MAJOR

Accounting personnel use corporate intranets and portals to consolidate transaction data from legacy systems to provide an overall view of internal projects. This view contains the current costs charged to each project, the number of hours spent on each project by individual employees, and an analysis of how actual costs compare to projected costs. Finally, accounting personnel use Internet access to government and professional Web sites to stay informed on legal and other changes affecting their profession.

FOR THE FINANCE MAJOR

Corporate intranets and portals can provide a model to evaluate the risks of a project or an investment. Financial analysts use two types of data in the model: historical transaction data from corporate databases via the intranet, and industry data obtained via the Internet. In addition, financial services firms can use the Web for marketing and to provide services.

FOR THE MARKETING MAJOR

Marketing managers use corporate intranets and portals to coordinate the activities of the sales force. Sales personnel access corporate portals via the intranet to discover updates on pricing, promotion, rebates, customer information, and information about competitors. Sales staff can also download and customize presentations for their customers. The Internet, particularly the Web, opens a completely new marketing channel for many industries. Just how advertising, purchasing, and information dispensation should occur appears to vary from industry to industry, product to product, and service to service.

FOR THE
PRODUCTION/OPERATIONS MANAGEMENT MAJOR

Companies are using intranets and portals to speed product development by providing the development team with three-dimensional models and animation. All team members can access the models for faster exploration of ideas and enhanced feedback. Corporate portals, accessed via intranets, enable managers to carefully supervise their inventories as well as real-time production on assembly lines. Extranets are also proving valuable as communication formats for joint research and design efforts among companies. The Internet is also a great source of cutting-edge information for POM managers.

FOR THE
HUMAN RESOURCES MANAGEMENT MAJOR

Human resources personnel use portals and intranets to publish corporate policy manuals, job postings, company telephone directories, and training classes. Many companies deliver online training obtained from the Internet to employees through their intranets. Human resources departments use intranets to offer employees healthcare, savings, and benefit plans, as well as the opportunity to take competency tests online. The Internet supports worldwide recruiting efforts, and it can also be the communications platform for supporting geographically dispersed work teams.

FOR THE MIS MAJOR

As important as the networking technology infrastructure is, it is invisible to users (unless something goes wrong). The MIS function is responsible for keeping all organizational networks up and running all the time. MIS personnel, therefore, provide all users with an "eye to the world" and the ability to compute, communicate, and collaborate anytime, anywhere. For example, organizations have access to experts at remote locations without having to duplicate that expertise in multiple areas of the firm. Virtual teaming allows experts physically located in different cities to work on projects as though they were in the same office.

>>> SUMMARY

1. Define the term *computer network*, and compare and contrast the two major types of networks.

A computer network is a system that connects computers via communications media so that data and information can be transmitted among them. The two major types of networks are local area networks (LANs) and wide area networks (WANs). LANs encompass a limited geographic area and are usually composed of one communications medium. In contrast, WANs encompass a broad geographical area and are usually composed of multiple communications media.

2. Describe the differences among the three types of wireline communications media, and discuss the main advantages and disadvantages of each type.

Twisted-pair wire, the most prevalent form of communications wiring, consists of strands of copper wire twisted in pairs. It is relatively inexpensive to purchase, widely available, and easy to work with. However, it is relatively slow for transmitting data, it is subject to interference from other electrical sources, and it can be easily tapped by unintended receivers.

Coaxial cable consists of insulated copper wire. It is much less susceptible to electrical interference than is twisted-pair wire, and it can carry much more data. However, coaxial cable is more expensive and more difficult to work with than twisted-pair wire. It is also somewhat inflexible.

Fiber-optic cables consist of thousands of very thin filaments of glass fibers that transmit information via light pulses generated by lasers. Fiber-optic cables are significantly smaller and lighter than traditional cable media. They also can transmit far more data, and they provide greater security from interference and tapping. Fiber-optic cable is often used as the backbone for a network, whereas twisted-pair wire and coaxial cable connect the backbone to individual devices on the network.

3. Differentiate between the Internet and the World Wide Web, and describe the most common methods for accessing the Internet.

The Internet is a global network of computer networks, using a common communications protocol, TCP/IP. The *World Wide Web* is a system that stores, retrieves, formats, and displays information accessible through a browser.

Methods for connecting to the Internet include dial-up, DSL, cable modem, satellite, wireless, and fiber to the home.

4. Identify six major categories of network applications, provide an example of each one, and explain how that application supports business functions.

> *Discovery* involves browsing and information retrieval, and provides users the ability to view information in databases, download it, and/or process it. Discovery tools include search engines, directories, and portals. Discovery tools enable business users to efficiently find needed information.

> Networks provide fast, inexpensive *communications*, via e-mail, call centers, chat rooms, voice communications, and blogs. Communications tools provide business users with a seamless interface among team members, colleagues, business partners, and customers.

> *Collaboration* refers to mutual efforts by two or more entities (individuals, groups, or companies) who work together to accomplish tasks. Collaboration is enabled by workflow systems. Collaboration tools enable business users to collaborate with colleagues, business partners, and customers.

> *E-learning* refers to learning supported by the Web. Distance learning refers to any learning situation in which teachers and students do not meet face-to-face. E-learning provides tools for business users to enable their lifelong learning.

> *Virtual universities* are online universities in which students take classes via the Internet at home or an off-site location. Virtual universities make it possible for students to obtain degrees while working full time, thus increasing their value to their firms.

> *Telecommuting* is the process whereby knowledge workers are able to work anywhere and anytime. Telecommuting provides flexibility for employees, with many benefits and some drawbacks.

>>> CHAPTER GLOSSARY

affinity portal A Web site that offers a single point of entry to an entire community of affiliated interests.

analog signals Continuous waves that transmit information by altering the amplitude and frequency of the waves.

asynchronous transfer mode (ATM) Data transmission technology that uses packet switching and allows for almost unlimited bandwidth on demand.

backbone networks High-speed central networks to which multiple smaller networks (such as LANs and smaller WANs) connect.

bandwidth The transmission capacity of a network, stated in bits per second.

broadband A transmission speed ranging from approximately one megabit per second up to several terabits per second.

broadcast media (also called wireless media) Communications channels that use electromagnetic media (the "airwaves") to transmit data.

browsers Software applications through which users primarily access the Web.

cable media (also called wireline media) Communications channels that use physical wires or cables to transmit data and information.

chat room A virtual meeting place where groups of regulars come to "gab" electronically.

client/server computing Form of distributed processing in which some machines (servers) perform computing functions for end-user PCs (clients).

clients Computers, such as users' personal computers, that use any of the services provided by servers.

coaxial cable Insulated copper wire; used to carry high-speed data traffic and television signals.

collaboration Mutual efforts by two or more individuals who perform activities in order to accomplish certain tasks.

commercial (public) portal A Web site that offers fairly routine content for diverse audiences; offers customization only at the user interface.

communications channel Pathway for communicating data from one location to another.

computer network A system that connects computers and other devices via communications media so that data and information can be transmitted among them.

corporate portal A Web site that provides a single point of access to critical business information located inside and outside of an organization.

digital signals A discrete pulse, either on or off, that conveys information in a binary form.

digital subscriber line (DSL) A high-speed, digital data-transmission technology using existing analog telephone lines.

distance learning (DL) Learning situations in which teachers and students do not meet face-to-face.

distributed processing Network architecture that divides processing work between two or more computers, linked together in a network.

domain name system (DNS) The system administered by the Internet Corporation for Assigned Names (ICANN) that assigns names to each site on the Internet.

domain names The name assigned to an Internet site, consisting of multiple parts, separated by dots, which are translated from right to left.

e-learning Learning supported by the Web; can be done inside traditional classrooms or in virtual classrooms.

enterprise network An organization's network composed of interconnected multiple LANs and WANs.

Ethernet A common local area network protocol.

extranet A network that connects parts of the intranets of different organizations.

fiber-optic cable A communications medium consisting of thousands of very thin filaments of glass fibers, surrounded by cladding, that transmit information via light pulses generated by lasers.

file server (also called network server) A computer that contains various software and data files for a local area network and contains the network operating system.

Hypertext Transport Protocol (HTTP) The communications standard used to transfer pages across the WWW portion of the Internet; defines how messages are formulated and transmitted.

industrywide portal A Web-based gateway to information and knowledge for an entire industry.

Internet (The Net) A massive global WAN that connects approximately 1 million organizational computer networks in more than 200 countries on all continents, including Antarctica, and features in the daily routine of almost 2 billion people. Participating computer systems include smart phones, PCs, LANs, databases, and mainframes.

Internet Protocol (IP) A set of rules responsible for disassembling, delivering, and reassembling packets over the Internet.

Internet Protocol (IP) address An assigned address that uniquely identifies a computer on the Internet.

Internet service provider (ISP) A company that provides Internet connections for a fee.

Internet telephony (Voice-over Internet Protocol or VoIP) The use of the Internet as the transmission medium for telephone calls.

Internet2 A new, faster telecommunications network that deploys advanced network applications such as remote medical diagnosis, digital libraries, distance education, online simulation, and virtual laboratories.

intranet A private network that uses Internet software and TCP/IP protocols.

local area network (LAN) A network that connects communications devices in a limited geographical region, such as a building, so that every user device on the network can communicate with every other device.

metasearch engine A computer program that searches several engines at once and integrates the findings of the various search engines to answer queries posted by users.

mobile portal A Web site that is accessible from mobile devices.

modem Device that converts signals from analog to digital and vice versa.

network access points (NAPs) Computers that act as exchange points for Internet traffic and determine how traffic is routed.

network server (see **file server**)

packet switching The transmission technology that divides blocks of text into packets.

peer-to-peer (P2P) processing A type of client/server distributed processing that allows two or more computers to pool their resources, making each computer both a client and a server.

portal A Web-based personalized gateway to information and knowledge that provides information from disparate information systems and the Internet, using advanced search and indexing techniques.

protocol The set of rules and procedures governing transmission across a network.

router A communications processor that routes messages from a LAN to the Internet, across several connected LANs, or across a wide area network such as the Internet.

search engine A computer program that searches for specific information by key words and reports the results.

servers Computers that provide access to various network services, such as printing, data, and communications.

synchronous optical network (SONET) An interface standard for transporting digital signals over fiber-optic lines; allows the integration of transmissions from multiple vendors.

T-carrier system A digital transmission system that defines circuits that operate at different rates, all of which are multiples of the basic 64 Kbps used to transport a single voice call.

telecommuting A work arrangement whereby employees work at home, at the customer's premises, in special workplaces, or while traveling, usually using a computer linked to their place of employment.

teleconferencing The use of electronic communication that allows two or more people at different locations to have a simultaneous conference.

Transmission Control Protocol/Internet Protocol (TCP/IP) A file transfer protocol that can send large files of information across sometimes unreliable networks with assurance that the data will arrive uncorrupted.

twisted-pair wire A communications medium consisting of strands of copper wire twisted together in pairs.

unified communications Common hardware and software platform that simplifies and integrates all forms of communications—voice, e-mail, instant messaging, location, and videoconferencing—across an organization.

uniform resource locator (URL) The set of letters that identifies the address of a specific resource on the Web.

videoconference A virtual meeting in which participants in one location can see and hear participants at other locations and can share data and graphics by electronic means.

virtual collaboration The use of digital technologies that enable organizations or individuals to collaboratively plan, design, develop, manage, and research products, services, and innovative information systems and electronic commerce applications.

virtual group (team) A work group whose members are in different locations and who meet electronically.

virtual universities Online universities in which students take classes via the Internet at home or an off-site location.

Voice-over Internet Protocol (VOIP; see **Internet telephony)**

Web site Collectively, all of the Web pages of a particular company or individual.

wide area network (WAN) A network, generally provided by common carriers, that covers a wide geographic area.

wireless media (see **broadcast media**)

wireline media (see **cable media**)

work group Two or more individuals who act together to perform some task, on either a permanent or temporary basis.

workflow The movement of information as it flows through the sequence of steps that make up an organization's work procedures.

World Wide Web (The Web, WWW, or W3) A system of universally accepted standards for storing, retrieving, formatting, and displaying information via a client/server architecture; it uses the transport functions of the Internet.

>>> DISCUSSION QUESTIONS

1. What are the implications of having fiber-optic cable to everyone's home?

2. What are the implications of BitTorrent for the music industry? For the motion picture industry?

3. Discuss the pros and cons of P2P networks.

4. Should the Internet be regulated? If so, by whom?

5. Discuss the pros and cons of delivering this book over the Internet.

6. Explain how the Internet works. Assume you are talking with someone who has no knowledge of information technology (in other words, keep it very simple).

7. How are the network applications of communication and collaboration related? Do communication tools also support collaboration? Give examples.

8. Access this article from The Atlantic: "Is Google Making Us Stupid?" (www.theatlantic.com/doc/200807/google). *Is* Google making us stupid? Support your answer.

>>> PROBLEM-SOLVING ACTIVITIES

1. Calculate how much bandwidth you consume when using the Internet every day. How many e-mails do you send daily, and what is the size of each? (Your e-mail program may have e-mail file size information.) How many music and video clips do you download (or upload) daily, and what is the size of each? If you view YouTube often, surf the Web to find out the size of a typical YouTube file. Add up the number of e-mail, audio, and video files you transmit or receive on a typical day. When you have calculated your daily Internet usage, determine if you are a "normal" Internet user or a "power" Internet user. What impact does network neutrality have on you as a "normal" user? As a "power" user?

2. Access several P2P applications, such as SETI@home. Describe the purpose of each application, and indicate which ones you would like to join.

3. Access http://ipv6.com and www.ipv6news.info and learn about more advantages of IPv6.

4. Access www.icann.org and learn more about this important organization.

5. Set up your own Web site using your name for the domain name (for example, KellyRainer).

   - Explain the process for registering a domain.
   - Which top-level domain will you use and why?

6. Access www.icann.org and obtain the name of an agency or company that can register a domain for the TLD that you selected. What is the name of that agency or company?

7. Access the Web site for that agency or company (in question 6) to learn the process that you must use. How much will it initially cost to register your domain name? How much will it cost to maintain that name in the future?

8. You plan to take a two-week vacation in Australia this year. Using the Internet, find information that will help you plan the trip. Such information includes, *but is not limited to,* the following:

   a. Geographical location and weather conditions at the time of your trip
   b. Major tourist attractions and recreational facilities
   c. Travel arrangements (airlines, approximate fares)
   d. Car rental; local tours
   e. Alternatives for accommodation (within a moderate budget) and food
   f. Estimated cost of the vacation (travel, lodging, food, recreation, shopping, etc.)

   g. Country regulations regarding the entrance of your dog
   h. Shopping
   i. Passport information (either to obtain one or to renew one)
   j. nformation on the country's language and culture
   k. What else do you think you should research before going to Australia?

9. From your own experience or from the vendor's information, list the major capabilities of Lotus Notes/Domino. Do the same for Microsoft Exchange. Compare and contrast the products. Explain how the products can be used to support knowledge workers and managers.

10. Visit Web sites of companies that manufacture telepresence products for the Internet. Prepare a report. Differentiate between telepresence products and videoconferencing products.

11. Access Google (or YouTube) videos and search for "Cisco Magic." This video shows Cisco's next-generation telepresence system. Compare and contrast it with current telepresence systems.

12. Access the Web site of your university. Does the Web site provide high-quality information (right amount, clear, accurate, etc.)? Do you think a high-school student who is thinking of attending your university would feel the same way?

13. Compare and contrast Google Sites (www.google.com/sites) and Microsoft Office Live (www.liveoffice.com). Which site would you use to create your own Web site? Explain your choice.

14. Access the Web site of the Recording Industry Association of America (www.riaa.com). Discuss what you find there regarding copyright infringement (that is, downloading music files). How do you feel about the RIAA's efforts to stop music downloads? Debate this issue from your point of view and from the RIAA's point of view.

15. Research the companies involved in Internet telephony (Voice-over IP). Compare their offerings as to price, necessary technologies, ease of installation, and so on. Which company is the most attractive to you? Which company might be the most attractive for a large company?

16. Access some of the alternative search engines at www.readwriteweb.com/archives/top_100_alternative_search_engines.php. Search for the same terms on several of the alternative search engines and on Google. Compare the results on breadth (number of results found) and precision (results are what you were looking for).

17. Second Life (www.secondlife.com) is a three-dimensional, online world built and owned by its residents. Residents of Second Life are avatars who have been created by real people. Access Second Life, learn about it, and create your own avatar to explore this world. Learn about the thousands of people who are making "real world" money from operations in Second Life.

18. Access the Yahoo! (http://babelfish.yahoo.com) or Google (www.google.com/language_tools) translation pages. Type in a paragraph in English and select, for example, English-to-French. When you see the translated paragraph in French, copy it into the text box, and select French-to-English. Is the paragraph that you first entered the same as the one you are looking at now? Why or why not? Support your answer.

>>> TEAM ASSIGNMENTS

1. Assign each group member to a collaboration product (e.g., Jive, Google Docs, SharePoint, or Quickr). Have each member visit the Web site of the product and obtain information about it. As a group, prepare a comparative table of the major similarities and differences among the products.

2. Each team will pick one of the following: YourStreet, Platial, Topix, or Google Earth. Compare and contrast these products as to features and ease-of-use. Present each product to the class. Each group will collaborate on writing a report on its product using Google Docs.

CLOSING **CASE 1 >** The Network Neutrality Wars

THE PROBLEM>>>

Analysts are bullish about Netflix (www.netflix.com), as the company moves from a DVD-delivery service to an on-demand entertainment provider. Netflix's 16 million subscribers stream so many movies that the company now accounts for 20 percent of all Internet traffic during the typical American evening, according to Sandvine (www.sandvine.com), which makes network-monitoring equipment.

The CEO of Netflix was asked whether the Internet's infrastructure can withstand the strain as his streaming business expands. He replied, "If there's anything you'd want to bet on, it's that technology will make bandwidth faster and cheaper."

That bet may not be as safe as it seems. Although the steady progress of communications technologies has led to bandwidth that meets demand in 2011, the explosion of streaming video and mobile technologies is beginning to cause problems. The Internet was built to transmit content such as e-mails and Web pages. In contrast, media items such as high-definition movies are magnitudes greater in size. To compound this problem, there are now more than 50 million smart phone users in the United States, many of whom stream video content to their phones.

In a widely cited estimate, Cisco Systems (www.cisco.com) predicted that Internet traffic will triple by 2014, to 64 exabytes (1 exabyte is 1 million terabytes) a month. (Monthly traffic in 2006 was 5 exabytes, enough to store every word ever spoken.) Moreover, by 2014, more than 90 percent of Internet traffic will consist of video. Market researcher Infonetics (www.infonetics.com) contends that Cisco's numbers may be conservative. Infonetics's worst-case scenario is that Internet backbone carriers will cease upgrading their technologies, leaving consumers with slow connections and hindering Internet innovation.

The issue is as much about economics as technology. Under the current system, consumers can send 1-kilobyte e-mails or watch the latest 30-gigabyte movie on their large-screen televisions for the same monthly broadband fee. In contrast to power and water bills, there is no meter to monitor high-bandwidth users.

A study from Juniper Networks (www.juniper.net) highlights this "revenue-per-bit" problem. The report predicts that Internet revenues for carriers such as AT&T (www.att.com) and Comcast (www.comcast.com) will grow by 5 percent per year through 2020. At the same time, traffic will increase by 27 percent annually, meaning that carriers will have to increase their investments by 20 percent per year just to keep up with demand. Using this math, the carriers' business models break down in 2014, when the total investment needed exceeds revenue growth.

Although few industry analysts expect carriers to stop investing in new capacity, a consensus has emerged that a financial crunch is coming. As traffic soars, analysts expect the revenue per megabit to fall from 43 cents in 2010 to just 2 cents in 2014. Those figures translate into a far lower return on investment. The carriers can find ways to increase their capacity, but it will be difficult for them to reap any benefits in terms of revenue.

Consider the problem that developed between Level 3 Communications (www.level3.com) and Comcast in late November 2010. Level 3, which operates Internet backbone networks, struck a deal with Netflix to help speed delivery of its streaming videos. The result was a sudden surge in Level 3's traffic. Ultimately, some of this traffic had to be rerouted through Comcast's cables to reach the company's subscribers. Level 3 accused Comcast of charging customers exorbitant rates to carry the additional traffic. Comcast replied that it had no obligation to bear the load for free. The exchange between the two companies gets to the heart of the problem: Even if the technology is up to the task of shipping huge amounts of data, no one is sure how to pay for it.

One possible solution is net neutrality. *Network neutrality* is the concept that Internet service providers (ISPs) must allow customers equal access to content and applications, regardless of the source or nature of the content. As of mid-2011, the Internet was neutral, meaning that Internet backbone carriers must treat all traffic equally on a first-come, first-serve basis. <<< **A NET NEUTRALITY SOLUTION**

Telecommunications and cable companies are not in favor of net neutrality, however. Instead, they want to be able to charge differentiated prices based on the amount of bandwidth consumed by the content being delivered over the Internet. They believe that differentiated pricing is the most equitable method to finance necessary investments in their network infrastructures.

To bolster their argument in favor of differentiated pricing, Internet service providers (ISPs) (Comcast is the nation's second-largest ISP) point to the huge amount of bandwidth that transmitting pirated content of copyrighted materials over the Internet requires. In fact, Comcast reported in 2010 that illegal file sharing of copyrighted material was consuming 50 percent of its network capacity. In 2008, the company slowed down transmission of BitTorrent (www.bittorrent.com) files, which are frequently used for piracy and illegal sharing of copyrighted materials. In response, the Federal Communications Commission (FCC) ruled that Comcast had to stop slowing down peer-to-peer traffic. Comcast then filed a lawsuit challenging the FCC's authority to enforce network neutrality.

Further, ISPs contend that mandating net neutrality will hinder U.S. competitiveness by decreasing innovation and discouraging capital expenditures for new network technologies. In this scenario, ISPs will be unable to handle the exploding demand for Internet and wireless data transmission.

In April 2010, a federal appeals court ruled in favor of Comcast, declaring that the FCC did not have the authority to regulate how an ISP manages its network. This ruling favored differentiated pricing of transmissions over the Internet and was a blow to net neutrality.

Meanwhile, proponents of net neutrality are petitioning Congress to regulate the industry to prevent network providers from adopting strategies like those of Comcast. They argue that the risk of censorship increases when network providers can selectively block or slow access to certain content, such as access to competing low-cost services such as Skype and Vonage. They also assert that a neutral network encourages everyone to innovate without permission from the phone and cable companies or other authorities, and that the neutral Internet has helped create many new businesses.

Most analysts expect that the users consuming the most data eventually will have to pay more, most likely in the form of tiered pricing plans. Americans, however, have never experienced limits on the amount of data they upload and download. Nevertheless, U.S. wireless networks have already moved in the direction of these plans. In June 2010, for example, AT&T discontinued its all-you-can-use $30 a month data plan, forcing mobile consumers to choose between two plans that cap usage at 0.2 gigabytes and 2 gigabytes per month, respectively. <<< **THE RESULTS**

Despite the court ruling of April 2010, on December 21, 2010, the FCC approved network neutrality rules, prohibiting broadband providers from blocking customer access to legal Web content. The new rules would bar wireline-based broadband providers—but not mobile broadband providers—from "unreasonable discrimination" against Web traffic. In January 2011, Verizon filed a legal appeal challenging the FCC's authority to enforce these new rules. As of mid-2011, the battle over network neutrality continues unabated.

1. How do you feel about the net neutrality issue? Should heavier bandwidth users pay for more bandwidth? Should wireless carriers operate under different rules than wireline carriers?

2. Should businesses get involved and monitor network usage? Do you think there is a problem with employees using company-purchased bandwidth for personal use?

SOURCES: L. Segall, "Verizon Challenges FCC Net Neutrality Rules," *CNN Money*, January 21, 2011; K. Corbin, "Net Neutrality 2011: What Storms May Come," *Internet News*, December 30, 2010; G. Gross, "FCC Approves Compromise Net Neutrality Rules," *Network World*, December 21, 2010; P. Burrows, "Will Video Kill the Internet, Too?" *Bloomberg BusinessWeek*, December 6–12, 2010; J. Nocera, "The Struggle for What We Already Have," *New York Times*, September 4, 2010; C. Miller, "Web Plan Is Dividing Companies," *New York Times*, August 11, 2010; A. Schatz and S. Ante, "FCC Web Rules Create Pushback," *Wall Street Journal*, May 6, 2010; www.comcast.com, accessed May 3, 2011.

CLOSING CASE 2 >

The City of Los Angeles Turns to Google Apps

THE PROBLEM>>> The City of Los Angeles (www.lacity.org), the second-largest city in the United States, has more than 30,000 employees and 44 different departments—police, fire, transportation, and many others. In 2009, the city's information technology (IT) agency, responsible for managing enterprise IT applications, faced a $400 million deficit. Until early 2009, the city had an aging e-mail system. The system did not work on some mobile devices, and city IT employees had to enforce inbox space quotas that city employees found limiting. In addition to e-mail, Los Angeles needed archiving and disaster-recovery capabilities to safeguard information. This functionality was particularly important in an area prone to earthquakes. Los Angeles faced a pressing need to modernize its IT applications. To achieve this objective, the city had to decide whether to upgrade its current Microsoft system or switch to Google Apps.

THE SOLUTION>>> In August 2009, the chief information officer of Los Angeles made her case for why the city should adopt Google Apps (www.google.com/apps/intl/en/business/index.html). She argued that the ability to get whatever information the city needs, whenever it is needed, on whatever device it is needed, would fundamentally change the way the city works and enhance productivity. She further noted that in a financial crisis it was difficult to find technology solutions that would save money without requiring a significant capital outlay.

The city ultimately agreed that Google Apps would provide the most feature-rich, cost-effective, and efficient communication solutions. In October 2009, the Los Angeles city council unanimously approved a $7.25 million contract that would move city employees to Google Apps by June 30, 2010. However, the implementation was delayed.

The key issue behind the delay was security concerns by the Los Angeles Police Department (LAPD). The LAPD, which must meet California Department of Justice security requirements, contended that although Google Apps would save the city money, it also poses certain security concerns. In particular, the LAPD expressed concerns about the system's data encryption, the segregation of city data from other data maintained by Google, and background checks for Google employees with access to LAPD information. One city councilman cautioned that sensitive police investigations could be compromised if data under Google's control were somehow exposed.

In addition, LAPD employees who had been using Google Apps on a pilot basis had experienced delays in receiving their e-mail. The LAPD is a 24/7 operation that relies on e-mail and Blackberry notifications for public-safety-related incidents across the city, and delays are not acceptable.

Acknowledging these concerns, the Los Angeles CIO made two key points. First, she stated that Los Angeles owned its data, not Google. Second, she maintained that Google's security was better than the city's Microsoft system. Ultimately, the CIO's comments and hard work by Google employees changed the attitude of the city council from skepticism to cautious acceptance of the contract with Google.

Los Angeles officials decided that 17,000 of the 30,000 city workers would migrate to Google Apps. The remaining 13,000 workers in the police department and the city attorney's office initially used only Gmail, but not the other Google Apps. To meet the security requirements for these two departments, Google had to provide additional levels of background checks for people authorized to access the data. They also had to offer an encryption option in which city officials held the encryption key. Further, Google had to add other functions to its e-mail service, such as auto-acknowledgement of receipt.

<<<THE RESULTS

Google Apps is saving Los Angeles $5.5 million over five years by enabling the city to shift resources currently dedicated to e-mail to other purposes. For example, moving to Google Apps has freed up nearly a hundred servers that were previously used for the city's old e-mail system. Interestingly, freeing up these servers produced an unanticipated benefit: It lowered the city's electricity bills by hundreds of thousands of dollars. Los Angeles found that Google's system availability was 99.9 percent and Google's service levels for response in the event of an issue were excellent.

Questions

1. Describe the reasons that Los Angeles decided to use Google Apps instead of upgrading its Microsoft system.

2. What are potential problems that could result from deploying Google Apps for such a large number of users?

SOURCES: J. Guynn and D. Sarno, "Google: Good Enough for Government Work," *Los Angeles Times*, July 27, 2010; T. Bradley, "Google Apps Project Delays Highlight Cloud Security Concerns," *PC World*, July 26, 2010; C. Huh, "Google—City of Los Angeles Deal Delayed," www.publicradio.org, July 26, 2010; S. Diaz, "Google, Los Angeles Hit Speed Bumps on Move to Cloud," *ZDNet*, July 23, 2010; M. Weinberger, "Google Apps Migration: City of Los Angeles Reality Check," www.mspmentor.net, May 3, 2010; L. Rao, "Los Angeles Bureaucrats Question the Transition to Google Apps," *TechCrunchIT*, April 30, 2010; E. Berridge, "Los Angeles Snubs Microsoft for Google," *The Inquirer*, April 29, 2010; A. Kameka, "Google Apps Has 50 Million Users . . . and Microsoft's Watchful Eye," www.gadgetell.com, March 29, 2010; T. Claburn, "Google's 'Gov Cloud' Wins $7.2 Million Los Angeles Contract," *InformationWeek*, October 28, 2009; D. Sarno, "Los Angeles Adopts Google E-Mail System for 30,000 City Employees," *Los Angeles Times*, October 27,2009; E. Mills, "Los Angeles Gets Its Google Apps Groove," *CNET News*, August 20, 2009; www.lacity.org, www.google.com, accessed March 2, 2011.

RUBY'S CLUB INTERNSHIP ASSIGNMENTS

Ruben and Lisa have questions, and they need answers. For now, it would be helpful if they understood the difference between DSL, cable, and fiber connections. They are especially interested in the up-front cost of installation, speed (amount of bandwidth), and monthly fee. In addition, they need to know how to wire their building. What cable medium would be best for them to use to wire their building for network access?

SPREADSHEET ACTIVITY

Objective: Creating charts and graphs is a really nice skill for you to have. Visual data can be shared more quickly, comprehended more easily, and displayed much more cleanly than simply numbers in a spreadsheet.

Chapter Connection: As you learn about network connections and speeds, this exercise will show you how to do an analysis on your own. It is possible that your Internet connection is not providing the speeds you are paying for! This tool is also useful when your Internet does not seem to be running as quickly as it should. Knowing how to test the speed will help you determine where the possible problem could be!

Prerequisites: There are no prerequisites for this activity.

Activity: Calculating return on investment (ROI) is extremely difficult when it comes to ROI for information systems. For example, when network administrators sense a strain on their network (from network diagnostics or user complaints), they may look into upgrading their network.

To get a feel for the type of information someone might see, create your own spreadsheet of data while watching your Internet connection at home. If you are not at home regularly, choose a computer in a convenient location and test the speed there. Go to http://speedtest.net where the network test will be on the home page asking you to "Begin Test." The test will take only a few minutes In a new spreadsheet, create columns for the following:

- Date
- Time
- Ping speed
- Upload speed
- Download speed
- Test location (not your location, but the host of the test)

Collect this data for a week, preferably three times a day (i.e., morning, afternoon, and evening). Once you have your 15 data points, create a chart that shows the change in bandwidth available over time.

This is exactly what a network administrator might see when trying to determine if it is necessary to upgrade the system.

Go to www.wiley.com/college/rainer to watch a short video on creating charts and graphs to help you create your final product.

Deliverables: The deliverable will be a line chart that shows data speeds over time.

Note: There is no correct answer, but there are wrong answers if you do not collect enough data or do not create the chart appropriately.

Quiz Questions:

1. Excel creates all of the following except:
   - (a) Line charts
   - (b) Pie charts
   - (c) Scatter plots
   - (d) Pareto chart
   - (e) Excel will make all of these charts.

2. Which of the following charts would be best used to show changes over time?
   - (a) Line charts
   - (b) Pie charts
   - (c) Scatter plots
   - (d) Pareto chart

3. A bar chart can show which of the following?
   - (a) Changes over time
   - (b) Comparisons
   - (c) Percentages
   - (d) All of the above

Discussion Questions:

1. What is it about a chart that makes it easier to comprehend than raw numbers?

2. Is it possible for charges and graphs to depict real data in a way that misleads the viewer?

DATABASE ACTIVITY: REPORTS I

Objective

In this activity, you will learn how to create an Access report, with grouping and summaries. A database is not useful if you cannot get information out of it. Reports are one way that users get information from a database. Reports can connect data from several tables, organize it, sort it, group it, summarize it, and more. Once designed, a report can be run as needed, reflecting the database content as of that instant.

Chapter Connection

Companies must monitor their network performance to make sure it is reliable, secure, and free of performance bottlenecks. Reports such as those in this activity help them do this.

The database in this activity tracks network problems. Users who notice problems submit "trouble tickets." These describe the problem and, later, its resolution. They identify the user who submitted it, the equipment involved, and the technician who fixed it.

Management can use reports derived from this database to identify problem devices and vendors, to evaluate technician performance, to identify users who are helpful in finding problems or who report nonexistent ones, and more.

Prerequisites:

None.

Activity:

In this activity, which you will find online, you will take a database and create multilevel reports from it. You will add summary fields to this report and reformat it to improve its appearance.

1. Download the Ch 04 NeTrouble database from www.wiley.com/college/rainer and open it. (You saw this database earlier if you did the Chapter 1 activity. This version does not include the report, query, or form you used there. Here, you will create other reports from the same underlying data.)

2. To create a new report, click the "Create" tab over the ribbon.

3. The section labeled "Reports" offers several reporting tools. We will use the Report Wizard, a compromise between the Report button (which does not offer much control) and Report Design (which forces us to do all the "heavy lifting" ourselves, without the head start that the Wizard can provide). Click on it.

4. The first screen lets us choose which tables we will base our report on and which fields from

those tables we want to use. (It also lets us base the report on *queries*. A query creates a temporary table, so for this purpose they are the same. You will create reports based on queries in later activities.) Our report will list trouble tickets by user, so start by selecting the UserTbl table.

5. The left box shows all fields in the selected table. To move a field into the report, select it and click ">." It moves into the right box. If you move a field you do not want, "<" moves it back. ">>" moves all the fields of that table into the report. This is useful when you want most of them, since ">>" followed by one or two "<" can be faster than moving all those you want individually. Finally, ">>" moves everything in this table out of the report and back to the table so you can start over.
   Here, move the user's name into the report.

6. Next, select DeptTbl, then move DeptName into the report.

7. Finally, select the TicketTbl table. Move TicketSubmitted, TicketResolved, and TicketStatus into the report. Click "Next."

8. This is the panel where you structure your report. Choose each of the three tables, one after another, and see how the report organization changes. For this report, select "by DeptTbl" and click "Next."

9. We do not need any more grouping levels. Click "Next."

10. Within each category, choose to sort the tickets by when they were submitted. Pull down the first sorting menu and select "TicketSubmitted." Click "Next."

11. Leave the layout unchanged here. Click "Next."

12. Change the title of the report to DeptRpt. Then click "Finish" and see the result.

Usage Hint: If you see "###" in any of the fields, the reason is almost certainly that the standard field width is not wide enough to show the data. Switch to Layout view by clicking the second icon from the right in the lower right corner of the window, click in each column field that has this problem to select it, and drag its right side, making it wide enough to the right until you can see the data. You may have to move column headers to keep them aligned with the data. Or, click on the data and shift-click on the heading to select them both, then make them wider together.

13. Our second report will add summary fields to this report. First, make a copy of the report so your instructor can see the version without summary fields. Right-click on the report in the navigation panel at the left of the Access window and select "Copy." Then click "Paste" in the ribbon. (It is under the "Home" tab, so click that tab if it

is not already selected.) Name the new report SumDeptRpt and confirm.

14. Open SumDeptRpt and select Layout view. Make sure the Design tab is selected, and click "Group & Sort" from the Grouping & Totals section.

Usage Hint: Access calls any kind of summary a "total." If you want an arithmetic total, you must ask for a *sum*. We will use the term *summary* rather than *total* here to avoid this common source of confusion, but you will see "total" on Access screens.

15. A new panel will open up at the bottom of the window. Its top row starts "Group on DeptID" and ends with "More" and a triangle pointing to the right. "More" hides many options. Click the triangle to see them.

16. We want to count the number of tickets each department submits. Pull down the triangle next to "with no totals." The first option lets us summarize TicketSubmitted, TicketStatus, or TicketResolved. We should count TicketSubmitted since every trouble ticket has a value in this field. Next, select either count. (They would be different if we counted a field that is blank for some tickets. Therefore, if we had selected TicketResolved or TicketStatus, we would use Count Records so that records that are blank in this field would be counted.) Check boxes to show the grand total and department totals in the group footer. When you click the triangle again to release the dialogue box, you will see department totals after each department with the grand total at the bottom. Your report should start like this:

DeptRpt				
DeptName	UserName	TicketSubmitted	TicketResolved	TicketStatus
Marketing				
	Adam			
		1/1/2011	1/5/2010	Closed
		5/5/2011		Open
	Betty			
		10/10/2010	10/11/2010	Closed
		2/2/2011	2/6/2010	Closed
		4		

If we had wanted to total by user, we would have clicked on the "More" triangle at that level in the panel at the bottom of the window.

Close your report, saving your changes.

17. Now we will improve the appearance of this report. Make a copy of SumDeptRpt. Call it FmtDeptRpt, open it, and go to Layout view. (Layout changes can also be made in Design view. Design view gives more control over some aspects of the layout, but Layout view can often suffice, and it gives immediate visual feedback when you make a change. It is preferable when it will do the job.)

18. First, change the column headings. Access sets them to the names of the database fields. However, database field names are for developers. Report headings should be for people who will read the report. Select each, just as in a word processing program, and change them to read "Department," "User," "Date Submitted," "Date Resolved" and "Status." Change the main report heading to "Trouble Tickets by Department and User." Shrink the width of the User column to bring the data elements closer together. Click "Logo" in the ribbon (Design tab, Header/Footer section), find a suitable picture, and insert. (By default, Access puts logos in the main heading area.) Switch to Report view. Your report should now start like this:

Trouble Tickets by Department and User				
Department	User	Date Submitted	Date Resolved	Status
Marketing				
	Adam			
		1/1/2011	1/5/2010	Closed
		5/5/2011		Open
	Betty			
		10/10/2010	10/11/2010	Closed
		2/2/2011	2/6/2010	Closed
		4		
Accounting				

19. Now it is your turn. Develop a report that shows trouble tickets by device. Group devices by vendor. Within a vendor, group by device type. Within a type, group by status: Closed, Open, or Cancelled. Provide counts for each category and for the entire report. Edit column headings and report title to be meaningful to business-oriented readers of the report. Name your report "DeviceRpt," and be sure to save it when you are done.

As with other aspects of Access, many videos on creating reports are available on the Web. You can find them by searching for "Access report," "Access report tutorial," or any similar string on a video hosting site such as YouTube, or using the general search engine of your choice while restricting its answers to videos.

Deliverables:

Your database with the four reports as specified above. Your instructor may add additional requirements.

Quiz Questions:

1. A report shows the content of the database as of:
   (a) The time the report is run (opened)
   (b) The time the report was designed
   (c) The time the user looks at the report
   (d) The time the user keys into the Report Effective Time field
2. True or False? A report can contain information from no more than two tables.
3. True or False? Report design can only be changed in Design view.

Discussion Questions:

1. Suppose you own or manage a restaurant. You have a typical restaurant computer system in which servers enter orders, which the kitchen uses to prepare orders, and which later creates bills and processes payments. Describe three reports that this system could prepare for your use. Draw, using paper and pencil, the top of each showing header, column headings, a few lines of sample data, and the first summary field.

2. Your instructor may have received a report with a class roster soon after the term started. It is based on two tables: a class table that lists the student IDs of everyone in the class, and a student table that gives the name, major, GPA, and so on for each student. Students are normally listed alphabetically by family name. (It is also based on a query, which finds only students in this class, but that is a separate topic.)
   (a) Discuss two ways this list could be organized, besides the usual order by name.
   (b) Discuss two summaries that this report, organized either in its usual way or in one of the two ways (your choice) in question a, could have.

3. Your e-mail program has an address list. Each entry in it includes an e-mail address. Some entries also include the sender's real name. A few may contain other information. Describe a report that could be produced from this list and other information that your e-mail program stores. Give it at least one summary field. Draw its first few rows.

5 | Business Intelligence

LEARNING OBJECTIVES >>>

1. Identify the phases in the decision-making process, and use a decision-support framework to demonstrate how technology supports managerial decision making.

2. Describe and provide examples of the three different ways that organizations use BI.

3. Specify the BI applications available to users for data analysis, and provide examples of how each one might be used to solve a business problem at your university.

4. Describe three BI applications that present the results of data analyses to users, and offer examples of how businesses and government agencies can use each of these technologies.

5. Describe corporate performance management, and provide an example of how your university could use CPM.

Occupational health and safety (OH&S) is an essential concern for Adelaide Brighton Cement (www.adelaidebrighton.com.au), an Australian company with just over 700 employees. The company provides cement to the Australian construction, engineering, and infrastructure industries. Its employees operate in a production environment defined by heavy machinery and high temperatures—a risky combination unless thorough safety measures are implemented.

Vince Aurora was promoted from production manager to plant manager of the firm's Angaston Plant. In his previous position he was responsible for the safety of the employees in the production department. As plant manager, however, he was now responsible for all departments within the plant. In his former job he had been using a company database to obtain hazard and injury reports. The database was hard to use, and he could not drill down into reports for greater detail. To monitor safety throughout the entire plant, he needed a better system.

 Aurora determined that an enterprise resource planning (ERP) system would be too costly and complicated for his needs. Instead, he selected myDIALS (www.mydials.com), a hosted business intelligence (BI) system. A hosted system means that the BI application runs on myDIALS servers—not on the cement company's servers—and the company obtains the results over the Internet. As a hosted

solution, myDIALS offered minimal risk at a low cost. In addition, myDIALS could be implemented without overhauling Adelaide's existing systems.

Since Adelaide implemented myDIALS, the company's incident hazard and reporting culture has improved dramatically. Vince can view information in ways never before possible. Previously his reports were generated only once a month. In contrast, myDIALS alerts him any time a new incident occurs. Vince can also drill down into reports to find more detailed information. Ultimately, he is able to keep a much closer watch on the safety operations of his plant with this new system simply because he has better and more-timely information.

Sources: Compiled from "Adelaide Brighton Cement," *myDIALS Case Study,* www.mydials.com, accessed April 11, 2011.

Questions

1. Provide specific examples of the advantages of the myDIALS package to Adelaide.

2. What were the reasons why Vince Aurora decided not to implement an ERP system? Was this an appropriate decision? Why or why not?

RUBY'S CLUB

As Ruben and Lisa prepare to reopen Ruby's Club for business, they need to establish some measurements to help them stay on track. They have a goal of a $300,000 net profit for their first year after their grand "reopening." This is an increase from $150,000 the previous year. One of the biggest problems they face is shrinkage.

>>> Shrinkage occurs when a bartender pours someone a little more alcohol than the drink recipe calls for, gives someone a free drink, or accidentally spills some alcohol on the floor. The result is that a bottle of alcohol that (for example) should provide enough alcohol to make 40 drinks actually brings in money for only 30 drinks. This shrinkage may not seem like much, but on a large scale (including food items) it can make a huge difference in profitability.

What Ruben and Lisa need is data and decision support. This chapter refers to this as business intelligence. They need to know how to set and measure monthly and weekly goals to know whether or not they are on track to make their overall goal of $300,000 net profit when they reopen.

INTRODUCTION

Business intelligence (BI) is a broad category of applications, technologies, and processes for gathering, storing, accessing, and analyzing data to help business users make better decisions. BI applications enable decision makers to quickly ascertain the status of a business enterprise by examining key information. Managers need current, timely, and accurate information that their current systems often cannot provide. Implementing BI applications can generate significant benefits throughout a company, supporting important decisions about the firm's overall business goals.

This chapter describes information systems that support *decision making*. You begin by reviewing the manager's job and the nature of modern managerial decisions. This discussion will help you to understand why managers need computerized support. You then learn about the concepts of business intelligence for supporting individuals, groups, and entire organizations.

It is impossible to overstate the importance of business intelligence to you. Recall from Chapter 1 that the essential goal of information systems is to provide the right information to the right person in the right amount at the right time in the right format. In essence, BI achieves this goal. BI systems provide business intelligence that you can act on in a timely fashion.

It is also impossible to overstate the importance of your input into the BI process within an organization, for several reasons. First, you (the user community) will decide what data should be stored in your organization's data warehouse. You will then work closely with the MIS department to obtain these data.

Going further, you will use your organization's BI applications, probably from your first day on the job. With some BI applications, such as data mining and decision support systems, you will decide how you want to analyze the data (user-driven analysis). With other BI applications such as dashboards, you will decide which data you want to see and in which format. Again, you will work closely with your MIS department to ensure that the dashboard meets your needs.

Much of this chapter is concerned with large-scale BI applications. However, you should keep in mind that smaller organizations, and even individual users, can implement small-scale BI applications as well. For example, Excel spreadsheets provide some BI functions, as do SQL queries of a database.

The most popular BI tool by far is Excel. For years, BI vendors "fought" against the use of Excel. Eventually, however, they decided to "join it" by designing their software so that it interfaces with Excel. How does this process work? Essentially, users download plug-ins that add functionality (e.g., the ability to list the top 10 percent of customers, based on sales) to Excel (or any of the Microsoft Office products). This process can be thought of as creating "Excel on steroids." Excel then connects to the vendor's application server—which provides additional data-analysis capabilities—which in turn connects to a back-end database, such as a data mart or warehouse. This arrangement gives Excel users the functionality and access to data that are typical of sophisticated BI products, while allowing users to work with a familiar client: Excel.

Microsoft has made similar changes to its product line. In particular, Excel can now be used with MS SQL Server (a database product), and it can be utilized in advanced BI applications, such as dashboards and data mining/predictive analysis.

After you finish this chapter, you will have a basic understanding of decision making, the business intelligence process, and BI applications in organizations today. This knowledge will enable you to immediately and confidently provide input into your organization's BI processes and applications. Further, the hands-on exercises in this chapter will familiarize you with the actual use of BI software. These exercises will enable you to use your organization's BI applications to effectively analyze data and thus make better decisions. Enjoy!

5.1 | Managers and Decision Making

Management is a process by which an organization achieves its goals through the use of resources (people, money, materials, and information). These resources are considered to be *inputs*. Achieving the organization's goals is the *output* of the process. Managers oversee this process in an attempt to optimize it. A manager's success is often measured by the ratio between inputs and outputs for which he or she is responsible. This ratio is an indication of the organization's **productivity**.

The Manager's Job and Decision Making

To appreciate how information systems support managers, you must first understand the manager's job. Managers do many things, depending on their position in the organization, the type and size of the organization, the organization's policies and culture, and the personalities of the managers themselves. Despite these variations, however, all managers perform three basic roles:

1. *Interpersonal roles:* figurehead, leader, liaison
2. *Informational roles:* monitor, disseminator, spokesperson, analyzer
3. *Decisional roles:* entrepreneur, disturbance handler, resource allocator, negotiator[1]

Early information systems primarily supported the informational roles. In recent years, information systems have been developed that support all three roles. In this chapter, you will focus on the support that IT can provide for decisional roles.

A **decision** refers to a choice among two or more alternatives that individuals and groups make. Decisions are diverse and are made continuously. Decision making is a systematic process. Economist Herbert Simon described decision making as composed of three major phases: intelligence, design, and choice.[2] Once the choice is made, the decision is implemented. Figure 5.1 illustrates this process, indicating which tasks are included in each phase. Note that there is a continuous flow of information from intelligence to design to choice (bold lines), but at any phase there may be a return to a previous phase (broken lines).

(*Sources:* Media Bakery; © Sigrid Olsson/Photo Alto/Age Fotostock; Image Source Limited; Artiga Photo/Masterfile)

[1]Mintzberg, H. (1973). *The Nature of Managerial Work.* New York: Harper & Row.
[2]Simon, H. A. (1977). *The New Science of Management Decision Making.* Upper Saddle River, NJ: Prentice Hall.

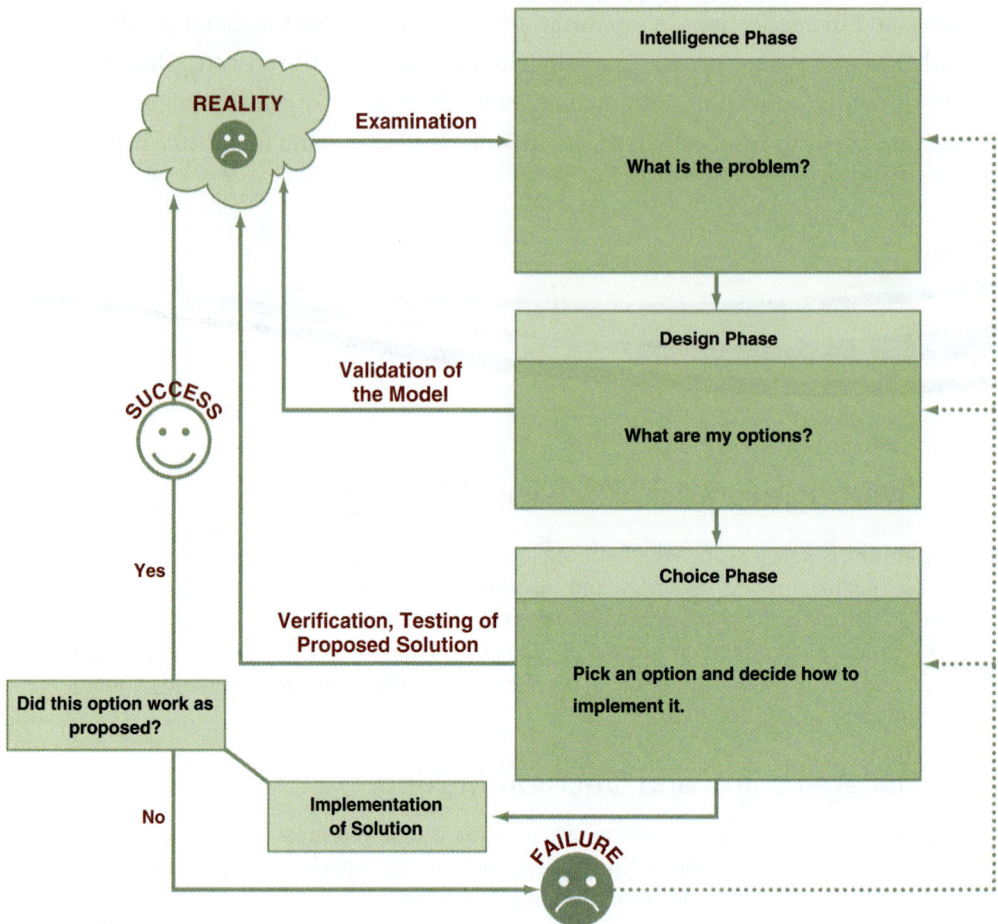

Figure 5.1 The process and phases of decision making.

This model of decision making is quite general. Undoubtedly, you have made decisions where you did not construct a model of the situation, validate your model with test data, or conduct a sensitivity analysis. The model we present here is intended to encompass all of the conditions that might occur when making a decision. For some decisions, some steps or phrases may be minimal, implicit (understood), or absent.

The decision-making process starts with the *intelligence phase*, in which managers examine a situation and identify and define the problem or opportunity. In the *design phase*, decision makers construct a model for the situation. They do this by making assumptions that simplify reality and by expressing the relationships among all the relevant variables. Managers then validate the model by using test data. Finally, decision makers set criteria for evaluating all of the potential solutions that are proposed. The *choice phase* involves selecting a solution or course of action that seems best suited to resolve the problem. This solution (the decision) is then implemented. Implementation is successful if the proposed solution solves the problem or seizes the opportunity. If the solution fails, then the process returns to the previous phases. Computer-based decision support assists managers in the decision-making process.

Why Managers Need IT Support

Making good decisions is very difficult without solid information. Information is vital for each phase and activity in the decision-making process. Even when information is available, however, decision making is difficult due to the following trends:

- The *number of alternatives* is constantly *increasing* due to innovations in technology, improved communications, the development of global markets, and the use of the Internet and e-business. A key to good decision making is to explore and compare many relevant alternatives. The more alternatives that exist, the more a decision maker needs computer-assisted searches and comparisons.

- Most decisions must be made *under time pressure*. It is often not possible to process information manually fast enough to be effective.

- Due to increased uncertainty in the decision environment, decisions are becoming more complex. It is usually necessary to *conduct a sophisticated analysis* in order to make a good decision.

- It is often necessary to rapidly access remote information, consult with experts, or conduct a group decision-making session, all without incurring large expenses. Decision makers can be situated in different locations, as can the information. Bringing them all together quickly and inexpensively can be a major challenge.

These trends create major difficulties for decision makers. Fortunately, as you will see throughout this chapter, a computerized analysis can be of enormous help.

What Information Technologies Are Available to Support Managers?

In addition to discovery, communication, and collaboration tools (Chapter 4) that provide indirect support to decision making, several other information technologies have been successfully used to support managers. As noted, these technologies are collectively referred to as business intelligence (BI). BI is closely linked to data warehousing, which provides the data needed for BI. You will now learn about additional aspects of decision making to place our discussion of BI in context. You will first look at the different types of decisions that managers face.

A Framework for Computerized Decision Analysis

To better understand BI, you will note that various types of decisions can be placed along two major dimensions: problem structure and the nature of the decision.[3] Figure 5.2 provides an overview of decision making along these two dimensions.

Nature of Decision

Type of Decision	Operational Control	Management Control	Strategic Planning	Support Needed
Unstructured	Accounts receivable, order entry [1]	Budget analysis, short-term forecasting, personnel reports, make-or-buy analysis [2]	Financial management (investment), warehouse location, distribution systems [3]	MIS, management science models, financial and statistical models
Semistructured	Production scheduling, inventory control [4]	Credit evaluation, budget preparation, plant layout, project scheduling, reward systems design [5]	Building new plant, mergers and acquisitions, new product planning, compensation planning, quality assurance planning [6]	DSS
Structured	Selecting a cover for a magazine, buying software, approving loans [7]	Negotiating, recruiting an executive, buying hardware, lobbying [8]	R & D planning, new technology development, social responsibility planning [9]	DSS, ES, neural networks
Support Needed	MIS, management science	Management science, DSS, EIS, ES	EIS, ES, neural networks	

Figure 5.2 Decision support framework. Technology is used to support the decisions shown in the column at the far right and in the bottom row.

[3]Gorry, G. A., & Scott Morton, M. S. (1971). "A Framework for Management Information Systems," *Sloan Management Review, 13*(1), pp. 55–70.

Problem Structure. The first dimension of decision making is *problem structure*, where decision-making processes fall along a continuum ranging from highly structured to highly unstructured (see the left column in Figure 5.2). *Structured decisions* refer to routine and repetitive problems for which standard solutions exist, such as inventory control. In a structured problem, the first three phases of the decision process—intelligence, design, and choice—are laid out in a particular sequence, and the procedures for obtaining the best (or at least a good enough) solution are known. Two basic criteria that are used to evaluate proposed solutions are minimizing costs and maximizing profits. These types of decisions are candidates for decision automation.

At the other extreme of problem complexity are *unstructured decisions*. These are "fuzzy," complex problems for which there are no cut-and-dried solutions. An unstructured problem is one in which there is no standardized procedure for carrying out any of the three phases. In such a problem, human intuition and judgment often play an important role in making the decision. Typical unstructured problems include planning new service offerings, hiring an executive, and choosing a set of research and development (R&D) projects for the coming year. Although BI cannot make unstructured decisions, it can provide information that assists decision makers.

Located between structured and unstructured problems are *semistructured* problems, in which only some of the decision process phases are structured. Semistructured problems require a combination of standard solution procedures and individual judgment. Examples of semistructured problems are evaluating employees, setting marketing budgets for consumer products, performing capital acquisition analysis, and trading bonds.

The Nature of Decisions. The second dimension of decision support deals with the *nature of decisions*. All managerial decisions fall into one of three broad categories:

1. *Operational control:* executing specific tasks efficiently and effectively
2. *Management control:* acquiring and using resources efficiently in accomplishing organizational goals
3. *Strategic planning:* the long-range goals and policies for growth and resource allocation

These categories are displayed along the top row of Figure 5.2.

Note: Strategic decisions define the context in which management control decisions are made. In turn, management control decisions define the context in which operational control decisions are made.

The Decision Matrix. The three primary classes of problem structure and the three broad categories of the nature of decisions can be combined in a decision-support matrix that consists of nine cells, as diagrammed in Figure 5.2. Lower-level managers usually perform tasks in cells 1, 2, and 4. The tasks in cells 3, 5, and 7 are usually the responsibility of middle managers and professional staff. Finally, tasks in cells 6, 8, and 9 are generally carried out by senior executives.

Computer Support for Structured Decisions. Examples of computer support that might be used for the nine cells in the matrix are displayed in the right-hand column and the bottom row of Figure 5.2. Structured and some semistructured decisions, especially of the operational and management control type, have been supported by computers since the 1950s. Decisions of this type are made in all functional areas, but particularly in finance and operations management.

Problems that lower-level managers encounter on a regular basis typically have a high level of structure. Examples are capital budgeting (for example, replacement of equipment), allocating resources, distributing merchandise, and controlling inventory. For each type of structured decision, prescribed solutions have been developed, which often include mathematical formulas that can often be used. This approach is called *management science* or *operations research*, and it is also executed with the aid of computers.

BEFORE *YOU GO ON . . .*

1. Describe the decision-making process proposed by Simon.

2. You are registering for classes next semester. Apply the decision-making process to your decision about how many and which courses to take. Is your decision structured, semistructured, or unstructured?

3. Consider your decision-making process when registering for classes next semester. Explain how information technology supports (or does not support) each phase of this process.

RUBY'S CLUB QUESTIONS

1. Discuss how the three roles of a manager (interpersonal, informational, and decisional) might play out as Ruben and Lisa tackle shrinkage. Will bartenders become defensive? Should they share financial information? How much should they monitor the bartenders?

2. Which of the four reasons that a manager needs IT support do you feel is most applicable in this situation? Is it that the number of alternatives is increasing? Time pressure? Uncertainty? Or the need to bring remote individuals and data into the picture?

3. Is the shrinkage problem a structured, semistructured, or unstructured situation? If it is structured, what controls may be put in place to handle it? If it is unstructured, what policies may be instituted to help rein in the problem?

4. Does this situation fall into operational control, management control, or strategic planning? Or does it fall into all three?

5. In what ways do you see that IT could provide help to Ruben and Lisa as they try to make their $300,000 net profit and control shrinkage?

Student Activity | 5.1

Objective: You will get a sense of how data are used in decision making using a situation to which everyone should be able to relate.

Chapter Connection: This activity relates to Section 5.1 and Learning Objective 1 in this chapter.

Prerequisites: You should have read Section 5.1

Activity:

View the video "Why Data Matters" and read the case at the bottom of the screen.

www.baselinemag.com/c/a/Business-Intelligence/
FDNY-Puts-Inspection-Data-to-Work-335129

Deliverables:

Prepare answers for the following questions:

What other data could the FDNY use, and how might they use them? Where would they get them? Think "outside the box."

Quiz Questions:

1. Information cannot give you a competitive advantage (True or False)

2. Tweets on Twitter are considered data. (True or False)

3. Capturing the data is not the problem anymore, _____ is.

Discussion Questions:

1. What kinds of data could your favorite sports team use to play a better game?

2. What kinds of data could your favorite café use to make your experience better?

5.2 | What Is Business Intelligence?

To provide users with access to corporate data, many organizations are implementing data warehouses and data marts, which you learned about in Chapter 3. Users analyze the data in warehouses and marts using a wide variety of BI tools. Many vendors offer integrated packages of these tools under the overall label of business intelligence (BI) software. Major BI vendors include SAS (www.sas.com), Hyperion (www.hyperion.com, now owned by Oracle), Business Objects (www.businessobjects.com, now owned by SAP), Information Builders (www.informationbuilders.com), SPSS (www.spss.com, now owned by IBM), and Cognos (www.ibm.com/cognos).

As has been shown, BI is vital to modern decision making and organizational performance. Let us now consider in greater detail the technical foundation for BI and the wide variety of ways that BI can be used.

The term *business intelligence* is relatively new. Business and IT analyst Howard Dresner coined the term in 1989 while he was an analyst at Gartner, a market research firm. The term is especially popular in industry, where it is used as an umbrella term that encompasses all decision support applications.

BI encompasses not only applications but also technologies and processes. It includes both "getting data in" (to a data mart or warehouse) and "getting data out" (through BI applications).

In addition, a significant change is taking place within the BI environment. In the past, organizations used BI only to support management. Today, however, BI applications are increasingly available to front-line personnel (e.g., call center operators), suppliers, customers, and even regulators. These groups rely on BI to provide them with the most current information.

The Scope of Business Intelligence

The use of BI in organizations varies considerably. In smaller organizations, BI may be limited to Excel spreadsheets. In larger ones, BI is often enterprisewide, and it includes applications such as data mining/predictive analytics, dashboards, and data visualization. It is important to recognize that the importance of BI to organizations continues to grow. It is not an exaggeration to say that for many firms, BI is now a requirement for competing in the marketplace, as illustrated in "IT's About Business 5.1."

IT's ABOUT BUSINESS | 5.1

Data Analytics Helps Kelley Blue Book Remain Competitive

Since 1926 Kelley Blue Book (www.kbb.com) essentially has been a publishing company known for its guide to used and new car values. In the 2000s, however, *Blue Book* sales began to decline, and the company needed to devise new strategies to generate revenue and compete with new online rivals, such as www.cars.com, www.edmunds.com, and home.autos.msn.com. As Kelley analyzed its situation, it concluded that data and information were products of the company, not just by-products. That is, Kelley realized that it was actually an "information company."

Kelley already possessed vast amounts of data on new and used cars. The company turned to data analytics to utilize those data more effectively. The first step was to update the company's data management infrastructure. Until that time, the company's appraisers had collected information by hand, recorded it in notebooks, and faxed it back to headquarters, where it was keyed into a database system.

Before Kelley could complete this update, it had to determine what data it actually had. To achieve this objective, the company performed an audit of its data, including both clickstream data collected from its Web site and third-party data.

Kelley invested in a data warehouse to collect, integrate, and house the data. In addition, it purchased business intelligence and data analytics software from MicroStrategy (www.microstrategy.com) and the SAS Institute (www.sas.com) in order to analyze its warehouse data more efficiently and effectively.

The next step was to determine how Kelley could utilize data analytics to improve its existing services. Kelley discovered, for example, that by using the software to integrate third-party data, it could refine its car value estimates on its Web site more quickly and accurately than ever before.

Kelley also developed applications to make money with its new data analytics capabilities. For instance, the company created an application designed to help car owners determine the best time to sell. This application uses historical data to estimate when a particular car make and model will need significant repairs. Thus, if a particular type of car usually needs a new water pump at a certain mileage mark, the owner may want to sell it before reaching that mark.

Kelley is also considering adding a widget to its Web site that will forecast likely care prices over a three-month period. This application will help potential buyers time their purchases when prices will be the lowest. Another application under development would help buyers understand how much negotiating room they have with dealers based on recent sales of similar cars in the same geographic region.

The bottom line is that data analytics has enabled Kelley to provide more rapid and accurate quotes. In addition, data analytics is helping Kelley develop new sources of revenue, which are essential if the company is to remain competitive with the online companies.

Questions

1. Provide specific examples of other revenue-generating applications that Kelley could develop from its data-mining application.

2. Analyze this case in terms of the three phases of the decision-making model (intelligence, design, and choice).

Sources: Compiled from L. Davidson, "Seller Beware: Don't Give Away the Store When Selling," *Forbes*, February 3, 2011; J. Kelly, "Data Analytics Software, Data Management Transforms Kelley Blue Book," *SearchBusinessAnalytics*, November 16, 2010; R. O'Regan, "How Kelley Blue Book Uses Web Analytics to Fuel Its Ad-Supported Model," www.emediavitals.com, October 6, 2010; H. Elliot, "The Easiest Cars to Bargain For," *Forbes*, August 10, 2010; www.kbb.com, www.microstrategy.com, www.sas.com, accessed April 5, 2011.

Not all organizations use BI in the same way. For example, some organizations employ a single or a few applications, while others utilize enterprisewide BI. The following subsections examine three specific BI targets that represent different levels of change:

- The development of a single or a few related BI applications
- The development of infrastructure to support enterprisewide BI
- Support for organizational transformation

These targets differ in terms of their focus; scope; level of sponsorship, commitment, and required resources; technical architecture; impact on personnel and business processes; and benefits.

The Development of a Single or a Few Related BI Applications. This BI target is often a point solution for a departmental need, such as campaign management in marketing. Sponsorship, approval, funding, impacts, and benefits typically occur at the departmental level. For this target, organizations usually create a data mart to store the necessary data. Organizations must be careful that the mart—an "independent" application—does not become a "data silo" that stores data that are inconsistent with and cannot be integrated with data used elsewhere in the organization. As you see in IT's About Business 5.2, North Carolina State University uses analytics in its Office of Technology Transfer.

IT's ABOUT BUSINESS | 5.2

North Carolina State University Uses Business Analytics to Monetize Intellectual Property

North Carolina State University (www.ncsu.edu) had a problem. The university needed a new process to make money from its huge number of scientific advancements and university-invented technologies by matching these innovations with appropriate research partners and sponsors. The Office of Technology Transfer at NC State (www.ncsu.edu/ott) is responsible for transferring university-developed innovations to the marketplace and interacting with partners.

The director of the office noted that the university has a huge portfolio of intellectual property (IP) assets, yet the office was understaffed. The office had 7 licensing professionals and 12 support professionals who managed some 3,000 technological innovations. The professionals were always considering what types of research partnerships the university could establish between an industry partner and a faculty member.

The office referred to the most time-consuming component of the technology-transfer process as *triage*. In triage, the licensing professionals review an innovation to assess its market potential, determine whether any patents already exist in that area, and, if necessary, seek patent protection in order to move early-stage technologies to market. The triage process typically took between two and four months. The licensing professionals spent much of that time trying to identify the right partners in a particular industry so they could be briefed on the project. This process required the professionals to search vast stores of documents, review Security and Exchange Commission (SEC) reports, keep up with blogs to see which company's research and development efforts

have been successful and which ones have failed, and attend industry trade meetings to gain knowledge of potential partners.

To alleviate the time-consuming technology-transfer process, the office decided to acquire IBM's "Big Data" analytics technology, which mines large amounts of unstructured Web data. The "Big Data" analysis is based on factors such as business relevancy, government policies, market needs, and trends. As input for the analytics package, the office identified key words, specific phrasing dedicated to those key words, and specific documents.

The analytics package interfaced with the university's technology transfer database. This database is used for all the agreement tracking, invention-disclosure tracking, compliance, and patent management for the university. The office also uses the database to launch marketing activities to potential partners.

IBM's analytics package discovered hidden business opportunities that the old triage system probably would not have, while condensing the triage process to 7 to 10 days. The package also ranks potential partners based on how they meet the university's specifications. For example, a team of researchers at the university is investigating new strains of *Salmonella* for use in vaccines. With IBM's technology, it took less than one week for the university to analyze 1.4 million Web pages, including opinion blogs, social networks, and documents.

The most outstanding benefit of the analytics software, however, has been to free up a large amount of time for the licensing professionals. These individuals can now focus on raising the university's technology profile and establishing new business opportunities. They also can help launch new companies based on some of the technologies developed within the university. In mid-2011, some 70 companies developed by faculty, staff, or students had been launched.

Questions

1. What advantages does the analytics software provide for the Office of Technology Transfer?

2. Should the analytics software in the Office of Technology Transfer be used in other departments in the university? Why or why not? Support your answer.

Sources: Compiled from D. Henschen, "IBM Analytics Help NC State Sell Tech Innovations," *InformationWeek*, August 20, 2010; S. Nunziata, "Business Analytics: Turning IP Into Opportunity," *CIO Insight*, August 17, 2010; S. Hamm, "Big Data Could Help NC State Bring Faculty Innovations to Market," *Building a Smarter Planet* ("A Smarter Planet Blog"), August 11, 2010; "IBM Analytics 'Search Engine' Helps N.C. State Save Money," *eSchool News*, August 11, 2010; www.ncsu.edu, www.ncsu.edu/ott, accessed April 7, 2011.

The Development of Infrastructure to Support Enterprisewide BI. This BI target supports current and future BI needs. A crucial component of BI at this level is an enterprise data warehouse. Because it is an enterprisewide initiative, senior management often provides sponsorship, approval, and funding. In addition, the impacts and benefits are felt throughout the organization.

An example of this target is the 3M corporation. Traditionally 3M's various divisions had operated independently and had utilized separate decision support platforms. Not only was this arrangement costly, but it also prevented 3M from integrating the data and presenting a "single face" to its customers. Thus, for example, sales representatives did not know whether or how business customers were interacting with other 3M divisions. The solution was to develop an enterprise data warehouse that enabled 3M to operate as an integrated company. As an added benefit, the cost of implementing this system was covered by savings resulting from the consolidation of the various platforms.

Support for Organizational Transformation. With this target, BI is used to fundamentally transform the ways in which a company competes in the marketplace. BI supports a new business model, and it enables the business strategy. Because of the scope and importance of these changes, critical elements such as sponsorship, approval, and funding originate at the highest organizational levels. The impact on personnel and processes can be significant, and the benefits are organizationwide.

Harrah's Entertainment provides a good example of this BI target. Traditionally, Harrah had managed its various properties as "independent fiefdoms." Then, in the early 1990s, gambling on riverboats and Indian reservations became legal. Harrah's senior management perceived this as an opportunity to expand the company's properties. In addition, the company decided to implement a new business model that would enable it to operate all of these properties in an integrated way. At the heart of this model was the collection and use of customer data and the creation of a customer loyalty program, known as Total Rewards, that encouraged customers to play across all of Harrah's casinos. To implement this strategy, Harrah's had to create a BI infrastructure (a data warehouse) that collected data from casino, hotel, and special event systems (e.g., wine-tasting weekends) across the various customer touchpoints (e.g., slot machines, table games, and Internet). Harrah's used these data to reward loyal customers and reach out to them in personal and appealing ways—for example, through promotional offers created using BI. As a result, the company became a leader in the gaming industry.

In Chapter 3, you studied the basics of data warehouses and data marts. In this section, you have seen how important data warehouses and marts are to the different ways that organizations use BI. In the next section, you will learn how the user community can analyze the data in warehouses and marts, how the results of these analyses are presented to users, and how organizations can use the results of these analyses.

BEFORE *YOU GO ON . . .*

1. Define BI.

2. Discuss the breadth of support provided by BI applications to organizational employees.

3. Identify and discuss the three basic targets of BI.

Student Activity | 5.2

Objective: Students need to understand how data can be used to provide intelligence. By looking at this application, you should begin to see how data must be captured, must be categorized, and must be flexible for reporting. The video illustrates the dimensions of a cube without calling it a cube, mentions a data warehouse as the repository of all the data, and shows "drill down" without calling it such.

Chapter Connection: This activity fits with Section 5.2 and Learning Objective 2 for this chapter.

Prerequisites: You should have read Section 5.2 before starting the activity. You also should be familiar with the notion of a Web page.

Activity:

Google Analytics is a free service offered by Google that generates detailed statistics about the visitors to a Web site. View the following video for insight into how the data are captured and made available with Google Analytics.

www.youtube.com/watch?v=Of3uc2Aum-o&feature=related

Deliverables:

Based on the terms that were introduced in the video, answer the following:

1. What is a bounce rate?

2. What is the difference between a visit and a new visit?

3. Define the three main categories of Web traffic.

4. What is the concept of a key word, and how is it used by Google Analytics?

Quiz Questions:

1. A _____ is how long a visitor stays on a Web site.

2. True or False? In Google Analytics, the number of new visits to a Web site is included in the number of visits to a Web site.

3. When a visitor gets to a Web site by typing in the address (or URL) of the Web site, it is considered which type of Web traffic?

   (a) Referring site
   (b) Indirect traffic
   (c) Direct traffic
   (d) Search engine
   (e) None of the above

Discussion Questions:

1. What is a "cookie," as referred to in the video?

2. The text of this chapter mentions the notion of "drill down." Did you see any evidence of drill down in the video?

3. The video addresses the visual of a cube holding data for business intelligence and a cube having dimensions. What do you think the dimensions are of the visit data cube in Google Analytics?

5.3 | Business Intelligence Applications for Data Analysis

A good strategy to study the ways in which organizations use business intelligence applications is to consider how the users analyze data, how the results of their analyses are presented to them, and how managers and executives implement these results. Recall from Chapter 3 that the data are stored in a data warehouse or data mart. The user community analyzes these data using a variety of BI applications. The results of these analyses can be presented to users via other BI applications. Finally, managers and executives put the overall results to good use. You will become familiar with data analysis, presentation, and use in depth in the next three sections.

A variety of BI applications for analyzing data are available. They include multidimensional analysis (also called online analytical processing, or OLAP), data mining, and decision support systems.

Multidimensional Analysis or Online Analytical Processing

Some BI applications include **online analytical processing (OLAP)** capabilities, also referred to as **multidimensional analysis**. OLAP involves "slicing and dicing" data stored in a dimensional format, drilling down the data to greater detail, and aggregating the data.

Consider our example from Chapter 3. Recall Figure 3.10 showing the data cube. The product is on the x-axis, geography is on the y-axis, and time is on the z-axis. Now, suppose you want to know how many nuts the company sold in the West region in 2009. You would slice and dice the cube using nuts as the specific measure for product, West as the measure for geography, and 2009 as the measure for time. The value(s) in the cell(s) that remain after our slicing and dicing is (are) the answer to our question. You might also want to know how many nuts were sold in January 2009; this is an example of drilling down. Alternatively, you might want to know how many nuts were sold during 2008–2010, which is an example of aggregation, also called "rollup."

Data Mining

Data mining refers to the process of searching for valuable business information in a large database, data warehouse, or data mart. Data mining can perform two basic operations: (1) predicting trends and behaviors and (2) identifying previously unknown patterns. BI applications typically provide users with a view of what has happened. Data mining helps to explain why it is happening, and it predicts what will happen in the future.

Regarding the first operation, data mining automates the process of finding predictive information in large databases. Questions that traditionally required extensive hands-on analysis can now be answered directly and quickly from the data. A typical example of a predictive problem is *targeted marketing*. Data mining can use data from past promotional mailings to identify those people who are most likely to respond favorably to future mailings. Another example of a predictive problem is forecasting bankruptcy and other forms of default.

Data mining can also identify previously hidden patterns in a single step. For example, it can analyze retail sales data to discover seemingly unrelated products that people often purchase together. The classic example is beer and diapers. Data mining found that young men tend to buy beer and diapers at the same time when they shop at a convenience store.

One significant pattern-discovery operation is detecting fraudulent credit card transactions. After you use your credit card for a time, a pattern emerges of the typical ways you use your card—the places you use your card, the amount you spend, and so on. If your card is stolen and used fraudulently, this usage is often different from your pattern. Data mining tools can discern this difference and bring this issue to your attention.

Numerous data mining applications are used in business and in other fields. According to a Gartner report (www.gartner.com), most of the Fortune 1000 companies worldwide currently use data mining, as the following representative examples illustrate. Note that in most cases the intent of data mining is to identify a business opportunity in order to create a sustainable competitive advantage.

- *Retailing and sales:* Predicting sales, preventing theft and fraud, and determining correct inventory levels and distribution schedules among outlets. For example, retailers such as AAFES (stores on military bases) use Fraud Watch from SAP (www.sap.com) to combat fraud by employees in their 1,400 stores.

- *Banking:* Forecasting levels of bad loans and fraudulent credit card use, predicting credit card spending by new customers, and determining which kinds of customers will best respond to (and qualify for) new loan offers.

- *Manufacturing and production:* Predicting machinery failures, and finding key factors that help optimize manufacturing capacity.

- *Insurance:* Forecasting claim amounts and medical coverage costs, classifying the most important elements that affect medical coverage, and predicting which customers will buy new insurance policies.

- *Policework:* Tracking crime patterns, locations, and criminal behavior; identifying attributes to assist in solving criminal cases.

- *Healthcare:* Correlating demographics of patients with critical illnesses, and developing better insights on how to identify and treat symptoms and their causes.

- *Marketing:* Classifying customer demographics that can be used to predict which customers will respond to a mailing or buy a particular product.

Decision Support Systems

Decision support systems (DSS) combine models and data in an attempt to analyze semi-structured and some unstructured problems with extensive user involvement. **Models** are simplified representations, or abstractions, of reality. DSS enable business managers and analysts to access data interactively, to manipulate these data, and to conduct appropriate analyses.

Decision support systems can enhance learning and contribute to all levels of decision making. DSS also employ mathematical models. In addition, they have the related capabilities of sensitivity analysis, what-if analysis, and goal-seeking analysis, which you will learn about next. You should keep in mind that these three types of analysis are useful for any type of decision support application. For example, Excel supports them.

Sensitivity Analysis. *Sensitivity analysis* is the study of the impact that changes in one or more parts of a decision-making model have on other parts. Most sensitivity analyses examine the impact that changes in input variables have on output variables.

Most models include two types of input variables: decision variables and environmental variables. "What is our reorder point for these raw materials?" is a decision variable (internal to the organization). "What will the rate of inflation be?" is an environmental variable (external to the organization). The output in this example would be the total cost of raw materials. The point of a sensitivity analysis is usually to determine the impact of environmental variables on the result of the analysis.

Sensitivity analysis is extremely valuable because it enables the system to adapt to changing conditions and to the varying requirements of different decision-making situations. It provides a better understanding of the model and the problem that the model purports to describe.

What-If Analysis. A model builder must make predictions and assumptions regarding the input data, many of which are based on the assessment of uncertain futures. The results depend on the accuracy of these assumptions, which can be highly subjective. *What-if analysis* attempts to predict the impact of a change in the assumptions (input data) on the proposed solution. For example, what will happen to the total inventory cost *if* the originally assumed cost of carrying inventories is not 10 percent but 12 percent? In a well-designed BI system, managers themselves can interactively ask the computer these types of questions as many times as needed.

Goal-Seeking Analysis. *Goal-seeking analysis* represents a "backward" solution approach. It attempts to find the value of the inputs necessary to achieve a desired level of output. For example, let's say that an initial BI analysis predicted a profit of $2 million. Management might want to know what sales volume would be necessary to generate a profit of $3 million. To find out, the company would perform a goal-seeking analysis.

However, managers cannot simply press a button that says "increase sales." Some action(s) will be necessary to make the sales increase possible. The action(s) could be to lower prices, to increase research and development, to provide a higher commission rate for the sales force, to increase advertising, to take some other action, or to implement some combination of these actions. Whatever the action is, it will cost money, and the goal-seeking analysis must take this into account.

BEFORE *YOU GO ON . . .*

1. Describe multidimensional analysis, and construct a data cube with information from "IT's About Business 5.1." (*Hint:* You must decide which three business dimensions you would like to analyze in your data cube.)
2. What are the two basic operations of data mining?
3. What is the purpose of decision support systems?

RUBY'S CLUB QUESTIONS

1. Ruben and Lisa hope to use Excel as their decision support tool. Which of the analyses would be best suited for their goal and shrinkage problem: the what-if analysis, the goal-seeking analysis, or the sensitivity analysis? Or do you think it would be a combination of all three?
2. What tools can you find in Excel that would support these analyses? (*Hint:* Google "Sensitivity Analysis Excel.")

Student Activity 5.3

Objective: This activity provides examples of data mining and stresses its mathematical nature.

Chapter Connection: This activity supports Section 5.3 and Learning Objective 3 of this chapter.

Prerequisites: You should have read Section 5.3 before beginning this activity.

Activity:

View the following video:

http://video.google.com/videoplay?docid=-7252045691453600738#

Deliverables:

Based on the terms that were introduced in the video, answer the following:

1. What is the goal of data mining?
2. What is classification?

3. What is clustering?
4. How does a person know if a model is right?

Quiz Questions:

1. _____ is discovering groups and structures that are somehow "similar."

2. _____ is generalizing a known structure to apply new data.

3. _____ _____ is used to uncover relationships among data.

Discussion Questions:

1. How do you feel about companies having access to your personal data?

2. What is the current Facebook policy on member privacy?

3. Some say the goal of data mining is to prove what relationships you already know and to find ones you didn't already know. What do you think of that statement?

4. Excel has a function called Pivot tables that can be used to summarize data in a data set to provide some insights into relationships within the data. View the following video about how to build them: www.youtube.com/watch?v=7zHLnUCtfUk&feature=related. How might you use Pivot tables with order data for a company?

5.4 | Business Intelligence Applications for Presenting Results

The results of the types of data analyses you just learned about can be presented with dashboards and data visualization technologies. Today, users increasingly rely on data that are real time or almost real time. Therefore, you will note a discussion of real-time BI in this section.

Dashboards

Dashboards evolved from executive information systems, which were information systems designed specifically for the information needs of top executives. However, as you saw in this chapter's opening case, today all employees, business partners, and customers can use digital dashboards.

A **dashboard** provides easy access to timely information and direct access to management reports. It is very user friendly and is supported by graphics. Of special importance, it enables managers to examine exception reports and drill down into detailed data. Table 5.1 summarizes the various capabilities that are common to many dashboards. In addition, some of the capabilities discussed in this section are now part of many BI products, as illustrated in Figure 5.3.

One outstanding example of a dashboard is the "Bloomberg." Bloomberg LLP (www.bloomberg.com), a privately held company, provides a subscription service that sells financial data, software to analyze these data, trading tools, and news (electronic, print, TV, and radio). All of this information is accessible through a color-coded Bloomberg keyboard that displays the desired information on a computer screen, either the user's

TABLE 5.1 The Capabilities of Dashboards

Capability	Description
Drill down	The ability to go to details, at several levels. Can be done through a series of menus or by clicking on a drillable portion of the screen.
Critical success factors (CSFs)	The factors most critical for the success of business. Can be organizational, industry, departmental, or for individual workers.
Key performance indicators (KPIs)	The specific measures of CSFs.
Status access	The latest data available on KPIs or some other metric, often in real time.
Trend analysis	Short-term, medium-term, and long-term trend of KPIs or metrics, which are projected using forecasting methods.
Exception reporting	Reports that highlight deviations larger than certain thresholds. Reports may include only deviations.

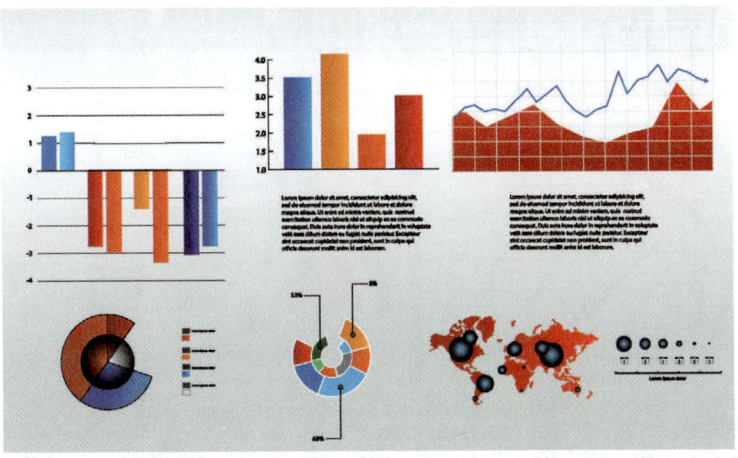

Figure 5.3 Sample performance dashboard. (*Source:* Dundas Software, www.dundas.com/dashboard/online-examples/screenshots/Marketing-Dashboard.aspx)

or one that Bloomberg provides. Users can also set up their own computers to access the service without a Bloomberg keyboard. The subscription service plus the keyboard is called the "Bloomberg." It literally represents a do-it-yourself dashboard, because users can customize their information feeds as well as the look and feel of those feeds (see Figure 5.4).

In another example, Figure 5.5 shows a human resources dashboard/scorecard developed by iDashboards, one of the leading BI software vendors. At a glance, users can see employee productivity, hours, team, department, and division performance in graphical, tabular, summary, and detailed form. The selector box to the left enables the user to easily change between specific analyst to compare their performance.

A unique and interesting application of dashboards to support the informational needs of executives is the Management Cockpit. Essentially, a Management Cockpit is a strategic management room containing an elaborate set of dashboards that enable top-level decision makers to pilot their businesses better. The goal is to create an environment that encourages more efficient management meetings and boosts team performance via effective communication. To help achieve this goal, the dashboard graphically displays key performance indicators and information relating to critical success factors on the walls of

Figure 5.4 A Bloomberg terminal. (*Source:* Corbis/Image Source Limited.)

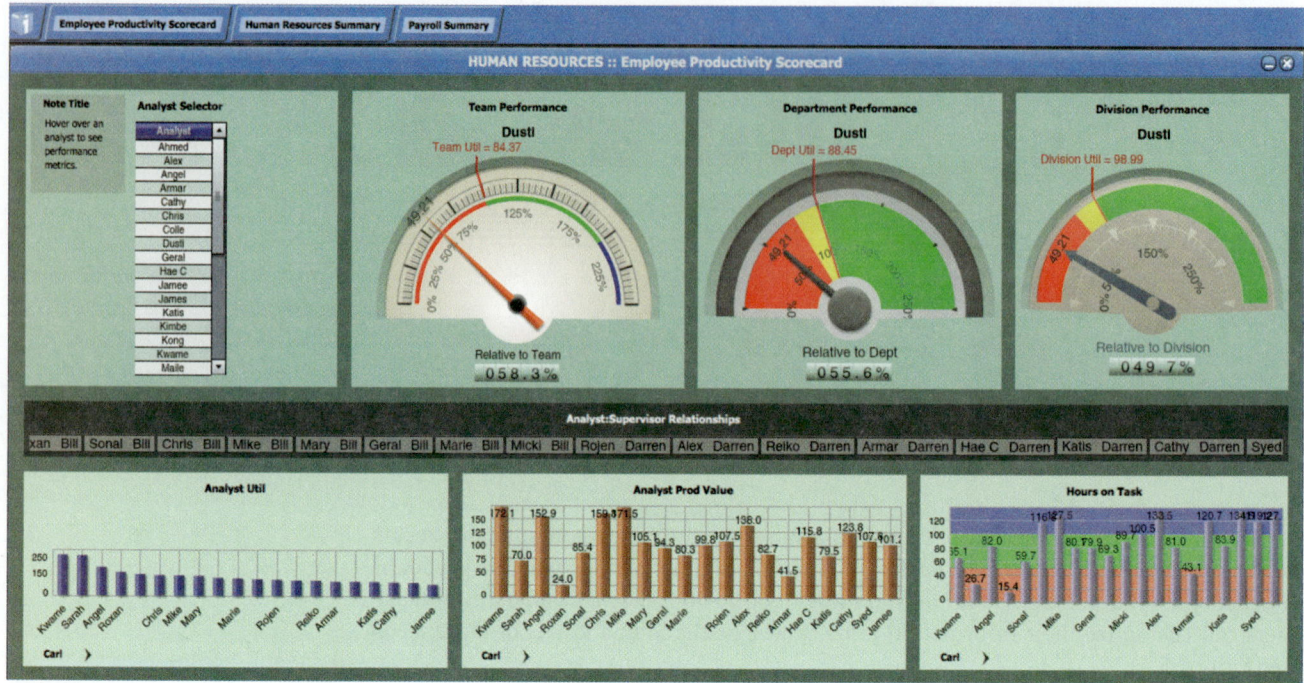

Figure 5.5 A human resource dashboard/scorecard. (*Source:* MicroStrategy.)

 a meeting room, called the Management Cockpit Room (see Figure 5.6). The cockpitlike arrangement of instrument panels and displays helps managers visualize how all the different factors in the business interrelate.

Within the room, the four walls are designated by color: Black, Red, Blue, and White. The Black Wall displays the principal success factors and financial indicators. The Red Wall measures market performance. The Blue Wall projects the performance of internal processes and employees. The White Wall indicates the status of strategic projects. The Flight Deck, a six-screen, high-end PC, enables executives to drill down to detailed information. External information needed for competitive analyses can easily be imported into the room.

Board members and other executives hold meetings in the Cockpit Room. Managers also meet there with the comptroller to discuss current business issues. For this purpose, the Management Cockpit can implement various what-if scenarios. It also provides a common basis for information and communication. Finally, it supports efforts to translate a corporate strategy into concrete activities by identifying performance indicators.

Figure 5.6 Management Cockpit. (*Source:* The Management Cockpit is a registered trademark of SAP, created by Professor M. Georges.)

Data Visualization Technologies

After data have been processed, they can be presented to users in visual formats such as text, graphics, and tables. This process, known as *data visualization*, makes IT applications more attractive and understandable to users. Data visualization is becoming more and more popular on the Web for decision support. A variety of visualization methods and software packages that support decision making are available. Two particularly valuable applications are geographic information systems and reality mining.

Geographic Information Systems. A **geographic information system (GIS)** is a computer-based system for capturing, integrating, manipulating, and displaying data using digitized maps. Its most distinguishing characteristic is that every record or digital object has an identified geographical location. This process, called *geocoding*, enables users to generate information for planning, problem solving, and decision making. In addition, the graphical format makes it easy for managers to visualize the data.

Today, relatively inexpensive, fully functional PC-based GIS packages are readily available. Representative GIS software vendors are ESRI (www.esri.com), Intergraph (www.intergraph.com), and Pitney Bowes Mapinfo (www.pbinsight.com/welcome/mapinfo). In addition, both government sources and private vendors provide diversified commercial GIS data. Some of these GIS packages are free—for example, CD-ROMs from Mapinfo and downloadable material from www.esri.com and http://data.geocomm.com.

There are countless applications of GISs to improve decision making in both the public and private sectors. The following example shows how the Environmental Systems Research Institute (ESRI; www.esri.com) impacts a huge number of organizations.

EXAMPLE

The mission of ESRI is to make it easier to turn complex data into understandable, insightful visual information, or to use GISs to understand how things are changing and to describe these changes in maps. ESRI has impacted any number of organizations in such areas as land use, urban planning, disaster response, sustainable development, mining and oil exploration, wildlife preservation, epidemic planning, and humanitarian relief.

ESRI recently adopted a policy of making its applications available to nonprofit organizations for free. As Jack Dangermond, ESRI's founder, explains, "Our world is evolving without consideration, and the result is a loss of biodiversity, energy issues, and congestion in cities. But geography, if used correctly, can be used to redesign sustainable and more livable cities."

Examples of nonprofit organizations using ESRI software abound. Residents of Glendale, California, can text the location of potholes, trash, and graffiti to city officials via an online ESRI map. During the BP disaster in the Gulf of Mexico, ESRI put up a Web site that combined data on wind and Gulf currents with Flickr photos and YouTube videos to map the spill and monitor the cleanup. BP and the Coast Guard used the site in setting up booms and sending in oil-skimming ships.

Sources: Compiled from M. Bahree, "A Sense of Where You Are," *Forbes*, October 11, 2010; www.esri.com, accessed April 2, 2011.

Reality Mining. One important emerging trend is the integration of GISs and global positioning systems (GPSs, discussed in Chapter 10). Using GISs and GPSs together can produce an interesting new type of technology, called reality mining. **Reality mining** allows analysts to extract information from the usage patterns of mobile phones and other wireless devices. If you want to catch a cab in New York City, the next example will show you how.

EXAMPLE

Is there some kind of secret formula for finding a cab in New York City? Yes. The most popular corners to catch a yellow cab in Manhattan can now be pinpointed at any hour of any day of the week, thanks to a record of

90 million actual taxi trips that have been tracked by the city. The city's Taxi and Limousine Commission (TLC) hopes the information can be used to create helpful tie-ins for customers, like the smart phone app that lets mobile users locate the ideal nearby corner to hail a cab.

Using the city's GPS data, Sense Networks (www.sensenetworks.com) examined the pickup point of every New York City cab ride taken in a six-month period. The result was a free mobile application called CabSense (www.cabsense.com). The app lets would-be taxi riders view a map of nearby street corners, ranked by the number of taxi hails they attract at that hour on that day of the week. The company has an algorithm to take into account parades, street construction, and other factors that could skew the results.

Here are two results from CabSense. The Upper East Side has a more cab-dependent culture than its neighbors across Central Park. More than 2 million trips started on the Upper East Side in May 2010, nearly twice as many as on the Upper West Side. Also, a neighborhood-by-neighborhood breakdown confirms what most New Yorkers already know: It is easier to get a cab below 96th Street in Manhattan, and much harder above 96th street.

Sources: Compiled from M. Grynbaum, "Need a Cab? New Analysis Shows Where to Find One," *New York Times*, April 2, 2010; www.sensenetworks.com, www.cabsense.com, accessed April 7, 2011.

Real-Time BI

Until recently, BI has focused on the use of historical data. This focus has changed with the emergence of technology for capturing, storing, and using real-time data. Real-time BI enables users to employ multidimensional analysis, data mining, and decision support systems to analyze data in real time. In addition, it helps organizations to make decisions and to interact with customers in new ways. It also influences how workers can be monitored and rewarded, as presented in "IT's About Business 5.3."

IT's ABOUT BUSINESS | 5.3

1-800 CONTACTS

1-800 CONTACTS (www.1800contacts.com) is the world's largest contact lens store, selling as many contact lenses as 2,500 retail optical shops combined. Customers can order over the Internet, by mail or fax, at Walmart, or by phone with nearly 300 customer service agents.

1-800 CONTACTS uses dashboards to monitor and motivate the customer service agents who handle sales calls. The company updates the dashboards every 15 minutes, and the service agents and their supervisors can measure their performance based on key metrics and compare their performance to other operators. The operators' compensation is based in part on this information.

Figure 5.7 presents a typical operator's dashboard. The gauges on the left are for the current day, and they indicate how the operator is performing on the closing ratio, average sale, and calls/hour metrics. The bar charts to the right show how the agent is performing throughout the day. The straight line displays the agent's average performance for the month for the three metrics. You can see that the operator is doing better than his monthly average on closing ratio and average sale, but only in the 1:00 PM hour has he done better on calls/hour. At the right of the screen is a customer testimony about favorable service. The ribbon at the bottom of the screen identifies the top five performers on various metrics.

In addition, the company calculates a Call Center Incentive (CCI) index for each operator, which it uses to determine the agents' monthly compensation. The CCI formula integrates a number of criteria: closing ratio index, average order size index, hours worked,

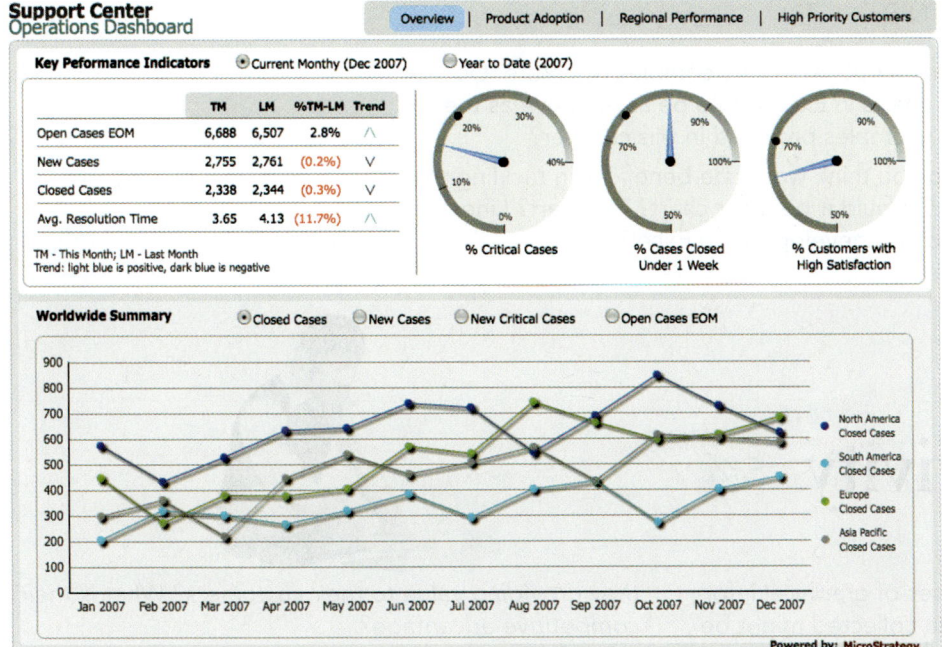

Figure 5.7 1-800 CONTACTS customers service agent dashboard.

bonus points for work such as setting up appointments, and a quality index that is based on audits of the quality of the operator's interactions with customers. The top 80 percent of agents receive monthly bonuses, which can exceed $1,000 for the very best agents.

Executive dashboards are used to indicate how the business is performing at any point during the day, how the business is performing relative to four weeks and a year ago, the performance of the various channels, and the predicted sales for the day. The last item is especially valuable. Based on an analysis of historical and current data, the company can generally predict by 10:00 AM each morning the end-of-the-day sales within a few thousand dollars. How can 1-800 CONTACTs utilize this capability? As one example, a marketing manager can monitor the effectiveness of a new campaign and quickly modify it if it is not producing results.

The operators' dashboards are highly effective. After implementing the dashboards, the company's revenues increased by $50,000 per month, and the quality of the service calls remained high. Call center management attributed the increase to the dashboards. Significantly, the operators have responded well to the dashboards. They appreciate the ability to monitor their performance and to compare it to the other agents. Every 15 minutes the agents can see how far they have "moved the needle."

Questions

1. Interpret the phrase "That which gets watched, gets done." Give an example from your personal life.

2. Would you like to work in a job where your compensation is based on your performance relative to your coworkers? Discuss.

Sources: Compiled from H. J. Watson and J. Hill, "What Gets Watched Gets Done: How Metrics Can Motivate," *Business Intelligence Journal* (September 2009), pp. 4–7.

BEFORE YOU GO ON . . .

1. What is a dashboard? Why are dashboards so valuable to employees?

2. Explain the difference between geographic information systems and reality mining, and provide examples of how each of these technologies can be used by businesses and government agencies.

3. What is real-time BI, and why is this technology valuable to an organization's managers and executives?

1. Dashboards are very nice but seem very complex to create. Do you think graphs and charts in Excel could be as effective as the elaborate dashboard examples provided in this chapter?

2. What type of chart do you think would be beneficial in tackling the problem of shrinkage? Would it be a bar chart? Pie chart? Line chart? How could Ruben and Lisa develop this in Excel?

Student Activity 5.4

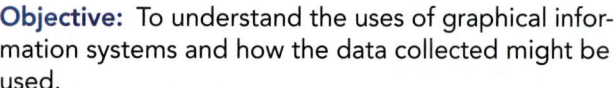

Objective: To understand the uses of graphical information systems and how the data collected might be used.

Chapter Connection: This activity relates to Section 5.4 and Learning Objective 4 in this chapter.

Prerequisites: You should read Sections 5.3 and 5.4 and should understand the terms *competitive advantage* and *revenue*.

Activity:

View the following two videos about location-tracking software:

www.youtube.com/watch?v=ZnCbZmhMGjg&feature=related

www.youtube.com/watch?v=Q-Oq-9enE-k

Both of these applications are based on location-aware technology that maps a mobile device to a GIS map, but each has a different business model.

Deliverables:

Prepare a paper contrasting the two business models. What is their product/service? How do they generate revenue? How are they attracting customers? How are they providing value to their customers? What is their competitive advantage?

Would you use either one? If not, why not? Under what scenario would you use either one?

Quiz Questions:

1. True or False? In Google's Latitude application, anyone can see where a member is.

2. True or False? Members can follow each other in Sense Network.

3. In Sense Network, a _____ is a group of members who share similar tastes as indicated by places they frequent.

Discussion Questions:

1. Do you see any ethical issues or privacy issues with either of these two software applications?

2. What can these companies do to maintain whatever competitive edge they have?

3. Are there any similar applications today? How do they compare?

5.5 | Business Intelligence in Action: Corporate Performance Management

Corporate performance management (CPM) is involved with monitoring and managing an organization's performance according to *key performance indicators* (KPIs) such as revenue, return on investment (ROI), overhead, and operational costs. For online businesses, CPM includes additional factors such as the number of page views, server load, network traffic, and transactions per second. BI applications allow managers and analysts to analyze data to obtain valuable information and insights concerning the organization's KPIs. The following example demonstrates corporate performance management at CiCi's.

CiCi's Enterprises (www.cicispizza.com), the eighth-largest pizza chain in the United States, operates 650 restaurants in 30 states and is expanding rapidly. As a result, CiCi's needed to access its data in a quicker and more structured manner so that everyone in the organization could make better decisions on a wide range of issues, including purchasing, development, distribution of food supplies, sales and marketing, and even detecting fraud.

CiCi's needed to improve its performance management with a system that could be accessed by a broad set of users. Because the company does business in an industry where sales and data from franchises change daily, CiCi's must be agile. The company had to consolidate its data in one place with easy access for all departments. To achieve this goal, CiCi's decided to implement IBM's Cognos (www.ibm.com/cognos) system.

The Cognos system has provided CiCi's with more accurate and timely budgets and forecasting, all in less time. For example, analysts can now determine more accurately the amount of food supplies used in specific stores at certain times. In fact, CiCi's can track item usage and average "tray cost" as they test a restructured buffet designed to reduce waste and increase profits. In addition, the company can now complete budgeting tasks in a few minutes that once took several hours.

CiCi's has enjoyed so many benefits from the Cognos system that the company is implementing Web dashboards for its regional managers. This process will enable even more executives to view firsthand how efficiently the company is being run and how it can be further improved.

Sources: Compiled from "IBM Cognos Solution Helps Keep CiCi's Fresh," *IBM Success Story* (www.ibm.com), accessed April 21, 2011.

BEFORE *YOU GO ON . . .*

1. What is corporate performance management?
2. How do BI applications contribute to corporate performance management?

Student Activity 5.5

Objective: To familiarize you with the concept and design of dashboards

Chapter Connection: This activity relates to Section 5.5 in the chapter.

Prerequisites: Students should have read Sections 5.4 and 5.5 and understand the concept of dashboards.

Activity:

View the following video:

www.youtube.com/watch?v=0H2OxFjnbv8&feature=related

Go to Arizona State University's site mentioned in the video (dashboards.asu.edu) and review the illustration about the drill-down process.

Deliverables:

Use PowerPoint or some other software that has drawing tools to design a dashboard for the Office of Residential Life (or its equivalent) at your university. Start by identifying the key performance indicators, and identify from where that data would come. Design a home page with four or five areas of interest for the staff in Office of Residential Life. Then for each of the areas on the home page, design its summary page (make up numbers). For two of these summary areas, design a data page. Indicate on the summary area if that summary number has a backup page (that is to say, that the design has a "drill-down" page). Look at some of the examples cited in Section 5.3 for ideas.

Quiz Questions:

1. KPI stands for key _____ indicators.
2. Drill-down means that a user can click on a number and get its source.

3. _____ reports highlight deviations larger than certain thresholds.

Discussion Questions:

1. Why does ASU have a procedure in place to grant access to its dashboards? Would you be able to get access?
2. How important is the use of color in a dashboard?
3. Why a summary page and a data page?

What's in IT for ME?

FOR THE ACCOUNTING MAJOR

 BI is used extensively in auditing to uncover irregularities. It is also used to uncover and prevent fraud. CPAs use BI for many of their duties, ranging from risk analysis to cost control.

FOR THE FINANCE MAJOR

 People have been using computers for decades to solve financial problems. Innovative BI applications have been created for activities such as making stock market decisions, refinancing bonds, assessing debt risks, analyzing financial conditions, predicting business failures, forecasting financial trends, and investing in global markets.

FOR THE MARKETING MAJOR

Marketing personnel utilize BI in many applications, from planning and executing marketing campaigns to allocating advertising budgets to evaluating alternative routings of salespeople. New marketing approaches such as targeted marketing and database marketing are heavily dependent on IT in general and on data warehouses and business intelligence applications in particular.

FOR THE PRODUCTION/OPERATIONS MANAGEMENT MAJOR

 BI supports complex operations and production decisions, from inventory control to production planning to supply chain integration.

FOR THE HUMAN RESOURCES MANAGEMENT MAJOR

 Human resources personnel use BI for many of their activities. For example, BI applications can find résumés of applicants posted on the Web and sort them to match needed skills and to support management succession planning.

FOR THE MIS MAJOR

MIS provides the data infrastructure used in BI. MIS personnel are also involved in building, deploying, and supporting BI applications.

>>> SUMMARY

1. **Identify the phases in the decision-making process, and use a decision-support framework to demonstrate how technology supports managerial decision making.**

When making a decision, either organizational or personal, the decision maker goes through a three-step process: intelligence, design, and choice. When the choice is made, the decision is implemented.

Several information technologies have been successfully used to directly support managers. Collectively, they are referred to as business intelligence information systems. Figure 5.2 provides a matrix that shows how technology supports the various types of decisions that managers must make.

2. **Describe and provide examples of the three different ways that organizations use BI.**

> *The development of a single or a few related BI applications.* This BI target is often a point solution for a departmental need, such as campaign management in marketing. A data mart is usually created to store necessary data.

> *The development of infrastructure to support enterprisewide BI.* This target supports current and future BI needs. A critical component is an enterprise data warehouse.

> *Support for organizational transformation.* With this target, BI is used to fundamentally change how a company competes in the marketplace. BI supports a new business model and enables the business strategy.

3. **Specify the BI applications available to users for data analysis, and provide examples of how each one might be used to solve a business problem at your university.**

Users have a variety of BI applications available to help them analyze data. These applications include multidimensional analysis, data mining, and decision support systems.

Multidimensional analysis, also called online analytical processing (OLAP), involves "slicing and dicing" data stored in a dimensional format, drilling down to greater data detail, and aggregating data. Data mining refers to the process of searching for valuable business information in a large database, data warehouse, or data mart. Decision support systems (DSS) combine models and data in an attempt to analyze semistructured and some unstructured problems with extensive user involvement. (The examples of using each application at your university, we leave to you.)

4. **Describe three BI applications that present the results of data analyses to users, and offer examples of how businesses and government agencies can use each of these technologies.**

A dashboard provides easy access to timely information and direct access to management reports. A geographic information system (GIS) is a computer-based system for capturing, integrating, manipulating, and displaying data using digitized maps. Reality mining analyzes information extracted from the usage patterns of mobile phones and other wireless devices. (Examples of how these technologies might be used by businesses and government agencies, we leave to you.)

5. **Describe corporate performance management, and provide an example of how your university could use CPM.**

Corporate performance management (CPM) is involved with monitoring and managing an organization's performance according to key performance indicators (KPIs) such as revenue, return on investment (ROI), overhead, and operational costs. (An example of how your university might use CPM, we leave to you.)

business intelligence A broad category of applications, technologies, and processes for gathering, storing, accessing, and analyzing data to help business users make better decisions.

corporate performance management The area of business intelligence involved with monitoring and managing an organization's performance, according to key performance indicators (KPIs) such as revenue, return on investment (ROI), overhead, and operational costs.

dashboard A BI application that provides rapid access to timely information and direct access to management reports.

data mining The process of searching for valuable business information in a large database, data warehouse, or data mart.

decision A choice among two or more alternatives that individuals and groups make.

decision support systems (DSS) Business intelligence systems that combine models and data in an attempt to solve semistructured and some unstructured problems with extensive user involvement.

geographic information system A computer-based system for capturing, integrating, manipulating, and displaying data using digitized maps.

management A process by which organizational goals are achieved through the use of resources.

models (in decision making) Simplified representations, or abstractions, of reality.

online analytical processing (OLAP) (or multidimensional data analysis) A set of capabilities for "slicing and dicing" data using dimensions and measures associated with the data.

productivity The ratio between the inputs to a process and the outputs from that process.

reality mining Extraction by analysts of information from the usage patterns of mobile phones and other wireless devices.

>>> DISCUSSION QUESTIONS

1. Your company is considering opening a new factory in China. List several typical activities involved in each phase of the decision (intelligence, design, and choice).

2. Recall that data mining found that young men tend to buy beer and diapers at the same time when they shop at a convenience store. Now that you know this relationship exists, can you provide a rationale for it?

3. American Can Company announced that it was interested in acquiring a company in the health maintenance organization (HMO) field. Two decisions were involved in this act: (1) the decision to acquire an HMO and (2) the decision of which HMO to acquire. How can the company use BI to assist it in this endeavor?

4. Discuss the strategic benefits of BI systems.

5. Will BI replace business analysts? (*Hint:* See W. McKnight, "Business Intelligence: Will Business Intelligence Replace the Business Analyst?" *DMReview*, February 2005).

>>> PROBLEM-SOLVING ACTIVITIES

1. The city of London (U.K.) charges an entrance fee for automobiles and trucks into the central city district. About a thousand digital cameras photograph the license plate of every vehicle passing by. Computers read the plate numbers and match them against records in a database of cars for which the fee has been paid for that day. If the computer does not find a match, the car owner receives a citation by mail. Examine the issues pertaining to how this process is accomplished, the mistakes it can make, and the consequences of those mistakes. Also examine how well the system is working by checking press reports. Finally, relate the process to business intelligence.

2. Enter www.cognos.com, and visit the demos on the right side of the page. Prepare a report on the various features shown in each demo.

3. Enter www.fico.com, and find products for fraud detection and risk analysis. Prepare a report.

4. Enter www.teradatastudentnetwork.com (TSN) (you will need a password), and find the paper titled "Data Warehousing Supports Corporate Strategy at First American Corporation" (by Watson, Wixom, and Goodhue). Read the paper and answer the following questions:

   a. What were the drivers for the data warehouse/business intelligence project in the company?

   b. What strategic advantages were realized?

   c. What were the critical success factors for the project?

5. Access www.ted.com/index.php/talks/view/id/92 to find the video of Hans Rosling's presentation. Comment on his data visualization techniques.

6. Enter www.visualmining.com. Explore the relationship between visualization and business intelligence. See how business intelligence is related to dashboards.

7. Access http://businessintelligence.ittoolbox.com. Identify all types of business intelligence software. Join a discussion group about topics discussed in this chapter. Prepare a report.

8. Visit the sites of some GIS vendors (such as www.mapinfo.com, www.esri.com, or www.autodesk.com).

Download a demo. What are some of the most important capabilities and applications?

9. Analyze Microsoft Virtual Earth (www.microsoft.com/virtualearth) as a business intelligence tool. (*Hint:* Access www.microsoft.com/Industry/government/solutions/virtual_earth/demo/ps_gbi.html). What are the business intelligence features of this product?

>>> TEAM ASSIGNMENTS

1. Using data mining, it is possible not only to capture information that has been buried in distant courthouses but also to manipulate and index it. This process can benefit law enforcement but invade privacy. In 1996, Lexis-Nexis, the online information service, was accused of permitting access to sensitive information on individuals. The company argued that it was unfairly targeted because it provided only basic residential data for lawyers and law enforcement personnel. Should Lexis-Nexis be prohibited from allowing access to such information? Debate the issue.

2. Use a search engine of your choice to find combined GIS/GPS applications. Also, look at various vendor sites to find success stories. For GPS vendors, look at http://biz.yahoo.com (directory) and Google. Each group will make a presentation of five applications and their benefits.

3. Each group will access a leading business intelligence vendor's Web site (for example, MicroStrategy, Oracle, Hyperion, Microsoft, SAS, SPSS, Cognos, and Business Objects). Each group will present a report on a vendor, highlighting each vendor's BI capabilities.

CLOSING **CASE 1** > Quality Assurance
at Daimler AG

German automaker Daimler AG's (www.daimler.com) divisions include Mercedes-Benz Cars, Daimler Trucks, Mercedes-Benz Vans, Daimler Buses, and Daimler Financial Services. The central tenet of Daimler's strategy is quality assurance, meaning that the company guarantees complete customer satisfaction. Daimler collects quality assurance data from the vehicles themselves, from garage service centers, and from related operations. In the past, the company relied upon a variety of data stored in separate databases: warranty and billing information, diagnostic data downloaded from on-board vehicle systems, and performance data gathered during service checks.

<<<**THE BUSINESS PROBLEM**

Dating back to the 1980s, Daimler's warranty data were housed on its Quality Information System (QUIS), a mainframe-based platform. In addition to using QUIS to conduct analysis, users from many departments also drew data from the system utilizing a variety of tools. The enormous demand for information combined with the use of different analytics tools created inconsistent information. Further, the users found the existing tools inadequate to meet user analysis requirements.

At the same time, because the diagnostic and warranty data were located in different information silos, they could not be evaluated together. Consequently, the organization was unable to take full advantage of the data. In addition, the diagnosis database had reached the limits of its capacity.

The obvious solution to this problem was to combine the various data sources into a single enterprise data warehouse. Over a three-year period, Daimler consolidated its data on a data warehouse, making these data available to users through a shared interface. The new system is called Advanced Quality Analysis (AQUA).

The company intended AQUA to provide support for two strategic goals: (1) to increase customer satisfaction and (2) to reduce costs. By creating a "single version of the truth"—a global, standardized perspective on all vehicle-related data—the new system could enable Daimler to better analyze both product and diagnostic effectiveness, as well as to ensure the quality of maintenance and repairs. In addition, sophisticated real-time analyses on AQUA would improve the existing early-warning systems, which detect the possible failure of a vehicular component such as the brakes. Finally, eliminating the existing, old systems would reduce IT operating costs.

<<<**THE IT SOLUTION**

Since early 2010, users have been receiving warranty and customer satisfaction reports via AQUA. Daimler used these data to implement an enhanced early-warning system that reports problems much faster than the previous system could. AQUA has also enabled Daimler to implement the "First Fixed Visit" tool, which identifies recurring repairs based on data collected in dealership service operations. Daimler maps those repairs back to its manufacturing processes so that the company can make improvements in those processes.

After Daimler integrated its data-mining tool into AQUA, the company no longer needed to copy data from one database to another. This arrangement dramatically lowered follow-on costs. By eliminating problems in the production stage, Daimler can avoid future warranty and goodwill costs. (If customers are not satisfied with their cars or with Daimler maintenance, then the company loses goodwill.)

Another feature of the new system, the AQUA Miner, provides a step-by-step approach to identifying the individual features that contribute to a high rate of part defects. Basically, the engineer selects a specific series type (of vehicle) and then chooses failure codes suspected of contributing to a particular defect. AQUA Miner then identifies subgroups of vehicles where such defects appear more frequently than in the remainder of the vehicle fleet.

Along with warranty and goodwill data, AQUA Miner also analyzes data on each vehicle's electronic control unit, such as revolutions per minute, vibration behavior, and temperature. These analyses help uncover the causes of defects based on actual driving experience. Daimler utilizes these data to improve the design of future vehicle models.

For the first time, Daimler has a data source that provides all quality-related information across its complete range of components and model lines. Developers and engineers employ these data to analyze thousands of variables, such as the repair frequency of all components. AQUA warns the engineers of any significant deviations from accepted standards, and it provides warnings up to two weeks faster than the previous system did. As a result, Daimler can pinpoint potential problems in vehicles that have been on the road for as briefly as one month, and it can adjust its production processes to eliminate these problems. This process is reducing long-term warranty costs.

AQUA has enabled Daimler to achieve deeper insights into how to optimize its production processes. Defects can be detected more quickly, resolved, and eliminated from future models. AQUA supports Daimler's strategic goals of quality leadership, customer satisfaction, and profitability.

Questions

1. Why is it so important to have a solid understanding of business intelligence and the possibilities that surround information-supported decision making?

2. Can you think of any situation you are in where you freely provide business intelligence to a company as its customer? Do you ever sign up for a discount card at your local grocery store? What do you think the stores does with your transaction history?

SOURCES: Compiled from S. DeCarlo, "The World's Biggest Companies," *Forbes*, April 20, 2011; H. Elliot, "Daimler's Dieter Zetsche: Sales Are Not Our No. 1 Priority," *Forbes*, January 11, 2011; A. Dullaghan, "Daimler Drives High Performance," *Teradata Magazine*, v. 11, no. 1, 2011; www.daimler.com, accessed April 5, 2011.

CLOSING **CASE 2** >

Norfolk Southern

Norfolk Southern is one of four large freight railroads in the United States. Each day, the company moves approximately 500 freight trains across 21,000 route miles in 22 eastern states, the District of Columbia, and Ontario, Canada. Norfolk Southern manages more than $26 billion in assets and employs more than 30,000 people.

For more than a century, the railroad industry was heavily regulated, and Norfolk Southern and its predecessor railroads made money by managing their costs. Managers focused on optimizing the use of railcars to get the maximum production out of their fixed assets. Then, in 1980 the industry was partially deregulated, which opened up opportunities for mergers and allowed companies to charge rates based on service and to enter into contracts with customers. On-time delivery became an important factor in the industry.

Over time, Norfolk Southern responded to these industry changes by becoming a "scheduled railroad." Put simply, the company would develop a fixed set of train schedules for cars to go between trains and yards. In this way, managers could predict when they could get a shipment to a customer.

Norfolk Southern had always used a variety of sophisticated systems to run its business. Becoming a scheduled railroad, however, required new systems that would use statistical models to determine the best routes and connections to optimize railroad performance and then apply the models to create the plan that would actually run the railroad operations. These new systems were called TOP, short for Thoroughbred Operating Plan. The railroad deployed TOP in 1992.

Norfolk Southern realized that in addition to implementing TOP, it had to monitor and measure its performance against the TOP plan. Norfolk Southern's numerous information systems generate millions of records about freight, railcars, train GPS information, train fuel levels, revenue information, crew management, and historical tracking records. Unfortunately, the company was not able to tap these data without jeopardizing the system's performance.

<<<**THE IT SOLUTION**

In 1995, the company invested in a 1-terabyte data warehouse in which the data are easy to access (using a Web browser) and can be manipulated for decision support. The warehouse data are collected from source systems that run the company. After the data are moved from the source systems' databases to the warehouse, users can access and use the data without the risk of impacting company operations.

In 2002, the data warehouse became a critical component of TOP. Norfolk Southern built a TOP dashboard application that pulls data from the data warehouse and then graphically depicts actual performance against the trip plan for both train performance and connection performance. The application uses visualization technology so that field managers can more easily interpret the large volumes of data (e.g., there are 160,000 weekly connections across the network).

Norfolk Southern has an enterprise data warehouse, which means that after data are placed in the warehouse, they become available across the company, not just for a single application or a single department. Although the company uses train and connection performance data primarily for the TOP application, it has been able to leverage that data for many other purposes as well. For example, the marketing department has developed an application called accessNS, which was created for Norfolk Southern customers who want visibility into the company's extensive transportation network. Customers want to know where their shipments are "right now." Sometimes they also want historical information: Where did my shipment come from? How long did it take to arrive? What were the problems along the route?

The accessNS app enables more than 14,500 users from 8,000 customer organizations to log in and access predefined and customer reports about their accounts at any time. Users can access current data, which is updated hourly, and they can also review data from the past three years. The app also provides alerting and RSS feed capabilities. In fact, accessNS pushes 4,500 reports to users daily. The self-service nature of accessNS has allowed Norfolk Southern to provide customers the information they want while reducing the number of people needed for customer service. Without accessNS, it would take approximately 47 people to support the current level of customer reporting.

Departments across the company—from engineering and strategic planning to accounting and human resources—use the enterprise data warehouse. One especially creative internal application was developed by human resources. The department needed to determine where to locate its field offices in order to best meet the needs of Norfolk

Southern's 30,000+ employees. By combining employee demographic data (e.g., zip codes) with geospatial data traditionally utilized by the engineering group, human resources was able to visually map out the employee population density, making it much easier to optimize the location of service offices.

THE RESULTS >>>

The Norfolk Southern data warehouse has evolved into a 6-terabyte system that manages a voluminous amount of information on the company's vast network of railroads and shipping services. Norfolk Southern uses the data warehouse to analyze trends, develop forecasting schedules, archive records, and facilitate customer self-service. The data warehouse provides information to more than 3,000 employees and 14,000 external customers and stakeholders. The number of missed connections has decreased by 60 percent since the application was implemented. Further, the amount of time it takes to unload a railcar, reload it, and attach it to another train has decreased by an entire day, which translates into millions of dollars in annual savings.

Norfolk Southern was the first railroad to offer self-service business intelligence, and this innovation served as an example that other railroads have followed. The company was also one of the first railroads to provide a large variety of historical data to external customers.

And the bottom line? Norfolk Southern reported revenues of approximately $8 billion in 2010 and made a profit of approximately $1 billion.

Questions

1. What is the importance of allowing external parties to access data in Norfolk Southern's data warehouse? What are the risks and rewards of allowing such access?

2. Describe other applications Norfolk Southern could develop using the data warehouse. (*Hint:* Remember that a railroad has to track trains, railcars, people, and cargo.)

SOURCES: Used with permission of Professors Barbara Wixom (University of Virginia), Hugh Watson (University of Georgia), and Jeff Hoffer (University of Dayton); www.nscorp.com, accessed March 23, 2011.

RUBY'S CLUB INTERNSHIP ASSIGNMENTS

Go to Wiley Plus (www.wileyplus.com) to download Ruben and Lisa's spreadsheet from last year as well as to watch tutorials that deal with using Excel for a goal-seeking analysis. This spreadsheet includes data on cover sales, food sales, and drink sales for each week. It also provides information on the type of music (genre, band, etc.) that was playing and what other type of events may have been going on that week.

Your task will be to use Excel as a platform for creating business intelligence and to provide Ruben and Lisa with projected ROI that will be required to meet their goals, based on the level of sales

they have. This ROI will then determine how closely they have to monitor shrinkage. For example, if sales are extremely high, shrinkage may not be a big concern. If sales are low and cutting costs is the only way to make the $300,000 goal, then shrinkage will be a major item. BI is the only way to determine what they need to manage and where they need to spend their time.

Finally, you will submit your spreadsheet and a written description to Ruben and Lisa (via your professor) in a professional business letter.

SPREADSHEET ACTIVITY

Objective: The objective of this activity is to help you understand that while spreadsheets are powerful, an interconnected workbook is even more so. You will learn how to write formulae that use information contained in different pages to help tie the workbook together.

Chapter Connection: Even though the opening case makes the point that spreadsheets are antiquated and often not able to keep up with the vast amounts of data needed to run an organization, spreadsheets still occupy an important place in smaller organizations. This activity brings business intelligence to the smaller mom-and-pop organizations.

Prerequisites: There are no prerequisites for this activity.

Activity: As you have seen, business intelligence is a huge concept. It can, however, also apply in much smaller ways to everyday business. Business intelligence can help small mom-and-pop organizations in tremendous ways. Consider the following example.

Ted is a 45-year-old full-time accountant. He loves his job and has had quite a successful career. He also takes great pride in working with his hands. Specifically, he has always enjoyed working with wood and making small rocking horses for children. For years he just made these for family and friends, but lately he has decided to start selling his work. The accountant side of him has kept detailed records of his inventory, costs, sales, hours, profits, losses, and so on. Now it is time to take his workbook and create business intelligence out of it.

Ted's spreadsheet contains some basic information but no formulas. Notes describe what he has done and the decisions he wants to make. You can download the spreadsheet from www.wiley.com/college/rainer. Specifically, Ted wants to know how much he has invested in each rocking horse. His time, materials, advertising, and other costs will definitely make a difference in his final price. Keep in mind that the point of this spreadsheet is to provide business intelligence. While spreadsheet skills are required, they are the means to an end of helping Ted set appropriate prices.

Deliverables: The final product will be a spreadsheet with Ted's data calculated to provide business intelligence in a small business scenario.

Quiz Questions:

1. Which of the following symbols is used to reference a specific cell in a spreadsheet?
   - **(a)** @
   - **(b)** $
   - **(c)** ^
   - **(d)** &
   - **(e)** *

2. Which of the following symbols is used as the multiply symbol in a formula?
   - **(a)** #
   - **(b)** X
   - **(c)** *
   - **(d)** ?
   - **(e)** /

3. Which of the following statements is the correct interpretation of the following formula?

$$" = B3/(B4 + B5) + 6$$

   - **(a)** B3 divided by B4, plus B5 and B6
   - **(b)** B3 divided by the sum of B4, B5, and B6
   - **(c)** B6 added to the division of B3 and the sum of B4 and B5
   - **(d)** B6 added to the division of B3 and B4 plus B5

Discussion Questions:

1. How does algebra play a role in writing formulas?
2. What happens to your data if you build a formula off of a previously incorrect formula?
3. If formulas are set up to predict or forecast (such as in regression), how many scenarios could be calculated?

DATABASE ACTIVITY: USING PIVOT TABLES

Objective

To learn how to turn a database into a *pivot table*, which is a structured representation of the database contents that lets you observe the relationships of any data field, or group of data fields, to others.

Chapter Connection

In this chapter you read how information systems can be used for better decisions. Most of what you read discussed specialized tools for organizing and presenting data. These are found mostly in medium-large and larger organizations. What's a small business to do?

Even a small business can use a database management system (DBMS) to organize and store information. In this module, we will see one way to use an Access database to support decision making: the pivot table.

This is a small-scale example of business intelligence (Section 5.2) and a BI application (Section 5.3).

Prerequisites

None.

Activity:

In this activity, which you will find online, you will use a sales database for a group of computer stores. You will analyze it for differences among stores, trends, and to see how the group could improve sales.

1. Download the Ch 05 CarlaComputerStores database from www.wiley.com/college/rainer and open it.
2. Open the OrderQry query by clicking on it in the Navigation Pane at the left of the Access window.

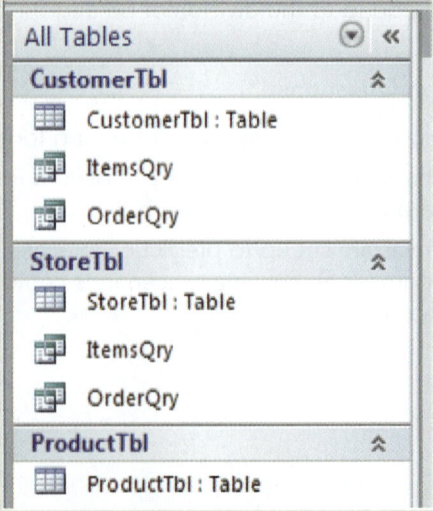

Usage Hint: If you do not see the navigation pane, but the words "Navigation Pane" run vertically at the far left of the window, click on those words or on the » above them to expand it.

Usage Hint: Depending on how your copy of Access is set up, navigation pane items may open with a single or double click. If a single click does not work, double-click. If you are using your own copy, you can set this preference in Options under the File tab. In the Current Database section, click "Navigation Options."

You will see what looks like a table with information about every sale since in this database. (Its first few rows are shown in the following screenshots.) As you will learn in the Chapter 10 activity, this "table" is not stored in the database. It is created as needed by combining data from other tables in a *query*. Those other tables are listed under Tables in the navigation pane. You can see how they are related to each other by clicking "Relationships" in the Database Tools ribbon.

OrderQry		
StoreCity	CustName	OrderPrice
Atlanta	Alice	$399.00
Atlanta	Alice	$438.99
Atlanta	Alice	$958.98
Atlanta	Alice	$1,737.98
Atlanta	Emily	$788.97
Atlanta	Emily	$549.94
Atlanta	Gladys	$1,137.97

These tables are a simplified version of what a real store would use. For example, a real database would include order date and method of payment. However, this database has purchase history: what each customer bought, when, at what store, and with what other items. That is what we will use here.

3. To analyze customer spending, look at this query in Pivot Table view. Select that view from the drop-down View menu at the left of the Home ribbon, or click the second icon from the left at the bottom right of the window.

Usage Hint: Access often provides multiple ways to do something. It usually does not matter which you choose. As you use Access more, you will develop preferences. They do not have to be the same as anyone else's.

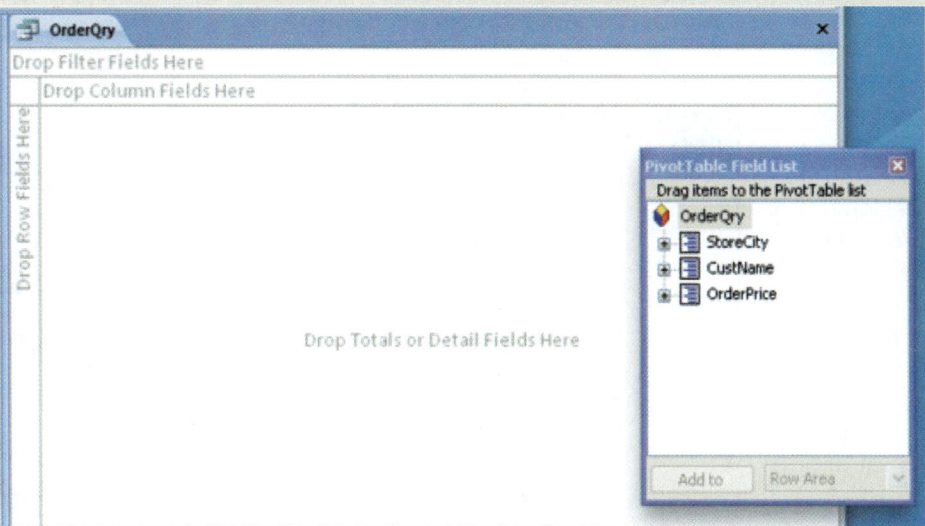

4. A windoid labeled "Pivot Table Field List" floats above the main Access window. It lists all the fields in the query, plus other items that can be derived from them. You will drag these into sections of the pivot table pane to analyze the data.

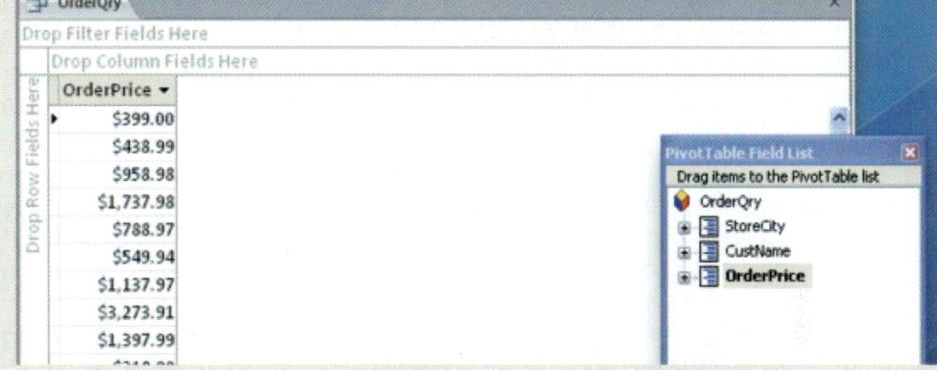

Usage Hint: If you do not see the Field List windoid, click the Field List icon in the Show/Hide section toward the left end of the ribbon.

Let us see if there are differences in order size among stores. Drag OrderPrice into the main area of the pane, labeled "Drop Totals or Detail Fields Here."

5. You will see all the order amounts in the central section of the pivot table. It is useless by itself. In terms of Chapter 1 concepts this is data, not information. To organize the amounts by store, drag StoreCity into the "Drop Row Fields Here" area at the left of the pane.

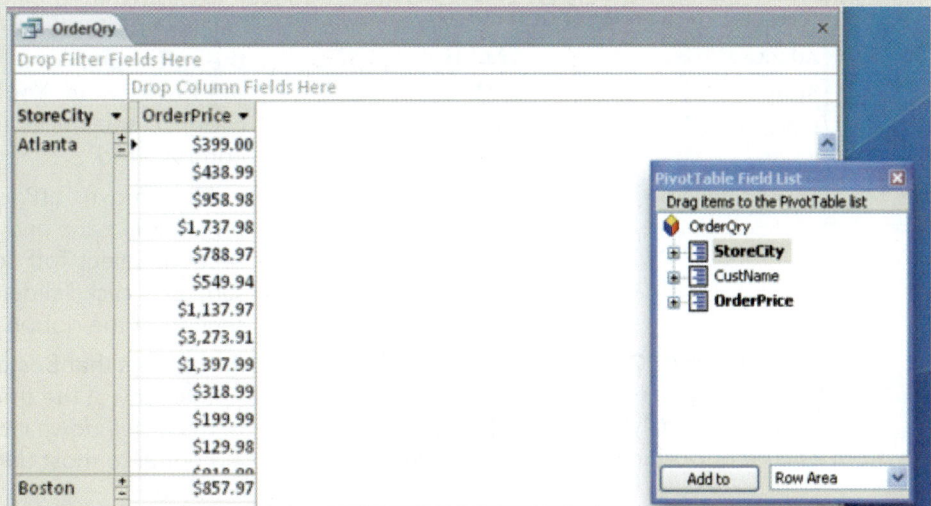

6. We want to see the average order size for each store. Select the OrderPrice column by clicking on its header. Then click the AutoCalc icon on the Design ribbon (Σ, the upper-case Greek letter sigma, a common mathematical symbol for summation). From the drop-down menu, select "Average." You will see each store's average order size below the list of orders.

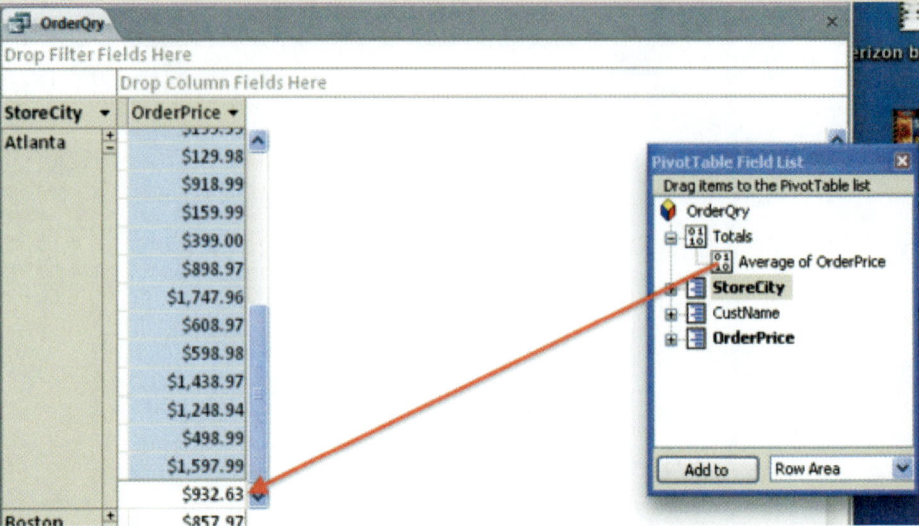

Usage Hint: The overall average is labeled "Grand Total." In everyday language, a "total" is what you get when you add several numbers. Access refers to that concept as a *sum*. To Access, a "total" is any summary calculation: sum, average, count, or any of the others listed under the AutoCalc icon.

Which city has the highest average sales? The lowest?

7. Suppose we only care about averages, not individual sales. To hide the details, select that column again and click "Hide Details" in the Show/Hide area at the left of the Design ribbon. "Show Details" in the same section will toggle them back on. You can hide or show details for one store by clicking "−" (hide) or "+" (show) under the store's city.

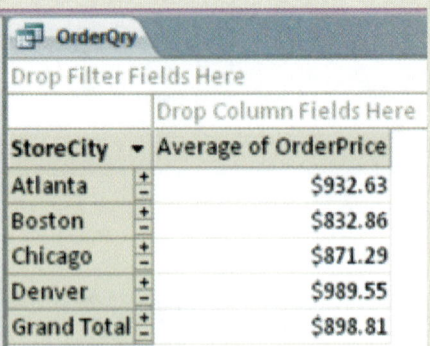

8. This is called a pivot table because you can *pivot* data from the top to the left and vice versa to make it easier to analyze. Drag the StoreCity label from its current position, above the city names, to the "Drop Column Fields Here" area at the top of the table. Hide and show details. See how the display changes.

9. Select Show Details, if they are not already showing, to display order prices. Select it by clicking OrderPrice near the top of any city column. Under AutoCalc, display the sum and the count. One store has the highest total sales but the smallest average sale. Why?

10. Close the query, saving changes when prompted.

11. We want to analyze our sales by city. Open ItemsQry. The TotPrice column in this table is not in the database. It is a calculated field: it is derived on the fly by multiplying the price of the product (in ProductTbl, for consistency across all orders) and the quantity in a given order. Switch to Pivot Table view.

Usage Hint: If you are curious about how calculated fields work, switch to Design View of the query and look at the rightmost column in the lower pane. You will have to make the column wider to see the entire formula, but it is not complicated.

Now, move TotPrice into the main section of the pivot table pane and StoreCity into the Row Fields section. Select TotPrice in the pivot table, add its sum, and click "Hide Details" in the Show/Hide section of the ribbon.

12. It seems that Boston sold more during the period than any of the other stores. To find out why, we must *drill down* into the data. (Drilling down is central to most data analysis.) Add ProdCategory

to the pivot table as a column field. What you get should look like this:

StoreCity ▼	ProdCategory ▼		Sum of TotPrice
⊟ Atlanta	CPU	±	$7,889.00
	Display	±	$2,851.00
	Memory	±	$959.87
	Portable	±	$4,891.00
	Printer	±	$2,419.89
	Storage	±	$2,439.68
	Total	±	$21,450.44
⊟ Boston	CPU	±	$10,085.00

Usage Hint: If your product categories ended up to the left of the city names, just select its name at the top of the column and drag it to the right until a thick blue line shows up to the right of the StoreCity column. Then release your mouse button.

13. You realize that this table is not easy to interpret. A chart would be better. Choose Pivot Chart view from the drop-down menu at the left end of the ribbon, or click the Pivot Chart icon at the bottom right of the Access window. Add a legend with the tool in the Show/Hide section of the Design ribbon.

14. You now realize that this is not the ideal chart design. It tells us that Atlanta, for example, got more revenue from CPUs than from memory, but anyone who knows computers would expect that. We would like to know how Atlanta compares with other stores in terms of memory revenue. Click "Switch Row/Column" in the Active Field section of the Design ribbon. You should get a chart whose lower left corner looks like this:

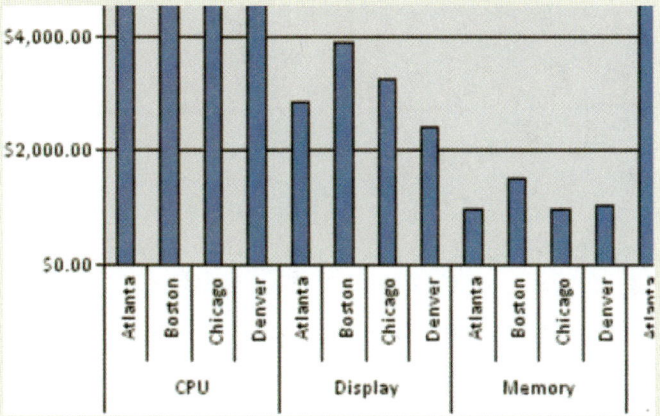

15. From the part of this chart above the screen shot, we see that Chicago's CPU sales are a concern. Before calling the Chicago store

manager, though, we need to do more research. Go back to PivotTable view and drag ProdDescrip into the row field area. Each category will be broken down by product. To see only products in the CPU category, click the down arrow next to ProdCategory to get a list of categories to filter. Uncheck everything except CPU and confirm.

Usage Hint: Rather than unchecking all the categories except the one we care about, it is easier to uncheck everything by clicking "All," then check "CPU."

16. Now look at the chart again. The Chicago store didn't sell any SuperCPUs! Its sales of the three slower models are more or less in line with expectations. We do not know the reason for this, of course. Maybe there are few gamers and graphic artists in the store's sales area. (These are two major markets for top-of-the-line systems.) Maybe the Chicago store ran a promotion for these during an earlier period, and most of its potential customers bought one then. Maybe a competitor is running such a promo now. We do, however, know what we want to ask when we call the Chicago store manager.

17. Close your database, saving changes when prompted.

Deliverables:

1. Your database, with the most recent pivot table and chart.
2. Answers to the preceding questions in items 6 and 9, in the form specified by your instructor.

Quiz Questions:

1. In Step 6, which store had the highest average order amount?
   (a) Atlanta
   (b) Boston
   (c) Chicago
   (d) Denver
2. A pivot table is a way of looking at this type of Access object:
   (a) Query
   (b) Table
   (c) Form
   (d) Either A or B
   (e) Either B or C
3. The central section of the pivot table pane contains this type of information:
   (a) Names of pivot table categories
   (b) Summary data for pivot table cells

(c) Individual data elements from the database, but not totals

(d) Links to the underlying Access tables

4. If a pivot table has only one column (that is, it has categories down the left but none across the top), then:

(a) You can create categories across the top by dragging categories from the side.

(b) You can create categories across the top by dragging new table fields into the "Drag Column Fields Here" area.

(c) You can analyze data in that column without having fields across the top.

(d) All of the above are correct.

Discussion Questions:

1. How could pivot tables be useful for someone in the kind of job you hope to have after you graduate? (Say what that job is.)

2. Describe a business decision for which pivot tables would *not* be helpful. Explain why you do not think they would help with it.

3. Suppose you worked for a large chain of photo stores. Your database has millions of rows with a few dozen columns in each, but its structure is much like the one in this activity. Would that change your approach to using pivot tables? If so, how? (Assume your computer is fast enough that the database size does not cause slow response times. In practice, that might not be true.)

Additional Resources:

An excellent resource for this activity is the following ten-minute video:
http://examples.oreilly.com/9780596527600/ch09/Pivot-Tables.html

As you watch it, keep in mind that Access has many ways to do almost anything. Matthew MacDonald does not always do things exactly as we did here. You can do them as he does them, as described here, and often in other ways as well.

6 | Ethics and Privacy

LEARNING OBJECTIVES

1. Define ethics, list and describe the three fundamental tenets of ethics, and describe the four categories of ethical issues related to information technology.

2. Identify three places that store personal data, and, for each one, discuss at least one potential threat to the privacy of the data stored there.

ShaNiqua had worked at the local bank for 10 years and had recently overheard a conversation between two employees regarding a customer's account. Being unsure what to do about it, she asked a co-worker because she felt this was not appropriate behavior.

The advice she received? Leave it alone because the bank's managers are trying to deal with the situation. ShaNiqua is afraid that if she tells what she knows she could get in trouble, and if she does not that they could be talking about her account next!

In this small town, everyone knows everyone. Usually, this situation is fine until curious bank tellers begin "snooping" into personal bank accounts. Although no one has ever reported theft by an employee or filed a consumer complaint, numerous rumors have spread of employees talking to their friends and family about various bank accounts, spending habits, and recent purchases. In addition, the number of new accounts at the bank in the past five years has steadily declined while competitors' accounts have grown.

Possible solutions include restricting access to bank accounts and hiring auditors to reconcile any unnecessary accessing of accounts and monitor all employee activity. Any decision is likely to have unanticipated results due to the delicate nature of balancing access to information needed for work and restricting access for security purposes. Ultimately, the solution may simply be to educate employees about the legal implications of misusing customer information and to create very strong policies to guard against this type of activity.

At the time of this writing, MidTown Bank managers have not determined exactly what to do. They have never been faced with this situation before and are having difficulty determining how to handle it.

Sources: Compiled from personal interviews with the author. Names have been changed at the request of the interviewees.

Questions

1. Do you feel that the co-worker's advice to ShaNiqua was correct? Why or why not?

2. How should the bank managers handle this problem? Are there other possibilities not mentioned in the case? If so, what are they?

RUBY'S CLUB

Ruben and Lisa have never developed an ethics and privacy statement for their club. Honestly, they never thought they would need one. But with their new systems that will collect customer data and establish memberships, they realize that it is now imperative that they develop a statement of this type.

Ruben and Lisa have both seen privacy statements. They get them in the mail from their credit card companies, and they agree to them anytime they create their own memberships online. However, they have never really paid attention to them and now have a lot of questions about their own privacy statement.

>>> Obviously, they know they need to deal with how they will handle the privacy of online information. However, they are unsure of how to deal with ethical issues in their club. Should they use their information systems to track the number of alcoholic beverages their customers purchase? If they do, is it ethical to limit a customer? Should they request a release form to continue to sell drinks after a certain point? Use the information in this chapter to help them make these decisions.

INTRODUCTION

You will study two major issues in this chapter: ethics and privacy. Both issues are closely related to IT and raise significant questions. For example, consider Chapter Closing Case 1. Are WikiLeaks' actions ethical? Does WikiLeaks violate the privacy of governments, organizations, and individuals? The answers to these questions are not straightforward. In fact, IT has made finding answers to these questions even more difficult.

You will encounter numerous ethical and privacy issues in your career, many of which will involve IT in some manner. This chapter will give you insights into how to respond to these issues. Further, it will help you to make immediate contributions to your company's code of ethics and its privacy policies. You will also be able to provide meaningful input concerning the potential ethical and privacy impacts of your organization's information systems on people inside and outside the organization.

For example, suppose your organization decides to adopt Web 2.0 technologies (presented in Chapter 8) to include business partners and customers in new product development. You will be able to analyze the potential privacy and ethical implications of implementing these technologies.

6.1 | Ethical Issues

Ethics refers to the principles of right and wrong that individuals use to make choices that guide their behaviors. Deciding what is right or wrong is not always easy or clear cut. Fortunately, many frameworks are available to help us make ethical decisions.

All ethical frameworks attempt to balance good for all. (*Source:* maxstockphoto/Shutterstock)

Ethical Frameworks

There are many sources for ethical standards. Here we consider four widely used standards: the utilitarian approach, the rights approach, the fairness approach, and the common good approach. There are many other sources, but these four are representative.

The *utilitarian approach* states that an ethical action is the one that provides the most good or does the least harm. The ethical corporate action would be the one that produces the greatest good and does the least harm for all affected parties—customers, employees, shareholders, the community, and the environment.

The *rights approach* maintains that an ethical action is the one that best protects and respects the moral rights of the affected parties. Moral rights can include the rights to make one's own choices about what kind of life to lead, to be told the truth, not to be injured, and to a degree of privacy. Which of these rights people are actually entitled to—and under what circumstances—is widely debated. Nevertheless, most people acknowledge that individuals are entitled to some moral rights. An ethical organizational action would be one that protects and respects the moral rights of customers, employees, shareholders, business partners, and even competitors.

The *fairness approach* posits that ethical actions treat all human beings equally, or, if unequally, then fairly, based on some defensible standard. For example, most people might believe it is fair to pay people higher salaries if they work harder or if they contribute a greater amount to the firm. However, there is less certainty regarding CEO salaries that are hundreds or thousands of times larger than those of other employees. Many people question whether this huge disparity is based on a defensible standard or whether it is the result of an imbalance of power and hence is unfair.

The *common good approach* highlights the interlocking relationships that underlie all societies. This approach argues that respect and compassion for all others is the basis for ethical actions. It emphasizes the common conditions that are important to the welfare of everyone. These conditions can include a system of laws, effective police and fire departments, health care, a public educational system, and even public recreation areas.

If we combine these four standards, we can develop a general framework for ethics or ethical decision making Figure 6.1. This framework consists of five steps.

The Bill of Rights is basically a legalized set of ethical standards. (*Source:* © Photri Images/SuperStock)

- Recognize an ethical issue.
  - Could this decision or situation damage someone or some group?
  - Does this decision involve a choice between a good and bad alternative?
  - Is this issue about more than what is legal? If so, how?

- Get the facts.
  - What are the relevant facts of the situation?
  - Do I know enough to make a decision?
  - Which individuals and/or groups have an important stake in the outcome?
  - Have I consulted all relevant persons and groups?

- Evaluate alternative actions.
  - Which option will produce the most good and do the least harm? (the utilitarian approach)
  - Which option best respects the rights of all stakeholders? (the rights approach)
  - Which option treats people equally or proportionately? (the fairness approach)
  - Which option best serves the community as a whole, and not just some members? (the common good approach)

- Make a decision and test it.
  - Considering all the approaches, which option best addresses the situation?

- Act and reflect on the outcome of your decision.
  - How can I implement my decision with the greatest care and attention to the concerns of all stakeholders?
  - How did my decision turn out, and what did I learn from this specific situation?

Now that we have created a general ethical framework, we will focus specifically on ethics in a corporate environment.

Ethics in the Corporate Environment

Many companies and professional organizations develop their own codes of ethics. A **code of ethics** is a collection of principles that are intended to guide decision making by members

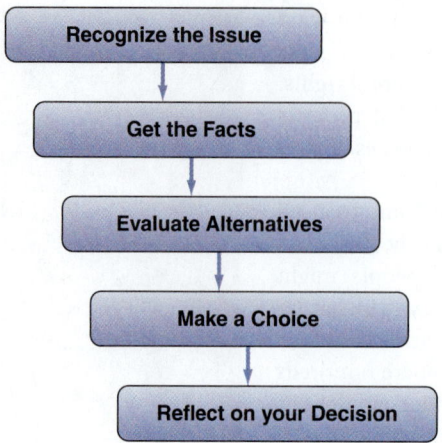

Figure 6.1 General framework for ethical decision making.

of the organization. For example, the Association for Computing Machinery (www.acm.org), an organization of computing professionals, has a thoughtful code of ethics for its members (see www.acm.org/constitution/code.html).

Keep in mind that different codes of ethics are not always consistent with one another. Therefore, an individual might be expected to conform to multiple codes. For example, a person who is a member of two large professional computing-related organizations may be required by one organization to comply with all applicable laws and at the same time be required by the other organization to refuse to obey unjust laws.

Fundamental tenets of ethics include responsibility, accountability, and liability. **Responsibility** means that you accept the consequences of your decisions and actions. **Accountability** refers to determining who is responsible for actions that were taken. **Liability** is a legal concept that gives individuals the right to recover the damages done to them by other individuals, organizations, or systems.

Before you go any further, it is very important that you realize that what is *unethical* is not necessarily *illegal*. For example, a bank's decision to foreclose on a home can be technically legal, but it can raise many ethical questions. In many instances, then, an individual or organization faced with an ethical decision is not considering whether to break the law. As the foreclosure example illustrates, however, ethical decisions can have serious consequences for individuals, organizations, and society at large.

In recent years we have witnessed a large number of extremely poor ethical decisions, not to mention outright criminal behavior. During 2001 and 2002, three highly publicized fiascos occurred at Enron, WorldCom, and Tyco, respectively. At each company, executives were convicted of various types of fraud for using illegal accounting practices. These actions led to the passage of the Sarbanes-Oxley Act in 2002. Sarbanes-Oxley requires publicly held companies to implement financial controls and company executives to personally certify financial reports.

More recently, the subprime mortgage crisis exposed unethical lending practices throughout the mortgage industry. The crisis also highlighted pervasive weaknesses in the regulation of the U.S. financial industry as well as the global financial system. It ultimately contributed to a deep recession in the global economy.

Improvements in information technologies have generated a new set of ethical problems. Computing processing power doubles about every two years, meaning that organizations are more dependent than ever before on their information systems. Organizations can store increasing amounts of data at decreasing cost, enabling them to store more data on individuals for longer periods of time. Computer networks, particularly the Internet, enable organizations to collect, integrate, and distribute enormous amounts of information on individuals, groups, and institutions. As a result, ethical problems are arising concerning the appropriate collection and use of customer information, personal privacy, and the protection of intellectual property, as "IT's About Business 6.1" illustrates.

Big Brother Is Watching You

People today live with a degree of surveillance that would have been unimaginable just a few generations ago. For example, surveillance cameras track you at airports, subways, banks, and other public venues. In addition, inexpensive digital sensors are now everywhere. They are incorporated into laptop webcams, video-game motion sensors, smart phone cameras, utility meters, passports, and employee ID cards. Step out your front door and you could be captured in a high-resolution photograph taken from the air or from the street by Google or Microsoft, as they update their mapping services. Drive down a city street, cross a toll bridge, or park at a shopping mall, and your license plate will be recorded and time-stamped.

Several developments are helping to increase the monitoring of human activity, including low-cost digital cameras, motion sensors, and biometric readers. In addition, the cost of storing digital data is decreasing. The result is an explosion of sensor data collection and storage.

In addition, technology to analyze the increasing amounts of digital sensor data is becoming more efficient as well as less expensive. For instance, Affectiva (www.affectiva.com) recently introduced biometric wristbands that are capable of monitoring tiny changes in sweat-gland activity to gauge emotional reactions. Marketing consultants are using the bands to discover what pleases or frustrates shoppers.

At the 2011 International Consumer Electronics Show, Intel and Microsoft introduced an in-store digital billboard that can memorize your face. These billboards can keep track of the products you are interested in based on purchases or your browsing behavior. One marketing analyst predicted that your experience in every store will soon be customized.

Clearly, privacy concerns must be addressed, particularly with the capacity for databases to share data and therefore to put together the pieces of a puzzle that can identify us in surprising ways. For example, attorneys have begun to use bridge toll records to establish travel patterns of spouses in divorce proceedings. Police looking to issue traffic citations now correlate photos, taken by cameras located at intersections, with vehicle ownership records.

One of the most troubling privacy problems is a practice advocated by Google and Facebook called *photo tagging*. The two companies are using facial-recognition software in their popular online photo-editing and sharing services, Google Picasa and Facebook Photo Albums. Both companies encourage users to assign names to people in photos, referred to as tagging. Facial-recognition software then indexes facial features. Once an individual in a photo is tagged, the software then looks for similar facial features in untagged photos. This process allows the user to quickly group photos in which the tagged person appears. Significantly, the individual is not aware of this process.

Once you are tagged in a photo, that photo could be used to search for matches across the entire Internet, or in private databases, including databases fed by surveillance cameras. The technology could be used by a car dealer who takes a picture of you when you step onto the car lot. The dealer could then quickly profile you on the Web, to gain an edge in making a sale. Even worse, a stranger in a restaurant could photograph you with a smart phone and then go online to profile you. One privacy attorney says that losing the right to anonymity would have a chilling effect on where you go, whom you meet, and how you live your life.

Another problem arises with smart phones equipped with global positioning system (GPS) sensors. These sensors routinely *geotag* photos and videos, embedding images with the longitude and latitude of the location shown in the image. You could be inadvertently supplying criminals with useful intelligence by posting personal images on social networks or photo-sharing Web sites. These actions would show the criminals exactly where you live.

Questions

1. Apply the general framework for ethical decision making to the practices of photo tagging and geotagging.

2. Discuss and provide examples of the benefits and the drawbacks of photo tagging and geotagging.

3. Are users responsible for their loss of privacy if they do not know that their photos can be tagged and that they can be located with GPS sensors?

Sources: Compiled from Autopia Blog, "Cellphone Networks and the Future of Traffic," *Wired*, March 2, 2011; "Hello, Big Brother: Digital Sensors Are Watching Us," *USA Today*, January 26, 2011; B. Acohido, "Helpful Digital Sensors," *USA Today*, January 25, 2011; D. Priest and W. Arkin, "Top Secret America," *Washington Post*, December 20, 2010; P. Elmer-DeWitt, "How the iPhone Spills Your Secrets," *Fortune*, December 18, 2010; T. Carmody, "The Internet of Cars: New R&D For Mobile Traffic Sensors," *Wired*, September 29, 2010; T. Harbert, "Beeps, Blips, and IT: Making Sense of Sensor Data," *Computerworld*, June 24, 2008; www.eff.org, accessed March 17, 2011.

Ethics and Information Technology

All employees have a responsibility to encourage ethical uses of information and information technology. Many of the business decisions you will face at work will have an ethical dimension. Consider these decisions you might have to make:

- Should organizations monitor employees' Web surfing and e-mail?
- Should organizations sell customer information to other companies?
- Should organizations audit employees' computers for unauthorized software or illegally downloaded music or video files?

The diversity and ever-expanding use of IT applications have created a variety of ethical issues. These issues fall into four general categories: privacy, accuracy, property, and accessibility.

1. *Privacy issues* involve collecting, storing, and disseminating information about individuals.
2. *Accuracy issues* involve the authenticity, fidelity, and accuracy of information that is collected and processed.
3. *Property issues* involve the ownership and value of information.
4. *Accessibility issues* revolve around who should have access to information and whether they should have to pay for this access.

Table 6.1 lists representative questions and issues for each of these categories. In addition, Online Appendix W6.1 presents 14 ethics scenarios for you to consider. These scenarios will provide a context for you to consider situations that involve ethical or unethical behavior.

Many of the issues and scenarios we have examined, such as photo tagging and geo tagging, involve privacy as well as ethics. In the next section, you will learn about privacy issues in more detail.

BEFORE *YOU GO ON . . .*

1. What does a code of ethics contain?
2. Describe the fundamental tenets of ethics.

RUBY'S CLUB QUESTIONS

1. Which framework do you think is the best for Ruby's Club: utilitarian, rights, fairness, or the common good? Why do you feel this way?

2. How do the concepts of responsibility, accountability, and liability play into the number of drinks an individual has consumed? At what point does Ruby's become responsible for the condition in which a customer leaves the club?

3. Since purchase does not necessarily equal consumption (perhaps the customer is buying drinks for a friend), should Ruby's limit the number of drinks a customer can purchase?

TABLE 6.1 A Framework for Ethical Issues

- **Privacy Issues**
  - What information about oneself should an individual be required to reveal to others?
  - What kind of surveillance can an employer use on its employees?
  - What types of personal information can people keep to themselves and not be forced to reveal to others?
  - What information about individuals should be kept in databases, and how secure is the information there?

- **Accuracy Issues**
  - Who is responsible for the authenticity, fidelity, and accuracy of the information collected?
  - How can we ensure that the information will be processed properly and presented accurately to users?
  - How can we ensure that errors in databases, data transmissions, and data processing are accidental and not intentional?
  - Who is to be held accountable for errors in information, and how should the injured parties be compensated?

- **Property Issues**
  - Who owns the information?
  - What are the just and fair prices for its exchange?
  - How should we handle software piracy (copying copyrighted software)?
  - Under what circumstances can one use proprietary databases?
  - Can corporate computers be used for private purposes?
  - How should experts who contribute their knowledge to create expert systems be compensated?
  - How should access to information channels be allocated?

- **Accessibility Issues**
  - Who is allowed to access information?
  - How much should companies charge for permitting accessibility to information?
  - How can accessibility to computers be provided for employees with disabilities?
  - Who will be provided with equipment needed for accessing information?
  - What information does a person or an organization have a right to obtain, under what conditions, and with what safeguards?

Student Activity | 6.1

Objective: You will be able to identify and categorize ethical issues dealing with information and data use.

Chapter Connection: This activity relates to Section 6.1 and Learning Objective 1 in this chapter.

Prerequisites: You should have read Section 6.1.

Activity:

You will review various articles in mainstream, business, and IS/IT-related sources and identify articles with an IT ethical issue in the article. Mainstream sources might include Time magazine, Newsweek, and the local newspaper. Business sources might include the Wall Street Journal and BusinessWeek. IS/IT-related sources might include Infoweek,

InfoWorld, and Computerworld. You should review five to ten articles from a mainstream source, a business source, and an IS/IT-related source, and then classify the articles based upon the four categories of ethical issues (privacy, property, accuracy, and accessibility) found in Section 6.1. Note that more than one category may apply to the same article.

Deliverables:

Prepare a table that identifies the following:

- Article's title
- Source of the article (mainstream, business, or IS/IT-related)
- Ethical category or categories in the article

You will also select the most interesting/eventful article and write/tell why. This may be turned in as a written assignment or posted blog style to a course site.

Quiz Questions:

1. True or False? An ethical issue will fall into only one of four categories: privacy, accuracy, property, or access.

2. True or False? The four ethical issues that the ever-expanding use of IT applications have created can be categorized as property, accuracy, theft, and embezzlement.

Discussion Questions:

1. Which IT-related ethical category seems to get the most coverage?

2. Which IT-related ethical category seems to get the least coverage?

3. Does ethical coverage seem to vary based on the source (i.e., does mainstream coverage of IT-related ethical issues differ from business coverage of IT-related ethical issues, or does business coverage of IT-related ethical issues differ from IS/IT-related coverage of IT-related ethical issues)?

4. Are ethical issues in business involving IS/IT any different from ethical issues in business that do not involve IS/IT? Why or why not?

6.2 | Privacy

In general, **privacy** is the right to be left alone and to be free of unreasonable personal intrusions. **Information privacy** is the right to determine when, and to what extent, information about you can be gathered and/or communicated to others. Privacy rights apply to individuals, groups, and institutions.

The definition of privacy can be interpreted quite broadly. However, court decisions in many countries have followed two rules fairly closely:

1. The right of privacy is not absolute. Privacy must be balanced against the needs of society.

2. The public's right to know supersedes the individual's right of privacy.

These two rules illustrate why determining and enforcing privacy regulations can be difficult. The right to privacy is recognized today in all U.S. states and by the federal government, either by statute or common law.

Rapid advances in information technologies have made it much easier to collect, store, and integrate data on individuals in large databases. On an average day, you generate data about yourself in many ways: surveillance cameras on toll roads, in public places, and at work; credit card transactions; telephone calls (landline and cellular); banking transactions; queries to search engines; and government records (including police records). These data can be integrated to produce a **digital dossier**, which is an electronic profile of you and your habits. The process of forming a digital dossier is called **profiling**.

Data aggregators, such as LexisNexis (www.lexisnexis.com) and Acxiom (www.acxiom.com), are good examples of profiling. These companies collect public data such as real estate records and published telephone numbers, in addition to nonpublic information such as Social Security numbers, financial data, and police, criminal, and motor vehicle records. They then integrate these data to form digital dossiers on most adults in the United States. They ultimately sell these dossiers to law enforcement agencies and companies that conduct background checks on potential employees. They also sell them to companies that want to know their customers better, a process called *customer intimacy*.

However, data on individuals can be used in more controversial manners. For example, a controversial new map in California identifies the addresses of donors who supported Proposition 8, the referendum that outlawed same-sex marriage in California (see www.eightmaps.com). Gay activists created the map by combining Google's satellite mapping technology with publicly available campaign records that listed Proposition 8 donors who contributed $100 or more. These donors are outraged, claiming that the map invades their privacy and could expose them to retribution.

Electronic Surveillance

According to the American Civil Liberties Union (ACLU), tracking people's activities with the aid of computers has become a major privacy-related problem. The ACLU notes that this monitoring, or **electronic surveillance**, is rapidly increasing, particularly with the emergence of new technologies. Electronic surveillance is conducted by employers, the government, and other institutions.

In general, employees have very limited legal protection against surveillance by employers. The law supports the right of employers to read their employees' e-mail and other electronic documents and to monitor their employees' Internet use. Today, more than three-fourths of organizations are monitoring employees' Internet usage. In addition, two-thirds use software to block connections to inappropriate Web sites, a practice called *URL filtering*. Further, organizations are installing monitoring and filtering software to enhance security by stopping malicious software and to increase productivity by discouraging employees from wasting time.

Electronic surveillance of employees is legal, but not of customers. But would you do it if you could make money off of the information? (*Source:* Bruce Rolff/Shutterstock)

In one organization, the chief information officer (CIO) monitored about 13,000 employees for three months to determine the type of traffic they engaged in on the network. He then forwarded the data to the chief executive officer (CEO) and the heads of the human resources and legal departments. These executives were shocked at the questionable Web sites the employees were visiting, as well as the amount of time they were spending on those sites. The executives quickly made the decision to implement a URL filtering product.

Surveillance is also a concern for private individuals regardless of whether it is conducted by corporations, government bodies, or criminals. Users in the United States are still struggling to define the appropriate balance between personal privacy and electronic surveillance, especially when threats to national security are involved.

Personal Information in Databases

Modern institutions store information about individuals in many databases. Perhaps the most visible locations of such records are credit-reporting agencies. Other institutions that store personal information include banks and financial institutions; cable TV, telephone, and utilities companies; employers; mortgage companies; hospitals; schools and universities; retail establishments; government agencies (such as the Internal Revenue Service, your state, your municipality); and many others.

There are several concerns about the information you provide to these record keepers. Some of the major concerns are these:

- Do you know where the records are?
- Are the records accurate?
- Can you change inaccurate data?
- How long will it take to make a change?
- Under what circumstances will personal data be released?
- How are the data used?
- To whom are the data given or sold?
- How secure are the data against access by unauthorized people?

Information on Internet Bulletin Boards, Newsgroups, and Social Networking Sites

Every day you see more and more *electronic bulletin boards, newsgroups, electronic discussions* such as chat rooms, and *social networking sites* (discussed in Chapter 8). These sites appear on the Internet, within corporate intranets, and on blogs. A *blog,* short for *Weblog,* is an informal, personal journal that is frequently updated and intended for general public reading. How does society keep owners of bulletin boards from disseminating information that may be offensive to readers or simply untrue? This is a difficult problem because it involves the conflict between freedom of speech on one hand and privacy on the other. This conflict is a fundamental and continuing ethical issue in U.S. society.

There is no better illustration of the conflict between free speech and privacy than the Internet. Many Web sites contain anonymous, derogatory information on individuals, who typically have little recourse in the matter. Approximately one-half of U.S. firms use the Internet in examining job applications, including searching for individuals on Google and on social networking sites. Consequently, derogatory information that can be found on the Internet can harm your chances of being hired. This problem has become serious enough that a company called Reputation Defender (www.reputationdefender.com) will search for damaging content online and destroy it on behalf of clients.

Social networking sites can also present serious privacy concerns. "IT's About Business 6.2" takes a look at Facebook's problems with its privacy policies.

IT's ABOUT BUSINESS | 6.2

Your Privacy on Facebook

In December 2009, Facebook adopted a new privacy policy that declared certain information, including lists of friends, to be publicly available, with no privacy settings. Previously, Facebook users could restrict access to this information. As a result of this change, users who had set their list of friends as private were forced to make the list public without even being informed. Further, the option to make the list private again was removed. For example, a user whose Family and Relationships information was set to be viewable by Friends Only would default to being viewable to Everyone (publicly viewable). Therefore, information such as the gender of your partner, relationship status, and family relations became viewable even to people who did not have a Facebook account. Facebook CEO Mark Zuckerberg justified this policy by asserting that privacy is no longer a social norm.

To compound this issue, the new Facebook policy can also expose your endorsements of various organizations and groups, which you make when you click the "Like" button. In addition, Facebook's "Instant Personalization" shares some of your data, without your advance permission, with other Web sites.

The results of the privacy fiasco? The Facebook privacy policy was protested by many people as well as privacy organizations such as the Electronic Frontier

Foundation (www.eff.org). In fact, Iranian dissidents began deleting their Facebook accounts so that the government could not track their contacts.

In another instance, four college students decided to build a social network that would not force people to surrender their privacy. They used an online Web site called Kickstarter (www.kickstarter.com), which helps creative people find support, to raise $10,000. When they introduced their project, called Diaspora (http://joindiaspora.com), in May 2010, they made the source code openly available. Users can employ this software to set up personal servers, create their own information hubs, and control the information they share. The Diaspora "crew" attracted more than 2,000 followers of "joindiaspora" on Twitter in just a few weeks.

Facebook responded by rolling back requirements that some content be public, such as promotional pages that users respond to, or "Like," in Facebook "language." Facebook is also providing a virtual one-click "off switch" that lets users block all access to their information from third-party applications and Web sites. Further, instead of being forced to customize every status update and photo for a "friend" or more broadly, users can put information such as employment history and vacation videos into buckets designated either for friends, friends of friends, or everyone on the Internet

In February 2011, Facebook revealed a new draft of its privacy policy. Although the revised policy does not modify the social network's data-handling practices, it contains information organized around more practical headings such as "your information and how it is used" and "how advertising works." Facebook maintains the new policy is much more of a user guide to how to manage your data.

Questions

1. Why did Facebook change its privacy policies in December 2009?

2. Make the argument in support of the privacy policy changes that Facebook instituted in December 2009.

3. Make the argument against the privacy policy changes that Facebook instituted in December 2009.

4. Discuss the trade-offs between conveniently sharing information and protecting privacy.

Sources: Compiled from J. Angwin and G. Fowler, "Microsoft, Facebook Offer New Approaches to Boost Web Privacy," *Wall Street Journal*, February 26–27, 2011; C. Kang, "Facebook CEO Announces Revamped Privacy Settings," *Washington Post*, May 27, 2010; M. Wagner, "Who Trusts Facebook Now?" *Computerworld Blogs*, May 27, 2010; J. Perez, "Facebook Earns Praise for Privacy Changes," *Computerworld*, May 26, 2010; S. Gaudin, "Amid Backlash, Facebook Unveils Simpler Privacy Controls," *Computerworld*, May 26, 2010; S. Gaudin, "Facebook CEO Says Mistakes Made, Privacy Changes Coming," *Computerworld*, May 24, 2010; R. Pegoraro, "Facebook Meets the 'Unlike' Button," *Washington Post*, May 17, 2010; J. Sutter, "Some Quitting Facebook as Privacy Concerns Escalate," *CNN.com*, May 13, 2010; J. Dwyer, "Four Nerds and a Cry to Arms Against Facebook," *New York Times*, May 11, 2010; B. Johnson, "Privacy No Longer a Social Norm, Says Facebook Founder," *The Guardian*, January 11, 2010.

Privacy Codes and Policies

Privacy policies or **privacy codes** are an organization's guidelines for protecting the privacy of its customers, clients, and employees. In many corporations, senior management has begun to understand that when an organization collects vast amounts of personal information, it must be protected. In addition, many organizations give their customers some voice in how their information is used by providing them with opt-out choices. The **opt-out model** of informed consent permits an entity to collect personal information until the individual specifically requests that the data not be collected. Privacy advocates prefer the **opt-in model** of informed consent, which prohibits an entity from collecting any personal information unless the individual specifically authorizes it.

One privacy tool currently available to consumers is the Platform for Privacy Preferences (P3P), a protocol that automatically communicates privacy policies between an electronic commerce Web site and visitors to that site. P3P enables visitors to determine the types of personal data that can be extracted by the Web sites they visit. It also allows visitors to compare a Web site's privacy policy to the visitors' preferences or to other standards, such as the Federal Trade Commission's (FTC) Fair Information Practices Standard or the European Directive on Data Protection.

Table 6.2 provides a sampling of privacy policy guidelines. The last section in Table 6.2, Data Confidentiality, refers to security, which you will explore in Chapter 7. It is important to note that all the good privacy intentions in the world are useless unless they are supported and enforced by effective security measures.

International Aspects of Privacy

As the number of online users has increased globally, governments throughout the world have enacted a large number of inconsistent privacy and security laws. This highly complex global legal framework is creating regulatory problems for companies. Approximately 50 countries have some form of data-protection laws. Many of these laws conflict with those of other countries, or they require specific security measures. Other countries have no privacy laws at all.

TABLE 6.2 Privacy Policy Guidelines: A Sampler

- **Data Collection**
  - Data should be collected on individuals only for the purpose of accomplishing a legitimate business objective.
  - Data should be adequate, relevant, and not excessive in relation to the business objective.
  - Individuals must give their consent before data pertaining to them can be gathered. Such consent may be implied from the individual's actions (e.g., applications for credit, insurance, or employment).

- **Data Accuracy**
  - Sensitive data gathered on individuals should be verified before they are entered into the database.
  - Data should, where and when necessary, be kept current.
  - The file should be made available so the individual can ensure that the data are correct.
  - If there is disagreement about the accuracy of the data, the individual's version should be noted and included with any disclosure of the file.

- **Data Confidentiality**
  - Computer security procedures should be implemented to ensure against unauthorized disclosure of data. These procedures should include physical, technical, and administrative security measures.
  - Third parties should not be given access to data without the individual's knowledge or permission, except as required by law.
  - Disclosures of data, other than the most routine, should be noted and maintained for as long as the data are maintained.
  - Data should not be disclosed for reasons incompatible with the business objective for which they are collected.

 The absence of consistent or uniform standards for privacy and security obstructs the flow of information among countries, which is called *transborder data flows*. The European Union (EU), for one, has taken steps to overcome this problem. In 1998 the European Community Commission (ECC) issued guidelines to all its member countries regarding the rights of individuals to access information about themselves. The EU data-protection laws are stricter than U.S. laws and thus could create problems for multinational corporations, which could face lawsuits for privacy violation.

The transfer of data in and out of a nation without the knowledge of either the authorities or the individuals involved raises a number of privacy issues. Whose laws have jurisdiction when records are stored in a different country for reprocessing or retransmission purposes? For example, if data are transmitted by a Polish company through a U.S. satellite to a British corporation, which country's privacy laws control the data, and when? Questions like these will become more complicated and frequent as time passes. Governments must make an effort to develop laws and standards to cope with rapidly changing information technologies in order to solve some of these privacy issues.

The United States and the EU share the goal of privacy protection for their citizens, but the United States takes a different approach. To bridge the different privacy approaches, the U.S. Department of Commerce, in consultation with the EU, developed a "safe harbor" framework to regulate the way that U.S. companies export and handle the personal data (such as names and addresses) of European citizens. See www.export.gov/safeharbor and http://ec.europa.eu/justice_home/fsj/privacy/index_en.htm.

BEFORE *YOU GO ON . . .*

1. Describe the issue of privacy as it is affected by IT.
2. Discuss how privacy issues can impact transborder data flows.

1. If privacy needs must be balanced against society's need to know information, at what point should Ruby's inform a customer's friends (on Facebook or Twitter) that he or she is about to leave the club a little too intoxicated?

2. With their new network, Ruben and Lisa hope to offer wireless Internet access. However, they are concerned about whether or not they should block certain Web sites. Obviously they do not want people watching pornography. While this is not illegal (assuming the customers are at least 18 years old), they do not find it appropriate or representative of the atmosphere they want to present in their club. What are your thoughts?

Student Activity 6.2

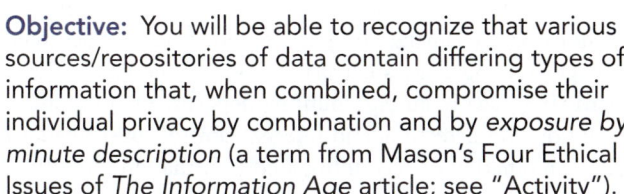

Objective: You will be able to recognize that various sources/repositories of data contain differing types of information that, when combined, compromise their individual privacy by combination and by *exposure by minute description* (a term from Mason's Four Ethical Issues of *The Information Age* article; see "Activity").

Chapter Connection: This activity relates to Section 6.2 and Learning Objective 2 in this chapter.

Prerequisites: You should have read Section 6.2

Activity:

Read the "Privacy" section of Richard Mason's "Four Ethical Issues of the Information Age" in Management Information Systems Quarterly *10(1), pp. 5–12. Make sure that you understand the concept of* exposure by minute description *from the article.*

Identify ten different sources/repositories/users of data about you, as a student, that are located on your campus.

Hint: Everywhere you have to pull out your student ID card or give your student ID number is probably a place that collects and stores data about you. List what information about you is actually stored by those places/users. If possible, ask someone to get the actual list of what is captured/stored.

What happens when you join all those pieces of data together into a single data source? What does it disclose about you that just one of the sources does not?

Can other data be inferred or created as sources are merged? For example, if A is known from one data source and B is known from another, can C, an additional piece of data not specifically contained in either of the sources, be created or figured out? For example, if this year is 2012 and I know that someone played football on a state championship team in 1970, then I know that person is roughly 55 to 58 years old (as the person was likely 15 to 18 years old in 1970).

Deliverables:

Develop a repository/data diagram that shows the following:

- Repository or user of the data
- List of data items stored in each repository
- List of inferred or created data

Quiz Questions:

1. Which of the following is true regarding opt-in/opt-out models?
   - **(a)** The opt-out model allows companies to collect personal information until the customer asks that data not be collected.
   - **(b)** The opt-in model prohibits companies from collecting data unless the customer specifically authorizes it.
   - **(c)** Privacy advocates prefer an opt-out model.
   - **(d)** A and B
   - **(e)** B and C

2. True or False? Transborder data flows are obstructed due to the absence of consistent or uniform standards for privacy and security.

1. Outside of school, identify several other sources/repositories/users of data about you. Develop a composite of that merged data. What data are common among the many sources/repositories/users? What data are specific to only one source/repository/user? What data can be created/inferred beyond that which are specifically stored?

   Hint: Think about places such as your bank, doctor, government agencies, employers, and so on.

2. Take a look at the privacy policy of a social networking site such as Facebook or Twitter. How private are your data? Are there gray areas that are not specific about how your data are or are not protected? What happens when you delete a picture from your account? Is it actually gone from the Internet? What would happen if you were unable to restrict who could see your wall on Facebook (i.e., what if potential employers could see your wall)? Would that change what you posted or allowed to be visible? Why or why not?

What's in IT for ME?

FOR THE ACCOUNTING MAJOR

Public companies, their accountants, and their auditors have significant information security responsibilities. Accountants are now being held professionally and personally responsible for reducing risk, eliminating fraud, increasing the transparency of transactions, and ensuring compliance with generally accepted accounting principles (GAAP). Regulatory agencies such as the SEC and the Public Company Accounting Oversight Board (PCAOB) require accounting departments to monitor information security, fraud prevention and detection, and internal controls over financial reporting. Forensic accounting, a combination of accounting and information security, is one of the most rapidly expanding areas in accounting today.

FOR THE FINANCE MAJOR

Because information security is essential to the success of modern organizations, it is no longer just the concern of the CIO. As a result of global regulatory requirements and the passage of Sarbanes-Oxley, responsibility for information security lies with the CEO and the chief financial officer (CFO) as well. Consequently, all aspects of the security audit, including the security of information and information systems, are key concerns for financial managers.

FOR THE MARKETING MAJOR

Marketing professionals have new opportunities to collect data about their customers—for example, through business-to-consumer electronic commerce (discussed in Chapter 9). Business ethics clearly mandate that these data should be used only within the company and should not be sold to anyone else. Marketers clearly do not want to be sued for invasion of privacy over data collected for the marketing database.

Customers expect their data to be properly secured. However, profit-motivated criminals want that data. Therefore, marketing managers must analyze the risks of their operations. Failure to protect corporate and customer data will cause significant public relations problems and outrage customers. Customer relationship management (discussed in Chapter 12) operations and tracking customers' online buying habits can expose data to misuse (if they are not encrypted) or result in privacy violations.

FOR THE
PRODUCTION/OPERATIONS MANAGEMENT MAJOR

POM professionals decide whether to outsource (or offshore) manufacturing operations. In some cases, these operations are sent overseas to countries that do not have strict labor laws. This situation raises serious ethical questions. For example, is it ethical to hire employees in countries with poor working conditions in order to reduce labor costs?

FOR THE
HUMAN RESOURCES MANAGEMENT MAJOR

Ethics are critically important to HR managers. HR policies explain the appropriate use of information technologies in the workplace. Questions such as these arise: Can employees use the Internet, e-mail, or chat systems for personal purposes while at work? Is it ethical to monitor employees? If so, how? How much? How often? HR managers must formulate and enforce such policies while at the same time maintaining trusting relationships between employees and management.

FOR THE MIS MAJOR

Ethics might be more important for MIS personnel than for anyone else in the organization, because these individuals have control of the information assets. They also have control over a huge amount of personal information on all employees. As a result, the MIS function must be held to the highest ethical standards. In fact, as you will see in the chapter-closing case about Terry Childs, regardless of what he actually did, what one thinks of what he did, and whether his conviction was justified, a person in his situation has the opportunity to behave improperly, and should not.

>>> SUMMARY

1. **Define *ethics*, list and describe the three fundamental tenets of ethics, and describe the four categories of ethical issues related to information technology.** The term *ethics* refers to the principles of right and wrong that individuals use to make choices that guide their behaviors.

Fundamental tenets of ethics include responsibility, accountability, and liability. Responsibility means that you accept the consequences of your decisions and actions. Accountability refers to determining who is responsible for actions that were taken. Liability is a legal concept that gives individuals the right to recover the damages done to them by other individuals, organizations, or systems.

The major ethical issues related to IT are privacy, accuracy, property (including intellectual property), and accessibility to information. Privacy may be violated when data are held in databases or transmitted over networks. Privacy policies that address issues of data collection, data accuracy, and data confidentiality can help organizations avoid legal problems.

2. **Identify three places that store personal data, and, for each one, discuss at least one personal threat to the privacy of the data stored there.** Privacy is the right to be left alone and to be free of unreasonable personal intrusions. Threats to privacy include advances in information technologies, electronic surveillance, and personal information in databases, Internet bulletin boards, newsgroups, and social networking sites. The personal threat in Internet bulletin boards, newsgroups, and social networking sites is that you might post too much information about yourself that many unknown people can see.

>>> CHAPTER GLOSSARY

accountability A tenet of ethics that refers to determining who is responsible for actions that were taken.

code of ethics A collection of principles that are intended to guide decision making by members of the organization.

digital dossier An electronic description of you and your habits.

electronic surveillance Tracking people's activities with the aid of computers.

ethics The principles of right and wrong that individuals use to make choices to guide their behaviors.

information privacy The right to determine when, and to what extent, information about you can be gathered and/or communicated to others.

liability A legal concept that gives individuals the right to recover the damages done to them by other individuals, organizations, or systems.

opt-in model A model of informed consent that prohibits an entity from collecting any personal information unless the individual specifically authorizes it.

opt-out model A model of informed consent that permits an entity from collecting personal information unless the individual specifically requests that the data not be collected.

privacy The right to be left alone and to be free of unreasonable personal intrusions.

privacy codes (see **privacy policies**)

privacy policies (also known as **privacy codes**) An organization's guidelines for protecting the privacy of customers, clients, and employees.

profiling The process of forming a digital dossier.

responsibility A tenet of ethics whereby you accept the consequences of your decisions and actions.

>>> DISCUSSION QUESTIONS

1. In 2008, the Massachusetts Bay Transportation Authority (MBTA) obtained a temporary restraining order barring three Massachusetts Institute of Technology (MIT) students from publicly displaying what they claimed to be a way to get "free subway rides for life." Specifically, the 10-day injunction prohibited the students from revealing vulnerabilities of the MBTA's fare card. The students were scheduled to present their findings in Las Vegas at the DEFCON computer hacking conference. Are the students' actions legal? Are their actions ethical? Discuss your answer from the perspective of the students and then from the perspective of the MBTA.

2. Frank Abagnale, the criminal played by Leonardo DiCaprio in the motion picture *Catch Me If You Can*, ended up in prison. However, when he left prison, he went to work as a consultant to many companies on matters of fraud.

    a. Why do companies hire perpetrators (if caught) as consultants? Is this a good idea?

    b. You are the CEO of a company. Discuss the ethical implications of hiring Frank Abagnale as a consultant.

>>> PROBLEM-SOLVING ACTIVITIES

1. An information security manager routinely monitored the Web surfing done by her company's employees. She discovered that many employees were visiting the "sinful six" Web sites. (*Note:* The sinful six are Web sites with material related to pornography, gambling, hate, illegal activities, tastelessness, and violence.) She then prepared a list of the employees and their surfing histories and gave the list to management. Some managers punished their employees. Some employees, in turn, objected to the monitoring, claiming that they should have a right to privacy.

    a. Is monitoring of Web surfing by managers ethical? (It is legal.) Support your answer.

    b. Is employee Web surfing on the "sinful six" ethical? Support your answer.

    c. Is the security manager's submission of the list of abusers to management ethical? Why or why not?

    d. Is punishing the abusers ethical? Why or why not? If yes, then what types of punishment are acceptable?

    e. What should the company do in this situation? (*Note:* There are a variety of possibilities here.)

2. Access the Computer Ethics Institute's "Ten Commandments of Computer Ethics" at the Web site of the Computer Professionals for Social Responsibility; www.cpsr.org/issues/ethics/cei. Study these ten rules, and decide if any others should be added.

3. Access the Association for Computing Machinery's code of ethics for its members at www.acm.org/constitution/code.html. Discuss the major points of this code. Is this code complete? Why or why not? Support your answer.

4. Access www.eightmaps.com. Is the use of data on this Web site illegal? Unethical? Support your answer.

5. The Electronic Frontier Foundation (www.eff.org) has a mission of protecting rights and promoting freedom in the "electronic frontier." Review the organization's suggestions about how to protect your online privacy, and summarize what you can do to protect yourself.

6. Access your university's guidelines for ethical computer and Internet use. Are there limitations as to the types of Web sites that you can visit and the types of material you can view? Are you allowed to change the programs on the lab computers? Are you allowed to download software from the lab computers for your personal use? Are there rules governing the personal use of computers and e-mail?

7. Access www.albion.com/netiquette/corerules.html. What do you think of this code of ethics? Should it be expanded? Is it too general?

8. Access www.cookiecentral.com and www.epubliceye.com. Do these sites provide information that helps you protect your privacy? If so, then explain how.

9. Do you believe that your university should be allowed to monitor e-mail sent and received on university computers? Why or why not? Support your answer.

>>> TEAM ASSIGNMENTS

Access www.ftc.gov/sentinel to learn how law enforcement agencies around the world work together to fight consumer fraud. Each team should obtain current statistics on one of the top five consumer complaint categories and prepare a report. Are any categories growing faster than others? Are any categories more prevalent in certain parts of the world?

CLOSING **CASE 1 >** What to Do About WikiLeaks?

<<<THE PROBLEM (?)

One of the major controversies generated by the Vietnam War occurred in 1971, when the *New York Times* and other sources publicized excerpts from a secret study commissioned by the Department of Defense—quickly labeled "The Pentagon Papers"—that detailed the history of U.S. involvement in Southeast Asia. These documents had been copied by defense analyst Daniel Ellsberg, one of the contributors to the study. Given the existing technologies, Ellsberg had to photocopy thousands of documents by hand. Today, whistle-blowers—employees with insider knowledge of an organization—can capture huge amounts of incriminating documents on a laptop, memory stick, or portable hard drive. They can send the information through personal e-mail accounts or online drop sites, or they can simply submit it directly to WikiLeaks (www.wikileaks.org).

WikiLeaks was officially unveiled in December 2006. Julian Assange, one of the founders, was reportedly inspired by the leak of the Pentagon Papers. Assange intended WikiLeaks to serve as a dropbox for anyone, anywhere, who disagreed with any organization's activities or secrets. According to its Web site, WikiLeaks focuses on material of ethical, political, and historical significance. In its first year, the organization's database expanded to 1.2 million documents. In addition, WikiLeaks receives approximately 10,000 new documents every day. Since its inception, WikiLeaks has had significant impacts on both businesses and governments. We discuss several examples here.

In January 2008, WikiLeaks posted documents alleging that the Swiss banking group Julius Baer (www.juliusbaer.com) hid its clients' profits from even the Swiss government by concealing them in what seemed to be shell companies in the Cayman Islands. The bank filed a lawsuit against WikiLeaks for publishing data that it claimed had been stolen from its clients. Baer later dropped the lawsuit—but only after generating embarrassing publicity for itself.

In October 2008, Iceland's Kaupthing Bank collapsed, saddling the country with $128 billion in debts. Ten months later, Bogi Ágústsson, the anchor for Icelandic national broadcaster RUV, appeared on the evening news and explained that a legal injunction had prevented the station from airing an exposé on the bank. Viewers who wanted to see the material, he suggested, should visit WikiLeaks. People who took Ágústsson's advice found a summary of Kaupthing's loans posted on the Web site, detailing more than $6 billion funneled from the bank to its owners and companies they owned, often with little or no collateral. WikiLeaks promptly became a household name in Iceland.

The following year, WikiLeaks published documents from a pharmaceutical trade group implying that its lobbyists were receiving confidential documents from, and exerting influence over, a World Health Organization (WHO) project to fund drug research in the developing world. The resulting attention helped to terminate the project.

In September 2009, commodities company Trafigura (www.trafigura.com) requested an injunction from the courts preventing the British media from mentioning a damaging internal report. The report indicated that the company had dumped tons of toxic waste in the Ivory Coast that sickened 100,000 local inhabitants. Although Trafigura could prevent the official media from reporting this story; however, it could not stop WikiLeaks from publishing the information. The public became aware of the transgression, and Trafigura eventually had to pay out more than $200 million in settlements.

As consequential as these business leaks were, probably the most controversial WikiLeaks exposé involved the U.S. government. From November 2009 to April 2010, U.S. Army Private First Class Bradley Manning downloaded hundreds of thousands of diplomatic cables to a CD at an outpost in Iraq. He then passed the information to WikiLeaks. In doing so, Manning violated 18 U.S. Code Section 1030(a)(1), which criminalizes unauthorized computer downloads. Beginning on November 28, 2010, WikiLeaks published the contents of more than 250,000 diplomatic cables, the largest unauthorized release of contemporary classified information in history. Among these cables were 11,000 documents marked secret. The U.S. government's definition of a secret document is one that, if released, would cause "serious damage to national security."

Diplomatic flaps quickly ensued. For example, North Korean leader Kim Jong Il learned that China would consider supporting the unification of the peninsula under the leadership of the South Korean government. Similarly, Iranian President Mahmoud Ahmadinejad discovered that his Arab neighbors were pleading with the U.S. to launch an attack against Tehran's nuclear program.

Not surprisingly, the release of the cables also had wide-ranging repercussions within the United States. The government ordered a clampdown on intelligence sharing between agencies, and it established new measures to control electronically stored documents. U.S. Secretary of State Hilary Clinton charged that the massive cable leak "puts people's lives in danger, threatens national security, and undermines our efforts to work with other countries to solve shared problems." From the opposite perspective, many individuals and groups supported WikiLeaks' actions, including Daniel Ellsberg.

The problem, then, boils down to this: How can governments, organizations, and even individuals prevent future disclosures. Is it possible to accomplish this task, given that the sources of WikiLeaks' information appear to be internal?

THE SOLUTION (?)>>>

In the initial moments after the release of the State Department cables, unknown hackers tried to shut down WikiLeaks by exposing its Web site to denial-of-service attacks (discussed in Chapter 7). It is unclear whether the hackers were working on behalf of the U.S. government, but they seemed to endorse the government's claims that the disclosures threatened national security.

WikiLeaks' supporters retaliated with anonymous hacktivism, attacking the Web sites of companies such as Amazon, which had thrown WikiLeaks off its servers, and MasterCard and PayPal, which had frozen the organization's accounts and prevented its supporters from donating to the cause.

Ultimately, all attempts to stifle WikiLeaks have proved futile. When the organization is blocked from one host server, it simply jumps to another. Further, the number of mirror Web sites—essentially clones of WikiLeaks' main content pages—had mushroomed to 1,300 by the end of 2010.

Prior to 9/11, the U.S. State Department had operated its own internal cable system and encrypted documents to ensure security. After the attacks, the State Department system was merged into a new digital records system controlled by the Department of Defense. Since the WikiLeaks disclosures, the State Department has temporarily severed its connection to the new system while it takes steps to prevent future unauthorized downloads.

In other attempts at thwarting WikiLeaks, governments and companies have turned to cybersecurity. Since 2007, every major security software vendor (for example, McAfee, www.mcafee.com; Symantec, www.symantec.com; and Trend Micro, www.trendmicro.com) has spent hundreds of millions of dollars to acquire companies in the data leak prevention (DLP) industry. These companies produce software that locates and tags sensitive information and then guards against its being stolen or illegally duplicated. Unfortunately, to date, DLP software has not been effective.

The failure of DLP software has prompted organizations to turn to *network forensics*, which is the process of constantly collecting every digital "fingerprint" on an organization's servers to trace and identify an intruder who has broken into the system. Although this software gathers data and makes them easily available, it does not identify the culprits.

<<<**THE RESULTS**

How can organizations and governments respond to WikiLeaks? Lawsuits will not work because WikiLeaks is legally protected in the United States by its role as a mere conduit for documents. Moreover, even if a company or a government somehow won a judgment against WikiLeaks, that would not shut down the company because its assets are spread all over the world.

In fact, WikiLeaks has a nation-sized ally: Iceland. Since WikiLeaks discovered the corrupt loans that helped destroy Iceland's biggest bank, the country has set out to become the conduit for a global flood of leaks. Birgitta Jónsdóttir, a member of Iceland's parliament, created the Icelandic Modern Media Initiative (IMMI). This initiative seeks to bring to Iceland all the laws that support protecting anonymous sources, freedom of information, and transparency from around the world. It would then set up a Nobel-style international award for activities supporting free expression. IMMI would also make Iceland the world's most friendly legal base for whistle-blowers. As of May 2011, IMMI had yet to become law.

Should WikiLeaks falter, other Web sites around the world are ready to take its place. For example, Greenleaks (www.greenleaks.org) is a Web site for whistle-blowers on environmental issues. Openleaks (www.openleaks.org) is a Web site that will not openly publish information sent to it, but will give it to reporters and human rights organizations to disseminate. Perhaps the most controversial site is Anonymous, the hacker collective.

What is the best protection against unauthorized leaks? Icelandic WikiLeaks staffer Kristinn Hrafnsson suggested, rather drily, that companies—and perhaps governments to some extent—reform their practices to avoid being targeted.

Questions

1. Given that the Constitution of the United States of America protects the freedom of speech, should the government that upholds the constitution restrict certain technologies in the name of security?

2. To what extent should unethical practices be punishable by law?

SOURCES: Compiled from R. Somaiya, "Former WikiLeaks Colleagues Forming New Web Site, OpenLeaks," *New York Times*, February 6, 2011; A. Greenberg, "WikiLeaks' StepChildren," *Forbes*, January 17, 2011; M. Calabresi, "Winning the Info War," *Time*, December 20, 2010; A. Greenberg, "WikiLeaks' Julian Assange," *Forbes*, December 20, 2010; J. Dougherty and E. Labott, "The Sweep: WikiLeaks Stirs Anarchy Online," *CNN.com*, December 15, 2010; E. Robinson, "In WikiLeaks Aftermath, An Assault on Free Speech," *Washington Post*, December 14, 2010; M. Calabresi, "The War on Secrecy," *Time*, December 13, 2010; I. Shapira and J. Warrick, "WikiLeaks' Advocates Are Wreaking 'Hacktivism'," *Washington Post*, December 12, 2010; F. Rashid, "WikiLeaks, Anonymous Force Change to Federal Government's Security Approach," *eWeek*, December 12, 2010; E. Mills, "Report: Ex-WikiLeakers to Launch New OpenLeaks Site," *CNET.com*, December 10, 2010; G. Keizer, "Pro-WikiLeaks Cyber Army Gains Strength; Thousands Join DDos Attacks," *Computerworld*, December 9, 2010; J. Warrick and R. Pegoraro, "WikiLeaks Avoids Shutdown as Supporters Worldwide Go on the Offensive," *Washington Post*, December 8, 2010; F. Rashid, "PayPal, PostFinance Hit by DoS Attacks, Counter-Attack in Progress," *eWeek*, December 6, 2010; "Holder: 'Significant'

Actions Taken in WikiLeaks Investigation," *CNN.com*, December 6, 2010; "WikiLeaks Back Online After Being Dropped by U.S. Domain Name Provider," *CNN.com*, December 3, 2010; "WikiLeaks Reports Another Electronic Disruption," *CNN.com*, November 30, 2010; "Feds Open Criminal Investigation into WikiLeaks Disclosures," *CNN.com*, November 29, 2010; L. Fadel, "Army Intelligence Analyst Charged in WikiLeaks Case," *Washington Post*, July 7, 2010; www.wikileaks.org, accessed February 11, 2011; G. Goodale, "WikiLeaks Q&A with Daniel Ellsberg, the Man Behind the Pentagon Papers," *Christian Science Monitor*, July 29, 2010, accessed May 12, 2011.

CLOSING **CASE 2** > You Be the Judge

THE PROBLEM>>>

Terry Childs worked in San Francisco's information technology department for five years as a highly valued network administrator. Childs, who holds a Cisco Certified Internetwork Expert certification, the highest level of certification offered by Cisco, built San Francisco's new multimillion-dollar computer network, the FiberWAN. He handled most of the implementation, including the acquisition, configuration, and installation of all the routers and switches that comprise the network. The FiberWAN contains essential city information such as officials' e-mails, city payroll files, confidential law enforcement documents, and jail inmates' booking information.

On July 13, 2008, Childs was arrested and charged with four felony counts of computer tampering. Authorities accused him of commandeering the FiberWAN by creating passwords that granted him exclusive access to the system. In addition to refusing to give city officials the passwords necessary to access the FiberWAN, Childs is accused of other actions. Authorities allege that he implemented a tracing system to monitor what administrators were saying and doing. Authorities also discovered dial-up and digital subscriber line (DSL) modems (discussed in Chapter 9) that would enable an unauthorized user to connect to the FiberWAN. They also found that he had placed a command on several devices on the network that would erase critical configuration data in the event that anyone tried to restore administrative access to the devices. Further, he allegedly collected pages of user names and passwords, including his supervisor's, to use their network login information. He was also charged with downloading terabytes of city data to a personal encrypted storage device. The extent of Childs's activities was not known until a June 2008 computer audit.

Childs had been disciplined on the job in the months leading up to his arrest, and his supervisors had tried to fire him. Those attempts were unsuccessful, in part because of his exclusive knowledge of the city's FiberWAN.

After his arrest, Childs kept the necessary passwords to himself for ten days, and then gave them to the mayor of San Francisco in a secret meeting in the city jail. What was he thinking? Had he become a rogue employee? His lawyer paints a different picture of the man and his situation.

Childs seems to have taken his job very seriously, to the point of arrogance. He worked very hard, including evenings and weekends, and he rarely took vacations. Because the FiberWAN was so complex and Childs did not involve any of the other network engineers in his unit, he was the only person who fully understood the network's configuration. He apparently trusted no one but himself with the details of the network, including its configuration and login information.

Childs had a poor relationship with his superiors, who were all managerially oriented rather than technically oriented. He considered his direct supervisor to be intrusive, incompetent, and obstructive, and he believed the managers above him had no real concept of the FiberWAN. In fact, he felt that his superiors were more interested in office politics than in getting anything done. He also complained that he was overworked and that many of his colleagues were incompetent freeloaders.

Childs's lawyer maintained that his client had been the victim of a "bad faith" effort to force him out of his post by incompetent city officials whose meddling was jeopardizing the network that Childs had built. He further charged that in the past Childs's supervisors and co-workers had damaged the FiberWAN themselves, hindered Childs's ability to maintain the system, and shown complete indifference to maintaining it themselves.

Childs was the only person in the department capable of operating the FiberWAN. Despite this fact, the department had established no policies as to the appropriate person to whom Childs could give the passwords. Childs maintains that no one who requested the passwords from him was qualified to have them.

Childs's lawyer raised the question, "How could the department say his performance was poor when he had been doing what no one else was able or willing to do?" Interestingly, the FiberWAN continued to run smoothly while Childs was holding the passwords.

As of May 2011, San Francisco officials maintained they had paid Cisco contractors almost $200,000 to fix the problems with the FiberWAN. The city has retained a security consulting firm, Secure DNA (www.secure-dna.com), to conduct a vulnerability assessment of its network. It has also set aside a further $800,000 to address potential ongoing problems.

On April 27, 2010, after nearly three days of deliberation, a jury convicted Childs of one count of felony computer tampering for withholding passwords to the city's FiberWAN network. On August 9, 2010, the judge sentenced Childs to four years in prison.

Questions

1. Do you agree with the jury that Childs is guilty of computer tampering?
   a. Discuss the case from the perspective of the prosecutor of the City of San Francisco.
   b. Discuss the case from the perspective of Childs's defense lawyer.

2. A single point of failure is a component of a system that, if it fails, will prevent the entire system from functioning. For this reason, a single point of failure is clearly undesirable, whether it is a person, a network, or an application. Is Childs an example of a single point of failure? Why or why not? If he is a single point of failure, then how should the City of San Francisco (or any organization) protect itself from such a person?

SOURCES: Compiled from R. McMillan, "Network Admin Terry Childs Gets 4-Year Sentence," *Bloomberg BusinessWeek*, August 7, 2010; J. Niccolai, "Terry Childs Is Denied Motion for Retrial," *PC World*, July 30, 2010; J. Vijayan, "After Verdict, Debate Rages in Terry Childs' Case," *Computerworld*, April 28, 2010; P. Venezia, "Slouching Toward Justice for Terry Childs," *InfoWorld*, March 1, 2010; J. Van Derbeken, "S.F. Officials Locked Out of Computer Network," *SFGate.com*, July 15, 2008; Z. Church, "San Francisco IT Hack Story Looks a Bit Too Much Like *Chinatown*," *SearchCIO-Midmarket.com*, July 16, 2008; P. Venezia, "Why San Francisco's Network Admin Went Rogue," *InfoWorld*, July 18, 2008; J. Van Derbeken, "Lawyer Says Client Was Protecting City's Code," *SFGate.com*, July 23, 2008; R. McMillan and P. Venezia, "San Francisco's Mayor Gets Back Keys to the Network," *Network World*, July 23, 2008; R. McMillan, "Parts of San Francisco Network Still Locked Out," *Network World*, July 23, 2008; J. Vijayan, "City Missed Steps to Avoid Network Lockout," *Computerworld*, July 28, 2008; A. Surdin, "San Francisco Case Shows Vulnerability of Data Networks," *Washington Post*, August 11, 2008; R. McMillan, "San Francisco Hunts for Mystery Device on City Network," *Computerworld*, September 11, 2008; B. Egelko, "S.F. Computer Engineer to Stand Trial," *SFGate.com*, December 27, 2008.

RUBY'S CLUB INTERNSHIP ASSIGNMENTS

To complete this assignment, Ruben and Lisa need suggestions on developing their ethics and privacy statement. Search Google (or another search engine) for clubs in your local area and see if any have an ethics and privacy statement online. Can you tell if they take the utilitarian, rights, fairness, or the common good approach to ethics? What seems to be the norm for clubs? Do any of them deal with the ethics of monitoring alcohol consumption?

Also look online for restaurants that offer WiFi access. Most of these make you agree to terms of use before accessing the network. Do any of them state anything regarding Web site or material that would be blocked or inappropriate?

Finally, prepare a statement for Ruben and Lisa to use as their rough draft as they prepare their own ethics and privacy statement. Submit it to them via your professor.

SPREADSHEET ACTIVITY

Objective: You will learn how to lock and protect spreadsheets to keep private information protected. You will also learn the difference between a "protected" spreadsheet and a secure database.

Chapter Connection: Ethics are a difficult subject in information systems. The tighter you keep a system, the less useful it is. However, the more freely you allow people to access data, the more privacy issues you have on your hands. The object of this exercise is to help establish the necessary balance between ethics, privacy, and data usefulness.

Prerequisites: There are no prerequisites for this activity.

Activity: Recently, a fraternity on campus made plans to host a party with a sorority and took reservations for T-shirt orders. One of the members was an MIS student who had set up a Google Survey for the orders and had exported all of the data into a spreadsheet. The data included name, address, shirt size, address, phone number, and so on. The university has asked the fraternity to keep this data confidential due to problems in the past.

Specifically, a year earlier, the same data were stored in an unsecured spreadsheet that was e-mailed around the fraternity. One of the fraternity brothers took some of the information and used it to exploit and make fun of a physically larger sorority sister. To ensure that this does not happen again, the university is asking the fraternity to show evidence that the spreadsheet is locked and will only be seen by those approved to deliver the T-shirts within the fraternity and the sorority.

As a member of those approved by the university to manage this information, your job is to take the data collected by the Google Survey and move

private information to the private page and lock it so that it cannot be used to exploit any member of either fraternity or sorority.

Go to www.wiley.com/college/rainer to download the spreadsheet. Then watch the accompanying video to learn how to make a spreadsheet secure.

Deliverables: The final product will be a spreadsheet with the survey data in a spreadsheet with the single page of data divided between a secure page and an "open" page.

Quiz Questions:

1. True or False? "Protection" in Excel is the same as "Security."

2. True or False? A password-protected spreadsheet is difficult to break into.

3. Reasons to lock cells include all of the following *except*:
   (a) To hide a formula
   (b) To hide the contents of the cell
   (c) To be able to quickly move through the spreadsheet by "tabbing"
   (d) To provide some level of protection

Discussion Questions:

1. How can a spreadsheet be helpful if it is so easy to secure and hack?

2. Are Google spreadsheets more secure than Excel spreadsheets?

3. If a sheet needs to be "very hidden," then why not go ahead and delete it?

DATABASE ACTIVITY: FILTERING AND SORTING

Objective

In this activity you will learn how to select only the useful rows of a table, hiding the others, and sort a table on any column in it. A database is useless if you cannot get information out of it. Access offers many ways to do that. Some are simple but limited. Others are more capable but require more work. Filtering and sorting a table are at the low end but are still often useful. We will start with them here, and go on to more complex (but more capable) methods in later activities.

Chapter Connection

All organizations keep critical information in databases. Security and privacy considerations govern who can access that database and what they are allowed to see there. This means being able to see some parts of a database but not others. Hence, the way people select parts of a database to see is closely connected to privacy and security considerations. Discussion questions 1 and 2 at the end of this activity go into this connection more deeply.

Prerequisites

None.

Activity:

In this activity, which you will find online, you will learn how to filter and sort an Access table to zero in on exactly the rows you want. The techniques are simple, but will be useful often.

The database you may have used with the Chapter 4 activity has information a company might use to track problems with network equipment. Its central element is the *trouble ticket*. A ticket is submitted by a user, who works in a department, and refers to a device (item of network equipment). A ticket is initially open. It is assigned to a technician, may go to "in process" or "on hold" (if there is any delay in resolving it), and is eventually closed or cancelled. That database has five tables: users, departments, technicians, devices, and trouble tickets. You can see how they are connected in the NeTrouble database on the Web site. Choose the Database Tools tab above the ribbon, and click on the relationship map.

Note: This version of the activity is for use with Access 2010. There is another version for Access 2007. Their content is identical, including the activities and their sequence. They differ where the two releases of the software differ: in screen shots and in some details of how specific operations are accomplished.

1. Download and open the Ch 06 NetSimple database from www.wiley.com/college/rainer. It has one table with the same information as in NeTrouble, minus some columns (such as employee date of birth and date of hire) to save screen space.

   This is usually a poor way to organize a database. It violates the normalization rules you learned in Chapter 3. However, this "flat file" data structure is common; it is not always bad; and it is where filtering works best.

2. Suppose you want to see the trouble tickets for all your routers. Open TroubleTbl in NetSimple. Make sure it is in Datasheet view. (It should open that way.) The second column of the table, DeviceName, gives the type of device.

3. Pull down the triangle to the right of the column name by clicking on it. You will see a list of all the different devices in the table, sorted alphabetically.

Note: You will see entries for both "Router" (correct) and "Rooter" (a misspelling). The chance of this sort of error is one reason that a flat file database is not a good option for anything but the simplest data storage requirements.

4. You will also see two entries in the table above the list of types: one that reads "Select All" and one that refers to blank (empty) cells in the datasheet. At this point all the boxes are checked. Click "Select All" to uncheck all the boxes. Then click "Bridge" and "OK."

5. All the rows have gone away except for those with Bridge in the DevName column (that is, except for all the trouble tickets that refer to bridges). You will see a small funnel next to the triangle in that column. It means the data you see are filtered on the content of that column.

6. Click the Home tab above the ribbon. In the Sort & Filter section toward the right side of the ribbon, Toggle Filter (a funnel icon) will be highlighted. Click it a few times to see what it does.

7. You can filter for more than one column at a time. Pull down the filtering menu for the Department column. It shows only the departments that are now visible—that is, those that reported a problem with a bridge. Since HR did not, it is not in the list.

   Now, click "Marketing." The Marketing box will be unchecked. So will the Select All box since all the choices are no longer selected. Click "OK." Trouble tickets from Marketing are now hidden, leaving those from all other departments. Both columns show funnels next to their triangles. The Toggle Filter button alternates between both filters on and both off. If you want to turn one of them off while leaving the other on, you must clear it individually.

8. To sort the visible trouble tickets by the date they were submitted, pull down the sorting and filtering menu of the TicketSubmitted column. Choose Sort Newest to Oldest and click "OK." The table now shows the trouble tickets with the newest at the top. This is useful if you need to find out about the latest problems.

Usage Hint: You also can sort by selecting a column and clicking one of the icons on the left side of the Sort & Filter section of the Home ribbon. The top icon sorts in ascending order; the middle one, sorts in descending order; and the last one clears any existing sorts on that column. This may be faster if the Home ribbon is selected, but not if you are working with a different ribbon.

9. Select the TicketSubmitted column of the table by clicking on its heading. Pull down its Sort & Filter menu and move your mouse pointer to Date Filters. (The type of filters you get here depends on the data type of the column you are working with.) Another menu will come out from the side of the main menu. Select "After . . . ," the fourth entry. In the dialogue box that appears, enter 3/1/2011.

10. Close this database, being sure to save your work.

Usage hint: If you open your database again at this point, it may seem that your sort and filters disappeared. They did not. They were saved with the database. They are just not applied. Clicking "Toggle Filters" will reactivate them.

11. Now, download and open the Ch 06 NeTrouble database from www.wiley.com/college/rainer. (You may have used a similar database in the Chapter 4 activity.) It is a better way to structure these data. However, as you will see, it is more awkward to filter on a multiple-table database. (That is why we will learn about other query techniques for such databases later, in the Chapter 10 activity.) To get the same result that was so easy to get, proceed as follows:

12. Open DeviceTbl. Find the Bridge row or rows. Since this table is short, you can scan it by eye in a couple of seconds. Record its primary key (DeviceID, its first column) and close it.

13. Open the TicketTbl. Find its Device column. Filter that column for the device key or keys you just recorded. This will select the trouble tickets for all bridges.

This is a lot of work to get a result that you obtained more easily the first time—and you only needed to use two tables, not seven or eight. That is one downside of multiple-table databases versus flat files. Their business advantages still outweigh their drawbacks. You will see how to get around those difficulties by using other query tools in future activities.

14. Close this database, being sure to save your work.

Deliverables:

1. Your Ch 06 NetSimple database, with the filters you applied
2. Your Ch 06 NeTrouble database, with the filters you applied

Quiz Questions:

1. True or False? Clicking on a "Sort" icon, with a table column selected, does exactly the same as selecting the corresponding Sort option from that column's pull-down filtering menu.

2. Consider the filter you applied to the single-table database in steps 3–5 of this activity. Could you have used the same basic method, but checking different boxes, to select:
   (a) All devices other than bridges?
   (b) All devices that are either bridges or switches?
   (c) All devices that are routers or rooters, to include misspellings?
   (d) Any of the above?

3. True or False? You apply a filter to a database table, close the database, then reopen it. When you look at that table in Datasheet view, its rows will still be filtered as they were.

4. The Sort & Filter section of the ribbon is found under which ribbon tab?
   (a) Home
   (b) Create
   (c) Database Tools
   (d) Datasheet

Discussion Questions:

1. Suppose you have the five-table version of this database (NeTrouble) and have been asked to analyze the distribution of trouble tickets by department. You understand the difficulty of doing this, as you did it for a different problem in activity steps 8–10, and you are willing to put up with that. However, for privacy reasons, you are not allowed to access the user table. Would this be a problem? Why or why not? If it would, suggest a solution.

2. Sometimes a person should see only certain rows of a table. Student access to grades is one example: You may see your own rows, but not those of other students. One way to make this happen is to create a copy of the table, filter for rows this person should *not* see, select them all, delete them, and then clear the filter to show the remaining rows. (This would have to be done automatically, or by someone who is allowed to see the entire table.) The result can then be e-mailed to the student, plugged into a Web page template, and so on.

   Think of two other situations where access to a table must be controlled on a row basis. Would this solution work for each of them? Why or why not?

3. The filtering menu of a column shows all data values in that column with check boxes. Rows containing checked values will remain visible when the filter is applied. Other rows will be hidden, but they can be shown by clearing the filter or toggling it off. More complex criteria can be applied by selecting [_____] Filters, where the blank specifies the data type of the column (e.g., text) and providing any parameters as in this activity's step 6.

   Choose any column of any table that contains text data. Select "Text Filters" from the drop-down menu. Consider the eight types of filters in the submenu that appears. Think of two situations in which those eight types do not meet the filtering needs. Be specific in explaining what these situations call for that they cannot handle.

7 | Information Security

LEARNING OBJECTIVES >>>

1. Discuss the five factors contributing to the increasing vulnerability of information resources, and give one specific example of each factor.

2. Compare and contrast human mistakes and social engineering, and give a specific example of each.

3. Describe the nine types of deliberate attacks.

4. Define the three risk mitigation strategies, and give an example of each in the context of you owning a home.

5. Identify the three major types of controls that organizations can use to protect their information resources, and give an example of each.

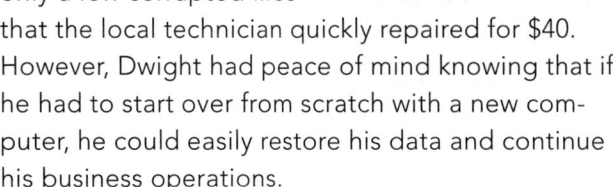

OPENING CASE > Thomas Tax Service

When Dwight Thomas tried to boot up his computer one morning, he realized he had a major problem. His tax service relied completely on the QuickBooks (http://quickbooks.intuit.com) program to maintain all of his customers' financial information. After multiple attempts to resurrect his computer, he called a local computer repair service. The technician determined that the motherboard was bad and he would require a $5,000 minimum charge to restore Dwight's data. And what was the worst part of it all? Dwight had no backup. So, he purchased a new computer and began the long and arduous process of manually restoring his data from his paper files.

After this incident, Dwight put a backup plan in place. All of his three employees now have a USB drive for QuickBooks file backups. Dwight also purchased a fireproof safe. Each Friday, he takes the USB drives out of the safe and all the employees back up their files, using the built-in backup system in QuickBooks. Dwight keeps the three most recent backups. When the employees back up each Friday, QuickBooks erases the oldest backup and creates a new one. Therefore, if there is a problem while the new backup is being created, two safe backups can still be accessed. Although this process seems simple, it is much more effective than not having a backup at all. Given the nature of Dwight's small business, his system is enough to keep his business going in spite of any computer failure.

Recently, Dwight experienced another computer failure. Fortunately, the problem turned out to be only a few corrupted files that the local technician quickly repaired for $40. However, Dwight had peace of mind knowing that if he had to start over from scratch with a new computer, he could easily restore his data and continue his business operations.

Sources: Compiled from author interview with Dwight Thomas, owner of Thomas Tax Service.

Questions

1. Why did Dwight restore his data manually by himself?
2. What are the advantages and disadvantages of Dwight's backup plan?

A solid backup plan is critical to information security. As you consider this case, think about your personal data—pictures, videos, schoolwork, financial information, or any digital files that you would like to have if you lost your computer. A duplicate backup is easy to keep, but you have to be diligent about backing up your essential files. For a small business, this process is even more important because any loss of data could mean lost customers and lost revenue.

RUBY'S CLUB

It seems that every day Ruben and Lisa hear of an attack where credit card information has been stolen, disgruntled employees have shared **passwords** (private combinations of characters that only the user should know) and stolen or sold customer data, computers have been physically stolen from behind locked doors, and other customer information has been compromised. They are very concerned about information security!

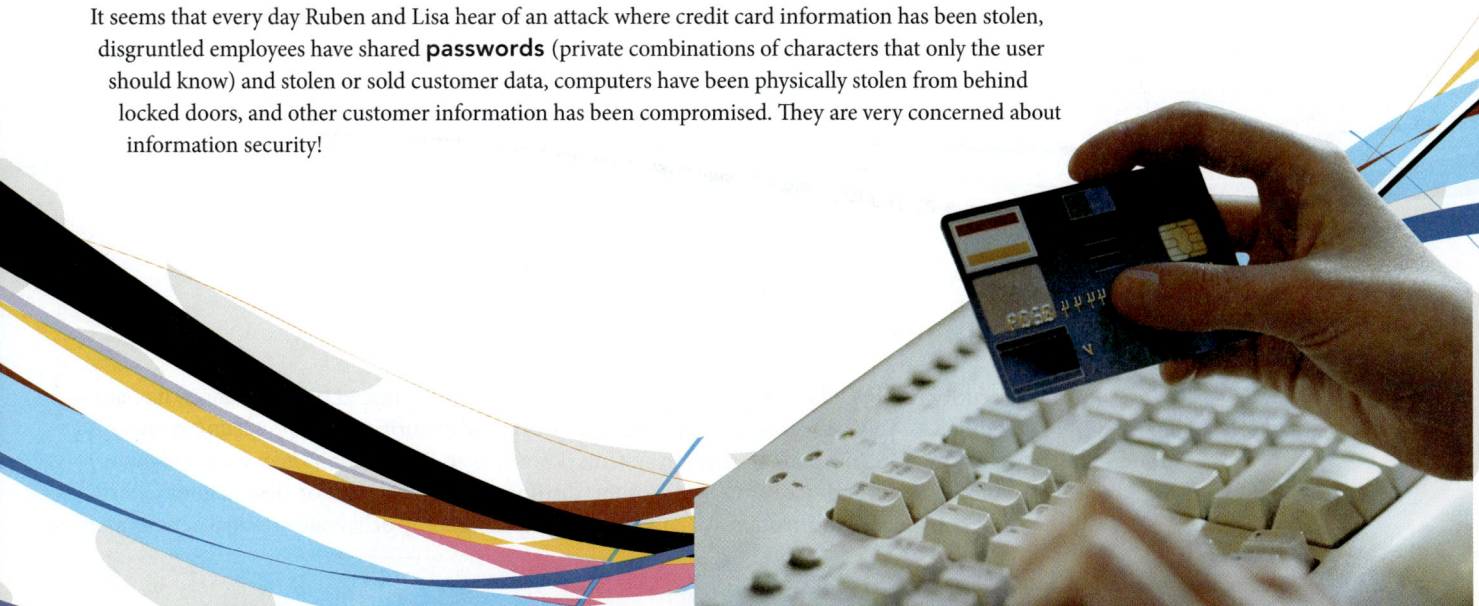

>>> Ruben and Lisa want to know what kind of threats are really out there and which threats might impact a nightclub. Can these threats be categorized so they can better understand them? In what ways might Ruby's be vulnerable to various information security threats? How much training do employees need to create a secure environment for their customers' private information?

INTRODUCTION

Information security is closely related to IT and raises significant questions. For example, how do organizations show due diligence in protecting sensitive, classified information? Is the cause of security breaches in organizations managerial, technological, or some combination of both? How should organizations protect their information more effectively? The most important question raised in this chapter, however, is whether it is possible to secure the Internet. The answer to this question impacts each and every one of us.

The answers to these and other questions are not clear. As you learn about information security in the context of information technology, you will acquire a better understanding of these issues, their importance, their relationships, and their trade-offs.

Information technologies, properly used, can have enormous benefits for individuals, organizations, and entire societies. So far, you have learned about diverse ways in which IT has made businesses more productive, efficient, and responsive to consumers. You have explored areas such as medicine and philanthropy in which IT has improved people's health and well-being. Unfortunately, information technologies can also be misused, often with devastating consequences. Consider the following:

- Individuals can have their identities stolen.
- Organizations' customer information can be stolen, leading to financial losses, erosion of customer confidence, and legal action.
- Countries face the threat of cyberterrorism and cyberwarfare. Cyberwarfare is a critical problem for the U.S. government. In fact, President Barack Obama's 2009 stimulus package contained billions of dollars to upgrade the government's digital defenses.

In fact, the misuse of information technologies has come to the forefront of any discussion of IT. For example, the Ponemon Institute (www.ponemon.org), a research firm, found that organizations spent an average of $6.75 million for each security breach in 2010.

The study measured the direct costs of a data breach, such as hiring forensic experts, notifying customers, setting up telephone hotlines to field queries from concerned or affected customers, offering free credit monitoring subscriptions, and discounts for future products and services. The study also measured more intangible costs of a breach, such as the loss of business from increased customer turnover (known as *customer churn*) and decreases in customer trust.

According to the study, employee negligence caused many of the data breaches. This finding confirms that organizational employees are a weak link in information security. As a result, it is very important for you to learn about information security so that you will be better prepared when you enter the workforce.

7.1 | Introduction to Information Security

Security can be defined as the degree of protection against criminal activity, danger, damage, and/or loss. Following this broad definition, **information security** means protecting an organization's information and information systems (known as an organization's *information resources*) from unauthorized access, use, disclosure, disruption, modification, or destruction. Clearly, information and information systems can be compromised by deliberate criminal actions and by anything that can impair the proper functioning of an organization's information systems.

Before you continue, let's look at these key terms. Organizations have huge amounts of information and numerous information systems that are subject to many threats. A **threat** to an information resource is any danger to which a system may be exposed. The **exposure** of an information resource is the harm, loss, or damage that can result if a threat compromises that resource. An information resource's **vulnerability** is the possibility that the system will suffer harm by a threat.

A number of factors are contributing to the increasing vulnerability of organizational information resources, making it much more difficult to secure them. Before you learn about these factors, they are listed here:

Human mistakes such as unattended equipment often leave resources vulnerable to theft. (*Source:* George Doyle/Image Source Limited)

- Today's interconnected, interdependent, wirelessly networked business environment
- Smaller, faster, cheaper computers and storage devices
- Decreasing skills necessary to be a computer hacker
- International organized crime taking over cybercrime
- Lack of management support

The first factor is the evolution of the information technology resource from mainframe only to today's highly complex, interconnected, interdependent, wirelessly networked business environment. The Internet now enables millions of computers and computer networks to freely and seamlessly communicate with one another. Organizations and individuals are exposed to a world of untrusted networks and potential attackers. A *trusted network*, in general, is any network within your organization. An *untrusted network*, in general, is any network external to your organization. In addition, wireless technologies enable employees to compute, communicate, and access the Internet anywhere and anytime. Significantly, wireless is an inherently nonsecure broadcast communications medium.

The second factor reflects the fact that modern computers and storage devices (e.g., thumb drives or flash drives) continue to become smaller, faster, cheaper, and more portable, with greater storage capacity. These characteristics make it much easier to steal or lose a computer or storage device that contains huge amounts of sensitive information. Also, many more people are able to afford powerful computers and connect inexpensively to the Internet, thus increasing the target size of an attack on information assets.

The third factor is that the computing skills necessary to be a hacker are *decreasing*. The reason is that the Internet contains information and computer programs (called *scripts*) that users with few skills can download and use to attack any information system connected to the Internet. (Security experts can also use these scripts for legitimate purposes, such as testing the security of various systems.)

The fourth factor is that international organized crime is taking over cybercrime. **Cybercrime** refers to illegal activities taking place over computer networks, particularly the Internet. VeriSign's iDefense Security Intelligence Services (http://labs.idefense.com) provides security information to governments and Fortune 500 companies. VeriSign states that groups of well-organized criminals have taken control of a global billion-dollar crime network. The network, powered by skillful hackers, targets known software security weaknesses. These crimes are typically nonviolent but quite lucrative. For example, the losses from armed robberies average hundreds of dollars, and those from white collar crimes average tens of thousands of dollars. In contrast, losses from computer crimes average hundreds of thousands of dollars. Also, these crimes can be committed from anywhere in the world, at any time, effectively providing an international safe haven for cybercriminals. Computer-based crimes cause billions of dollars in damages to businesses each year, including the costs to repair information systems and the costs of lost business.

The fifth, and final, factor is lack of management support. For the entire organization to take security policies and procedures seriously, senior managers must set the tone. Ultimately, however, lower-level managers may be even more important. These managers are in close contact with employees every day and thus are in a better position to determine whether employees are following security procedures.

BEFORE *YOU GO ON . . .*

1. Define information security.
2. Define a threat, an exposure, and a vulnerability.
3. Why are the skills needed to be a hacker decreasing?

Student Activity | 7.1

Objective: The objective of this exercise is to become familiar with information security and how it is done.

Chapter Connection: This case relates to Chapter 7, Section 7.1, and the importance of information security. When doing business over the Web, it is important to protect an organization's information and information systems (known as an organization's *information resources*) from unauthorized access, use, disclosure, disruption, modification, or destruction.

Prerequisites: You should read Section 7.1 before doing this exercise to become familiar with security.

Activity:

Identity theft has become a major concern for those buying merchandise via Web sites. We all want to be sure our personal data is transferred securely. VeriSign is a company that is in the business of protecting Web sites and Web users. Visit the following Web site to read about it:

www.verisign.com/ssl/ssl-information-center/how-ssl-security-works

Deliverables:

Read the article and then answer the following questions.

1. Describe the five steps that occur when a browser connects to a *secure* Web site.
2. What are SSL certificates?
3. What are the normal visual cues that a connection is secure?
4. What is the extended verification that is seen on some sites?

Multiple Choice Questions:

1. How does an SSL certificate protect sites?
   - (a) It enables encryption of sensitive information.
   - (b) It is a unique credential.
   - (c) It authenticates the owner.
   - (d) All of the above.

2. What is the first step in setting up a secure connection?
   - (a) Server sends back digital acknowledgement.
   - (b) Browser checks if it trusts SSL certificate.
   - (c) Encrypted data are shared.
   - (d) Browser requests the server identify itself.

3. What is the last step of setting up a secure connection?
   - (a) Server sends back digital acknowledgement.
   - (b) Browser checks if it trusts SSL certificate.
   - (c) Encrypted data are shared.
   - (d) Browser requests the server to identify itself.

4. Strong encryption is how many bits?
   - (a) 8
   - (b) 64
   - (c) 128
   - (d) 256

5. What company is in the identity and authentication security business to secure and certify Web sites?
   - (a) Microsoft
   - (b) IBM
   - (c) InfoSys
   - (d) VeriSign

Discussion Question:

Discuss the benefits of using VeriSign on a business Web site for both the company and the user.

7.2 | Unintentional Threats to Information Systems

Information systems are vulnerable to many potential hazards and threats, as you see in Figure 7.1. The two major categories of threats are unintentional threats and deliberate threats. In this section you will learn about unintentional threats. The next section addresses deliberate threats.

Unintentional threats are those acts with no malicious intent. Human errors are unintentional and represent a serious threat to information security.

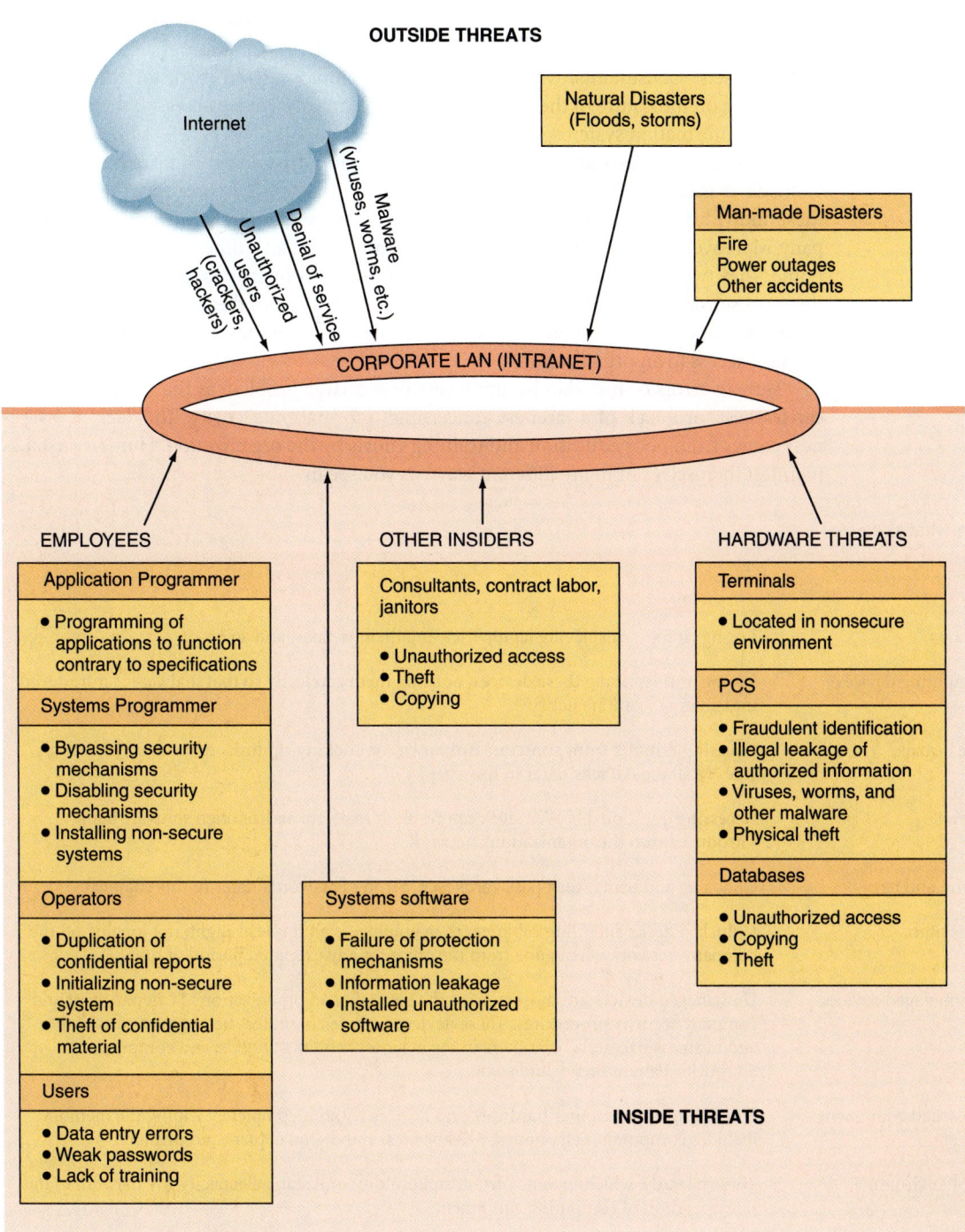

Figure 7.1 Security threats.

Human Errors

Organizational employees span the breadth and depth of the organization, from mail clerks to the CEO, and across all functional areas. There are two important points to be made about employees. First, the higher the level of employee, the greater the threat the employee poses to information security. This situation exists because higher-level employees typically have greater access to corporate data and enjoy greater privileges on organizational information systems. Second, employees in two areas of the organization pose significant threats to information security: human resources and information systems. Human resources employees generally have access to sensitive personal information about all employees. Likewise, information systems employees not only have access to sensitive organizational data, but they also often control the means to create, store, transmit, and modify that data.

Other employees include contract labor, consultants, and janitors and guards. Contract labor, such as temporary hires, may be overlooked in information security. However, these employees often have access to the company's network, information systems, and information assets. Consultants, while technically not employees, do work for the company. Depending on the nature of their work, these people may also have access to the company's network, information systems, and information assets.

Janitors and guards are the most frequently ignored people in information security. Companies might outsource their security and janitorial services, meaning that, although these individuals technically are not employees, they nevertheless do work for the company. Moreover, they are usually present when most—if not all—other employees have gone home. They typically have keys to every office, and nobody questions their presence in even the most sensitive parts of the building. In fact, an article from the Winter 1994 edition of *2600: The Hacker Quarterly* described how to get a job as a janitor for the purpose of gaining physical access to an organization.

Human errors or mistakes by employees pose a large problem as the result of laziness, carelessness, or a lack of awareness concerning information security. This lack of awareness comes from poor education and training efforts by the organization. Human mistakes manifest themselves in many different ways, as you see in Table 7.1.

TABLE 7.1 Human Mistakes

Mistake	Description and Examples
Carelessness with laptops	Losing laptops, misplacing laptops, leaving them in taxis, and so on.
Carelessness with computing devices	Losing or misplacing these devices, or using them carelessly so that malware is introduced into an organization's network.
Opening questionable e-mails	Opening e-mails from someone unknown, or clicking on links embedded in e-mails (see "Phishing Attacks" later in this chapter).
Careless Internet surfing	Accessing questionable Web sites; can result in malware and/or alien software being introduced into the organization's network.
Poor password selection and use	Choosing and using weak passwords (see "Strong Passwords" later in this chapter).
Carelessness with one's office	Unlocked desks and filing cabinets when employees go home at night; not logging off the company network when gone from the office for any extended period of time.
Carelessness using unmanaged devices	Unmanaged devices are those outside the control of an organization's IT department and company security procedures. These devices include computers belonging to customers and business partners, computers in the business centers of hotels, and computers in Starbucks, Panera Bread, and so on.
Carelessness with discarded equipment	Discarding old computer hardware and devices without completely wiping the memory; includes computers, cell phones, Blackberries, and digital copiers and printers.
Careless monitoring of environmental hazards	These hazards, which include dirt, dust, humidity, and static electricity, are harmful to the safe operation of computing equipment.

Who is real and who is engaged in social engineering? Can you tell? (*Source:* Blend/Image Source Limited)

The human errors that you have just studied are unintentional on the part of the employee. However, employees can also make unintentional mistakes as a result of actions by an attacker. Attackers often employ social engineering to induce individuals to make unintentional mistakes and disclose sensitive information.

Social Engineering

In a **social engineering** attack, the perpetrator uses social skills to trick or manipulate a legitimate employee into providing confidential company information such as passwords. The most common example of social engineering occurs when the attacker impersonates someone else on the telephone, such as a company manager or information systems employee. The attacker claims to have forgotten the password and asks the legitimate employee to provide a password to use. Other common exploits include posing as an exterminator, an air conditioning technician, or a fire marshal. Examples of social engineering abound.

In one company, a perpetrator entered a company building wearing a company ID card that looked legitimate. He walked around and put up signs on bulletin boards saying, "The help desk telephone number has been changed. The new number is 555-1234." He then exited the building and began receiving calls from legitimate employees thinking they were calling the company help desk. Naturally, the first thing the perpetrator asked for was user name and password. He now had the information necessary to access the company's information systems.

Two other social engineering techniques include tailgating and shoulder surfing. *Tailgating* is a technique designed to allow the perpetrator to enter restricted areas that are controlled with locks or card entry. The perpetrator follows closely behind a legitimate employee and, when the employee gains entry, asks the person to "hold the door." *Shoulder surfing* occurs when a perpetrator watches the employee's computer screen over that person's shoulder. This technique is particularly successful in public areas such as airports and commuter trains and on airplanes.

Piracy is theft. Would you steal a DVD? (*Source:* © Creasource/Corbis)

┌─▶ **BEFORE** *YOU GO ON . . .*
│
│   **1.** What is an unintentional threat to an information system?
│   **2.** Provide other examples of social engineering attacks.

RUBY'S CLUB QUESTIONS

1. Provide an example of a social engineering attack on Ruby's and how the club might counter the attack.

2. USB storage devices are small and can store huge amounts of information. What type of policy should Ruby's implement to avoid information being stolen with such a device?

Student Activity | 7.2

Objective: The objective of this exercise is to become familiar with some threats to information security that are often committed unintentionally.

Chapter Connection: This case relates to Chapter 7, Section 7.2, on unintentional threats to information systems. Information systems are vulnerable to many potential hazards and threats. The two major categories of threats are unintentional threats and deliberate threats. In this section we discuss unintentional threats.

Prerequisites: You should read Section 7.2 before doing this exercise to become familiar with security threats.

Activity:

Go to the following Web address, read the background information in the article, and then watch the video clip.

http://blogs.techrepublic.com.com/itdojo/?p=1700&tag=content;col1 (Copiers)

Deliverables:

Write a paragraph summarizing what happened and what was discussed in this video.

1. Ask some people who work in your school library or some people you know who work in industry

if they are aware if the copiers they use are periodically "cleaned" by the hard drives being deleted of any sensitive data.

2. Report on your findings.

Multiple Choice Questions:

1. Based on the article and narrative, why are companies NOT cleaning the hard drives of their copiers?

   (a) Not aware of risk
   (b) Too much effort
   (c) Not verifying data erased
   (d) All of the above

2. Who reported this happening?

   (a) CNN
   (b) CBS
   (c) NBC
   (d) TNN

Discussion Questions:

Discuss some of the uses you have made of copiers in school or at the library. Have you ever copied personal data? How would you feel if this were made available to the wrong people? What do you think should be done?

7.3 | Deliberate Threats to Information Systems

There are so many types of deliberate acts that a brief list is provided here for your convenience:

- Espionage or trespass
- Information extortion
- Sabotage or vandalism
- Theft of equipment or information
- Identity theft
- Compromises to intellectual property
- Software attacks
- Alien software
- Supervisory control and data acquisition (SCADA) attacks
- Cyberterrorism and cyberwarfare

Espionage or Trespass

Espionage or trespass occurs when an unauthorized individual attempts to gain illegal access to organizational information. It is important to distinguish between competitive intelligence and industrial espionage. Competitive intelligence consists of legal information-gathering techniques, such as studying a company's Web site and press releases, attending trade shows, and so on. In contrast, industrial espionage crosses the legal boundary.

Information Extortion

Information extortion occurs when an attacker either threatens to steal, or actually steals, information from a company. The perpetrator demands payment for not stealing the information, for returning stolen information, or for agreeing not to disclose the information.

Sabotage or Vandalism

Sabotage and vandalism are deliberate acts that involve defacing an organization's Web site, possibly causing the organization to lose its image and its customers to experience a loss of confidence. One form of online vandalism is a hacktivist or cyberactivist operation. These are cases of high-tech civil disobedience to protest the operations, policies, or actions of an organization or government agency.

Theft of Equipment and Information

Computing devices and storage devices are becoming smaller yet more powerful with vastly increased storage (e.g., laptops, BlackBerrys, personal digital assistants, smart phones, digital cameras, thumb drives, and iPads). As a result, these devices are becoming easier to steal and easier for attackers to use to steal information.

Table 7.1 points out that one type of human mistake is carelessness with laptops. In fact, such carelessness often leads to laptops being stolen. The cost of a stolen laptop includes the loss of data, the loss of intellectual property, laptop replacement, legal and regulatory costs, investigation fees, and lost productivity.

One form of theft, known as *dumpster diving,* involves the practice of rummaging through commercial or residential trash to find information that has been discarded. Paper files, letters, memos, photographs, IDs, passwords, credit cards, and other forms of information can be found in dumpsters. Unfortunately, many people never consider that the sensitive items they throw in the trash may be recovered. Such information, when recovered, can be used for fraudulent purposes.

Software attacks are frustrating, can be embarrassing, and often stop productivity. (*Source:* FSTOP/Image Source Limited)

Dumpster diving is not necessarily theft, because the legality of this act varies. Because dumpsters are usually located on private premises, dumpster diving is illegal in some parts of the United States. Even in these cases, however, the relevant laws are enforced with varying degrees of rigor.

Identity Theft

Identity theft is the deliberate assumption of another person's identity, usually to gain access to his or her financial information or to frame him or her for a crime. Techniques for obtaining information include:

- stealing mail or dumpster diving;
- stealing personal information in computer databases;
- infiltrating organizations that store large amounts of personal information (e.g., data aggregators such as Acxiom, www.acxiom.com); and
- impersonating a trusted organization in an electronic communication (**phishing**).

Recovering from identity theft is costly, time consuming, and difficult. Victims also report problems in obtaining credit and obtaining or holding a job, as well as adverse effects on insurance or credit rates. In addition, victims state that it is often difficult to remove negative information from their records, such as their credit reports.

Anyone's personal information can be compromised in other ways. For example, an identity can be uncovered just from examining searches in a search engine. The ability to analyze all searches by a single user can enable a criminal to identify who the user is and what he or she is doing. As just one example, the *New York Times* tracked down a particular person based solely on her AOL searches.

Compromises to Intellectual Property

Protecting intellectual property is a vital issue for people who make their livelihood in knowledge fields. **Intellectual property** is the property created by individuals or corporations that is protected under *trade secret*, *patent*, and *copyright* laws.

A **trade secret** is an intellectual work, such as a business plan, that is a company secret and is not based on public information. An example is a corporate strategic plan. A **patent** is a document that grants the holder exclusive rights on an invention or process for 20 years. **Copyright** is a statutory grant that provides the creators of intellectual property with ownership of the property for the life of the creator plus 70 years. Owners are entitled to collect fees from anyone who wants to copy the property. It is important to note that these are definitions under U.S. law. There is some international standardization, but it is far from total. Therefore, differences may be found between U.S. law and other countries' laws.

The most common intellectual property related to IT deals with software. The U.S. Federal Computer Software Copyright Act (1980) provides protection for *source* and *object code* of computer software, but the law does not clearly identify what is eligible for protection. For example, copyright law does not protect similar concepts, functions, and general features such as pull-down menus, colors, and icons. However, copying a software program without making payment to the owner—including giving a disc to a friend to install on his or her computer—is a copyright violation. Not surprisingly, this practice, called **piracy**, is a major problem for software vendors. The global trade in pirated software amounts to billions of dollars.

Software Attacks

Software attacks have evolved from the outbreak era—during which malicious software (**malware**) tried to infect as many computers worldwide as possible—to the profit-driven, Web-based attacks of today. Cybercriminals are heavily involved with malware attacks to make money, and they use sophisticated, blended attacks typically via the Web. Table 7.2 shows a variety of software attacks. You will see that software attacks are grouped into three categories: remote attacks needing user action; remote attacks needing no user action; and software attacks by programmers during the development of a system. "IT's About Business 7.1" provides an example of a software attack.

TABLE 7.2 Types of Software Attacks

Type	Description
(1) Remote Attacks Needing User Action	
Virus	Segment of computer code that performs malicious actions by attaching to another computer program.
Worm	Segment of computer code that performs malicious actions and will replicate and will replicate, or spread, by itself (without requiring another computer program).
Phishing Attack	Phishing attacks use deception to acquire sensitive personal information by masquerading as official-looking e-mails or instant messages.
Spear Phishing Attack	Phishing attacks target large groups of people. In spear phishing attacks, the perpetrators find out as much information about an individual as possible to improve their chances that phishing techniques will be able to obtain sensitive, personal information.
(2) Remote Attacks Needing No User Action	
Denial-of-Service Attack	Attacker sends so many information requests to a target computer system that the target cannot handle them successfully and typically crashes (ceases to function).
Distributed Denial-of-Service Attack	An attacker first takes over many computers, typically by using malicious software. These computers are called *zombies*, or *bots*. The attacker uses these bots (which form a *botnet*) to deliver a coordinated stream of information requests to a target computer, causing it to crash.
(3) Attacks by Programmer Developing a System	
Trojan Horse	Software programs that hide in other computer programs and reveal their designed behavior only when they are activated.
Back Door	Typically a password, known only to the attacker, that allows him or her to access a computer system at will, without having to go through any security procedures (also called a *trap door*).
Logic Bomb	Segment of computer code that is embedded within an organization's existing computer programs and is designed to activate and perform a destructive action at a certain time or date.

IT's ABOUT BUSINESS | 7.1

 ## Virus Attack Hits the University of Exeter

A massive virus attack impacted the University of Exeter (www.exeter.ac.uk), located in southwestern England. The university has 16,000 students on three campuses, two in Exeter and one in Cornwall. The virus attack, which exploited computers running Microsoft Windows Vista Service Pack 2, caused the university to temporarily take its entire network offline. University officials stated that this measure was necessary in order to scan and repair all university computers. The university also scanned nonuniversity-owned Vista personal computers, which were used by students who had connected to the university's network. In addition, the Cornwall campus was isolated from the main campuses in Exeter to avoid spreading the virus.

The virus caused problems for university faculty. The interactive teaching boards in all classrooms were inoperable, meaning that professors could not use PowerPoint presentations or access the Internet in class. Also, the university's voice-over-Internet Protocol (VoIP) telephone system was inoperable.

One of the biggest issues for the university's students is that they had no access to the virtual learning environment (VLE). This lack of access presented a large problem for students who had assignments or papers due, and could not obtain access to online versions stored in the VLE. Further, students could not access any data stored in the VLE.

The university faculty did promise to make allowances for students and arranged short-term extensions to deadlines. Interestingly, computers in student residence halls were the last to be added back to the operational university network.

It took three days to clean infected computers and bring the network back into operation. In early 2011, no one knows for certain how the virus entered the university network or who the perpetrators were. However, an internal university e-mail suggested that someone had not applied appropriate patches for the security software in a timely fashion, leading to the massive attack.

Questions

1. What other actions could the university have taken to prevent the attack?
2. What actions should the university now perform to prevent future attacks?

Sources: Compiled from "University of Exeter Shuts Down Its Network Because of the Attack of a Virus," www.2-viruses, January 21, 2010; L. Constatin, "Mystery Computer Virus Hits UK University," www.softpedia.com, January 21, 2010; J. Leyden, "Exeter Uni Goes Offline to Fight Mystery Malware," *The Register*, January 21, 2010; Z. Whittaker, "Virus Attack Hits Vista Machines, Cripples University Network," *ZDNet.com*, January 20, 2010; "University of Exeter Malware Outbreak," www.ja.net, January 20, 2010; www.exeter.ac.uk, accessed February 9, 2011.

Alien Software

Many personal computers have alien software (also called *pestware*) running on them that the owners do not know about. **Alien software** is clandestine software that is installed on a computer through duplicitous methods. Alien software is typically not as malicious as viruses, worms, or Trojan horses, but it does use up valuable system resources. In addition, it can report on your Web surfing habits and other personal behavior.

The vast majority of pestware is **adware**—software that is designed to help pop-up advertisements appear on your screen. Adware is so common because it works. According to advertising agencies, for every 100 people who delete such an ad, three click on it. This "hit rate" is extremely high for Internet advertising.

Spyware is software that collects personal information about users without their consent. Two types of spyware are addressed here: keystroke loggers and screen scrapers.

Keystroke loggers (also called *keyloggers*) record keystrokes and record Internet Web browsing history. The purposes range from criminal (e.g., theft of passwords and sensitive personal information such as credit card numbers) to annoying (e.g., recording Internet search history for targeted advertising).

Companies have attempted to counter key loggers by switching to other forms of input for authentication. For example, all of us have been forced to look at wavy, distorted letters and type them correctly into a box. That string of letters is called a CAPTCHA, and it is a test. The point of CAPTCHA is that reading those distorted letters is something that computers cannot do accurately (yet). The fact that you can transcribe them means that you are probably not a software program run by an unauthorized person, such as a spammer. As a result, attackers have turned to *screen scrapers* (or *screen grabbers*), software that records a continuous "movie" of a screen's contents rather than simply recording keystrokes.

Spamware is pestware that is designed to use your computer as a launch pad for spammers. **Spam** is unsolicited e-mail, usually for the purpose of advertising for products and services. When your computer is used this way, e-mails from spammers appear to come from you. Even worse, spam will be sent to everyone in your e-mail address book.

Not only is spam a nuisance, but it wastes time and money. Spam costs U.S. companies billions of dollars per year. These costs come from productivity losses, clogged e-mail systems, additional storage, user support, and antispam software. Spam can also carry viruses and worms, making it even more dangerous.

Cookies are small amounts of information that Web sites store on your computer, temporarily or more-or-less permanently. In many cases, cookies are useful and innocuous. For example, some cookies store passwords and user IDs that you do not have to retype every time you load a new page at the Web site that issued the cookie. Cookies are also necessary if you want to shop online, because they are used for your shopping carts at various online merchants.

Tracking cookies, however, can be used to track your path through a Web site, the time you spend there, what links you click on, and other details that the company wants to record, usually for marketing purposes. Tracking cookies can also combine this information with your name, purchases, credit card information, and other personal data, to develop an intrusive profile of your spending habits.

Most cookies can be read only by the party that created them. However, some companies that manage online banner advertising are, in essence, cookie-sharing rings. These companies can track information such as which pages you load and which ads you click on. They then share this information with their client Web sites (which may number in the thousands). For a cookie demonstration, see http://privacy.net/track.

Supervisory Control and Data Acquisition (SCADA) Attacks

SCADA refers to a large-scale, distributed, measurement and control system. SCADA systems are used to monitor or to control chemical, physical, or transport processes such as oil refineries, water and sewage treatment plants, electrical generators, and nuclear power plants. Essentially, SCADA systems provide the link between the physical world and the electronic world.

SCADA systems consist of multiple sensors, a master computer, and communications infrastructure. The sensors connect to physical equipment and read status data such as the open/closed status of a switch or a valve, as well as measurements such as pressure, flow, voltage, and current. By sending signals to equipment, sensors control that equipment, such as opening or closing a switch or valve or setting the speed of a pump.

The sensors are connected in a network, and each sensor typically has an Internet (Internet Protocol, or IP) address. (You studied about IP addresses in Chapter 4.) If an attacker can gain access to the network, he or she can disrupt the power grid over a large area or disrupt the operations of a large chemical plant. Such actions could have catastrophic results, as you can see in "IT's About Business 7.2."

Cyberterrorism and Cyberwarfare

With both **cyberterrorism** and **cyberwarfare**, attackers use a target's computer systems, particularly via the Internet, to cause physical, real-world harm or severe disruption, usually

The Stuxnet Worm

Stuxnet is the name of a worm, discovered in July 2010, that targets SCADA systems. In particular, Stuxnet targets only Siemens SCADA systems that are configured to control and monitor specific industrial processes. In fact, security experts around the world suspect that the worm's target was the uranium enrichment industrial infrastructure in Iran. On November 29, 2010, Iran confirmed that its nuclear program had been damaged by Stuxnet. Thus, the worm may have damaged Iran's nuclear facilities in Natanz, and eventually delayed the startup of Iran's Bushehr nuclear power plant.

Construction of the Stuxnet worm required an in-depth knowledge of nuclear industrial processes. The worm fakes industrial process control sensor signals so that an infected system does not shut down due to abnormal behavior. The worm appears to impair Iran's computer-controlled uranium centrifuges, which mysteriously lost 30 percent of their production capacity, thereby delaying any plans to produce a nuclear weapon. The worm adjusts the user interface for the centrifuge control systems to make it appear that the centrifuges are operating normally. Stuxnet changes the speed of the motors that spin the centrifuges from very high to very low, and back again. This process stops the uranium from being enriched and damages the motors.

Security experts from Symantec (www.symantec. com), a leading vendor of information security systems, think that the group that developed Stuxnet was well funded, consisted of five to ten people, and took six months to create the worm. The *New York Times* reported that experts studying Stuxnet feel that the complexity of the worm indicates that only a nation-state would have the capabilities to produce it.

In response to the infection, Iran assembled a team to combat the worm, which spread rapidly in that country, affecting more than 30,000 IP addresses there. This problem has been compounded by the ability of Stuxnet to mutate, meaning that new versions of the worm continue to spread. In addition, no one knows who created the worm and no one has taken credit for creating it. A security expert noted that it was impossible to definitively state where Stuxnet originated.

Stuxnet heralds a frightening new era in cyberwarfare. China, Russia, the United States, and other nations have been quietly engaging in cyberwarfare for several years, but this worm represents a major technological escalation. One security expert noted that worms such as Stuxnet are what nation-states build if their only other option is to go to war.

Questions

1. Describe the implications of the precisely targeted nature of the Stuxnet attack.
2. What does the statement mean that "nations use malware such as the Stuxnet worm when their only alternative is to go to war."

Sources: Compiled from M. Schwartz, "Stuxnet Iran Attack Launched from 10 Machines," *InformationWeek*, February 14, 2011; G. Keizer, "Stuxnet Struck Five Targets in Iran, Say Researcher," *Computerworld*, February 11, 2011; M. Schwartz, "Symantec Finds Stuxnet Targets Iranian Nuclear Enrichment," *InformationWeek*, November 16, 2010; "Stuxnet: Declaring Cyberwarfare on Iran," *The Week*, October 8, 2010; E. Messmer, "Is Stuxnet an Israeli-Invented Attack Against Iran?" *NetworkWorld*, September 30, 2010; T. Claburn, "Iran Denies Stuxnet Worm Hurt Nuclear Plant," *InformationWeek*, September 27, 2010; D. Goodin, "SCADA Worm a Nation-State Search-and-Destroy Weapon," *The Register*, September 22, 2010; M. Clayton, "Stuxnet Malware: Is 'Weapon' Out to Destroy . . . Iran's Bushehr Nuclear Plant?" *Christian Science Monitor*, September 21, 2010; J. Kirk, "Eset Discovers Second Variation of Stuxnet Worm," *NetworkWorld*, July 20, 2010; www. symantec.com, accessed February 16, 2011.

to carry out a political agenda. Cyberterrorism and cyberwarfare range from gathering data to attacking critical infrastructure (via SCADA systems). The two types of attacks are discussed synonymously here, even though cyberterrorism typically is carried out by individuals or groups, whereas cyberwarfare involves nations. Following are examples of cyberattacks against Estonia and the Republic of Georgia.

EXAMPLE

In 2007, a three-week wave of massive distributed denial-of-service (DDoS) cyberattacks against the Baltic country of Estonia disabled the Web sites of government ministries, political parties, newspapers, banks, and companies. One of the most wired societies in Europe, Estonia is a pioneer of e-government. As a result, the country is highly vulnerable to cyberattack. In the early phase of the DDoS attack, some perpetrators were identified by their IP addresses. Many of these addresses were Russian, and some of them were from Russian state institutions.

In August 2008, Russian troops entered the Republic of Georgia's province of South Ossetia to crush a Georgian attempt to control a breakaway by that region. DDoS attacks on Georgian Web sites were apparently synchronized with the Russian invasion. The cyberattack shut down the Web site of the Georgian president, Mikheil Saakashvili, for 24 hours and defaced the Georgian parliament Web site with images of Adolf Hitler. Saakashvili blamed Russia for the attacks, but the Russian government denied the charges.

Terrorist groups around the world have expanded their activities on the Internet, increasing the sophistication and volume of their videos and messages, in an effort to recruit new members and raise money. In response, the U.S. military is expanding its offensive capabilities to attack terrorists' Web sites, rather than just monitor them.

BEFORE *YOU GO ON . . .*

1. Why has the theft of computing devices become more serious over time?
2. What are the three types of software attacks?
3. Define alien software.
4. What is a SCADA system?

RUBY'S CLUB QUESTIONS

1. You saw four examples of methods used to steal identities. Which of these are most important for Ruby's to consider? For each method that you choose, discuss how Ruby's can protect its customers and employees from identity theft.

2. Because Ruby's is redesigning the physical layout of the club, where should it house its "back office" operations to help deter theft of equipment and/or information?

Student Activity | 7.3

Objective: The objective of this exercise is to become familiar with information security and deliberate threats that could result in identity theft or otherwise compromise information.

Chapter Connection: This case relates to Chapter 7, Section 7.3 and the importance of protecting information from deliberate threats.

Prerequisites: Read Section 7.3 before doing this exercise to become familiar with types of threats.

Activity:

Many types of deliberate acts can threaten the **privacy** of personal information, such as espionage, information extortion, sabotage or vandalism, theft of equipment or information, identity theft, software attacks, cyberterrorism, and cyberwarfare.

Watch the video at the following link:

http://deliveringtrust.com *by clicking the arrow in the middle of the screen.*

Then click on "Learn" and click the icons at the right to learn about various types of threats.

Deliverables:

Answer the following:

1. What is Internet fraud?
2. What is identity theft?
3. What is telemarketing fraud?
4. What is cross-border fraud?

Multiple Choice Questions:

1. Phishing is what happens when:
   (a) Someone sends you unwanted e-mails attempting to sell products or services.
   (b) Someone illegally blocks your access to a Web site.
   (c) Someone pretends to be a trustworthy source to steal your personal information.

2. If a stranger tries to "friend" you on a social media Web site such as MySpace or Facebook, you should:
   (a) Introduce yourself.
   (b) Ask the person to contact you at your e-mail address.
   (c) Ignore the person.

3. The "London Scam" is what happens when:
   (a) Someone promises to send you a large sum of money if you provide your bank account number.
   (b) Someone pretends to be stranded outside the United States and asks for your help.
   (c) A domestic Web site registers under a false foreign domain.

4. If you get a message from a friend on MySpace or Facebook that is blank except for a Web link, what should you do?
   (a) Ignore it. It may be a "phishing" scam.
   (b) Click on the link, but do not provide any information to the linked site.
   (c) Reply and ask the friend if he or she really sent the link.

5. You should change your online password:
   (a) Every day.
   (b) Frequently.
   (c) Once a year.

Discussion Question:

Discuss the various types of deliberate threats that can happen. Has anyone been a victim of any of these?

7.4 | What Companies Are Doing to Protect Information Resources

Why is it so difficult to stop cybercriminals? Table 7.3 lists the major difficulties involved in protecting information. Because organizing an appropriate defense system is so important to the entire enterprise, it is one of the major responsibilities of any prudent CIO as well as the functional managers who control information resources. In fact, IT security is the business of *everyone* in an organization.

Another reason why it is difficult to protect information resources is that the online commerce industry is not particularly willing to install safeguards that would make it harder to complete transactions. It would be possible, for example, to demand passwords or personal identification numbers for all credit card transactions. However, these requirements might discourage people from shopping online. Also, there is little incentive for companies like AOL to share leads on criminal activity either with one another or with the FBI. For credit card companies, it is cheaper to block a stolen credit card and move on than to invest time and money on a prosecution.

Despite these difficulties, the information security industry is battling back. Companies are developing software and services that deliver early warnings of trouble on the Internet.

TABLE 7.3 The Difficulties in Protecting Information Resources

Hundreds of potential threats exist.
Computing resources may be situated in many locations.
Many individuals control information assets.
Computer networks can be located outside the organization and are thus difficult to protect.
Rapid technological changes make some controls obsolete as soon as they are installed.
Many computer crimes are undetected for a long period of time, so it is difficult to learn from experience.
People tend to violate security procedures because the procedures are inconvenient.
The amount of computer knowledge necessary to commit computer crimes is usually minimal. As a matter of fact, one can learn hacking, for free, on the Internet.
The cost of preventing hazards can be very high. Therefore, most organizations simply cannot afford to protect against all possible hazards.
It is difficult to conduct a cost-benefit justification for controls before an attack occurs because it is difficult to assess the value of a hypothetical attack.

Unlike traditional antivirus software, which is reactive, early-warning systems are proactive, scanning the Web for new viruses and alerting companies to dangers.

Organizations spend a great deal of time and money protecting their information resources. Before doing so, they perform risk management.

Risk is the probability that a threat will impact an information resource. The goal of **risk management** is to identify, control, and minimize the impact of threats. In other words, risk management seeks to reduce risk to acceptable levels. Risk management encompasses three processes: risk analysis, risk mitigation, and controls evaluation.

Risk analysis is the process by which an organization assesses the value of each asset being protected, estimates the probability that each asset will be compromised, and compares the probable costs of the asset's being compromised with the costs of protecting that asset. Organizations perform risk analysis to ensure that their information systems' security programs are cost effective. The risk analysis process prioritizes the assets to be protected based on each asset's value, its probability of being compromised, and the estimated cost of its protection. The organization then considers how to mitigate the risk.

In **risk mitigation**, the organization takes concrete actions against risks. Risk mitigation has two functions: (1) implementing controls to prevent identified threats from occurring and (2) developing a means of recovery should the threat become a reality. Several risk mitigation strategies may be adopted by organizations. The three most common are risk acceptance, risk limitation, and risk transference.

- **Risk acceptance:** Accept the potential risk, continue operating with no controls, and absorb any damages that occur.
- **Risk limitation:** Limit the risk by implementing controls that minimize the impact of the threat.
- **Risk transference:** Transfer the risk by using other means to compensate for the loss, such as by purchasing insurance.

In controls evaluation, the organization examines the costs of implementing adequate control measures against the value of those control measures. If the costs of implementing a control are greater than the value of the asset being protected, then control is not cost effective. In the next section, you will study the various controls that organizations use to protect their information resources.

BEFORE YOU GO ON . . .

1. Describe several reasons why it is difficult to protect information resources.
2. Compare and contrast risk management and risk analysis.

RUBY'S CLUB QUESTIONS

1. Risk analysis is crucial for Ruby's. Is the database crucial to Ruben and Lisa's business plan? Perform a risk analysis of their database. Which risk mitigation strategy should Ruby's use? Support your answer.
2. Ruben and Lisa also want to know how they can test their security against intentional and unintentional threats.

Student Activity 7.4

Objective: The objective of this exercise is to become familiar with the Fair Information Practices Principles and relate them to business procedures to protect personal data.

Chapter Connection: This case relates to Chapter 7, Section 7.4 on protecting information resources. It is the responsibility of the organization to protect the information resources it needs to successfully conduct business. The organization should also inform the customer what information is collected and how it is being used. These both relate to the Fair Information Practices.

Prerequisites: You should read Section 7.4 before doing this exercise to become familiar with data privacy issues and procedures recommended to secure the data.

Activity:

The heart of information systems is the data used in processing transactions and making business decisions. However, often this data is private information about individuals and companies. It is important that this data and information be used wisely and protected. The Federal Trade Commission (FTC) has established a set of Fair Information Practices Principles as guidelines for government agencies' collection and use of personal information. These same guidelines also should be a basis for business use of data.

Review the Fair Information Practices Principles for protecting America's consumers at ftc.gov/reports/privacy3/fairinfo.shtm.

Deliverables:

Open a Word document and summarize in your own words the key points for the following five guidelines. Check with you instructor on how to submit your answers.

1. Notice/Awareness
2. Choice/Consent
3. Access/Participation
4. Integrity/Security
5. Enforcement/Redress

Watch the Pizza Ordering Video at www.youtube.com/watch?v=RNJl9EEcsoE *with the Fair Information Practices Principles in mind. Based on the video and the FTC guidelines, answer the following questions.*

Multiple Choice Questions:

1. Making data available to the consumer so they can verify its correctness is an example of:
   (a) Notice/Awareness
   (b) Choice/Consent
   (c) Access/Participation
   (d) Integrity/Security

2. Giving consumers the right to opt-in or opt-out of how their information is used is an example of:
   (a) Notice/Awareness
   (b) Choice/Consent
   (c) Access/Participation
   (d) Integrity/Security

3. Informing the consumer what data is being collected and how it will be used is an example of:
   (a) Notice/Awareness
   (b) Choice/Consent
   (c) Access/Participation
   (d) Integrity/Security

4. Having the data collector protect the information from unauthorized use or disclosure is an example of:
   (a) Notice/Awareness
   (b) Choice/Consent
   (c) Access/Participation
   (d) Integrity/Security

5. Which of these mechanisms is/are in place to enforce fair information practices?
   (a) Self-regulation
   (b) Private remedies
   (c) Government enforcement
   (d) All of the above.

Discussion Questions:

1. How would following the Fair Information Practices Principles prevent some of what you viewed in the pizza video from happening? Identify ways in which the five core principles are not followed.

2. Have you or a family member ever experienced identity theft? If so, did the company that had the information breech provide some future protection to those whose data was compromised?

3. What can you do to protect yourself from identity theft?

7.5 | Information Security Controls

To protect their information assets, organizations implement **controls**, or defense mechanisms (also called *countermeasures*). **Information security controls** are designed to protect all of the components of an information system, including data, software, hardware, and networks. Because there are so many diverse threats, organizations utilize layers of controls, or defense-in-depth.

Controls are intended to prevent accidental hazards, deter intentional acts, detect problems as early as possible, enhance damage recovery, and correct problems. Before you study controls in more detail, it is important to emphasize that the single most effective control is user education and training, leading to increased awareness of the vital importance of information security on the part of every organizational employee.

The three major types of controls are physical controls, access controls, and communications controls. Figure 7.2 illustrates these controls. In addition to applying controls, organizations plan for business continuity in case of a disaster and audit their information resources.

Physical Controls

Physical controls prevent unauthorized individuals from gaining access to a company's facilities. Common physical controls include walls, doors, fencing, gates, locks, badges, guards, and alarm systems. More sophisticated physical controls include pressure sensors, temperature sensors, and motion detectors. One weakness of physical controls is that they can be inconvenient to employees.

Guards deserve special mention because they have very difficult jobs for at least two reasons. First, their jobs are boring and repetitive and generally do not pay well. Second, if they do their jobs thoroughly, other employees harass them, particularly if their being conscientious slows up the process of entering a facility.

Organizations also put other physical security considerations in place. Such controls limit users to acceptable login times and locations. These controls also limit the number of unsuccessful login attempts, and they require all employees to log off their computers when

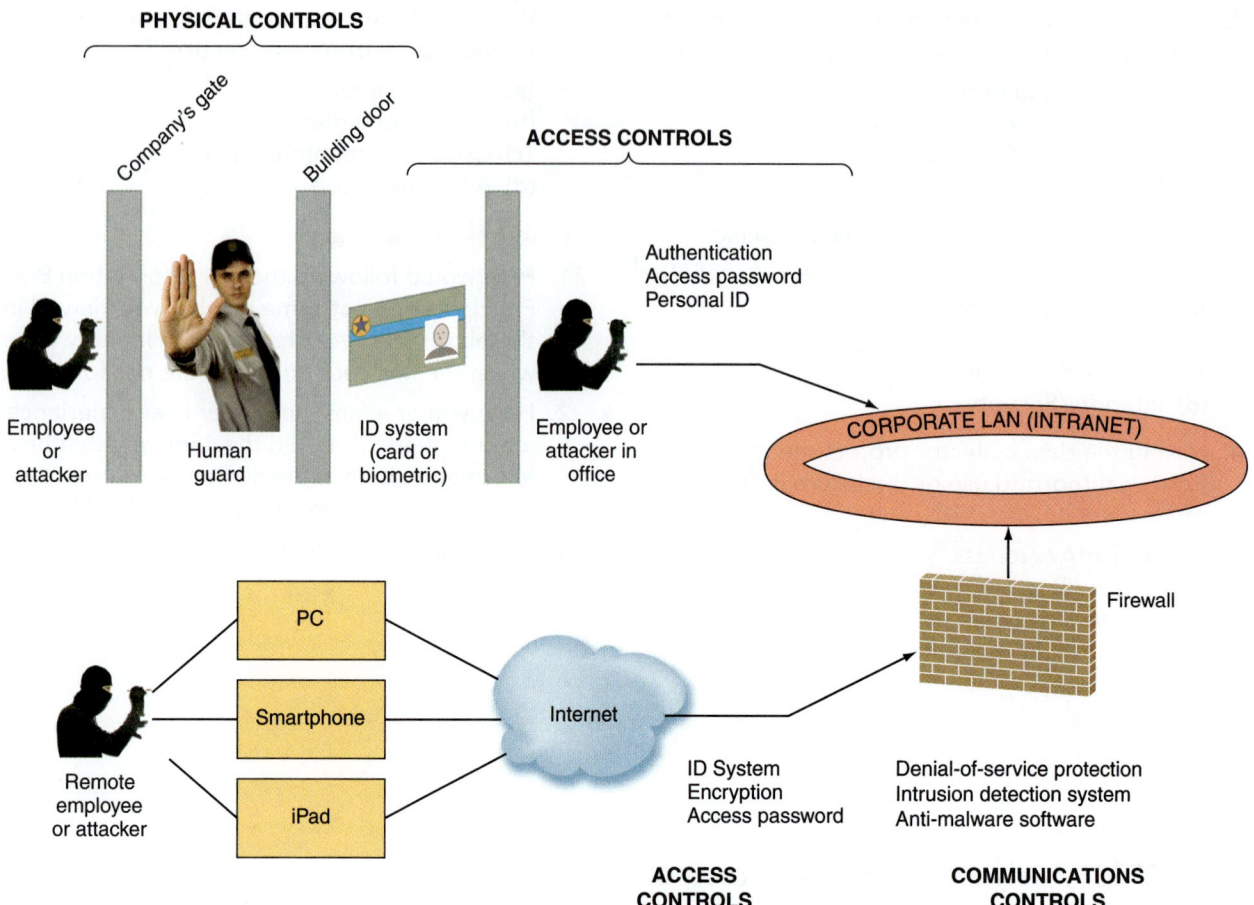

Company's gate

Building door

ACCESS CONTROLS

Authentication
Access password
Personal ID

Employee
or
attacker

Human
guard

ID system
(card or
biometric)

Employee or
attacker in
office

CORPORATE LAN (INTRANET)

PC

Smartphone

iPad

Internet

Firewall

Remote
employee
or attacker

ID System
Encryption
Access password

Denial-of-service protection
Intrusion detection system
Anti-malware software

ACCESS
CONTROLS

COMMUNICATIONS
CONTROLS

Figure 7.2 Where defense mechanisms are located. (*Sources:* © Sergey Titov/iStockphoto; fatihhoca/iStockphoto)

they leave for the day. In addition, computers are set to automatically log off the user after a certain period of disuse.

Access Controls

Access controls restrict unauthorized individuals from using information resources. These controls involve two major functions: authentication and authorization. **Authentication** determines the identity of the person requiring access. After the person is authenticated (identified), authorization is applied. **Authorization** determines which actions, rights, or privileges the person has, based on verified identity.

Authentication. To authenticate (identify) authorized personnel, an organization can use one or more of the following methods: something the user is, something the user has, something the user does, and/or something the user knows.

Something the user is (also known as **biometrics**), is an authentication method that examines a person's innate physical characteristics. Common biometric applications are fingerprint scans, palm scans, retina scans, iris recognition, and facial recognition. Of these, fingerprints, retina scans, and iris recognition provide the most definitive identification.

Something the user has is an authentication mechanism that includes regular identification (ID) cards, smart ID cards, and tokens. *Regular ID cards,* or *dumb cards,* typically have the person's picture, and often his or her signature. *Smart ID cards* have a chip embedded in them with pertinent information about the user. (Smart ID cards used for identification differ from smart cards used in electronic commerce (see Chapter 9). Both types of card have embedded chips, but they are used for different purposes). *Tokens* have embedded chips and a digital display that presents a login number that the employees use to access the organization's network. The number changes with each login.

Something the user does is an authentication mechanism that includes voice and signature recognition. In **voice recognition**, the user speaks a phrase (e.g., his or her name and department) that has been previously recorded under controlled, monitored conditions. The voice recognition system matches the two voice signals. In **signature recognition**, the user signs his or her name, and the system matches this signature with one previously recorded under controlled, monitored conditions. Signature recognition systems also match the speed of the signature and the pressure of the signature.

Something the user knows is an authentication mechanism that includes passwords and passphrases. Passwords present a huge information security problem in all organizations. All users should use strong passwords so that the password cannot easily be discovered. **Strong passwords** have the following characteristics:

- They should be difficult to guess.
- They should be longer rather than shorter.
- They should contain uppercase letters, lowercase letters, numbers, and special characters.
- They should not be a recognizable word.
- They should not be the name of anything or anyone familiar, such as family names or names of pets.
- They should not be a recognizable string of numbers, such as a Social Security number or birthday.

Unfortunately, strong passwords are irritating. If the organization mandates longer (stronger) passwords and/or frequent password changes, they become more difficult to remember, causing employees to write them down. What is needed is a way for a user to create a strong password that is easy to remember. A passphrase can help, either by being a password itself, or by helping you create a strong password.

A **passphrase** is a series of characters that is longer than a password but can be memorized easily. Examples of passphrases are "maytheforcebewithyoualways," "goaheadmakemyday," "livelongandprosper," and "aman'sgottoknowhislimitations." A user can turn a passphrase into a strong password in this manner. Start with the last passphrase above, and use the first letter of each word. You will have amgtkhl. Then capitalize every other letter, to have AmGtKhL. Then add special characters and numbers, to have 9AmGtKhL//*. Now you have a strong password that you can remember.

Many organizations are using *multifactor authentication* (more than one type of authentication) to more efficiently and effectively identify authorized users. This type of authentication is particularly important when users are logging in from remote locations.

Single-factor authentication, which is notoriously weak, commonly consists simply of a password. Two-factor authentication consists of a password plus one type of biometric identification (e.g., a fingerprint). Three-factor authentication is any combination of three authentication methods. You should keep in mind that stronger authentication is more expensive and can be irritating to users as well.

Authorization. Once users have been properly authenticated, then the rights and privileges that they have on the organization's systems are established, a process called *authorization*. Companies use the principle of least privilege for authorization purposes. A **privilege** is a collection of related computer system operations that can be performed by users of the system. **Least privilege** is a principle that users be granted the privilege for some activity only if there is a justifiable need to grant this authorization. As you see in "IT's About Business 7.3," granting the rights and privileges that users have on an organization's information systems can be complicated.

Communications Controls

Communications (network) controls secure the movement of data across networks. Communications controls consist of firewalls, anti-malware systems, whitelisting and blacklisting, encryption, virtual private networking (VPN), secure socket layer (SSL), and employee monitoring systems.

Information Security at City National Bank & Trust

City National Bank & Trust (www.cnbok.com) has 32 branches throughout Oklahoma and is continuing to expand the scope of its operations. Many of the bank's new branches are located in Walmart Supercenters. In addition to its new branches, the bank implemented CityNET, its online banking service. CityNET is designed to make banking easy for its customers wherever they are. The bank also implemented services for improved customer convenience, including banking by phone and access to its statewide ATM system. During this expansion, the bank doubled the number of employees and quadrupled the size of its network.

The bank's rapid growth in branches and customer service offerings, coupled with the global increase in malicious software, put the bank's networks and employees at much greater risk. The security risks increased as growing numbers of employees needed access to the Web.

Before its expansion, the bank had appropriate controls in place to prevent employees from installing software. In addition, the bank strictly controlled the number of users with access to the Web. The bank could run reports to see what Web sites those employees were visiting and whether or not malware had been downloaded inadvertently. However, the IT group could only prevent such malware intrusions with antivirus software on desktops, not at the gateway to the bank's network.

The IT group was also spending too much time constantly making small security policy changes. These changes included accepting a sender as friendly and blocking or adding a specific Web site. In short, the bank needed an enterprise security solution, not its current piecemeal security system.

The bank selected M86 Security (www.m86security.com) for its strong content filtering capabilities and its capability to dynamically set and change security policies. In weeks, the security system was protecting the bank from e-mail and Web-based malware and offensive content.

The bank quickly applied policy-based standards throughout its network. For example, it set a policy to block e-mail messages with attached batch, executable, and .zip files. Another policy stopped employees from downloading potentially dangerous files and blocked access to offensive Web sites. With this level of control, the IT group can apply basic security policies to all employees and feel secure that employees cannot accidentally download malware.

The M86 Security system also helps the bank comply with the Sarbanes-Oxley Act. For example, the IT group can sample information to make sure that customers' confidential information, such as credit card numbers, is not leaving the company unencrypted.

The bank occasionally receives malware threats for which there are no antivirus digital signatures. In these cases, the threat is scanned and sent to the M86 Security content system. This system subjects the threat to the bank's security policies. Threats that do not clear all policies are automatically quarantined.

The company's e-mail policies are also stringent. For an employee to have external e-mail access, it must have a business justification. This policy leaves 60 percent of the bank's employees with only internal e-mail access, which presents a problem for those who need to obtain information and electronic statements about their retirement funds and 401(k) accounts via e-mail under the bank's benefits plan.

The IT group can now provide this access to individuals without extending full external e-mail rights. This is an example of how the M86 Security system can help the bank create situation-by-situation policies without compromising the bank's security standards.

The M86 Security system also provides excellent dynamic Web site categorization. If an employee accesses a Web site that has not already been classified as pornographic, the security system scans all the content on the Web site and looks for characteristics that would indicate that the site is pornographic. If the site has those characteristics, access to it is blocked immediately, and the site is blacklisted.

Since installing the M86 Security system, the bank has gone from receiving a few thousand e-mail messages per day to five million messages per month. Because the system is enterprisewide and centralized, the bank can easily extend Web and internal and external e-mail protection to its new branches. Further, the bank can implement security policies that protect its entire organization from one centralized management console.

Questions

1. Why is it so important for organizations to establish enterprisewide security policies?

2. Are the bank's e-mail policies too stringent? Why or why not? Support your answer.

Sources: Compiled from T. Austin, "How Banks Are Fighting Fraud," *Bank Info Security*, February 1, 2011; M. Meason, "Bank Protects More Than Money," *Baseline Magazine*, May 19, 2009; "Information Security Policies Are Your First Line of Defense," *BankersOnline.com*, April 20, 2009; T. Claburn, "Most Bank Sites Are Insecure," *InformationWeek*, July 23, 2008; www.cnbok.com, accessed February 6, 2011; www.m86security.com, accessed February 9, 2011.

Firewalls. A **firewall** is a system that prevents a specific type of information from moving between untrusted networks, such as the Internet, and private networks, such as your company's network. Put simply, firewalls prevent unauthorized Internet users from accessing private networks. All messages entering or leaving your company's network pass through a firewall. The firewall examines each message and blocks those that do not meet specified security rules. Firewalls filter network traffic according to categories of activities likely to cause problems, whereas anti-malware systems filter traffic according to a database of specific problems.

Firewalls range from simple, for home use, to very complex for organizational use. Figure 7.3a shows a basic firewall for a home computer. In this case, the firewall is implemented as software on the home computer. Figure 7.3b shows an organization that has implemented an external firewall, which faces the Internet, and an internal firewall, which faces the company network. Corporate firewalls typically consist of software running on a computer dedicated to the task. A **demilitarized zone (DMZ)** is located between the two firewalls. Messages from the Internet must first pass through the external firewall. If they conform to the defined security rules, then they are sent to company servers located in the DMZ. These servers typically handle Web page requests and e-mail. Any messages designated for the company's internal network (e.g., its intranet) must pass through the internal firewall, again with its own defined security rules, to gain access to the company's private network.

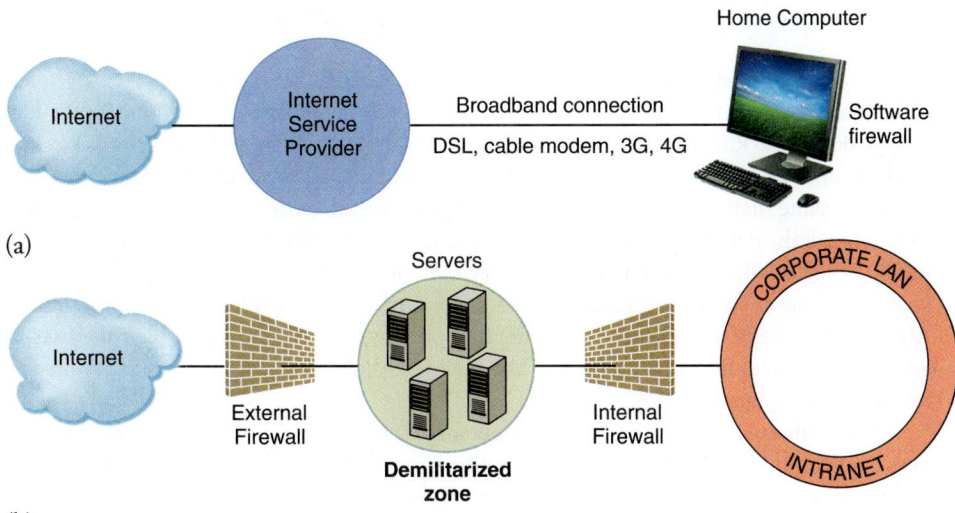

Figure 7.3 (a) Basic firewall for home computer. (b) Organization with two firewalls and demilitarized zone. (*Source:* © Dmitry Rukhlenko-Fotolia.com)

The danger from viruses and worms is so severe that many organizations are placing firewalls at strategic points *inside* their private networks. In this way, if a virus or worm does get through both the external and internal firewalls, then the internal damage may be contained.

Anti-malware Systems. **Anti-malware systems (antivirus software)**, also called AV, are software packages that attempt to identify and eliminate viruses, worms, and other malicious software. This software is implemented at the organizational level by the information systems department. Hundreds of AV software packages are currently available. Among the best known are Norton Antivirus (www.symantec.com), McAfee Virusscan (www.mcafee.com), and Trend Micro PC-cillin (www.trendmicro.com).

Anti-malware systems are generally reactive. They work by creating definitions, or signatures, of various types of malware, and then updating these signatures in their products. The anti-malware software then examines suspicious computer code to see if it matches a known signature. If it does, then the anti-malware software will remove it. This is the reason why organizations update their malware definitions so often. (See Chapter Closing Case 2.)

Because malware is such a serious problem, the leading vendors are rapidly developing anti-malware systems that function proactively as well as reactively. These systems evaluate behavior rather than relying on signature matching. In theory, therefore, it is possible to catch malware before it can infect systems.

Whitelisting and Blacklisting. A report by the Yankee Group (www.yankeegroup. com), a technology research and consulting firm, stated that 99 percent of organizations had anti-malware systems installed, but 62 percent of companies still suffered successful malware attacks. As you have noted, anti-malware systems are usually reactive, and malware continues to infect companies.

One solution to this problem is whitelisting. **Whitelisting** is a process in which a company identifies the software that it will allow to run and does not try to recognize malware. Whitelisting permits acceptable software to run and either prevents anything else from running or lets new software run in a quarantined environment until the company can verify its validity.

Whereas whitelisting allows nothing to run unless it is on the whitelist, **blacklisting** allows everything to run unless it is on the blacklist. A blacklist, then, includes certain types of software that are not allowed to run in the company environment. For example, a company might blacklist peer-to-peer file sharing on its systems. In addition to software, people, devices, and Web sites can also be whitelisted and blacklisted.

Encryption. When organizations do not have a secure channel for sending information, they use encryption to stop unauthorized eavesdroppers. **Encryption** is the process of converting an original message into a form that cannot be read by anyone except the intended receiver.

All encryption systems use a key, which is the code that scrambles, and then decodes, the messages. The majority of encryption systems use public-key encryption. **Public-key encryption**—also known as *asymmetric encryption*—uses two different keys: a public key and a private key (see Figure 7.4). The public key and the private key are created simultaneously using the same mathematical formula or algorithm. Because the two keys are mathematically related, the data encrypted with one key can be decrypted by using the other key. The public key is publicly available in a directory that all parties can access. The private key is kept secret, never shared with anyone, and never sent across the Internet. In this system, if Alice wants to send a message to Bob, she first obtains Bob's public key, which she uses to encrypt (scramble) her message. When Bob receives Alice's message, he uses his private key to decrypt (unscramble) it.

Although this system is adequate for personal information, organizations doing business over the Internet require a more complex system. In such cases, a third party, called a **certificate authority**, acts as a trusted intermediary between companies. As such, the certificate authority issues digital certificates and verifies the worth and integrity of the certificates. A **digital certificate** is an electronic document attached to a file certifying

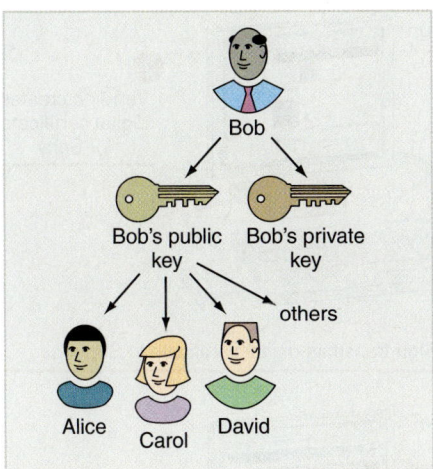

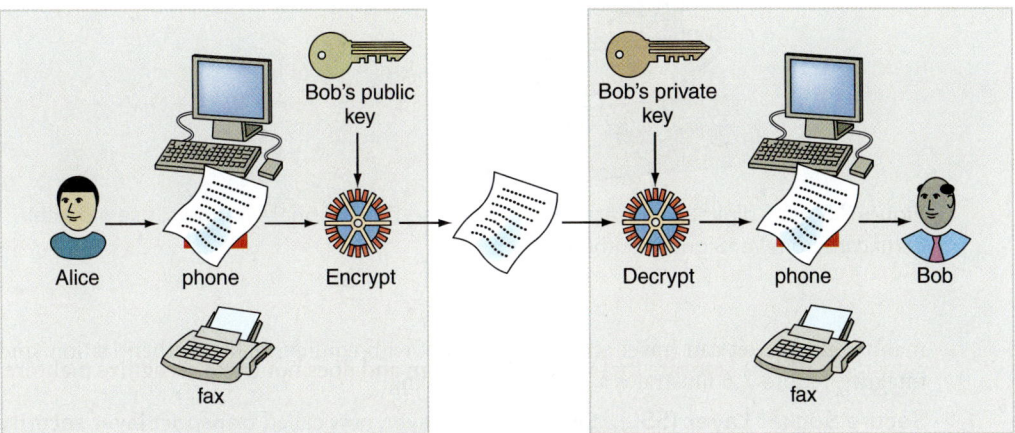

Figure 7.4 How public key encryption works. (Omnisec AG.)

that the file is from the organization it claims to be from and has not been modified from its original format. As you can see in Figure 7.5, Sony requests a digital certificate from VeriSign, a certificate authority, and uses this certificate when doing business with Dell. Note that the digital certificate contains an identification number, the issuer, validity dates, and the requester's public key. For examples of certificate authorities, see www. entrust.com, www.verisign.com, www.cybertrust.com, www.secude.com, and www. thawte.com.

Virtual Private Networking. A **virtual private network (VPN)** is a private network that uses a public network (usually the Internet) to connect users. As such, VPNs integrate the global connectivity of the Internet with the security of a private network and thereby extend the reach of the organization's networks. VPNs are called "virtual" because they have no separate physical existence. They use the public Internet as their infrastructure. They create a *virtual private* network by using log-ins, encryption, and other techniques to enhance privacy.

VPNs have several advantages. First, they allow remote users to access the company network. Second, they allow flexibility. That is, mobile users can access the organization's network from properly configured remote devices. Third, organizations can impose their security policies through VPNs. For example, an organization may dictate that only corporate e-mail applications are available to users when they connect from unmanaged devices.

To provide secure transmissions, VPNs use a process called tunneling. **Tunneling** encrypts each data packet to be sent and places each encrypted packet inside another packet. In this

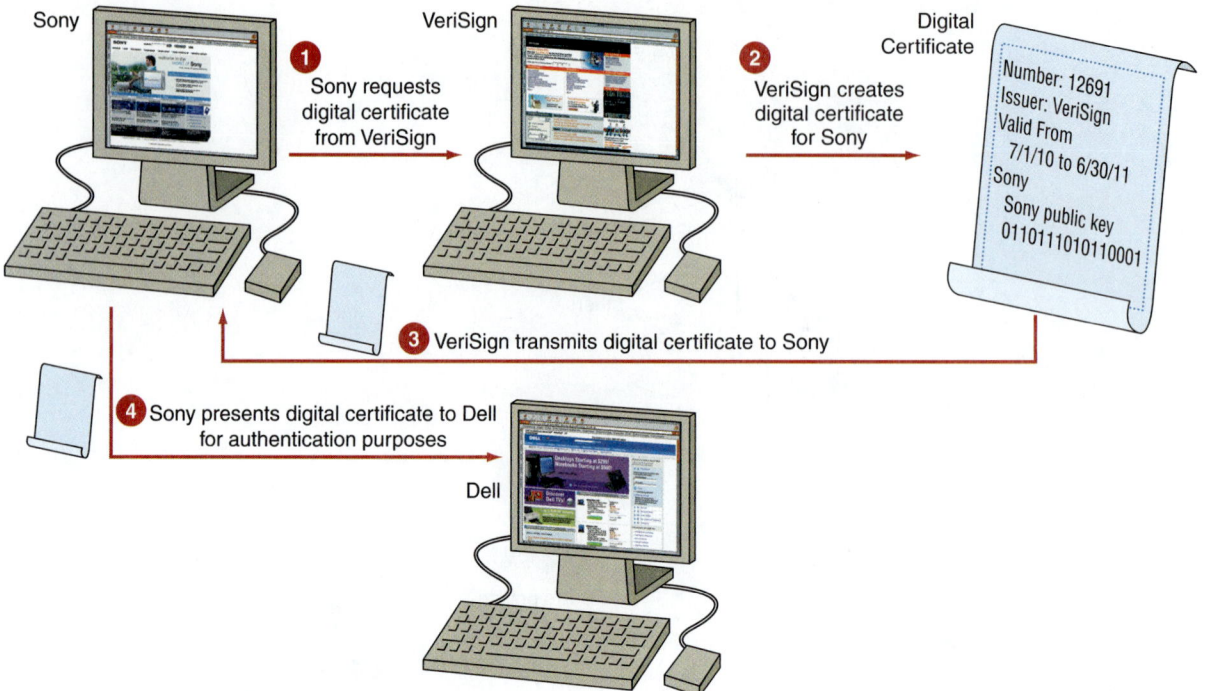

Figure 7.5 How digital certificates work. Sony and Dell, business partners, use a digital certificate from VeriSign for authentication.

manner, the packet can travel across the Internet with confidentiality, authentication, and integrity. Figure 7.6 illustrates a VPN and tunneling.

Secure Socket Layer (SSL). **Secure socket layer**, now called **transport layer security (TLS)**, is an encryption standard used for secure transactions such as credit card purchases and online banking. TLS encrypts and decrypts data between a Web server and a browser end to end.

TLS is indicated by a URL that begins with https rather than http, and it often includes a small padlock icon in the browser's status bar. Using a padlock icon to indicate a secure connection, and placing this icon in a browser's status bar, are artifacts of specific browsers. Other browsers use other icons (e.g., a key that is either broken or whole). The important thing to remember here is that browsers usually provide visual confirmation of a secure connection.

Employee Monitoring Systems. Many companies are taking a proactive approach to protecting their networks from what they view as one of their major security threats, namely employee mistakes. These companies are implementing **employee monitoring systems**, which monitor their employees' computers, e-mail activities, and Internet surfing activities.

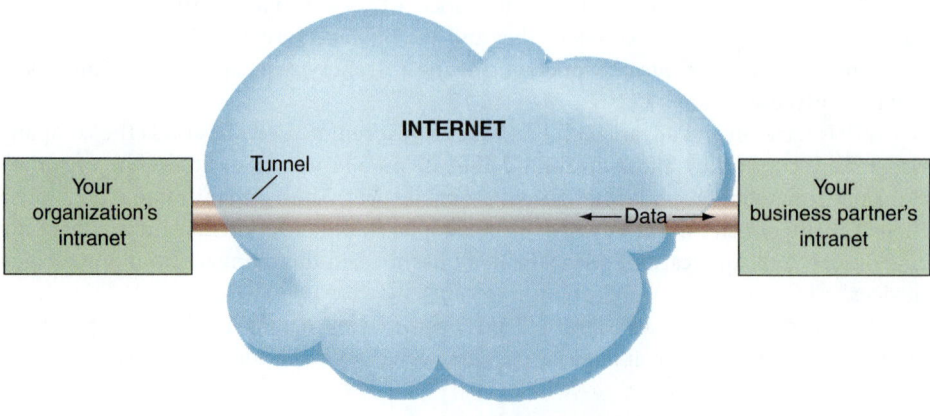

Figure 7.6 Virtual private network and tunneling.

These products are useful to identify employees who spend too much time surfing on the Internet for personal reasons, who visit questionable Web sites, or who download music illegally. Vendors that provide monitoring software include SpectorSoft (www.spectorsoft.com) and Websense (www.websense.com).

Business Continuity Planning

An important strategy for organizations is to be prepared for any eventuality. A critical element in any security system is a business continuity plan, also known as a disaster recovery plan.

Business continuity is the chain of events linking planning to protection and to recovery. The purpose of the business continuity plan is to provide guidance to people who keep the business operating after a disaster occurs. Using this plan, employees prepare for, react to, and recover from events that affect the security of information assets and the subsequent restoration to normal business operations. The plan helps to ensure that critical business functions continue.

In the event of a major disaster, organizations can employ several strategies for business continuity. These strategies include hot sites, warm sites, and cold sites. A **hot site** is a fully configured computer facility, with all services, communications links, and physical plant operations. A hot site duplicates computing resources, peripherals, telephone systems, applications, and workstations. A **warm site** provides many of the same services and options of the hot site. However, a warm site typically does not include the actual applications the company needs. A warm site does include computing equipment such as servers, but it often does not include user workstations. A **cold site** provides only rudimentary services and facilities, such as a building or room with heating, air conditioning, and humidity control. This type of site provides no computer hardware or user workstations. The point of a cold site is that it takes care of long lead-time issues. Building, or even renting, space takes a long time. Installing high-speed communication lines, often from two or more carriers, takes a long time. Installing high-capacity power lines takes a long time. By comparison, buying and installing servers should not take a particularly long time.

Hot sites reduce risk to the greatest extent, but they are the most expensive option. Conversely, cold sites reduce risk the least, but they are the least expensive option.

Information Systems Auditing

Companies implement security controls to ensure that information systems work properly. These controls can be installed in the original system, or they can be added after a system is in operation. Installing controls is necessary but not sufficient to provide adequate security. In addition, people responsible for security need to answer questions such as these: Are all controls installed as intended? Are they effective? Has any breach of security occurred? If so, what actions are required to prevent future breaches?

These questions must be answered by independent and unbiased observers. Such observers perform the task of *information systems auditing*. In an IS environment, an **audit** is an examination of information systems, their inputs, outputs, and processing.

Types of Auditors and Audits. The two types of auditors and audits are internal and external. IS auditing is usually a part of accounting *internal auditing*, and it is frequently performed by corporate internal auditors. An *external auditor* reviews the findings of the internal audit as well as the inputs, processing, and outputs of information systems. The external audit of information systems is frequently a part of the overall external auditing performed by a certified public accounting (CPA) firm.

IS auditing considers all potential hazards and controls in information systems. It focuses on topics such as operations, data integrity, software applications, security and privacy, budgets and expenditures, cost control, and productivity. Guidelines are available to assist auditors in their jobs, such as those from ISACA (formerly the Information Systems Audit and Control Association, www.isaca.org).

How Is Auditing Executed? IS auditing procedures fall into three categories: (1) auditing around the computer, (2) auditing through the computer, and (3) auditing with the computer.

Auditing around the computer means verifying processing by checking for known outputs using specific inputs. This approach is best used in systems with limited outputs. In *auditing through the computer*, inputs, outputs, and processing are checked. Auditors review program logic and test data. *Auditing with the computer* means using a combination of client data, auditor software, and client and auditor hardware. This approach allows the auditor to perform tasks such as simulating payroll program logic using live data.

BEFORE *YOU GO ON . . .*

1. What is the single most important information security control for organizations?
2. Differentiate between authentication and authorization. Which one of these always comes first?
3. Compare and contrast whitelisting and blacklisting.
4. What is the purpose of a disaster recovery plan?
5. What is information system auditing?

RUBY'S CLUB QUESTIONS

1. What security controls should Ruben and Lisa put in place to help ensure the safety of sensitive customer information?
2. Should Ruben and Lisa put these controls in place, or should they hire a third-party vendor to put them in place?

Student Activity | 7.5

Objective: The objective of this exercise is to become familiar with security controls.

Chapter Connection: This case relates to Chapter 7, Section 7.5 on information security controls. *Security controls* are designed to protect all of the components of an information system, including data, software, hardware, and networks. Because there are so many diverse threats, organizations utilize layers of controls. This activity focuses on one of these.

Prerequisites: Before doing this exercise, you should read Section 7.5 to become familiar with security controls.

Activity:

Public key encryption is used in sending data you want to keep secure.

View the following video: http://www.youtube.com/watch?v=a72fHRr6MRU

Read about public key encryption: http://computer.howstuffworks.com/encryption3.htm

Deliverables:

Prepare answers to the following questions:

1. What is the difference between the public key and the private key? How is each used?
2. Public key encryption requires how many keys to work?
3. What is encryption?
4. What is the problem with using only one key or private key encryption?

Multiple Choice Questions:

1. How many keys does public key encryption use?
   (a) 1
   (b) 2
   (c) 3
   (d) 4

2. Who knows the private key?
   (a) The company
   (b) The computer

(c) The receiver
(d) All of the above

3. Who knows the public key?

   (a) Only the computer
   (b) Only the receiver
   (c) Only the customers
   (d) All who want to communicate securely with the receiver

4. The key pairs are based on

   (a) Only even numbers
   (b) Only odd numbers

(c) Only prime numbers
(d) Only numbers divisible by 5

Discussion Questions:

Discuss the benefits of public key encryption (two keys) over private key encryption (one key). What is the problem with using only one key? What is the benefit of using two keys?

What's in IT for ME?

FOR THE ACCOUNTING MAJOR

Public companies, their accountants, and their auditors have significant information security responsibilities. Accountants are now being held professionally responsible for reducing risk, ensuring compliance, eliminating fraud, and increasing the transparency of transactions according to generally accepted accounting principles (GAAP). The Securities and Exchange Commission (SEC) and the Public Company Accounting Oversight Board (PCAOB), among other regulatory agencies, require information security, fraud prevention and detection, and internal controls over financial reporting. Forensic accounting, a combination of accounting and information security, is one of the most rapidly growing areas in accounting today.

FOR THE FINANCE MAJOR

Because information security is essential to the success of organizations today, it is no longer just the concern of the chief information officer (CIO). As a result of global regulatory requirements and the passage of Sarbanes-Oxley, responsibility for information security lies with the chief executive officer (CEO) and chief financial officer (CFO). Consequently, all aspects of the security audit, including the security of information and information systems, are a key concern for financial managers.

In addition, CFOs and treasurers are increasingly involved with investments in information technology. They know that a security breach of any kind can have devastating financial effects on a company. Banking and financial institutions are prime targets for computer criminals. A related problem is fraud involving stocks and bonds that are sold over the Internet. Finance personnel must be aware of both the hazards and the available controls associated with these activities.

FOR THE MARKETING MAJOR

Marketing professionals have new opportunities to collect data on their customers (e.g., through business-to-consumer electronic commerce). Customers expect their data to be properly secured. However, profit-motivated criminals want that data. Therefore, marketing managers must analyze the risk of their operations. Failure to protect corporate and customer data will cause significant public relations problems and make customers very angry. Customer relationship management (CRM) operations and tracking customers' online buying habits can expose data to misuse (if they are not encrypted) or result in privacy violations.

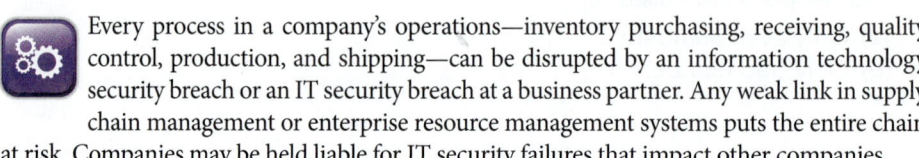

FOR THE
PRODUCTION/OPERATIONS MANAGEMENT MAJOR

Every process in a company's operations—inventory purchasing, receiving, quality control, production, and shipping—can be disrupted by an information technology security breach or an IT security breach at a business partner. Any weak link in supply chain management or enterprise resource management systems puts the entire chain at risk. Companies may be held liable for IT security failures that impact other companies.

FOR THE
HUMAN RESOURCES MANAGEMENT MAJOR

HR managers have responsibilities to secure confidential employee data. In addition, they must ensure that all employees explicitly verify that they understand the company's information security policies and procedures.

FOR THE MIS MAJOR

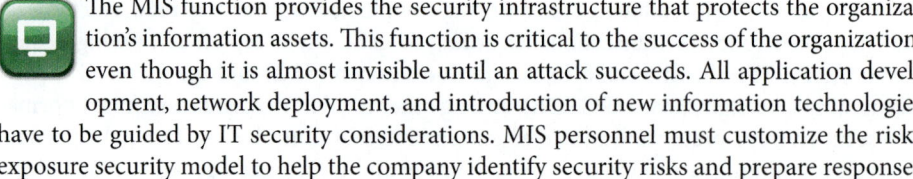

The MIS function provides the security infrastructure that protects the organization's information assets. This function is critical to the success of the organization, even though it is almost invisible until an attack succeeds. All application development, network deployment, and introduction of new information technologies have to be guided by IT security considerations. MIS personnel must customize the risk-exposure security model to help the company identify security risks and prepare responses to security incidents and disasters.

Senior executives of publicly held companies look to the MIS function for help in meeting Sarbanes-Oxley requirements, particularly in detecting "significant deficiencies" or "material weaknesses" in internal controls and remediating them. Other functional areas also look to the MIS function to help them meet their security responsibilities.

>>> SUMMARY

1. Discuss the five factors contributing to the increasing vulnerability of information resources and give one specific example of each factor.

The five factors are:

> Today's interconnected, interdependent, wirelessly networked business environment

>> Example: the Internet

> Smaller, faster, cheaper computers and storage devices

>> Examples: netbooks, thumb drives, iPads

> Decreasing skills necessary to be a computer hacker

>> Example: information system hacking programs circulating on the Internet

> International organized crime taking over cybercrime

>> Example: Organized crime has formed transnational cybercrime cartels. Because it is difficult to know exactly where cyberattacks originate, these cartels are extremely hard to bring to justice.

> Lack of management support

>> Example: Suppose that your company spent $10 million on information security countermeasures last year and experienced no successful attacks on information resources. Shortsighted management might conclude that the company could spend less during the next year and obtain the same results. Bad idea.

2. Compare and contrast human mistakes and social engineering, and give a specific example of each.

Human mistakes are unintentional errors. However, employees can also make unintentional mistakes as a result of actions by an attacker, such as social engineering. *Social engineering* is an attack in which the perpetrator uses social skills to trick or manipulate a legitimate employee into providing confidential company information.

An example of a human mistake is tailgating. An example of social engineering is when an attacker calls an employee on the phone and impersonates a superior in the company.

3. Describe the types of deliberate attacks.

The types of deliberate attacks are:

> *Espionage or trespass* occurs when an unauthorized individual attempts to gain illegal access to organizational information.

> *Information extortion* occurs when an attacker either threatens to steal, or actually steals, information from a company. The perpetrator demands payment for not stealing the information, for returning stolen information, or for agreeing not to disclose the information.

> *Sabotage and vandalism* are deliberate acts that involve defacing an organization's Web site, possibly causing the organization to lose its image and experience a loss of confidence by its customers due to sabotage or vandalism.

> Computing devices and storage devices are becoming smaller yet more powerful with vastly increased storage, making these devices easier and more valuable to *steal*.

> *Identity theft* is the deliberate assumption of another person's identity, usually to gain access to his or her financial information or to frame him or her for a crime.

> *Protecting intellectual property* is a vital issue for people who make their livelihood in knowledge fields. Protecting intellectual property is particularly difficult when that property is in digital form.

> *Software attacks* occur when malicious software penetrates a computer system. Today, these attacks are typically profit driven and Web based.

> *Alien software* is clandestine software that is installed on a computer through duplicitous methods. Alien software uses valuable system resources and can report on your Web surfing habits and other personal behavior.

> Supervisory control and data acquisition (SCADA) refers to a large-scale, distributed, measurement and control system. SCADA systems are used to monitor or to control chemical, physical, or transport processes. A *SCADA attack* attempts to compromise such a system in order to cause damage to the real-world processes that the system controls.

> With both *cyberterrorism* and *cyberwarfare*, attackers use a target's computer systems, particularly via the Internet, to cause physical, real-world harm or severe disruption, usually to carry out a political agenda.

4. Define the three risk mitigation strategies, and give an example of each in the context of you owning a home.

The three risk mitigation strategies are:

> With *risk acceptance*, the organization accepts the potential risk, continues operating with no controls, and absorbs any damages that occur. If you own a home, you may decide not to insure it. Thus, you are practicing risk acceptance. Clearly, this is a bad idea.

> With *risk limitation*, the organization limits the risk by implementing controls that minimize the impact of threats. As a home owner, you practice risk limitation by putting in an alarm system or by cutting down weak trees near your house.

> With *risk transference*, the organization transfers the risk by using other means to compensate for the loss, such as by purchasing insurance. The vast majority of home owners practice risk transference by purchasing insurance on their houses and contents.

5. Identify the three major types of controls that organizations can use to protect their information resources, and give an example of each.

Physical controls prevent unauthorized individuals from gaining access to a company's facilities. Common physical controls include walls, doors, fencing, gates, locks, badges, guards, and alarm systems. More sophisticated physical controls include pressure sensors, temperature sensors, and motion detectors.

Access controls restrict unauthorized individuals from using information resources. These controls involve two major functions: authentication and authorization. Authentication determines the identity of the person requiring access. As an example, authentication can be established through the use of biometrics. After the person is authenticated (identified), authorization is applied. Authorization determines which actions, rights, or privileges the person has, based on verified identity. As an example, authorization is based on least privilege.

Communications (network) controls secure the movement of data across networks. Communications controls consist of firewalls, anti-malware systems, whitelisting and blacklisting, encryption, virtual private networking (VPN), secure socket layer (SSL), and vulnerability management systems.

>>> CHAPTER GLOSSARY

access controls Controls that restrict unauthorized individuals from using information resources and are concerned with user identification.

adware Alien software designed to help pop-up advertisements appear on your screen.

alien software Clandestine software that is installed on a computer through duplicitous methods.

anti-malware systems (antivirus software) Software packages that attempt to identify and eliminate viruses, worms, and other malicious software.

audit An examination of information systems, their inputs, outputs, and processing.

authentication A process that determines the identity of the person requiring access.

authorization A process that determines which actions, rights, or privileges the person has, based on verified identity.

back door (also known as *trap door*) Typically a password, known only to the attacker, that allows the attacker to access the system without having to go through any security procedures.

biometrics The science and technology of authentication (i.e., establishing the identity of an individual) by measuring the subject's physiologic or behavioral characteristics.

blacklisting A process in which a company identifies certain types of software that are not allowed to run in the company environment.

certificate authority A third party that acts as a trusted intermediary between computers (and companies) by issuing digital certificates and verifying the worth and integrity of the certificates.

cold site A backup location that provides only rudimentary services and facilities.

communications (network) controls Controls that deal with the movement of data across networks.

controls Defense mechanisms (also called *countermeasures*).

cookies Small amounts of information that Web sites store on your computer, temporarily or more-or-less permanently.

copyright A grant that provides the creator of intellectual property with ownership of it for the life of the creator plus 70 years.

cybercrime Illegal activities executed on the Internet.

cyberterrorism Can be defined as a premeditated, politically motivated attack against information, computer systems, computer programs, and data that results in violence against noncombatant targets by subnational groups or clandestine agents.

cyberwarfare War in which a country's information systems could be paralyzed from a massive attack by destructive software.

demilitarized zone (DMZ) A separate organizational local area network that is located between an organization's internal network and an external network, usually the Internet.

denial-of-service attack A cyberattack in which an attacker sends a flood of data packets to the target computer, with the aim of overloading its resources.

digital certificate An electronic document attached to a file certifying that this file is from the organization it claims to be from and has not been modified from its original format or content.

distributed denial-of-service (DDoS) A denial-of-service attack that sends a flood of data packets from many compromised computers simultaneously.

employee monitoring systems Systems that monitor employees' computers, e-mail activities, and Internet surfing activities.

encryption The process of converting an original message into a form that cannot be read by anyone except the intended receiver.

exposure The harm, loss, or damage that can result if a threat compromises an information resource.

firewall A system (either hardware, software, or a combination of both) that prevents a specific type of information from moving between untrusted networks, such as the Internet, and private networks, such as your company's network.

hot site A fully configured computer facility, with all information resources and services, communications links, and physical plant operations, that duplicate a company's computing resources and provide near real-time recovery of IT operations.

identity theft Crime in which someone uses the personal information of others to create a false identity and then uses it for some fraud.

information security Protecting an organization's information and information systems from unauthorized access, use, disclosure, disruption, modification, or destruction.

information systems controls The procedures, devices, or software aimed at preventing a compromise to a system.

intellectual property The intangible property created by individuals or corporations that is protected under trade secret, patent, and copyright laws.

keystroke loggers (keyloggers) Hardware or software that can detect all keystrokes made on a compromised computer.

least privilege A principle that users be granted the privilege for some activity only if there is a justifiable need to grant this authorization.

logic bomb Segments of computer code embedded within an organization's existing computer programs.

malware malicious software such as viruses and worms.

network controls (*see* **communications controls**).

passphrase A series of characters that is longer than a password but that can be memorized easily.

passwords Private combinations of characters that only the user should know.

patent A document that grants the holder exclusive rights on an invention or process for 20 years.

phishing attack An attack that uses deception to fraudulently acquire sensitive personal information by masquerading as an official-looking e-mail.

physical controls Controls that restrict unauthorized individuals from gaining access to a company's computer facilities.

piracy Copying a software program (other than freeware, demo software, etc.) without making payment to the owner.

privacy The right to be left alone and to be free of unreasonable personal intrusion.

privilege A collection of related computer system operations that can be performed by users of the system.

public-key encryption (also called *asymmetric encryption*) A type of encryption that uses two different keys: a public key and a private key.

risk The likelihood that a threat will occur.

risk acceptance A strategy in which the organization accepts the potential risk, continues to operate with no controls, and absorbs any damages that occur.

risk analysis The process by which an organization assesses the value of each asset being protected, estimates the probability that each asset might be compromised, and compares the probable costs of each being compromised with the costs of protecting it.

risk limitation A strategy in which the organization limits its risk by implementing controls that minimize the impact of a threat.

risk management A process that identifies, controls, and minimizes the impact of threats, in an effort to reduce risk to manageable levels.

risk mitigation A process whereby the organization takes concrete actions against risks, such as implementing controls and developing a disaster recovery plan.

risk transference A process in which the organization transfers the risk by using other means to compensate for a loss, such as by purchasing insurance.

SCADA (Supervisory Control and Data Acquisition) Large-scale, distributed, measurement and control systems used to monitor or to control chemical, physical, or transport processes.

secure socket layer (SSL) (also known as *transport layer security*) An encryption standard used for secure transactions such as credit card purchases and online banking.

security The degree of protection against criminal activity, danger, damage, and/or loss.

signature recognition The user signs his or her name, and the system matches this signature with one previously recorded under controlled, monitored conditions.

social engineering Getting around security systems by tricking computer users inside a company into revealing sensitive information or gaining unauthorized access privileges.

spam Unsolicited e-mail.

spamware Alien software that uses your computer as a launch platform for spammers.

spyware Alien software that can record keystrokes and/or capture passwords.

strong passwords Passwords that are difficult to guess; longer rather than shorter; contain uppercase and lowercase letters, numbers, and special characters; and are not a recognizable word or string of numbers.

threat Any danger to which an information resource may be exposed.

trade secret Intellectual work, such as a business plan, that is a company secret and is not based on public information.

transport layer security (TLS) (*see* **secure socket layer**).

trap doors (*see* **back door**).

Trojan horse A software program containing a hidden function that presents a security risk.

tunneling A process that encrypts each data packet to be sent and places each encrypted packet inside another packet.

virtual private network (VPN) A private network that uses a public network (usually the Internet) to securely connect users by using encryption.

virus Malicious computer code that can attach itself to (or "infect") other computer programs without the owner of the program being aware of the infection.

voice recognition The user speaks a phrase that has been previously recorded under controlled, monitored conditions, and the voice recognition system matches the two voice signals.

vulnerability The possibility that an information resource will suffer harm by a threat.

warm site A site that provides many of the same services and options of a hot site but does not include the company's applications.

whitelisting A process in which a company identifies acceptable software and permits it to run, and either prevents anything else from running or lets new software run in a quarantined environment until the company can verify its validity.

worm Destructive computer code that replicates itself without requiring another program to provide a safe environment for replication.

>>> DISCUSSION QUESTIONS

1. Why are computer systems so vulnerable?

2. Why should information security be of prime concern to management?

3. Is security a technical issue? A business issue? Both? Support your answer. Hint: Read Kim Nash, "Why Technology Isn't the Answer to Better Security," *CIO* (www.cio.com), October 15, 2008.

4. Compare information security in an organization with insuring a house.

5. Why are authentication and authorization important to e-commerce?

6. Why is cross-border cybercrime expanding rapidly? Discuss possible solutions.

7. Discuss why the Sarbanes-Oxley Act is having an impact on information security.

8. What types of user authentication are used at your university and/or place of work? Do these authentication measures seem to be effective? What if a higher level of authentication were implemented? Would it be worth it, or would it decrease productivity?

9. Why are federal government authorities so worried about SCADA attacks?

>>> PROBLEM-SOLVING ACTIVITIES

1. A critical problem is assessing how far a company is legally obligated to go in order to secure personal data. Because there is no such thing as perfect security (i.e., there is always more that can be done), resolving this question can significantly affect cost.

   a. When are security measures that a company implements sufficient to comply with its obligations?

   b. Is there any way for a company to know if its security measures are sufficient? Can you devise a method for any organization to determine if its security measures are sufficient?

2. Assume that the daily probability of a major earthquake in Los Angeles is .07 percent. The chance of your computer center being damaged during such a quake is 5 percent. If the center is damaged, the average estimated damage will be $4.0 million.

   a. Calculate the expected loss in dollars.

   b. An insurance agent is willing to insure your facility for an annual fee of $25,000. Analyze the offer, and discuss whether to accept it.

3. Enter www.scambusters.org. Find out what the organization does. Learn about e-mail scams and Web site scams. Report your findings.

4. Visit www.dhs.gov/index.shtm (Department of Homeland Security). Search the site for "National Strategy to Secure Cyberspace," and write a report on the agency's agenda and accomplishments to date.

5. Enter www.alltrustnetworks.com and other vendors of biometrics. Find the devices they make that can be used to control access into information systems. Prepare a list of products and major capabilities of each.

6. Software piracy is a global problem. Access the following Web sites: www.bsa.org and www.microsoft.com/piracy. What can organizations do to mitigate this problem? Are some organizations dealing with the problem better than others?

7. Investigate the Sony Playstation Network hack that occurred in April 2011.

   a. What type of attack was it?

   b. Was the success of the attack due to technology problems at Sony, management problems at Sony, or a combination of both? Provide specific examples to support your answer.

   c. Which Sony controls failed?

   d. Could Sony have prevented the hack? If so, how?

   e. Discuss Sony's response to the hack.

   f. Describe the damages that Sony incurred from the successful hack.

>>> TEAM ASSIGNMENTS

1. Access www.ftc.gov/sentinel to learn more about how law enforcement agencies around the world work together to fight consumer fraud. Each team should obtain current statistics on one of the top five consumer complaint categories and prepare a report. Are any categories growing faster than others? Are any categories more prevalent in certain parts of the world?

2. Read "In the Matter of BJ's Wholesale Club, Inc., Agreement containing Consent Order, FTC File No. 042 3160, June 16, 2005" at www.ftc.gov/opa/2005/06/bjswholesale.htm. Describe the security breach at BJ's

Wholesale Club. What was the reason for this agreement? Identify some of the causes of the security breach and how BJ's can better defend itself against hackers and legal liability.

3. Read the article "The Security Tools You Need" at http://www.pcworld.com/downloads/collection/collid,1525/files.html. Each team should download a product and discuss its pros and cons for the class. Be sure to take a look at all the comments posted about this article.

CLOSING **CASE 1 >** Cybercriminals Use Social Networks for Targeted Attacks

Each infected personal computer in a corporate network represents a potential point of access to valuable intellectual property, such as customer information, patents, and strategic documents. The attackers who breached Google and 30 other technology, media, defense, and financial companies from mid- to late 2009 were after these kinds of information. Dubbed Operation Aurora by cyber security company McAfee (www.mcafee.com), the attacks were likely initiated by fake friendly messages sent to specific employees at the targeted companies. How do such attacks work? Take a look at the following example.

<<<**THE PROBLEM**

Bob works for a large U.S. financial company. Somehow, attackers gained access to Bob's Facebook account, logged into it, grabbed his contact list of 50 to 60 friends, and began manually reviewing messages and postings on his profile page. The attackers noted discussions about a recent company picnic and sent individual messages to Bob's friends who worked at his company.

Alice, one of Bob's co-workers, received a Facebook message from Bob, asking her to take a look at pictures from the company picnic. She had, in fact, attended the picnic with Bob. When she clicked on the accompanying Web link, she expected to see Bob's pictures, but the message had come from the attackers and the link carried malicious software (malware).

Upon clicking on the link, Alice unknowingly downloaded a keystroke logger, which was designed to save everything she typed at her keyboard and, once per hour, send a text file of all her keystrokes to a free Gmail account controlled by the attackers. (The keystroke logger was available free on the Internet.) The attackers reviewed Alice's hourly keystroke reports and noted when she logged into a virtual private network account to access her company's network. With her username and password, the attackers logged on to the financial firm's network and gained access to the company's servers and all the sensitive information they contain. The attackers also took control of Alice's computer without her knowing it. As such, her computer became a zombie computer, under the control of the attackers.

Successful breaches, such as the preceding example, illustrate a shift in the way cybercriminals attack their targets. They are aggressively taking advantage of an unanticipated hole in corporate defenses: the use of social networks in corporate settings. They are using the personal information provided by individuals communicating on social networks.

These networks provide a rich repository of information that cybercriminals can use to more precisely target individual corporate employees through phishing attacks. (A phishing attack is an attack that uses deception to fraudulently acquire sensitive information by masquerading as an authentic-looking e-mail.) In fact, the attacks are so precisely targeted that they have a new name, spear fishing. (Spear fishing attacks are phishing attacks that target specific individuals.)

In addition to copying or stealing sensitive personal and corporate information, attackers combine many zombie computers into botnets, which can contain millions of computers. The attackers then use these botnets to execute all forms of cybercrime.

In just four weeks in early 2010, cyberthieves known as the Kneber gang stole 3,644 usernames and passwords for Facebook accounts from individuals in over 2,000 companies. Stolen credentials like these flow into hacking Web sites where a batch of 1,000 Facebook username and password pairs, guaranteed valid, sell for $75 to $200, depending on the number of "friends" tied to the accounts. From each account, thieves can gather up e-mail addresses, contact lists, birth dates, hometowns, mothers' maiden names, photos, and recent gossip—all useful for targeting specific victims and turning their computers into zombies.

In another example of attacks on social networking sites, the Koobface worm targets users of social networking Web sites, including Facebook (its name is an anagram of Facebook), Twitter, MySpace, hi5, Bebo, Friendster, and others. A study by the Information Warfare Monitor (www.infowar-monitor.net) revealed that the operators of the Koobface worm generated over $2 million in revenue from June 2009 to June 2010. Kaspersky Labs (http://usa.kaspersky.com), a security firm, estimates that 500,000 Koobface-controlled personal computers are active on the Internet on any given day.

AN ATTEMPTED SOLUTION>>>

Facebook, the dominant social network and, therefore, the biggest target, is partnering with Microsoft and security firm McAfee to help filter malicious programs. A Facebook spokesperson said that this process should keep compromised accounts to a minimum. The spokesperson went on to say that Facebook is "constantly working to improve complex systems that quickly detect and block suspicious activity, delete malicious links, and help people restore access to their accounts."

THE RESULTS>>>

Unfortunately, vulnerabilities in social networking Web sites continue to be exploited. Many owners of infected zombie computers do not know that their computers are compromised. The best solution that will yield the best results is for all users of social networks to be extremely careful of what information they post on their pages. Further, all computer users must not click on any link in an e-mail, even if that e-mail comes from a supposedly trusted source.

However, there is some good news. Social networking users in the United States, more than any other country, limit the personal information they post and set privacy settings to restrict who can view their information. This finding comes from the 2010 Unisys Security Index, a bi-annual study conducted by market research company Lieberman Research Group (www.liebermanresearch.com).

Questions

1. Describe the difference between phishing attacks and spear fishing attacks. Which attack is the most dangerous? Be specific as you support your answer.

2. What are specific actions that you can take to decrease your vulnerability to such attacks?

SOURCES: Compiled from "Information Security Experts at Facebook Fix Vulnerability Discovered by Indiana University Students," *EzineMark.com*, February 3, 2011; R. McMillan, "Five 2010 Stories That Nobody Predicted," *CIO*, January 3, 2011; T. Eston, "Social Networks' Threat to Security," *InformationWeek*, October 30, 2010;

M. Schwartz, "Americans Maximize Social Network Security," *InformationWeek*, October 27, 2010; A. Freed, "Enterprise Information Security and Social Networks," *Infosec Island*, October 25, 2010; M. Schwartz, "Social Networks Pose Security Risks to SMBs," *InformationWeek*, September 14, 2010; A. Diana, "Employees Flout Social Network Security Policies," *InformationWeek*, July 23, 2010; M. Schwartz, "Social Network Security Policies Lacking," *InformationWeek*, June 28, 2010; "Facebook Fixes Bug That Exposed Private Chats," *CIO*, May 5, 2010; N. Roiter, "Tweet This: Social Network Security Is Risky Business," *Computerworld*, March 4, 2010; B. Acohido, "An Invitation to Crime," *USA Today*, March 4, 2010; Admin, "Hacking a Corporate Network with Facebook," *Information Security Resources*, January 12, 2010.

CLOSING **CASE 2** >

Who Is Minding the Security Store?

On Wednesday, April 21, 2010, computers in companies, hospitals, and schools around the world got stuck repeatedly rebooting themselves after an antivirus program from security vendor McAfee (www.mcafee.com) identified a normal Windows file as a virus. Only computers running Windows XP Service Pack 3 in combination with McAfee VirusScan 8.7 were affected. The problems were widespread.

<<<**THE PROBLEM**

- About a third of the hospitals in Rhode Island had to postpone elective surgeries and stop treating patients without traumas in emergency rooms.
- In Kentucky, state police officers were told to shut down the computers in their patrol cars as technicians tried to fix the problem.
- The National Science Foundation in Arlington, Virginia, lost computer access.
- At Illinois State University in Normal, Illinois, dozens of computers in the College of Business became inoperable.

McAfee pushes daily updates to its corporate customers, and the April 21, 2010, update was intended to detect and destroy a minor threat, the "W32/wecorl.a" virus. However, the update incorrectly identified the critical "svchost.exe" file in Windows XP Service Pack 3 as malicious software and then quarantined it. In some cases, the update actually deleted the file. Without svchost.exe a Windows personal computer will not boot (start up) correctly.

When users applied the McAfee update and then rebooted their computers, the computers crashed and rebooted repeatedly. Most of these computers lost all network capability as well. Adding to these problems, some computers became unable to recognize their own USB drives. This problem turned out to be major, since recovery required the reinstallation of svchost.exe, a process that could be done more easily by walking a flash drive from one crippled computer to the next.

 Because virtually all the affected personal computers were unable to connect to a network, corporate IT personnel had to manually fix each machine. (Of course, this process became much more difficult if the affected computers could not even recognize their own USB drives.)

<<<**THE SOLUTION**

Later on Wednesday, McAfee spelled out the steps to take in a document on its Web site. On Thursday, the company made available a semi-automated tool that should be run on affected computers after entering Windows' Safe Mode.

McAfee took two days (until April 23, 2010) to post on its Web site an FAQ (list of frequently asked questions) concerning the update disaster. Late on April 23, McAfee's home page contained a link to a blog post by McAfee's Barry McPherson, which attempted to minimize the issue. (Interestingly, McPherson was McAfee's executive vice president of support and customer service, not its CEO.) McPherson pledged that McAfee would improve its quality assurance processes to see that this problem did not reoccur.

<<<**THE RESULTS**

Most large McAfee customers had their computers up and running in two days or less. However, a number of small businesses that did not have IT departments were still trying to fix their computers several days later.

Interestingly, perhaps modern organizations are somewhat to blame for this problem. Today, organizations are pushing for more rapid updates to their antivirus software to minimize their exposure time to new malware threats. Correspondingly, antivirus vendors have speeded up the delivery of their software updates in an attempt to match the pace of new malware development by hackers. These rapid updates could cause security vendors to make mistakes in their quality control procedures, which you have seen happened to McAfee.

Questions

1. Discuss McAfee's handling of the update disaster. Should McAfee have done anything differently? If so, what? Support your answer.

2. What should organizations do to prevent such problems in the future?

SOURCES: Compiled from G. Keizer, "McAfee Apologizes for Crippling PCs with Bad Update," *Computerworld*, April 23, 2010; "McAfee Antivirus Program Goes Berserk, Freezes PCs," *The Economic Times*, April 22, 2010; A. Kingsley-Hughes, "McAfee Issues Fix, and Apology, for Hosed XP SP3 PCs," *ZDNET.com*, April 22, 2010; G. Keizer, "The McAfee Update Mess Explained," *PC World*, April 22, 2010; E. Bott, "McAfee Admits 'Inadequate' Quality Control Caused PC Meltdown," *ZDNET.com*, April 22, 2010; S. Choney, "Some Still Recovering from McAfee PC Problem," *MSNBC.com*, April 22, 2010; "McAfee Program Goes Berserk, Reboots PCs," *MSNBC.com*, April 21, 2010.

RUBY'S CLUB INTERNSHIP ASSIGNMENTS

Ruben and Lisa have decided to employ a third party to handle their electronic commerce transactions (electronic commerce is presented in Chapter 9). They do not want to store any customer payment information on their Web site. While they realize they are losing some money on each transaction in fees to the e-commerce provider, they consider this fee cost-effective risk transfer for them.

Specifically, they are considering the Google Checkout, Amazon Stores, eBay Stores, Yahoo! Business, and PayPal as viable possibilities for handling Ruby's transactions. As their intern, they

want you to research these five companies and provide feedback on each. Have any of them had any recent security breaches? If so, how were they handled, and what were the ramifications to customers (the companies provided with the e-commerce tools and the customers of that company)? What do their security policies state?

After you do your research, write Ruben and Lisa a letter (in business format) and make a suggestion as to which company would best suit their needs.

SPREADSHEET ACTIVITY

Objective: This activity will bring together the ideas of security and formula writing in a spreadsheet. Upon completion, you will be able to take data presented in written form, translate it into numbers, create formulas, and then rank security issues based on the spreadsheet you create.

Chapter Connection: Security issues are not all created equal. Some are frequent and inexpensive to overcome; others are rare and costly. Intentional and unintentional threats must be dealt with. But as a network manager, how do you know what deserves the most resources? Given that you never know where the next threat will come from, how will you allocate resources? This activity will bring this discussion to a spreadsheet and help you apply your math and spreadsheet skills to this very "real-world" situation.

Prerequisites: There are no prerequisites for this activity.

Activity: Consider the following situation. You are the network manager at a local bank. A number of security issues must be dealt with. However, like everyone else, you have limited resources. You only have $10,000 in your budget to allocate to security. This money can be spent on hardware, software, training, or anything else you deem worthy of this money. Here is a list of potential threats.

- *Malware.* If malware ends up installed on a computer in the system, it could easily spread to the other machines without anyone knowing it is there. The expense of repairing the machines and restoring data are minimal when compared to the cost of rebuilding trust in the consumer. Estimated total cost of marketing and repairing customer trust: $25,000. Probability of occurring: 35 percent. Cost of preventative maintenance and training: $3,500.

- *Careless employees.* Judy has to run to the restroom. Since she trusts everyone she works with, she walks away from her computer without locking it. While she is away from her desk and her computer is unlocked, Johnny walks in. No one thinks anything about Johnny on Judy's computer because he is the local "computer guru" even though he is a janitor. While Judy is away and Johnny is on her computer, he transfers a total of $7,500 from over 150 total accounts by running a script in the computer system. When Judy returns, she sees Johnny on the computer and thanks him for watching it, laughing about how she accidentally left it unlocked. Probability of occurring: 5 percent. Cost of preventative maintenance and training: $2,000.

- *Cloud computing.* Banks rely on many software packages to accomplish their goals. Not the least of these are the many packages run by the home office. These are accessed over the Internet, and private data are transferred back and forth. A hacker who is able to hack into the local system would by default have access to the cloud. The cost of this is monumental. Customer data from across the nation would be compromised. Having a backup of all data is imperative. Keeping employees trained on using the system, avoiding social engineering, changing passwords, and other issues are paramount to help protect the home office and the local office. Total potential loss: $2.5 million. Probability of occurrence: 2.5 percent. Cost of preventative maintenance and training: $7,000.

- *Fire.* This always a threat. If a fire breaks out it could be devastating. Loss of technology equipment alone would run close to $20,000. Loss of records would be almost unrecoverable. However, the chance of fire is relatively low. At a 2 percent chance of fire, this is a minimal concern. The cost of preventative maintenance is not cheap. Sprinklers have to be inspected, fire retardant material must be tested, and fire extinguishers must be replaced. Total preventative maintenance cost is $1,500. However the total potential loss is a devastating $250,000.

Given that most people agree that risk (R) is equal to the consequence (C) multiplied by the probability of occurrence (P):

$$R = C*P$$

Create a spreadsheet that calculates this formula. Then use your estimated risk to figure the return on security investment (ROSI) that most consider to be equal to risk avoided (R; hopefully it will be avoided by the investment) divided by the cost of preventative maintenance (PM).

$$ROSI = R/PM$$

This number represents the "impact" of an investment and can be used to help determine how to create a budget so that the return is maximized. The higher the number, the more of the risk is covered by the investment. Use this number to prioritize where to make security investments.

Since your budget is only $10,000, you will need to determine where to spend your money. According to this scenario, total coverage would cost $14,000. Use the ROSI to recommend a budget. Also provide your spreadsheet for justification of the budget.

Deliverables: The final product will be a spreadsheet formula, ranking, and presentation of a suggested budget.

Quiz Questions:

1. Are all security threats intentional?

2. When building a spreadsheet in Microsoft Excel and copying formula down from the top of a column to the bottom, you move your cursor to

   (a) The top left corner

   (b) The top right corner

   (c) The bottom right corner

   (d) The bottom left corner

   (e) You just click and drag anywhere in the cell you desire to copy.

3. Correct formula writing is very important because of which of the following?

   (a) An incorrect formula will provide incorrect data and wrong decisions may be made.

(b) If an incorrect formula is copied to other cells, the mistake will be multiplied.

(c) If other formulas are built on the answer created by this formula, then the mistake will be compounded.

(d) All of the above.

Discussion Questions:

1. Discuss the advantages and disadvantages of building a formula once and copying it to multiple rows or columns.

2. Discuss the importance of taking verbal or written clues and being able to build a spreadsheet. Is a spreadsheet the ultimate combination of math and business?

3. Given that no one has unlimited resources, is it possible to ever cover all the bases and ensure security? What type of agreement must there be between the business and the consumer for this situation to exist and be acceptable?

DATABASE ACTIVITY: TABLES II

Objective

Information systems need checks to catch errors in the entry of data. Not all errors can be caught, but many can be. You'll learn a few of the methods here using the following features of Microsoft Access:

- Default values
- Range checks
- Value checks against a list

Chapter Connection

Security includes keeping bad data out of databases. Checking data as entered can prevent many errors and some mischief. Here, you'll see how Access checks data as it is entered. Other database management systems work in much the same way.

Prerequisites

Before you begin this activity, you will need to familiarize yourself with and practice three concepts: default values, validation checks based on a range of valid data, and validation checks against a list. The following sections introduce these concepts and provide practice in dealing with them. Read these sections and complete the brief practice items before moving to the larger activity.

DEFAULT VALUES

A *default value* is the value a data item has if no other value is entered. Say an Ohio college attracts primarily

students from the Dayton area. Most of its applicants have a home phone in area code 937. A database could pre-enter 937 as the area code of new applicants. The work-study student who enters applicant information into a database can change it for those with different area codes, but having it saves time and reduces errors overall.

To enter a default value for a field in an Access table:

1. Open the table in Design view.
2. Select the field for which you want to specify a default value.
3. Find the Default Value row in the Field Properties pane, under the General tab.
4. Click on the right side of this row and key in the desired value, as shown in Figure 7A.1.

Usage Hint: You can also assign default values and perform validation checks on fields in forms instead of in tables. In the form's Layout or Design view, open its Property Sheet, select a field, select the Data or All tab on the Property Sheet, and continue as above. The check will be applied only to data entered via that form. Checks entered in table definitions are applied to all data entered in any way.

5. Go to Datasheet view to confirm that the default value was entered correctly. You should see the value in the bottom (New) row of the table. If you enter a default value in a form, you won't see it in the table's Datasheet view, but you will see it if you enter a new record via the form.

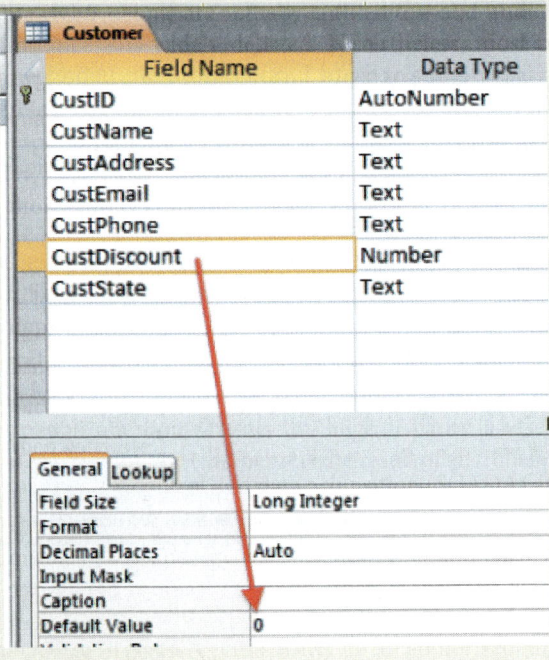

Figure 7A.1

RANGE CHECKS

Database designers often need to make sure data are in an allowable range. For example, the quantity of something in an order must be greater than zero, or the year of birth of a pupil entering kindergarten in September 2011 might have to be 2006.

This, by the way, shows one reason for putting checking in a form rather than in the table on which the form is based. Suppose an occasional student born outside the usual year enters kindergarten. The school principal might have a different form, in which it can be 2005–07. Supervisors can often override data entry checks that apply to the workers they supervise.

To enter a range check for a field in an Access table:

1. Open the table in Design view.

2. Select the field for which you want to enter a range check.

3. In the Field Properties pane below the list of fields, under the General tab, find the Validation Rule row.

4. In the right side of this row, enter an expression that will evaluate to True or False, and is True for valid data. For example, the expression ">5" (without quotation marks) means the value entered in the field must be greater than 5. The data the user enters is implied to the left of the ">."

These comparison operators are used in validation expressions:

= (equal to) Seldom useful by itself. If you know what a value must be, why enter it?

> (greater than)

< (less than)

>= (greater than or equal to)

<= (less than or equal to)

<> (less than or greater than; that is, *not* equal to)

In addition, these are often useful in validation and other expressions:

AND requires *both* the condition on its left and the condition on its right to be met. ">= 0 AND <=10" requires a value of at least zero but no more than ten.

OR requires *either* the condition on its left or the one on its right, possibly both, to be met. "<5 OR >50" excludes numbers from 5 to 50 but allows all others. (Be sure you understand why the expression means this.)

BETWEEN . . . AND . . . means just what you would think. "BETWEEN 0 AND 10" is another way to write the condition that was used as an example for AND.

IS NULL lets you leave a field blank. Some versions of Access won't let you leave one blank if it has a validation rule, since blank data does not satisfy the rule. If you want to allow the field to be left empty, write "IS NULL OR . . ." where the rest of the rule is whatever you want as validation if anything at all is entered.

If you want to use a date in a condition, enclose it between #s. ">=#1/1/2010#" (without quotation marks) will accept any date in 2010 or later.

Instead of an actual date, you can write "DATE()" to mean today's date. ">DATE()" will accept any date in the future. This can be useful, for example, for delivery date estimates. It does not guarantee that the order will arrive then, but it prevents a promise to deliver something last week.

There is more. For example, you could make sure an account number consists of a letter followed by five digits, the last of which is even. Once you understand how validation rules work, you can read up on the rest if you need to.

5. Optionally, but a good practice, enter an error message in the right side of the Validation Text row. Access will display it to the user if the test fails. A few suggestions:

• Make messages informative. Use "Quantity must be greater than zero," not "Quantity error."

• Do not try to be funny. It is nearly impossible to do this well. Even a genuinely funny message loses its humor after someone has seen it five times.

• Do not insult the user. (The user might be your boss.)

- Do not end the message with an exclamation point. "Must be from 1 to 5" is fine. "Must be from 1 to 5!" is scolding. Nobody likes to be scolded.

  If you do not provide a message, Access will display the rule that the data did not satisfy in a standard message format. Some users will be able to figure out the problem from this, but many nontechnical people will find it confusing.

6. Test your work by going to Datasheet view, entering sample data values, and confirming that valid ones are accepted but invalid ones are not. Pick values that provide good tests. Try values at the limits: If a number is supposed to be *less than* 10, not *less than or equal to* 10, make sure 10 is rejected.

Usage Hint: Access does not apply validation checks to default values. This can lead to problems when a user changes a default, realizes that the change was in error, and tries to change it back. If there are both a default and a validation rule for the same field, be sure the validation rule allows the default value. That way, you can restore the default value if you change it by mistake.

Checking Values Against a List

Sometimes there is no simple formula to define valid data, but there is a list of valid values. For example, you might require a state code in a U.S. postal address to be one of the 50+ that the U.S. Postal Service recognizes, or you might require a department name to be one of those in your company.

The simplest way to handle this is to list them in the rule. The expression "IN (a, b, c, . . .)" does this. This evaluates as True if the entered value is a, b, c, up to as many as you have. (Replace a, b, c and so on with the valid values.) If items are text, put them in quotation marks. A rule to see if a location is one of your firm's offices might look like this:

    IN ("Boston", "Paris", "Sydney", "Santiago")

Usage Hint: If you're in North America, you were taught that commas go inside quotation marks in English writing. That does not apply to Access functions!

Longer lists should be in tables. (This is a flexible concept that can do more than reduce data entry errors.) To get a pull-down list with all valid values:

1. Create a new table with one field. Give it the same data type as the field whose data you want to validate. Enter all valid data values into this column. Save the table, giving it a suitable name, and close it. You can change it whenever the list of valid data values changes.

2. Open the table that contains the field you want to check against this list. In Design view, select that field. Select its Data Type column, and change its data type to "Lookup Wizard . . ."

3. On the first page of the wizard, tell it you want to look up values in a table or query.

4. On the next page, select the table you just created.

5. On the next page, select the only column this table has and move it to the right-hand pane by clicking the "]" symbol. Click "Next" a few times until the wizard exits Figure 7A.2.

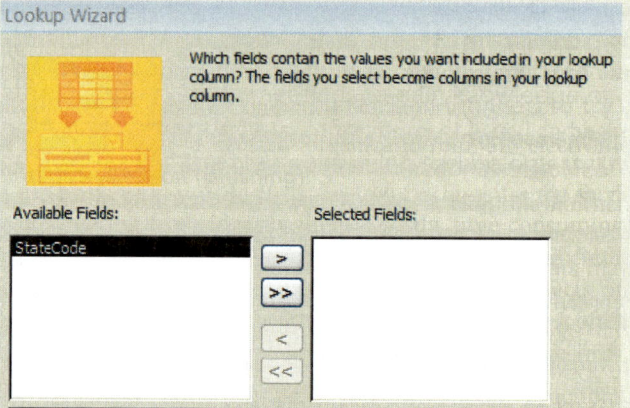

Figure 7A.2

6. A value list created this way lets the user select values from a pull-down list. It also lets the user enter a value that is not in the list. If you want to prevent that, while this field is still selected, click the Lookup tab in the Field Properties pane. Change "Limit to list" to "Yes" via the down arrow at the right of the row. (If you do not do this now, you can do it later.)

7. Switch to Datasheet view to confirm that the field behaves correctly.

8. You can click the Database Tools ribbon tab and look at the relationship map. If it does not show the new table, click Show Table and add it to the map. You'll see a link between the new table and the table that contains the data to be validated against it.

Activity:

1. Download the Ch 07 CustOrder database from the Web site and open it. It has tables for customers, orders, line items, and products. Its structure resembles the example in Section 3.3 of this book. The Ordered Parts table there corresponds to the Line Item table here.

2. Open the Line Item table and specify a default value of 1 for Quantity.

3. Open the Customer table and enter a default value of 0 for customer discount. Also, for the same field, add a rule to limit the discount to a range of 0 to 25 percent. (Enter the upper limit as 0.25, not 25. Access can display fractions as percentages, but that is just for display. It treats them as fractions internally and validates them that way.)

4. Add a validation rule to the payment date: It must be no later than today. (The limiting value, today, is allowable.)

5. Create a table CountryList with one column: countries from which you expect orders. Enter ten countries into it, including your home country, the others in the sample data, and seven others of your choice (or six, if your home country is not in the sample data). Link the table to the Country field in the Customer table. The user should be allowed to enter a new country in the Customer table if a customer's country is not in the list.

Deliverables:

Your completed database, with the above changes.

Quiz Questions:

1. True or False? A person entering data into an Access database can change a default value.

2. In which of the following places can you specify a default value for a data element?

   2.1. In a table, in Datasheet view

   2.2. In a table, in Design view

   2.3. In a report

   2.4. In a form

Choose one of the following four answers:

(a) 2.2

(b) 2.2 and 2.4

(c) 2.1 and 2.4

(d) 2.2 and 2.3

3. Which of the following validation rules will allow only dates between July 13 and December 16, 2011 (including both endpoints)?

(a) >#7/12/2011# AND <#12/17/2011#

(b) BETWEEN #7/13/2011 AND #12/16/2011#

(c) >= #7/13/2011# AND <= #12/16/2011#

(d) All of the above.

4. If a validation rule has no validation text, which of the following will happen?

(a) The rule will not be applied. Any data can be entered without checking.

(b) The rule will be applied to Number and Date data, but not to Text data.

(c) The rule will be applied, but the error message may not be informative.

(d) The rule will be applied to new data, but not to data that someone changes later.

Discussion Questions:

1. How would you write a validation rule that permits a data value to be either 0 or any number from 5 through 10?

2. What is the purpose of Validation Text in an Access table definition?

3. How would you write a validation rule that requires a data value to be one of the six letters A, B, C, D, F or I?

8 | Web 2.0 and Social Networks

LEARNING OBJECTIVES >>>

1. Describe the differences between Web 1.0 and Web 2.0, and explain the benefits of three information technologies used by Web 2.0.

2. Identify five prominent Web 2.0 applications, and provide at least one example of how each one can be utilized in a business setting.

3. Discuss the three categories of Web 2.0 sites, and provide at least one example of how each one can improve business efficiency and profitability.

OPENING **CASE** > Making Money with YouTube Videos

Rhett McLaughlin and Link Neal, the comedians known professionally as Rhett & Link (www.rhettandlink.com), wanted to be television stars. They were on the verge of achieving that goal in 2008 when the CW television network canceled their variety show after only four episodes. In response, Rhett & Link set out to create a business centered on YouTube videos. They persuaded AJJ Cornhole (www.ajjcornhole.com), a toy company, to sponsor them in making a music video—really an advertisement—about a beanbag tossing game. Although the video generated more interest than money, it led to more work for the duo. Since then, Alka Seltzer, McDonald's, the Food Network, Cadillac, and other brands have sponsored Rhett & Link videos.

In the summer of 2010, the Web analytics company TubeMogul (www.tubemogul.com) released a study estimating that the top independent video producers on YouTube earn more than $100,000 in annual advertising revenue alone. In 2010, Rhett & Link videos averaged approximately 120,000 views per day, according to Tube-Mogul. However, what really sets the comedians apart is their leadership in company sponsorships. In some Rhett & Link videos, products appear on screen. In other videos, the name of the company is flashed at the end.

Rhett & Link receive two streams of income from You-Tube. In addition to the sponsorship money, which is entirely theirs, they receive advertising income because Rhett & Link have been designated an official YouTube partner (www.youtube.com/partners). Creators must apply to become partners, and by early 2011 YouTube had accepted about 10,000 partners. Partners receive a percentage of the advertising sales on their channel. The ads are sold by Google, which owns YouTube.

McLaughlin and Neal are making money from their YouTube videos. YouTube partners are contractually forbidden to discuss their ad earnings. Rhett & Link concede, however, that they are no longer scrambling for survival.

For most participants, the YouTube partner program does not provide enough money on which to survive. As a result, video makers hustle on multiple fronts. They sell T-shirts and mugs to fans on their YouTube pages. Musicians use videos to sell songs on iTunes and tickets for live performances.

Sources: Compiled from M. Humphrey, "YouTube: Five Tips for Building Your Own Video Career," *Forbes*, March 30, 2011; J. Ribeiro, "YouTube Acquires Next New Networks to Aid Video Creators," *Computerworld*, March 8, 2011; F. Gillette, "On YouTube, Seven-Figure Views, Six-Figure Paychecks," *Bloomberg BusinessWeek*, September 27–October 3, 2010; T. Claburn, "YouTube Promises 15 Minutes of Fame," *InformationWeek*, July 29, 2010; www.youtube.com/partners, www.rhettandlink.com, accessed April 2, 2011.

Questions

1. Access the *Forbes* article "YouTube: Five Tips for Building Your Own Video Career." Provide examples of how McLaughlin and Neal have followed each tip.

2. What are the difficulties involved in building your own brand on YouTube? Give specific examples of these difficulties.

RUBY'S CLUB

Ruby's Club introduced its Web site only five years ago. Since then, it has been a very basic Web 1.0 site, containing static information that has changed very little over time. Now, with the emergence of Web 2.0 technologies and social networks, coupled with the growing skills of Internet users, it seems natural that Ruben and Lisa use these technologies to reach their customers.

>>> While Ruben and Lisa are aware of these technologies, neither of them is very experienced with them. Ruben only joined Facebook last year because he was trying to learn more about a band that was coming to perform at the club. He has not explored Facebook from a business standpoint and really does not know what is possible. And Twitter is not even on their radar yet.

In addition, they want to explore options such as blogs, wikis, and other Web 2.0 technologies. But where do they go? What should they hope to accomplish?

INTRODUCTION

Organizations today are using Web 2.0 technologies and applications in a variety of innovative ways. You begin this chapter with a discussion of Web 2.0 technologies and applications. You will then take a look at three widespread categories of Web 2.0 sites.

When you complete this chapter, you will have a thorough understanding of Web 2.0 technologies, applications, and Web sites and the ways in which modern organizations use them. You will be familiar with their advantages and disadvantages and the risks and rewards they can bring to your organization. Most of you already have pages on social networking sites, so you are familiar with the benefits and drawbacks of such sites. This chapter will enable you to apply this knowledge to your organization's efforts in the Web 2.0 arena. You will be in a position to contribute to your organization's policies on social network use while at work. You will also be able to help your organization design its own strategy for social networking.

Significantly, social networking technologies can help you start your own business. In fact, many entrepreneurs have developed successful businesses on YouTube (www.youtube.com), the popular video-sharing social networking Web site (see this chapter's opening case).

8.1 | Web 2.0 Underlying Technologies

The World Wide Web, which you learned about in Chapter 4, first appeared in 1990. Web 1.0 was the first generation of the Web. We did not use this term in Chapter 4 because there was no need to say "Web 1.0" until we presented Web 2.0.

The key developments of Web 1.0 were the creation of Web sites and the commercialization of the Web. Users typically have minimal interaction with Web 1.0 sites. Rather, they passively receive information from those sites.

Web 2.0 is a popular term that has proved difficult to define. According to Tim O'Reilly, a noted blogger (see www.oreillynet.com/lpt/a/6228), **Web 2.0** is a loose collection of information technologies and applications, plus the Web sites that use them. These Web sites enrich the user experience by encouraging user participation, social interaction, and collaboration. Unlike Web 1.0 sites, Web 2.0 sites are not so much online places to visit as Web locations that facilitate information sharing, user-centered design, and collaboration. Web 2.0 sites often harness collective intelligence (for example, wikis); deliver functionality as services, rather than packaged software (for example, Web services); and feature remixable applications and data (for example, mashups).

You begin your exploration of Web 2.0 by examining the various Web 2.0 information technologies. Among the most widely used technologies are AJAX, tagging, and Really Simple Syndication (RSS).

AJAX

AJAX is a Web development technique that enables portions of Web pages to reload with fresh data instead of requiring the entire Web page to reload. This process speeds up response time and increases user satisfaction.

Tagging

A **tag** is a keyword or term that describes a piece of information—for example, a blog, a picture, an article, or a video clip. Users typically choose tags that are meaningful to them. Tagging allows users to place information in multiple, overlapping associations rather than in rigid categories. For example, a photo of a car might be tagged with "Corvette," "sports car," and "Chevrolet." Tagging is the basis of *folksonomies*, which are user-generated classifications that use tags to categorize and retrieve Web pages, photos, videos, and other Web content.

As one example, the Web site Delicious (www.delicious.com) provides a system for organizing not just individuals' information but the entire Web. Delicious is basically a tagging system, or a place to store links that do not fit in a "Favorites" folder. This system not only collects your links in one place, but it organizes them as well.

One critical feature of Delicious is that it has no rules governing how its users create and use tags. Instead, each person designs his or her own rules. Nevertheless, the product of all those individual decisions is well organized. That is, if you conduct a search on Delicious for all the pages that are tagged with a particular word, you will likely come up with a very good selection of related Web sources.

One specific form of tagging, known as *geo-tagging*, refers to tagging information on maps. For example, Google Maps allows users to add pictures and information, such as restaurant or hotel ratings, to maps. Therefore, when users access Google Maps, their experience is enriched because they can see pictures of attractions, reviews, and things to do, all related to the map location they are viewing.

Really Simple Syndication (RSS)

Really Simple Syndication (RSS) allows you to receive the information you want (customized information), when you want it, without having to surf thousands of Web sites. RSS allows anyone to syndicate (publish) his or her blog, or any other content, to anyone who has an interest in subscribing. When changes to the content are made, subscribers receive a notification of the changes and an idea of what the new content contains. Subscribers can then click on a link that will take them to the full text of the new content.

For example, CNN.com provides RSS feeds for each of its main topic areas, such as world news, sports news, technology news, and entertainment news. NBC uses RSS feeds to allow viewers to download the most current version of shows such as *Meet the Press* and *NBC Nightly News*.

You can find thousands of Web sites that offer RSS feeds at Syndic8 (www.syndic8. com) and NewsIsFree (www.newsisfree.com). Figure 8.1 illustrates how an RSS can be searched and how RSS feeds can be located.

To use RSS, you can utilize a special news reader that displays RSS content feeds from Web sites you select. Many such readers are available, several of them for free. Examples are AmphetaDesk (www.disobey.com/amphetadesk) and Pluck (www.pluck.com). In addition, most browsers have built-in RSS readers. For an excellent RSS tutorial, visit www.mnot.net/rss/tutorial.

⌐ BEFORE *YOU GO ON . . .*

1. Differentiate between Web 1.0 and Web 2.0.
2. Explain how AJAX, tagging, and RSS have made the Web more interactive and informative.

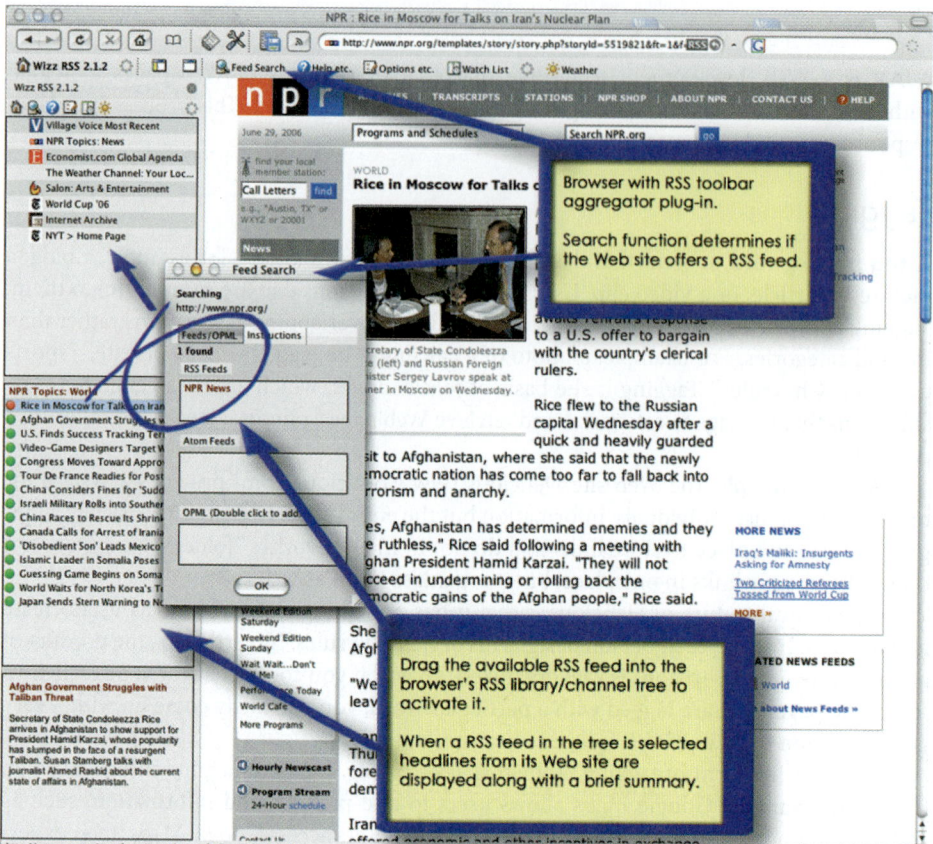

Figure 8.1 The Web site of National Public Radio (NPR) with RSS toolbar aggregator and search function. (Courtesy of NPR. Used with permission.)

RUBY'S CLUB QUESTIONS

1. Search engine optimization is a useful skill that uses tags and key words. What key words would people search for that would help them find Ruby's Club?

2. Search for RSS feeds and see how most people use them. Are they for advertising? Newsletters? Articles? New products? Promotions?

3. Are any bars or clubs in your area using RSS feeds? What seems to be their purpose?

Student Activity | 8.1

Objective: You will be able to identify Web 2.0 technologies/applications on popular Web sites.

Chapter Connection: This activity relates to Section 8.1 and Learning Objective 1 in this chapter.

Prerequisites: You should have read Section 8.1

Activity:

View the following video: www.youtube.com/user/danaehowetech#p/u/7/Pn8j9QCX_Mw

Then identify Web 2.0 technologies/applications that are being used by the Fortune 10 (or 20). A list of the companies in the Fortune 500 for 2010 can be found at this Web site:

http://money.cnn.com/magazines/fortune/fortune500/2010

In some cases, you may be able to discern these directly from the company's Web site.

Deliverables:

Prepare a table that identifies the following about the Fortune 10 (or 20):

- The company's name
- The company's rank
- The type of company (e.g., retail, consulting services, communications, etc.)
- A list of the Web 2.0 technologies/applications that are being used by each company
- A brief description of the ways that each of the Web 2.0 technologies/applications are being used by the company

Quiz Questions:

1. True or False? Web 2.0 is more user driven or user produced.

2. True or False? Even though Web 2.0 encourages user participation in commenting, it is not very good at enabling collaboration.

3. Which of the following is considered a Web 2.0 technology?
   - (a) HTML
   - (b) Tagging
   - (c) RSS
   - (d) A and B

4. Which of the following are correct analogies of the differences between Web 1.0 and Web 2.0 technology?
   - (a) Web 1.0 is more like a lecture, whereas Web 2.0 is more like a conversation.
   - (b) In Web 1.0, the news looks for you, and in Web 2.0, you look for the news.
   - (c) Web 1.0 tends to be machine independent, while Web 2.0 is more machine specific.
   - (d) A and B
   - (e) B and C

Discussion Questions:

1. Are particular company types (or particular industries) more or less likely to use Web 2.0 technologies/applications?

2. Does a particular Web 2.0 technology/application tend to be the most used? Least used? In your opinion, why is that the case?

3. From your research or that of your class, pick a company that is weak in the use of Web 2.0 and think of them as your client. What suggestions would you make to the company about the potential uses of Web 2.0 in its business practices?

8.2 | Web 2.0 Applications

Web 2.0 applications use some or all of the technologies you have just seen. These applications include blogs, wikis, netcasting, printing-on-demand, and crowdsourcing. In this section, you will learn about these applications and the various ways in which businesses utilize them.

Blogs and Blogging

A **weblog** (**blog** for short) is a personal Web site, open to the public, in which the site creator expresses his or her feelings or opinions via a series of chronological entries. *Bloggers*—people who create and maintain blogs—write stories, convey news, and provide links to other articles and Web sites that are of interest to them. The simplest method of creating a blog is to sign up with a blogging service provider, such as www.blogger.com (now owned by Google), www.xanga.com (see Figure 8.2), and www.sixapart.com. The **blogosphere** is the term for the millions of blogs on the Web.

Companies employ blogs in different ways. Some companies listen to the blogosphere for marketing purposes. Others open themselves up to the public for input into their processes and products.

Many companies listen to consumers in the blogosphere who express their views on the companies' products. In marketing, these views are called *consumer-generated media*. Two companies, Cymfony (www.cymfony.com) and BuzzMetrics (www.nielsenbuzzmetrics.com), "mine" the blogosphere for their clients to provide information in several areas. For example, they help their clients find ways to serve potential markets, ranging from broad-based to niche

Figure 8.2 Community blogs or discussion boards are used in mainstream media. (*Source:* Fancy/Image Source Limited)

markets. They also help their clients detect false rumors before these rumors appear in the mainstream press, and they gauge the potency of a marketing push or the popularity of a new product.

Blogs also have become influential in the mainstream media. Many traditional media companies, such as CNN, now use blogs to provide a richer version of the stories they cover. For example, Anderson Cooper, one of CNN's anchors, edits and writes for CNN's flagship blog called "Anderson Cooper 360." Further, many corporations maintain blogs. For example, many company executives use Google's Corporate Blog to present their views on their industry and their organization.

Blogs can also influence public opinion. One example of the power of blogging occurred during the 2004 election and came to be known as "Rathergate." Dan Rather, appearing on *60 Minutes*, reported on some suspect findings concerning President George W. Bush's record of military service. Bloggers soon after (correctly) reported that the documents used in this news story were falsified. Without the bloggers' input, this misrepresentation may have not surfaced publicly. Because of the bloggers' reports, Dan Rather resigned from *60 Minutes*, and some analysts claim that this scandal eventually caused his dismissal from CBS News.

Although blogs can be very useful, they also have shortcomings. Perhaps the primary value of blogs is their ability to bring current, breaking news to the public in the fastest time possible. Unfortunately, in doing so, bloggers sometimes cut corners, and their blogs can be inaccurate. For example, in May 2007, Engadget.com (a technology blog) reported that Apple's iPhone and OS X operating system were going to be delayed. This news caused Apple's stock price to drop by 4 percent in less than 20 minutes. When this report was challenged, Engadget.com retracted it.

Regardless of their various problems, blogs have transformed the ways in which people gather and consume information. In fact, many readers have canceled their newspaper subscriptions and rely instead on free information from blogs and other online sources. In turn, decreasing readership has caused advertisers to withdraw business from traditional newspapers. This withdrawal has led to layoffs at many well-known newspapers, such as the *San Francisco Chronicle* and the *New York Times*. This problem is so widespread that Google Maps now provides a Web service that visually displays where layoffs are occurring at newspapers across the United States (see http://papercuts.graphicdesignr.net). In fact, blogs have actually replaced the mainstream media in northern Mexico, as you can see in "IT's About Business 8.1."

Wikis

A **wiki** is a Web site on which anyone can post material and make changes to already posted material. Wikis have an "edit" link on each page that allows anyone to add, change, or delete material, fostering easy collaboration.

The Blog del Narco

Normally, people expect the mainstream press to provide news. In many parts of Mexico, however, especially in the north, the media have effectively ceased to function. More than 30 journalists have been murdered or have gone missing since 2006, according to a report released in September 2010 by the Committee to Protect Journalists.

For example, the July 17, 2010, edition of the Nuevo Laredo daily newspaper *Primera Hora* was filled with very bland news. Readers would have been unaware that a vicious clash had erupted the previous day between drug cartels and the Mexican military. The street battle had lasted for five hours, shut down large parts of the city, and left at least 12 people dead and 21 injured. Not a word of this battle appeared in Nuevo Laredo's other newspapers either, nor on its radio or television stations. The reason: In Nuevo Laredo, the press does not report what the cartels do not want people to know.

Despite this imposed blackout, however, local residents could obtain information about these events by logging on to the Blog del Narco (www.blogdelnarco.com). There, they learned which streets to avoid and where wounded shooting victims were being treated. They read that the U.S. consulate was urging people to stay indoors and that Mexican soldiers had arrested members of the Zetas, a drug-trafficking group. They saw photos of avenues blocked by large trucks commandeered by the drug cartels. They watched videos of bullet-riddled pickup trucks and corpses. They found, in other words, valuable reporting—all of it compiled by a college student working anonymously somewhere in northern Mexico.

The Blog del Narco has become the go-to Web site for cartel-related news in Mexico, drawing about 3 million hits per week. In addition to everyday citizens, its followers include members of the military and the police, as well as the drug traffickers themselves. Despite the blog's popularity, however, the identity of the blogger remains unknown. He describes himself as a computer science student at a university in northern Mexico. He administers the site on his own, from a laptop he carries with him wherever he goes. Every day, he receives 70 to 100 anonymous e-mails, some of them containing graphic photos and videos. He posts whatever he receives, unedited and unverified.

The postings on Blog del Narco periodically yield important pieces of intelligence. In fact, the blogger may have helped solve one case after he posted a video confession implicating a prison warden who allegedly freed armed inmates at night so they could carry out cartel-ordered murders.

Questions

1. What are the advantages of the Blog del Narco?
2. What are the disadvantages of the Blog del Narco?

Sources: Compiled from A. Campo-Flores, "Hiding Behind the Web," *Newsweek*, October 11, 2010; Mail Foreign Service, "The REAL City of God: Student Risks Life Documenting Mexico's Drug War in Gritty, Blood-Soaked Blog," *The Daily Mail*, August 14, 2010; www.blogdelnarco.com, accessed May 7, 2011.

Wikis harness the collective intelligence of Internet users, meaning that wikis take advantage of the combined input of many individuals. Consider Wikipedia (www.wikipedia.org), the online encyclopedia, which is the largest wiki in existence. Wikipedia contains more than 3.4 million articles in English, which are viewed almost 500 million times every day. Wikipedia's volunteer administrators enforce a neutral point of view and encourage users to delete copy displaying clear bias. Nevertheless, the fundamental question concerning Wikipedia remains: How reliable and accurate are the articles? Many educators do not allow students to cite references from Wikipedia because content can be provided by anyone at any time. Moreover, Wikipedia does not provide any quality assessment or fact checking by experts. This process leads to questions about the authenticity of the content.

The reliability of content on Wikipedia, compared to encyclopedias and more specialized sources, is assessed in several ways by outside groups, including statistically, by comparative

A Wiki allows open contribution to a document. (*Source:* © esolla/iStockphoto)

review, and by analysis of the strengths and weaknesses inherent in the Wikipedia process.

Organizations use wikis in several ways. In project management, for example, wikis provide a central repository for capturing constantly updated product features and specifications, tracking issues, resolving problems, and maintaining project histories. In addition, wikis enable companies to collaborate with customers, suppliers, and other business partners on projects. Wikis are also valuable in knowledge management. For example, companies use wikis to keep enterprisewide documents, such as guidelines and frequently asked questions, accurate and current.

Netcasting

In many cases, access to blogs and other Web resources, which consist of written content, is often impractical (e.g., when traveling or exercising). Today, however, technologies such as Apple's iPods, Microsoft's Zune, and other digital music players, which have transformed the way people listen to music while on the go, are also enabling users to consume information that was previously available only when they accessed the Internet.

Netcasting, the distribution of digital media via syndication feeds for playback on digital media players and personal computers, includes **podcasting** (primarily audio files) and **videocasting** (primarily video files). Interestingly, the term *podcasting*, derived from combining the terms *iPod* and *broadcasting*, is a misnomer because netcasts (or podcasts) can be played on a variety of devices in addition to iPods.

Netcasting has become increasingly prevalent, with traditional media organizations now podcasting a wide variety of content, from National Public Radio shows to the *Oprah Winfrey Show*. In addition to traditional media, educational institutions use netcasts to provide students with access to lectures, lab demonstrations, and sports events. These netcasts enable students to review lectures or prepare for class during their morning and evening commutes and while exercising at the gym. In 2007, Apple launched iTunes U, which offers free content provided by major U.S. universities such as Stanford and MIT.

Web 2.0 Media

Web 2.0 media sites have a powerful presence on the Internet. These Web sites allow people to come together and share digital media, such as pictures, audio, and video. **Web 2.0 media** can be defined as any Web site that provides user-generated media content and promotes tagging, rating, commenting, and other interactions among users and their media contributions. Web 2.0 media provide a variety of content, including the following:

- Video (Amazon Video on Demand, YouTube, Hulu, Facebook)
- Music (Amazon MP3, Last.fm, Rhapsody, Pandora, Facebook, iTunes)
- Photographs (Photobucket, Flickr, Shutterfly, Picasa, Facebook)

Photo-sharing Web sites combine the features of social networking with photo sharing. "IT's About Business 8.2" presents examples of photo-sharing sites.

Printing-on-Demand

Web 2.0 helps users to publish their own material. Traditionally, self-publishing was largely restricted to authors who published original materials (e.g., books). This endeavor was risky because the author incurred high costs for producing the books and had to sell enough books to recover his or her costs before making a profit.

Today, however, **printing-on-demand**, which is customized printing done in small batches, is becoming increasingly popular. Open-source versions of software for text editing

Share Your Life in Pictures

The market for photo-sharing services on the Internet is changing rapidly. Photo-upload Web sites such as Ofoto (now Kodak Gallery; www.kodakgallery.com) and Shutterfly (www.shutterfly.com) dominated the field in the late 1990s as people uploaded digital pictures to the Web primarily so they could have them printed. Then, in 2004, Flickr (www.flickr.com) emerged and was acquired by Yahoo! in 2005, giving serious photographers a place to publish and show high-resolution images. Other Web sites, such as Google's Picasa (http://picasa.google.com), Myspace's Photobucket (www.photobucket.com), and, more recently, Facebook, provide photo-sharing and photo-editing services.

More recently, a new photo service/social network for the iPhone named Instagram (www.instagram.com) has emerged. In its first four months, Instagram attracted more than 1.75 million users who were uploading almost 300,000 photos per day.

Instagram offers free accounts and enables members to snap pictures with their phones and then add visual effects that give images the classic look of photographs captured on traditional film and developed with chemicals. Users can then post their images to their Instagram accounts or to social networks such as Facebook and Twitter. They can also browse and comment on collections from other photographers. When users post their images, the community provides instant feedback.

Instagram's explosive growth has been spurred by a new wave of people who have smart phones, like to take photos of parts of their day, and share them. Instagram is also benefitting from the emergence of smart phones such as the iPhone 4 that take relatively high-quality images and have fast and reliable wireless networks that enable people to easily upload their images. Instagram represents a new kind of Web startup, whose rapidly increasing popularity, thanks to platforms such as Apple's App Store, has come before it has evolved into a real company with corporate trappings such as financing and office space.

Another photo-sharing smart phone app, Color (www.color.com), from Color Labs, integrates location-based technology with social media. Color shares images, comments, and videos with other users located within 50 feet of the sender. It thus creates a network of Color users based only on proximity. Users load the free iPhone or Android app and take photographs. The app then locates nearby phones, combines these photos with other users' photos from the same location, stores the shots on a cloud-based server, and makes all the photos available on social media Web sites such as Twitter.

Color has no password, does not enable friending, and does not allow users to limit private content to specific individuals. The founder of Color Labs maintains that this is the post-PC world and that Color is a new way of sharing.

 The Color app removes any concept of user privacy. (The company spells out this policy in its privacy statement.) When a user creates content with Color, that content is immediately published to any nearby user who has the app open, and often to unique users with whom the user has had previous contact, whether they are geographically close or not. That content is also published and available for viewing through various social media sites. Unique users can view your content and can send anyone a link to your content, the content of other unique users, and collections that include your content. Therefore, your content can be sent to *anyone*.

Questions

1. Explain how and why a startup can survive if it becomes "wildly popular" before it evolves into a real, profit-making business.

2. What are some potential disadvantages to photo-sharing Web sites such as Instagram and Color?

Sources: Compiled from A. Diana, "Color Labs Offers Location-Based Photo Sharing App," *InformationWeek*, March 24, 2011; B. Stone, "Zero Revenue. Four Staffers. 1.74 Million Users," *Bloomberg BusinessWeek*, February 7–13, 2011; J. Evans, "Collected: What We Know About the Mac App Store," *Computerworld*, January 6, 2011; M. Isaac, "New Social Network Path = iPhone + Instagram + Facebook—499,999,950 Friends," *Forbes*, November 2010; www.instagram.com, www.color.com, accessed March 30, 2011.

and typesetting are available in word processing programs and on the Internet. Another important innovation is small-book printing machines, which minimize setup and per print run costs. These technologies have significantly reduced the costs of print-on-demand, making this process very attractive to first-time authors. Leading print-on-demand companies include CreateSpace (www.createspace.com), Lulu (www.lulu.com), and Blurb (www.blurb.com). Many of these companies also offer distribution services. For example, CreateSpace (owned by Amazon.com) provides end-to-end service where authors submit their manuscripts and the online publisher edits, formats, prints, and sells the work. Publishers provide these services for a sales commission, and the remainder of the revenue from book sales goes to the author.

Crowdsourcing

Suppose an organization has a problem it needs to solve. Why not offer the problem to a crowd to determine whether their collective knowledge and wisdom can come up with a solution? This process, called **crowdsourcing**, involves taking a job traditionally performed by an employee or a consultant and outsourcing it to an undefined group of people in the form of an open call. Can crowds really outperform experts employed by a company? (See Figure 8.3) Let's look at some examples where they have done so.

- Tongal (http://tongal.com) pays people to create online videos for companies such as Mattel and Allstate. Companies typically pay $15,000 to $20,000 for each project they post on Tongal's Web site. Tongal runs the projects like contests. Instead of a winner-take-all approach, the company breaks up the projects into stages, such as ideas and videos. It rewards the top five ideas with cash. Participants in the video phase are then free to use any of those five ideas to create the video.

- Amazon's Mechanical Turk (www.amazon.com/mturk) provides a Web site where anyone with a task to be completed or a problem to be solved can put it on the site, naming the price for completion or a solution. For performing this role, Amazon takes a small cut of each transaction.

- Pharmaceutical giant Eli Lilly (www.lilly.com) created a Web site called InnoCentive (www.innocentive.com) where companies can post scientific problems and everyone can try to solve them.

Figure 8.3 Crowdsourcing.
(*Source:* Scott Maxwell/
LuMaxArt/Shutterstock)

- Until a few years ago, book publishers had to rely on stock photography for many of the images used in their books. These photos were taken by professional photographers and were quite expensive. Today, high-quality digital cameras cost less than $1,000, and, with available photo editing software, amateur photographers can create images that almost match those of the professionals. The amateurs can upload their pictures to image-sharing Web sites such as iStockphoto (www.istockphoto.com), where interested parties can license and download the images for $1 to $5 per image, which is a fraction of the price of a regular stock photo. Because overhead costs are extremely low, iStockphoto can make a profit while still sharing part of the revenue with the pictures' creators.

- Amazon and Barnes and Noble (www.barnesandnoble.com) sell the same products, and they receive the same product descriptions and editorial content from their vendors. However, Amazon has led all bookstores in soliciting user input in the form of user editorial reviews. As a result, most Amazon users go directly to the user reviews when they are deciding whether to buy a book.

The benefits of crowdsourcing to companies include finding large numbers of workers to complete projects quickly, attracting niche expertise, saving money, and making better use of in-house resources. For the workers, crowdsourcing provides unprecedented flexibility to work almost anywhere at any time.

BEFORE *YOU GO ON . . .*

1. Differentiate between blogs and wikis.
2. What is netcasting?
3. Discuss the business benefits of crowdsourcing.

RUBY'S CLUB QUESTIONS

1. Blogs allow for posts and comments. While it creates a space for interaction, comments, and praise, it also allows for negative comments. Is a blog something Ruby's could benefit from? Can you find other bars/clubs that use blogs? How do they seem to be incorporated into their strategy?

2. Wikipedia often has pages regarding businesses. Can you find any bars/clubs on Wikipedia? Is there any information there that you can find helpful?

Student Activity 8.2

Web 2.0 Applications

Objective: You will be able to understand how Web 2.0 technologies can empower consumers.

Chapter Connection: This activity relates to Section 8.2 and Learning Objective 2 in this chapter.

Prerequisites: You should have read Section 8.2

Activity:

View the Wikipedia entry concerning United Breaks Guitars:

http://en.wikipedia.org/wiki/United_Breaks_Guitars.

Then read Dave Carroll's story about how the song came about:

www.davecarrollmusic.com/ubg/story

Also view the YouTube video for the first song of the United Breaks Guitars trilogy, "United Breaks Guitars":

www.youtube.com/user/sonsofmaxwell#p/u/3/
5YGc4zOqozo

And the third song of the trilogy, "United We Stand":

www.youtube.com/user/sonsofmaxwell#p/u/0/
P45E0uGVyeg

Identify other ramifications or outcomes from Dave Carroll's experiences with United Airlines. These may be directly affecting Dave Carroll (or the Sons of Maxwell), United Airlines, or other third parties.

Deliverables:

Prepare a table that identifies the following:

- Who was affected
- What they did
- What was the outcome

Post these results to a wiki that has been created for the course/class.

Quiz Questions:

1. True or False? United Airlines offered Dave Carroll flight vouchers to compensate for his _____.

2. True or False? It only took six months for the first video of Dave Carroll's United Breaks Guitars trilogy to garner one million views on YouTube.

3. Which of the following is true concerning Dave Carroll and his United Airlines experience?
   - (a) His guitar was broken in transit by airline employees.
   - (b) His flight was delayed, which caused his band to miss a big concert.
   - (c) His name showed up on a no-fly list and, despite being a law-abiding citizen, he was not allowed to board the plane.
   - (d) All of the above statements are true.
   - (e) None of the above is true.

4. Which is true about the first of the Dave Carroll songs about his United Airlines experience?
   - (a) It was featured in *Time* magazine's Top 10 Viral Videos of 2009.
   - (b) A spokesman from United Airlines apologized to Carroll and asked if United could use the video internally for training.
   - (c) In slightly more than a year, the song had garnered more than 9 million hits on YouTube.
   - (d) A and C are true.
   - (e) A, B, and C are true.

Discussion Questions:

1. What other types of Web 2.0 has, or could have, Dave Carroll used to wage his campaign against United Airlines. How would (did) he use them?

2. How are consumers more empowered today than, say, ten years ago, and how does Web 2.0 technology influence that empowerment?

8.3 | Categories of Web 2.0 Sites

There are literally thousands of Web 2.0 sites, and each one uses some or all of the Web 2.0 technologies and applications that you have just studied. In this section, you will focus on the three major categories of Web 2.0 sites: social networking, aggregators, and mashups.

Social Networking

Social networking Web sites allow users to upload their content to the Web in the form of text (for example, blogs), voice (for example, podcasts), images, and videos (for example, videocasts). These sites provide an easy, interactive tool for communicating and collaborating with other people on the Web. They help users find like-minded people online, either to pursue an interest or a goal or just to establish a sense of community among people who may never meet in the real world.

Social Networking allows convenient connections to those of similar interest. (*Source:* © Ben Legend-Fotolia.cpm)

Social networks are also highly valuable business tools. The following example illustrates how Adagio Teas uses social networking tools to build its business.

EXAMPLE

Adagio Teas (www.adagio.com) is a retailer that sells premium teas online and in Chicago area stores. The company's Web site offers many social media features. Customers can post product reviews and ratings, read blogs, participate in "Tea Chat" discussion groups, share information about teas with friends who input their Gmail address and password (the Web site automatically promotes "friend" selections and preferences), and receive tweets for their order and shipment status.

One practice that makes Adagio unusual is that the company does not filter reviews for the 200 teas and other products it sells. Everything is displayed in real time. Once a customer orders from the company and has an account, he or she can post on the Web site. This approach, which many companies avoid, benefits Adagio. The company incorporates the data into its market research, and it makes decisions about which teas to offer and which to "kill off" based on a combination of sales data and customer feedback.

Adagio has also integrated other capabilities. For example, customers can create custom tea blends, which the site then shares with other customers. When another customer buys a custom blend, the creator receives points that lead to a gift certificate. Adagio also offers points and discounts for sending friends a free $5 gift certificate (once it is redeemed) via e-mail, Facebook, and Twitter. Finally, Adagio provides a Facebook "Like" button for all its products, and it uses Twitter to engage customers more fully.

Sources: Compiled from S. Greengard, "Winning Business with Social Media," *Baseline Magazine*, April 6, 2011; www.adagio.com, accessed April 18, 2011.

One of the most powerful features of most social networks is the feed (or newsfeed). *Feeds* provide timely updates on the activities of people or topics with which an individual is associated. These feeds are inherently viral. By displaying other peoples' activities on a social network, feeds can rapidly mobilize populations and dramatically spread the adoption of applications. For example, by leveraging feeds, the Facebook group Support the Monks' Protest in Burma was able to attract more than 160,000 Facebook members in just 10 days. Feeds also helped the music app iLike acquire 3,000,000 Facebook users just 2 weeks after its launch.

Feeds are also controversial, however. Many users react negatively to having their online activities broadcast publicly. Going further, mismanaged feeds can create public relations fiascos, spur user discontent, and lead to legal actions. For example, Facebook initially experienced a massive user outcry when it launched its feeds, and it faced a subsequent backlash when its Beacon service broadcast its user purchases without first explicitly asking for the users' permission.

Despite the potential pitfalls, many organizations are finding useful ways to employ social networks to pursue strategic objectives. For example, many employees have organized work groups using publicly available social networking sites because their companies do not offer similar tools. In response, many firms are meeting this demand by implementing internal social network platforms that are secure and are tailored to company needs. These networks typically replace the traditional employee directory. Social network listings are easy to update and expand, and employees are encouraged to add their own photos, interests, and expertise.

Companies such as Deloitte, Dow Chemical, and Goldman Sachs have created social networks for their "alumni" who have left the firm or are retired. These networks are useful in maintaining contacts for future business opportunities, rehiring former employees, and recruiting retired staff to serve as contractors. IBM's internal social network makes it easier to locate employee expertise within the company, thereby helping project leaders find needed talent anywhere in the organization.

Well-known social networking sites include these:

- Facebook (www.facebook.com), Myspace (www.myspace.com), and Google+ (https://plus.google.com): popular social networking Web sites (as of August 2011, Facebook had more than 700 million members, Myspace had more than 80 million members, and Google+ had more than 32 million members, according to Alexa.com).

- Flickr (www.flickr.com): a photo-sharing Web site, widely used by bloggers as a photo repository.

- LinkedIn (www.linkedin.com): a business-oriented social networking site that is valuable for recruiting, sales, and investment. The company makes money from advertising and services. People—primarily the site's 60,000 recruiters—pay an average of $3,600 per year for premium features such as sending messages to LinkedIn members outside their own networks. Corporate members pay fees of up to six figures for access to the network.

- YouTube (www.youtube.com): a social networking site for video uploads.

- Twitter (http://twitter.com): allows users to post short updates (called "tweets") on a topic of interest (no more than 140 characters) via the Web site, instant messaging, or mobile devices. The following example illustrates the potential power of Twitter.

EXAMPLE

Twitter has become so pervasive that in May 2010, the Library of Congress acquired Twitter's entire archive of public tweets. Some 50 million new Tweets are posted every day. All of the public ones will become available to the library 6 months after they are posted.

For centuries, history has been biased toward powerful and prominent individuals, such as presidents, kings, and movie stars. A major reason for this bias is that "ordinary people" did not generally document their lives. Historians can find material about extraordinary people during ordinary times because someone always keeps your letters when you are famous. They can also find some material about ordinary people during extraordinary times when "average" people keep records (e.g., Anne Frank's diary). The most imposing challenge is finding material about ordinary people during ordinary times. Historians believe this is why Twitter will become so important. In short, Twitter provides a deeply personal insight into the daily lives of average individuals—on a completely unprecedented scale.

The Library of Congress has created teams of librarians, linguists, historians, and computer scientists to coherently catalog the tweets. After they develop a searchable Twitter archive, historians will be able to search this archive for useful information.

Sources: Compiled from M. Hesse, "Twitter Archive at Library of Congress Could Help Redefine History's Scope," *Washington Post*, May 6, 2010; "Twitter Donates Entire Tweet Archive to Library of Congress," www.loc.gov, April 15, 2010; www.loc.gov, accessed March 2, 2011.

One interesting type of social network is online games. As you see in "IT's About Business 8.3," online gaming can be a successful business model.

IT's ABOUT BUSINESS | 8.3

Online Games Are Big Business

Globally, more than 200 million people play social games every month, and their numbers are rapidly increasing. In fact, online games just passed e-mail as the second most popular online activity, behind social networking.

Not surprisingly, many companies are entering the online gaming industry. In July 2010, for example, Disney paid $563 million to purchase the social game developer Playdom (www.playdom.com). Meanwhile, Google announced the creation of its Google Game Developer Center, an online resource specifically designed to promote Google-related game technology and infrastructure. Why all the interest? The answer is that companies have noticed that 40 percent of Facebook's 600 million users regularly play social games.

One popular Facebook game, Scrabble, is as simple as the original 1948 game that is played on cardboard. The most popular game on Facebook, FarmVille, requires clicking around an imaginary farm to plant crops and take care of animals. In Happy Aquarium, users feed fish and clean tanks. Millions of women throw parties together on Sorority Life. Men can act out their Tony Soprano fantasies by "capping" people in Mafia Wars.

For Facebook and the gaming companies, the business opportunity is enormous, even though playing the games is free. Users can buy add-ons and move through game levels faster by spending very small amounts of money on what amounts to virtual objects on a screen. Analysts estimated that these transactions exceeded $835 million in 2010.

Consider the case of Zynga (www.zynga.com). More than 120 million people play Zynga's online social games, such as FarmVille and Mafia Wars. In 2010 the company's revenue surpassed $450 million.

As impressive as these numbers are, however, Zynga's success depends on the good graces of Facebook, where almost all Zynga games are played. In March 2010, Facebook prohibited Zynga and other app creators from promoting games in the "Notifications" menu that users see each time they log on. Facebook claimed that users were complaining about spamlike messages that appeared every time one of their game-playing friends performed an action in an online game. In fact,

5 million Facebook users organized a protest group that called itself "I Don't Care About Your Farm, Or Your Fish, Or Your Park, Or Your Mafia!"

Zynga claims that the policy change hurt its business by reducing traffic to its games. Nevertheless, Zynga insists it can help Facebook (and vice versa) because Zynga's games increase the time that users spend on Facebook.

Facebook does receive income from Zynga. Any time a game appears to be a hit, Zynga spends millions of dollars on ads promoting it to Facebook members. In total, Zynga spends between $5 million and $8 million per month for banner ads on Facebook, according to industry analysts.

More than 90 percent of Zynga's revenues come from users converting real cash into proprietary virtual currency. FarmVille, for example, has Farm Coins. If you buy a tractor for 5,000 Farm Coins, that equals about $3.30. In the past, Zynga paid less than 10 percent of that revenue to a third-party transaction handler such as PayPal, and it kept the rest. However, Facebook has developed a service called Facebook Credits that offers a single virtual currency for use

on many different apps. In May 2010, Facebook and Zynga agreed to a five-year deal in which Zynga agreed to use Facebook Credits. As a result, Zynga pays Facebook up to 30 percent of every transaction.

Questions

1. From Zynga's perspective, discuss the advantages and disadvantages of the company's close relationship with Facebook.

2. What kinds of actions could Zynga take to minimize its dependence on Facebook? Be specific, and provide examples.

Sources: Compiled from T. Claburn, "Google Gets Gaming," *InformationWeek*, March 3, 2011; A. Diana, "Facebook Makes Credits Sole Legal Currency," *InformationWeek*, January 25, 2011; D. MacMillan, "Inside Zynga's Hit Factory," *Bloomberg BusinessWeek*, November 22–28, 2010; M. Rosenwald, "FarmVille, Other Online Social Games Mean Big Business, and Bonding," *Washington Post*, August 3, 2010; A. Gonsalves, "Facebook, Zynga Ink Five Year Deal," *InformationWeek*, May 19, 2010; D. MacMillan, "Zynga and Facebook: It's Complicated," *Bloomberg BusinessWeek*, April 26–May 2, 2010; www.zynga.com, accessed March 29, 2011.

Social Commerce

Social commerce is a type of electronic commerce (discussed in Chapter 9) that uses social media to assist in the online buying and selling of products and services. Social commerce taps into a community of enthusiasts, builds relationships, anticipates needs, and promotes products with special deals for the community's members. Social commerce efforts include shareable coupons, refer-a-friend programs, loyalty incentives, group promotions, and time-sensitive offers.

The biggest advantage that social commerce enjoys over traditional e-commerce and even Google Search is the ability to predict buying habits based on real-time information as opposed to historical data. Google Search cannot anticipate one person's needs very well. In contrast, that person's friends would know, for example, that she is going to be a grandmother and will probably be shopping for baby products. Social commerce focuses squarely on one-to-one relationships. Still another advantage is that social commerce analyzes relationships and interactions within a social community, enabling companies to bring new exciting new products to the market more effectively.

This chapter's Closing Case 1 on Groupon demonstrates how the company uses social networking to build its social commerce business model. That is, Groupon realized that social networking technologies can provide a direct link between businesses and their customers.

Aggregators

Aggregators are Web sites that provide collections of content from the Web. Well-known aggregator Web sites include the following:

- Bloglines (www.bloglines.com): Collects blogs and news from all over the Web and presents the material in one, consistent, updated format.

- Digg (www.digg.com): A news aggregator that is part news site, part blog, and part forum. Users suggest and rate news stories, which are then ranked based on this feedback.
- Simply Hired (www.simplyhired.com): This site searches some 4.5 million listings on job and corporate Web sites and contacts subscribers via an RSS feed or an e-mail alert when a job appears that meets their criteria.
- Technorati (http://technorati.com): Contains information on all blogs in the blogosphere. It indicates how many other blogs link to a particular blog, and it ranks blogs by topic.

Mashups

Mashup means to "mix and match" content from other parts of the Web. A **mashup** is a Web site that takes different content from a number of other Web sites and mixes them together to create a new kind of content. The launch of Google Maps is credited with providing the start for mashups. A user can take a map from Google, add his or her own data, and then display a map mashup on his or her Web site that plots crime scenes, cars for sale, or virtually any other subject.

There are many examples of mashups (for a complete list of mashups, see www.programmableweb.com):

- Craigslist developed a dynamic map of all available apartments in the United States that are listed on Craigslist (www.housingmaps.com).
- Everyblock.com is a mashup of Web services that integrates content from newspapers, blogs, and government databases to enable citizens of cities such as Chicago, New York, and Seattle to find out what is happening in their neighborhoods. Available information includes crime information, restaurant inspections, and local photos posted on Flickr.

New tools are emerging to build location mashups. For example, Pipes from Yahoo! (http://pipes.yahoo.com) is a service that lets users visually remix data feeds and create mashups, using drag-and-drop features to connect multiple Web data sources. "IT's About Business 8.4" describes an interesting mashup named Foursquare.

IT's ABOUT BUSINESS | 8.4

Location, Location, Location

Consider this scenario: At 6:00 PM your smart phone alerts you to your evening's plans. It has already checked your friends' calendars and knows who is free tonight, so it suggests a restaurant that you have all wanted to try. Your phone notes when a table is available and informs you that three other friends are planning to meet you for dinner.

Harnessing GPS-enabled mobile technology to let users broadcast their location is not a new idea.

Loopt (www.loopt.com), Google's Latitude (www.google.com/latitude), and Facebook Places (www.facebook.com/places) all offer location-based, friend-locating apps. Foursquare (http://foursquare.com) adds a gamelike twist: Its 1 million-plus users earn badges by "checking in" at certain bars, restaurants, and other venues by pressing a button on the app when they arrive. A user can earn a "mayor" icon from an establishment if he or she has checked in more than anyone else during the previous 60 days.

Foursquare's business model is simple: Generate as big a user base as possible, and sell national brands and local merchants on the possibilities of marketing to people as they gather—ready to eat, shop, or spend. In mid-2011, more than 3,000 restaurants, bars, and other establishments used Foursquare to attract customers with promotions.

PepsiCo, Zagat, and more than a dozen other well-known brands have signed paid-partnership deals with Foursquare. The cable television network Bravo (www.bravotv.com) launched its partnership with Foursquare in February 2010. The more than 10,000 viewers who have been participating in Bravo's Foursquare promotion can "unlock" badges by checking in at locations linked to Bravo shows. The venues range from restaurants favored by some of the celebrities on *Top Chef* to retailers popular with the women on *Real Housewives*. Participants also get tips on what to do or what to buy at the locations, and, in some cases, they earn prizes for getting there first.

PepsiCo teamed up with Foursquare in December 2009 for a charity drive in New York City. Every time someone checked in within the city limits, Pepsi donated 4 cents to a nonprofit organization named CampInteractive (www.campinteractive.org), up to a maximum of $10,000. Pepsi's global director of digital and social media was impressed with the user response on that marketing campaign.

It remains to be seen if Foursquare's check-in feature is enough to build a sustainable business. Gowalla (http://gowalla.com), Brightkite (http://brightkite.com), and Geoloqi (http://geoloqi.com) have implemented rival networks, each with check-in features. In addition, established companies such as Twitter and Yelp have created location-based tools. Despite this competition, however, Foursquare was valued at $250 million in January 2011, and the company anticipated reaching 10 million users by June 2011.

Questions

1. What are some possible disadvantages of being a member of Foursquare? Would you join Foursquare? Why or why not?

2. Analyze the differences between social networking and social location networking, using specific examples.

Sources: Compiled from S. Denning, "Social Location Marketing," *Forbes*, April 15, 2011; A. Diana, "Foursquare, AMEX Partner on Offer Program at SXSW," *InformationWeek*, March 11, 2011; A. Diana, "Foursquare Value Checks In at $250 Million," *InformationWeek*, January 24, 2011; M. Copeland, "Facebook Is Going Places. Where Will Foursquare Go?" *Fortune*, August 18, 2010; D. Brady, "Social Media's New Mantra: Location, Location, Location," *Bloomberg BusinessWeek*, May 10–16, 2010; G. Moran, "My Smartphone Sent Me," *InformationWeek*, May 6, 2010; www.foursquare.com, accessed April 14, 2011.

BEFORE *YOU GO ON . . .*

1. What are social networks, and how are organizations using them?
2. What are aggregators, and what is their greatest value to Web 2.0 users?
3. Describe mashups, and discuss their business value.

RUBY'S CLUB QUESTIONS

1. Social media is taking our world by storm. Many companies use Facebook to connect to customers. Facebook pages allow them to advertise products, promotions, and target only those customers who have "liked" them on Facebook. How could Ruben and Lisa use this tool to help create their community feel? What type of privacy issues would arise from posting pictures?

2. Twitter is also becoming a powerful tool for customer contact. What are the main differences between Twitter and Facebook? How might these two social media outlets complement each other?

Student Activity | 8.3

Objective: You will be able to understand the breadth and potential reach and implications of social media from a business perspective.

Chapter Connection: This activity relates to Section 8.3 and Learning Objective 3 in this chapter.

Prerequisites: You should have read Section 8.3.

Activity:

View the video "Social Media Revolution 2 (Refresh)":

www.youtube.com/watch?v=lFZ0z5Fm-Ng)

Two students (or two student teams or split the class in half) will square off and discuss the advantages/ disadvantages of social media. Is it a fad or something that is here to stay? One student (or student team or side of the class) will then address the pros and cons from a consumer perspective and the other from the business perspective.

- For the discussion/debate, maintain a table of advantages/disadvantages as well as pros and cons for businesses and consumers during the discussion that will be posted/provided to the students afterward.

- For open class discussion, keep a cumulative rating. Keep a log of companies and how they are or are not successfully incorporating social media into their business practices.

Quiz Questions:

1. True or False? According to the "Social Media Revolution" video on YouTube, Facebook has more weekly traffic than Google.

2. True or False? According to the "Social Media Revolution" video on YouTube, the majority of articles on Wikipedia are in English.

3. True or False? According to the "Social Media Revolution" video on YouTube, studies have shown that it is as accurate as the *Encyclopedia Britannica*.

4. According to the "Social Media Revolution" video on YouTube, which of the following is *false*?

   (a) Before social media, pornography was the number-one activity on the Web.

   (b) Today, one out of eight couples married in the United States met via social media.

   (c) If Facebook were a country, it would be bigger than every country except for India and China.

   (d) Roughly 25 percent of companies use social media for recruitment.

   (e) Some celebrities have more followers on Twitter than the entire populations of countries such as Sweden and Norway.

5. According to the "Social Media Revolution" video on YouTube, which of the following is true?

   (a) Half of mobile Internet traffic in the United Kingdom is for Facebook.

   (b) Because many Generation Y and Generation X members consider e-mail passé, some universities have stopped distributing e-mail accounts.

   (c) YouTube is the second-largest search engine in the world.

   (d) A and B are true.

   (e) A, B, and C are true.

6. According to the "Social Media Revolution" video on YouTube, which of the following is true?

   (a) People care more about how their social graph ranks products and services than how Google ranks them.

   (b) A majority of traditional TV campaigns generate a positive return on investment (ROI).

   (c) People trust peer recommendations and company advertisements about the same.

   (d) A and B are true.

   (e) B and C are true.

Discussion Questions:

1. In your opinion, among Facebook, YouTube, and Twitter, which one would be the most effective social media for businesses to focus on? Why?

2. Pick a Fortune 500 company that you think could be doing a much better job of using social media. What suggestions would you make to its staff? What social media would you suggest, and how would you suggest that they use it? Are there any social media that you would suggest that they avoid either because of their company/product/clientele or because of the social media itself? Why?

What's in **IT** for ME?

FOR THE ACCOUNTING MAJOR

 Audit teams use social networking technologies internally to stay in touch with team members who are working on multiple projects. These technologies serve as a common channel of communications. For example, an audit team manager can create a group, include his or her team members as subscribers, and then push information regarding projects to all members at once. Externally, these technologies are useful in interfacing with clients and other third parties for whom the firm and its staff provide services.

FOR THE FINANCE MAJOR

 Many of the popular social networking sites have users who subscribe to finance-oriented subgroups. Among these groups are finance professionals who collaborate and share knowledge as well as nonfinancial professionals who are potential clients.

FOR THE MARKETING MAJOR

 Web 2.0 applications enable marketing professionals to become closer to their customers in a variety of ways, including blogs, wikis, ratings, and recommendations. Marketing professionals now receive almost real-time feedback on products.

FOR THE
PRODUCTION/OPERATIONS MANAGEMENT MAJOR

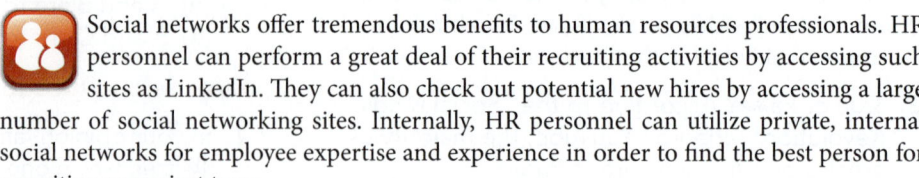 Web 2.0 applications allow production personnel to "enlist" business partners and customers in product development activities.

FOR THE
HUMAN RESOURCES MANAGEMENT MAJOR

Social networks offer tremendous benefits to human resources professionals. HR personnel can perform a great deal of their recruiting activities by accessing such sites as LinkedIn. They can also check out potential new hires by accessing a large number of social networking sites. Internally, HR personnel can utilize private, internal social networks for employee expertise and experience in order to find the best person for a position or project team.

FOR THE MIS MAJOR

 The MIS department is responsible for two aspects of Web 2.0 usage: (1) monitoring employee usage of Web 2.0 applications while at work, both time and content, and (2) developing private, internal social networks for company employees and then monitoring the content of these networks.

>>> SUMMARY

1. Describe the differences between Web 1.0 and Web 2.0, and explain the benefits of three information technologies used by Web 2.0.

Web 1.0 was the first generation of the Web. Key developments of Web 1.0 were the creation of Web sites and the commercialization of the Web. Users typically have minimal interaction with Web 1.0 sites, which provide information that users receive passively.

Web 2.0 is a loose collection of information technologies and applications, plus the Web sites that use them. These Web sites enrich the user experience by encouraging user participation, social interaction, and collaboration. Unlike Web 1.0 sites, Web 2.0 sites are not so much online places to visit as sites that facilitate information sharing, user-centered design, and collaboration. Web 2.0 sites often harness collective intelligence (for example, wikis); deliver functionality as services rather than packaged software (for example, Web services); and feature remixable applications and data (for example, mashups).

AJAX is a Web development technique that enables portions of Web pages to reload with fresh data instead of requiring the entire Web page to reload. This process speeds up response time and increases user satisfaction.

A *tag* is a key word or term that describes a piece of information (for example, a blog, a picture, an article, or a video clip). Users typically choose tags that are meaningful to them.

Really Simple Syndication (RSS) allows you to receive the information you want (customized information), when you want it, without having to surf thousands of Web sites.

2. Identify five prominent Web 2.0 applications, and provide at least one example of how each one can be utilized in a business setting.

A *weblog* (*blog* for short) is a personal Web site, open to the public, in which the site creator expresses his or her feelings or opinions with a series of chronological entries. Companies are using blogs in different ways. Some companies listen to the blogosphere for marketing purposes. Others open themselves up to the public for input into their processes and products.

A *wiki* is a Web site on which anyone can post material and make changes to already posted material. Wikis foster easy collaboration, and they harness the collective intelligence of Internet users.

Organizations use wikis in several ways. In project management, for example, wikis provide a central repository for capturing constantly updated product features and specifications, tracking issues, resolving problems, and maintaining project histories. In addition, wikis enable companies to collaborate with customers, suppliers, and other business partners on projects. Wikis are also useful in knowledge management.

Netcasting is the distribution of digital media, such as audio files (*podcasting*) and video files (*videocasting*), via syndication feeds for playback on digital media players and personal computers. Educational institutions use netcasts for providing students with access to lectures, lab demonstrations, and sports events.

Printing-on-demand is customized printing performed in small batches. For example, CreateSpace (owned by Amazon.com) provides end-to-end service where authors submit their manuscripts and the online publisher edits, formats, prints, and sells the work. Publishers provide these services for a sales commission, and the remainder of the revenue from book sales goes to the author.

Crowdsourcing is the process of taking a job traditionally performed by an employee or a consultant and outsourcing it to an undefined group of people in the form of an open call.

3. Discuss the three categories of Web 2.0 sites, and provide at least one example of how each one can improve business efficiency and profitability.

Social networking Web sites allow users to upload their content to the Web in the form of text (for example, blogs), voice (for example, podcasts), images, and videos (for example, videocasts). Organizations can use social networking to get closer to customers (achieve customer intimacy), business partners, and suppliers.

Aggregators are Web sites that provide collections of content from the Web. Organizations can post job openings on aggregator Web sites for increased exposure. Organizations can also scan aggregator news sites for information on the organization that is pulled from sites across the Web.

A *mashup* is a Web site that takes different content from a number of other Web sites and mixes them together to create a new kind of content. Many organizations use mashups to deliver valuable information to their customers. For example, many governments are using mashups to deliver information to their constituents, such as crime information, housing information, and health information.

>>> CHAPTER GLOSSARY

aggregators Web sites that provide collections of content from the Web.

AJAX A Web development technique that allows portions of Web pages to reload with fresh data rather than requiring the entire Web page to reload.

blog (weblog) A personal Web site, open to the public, in which the site creator expresses his or her feelings or opinions with a series of chronological entries.

blogosphere The term for the millions of blogs on the Web.

crowdsourcing The process of taking a job traditionally performed by an employee or consultant and outsourcing it to an undefined group of people in the form of an open call.

mashup Web site that takes different content from a number of other Web sites and mixes them together to create a new kind of content.

netcasting The distribution of digital media via syndication feeds for playback on digital media players and personal computers.

podcasting The distribution of digital audio media via syndication feeds for playback on digital media players and personal computers.

printing-on-demand Customized printing done in small batches.

Really Simple Syndication (RSS) A technology that allows users to receive the information they want, when they want it, without having to surf thousands of Web sites.

social networking sites Web sites that allow users to upload their content to the Web in the form of text, voice, images, and videos.

tag A keyword or term that describes a piece of information.

videocasting The distribution of digital video media via syndication feeds for playback on digital media players and personal computers.

Web 2.0 A loose collection of information technologies and applications, plus the Web sites that use them.

Web 2.0 media Any Web site that provides user-generated media content, and promotes tagging, rating, commenting, and other interactions among users and their media contributions.

weblog (see **blog**)

wiki A Web site on which anyone can post material and make changes to other material.

>>> DISCUSSION QUESTIONS

1. How would you describe Web 2.0 to someone who has not taken a course in information systems?

2. If you were the CEO of a company, would you pay attention to blogs about your company? Why or why not? If yes, would you consider some blogs to be more important or more reliable than others? If so, which ones? How would you find blogs relating to your company?

3. Do you have a page on a social networking Web site? If yes, why? If no, what is keeping you from creating one? Is there any content that you definitely would *not* post on such a page?

4. How can an organization best employ Web 2.0 technologies and applications to benefit its business processes?

5. What factors might cause an individual, an employee, or a company to be cautious in the use of social networks?

6. What risks does a company expose itself to if it leverages feeds? How might the company mitigate these risks?

7. What sorts of restrictions or guidelines should firms place on the use of social networks by employees? Are these Web 2.0 sites a threat to security? Can they tarnish a firm's reputation? If so, how? Can they enhance a firm's reputation? If so, how?

>>> PROBLEM-SOLVING ACTIVITIES

1. Enter www.programmableweb.com, and study the various services that the Web site offers. Learn how to create mashups, and then propose a mashup of your own. Present your mashup to the class.

2. Go to Amazon's Mechanical Turk Web site (www.mturk.com). View the available HITs. Are there any HITs that you would be interested in to make some extra money? Why or why not?

3. Access Mojofiti (www.mojofiti.com). What is interesting about this social networking site?

4. Access ChatRoulette (www.chatroulette.com). What is interesting about this social networking site?

5. Using a search engine, look up the following:

   - *Most popular or most visited blogs.* Pick two, and follow some of the posts. Why do you think these blogs are popular?

   - *Best blogs* (try www.bloggerschoiceawards.com). Pick two, and consider why they might be the "best blogs."

6. Research how to be a successful blogger. What does it take to be a successful blogger? What time commitment might be needed? How frequently do successful bloggers post?

7. Design a mashup for your university. Include the purpose of the mashup, sources of data, and intended audience.

1. Each team will visit a major social networking site. Discover features that distinguish each site. Present the pros, cons, and distinguishing features of each site to the class.

2. Each team should pick a subject that needs aggregation. Set up the plans for an aggregator Web site to accomplish this goal. Present the aggregators to the class.

3. Enter www.podcasting-tools.com. Explain how to record a podcast. Each team will create a podcast on some idea in the course and make it available on your class Web site.

4. Each team will independently take on the following problem: You are an external consulting company with experience in corporate Web 2.0 implementation.

Create a PowerPoint presentation that sells Web 2.0 to the following company while addressing the following concerns:

- The company is a credit card and payment-processing firm that has 100 employees. Many of the employees are not very literate on the Internet, and most have not heard of Web 2.0. It is believed that some employees will be resistant to any proposed changes.

- The company CIO would like to implement Web 2.0 technologies and applications to enhance employee life and perhaps venture into new ways of marketing the company's services.

Each team will conduct its research independently and present the results to the class.

CLOSING **CASE 1 >** From Social Networks
to Social Commerce

Every year companies spend about $100 billion annually on local advertising in the United States alone. Much of that money is wasted, because local commerce is highly segmented and inefficient. A small company cannot acquire customers or advertise with the efficiency of a large chain that has multiple locations in the same town. The problem, therefore, is how to make local advertising more efficient and effective for small businesses.

<<<**THE PROBLEM**

The solution may lie in the emerging area of social commerce, as illustrated by Groupon (www.groupon.com). Groupon offers its subscribers—who numbered more than 70 million in March 2011 and are growing at a rate of 3 million per month—discounts on goods and services, but only if a critical mass of people agrees to buy the deals that are e-mailed to them each day. The discount could be up to 90 percent off on a car wash, a restaurant meal, a cooking class, dental work, or just about any product or service available in the 500 cities and 35 countries where Groupon operates. Groupon's social commerce model pays off in three ways: (1) The subscriber gets a better price, (2) the merchant is guaranteed additional business and potential new customers, and (3) Groupon receives a share of the revenues generated by the deals.

The first phase of Groupon's business model connected local merchants with local customers, using blasts of discounts that were not precisely targeted. When Groupon launched its operation, the business limited itself to promoting one deal per day because it did not have any merchant relationships. As Groupon became more popular, however, demand became so great that merchants were waiting months for their deal to be featured on the site. To solve this problem, Groupon created Groupon Stores and the Deal Feed.

<<<**THE SOLUTION**

Groupon Stores lets businesses create and launch their own deals whenever they want to and as frequently as they want to, without waiting to be featured as the deal of the day. Participating merchants create Groupon stores, and Groupon then promotes their deals via e-mail, Twitter, and Facebook. There is no upfront fee, and businesses receive 70 percent of each promoted Groupon sale. When people visit a merchant's Groupon Store, they have the option to "follow" it, just as they would on Twitter. This process is called the Deal Feed. Merchants can therefore inform their followers about new deals or special offers. Each day, Groupon selects the best deals from Groupon Stores and matches them with customers using Groupon's proprietary personalization technology.

Groupon labels the next phase of its business model *hyperlocal*. This phase involves knowing where subscribers live and what their interests are, becoming familiar with their commercial experiences, and sharing this knowledge with their friends. Put simply, Groupon knows not just what you like but also what deals might trigger your curiosity. The company can thus inform you directly of these deals via your cell phone. It can also integrate and popularize deals offered to various individuals through social networking sites such as Twitter and Facebook.

Groupon calls the third phase of its business model Groupon Now. This service features two choices: "I'm hungry" and "I'm bored." When a Groupon subscriber clicks the "I'm hungry" button, Groupon displays a list of deals from nearby restaurants. Similarly, when he or she clicks "I'm bored," Groupon displays a list of local activities occurring nearby.

One objective of Groupon Now is to help eliminate perishable inventory—food products, labor hours, and anything else that is wasted if it not used immediately. Groupon claims that Groupon Now will enable small businesses to become more like airlines, matching supply against demand to maximize revenues. For example, a spa could send out a deal on a massage because a customer canceled, or a gym could run several days of coupons to fill the class of a new yoga instructor.

THE RESULTS >>>

Groupon's business model has been wildly successful. The company has about 6,000 employees and sends out more than 900 deals each day in 550 markets. The company, which launched in 2008, gained 1 million subscribers within a year and went from zero to $500 million in sales within 18 months. Groupon is on track to generate some $3 billion in revenue in 2011, a dramatic increase from the $750 million it earned in 2010.

Groupon's success has created intense competition. Today, more than 500 companies around the world offer similar services. For example, when Google tried to purchase Groupon in December 2010 for $6 billion, Groupon turned down the offer. Google promptly became a competitor and developed plans for its own social commerce site, called Google Offers. Groupon's biggest rival, LivingSocial (www.livingsocial.com), received an infusion of $175 million from Amazon in 2010 because Amazon wanted a foothold in social commerce. This investment enabled LivingSocial to develop a technology platform from which to expand its base of 10 million subscribers.

In addition to competition, Groupon has other problems. As some small businesses have learned the hard way, running a discounted deal can attract so many customers that the deal can actually cost them money. A recent study surveyed 150 small to midsize businesses that had used Groupon. Of the respondents, 63 percent replied that their Groupon deal was profitable, whereas 32 percent found it unprofitable. Further, 40 percent of the respondents asserted that they would not use Groupon again, in large part because small businesses did not know what to expect from each Groupon deal. These businesses could be overwhelmed with customers or not have any customers show up at all.

Questions:

1. Do you think social commerce is less irritating than viral marketing? Is it just a new wave of electronic marketing, or is this a new and better way to reach customers?

2. What are the advantages and disadvantages of social commerce?

SOURCES: Compiled from B. Stone and D. MacMillan, "Are Four Words Worth $25 Billion for Groupon?" *Bloomberg BusinessWeek*, March 17, 2011; B. Saporito, "The Groupon Clipper," *Time*, February 21, 2011; L. Indvik, "Groupon Goes from Local to Hyperlocal with New Ad Campaign," *Forbes*, January 25, 2011; J. O'Dell, "The History of Groupon," *Forbes*, January 7, 2011; E. Anderson, "Groupon Getting It Right," *Forbes*, January 7, 2011; S. Purewal, "Groupon Nightmares (and How to Avoid Them)," *Entrepreneur*, December 10, 2010; S. Gaudin, "Google Expected to Buy or Eclipse Groupon," *Computerworld*, December 6, 2010; K. Burnham, "Groupon 2.0: More Deals and a Personalized Feed," *CIO*, December 1, 2010; J. Galante, "Groupon Coupons: The Small-Biz Challenge," *Bloomberg BusinessWeek*, June 10, 2010; www.groupon.com, www.livingsocial.com, accessed February 21, 2011.

CLOSING **CASE 2 >**

Marketing with Facebook

Almost a hundred years ago, John Wanamaker coined the advertiser's dilemma: "Half the money I spend on advertising is wasted; the trouble is I don't know which half." Until the advent of the Web, it was difficult to argue that these percentages, or even an advertiser's ability to track these percentages, had improved much. However, the Web has advanced to the point that most large sites can serve ads based on a user's browsing history. For example, Google (www.google.com) has developed its brand of targeted advertising so effectively that the company reported some $28 billion in revenues in 2010.

<<<**THE PROBLEM**

Marketers have long hoped to turn the Web into the perfect advertising medium. Pop-ups on AOL, banners on Yahoo!, and search ads on Google were steps along that path. Facebook, however, is pioneering targeted advertising.

Facebook (www.facebook.com) has developed a powerful kind of targeted advertising that is more personal, or more "social," than any previous type. For example, if you recently became engaged and you updated your Facebook status to reflect that fact, you might start seeing ads from local jewelers. Those jewelers have likely used Facebook's automated ad system to target recently engaged couples living in the area.

<<<**THE SOLUTION**

Consider David Belden, founder of Residential Solar 101 (www.residentialsolar101.com), a San Francisco-based reseller of solar panels. Belden knows exactly who his customer is: male, around 55 years old, with an environmental conscience that is often demonstrated in the ownership of a hybrid car. Such details are exactly what Facebook can provide for Belden.

However, ads on Facebook's Web site (say for Belden's Residential Solar 101) are located on the far right of the page and are clicked on by less than one-tenth of 1 percent of the site's users. In contrast, Google ads, which are triggered by searches for specific topics, can draw clicks from up to 10 percent of all searchers. However, they are also far more expensive than Facebook ads.

Facebook's extremely low click-through rates limit the effectiveness of the site's targeted ads, which would matter much more if Facebook were only selling clicks. However, Facebook ads can evolve into conversations among friends, colleagues, and family members, and advertisers want to be involved in these conversations.

The entire premise for Facebook's model of advertising is that advertisements are more valuable when they are reinforced by your friends' behaviors. If enough of your friends like or comment on an ad, that ad can move into your main news feed, along with the names of your friends and all the conversations about the ad. The advertiser pays nothing for this movement.

Facebook's promise to advertisers is not to get consumers to buy their products—or even to get them to visit the advertiser's Web site. Instead, Facebook wants to subtly place the advertiser's brand in the user's consciousness and provoke a purchase at a later time. More immediately, Facebook wants you to "like" the brand itself. When you do this, it serves as a type of opt-in, allowing the advertiser to insert future messages into your feed.

Nielsen (www.nielsen.com), the marketing research firm, notes that if users discover that their friends "like" an ad or have commented on it positively or negatively, they are up to 30 percent more likely to recall the ad's message. Consider Nike's (www.nike.com) 3-minute

<<<**THE RESULTS**

commercial at the FIFA World Cup in the summer of 2010. Hundreds of millions of people saw the commercial on television. However, before the commercial even appeared on television, Nike launched it on Facebook.

The commercial started as a video on Facebook and then was passed from friend to friend, often with comments and recommendations. Facebook users played and commented on the commercial more than 9 million times. This activity helped Nike double its number of Facebook fans from 1.6 million to 3.1 million over a single weekend. Nike officials said that placing the ad on Facebook cost "a few million dollars." However, passing around the ad did not cost Nike anything. David Grasso, Nike's chief marketing officer, noted that Facebook was the equivalent for Nike of what TV was for marketers in the 1960s. Facebook is now an integral part of Nike's marketing strategy.

Ford, 7-Eleven, and McDonald's have unveiled products on their Facebook pages, in some cases using their fan groups to help design those items in advance. Starbucks offers coupons and free pastries to its 14 million fans. Other brands use Facebook to pursue what they describe as their products' "service mission." For example, Special K's page provides nutritional tips, and Nature Valley's page discusses national parks and nature photography. Coca-Cola, which has more than 12 million Facebook fans, also relies and focuses on Facebook.

And the bottom line for Facebook? The company reported revenue of $1.86 billion in 2010 and was valued at $82.9 billion in January 2011.

Even though Facebook's bottom line looks good, the company's success is creating competition. Google is adding a feature to its Web searches that enables users to recommend useful search results to friends. This process could lead Google to rank Web sites based on what users and their friends find useful rather than using only Google's PageRank algorithm. Google's social search effort is called Google+. Google and Facebook increasingly appear to be on a collision course for online advertising dollars.

Questions

1. Describe the advantages enjoyed by advertisers who place ads on Facebook.

2. Discuss disadvantages that users may encounter when advertisers target them on Facebook.

Sources: Compiled from A. Efrati, "Google Wants Search to Be More Social," *Wall Street Journal*, March 31, 2011; T. Team, "Squint Your Eyes and Facebook Looks Like a $55 Billion Biz," *Forbes*, February 16, 2011; A. Levy, "Facebook Valuation Tops Amazon.com, Trailing Only Google on Web," *Bloomberg BusinessWeek*, January 29, 2011; A. Diana, "Facebook Ad Spending to Hit $4.05 Billion in 2011," *InformationWeek*, January 20, 2011; L. Horn, "How Facebook Earned $1.86 Billion Ad Revenue in 2010," *PC Magazine*, January 18, 2011; B. Stone, "Sell Your Friends," *Bloomberg BusinessWeek*, September 27–October 3, 2010; A. Ostrow, "Spending a Lot on Facebook," *Forbes*, August 31, 2010; T. Bradley, "Facebook Set to Challenge Google Ad Empire," *CIO*, March 22, 2010; www. facebook.com, accessed April 2, 2011.

RUBY'S CLUB INTERNSHIP ASSIGNMENTS

The end-of-section discussion questions have already asked you to consider many facets of Web 2.0 and social media. RSS feeds, Facebook, Twitter, blogs, and wikis provide multiple ways for businesses to connect with their customers. How are other bars/clubs using these tools? If you have not already searched this to answer the section questions, search now and see what you can find.

Remember that Ruby's strategy is to create a relaxing "community" environment where customers come for nice music and good

drinks. Can social media help Ruben and Lisa create this? Will more privacy issues be brought up than this is worth?

Finally, write a letter to Ruben and Lisa explaining the different social media and how they may use them in their grand reopening to help promote their club. Do not take for granted that they are familiar with each social network and how it works. Remember, Ruben is a "newbie" when it comes to Facebook and does not even have a Twitter account! Submit this letter to Ruben and Lisa via your professor.

SPREADSHEET ACTIVITY

Objective: When someone uses the phrase "social network" we generally think of MySpace or Facebook. However, many online tools allow people to collaborate and work together on projects. Google Docs is one of these. This activity will introduce the Google Spreadsheet Survey tool.

Chapter Connection: While Google Spreadsheets are not social networks like Facebook and MySpace, they are definitely examples of Web 2.0. They allow multiple people to work together and collaborate on many projects. The Google Spreadsheet Survey tool is no exception. It allows for the easy collection and sharing of data.

Prerequisites: There are no prerequisites for this activity.

Activity: Consider the following scenario. You are the marketing officer for "Students for Better Campus Lunches" and have been charged with a campuswide survey to find out how people feel about the current food offerings and their desires for future possibilities. You decide to use a Google Form because the data are automatically saved in a Google Spreadsheet and will be easy for you to analyze. The following questions have been recommended. You will likely need to reword some of these so they will fit a multiple-choice question format. You also may want to have a couple of open-ended questions to allow for comments.

1. How often do you eat on campus?
2. Which meals do you eat?
3. Are you satisfied with the current choices?
4. What cuisines would you like to see more of?
5. What do you think we could do without?
6. Is eating on campus too expensive?
7. Do you have any general recommendations for food on campus?

To complete this exercise you will need to create a Google account if you do not already have one. Then log in to docs.google.com and create a new form. Go to the Google Docs Web site and watch the tutorials on how to create Google Forms. Or simply search Google for "Google Form Videos" and have a look at the tutorials.

Once you have created your form, have some friends complete your survey and have a look at the data in your spreadsheet. Download this spreadsheet and submit it to your professor in whatever form requested.

Deliverables: The final product will be a workable survey/form built in Google Docs.

Quiz Questions:

1. True or False? When creating a Google Form, a Google database is automatically created to capture the data.

2. To create a survey using Google Docs, you need to log in to Google Docs and click on "Create New _____."
   (a) Document
   (b) Spreadsheet
   (c) Presentation
   (d) Form

3. True or False? Google Docs does not give you the option to make a question "required." If you wanted to change the text that is displayed to the user upon completion of a form, you would click on"
   (a) More actions → Theme → New Thank You
   (b) More actions → Embed
   (c) Theme → Finance Chart
   (d) More actions → Edit Confirmation

Discussion Questions:

1. Discuss the advantages and disadvantages of using this type of tool. For example, how do you know how many times someone completes the survey? Given this lack of control, in how many situations would this truly be useful?

2. If you were to embed a Google Form into another Web page, do you think you should tell people that your form was created on a Google site? Should you explain the security levels available? How much do you want them to know about how easily they could take and retake the survey?

DATABASE ACTIVITY: FORMS I

Objective

In this activity you will learn how to use forms that select columns of interest from one or more related tables, to view or to enter new data. So far we have entered all our data directly into our tables and looked at them that way too (or in reports). We opened tables in Datasheet view, selected a row, and keyed in the data or examined it. In this activity, you will learn a better way to enter or view data.

Working with one table at a time is not ideal for two main reasons:

1. Understanding information in a meaningful way often means looking at more than one table. Registering for a new course may involve a registration table, a student table, a course table, and perhaps others.

2. Looking at a table shows all its columns. A real table may have hundreds of columns. Most database uses do not need all, or even most, of them. Grouping those needed for one purpose will not be ideal for a different one.

Using forms solves both of these problems. In this activity, you will see how.

Chapter Connection

The unifying characteristic of social network applications is that users, not site owners, provide the content. For this to work, the interfaces they use must hide the underlying complexity of the database. Forms can do this.

Prerequisites

None

Activity:

In this activity, which you will find online, you will learn about creating forms with the Form tool and the Form Wizard. You will create complex forms, using up to three tables.

1. Download and open the Ch 08 PhotoNet database from www.wiley.com/college/rainer. It contains three tables: members, photos, and comments. Each comment is by a member, about a photo posted by a member. (They may be the same; that is, a member may comment on his or her own photo.) Open the relationship map, under the Database Tools ribbon tab, to see how they are related.

2. We will start with a one-table form to provide a user-friendly data entry environment. To create a form based on the Member table, open it and make sure it is in front so Access will know which table to base the form on. Then click the "Create" ribbon tab, find the Forms section, and click "Form." A simple form based on MemberTbl will show up.

3. The form will be in Layout view. In the Chapter 9 activity you will learn to modify a form in this view. Here, just close the form. When prompted, name it NewMemberFrm.

4. Open it again. It will be in Form view, showing data for Member 1. Use the navigation tools at the bottom to move through the rows of MemberTbl. Tool tips on each symbol tell what it does. You can also enter a record number in the field that says "*n* of *m*," where *n* is the number of the current record (table row) and *m* is the number of records in the table.

5. Enter a new record by, first, clicking the far right icon in the navigation area at the bottom of the form. Enter yourself as a new member, with today's date as your joining date. Fill the other fields with data of your choice.

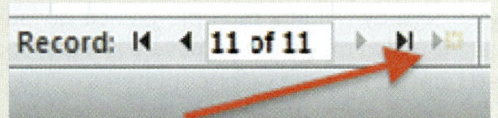

6. Suppose we want to see all of a member's photos. PhotoTbl lists them by MemberID. People do not know members by their IDs. We use names in the real world, handles on most Web sites. These are in MemberTbl. So, a form to show a member's handle and photos must use two tables. To create this form, again click the "Create" ribbon tab. This time, select the Form Wizard. If your window is not wide enough for Access to display its label, it is the icon in that section with the wizard's wand sprinkling magic dust.

7. The Wizard asks you to select tables and columns for this form. First, select MemberTbl from the Tables/Queries pull-down list. When its fields are showing, move MemberHandle to the right panel ("Selected Fields") by selecting it and

clicking ">." Then select PhotoTbl from the pull-down list, and move PhotoTitle and PhotoLink into the form. Then click "Next."

8. Since we want to list each member with his or her photos, view it by MemberTbl. (If we view by photo, the form will treat member data as an extension of photo data.) Click "Next."

9. A Datasheet view of the subform means that, within each member form, the member's photos will be listed in an embedded datasheet. Select this option, and click "Next."

10. Title the main form "Photos by Member" and the subform "Photo List." Select "Open the form to view or enter information," and click "Finish" to see the form you created.

11. You will see a form with Member 1's photos. The navigation tools at the bottom of the subform go through them. Those at the bottom of the entire window go through members. As you change members, the subform changes to show

each one's photos. To enter a new photo, find the desired member and add it to the subform. Access will enter the correct MemberID in PhotoTbl. Confirm this: Enter a new photo for the first user, then open PhotoTbl. Your new item will be at the end, with that user's MemberID.

12. If a member forgets to add a photo link, the post should display a photo of the founder's dog. To make this happen, do either (a) or (b) in the following list. Method a, using the table, will enter this link whenever a new member is added in any way. Method b, using the form, will enter it only when a new member is added via this form.

(a) Open PhotoTbl in Design view. Select the PhotoLink row. Enter "www.photosite.com/dog.jpg" (*with* the quotation marks) in the Default Value row as shown in the following screen shot. Close the table.

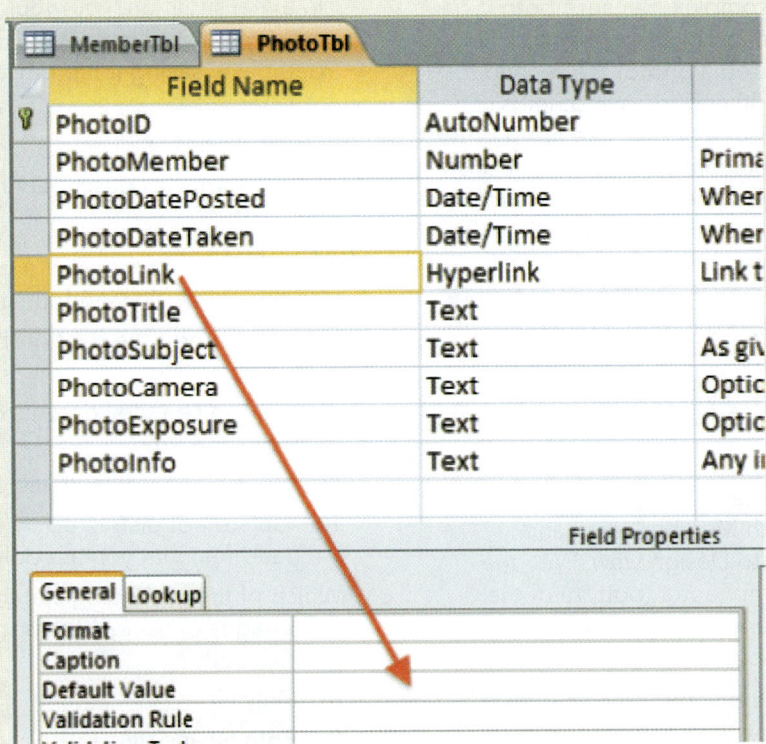

(b) Open the Photos by Member form in either Design or Layout view. (Layout view is shown in the following screen shot, but either one works as well as the other.) In either view, click the "Design" tab. Then click the "Property Sheet" icon at the far right. On that sheet, select its "Data" tab. Enter "www.photosite.

com/dog.jpg" (*with* the quotation marks) in the Default Value row. Then return to Form view. The property sheet will vanish, since it is not usable in Form view. This URL will be in the "New" row of the table. Since it is a default, not a fixed value, a user can replace it with a real link.

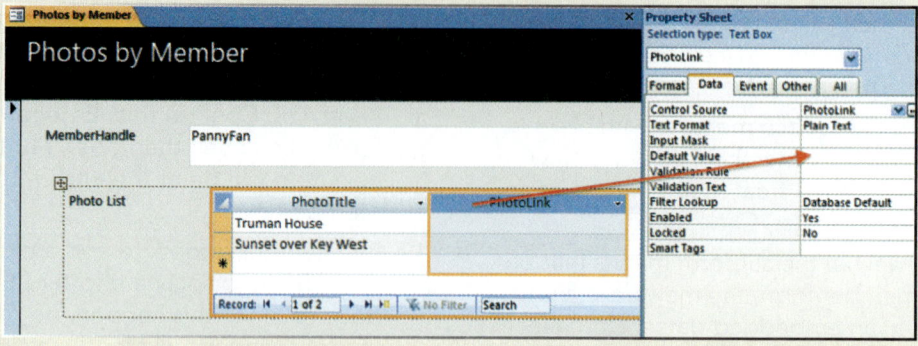

Usage Hint: An Access object's property sheet describes it in full. It is the "go-to place" for when all other attempts to change something about an object fail, to set precise dimensions that cannot be set as accurately by dragging on the screen, or to change some object characteristics that are not visible anywhere else.

13. The third form, to show members, photos, and comments, is more complex. Because both PhotoTbl and CommentTbl link to MemberTbl (the first for who posted a photo, the second for who commented on it) and to each other (since each comment is about a photo), the Form Wizard cannot figure out their connections. We must do this form in stages. First, we will create a *subform* to show photos and their comments. Then, we will put it into a form with member information. For the subform, use the Form Wizard as before using all three tables, organizing it by PhotoTbl. You will see member data treated as part of the comment data. This time, in what was step 9 (above), choose "Tabular" format. Save this as PhotoSubform.

14. Again using Form Wizard, create a form from only MemberTbl, with MemberName and MemberHandle. Go to Design view. With the mouse, grab the Form Footer (bottom of the form) by its top edge and drag it down to make as much space as possible for the subform.

15. Select the Design ribbon, and click "Subform" in the Controls section. (It is probably at the bottom of the left column of three small icons, but Access will sometimes rearrange ribbons to fit the window. Mouse around until you get a Subform/ Subreport tool tip.) The mouse pointer will become a + when you move it to the form design area. Drag it over the space you created when you expanded the form to create a rectangle where the subform will go.

16. Click the "Property Sheet" icon at the right of the ribbon, or double-click the edge of the rectangle

you just drew. (Hitting the edge takes precise positioning.) The first row under the Data tab reads "Source Object." Pull down the menu of possible source objects via the down arrow at the right of that row, and select "PhotoSubform." It will appear in the rectangle.

17. Switch to Form view, and see what you created. You probably feel that you can improve its layout. In a real situation, you would. In the Chapter 9 activity, you will learn how. For now, close your database, saving it if prompted.

Deliverables:

Your three forms, as described in the problem.

Quiz Questions:

1. Consider the following four statements:
   i. You can edit the relationships among database tables.
   ii. You can see the contents of more than one table at a time.
   iii. You can set a default value for a data field.
   iv. You are not distracted by data fields you do not need for what you are doing.

   Which of the preceding statements describe(s) the advantages of using Access forms over using a table directly?
   (a) Only (ii)
   (b) Both (ii) and (iv)
   (c) Both (ii) and (iii)
   (d) All of the listed items are advantages of Access forms over using a table directly.

2. True or False? When table relationships are simple, the Form Wizard can figure out which rows of one table are associated with a row in another table.

3. True or False? The Form button in the Access Create ribbon can create a form that uses data from more than one table.

4. Which of the following *cannot* be done in the Form Wizard?

(a) Selecting tables on which to base the form being designed

(b) Selecting a design theme/color scheme for the form being designed

(c) Selecting totals to be placed in the form being designed

(d) None of the above (All three can be done in the Form Wizard.)

Discussion Questions:

1. Consider the on-screen grade report you get at the end of each term. It is a form, though your school's course information system probably does not use Access. It is based on tables that contain student information such as your name, course information such as full course titles, and a table with grades that connects your record in the student table to the records of your courses in the course table.

   Suppose you were designing this form in the Form Wizard. Describe, in words, the steps you would go through. Invent table names and column names as necessary.

2. Go to www.dpreview.com (Digital Photography Review). At the top, click "Forums." Select any camera type forum from the menu that drops down. In the list of threads for that forum, select any thread with at least ten messages (in the rightmost column of the thread listing). You will see that replies to other messages are listed, indented, under the message to which they reply. A long thread can have many levels of indentation.

   What additional information must be added to the CommentTbl of this activity's database to make this possible? (Ignore the complexities of actually displaying things this way, whether in an Access form or anywhere else. It takes a lot of programming to make it work. Just discuss the information a program would need in order to do this at all.)

3. A city tax department has a table of real estate properties and a table of property owners. A property belongs to only one owner. An owner may own more than one property. Using paper and pencil (or other tools that your instructor may specify), draw a form it could use to show all of one owner's properties. Make reasonable assumptions about the columns in both tables.

9 | E-Business and E-Commerce

LEARNING OBJECTIVES >>>

1. Describe the six common types of electronic commerce; provide specific *personal* examples of how you have used or could use B2C, C2C, G2C, and mobile commerce; and offer a specific example of B2B and G2B.

2. Discuss the five online services of business-to-consumer electronic commerce, provide a specific example of each service, and state how you have used or would use each service.

3. Describe the three business models for business-to-business electronic commerce, and provide a specific example of each model.

4. Describe the four types of electronic payments, provide a specific example of each one, and explain whether you would use each type.

5. Illustrate the ethical and legal issues related to electronic commerce with two specific examples of each issue, and describe how you would respond or react to the four examples you have provided.

Treat America Food Services (http://treatamerica.com) is, among other things, a vending machine company. Doctors' offices, colleges, hospitals, and other organizations contract with Treat America to provide vending services to their customers and employees. The problem is that Treat America's vending machines are unstaffed most of the time. The company has no idea how much money or product is in each machine, or even if someone has broken into it. With gas prices rapidly increasing, it is becoming prohibitively expensive for Treat America to monitor vending machines by driving to each machine's location. Many of the firm's competitors have simply raised prices. However, Treat America found a better solution: e-business.

E-business refers to performing any "normal" business activity with the assistance of computer-based information systems and networks. Treat America determined that it essentially needs only a few simple pieces of information. Consequently, the company installed a small device on the top of each machine that communicates with headquarters via a cellular connection. The device reports the amount of money in the machine at any given minute, the amount of product inventory remaining, whether the machine has been moved, and whether the door has been opened past business hours.

The company's efforts paid off. In one Phoenix location, for example, when thieves broke into a vending machine, the attached device automatically alerted the customer and the police that the door was open after hours. Police caught the culprits in action and arrested them. In a New Orleans store, several employees quit when they could no longer steal from the vending machine. As an added benefit, Treat America's customers are using less gas because they can check inventory online without having to drive to the machine to check quantities and then return to restock. This online feature costs Treat America's customers approximately $150 per machine per year—a minimal cost considering how much money the system saves customers in theft and fuel.

Sources: Compiled from J. Smith, "Vending Machines Go High-Tech with Wireless, Web-Based Systems," *Kansas City Star*, April 10, 2011; http://treatamerica.com, accessed April 21, 2011.

Questions

1. Provide two examples of how the technology added to the vending machines gives Treat America a competitive advantage.

2. Is this competitive advantage sustainable for any length of time? Why or why not? Support your answer.

RUBY'S CLUB

Ruben and Lisa are ready to implement e-commerce on their Web site. They intend to sell hats, shirts, bracelets, necklaces, shot glasses, tumblers, coffee mugs, special event T-shirts, and other paraphernalia. They do not need a complicated site because they will only sell about 20 items.

They have decided to use PayPal as the payment mechanism. It appears that PayPal provides a set of e-commerce tools that Ruben and Lisa can integrate into their site. In addition, many people already have a PayPal account. This fact will allow Ruby's Club to tap into an existing set of customers without having to develop a payment mechanism. It will also give the club instant credibility in the online marketplace.

>>> Given this decision, Ruben and Lisa want you to learn about the e-commerce market. Use this chapter's material to help them understand how they can use these tools to create an online retail store. By the end of the chapter, they hope you can give them an idea of the problems they may face as they move to this system. Also, they want some specific directions on implementing PayPal on their site.

INTRODUCTION

One of the most profound changes in the modern world of business is the emergence of electronic commerce, also known as e-commerce (EC). E-commerce is transforming all business functional areas and their fundamental tasks, from advertising to paying bills. Its impact is so widespread that it is affecting almost every organization. This means that, regardless of where you land a job, your organization likely will be practicing electronic commerce.

Electronic commerce impacts organizations in many significant ways. First, it increases an organization's reach, defined as the number of potential customers to whom the company can market its products. In fact, e-commerce provides unparalleled opportunities for companies to expand worldwide at a small cost, to increase market share, and to reduce costs. By utilizing electronic commerce, many small businesses can now operate and compete in market spaces once dominated by larger companies.

Another major impact of electronic commerce has been to remove many of the barriers that previously impeded entrepreneurs seeking to start their own businesses. E-commerce offers amazing opportunities for you to open your own business by developing an e-commerce Web site.

"IT's About Business 9.1" shows you how one person used e-commerce to start an extremely successful business.

IT's ABOUT BUSINESS | 9.1

Minecraft

Markus Persson is the lone developer of Minecraft (www.minecraft.net), the no-frills video game that has sold close to 2 million copies. What makes these numbers even more impressive is the fact that Persson has not spent any money to market Minecraft. Further, unlike iPhone bestsellers such as Angry Birds, Minecraft has not benefited from the distribution muscle of Apple or any other company.

The only place to buy Minecraft is on Persson's Web site, where it sells for about $21. The game is played through a Web browser. Minecraft places users inside a vast landscape. The goal—to the extent there is one—is to avoid being eaten by monsters that come out after dark. All the fun, however, lies in using square blocks of materials like dirt, gravel, and clay to build elaborate caves, towers, and fortresses.

Persson wrote the computer program for Minecraft in 2009, looking for a side project when he came home from working on his day job at King. com, a gaming Web site. By the end of January 2010, he was selling about 7,000 copies on an average day.

As Persson observed, "Once (sales) got up to fifteen copies a day, that was enough for me to have a salary." One source stated that by late 2010 Minecraft was earning $350,000 per day. In March 2010 the Independent Games Festival awarded Minecraft its grand prize.

In late 2010, Persson founded a gaming company called Mojang (www.mojang.com), Swedish for "gadget." He and seven employees split their time between continuing to develop Minecraft and working on a new video game called Scrolls. In addition, Mojang is creating versions of Minecraft for iPhones, iPads, and Android phones that will be available in late 2011. These versions will be sold through third-party app stores such as Apple's iTunes.

Questions

1. Provide two specific examples of how electronic commerce enabled Persson's business to be so successful.

2. Provide two specific examples of potential disadvantages that Persson might encounter by using electronic commerce.

Sources: Compiled from "The Improbable Rise of Minecraft," *Bloomberg BusinessWeek*, April 11–17, 2011; L. Westbrook, "Minecraft Makes $350,000 Per Day," *The Escapist Magazine*, September 28, 2010; www.minecraft.net, www.mojang.com, accessed April 19, 2011.

Electronic commerce is also drastically changing the nature of competition, due to the development of new online companies, new business models, and the diversity of EC-related products and services. Recall your study of competitive strategies in Chapter 2, particularly the impact of the Internet on Porter's five forces. You learned that the Internet can both endanger and enhance a company's position in a given industry.

"Chapter Closing Case 1" shows you that e-commerce has fundamentally altered the nature of competition in the futures markets and stock markets. Despite all the advantages of e-commerce, the Flash Crash demonstrates that the reliance on computers (and thus on e-commerce) can lead to disaster if the process is not properly monitored by humans.

It is important for you to have a working knowledge of electronic commerce because your organization almost certainly will be employing e-commerce applications that impact the firm's strategy and business model. This knowledge will make you more valuable to your organization and will enable you to quickly contribute to e-commerce applications in your functional area. As you read "What's In IT For Me?" at the end of the chapter, envision yourself performing the activities discussed in your functional area.

Going further, you may decide to become an entrepreneur and start your own business. In this case, it is even more essential for you to understand electronic commerce, because e-commerce, with its broad reach, will probably be critical for your business to survive and thrive.

In this chapter you will discover the major applications of e-business and will be able to identify the services that are necessary for its support. You then study the major types of electronic commerce: business-to-consumer (B2C), business-to-business (B2B), consumer-to-consumer (C2C), business-to employee (B2E), and government-to-citizen (G2C). You conclude by examining several legal and ethical issues that have arisen as a result of the rapid growth of e-commerce.

9.1 | Overview of E-Business and E-Commerce

Any entrepreneur or company that decides to practice electronic commerce must develop a strategy to do so effectively. The first step is to determine exactly *why* you want to do business over the Internet using a Web site. There are several reasons for employing Web sites:

- To sell goods and services
- To induce people to visit a physical location
- To reduce operational and transaction costs
- To enhance your reputation

A Web site can accomplish any and all of these goals. Unless a company (or you) has substantial resources, however, it is difficult to accomplish all of them at the same time. The appropriate Web site for achieving each goal will be somewhat different. As you set up your Web site, you must consider how the site will generate and retain traffic, as well as a host of other issues. The point here is that, when you are studying the various aspects of electronic commerce, keep the strategy of the organization or entrepreneur in mind, and you will have a good idea as to the type of Web site to use.

This section examines the basics of e-business and e-commerce. First, you define these two concepts and then become familiar with pure and partial electronic commerce. You then take a look at the various types of electronic commerce. Next, you focus on e-commerce mechanisms, which are the ways that businesses and people buy and sell over the Internet. You conclude this section by considering the benefits and limitations of e-commerce.

Definitions and Concepts

Electronic commerce (**EC** or **e-commerce**) describes the process of buying, selling, transferring, or exchanging products, services, or information via computer networks, including the Internet. **E-business** is a somewhat broader concept. In addition to the buying and selling of goods and services, e-business also refers to servicing customers, collaborating with business partners, and performing electronic transactions within an organization.

Electronic commerce can take several forms depending on the degree of digitization involved. The *degree of digitization* is the extent to which the commerce has been transformed from physical to digital. This concept can relate to both the product or service being sold and the delivery agent or intermediary. In other words, the product can be either physical or digital, and the delivery agent can be either physical or digital.

In traditional commerce both dimensions are physical. Purely physical organizations are referred to as **brick-and-mortar organizations.** (You may also see the term *bricks-and-mortar*.) In contrast, in *pure EC* all dimensions are digital. Companies engaged only in EC are considered **virtual** (or **pure-play**) **organizations**. All other combinations that include a mix of digital and physical dimensions are considered *partial* EC (but not pure EC). **Clicks-and-mortar organizations** conduct some e-commerce activities, yet their primary business is carried out in the physical world. A common alternative to the term *clicks-and-mortar* is *clicks-and-bricks*. You will encounter both terms. Therefore, clicks-and-mortar organizations are examples of partial EC. E-commerce is now so well established that people generally expect companies to offer this service in some form.

Purchasing a shirt at Walmart Online or a book from Amazon.com is partial EC because the merchandise, although bought and paid for digitally, is physically delivered by FedEx or UPS. In contrast, buying an e-book from Amazon.com or a software product from Buy.com is pure EC because the product itself as well as its delivery, payment, and transfer are digital. To avoid confusion, we use the term *electronic commerce* to denote both pure and partial EC.

Types of E-Commerce

E-commerce can be conducted between and among various parties. In this section, you will identify the six common types of e-commerce, and learn about three of them—C2C, B2E, and e-government—in detail. You then consider B2C and B2B in separate sections because they are very complex.

- **Business-to-consumer electronic commerce (B2C).** In B2C, the sellers are organizations, and the buyers are individuals. You learn about B2C electronic commerce in Section 9.2.

- **Business-to-business electronic commerce (B2B).** In B2B transactions, both the sellers and the buyers are business organizations. The vast majority of EC volume is of this type. You will learn more about B2B electronic commerce in Section 9.3. Figure 1.5 also illustrates B2B electronic commerce.

- **Consumer-to-consumer electronic commerce (C2C).** In C2C (also called customer-to-customer), an individual sells products or services to other individuals. The major strategies for conducting C2C on the Internet are auctions and classified ads.

In dozens of countries, C2C selling and buying on auction sites are exploding. Most auctions are conducted by intermediaries such as eBay (www.ebay.com). Consumers can select general sites such as www.auctionanything.com, a company that sells software and services that help individuals and organizations conduct their own auctions. In addition, many individuals are conducting their own auctions. Similarly, www.greatshop.com provides software to create online C2C reverse auction communities as just one offering from its broad product line. (You will learn about reverse auctions, in which buyers solicit bids from sellers, later in this section.)

The major categories of online classified ads are similar to those found in print ads: vehicles, real estate, employment, pets, tickets, and travel. Classified ads are available through most Internet service providers (AOL, MSN, etc.), at some portals (Yahoo!, etc.), and from Internet directories and online newspapers. Many of these sites contain search engines that help shoppers narrow their searches. Craigslist (www.craigslist.org) is the largest online classified ad provider.

Internet-based classified ads have one big advantage over traditional types of classified ads: They provide access to an international, rather than a local, audience. This wider audience greatly increases both the supply of goods and services and the number of potential buyers. It is important to note that the value of expanded geographic reach depends greatly on what is being bought or sold. For example, you might buy software from a company located 1,000 miles away from you, but you would not buy firewood from someone at such a distance.

- **Business-to-employee (B2E).** In B2E, an organization uses EC internally to provide information and services to its employees. For example, companies allow employees to manage their benefits and to take training classes electronically. In addition, employees can buy discounted insurance, travel packages, and tickets to events on the corporate intranet. They also can order supplies and materials electronically. Finally, many companies have electronic corporate stores that sell the company's products to its employees, usually at a discount.

- **E-government.** E-government is the use of Internet technology in general and e-commerce in particular to deliver information and public services to citizens (called government-to-citizen or G2C EC) and to business partners and suppliers (called government-to-business or G2B EC). G2B EC is much like B2B EC, usually with an overlay of government procurement regulations. That is, G2B EC and B2B EC are similar conceptually. However, the functions of G2C EC are conceptually different from anything that exists in the private sector (e.g., B2C EC).

  E-government is also an efficient way of conducting business transactions with citizens and businesses and within the governments themselves. E-government makes government more efficient and effective, especially in the delivery of public services. An example of G2C electronic commerce is electronics benefits transfer, in which governments transfer benefits, such as Social Security and pension payments, directly to recipients' bank accounts.

- **Mobile commerce (m-commerce).** The term *m-commerce* refers to e-commerce that is conducted entirely in a wireless environment. An example is using cell phones to shop over the Internet. You will learn about m-commerce in Chapter 10.

Each type of EC is executed in one or more business models. A **business model** is the method by which a company generates revenue to sustain itself. Table 9.1 summarizes the major EC business models.

E-Commerce and Search

The development of e-commerce has proceeded in phases. Offline and online brands were initially kept distinct and then were awkwardly merged. Initial e-commerce efforts

TABLE 9.1 E-Commerce Business Models

EC Model	Description
Online direct marketing	Manufacturers or retailers sell directly to customers. Very efficient for digital products and services. Can allow for product or service customization. (www.dell.com)
Electronic tendering system	Businesses request quotes from suppliers. Uses B2B with a reverse auction mechanism.
Name-your-own-price	Customers decide how much they are willing to pay. An intermediary tries to match a provider. (www.priceline.com)
Find-the-best-price	Customers specify a need; an intermediary compares providers and shows the lowest price. Customers must accept the offer in a short time or may lose the deal. (www.hotwire.com)
Affiliate marketing	Vendors ask partners to place logos (or banners) on partner's site. If customers click on logo, go to vendor's site, and buy, then vendor pays commissions to partners.
Viral marketing	Receivers send information about your product to their friends.
Group purchasing (e-coops)	Small buyers aggregate demand to get a large volume; then the group conducts tendering or negotiates a low price.
Online auctions	Companies run auctions of various types on the Internet. Very popular in C2C, but gaining ground in other types of EC. (www.ebay.com)
Product customization	Customers use the Internet to self-configure products or services. Sellers then price them and fulfill them quickly (*build-to-order*). (www.jaguar.com)
Electronic marketplaces and exchanges	Transactions are conducted efficiently (more information to buyers and sellers, less exchanges transaction cost) in electronic marketplaces (private or public).
Bartering online	Intermediary administers online exchange of surplus products and/or company receives "points" for its contribution, and the points can be used to purchase other needed items. (www.bbu.com)
Deep discounters	Company offers deep price discounts. Appeals to customers who consider only price in their purchasing decisions. (www.half.com)
Membership	Only members can use the services provided, including access to certain information, conducting trades, etc. (www.egreetings.com)

consisted of flashy brochure sites, with rudimentary shopping carts and checkout systems. They were replaced with systems that tried to anticipate customer needs and accelerate checkout.

From Google's perspective, though, one of the biggest changes has been the growing importance of the search function. Google managers point to a huge number of purchases that follow successful Web searches as well as abandoned shopping carts that immediately followed an unproductive search.

Google is confident that in the future retailers will post tremendous amounts of additional details. Merchants will pour continuous structured feeds of data—including product listings, daily inventory, and hours of operation—into public search engines such as Google. Google is currently using Google Base, the company's online database, to work on this process. This process would allow customers to access much more specific and relevant search results.

Major E-Commerce Mechanisms

Businesses and customers can buy and sell on the Internet through a number of mechanisms. The most widely used are electronic catalogs, electronic auctions, e-storefronts, e-malls, and e-marketplaces.

Catalogs have been printed on paper for generations. Today, however, they are available on CD-ROM and the Internet. Electronic catalogs consist of a product database, directory and search capabilities, and a presentation function. They are the backbone of most e-commerce sites.

An **auction** is a competitive process in which either a seller solicits consecutive bids from buyers or a buyer solicits bids from sellers. The primary characteristic of auctions is that prices are determined dynamically by competitive bidding. Electronic auctions (e-auctions) generally increase revenues for sellers by broadening the customer base and shortening the cycle time of the auction. Buyers generally benefit from e-auctions because they can bargain for lower prices. In addition, they do not have to travel to an auction at a physical location.

The Internet provides an efficient infrastructure for conducting auctions at lower administrative costs and with many more involved sellers and buyers. Individual consumers and corporations alike can participate in auctions. The two major types of auctions are forward and reverse.

Forward auctions are auctions that sellers use as a channel to many potential buyers. Usually, sellers place items at sites for auction, and buyers bid continuously for them. The highest bidder wins the items. Both sellers and buyers can be individuals or businesses. The popular auction site eBay.com is a forward auction.

In **reverse auctions**, one buyer, usually an organization, wants to buy a product or a service. The buyer posts a request for quotation (RFQ) on its Web site or on a third-party site. The RFQ provides detailed information on the desired purchase. The suppliers study the RFQ and then submit bids electronically. Everything else being equal, the lowest-price bidder wins the auction. The reverse auction is the most common auction model for large purchases (in terms of either quantities or price). Governments and large corporations frequently use this approach, which may provide considerable savings for the buyer.

Auctions can be conducted from the seller's site, the buyer's site, or a third party's site. For example, eBay, the best-known third-party site, offers hundreds of thousands of different items in several types of auctions. Overall, more than 300 major companies, including Amazon.com and Dellauction.com, offer online auctions.

An *electronic storefront* is a Web site that represents a single store. An *electronic mall*, also known as a *cybermall* or *e-mall*, is a collection of individual shops under one Internet address. Electronic storefronts and electronic malls are closely associated with B2C electronic commerce. You study each one in more detail in Section 9.2.

An **electronic marketplace** (e-marketplace) is a central, virtual market space on the Web where many buyers and many sellers can conduct e-commerce and e-business activities. Electronic marketplaces are associated with B2B electronic commerce. You learn about electronic marketplaces in Section 9.3.

Benefits and Limitations of E-Commerce

Few innovations in human history have provided as many benefits to organizations, individuals, and society as e-commerce has. E-commerce benefits organizations by making national and international markets more accessible and by lowering the costs of processing, distributing, and retrieving information. Customers benefit by being able to access a vast number of products and services, around the clock. The major benefit to society is the ability to easily and conveniently deliver information, services, and products to people in cities, rural areas, and developing countries.

Despite all these benefits, EC has some limitations, both technological and nontechnological, that have restricted its growth and acceptance. One major technological limitation is the lack of universally accepted security standards. Also, in less-developed countries, telecommunications bandwidth often is insufficient, and accessing the Web is expensive.

Nontechnological limitations include the perceptions that EC is insecure, has unresolved legal issues, and lacks a critical mass of sellers and buyers. As time passes, the limitations, especially the technological ones, will diminish or be overcome.

BEFORE *YOU GO ON . . .*

1. Define e-commerce, and distinguish it from e-business.
2. Differentiate among B2C, B2B, C2C, and B2E electronic commerce.
3. Define e-government.
4. Discuss forward and reverse auctions.
5. Identify some benefits and limitations of e-commerce.

RUBY'S CLUB QUESTIONS

1. Ruby's Club is definitely not a pure e-commerce business. Its main product is entertainment, and Ruben and Lisa simply want to sell their brand via hats, T-shirts, and other paraphernalia. To what degree can they digitize the entertainment aspect of their product?
2. In what ways might Ruby's utilize B2B or B2E e-commerce?

Student Activity | 9.1

Objective: You will understand what e-commerce is and its benefits and limitations.

Chapter Connection: This activity relates to Section 5.1, which sets the stage for the rest of this chapter.

Prerequisites: You should have read Section 5.1 before doing this activity.

Activity:

Read all of the sections of this article on e-commerce in "How E-Commerce Works":

http://communication.howstuffworks.com/ecommerce.htm

Read the following article, which compares e-business and e-commerce:

http://scm.ncsu.edu/public/lessons/less021127.html

Deliverables:

Write a two- to three-page paper that considers the following questions:

1. Can a business be an e-business without being an e-commerce business? Give examples of why that would be true or why that would be false.

2. Why would a pure e-commerce business become a partial e-commerce business?

3. Bennett runs a BBQ restaurant named B's BBQ, which also has a catering business. Could Bennett be an e-business even if he chose not to be an e-commerce business? Why or why not? If so, what processes could he use that would fall under the definition of e-business?

4. Can Bennett be an e-commerce business? Why or why not? If he chose to be an e-commerce business, what steps would he have to go through? Develop a list of development activities, maybe working the list around questions Bennett will need to answer about what his Web site will (or will not) do.

Quiz Questions:

1. Which of the following is a lure of e-commerce?
   (a) Limited number of products offered to customers
   (b) Easy fulfillment
   (c) Lower transaction costs
   (d) No returns
   (e) All of the above

2. Customers can order products online from BestBuy and buy the same products at a BestBuy store. This is an example of:
   (a) Pure e-commerce
   (b) Partial e-commerce

3. Which of the following statements is false?
   (a) E-business means using Internet technologies.
   (b) E-business is internally focused

   (c) E-business integrates all company functions into one IT infrastructure.
   (d) The customer sees no benefit from e-business.

Discussion Questions:

1. Can a business survive without e-commerce?

2. Do service businesses have e-commerce on their Web sites?

3. What are the advantages for companies that have partial e-commerce?

4. It is harder to differentiate when many stores are selling the same products for nearly the same price. One way to differentiate is the services provided to customers via the Web presence. Can you think of any?

9.2 Business-to-Consumer (B2C) Electronic Commerce

B2B EC is much larger than B2C EC by volume, but B2C EC is more complex. The reason is that B2C involves a large number of buyers making millions of diverse transactions per day with a relatively small number of sellers. As an illustration, consider Amazon, an online retailer that offers thousands of products to its customers. Each customer purchase is relatively small, but Amazon must manage that transaction as if that customer were its most important one. Each order must be processed quickly and efficiently, and the products must be shipped to the customer in a timely manner. In addition, returns must be managed. Multiply this simple example by millions, and you get an idea of the complexity of B2C EC. Overall, B2B complexities tend to be more business related, whereas B2C complexities tend to be more technical and volume related.

This section addresses the primary issues in B2C EC. You begin by studying the two basic mechanisms that customers utilize to access companies on the Web: electronic storefronts and electronic malls. In addition to purchasing products over the Web, customers also access online services. Therefore, the next section covers several online services, such as banking, securities trading, job searching, and travel. The complexity of B2C EC creates two major challenges for sellers: channel conflict and order fulfillment. You examine these two topics in detail. Finally, companies engaged in B2C EC must "get the word out" to prospective customers. Therefore, you conclude this section with a look at online advertising.

Electronic Storefronts and Malls

For several generations, home shopping from catalogs, and later from television shopping channels, has attracted millions of customers. Today, shopping online offers an alternative to catalog and television shopping. **Electronic retailing (e-tailing)** is the direct sale of products and services through electronic storefronts or electronic malls, usually designed around an electronic catalog format and/or auctions.

Like any mail-order shopping experience, e-commerce enables you to buy from home and to do so 24 hours a day, 7 days a week. However, EC offers a wider variety of products and services, including the most unique items, often at lower prices. Furthermore, within seconds, shoppers can access very detailed supplementary product information. In addition, they can easily locate and compare competitors' products and prices. Finally, buyers can find hundreds of thousands of sellers. Two popular online shopping mechanisms are electronic storefronts and electronic malls.

Electronic Storefronts. As noted earlier, an **electronic storefront** is a Web site that represents a single store. Hundreds of thousands of electronic storefronts can be found on the Internet. Each one has its own uniform resource locator (URL), or Internet address, at which buyers can place orders. Some electronic storefronts are extensions of physical stores such as Hermes, The Sharper Image, and Walmart. Others are new businesses started by entrepreneurs who discovered a niche on the Web (e.g., Restaurant.com and Alloy.com). Manufacturers (e.g., www.dell.com) and retailers (e.g., www.officedepot.com) also use storefronts.

Despite the proliferation of e-businesses, questions have lingered about whether selling luxury goods online would be successful. "IT's About Business 9.2" answers this question.

IT's ABOUT BUSINESS | 9.2

Luxury Goods Turn to E-Commerce

Major luxury goods companies such as Richemont (www.richemont.com), Burberry (www.burberry.com), and Moët Hennessy Louis Vuitton (LVMH, www.lvmh.com) have turned their attention to electronic commerce. Recognizing that shoppers are increasingly willing to buy very expensive products over the Web, the big luxury brands are making digital retailing a higher priority. High-end retail Web sites such as Net-a-Porter (www.net-a-porter.com) and Yoox (www.yoox.com), as well as discount luxury flash sales Web sites such as Gilt Groupe (www.gilt.com) and Rue La La (www.ruelala.com), have forced executives in the well-known luxury brands to rethink the benefits of online sales. In fact, Bain & Co. (www.bain.com) estimates that the $5-billion online luxury market grew by 20 percent in 2009.

However, selling $1,000 dresses online is different from selling books and DVDs. Customers want a guiding hand to replace the in-store salesperson and to signal which fashions are in style. To provide this guiding hand, Swiss luxury goods maker Richemont purchased Net-a-Porter. Richemont is the owner of brands such as Cartier (www.cartier.com), Montblanc (www.montblanc.com), Van Cleef & Arpels (www.vancleef-arpels.com), and Chloe (www.chloe.com). With this purchase, Richemont is making a commitment to increasing its presence in the online luxury market.

Net-a-Porter is an interactive shopping fashion magazine that publishes 52 weeks of editorial content each year in addition to its designer clothes sales operations. The company is planning to double its operation in the United States and to open a new distribution center in Southeast Asia.

In 2009, Net-a-Porter launched a sister Web site, theOutnet.com (www.outnet.com), which offers discounted designer clothes. This move enables Net-a-Porter to compete with other companies that operate flash sales of high-end merchandise. Competitors include Gilt Groupe, Rue La La, and eBay (www.ebay.com).

Let us use the Gilt Groupe to illustrate how flash sales Web sites operate. The Gilt Groupe operates an invitation-only Web site, which brings the real-life, exclusive, frenzied New York City sample-sale experience online to a mass audience. Shortly before noon, Gilt sends an e-mail to its nearly 3 million members, alerting them of the day's sales. Shoppers have only 36 hours to snap up the limited number of deeply discounted designer clothes, jewelry, and other luxury goods advertised in the e-mail. This process creates strong incentives to buy quickly.

The Gilt Groupe (and companies like it) has had an enormous impact on how well-known luxury brands view electronic commerce. First, Gilt has forced luxury brands to embrace the Internet. For example, Marc Jacobs (www.marcjacobs.com), Jimmy Choo (www.jimmychoo.com), and Donna Karan (www.donnakaran.com) added retail sales to their Web sites in 2010. Burberry now offers select pieces from its runway presentations for a limited time on its Web site just hours after its Fashion Week show. Second, these companies have changed how the fashion industry works, allowing smaller brands that, unlike the better-known brands, do not have large retail outlets to sell older merchandise at a discount. Third, these companies have democratized fashion, giving consumers everywhere access to the most exclusive brands at insider prices that shoppers could formerly get only in New York City. Finally, these firms have changed the way we shop. As we work more and more hours, it makes sense that we do an increasing amount of shopping on the Internet.

The end result for the luxury goods market? These firms are embracing the 21st century model for luxury fashion retailing—namely, electronic commerce.

Questions

1. Provide two specific examples of luxury shoppers' requirements that a Web site could not provide.

2. What are the features provided by online luxury retailers that overcome the problems you mentioned in question 1?

Sources: Compiled from R. Laneri, "Gilt Groupe Founders: The Most Powerful People in Fashion?" *Forbes*, November 9, 2010; P. Sonne, "Richemont to Buy Net-a-Porter," *Wall Street Journal*, April 2, 2010; A. Lee, "Luxury Goes Digital: Fashion House Richemont Embraces E-Commerce," *Fast Company*, April 1, 2010; A. Rice, "What's a Dress Worth," *New York*, February 14, 2010.

Electronic Malls. Whereas an electronic storefront represents a single store, an **electronic mall**, also known as a *cybermall* or an *e-mall*, is a collection of individual shops grouped under a single Internet address. The basic idea of an electronic mall is the same as that of a regular shopping mall: to provide a one-stop shopping place that offers a wide range of products and services. A cybermall may include thousands of vendors. For example, Microsoft Shopping (now Bing shopping, www.bing.com/shopping) includes tens of thousands of products from thousands of vendors.

There are two types of cybermalls. In the first type, known as *referral malls* (for example, www.hawaii.com), you cannot buy anything. Instead, you are transferred from the mall to a participating storefront. In the second type of mall (for example, http://shopping.google.com), you can actually make a purchase (see Figure 9.1). At this type of mall, you might shop from several stores, but you make only one purchase transaction at the end. You use an *electronic shopping cart* to gather items from various vendors and then pay for them all together in a single transaction. The mall organizer, such as Google!, takes a commission from the sellers for this service.

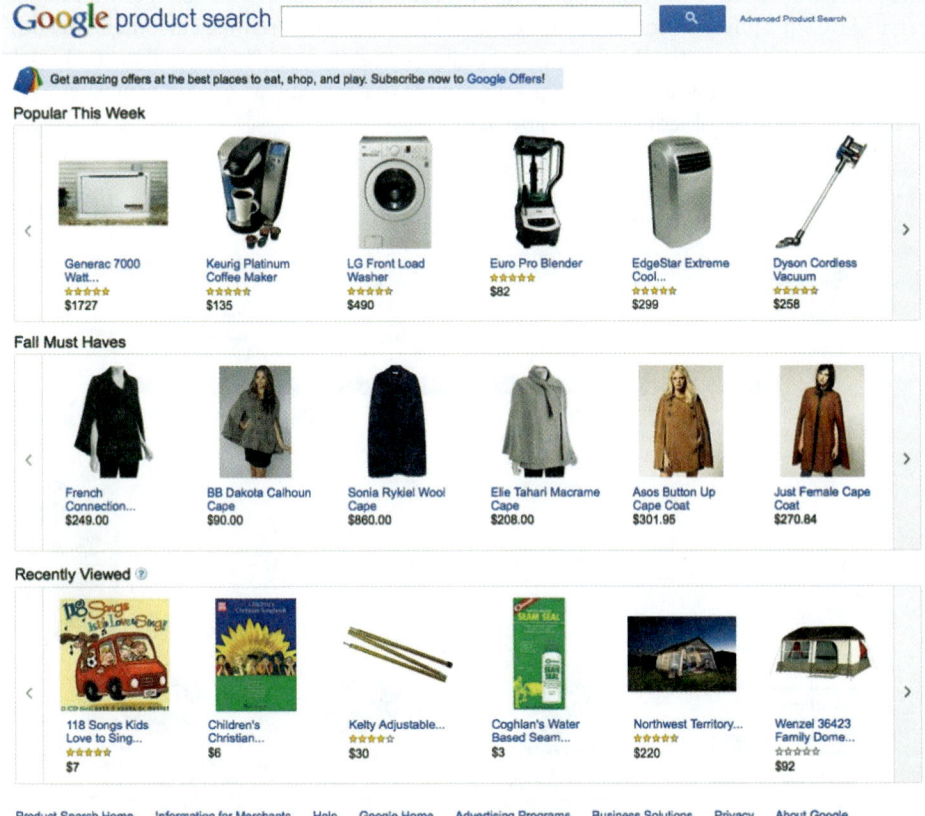

Figure 9.1 Electronic malls include products from many vendors.

Online Service Industries

In addition to purchasing products, customers can also access needed services via the Web. Selling books, toys, computers, and most other products on the Internet can reduce vendors' selling costs by 20 to 40 percent. Further reduction is difficult to achieve because the products must be delivered physically. Only a few products, such as software or music, can be digitized and then delivered online for additional savings. In contrast, services, such as buying an airline ticket and purchasing stocks or insurance, can be delivered entirely through e-commerce, often with considerable cost reduction. Not surprisingly, then, online delivery of services is growing very rapidly, with millions of new customers being added each year.

One of the most pressing EC issues relating to online services (as well as in marketing tangible products) is disintermediation. Intermediaries, also known as middlemen, have two functions: (1) They provide information, and (2) they perform value-added services such as consulting. The first function can be fully automated and most likely will be assumed by e-marketplaces and portals that provide information for free. When this occurs, the intermediaries who perform only (or primarily) this function are likely to be eliminated. This process is called **disintermediation**.

In contrast, performing value-added services requires expertise. Unlike the information function, then, this function can be only partially automated. Thus, intermediaries who provide value-added services not only are likely to survive, but they may actually prosper. The Web helps these employees in two situations: (1) when the number of participants is enormous, as with job searches, and (2) when the information that must be exchanged is complex.

In this section, you will examine some leading online service industries: banking, trading of securities (stocks, bonds), job matching, travel services, and online advertising.

Cyberbanking. *Electronic banking*, also known as **cyberbanking**, involves conducting various banking activities from home, at a place of business, or on the road instead of at a physical bank location. Electronic banking has capabilities ranging from paying bills to applying for a loan. For customers, it saves time and is convenient. For banks, it offers an inexpensive alternative to branch banking—for example, about 2 cents cost per transaction versus $1.07 at a physical branch. It also enables banks to attract remote customers. In addition to regular banks with added online services, **virtual banks**, which are dedicated solely to Internet transactions, are emerging. An example of a virtual bank is First Internet Bank of Indiana (www.firstib.com) (see Figure 9.2).

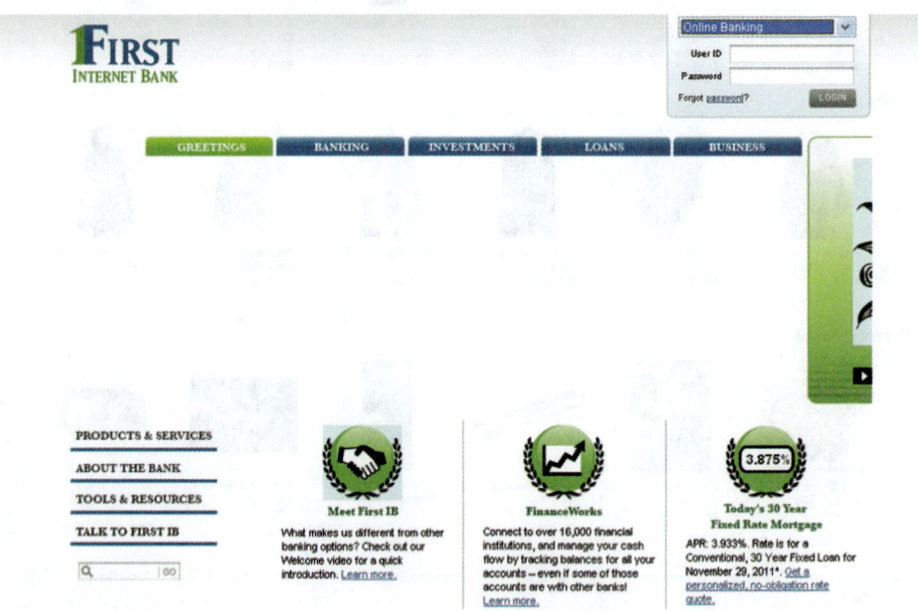

Figure 9.2 First Internet Bank of Indiana.

International banking and the ability to handle trading in multiple currencies are critical for international trade. Transfers of electronic funds and electronic letters of credit are important services in international banking. An example of support for EC global trade is provided by TradeCard, in conjunction with MasterCard. TradeCard is an international company that provides a secure method for buyers and sellers to make digital payments anywhere on the globe (see the demo at www.tradecard.com). In another example, banks and companies such as Oanda (www.oanda.com) provide conversions of more than 160 currencies.

Online Securities Trading. Emarketer.com estimates that some 40 million people in the United States use computers to trade stocks, bonds, and other financial instruments. In fact, several well-known securities companies, including E*Trade, Ameritrade, and Charles Schwab, offer only online trading. In Korea, more than half of stock traders are already using the Internet for that purpose. Why? Because it is cheaper than a full-service or discount broker. On the Web, investors can find a considerable amount of information regarding specific companies or mutual funds in which to invest (for example, http://money.cnn.com and www.bloomberg.com).

For example, let's say you have an account with Scottrade. You access Scottrade's Web site (www.scottrade.com) from your personal computer or your Internet-enabled mobile device, enter your account number and password to access your personalized Web page, and then click on "stock trading." Using a menu, you enter the details of your order—buy or sell, margin or cash, price limit, market order, and so on. The computer informs you of the current "ask" and "bid" prices, much as a broker would do over the telephone. You can then approve or reject the transaction.

The Online Job Market. The Internet offers a promising new environment for job seekers and for companies searching for hard-to-find employees. Thousands of companies and government agencies advertise available positions, accept resumes, and take applications via the Internet.

Job seekers use the online job market to reply online to employment ads, to place resumes on various sites, and to use recruiting firms (for example, www.monster.com, www.simplyhired.com, www.linkedin.com, and www.truecareers.com). Companies that have jobs to offer advertise these openings on their Web sites, and they search the bulletin boards of recruiting firms. In many countries, governments must advertise job openings on the Internet.

Travel Services. The Internet is an ideal place to plan, explore, and arrange almost any trip economically. Online travel services allow you to purchase airline tickets, reserve hotel rooms, and rent cars. Most sites also offer a fare-tracker feature that sends you e-mail messages about low-cost flights. Examples of comprehensive online travel services are Expedia.com, Travelocity.com, and Orbitz.com. Online services are also provided by all major airline vacation services, large conventional travel agencies, car rental agencies, hotels (e.g., www.hotels.com), and tour companies. In a variation of this process, Priceline.com allows you to set a price you are willing to pay for an airline ticket or hotel accommodations. It then attempts to find a vendor that will match your price.

One costly problem that e-commerce can cause is "mistake fares" in the airline industry. For example, over the weekend of May 4–6, 2007, United Airlines offered a $1,221 fare for a U.S.-to-New Zealand round-trip in business class. This price was incorrect; the actual price was higher. By the time United noticed the mistake and pulled the fare, however, hundreds of tickets had been sold, thanks in part to online travel discussion groups.

Online Advertising. *Advertising* is the practice of disseminating information in an attempt to influence a buyer–seller transaction. Traditional advertising on TV or in newspapers is impersonal, one-way mass communication. In contrast, direct-response marketing, or telemarketing, contacts individuals by direct mail or telephone and requires them to respond in order to make a purchase. The direct-response approach personalizes advertising and marketing. At the same time, however, it can be expensive, slow, and ineffective. It can also be extremely annoying to the consumer.

Banner (468 x 60)

Figure 9.3 When customers click on a banner ad, they are transferred to the vendor's home page.

Internet advertising redefines the advertising process, making it media-rich, dynamic, and interactive. It improves on traditional forms of advertising in a number of ways. First, Internet ads can be updated any time at minimal cost and therefore can be kept current. In addition, these ads can reach very large numbers of potential buyers all over the world. Further, they are generally cheaper than radio, television, and print ads. Finally, Internet ads can be interactive and targeted to specific interest groups and/or individuals.

Advertising Methods. The most common online advertising methods are banners, pop-ups, and e-mail. **Banners** are simply electronic billboards. Typically, a banner contains a short text or graphical message to promote a product or a vendor. It may even contain video clips and sound. When customers click on a banner, they are transferred to the advertiser's home page. Banner advertising is the most commonly used form of advertising on the Internet (see Figure 9.3).

A major advantage of banners is that they can be customized to the target audience. If the computer system knows who you are or what your profile is, it might send you a banner that is supposed to match your interests. A major disadvantage of banners is that they can convey only limited information due to their small size. Another drawback is that many viewers simply ignore them.

Pop-up and pop-under ads are contained in a new browser window that is automatically launched when you enter or exit a Web site. A **pop-up ad** appears in front of the current browser window. A **pop-under ad** appears underneath the active window; when users close the active window, they see the ad. Many users strongly object to these ads, which they consider intrusive. Modern browsers let users block pop-up ads, but this feature must be used with caution because some Web sites depend on pop-up capabilities to present content other than advertising. For example, when you log on to your Verizon e-mail page, you also see a brief (one line each) summary of recent news stories. If you hover your mouse over one of them, you get a pop-up window with an extended summary (a few paragraphs) of that story. Another example is the WebCT Vista software for online instruction, where discussion group posts appear in pop-up windows. Blocking pop-ups would make the first of these two examples less useful and would eliminate important functionality from the second example.

E-mail is emerging as an Internet advertising and marketing channel. It is generally cost-effective to implement, and it provides a better and quicker response rate than other advertising channels. Marketers develop or purchase a list of e-mail addresses, place them in a customer database, and then send advertisements via e-mail. A list of e-mail addresses can be a very powerful tool because the marketer can target a group of people or even individuals.

As you have probably concluded by now, there is a potential for misuse of e-mail advertising. In fact, some consumers receive a flood of unsolicited e-mail, or *spam*. **Spamming** is the indiscriminate distribution of electronic ads without the permission of the receiver. Unfortunately, spamming is becoming worse over time.

Two important responses to spamming are permission marketing and viral marketing. **Permission marketing** asks consumers to give their permission to voluntarily accept online advertising and e-mail. Typically, consumers are asked to complete an electronic form that asks what they are interested in and requests permission to send related marketing information. Sometimes, consumers are offered incentives to receive advertising.

Permission marketing is the basis of many Internet marketing strategies. For example, millions of users periodically receive e-mails from airlines such as American and Southwest. Users of this marketing service can ask to be notified of low fares from their hometown or to their favorite destinations. Significantly, they can easily unsubscribe at any time. Permission marketing is also extremely important for market research (for example, search for "Media Metrix" at www.comscore.com).

In one particularly interesting form of permission marketing, companies such as Clickdough.com, ExpressPaidSurveys.com, and CashSurfers.com have built customer lists of millions of people who are happy to receive advertising messages whenever they are on the Web. These customers are paid $0.25 to $0.50 an hour to view messages while they do their normal surfing.

Viral marketing refers to online word-of-mouth marketing. The strategy behind viral marketing is to have people forward messages to friends, family members, and other acquaintances suggesting they "check this out." For example, a marketer can distribute a small game program embedded with a sponsor's e-mail that is easy to forward. The marketer releases only a few thousand copies, with the expectation that the recipients in turn will forward the program to many more thousands of potential customers. In this way, viral marketing enables companies to build brand awareness at a minimal cost without having to spam millions of uninterested users.

Online Advertising on Social Networks. Online advertising on social networks has become more successful over time. This type of advertising takes several forms, including self-service advertising, brand advertising, performance-based advertising and impression-based advertising.

Self-service advertising is advertising that is purchased without the assistance of a sales representative. By eliminating the expense of a sales representative, a social networking company can offer smaller minimum ad buys than would otherwise be practical or profitable. Also, by using text ads rather than banner ads, self-service advertising is easier for small businesses that do not have compelling graphical ads. Self-service advertising enables companies to carefully target very small groups. For example, Facebook allows advertisers to target "Americans who are married or engaged and are avid flyfishers."

Brand advertising relies on large advertising campaigns that emphasize the company's brand and utilize special features such as fan pages that are unique to Facebook and other social networking sites. Typically, a company that runs a brand advertising campaign on a social networking site will create a fan page for free. The advertising company pays the social networking site for premium ad placement that drives users to the fan page where they can interact with the brand.

With *performance-based advertising*, the advertising company pays only for measurable results—that is, when someone clicks on a company's ad and goes on to purchase something. Consider the University of Phoenix, an online higher education company. The university places precisely targeted ads on Facebook. The right sorts of people view the ads, click on them, and sign up for online courses. Facebook is paid only when customers actually enroll for classes.

Impression-based advertising occurs when a company purchases a set amount of impressions. An *impression* is a single instance of an ad appearing on a Web site. Impression-based advertising is typically cheaper than *click-through advertising*, where a company pays only when someone clicks on its ad.

Issues in E-Tailing

Despite e-tailing's increasing popularity, many e-tailers continue to face serious issues that can restrict their growth. Perhaps the two major issues are channel conflict and order fulfillment.

Clicks-and-mortar companies may face a conflict with their regular distributors when they sell directly to customers online. This situation, known as **channel conflict**, can alienate the distributors. Channel conflict has forced some companies to avoid direct online sales. For example, Walmart, Lowe's, and Home Depot would rather have customers come to their stores. Therefore, although all three companies maintain e-commerce Web sites, their sites place more emphasis on providing information—products, prices, specials, and store locations—than on online sales.

Channel conflict can arise in areas such as pricing and resource allocation—for example, how much money to spend on advertising. Another potential source of conflict involves the logistics services provided by the offline activities to the online activities. For example, how should a company handle returns of items purchased online? Some companies have completely separated the "clicks" (the online portion of the organization) from the "mortar" or "bricks" (the traditional bricks-and-mortar part of the organization). However, this approach can increase expenses and reduce the synergy between the two organizational channels. As a result, many companies are integrating their online and offline channels, a process known as **multichanneling**. "IT's About Business 9.3" illustrates how the online channel is causing problems for the Hong Kong Jockey Club.

IT's ABOUT BUSINESS | 9.3

Hong Kong's Jockey Club in a Race

 For decades, the Hong Kong Jockey Club (www.hkjc.com) has been at the peak of politics, business, and society in one of the world's richest cities. In Hong Kong, clubs are at the center of high society. But the Jockey Club, established in 1884 under British rule, has stood apart from the rest of the clubs as a money-maker. The club, a nonprofit organization, enjoys a government-granted monopoly on horse racing and lotteries. In turn, it is Hong Kong's single-largest taxpayer, accounting for approximately 8 percent of the government's total revenues.

In the year that ended in March 2010, Jockey Club customers bet approximately $15 billion. Some 82 percent was returned to winning betters as dividends and payouts. The club claimed the remaining $2.7 billion as revenue, and it paid 64 percent of this total ($1.7 billion) to the government. That is one of the highest tax rates for the industry, and it is part of the bargain struck decades ago when the government legalized betting. The Jockey Club claims it spent another $193 million on charity, and it employed almost 27,000 full- and part-time employees, making it one of the largest private employers in Hong Kong.

Over the course of its existence, the Jockey Club has survived equine flu, the Japanese occupation, bribery scandals, and the end of British colonial rule.

Now the club must cope with its biggest challenge yet: the Internet. Although its members still gather at the club's two tracks to bet on the races, a growing share of the money wagered is bypassing the club in favor of unauthorized betting Web sites. In short, the club's competitiveness is at risk due to the Internet.

Unauthorized bookmakers take bets on Hong Kong horse races equal to somewhere between 33 percent and 100 percent of the club's receipts, according to estimates by the club itself. Further, because betting sites pay neither Hong Kong taxes nor track expenses, they can offer more attractive odds. Many of these sites are based in overseas locations such as the South Pacific island of Vanuatu and Curacao in the Caribbean, so authorities are powerless to go after them.

The Jockey Club is no stranger to the Internet. Some 35 percent of the club's bets on horse racing now come through its Web site or mobile devices. The club's solid reputation as Hong Kong's only track operator could help it build its online business because many gamblers may not trust unregulated Web sites.

Another option for the club to fight online bookmakers is to link up with racing courses elsewhere to pool bets, a system that lets track operators offer better odds because more money is at stake. In Hong Kong, however, the Jockey Club's overseas revenue would be taxed both at home and in the country where the bet was made, eliminating any profit. To solve this problem, the Hong Kong government would have to consider a change in its tax policy.

Questions

1. What competitive advantages does the Hong Kong Jockey Club already have in its competition with online betting Web sites?

2. Use specific examples to describe other measures that the Hong Kong Jockey Club might take to compete with online betting Web sites.

Sources: Compiled from "For Hong Kong's Jockey Club, the Race is Online," *Bloomberg BusinessWeek*, February 21–27, 2011; S. Oster, "Scandal Hits Hong Kong's Exclusive Jockey Club," *Wall Street Journal*, December 2, 2010; www.hkjc.com, accessed March 19, 2011.

The second major issue confronting e-commerce is order fulfillment, which can create problems for e-tailers as well. Any time a company sells directly to customers, it is involved in various order-fulfillment activities. It must perform the following activities: quickly find the products to be shipped; pack them; arrange for the packages to be delivered speedily to the customer's door; collect the money from every customer, either in advance, by COD, or by individual bill; and handle the return of unwanted or defective products.

It is very difficult to accomplish these activities both effectively and efficiently in B2C because a company has to ship small packages to many customers and do it quickly. For this reason, companies involved in B2C activities often experience difficulties in their supply chains.

In addition to providing customers with the products they ordered and doing it on time, order fulfillment also provides all related customer services. For example, the customer must receive assembly and operation instructions for a new appliance. In addition, if the customer is not happy with a product, an exchange or return must be arranged. (Visit www.fedex.com to see how returns are handled via FedEx.)

In the late 1990s, e-tailers faced continuous problems in order fulfillment, especially during the holiday season. These problems included late deliveries, delivering wrong items, high delivery costs, and compensation to unhappy customers. For e-tailers, taking orders over the Internet is the easy part of B2C e-commerce. Delivering orders to customers' doors is the hard part. In contrast, order fulfillment is less complicated in B2B. These transactions are much larger, but they are fewer in number. In addition, these companies have had order fulfillment mechanisms in place for many years.

BEFORE *YOU GO ON . . .*

1. Describe electronic storefronts and malls.
2. Discuss various types of online services, such as cyberbanking, securities trading, job searches, travel services, and so on.
3. Discuss online advertising, its methods, and its benefits.
4. Identify the major issues relating to e-tailing.
5. What are spamming, permission marketing, and viral marketing?

RUBY'S CLUB QUESTIONS

1. Would it make sense for Ruby's Club to have a presence in an electronic mall? Why or why not?
2. How might Ruby's use multichanneling since most of its online customers would also be in the same geographical area?

Student Activity | 9.2

Objective: To familiarize you with business-to-consumer e-commerce and viral marketing.

Chapter Connection: This activity relates to Section 9.2 of this chapter, which focuses on the customer side of e-commerce.

Prerequisites: You should have read Sections 5.1 and 5.2 before doing this activity.

Activity:

At this point in your buying career, you have probably bought something online, gone to an auction site and possibly won a bid, and done online banking. Your generation is very comfortable with the retail side of e-commerce.

You are getting e-mails promoting a product, you see pop-up ads promoting products, you see ads when you search. Companies now want you to do their advertising for them. Watch this video on viral marketing: www.5min.com/Video/How-to-sell-soap---about-viral-marketing-1107.

Deliverable:

Bennett's BBQ restaurant, B's BBQ, also has a catering business. Write a paper explaining how Bennett might use viral marketing to increase his sales. Explain what Bennett would have to do to conduct this type of online marketing.

Quiz Questions:

1. True or False? Viral marketing uses direct marketing materials.
2. True or False? Viral marketing results in improved sales.
3. True or False? Viral marketing can be online or offline.

Discussion Questions:

Why are businesses putting their products in online auctions? What is the benefit of doing so?

9.3 | Business-to-Business (B2B) Electronic Commerce

In *business to business (B2B)* e-commerce, the buyers and sellers are business organizations. B2B comprises about 85 percent of EC volume. It covers a broad spectrum of applications that enable an enterprise to form electronic relationships with its distributors, resellers, suppliers, customers, and other partners. Organizations can use B2B to restructure their supply chains and their partner relationships.

B2B applications utilize any of several business models. The major models are sell-side marketplaces, buy-side marketplaces, and electronic exchanges.

Sell-Side Marketplaces

In the **sell-side marketplace** model, organizations attempt to sell their products or services to other organizations electronically from their own private e-marketplace Web site and/or from a third-party Web site. This model is similar to the B2C model in which the buyer is expected to come to the seller's site, view catalogs, and place an order. In the B2B sell-side marketplace, however, the buyer is an organization.

The key mechanisms in the sell-side model are electronic catalogs that can be customized for each large buyer and forward auctions. Sellers such as Dell Computer (www.dellauction.com) use auctions extensively. In addition to conducting auctions from their own Web sites, organizations can use third-party auction sites, such as eBay, to liquidate items. Companies such as Ariba (www.ariba.com) are helping organizations to auction old assets and inventories.

The sell-side model is used by hundreds of thousands of companies. It is especially powerful for companies with superb reputations. The seller can be either a manufacturer (for example, Dell or IBM), a distributor (for example, www.avnet.com), or a retailer (for example, www.bigboxx.com). The seller uses EC to increase sales, reduce selling and advertising expenditures, increase delivery speed, and lower administrative costs. The sell-side model is especially suitable to customization. Many companies allow their customers to configure their orders online. For example, at Dell (www.dell.com), you can determine the exact type of computer that you want. You can choose the type of chip (for example, Itanium 2), the size of the hard drive (for example, 1 terabyte), the type of monitor (for example, 22-inch flat screen), and so on. Similarly, the Jaguar Web site (www.jaguar.com) allows you to customize the Jaguar you want. Self-customization greatly reduces any misunderstandings concerning what customers want, and it encourages businesses to fill orders more quickly.

Buy-Side Marketplaces

The **buy-side marketplace** is a model in which organizations attempt to buy needed products or services from other organizations electronically. A major method of buying goods and services in the buy-side model is the reverse auction.

The buy-side model uses EC technology to streamline the purchasing process. The goal is to reduce both the costs of items purchased and the administrative expenses involved in purchasing them. In addition, EC technology can shorten the purchasing cycle time. Procurement includes purchasing goods and materials as well as sourcing (finding goods), negotiating with suppliers, paying for goods, and making delivery arrangements. Organizations now use the Internet to accomplish all of these functions.

Purchasing by using electronic support is referred to as **e-procurement**. E-procurement uses reverse auctions, particularly group purchasing. In **group purchasing**, multiple buyers combine their orders so that they constitute a large volume and therefore attract more seller attention. In addition, when buyers place their combined orders on a reverse auction, they can negotiate a volume discount. Typically, the orders of small buyers are aggregated by a third-party vendor, such as the United Sourcing Alliance (www.usa-llc.com).

Electronic Exchanges

Private exchanges have one buyer and many sellers. E-marketplaces, called **public exchanges** or just **exchanges**, are independently owned by a third-party and connect many sellers and many buyers. Public exchanges are open to all business organizations. They frequently are owned and operated by a third party. Public exchange managers provide all the necessary information systems to the participants. Thus, buyers and sellers merely have to "plug in" in order to trade. B2B public exchanges are often the initial point for contacts between business partners. Once the partners make contact, they may move to a private exchange or to private trading rooms provided by many public exchanges to conduct their subsequent trading activities.

Some electronic exchanges deal in direct materials, and others in indirect materials. *Direct materials* are inputs to the manufacturing process, such as safety glass used in automobile windshields and windows. *Indirect materials* are those items, such as office supplies, that are needed for maintenance, operations, and repairs (MRO). There are three basic types of public exchanges: vertical, horizontal, and functional. All three types offer diversified support services, ranging from payments to logistics.

Vertical exchanges connect buyers and sellers in a given industry. Examples of vertical exchanges are www.plasticsnet.com in the plastics industry, www.papersite.com in the paper industry, www.chemconnect.com in the chemical industry, and www.isteelasia.com in the steel industry.

Vertical exchanges are frequently owned and managed by a *consortium*, a term for a group of major players in an industry. For example, Marriott and Hyatt own a procurement consortium for the hotel industry, and ChevronTexaco owns an energy e-marketplace. The vertical e-marketplaces offer services that are particularly suited to the community they serve.

Horizontal exchanges connect buyers and sellers across many industries and are used primarily for MRO materials. Examples of horizontal exchanges are EcEurope (www.eceurope.com), Globalsources (www.globalsources.com), and Alibaba (www.alibaba.com).

In *functional exchanges*, needed services such as temporary help or extra office space are traded on an "as-needed" basis. For example, Employease (www.employease.com) can find temporary labor by searching employers in its Employease Network.

·BEFORE *YOU GO ON* . . .

1. Briefly differentiate between the sell-side marketplace and the buy-side marketplace.
2. Briefly differentiate among vertical exchanges, horizontal exchanges, and functional exchanges.

Student Activity | 9.3

Objective: To understand how B2B differs from other forms of e-business.

Chapter Connection: This activity relates to Section 9.3 of the text.

Prerequisites: Students should have read Sections 5.1, 5.2, and 5.3 before doing this activity.

Activity:

The text talks about the sell-side of B2B and the buy-side of B2B. Let us start out by thinking about the buyer's behavior by watching this video:

http://video.blogmyway.org/video/How-Customers-Think-the-B2B-and

Also read this article on the difference between B2B and B2C:

www.yourdictionary.com/answers/what/difference-between-b2-b-and-b2-c.html

Complete your research by looking at two Exchange sites mentioned in the text:

www.papersite.com

www.worldbid.com

Deliverables:

Write a two- to three-page paper that addresses the following:

1. In B2B the customer is another business. In B2C the customer is the ultimate consumer. Can a business be both a B2B and B2C company?

2. Outline the differences in sales and marketing between a B2B and B2C company.

3. Why do exchanges work?

4. Why do maintenance, operations, and repair supplies work best in Horizontal exchanges like www.worldbid.com?

5. When you look at these sites, what differences do you see between them and sites you look at like Amazon.com and BestBuy.com?

Quiz Questions:

1. True or False? Buying decisions in a B2C model use emotion and no logic.

2. True or False? Buying decisions in a B2B model are based entirely on logic.

3. Two questions a buyer in a B2B purchase would be asking are
   (a) When can I get it?
   (b) Will it make me money?
   (c) Will it save me money?
   (d) A and C
   (e) B and C

4. True or False? Target markets are the same for B2B and B2C sales.

5. With _____ sales, the sale is almost instantaneous.
   (a) B2C
   (b) B2B

(c) Both B2C and B2B

(d) Neither B2C nor B2B

6. True or False? The length of time that is required to complete a sale is the same in both B2C and B2B.

Discussion Questions:

1. Is eBay an exchange based on the text definition (not originally when it was C2C, but many businesses are now posting product in eBay)?

2. What about craigslist?

9.4 | Electronic Payments

Implementing EC typically requires electronic payments. **Electronic payment systems** enable buyers to pay for goods and services electronically, rather than writing a check or using cash. Payments are an integral part of doing business, whether in the traditional manner or online. Traditional payment systems have typically involved cash and/ or checks.

In most cases, traditional payment systems are not effective for EC, especially for B2B. Cash cannot be used because there is no face-to-face contact between buyer and seller. Not everyone accepts credit cards or checks, and some buyers do not have credit cards or checking accounts. Finally, contrary to what many people believe, it may be *less* secure for the buyer to use the telephone or mail to arrange or send payments, especially from another country, than to complete a secured transaction on a computer. For all of these reasons, a better way is needed to pay for goods and services in cyberspace. This better method is electronic payment systems. Let us now take a closer look at four types of electronic payment: electronic checks, electronic credit cards, purchasing cards, and electronic cash.

Electronic Checks

Electronic checks (*e-checks*) are similar to regular paper checks. They are used primarily in B2B. A customer who wishes to use e-checks must first establish a checking account with a bank. Then, when the customer buys a product or a service, he or she e-mails an encrypted electronic check to the seller. The seller deposits the check in a bank account, and funds are transferred from the buyer's account into the seller's account.

Like regular checks, e-checks carry a signature (in digital form) that can be verified (see www.authorize.net). Properly signed and endorsed e-checks are exchanged between financial institutions through electronic clearinghouses. (See www.eccho.org and www.troygroup.com for details.)

Electronic Credit Cards

Electronic credit (*e-credit*) *cards* allow customers to charge online payments to their credit card account. These cards are used primarily in B2C and in shopping by small-to-medium enterprises (SMEs). Here is how e-credit cards work (see Figure 9.4).

- Step 1: When you buy a book from Amazon, for example, your credit card information and purchase amount are encrypted in your browser. This way the information is safe while it is "traveling" on the Internet to Amazon.

- Step 2: When your information arrives at Amazon, it is not opened. Rather, it is transferred automatically (in encrypted form) to a *clearinghouse*, where it is decrypted for verification and authorization.

- Step 3: The clearinghouse asks the bank that issued you your credit card (the card issuer bank) to verify your credit card information.

- Step 4: Your card issuer bank verifies your credit card information and reports this to the clearinghouse.

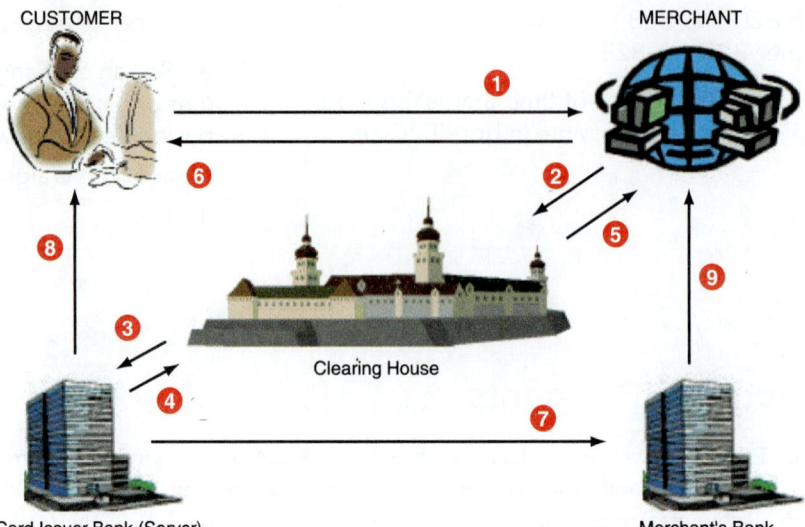

CUSTOMER   MERCHANT

Clearing House

Card Issuer Bank (Server)   Merchant's Bank

Figure 9.4 How e-credit cards work. (The numbers 1–9 indicate the sequence of activities.)

- Step 5: The clearinghouse reports the result of the verification of your credit card to Amazon.
- Step 6: Amazon reports a successful purchase and amount to you.
- Step 7: Your card issuer bank sends funds in the amount of the purchase to Amazon's bank.
- Step 8: Your card issuer bank notifies you (either electronically or in your monthly statement) of the debit on your credit card.
- Step 9: Amazon's bank notifies Amazon of the funds credited to its account.

Several major credit card issuers are offering customers the option of shopping online with *virtual, single-use credit card numbers* (see Figure 9.5). The goal is to thwart criminals by using a different, random card number every time you shop online. A virtual number is good only on the Web site where you make your purchase. An online purchase made with a virtual card number shows up on your bill just like any other purchase.

Purchasing Cards

The B2B equivalent of electronic credit cards is *purchasing cards* (see Figure 9.6). In some countries, purchasing cards are the primary form of payment between companies. Unlike credit cards, where credit is provided for 30 to 60 days (for free) before payment is made to the merchant, payments made with purchasing cards are settled within a week.

Purchasing cards typically are used for unplanned B2B purchases, and corporations generally limit the amount per purchase, usually $1,000 to $2,000. Purchasing cards can be used on the Internet, much like regular credit cards.

Figure 9.5 Example of virtual credit card.

Figure 9.6 Example of purchasing card. (*Source:* Mike Clarke/AFP/GettyImages/NewsCom)

Electronic Cash

Despite the growth of credit cards, cash remains the most common mode of payment in offline transactions. However, many EC sellers, and some buyers, prefer electronic cash. *Electronic cash* (*e-cash*) appears in three major forms: stored-value money cards, smart cards, and person-to-person payments.

Stored-Value Money Cards. Although **stored-value money cards** resemble credit cards, they actually are a form of e-cash. The cards that you use to pay for photocopies in your library, for transportation, and for telephone calls are stored-value money cards. They are called "stored-value" because they allow you to store a fixed amount of prepaid money and then spend it as necessary. Each time you use the card, the amount is reduced by the amount you spent. Figure 9.7 shows a New York City Metro (subway and bus) card.

Smart Cards. Although some people refer to stored-value money cards as "smart cards," they are not really the same. True **smart cards** contain a chip that can store a considerable amount of information—more than a hundred times that of a stored-value money card (see Figure 9.8). Smart cards are frequently multipurpose—that is, you can use them as a credit card, a debit card, a stored-value money card, or a loyalty card. Smart cards are ideal for *micropayments*, which are small payments of a few dollars or less.

Person-to-Person Payments. **Person-to-person payments** are a form of e-cash that enables two individuals, or an individual and a business, to transfer funds without using a credit card. Person-to-person payments can be used for a variety of purposes, such as sending money to students at college, paying for an item purchased at an online auction, or sending a gift to a family member.

One of the first companies to offer this service was PayPal (an eBay company). Today, AOL QuickCash, and One's Bank eMoneyMail, and all compete with PayPal.

Virtually all of these person-to-person payment services work in a similar way. First, you select a service and open up an account. Basically, this process entails creating a user name, selecting a password, and providing the service with a credit card or bank account number. Next, you transfer funds from your credit card or bank account to your new

Figure 9.7 The New York City Metro card. (*Source:* © Clarence HolmesPhotography/AlamyLimited)

Figure 9.8 Smart cards are frequently multipurpose. (*Source:* © MARKA/Alamy Limited)

account. Now you are ready to send money to someone over the Internet. You access the service—for example, PayPal—with your user name and password, and you specify the e-mail address of the person to receive the money, along with the dollar amount that you want to send. The service then sends an e-mail to the payee's e-mail address. The e-mail contains a link back to the service's Web site. When the recipient clicks on the link, he or she is taken to the service. There, the recipient is asked to set up an account to which the money that you sent will be credited. The recipient can then credit the money from this account to either a credit card or a bank account. The service charges the payer a small amount, roughly $1 per transaction.

An attractive security feature of PayPal is that you have to put only enough money in the account to cover any upcoming transactions. Therefore, if anyone should gain access to your account, they will not have access to all of your money.

BEFORE *YOU GO ON . . .*

1. List the various electronic payment mechanisms. Which of these mechanisms are most often used for B2B payments?
2. What are micropayments?

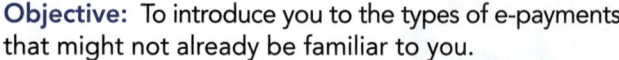

Student Activity | 9.4

Objective: To introduce you to the types of e-payments that might not already be familiar to you.

Chapter Connection: This activity relates to Section 9.4 in this chapter.

Prerequisites: You should have read Sections 9.2, 9.3, and 9.4 before doing this activity.

Activity:

Think about all of the times you have done electronic payments—debit card at the grocery store, a

contactless payment device at the gas station, a stored-value card for a metro transportation system, and, of course, PayPal online.

Go to the following Intuit site:

http://intuit-gopayment.com/gp?cid5ppc_google_GoPay-TopIPS-NB_electronic-payments_Exact&ef_id=2425:3:s_c48730c915275aa020e672aa17dc642a_6503146389:TIzidAqoEGQAADAKIugAAA0W:20100912142348

Then click on "View Demo."

Deliverables:

Write a one-page paper outlining how Bennett should use electronic payments for B's BBQ and what the advantages are to Bennett. If Bennett wanted to justify costs for such use, what savings do you think he would see?

Quiz Questions:

1. True or False? Electronic payments can only be used for online purchases.

2. True or False? A stored value card can be used like a credit card.

3. True or False? Online payment options are for the convenience of the consumer.

Discussion Questions:

1. Compile a list of all the electronic payments you make regularly. How many of these do you consciously think about? How many do you make without thinking?

2. Would you call for deliveries from a pizza shop that did not take credit/debit cards for the delivery? Why/why not? Would you care if you received a receipt?

9.5 | Ethical and Legal Issues in E-Business

Technological innovation often forces a society to reexamine and modify its ethical standards. In many cases the new standards are incorporated into law. In this section, you will learn about two important ethical considerations—privacy and job loss—as well as various legal issues arising from the practice of e-business.

Ethical Issues

Many of the ethical and global issues related to IT also apply to e-business. Here you will learn about two basic issues: privacy and job loss.

By making it easier to store and transfer personal information, e-business presents some threats to privacy. First, most electronic payment systems know who the buyers are. It may be necessary, then, to protect the buyers' identities. Businesses frequently use encryption to provide this protection.

Another major privacy issue is tracking. For example, individuals' activities on the Internet can be tracked by cookies (discussed in Chapter 7). Cookies store your tracking history on your personal computer's hard drive, and any time you revisit a certain Web site, the server recognizes the cookie (see http://netinsight.unica.com). In response, antivirus software packages routinely search for potentially harmful cookies.

In addition to compromising individual privacy, the use of EC may eliminate the need for some of a company's employees, as well as brokers and agents. The manner in which these unneeded workers, especially employees, are treated can raise ethical issues: How should the company handle the layoffs? Should companies be required to retrain employees for new positions? If not, how should the company compensate or otherwise assist the displaced workers?

Legal and Ethical Issues Specific to E-Commerce

There are many legal issues that are related specifically to e-commerce. When buyers and sellers do not know one another and cannot even see one another, there is a chance that dishonest people will commit fraud and other crimes. During the first few years of EC, the public witnessed many such crimes. These illegal actions ranged from creating a virtual bank that disappeared along with the investors' deposits to manipulating stock prices on the Internet. Unfortunately, fraudulent activities on the Internet are increasing. In the following section, you explore some of the major legal issues that are specific to e-commerce.

Fraud on the Internet. Internet fraud has grown even faster than Internet use itself. In one case, stock promoters falsely spread positive rumors about the prospects of the companies they touted in order to boost the stock price. In other cases the information provided might have been true, but the promoters did not disclose that they were paid to talk up the companies. Stock promoters specifically target small investors who are lured by the promise of fast profits.

Stocks are only one of many areas where swindlers are active. Auctions are especially conducive to fraud, by both sellers and buyers. Other types of fraud include selling bogus investments and setting up phantom business opportunities. Due to the growing use of e-mail, financial criminals now have access to many more people. The U.S. Federal Trade Commission (FTC, www.ftc.gov) regularly publishes examples of scams that are most likely to be spread via e-mail or to be found on the Web. Later in this section you will see some ways in which consumers and sellers can protect themselves from online fraud.

Domain Names. Another legal issue is competition over domain names. Domain names are assigned by central nonprofit organizations that check for conflicts and possible infringement of trademarks. Obviously, companies that sell goods and services over the Internet want customers to be able to find them easily. In general, the closer the domain name matches the company's name, the easier the company is to locate.

A domain name is considered to be legal when the person or business who owns the name has operated a legitimate business under that name for some time. Companies such as Christian Dior, Nike, Deutsche Bank, and even Microsoft have had to fight or pay to get the domain name that corresponds to their company's name. Consider the case of Delta Air Lines. Delta originally could not obtain the Internet domain name delta.com because Delta Faucet had purchased it first. Delta Faucet had been in business under that name since 1954 and therefore had a legitimate business interest in the domain name. Delta Air Lines had to settle for delta-airlines.com until it bought the domain name from Delta Faucet. Delta Faucet is now at deltafaucet.com. Several cases of disputed domain names are already in court.

Cybersquatting. **Cybersquatting** refers to the practice of registering or using domain names for the purpose of profiting from the goodwill or the trademark that belongs to someone else. The Anti-Cybersquatting Consumer Protection Act (1999) permits trademark owners in the United States to sue for damages in such cases.

However, some practices that could be considered cybersquatting are not illegal, although they may well be unethical. Perhaps the more common of these practices is "domain tasting." Domain tasting lets registrars profit from the complex money trail of pay-per-click advertising. The practice can be traced back to the policies of the organization responsible for regulating Web names, the Internet Corporation for Assigned Names and Numbers

Figure 9.9 Internet Corporation for Assigned Names and Numbers (ICANN) Web site (*Source:* www.icann.org).

(ICANN) (www.icann.org). In 2000, ICANN established the "create grace period," a five-day period during which a company or person can claim a domain name and then return it for a full refund of the $6 registry fee. ICANN implemented this policy to allow someone who mistyped a domain to return it without cost. In some cases, companies engage in cybersquatting by registering domain names that are very similar to their competitors' domain names in order to generate traffic from people who misspell Web addresses.

Domain tasters exploit this policy by claiming Internet domains for five days at no cost. These domain names frequently resemble those of prominent companies and organizations. The tasters then jam these domains full of advertisements that come from Yahoo! and Google. Because this process involves zero risk and 100 percent profit margins, domain tasters register millions of domain names every day—some of them over and over again. Experts estimate that registrants ultimately purchase less than 2 percent of the sites they sample. In the vast majority of cases, they use the domain names for only a few days to generate quick profits.

Humorous - but not true. Most laws only allow copyright for a specified period. (*Source:* www. CartoonStock.com)

Taxes and Other Fees. In offline sales, most states and localities tax business transactions that are conducted within their jurisdiction. The most obvious example is sales taxes. Federal, state, and local authorities now are scrambling to create some type of taxation policy for e-business. This problem is particularly complex for interstate and international e-commerce. For example, some people claim that the state in which the *seller* is located deserves the entire sales tax (in some countries, it is a value-added tax, or VAT). Others contend that the state in which the *server* is located also should receive some of the tax revenues.

In addition to the sales tax, there is a question about where—and in some cases, whether—electronic sellers should pay business license taxes, franchise fees, gross-receipts taxes, excise taxes, privilege taxes, and utility taxes. Furthermore, how should tax collection be controlled? Legislative efforts to impose taxes on e-commerce are opposed by an organization named the Internet Freedom Fighters. So far, their efforts have been successful. As of mid-2011, the United States and several other countries had imposed a ban on imposing a sales tax on business conducted on the Internet. In addition, buyers were exempt from any tax on Internet access.

Copyright. Recall from Chapter 6 that intellectual property is protected by copyright laws and cannot be used freely. This point is significant because many people mistakenly believe that once they purchase a piece of software, they have the right to share it with others. In fact, what they have bought is the right to *use* the software, not the right to *distribute* it. That right remains with the copyright holder. Similarly, copying material from Web sites without permission is a violation of copyright laws. Protecting intellectual property rights in e-commerce is extremely difficult, however, because it involves hundreds of millions of people in some 200 countries with differing copyright laws who have access to billions of Web pages.

▸ BEFORE *YOU GO ON . . .*

1. List and explain some ethical issues in EC.
2. Discuss the major legal issues of EC.
3. Describe buyer protection and seller protection in EC.

RUBY'S CLUB QUESTIONS

1. Describe the privacy issues that Ruben and Lisa must consider before they use PayPal.
2. Which of the payment forms (electronic checks, electronic cards, etc.) do you recommend that Ruben and Lisa use?

Student Activity | 9.5

Objective: This activity addresses some legal issues specific to e-Commerce.

Chapter Connection: This activity relates to Section 9.5: Ethical and Legal Issue in e-Commerce.

Prerequisites: You should have read Section 9.5 before doing this activity.

Activity:

Read "Case 1: Security" and its related questions at the following link:

http://www2.harpercollege.edu/~tmorris/ekin/case1.htm

The Web site refers to this as a group assignment, but for us it is an individual assignment.

Deliverables:

Write a two- to three-page paper that addresses the questions.

Quiz Questions:

1. E-Kin's CIO is worried about implementing the Web site so early because:
   (a) He is worried that it might not work.
   (b) He is worried that the timing might not be right.
   (c) He is worried that it will not be secure.
   (d) He is worried that it will not bring in enough revenue.
   (e) All of the above.

2. E-Kin's sales and marketing director wants to release the e-commerce option early so that:
   (a) The company can open into new markets.
   (b) The company can realize a huge revenue increase for the short term and long term.
   (c) The company will lose customers to competitors with an e-commerce feature on their site.
   (d) The company can attract angel investors.
   (e) All of the above.

3. Which of the following is *not* an issue that could result if the site is rolled out and is not secure?
   (a) Bad press
   (b) Run out of inventory
   (c) Lost customers and customer loyalty
   (d) Company's reputation
   (e) Stealing of customer information

Discussion Questions:

How would you feel about a delivery person swiping your card on a mobile device attached to a cell phone? What issues would that raise for you?

What's in **IT** for ME?

FOR THE ACCOUNTING MAJOR

Accounting personnel are involved in several EC activities. Designing the ordering system and its relationship with inventory management requires accounting attention. Billing and payments are also accounting activities, as are determining cost and profit allocation. Replacing paper documents with electronic means will affect many of the accountant's tasks, especially the auditing of EC activities and systems. Finally, building a cost-benefit and cost-justification system to determine which products/services to take online and creating a chargeback system are critical to the success of EC.

FOR THE FINANCE MAJOR

 The worlds of banking, securities and commodities markets, and other financial services are being reengineered due to EC. Online securities trading and its supporting infrastructure are growing more rapidly than any other EC activity. Many innovations already in place are changing the rules of economic and financial incentives for financial analysts and managers. Online banking, for example, does not recognize state boundaries, and it may create a new framework for financing global trades. Public financial information is now accessible in seconds. These innovations will dramatically change the manner in which finance personnel operate.

FOR THE MARKETING MAJOR

 A major revolution in marketing and sales is taking place due to EC. Perhaps its most obvious feature is the transition from a physical to a virtual marketplace. Equally important, though, is the radical transformation to one-on-one advertising and sales and to customized and interactive marketing. Marketing channels are being combined, eliminated, or recreated. The EC revolution is creating new products and markets and significantly altering existing ones. Digitization of products and services also has implications for marketing and sales. The direct producer-to-consumer channel is expanding rapidly and is fundamentally changing the nature of customer service. As the battle for customers intensifies, marketing and sales personnel are becoming the most critical success factor in many organizations. Online marketing can be a blessing to one company and a curse to another.

FOR THE PRODUCTION/OPERATIONS MANAGEMENT MAJOR

 EC is changing the manufacturing system from product-push mass production to order-pull mass customization. This change requires a robust supply chain, information support, and reengineering of processes that involve suppliers and other business partners. Suppliers can use extranets to monitor and replenish inventories without the need for constant reorders. In addition, the Internet and intranets help reduce cycle times. Many production/operations problems that have persisted for years, such as complex scheduling and excess inventories, are being solved rapidly with the use of Web technologies. Companies can now use external and internal networks to find and manage manufacturing operations in other countries much more easily. Also, the Web is reengineering procurement by helping companies conduct electronic bids for parts and subassemblies, thus reducing cost. All in all, the job of the progressive production/operations manager is closely tied in with e-commerce.

FOR THE HUMAN RESOURCES MANAGEMENT MAJOR

 HR majors need to understand the new labor markets and the impacts of EC on old labor markets. Also, the HR department may use EC tools for such functions as procuring office supplies. Also, becoming knowledgeable about new government online initiatives and online training is critical. In addition, HR personnel must be familiar with the major legal issues related to EC and employment.

FOR THE MIS MAJOR

 The MIS function is responsible for providing the information technology infrastructure necessary for electronic commerce to function. In particular, this infrastructure includes the company's networks, intranets, and extranets. The MIS function is also responsible for ensuring that electronic commerce transactions are secure.

>>> SUMMARY

1. Describe the six common types of electronic commerce; provide specific *personal* examples of how you have used or could use B2C, C2C, G2C, and mobile commerce; and offer a specific example of B2B and G2B.

In *business-to-consumer* (B2C) electronic commerce, the sellers are organizations and the buyers are individuals. In *business-to-business* (B2B) electronic commerce, the sellers and the buyers are businesses. In *consumer-to-consumer* (C2C) electronic commerce, an individual sells products or services to other individuals. In *business-to-employee* (B2E) electronic commerce, an organization uses EC internally to provide information and services to its employees. *E-government* is the use of Internet technology in general and e-commerce in particular to deliver information and public services to citizens (called government-to-citizen or G2C EC) and business partners and suppliers (called government-to-business or G2B EC). *Mobile commerce* refers to e-commerce that is conducted entirely in a wireless environment. We leave the examples of each type to you.

2. Discuss the five online services of business-to-consumer electronic commerce, provide a specific example of each service, and state how you have used or would use each service.

Electronic banking, also known as cyberbanking, involves conducting various banking activities from home, at a place of business, or on the road instead of at a physical bank location.

Online securities trading involves buying and selling securities over the Web.

Online job matching over the Web offers a promising environment for job seekers and for companies searching for hard-to-find employees. Thousands of companies and government agencies advertise available positions, accept resumes, and take applications via the Internet.

Online travel services allow you to purchase airline tickets, reserve hotel rooms, and rent cars. Most sites also offer a fare-tracker feature that sends you e-mail messages about low-cost flights. The Internet is an ideal place to plan, explore, and arrange almost any trip economically.

Online advertising over the Web makes the advertising process media-rich, dynamic, and interactive.

We leave the examples to you.

3. Describe the three business models for business-to-business electronic commerce, and provide a specific example of each model.

In the *sell-side marketplace* model, organizations attempt to sell their products or services to other organizations electronically

from their own private e-marketplace Web site and/or from a third-party Web site. Sellers such as Dell Computer (www.dellauction.com) use sell-side auctions extensively. In addition to auctions from their own Web sites, organizations can use third-party auction sites, such as eBay, to liquidate items.

The *buy-side marketplace* is a model in which organizations attempt to buy needed products or services from other organizations electronically.

E-marketplaces, in which there are many sellers and many buyers, are called *public exchanges*, or just exchanges. Public exchanges are open to all business organizations. They frequently are owned and operated by a third party. There are three basic types of public exchanges: vertical, horizontal, and functional. *Vertical exchanges* connect buyers and sellers in a given industry (e.g., www.plasticsnet.com in the plastics industry). *Horizontal exchanges* connect buyers and sellers across many industries (e.g., EcEurope, www.eceurope.com). In *functional exchanges*, needed services such as temporary help or extra office space are traded on an "as-needed" basis (e.g., Employease, www.employease.com).

4. Describe the four types of electronic payments, provide a specific example of each one, and explain whether you would use each type.

Electronic checks (*e-checks*) are similar to regular paper checks. They are used mostly in B2B.

Electronic credit (*e-credit*) *cards* allow customers to charge online payments to their credit card account. Electronic credit cards are used primarily in B2C and in shopping by small-to-medium enterprises.

The B2B equivalent of electronic credit cards is *purchasing cards*. Unlike credit cards, where credit is provided for 30 to 60 days (for free) before payment is made to the merchant, payments made with purchasing cards are settled within a week. Purchasing cards typically are used for unplanned B2B purchases, and corporations generally limit the amount per purchase (usually $1,000 to $2,000).

Electronic cash (*e-cash*) appears in four major forms: stored-value money cards, smart cards, person-to-person payments, and digital wallets. Although they resemble credit cards, *stored-value money cards* allow you to store a fixed amount of prepaid money and then spend it as necessary. Each time you use the card, the amount is reduced by the amount you spent. *Smart cards* contain a chip that can store a considerable amount of information. You can use them as a credit card, a debit card, or a stored-value money card. *Person-to-person payments* enable two individuals or an individual and a business to transfer funds without using a credit card. **Digital wallets** (or **e-wallets**) are software mechanisms that provide security measures, combined with convenience, to EC purchasing. The wallet stores the financial information of the buyer, such as credit card number, shipping information, and so on. Thus, the buyer does not need to reenter sensitive information for each purchase.

We leave the examples to you.

5. **Illustrate the ethical and legal issues relating to electronic commerce with two specific examples of each issue, and describe how you would respond or react to the four examples you have provided.**

E-business presents some threats to privacy. First, most electronic payment systems know who the buyers are. It may be necessary then to protect the buyers' identities with encryption. Another major privacy issue is tracking, where individuals' activities on the Internet can be tracked by cookies.

The use of EC may eliminate the need for some of a company's employees, as well as brokers and agents. The manner in which these unneeded workers, especially employees, are treated can raise ethical issues: How should the company handle the layoffs? Should companies be required to retrain employees for new positions? If not, how should the company compensate or otherwise assist the displaced workers?

We leave the descriptions to you.

>>> CHAPTER GLOSSARY

auction A competitive process in which either a seller solicits consecutive bids from buyers or a buyer solicits bids from sellers, and prices are determined dynamically by competitive bidding.

banners Electronic billboards, which typically contain a short text or graphical message to promote a product or a vendor.

brick-and-mortar organizations Organizations in which the product, the process, and the delivery agent are all physical.

business model The method by which a company generates revenue to sustain itself.

business-to-business electronic commerce (B2B) Electronic commerce in which both the sellers and the buyers are business organizations.

business-to-consumer electronic commerce (B2C) Electronic commerce in which the sellers are organizations and the buyers are individuals; also known as e-tailing.

business-to-employee electronic commerce (B2E) An organization using electronic commerce internally to provide information and services to its employees.

buy-side marketplace B2B model in which organizations buy needed products or services from other organizations electronically, often through a reverse auction.

channel conflict The alienation of existing distributors when a company decides to sell to customers directly online.

clicks-and-mortar organizations Organizations that do business in both the physical and digital dimensions.

consumer-to-consumer electronic commerce (C2C) Electronic commerce in which both the buyer and the seller are individuals (not businesses).

cyberbanking Various banking activities conducted electronically from home, a business, or on the road instead of at a physical bank location; also known as *electronic banking*.

cybersquatting Registering domain names in the hope of selling them later at a higher price.

digital wallets (e-wallets) Software components in which a user stores secured personal and credit card information for one-click reuse.

disintermediation Elimination of intermediaries in electronic commerce.

e-government The use of electronic commerce to deliver information and public services to citizens, business partners, and suppliers of government entities, and those working in the public sector.

electronic business (e-business) A broader definition of electronic commerce, including buying and selling of goods and services, and also servicing customers, collaborating with business partners, conducting e-learning, and conducting electronic transactions within an organization.

electronic commerce (EC or e-commerce) The process of buying, selling, transferring, or exchanging products, services, or information via computer networks, including the Internet.

electronic mall A collection of individual shops under one Internet address; also known as a *cybermall* or an *e-mall*.

electronic marketplace A virtual market space on the Web where many buyers and many sellers conduct electronic business activities.

electronic payment systems Computer-based systems that allow customers to pay for goods and services electronically, rather than writing a check or using cash.

electronic retailing (e-tailing) The direct sale of products and services through storefronts or electronic malls, usually designed around an electronic catalog format and/or auctions.

electronic storefront The Web site of a single company, with its own Internet address, at which orders can be placed.

e-procurement Purchasing by using electronic support.

e-wallets (see **digital wallets**)

exchanges (see **public exchanges**)

forward auctions Auctions that sellers use as a selling channel to many potential buyers; the highest bidder wins the items.

group purchasing The aggregation of purchasing orders from many buyers so that a volume discount can be obtained.

mobile commerce (m-commerce) Electronic commerce conducted in a wireless environment.

multichanneling A process in which a company integrates its online and offline channels.

permission marketing Method of marketing that asks consumers to give their permission to voluntarily accept online advertising and e-mail.

person-to-person payments A form of electronic cash that enables the transfer of funds between two individuals, or between an individual and a business, without the use of a credit card.

pop-under ad An advertisement that is automatically launched by some trigger and appears underneath the active window.

pop-up ad An advertisement that is automatically launched by some trigger and appears in front of the active window.

public exchanges (or **exchanges**) Electronic marketplace in which there are many sellers and many buyers, and entry is open to all; it is frequently owned and operated by a third party.

reverse auctions Auctions in which one buyer, usually an organization, seeks to buy a product or a service, and suppliers submit bids; the lowest bidder wins.

sell-side marketplace B2B model in which organizations sell to other organizations from their own private e-marketplace and/or from a third-party site.

smart cards Cards that contains a microprocessor (chip) that enables the card to store a considerable amount of information (including stored funds) and to conduct processing.

spamming Indiscriminate distribution of e-mail without the receiver's permission.

stored-value money cards A form of electronic cash on which a fixed amount of prepaid money is stored; the amount is reduced each time the card is used.

viral marketing Online word-of-mouth marketing.

virtual banks Banking institutions dedicated solely to Internet transactions.

virtual (or **pure play**) **organizations** Organizations in which the product, the process, and the delivery agent are all digital.

>>> DISCUSSION QUESTIONS

1. Discuss the major limitations of e-commerce. Which of these limitations are likely to disappear? Why?
2. Discuss the reasons for having multiple EC business models.
3. Distinguish between business-to-business forward auctions and buyers' bids for RFQs.
4. Discuss the benefits to sellers and buyers of a B2B exchange.
5. What are the major benefits of G2C electronic commerce?
6. Discuss the various ways to pay online in B2C. Which method(s) would you prefer and why?
7. Why is order fulfillment in B2C considered difficult?
8. Discuss the reasons for EC failures.
9. Should Mr. Coffee sell coffeemakers online? *Hint:* Take a look at the discussion of channel conflict in this chapter.
10. In some cases, individuals engage in cybersquatting so that they can sell the domain names to companies expensively. In other cases, companies engage in cybersquatting by registering domain names that are very similar to their competitors' domain names in order to generate traffic from people who misspell Web addresses. Discuss each practice in terms of its ethical nature and legality. Is there a difference between the two practices? Support your answer.

>>> PROBLEM-SOLVING ACTIVITIES

1. Assume you are interested in buying a car. You can find information about cars at numerous Web sites. Access five Web sites for information about new and used cars, financing, and insurance. Decide which car you want to buy. Configure your car by going to the car manufacturer's Web site. Finally, try to find the car from www.autobytel.com. What information is most supportive of your decision-making process? Write a report about your experience.

2. Compare the various electronic payment methods. Specifically, collect information from the vendors cited in this chapter, and find additional vendors using google.com. Pay attention to security level, speed, cost, and convenience.

3. Conduct a study on selling diamonds and gems online. Access such sites as www.bluenile.com, www.diamond.com, www.thaigem.com, www.tiffany.com, and www.jewelryexchange.com.

   a. What features do these sites use to educate buyers about gemstones?

   b. How do these sites attract buyers?

   c. How do these sites increase customers' trust in online purchasing?

   d. What customer service features do these sites provide?

4. Access www.nacha.org. What is NACHA? What is its role? What is the ACH? Who are the key participants in an ACH e-payment? Describe the "pilot" projects currently underway at ACH.

5. Access www.espn.com. Identify at least five different ways the site generates revenue.

6. Access www.queendom.com. Examine its offerings and try some of them. What type of electronic commerce is this? How does this Web site generate revenue?

7. Access www.ediets.com. Prepare a list of all the services the company provides. Identify its revenue model.

8. Access www.theknot.com. Identify the site's revenue sources.

9. Access www.mint.com. Identify the site's revenue model. What are the risks of giving this Web site your credit and debit card numbers, as well as your bank account number?

10. Research the case of www.nissan.com. Is Uzi Nissan cybersquatting? Why or why not? Support your answer. How is Nissan (the car company) reacting to the www.nissan.com Web site?

11. Access the Stock Market Game (www.smgww.org). You will be bankrolled with $100,000 in a trading account every month. Play the game, and relate your experiences with regard to information technology.

12. Enter www.alibaba.com. Identify the site's capabilities. Look at the site's private trading room. Write a report. How can such a site help a person who is making a purchase?

13. Enter www.campusfood.com. Explore the site. Why is the site so successful? Could you start a competing site? Why or why not?

14. Enter www.dell.com, go to "Desktops," and configure a system. Register to "My Cart" (no obligation). What calculators are used there? What are the advantages of this process as compared with buying a computer in a physical store? What are the disadvantages?

15. Enter www.checkfree.com and www.lmlpayment.com to identify their services. Prepare a report.

16. Access various travel sites such as www.travelocity.com, www.orbitz.com, www.expedia.com, www.kayak.com, and www.pinpoint.com. Compare these Web sites for ease of use and usefulness. Note differences among the sites. If you ask each site for the itinerary, which one gives you the best information and the best deals?

17. Access www.outofservice.com, and answer the musical taste and personality survey. When you have finished, click on "Results" and see what your musical tastes say about your personality. How accurate are the findings about you?

>>> TEAM ASSIGNMENTS

1. Assign each team to one industry vertical. (An industry vertical is a group of industries in the "same" business, such as financial services, insurance, healthcare, manufacturing, retail, telecommunications, pharmaceuticals and chemicals, and so on.) Each team will find five real-world applications of the major B2B models listed in this chapter. (Try success stories of vendors and EC-related magazines.) Examine the problems they solve or the opportunities they exploit.

2. Have teams investigate how B2B payments are made in global trade. Consider instruments such as electronic letters of credit and e-checks. Visit www.tradecard.com, and examine its services to small and medium-size enterprises (SMEs). Also, investigate what Visa and MasterCard are offering. Finally, check Citicorp and some German and Japanese banks.

CLOSING **CASE 1 >** The Flash Crash

On May 6, 2010, the U.S. stock market experienced a crash in which the Dow Jones Industrial Average lost almost 9 percent of its total value, only to recover those losses within minutes. It was the second-largest point swing—1,010.14 points—and the biggest one-day point decline—998.5 points—on an intraday basis in the history of Dow Jones. This crash became known as the Flash Crash.

That day, the market was already under pressure as a result of a massive debt crisis in Greece. Then, an automated sale of a large block of futures touched off a chain reaction of events. A mutual fund's computer program began selling $4.1 billion of futures contracts. A futures contract is an agreement, traded on an exchange, to buy or sell assets—particularly commodities or shares of stock—at a fixed price but to be delivered and paid for later.

Normally, a sale of this size would take place over as many as 5 hours. In this case, however, the sell algorithm installed on the mutual fund's computer placed 75,000 contracts on the market in 20 minutes. The algorithm was programmed to execute the trade "without regard to price or time," which meant that it continued to sell even as prices dropped rapidly.

Many of the contracts sold by the algorithm were purchased by high-frequency traders (HFTs). HFTs are computerized traders who buy and sell at high speed. They account for a large percentage of overall trading in today's markets. The HFT programs detected that they had amassed excessive "long" positions, meaning that they purchased stock with the expectation that its price would rise. They immediately began to sell these stocks aggressively, which in turn caused the mutual fund's algorithm to accelerate selling. As

<<<**THE BUSINESS PROBLEM**

the HFT and mutual fund programs traded contracts back and forth, they created a "hot potato" effect, where contracts changed hands 27,000 times in 14 seconds. Despite this frenzied trading, however, only 200 contracts were actually bought or sold. In most cases the same contracts moved back and forth between the mutual funds and the HFTs in microseconds.

The only buy orders originated from automated systems, which were submitting orders known as "stub quotes." Stub quotes are offers to buy stocks at prices so low that the purchasers are unlikely to ever be the only buyers of that stock. However, during the flash crash, the stub quotes were the only offers from buyers. When the only offer to buy available is a penny-priced stub quote, a market order, by definition, will buy the stock at that price. In this respect, automated trading systems will follow their algorithms regardless of the outcome. This process caused shares of some prominent companies, such as Procter & Gamble and Accenture, to trade down as low as a penny per share. Significantly, human involvement probably would have prevented these orders from executing at absurdly low prices.

A STOPGAP SOLUTION>>>

The U.S. Securities and Exchange Commission (SEC) responded to the crash by instituting, on all stocks in the S & P 500 stock index, circuit breakers—which halt trading in a stock for five minutes if the price moves by 10 percent or more in a five-minute period. After a short time, the SEC expanded the circuit breakers to include a broader range of stocks. However, no one knows if the circuit breakers can prevent any future "flash crash."

Lawmakers are proposing another possible solution: namely, enacting a small tax on each equity trade. Such a tax would likely discourage some high-frequency trading, slow the market's overall pace, and raise billions of dollars in revenue for the federal government. Some of the tax revenues could be used to enhance the SEC's monitoring efforts.

THE RESULTS>>>

The circuit breakers are in place, but the Flash Crash raises a larger question about the stock market. In recent years, the market has grown exponentially faster and more diverse. The primary venue for stock trading is no longer the New York Stock Exchange, but, rather, computer servers run by companies around the world. This diversity has made stock trading cheaper, which benefits both institutional and individual investors. Unfortunately, it has also made it more difficult to ensure an orderly market.

A major danger is that regulators, politicians, and industry leaders—already distracted by the major challenge of reforming Wall Street in the wake of the broader credit crisis of 2008—will shrug off the Flash Crash as an aberration requiring no fundamental rethinking of how human, machine, and market interact.

The bottom line? Wall Street's computer models tend to fail when unpredictable disasters overlap, meaning that flash crashes can happen again.

Questions

1. Do you think information technology has made it easier to do business? Or has IT only raised the bar on what is required to be able to conduct business in the 21st century? Support your answer with specific examples.

2. With the rise of electronic commerce, what do you think will happen to those without computer skills, Internet access, computers, smart phones, and so on. Will they be able to survive and advance by hard work?

SOURCES: Compiled from E. Macbride, "Flash Crash Update: Why the Multi-Asset Meltdown Is a Real Possibility," *Forbes*, March 2, 2011; Spicer, J. "Special Report: Globally, the Flash Crash Is No Flash in the Pan," *Reuters*, October 15, 2010; E. Lambert, "The Truth About the Flash Crash," *Forbes*, October 1, 2010; S. Schaefer, "Dissecting the Flash Crash," *Forbes*, October 1, 2010; L. Mearian, "Regulators Blame Computer Algorithm for Stock Market 'Flash Crash'," *Computerworld*, October 1, 2010; G. Bowley, "Lone $4.1 Billion Sale Led to 'Flash Crash' in May," *New York Times*, October 1, 2010; S. Patterson, "Letting the Machines Decide," *Wall Street Journal*, July 13, 2010; N. Mehla, "The Machines That Ate the Market," *Bloomberg BusinessWeek*, May 20, 2010; S. Patterson,

"How the 'Flash Crash' Echoed Black Monday," *Wall Street Journal*, May 17, 2010; L. Harris, "How to Prevent Another Trading Panic," *Wall Street Journal*, May 12, 2010; E. Wyatt, "Regulators Vow to Find Way to Stop Rapid Dives," *New York Times*, May 10, 2010; S. Patterson and T. Lauricella, "Did a Big Bet Help Trigger 'Black Swan' Stock Swoon?" *Wall Street Journal*, May 10, 2010; A. Lucchetti, "Exchanges Point Fingers Over Human Hands," *Wall Street Journal*, May 9, 2010.

CLOSING **CASE 2** >

eBay Finds a Way into China

By 2010 the number of Chinese Internet users had grown to 457 million. In 2005, e-commerce in China amounted to $2 billion; by 2010, that number had increased to $76 billion. The Chinese market is simply too vast for any company to ignore.

<<<THE PROBLEM

And eBay is just one of many foreign e-commerce companies seeking to expand into China. For example, Groupon (www.groupon.com) announced the launch of a Chinese version of its group buying service, teaming up with Tencent Holdings (www.tencent.com), an instant messaging operator that is China's largest Internet company. Russia's Digital Sky Technologies invested $500 million in 360buy (www.360buy.com), a Chinese online retailer.

In 2003, eBay paid $150 million to purchase EachNet, China's top e-commerce Web site at that time. Later eBay invested an additional $100 million in the operation, but a combination of management mistakes—for example, not giving enough power to local executives—and intense competition from local competitor Taobao (www.taobao.com) crippled the business. By 2006, eBay gave up and folded eBay EachNet into a joint venture with Tom Online (www.tom.com). Taobao, which, unlike eBay, does not charge commissions, has maintained its lead.

Although eBay is no longer trying to challenge Taobao, it does have a plan for China. The plan is to link Chinese entrepreneurs and exporters to eBay consumers located elsewhere. Their strategy centers on sellers such as Tang Fengyan. In 2007, Tang started her own dress business. She found eBay an ideal medium for selling her $50 cocktail and rockabilly swing dresses. In 2010 alone, her sales totaled $700,000. Although eBay has minimal presence inside China, Tang does not mind because she is looking to attract global customers. To reach them, eBay makes the most sense for her.

<<<THE SOLUTION

In fact, eBay searched for segments of the Chinese electronic commerce market that were not dominated by Taobao's boss, Jack Ma, and his Alibaba Group (www.alibaba.com). Taobao is dominant in China but has little consumer reach outside the country. Alibaba, a site connecting small and midsize importers and exporters worldwide, does not cater much to consumers, and eBay saw an opening and quickly moved in and now has 150 service agents catering to Chinese sellers. In 2010, eBay launched a service, together with China Post and the U.S. Postal Service, to provide a way for foreign buyers to track their China purchases and also to allow sellers on the mainland to offer free shipping.

Thanks to its new business model and exporters like Tang Fengyan, eBay now operates a successful business in China. Transactions from China and Hong Kong on eBay and its PayPal unit amounted to $4 billion in 2010, making China eBay's fifth-largest market behind the United States, Germany, Britain, and South Korea.

<<<THE RESULTS

Despite this success, eBay continues to be concerned about Alibaba. In 2010, Alibaba launched a service called AliExpress that makes it easier for Chinese-based companies to sell to consumers outside China.

uestions

1. Research the reasons (besides the one listed in this case) why eBay was unsuccessful when it purchased EachNet.

2. Is the competitive advantage eBay has gained by providing a service for Chinese exporters a sustainable competitive advantage? Why or why not? Support your answer.

SOURCES: Compiled from B. Einhorn, "eBay Finds a Secret Door to China," *Bloomberg BusinessWeek*, April 18–24, 2011; L. Chao, "Taobao to Launch Local Deals on Group-Buying Website," *Wall Street Journal*, February 23, 2011; J. Mangalindan, "Can Groupon Crack the China Puzzle?" *Fortune*, February 23, 2011; G. Epstein, "The Biggest Winner in China in 2015? E-Commerce," *Forbes*, January 4, 2011; H. Wang, "How eBay Failed in China," *Forbes*, September 12, 2010; "eBay Finds It Hard to Topple Alibaba in China," *Forbes*, September 10, 2010; G. Epstein, "eBay Chief Visits His Chinese Conqueror," *Forbes*, September 9, 2010.

>>> INTERACTIVE LEARNING

Opening Up E-Wallets on Amazon.com

Go to the Interactivities section on the *WileyPLUS* Web site (www.wileyplus.com) and access Chapter 9: E-Business and E-Commerce. There you will find an interactive simulation of the technologies used for the electronic wallets used by Amazon.com's customers, as well as some hands-on activities that visually explain business concepts in this chapter.

E-commerce at Club IT

Go to the Club IT link on the *WileyPLUS* Web site www.wileyplus.com to find assignments that will ask you to help club owners leverage e-commerce.

Tips for Safe Electronic Shopping

- Look for reliable brand names at sites such as Walmart Online, Disney Online, and Amazon. Before purchasing, make sure that the site is authentic by entering the site directly and not from an unverified link.
- Search any unfamiliar selling site for the company's address and phone and fax numbers. Call up and quiz the employees about the seller.

- Check out the vendor with the local Chamber of Commerce or Better Business Bureau (www.bbbonline.org). Look for seals of authenticity such as TRUSTe.
- Investigate how secure the seller's site is by examining the security procedures and by reading the posted privacy policy.
- Examine the money-back guarantees, warranties, and service agreements.
- Compare prices with those in regular stores. Too-low prices are too good to be true, and some catch is probably involved.
- Ask friends what they know. Find testimonials and endorsements on community Web sites and well-known bulletin boards.
- Find out what your rights are in case of a dispute. Consult consumer protection agencies and the National Consumer League's Fraud Center (www.fraud.org).
- Check Consumerworld (www.consumerworld.org) for a collection of useful resources.
- For many types of products, www.resellerratings.com is a useful resource.

RUBY'S CLUB INTERNSHIP ASSIGNMENTS

Visit PayPal.com and investigate their Business Payment Solutions. Give Ruben and Lisa feedback on exactly what their Web site will be. Define it by the type of e-commerce (pure versus partial) they will be engaging (B2B, B2C, etc.). Then give examples of how other businesses in the same category conduct business? How can PayPal support this model? What benefits will they have from using PayPal? What potential ethical and legal problems might they face?

Finally, provide instructions on how they can utilize this technology. Go to the Business tab and review all of their merchant services. Determine which one is the best for Ruben and Lisa's needs, and gather the instructions on how to implement this system. Finally, let them know the percentage PayPal will take from each transaction, but present it as an opportunity cost to quickly and safely provide e-commerce on their site. Be sure to reference any training materials PayPal may offer.

SPREADSHEET ACTIVITY

Objective: Graphs and charts are helpful tools within most spreadsheet applications. This activity will place you in a business scenario where graphs and charts are extremely helpful in determining customer patterns and preferences.

Chapter Connection: E-business and e-commerce are much more than simply buying and selling via the Internet. Amazon.com is a perfect example of a company that has leveraged the power of the Web to make product suggestions to customers and help them find the right product. This activity builds on this concept and applies spreadsheet tools to help provide this type of business data and make it useful even in a traditional bricks-and-mortar scenario.

Prerequisites: There are no prerequisites for this activity.

Activity: Go to Amazon.com and search for a Coleman Sundome 10 × 10 tent. At the time of this writing, customers are shown items that are frequently purchased with the tent, items that customers often buy with it (but not as frequently as the other group), and finally a list of related products. This type of information is very helpful to consumers, especially when combined with customer ratings.

Another type of feedback provided by Amazon.com is the list of items that are most frequently purchased after shopping for a particular item. This type of information is invaluable to consumers and can only be provided in an online environment. Walmart cannot tell customers what most people buy when they are standing in the aisle, so consumers are blind and have to make a choice based on either information they found before they arrived or on what is said on the box.

Imagine if you work for a small bookstore. You would like to post a chart next to a book showing that it is one of the more popular books purchased, or possibly to direct someone to a more popular book (that you also sell). Search Amazon.com for five books (pick your own genre) and find Amazon's "What do customers ultimately buy after viewing this item" section. You may have to search for more than one book to find it because they do not list it on every page. Collect the percentage data and place it in a spreadsheet. Then use the tools provided in Microsoft Excel to create at least three different types of charts based on your data. Take each chart and copy and paste it in a Word document that you could place on the shelf in your bookstore to help

drive customers to the right product. If you need some help with charts, try searching for "Microsoft Excel Charts" and watch some tutorials. Some tools are available on Microsoft's Web site that are easy to find if you search for them.

Deliverables: The final product will be five separate Word documents that the owner of the small bookstore could place on the shelf in front of a product. The chart will show the percentage of Amazon.com customers who buy that product as well as what other books they purchase. The final documents demonstrate how traditional businesses can leverage the power of e-business and e-commerce in their stores with public information.

Quiz Questions:

1. Amazon.com provides excellent data to its customers via e-business tools. This data includes all of the following sections *except*:
   (a) Frequently purchased together
   (b) What customers purchase after viewing
   (c) Where to purchase offline
   (d) Related items

2. True or False? For businesses to engage in e-commerce and e-business, very sophisticated systems are required in order to provide information to consumers.

3. Which of the following graphs/charts can Excel make?
   (a) Pie
   (b) Bubble
   (c) Scatter
   (d) Area
   (e) All of the above

Discussion Questions:

1. Given the complexity of e-business and e-commerce, is it something that everyone should engage in? Is the future of business to have a Web site and sell everything online? Will there always be a place for traditional bricks-and-mortar stores?

2. Online shopping provides many advantages to consumers. Other than the example provided in this exercise, what other ways can you think of that will help traditional businesses leverage the power of online tools for their in-store customers?

DATABASE ACTIVITY: FORMS II

Objective

To learn how to create a three-table form directly, using the Form Wizard, and how to improve the appearance of your forms. You were introduced to forms in the Chapter 8 activity. There, you created three forms: one based on a single table, one based on two tables, and one based on three tables where you had to create a subform yourself to deal with complex table relationships. Here, you will extend what you know to more complex form design issues.

Chapter Connection

This chapter of the book is about electronic commerce. E-commerce runs on forms. With the knowledge you will gain here, you will be able to develop forms that need only be connected to the Web and a database to be used in that area.

Prerequisites

Chapter 8 database activity (Forms I).

Activity:

In this activity, which you will find online at www.wiley.com/college/rainer, you will work with a new database to create more advanced types of forms.

1. Download the Ch 09 ItemSales database from www.wiley.com/college/rainer and open it. A store might use a database like this. It has data on items it sells, their manufacturers, and the distributors from which it gets them. A distributor may supply items from several manufacturers. The relationship map, accessed via the Database Tools ribbon, shows the table relationships.

2. The first form will show all three tables. Open the Form Wizard. From DistTbl, select the distributor's name, city, and state. (You should not have any trouble figuring out the correct column names for these.) From MfrTbl, select the manufacturer's name and country. From ProdTbl, select the item number, description, shipping weight, and selling price. Organize the form by DistTbl.

3. In the next step, specify "Form with subforms." Then finish creating it as you did in the previous activity. Save the form as DistForm. Save its subforms as MfrSubform and ProdSubform. Open it to enter data.

4. You will see that there are two subforms inside the main form here. This is how the Form Wizard creates a three-table form. While the lower one is not nested physically within the upper one, it behaves as though it is. When you move through the manufacturers supplied by the first distributor, in the upper subform, the lower subform changes to show each manufacturer's products.

5. This form looks exactly as the wizard created it. Now we will change its appearance. Repeat the form creation process, this time naming your form DistForm2, its subforms MfrSubform2 and ProdSubform2.

Usage Hint: You might wonder why you do not just copy the form. You could. You would have to make copies of the subforms, too. Then, you would have to go into the forms and change their source data to refer to the copies. It is easier to create a new set.

6. Let us start with labels:

   (a) The form header shows the form's name in the database, DistForm. Click on it to edit and change it to "Distributors with Manufacturers and Products" (without quotation marks). This may make its box several lines deep. If it does, drag its right edge with your mouse and drag it far enough to the right to fit the header on one line. Then drag its bottom edge and move it up as far as possible without covering any of the text.

   (b) Click in the field names in the top portion of the form and change them to "Distributor," "City," and "State." The original names were chosen for database developers. These names make more sense to the people who will use this form.

   (c) Shrink those fields vertically to one line each.

   (d) If you are used to shrinking the state field and putting it on the same line with the city, do it. If you are using an earlier version of Access, you may know that you cannot adjust that one field without adjusting the other two. The reason is that Access links the fields on the layout, which changes the others unless you remove the layout controls. This is no longer necessary in Access 2010; you can adjust the fields now. So, shrink the State field in width until it is about the right size for a few letters. Shrink the City field until it is long enough for a long city name. Then select the State field and its label (click one, then shift-click the other) together so they will move as a unit, and position them to the right of the city field.

Usage Hint: It can be hard to get the City and State fields to line up precisely. Design view has a grid to make this easier, but most things are easier done in Layout view. In that view, you can open the form's Property Sheet, under the Arrange ribbon tab. Click a field whose position is okay—say, the City field. Note the value of its Top attribute (under the Property Sheet's Format tab). To align other fields with it, select them and set their Top to that value. Another option is to use the Control Alignment tools in the Arrange ribbon. They are fine when they work, but their behavior can be nonintuitive. Try them if you want. There is an Undo button if you do not like the result.

(e) Edit the labels of the two subforms to read "Manufacturer" and "Product" in full. (This sometimes works better in Design view than in Layout view.) Using the Font tools under either the Format or the Home ribbon tab, make them bold and increase their size to 14 points.

(f) Shrink the fields ProdID and ProdPrice to reasonable widths for their contents. (You have to grab the column divider in the header row, not farther down.) Then shrink/adjust the subform widths to what is now required. You will see that both subforms shrink together, since their layouts are still linked. We could unlink them if we wanted to, but there is no reason to do that here. Also, move them up to use some of the space freed up when you put the distributor's city and state on a single line. (Forms that are unnecessarily spread out are hard to use, and they can take up an annoyingly large amount of screen space when several windows are open.)

(g) Find a picture on the Web and download it. Click "Logo" in the Format ribbon, navigate to the picture, and select it. It will appear in your form's header. Move it to the right of the text.

(h) Go to Design view if you are not already in it. Click the Rectangle tool near the center in the Controls section of the Design ribbon. (You may have to scroll the set of icons down to see it.) You will see other tools that are not in Layout view, too. Draw a rectangle around all the distributor data at the top of the form.

(i) Switch back to Form view and admire your work. At work, you might do more. You know about some of the tools you could use. Close the form, saving if prompted.

7. Your third form will be one that a firm could use to review customer orders. Download the database from www.wiley.com/college/rainer. It has four tables: customers, products, orders, and line items. You can see their relationships in the relationship map of the database. (It resembles the example in Section 3.3 of this chapter, minus its supplier table. Its Line Item table is called Ordered Parts there.)

8. Open the Form Wizard and create a form using all four tables. Organize it by customer. Show all the customer information except CustomerID, order date and total, line item quantity, and product name and price. Use Tabular form for the Order subform (the first one), Datasheet form for the line item/product subform (the second).

9. Open the form in Layout view and improve its arrangement as you did previously.

10. This form could be used by customers. Customers need instructions. To put them on the form, go to Design view. (Layout view will not do this.) Choose the Label tool from the middle of the Design ribbon, the third item from the left in the Controls section. The mouse pointer becomes crosshairs. Draw a rectangle in any free space on the form. (You can move form elements to free up space.) Enter any text in it—we are not practicing instruction writing. In Form view, confirm that it shows up.

11. It can be hard to remember customer names or key them in without error. Access offers two ways to make it unnecessary. One, a *list box*, restricts selections to data in the list. We will use that here. The other, a *combo box*, lets users enter a new value in addition to those.

   To begin, make room for the box where the CustName field is now. In Design view, delete it and its label. (You may have to remove its control layout first. See 6d.) If any other fields move up to fill its space, select them and move them back down.

12. To create a list box, go to Design view and the Design ribbon. If "Use Control Wizards" toward the right is not highlighted, click it. Click the downward triangle with the line over it at the right of the Controls section to confirm that Use Control Wizards is selected. If it is not, select it. Then click the List Box tool, shown in the following figure, on the ribbon. (You may have to scroll up or down the list, or display the entire set via the same downward triangle with the line over it, to see this tool. You can also identify it by holding the mouse over it to see its tool tip.)

Draw a rectangle with the crosshairs where the customer name field used to be. Make it wide enough for a couple of data fields, deep enough for a few rows.

13. In the first step of the wizard, select "Find a record on my form based on the value I selected in my list box," since this is what you want to do. Click "Next."

14. Since you will pick a customer name, select "CustTbl" as the source of the values. Click "Next."

15. Move CustID and CustName into the Selected Fields pane. You will need CustID to identify the correct record uniquely, CustName for people to read. Click "Next."

16. Make sure the box to hide the key column is checked—your users do not need customer numbers—and expand the field width to permit longer names in the future. Click "Next."

17. Choose the label Customer Name. Click "Finish."

18. Go to Form view. You will see customer names in the list box, with scroll bar and arrows to move through the list. Select a customer name, and his or her orders will appear below it. Select one of that customer's orders, and its line items will appear in the bottom subform.

19. Close this form, saving if prompted. Name it CustOrderForm.

Deliverables:

The two databases—ItemSales and DaffyDonuts—with their new forms.

Quiz Questions:

1. True or False? In a list box, if you do not see the value you want, you can enter it.

2. To draw a new rectangle on a form, you would use:
   (a) Form view
   (b) Layout view
   (c) Design view
   (d) Pivot chart view

3. True or False? In creating a form with subforms with the Form Wizard, all the data fields on the subforms must be in the tables that are chosen for the form.

4. In formatting data fields in Layout mode, the tools in the ribbon do all of the following *except*:
   (a) Highlight text
   (b) Change text size
   (c) Change font
   (d) Put text in italics

Discussion Questions:

1. The last form mentioned in this activity was described as being used to review customer orders. Therefore, its users do not need to be able to change order data. A company's order entry personnel, or customers directly, could use a similar form to enter new orders. They would first enter information, such as date, about a new order, then its line items. Discuss where one or more additional list boxes and/or combo boxes might be helpful for this new purpose. (Do not add them to the database. Just discuss where you would add them and what they would do.)

2. Search the Web for information on form usability. (The phrase "ease of use" can be useful in your search strings.) Find four guidelines for easy-to-use forms. For each guideline, state whether the forms you developed here follow it, do not follow it, or it does not apply. (Your answers can differ for the two forms.) If they do not follow it, say what would have to change to follow it. If they do not apply, explain why.

3. If you were a market analyst for DaffyDonuts and you wanted to analyze which of your products sell best in different stores and at different times, what additional data might you want that is not in the second form you developed here? Suggest three items. Do not limit your thinking to what is in the tables of this database but not on the form. Think more broadly. Discuss how you might use each of the additional data fields.

10 | Wireless, Mobile Computing, and Mobile Commerce

LEARNING OBJECTIVES >>>

1. Describe the four main types of wireless transmission media, and identify at least one advantage and one disadvantage of each type.

2. Discuss the basic purposes of short-range, medium-range, and long-range networks, and explain how businesses can use at least one technology employed by each type of network.

3. Discuss the five major m-commerce applications, and provide a specific example of how each application can benefit a business.

4. Define pervasive computing, describe two technologies that underlie this technology, and provide at least one example of how a business can utilize each one.

5. Identify the four major threats to wireless networks, and explain, with examples, how each one can damage a business.

OPENING CASE > Tacos, Trucks, and Tweets?

Mark Manguera had a great idea. He thought that Korean BBQ would taste great on a taco. Sound odd? Mark actually took this idea one step further by planning to sell his concoction like ice cream from a taco truck! But, how would he go about letting people know where he would be, so they could find his truck and buy his tacos? Mark's concept involves a number of variables. The location and menu change daily, and so do the customers. Good communication would be critical to a successful operation.

The answer to Mark's dilemma was simply to tweet his location. (Twitter is discussed in Chapters 8 and 12.) Mark's family and friends began blogging and tweeting about his tacos. By leveraging Twitter and mobile connectivity via smart phones, Mark obtained access to all cellular networks and devices because they all accept text messages. His story went viral—meaning that it spread rapidly—and it attracted a large number of followers.

Using Twitter to reach customers across mobile networks, Mark began to share his location and to ask others to forward it. As a result, his truck draws between 300 and 800 people each time it parks. Mark now operates out of five trucks and one bar. He updates his Twitter feed constantly, informing customers where the trucks are and where they are going. His Web site provides this information ahead of time and even suggests locations where customers can sit down to enjoy the food.

Not only were Mark's BBQ tacos a hit, but they gave birth to a cultural phenomenon. "Kogi culture," as it is known in Los Angeles, refers to the large crowds of people who congregate around the truck. It brings people out in neighborhoods where otherwise they would stay indoors. He was even contacted by an entertainment company because his crowds create mini street parties and have opened the doors to other entrepreneurs.

Sources: Compiled from "Kogi BBQ—A Combination of Chipotle and Korean Food on Wheels!" *The Howler Online*, January 20, 2011; J. Gelt, "Kogi Korean BBQ, a Taco Truck Brought to You by Twitter," *Los Angeles Times*, February 11, 2009; http://kogibbq.com, accessed April 27, 2011.

Questions

1. Provide specific examples of the advantages that mobile communications provided to Mark.

2. Which technology—Twitter or mobile communications—enables the other? Support your answer.

RUBY'S CLUB

Imagine this scenario. A customer arrives at Ruby's Club and is catching up with some friends. Rather than leaving the conversation and going to the bar, he gets out his smart phone, goes to Ruby's mobile site, and places a drink order. Payment is made on PayPal's mobile site. The completed order information, including an order ID, is transmitted to the bartender and the customer at the same time. Customers also receive a reminder that they will have to show their ID when they pick up the order, or it will not be delivered and their money will not be refunded.

In just a few minutes, customers receive a text message that their drink is ready. They approach the "Web order" end of the bar, show their text message and their ID, and pick up their drink.

Is this feasible? What technology should they use to deliver this wireless content? They have already discussed a Wi-Fi network, but they wonder what other alternatives might allow this type of interaction with their customer.

INTRODUCTION

The old, traditional working environment that required users to come to a wired computer was ineffective and inefficient. The solution was to build computers that are small enough to carry or wear and can communicate via wireless networks. The ability to communicate anytime and anywhere provides organizations with a strategic advantage by increasing productivity and speed and improving customer service. **Wireless** is a term that is used to describe telecommunications in which electromagnetic waves, rather than some form of wire or cable, carry the signal between communicating devices such as computers, smart phones, and iPads.

Before you continue, it is important to distinguish between the terms *wireless* and *mobile*, because they can mean different things. The term *wireless* means exactly what it says: without wires. In contrast, *mobile* refers to something that changes its location over time. Some wireless networks, such as MiFi (discussed later in this chapter), are also mobile. Others, however, are fixed. For example, microwave towers form fixed wireless networks.

Wireless technologies enable individuals and organizations to conduct mobile computing, mobile commerce, and pervasive computing. These terms are defined here, and then each one is discussed in detail later in the chapter.

Mobile computing refers to a real-time, wireless connection between a mobile device and other computing environments, such as the Internet or an intranet. *Mobile commerce*—also known as *m-commerce*—refers to e-commerce (EC) transactions that are conducted with a mobile device. *Pervasive computing*, also called *ubiquitous computing*, means that virtually every object has processing power with wireless or wired connections to a global network.

Wireless technologies and mobile commerce are spreading rapidly, replacing or supplementing wired computing. In fact, Cisco (www.cisco.com) predicts that the volume of mobile Web traffic will double every year until 2013.

As illustrated in the opening case, there is a huge battle underway to provide you with a mobile, digital wallet and to enable you to get rid of your physical wallet altogether, including all of the credit and debit cards you have in it. Billions of dollars are at stake, further highlighting the importance of wireless to you and your organizations.

Almost all (if not all) organizations utilize wireless computing. Therefore, when you begin your career, you likely will be assigned a company smart phone and a wirelessly enabled computer. Clearly, then, it is important for you to learn about wireless computing not only because you will be using wireless applications but also because wireless computing will be so important to your organization. In your job, you will be involved with customers who conduct wireless transactions, with analyzing and developing mobile commerce applications, and with wireless security. And the list goes on.

Simply put, an understanding of wireless technology and mobile commerce applications will make you more valuable to your organization. When you look at "What's In IT For Me?" at the end of this chapter, envision yourself performing the activities discussed in your functional area. An understanding of wireless technology can also help you start and grow your own business, as illustrated in the chapter opening case.

The wireless infrastructure upon which mobile computing is built may reshape the entire IT field. The technologies, applications, and limitations of mobile computing and mobile commerce are the main focus of this chapter. You begin the chapter by learning about wireless devices and wireless transmission media. You continue by examining wireless computer networks and wireless Internet access. You then look at mobile computing and mobile commerce, which are made possible by wireless technologies. Next, you turn your attention to pervasive computing and conclude the chapter by familiarizing yourself with a critical component of the wireless environment—namely, wireless security.

10.1 | Wireless Technologies

Wireless technologies include both wireless devices, such as smart phones, and wireless transmission media, such as microwave, satellite, and radio. These technologies are fundamentally changing the ways organizations operate.

Individuals are finding wireless devices convenient and productive to use, for several reasons. First, they can make productive use of time that was formerly wasted—for example, while commuting to work on public transportation. Second, because they can take these devices with them, their work locations are becoming much more flexible. Third, wireless technology enables them to schedule their working time around personal and professional obligations.

Wireless Devices

Wireless devices provide three major advantages to users:

- They are small enough to easily carry or wear.
- They have sufficient computing power to perform productive tasks.
- They can communicate wirelessly with the Internet and other devices.

Modern *smart phones* provide capabilities that include cellular telephony, Bluetooth, Wi-Fi, a digital camera for images and video, Global Positioning System (GPS), an organizer, a scheduler, an address book, a calculator, access to e-mail and Short Message Service (SMS, sending and receiving short text messages up to 160 characters in length), instant messaging, text messaging, an MP3 music player, a video player, Internet access with a full-function browser, and a QWERTY keyboard.

One downside of smart phones is that people can use them to copy and pass on confidential information. For example, if you were an executive at Intel, would you want workers snapping pictures of their colleagues with your secret new technology in the background? Unfortunately, managers think of these devices as phones, not as digital cameras that can transmit wirelessly. New jamming devices are being developed to counter the threat. Some companies, such as Samsung (www.samsung.com), have recognized the danger and have banned the devices from their premises altogether. Regardless of any disadvantages, cell phones, and particularly smart phones, have far greater impact on human society than most of us realize, as you can see in Table 10.1.

TABLE 10.1 Do Not Underestimate the Power of Cell Phones!

- In January 1982, the first 100 hand-held cell phones in Washington, D.C., each weighing two pounds, were put into service. By mid-2009, there was one cell phone for every two humans on Earth. This represents the fastest global diffusion of any technology in human history. Cell phones have transformed the world faster than did electricity, automobiles, refrigeration, credit cards, and television.

- Cell phones have made even a bigger difference in less time in underdeveloped areas where land lines have been scarce. As shown in the opening case in Chapter 1, cell phones have become the driving force behind many modernizing economies. Cell phones are the first telecommunications technology in history to have more users in the developing world— 60 percent of all users—than in the developed nations. In just one example, cell phone usage in Africa has been growing at 50 percent annually, faster than any other region.

- Cell phones can heavily influence politics. As you read in "Chapter Closing Case 1" about the Arab Spring, cell phones played a critical role in the revolutions that erupted across the Middle East in 2011.

- Your cell phone now can be your wallet. As "Chapter Closing Case 1" of this chapter demonstrates, there is almost nothing in your wallet that you cannot put in your cell phone— for example, pictures of spouses and children, credit cards, bus tickets, and many other items.

- In neighborhoods around Cambridge, England, bicycle couriers monitor air pollution using cell phones equipped with global position technology.

- Scientists at Purdue University want to network the United States with millions of cell phones equipped with radiation sensors to detect terrorists trying to assemble dirty bombs.

TABLE 10.1 *(Continued)*

- In the San Francisco Bay area, cell phones are being used to transmit real-time traffic information, such as automobile speeds, the extent of traffic jams, and travel time.

- And there is more to come! Even with all their power, cell phones have problems such as haphazard sound quality, dropped calls, slow downloads, and annoying delays between speaking and being heard. To help solve these problems, a company called picoChip (www.picochip.com) is placing miniature cellular base stations, called femtocells, in every home or office that wants better reception. Femtocells work with any cell phone, and they relieve congestion on cell towers and cellular frequencies by creating extra capacity at very small cost. The transmitter is cheap, the broadband connection is free (most houses and offices have existing idle broadband connections), and the low-power signal does not interfere with other frequencies.

Yet the latest version of cell phones—smart phones—can cause problems despite all their advantages. The following example demonstrates how smart phones can disrupt the court system.

EXAMPLE

Smart Phones in Court

Smart phones are now present in U.S. jury boxes, raising serious questions about juror impartiality and the ability of judges to control courtrooms. A Reuters legal analysis found that jurors' forays onto the Internet via smart phones have resulted in dozens of mistrials, appeals, and overturned verdicts.

For decades, courts have instructed jurors not to seek information about cases outside of the evidence introduced at trial, and jurors are routinely warned not to communicate about a case with anyone before they reach a verdict. Today, however, jurors can, with a few clicks on their smart phones, look up definitions of legal terms on Wikipedia, view crime scenes via Google Earth, and communicate on their Facebook pages.

The consequences can be significant. In September 2010, for example, a Florida court overturned the manslaughter conviction of a man charged with killing his neighbor, citing the jury foreman's use of an iPhone to look up the definition of *prudent* in an online dictionary. That same month, the Nevada Supreme Court granted a new trial to a defendant convicted of sexually assaulting a minor, because the foreman had used his smart phone to search online for information about the types of physical injuries suffered by young victims of sexual assaults.

Courts are exploring ways to keep jurors "unplugged." Some judges now confiscate all smart phones from jurors when they enter a courtroom. In 2009, California updated its civil jury instructions to bar jurors from "all forms of electronic communication." From a different perspective, some legal experts argue that rather than try to stifle jurors from pursuing information on the Internet, courts need to figure out how to help them do so in a responsible way.

Sources: Compiled from "Juries and the Internet: Justice Online," *The Guardian*, January 3, 2011; "As Jurors Go Online, U.S. Trials Go Off Track," *Reuters*, December 8, 2010.

Wireless Transmission Media

Wireless media, or broadcast media, transmit signals without wires. The major types of wireless media are microwave, satellite, radio, and infrared. Table 10.2 lists the advantages and disadvantages of each type.

Microwave. **Microwave transmission** systems transmit data via electromagnetic waves. These systems are used for high-volume, long-distance, line-of-sight communication. *Line-of-sight* means that the transmitter and receiver are in view of each other. This requirement creates problems because Earth's surface is curved rather than flat. For this reason, microwave towers usually cannot be spaced more than 30 miles apart.

TABLE 10.2 Advantages and Disadvantages of Wireless Media

Channel	Advantages	Disadvantages
Microwave	High bandwidth Relatively inexpensive	Must have unobstructed line of sight Susceptible to environmental interference
Satellite	High bandwidth Large coverage area	Expensive Must have unobstructed line of sight Signals experience propagation delay Must use encryption for security
Radio	High bandwidth Signals pass through walls Inexpensive and easy to install	Creates electrical interference problems Susceptible to snooping unless encrypted
Infrared	Low to medium bandwidth Used only for short distances	Must have unobstructed line of sight

Clearly then, microwave transmissions offer only a limited solution to data communications needs, especially over very long distances. In addition, microwave transmissions are susceptible to environmental interference during severe weather such as heavy rain and snowstorms. Although long-distance microwave data communications systems are still widely used, they are being replaced by satellite communications systems.

Satellite. Satellite transmission systems make use of communication satellites. Currently, there are three types of satellites circling Earth: geostationary (GEO), medium-earth-orbit (MEO), and low-earth-orbit (LEO). Each type has a different orbit, with the GEO being farthest from Earth and the LEO the closest. In this section you examine the three types of satellites and then discuss two major satellite applications: Global Positioning Systems and Internet transmission via satellites. Table 10.3 compares and contrasts the three types of satellites.

TABLE 10.3 Three Basic Types of Telecommunications Satellites

Type	Characteristics	Orbit	Number	Use
GEO	• Satellites stationary relative to point on Earth. • Few satellites needed for global coverage • Transmission delay (approximately .25 second) • Most expensive to build and launch • Longest orbital life (many years)	22,300 miles	8	TV signal
MEO	• Satellites move relative to point on Earth. • Moderate number needed for global coverage • Requires medium-powered transmitters • Negligible transmission delay • Less expensive to build and launch • Moderate orbital life (6–12 years)	6,434 miles	10–12	GPS
LEO	• Satellites move rapidly relative to point on Earth. • Large number needed for global coverage • Requires only low-power transmitters • Negligible transmission delay • Least expensive to build and launch • Shortest orbital life (as low as 5 years)	400–700 miles	Many	Telephone

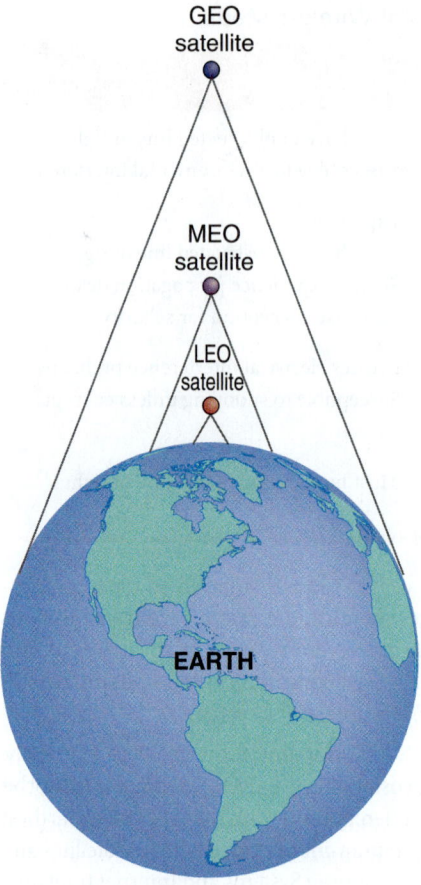

GEO
satellite

MEO
satellite

LEO
satellite

EARTH

Figure 10.1 Comparison of
satellite footprints.
(*Source:* Drawn by Kelly Rainer.)

As with microwave transmission, satellites must receive and transmit data via line-of-sight. However, the enormous *footprint*—the area of Earth's surface reached by a satellite's transmission—overcomes the limitations of microwave data relay stations. The most basic rule governing footprint size is simple: The higher a satellite orbits, the larger its footprint. Thus, medium-earth-orbit satellites have a smaller footprint than geostationary satellites, and low-earth-orbit satellites have the smallest footprint of all. Figure 10.1 compares the footprints of the three types of satellite.

In contrast to line-of-sight transmission with microwave, satellites use *broadcast* transmission, which sends signals to many receivers at one time. So, even though satellites are line-of-sight like microwave, they are high enough for broadcast transmission, thus overcoming the limitations of microwave.

Types of Orbits. *Geostationary earth orbit (GEO) satellites* orbit 22,300 miles directly above the equator. These satellites maintain a fixed position above Earth's surface because, at their altitude, their orbital period matches the 24-hour rotational period of Earth. For this reason, receivers on Earth do not have to track GEO satellites. GEO satellites are excellent for sending television programs to cable operators and for broadcasting directly to homes.

One major limitation of GEO satellites is that their transmissions take a quarter of a second to send and return. This brief pause, one kind of **propagation delay**, makes two-way telephone conversations difficult. Also, GEO satellites are large and expensive, and they require substantial amounts of power to launch.

Medium-earth-orbit (MEO) satellites are located about 6,000 miles above Earth's surface. MEO orbits require more satellites to cover Earth than GEO orbits because MEO footprints are smaller. MEO satellites have two advantages over GEO satellites: They are less expensive, and they do not have an appreciable propagation delay. However, because MEO satellites move with respect to a point on Earth's surface, receivers must track these satellites. (Think of a satellite dish slowly turning to remain oriented to a MEO satellite).

Low-earth-orbit (LEO) satellites are located 400 to 700 miles above Earth's surface. Because LEO satellites are much closer to Earth, they have little, if any, propagation delay.

Like MEO satellites, however, LEO satellites move with respect to a point on Earth's surface and therefore must be tracked by receivers. Tracking LEO satellites is more difficult than tracking MEO satellites because LEO satellites move much more quickly than MEO satellites relative to a point on Earth.

Unlike GEO and MEO satellites, LEO satellites can pick up signals from weak transmitters. This characteristic makes it possible for satellite telephones to operate via LEO satellites, because they can operate with less power and smaller batteries. Another advantage of LEO satellites is that they consume less power and cost less to launch than GEO and MEO satellites.

At the same time, however, the footprints of LEO satellites are small, which means that many of them are required to cover the planet. For this reason a single organization often produces multiple LEO satellites, known as *LEO constellations*. Two examples are Iridium and Globalstar.

Iridium (www.iridium.com) has placed a LEO constellation in orbit that consists of 66 satellites and 12 in-orbit spare satellites. The company maintains that it provides complete satellite communications coverage of Earth's surface, including the polar regions. Globalstar (www.globalstar.com) also has a LEO constellation in orbit.

Global Positioning Systems. The **Global Positioning System (GPS)** is a wireless system that utilizes satellites to enable users to determine their position anywhere on Earth. GPS is supported by 24 MEO satellites that are shared worldwide. The exact position of each satellite is always known because the satellite continuously broadcasts its position along with a time signal. By using the known speed of the signals and the distance from three satellites (for two-dimensional location) or four satellites (for three-dimensional location), it is possible to find the location of any receiving station or user within a range of 10 feet. GPS software can also convert the user's latitude and longitude to an electronic map.

Most of you are probably familiar with GPS in automobiles, which "talks" to drivers when giving directions. Figure 10.2 illustrates two ways for drivers to obtain GPS information in a car: a dashboard navigation system and a GPS app (in this case, TomTom; www.tomtom.com) on an iPhone.

Commercial use of GPS for activities such as navigating, mapping, and surveying has become widespread, particularly in remote areas. Cell phones in the United States now must have a GPS embedded in them so that the location of a person making an emergency call (for example, 911, known as **wireless 911**) can be detected immediately. (For a GPS tutorial, visit www.trimble.com/gps.)

Three other global positioning systems are either planned or operational. The Russian GPS, *GLONASS*, was completed in 1995. However, the system fell into disrepair with the collapse of the Soviet economy. In 2010, GLONASS achieved 100 percent coverage of Russian territory. The European Union GPS, *Galileo*, has an anticipated completion date of 2015. China expects to complete its GPS, *Beidou*, by 2020.

Internet over Satellite (IoS). In many regions of the world, Internet over Satellite (IoS) is the only option available for Internet connections because installing the necessary cables is either too expensive or physically impossible. IoS enables users to access the Internet via GEO satellites from a dish mounted on the side of their homes. Although IoS makes the Internet available to many people who otherwise could not access it, it has its drawbacks. Not only do GEO satellite transmissions entail a propagation delay, but they can be disrupted by environmental influences such as thunderstorms.

Dashboard GPS

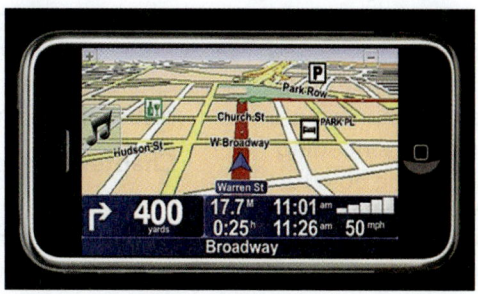

TomTom app on iPhone

Figure 10.2 Obtaining GPS information in an automobile. (*Source:* Image Source)

Radio. **Radio transmission** uses radio-wave frequencies to send data directly between transmitters and receivers. Radio transmission has several advantages. First, radio waves travel easily through normal office walls. Second, radio devices are fairly inexpensive and easy to install. Third, radio waves can transmit data at high speeds. For these reasons, radio increasingly is being used to connect computers to both peripheral equipment and local area networks (LANs; discussed in Chapter 4).

As with other technologies, however, radio transmission also has its drawbacks. First, radio media can create electrical interference problems. Also, radio transmissions are susceptible to snooping by anyone who has similar equipment that operates on the same frequency.

Another problem with radio transmission is that when you travel too far away from the source station, the signal breaks up and fades into static. Most radio signals can travel only 30 to 40 miles from their source. However, *satellite radio* overcomes this problem. **Satellite radio** (or **digital radio**) offers uninterrupted, near CD-quality transmission that is beamed to your radio, either at home or in your car, from space. In addition, satellite radio offers a broad spectrum of stations, including many types of music, news, and talk.

XM Satellite Radio and Sirius Satellite Radio were competitors that launched satellite radio services. XM broadcast its signals from GEO satellites, while Sirius used MEO satellites. In July 2008 the two companies merged to form Sirius XM (www.siriusxm.com). Listeners subscribe to the service for a monthly fee.

Infrared. The final type of wireless transmission is infrared transmission. **Infrared** light is red light that is not commonly visible to human eyes. Common applications of infrared light are found in remote control units for televisions, VCRs, and DVD and CD players. In addition, like radio transmission, infrared transceivers are used for short-distance connections between computers and peripheral equipment and local area networks. A *transceiver* is a device that can transmit and receive signals.

BEFORE *YOU GO ON . . .*

1. Describe the most common types of wireless devices.
2. Describe the various types of transmission media.

RUBY'S CLUB QUESTIONS

1. What qualities of wireless transmission via radio waves would make it most ideal for Ruby's Club?
2. Which business models would work best with satellite transmissions?

Student Activity 10.1

Objective: This activity is designed to make you aware of a fifth choice on wireless communication, mainly for long distance communications needing very high-speed data rate. You should be able to define Free Space Optics and how it relates to wireless communications and list at least two advantages and disadvantages of using the free space optics as communications media. You should also be able to

critically examine its viability as a medium for short-distance and short-range data communications.

Chapter Connection: This activity relates to Section 10.1 in the chapter and connects to Learning Objective 10.1

Prerequisites: You should have read Section 10.1 of this chapter.

Deliverables:

Prepare answers to the following questions:

1. What is the maximum speed that FSO can attain? Under what condition will that speed be reduced?

2. The "Last Mile Problem" in telecommunications refers to connecting the last part of the household to the high-speed network. Currently, wire-based media (cable, telephone lines, and fiber optics in limited cases) are used for it, but most of them are limited in capacity and speed, and fiber optics installations are expensive. Do you think FSO can solve the last mile problem? Provide two arguments for and two arguments against using FSO as the "Last Mile Solution."

Quiz Questions:

1. The requirements for FSO to work include:
   (a) Access to microwave spectrum
   (b) Electromagnetic reflectors to make the beams narrow
   (c) A clear line of sight between two FSO stations
   (d) All of the above

2. The advantage(s) of FSO is (are):
   (a) It is immune to electromagnetic interferences.
   (b) There is no licensing to be obtained for the spectrum.
   (c) It can transmit at gigabit speed.
   (d) All of the above.

3. The _____ speed possible to obtain in an FSO network is the _____ range.

4. FSO uses a _____ beam of _____ light, thus making it highly _____.

Discussion Question:

Can FSO replace satellites as a medium of communication? Why or why not? Provide at least three reasons.

10.2 | Wireless Computer Networks and Internet Access

You have learned about various wireless devices and how these devices transmit wireless signals. These devices typically form wireless computer networks, and they provide wireless Internet access. Next, you will categorize wireless networks by their effective distance: short-range, medium-range, and wide-area.

Short-Range Wireless Networks

Short-range wireless networks simplify the task of connecting one device to another, and they eliminate wires and enable users to move around while they use the devices. In general, short-range wireless networks have a range of 100 feet or less. In this section you consider three basic short-range networks: Bluetooth, ultra-wideband (UWB), and near-field communications (NFC).

Bluetooth. **Bluetooth** (www.bluetooth.com) is an industry specification used to create small personal area networks. A **personal area network** is a computer network used for communication among computer devices—for example, telephones, personal digital assistants, and smart phones—located close to one person. Bluetooth 1.0 can link up to eight devices within a 10-meter area (about 30 feet) with a bandwidth of 700 Kbps (kilobits per second) using low-power, radio-based communication. Bluetooth 2.0 can transmit up to 2.1 Mbps (megabits per second) and, at greater power, up to 100 meters. Ericsson, the Scandinavian mobile handset company that developed this standard, called it Bluetooth after the tenth-century Danish King Harald Blatan (*Blatan* means "Bluetooth"). Ericsson named the standard after Blatan because he unified previously separate islands into the nation of Denmark.

Common applications for Bluetooth are wireless handsets for cell phones and portable music players. Advantages of Bluetooth include low power consumption and the fact that

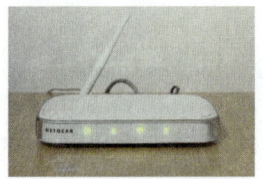

Figure 10.3 Wireless access point. (*Source:* © Pearl Bucknall/Age Fotostock America, Inc.)

it uses omnidirectional radio waves—that is, waves that are emitted in all directions from a transmitter. For this reason you do not have to point one Bluetooth device at another for a connection to occur.

Ultra-Wideband. Ultra-wideband (UWB) is a high-bandwidth wireless technology with transmission speeds in excess of 100 Mbps. This very high speed makes UWB a good choice for applications such as streaming multimedia from, say, a personal computer to a television.

Time Domain (www.timedomain.com), a pioneer in ultra-wideband technology, has developed many UWB applications. One interesting application is the PLUS Real-Time Location System (RTLS). An organization can utilize PLUS to locate multiple people and assets simultaneously. Employees, customers, and/or visitors wear the PLUS Badge Tag. PLUS Asset Tags are placed on equipment and products. PLUS is extremely valuable for healthcare environments, where real-time location of caregivers (e.g., doctors, nurses, technicians) and mobile equipment (e.g., laptops, monitors) is critical.

Near-Field Communications. Near-field communications (NFC) has the smallest range of any short-range wireless networks. It is designed to be embedded in mobile devices such as cell phones and credit cards. For example, using NFC, you can swipe your device or card within a few centimeters of point-of-sale terminals to pay for items.

Medium-Range Wireless Networks

Medium-range wireless networks are the familiar wireless local area networks (WLANs). The most common type of medium-range wireless network is Wireless Fidelity, or Wi-Fi. WLANs are useful in a variety of settings, some of which may be challenging.

Wireless Fidelity (Wi-Fi). Wireless Fidelity (Wi-Fi) is a medium-range **wireless local area network (WLAN)**, which is basically a wired LAN but without the cables. In a typical configuration, a transmitter with an antenna, called a **wireless access point**, connects to a wired LAN or to satellite dishes that provide an Internet connection. Figure 10.3 displays a wireless access point. A wireless access point provides service to a number of users within a small geographical perimeter (up to a couple of hundred feet), known as a **hotspot**. Supporting a larger number of users across a larger geographical area requires multiple wireless access points. To communicate wirelessly, mobile devices, such as laptop PCs, typically have a built-in wireless network interface capability.

Wi-Fi provides fast and easy Internet or intranet broadband access from public hotspots located at airports, hotels, Internet cafés, universities, conference centers, offices, and homes (see Figure 10.4). Users can access the Internet while walking across a campus, to their office, or through their homes. In addition, users can access Wi-Fi with their laptops, desktops, or PDAs by adding a wireless network card. Most PC and laptop manufacturers incorporate these cards in their PCs.

Figure 10.4 Starbucks' patrons using Wi-Fi. (*Source:* Marianna Day Massey/Zuma Press.)

The Institute of Electrical and Electronics Engineers (IEEE) has established a set of standards for wireless computer networks. The IEEE standard for Wi-Fi is the 802.11 family. There are four standards in this family: 802.11a, 802.11b, 802.11g, and 802.11n.

Today, many WLANs use the 802.11n standard, which can transmit up to 600 Mbps and has a range of about 800 feet. There are many 802.11n products. One example is Netgear's (www.netgear.com) RangeMax Wireless-N router.

The major benefits of Wi-Fi are its low cost and its ability to provide simple Internet access. It is the greatest facilitator of the wireless Internet—that is, the ability to connect to the Internet wirelessly.

Corporations are integrating Wi-Fi into their strategies. For example, Starbucks, McDonald's, Panera, and Barnes & Noble offer customers Wi-Fi in many of their stores, primarily for Internet access.

Although Wi-Fi has become extremely popular, it is not without problems. Three factors are preventing the commercial Wi-Fi market from expanding even further: roaming, security, and cost. Regarding the first factor. At this time users cannot roam from hotspot to hotspot if the hotspots use different Wi-Fi network services. Unless the service is free, users have to log on to separate accounts and, where required, pay a separate fee for each service. (Some Wi-Fi hotspots offer free service, while others charge a fee.)

Security is the second barrier to greater acceptance of Wi-Fi. Because Wi-Fi uses radio waves, it is difficult to shield from intruders. The final limitation to greater Wi-Fi expansion is cost. Even though Wi-Fi services are relatively inexpensive, many experts question whether commercial Wi-Fi services can survive when so many free hotspots are available to users.

Wi-Fi Direct. Until late 2010, Wi-Fi required the presence of a wireless antenna at the center of a hotspot, and ad-hoc connections among individual computers or other devices were somewhat limited. Because of these limitations, organizations have typically used Wi-Fi for communications of up to about 800 feet, and they have used Bluetooth for shorter, ad-hoc connections.

Wi-Fi Direct is a new iteration of Wi-Fi. It enables peer-to-peer communications, so devices can connect directly. Wi-Fi Direct enables users to transfer content among devices, even without a wireless antenna. It can connect pairs or groups of devices at Wi-Fi speeds of up to 250 Mbps and at distances of up to 800 feet. Further, devices with Wi-Fi Direct can broadcast their availability to other devices just as Bluetooth devices can. Finally, Wi-Fi Direct is compatible with the more than 1 billion Wi-Fi devices currently in use.

Wi-Fi Direct will probably challenge the dominance of Bluetooth in the area of device-to-device networking. It offers a similar type of connectivity but with greater range and much faster data transfer.

MiFi. MiFi is a small, portable wireless device that provides users with a permanent Wi-Fi hotspot wherever they go. Thus, users are always connected to the Internet. The range of the MiFi device is about 10 meters. Developed by Novatel, the MiFi device is also called an intelligent mobile hotspot. Accessing Wi-Fi through the MiFi device allows up to five persons to be connected at the same time, sharing the same connection.

MiFi provides broadband Internet connectivity anywhere there is 3G cellular network coverage. MiFi also allows users to use voice-over-IP technology to make free (or cheap) calls, both locally and internationally. One drawback with MiFi is the cost, both for acquiring it and for using it.

Wireless Mesh Networks. **Mesh networks** use multiple Wi-Fi access points to create a wide area network that can be quite large. Mesh networks could have been included in the long-range wireless section, but you see them here because they are essentially a series of interconnected local area networks.

Around the United States, public wireless mesh programs are stalling and failing (for example, in Philadelphia, Boston, and Long Island). Service providers that partnered with cities to maintain the systems are dropping out, largely because the projects' costs are escalating and the revenue models are unclear.

Despite these problems, there are many examples of successful mesh-network applications. Consider the following:

- U.S. military forces are using wireless mesh networks to connect their laptops in field operations.

- Electric meters are now being placed on residences to transfer their readings to the central office for billing, without the need for human readers or the need to connect the meters with cables.
- The LEO Iridium constellation operates as a mesh network, with wireless links among adjacent satellites. Calls between two satellite phones are routed through the mesh, from one satellite to another across the constellation, without having to go through an Earth-based station. As a result, the signal travels a shorter distance, reducing any transmission lag. In addition, the constellation can operate with fewer Earth stations.

Wide-Area Wireless Networks

Wide-area wireless networks connect users to the Internet over a geographically dispersed territory. These networks typically operate over the licensed spectrum—that is, they use portions of the wireless spectrum that are regulated by the government. In contrast, Bluetooth and Wi-Fi operate over the unlicensed spectrum and are therefore more prone to interference and security problems. In general, wide-area wireless network technologies fall into two categories: cellular radio and wireless broadband.

Cellular Radio. Cellular telephones (cell phones) provide two-way radio communications over a cellular network of base stations with seamless handoffs. Cellular telephones differ from cordless telephones, which offer telephone service only within a limited range through a single base station attached to a fixed land line—for example, within a home or an office.

The cell phone communicates with radio antennas, or towers, placed within adjacent geographic areas called *cells* (see Figure 10.5). A telephone message is transmitted to the local cell—that is, the antenna—by the cell phone and then is passed from cell to cell until it reaches the cell of its destination. At this final cell, the message either is transmitted to the receiving cell phone or it is transferred to the public switched telephone system to be transmitted to a wireline telephone. This is why you can use a cell phone to call other cell phones as well as standard wireline phones.

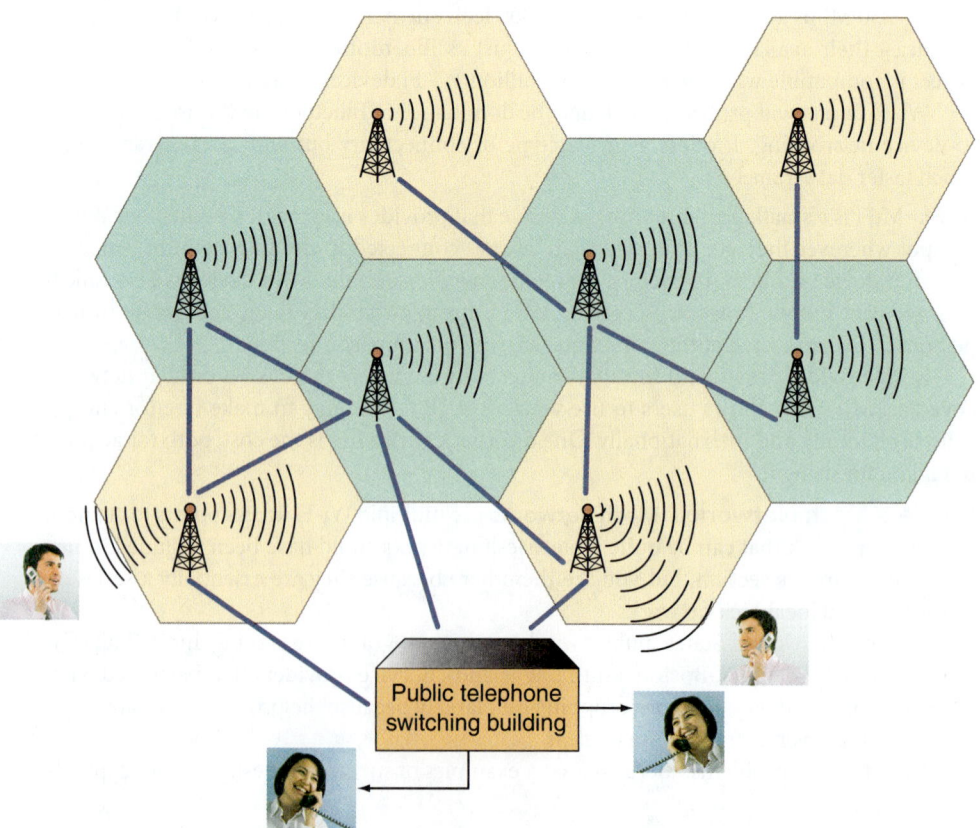

Public telephone switching building

Figure 10.5 The cell phone communicates with radio antennas, or towers, placed within adjacent geographic areas called *cells*. (*Sources*: Image Source; © Engine Images-Fotolia.com)

Until early 2011, large cell towers have been a "given" for cellular technology. The following example introduces an exciting new technology from Alcatel-Lucent (www. alcatel-lucent.com) that aims to replace these towers.

EXAMPLE

lightRadio

The global wireless industry is spending $210 billion per year to operate their networks and $50 billion per year to upgrade them. Despite all that spending and pressure on consumers to curb their data usage, the networks are fighting a losing battle. Mobile data usage is expected to grow 30 times by 2015 and 500 times by 2020. With a combination of miniaturization and cloud technology (discussed in Plug IT In 3), lightRadio might be able to help wireless carriers keep pace with their customers.

A lightRadio is a 2.3-inch cube that contains all of the components of a cell tower. Alcatel-Lucent's engineers stripped out all the heavy power equipment that controls cell towers and moved it to centralized stations. Consequently, the lightRadio cubes are small enough to be deployed virtually anywhere and almost inconspicuously—for example, on top of bus station awnings, on the sides of buildings, and on lampposts.

Not only are lightRadio cubes much smaller and less conspicuous than cell towers; they also are 30 percent more efficient. Wireless carriers can assess live data about who is using the cubes and then adjust the antennas' directional beams to maximize their potential. For example, antennas may be pointed in one direction as people are coming to work in the morning and in another direction when they are going home. In addition, the cubes contain multigenerational antennas that can relay 2G, 3G, and 4G network signals (discussed next), all from the same cube.

Each lightRadio cube powers about a two-block radius, so in urban areas they can be deployed throughout the city and stacked in stadiums or other areas that need extra capacity. In rural areas, they can be deployed on top of existing cell towers.

Sources: Compiled from D. Goldman, "The Tiny Cube That Could Cut Your Phone Bill," *CNNMoney*, March 21, 2011; C. Babcock, "Alcatel Lucent Shrinks Cell Phone Towers," *InformationWeek*, February 7, 2011; www.alcatel-lucent.com, accessed May 11, 2011.

Cellular technology is quickly evolving, moving toward higher transmission speeds and richer features. The technology has progressed through several stages:

- *First generation (1G)* cellular used analog signals and had low bandwidth (capacity).
- *Second generation (2G)* uses digital signals primarily for voice communication; it provides data communication up to 10 Kbps.
- *2.5G* uses digital signals and provides voice and data communication up to 144 Kbps.
- *Third generation (3G)* uses digital signals and can transmit voice and data up to 384 Kbps when the device is moving at a walking pace, 128 Kbps when it is moving in a car, and up to 2 Mbps when it is in a fixed location. 3G supports video, Web browsing, and instant messaging.

Third-generation cellular service does have disadvantages. Perhaps the most fundamental problem is that cellular companies in North America use two separate technologies: Verizon and Sprint use Code Division Multiple Access (CDMA), while Cingular and others use Global System for Mobile Communications (GSM). CDMA companies are currently using *Evolution-Data Optimized* (*EV-DO*) technology, which is a wireless broadband cellular radio standard.

In addition, 3G is relatively expensive. In fact, most carriers limit how much information you can download and for what the service can be used. For instance, some carriers prohibit downloading or streaming audio or video. If you go beyond the limits, the carriers reserve the right to cut off your service.

- *Fourth generation (4G)* is still under development and is not one defined technology or standard. The International Telecommunications Union has specified speed requirements for 4G: 100 Mbps (million bits per second) for high-mobility communications such as cars and trains, and 1 Gbps (billion bits per second) for low-mobility communications such as pedestrians. A 4G system is expected to provide a secure all-IP (Internet Protocol)-based mobile broadband system to all types of mobile devices.

Wireless Broadband or WiMAX. Worldwide Interoperability for Microwave Access, popularly known as WiMAX, is the name for IEEE Standard 802.16. WiMAX has a wireless access range of up to 31 miles, compared to 300 feet for Wi-Fi. WiMAX also has a data-transfer rate of up to 75 Mbps. It is a secure system, and it offers features such as voice and video. WiMAX antennas can transmit broadband Internet connections to antennas on homes and businesses miles away. The technology can therefore provide long-distance broadband wireless access to rural areas and other locations that are not currently being served, as "IT's About Business 10.1" shows.

IT's ABOUT BUSINESS | 10.1

WiMAX Helps the People of Northern Thailand

The Thailand National Telecommunications Commission (NTC) and Mae Fah Luang (MFL) University are deploying WiMAX to deliver broadband communications to schools and villages in a remote region of northern Thailand. The project is benefiting not only students and teachers through an e-learning program, but also rural residents of the area, some of whom have never used a personal computer or the Internet.

The NTC and MFL University selected Cisco as the project's vendor because Cisco's Advanced Antenna System (AAS) provided increased data transmission volume and operated over greater distances than its competitors. The AAS takes advantage of multiple antennas to send and receive data. Using multiple wireless data streams decreases the likelihood that data will be lost. The network requirements were that Cisco provide a minimum of 3 Mbps (3 megabits per second, or 3 million bits per second) upload and download throughput. Cisco's actual transmission results were between 4.5 Mbps and 5 Mbps.

After the WiMAX system was deployed, the next challenge was to create useful content for the students and communities. Accordingly, MFL University developed an educational program for the surrounding schools. University staff members are responsible for training teachers at the rural schools on how to develop educational content in the form of e-books. These e-books focus on core subjects such as math, science, English, and social studies. The teachers are initially trained on the basics of e-book publishing, using text and images. After several months of training, teachers are capable of developing elaborate e-books with embedded voice and video using various software applications.

The teachers then return to their respective schools and continue developing educational content. E-book content development has been highly successful, according to MFL University faculty members. The e-books are stored on a server farm (discussed in "Plug IT In 3") located on the MFL University campus. Individual classes utilize the network to acquire e-book material created by all the schools. The ability of the various village schools using the WiMAX technology to collaborate with one another has helped create a sense of community throughout the region.

An even larger challenge for the project was to provide the information in the e-books to everyone else in the outlying villages. These villages are comprised primarily of farmers who grow rice, pineapple, coffee, and tea. Prior to the WiMAX deployment, villages relied on standard radio communication for information. Now, teachers and schoolchildren compile information using the Internet as a research tool. Not surprisingly, much of this information relates to agriculture and healthcare. This content is developed into a script that is read by the announcers at the radio stations. The underlying concept is to use a current technology to introduce a new medium to the villagers. According to the MFL University staff, this process has been hugely successful. In fact, many villagers are learning to use computers and to access the Internet themselves for the first time in their lives.

What lessons can we learn from the WiMAX project in northern Thailand? First, WiMAX clearly is capable of handling mobile wireless data transmission at a very low total cost of ownership. Second, WiMAX can be implemented faster than wireline solutions.

Questions

1. Provide specific examples of other advantages that WiMAX can deliver to the villagers.
2. Provide specific examples of the advantages of WiMAX compared to wireline communications.

Sources: Compiled from A. Pornwasin, "Thailand Needs to Make Urgent WiMAX Decision," *The Nation*, March 16, 2010; A. Froehlich, "WiMAX Changes Lives in Rural Thailand," *Network World*, May 25–June 1, 2009; http://eng.ntc.or.th, www.mfu.ac.th, accessed April 19, 2011.

BEFORE YOU GO ON . . .

1. What is Bluetooth? What is a WLAN?
2. Describe Wi-Fi, cellular service, and WiMAX.

RUBY'S CLUB QUESTIONS

1. For Ruby's Club, what is a significant difference in the way Bluetooth operates compared to infrared transmission that would make it more feasible for Ruben and Lisa's choice of technology?

2. Obviously, Ruben and Lisa want to create a WLAN with some type of wireless technology. Based on the options discussed in Section 10.2, which one do you think would be the most worthwhile? Keep in mind that for it to be useful to customers, devices must be compatible with the club's network.

Student Activity | 10.2

Objective: To make you aware of the "net neutrality" issue related to Internet access. You should be able to describe net neutrality and how the movement to higher speed may or may not alleviate the issue. You should also be able to define Quality of Service (QoS) for computer networks and see its role in serving content in high-speed broadband wireless networks.

Chapter Connection: This activity relates to Section 10.2 in this chapter.

Prerequisites: You should have read Section 10.2 of this chapter.

10.3 | Mobile Computing and Mobile Commerce

In the traditional computing environment users come to a computer, which is connected with wires to other computers and to networks. Because these networks need to be linked by wires, it is difficult or even impossible for people on the move to use them. In particular, salespeople, repair people, service employees, law enforcement agents, and utility workers can be more effective if they can use IT while in the field or in transit. Thus, mobile computing was designed for workers who travel outside the boundaries of their organizations as well as for anyone traveling outside his or her home.

Mobile computing refers to a real-time connection between a mobile device and other computing environments, such as the Internet or an intranet. This innovation is revolutionizing how people use computers. It is spreading at work and at home; in education, healthcare, and entertainment; and in many other areas.

Mobile computing has two major characteristics that differentiate it from other forms of computing: mobility and broad reach. *Mobility* means that users carry a device with them and can initiate a real-time contact with other systems from wherever they happen to be. *Broad reach* refers to the fact that when users carry an open mobile device, they can be reached instantly, even across great distances.

These two characteristics, mobility and broad reach, create five value-added attributes that break the barriers of geography and time: ubiquity, convenience, instant connectivity, personalization, and localization of products and services. A mobile device can provide information and communication regardless of the user's location (*ubiquity*). With an Internet-enabled mobile device, users can access the Web, intranets, and other mobile devices quickly and easily, without booting up a PC or placing a call via a modem (*convenience* and *instant connectivity*). A company can customize information and send it to individual consumers as an SMS (*customization*). And, knowing a user's physical location helps a company advertise its products and services (*localization*). Mobile computing provides the foundation for mobile commerce (m-commerce).

Mobile Commerce

In addition to affecting our everyday lives, mobile computing is also transforming the way organizations conduct business by allowing businesses and individuals to engage in mobile commerce. As you saw at the beginning of this chapter, **mobile commerce** (or **m-commerce**) refers to electronic commerce (EC) transactions that are conducted in a wireless environment, especially via the Internet. Like regular EC applications, m-commerce can be transacted via the Internet, private communication lines, smart cards, and other infrastructures. M-commerce creates opportunities for businesses to deliver new services to existing customers and to attract new customers. To see how m-commerce applications are classified by industry, see www.wirelessresearch.eu.

The development of m-commerce is driven by the following factors:

- *Widespread availability of mobile devices.* By mid-2011, more than 5 billion cell phones were in use throughout the world. Experts estimate that within a few years about 70 percent of cell phones in developed countries will have Internet access. Going further, as already discussed in this chapter, cell phones are spreading even more quickly in developing countries. Thus, a potential mass market is developing for mobile computing and m-commerce.

- *No need for a PC.* Because users can access the Internet via a smart phone or other wireless device, they do not need a PC to go online. Even though the cost of a PC that is used primarily for Internet access can be less than $300, that amount is still a major expense for the vast majority of people in the world, particularly in developing countries.

- *The "cell phone culture."* The widespread use of cell phones is a social phenomenon, especially among young people. The use of SMS and instant messaging has increased enormously in European and Asian countries. The members of the "cell phone culture" will constitute a major force of online buyers once they begin to make and spend more money.

- *Declining prices.* The price of wireless devices is declining and will continue to decline.

- *Bandwidth improvement.* To properly conduct m-commerce, you need sufficient bandwidth for transmitting text, voice, video, and multimedia. Wi-Fi, 3G cellular technology, and WiMAX provide the necessary bandwidth.

Mobile computing and m-commerce include many applications. These applications result from the capabilities of various technologies. You will examine these applications and their impact on business activities in the next section.

Mobile Commerce Applications

Mobile commerce applications are many and varied. The most popular applications include location-based applications, financial services, intrabusiness applications, accessing information, and telemetry. The rest of this section examines these various applications and their effects on the ways people live and do business.

Location-Based Applications and Services. M-commerce B2C applications include location-based services and location-based applications. Location-based mobile commerce is called **location-based commerce** (or **L-commerce**).

Location-based services provide information that is specific to a given location. For example, a mobile user can (1) request the nearest business or service, such as an ATM or a restaurant; (2) receive alerts, such as a warning of a traffic jam or an accident; and (3) find a friend. Wireless carriers can provide location-based services such as locating taxis, service personnel, doctors, and rental equipment; scheduling fleets; tracking objects such as packages and train boxcars; finding information such as navigation, weather, traffic, and room schedules; targeting advertising; and automating airport check-ins.

Consider, for example, how location-based advertising can make the marketing process more productive. Marketers can use this technology to integrate the current locations and preferences of mobile users. They can then send user-specific advertising messages concerning nearby shops, malls, and restaurants to consumers' wireless devices. "IT's About Business 10.2" illustrates how shopping malls are using location-based apps to attract the increasing number of people who shop online rather than visiting malls.

Location-Based Services at Shopping Malls

The rapid growth of online retail shopping is threatening shopping malls. Consequently, malls are experimenting with mobile applications to help consumers navigate their stores and parking lots and to find sales and special discounts. The mall industry does not expect these efforts to entirely prevent malls from losing more shoppers to online retailers. However, they view the apps as vital at a time when shoppers increasingly consult mobile devices to plan their shopping excursions.

Mall apps are emerging at a time when malls face a huge challenge. Online sales still account for just a fraction of overall retail sales, but they are growing rapidly. In fact, they increased by more than 10 percent in 2010, reaching a total of $176 billion, and they are expected to increase at a compound annual rate of 10 percent through 2015. By contrast, sales at brick-and-mortar stores, excluding gasoline and vehicles, increased by only 3.7 percent in 2011 to $2.37 trillion.

The current generation of mall apps do little more than help shoppers remember where they parked and provide store directories and movie times. Some apps also offer reward points for visiting certain stores. As an example, consider the Simon Property Group, the nation's biggest mall owner.

The Simon Property Group offers Shopkick's shopper-rewards app in about half of its 338 properties. Shopkick is one of the leading mobile apps for shopping, with more than 1 million users. On average, a Shopkick user obtains 60 to 150 Shopkick reward points for visiting a participating store. The user can redeem 875 points for a $25 gift certificate from any one of the retailers.

The Simon Property Group is also developing its own app to offer group discounts. The company would like the app to emulate Groupon (discussed in Chapter 8). The company's CEO envisions the app as a loyalty program coupled with an offer program for the mall environment. Mall retailers would participate in the app. The Simon Group and several retailers, including Target and American Eagle Outfitters, have signed up to offer shoppers rewards through the app, which is free and accessible via the iPhone as well as Android devices.

The bottom line? It remains to be seen whether mobile apps will help slow the decline in the number of mall shoppers.

Questions

1. Are the advantages of the mall apps discussed in this case enough to entice you to go to a mall? Why or why not? Support your answer.

2. Identify two specific benefits that you would add to mall apps to make them functional enough to attract shoppers to the mall.

Sources: Compiled from K. Hudson, "Malls Test Apps to Aid Shoppers," *Wall Street Journal*, April 26, 2011; E. Byron, "In-Store Sales Begin at Home," *Wall Street Journal*, April 25, 2011; E. Morphy, "Don't Be Evil When You Sell, and Other Retail Resolutions," *Forbes*, December 31, 2010; E. Woyke, "A Rewarding Life Through Apps," *Forbes*, October 1, 2010; G. Fowler, "The Green Side of Online Shopping," *Wall Street Journal*, March 3, 2009; www.simon.com, www.shopkick.com, accessed April 28, 2011.

Financial Services. Mobile financial applications include banking, wireless payments and micropayments, money transfers, wireless wallets, and bill-payment services. The bottom line for mobile financial applications is to make it more convenient for customers to transact business regardless of where they are or what time it is. Harried customers are demanding such convenience.

In many countries, banks increasingly offer mobile access to financial and account information. For example, Citibank (www.citibank.com) alerts customers on their digital cell phones about changes in their account information.

Wireless payment systems transform mobile phones into secure, self-contained purchasing tools capable of instantly authorizing payments over the cellular network. In the

United States, CPNI (www.cpni-inc.com) allows people to transfer money instantly to individuals and to make payments to businesses anywhere in the world with any wireline or mobile phone.

At Atlanta's Philips Arena, for example, season ticket holders with Chase-issued Visa credit accounts and Cingular wireless accounts can make contactless payments at concession stands throughout the arena using Nokia cell phones enabled with near-field communications. Customers wave the phone within an inch or two of a radio-frequency reader, without the need for a PIN or a signature. This process speeds up customer flow and frees up workers to help other customers.

If you took a taxi ride in Frankfurt, Germany, you could use your cell phone to pay the taxi driver. Such very small purchase amounts (generally less than $10) are called *micropayments*.

Web shoppers historically have preferred to pay with credit cards. Because credit card companies sometimes charge fees on transactions, however, credit cards are an inefficient way to make very small purchases. The growth of relatively inexpensive digital content, such as music (for example, iTunes), ring tones, and downloadable games, is driving the growth of micropayments, as merchants seek to avoid paying credit card fees on small transactions.

Ultimately, however, the success of micropayment applications will depend on the costs of the transactions. Transaction costs will be small only when the volume of transactions is large. One technology that can increase the volume of transactions is wireless mobile wallets, as you see in this chapter's "Closing Case 1."

Various companies offer **mobile wallet (m-wallet)** technologies that enable cardholders to make purchases with a single click from their mobile devices. One example is the Nokia wallet. This application securely stores information such as credit card numbers in the customer's Nokia phone for use in making mobile payments. People can also use this information to authenticate transactions by signing them digitally. Microsoft also offers an m-wallet, Passport, for use in a wireless environment.

In China, SmartPay allows users to use their mobile phones to pay their phone bills and utility bills, buy lottery tickets and airline tickets, and make other purchases. SmartPay launched 172.com (see www.172.com), a portal that centralizes the company's mobile, telephone, and Internet-based payment services for consumers. The portal is designed to provide a convenient, centralized source of information for all these transactions.

Intrabusiness Applications. Although business-to-consumer (B2C) m-commerce gets considerable publicity, most of today's m-commerce applications actually are used *within* organizations. In this section you will see how companies use mobile computing to support their employees.

Mobile devices increasingly are becoming an integral part of workflow applications. For example, companies can use nonvoice mobile services to assist in dispatch functions—that is, to assign jobs to mobile employees, along with detailed information about the job. Target areas for mobile delivery and dispatch services include transportation (e.g., delivery of food, oil, newspapers, cargo; courier services; tow trucks; taxis), utilities (e.g., gas, electricity, phone, water), field service (e.g., computer, office equipment, home repair), healthcare (e.g., visiting nurses, doctors, social services), and security (e.g., patrols, alarm installation). The following example illustrates an exciting intrabusiness application, telematics, that is being utilized at UPS.

EXAMPLE

Telematics

UPS (www.ups.com) was a pioneer in adopting information technology. It currently has an IT budget of $1 billion. The company has been using telematics in its trucks for 20 years. *Telematics* refers to the wireless communication of location-based information and control messages to and from vehicles and other mobile assets. UPS launched a major program in 2009 to capture more data and better utilize them to cut fuel costs, maintain trucks more effectively, and improve safety. UPS employs Global Positioning Systems to obtain data on more than 200 engine measurements, from speed to number of starts to oil pressure. It also acquires data on seat belts, cargo doors, and reverse gears in transmissions from sensors located all over the vehicle.

UPS then combines these data with mapping software to provide its managers with a tool for modifying driver behaviors in ways that cut costs, improve safety, and reduce the environmental impact. The company can literally "re-create a driver's day." By analyzing these data, UPS has been able to reduce the need for truck drivers to use reverse gear by 25 percent, thereby diminishing the risk of accidents. UPS has also been able to reduce idling time by 15 minutes per driver per day. Although this step might not sound significant, in fact idling burns one gallon of gas per hour and generates 20 percent more pollution than a truck running at 32 miles per hour. Therefore, the savings are substantial for both UPS and the environment. Finally, mechanics now make engine repairs based on actual vehicle use rather than according to set schedules—that is, they change a starter based on the number of starts rather than every 2 years regardless of use.

Sources: Compiled from E. Sperling, "What's Deep Inside Big Brown's Trucks," *Forbes*, June 7, 2010; C. Murphy, "UPS: Positioned for the Long Haul," *InformationWeek*, January 17, 2009; www.ups.com, accessed February 5, 2009.

Accessing Information. Mobile portals and voice portals are designed to aggregate and deliver content in a form that will work within the limited space available on mobile devices. These portals provide information anywhere and anytime to users.

A **mobile portal** aggregates and provides content and services for mobile users. These services include news, sports, and e-mail; entertainment, travel, and restaurant information; community services; and stock trading. The world's best-known mobile portal—i-mode from NTT DoCoMo (www.nttdocomo.com)—has more than 40 million subscribers, primarily in Japan. Major players in Europe are Vodafone, O2, and T-Mobile. Some traditional portals—for example, Yahoo, AOL, and MSN—have mobile portals as well.

A **voice portal** is a Web site with an audio interface. Voice portals are not Web sites in the normal sense because they can also be accessed through a standard phone or a cell phone. A certain phone number connects you to a Web site, where you can request information verbally. The system finds the information, translates it into a computer-generated voice reply, and tells you what you want to know. Most airlines provide real-time information on flight status this way.

An example of a voice portal is the voice-activated 511 travel-information line developed by Tellme.com. It enables callers to inquire about weather, local restaurants, current traffic, and other handy information. In addition to retrieving information, some sites provide true interaction. For example, iPing (www.iping.com) is a reminder and notification service that allows users to enter information via the Web and receive reminder calls. This service can even call a group of people to notify them of a meeting or conference call.

Telemetry Applications. Telemetry is the wireless transmission and receipt of data gathered from remote sensors. Telemetry has numerous mobile computing applications. For example, technicians can use telemetry to identify maintenance problems in equipment. As another example, doctors can monitor patients and control medical equipment from a distance.

Car manufacturers use telemetry applications for remote vehicle diagnosis and preventive maintenance. For instance, drivers of many General Motors cars use its OnStar system (www.onstar.com) in numerous ways, as you see in "IT's About Business 10.3."

Your Car Becomes a Smart Phone

General Motors (www.gm.com) has big ambitions for OnStar (www.onstar.com). The company wants to expand the communications service by increasing the number of GM car owners who continue to subscribe after their free 6 months of service ends. OnStar is the market leader, with 6 million users. More than 4 million of these users pay an average of $240 per year. Add in the mobile-phone minutes from Verizon that OnStar resells, and the GM unit logs more than $1 billion per year in revenue. Its staff of 2,200 agents answers 99.7 percent of emergency calls within one second.

OnStar provides a wide range of features to owners of GM cars. The system can alert owners to most malfunctions in the vehicle and schedule repairs at a dealership. It can also unlock doors remotely and slow down cars if they have been stolen. In addition, it automatically alerts an OnStar operator when an air bag deploys. Drivers can also call OnStar with questions about a warning light that appears on their dashboard.

GM has also launched OnStar for its vehicles in China, complete with Mandarin-speaking agents. The subscriber base reached 200,000 in February 2011, and is growing by 40,000 per month.

Despite these impressive numbers, GM may have waited too long to keep its competitive advantage. OnStar has earned a reputation for security and safety, thanks to features that alert police if a connected car is stolen or involved in an accident. However, Ford has jumped ahead of GM in the market for in-car entertainment content. Ford's Sync system plays music on voice command and even reads tweets to drivers. Further, Hyundai Motor launched a system called Blue Link to compete with OnStar for safety and security features.

Questions

1. Explain why OnStar, Sync, and Blue Link are telemetry applications.
2. Provide specific examples of the disadvantages of OnStar, Sync, and Blue Link.

Sources: Compiled from D. Welch, "OnStar Wants to Turn Your Car into a Smartphone," *Bloomberg BusinessWeek*, March 14–20, 2011; "Hyundai Blue Link Tackles OnStar and Sync," *Edmunds Inside Line*, January 5, 2011; www.gm.com, www.onstar.com, www.ford.com/technology/sync, www.hyundaiusa.com/bluelink/index.aspx, accessed April 19, 2011.

An interesting telemetry application for individuals is an iPhone app called Find My iPhone. Find My iPhone is a part of MobileMe, a service from Apple (www.apple.com) that synchronizes your e-mail, contacts, and calendars wirelessly across all your devices. MobileMe assigns you an address on www.me.com, a Web site that gives you access to your information—e-mail, contacts, calendars, photos, and files—from one place on the Web. Any changes you make on me.com are stored in the cloud, so you can see these changes on all your other devices.

Find My iPhone provides several very helpful telemetry functions. If you lose your iPhone, there are two ways to see its approximate location on a map: You can sign into me.com from any computer or you can use the Find My iPhone app on another iPhone, iPad, or iPod touch.

If you have left your iPhone somewhere you remember, you can write a message and display it on your iPhone's screen. The message might say, "Left my iPhone. Please call me at 301-555-1211." Your message appears on your iPhone, even if the screen is locked. And, if the map shows your iPhone is nearby—perhaps in your office under a pile of papers—you can tell Find My iPhone to play a sound that overrides the volume or silent setting.

If you left your iPhone in a public place, you may want to protect its contents. You can remotely set a four-digit passcode lock to prevent people from using your iPhone, accessing your personal information, or tampering with your settings.

You can initiate a remote wipe (erase all contents) to restore your iPhone to its factory settings. If you eventually find your iPhone, you can connect it to your computer and use iTunes to restore the data from your most recent backup.

If you have lost your iPhone and do not have access to a computer, you can download the Find My iPhone app to a friend's iPhone, iPad, or iPod touch and sign in to access all the Find My iPhone features.

BEFORE *YOU GO ON . . .*

1. What are the major drivers of mobile computing?
2. Describe mobile portals and voice portals.
3. Describe wireless financial services.
4. List some of the major intrabusiness wireless applications.

RUBY'S CLUB QUESTIONS

1. Ruben and Lisa's idea for the mobile ordering of drinks is a form of location-based m-commerce. What other advantages (aside from mobile ordering and paying for drinks) can you think of that Ruben and Lisa can tap into?

2. Mobile commerce offers five value-added attributes that break the barriers of geography and time: ubiquity, convenience, instant connectivity, personalization, and localization of products and services. Which of these do you think is most important for Ruben's idea of the mobile ordering system?

Student Activity | 10.3

Objective: You should be able to describe a few environmental factors that can influence the success of mobile services and m-commerce.

Chapter Connection: This activity relates to Section 10.3 in this chapter.

Prerequisites: You should have read Section 10.3 of this chapter.

Activity:

Read the following excerpts on NTT DoCoMo and also visit the following Web sites:

www.nttdocomo.com/services/imode/history/index.html

www.nttdocomo.com/services/index.html

www.getjar.com

NTT DoCoMo, i-mode, and Smart Phones

In 1991, the Japanese incumbent giant Nippon Telegraph and Telephone entered the mobile phone market by creating a subsidiary and named it NTT DoCoMo (henceforth referred to as DoCoMo, which means "anywhere" in Japanese). Initially, the company offered voice communication services to Japanese consumers, but it became a worldwide sensation in the mobile business area with the launch of its i-mode service in 1999 that allowed DoCoMo customers to connect to Internet and data services through a company portal for downloading various types of content. The phenomenal growth that followed made NTT DoCoMo the greatest icon of mobile business success. By 2001, the subscriber base reached 30 million plus, covering approximately 40 percent of the Japanese market. The company also managed to get average revenue per user (ARPU) of 10400 yen (US$77.8), a very high number by the industry standard. The company and its i-mode have since been researched by many in an effort to understand the factors that led to such a tremendous success. It appears that a combination of social culture, technological innovation and support, economic environment, lack of cheaper alternatives to connect to the Internet, and some crucial decisions by the company in creating the business models led to such success. The commuting time in Japan is rather lengthy, and the commuters mainly use public transportation. This creates an idle-time opportunity for consumption on mobile phones of content such as news, games, and other entertainment items. Furthermore, the polite nature of Japanese society that inhibits talking loudly in public places fueled the growth of text-based communications in subways, buses, and other public places. The i-mode service also provided a way for Japanese consumers to connect to information services that otherwise were not readily available to them due to the low penetration of personal computers and the high cost of Internet connections from home. A strong Japanese economy with significant disposable income and a growing youth segment also facilitated the growth of paid premium content.

The business model of DoCoMo also played a significant role in the success of i-mode. The company created specially designed "cool" i-mode phones, preconfigured them with all relevant parameters and one-button push connection to i-mode (iPhone started this in the smart phone era, but this happened long before smart phones came into existence) and made the basic service relatively cheap with a charge of only 100–300 yen per month (about US$1–3). DoCoMo also realized early on that it cannot be a successful content creator and thus must allow others to generate attractive content for its customers and be an efficient channel and a facilitator for distribution of such content. It adopted cHTML (compact hypertext markup language), a variation of the standard HTML that is used for creating Web pages, as the standard for creating the content pages so that the content creators would have a low learning curve for adapting to or creating i-mode sites. DoCoMo also filtered the contents to make sure that they had compelling value to the end users, and it provided an integrated billing system that allows customers to make micropayments for consuming content. In addition, i-mode was an open portal that allowed users the freedom to browse to any i-mode-compatible site beyond DoCoMo's official list of i-mode sites. DoCoMo charged only a 9 percent commission to the content creators (in other markets, the mobile operators typically charge between 15 and 40 percent) for hosting their contents on the i-mode portal and providing the billing service. The content providers thus could keep 91 percent of the revenue generated from their content and thus could run a profitable business. This model created a win–win situation for both DoCoMo and content providers, and it created

a positive feedback loop by attracting more content, which in turn attracted more subscribers.

The hypergrowth enjoyed by DoCoMo, however, started flattening out after 2003 with serious competition from other mobile operators and market saturation. It actually saw decline in its average monthly ARPU for the last few years. Currently, the company has about 55 million customers with an average revenue per user that is close to 5000 yen (about US$50). Recently, the company, among other ventures, entered the U.S. market in collaboration with some of the largest mobile phone operators in the United States to offer services like i-mode. However, this effort met with very limited success. The proliferation of smart phones and their ability to easily download apps and connect to the Internet diminished the attractiveness of the value offerings of DoCoMo. In the current era of smart phone and apps, NTT DoCoMo sees itself as an "exchange hub" for apps developers and smart phone users, and it plans to leverage its experience with i-mode to make that happen. DoCoMo realized that the volatile growth of the apps since 2007 (as of December 2010, the Apple Store reports about 366,000 apps and Android Market reports about 100,000 apps) will soon make discovering the apps a huge challenge for consumers, and it wants to reduce that difficulty by creating a Web portal "DoCoMo market" that aggregates apps and content from other app store platforms to make them more easily discoverable for users. This is indeed becoming an increasingly lucrative market as it offers revenue opportunities through advertising and search-related charges. Getjar.com is an early entrant into the market for such services with its offer of preferential listings to apps developers who are willing to pay for key words on a per-click basis.

Sources: Compiled from "NTT DoCoMo: A Love Story", from www.accenture.com/Global/Services/By_Industry/Communications/Access_Newsletter/Article_Index/NttStory.htm, accessed December 2, 2010; "3Q10 Japan Mobile Operator Forecast, 2010–2014: Japan to Have 130 Million Mobile Subscriber Connections in 2014 with SoftBank Taking Market Share of 20.8 Percent," from www.mindbranch.com/listing/product/R735-1139.html, accessed December 2, 2010; John C. Tanner, "NTT DoCoMo Leverages i-mode Success for Smartphone Apps," *CommunicAsia Show Daily*, June 16, 2010, accessed from www.telecomasia.net/content/ntt-docomo-leverages-i-mode-success-smartphone-apps, accessed December 2, 2010; www.nttdocomo.com/services/imode/history/index.html and www.nttdocomo.com/services/index.html, accessed December 2, 2010.

Deliverables:

Provide answers for the following questions:

1. List at least four factors that led to the success of NTT DoCoMo's i-mode services.

2. What may have been some of the reasons for DoCoMo's lack of success in the U.S. market?

3. The NTT DoCoMo Web site (www.nttdocomo.com/services/index.html) shows a progression of the role of the mobile phone in our lives. Where do you think the U.S. consumers are along that timeline? Is that position different between smart phone users and users without smart phones? Explain your answer briefly.

4. What is Getjar.com's business model? How does it add value to an end user? How do you think it generates revenue? Do you think NTT DoCoMo's Web portal will be a competitor to Getjar.com? Why or why not?

Quiz Questions:

1. The measure of revenue generated from a subscriber is typically referred to as _____ by mobile operators.

2. One of the reasons for i-mode's success is its ability to provide _____ content during the relatively long _____ time of Japanese consumers using public transport.

3. The Web site (mentioned in the excerpt) that allows users to search and download apps for various types of phones and operating system and also allows apps developers to pay for getting preferential listing is _____ .

4. According to the excerpt, which of the following is *not* a reason for DoCoMo's i-mode success?

(a) The lengthy commuting time and polite nature of Japanese consumers

(b) The fact that DoCoMo is a subsidiary of the largest telecommunications company in Japan and thus had a lot of financial support

(c) A relatively low percentage for the service charge levied by DoCoMo to content providers

(d) The relatively high disposable income of Japanese consumers

5. Which of the following is *not* a reason for DoCoMo's decline in ARPU in recent years?

(a) Increasing competitive pressure

(b) Saturation in the available number of customers in the marketplace

(c) Lack of innovation in the i-mode services

(d) DoCoMo's attempt to create a lifestyle device for the end users

Discussion Question:

We claim that the success of Apple's iPhone can be attributed to factors similar to those of DoCoMo's i-mode service. For example, just like DoCoMo, Apple created a compelling value for users by providing a device with excellent design and features that were not available before in the U.S. mobile market and helped in easy connection with the Internet. Can you identify other similarities? (Hint: Apple Store and iTunes.)

10.4 | Pervasive Computing

Key fobs are a simple example of how wireless technologies have changed our lives. (*Source:* Media Bakery)

A world in which virtually every object has processing power with wireless or wired connections to a global network is the world of **pervasive computing** (or **ubiquitous computing**). Pervasive computing is invisible "everywhere computing" that is embedded in the objects around us—the floor, the lights, our cars, the washing machine, our cell phones, our clothes, and so on.

For example, in a *smart home*, your home computer, television, lighting and heating controls, home security system, and many appliances can communicate with one another via a home network. You can control these linked systems through various devices, including your pager, cell phone, television, home computer, PDA, and even your automobile. One of the key elements of a smart home is the *smart appliance*, an Internet-ready appliance that can be controlled by a small handheld device or a desktop computer via a home network, either wireline or wireless. Two technologies provide the infrastructure for pervasive computing: radio-frequency identification (RFID) and wireless sensor networks (WSNs).

Radio-Frequency Identification (RFID)

Radio-frequency identification (RFID) technology allows manufacturers to attach tags with antennas and computer chips on goods and then track their movement through radio signals. RFID was developed to replace bar codes. A typical bar code, known as the *Universal Product Code (UPC)*, is made up of 12 digits that are batched in various groups. The first digit identifies the item type, the next 5 digits identify the manufacturer, and the next 5 identify the product. The last digit is a check digit for error detection. Bar codes have worked well, but they have limitations. First, they require line-of-sight to the scanning device. This system works well in a store, but it can pose substantial problems in a manufacturing plant or a warehouse or on a shipping/receiving dock. Second, because bar codes are printed on paper, they can be ripped, soiled, or lost. Third, the bar code identifies the manufacturer and product but not the actual item. Two systems are being developed to replace bar codes: *QR (for quick response) codes* and RFID systems. Figure 10.6 shows bar codes, QR codes, and an RFID tag.

A QR code is a two-dimensional code, readable by dedicated QR readers and camera phones. QR codes have several advantages over bar codes:

- QR codes can store much more information than bar codes.
- Data types stored in QR codes include numbers, text, URLs, and even Japanese characters.
- The size of QR codes is small because these codes store information horizontally and vertically.
- QR codes are more resistant to damage than bar codes.
- QR codes can be read from any direction or angle, so the possibility of a failure in reading a QR code is reduced.

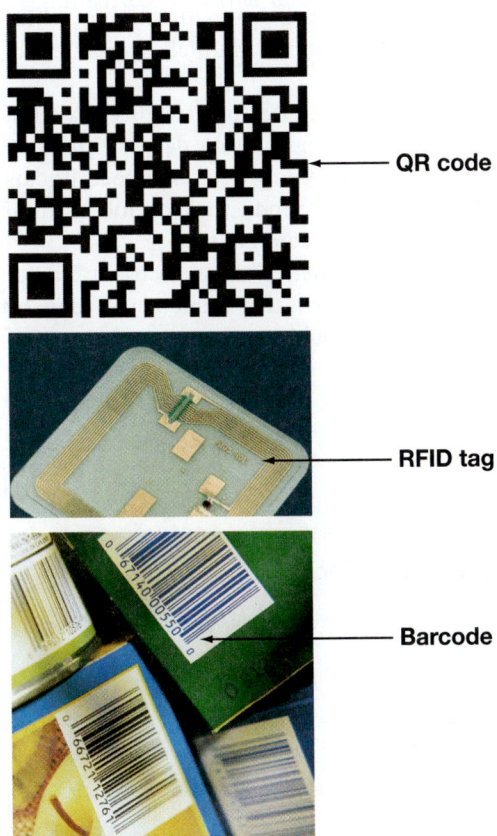

QR code

RFID tag

Barcode

Figure 10.6 Bar codes, RFID tags, and QR codes. (*Sources:* © Patrick Duinkerke/iStockphoto; © raphotography/iStockphoto; Media Bakery)

Figure 10.7 Small RFID tag. (*Source:* © Ecken, Dominique/ Keystone Pressedienst/Zuma Press)

RFID systems use tags with embedded microchips, which contain data, and antennas to transmit radio signals over a short distance to RFID readers. The readers pass the data over a network to a computer for processing. The chip in the RFID tag is programmed with information that uniquely identifies an item. It also contains information about the item such as its location and where and when it was made. Figure 10.7 shows an RFID reader and an RFID tag on a pallet.

There are two basic types of RFID tags: active and passive. *Active RFID tags* use internal batteries for power, and they broadcast radio waves to a reader. Because active tags contain batteries, they are more expensive than passive RFID tags and can be read over greater distances. Active tags, therefore, are used for more expensive items. *Passive RFID tags* rely entirely on readers for their power. They are less expensive than active tags and can be read only up to 20 feet. They are generally applied to less-expensive merchandise. Problems with RFID include expense and the comparatively large size of the tags.

Wireless Sensor Networks

Wireless sensor networks (WSNs) are networks of interconnected, battery-powered, wireless sensors called *motes* (analogous to nodes) that are placed into the physical environment. The motes collect data from many points over an extended space. Each mote contains processing, storage, and radio-frequency sensors and antennas. Each mote "wakes up" or activates for a fraction of a second when it has data to transmit. It then relays those data to its nearest neighbor. So, instead of every mote transmitting its data to a remote computer at a base station, the data are moved mote by mote until they reach a central computer where they can be stored and analyzed. An advantage of a wireless sensor network is that if one mote fails then another one can pick up the data. This process makes WSNs very efficient and reliable. Also, if the network requires more bandwidth, it is easy to boost performance by placing new motes when and where they are required.

The motes provide information that enables a central computer to integrate reports of the same activity from different angles within the network. Therefore, the network can determine with much greater accuracy information such as the direction in which a person is moving, the weight of a vehicle, and the amount of rainfall over a field of crops.

One kind of wireless sensor network is ZigBee (www.ZigBee.org). ZigBee is a set of wireless communication protocols that target applications requiring low data-transmission rates and low power consumption. ZigBee can handle hundreds of devices at once. Its current focus is to wirelessly link sensors that are embedded into industrial controls, medical devices, smoke and intruder alarms, and building and home automation.

A promising application of ZigBee is reading utility meters, such as electricity. ZigBee sensors embedded in these meters would send wireless signals that could be picked up by utility employees driving by your house. The employees would not even have to get out of their trucks to read your meter.

• BEFORE *YOU GO ON . . .*

1. Define pervasive computing, RFID, and wireless sensor networks.
2. Provide two specific business uses of RFID technology.

RUBY'S CLUB QUESTIONS

1. How might Ruby's Club utilize telemetry to measure and account for its problem with shrinkage (the problem of a bartender pouring a little more alcohol than the customer paid for)?

2. Is there a mobile portal that could help Ruben and Lisa reach their customers?

Student Activity 10.4

Objective: You should be able to provide a short definition of pervasive computing and describe some of the latest research and development going on in that area. You should also be able to describe with at least two concrete examples how this technology can be used for business, and you should be able to list at least two concerns/issues with pervasive computing from both the technological and social perspectives.

Chapter Connection: This activity relates to Section 10.4 and Learning Objective 4 of this chapter.

Prerequisites: You should have read Section 10.4 of this chapter.

Activity:

View the video on SixthSense technology at the TED Web site and visit MIT's Project Oxygen Web site:

Sixth sense demonstration: www.ted.com/talks/pranav_mistry_the_thrilling_potential_of_sixthsense_technology.html

Project Oxygen Web site: http://oxygen.lcs.mit.edu/Overview.html

Deliverables:

Prepare answers to the following questions:

1. List the five different types of technologies described in MIT's Project Oxygen with a very short definition of each.
2. Describe the roles of the SixthSense technology and various types of wireless connections, including mobile phones, in creating a pervasive computing environment. You can use some of the terminologies or framework used in Project Oxygen.
3. Describe two business applications of the SixthSense technology.

Quiz Questions:

1. According to the Project Oxygen Web site, one of the requirements of pervasive computing is that it should be:
   (a) RFID technology
   (b) Eternal
   (c) Device independent
   (d) Exclusively gesture oriented

2. One of the concerns of SixthSense technology is that it can easily project information in public places thus violating:
   (a) Government law
   (b) Privacy issues
   (c) Knowledge access
   (d) Face-to-face communications

3. The name of the main person working on the SixthSense project is _____.

4. The name of the network-level technology described in Project Oxygen is _____.

Discussion Question:

List at least one technological concern and one social concern if the SixthSense technology indeed becomes a part of pervasive computing.

10.5 | Wireless Security

Clearly, wireless networks provide numerous benefits for businesses. However, they also present a huge challenge to management—namely, their inherent lack of security. Wireless is a broadcast medium, and transmissions can be intercepted by anyone who is close enough and has access to the appropriate equipment. There are four major threats to wireless networks: rogue access points, war driving, eavesdropping, and RF jamming.

A *rogue access point* is an unauthorized access point to a wireless network. The rogue could be someone in your organization who sets up an access point meaning no harm but fails to inform the IT department. In more serious cases the rogue is an "evil twin"—someone who wishes to access a wireless network for malicious purposes.

In an evil twin attack, the attacker is in the vicinity with a Wi-Fi-enabled computer and a separate connection to the Internet. Using a hotspotter—a device that detects wireless networks and provides information on them (see www.canarywireless.com)—the attacker simulates a wireless access point with the same wireless network name, or SSID, as the one that authorized users expect. If the signal is strong enough, users will connect to the attacker's system instead of the real access point. The attacker can then serve them a Web page asking for them to provide confidential information such as user names, passwords, and account numbers. In other cases the attacker simply captures wireless transmissions. These attacks are more effective with public hotspots (for example, McDonald's and Starbucks) than with corporate networks.

War driving is the act of locating WLANs while driving (or walking) around a city or elsewhere. To war drive or walk, you simply need a Wi-Fi detector and a wirelessly enabled computer. If a WLAN has a range that extends beyond the building in which it is located, then an unauthorized user might be able to intrude into the network. The intruder can then obtain a free Internet connection and possibly gain access to important data and other resources.

Eavesdropping refers to efforts by unauthorized users to access data that are traveling over wireless networks.

In *radio-frequency (RF) jamming*, a person or a device intentionally or unintentionally interferes with your wireless network transmissions.

As you see, wireless systems can be difficult to secure. "Plug IT In 6" discusses a variety of techniques and technologies that you should implement to help you avoid these threats. "IT's About Business 10.4" demonstrates how important protecting wireless networks is at Brigham Young University–Hawaii.

IT's ABOUT BUSINESS | 10.4

Protecting an Open Wireless Network at Brigham Young University–Hawaii

The 2,500 students and 500 faculty and staff at Brigham Young University–Hawaii use the university's open wireless campus network. In addition to the obvious problem that anyone and any computer could connect to the network, another big issue was the university's inability to capture important information about the wireless users who were accessing the campus network. The IT team, which consisted of only three people, had no way of knowing who was on the network or how the network was being utilized.

In a specific example, the team realized the importance of identifying users who were using network resources inappropriately. All BYU–Hawaii students are required to sign an honor code of conduct. If someone violates a conduct policy, such as downloading inappropriate material, the IT team needed a way to identify the student as required by

the Honor Code Office. With no way to identify users, reporting violators was almost impossible.

The team decided to add greater authentication (i.e., identification) and authorization (discussed in Chapter 7) to restrict access to campus resources. The challenge was finding the best strategy for deploying the new system while limiting service disruptions to the users. To address these issues, the IT team first had to authenticate the users.

Being a Cisco customer, BYU–Hawaii tried to use the Cisco Clean Access solution to authenticate network users. However, with that system, anyone could still connect to the network as a guest. The IT team decided to use Avenda (www.avendasys.com) because this system works with both wireless networks and wired networks, and it provides virtual private networking for off-campus users.

Avenda automatically provides authorization privileges after a user is authenticated. That is, once a user is identified, the system provides access only to those systems necessary for that user to do his or her job, a process called *least privilege* (discussed in Chapter 7).

As a result of implementing the Avenda system, the IT team members now control and differentiate access to the wireless network. In addition, they can determine what users are doing on the network. The team is also able to collect user information and details about network usage and the overall performance of the campus wireless network in only minutes.

Questions

1. What are the advantages of the Avenda system to the users?
2. Are any user privacy issues associated with the Avenda system? If so, provide specific examples.

Sources: Compiled from M. Aughenbaugh and J. Call, "Wireless Networking Case Study," *Baseline Magazine*, April 26, 2011; www.byuh.edu, www.avendasys.com, accessed May 5, 2011.

BEFORE YOU GO ON . . .

1. Describe the four major threats to the security of wireless networks.
2. Which of these threats is the most dangerous for a business? Which is the most dangerous for an individual? Support your answers.

RUBY'S CLUB QUESTIONS

1. Wireless security is going to be very important at Ruby's Club. Ruben and Lisa only want customers who have paid the cover fee to be able to access the network. What ideas can you give them to help manage this need?
2. How do hotels and restaurants handle this problem? Would their model work for Ruby's Club?

Student Activity | 10.5

Objective: You should be able to list at least two security issues with mobile phones beyond the ones discussed in the chapter and their implications on businesses. You should also be able to do a critical analysis of the pros and cons of open versus closed operating systems for mobile phones.

Chapter Connection: This activity relates to Section 10.5 and Learning Objective 5 of this chapter.

Prerequisites: You should have read Section 10.5 of this chapter.

Activity:

Read the two articles available at the following links:

"Security Issues for Mobile Phones": www.mobilephonesandsafety.co.uk/security-issues-for-mobile-phones.html
"Android Vulnerable to Data Theft Exploit": www.informationweek.com/news/security/vulnerabilities/showArticle.jhtml?articleID=228400108

Deliverables:

Prepare answers to the following questions:

1. Explain why the following statement is true, and provide at least two specific examples of security risks that are not present for laptops or desktops: "Increased capabilities

of smart phones made it possible to use them as substitute for desktops and laptops but increased the security risks."

2. Use Internet search engines to find at least three ways to address the security issues for mobile phones, and list your findings.

Quiz Questions:

1. According to the article on the security issues for mobile phones, which of the following will be an important security feature for mobile phones for sensitive applications such as mobile banking?

   (a) RFID technology
   (b) Fingerprinting and biometrics
   (c) IP profiling
   (d) Electronic cell phone lock

2. Increasingly, mobile phone operators are providing services that can lock out everything in a phone if a phone is reported stolen. For that the service providers must know

   (a) The SIM card number
   (b) The model and make of the phone
   (c) IEMI
   (d) None of the above

3. The Android attack can read information from the phone as well as from _____ card using _____ exploits.

4. New features, such as _____, video recording facility, and so on, are making mobile phones more _____ and thus vulnerable to _____.

Discussion Question:

The InformationWeek *article shows the vulnerability of Android to a programming attack. Do you think iPhones are equally at risk for such attacks? Why or why not? (Hint:* Open vs. closed OS)

What's in IT for ME?

FOR THE ACCOUNTING MAJOR

Wireless applications help accountants to count and audit inventory. They also expedite the flow of information for cost control. Price management, inventory control, and other accounting-related activities can be improved with the use of wireless technologies.

FOR THE FINANCE MAJOR

Wireless services can provide banks and other financial institutions with a competitive advantage. For example, wireless electronic payments, including micropayments, are more convenient (anywhere, anytime) than traditional means of payment, and they are also less expensive. Electronic bill payment from mobile devices is becoming more popular, increasing security and accuracy, expediting cycle time, and reducing processing costs.

FOR THE MARKETING MAJOR

Imagine a whole new world of marketing, advertising, and selling, with the potential to increase sales dramatically. Such is the promise of mobile computing. Of special interest for marketing are location-based advertising as well as the new opportunities resulting from pervasive computing and RFIDs. Finally, wireless technology also provides new opportunities in sales force automation (SFA), enabling faster and better communications with both customers (CRM) and corporate services.

FOR THE
PRODUCTION/OPERATIONS MANAGEMENT MAJOR

 Wireless technologies offer many opportunities to support mobile employees of all kinds. Wearable computers enable off-site employees and repair personnel working in the field to service customers faster, better, and less expensively. Wireless devices can also increase productivity within factories by enhancing communication and collaboration as well as managerial planning and control. In addition, mobile computing technologies can improve safety by providing quicker warning signs and instant messaging to isolated employees.

FOR THE
HUMAN RESOURCES MANAGEMENT MAJOR

 Mobile computing can improve HR training and extend it to any place at anytime. Payroll notices can be delivered as SMSs. In addition, wireless devices can make it even more convenient for employees to select their own benefits and update their personal data.

FOR THE MIS MAJOR

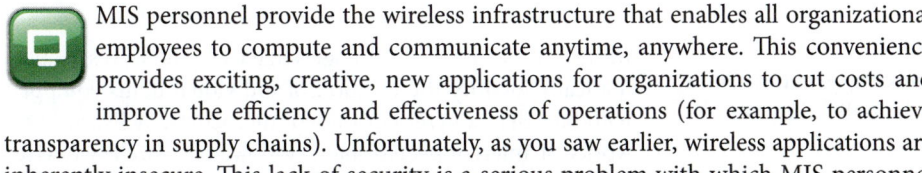 MIS personnel provide the wireless infrastructure that enables all organizational employees to compute and communicate anytime, anywhere. This convenience provides exciting, creative, new applications for organizations to cut costs and improve the efficiency and effectiveness of operations (for example, to achieve transparency in supply chains). Unfortunately, as you saw earlier, wireless applications are inherently insecure. This lack of security is a serious problem with which MIS personnel must contend.

>>> SUMMARY

1. Describe the four main types of wireless transmission media, and identify at least one advantage and one disadvantage of each type.

Microwave transmission systems are used for high-volume, long-distance, line-of-sight communication. One advantage is the high volume. A disadvantage is that microwave transmissions are susceptible to environmental interference during severe weather such as heavy rain and snowstorms.

Satellite transmission systems make use of communication satellites, and they receive and transmit data via line-of-sight. One advantage is that the enormous footprint—the area of Earth's surface reached by a satellite's transmission—overcomes the limitations of microwave data-relay stations. Like microwaves, satellite transmissions are susceptible to environmental interference during severe weather.

Radio transmission systems use radio-wave frequencies to send data directly between transmitters and receivers. An advantage is that radio waves travel easily through normal office walls. A disadvantage is that radio transmissions are susceptible to snooping by anyone who has similar equipment that operates on the same frequency.

Infrared light is red light that is not commonly visible to human eyes. Common applications of infrared light are in remote-control units for televisions, VCRs, and DVD and CD players. An advantage of infrared is that it does not penetrate walls and so does not interfere with other devices in adjoining rooms. A disadvantage is that infrared signals can be easily blocked by furniture.

2. Discuss the basic purposes of short-range, medium-range, and long-range networks, and explain how businesses can use at least one technology employed by each type of network.

Short-range wireless networks simplify the task of connecting one device to another, eliminating wires and enabling users to move around while they use the devices. In general, short-range wireless networks have a range of 100 feet or less. Short-range wireless networks include Bluetooth, ultra-wideband, and near-field communications. A business application of ultra-wideband is the PLUS Real-Time Location System from Time Domain. Using PLUS, an organization can locate multiple people and assets simultaneously.

Medium-range wireless networks include Wireless Fidelity (Wi-Fi) and mesh networks. *Wi-Fi* provides fast and easy Internet or intranet broadband access from public hotspots located at airports, hotels, Internet cafés, universities, conference centers, offices, and homes. *Mesh networks* use multiple Wi-Fi access points to create a wide area network that can be quite large.

Wide-area wireless networks connect users to the Internet over geographically dispersed territory. They include cellular telephones and wireless broadband. *Cellular telephones* provide two-way radio communications over a cellular network of base stations with seamless handoffs. *Wireless broadband* (WiMAX) has a wireless access range of up to 31 miles and a data-transfer rate of up to 75 Mbps. WiMAX can provide long-distance broadband wireless access to rural areas and remote business locations.

3. Discuss the five major m-commerce applications, and provide a specific example of how each application can benefit a business.

Location-based services provide information specific to a location. For example, a mobile user can (1) request the nearest business or service, such as an ATM or restaurant; (2) receive alerts, such as a warning of a traffic jam or an accident; and (3) find a friend. With *location-based advertising*, marketers can integrate the current locations and preferences of mobile users. They can then send user-specific advertising messages about nearby shops, malls, and restaurants to wireless devices.

Mobile financial applications include banking, wireless payments and micropayments, money transfers, wireless wallets, and bill-payment services. The bottom line for mobile financial applications is to make it more convenient for customers to transact business regardless of where they are or what time it is.

Intrabusiness applications consist of m-commerce applications that are used *within* organizations. Companies can use nonvoice mobile services to assist in dispatch functions—that is, to assign jobs to mobile employees, along with detailed information about the job.

When it comes to *accessing information,* mobile portals and voice portals are designed to aggregate and deliver content in a form that will work within the limited space available on mobile devices. These portals provide information anywhere and anytime to users.

Telemetry is the wireless transmission and receipt of data gathered from remote sensors. Company technicians can use telemetry to identify maintenance problems in equipment. Car manufacturers use telemetry applications for remote vehicle diagnosis and preventive maintenance.

4. Define pervasive computing, describe two technologies that underlie this technology, and provide at least one example of how a business can utilize each one.

Pervasive computing is invisible and everywhere computing that is embedded in the objects around us. Two technologies provide the infrastructure for pervasive computing: *radio-frequency identification* (*RFID*) and *wireless sensor networks* (*WSNs*).

RFID is the term for technologies that use radio waves to automatically identify the location of individual items equipped with tags that contain embedded microchips. WSNs are networks of interconnected, battery-powered, wireless devices placed in the physical environment to collect data from many points over an extended space.

5. Identify the four major threats to wireless networks, and explain, with examples, how each one can damage a business.

The four major threats to wireless networks are rogue access points, war driving, eavesdropping, and radio-frequency jamming. A *rogue access point* is an unauthorized access point to a wireless network. *War driving* is the act of locating WLANs while driving around a city or elsewhere. *Eavesdropping* refers to efforts by unauthorized users to access data that are traveling over wireless networks. *Radio-frequency jamming* occurs when a person or a device intentionally or unintentionally interferes with wireless network transmissions.

>>> CHAPTER GLOSSARY

bluetooth Chip technology that enables short-range connection (data and voice) between wireless devices.

cellular telephones (cell phones) Phones that provide two-way radio communications over a cellular network of base stations with seamless handoffs.

Global Positioning System (GPS) A wireless system that uses satellites to enable users to determine their position anywhere on earth.

hotspot A small geographical perimeter within which a wireless access point provides service to a number of users.

infrared A type of wireless transmission that uses red light not commonly visible to human eyes.

location-based commerce (l-commerce) Mobile commerce transactions targeted to individuals in specific locations, at specific times.

mesh networks Networks composed of multiple Wi-Fi access points that create a wide area network that can be quite large.

microwave transmission A wireless system that uses microwaves for high-volume, long-distance, point-to-point communication.

mobile commerce (or **m-commerce**) Electronic commerce transactions that are conducted with a mobile device.

mobile computing A real-time connection between a mobile device and other computing environments, such as the Internet or an intranet.

mobile portal A portal that aggregates and provides content and services for mobile users.

mobile wallet (m-wallet) A technology that allows users to make purchases with a single click from their mobile devices.

near-field communications (NFC) The smallest of the short-range wireless networks that is designed to be embedded in mobile devices such as cell phones and credit cards.

personal area network A computer network used for communication among computer devices close to one person.

pervasive computing (or **ubiquitous computing**) A computer environment where virtually every object has processing power with wireless or wired connections to a global network.

propagation delay Any delay in communications due to signal transmission time through a physical medium.

radio-frequency identification (RFID) technology A wireless technology that allows manufacturers to attach tags with antennas and computer chips on goods and then track their movement through radio signals.

radio transmission Uses radio-wave frequencies to send data directly between transmitters and receivers.

satellite radio (or **digital radio**) A wireless system that offers uninterrupted, near CD-quality music that is beamed to your radio from satellites.

satellite transmission A wireless transmission system that uses satellites for broadcast communications.

telemetry The wireless transmission and receipt of data gathered from remote sensors.

ubiquitous computing (see **pervasive computing**)

ultra-wideband (UWB) A high-bandwidth wireless technology with transmission speeds in excess of 100 Mbps that can be used for applications such as streaming multimedia from, say, a personal computer to a television.

voice portal A Web site with an audio interface.

wireless Telecommunications in which electromagnetic waves carry the signal between communicating devices.

wireless 911 911 emergency calls made with wireless devices.

wireless access point An antenna connecting a mobile device to a wired local area network.

Wireless Fidelity (Wi-Fi) A set of standards for wireless local area networks based on the IEEE 802.11 standard.

wireless local area network (WLAN) A computer network in a limited geographical area that uses wireless transmission for communication.

wireless sensor networks (WSNs) Networks of interconnected, battery-powered, wireless sensors placed in the physical environment.

>>> DISCUSSION QUESTIONS

1. Discuss how m-commerce can expand the reach of e-business.

2. Discuss how mobile computing can solve some of the problems of the digital divide.

3. List three to four major advantages of wireless commerce to consumers, and explain what benefits they provide to consumers.

4. Discuss the ways in which Wi-Fi is being used to support mobile computing and m-commerce. Describe the ways in which Wi-Fi is affecting the use of cellular phones for m-commerce.

5. You can use location-based tools to help you find your car or the closest gas station. However, some people see location-based tools as an invasion of privacy. Discuss the pros and cons of location-based tools.

6. Discuss the benefits of telemetry in healthcare for the elderly.

7. Discuss how wireless devices can help people with disabilities.

8. Some experts say that Wi-Fi is winning the battle with 3G cellular service. Others disagree. Discuss both sides of the argument, and support each one.

9. Which of the applications of pervasive computing do you think are likely to gain the greatest market acceptance over the next few years? Why?

>>> PROBLEM-SOLVING ACTIVITIES

1. Investigate commercial applications of voice portals. Visit several vendors (e.g., www.tellme.com, www.nuance.com, and so on). What capabilities and applications do these vendors offer?

2. Using a search engine, try to determine whether there are any commercial Wi-Fi hotspots in your area. (*Hint:* Access http://v4.jiwire.com/search-hotspot-locations.htm.) Also check www.boingo.com.

3. Examine how new data-capture devices such as RFID tags help organizations accurately identify and segment their customers for activities such as targeted marketing. Browse the Web, and develop five potential new applications not listed in this chapter for RFID technology. What issues would arise if a country's laws mandated that such devices be embedded in everyone's body as a national identification system?

4. Investigate commercial uses of GPS. Start with http://gpshome.ssc.nasa.gov; then go to www.neigps.com. Can some of the consumer-oriented products be used in industry? Prepare a report on your findings.

5. Access www.bluetooth.com. Examine the types of products being enhanced with Bluetooth technology. Present two of these products to the class, and explain how they are enhanced by Bluetooth technology.

6. Explore www.nokia.com. Prepare a summary of the types of mobile services and applications Nokia currently supports and plans to support in the future.

7. Enter www.ibm.com. Search for "wireless e-business." Research the resulting stories to determine the types of wireless capabilities and applications IBM's software and hardware support. Describe some of the ways these applications have helped specific businesses and industries.

8. Research the status of 3G and 4G cellular service by visiting www.itu.int, www.4g.co.uk, and www.huffingtonpost.com/2011/06/19/4g-network-what-you-should-know_n_879609.html. Prepare a report on the status of 3G and 4G based on your findings.

9. Enter Pitney-Bowes Business Insight (www.pbinsight.com). Click on "MapInfo Professional," then click on the "Resources" tab, then on the "Demos" tab. Look for the location-based services demos. Try all the demos. Summarize your findings.

10. Enter www.packetvideo.com. Examine the demos and products, and list their capabilities.

11. Enter www.onstar.com. What types of *fleet* services does OnStar provide? Are these any different from the services OnStar provides to individual car owners? (Play the movie.)

12. Access www.itu.int/osg/spu/publications/internetofthings/InternetofThings_summary.pdf. Read about the Internet of Things. What is it? What types of technologies are necessary to support it? Why is it important?

>>> TEAM ASSIGNMENTS

1. Each team should examine a major vendor of mobile devices (Nokia, Kyocera, Motorola, Palm, BlackBerry, Apple, and so on). Each team will research the capabilities and prices of the devices offered by each company and then make a class presentation, the objective of which is to convince the rest of the class they should buy that company's products.

2. Each team should explore the commercial applications of m-commerce in one of the following areas: financial services, including banking, stocks, and insurance; marketing and advertising; manufacturing; travel and transportation; human resources management; public services; and healthcare. Each team will present a report to the class based on their findings. (Start at www.mobiforum.org.)

3. Each team should take one of the following areas—homes, cars, appliances, or other consumer goods like clothing—and investigate how embedded microprocessors are currently being used and will be used in the future to support consumer-centric services. Each team will present a report to the class based on their findings.

CLOSING **CASE 1 >** The Battle for the Mobile Wallet

THE PROBLEM>>> Customers today are in more of a hurry today than ever before. To satisfy them and keep their business, retailers are looking for strategies to speed up the checkout process and improve the overall customer experience. One strategy is to rely on customers' smart phones as a replacement for all of their credit and debit cards. Instead of swiping a plastic card at the checkout counter, consumers merely wave their phones a few inches above a payment terminal. This process uses a contact-free technology called near-field communications (NFC).

The technology described in the preceding paragraph, known as the mobile wallet, is already being installed in millions of phones both in the United States and overseas. However, wide adoption of this technology in the United States is being hindered by a major battle among large corporations.

In one camp are the established credit card companies such as MasterCard, Visa, and American Express, along with the banks that actually issue the cards to customers. These businesses want to maintain their traditional position at the center of any payment system and to continue to collect their fees from merchants. However, they are facing intense competition from technology companies such as Google and PayPal whose goal is to become major players in the new payment system. In addition, Apple and the mobile carriers such as Verizon, AT&T, and T-Mobile want to collect fees through their control of the phones themselves. Adding to the competitive mix are individual companies such as Starbucks that are developing proprietary mobile wallet technologies.

In the middle, and perhaps playing a deciding role, are the retailers. They have to install terminals that accept mobile payments. Consumer advocates, meanwhile, are concerned that a mobile system will bring higher fees, which, of course, would be passed along to customers.

The stakes in this competition are enormous because the small fees that are generated every time consumers swipe their cards add up to tens of billions of dollars annually in the United States alone. Before these companies make any money, they need to sort out what role each one will play and who will collect the lucrative transaction fees from retailers.

<<<A VARIETY OF SOLUTIONS

Mobile Phone Carriers. In 2010, three of the big four providers—AT&T, T-Mobile, and Verizon, but not Sprint—along with Discover (www.discovercard.com) and Barclays Bank (www.barclays.co.uk) formed a joint venture named Isis. Their intention was to create a new payment network that encompassed credit card companies and card-issuing banks. Isis creates a digital wallet into which customers of card-issuing banks can easily move their accounts. Consumers would interface with Isis through a mobile app, which would give them access to multiple credit and debit accounts. Retailers would participate by offering targeted offers to loyalty members through Isis, while product companies and brands could also offer discounts to customers who opt in.

Credit Card Issuers. In 2010, Visa, MasterCard, and American Express spent nearly $3 billion to buy Internet-based payment processors. For example, in August 2010, MasterCard bought payment company DataCash Group (www.datacash.com) for $526 million. All three card issuers have mobile applications: MasterCard has MasterCard PayPass, Visa has Visa Mobile, and American Express has American Express Mobile. In addition, credit card companies have been experimenting with wave-and-pay systems that use NFC-enabled credit or debit cards (e.g., the Visa Wave).

The credit card companies claim that their mobile applications enable consumers to make online payments quickly, without having to enter a card number and billing address over and over. For example, a smart phone game could allow players to buy add-ons, such as new weapons or extra ammunition, by clicking a Visa logo. A caterer might be able to e-mail a bill with a button that allows a client to pay with one click. Payers would authorize the transaction simply by entering a name and password.

Technology Companies. Google has its own payment system, called Google Checkout (http://checkout.google.com). The company claims that it will be willing to partner with payment processors to handle purchases made with its smart phones. Interestingly, if future models of the iPhone incorporate NFC, the device may route payments through Apple's iTunes store, which already has 200 million accounts tied to credit cards. Both Google Checkout and Apple's iTunes could be turned into mobile wallets. Both systems, however, would need access to the smart phone chips and to the merchants' terminals. Apple could manufacture its own smart phone chips, but Google could not because it makes only Android smart phone software, not the phones themselves.

PayPal has developed PayPal X (www.x.com/index.jspa), software used by entrepreneurs to develop apps for PayPal. For example, if you are at the ballpark and you want to skip the long lines at the concession stand, just download the iConcessionStand (www.iconcessionstand.com) smart phone app. The app lets sports fans order hot dogs and cold beer from their mobile phones and pay by transferring money from PayPal (www.paypal.com) to a nearby food vendor. An alert pops up when the order is ready. PayPal, a unit of eBay, earns about 3 percent on each transaction. The iConcessionStand app is 1 of more than 1,000 developed by entrepreneurs using PayPal X. In addition, new technology startups, such as Zong (www.zong.com) and Obopay (www.obopay.com), are developing applications to make online and mobile payments easier.

Individual Companies. In January 2011 Starbucks (www.starbucks.com) announced that customers could use a bar-code app on their phones to buy coffee in almost 7,000 of its stores. This is the first major pay-by-phone initiative in the United States. Customers can download the free Starbucks Card app and hold their phones in front of a scanner at Starbucks cash registers. The money is subtracted from customers' Starbucks accounts, which they can load with credit cards, or, on iPhones, with PayPal funds. Customers can also use the Starbucks app to check their balances, find nearby stores, and earn stars to qualify for free drinks.

THE RESULTS >>>

The battle for the transaction fees from your mobile wallet is ongoing, and the results will be several years in arriving. However, the potential for large revenue streams is real, because mobile wallets have clear advantages. For example: Which are you more likely to have with you at any given moment—your phone or your wallet? Also, keep in mind that if you lose your phone, it can be located on a map and remotely deactivated. Plus, your phone can be password protected. Your wallet cannot do these things.

Questions

1. Given that you can lose a cell phone as easily as a wallet, which do you feel is a more secure way of carrying your personal data? Support your answer.

2. If mobile computing is the next wave of technology, would you ever feel comfortable with handing a waiter or waitress your cell phone to make a payment at a restaurant the way you currently hand over your credit or debit card? Why or why not?

SOURCES: Compiled from R. Kim, "Isis: Respect the Carriers; We'll Be Key to NFC Success," *GigaOM*, May 6, 2011; S. Marek, "AT&T, Verizon Wireless and T-Mobile Backpedal on Isis Joint Venture," *FierceWireless*, May 4, 2011; R. Sidel and S. Raice, "Pay By Phone Dialed Back," *Wall Street Journal*, May 4, 2011; T. Team, "American Express and Visa Squeeze PayPal's Crown Jewels," *Forbes*, April 4, 2011; A. Efrati and R. Sidel, "Google Sets Role in Mobile Payment," *Wall Street Journal*, March 28, 2011; T. Bernard and C. Miller, "Swiping Is the Easy Part," *New York Times*, March 23, 2011; D. Aamoth, "Pay Phone," *Time*, February 21, 2011; D. MacMillan, "Turning Smartphones into Cash Registers," *Bloomberg BusinessWeek*, February 14–20, 2011; K. Eaton, "The Race Is On to Make NFC Wireless Credit Card Dreams Come True (and Win Market Share)," *Fast Company*, February 2, 2011; M. Hamblen, "NFC: What You Need to Know," *Computerworld*, January 28, 2011; K. Heussner, "Is Your Next Credit Card Your Cell Phone?" *ABC News*, January 26, 2011; S. Greengard, "Mobile Payment, Please," *Baseline Magazine*, January 26, 2011; E. Zemen, "Will Apple, Google Lead Mobile Payment Revolution?" *InformationWeek*, January 25, 2011; B. Ellis, "The End of Credit Cards Is Coming," *CNNMoney*, January 24, 2011; C. Miller, "Now at Starbucks: Buy a Latte by Waving Your Phone," *New York Times*, January 18, 2011; O. Kharif, "In the Works: A Google Mobile Payment Service?" *Bloomberg BusinessWeek*, January 4, 2011; R. King, "Wells Fargo to Employees: Leave Wallets Home, Pay by Phone," *Bloomberg BusinessWeek*, January 4, 2011; H. Shaughnessy, "Banking Gets Mobile and Social," *Forbes*, November 22, 2010; J. Galante and P. Eichenbaum, "Card Companies Are Wooing Programmers," *Bloomberg BusinessWeek*, November 22–28, 2010; P. Pachal, "U.S. Carriers Create Pay-by-Phone System, for Real This Time," *PC Magazine*, November 16, 2010; T. Claburn, "Web 2.0: Google CEO Sees Android Phones Replacing Credit Cards," *InformationWeek*, November 16, 2010; E. Zeman, "Starbucks Mobile Pay Now in NYC," *InformationWeek*, November 1, 2010; www.iconcessionstand.com, www.paypal.com, www.x.com/index.jspa, accessed April 28, 2011.

CLOSING **CASE 2 >**

A Mobile Application for Home Depot

Home Depot (www.homedepot.com), the world's largest retailer of home improvement and construction products and services, has been lagging in information technology. In fact, IT was an afterthought at Home Depot for years because the company's primary emphasis was opening new stores. Today, Home Depot has more than 2,000 retail outlets.

Until 2010, employees stocked shelves as they had for 15 years, using computers powered by motorboat batteries and rolled around stores on bulky carts. In early 2011, Home Depot still did not offer customers the option to order online and pick up merchandise in stores, as Lowe's (www.lowes.com), Home Depot's biggest competitor, already did. Further, when Home Depot employees processed special orders for customers, they had to rely on outdated information systems. This arrangement hurt both sales and service.

In 2007, Frank Blake became Home Depot's new CEO. Blake shifted the company's focus to increasing profits from existing stores. Inventory turns—a measure of how well a retailer turns goods into sales—began to increase. However, Home Depot did not have the information systems to enable this change in corporate strategy. Therefore, the company had to modernize its information systems to improve in-store technology.

Another component of Home Depot's new strategy was to attract younger customers who are accustomed to shopping online, often with devices they carry in their pockets or handbags—that is, the company wanted to increase online transactions. (In 2010, online transactions amounted to roughly 1.5 percent of Home Depot's total sales.) Unfortunately, the company's Web site was unattractive, difficult to navigate, and did not provide for a seamless shopping experience. Therefore, the company had to improve its site to capture the attention of the numerous customers who browse online before they go to the store.

<<<**THE BUSINESS PROBLEM**

During fiscal year 2010, which ended on January 30, 2011, Home Depot spent $350 million on information technology, which amounted to one-third of the company's total capital expenditures. One of the new IT applications involved mobility. The company spent $60 million to buy 40,000 handheld devices, called "First Phones," to replace the old in-store computers. First Phones enable Home Depot associates to manage inventory and help customers find products. These devices not only act as a phone, but they replace walkie-talkies. In addition, with its credit card reader, the device becomes a mobile cash register. Further, associates can check inventory in their store and in other stores from any location on the floor.

Home Depot also launched a blogging site on its Web site where employees answer customer questions on all home improvement and home construction matters. Further, as part of a broader upgrade of its checkout systems, the company's U.S. stores installed contactless scanners for reading credit card information on customers' smart phones.

<<<**THE IT SOLUTION**

It is too soon to predict the results of these new policies. Interestingly, Home Depot's IT initiatives could be complicated by the preference of most older contractors and do-it-yourself homeowners to buy in person at a store. Home Depot recognizes that the company has to serve customers the way they want to be served. However, the company feels that over the long run, customers are going to become much more comfortable using their smart phones on a real-time basis outside or inside the store.

<<<**THE RESULTS**

$\mathcal{Q}$uestions

1. Provide two specific reasons why Home Depot felt it necessary to deploy wireless handheld devices.

2. Identify two potential disadvantages of deploying wireless handhelds at Home Depot.

SOURCES: Compiled from C. Burritt, "Home Depot's Fix-It Lady," *Bloomberg BusinessWeek*, January 17–January 23, 2011; A. Blair, "Home Depot's $64 Million Mobile Investment Rolls Out to 1,970 Stores," *Mobile Redirect*, December 7, 2010; G. Tsirulnik, "Home Depot Adds Commerce Functionality to App in Time for Holidays," *Mobile Commerce Daily*, November 23, 2010; E. Zemen, "Mobile Shopping to Take Off for Holidays," *InformationWeek*, November 10, 2010; E. Shein, "Bank of America, Visa Pilot Mobile Payments," *InformationWeek*, August 23, 2010; T. Parry, "Home Depot's Mobile Site Could Be Better," *The Big Fat Marketing Blog*, April 5, 2010; "Rating Retailers' iPhone Apps: Amazon, Best Buy, Home Depot, Target, Walmart," *Mobile Commerce Daily*, January 19, 2010; "Home Depot App Takes Mobile Commerce on the Job," www.cell-phone-plans.net, accessed February 11, 2011; www.homedepot.com, www.lowes.com, accessed February 12, 2011.

RUBY'S CLUB INTERNSHIP ASSIGNMENTS

Search the Web for "pay-by-phone" applications, or for companies that promote mobile, online ordering systems. Ruben and Lisa are most interested in a method to keep customers outside the store from ordering drinks to be picked up by someone else, particularly a minor.

How could they control this? Can you think of any policies or procedures they could put in place to keep this from becoming a problem? Also, can you find any examples of mobile devices being used for restaurants, clubs, or bars? Is there any way to restrict orders to customers currently in the store?

After you do your research, prepare a report for Ruben and Lisa that will help them understand what they may be up against with this mobile ordering system.

SPREADSHEET ACTIVITY

Objective: Spreadsheets are powerful tools, but part of their power comes from the user interface (UI). This activity will use online demonstrations to allow you to experience spreadsheets in a mobile environment.

Chapter Connection: This activity puts wireless spreadsheets into the palm of your hand. While the demonstrations used here are based on spreadsheet tools, the implications of mobile user interface will apply in many situations. While mobile tools are very useful, they are also limited. This activity will help you see the difference in interacting with spreadsheets based on the method used to connect to them.

Prerequisites: There are no prerequisites for this activity.

Activity: Many online tools are available today. Microsoft has now released an online version of its Office Suite, though Google is by far the leader in online document creation. A single account with Google gives users access to e-mail, calendars, documents, YouTube, and much more. While online document creation, editing, and storing offers lots of advantages, there are drawbacks, especially when these tools are used in a mobile environment.

There are three steps to this activity. First, you will create a Microsoft Excel spreadsheet that will track fuel mileage for your company vehicle. This sheet needs columns for the date, odometer reading, gallons pumped, and miles per gallon. The last column will be calculated based on the difference in the previous and current odometer reading and the number of gallons pumped. For this part of the exercise, you need at least five entries to be sure your spreadsheet is working properly.

Once you are satisfied that your spreadsheet is calculating appropriately, create a Google account and log into GoogleDocs in a Web browser. Upload your spreadsheet, and add five more entries online.

Finally, log into the mobile version of Google Docs on your mobile phone. If you do not have an Internet-enabled phone, search Google for "Opera Mini Demo," and use the demo of Opera's mobile Internet browser. Whether from your phone or the demo browser, add two more entries to your spreadsheet.

Keep a detailed diary of your experience, noting which method worked best. Be sure to explain the advantages and disadvantages of each method of accessing and editing the spreadsheet. Finally, open your Google spreadsheet in a browser, and get the URL to share the document. Add this link to your diary, and submit your document to your professor along with your original Excel spreadsheet.

Deliverables: You will submit both an Excel spreadsheet and a Word document. The spreadsheet should have at least five entries that calculate gas mileage. The document will be the diary detailing each of the three methods of accessing this spreadsheet.

Quiz Questions:

1. True or False? All features available in Google Docs are also available in the mobile version of the documents.
2. True or False? Data entry operates the same in the mobile version of Google Docs.
3. Which of the following are available for Google Docs but not for Microsoft Excel?
   (a) Online document sharing
   (b) Formula editing
   (c) Complete revision history
   (d) Graphs and charts

Discussion Questions:

1. What do you think needs to change in the mobile and Web-based environments for them to match the traditional Excel experience? Or do they even need to match?
2. Recently it was reported that Google was going to release an operating system that ran in the "cloud" that would bring us closer to a fully "cloud-based" computing experience. Based on your diary thoughts, what improvements can you see that will need to be made in networks, computer interaction devices, storage speeds, and so on for this to be successful?

DATABASE ACTIVITY: QUERIES I

Objective:

In this activity, you will learn how to create a query based on more than one table, with multiple criteria. In the Chapter 6 activity you selected records from a table by filtering. Sometimes selection criteria are too complex for that approach, especially if more than one table is involved. Or, perhaps you would like to set up a database so a user who is not familiar with Access can accomplish the same thing. Queries let you do that.

Chapter Connection:

You will see how queries can be useful in a mobile e-commerce situation.

Prerequisites:

None, although the Chapter 6 activity (Filters) will provide useful background.

Activity:

In this activity, which you will find online at www.wiley.com/college/rainer, you will create queries that combine data from more than one table to find information that, in the database, is spread across all of them.

Note: This version of the activity is for use with Access 2010. There is another version for Access 2007. The contents of both are identical, including the activities and their sequence. They differ where the two releases of the software differ: in screen shots and in some details of how specific operations are accomplished.

1. Download and open the Ch 10 DizzyDonuts database from www.wiley.com/college/rainer. It belongs to a chain of donut shops. Much of their business comes from people driving or walking by their stores. The stores have a "smart phone" application that determines customer location from the phone's GPS data, lets a customer order online and pay by credit card, sends a bar code to the phone as a graphic, and then lets the customer pick up the order by holding the bar code up to a reader at the counter or drive-in window.

   The database you will work with here supports that application. It has five tables: stores, customers, products, orders, and line items. You can see their relationships in the relationship map of the database. (This database resembles the Ch 09 DaffyDonuts database you may have used, plus a new store table with location information to support this app.)

2. The first query will be used to find out how often a given customer uses this service. We know the customer's name, but not his or her number, so we need to use both CustTbl and OrderTbl in this query. To start, click the "Create" ribbon tab. In the Other section toward the right, click "Query Design."

Usage Hint: In contrast to Design view for most other Access objects, Design view for queries is easy to use and adds important capabilities. Therefore, we will use it rather than a wizard here.

3. The first thing you see there is a Show Table box, similar to the one you may have used in creating the database relationship map in the Chapter 2 activity. You use it to specify which tables you will use in this query. You must include three types of tables:

   • All tables that the query checks to select data to display in response to the query, even if no data from those tables will show up in the reply

   • All tables that provide data to display in the reply to the query, even if no data from those tables is used in selecting records to display

   • All tables that sit between any of the others in the database relationship map, since Access needs them to figure out how to connect the others

Usage Hint: Selecting the wrong tables will cause a query to fail or return erroneous results. If your query has problems, this is one place to check. If the tables are not all connected to each other in the top pane of the query design window, you left one out or (less

likely) your database does not have all the necessary table relationships.

Here, add the Customer and Order tables. You will see a line between them. That means Access does not need any other tables to connect them. Close the Show Table windoid.

4. Click in the top row of the first column of the query design grid if it is not already selected. Enter "CustName" (the quotation marks are optional; if you leave them off, Access will supply them), or select CustName from the pull-down list under the arrow. When you tab out of that field or click somewhere else, Access will fill in CustTbl as the table name directly underneath it.

Usage Hint: Easier—You can also drag a field name from any table in the upper pane of the design window into the grid. Even easier—Double-click a field name in the upper pane, and it will appear in the next empty grid column.

By the way, this grid is sometimes referred to as the *Query by Example* or *QBE* grid because you use it to create an example of what you are looking for. The name is not entirely appropriate; it was first used at a time when the grid was a real example of data to be found, but it is still around.

5. In the Criteria row of that column, enter "Adam" as the customer name. This will be the selection criterion for this query.

Usage Hint (for English usage, not Access): *Criteria* is the plural form. Use it only when there are two or more. If you only have one, it is a *criterion*.

6. In the top row of the next two columns, enter OrderDate, OrderStore, and OrderTotal. Do not enter any selection criteria here. We want to see all of Adam's orders, no matter what date they were on or what store they were at.

7. Click "Run," the large red exclamation point near the left of the ribbon, to see the result. It should be correct, but its structure and appearance leave a lot to be desired. If you do the Chapter 11 activity, you will see how to put this result into a better-organized, nicer-looking report.

If you got an empty table—no matching records—the most likely reason is an error in keying in "Adam" as the selection criterion or entering it in the wrong column. Go back to Design view and check those.

Usage Hint: The tablelike results of a query are called a *dynaset*, for "dynamic set." When data in a table change, the dynaset changes dynamically but records are not rescreened. If changes affect selection criteria, the affected records will not move in or out of the dynaset but will show the new data. For example, if you select all items priced under $100 and then change a price to $109.99, that item will still be displayed with its new, higher price. To update the selection for the new data, rerun the query.

8. Return to Design view. Change the customer name to "Belina." Run the query again.

9. Close the query, saving it as "CustOrderQry" when prompted.

10. The next query will find all customers who shopped at a given store. Create a new query in Design view. Enter CustTbl and StoreTbl into the upper pane of the query design window. You will see that they are not connected. The database relationship map shows why: They must be linked via the Order table. Reopen the Show Table box if you closed it (near the middle of the Design ribbon) and add OrderTbl to the query. The tables are now connected.

11. Select fields for this query: store city, customer name, order date, and order total.

12. As a selection criterion, enter "Boston" as the store city.

13. Run the query, showing all the orders for the Boston store.

14. Close the query, saving it as "StoreOrderQry" when prompted.

15. The third query can be used to find out who orders expensive products. ("Expensive" is a relative concept. Nothing that a donut shop sells would be considered expensive at an art gallery.) As before, open a new query design window. This time you must connect products and customers. To do this, you will need to show additional tables in the query. Enter them in the upper pane from the Show Table list. You should see a total of four tables here. If you arrange them in a line with the Customer table at one end and the Product table at the other, the tables in that line should be connected from one end to the other.

16. In the first column of the query design grid, enter ProdPrice and a criterion of "> 1.6" (without the quotation marks). Selection criteria can include comparisons, as well as other options. We will get to some of them later here and in future activities.

Usage Hint: Criteria involving currency amounts must be entered as numbers. Access stores currency amounts that way. Specifying Currency data type controls how they are displayed, but does not affect the underlying data. Using a currency symbol in a query criterion will result in an error message. If this happens, dismiss the message, remove the dollar sign, remove the quotation marks that Access supplied because it thought you entered a character string, and continue.

17. In the next two columns, enter ProdName and CustName. Run the query.

18. Close the query, saving it as "ExpensiveProdQry" when prompted.

19. Make a copy of ExpensiveProdQry and open it in Design view. Add the Store table to the query. Add StoreCity to the first empty column of the query design grid. Enter a selection criterion of "Boston" for it, in the same row as the price criterion. Run the query. The result shows customers who ordered expensive (that is, over $1.60) items from the Boston store.

Note: Criteria in the same row of the query grid, but in different columns, are combined via an implied "And."

20. Close the query, saving it as "ExpensiveProdStoreQry" when prompted. (Depending on how you created the copy, you may have had a chance to name it earlier.)

21. Make a copy of ExpensiveProdStoreQry, which you just saved, and open it in Design view. Delete the Boston criterion from the grid cell it is in, and re-enter it in the same column, one row down. Run the query. This time, you will see all the customers who ordered expensive products at any store, and in addition all the customers who ordered anything at all from the Boston store.

Note: Criteria in different rows of the query grid are combined via an implied "Or."

20. Close the query, saving it as "ExpensiveTestQry" when prompted. (Depending on how you created the copy, you may have had a chance to name it earlier.)

21. Close the database.

Deliverables:

Your database, with the preceding five queries.

Quiz Questions:

1. The relationship between Orders and Products in this database is:
   (a) One-to-one
   (b) Many-to-one
   (c) Many-to-many
   (d) One-to-many

2. When criteria are entered on the same row of different columns in the query design grid:
   (a) The query will display result rows in which all criteria are true.
   (b) The query will display result rows in which at least one of the criteria is true.

(c) The query will display result rows in which at least two of the criteria are true.

(d) Something else.

3. The table pane of the query design grid should show:

   (a) Only tables whose values are tested by query criteria

   (b) All tables in the database

   (c) Only tables whose data we want to see in the query results

   (d) None of the above

4. True or False? A query must use a minimum of two tables.

Discussion Questions:

1. Consider a three-table database of students, grades, and courses, such as your school probably has. Suppose you want to display a student's grades. What would you put in the query design grid? (Make reasonable assumptions about the columns in the three tables.)

2. Suppose you are Director of Business Planning for Dizzy Donuts. You suspect that order patterns for the morning differ from those in the afternoon. (Access can compare times, though we did not use that here.) What sort of query could you design to help you confirm or deny this suspicion? Draw a sample page of how its results might look. You do not have to use real data from this database.

3. Some database management systems do not treat Currency as a data type when you define a table. Instead, currency amounts are first specified as "Number." Currency formatting is available as an option for numeric data, but it is treated as a formatting option like the use of commas to separate groups of three digits.

4. Do you prefer this approach or the Access approach? Why?

11 | Information Systems Within the Organization

LEARNING OBJECTIVES >>>

1. Explain the purposes of transaction processing systems, and provide at least one example of how businesses use these systems.

2. Define functional area information systems, and provide an example of the support they provide for each functional area of the organization.

3. Explain the purpose of enterprise resource planning systems, and identify four advantages and four drawbacks to implementing an ERP system.

4. Discuss the three major types of reports generated by the functional area information systems and enterprise resource planning systems, and provide an example of each type.

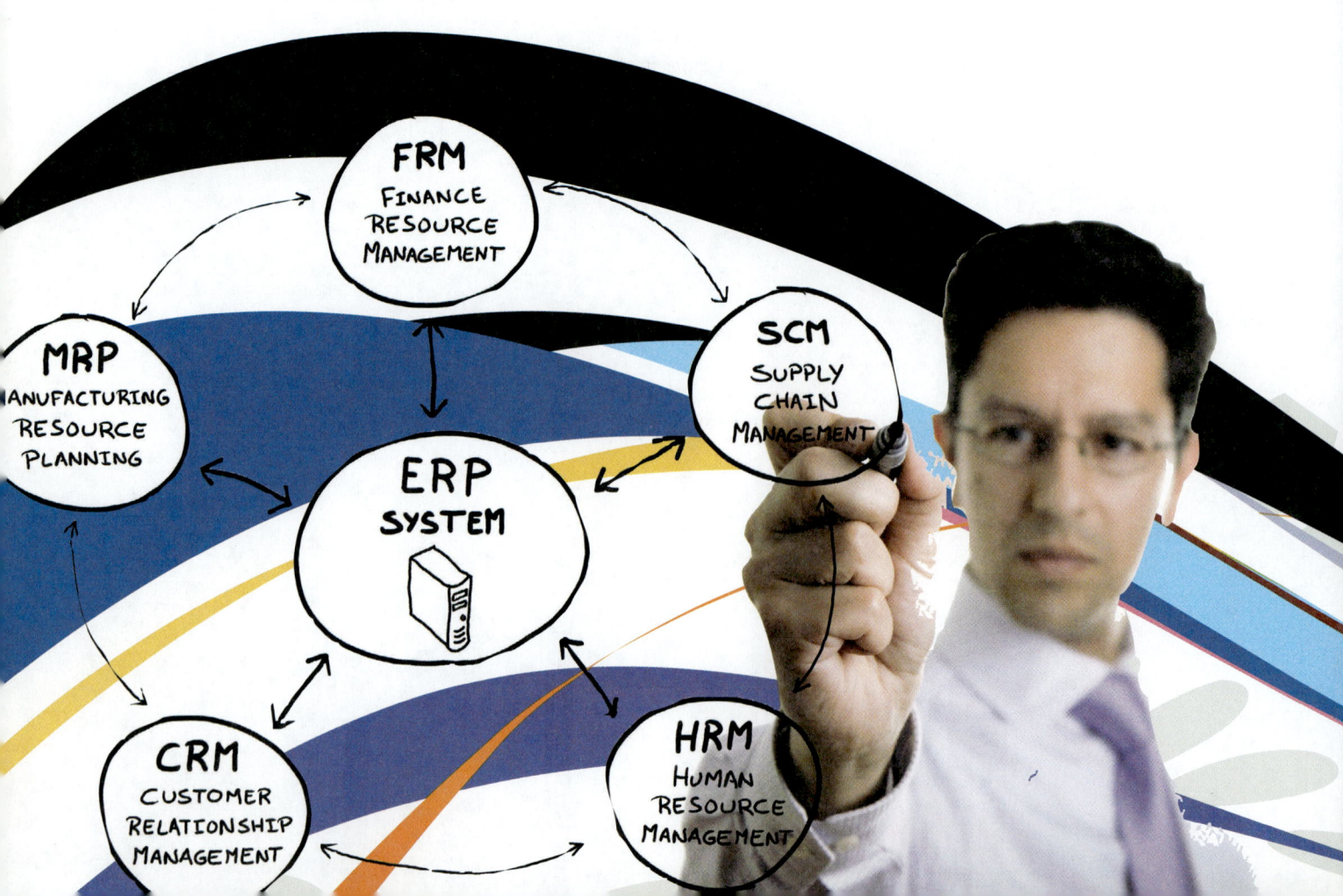

OPENING **CASE** > USA Cycling

Cycling teams are located around the country and the world. As they travel, they take supplies with them. When teams need to restock tires, seats, chains, parts, and other items, however, they must take time to gather inventory information from various locations to determine which items they need to reorder. This lack of information results in poor planning. This situation was not a problem when USA Cycling was a small group. Today, however, the organization has more than 6,600 members and 2,600 sponsored practice days, so inventory management has become vital to its success.

SmartTurn (www.smartturn.com) provides an on-demand inventory and warehouse management system that allows customers in different locations to manage inventory in a single system. The system is delivered as software-as-a-service (SaaS). (Refer to Chapter 14 for a detailed discussion of SaaS.) Smart-Turn allows cycling teams across the globe to update their inventory so that the home office can instantly see which supplies their various teams have and which supplies they need. In that way, headquarters can be sure that all of the cyclists are well stocked for their events.

USA Cycling staff members now have all the information they need right at their fingertips. No matter where they are, they can view inventory levels and make important purchasing decisions for their teams as they travel around the world. Gregory Cross, Director of Logistics and Operations for USA Cycling, said that cycling teams can now "rest assured that [they] are well equipped and receiving the necessary support wherever they are in the world. Additionally, with increased visibility, we can now better manage our assets to minimize lost equipment, further reducing costs."

Sources: Compiled from "SmartTurn Warehouse Management System Helps Bring Competitive Edge," *USA Cycling*, April 5, 2010; www.usacycling.org, www.smartturn.com/customers/index.jsp, accessed April 22, 2011.

Questions

1. Why did USA Cycling need an inventory system?

2. What advantages did the SmartTurn system provide for USA Cycling?

RUBY'S CLUB

Each month, Ruben and Lisa sit down to a table of receipts. They know there is a lot of information in there, but they have a terrible time sorting their way through the piles to find it. They know there has to be a better way. This is part of the reason for integrating IT into their remodeled and restructured business. They hope that their new information systems will provide them with more accurate, timely, helpful information so they can go about making decisions.

Specifically, they hope their transaction processing system will capture and collect data on customers' entry and departure times, food and beverage items purchased, bands playing when attending, and so on to help them make plans for the future. As you read through this chapter, consider how Ruby's Club could utilize the different information systems presented.

INTRODUCTION

USA Cycling needed an inventory system, and Smart-Turn matched the organization's needs. As the opening case demonstrates, "information systems within organizations" do not have to be owned by the organization itself. Instead, organizations can deploy very productive "internal" information systems that are owned by an external vendor. The important point here is that "information systems within an organization" are intended to support internal processes, regardless of who actually owns the systems.

There are an astonishing variety of information systems (ISs) that you will learn about in this chapter. Information systems are everywhere, and they impact organizations in countless ways. Who would have thought that an IS could help a large organization like professional baseball become more like a science? Information systems also impact small organizations, as illustrated by the chapter opening case.

It is important for you to have a working knowledge of information systems within your organization, for a variety of reasons. First, in your job you will be accessing corporate data that are largely supplied by your firm's transaction processing systems and enterprise resource planning systems. Second, you will have a great deal of input into the format and content of the reports that you receive from these systems. Third, you will use the information in these reports to perform your job more productively.

In this chapter you will see the various systems within the organization. You begin by considering transaction processing systems, the most fundamental information systems within organizations. You continue with the functional area management information systems, and then with the enterprise resource planning systems.

11.1 | Transaction Processing Systems

Millions (sometimes billions) of transactions occur in large organizations every day. A **transaction** is any business event that generates data worthy of being captured and stored in a database. Examples of transactions are a product manufactured, a service sold, a person hired, and a payroll check generated. In another example, when you are checking out of Walmart, each time the cashier swipes an item across the bar code reader, that is one transaction.

A **transaction processing system (TPS)** supports the monitoring, collection, storage, and processing of data from the organization's basic business transactions, each of which generates data. The TPS collects data continuously, typically in *real time*—that is, as soon as the data are generated—and it provides the input data for the corporate databases. The TPSs are critical to the success of any enterprise because they support core operations.

In the modern business world, TPSs are inputs to the functional area information systems and business intelligence systems, as well as business operations such as customer relationship management, knowledge management, and e-commerce. TPSs have to handle both high volume and large variations in volume (for example, during peak times) of data efficiently. In addition, they must avoid errors and downtime, record results accurately and securely, and maintain privacy and security. Figure 11.1 shows how TPSs manage data. Consider these examples of how TPSs manage the complexities of transactional data:

- When more than one person or application program can access the database at the same time, the database has to be protected from errors resulting from overlapping updates. The most common error is for the results of one of the updates to be lost.

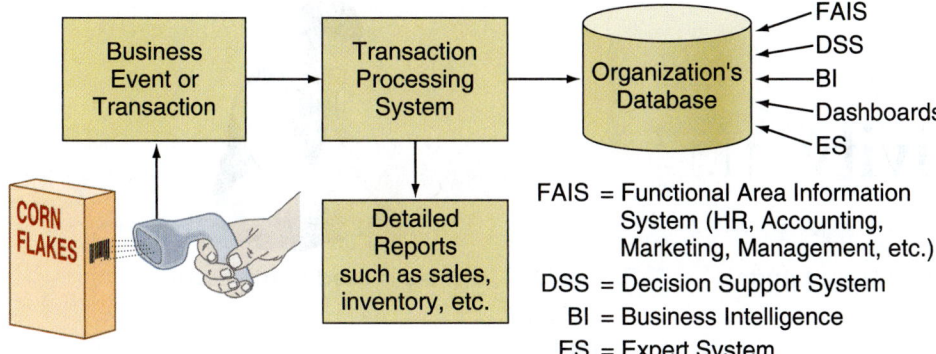

Figure 11.1 How transaction processing systems manage data.

FAIS = Functional Area Information
System (HR, Accounting,
Marketing, Management, etc.)
DSS = Decision Support System
BI = Business Intelligence
ES = Expert System

- When processing a transaction involves more than one computer, the database and all users must be protected against inconsistencies arising from a failure of any component at any time. For example, if an error occurs at some point in an ATM withdrawal, the customer could receive cash while the bank's computer indicates that he did not. (Conversely, the customer might not receive cash while the bank's computer indicates that he did.)

- It must be possible to reverse a transaction in its entirety if it turns out to have been entered in error. It is also necessary to reverse a transaction when a purchased item is returned.

- It may be important to preserve an audit trail. In fact, for certain transactions an audit trail may be legally required.

These and similar issues explain why organizations spend millions of dollars on expensive mainframe computers. In today's business environment, firms must have the dependability, reliability, and processing capacity of these computers to handle their transaction processing loads.

Regardless of the specific data processed by a TPS, the actual process tends to be standard, whether it occurs in a manufacturing firm, a service firm, or a government organization. First, data are collected by people or sensors and are entered into the computer via any input device. Generally speaking, organizations try to automate the TPS data entry as much as possible because of the large volume involved, a process called *source data automation*.

Next, the system processes data in one of two basic ways: batch processing and online processing. In **batch processing**, the firm collects data from transactions as they occur, placing them in groups or *batches*. The system then prepares and processes the batches periodically (say, every night).

In **online transaction processing (OLTP)**, business transactions are processed online as soon as they occur. For example, when you pay for an item at a store, the system records the sale by reducing the inventory on hand by one unit, increasing sales figures for the item by one unit, and increasing the store's cash position by the amount you paid. The system performs these tasks in real time by means of online technologies.

BEFORE *YOU GO ON* . . .

1. Define TPS.
2. List the key functions of a TPS.

RUBY'S CLUB QUESTIONS

1. How might Ruby's benefit from a TPS that provides an audit trail?
2. Is Ruby's Club subject to inconsistencies? Where might they come from, and how could a TPS help protect the club from this problem?
3. Considering the processing methods of OLTP and batch processing, which seems most likely to be used at Ruby's Club?

Student Activity | 11.1

Objective: To understand how software supports transaction processing systems.

Chapter Connection: This section is very short so the exercise builds on the fact that you have been generating transactions for companies.

Prerequisites: You should have read Section 11.1 of this chapter before doing this activity.

Activity:

Watch the following video, which illustrates the process for creating purchase orders and subsequently recording receipt of the ordered goods and paying the vendor using QuickBooks:

www.youtube.com/user/offtheshelfsystems?feature=pyv&ad=5802924234&kw=QuickBooks#p/u/0/MzblbOaAcrg

Refer again to the Web site pages (in order) that you looked at for "Student Activity 11.1" that explain what a data flow diagram is.

Deliverables:

Transaction processing systems manage data. They capture it at input, they process it, they store it, they report it. Draw a data flow diagram that follows the flow of the data as illustrated in the YouTube video on QuickBooks that you watched.

Quiz Questions:

1. Data flow diagrams are used to show how _____ flow through a system.

   (a) People
   (b) Paper
   (c) Data
   (d) B and C
   (e) None of the above

2. In a DFD, a circle is used to represent _____.

   (a) People
   (b) Paper
   (c) Data
   (d) B and C
   (e) None of the above

3. In a DFD, a line is used to show the flow of _____.

   (a) People
   (b) Paper
   (c) Data
   (d) B and C
   (e) None of the above

4. In a DFD, a _____ represents an activity that transforms or manipulates the data.

   (a) Circle
   (b) Arrow
   (c) Parallel lines
   (d) Square
   (e) None of the above

5. True or False? QuickBooks automatically prints a check when the user indicates that goods have been received.

6. True or False? A purchase order is sent to a customer.

Discussion Questions:

1. For the QuickBooks exercise, where do the data come from in all the drop-down menus?

2. Why is it important to have a copy of the internal purchase order?

11.2 | Functional Area Information Systems

Each department or functional area within an organization has its own collection of application programs, or information systems. Each of these **functional area information systems** supports a particular functional area in the organization by increasing each area's internal efficiency and effectiveness. FAISs often convey information in a variety of reports, which you will see in Section 11.4. Examples are accounting IS, finance IS, production/operations management (POM) IS, marketing IS, and human resources IS.

As illustrated in Figure 11.1, the FAISs access data from the corporate databases. In the next sections, you study the support that functional area information systems provide for these functional areas.

Information Systems for Accounting and Finance

A primary mission of the accounting and finance functional areas is to manage money flows into, within, and out of organizations. This mission is very broad because money is involved in all organizational functions. Therefore, accounting and finance information systems are very diverse and comprehensive. In this section you focus on certain selected activities of the accounting/finance functional area.

Financial Planning and Budgeting. Appropriate management of financial assets is a major task in financial planning and budgeting. Managers must plan for both acquiring and utilizing resources.

- *Financial and economic forecasting.* Knowledge about the availability and cost of money is a key ingredient for successful financial planning. Cash flow projections are particularly important because they inform organizations what funds they need, when they need them, and how they will acquire them.

  Funds for operating organizations come from multiple sources, including stockholders' investments, bond sales, bank loans, sales of products and services, and income from investments. Decisions concerning funding for ongoing operations and for capital investment can be supported by decision support systems, business intelligence applications (discussed in Chapter 5), and expert systems (discussed in "Plug IT In 4"). In addition, numerous software packages for conducting economic and financial forecasting are available. Many of these packages can be downloaded from the Internet, some of them for free.

- *Budgeting.* An essential part of the accounting/finance function is the annual budget, which allocates the organization's financial resources among participants and activities. The budget allows management to distribute resources in the way that best supports the organization's mission and goals.

  Several software packages are available to support budget preparation and control and to facilitate communication among participants in the budget process. These packages can reduce the time involved in the budget process. Further, they can automatically monitor exceptions for patterns and trends.

Managing Financial Transactions. Many accounting/finance software packages are integrated with other functional areas. For example, Peachtree by Sage (www.peachtree.com) offers a sales ledger, purchase ledger, cash book, sales order processing, invoicing, stock control, fixed assets register, and more.

Companies involved in electronic commerce need to access customers' financial data (e.g., credit line), inventory levels, and manufacturing databases (to see available capacity, to place orders). For example, Microsoft Dynamics GP (formerly Great Plains Software; www.microsoft.com/dynamics/gp/default.mspx) offers 50 modules that meet the most common financial, project, distribution, manufacturing, and e-business needs.

Organizations, business processes, and business activities operate with, and manage, financial transactions. Consider these examples:

- *Global stock exchanges.* Financial markets operate in global, 24/7/365, distributed electronic stock exchanges that use the Internet both to buy and sell stocks and to broadcast real-time stock prices.

- *Managing multiple currencies.* Global trade involves financial transactions in different currencies. The conversion ratios of these currencies are constantly in flux. Financial and accounting systems take financial data from different countries and convert the currencies from and to any other currency in seconds. Reports based on these data, which used to take days to generate, now take seconds to produce. These systems manage multiple languages as well.

- *Virtual close.* Companies traditionally closed their books (accounting records) quarterly, usually to meet regulatory requirements. Today, many companies want to be able to close their books at any time, on very short notice. Information systems make it possible to close the books quickly in what is called a *virtual close.* This process provides almost real-time information on the organization's financial health.

- *Expense management automation.* Expense management automation (EMA) refers to systems that automate the data entry and processing of travel and entertainment expenses. EMA systems are Web-based applications that enable companies to quickly and consistently collect expense information, enforce company policies and contracts, and reduce unplanned purchases as well as airline and hotel services. They also allow companies to reimburse their employees more quickly because expense approvals are not delayed by poor documentation.

Investment Management. Organizations invest large amounts of money in stocks, bonds, real estate, and other assets. Managing these investments is a complex task, for several reasons. First, there are literally thousands of investment alternatives, and they are dispersed throughout the world. In addition, these investments are subject to complex regulations and tax laws, which vary from one location to another.

Investment decisions require managers to evaluate financial and economic reports provided by diverse institutions, including federal and state agencies, universities, research institutions, and financial services firms. In addition, thousands of Web sites provide financial data, many of them for free.

To monitor, interpret, and analyze the huge amounts of online financial data, financial analysts employ two major types of IT tools: (1) Internet search engines and (2) business intelligence and decision support software.

Control and Auditing. One major reason why organizations go out of business is their inability to forecast and/or secure a sufficient cash flow. Underestimating expenses, overspending, engaging in fraud, and mismanaging financial statements can lead to disaster. Consequently, it is essential that organizations effectively control their finances and financial statements. Let us examine some of the most common forms of financial control.

- *Budgetary control.* Once an organization has finalized its annual budget, it divides those monies into monthly allocations. Managers at various levels monitor departmental expenditures and compare them against the budget and the operational progress of the corporate plans.

- *Auditing.* Auditing has two basic purposes: (1) to monitor how the organization's monies are being spent and (2) to assess the organization's financial health. Internal auditing is performed by the organization's accounting/finance personnel. These employees also prepare for periodic external audits by outside CPA firms.

- *Financial ratio analysis.* Another major accounting/finance function is to monitor the company's financial health by assessing a set of financial ratios. Included here are liquidity ratios (the availability of cash to pay debt), activity ratios (how quickly a firm converts noncash assets to cash assets), debt ratios (measure the firm's ability to repay long-term debt), and profitability ratios (measure the firm's use of its assets and control of its expenses to generate an acceptable rate of return).

Information Systems for Marketing

It is impossible to overestimate the importance of customers to any organization. Therefore, any successful organization must understand its customers' needs and wants and then develop its marketing and advertising strategies around them. Information systems provide numerous types of support to the marketing function. In fact, customer-centric organizations are so important that Chapter 12 (Extending the Organization to Customers) is devoted to this topic.

Information Systems for Production/Operations Management

The production and operations management (POM) function in an organization is responsible for the processes that transform inputs into useful outputs as well as for the overall operation of the business. Because of the breadth and variety of POM functions, you see only four here: in-house logistics and materials management, planning production and operation, computer-integrated manufacturing (CIM), and product life cycle management (PLM).

The POM function is also responsible for managing the organization's supply chain. Because supply chain management is vital to the success of modern organizations, Chapter 13 (Extending the Organization Along the Supply Chain) covers this topic in detail.

A "Quality Guarentee" requires data collection and analysis throughout production to maintain standards. (*Source:* Zoom Team/Shutterstock)

In-House Logistics and Materials Management. Logistics management deals with ordering, purchasing, inbound logistics (receiving), and outbound logistics (shipping) activities. Related activities include inventory management and quality control.

Inventory Management. As the name suggests, inventory management determines how much inventory to maintain. Both excessive inventory and insufficient inventory create problems. Overstocking can be expensive, due to storage costs and the costs of spoilage and obsolescence. However, keeping insufficient inventory is also expensive, due to last-minute orders and lost sales.

Operations personnel make two basic decisions: when to order and how much to order. Inventory models, such as the economic order quantity (EOQ) model, support these decisions. A large number of commercial inventory software packages that automate the application of these models are available.

Many large companies allow their suppliers to monitor their inventory levels and ship products as they are needed. This strategy, called *vendor-managed inventory* (VMI), eliminates the need for the company to submit purchasing orders.

Quality Control. Quality-control systems used by manufacturing units provide information about the quality of incoming material and parts, as well as the quality of in-process semifinished products and finished products. Such systems record the results of all inspections and compare the actual results to established metrics. These systems also generate periodic reports containing information about quality—for example, the percentage of defects and the percentage of necessary rework. Quality control data can be collected by Web-based sensors and interpreted in real time, or they can be stored in a database for future analysis.

Planning Production and Operations. In many firms, POM planning is supported by IT. POM planning has evolved from material requirements planning (MRP), to manufacturing resource planning (MRP II), to enterprise resource planning (ERP). We briefly discuss MRP and MRP II here, and we examine ERP in detail later in this chapter.

Inventory systems that use an EOQ approach are designed for items for which demand is completely independent—for example, the number of identical personal computers a computer manufacturer will sell. In manufacturing operations, however, the demand for some items is interdependent. Consider, for example, a company that makes three types of chairs, all of which use the same screws and bolts. In this case, the demand for screws and bolts depends on the total demand for all three types of chairs and their shipment schedules. The planning process that integrates production, purchasing, and inventory management of interdependent items is called *material requirements planning* (MRP).

MRP deals only with production scheduling and inventories. More complex planning also involves allocating related resources, such as money and labor. For these cases, more complex, integrated software, called *manufacturing resource planning* (MRP II), is available. MRP II integrates a firm's production, inventory management, purchasing, financing, and labor activities. Thus, MRP II adds functions to a regular MRP system. In fact, MRP II has evolved into enterprise resource planning (ERP).

Computer-Integrated Manufacturing. Computer-integrated manufacturing (**CIM**; also called *digital manufacturing*) is an approach that integrates various automated factory systems. CIM has three basic goals: (1) to simplify all manufacturing technologies and techniques, (2) to automate as many of the manufacturing processes as possible, and (3) to integrate and coordinate all aspects of design, manufacturing, and related functions via computer systems.

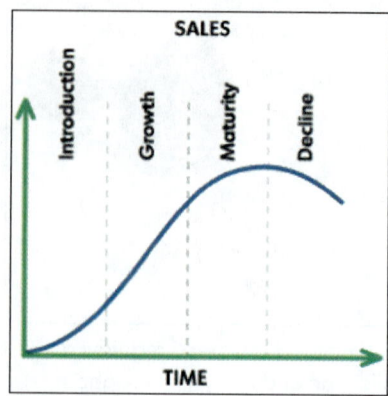

Product life-cycle.

Product Life Cycle Management. Even within a single organization, designing and developing new products can be expensive and time consuming. When multiple organizations are involved, the process can become very complex. *Product life cycle management* (PLM) is a business strategy that enables manufacturers to share product-related data that support product design and development and supply chain operations. PLM applies Web-based collaborative technologies to product development. By integrating formerly disparate functions, such as a manufacturing process and the logistics that support it, PLM enables these functions to collaborate, essentially forming a single team that manages the product from its inception through its completion.

Information Systems for Human Resource Management

Initial human resource information system (HRIS) applications dealt primarily with transaction processing systems, such as managing benefits and keeping records of vacation days. As organizational systems have moved to intranets and the Web, however, so have HRIS applications.

Many HRIS applications are delivered via an HR portal. For example, numerous organizations use their Web portals to advertise job openings and conduct online hiring and training. In this section, you consider how organizations are using IT to perform some key HR functions: recruitment, HR maintenance and development, and HR planning and management.

Recruitment. Recruitment involves finding potential employees, evaluating them, and deciding which ones to hire. Some companies are flooded with viable applicants; others have difficulty finding the right people. IT can be helpful in both cases. In addition, IT can assist in related activities such as testing and screening job applicants.

With millions of resumes available online, it is not surprising that companies are trying to find appropriate candidates on the Web, usually with the help of specialized search engines. Companies also advertise hundreds of thousands of jobs on the Web. Online recruiting can reach more candidates, which may bring in better applicants. In addition, the costs of online recruitment are usually lower than traditional recruiting methods such as advertising in newspapers or in trade journals.

Human Resources Development. After employees are recruited, they become part of the corporate human resources pool, which means they must be evaluated and developed. IT provides support for these activities.

Most employees are periodically evaluated by their immediate supervisors. Peers or subordinates may also evaluate other employees. Evaluations are typically digitized and are used to support many decisions, ranging from rewards to transfers to layoffs.

IT also plays an important role in training and retraining. Some of the most innovative developments are taking place in the areas of intelligent computer-aided instruction and the application of multimedia support for instructional activities. For example, companies conduct much of their corporate training over their intranet or via the Web.

Human Resources Planning and Management. Managing human resources in large organizations requires extensive planning and detailed strategy. The following three areas are where IT can provide support:

- *Payroll and employees' records.* The HR department is responsible for payroll preparation. This process is typically automated with paychecks being printed or money being transferred electronically into employees' bank accounts.

- *Benefits administration.* Employees' work contributions to their organizations are rewarded by wages, bonuses, and other benefits. Benefits include health and dental care, pension contributions, wellness centers, and child care centers.

    Managing benefits is a complex task, due to the multiple options offered and the tendency of organizations to allow employees to choose and trade off their benefits.

In many organizations, employees can access the company portal to self-register for specific benefits.

- *Employee relationship management.* In their efforts to better manage employees, companies are developing *employee relationship management* (ERM) applications. A typical ERM application is a call center for employees' problems.

Table 11.1 provides an overview of the activities that the functional area information systems support. Figure 11.2 diagrams many of the information systems that support these five functional areas.

TABLE 11.1 Activities Supported by Functional Area Information Systems

Accounting and Finance

Financial planning—availability and cost of money

Budgeting—allocates financial resources among participants and activities

Capital budgeting—financing of asset acquisitions

Managing financial transactions

Handling multiple currencies

Virtual close—ability to close books at any time on short notice

Investment management—managing organizational investments in stocks, bonds, real estate, and other investment vehicles

Budgetary control—monitoring expenditures and comparing against budget

Auditing—ensuring the accuracy and condition of financial health of organization

Payroll

Marketing and Sales

Customer relations—know who customers are and treat them like royalty

Customer profiles and preferences

Sales force automation—using software to automate the business tasks of sales, thereby improving the productivity of salespeople

Production/Operations and Logistics

Inventory management—how much inventory to order, how much inventory to keep, and when to order new inventory

Quality control—controlling for defects in incoming material and defects in goods produced

Materials requirements planning—planning process that integrates production, purchasing, and inventory management of interdependent items (MRP)

Manufacturing resource planning—planning process that integrates an enterprise's production, inventory management, purchasing, financing, and labor activities (MRP II)

Just-in-time systems—principle of production and inventory control in which materials and parts arrive precisely when and where needed for production (JIT)

Computer-integrated manufacturing—manufacturing approach that integrates several computerized systems, such as computer-assisted design (CAD), computer-assisted manufacturing (CAM), MRP, and JIT

Product life cycle management—business strategy that enables manufacturers to collaborate on product design and development efforts, using the Web

Human Resource Management

Recruitment—finding employees, testing them, and deciding which ones to hire

Performance evaluation—periodic evaluation by superiors

Training

Employee records

Benefits administration—medical, retirement, disability, unemployment, etc.

				STRATEGIC
Profitability Planning	Financial Planning	Employment Planning, Outsourcing	Product Life Cycle Management	Sales Forecasting, Advertising Planning
Auditing, Budgeting	Investment Management	Benefits Administration, Performance Evaluation	Quality Control, Inventory Management	Customer Relations, Sales Force Automation	TACTICAL
Payroll, Accounts Payable, Accounts Receivable	Manage Cash, Manage Financial Transactions	Maintain Employee Records	Order Fulfillment, Order Processing	Set Pricing, Profile Customers	OPERATIONAL
ACCOUNTING	FINANCE	HUMAN RESOURCES	PRODUCTION/ OPERATIONS	MARKETING

Figure 11.2 Examples of information systems supporting the functional areas.

BEFORE *YOU GO ON . . .*

1. What is a functional area information system? List its major characteristics.
2. How do information systems benefit the finance and accounting functional area?
3. Explain how POM personnel use information systems to perform their jobs more effectively and efficiently.
4. What are the most important HRIS applications?

RUBY'S CLUB QUESTIONS

1. Do you think Ruby's Club is big enough to need a different system for finance, accounting, HR, and marketing? Or, would different views of the club's data suffice for Ruben and Lisa's small business?
2. How might Ruben and Lisa best tackle the difficulty of measuring shrinkage within their club (bartenders pouring more alcohol than the customer paid for)? With an inventory management system or a quality control system?
3. What are some benefits of replacing their old time-card system (they actually still use a card to "clock in and clock out") with a newer HR system that tracks this data in a computer rather than on a card?

Student Activity | 11.2

Objective: To help you understand functional area information systems as self-contained.

Chapter Connection: This section should set the stage for enterprise resource management systems. It is important that you understand that each functional area has transactions and each has its own set of processes for handling those transactions.

Prerequisites: You should have read Section 1 and Section 2 of this chapter.

Activity:

Watch the following videos on how to set up and use the payroll features of QuickBooks:

Payroll reports: www.youtube.com/watch?v=s42Amp4fA2g&feature=related

Enter time from timesheets: www.youtube.com/watch?v=Kd9pzkjY9xA&feature=related

Process paychecks: www.youtube.com/watch?v=pC-aIY_7Qgs&feature=related

Edit paychecks: www.youtube.com/watch?v=UHF2pWfvKzA&playnext=1&videos=aa0uGNbFMgg&feature=mfu_in_order

Print checks: www.youtube.com/watch?v=HeEQG0AYg9k&playnext=1&videos=N8Gol1WPqKo&feature=mfu_in_order

Print pay stubs: www.youtube.com/watch?v=O5PiajO6thI&playnext=1&videos=3cYYKOUZDdE&feature=mfu_in_order

Print payroll reports: www.youtube.com/watch?v=s42Amp4fA2g&feature=related

Refer again to the Web site pages (in order) that you looked at for "Student Activity 11.1" that explain what a data flow diagram is:

www.freetutes.com/systemanalysis/sa5-data-flow-diagrams.html

www.freetutes.com/systemanalysis/sa5-elements-of-data-flow-diagrams.html

www.freetutes.com/systemanalysis/sa5-dfd-system-pays-workers.html

Deliverables:

A payroll application is an example of a transaction processing system for the human resources functional area. As you see from the series of videos it is a multistep process. The data from the payroll application are fed to the accounting and finance functional area. The company needs to track the payroll expense and the cash.

Draw a data flow diagram that follows the flow of the data as illustrated in the videos on QuickBooks.

Quiz Questions:

1. True or False? A user can enter time for an employee before the employee is added to QuickBooks.

2. True or False? Once timesheet data have been entered in QuickBooks, pay checks are automatically generated.

3. True or False? Paychecks are not printed when they are generated.

Discussion Questions:

Compare several diagrams, and note any differences in flows that you see. What accounts for these differences?

11.3 | Enterprise Resource Planning Systems

Historically, the functional area information systems were developed independently of one another, resulting in *information silos*. These silos did not communicate well with one another, and this lack of communication and integration made organizations less efficient. This inefficiency was particularly evident in business processes that involve more than one functional area.

Enterprise resource planning (ERP) systems are designed to correct a lack of communication among the functional area ISs. ERP systems resolve this problem by tightly integrating the functional area ISs via a common database. For this reason, experts credit ERP systems with greatly increasing organizational productivity. **Enterprise resource planning (ERP) systems** adopt a business process view of the overall organization to integrate the planning, management, and use of all of an organization's resources, employing a common software platform and database.

The major objectives of ERP systems are to tightly integrate the functional areas of the organization and to enable information to flow seamlessly across them. Tight integration means that changes in one functional area are immediately reflected in all other pertinent functional areas. In essence, ERP systems provide the information necessary to control the business processes of the organization.

It is important to understand here that ERP systems are an evolution of FAISs. That is, ERP systems have much the same functionality as FAIS and produce the same reports. ERP systems simply integrate the functions of the various FAIS.

Although some companies have developed their own ERP systems, most organizations use commercially available ERP software. The leading ERP software vendor is SAP (www. sap.com), which features its SAP R/3 package. Other major vendors include Oracle (www. oracle.com) and PeopleSoft (www.peoplesoft.com), now an Oracle company. (With more than 700 customers, PeopleSoft is the market leader in higher education.) For up-to-date information on ERP software, visit http://erp.ittoolbox.com.

Although ERP systems can be difficult to implement because they are large and complicated, many companies have done so successfully. "IT's About Business 11.1" recounts a successful SAP deployment at Airgas.

IT's ABOUT BUSINESS | 11.1

SAP at Airgas

Airgas (www.airgas.com), which sells medical, industrial, and specialized gases and related equipment, defines its "highly customized" implementation of SAP as a huge success. Airgas chose approximately 300 subject-matter experts from the 14,000-person company to identify which new functionalities were required in the SAP system. These experts worked side by side with a 120-member, full-time project team composed of Deloitte consultants and Airgas executives.

 In July 2010, Airgas switched over its hard-goods supply chain operation to SAP. The supply chain touches nearly every area of Airgas. The company plans to speed up the remaining areas of the implementation so that the entire project will be completed by the end of 2012. The accelerated schedule will cost another $20 million over the original $85 million budget, but the cost overrun will be more than offset by the economic benefits that will begin to accrue during the conversion process from the company's present legacy information systems to the SAP system.

The SAP deployment is expected to generate between $75 and $125 million in additional operating income each year, thanks to improved sales, better price management, and leaner operating costs. Airgas expects to find additional benefits as the project moves forward.

Airgas appears to have been making a calculated response to rival Air Products' ongoing bid to take over the company. The Airgas CEO stated, "In response to Air Products' offer to acquire Airgas, we have consistently stated that it is all about value, and we believe the substantial economic benefits of our robust, customized SAP system should be reflected in any valuation of the company."

Questions

1. What actions did Airgas take to help ensure the successful implementation of SAP?

2. What benefits does Airgas expect to receive from its deployment of SAP?

Sources: Compiled from C. Kanaracus, "Gas Distributor Says Its SAP Project Expected to Succeed," *Computerworld*, August 31, 2010; C. Gutierrez, "Air Products Makes Latest Bid for Airgas," *Forbes*, September 7, 2010; www.airgas.com, accessed May 1, 2011.

Evolution of ERP Systems

ERP systems were originally deployed to facilitate business processes associated with manufacturing, such as raw materials management, inventory control, order entry, and distribution. However, these early ERP systems did not extend to other functional areas, such as sales and marketing. They also did not include any customer relationship management (CRM) capabilities that would allow organizations to capture customer-specific information. Further, they did not provide Web-enabled customer service or order fulfillment.

Over time, ERP systems evolved to include administrative, sales, marketing, and human resources processes. Companies now employ an enterprisewide approach to ERP that utilizes the Web and connects all facets of the value chain. These systems are called ERP II.

ERP II Systems

ERP II systems are interorganizational ERP systems that provide Web-enabled links among a company's key business systems—such as inventory and production—and its customers, suppliers, distributors, and others. These links integrate internal-facing ERP applications with the external-focused applications of supply chain management and customer relationship management. Figure 11.3 illustrates the organization and functions of an ERP II system.

The various functions of ERP II systems are now delivered as e-business suites. The major ERP vendors have developed modular, Web-enabled software suites that integrate ERP, customer relationship management, supply chain management, procurement, decision support, enterprise portals, and other business applications and functions. Examples are Oracle's e-Business Suite and SAP's mySAP. The goal of these systems is to enable

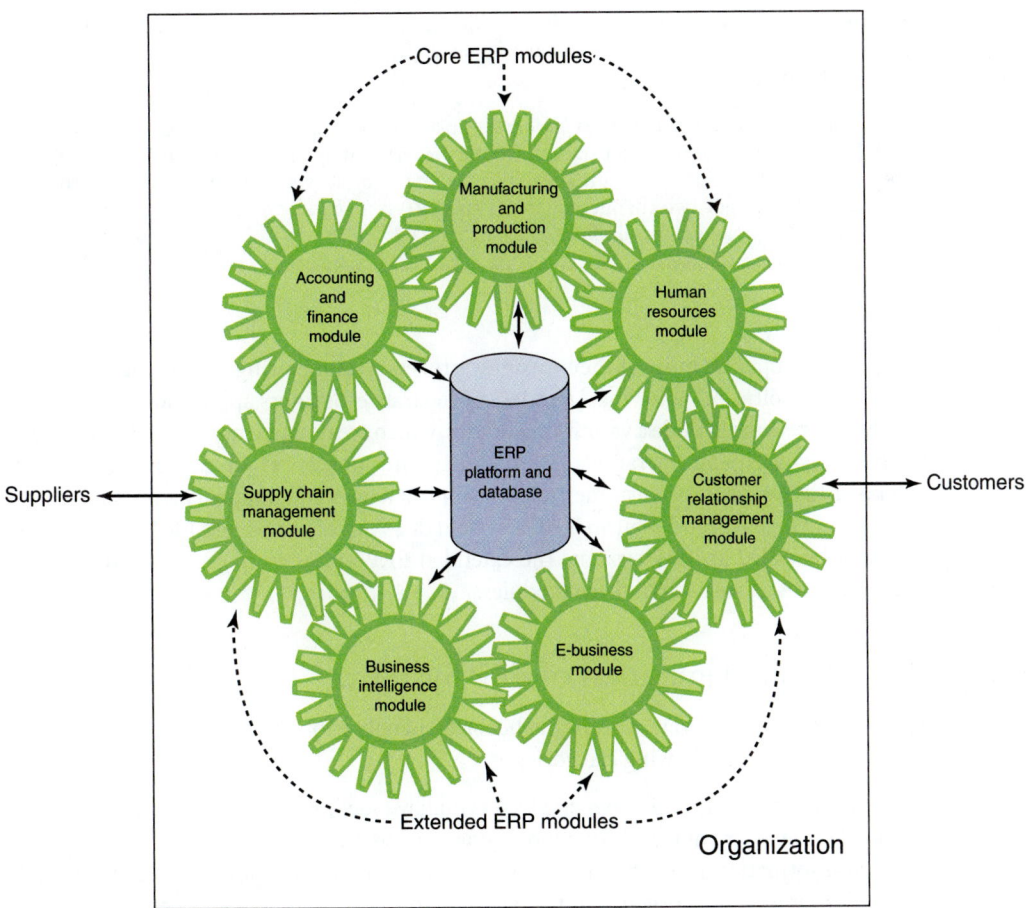

Figure 11.3 ERP II system.

TABLE 11.2 ERP Modules

Core ERP Modules

Financial Management. These modules support accounting, financial reporting, performance management, and corporate governance. They manage accounting data and financial processes such as general ledger, accounts payable, accounts receivable, fixed assets, cash management and forecasting, product-cost accounting, cost-center accounting, asset accounting, tax accounting, credit management, budgeting, and asset management.

Operations Management. These modules manage the various aspects of production planning and execution such as demand forecasting, procurement, inventory management, materials purchasing, shipping, production planning, production scheduling, materials requirements planning, quality control, distribution, transportation, and plant and equipment maintenance.

Human Resource Management. These modules support personnel administration (including workforce planning, employee recruitment, assignment tracking, personnel planning and development, and performance management and reviews), time accounting, payroll, compensation, benefits accounting, and regulatory requirements.

Extended ERP Modules

Customer Relationship Management. (Discussed in detail in Chapter 12.) These modules support all aspects of a customer's relationship with the organization. They help the organization to increase customer loyalty and retention, and thus improve its profitability. They also provide an integrated view of customer data and interactions, enabling organizations to be more responsive to customer needs.

Supply Chain Management. (Discussed in detail in Chapter 13.) These modules manage the information flows between and among stages in a supply chain to maximize supply chain efficiency and effectiveness. They help organizations plan, schedule, control, and optimize the supply chain from the acquisition of raw materials to the receipt of finished goods by customers.

Business Intelligence. (Discussed in detail in Chapter 5.) These modules collect information used throughout the organization, organize it, and apply analytical tools to assist managers with decision making.

E-Business. (Discussed in detail in Chapter 9.) Customers and suppliers demand access to ERP information including order status, inventory levels, and invoice reconciliation. Further, they want this information in a simplified format that can be accessed via the Web. As a result, these modules provide two channels of access into ERP system information—one channel for customers (B2C) and one for suppliers and partners (B2B).

companies to operate most of their business processes using a single Web-enabled system of integrated software rather than a variety of separate e-business applications.

ERP II systems include a variety of modules, which are divided into core ERP modules—financial management, operations management, and human resource management—and extended ERP modules—customer relationship management, supply chain management, business intelligence, and e-business. If a system does not have the core ERP modules, then it cannot be called an ERP system. The extended ERP modules, in contrast, are optional. Table 11.2 describes each of these modules.

Benefits and Limitation of ERP Systems

ERP systems can generate significant business benefits for an organization. The major benefits fall into the following categories:

- *Organizational flexibility and agility.* As you have seen, ERP systems break down many former departmental and functional silos of business processes, information systems, and information resources. In this way they make organizations more flexible, agile, and adaptive. The organizations can therefore react quickly to changing business conditions and also capitalize on new business opportunities.

- *Decision support.* ERP systems provide essential information on business performance across functional areas. This information significantly improves managers' ability to make better, more timely decisions.

- *Quality and efficiency.* ERP systems integrate and improve an organization's business processes, resulting in significant improvements in the quality of customer service, production, and distribution.

Despite all of their benefits, ERP systems have drawbacks. The business processes in ERP software are often predefined by the best practices that the ERP vendor has developed. *Best practices* are the most successful solutions or problem-solving methods for achieving a business objective. As a result, companies may need to change existing business processes to fit the predefined business processes of the software. For companies with well-established procedures, this requirement can be a huge problem. It is important to note that best practices, by definition, are appropriate for *most* organizations. However, organizations differ. Therefore, a particular "best practice" might not be the "best" one for your company.

In addition, ERP systems can be extremely complex, expensive, and time consuming to implement. In fact, the costs and risks of failure in implementing a new ERP system are substantial. Quite a few companies have experienced costly ERP implementation failures. Large losses in revenue, profits, and market share have resulted when core business processes and information systems failed or did not work properly. In many cases, orders and shipments were lost, inventory changes were not recorded correctly, and unreliable inventory levels caused major-stock outs to occur. Companies such as Hershey Foods, Nike, A-DEC, and Connecticut General sustained losses in amounts up to hundreds of millions of dollars. In the case of FoxMeyer Drugs, a $5 billion pharmaceutical wholesaler, a failed ERP implementation caused the company to file for bankruptcy protection.

In almost every ERP implementation failure, the company's business managers and IT professionals underestimated the complexity of the planning, development, and training that were required to prepare for a new ERP system that would fundamentally change their business processes and information systems. Failure to involve affected employees in the planning and development phases and in change management processes, and trying to do too much too fast in the conversion process, were typical causes of unsuccessful ERP projects. Insufficient training in the new work tasks required by the ERP system and the failure to perform proper data conversion and testing for the new system also contributed to unsuccessful implementations. The cases at the end of this chapter highlight many of the difficulties involved in implementing and maintaining ERP systems.

Enterprise Application Integration

For some organizations, ERP systems are inappropriate. This is particularly true for non-manufacturing companies as well as manufacturing companies that find the process of converting from their existing system too difficult, time consuming, or expensive.

Such companies, however, may still have isolated information systems that need to be connected with one another. To accomplish this task some of these companies use enterprise application integration. An **enterprise application integration (EAI) system** integrates existing systems by providing layers of software that connect applications together. These layers of software are called *middleware*. In essence, the EAI system allows existing applications to communicate and share data, thereby enabling organizations to use existing applications while eliminating many of the problems caused by isolated information systems.

⌐→ **BEFORE** *YOU GO ON . . .*
 1. Define ERP, and describe its functionalities.
 2. What are ERP II systems?
 3. Differentiate between core ERP modules and extended ERP modules.
 4. List some drawbacks of ERP software.

Student Activity | 11.3

Objective: To understand how an ERP system integrates all of the functional systems.

Chapter Connection: ERP as a concept is difficult to understand without understanding what functional areas an organization has.

Prerequisites: You should have read Sections 11.1, 11.2, and 11.3 of this chapter.

Activity:

View the following video:

www.youtube.com/watch?v=CzL1u7h0kgE&feature=related

Refer again to the Web site pages (in order) that you looked at for "Student Activity 11.1" that explain what a data flow diagram is.

Deliverables:

Draw a data flow diagram that shows all of the functional areas illustrated in the video. Your diagram should show the data coming from and going into the functional area as well as the data coming from the customer and going to the customer.

Quiz Questions:

1. True or False? SAP Business One is for large businesses.
2. True or False? When a customer places an order, the amount of the order is deducted from the customer's balance.
3. True or False? The purchasing department sends an e-mail to the customer alerting the customer that the order is on its way.

Discussion Questions:

1. How easy do you think it is to install an ERP system?
2. What problems might arise when an organization begins planning for an ERP?
3. Review the drill-down concept.
4. Discuss the dashboard shown.
5. Review customer relationship management.

11.4 | Reports

All information systems produce reports: transaction processing systems, functional area information systems, ERP systems, customer relationship management systems, business intelligence systems, and so on. We discuss reports here because they are so closely associated with FAISs and ERP systems. However, the important point is that *all* information systems produce reports. These reports generally fall into three categories: routine, ad-hoc (on-demand), and exception.

Routine reports are produced at scheduled intervals. They range from hourly quality control reports to daily reports on absenteeism rates. Although routine reports are extremely valuable to an organization, managers frequently need special information that is not included in these reports. Other times they need the information but at different times ("I need the report today, for the last three days, not for one week").

Such out-of-the routine reports are called **ad-hoc (on-demand) reports**. Ad-hoc reports also can include requests for the following types of information:

- **Drill-down reports** display a greater level of detail. For example, a manager might examine sales by region and decide to "drill down to more detail" to look at sales by store and then by salesperson.

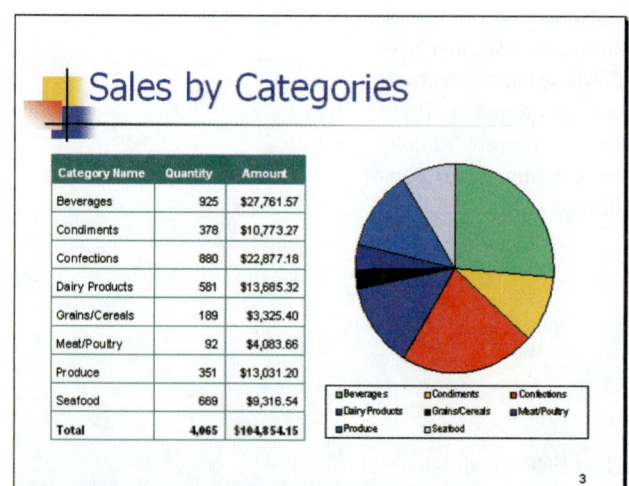

Monthly sales report.

- **Key-indicator reports** summarize the performance of critical activities. For example, a chief financial officer might want to monitor cash flow and cash on hand.
- **Comparative reports** compare, for example, performances of different business units or of a single unit during different time periods.

Some managers prefer **exception reports**. Exception reports include only information that falls outside certain threshold standards. To implement *management by exception*, management first creates performance standards. The company then sets up systems to monitor performance (via the incoming data about business transactions such as expenditures), compare actual performance to the standards, and identify exceptions to the standards. The system alerts managers to the exceptions via exception reports.

Let us use sales as an example. First, management establishes sales quotas. The company then implements an FAIS that collects and analyzes all of the sales data. An exception report would identify only those cases where sales fell outside an established threshold—for example, more than 20 percent short of the quota. It would *not* report expenditures that fell *within* the accepted range of standards. By leaving out all "acceptable" performances, exception reports save managers time and help them focus on problem areas.

BEFORE YOU GO ON . . .

1. Compare and contrast the three major types of reports.
2. Compare and contrast the three types of on-demand reports.

RUBY'S CLUB QUESTIONS

1. What types of report do you think Ruben and Lisa will benefit most from: routine, ad-hoc, drill-down, key-indicator, comparative, or exception? Why?
2. What would be some key indicators Ruben and Lisa should look for? Cover charges? Drinks? Food sold? What if they sell more food when there are fewer people and more drinks when there are more people? How could they use this data?

Student Activity 11.4

Objective: To demonstrate that reports (outputs) serve a variety of purposes and the format needs to fit that purpose.

Chapter Connection: This activity relates to Section 11.4 of this chapter.

Prerequisites: You should have read Section 11.4 of this chapter.

Activity:

View the following video on how a user can use Crystal Reports to create reports:

www.youtube.com/watch?v=_CsgT4kVHPU

Then view this video, which illustrates how a dashboard could be used:

www.youtube.com/watch?v=BzOYt2P5ka4&feature=related

Write a two-page report that addresses the following questions:

- Why do users need to do ad-hoc reporting using a tool such as Crystal Reports?
- Why do users review comparison reports? Give examples.

- Explain how performance standards are used for reporting. Give examples.
- What is the purpose of a dashboard?
- How does a dashboard use color? Give examples.

Deliverables:

The Crystal Reports video shows how ad-hoc reporting can be done by the end user. The dashboard video shows exception reporting (usually in colors) and comparison reporting.

Quiz Questions:

1. _____ are produced at scheduled intervals.
   - (a) Exception reports
   - (b) Drill-down reports
   - (c) Routine reports
   - (d) Ad-hoc reports
   - (e) Comparative reports

2. _____ show different sets of data side by side.
   - (a) Exception reports
   - (b) Drill-down reports
   - (c) Routine reports
   - (d) Ad-hoc reports
   - (e) Comparative reports

3. _____ are based on performance standards.
   - (a) Exception reports
   - (b) Drill-down reports
   - (c) Routine reports
   - (d) Ad-hoc reports
   - (e) Comparative reports

4. _____ are produced on demand with specific data requirements.
   - (a) Exception reports
   - (b) Drill-down reports
   - (c) Routine reports
   - (d) Ad-hoc reports
   - (e) Comparative reports

5. You would expect _____ in a dashboard.
   - (a) Exception reports
   - (b) Drill-down reports
   - (c) Routine reports
   - (d) Ad-hoc reports
   - (e) Comparative reports

Discussion Questions:

Design a dashboard for a payroll application. Be sure to show how color would be used and how drill-down would be supported. Remember the first thing to understand is what the key indicators are and which data elements management might need to manage by exception.

What's in IT for ME?

FOR THE ACCOUNTING MAJOR

 Understanding the functions and outputs of TPSs effectively is a major concern of any accountant. It is also necessary to understand the various activities of all functional areas and how they are interconnected. Accounting information systems are a central component in any ERP package. In fact, all large CPA firms actively consult with clients on ERP implementations, using thousands of specially trained accounting majors.

FOR THE FINANCE MAJOR

IT helps financial analysts and managers perform their tasks better. Of particular importance is analyzing cash flows and securing the financing required for smooth operations. In addition, financial applications can support such activities as risk analysis, investment management, and global transactions involving different currencies and fiscal regulations.

Finance activities and modeling are key components of ERP systems. Flows of funds (payments), at the core of most supply chains, must be executed efficiently and effectively.

Financial arrangements are especially important along global supply chains, where currency conventions and financial regulations must be considered.

FOR THE MARKETING MAJOR

Marketing and sales expenses are usually targets in a cost-reduction program. Also, sales force automation not only improves salespeople's productivity (and thus reduces costs), but it also improves customer service.

FOR THE PRODUCTION/OPERATIONS MANAGEMENT MAJOR

Managing production tasks, materials handling, and inventories in short time intervals, at a low cost, and with high quality is critical for competitiveness. These activities can be achieved only if they are properly supported by IT. In addition, IT can greatly enhance interaction with other functional areas, especially sales. Collaboration in design, manufacturing, and logistics requires knowledge of how modern information systems can be connected.

FOR THE HUMAN RESOURCES MANAGEMENT MAJOR

Human resources managers can increase their efficiency and effectiveness by using IT for some of their routine functions. Human resources personnel need to understand how information flows between the HR department and the other functional areas. Finally, the integration of functional areas via ERP systems has a major impact on skill requirements and scarcity of employees, which are related to the tasks performed by the HRM department.

FOR THE MIS MAJOR

The MIS function is responsible for the most fundamental information systems in organizations: the transaction processing systems. The TPSs provide the data for the databases. In turn, all other information systems use these data. MIS personnel develop applications that support all levels of the organization (from clerical to executive) and all functional areas. The applications also enable the firm to do business with its partners.

>>> SUMMARY

1. **Explain the purposes of transaction processing systems, and provide at least one example of how businesses use these systems.**

TPSs monitor, store, collect, and process data generated from all business transactions. These data provide the inputs into the organization's database.

2. **Define functional area information systems, and provide an example of the support they provide for each functional area of the organization.**

The major business functional areas are production/operations management, marketing, accounting/finance, and human resources management. Table 11.1 provides an overview of the many activities in each functional area supported by FAISs.

3. Explain the purpose of enterprise resource planning systems, and identify four advantages and four drawbacks to implementing an ERP system.

Enterprise resource planning (ERP) systems integrate the planning, management, and use of all of the organization's resources. The major objective of ERP systems is to tightly integrate the functional areas of the organization. This integration enables information to flow seamlessly across the various functional areas.

4. Discuss the three major types of reports generated by the functional area information systems and enterprise resource planning systems, and provide an example of each type.

Routine reports are produced at scheduled intervals. They range from hourly quality control reports to daily reports on absenteeism rates.

Out-of-the routine reports are called *ad-hoc (on-demand) reports*. For example, a chief financial officer might want to monitor cash flow and cash on hand.

Exception reports include only information that falls outside certain threshold standards. An exception report might identify only those cases where sales fell outside an established threshold—for example, more than 20 percent short of the quota.

>>> CHAPTER GLOSSARY

ad-hoc (on-demand) reports Nonroutine reports that often contain special information that is not included in routine reports.

batch processing Transaction processing system (TPS) that processes data in batches at fixed periodic intervals.

comparative reports Reports that compare performances of different business units or time periods.

computer-integrated manufacturing (CIM) An information system that integrates various automated factory systems; also called *digital manufacturing*.

drill-down reports Reports that show a greater level of detail than is included in routine reports.

enterprise application integration (EAI) system A system that integrates existing systems by providing layers of software that connect applications together.

enterprise resource planning (ERP) systems Information systems that take a business process view of the overall organization to integrate the planning, management, and use of all of an organization's resources, employing a common software platform and database.

ERP II systems Interorganizational ERP systems that provide Web-enabled links among key business systems (such as inventory

and production) of a company and its customers, suppliers, distributors, and others.

exception reports Reports that include only information that exceeds certain threshold standards.

functional area information systems (FAISs) Systems that provide information to managers (usually mid-level) in the functional areas, in order to support managerial tasks of planning, organizing, and controlling operations.

key-indicator reports Reports that summarize the performance of critical activities.

online transaction processing (OLTP) Transaction processing system (TPS) that processes data after transactions occur, frequently in real time.

routine reports Reports produced at scheduled intervals.

transaction Any business event that generates data worth capturing and storing in a database.

transaction processing system (TPS) Information system that supports the monitoring, collection, storage, and processing of data from the organization's basic business transactions, each of which generates data.

>>> DISCUSSION QUESTIONS

1. Consider "Chapter Closing Case 1." What are the advantages that FIELDf/x provides for the owners of professional baseball teams? What are the advantages that FIELDf/x provides for professional baseball players? Are there disadvantages for the players? Support your answers.

2. Why is it logical to organize IT applications by functional areas?

3. Describe the role of a TPS in a service organization.

4. Describe the relationship between TPS and FAIS.

5. Discuss how IT facilitates the budgeting process.

6. How can the Internet support investment decisions?

7. Describe the benefits of integrated accounting software packages.

8. Discuss the role that IT plays in support of auditing.

9. Investigate the role of the Web in human resources management.

10. What is the relationship between information silos and enterprise resource planning?

>>> PROBLEM-SOLVING ACTIVITIES

1. Finding a job on the Internet is challenging as there are almost too many places to look. Visit the following sites: www.careerbuilder.com, www.craigslist.org, www.linkedin.com, www.careermag.com, www.jobcentral.com, and www.monster.com. What does each of these sites provide you as a job seeker?

2. Enter www.sas.com and access *revenue optimization* there. Explain how the software helps in optimizing prices.

3. Enter www.eleapsoftware.com and review the product that helps with online training (training systems). What are the most attractive features of this product?

4. Enter www.microsoft.com/dynamics/sl/product/demos.mspx. View three of the demos in different functional areas of your choice. Prepare a report on each product's capabilities.

>>> WEB ACTIVITIES

1. Examine the capabilities of the following (and similar) financial software packages: Financial Analyzer (from Oracle) and CFO Vision (from SAS Institute). Prepare a report comparing the capabilities of the software packages.

2. Surf the Net and find free accounting software. (Try www.shareware.com, www.rkom.com, www.tucows.com, www.passtheshareware.com, and www.freeware-guide.com.) Download the software and try it. Compare the ease of use and usefulness of each software package.

3. Examine the capabilities of the following financial software packages: TekPortal (from www.tekknowledge.com), Financial Analyzer (from www.oracle.com), and Financial

Management (from www.sas.com). Prepare a report comparing the capabilities of the software packages.

4. Find Simply Accounting Basic from Sage Software (http://us.simplyaccounting.com). Why is this product recommended for small businesses?

5. Enter www.halogensoftware.com and www.successfactors.com. Examine their software products and compare them.

6. Enter www.iemployee.com and find the support it provides to human resources management activities. View the demos and prepare a report on the capabilities of the products.

>>> TEAM ASSIGNMENTS

1. The class is divided into groups. Each group member represents a major functional area: accounting/finance, sales/marketing, production/operations management, and human resources. Find and describe several examples of processes that require the integration of functional information systems in a company of your choice. Each group will also show the interfaces to the other functional areas.

2. Each group is to investigate an HRM software vendor (Oracle, Peoplesoft [now owned by Oracle], SAP, Lawson Software, and others). The group should prepare a list of all HRM functionalities supported by the software. Then

each of the groups makes a presentation to convince the class that its vendor is the best.

3. Each group in the class will be assigned to a major ERP/SCM vendor such as SAP, Oracle, Lawson Software, and others. Members of the groups will investigate topics such as (a) Web connections, (b) use of business intelligence tools, (c) relationship to CRM and to EC, and (d) major capabilities by the specific vendor. Each group will prepare a presentation for the class, trying to convince the class why the group's software is best for a local company known to the students (for example, a supermarket chain).

CLOSING CASE 1 > Is Baseball a Science

The last remaining nonscientific frontier in baseball is fielding. John Dewan, the owner of Baseball Info Solutions (BIS, www.baseballinfosolutions.com), knows this better than anyone. Dewan has spent many years building the current standard in fielding metrics. He estimates that game analysts are collectively about 90 percent along the way to creating a complete picture of hitters, and almost 85 percent with pitchers.

<<< THE PROBLEM

When it comes to fielders, however, Dewan contends that analysts began with a severe handicap. For more than a hundred years, scorekeepers have described a player's work in the field based only on what he does after he gets to the ball. If a shortstop gathers in a grounder and throws it to first in time to make the out, he is credited with an assist. If he

bobbles the grounder and cannot make the throw in time, he gets an error. The standard fielding average simply reflects the percentage of plays that a fielder executes successfully—that is, without making an error. According to Dewan, this basic accounting captures only about 5 percent of what fielding is all about.

Dewan looked for a better way to assess fielding, or defense, in baseball. He divided the field into 3,000 zones and then counted how often fielders were able to make outs on balls hit into each zone. He then measured each fielder against the average of all fielders at that position. If a center fielder, for instance, made a catch on a ball that 70 percent of major leaguers would also catch, he was credited with .3 toward what Dewan called his Ultimate Zone Rating. Dewan then converted the zone rating into the number of runs saved by a fielder's play.

At BIS, compiling all these numbers is a laborious task. The company employs roughly 20 video scouts. They watch videos of every game at least three times, and they tag every batted ball with a direction (from 135 to 225 degrees), distance (0 to about 400 feet, depending on the size of the ballpark), pace (hard, medium, or soft), and type (grounder, fly ball, line drive, or "fliner"). The results provide information that major league teams pay to see.

The BIS data, however, are limited. For example, they do not indicate where a fielder was standing when the ball was hit. In addition, the data are susceptible to human error, with a margin of 15 to 20 feet on some plays. Dewan himself estimated that BIS and its video scouts could measure only 60 percent of a fielder's ability.

THE >>> SOLUTION

Enter Sportvision (www.sportvision.com), a leader in sports broadcasting technology. Sportvision created FIELDf/x, a motion-capture or optical tracking system, that promises to rid sports of the biases of the human eye and quantify the formerly unquantifiable art of being in the right place at the right time. Sportvision claims that FIELDf/x is accurate to within 1 foot.

FIELDf/x uses four cameras placed high above the field to track players and the ball, and log their movements. The system collects movement data and produces valuable information such as a fielder's reaction time, his path to the ball, the base runner's speed, and the arc of a fly ball. The system generates more than 2.5 million records per game, or 2 terabytes of data. When Fiedlf/x is installed at all major league baseball parks, it will create a digital catalog of virtually every movement of every fielder at every Major League Baseball game.

THE RESULTS >>>

In mid-2011, FIELDf/x was in place at San Francisco's AT&T Park, and it was being installed in four more parks that year. The current goal is to install the system in every Major League park by 2012. Tom Tippett, the director of baseball information services for the Boston Red Sox, is responsible for gathering and analyzing data to put together a winning team in Boston. He asserts that FIELDf/x will essentially make all other fielding statistics irrelevant.

In summer 2010, Sportvision invited six baseball analysts to see what they could find in FIELDf/x data from 13 games. Even with that small amount of data, the analysts were able to distinguish between plays made because a fielder was already standing in the right place and plays made because a player was exceptionally quick in getting to the ball.

Ultimately, FIELDf/x will generate new baseball metrics, such as degree-of-difficulty fielding ratings. FIELDf/x will also make coaching more precise. For example, coaches will be able to better position their fielders, depending on the hitter and the pitch being thrown (e.g., fast ball versus slow curve ball). Finally, the system will enhance the process by which clubs evaluate—and pay—their players.

Questions

1. Describe the advantages and disadvantages of FIELDf/x for a team owner. Now, describe the advantages and disadvantages of FIELDf/x for a player.

2. In sports, paper-based systems have ruled for years. Coaches used to mail VHS tapes of their team to their opponent so they could scout each other's teams. Given the availability of computer-based information systems, how many ways can this process improved?

SOURCES: Compiled from I. Boudway, "Running the Numbers," *Bloomberg BusinessWeek*, April 4–10, 2011; J. Dubox, "New System Tries to Measure Pitchers Command," *Forbes*, April 1, 2011; K. Bhasin, "FIELDf/x: The Amazing Tracking Technology That's About to Change Baseball Forever," *Business Insider*, March 31, 2011; www.sportvision.com, accessed March 14, 2011.

CLOSING **CASE 2 >**

Difficulties in Managing Enterprise Resource Planning Systems

Companies initially installed ERP systems to make sense of their complicated operations. In doing so, they were able to operate better and faster than their competition, at least until the competition caught up. In many of these companies, the ERP systems are still essential. However, they no longer provide a competitive advantage. Further, they are not helping to bring in new revenue, and managing them is absorbing an increasing share of the company's IT budget. However, companies are not getting rid of ERP systems because they still need them to manage their supply chain, financial, and employee data. Nevertheless, ERP systems are causing problems for many organizations.

Kennametal (www.kennametal.com), a $2 billion manufacturer of construction tools, has spent $10 million on SAP maintenance contracts since 1998. Throughout this entire period, however, the company has been unable to take advantage of any upgrades in the SAP software. The reason is that, over the years, Kennametal made more than 6,000 customizations to its SAP system. Consequently, the company could not implement any new technology that SAP built into its software. The firm's SAP implementation was simply too customized. The time and effort needed to install and test the upgrades outweighed any benefits. In late 2009, Kennametal inquired about the costs of hiring consultants to assist with an SAP reimplementation. The company was shocked by the estimates, which ranged from $15 million to $54 million. Kennametal's CIO charged that not only SAP, but all the major ERP packages, are "old and inflexible, and the vendors cannot build flexibility into their packages."

<<<**THE FIRST PROBLEM: LACK OF FLEXIBILITY**

Even if Kennametal could afford to pay up to $54 million for consultants to help the company upgrade to the latest version of its SAP software, the CIO does not want to spend this amount of money. Instead, he plans to turn Kennametal's old ERP strategy upside down by installing as generic a version of SAP as possible. He and Kennametal's CEO are willing to change the company's internal business processes to match the way SAP works, rather than modifying the SAP software to match Kennametal's business processes.

<<<**A POTENTIAL SOLUTION**

Kennametal will also perform the implementation itself. The company hired IBM to consult about requirements and to identify business processes that must be reworked to conform to SAP's procedures. In fact, Kennametal planned to implement at least 90 percent of the SAP software unmodified.

Haworth (www.haworth.com), a $1.7 billion office furniture manufacturer, is another company that decided to make no customer changes to the core SAP code. The company uses tools from iRise (www.irise.com) to visually plant its SAP rollouts in its major offices on four continents. The iRise tools will simulate how the finished SAP system will look to employees, to get them accustomed to changes before the actual rollout. The company also uses a sales compensation application from Vertex (www.vertex.com) because SAP does not support the complicated, multitiered compensation model that Haworth uses to pay its salespeople.

Implementing the core code of an ERP system without any significant modifications minimized both the costs of the system and the time devoted to the system for Kennametal

<<<**THE RESULT**

and Haworth. However, there is a trade-off: Both companies had to spend time and money reworking their business processes to meet the procedures established by their ERP systems.

THE SECOND >>>
PROBLEM: HIGH
MAINTENANCE
FEES

 Dana Holding (www.dana.com) is an $8.1 billion auto parts supplier. Dana's CIO discovered that 90 percent of the fees the company paid to maintain its ERP system were pure profit for the ERP vendor. When the auto market hit tough times, Dana wanted its ERP vendor to work with the company to reduce maintenance fees, but the vendor objected. To persuade Dana that its maintenance fees were justifiable, the vendor analyzed Dana's use of its support. The analysis concluded that Dana made 21,000 requests to the vendor over a 9-month period. Dana countered that 98 percent of the requests did not involve human interaction but were automated lookups on the vendor's knowledge base.

DANA'S >>>
SOLUTION

Dana stopped making maintenance payments to its ERP vendor. The risks to any company that decides to stop paying maintenance fees include being hit with penalties assessed by the vendor for breaking a contract and being left without technical support in an emergency. Dana's lawyers studied the contracts with the vendor and felt comfortable that the firm would not be violating any terms by terminating the payments. Then, Dana's IT team explored ways to obtain support for their ERP system through other avenues. They found many alternatives, including online user forums, books, and consultants.

THE RESULTS >>>

One result of the move away from provider support is that Dana's IT group has to be more knowledgeable about the company's ERP system so they can fix whatever goes wrong. However, Dana's CIO notes that there have been no technology disasters with its ERP system because the system is mature and reliable. In addition eliminating maintenance saves money, because Dana is no longer paying for a service of questionable value.

Questions

1. Describe what it means for an ERP system to be inflexible.

2. Describe the pros and cons of tailoring your organization's business processes to align with the procedures in an ERP system.

Sources: Compiled from K. Nash, "ERP: How and Why You Need to Manage It Differently," *CIO*, January 27, 2010; www.kennametal.com, www.sap.com, www.haworth.com, www.dana.com, accessed May 9, 2011.

RUBY'S CLUB INTERNSHIP ASSIGNMENTS

Last week Lisa stayed up late to take data from individual receipts and put them in a spreadsheet. She and Ruben want to see what kind of graphs or charts they might be able to get out of a more sophisticated IS. While this is just a basic spreadsheet, the principle of taking large amounts of data and analyzing them with a visual aid still applies.

Specifically, this sheet shows entry and departure times for customers. It also lists the number of drinks they purchased. They hope to use this information to know when to run a "house special"

that will hopefully keep customers a little longer and get them to buy one or two more drinks.

Go to www.wiley.com/college/rainer and download the spreadsheet to look over the data. Specifically, you will need to use the "Total Number of Hours" and "Total Drinks" columns. Create a scatter plot that shows the number of drinks people buy based on the amount of time they stay at the club. Then make a recommendation as to what hour needs to be the "Happy Hour" that will, hopefully, keep their customers in the club!

SPREADSHEET ACTIVITY

Objective: Microsoft Excel is powerful for more than just keeping up with numbers. With the right add-ons you can run elaborate statistical analysis. This activity will introduce simple regression within Microsoft Excel.

Chapter Connection: Transaction processing systems are just the beginning. They provide data to many systems throughout an organization. Ultimately, the data they provide are used to plan and forecast for years ahead. This activity ties the spreadsheet tool to the data found in the various systems within the organization.

Prerequisites: There are no prerequisites for this activity.

Activity: Imagine that you are an intern for a local restaurant/bar/club (the focus tends to change as it gets later in the evening). You have been asked to help the owners with a serious problem: managing their supply chain.

Forecasting has always been a problem for them. One week they are booming and another week things are dead. Really, they expect as much since they are in a college town. But there are weekends when people should be in and they are not, and weekends you would expect everyone to be gone and they are packed.

They have put together a spreadsheet for you to use to help them understand their demand and how to better match their food and drink supplies to what the demand will be. For a restaurant owner there is nothing worse than telling customers that you are out of something or throwing away unsold goods that spoiled. The owners need better forecasting.

Please go to www.wiley.com/college/rainer and watch the tutorial videos. One describes an "Add-In" you may have to install for Excel to run a regression, and the other is about regression analysis itself. You will use this tool in Excel to help your employers better understand the situation they are in. Ultimately you will complete your analysis to determine which variables have the most statistically significant impact on their demand. Finally, you will write a short memo to your employers (your professor) to explain your findings in a way they can understand it.

The spreadsheet you will download has lots of 1's and 0's in it. A "1" means an event was "true." For example, under "Jazz" a "1" would mean that jazz was the genre of music playing that night in the club. A "0" would mean that jazz was not played that night. Most of the variables are considered independent variables. This means that whether jazz was playing is not dependent on any other variables. You use these independent factors to help understand the *dependent* variables that you are most concerned about: cover sales, food sales, and drink sales.

Video Files: Please use Videos 1 and 2 for Chapter 10 of the Ruby's Club for Rainer 3e: the Interactive Case. Both need to be made available.

Deliverables: Your work will include a spreadsheet that includes the regression analysis as well as a Word document that shows the interpretation of that analysis. The Word document will also (based on the interpretation) offer suggestions that will help the restaurant owners understand their demand and better schedule their food and drink purchases.

Quiz Questions:

1. What is the best definition of R-square?
   - (a) The amount of data not explained by the regression
   - (b) The amount of data undetectable in the regression
   - (c) The amount of variance not explained by the regression
   - (d) The amount of variance explained by the regression

2. Which of the following would be a good p-value?
   - (a) 100 percent
   - (b) 5.0
   - (c) 0.019
   - (d) 0.874

3. Which of the following is the best interpretation of a statistically significant coefficient of 3.5 under "Karaoke" when "Cover Sales" is the dependent variable?
   - (a) As cover sales go up by $3.50, more people will come to sing karaoke.
   - (b) As cover prices go down by $3.50, more people will come to sing karaoke.
   - (c) On nights when karaoke is available, cover sales increase 350 percent.
   - (d) On nights when karaoke is available, only 3.5 people show up.

Discussion Questions:

1. Given the simplicity of running a regression in Excel, why do so many people look for more elaborate systems? What do the expensive systems do that a regression in Excel cannot do?

2. Outside of the food industry, what other local businesses can you think of that would benefit from the use of regression in forecasting?

DATABASE ACTIVITY: REPORTS II

Objective

In this activity, you will learn how to create a report that uses a query, rather than tables, as its data source. The Chapter 10 database activity gave you the tools to create something like your grade report: the ability to combine data from more than one table, then to select the rows of combined data that you want. A real grade report, however, is formatted nicely and probably has summary calculations such as GPA. This activity adds those capabilities to your toolkit.

Chapter Connection

Organizational information systems, such as those this chapter discusses, are a primary source of information for management. The methods used in this activity are how the information is organized and presented to them.

Prerequisites

Before starting this activity, you should complete the database activities for Chapter 4 (Reports I) and Chapter 10 (Queries I).

Activity:

In this activity, which you will find online at www.wiley.com/college/rainer, you will combine the selection and table-joining capabilities of queries with the layout and summary capabilities of reports. This creates a powerful tool for presenting data to businesspeople who need to use it.

1. Download the Ch 11 DizzyDonuts database from www.wiley.com/college/rainer and open it. It is the end product of the Chapter 10 database activity, with the queries described there. If you did that activity, you can use what you did there as the basis for this one.

2. Open StoreOrderQry. It shows all the orders placed at the Boston store. Go to Design view and add a column to the query for OrderStatus, since we want to ignore discarded orders in our analysis. Enter "<>Discarded" (without the quotation marks; Access will supply them around the character string part) for "not equal to 'Discarded'" in the Criteria section, on the same row as the store name. Run the query.

3. You will see that the result table is shorter and shows no orders with Discarded status. However, we do not need to display this column. Unnecessary content in user reports is clutter: It gets in the way of focusing quickly on the important parts. Go back to Design view, and uncheck the "Show" box in the OrderStatus column. Rerun the query. It still excludes discarded orders, but it no longer reminds us on every line. (If we cared about order status we could leave that column in, but let us assume we do not.) Close the query.

4. Now click the "Create" ribbon tab, and open the Report Wizard. The Tables/Queries menu in the first step includes both the tables and the queries in the database. We will base our new report on StoreOrderQry. Select it from the menu. Move CustName, OrderDate, and OrderTotal into the Selected Fields panel. Then click "Next."

Usage Hint: If we had left OrderStatus in the query results, we could choose not to move it to Selected Fields here. We would end up with exactly the same report.

5. Organize the report by CustTbl. That will group all the orders of each customer. Click "Next" twice, since you do not want to add any grouping levels.

6. In the next dialogue box, click "Summary Options." Since OrderTotal is the only field that the Report Wizard knows how to summarize, only it will show. (Access can do more, as you may recall from the Chapter 6 activity, but the Wizard cannot.) Check the Sum box to total each customer's orders. Select "Detail" and "Summary" at the right. Click "OK," then "Next."

7. If you carried out all of the preceding steps properly, the report will contain the correct content. Its first few lines should look something like the following. Yours may not look exactly like this because you may have made different design choices in the Wizard.

CustTbl		
CustName	OrderDate	OrderTotal
Belina		
	9/26/2010	$5.56
	9/13/2010	$3.08
	6/6/2010	$4.27
Summary for 'CustName' = Belina (3 detail records)		
Sum		$12.91
Cameron		

This appearance leaves a lot to be desired. So, switch to Layout view, and:

(a) Select the label that starts "Summary for 'CustName . . ." and delete it.

(b) Select the sum fields (customer sum and overall sum), and move them to the left, closer to the data on which they are based.

(c) Edit the report heading to be more descriptive.

(d) Edit the column headings to have meaningful labels, not database field names.

(e) Change the word "Sum" to "Customer Total."

8. Switch to Report view to make sure you are happy with the results. When you are, close the report. If you were not prompted to give it a name, name it OrderSummaryRpt, renaming it in the navigation pane if necessary. (Right-click on its name for the Rename option.)

9. You realize that this report is just for one city. However, nothing about it identifies that city. Its name is only in the query design. To redo the report to show that, go back to step 4, this time moving all the fields into the Selected Fields pane. Organize the report by StoreTbl, and click "Next."

10. In the following dialogue box, add a grouping level by customer by selecting "CustName" and clicking.

11. Continue as before, inserting a sum on OrderTotal, until you click "Finish."

12. You now have a report grouped by city. However, there is only one city in it, so that is not ideal. We would rather state the city in the header, with the report body much as it was before. This must be done in Design view, as Layout view does not allow moving report elements from one area to another. Change to that view.

13. Edit the report header to read "Customers in City:" (without the quotation marks).

14. Delete the StoreCity column heading. Select the StoreCity data field. In the Home ribbon tab, click "Cut" (pair of scissors, near the left) or press "Control-X." Click in the Report Header section of the report design, and click "Paste" (large icon with a sheet of paper sliding off a clipboard, in the same area), or press "Control-V." (If you are really good with your mouse or trackpad, you can avoid the cutting and pasting by selecting and moving it while the mouse pointer is a four-headed arrow.)

15. Click the Format Painter in the Clipboard section of the Home ribbon tab or the Font section of the Format tab. (You may be familiar with it from other parts of Microsoft Office.) Click in

the report header to copy its format, then in the StoreCity field you just moved to give it the same format.

Usage Hint: If you prefer, click in the report header. Note its font, size, and color in the Font section of the ribbon, under either the Home or the Format tab. Then select the StoreCity field, and format it the same way. The result will be the same.

16. Format this report as you formatted the previous one. You can do most of the formatting in Layout view if you prefer. Also:

(a) Drag CustName Header up to remove the space that the store city used to occupy. (This is easiest to do in Design view.)

(b) Delete the heading for "StoreCity" in the page header.

(c) Move all the remaining column headings and data fields to the left, into the space that the city name used to occupy.

(d) Delete the total at the city level. With just one city, it duplicates the grand total.

17. Name the report "ImprovedCityRpt," and close it.

18. Open StoreOrderQry, change the city to Chicago, and close it, saving when prompted.

19. Open ImprovedCityRpt. It should say "Chicago" in the header and reflect Chicago data.

Quiz Questions:

1. A report can display data from:

(a) More than one table

(b) More than one query

(c) A combination of tables and queries

(d) All of the above

2. True or False? When a report is based on a query, the query is rerun with new selection criteria, and the new query result is saved; opening the report will redisplay the original data.

3. Open any Access report (an existing one or a new one you create to play with; it does not matter) in Layout view. Try several Themes (near the left of the Design ribbon). Which of the following do Themes *not* modify?

(a) Report fonts

(b) Report column headings

(c) Report font sizes

(d) Report colors

4. True or False? Clicking "Cut," as you did in step 14, lets you remove a column heading while leaving that column's data in place.

Discussion Questions:

1. You are developing an information system for inventory management, which is discussed in the "In-House Logistics and Materials Management" section of this chapter. You want to identify all items that are at 1.0 to 1.5 times their reorder point for human review. (If an item is below its reorder point, it has already been reordered, or someone decided not to reorder it.) You decide to do this with a query. Its selection criteria will specify these comparisons. Access will then create a report for the purchasing manager. Draw this report, with suitable data columns, groupings, and summaries. Try to put yourself in the purchasing manager's position, asking what information this person needs to make reordering decisions and how that information can best be presented. Make any necessary assumptions about the content of your company's inventory database.

2. Section 11.4 of this chapter, "Reports," discusses five types of reports: routine, drill-down, key-indicator, comparative, and exception. Give an example of each, not repeating examples from that section, and discuss how a query could be used as the basis for it. If it cannot be used for that purpose, explain why.

3. You work for a university radio station. Your funding comes from several sources: the university, paid memberships, selling merchandise such as logo coffee mugs and soda can holders, and donations. Donations and merchandise sales often come from members, and members often renew year after year. You have a database that stores this information, as well as results of surveys about favorite musicians and music genres. Many, but not all, of the surveys identify the respondent.

   (a) Draw an ERD for this database. If you did not study ER diagramming in Chapter 3, draw an Access relationship map for it. Show its tables, their data fields (columns), and their relationships.

   (b) You want to use this information to help the station raise funds by matching its programming to what its supporters want and in other ways. How could you use query-driven reports to do this? Use your imagination. Be creative. Make any necessary assumptions about the content of the station's database.

12 | Extending the Organization to Customers

LEARNING OBJECTIVES >>>

1. Define customer relationship management and collaborative CRM, and identify the primary functions of both processes.

2. Describe the two major components of operational CRM systems, list three applications used in each component, and provide at least one example of how businesses use each application.

3. Define analytical CRM systems, and describe four purposes for which businesses use these systems.

4. Define mobile CRM systems, on-demand CRM systems, and open-source CRM systems, and identify one main advantage and one main drawback of each one.

Charles Mack and his son, Charles Mack, Jr., started an auto detailing business more than 25 years ago, providing the Washington, D.C., area with the "highest possible quality auto detail and auto electronics service." Their customers love their service and rave about them on the Macks' Web site. However, after 25 years and random IT upgrades, their various information systems created so much paperwork that they barely had time for their customers. They realized they needed to place more emphasis on relationships and less on paperwork. They initially considered hiring another person to perform this job. Ultimately, however, they decided to purchase software that could help them manage their customers throughout the initial contact, sale, service, payment, and continued-relationship cycle.

Charles Jr. decided on a small-business customer relationship management tool called Infusionsoft. This software allowed Charles Sr. and Charles Jr. to integrate their systems to provide a better customer experience for their clients. The Macks now have easier access to their clients' information and more time to interact with them. Scheduling, billing, and e-mail are all more efficient as well.

Within the first 3 months of implementation, Charles Jr. and his father enjoyed a 17 percent increase in sales. Those numbers continued to increase, and by mid-2011, their sales had increased by 50 percent.

Sources: Compiled from www.vipautoappearance.com, www.infusionsoft.com, accessed May 12, 2011.

Questions

1. Why did the Macks purchase a software package instead of hiring another person?

2. Describe the advantages that the Macks gained from their new software package

RUBY'S CLUB

Ruben and Lisa realize that this generation is much more connected than any before. Facebook, Twitter, MySpace, text messaging, instant messaging, and so on have all connected people anywhere, anytime. They also feel that they need to tap into this social market, but they are not sure how.

They know that many of their customers are on Facebook. However, they think that Facebook is more for personal use and do not want their customers to feel invaded by receiving advertisements from them on Facebook. Twitter seems more popular for business promotions, but they wonder how many of their customers are regulars on Twitter.

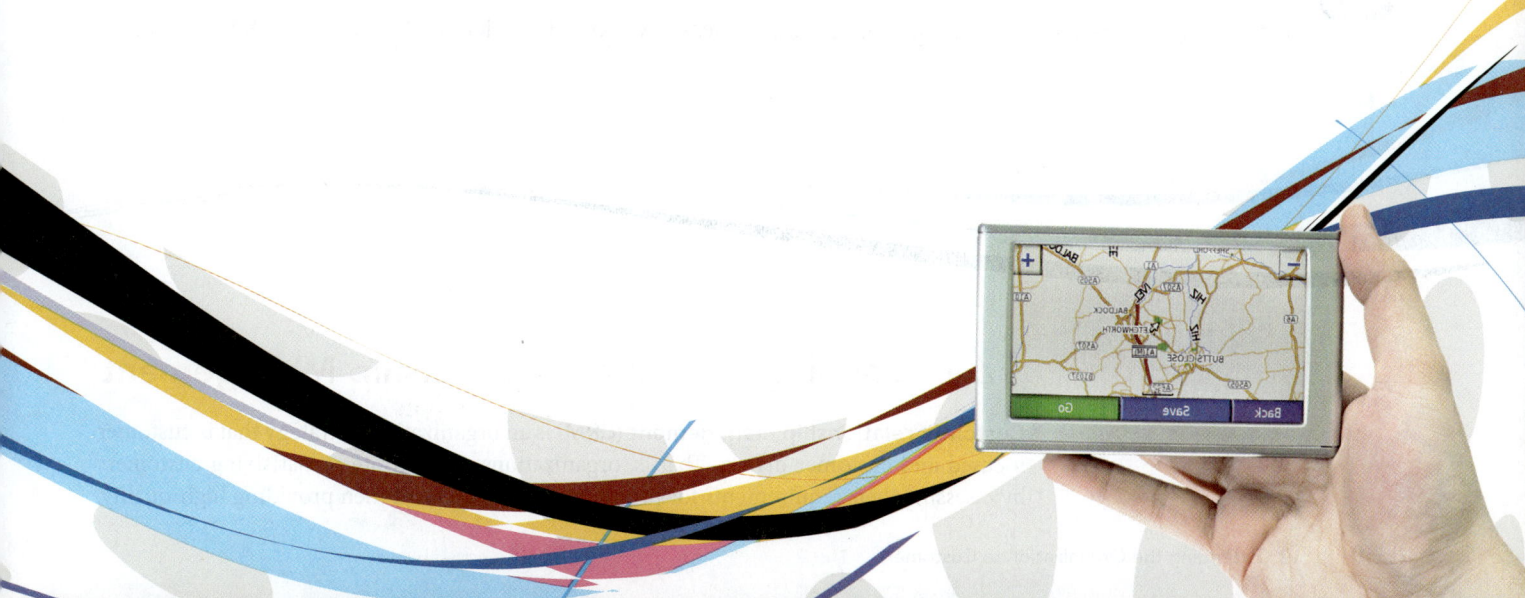

>>> As you learn about customer relationship management, consider their dilemma. Maintaining customers is about balance. Communicate at the right time, place, and manner, and Ruben and Lisa can win with their customers. However, if they cross a boundary, they may lose the community atmosphere in their club because of a virtual communication.

INTRODUCTION

Before the supermarket, the mall, and the automobile, people went to their neighborhood stores to purchase goods. The owner and employees recognized customers by name and knew their preferences and wants. For their part, customers remained loyal to the store and made repeated purchases. Over time, however, this personal customer relationship became impersonal as people moved from farms to cities, consumers became mobile, and supermarkets and department stores were established to achieve economies of scale through mass marketing efforts. Although prices were lower and products were more uniform in quality, the relationship with customers became nameless and impersonal.

The customer relationship has become even more impersonal with the rapid growth of the Internet and the World Wide Web. In today's hypercompetitive marketplace, customers are increasingly powerful. If they are dissatisfied with a product and/or a service from one organization, a competitor is often just one mouse click away. Further, as more and more customers shop on the Web, an enterprise does not even have the opportunity to make a good first impression *in person*.

 Customer relationship management (CRM) returns to personal marketing. That is, rather than market to a mass of people or companies, businesses market to each customer individually. By employing this approach, businesses can use information about each customer—for example, previous purchases, needs, and wants—to create offers that customers are more likely to accept. That is, the CRM approach is designed to achieve *customer intimacy*. This CRM approach is enabled by information technology in the form of a variety of CRM systems and applications.

Customer relationship management is not only about the software. Sometimes the problem with managing relationships is simply time and information. Old legacy systems may contain the information, but it may take too long to access it, and the information may not be usable across a variety of applications. The result is reduced time to spend with customers. Charles Mack and his son employed a CRM tool that manages e-mail distribution, scheduling, billing, and customer information. This tool enables them to find everything they need in one place so they can focus on what their business is really about: providing their customers with excellent service. The Macks are emphasizing a customer-centric approach to their business practices because they know that sustainable value is found in long-term customer relationships that extend beyond today's business transaction.

However, you may be asking yourself this: Why should I learn about CRM? As you will see in this chapter, customers are supremely important to *all* organizations. Regardless of the particular job you perform, you will have either a direct or an indirect impact on managing your firm's customers. As you read the "What's In IT For Me?" feature, you will encounter a number of opportunities in which you can make immediate contributions on your first job. Therefore, it is important that you possess a working knowledge of CRM and CRM systems.

12.1 | Defining Customer Relationship Management

Customer relationship management (CRM) is an organizational strategy that is customer focused and customer driven. That is, organizations concentrate on satisfying customers by assessing their requirements for products and services and then providing high-quality, responsive service. CRM is not a process or a technology per se; rather, it is a way of thinking and acting in a customer-centric fashion. The focus of organizations today has shifted from conducting business transactions to managing customer relationships. In general, organizations recognize that customers are the core of a successful enterprise, and the success of the enterprise depends on effectively managing relationships with them.

CRM builds sustainable long-term customer relationships that create value for the company as well as for the customer. That is, CRM helps companies acquire new customers, retain existing profitable customers, and grow the relationships with existing customers. This last CRM function is particularly important because repeat customers are the largest generator of revenue for an enterprise. Also, organizations have long understood that getting a customer back after he or she has switched to a competitor is vastly more expensive than keeping that customer satisfied in the first place.

Figure 12.1 depicts the CRM process. The process begins with marketing efforts, where the organization solicits prospects from a target population of potential customers. A certain number of prospects will make a purchase, thus becoming customers. Of the organization's customers, a certain number will become repeat customers. The organization then segments its repeat customers into low-value and high-value repeat customers. An organization's overall goal is to maximize the *lifetime value* of a customer, which is that customer's potential revenue stream over a number of years.

The organization inevitably will lose a certain percentage of customers, a process called *customer churn*. The optimal result of the organization's CRM efforts is to maximize the number of high-value repeat customers while minimizing customer churn.

CRM is basically a simple idea: Treat different customers differently because their needs differ and their value to the company also may differ. A successful CRM strategy not only improves customer satisfaction, but it also makes the company's sales and service employees more productive, which in turn generates increased profits. In fact, researchers at the National

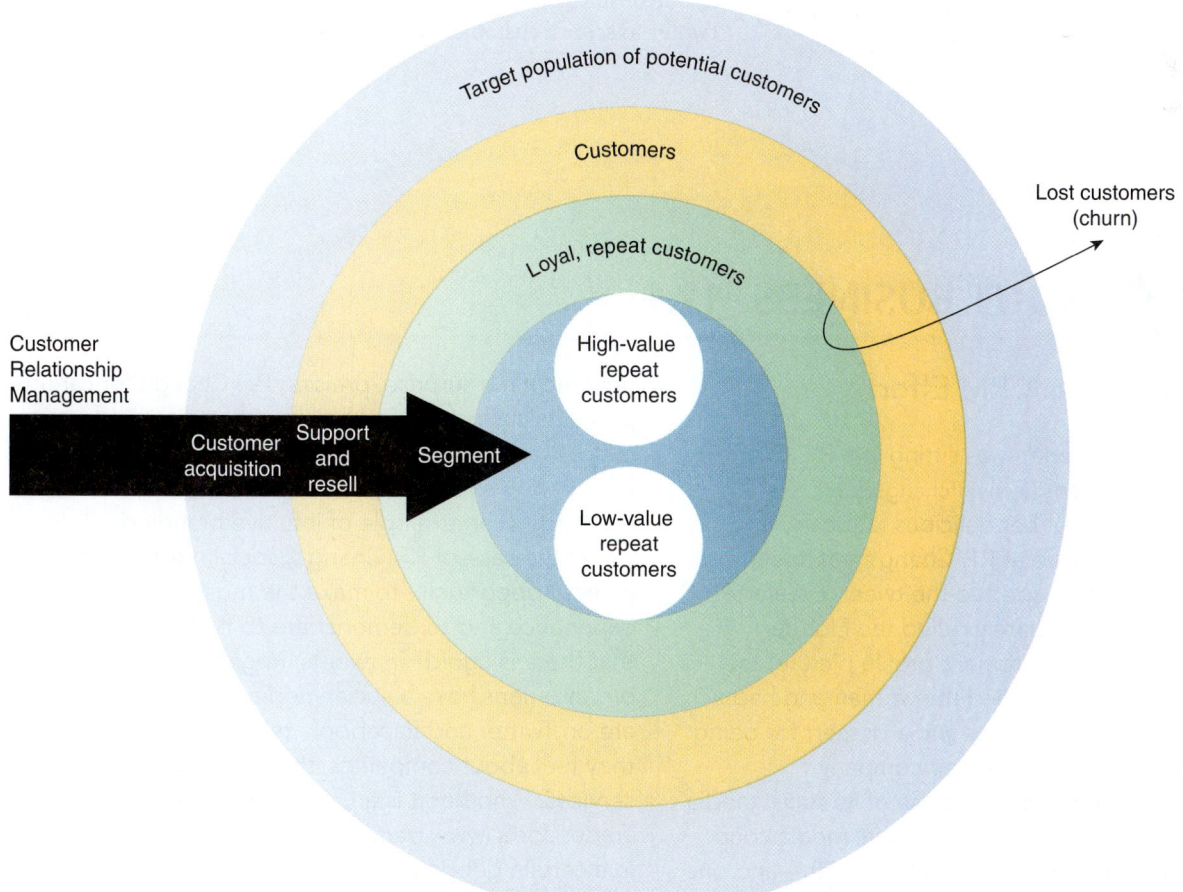

Figure 12.1 The customer relationship management process.

Coupon Kiosks are an attempt to build loyalty among customers. (*Source:* © Spencer Grant/PhotoEdit)

Quality Research Center at the University of Michigan found that a 1 percent increase in customer satisfaction can lead to as much as a 300 percent increase in a company's market capitalization, defined as the number of shares of the company's stock outstanding multiplied by the price per share of the stock. Put simply, a minor increase in customer satisfaction can lead to a major increase in a company's overall value.

Up to this point, you have been looking at an organization's CRM strategy. It is important to distinguish between a CRM *strategy* and CRM *systems*. Basically, CRM systems are information systems designed to support an organization's CRM strategy. For organizations to pursue excellent relationships with their customers, they need to utilize CRM systems that provide the necessary infrastructure to support those relationships. Because customer service and support are essential to a successful business, organizations must place a great deal of emphasis on both their CRM strategy and their CRM systems.

Broadly speaking, CRM systems can be placed along a continuum, from low-end CRM systems—designed for enterprises with many small customers—to high-end CRM systems—for enterprises with a few large customers. An example of a low-end system is when Amazon uses its CRM system to recommend books to returning customers. An example of a high-end system is when Boeing uses its CRM system to coordinate staff activities in a campaign to sell its new 787 aircraft to Delta Airlines. As you go through the cases and examples in this chapter, consider where on the continuum a particular CRM system would fall.

There are many examples of organizations that have gone beyond what is merely expected in their efforts to be customer-centric. "IT's About Business 12.1" illustrates how P.F. Chang's China Bistro used Twitter to score a customer-relationship coup.

IT's ABOUT BUSINESS | 12.1

An Instantaneous CRM Effort

While a woman in Florida was sitting in a P.F. Chang's China Bistro restaurant (www.pfchangs.com), she sent out a tweet about her delicious lettuce-wrap appetizer. An employee at P.F. Chang's headquarters in Scottsdale, Arizona, spotted the tweet. He alerted a manager, who immediately called the Florida restaurant. Using the customer's profile picture, the restaurant manager identified the woman and had a server bring her lettuce wraps and a dessert for being an enthusiastic supporter of their company.

By having its finger on the pulse of its social media branding, P.F. Chang's executed a social media coup. Not only did the restaurant earn a fan for life—and one who has an active Twitter account—but the customer undoubtedly told her friends and co-workers about

her lunchtime surprise, praising P.F. Chang's for caring about its customers. Further, in a short time, marketing executives in many organizations were presenting P.F. Chang's and its lettuce wraps in conferences and meetings as an example of intuitive branding.

In the case of P.F. Chang's, social media presented an easy opportunity to make the most of the customer experience and to demonstrate to the organization that there is "gold" in tweets. Regardless of whether organizations have a social media strategy, customers are on Twitter and Facebook, telling the world how they feel about companies, their products, and their services. Whether it is a Facebook group begging Trader Joe's (www.traderjoes.com) to open a store in a certain geographic location or a blogger with a million followers complaining about his or her washing machine, companies ignore social media at their peril.

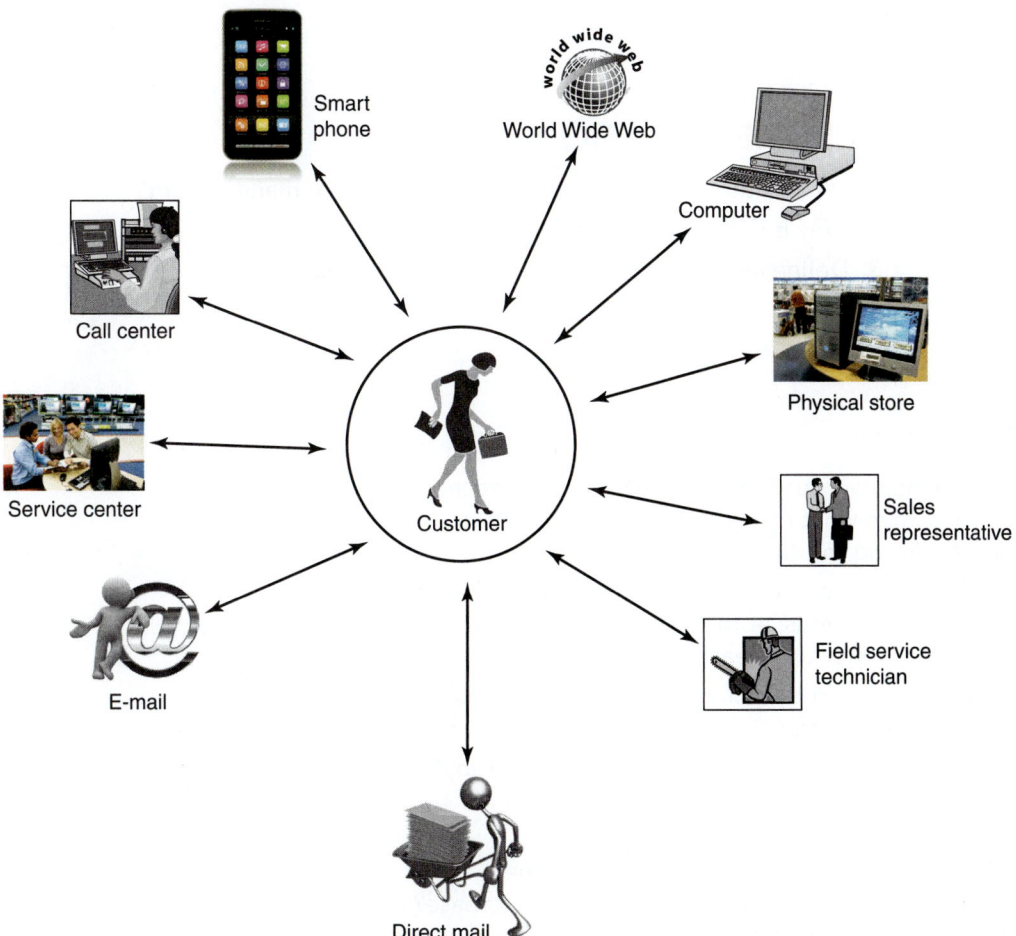

Questions

1. Provide two examples of specific actions a company could take to utilize social media in its CRM efforts.

2. Should all organizations include a social media component in their CRM strategy? Why or why not? Support your answer.

Sources: Compiled from W. Schuchart, "How P.F. Chang's Turned a Plate of Lettuce Wraps into a Twitter Win," *IT Knowledge Exchange*, March 16, 2011; www.pfchangs.com, accessed April 17. 2011.

Although CRM varies according to circumstances, all successful CRM policies share two basic elements. First, the company must identify the many types of customer touch points. Second, it needs to consolidate data about each customer. Let us examine these two elements in more detail.

Customer Touch Points

Organizations must recognize the numerous and diverse interactions that they have with their customers. These various types of interactions are referred to as **customer touch points**. Traditional customer touch points include telephone contact, direct mailings, and actual physical interactions with customers during their visits to a store. However, organizational CRM systems must manage many additional customer touch points that occur through the use of popular personal technologies. These touch points include e-mail, Web sites, and communications via smart phones (see Figure 12.2).

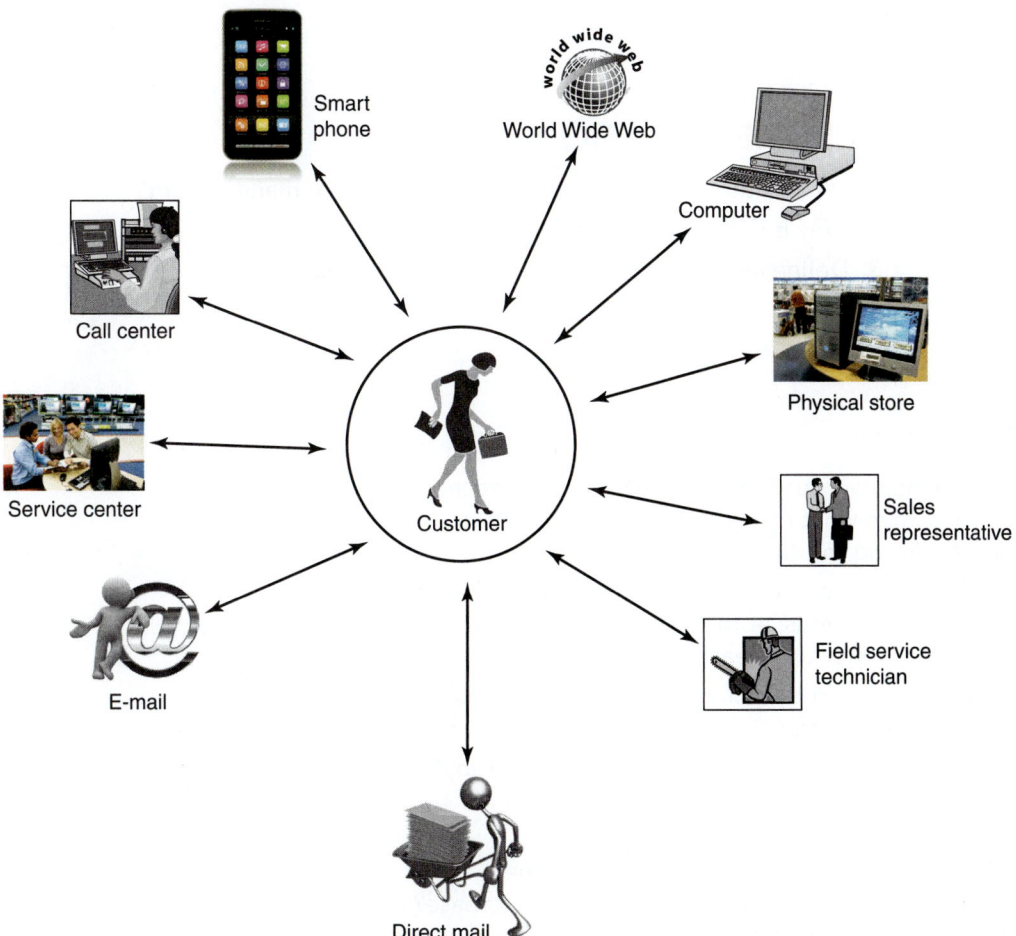

Figure 12.2 Customer touch points. (*Sources:* Smartphone-Oleksiy Mark/Shutterstock; Service center-Media Bakery; Physical store-Media Bakery)

Data Consolidation

Data consolidation is also critical to an organization's CRM efforts. Customer data must be managed effectively by the organization's CRM systems. In the past, customer data were located in isolated systems in different functional areas across the business. For example, it was not uncommon to find customer data stored in separate databases in the finance, sales, logistics, and marketing departments. Even though all of these data related to the same customer, it was difficult to share them across the various functional areas.

As you saw in Chapter 5, modern, interconnected systems built around a data warehouse now make all customer-related data available to every unit of the business. This complete data set on each customer is called a *360-degree view* of that customer. By accessing this 360-degree view, a company can enhance its relationship with its customers and ultimately make more productive and profitable decisions.

Data consolidation and the 360-degree view of the customer enable the organization's functional areas to readily share information about customers. This information sharing leads to collaborative CRM. **Collaborative CRM systems** provide effective and efficient interactive communication with the customer throughout the entire organization. That is, collaborative CRM systems integrate communications between the organization and its customers in all aspects of marketing, sales, and customer support. Collaborative CRM systems also enable customers to provide direct feedback to the organization. As you read in Chapter 9, Web 2.0 applications such as blogs and Wikis are very important to companies that value customer input into their product and service offerings as well as into new product development.

A CRM system in an organization contains two major components: operational CRM systems and analytical CRM systems. You learn about these components in the next two sections.

• BEFORE *YOU GO ON . . .*

1. What is the definition of customer relationship management?

2. Why is CRM so important to any organization?

3. Define and provide examples of customer touch points.

RUBY'S CLUB QUESTIONS

1. Ruby's Club seeks to maintain customers. If CRM is not a technology but a way of thinking, then what role could technology play to support this way of thinking for Ruben and Lisa?

2. Look at Figure 12.1, the CRM process. Ethically, when should Ruby's Club begin marketing to students: at the beginning of their 4 to 6 years of college or only after they reach the age of 21?

3. If CRM were implemented at Ruby's Club, would Ruben and Lisa need a low-end or high-end system?

4. What do you think are the most common touch points for Ruby's Club customers? Cell phones? Facebook? E-mail? Twitter? Telephone? USPS? Campus flyers?

5. Would Ruben and Lisa have a true 360-degree view of their customers if each order entry area operated on its own database? What would be the problem with having customer data spread over several computers?

Student Activity | 12.1

Objective: You will learn how an online retailer, www.REI.com, implements its CRM system and how the system supports the company's CRM strategy.

Chapter Connection: This activity relates to Section 12.1 and Learning Objective 1.

Prerequisites: You should read Section 12.1 prior to completing this activity.

Activity:

Watch the following video clip about REI's CRM system:

www.youtube.com/watch?v=fUSEtLlwzNg

Then visit the company's Web site:

www.rei.com.

Deliverables:

Prepare written answers (e.g., in MS Word document, posted on blogs or online discussion boards) to the following quiz and discussion questions.

Quiz Questions:

1. What are the main purposes of implementing a CRM system?
2. Would you categorize REI's CRM system as a low-end or high-end system? Why or why not?

Discussion Questions:

1. What are REI's main objectives in implementing its CRM system?
2. What features on REI's Web sites did you consider part of its CRM strategy?
3. How do you think the CRM features on REI's Web site will help acquire new customers and retain and build a long-term relationship with its existing customers?

12.2 | Operational Customer Relationship Management Systems

Operational CRM systems support front-office business processes. Front-office processes are those that directly interact with customers—that is, sales, marketing, and service. The two major components of operational CRM systems are customer-facing applications and customer-touching applications.

Customer-Facing Applications

Customer-facing CRM applications are those applications where an organization's sales, field service, and customer interaction center representatives interact directly with customers. These applications include customer service and support, sales force automation, marketing, and campaign management.

Customer Service and Support. Customer service and support refers to systems that automate service requests, complaints, product returns, and requests for information. Today, organizations have implemented **customer interaction centers (CIC)**, where organizational representatives use multiple communication channels such as the Web, telephone, fax, and face-to-face interactions to support the communication preferences of customers. The CIC manages several different types of customer interaction.

One of the most well-known customer interaction centers is the *call center*. A call center is a centralized office used for the purpose of receiving and transmitting a large volume of requests by telephone. Call centers enable companies to respond to a large variety of questions, including product support and complaints.

Organizations use the CIC to create a call list for the sales team, whose members contact sales prospects. This type of interaction is called *outbound telesales*. In these interactions, the customer and the sales team collaborate in discussing products and services that can satisfy customers' needs and generate sales.

Customers can communicate directly with the CIC to initiate a sales order, inquire about products and services before placing an order, and obtain information about a transaction that they have already made. These interactions are referred to as *inbound teleservice*. Teleservice representatives respond to requests either by utilizing service instructions found in an organizational knowledge base or by noting incidents that cannot be handled through the CIC but must be addressed by field service technicians.

The CIC also provides the information help desk. The help desk assists customers with their questions concerning products or services, and it also processes customer complaints. Complaints generate follow-up activities such as quality-control checks, delivery of replacement parts or products, service calls, generation of credit memos, and product returns.

New technologies are extending the functionality of the traditional CIC to include e-mail and Web interaction. For example, Epicor (www.epicor.com) provides software solutions that combine Web channels, such as automated e-mail reply, and Web knowledge bases. The information the software provides is available to CIC representatives and field service personnel. Another new technology, live chat, allows customers to connect to a company representative and conduct an instant messaging session. The advantage of live chat over a telephone conversation is the ability to show documents and photos (see www. livechatinc.com and www.websitealive.com). Some companies conduct the chat with a computer rather than a real person using natural language processing.

Sales Force Automation. **Sales force automation (SFA)** is the component of an operational CRM system that automatically records all of the components in a sales transaction process. SFA systems include a *contact management system*, which tracks all contacts that have been made with a customer, the purpose of each contact, and any follow-up that might be necessary. This system eliminates duplicated contacts and redundancy, which in turn reduces the risk of irritating customers. SFA also includes a *sales lead tracking system*, which lists potential customers or customers who have purchased related products.

Other elements of an SFA system can include a *sales forecasting system*, which is a mathematical technique for estimating future sales, and a *product knowledge system,* which is a comprehensive source of information regarding products and services. More-developed SFA systems also have online product-building features (called *configurators*) that enable customers to model the product to meet their specific needs. For example, you can customize your own running shoe at NikeID (http://nikeid.nike.com). Finally, many of the current SFA systems provide for remote connectivity for the salesperson in the field via Web-based interfaces that can be displayed on smart phones.

Marketing. Thus far you have focused primarily on how sales and customer service personnel can benefit from CRM systems. However, CRM systems have many important applications for an organization's marketing department as well. For example, they enable marketers to identify and target their best customers, to manage marketing campaigns, and to generate quality leads for the sales teams. In addition, CRM marketing applications provide opportunities to sift through volumes of customer data—a process known as data mining—and develop *purchasing profiles*—a snapshot of a consumer's buying habits—that may lead to additional sales through cross-selling, up-selling, and bundling.

Cross-selling is the practice of marketing additional related products to customers based on a previous purchase. This sales approach has been used very successfully by the world's largest online retailer, Amazon (www.amazon.com). For example, if you have purchased several books on Amazon, the next time you visit the Web site, Amazon will provide recommendations of other books you might like to purchase.

Up-selling is a sales strategy whereby the business person will provide to customers the opportunity to purchase higher-value related products or services as opposed to or along with the consumer's initial product or service selection. For example, if a customer goes into an electronics store to buy a new television, a salesperson may show him a 1080i high-definition LCD next to non-HD TV in the hope of selling the more expensive set (assuming the customer is willing to pay the extra cost for a sharper picture). Other common examples of up-selling are warranties on electronics purchases and the purchase of a car wash after you purchased gas at the gas station.

Bundling is a form of cross-selling whereby a business sells a group of products or services together at a price that is lower than the combined individual prices of the products. For example, your cable company might offer a bundle price that includes basic cable TV, broadband Internet access, and local telephone service at a lower price than if you acquired each service separately.

Campaign Management. Campaign management applications help organizations plan campaigns so that the right messages are sent to the right people through the right channels. Organizations manage their customers very carefully to avoid targeting people who have opted out of receiving marketing communications. Further, companies use these applications to personalize individual messages for each particular customer.

Customer-Touching Applications

Corporations have used manual CRM systems for many years. The term electronic *CRM* (or *e-CRM*) appeared in the mid-1990s, when organizations began using the Internet, the Web, and other electronic touch points (e.g., e-mail, point-of-sale terminals) to manage customer relationships. Customers interact directly with these technologies and applications rather than interact with a company representative as is the case with customer-facing applications. Such applications are called **customer-touching CRM applications** or **electronic CRM (e-CRM) applications**. Using these applications, customers typically are able to help themselves. There are many types of e-CRM applications. Some of the major applications are presented in this section.

Search and Comparison Capabilities. With the vast array of products and services available on the Web, it is often difficult for customers to find what they want. To assist customers, many online stores and malls offer search and comparison capabilities, as do independent comparison Web sites (see www.mysimon.com).

Technical and Other Information and Services. Many organizations offer personalized experiences to induce a customer to make a purchase or to remain loyal. For example, Web sites often allow customers to download product manuals. One example is General Electric's Web site (www.ge.com), which provides detailed technical and maintenance information and sells replacement parts for discontinued models for customers who need to repair outdated home appliances. Another example is Goodyear's Web site (www.goodyear.com), which provides information about tires and their use.

Customized Products and Services. Another customer-touching service that many online vendors use is mass customization, a process in which customers can configure their own products. For example, Dell Computer (www.dell.com) allows customers to configure their own computer systems. The Gap (www.gap.com) allows customers to "mix and match" an entire wardrobe. Web sites such as Hitsquad (www.hitsquad.com) and Surprise (www.surprise.com) allow customers to pick individual music titles from a library and customize a CD, a feature that traditional music stores do not offer.

In addition, customers can now view their account balances or check the shipping status of their orders from their computers or smart phones at any time. If you order books from Amazon, for example, you can look up the anticipated arrival date. Many other companies follow this model and provide similar services (see www.fedex.com and www.ups.com).

Personalized Web Pages. Many organizations permit their customers to create their own personalized Web pages. Customers use these pages to record purchases and preferences, as well as problems and requests. For example, American Airlines generates personalized Web pages for each of approximately 800,000 registered travel-planning customers.

FAQs. Frequently asked questions (FAQs) are a simple tool for answering repetitive customer queries. Customers who find the information they need by using this tool do not need to communicate with an actual person.

E-mail and Automated Response. The most popular tool for customer service is e-mail. Inexpensive and fast, e-mail is used not only to answer inquiries from customers but also to

Discounts and coupons are also a way to collect shopping data for CRM tools. (*Source:* © Amy Eira/PhotoEdit)

disseminate information, send alerts and product information, and conduct correspondence regarding any topic.

Loyalty Programs. **Loyalty programs** recognize customers who repeatedly use a vendor's products or services. Loyalty programs are appropriate when two conditions are met: a high frequency of repeat purchases and little product customization for each customer.

The purpose of loyalty programs is not to reward past behavior but to influence future behavior. It is important to note here that the most profitable customers are not necessarily those whose behavior can be influenced the most easily. As one example, most major U.S. airlines provide some "elite" benefits to anyone who flies 25,000 miles with them and their partners over the course of a year. Customers who fly on paid first-class tickets pay many times as much for a given flight as one who flies in discount economy. But, the first-class flyers will reach elite status only 1.5 to 2 times faster than economy-class passengers. The reason is that, although first-class passengers are far more profitable than discount seekers, they are also less influenced by loyalty programs. Discount flyers respond much more enthusiastically to the benefits of frequent flyer programs. Therefore, airlines award discount flyers more benefits than they offer first-class flyers (relative to their spending).

Perhaps the best-known loyalty programs are the airlines' frequent flyer programs. In addition, casinos use their players' clubs to reward their frequent players, and supermarkets use similar programs to reward frequent shoppers. Loyalty programs use a database or data warehouse to keep a record of the points (or miles) a customer has accrued and the rewards to which he or she is entitled. The programs then use analytical tools to mine the data and learn about customer behavior.

Operational CRM systems provide the following benefits:

- Efficient, personalized marketing, sales, and service
- A 360-degree view of each customer
- The ability of sales and service employees to access a complete history of customer interaction with the organization, regardless of the touch point

Another example of an operational CRM system involves Caterpillar, Inc. (www.cat.com), an international manufacturer of industrial equipment. Caterpillar uses its CRM tools to accomplish the following objectives:

- Assist the organization in improving sales and account management by optimizing the information shared by multiple employees and by streamlining existing processes (for example, taking orders using mobile devices)
- Form individualized relationships with customers, with the aim of improving customer satisfaction and maximizing profits
- Identify the most profitable customers, and provide them the highest level of service
- Provide employees with the information and processes necessary to know their customers
- Understand and identify customer needs, and effectively build relationships among the company, its customer base, and its distribution partners

BEFORE *YOU GO ON . . .*

1. Differentiate between customer-facing applications and customer-touching applications.
2. Other than the examples in the book, provide an example of cross-selling, up-selling, and bundling.

1. Do you think there would there be any legal or ethical issues with up-selling alcoholic beverages? What about cross-selling alcohol with food?

2. Campaign management seems to be the issue Ruben and Lisa are really concerned about. How do they touch their customer on the right touch point, at the right time, in the right way? What examples can you find online that show how other clubs/bars handle campaign management?

3. What type of loyalty club could Ruben and Lisa create? What advantages could they create for their customer with this type of club?

Student Activity | 12.2

Objective: You will apply your knowledge from Section 12.2 to identify features of operational CRM systems on retail Web sites.

Chapter Connection: This activity relates to Section 12.2 and Learning Objective 2. It also reinforces the materials covered in Section 12.1 and Learning Objective 1.

Prerequisites: You should read Sections 12.1 and 12.2 prior to completing this activity.

Activity:

Visit one of the following Web sites (or the Web site chosen by the instructor), and identify and explore CRM features on these leading online retail stores:

Lands' End: www.landsend.com

Dell: www.dell.com

Zappos: www.zappos.com

1-800-Flowers: www.1800flowers.com

Deliverables:

Prepare written answers (e.g., in an MS Word document, posted on blogs or online discussion boards) to the following quiz and discussion questions.

Quiz Questions:

1. Which of the following Web site functionalities best describes an example of a customer-facing application in an operational CRM system?
   - (a) Live chat
   - (b) Mass customization features
   - (c) Search capabilities
   - (d) Personalized Web pages
   - (e) Loyalty program

2. Identify three examples of customer-touching applications implemented on the Web site you visited.

3. Identify three features on the Web site you visited that are examples of a customer-facing application.

Discussion Questions:

1. What are the main differences between customer-facing and customer-touching applications on an operational CRM system?

2. What potential benefits do you think online retailers such as Lands' End, Dell, Zappos, and 1-800-Flowers can gain from their online CRM systems?

12.3 | Analytical Customer Relationship Management Systems

Whereas operational CRM systems support front-office business processes, **analytical CRM systems** analyze customer behavior and perceptions in order to provide actionable business intelligence. For example, analytical CRM systems typically provide information on customer requests and transactions, as well as on customer responses to an organization's marketing, sales, and service initiatives. These systems also create statistical models of customer behavior and the value of customer relationships over time, as well as forecasts about acquiring, retaining, and losing customers. Figure 12.3 illustrates the relationship between operational CRM systems and analytical CRM systems.

Important technologies in analytical CRM systems include data warehouses, data mining, decision support, and other business intelligence technologies (discussed in Chapter 12). Once systems have completed the various analyses, information to the organization is available in the form of reports and digital dashboards.

Analytical CRM systems analyze customer data for a variety of purposes, including these:

- Designing and executing targeted marketing campaigns
- Increasing customer acquisition, cross-selling, and up-selling
- Providing input into decisions relating to products and services (e.g., pricing and product development)
- Providing financial forecasting and customer profitability analysis

BEFORE *YOU GO ON . . .*

1. What is the relationship between operational CRM systems and analytical CRM systems?
2. What are some of the functions of analytical CRM systems?

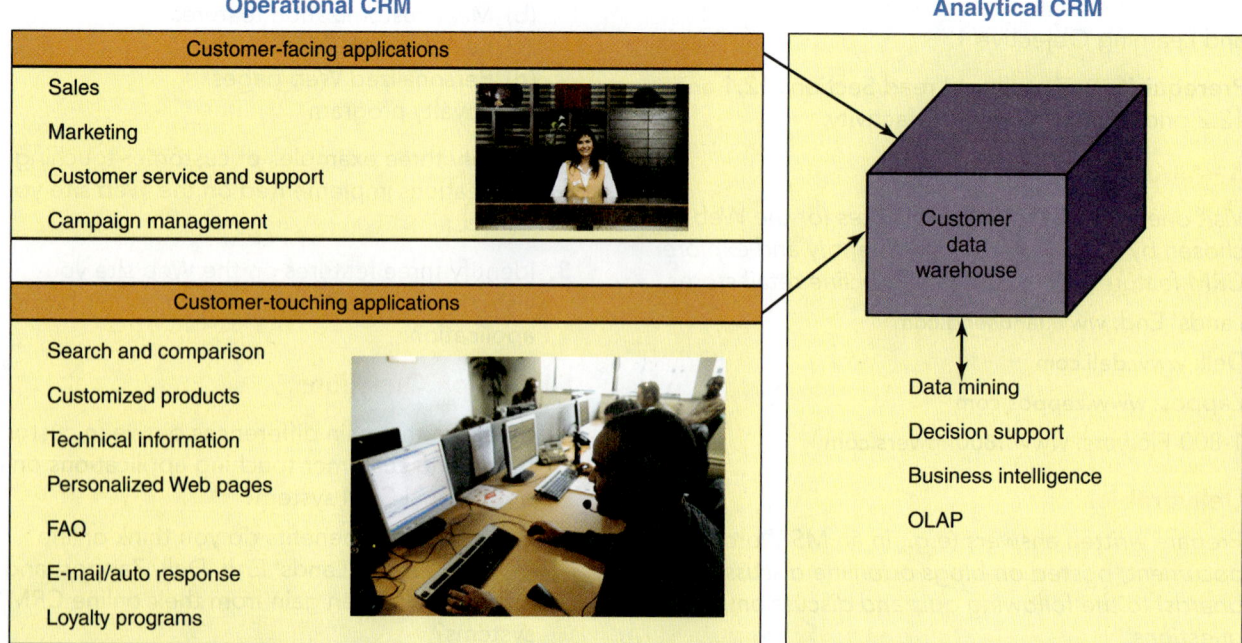

Figure 12.3 The relationship between operational CRM and analytical CRM. (*Source:* Image Source Limited; J-C & D. PRATT/PhotoNonStop/Glow Images)

Student Activity | 12.3

Objective: You will apply your knowledge from Section 12.3 to identify and discuss features and potential benefits of analytical CRM systems.

Chapter Connection: This activity relates to Section 12.3 and Learning Objective 3. It also reinforces the materials covered in Section 12.2 and Learning Objective 2.

Prerequisites: You should read Sections 12.1, 12.2, and 12.3 prior to undertaking this activity.

Activity:

Read the case study, and watch the accompanying video about how 1-888-Trash-It uses its CRM system to enhance its business analytics. The case study can be found here:

www.microsoft.com/casestudies/Microsoft-Dynamics-CRM-4.0/1-888-TRASH-IT/Junk-Removal-Service-Finds-Gold-with-Microsoft-Dynamics-CRM-Online/4000001895

Deliverables:

Prepare written answers (e.g., in an MS Word document, posted on blogs or online discussion boards) to the following quiz and discussion questions.

Quiz Questions:

1. Which of the following best describes one of the purposes of implementing an analytical CRM system?

 (a) To enhance financial forecasting and customer profitability analysis
 (b) To keep records of day-to-day business transactions
 (c) To improve the scalability of the corporate database
 (d) To integrate an organization's information system with those of its suppliers
 (e) To allow a company to streamline its logistical operations in its supply chain

2. Identify the essential technologies that enable an analytical CRM system.

Discussion Questions:

1. Describe the main difference between operational and analytical CRM systems.

2. Identify and describe *analytical* features of the CRM system at 1-888-Trash-It. How do these features help the company strengthen its relationship with its customers?

3. Identify and discuss the benefits that can be gained from implementing an analytical CRM system. What actual benefits did 1-888-Trash-It gain from its CRM implementation?

12.4 | Other Types of Customer Relationship Management Systems

Now that you have examined operational and analytical CRM systems, you focus on other types of CRM systems. Three exciting developments in this area are on-demand CRM systems, mobile CRM systems, and open-source CRM systems.

On-Demand CRM Systems

Customer relationship management systems may be implemented as either *on premise* or *on demand*. Traditionally, organizations utilized on-premise CRM systems, meaning that they purchased the systems from a vendor and then installed them on site. This arrangement was expensive, time consuming, and inflexible. Some organizations, particularly smaller ones, could not justify the cost.

On-demand CRM systems became a solution for the drawbacks of on-premise CRM systems. An **on-demand CRM system** is a CRM system that is hosted by an external vendor in the vendor's data center. This arrangement spares the organization the costs associated with purchasing the system. In addition, because the vendor creates and maintains the system, the organization's employees need to know only how to access and utilize it. The concept of on demand is also known as utility computing (see "Plug IT In 2") or software-as-a-service (SaaS; see "Plug IT In 3").

Despite their benefits, on-demand CRM systems have potential problems. First, the vendor could prove to be unreliable, in which case the company would have no CRM functionality at all. Second, hosted software is difficult or impossible to modify, and only the vendor can upgrade it. Third, vendor-hosted CRM software may be difficult to integrate with the organization's existing software. Finally, giving strategic customer data to vendors always carries risks.

Salesforce (www.salesforce.com) is the best-known on-demand CRM vendor. The goal of Salesforce is to provide a new business model that allows companies to rent the CRM software instead of buying it. The secret to Salesforce's success appears to be that CRM has common requirements across many customers.

One Salesforce customer is Minneapolis-based Häagen-Dazs (www.haagen-dazs.com). Häagen-Dazs estimated that it would have had to spend $65,000 for a custom-designed database to remain in close contact with its retail franchises. Rather than make this expenditure, the company spent an initial $20,000 to establish service with Salesforce. It now pays $125 per month for 20 users to remotely monitor, via the Web or their smart phones, all the Häagen-Dazs franchises across the United States.

Other vendors also offer on-demand CRM software. The following example demonstrates the advantages that McKesson Specialty (www.mckesson.com) gained from deploying the Oracle on-demand CRM application.

EXAMPLE

McKesson Specialty, a division of the McKesson Corporation (www.mckesson.com), delivers the approaches and solutions needed to ensure success in the evolving specialty pharmaceutical market. The division's services include reimbursement support services for patients and physicians, reimbursement strategies for pharmaceutical manufacturers, specialty distribution and pharmacy services, oncology services, and patient support services including clinical support and patient assistance programs.

McKesson Specialty wanted a CRM system that would enable it to perform the following functions:

- Make sales activities and customer accounts more visible to the corporation.
- Standardize and automate sales and CRM processes.
- Track reported problems, inconsistent processes, and resolution time.

In addition, the system had to be easy to use. McKesson Specialty ultimately implemented Oracle's CRM On Demand application to standardize the sales and marketing systems across all of its product lines. The new system enabled the company to consolidate reporting across product lines, and it provided the necessary flexibility to accommodate multiple sales processes. Further, it allowed the organization to monitor and track issues that arose in the resolution process.

In essence, Oracle's CRM On Demand application provided McKesson Specialty with a 360-degree view of customer account information across the entire organization, which has proved to be very useful. In addition, McKesson Specialty was able to deploy the system in less than 90 days.

Sources: Compiled from "McKesson Specialty: Oracle Customer Snapshot," www.oracle.com, accessed August 15, 2011; "McKesson Specialty Standardizes Sales and Marketing Processes and Increases Customer Visibility," http://techrepublic.com, accessed August 15, 2011.

Mobile CRM Systems

A **mobile CRM system** is an interactive CRM system that enables an organization to conduct communications related to sales, marketing, and customer service activities through a mobile medium for the purpose of building and maintaining relationships with its customers. Put simply, mobile CRM systems involve interacting directly with consumers through their own portable devices, such as smart phones. Many forward-thinking companies believe mobile CRM systems hold tremendous promise as an avenue to create a personalized customer relationship that may be accessed anywhere and at any time. In fact, the potential opportunities provided through mobile marketing appear so rich that a host of companies have already identified mobile CRM systems as a cornerstone of their future marketing activities. "IT's About Business 12.2" discusses a mobile CRM application at the Hard Rock Hotel and Casino.

Open-Source CRM Systems

As explained in "Plug IT In 2," the source code for open-source software is available at no cost to developers or users. An **open-source CRM system**, therefore, is a CRM system whose source code is available to developers and users.

IT's ABOUT BUSINESS | 12.2

Mobile CRM on a Smart Phone

On busy weekends in Las Vegas, getting a drink at bars and nightclubs can be a full-contact sport. First, you muscle your way through a crowd to get near the bar. Then, you shout your order and hope the bartender hears it correctly. The Hard Rock Hotel and Casino (www.hardrockhotel.com) has developed

a unique approach to this problem. In April 2011, the hotel deployed a system that enables customers to use their smart phones to order food and drinks, which are then delivered to their location by a server. The technology, called Kickback, is a product of Kickback Mobile (www.kickbackmobile.com).

To participate, customers download a free app to their smart phones and register with their credit card information. At that point, Kickback uses Global Positioning System (GPS) technology to determine which of the seven Hard Rock venues the customer is visiting, and it pushes menu options to the customer's smart phone accordingly. Customers can also use the app for room service.

Kickback offers a number of benefits. For customers, ordering food and drinks at the resort's pool, concert venue, and food and beverage outlets no longer requires trips to the bar. Hard Rock gains

full integration with its CRM and point-of-sale systems as well as the capability to track the purchases of big spenders. Hard Rock also hopes to use Kickback to develop and push promotions—for example, a marketing campaign for a particular liquor—based on a customer's preferences, spending habits, and location within the resort.

Kickback uses a technology called geo-fencing, which employs a smart phone's GPS capabilities and location in relation to nearby cellular towers to estimate where a customer is located when he or she places an order. Customers select where the server should deliver the order using a predefined list. They can even purchase food or drinks when they are not at a Hard Rock venue and have the order delivered to friends who are there.

Questions

1. What are the disadvantages of the Kickback mobile CRM application?
2. Identify two additional advantages of the Kickback mobile CRM application.

Sources: Compiled from M. Villano, "CRM on a Smart Phone," *CIO*, April 27, 2011; www.hardrockhotel.com, www.kickbackmobile.com, accessed May 9, 2011.

Open-source CRM systems do not provide more or fewer features or functions than other CRM software, and they may be implemented either on premise or on demand. Leading open-source CRM vendors include SugarCRM (www.sugarcrm.com), Concursive (www.concursive.com), and vtiger (www.vtiger.com).

The benefits of open-source CRM systems include favorable pricing and a wide variety of applications. In addition, these systems are very easy to customize. This is an attractive feature for organizations that need CRM software designed for their specific needs. Finally, updates and bug (software error) fixes for open-source CRM systems occur rapidly, and extensive support information is available free of charge.

Like all software, however, open-source CRM systems have certain risks. The most serious risk involves quality control. Because open-source CRM systems are created by a large community of unpaid developers, there sometimes is no central authority that is responsible for overseeing the quality of the product. Further, for best results, companies must have the same information technology platform in place as the platform on which the open-source CRM system was developed.

BEFORE *YOU GO ON . . .*

1. Define on-demand CRM.
2. Define mobile CRM.
3. Define open-source CRM.

Student Activity | 12.4

Objective: You will explore the possibilities and potential benefits of on-demand CRM systems and how they differ from traditional on-premise CRM systems.

Chapter Connection: This activity relates to Section 12.4 and Learning Objective 4.

Prerequisites: You should read Section 12.4 prior to completing this activity.

Activity:

Watch the video clip about Salesforce.com's CRM system:

www.youtube.com/watch?v=_r1H7OK8lzY

Then visit the Salesforce Web site to explore the CRM solutions for clients in the retail industry:

www.Salesforce.com

Deliverables:

Prepare written answers (e.g., in an MS Word document, posted on blogs or an online discussion board) to the following quiz and discussion.

Quiz Questions:

1. What is an on-demand CRM system?
2. List two potential benefits and drawbacks to on-demand CRM systems.

Discussion Questions:

1. Identify and describe CRM features that are provided by Salesforce.com.
2. What are the potential benefits and problems of using an on-demand CRM system such as the one provided by Salesforce.com in the retail industry?

What's in **IT** for ME?

FOR THE ACCOUNTING MAJOR

CRM systems can help companies establish controls for financial reporting related to interactions with customers in order to support compliance with legislation. For example, the Sarbanes-Oxley Act requires companies to establish and maintain an adequate set of controls for accurate financial reporting that can be audited by a third party. Other sections of the law [302 and 401(b)] have implications for customer activities, including the requirements that sales figures reported for the prior year are correct. Section 409 requires companies to report material changes to financial conditions, such as the loss of a strategic customer or significant customer claims about product quality.

CRM systems can track document flow from a sales opportunity, to a sales order, to an invoice, to an accounting document, thus enabling finance and accounting managers to monitor the entire flow. CRM systems that track sales quotes and orders can be used to incorporate process controls that identify questionable sales transactions. CRM systems can provide exception-alert capabilities to identify instances outside defined parameters that put companies at risk.

FOR THE FINANCE MAJOR

CRM systems allow companies to track marketing expenses, collecting appropriate costs for each individual marketing campaign. These costs can then be matched to corporate initiatives and financial objectives, demonstrating the financial impact of the marketing campaign.

Pricing is another key area that impacts financial reporting. For example, what discounts are available? When can a price be overridden? Who approves discounts? CRM systems can put controls into place for these issues.

FOR THE MARKETING MAJOR

CRM systems are an integral part of every marketing professional's work activities. CRM systems contain the consolidated customer data that provide the foundation for making informed marketing decisions. Using this data, marketers develop well-timed and targeted sales campaigns with customized product mixes and established price points that enhance potential sales opportunities and therefore increase revenue. CRM systems also support the development of forecasting models for future sales to existing clients through the use of historical data captured from previous transactions.

FOR THE
PRODUCTION/OPERATIONS MANAGEMENT MAJOR

Production is heavily involved in the acquisition of raw materials, conversion, and distribution of finished goods. However, all of these activities are driven by sales. Increases or decreases in demand for goods results in a corresponding increase or decrease in a company's need for raw materials. Integral to a company's demand is forecasting future sales, an important part of CRM systems. Sales forecasts are created through the use of historical data stored in CRM systems.

This information is critically important to a production manager who is placing orders for manufacturing processes. Without an accurate future sales forecast, production managers may face inventory problems (discussed in detail in this chapter). The use of CRM systems for production and operational support is critical to efficiently managing the resources of the company.

FOR THE HUMAN RESOURCES MAJOR

As companies try to enhance their customer relationships, they must recognize that employees who interact with customers are critical to the success of CRM strategies. Essentially, CRM will be successful based on the employees' desire and ability to promote the company and its CRM initiatives. In fact, research analysts have found that customer loyalty is largely based on employees' capabilities and their commitment to the company.

As a result, human resource managers know that if their company desires valued customer relationships, then it needs valued relationships with its employees. Therefore, HR managers are implementing programs to increase employee satisfaction and are providing training for employees so that they can execute CRM strategies.

FOR THE MIS MAJOR

The IT function in the enterprise is responsible for the corporate databases and data warehouse, and the correctness and completeness of the data in them. That is, the IT department provides the data used in a 360-degree view of the customer. Further, IT personnel provide the technologies underlying the customer interaction center.

>>> SUMMARY

1. Define customer relationship management and collaborative CRM, and identify the primary functions of both processes.

Customer relationship management (CRM) is an organizational strategy that is customer focused and customer driven. That is, organizations concentrate on satisfying customers by assessing their requirements for products and services and then providing high-quality, responsive service. CRM functions include acquiring new customers, retaining existing customers, and growing the relationships with existing customers.

Collaborative CRM is an organizational CRM strategy whereby data consolidation and the 360-degree view of the customer enable the organization's functional areas to readily share information about customers. The functions of collaborative CRM include integrating communications between the organization and its customers in all aspects of marketing, sales, and customer support processes, and enabling customers to provide direct feedback to the organization.

2. Describe the two major components of operational CRM systems, list three applications used in each, and provide at least one example of how businesses use each application.

Operational CRM systems support the front-office business processes that interact directly with customers (i.e., sales,

marketing, and service). The two major components of operational CRM systems are customer-facing applications and customer-touching applications.

Customer-facing CRM applications include customer service and support, sales force automation, marketing, and campaign management. *Customer-touching applications* include search and comparison capabilities, technical and other information and services, customized products and services, personalized Web pages, FAQs, e-mail and automated response, and loyalty programs.

3. Define analytical CRM systems, and describe four purposes for businesses using these systems.

Analytical CRM systems analyze customer behavior and perceptions in order to provide business intelligence. Organizations use analytical systems for many purposes, including designing and executing targeted marketing campaigns; increasing customer acquisition, cross-selling, and up-selling; providing input into decisions relating to products and services (e.g., pricing and product development); and providing financial forecasting and customer profitability analysis.

4. Define mobile CRM systems, on-demand CRM systems, and open-source CRM systems, and identify one main advantage and one main drawback of each one.

On-demand CRM systems are CRM systems hosted by an external vendor in the vendor's data center. Advantages of on-demand CRM systems include lower costs and a need for employees to know only how to access and utilize the software. Drawbacks include possibly unreliable vendors, difficulty in modifying the software, and difficulty in integrating vendor-hosted CRM software with the organization's existing software.

Mobile CRM systems are interactive CRM systems whereby communications related to sales, marketing, and customer service activities are conducted through a mobile medium for the purpose of building and maintaining customer relationships between an organization and its customers. Advantages of mobile CRM systems include convenience for customers and the chance to build a truly personal relationship with customers. A drawback could be difficulty in maintaining customer expectations. That is, the company must be extremely responsive to customer needs in a mobile, near-real-time environment.

Open-source CRM systems are CRM systems whose source code is available to developers and users. The benefits of open-source CRM systems include favorable pricing, a wide variety of applications, easy customization, rapid updates and bug (software error) fixes, and extensive free support information. The major drawback of open-source CRM systems is quality control.

>>> CHAPTER GLOSSARY

analytical CRM systems CRM systems that analyze customer behavior and perceptions in order to provide actionable business intelligence.

bundling A form of cross-selling whereby an enterprise sells a group of products or services together at a lower price than the combined individual price of the products.

campaign management applications CRM applications that help organizations plan marketing campaigns so that the right messages are sent to the right people through the right channels.

collaborative CRM systems CRM systems in which communications between the organization and its customers are integrated across all aspects of marketing, sales, and customer support processes.

cross-selling The practice of marketing additional related products to customers based on a previous purchase.

customer-facing CRM applications Areas where customers directly interact with the organization, including customer service and support, sales force automation, marketing, and campaign management.

customer interaction centers CRM operations where organizational representatives use multiple communication channels to interact with customers in functions such as inbound teleservice and outbound telesales.

customer relationship management (CRM) A customer-focused and customer-driven organizational strategy that concentrates on satisfying customers by addressing their requirements for products and services, and then by providing high-quality, responsive service.

customer-touching CRM applications (or **electronic CRM** or **e-CRM applications**) Applications and technologies with which customers interact and typically help themselves.

customer touch points Any interactions between a customer and an organization.

electronic CRM (e-CRM) (see **customer-touching CRM applications**)

loyalty programs Programs that offer rewards to customers to influence future behavior.

mobile CRM system An interactive CRM system where communications related to sales, marketing, and customer service activities are conducted through a mobile medium for the purpose of building and maintaining customer relationships between an organization and its customers.

on-demand CRM system A CRM system that is hosted by an external vendor in the vendor's data center.

open-source CRM system CRM software whose source code is available to developers and users.

operational CRM systems Components of CRM that support the front-office business processes that directly interact with customers (i.e., sales, marketing, and service).

sales force automation The component of an operational CRM system that automatically records all the aspects in a sales transaction process.

up-selling A sales strategy whereby the organizational representative will provide to customers the opportunity to purchase higher-value related products or services as opposed to or along with the consumer's initial product or service selection.

>>> DISCUSSION QUESTIONS

1. How do customer relationship management systems help organizations achieve customer intimacy?

2. What is the relationship between data consolidation and CRM systems?

3. Discuss the relationship between CRM and customer privacy.

4. Distinguish between operational CRM systems and analytical CRM systems.

5. Differentiate between customer-facing CRM applications and customer-touching CRM applications.

6. Explain why Web-based customer interaction centers are critical for successful CRM systems.

7. Why are companies so interested in e-CRM applications?

8. Discuss why it is difficult to justify CRM applications.

9. You are the CIO of a small company with a rapidly growing customer base. Which CRM system would you use: on-premise CRM system, on-demand CRM system, or open-source CRM system? Remember that open-source CRM systems may be implemented either on premise or on demand. Discuss the pros and cons of each type of CRM system for your business.

>>> PROBLEM-SOLVING ACTIVITIES

1. Enter www.anntaylor.com, www.hermes.com, and www.tiffany.com. Compare and contrast the customer service activities offered by these companies on their Web sites. Do you see marked similarities? Differences?

2. Access your university's Web site. Investigate how your university provides for customer relationship management. *Hint:* First decide who your university's customers are.

3. Access www.sugarcrm.com, and take the interactive tour. Prepare a report on SugarCRM's functionality to the class.

4. Enter the Teradata Student Network (www.teradatauniversitynetwork.com/tun), and find the First American Corporation case (by Watson, Wixom, and Goodhue), which focuses on CRM implementation. Answer the questions at the end of the case.

>>> TEAM ASSIGNMENTS

1. Each group will be assigned to an open-source CRM vendor. Each group should examine the vendor, its products, and the capabilities of those products. Each group will make a presentation to the class detailing how its vendor product is superior to the other open-source CRM products. See SugarCRM (www.sugarcrm.com), Concursive (www.concursive.com), vtiger (www.vtiger.com), SplendidCRM Software (www.splendidcrm.com), Compiere (www.compiere.com), Hipergate (http://sourceforge.net/projects/hipergate), and openCRX (www.opencrx.com).

2. Each group will be assigned to an on-demand CRM vendor. Each group should examine each vendor, its products, and the capabilities of those products. Each group will make a presentation to the class detailing how its vendor product is superior to the other open-source CRM products. See Salesforce (www.salesforce.com), Oracle (http://crmondemand.oracle.com), Aplicor (www.aplicor.com), NetSuite (www.netsuite.com),

SalesNexus (www.salesnexus.com), SageCRM (www.sagecrm.com), Commence (www.commence.com), Soffront (www.soffront.com), and eSalesTrack (www.esalestrack.com).

3. Create groups to investigate the major CRM applications and their vendors.

- Sales force automation (Microsoft Dynamics, Oracle, FrontRange Solutions, RightNow Technologies, Maximizer Software)
- Call centers (LivePerson, Cisco, Oracle)
- Marketing automation (SalesNexus, Marketo, Chordiant, Infor, Consona, Pivotal, Oracle)
- Customer service (Oracle, Amazon, Dell, Sage)

Start with www.searchcrm.com and www.customerthink.com (to ask questions about CRM solutions). Each group will present arguments to convince the class members to use the product(s) the group investigated.

CLOSING **CASE 1 >** The Next Step in Customer Relationship Management

Welcome, [Your First Name Here], to the era of personalization. Amazon recommends books you might like. Netflix tailors your movie menu. Google customizes your news. In exchange for this friendly assistance, targeted ads follow you wherever you navigate online. This process is called *taste profiling*.

Many, many people have accepted this bargain. It turns out, however, that taste profiling is only the beginning. A technique called *persuasion profiling* is rapidly evolving. This technique goes well beyond suggesting content that you might enjoy. It actually figures out how you think.

Today, most recommendation and targeting systems focus on products. For example, e-commerce Web sites analyze our consumption patterns and use that information to determine that, for instance, viewers of *Iron Man* also watch *The Dark Knight*. However, new research suggests that that retailers and advertisers can use another factor. Specifically, these professionals can personalize not only the products they advertise to potential customers but also the strategies they employ to advertise them.

The research indicates that different people respond to different approaches, or pitches. For example, in a bookstore, different pitches might look like this:

- *Appeal to authority:* "Another famous author says that you will like this book."
- *Social proof:* "All your friends on Facebook are buying this book."
- *High need for cognition:* Smart, subtle points that require some thinking to realize, such as "*The Hunger Games* is the *Inferno* of children's literature."
- *Hit over the head:* A simple message such as "*The Hunger Games* is a fun, fast read!"

Researchers are able to track which pitch is the most persuasive for each person. By eliminating persuasion styles that did not work on a particular individual, a retailer can increase the effectiveness of recommendations by 30 to 40 percent. Most significantly, people respond to the same pitch across multiple domains. In other words, if marketers figure out how to sell books to particular customers, then they can use the same techniques to sell them clothes.

As you probably have figured out by now, your persuasion profile will be worth quite a bit of money to many companies. Once a company like Amazon has determined your profile by suggesting products in a variety of ways over time and analyzing your responses, there is nothing to prevent that company from selling this information to other companies. That is, if you respond a few times to a "50 percent off in the next 10 minutes!" deal, you could find yourself surfing a Web filled with blaring red headlines and countdown clocks.

Persuasion profiling can provide many benefits. Consider DirectLife (www.directlife. phillips.com), a wearable coaching device manufactured by Phillips that uses human coaches to determine which arguments motivate a particular individual to eat a healthier diet and exercise more regularly. However, DirectLife also highlights one of the core challenges of persuasion profiling: It works best when it is invisible to the user.

Whereas DirectLife is intended to improve your health, most companies that buy and sell your persuasion profile most likely will not have your well-being at heart. If persuasion profiling makes it possible for a coaching device to shout "You can do it" to people who need positive reinforcement, in theory the technique could also enable politicians to make personalized appeals based on each voter's particular fears. For example, if your persuasion profile indicates that you are vulnerable to social pressure, then a candidate could target you with ads on your Facebook page claiming that your friends are all voting for him or her.

Persuasion profiling offers quick, easily transferable, targeted access to your personal psychological weak spots. How can you protect yourself from this technique? The best way is to be aware that retailers are practicing persuasion profiling, keep an eye out for it, and view all marketing arguments with the skepticism they deserve.

Persuasion profiling can cause another problem. *Micro-profiling*, or micro-personalization, can encase individuals in a silent, subtle bubble, thereby isolating them from discoveries and insights that fall outside their usual tastes and interests. This filter bubble is invisible. People are unaware of how their Internet and the Web sites they visit differ from what other people see. In fact, several years ago, when people searched a particular topic, everyone would get the same result. Today, different people who Google the same topic can get different results. These different results are based on the enormous amount of data (through Google Search, Gmail, Google Maps, and other Google services) that Google maintains on its users.

Questions

1. Describe taste profiling and persuasion profiling.

2. Discuss the benefits of persuasion profiling.

3. Describe the dangers of persuasion profiling.

SOURCES: "What the Internet Is Hiding from You," *CNN.com*, May 19, 2011; E. Pariser, "Mind Reading," *Wired*, May, 2011.

CLOSING **CASE 2 >**

Refining the Call Center

Call centers are expensive. An average call center seat (representative) costs about $50,000 per year to maintain. The biggest companies, such as AT&T, with 100,000 seats, spend billions of dollars to placate irritated customers. ELoyalty (www.eloyalty.com) provides complex software that not only can define a specific complaint, but can also analyze a caller's personality.

ELoyalty has analyzed 600 million conversations, and its 1,000 servers store 600 terabytes of customer data. (By way of comparison, the entire print collection of the Library of Congress would require 10 terabytes of storage.) Based on this analysis, the software categorizes people into one of six personality types, and it looks for telltale phrases that provide clues as to what the customer's specific complaint might be. It then routes callers to the service representative who is most qualified to handle that combination of problem and personality.

The six personality types identified by ELoyalty software are these:

- *Emotions-driven* (30 percent of the population): These customers forge relationships with agents before getting into the problem.
- *Thoughts-driven* (25 percent of the population): These customers want facts and analysis and do not waste time on pleasantries.
- *Reactions-driven* (20 percent of the population): These customers either love something or hate it. "This product is so cool," they might say.
- *Opinions-driven* (10 percent of the population): These customers' language is full of imperatives, and their minds are made up.
- *Reflections-driven* (10 percent of the population): These customers are introverts who live in their own worlds, prefer silence to banter, and often skip personal pronouns in their speech.
- *Actions-driven* (5 percent of the population): These customers want movement and progress. Think Donald Trump.

ELoyalty's software looks for key words, such as *cancel* and *disappointed*, indicating that a customer might want to close an account. If a customer has called in the past, call center systems flag her personality for representatives and assess the chances that she is calling to cancel her account. The systems also offer hints as to how to deal with her. The software even integrates with company accounts that indicate how valuable the caller might be. For example, customers who carry large balances on their credit cards and pay on time receive higher priority than infrequent users.

Research revealed that when callers were paired with a representative with a similar personality, their calls averaged just over 5 minutes, and the parties reached a satisfactory resolution 92 percent of the time. In contrast, when customers spoke with a representative with a different type of personality from themselves, calls averaged nearly 10 minutes, and the parties reached resolution only 47 percent of the time.

Pairing callers with like-minded representatives offers four benefits to companies: (1) It saves them a great deal of money, (2) it enables company representatives to resolve issues for more customers, (3) it increases customer satisfaction, and (4) it reduces *customer churn* (turnover). According to ELoyalty's clients, the software has reduced their call center expenses by up to 20 percent by making the calls shorter and more productive.

1. Review the six categories of customers. Which kind of customer are you? Do you think it would be advantageous to you if you could speak with a customer service representative who had a similar personality? Why or why not?

2. Should companies inform customers about the use of ELoyalty software in their call centers? Why or why not? Support your answer.

SOURCES: Compiled from M. Schroeck, "Why the Call Center Isn't Dead," *Forbes*, March 15, 2011; C. Steiner, "He Feels Your Pain," *Forbes*, February 14, 2011; C. Steiner, "Making Call Centers Really Hum," *Forbes*, January 26, 2011; www.eloyalty.com, accessed March 14, 2011.

RUBY'S CLUB INTERNSHIP ASSIGNMENTS

Excel is a spreadsheet, and it can be used to support CRM efforts. Recently, Ruben and Lisa teamed up with one of their college professors and created a survey to find out about student use of different media. Visit the following link to view a video about the survey:

http://higheredbcs.wiley.com/legacy/college/rainer/0470473525/interactive/ch06/chapter6_video2/index.html

This video will also teach you to how to use the filtering and pivot table tools to find useful information in a spreadsheet.

For your analysis, Ruben and Lisa want you to look specifically for the social networks used by students with three or more free nights a week. Their idea is that if they can get the people with more free time as customers, those people will become regulars and bring their friends. So Ruben and Lisa want to connect with their potential customers on the right social network and establish loyalty through that channel.

SPREADSHEET ACTIVITY

Objective: Customer relationship management is very important in today's market. Competition is reaching new frontiers with global companies doing business in rural areas that have traditionally been served by small mom-and-pop companies. How, exactly, can these smaller companies survive without the complex customer relationship management tools available to the "big box" companies?

Chapter Connection: Customer relationship management (CRM) is an excellent use of technology. It is easy to understand because the students are often on the "receiving" end of this particular system. However, students also experience many of its flaws because they receive invitations and coupons that they do not use. This money ends up being wasted because it did not bring its target customer into the store. This activity teaches students how they can utilize a simple spreadsheet to create their own basic CRM. While it is a very basic function and a poor example of a CRM solution, it does show how simple tools such as Excel and Word can be utilized to create helpful systems.

Prerequisites: There are no prerequisites for this activity.

Activity: A year ago, Dustin was very busy in his shop. That was before Walmart opened its Tire & Lube Express. Now a lot of Dustin's customers have switched to Walmart for the convenience of having their vehicle serviced while they shop. However, Dustin has an idea. He has created a spreadsheet of data from everyone who has brought their car to him on a regular basis. He wants to contact them with a personal letter to try and win back their service.

Dustin wants to thank his customers for past business and draw on their hometown emotions to pull them back to him in spite of Walmart's convenience and lower price. While he cannot afford an expensive CRM tool, he does remember something about Microsoft Excel having a mail-merge feature that would allow him to rapidly produce customized letters for the mail.

Visit the Microsoft Web site and search for the tutorial concerning Mail Merge. It is a simple process, and it is explained online in just a couple of pages. Once you feel comfortable with the concept, visit www.wiley.com/college/rainer, and download the file MIS—Chapter 12.zip, which contains the spreadsheet and the MS Word document Dustin plans to mail out. You will connect the two such that the letters will be automatically created for multiple customers at one time.

Deliverables: You will need to open the .zip file and the MS Word document and produce a batch of letters ready to send out to the customers. You will also need to submit your spreadsheet and Word document, which are linked such that your work can be checked. Your instructor will choose how many letters need to be submitted.

Quiz Questions:

1. Mail Merge uses which two Microsoft programs?
   (a) Word and PowerPoint
   (b) Word and Excel
   (c) Excel and PowerPoint
   (d) Word and Access
   (e) Excel and Access

2. True or False? It is best to create your spreadsheet first and then build your Mail Merge document from that existing data set.

3. True or False? Mail Merge is meant to pull information from Word documents into Excel spreadsheets.

Discussion Questions:

1. CRM does not have to be complicated; it is simply an effort to reach out to the customer to develop and/or maintain loyalty. As such, simple tools like Mail Merge can be used to touch customers on a personal basis. In what other ways could this tool be used in place of a more complex and more expensive CRM?

2. What do you think should be the determining factor regarding the type of CRM to use? Given that simple Excel tools can be used to reach customers, why would a company spend lots of time and energy implementing a system that may not reach more customers than the Excel tools would? What creates the "breaking point" of when things need to change?

DATABASE ACTIVITY: QUERIES II

Objective

In this activity, you will learn how to use parameters to simplify entering query selection criteria. When you needed Adam's orders from DizzyDonuts, you entered his name in the query design grid. That is not ideal for casual users. This activity will show you how using query *parameters* avoids this step.

Chapter Connection

People who work with customer information must often specify whose information they need to review.

Queries can do that, but a customer service agent should not have to modify the query design for each question!

Prerequisites

Before starting this activity, you should complete the database activity for Chapter 10 (Queries I).

Activity:

In this activity, which you will find online, you will provide a simple interface to enter data for a query. For example, a database user could ask for information on sales between June 1 and August 31 one time, September 1–30 another, without needing to alter the query itself.

1. Download and open the Ch 12 DizzyDonuts database from www.wiley.com/college/rainer. This is a fresh copy of the database you used in the Chapter 10 activity.

2. The first query you developed there was to find out how often a given customer uses the mobile ordering service. This one will be similar. Create a new Query Design with Customer, Order, and Store tables. Enter CustName, StoreCity, OrderDate, and OrderTotal in the grid.

3. In the Chapter 10 activity, you entered "Adam" as the CustName selection criterion. Here, we will use a *parameter* instead. Each time the query is run, Access will prompt the user to enter a value. No fixed value, Adam or anything else, is built into the query.

   To enter a parameter, instead of entering the desired value in the Criteria section of the grid, enter a *prompt string* there between square brackets, like this:

Field:	CustName	OrderDate	StoreCity
Table:	CustTbl	OrderTbl	StoreTbl
Sort:			
Show:	✔	✔	✔
Criteria:	[Enter customer name]		

Run the query. You will see a dialogue box like this:

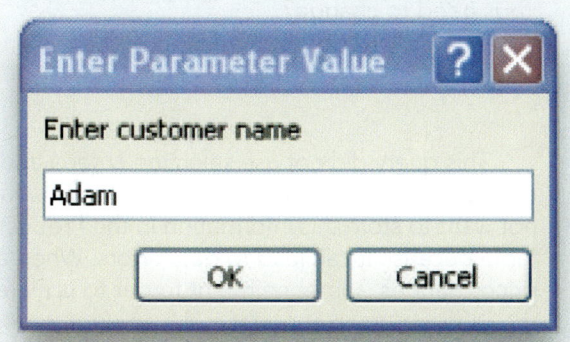

into which you can enter a customer name. The text above the data entry box is between the brackets in the query design grid. Enter "Adam," as shown, and click "OK." You should see a list of all Adam's orders, with cities, dates, and totals.

Usage Hint: There are a few rules about what you put in a prompt string. It must fit on one line (about 40 characters), it cannot be a field name, and it cannot use "." (period), "!" (exclamation point), "&" (ampersand), "[" or "]" (square brackets).

If your query uses multiple criteria, you can have parameters in several of them. Here, you could look for all the orders from a specific customer (one parameter) after a specific date (a second parameter) at a specific store (a third one).

4. To rerun the query, select "Refresh All" from the middle of the Home ribbon. (If the icon reads "Refresh," click the down arrow for other options and select "Refresh All.") You will see the dialogue box for entering a parameter value again. Now, enter "Belina" to see her orders.

5. Close the query, saving it as CustOrderParamQry.

6. Parameters are not limited to finding exact matches. Any type of comparison that can be done in a query criterion can use parameters. Before Access does the comparison, it gets values for all the parameters in it and replaces the parameter indicators with those values. Entering a parameter value "Adam" is the same as entering "Adam" in the query design grid.

   Re-create ExpensiveProdQry from Chapter 10. As the query's only criterion, however, do not use the earlier ">1.6." Instead, enter ">[Products over what amount?]" (without the quotation marks).

Usage Hint: Comparison operators include, besides ">" for "greater than," these symbols:

< less than

>= greater than or equal to

<= less than or equal to

<> not equal to

= equal to (assumed if no comparison sign is entered)

IN followed by a list of text strings separated by commas, will match anything in the list

BETWEEN . . . AND . . . does what you would expect. This, by the way, is an example of where you might want to use two parameters in the same criterion—for example, a starting date and an ending date.

There are more criteria, but these are enough for now. You know enough to understand and use what you will find in a Web search for more in this area.

7. Run this query twice: first with a cutoff of $1.50, then with a cutoff of $5.

Usage Hint: If you use a dollar sign when you enter a currency amount in a parameter entry box, Access is smart enough to ignore it.

8. Close the query, saving it as ExpensiveProdParamQry.

Queries can calculate a column based on other data in the same row. This can be data you choose not to show, as long as it comes from a table in the query. Let us create a query to help our staff price out orders for more than one of an item. (In a real store this would be done electronically, but the query is still a good example.) Open a new query in Design view, select "ProdTbl" as its data source, and enter "ProdName" and "ProdPrice" into the design grid.

9. In the top row of the first empty column, enter "2*ProdPrice" (without quotation marks), make sure that column's Show box is checked, and run the query. You will see something like this:

ProdName ▾	ProdPrice ▾	Expr1 ▾
Plain Donut	$1.19	$2.38
Blueberry Muffin	$1.29	$2.58
Sm Coffee	$1.29	$2.58
Lg Coffee	$1.69	$3.38

The calculated values are in the column where you entered the expression.

10. Return to Design view, and look at the expression again. Access changed it in two ways:

  (a) Access created the name we saw as its column name, Expr1. It precedes the expression, separated by a colon. If we do not like this name, we can change it. If we know what we want ahead of time, we can enter it when we define the calculated field.

  (b) Access put square brackets around the field name. These are only required when there are spaces in the field name, but Access plays it safe and puts them in every time.

11. Change the column name "Expr1" to read "2x."

12. Enter expressions for 3x, 4x, and 5x. (It may be easier to copy and paste the 2x column, then edit its column name and the multiplier in its calculation, than to key in each one from scratch. It is definitely less error prone.)

13. Run the query to confirm that it works. Then close it, saving it as "ProdPriceQry."

This query did not use selection criteria and did not combine tables, but it is still useful. We would not want to store this information in the Product table because it can lead to data errors: When a price changes, someone might forget to update the other columns or might make an error in one of them. (A specialist would say such a table *violates normalization rules* by having columns whose value depends only on other columns of the same table.)

14. It is easier to build complicated expressions with the Expression Builder. Create a new query, using the same two fields from ProdTbl as above. In Design view, click the top row of the first empty column and then "Builder" in the Query Setup section of the Design ribbon. The Expression Builder will open. It has two main sections as shown here:

• A window in which to build an expression.

• A series of three areas to select expression elements without keying them in. (That is always an option, though.) If you click "<<Less," this area is hidden, and the button changes to "More>>" so you can display it again.

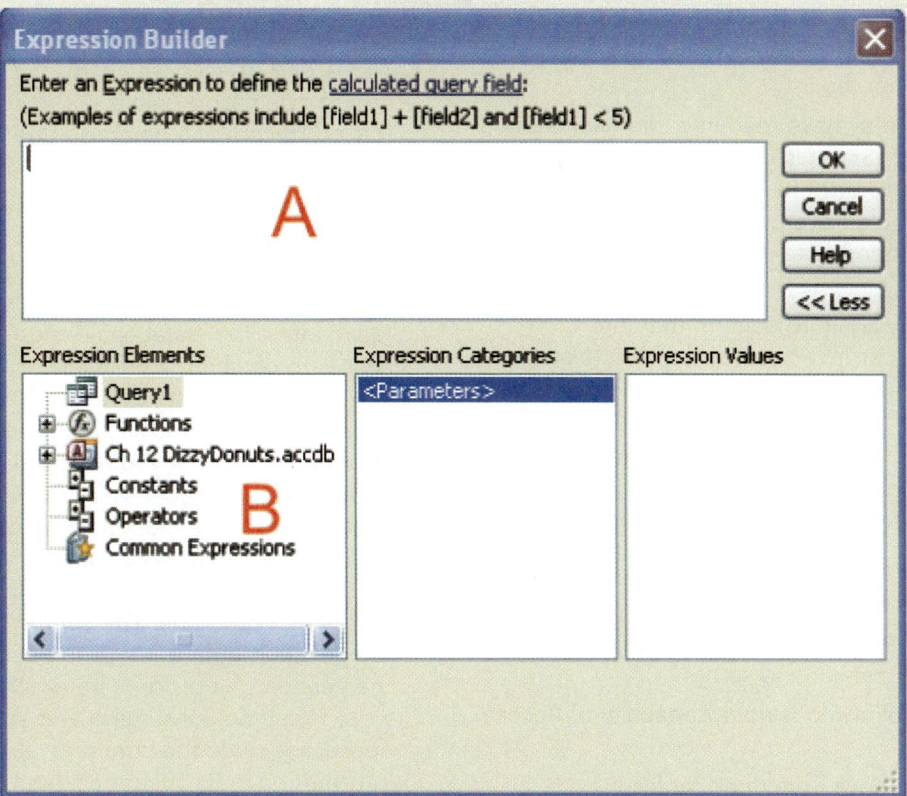

15. We will create an expression to round up each product price to the next whole dollar. Expand Functions in the left pane of the bottom area, and select "Built-In Functions."

16. In the middle pane, double-click "Math" as the type of function.

17. In the right pane, double-click "Int." The Int function takes the integer part of a number: given 1.79, it will return 1. It appears in the top pane, with a placeholder for the number.

18. Click the placeholder to select it. Then expand the database name in region B, expand Tables, select "ProdTbl" in the list of tables that drops down, and double-click "ProdPrice" in the list of fields for that table in the middle pane. It will replace «Number» in the expression.

19. Since Int gives the integer *below* the price, and we want the next whole dollar *above* it, we must add 99¢ to the value it takes the Int of. (If we added $1, a price in whole dollars such as $2.00 would become the next higher dollar amount, in this case $3.00. We do not want that to happen.) With the insertion point between ProdPrice and the right parenthesis of Int, select "Operators" in Region B.

In the middle pane, select either "<All>" or "Arithmetic." In the right pane, double-click the plus sign. It will show up in your expression where the insertion point was. «Expr» shows where it needs something to add. Click "«Expr»" to select it, and type "0.99" (without the quotation marks). Then click "OK."

Usage Hint: In this case it would probably have been easier to just key in "+0.99" rather than going to the list of operators and then replacing "Expr." However, it is important to know where to find the full process and how to go through it, because it is often the best way to get something done.

20. Back in the design grid, replace the name of this column, which Access has set to its default of Expr1, to "Rounded Up." (It may be easier to do this if you widen the column.)

21. Run the query. It shows 2 for every item priced from $1.01 to $2.00, and so on.

22. The new column would look better formatted as currency. Return to Design view, select the expression, and open the query's Property Sheet (at the right end of the ribbon, in the Show/Hide section, under the Design tab). Under the General

tab of the property sheet, click in the "Format" row (the second one down). Select "Currency" formatting from the list.

Usage Hint: You may have read in earlier activities that the Property Sheet is the "go-to place" for most things that do not have ribbon icons. This is an example. We could have used Expression Builder's formatting functions instead, but they are more work.

23. Run the query again to confirm that the formatting is correct, close, and save it. Name it "ProdPriceRoundUpQry" if you did not do so previously.

Deliverables:

Your database, with the three preceding queries.

Quiz Questions:

1. True or False? Access always names calculated fields as Expr1, Expr2, and so on.

2. Which of the following is *not* a capability of Access queries?

   (a) Combining data from three tables

   (b) Choosing all records that have a date field with a value after June 6, 1944

   (c) Displaying the cosine of a number that the query finds

   (d) None of the above (Access can do all of them.)

3. True or False? You can set the formatting of a calculated field to Currency by clicking the $ sign in the ribbon.

4. A parameter, in the context of an Access query, is:

   (a) A characteristic of an Access object on the screen, such as font, height, or color

   (b) A distance of slightly less than 6 feet, 7 inches, scaled to the window size

   (c) A query criterion data item that a user can enter

   (d) The fraction of available RAM that the currently open database is using

Discussion Questions:

1. At the end of every semester, you probably read your grade report online. As you now understand, it is produced by a database query. What are that query's two parameters?

2. If you develop a database in Access 2007, anyone who uses it can see everything in it. In some situations this is unacceptable. Other database management systems, including some from Microsoft, allow database designers to restrict access to certain rows (for example, only you can see your grade data, other students cannot) or columns (a faculty advisor can see your academic information but not your medical or financial information). Suppose you are designing a query for a software company's technical support staff. The company receives e-mails and phone calls from customers with questions about this company's products. The support staff may need to know something about the customer, such as the version of a product he or she has. Asking would be time consuming and should not be necessary, since the company already has the information in its customer database. Discuss the row-level and column-level restrictions you might place on a query to be used for this purpose. Make any reasonable assumptions about the content and organization of the company's database.

3. The DizzyDonuts database has a field in the Order table that stores the total amount of each order. This could be calculated each time the order is displayed: A calculated field will multiply price × quantity for each line item, and the Sum function of the report could add them up. When asked why they designed the database this way, the DizzyDonut database designers explained that they wanted to store how much orders cost when they are placed, not how much they might cost when a report is run later if prices changed in the meantime. Do you agree with their logic? Why or why not?

13 | Extending the Organization Along the Supply Chain

LEARNING OBJECTIVES >>>

1. Define the term *supply chain*, and describe the three components and the three flows of a supply chain.

2. Identify two major challenges in setting accurate inventory levels throughout the supply chain, and describe three popular strategies to solve supply chain problems.

3. Define the terms *electronic data interchange (EDI)*, *extranet*, and *portal*, and explain how each of these applications helps support supply chain management.

OPENING **CASE** > Swagelok Implements an ERP System

Swagelok (www.swagelok.com) is a major company in the fluid systems industry. Specifically, it produces tube fittings, hoses, regulators, and other parts that are vital to high-pressure fluid systems in industries that range from power generation to biopharmaceuticals. After more than 50 years of business, Swagelok had 25 facilities, each with one or two supply chain schedulers. This situation meant that the company had some 40 supply chain decision makers who were managing the company's supply chain just for their facility, without the full picture of the firm's supply chain operations.

Greg Houdek, Director of Supply Chain Planning, realized that Swagelok needed to improve its forecasting and distribution processes within the organization, as well as with its suppliers, so it could operate with less inventory and be more cost efficient. To improve business processes and reduce inventory, it had to update its supply chain systems as well as help its suppliers improve their own planning processes.

Swagelok decided to implement a new enterprise resource planning system, rather just update its existing system. JDA (www.jda.com) offered the company a solution that would operate with its existing system and offer improvements at a lower cost. This new solution would provide more options to the company's supply chain planners and allow more accurate and timely information sharing.

Inventory levels dropped immediately upon implementation. Houdek reported that Swagelok was able to eliminate about 50 percent of its inventory due to more efficient planning. In addition, lower inventories meant less warehouse space needed to house the inventory. Just as important, Swagelok's suppliers have been able to lower their inventories with the improved methods of calculating and planning for production.

The JDA software enabled more effective communication within the organization and with suppliers. Further, the system helped to lower inventories across the supply chain and increase customer service levels.

Sources: Compiled from www.jda.com, www.swagelok.com/about-swagelok.aspx, www.jda.com/company/display-collateral/pID/1180, accessed June 16, 2011.

Questions

1. Describe the problems that led to Swagelok's decision to implement a new ERP system.

2. Why is it so important for Swagelok to include its supply chain partners when the company is improving its internal business processes?

RUBY'S CLUB

Ruben and Lisa always have trouble scheduling their inventory. It is especially difficult in a college town where their customers pour in one week and leave a ghost town behind the next week.   It seems that lots of factors influence their customer base on any given night. Obviously, the school schedule is a big factor, as are community events, athletic events, and more, but how much does each of these impact the number of customers they will have?

More than once Ruben and Lisa have had to throw away perishable goods because they were not able to use all that they had ordered before its expiration date, or they ran out of food when they had more customers than they expected. Neither of these situations is desirable because they both mean lost profits.

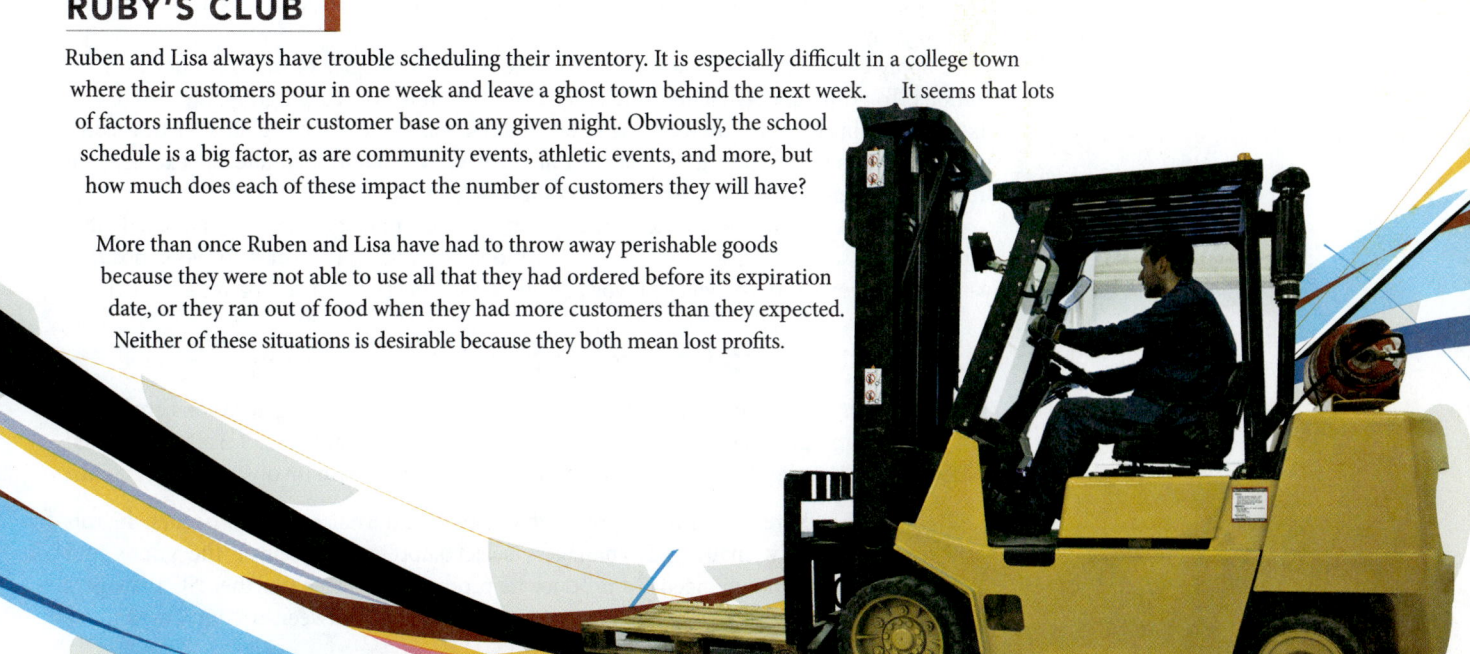

13.1 | Supply Chains

Modern organizations are increasingly concentrating on their core competencies and on becoming more flexible and agile. To accomplish these objectives, they are relying on other companies to supply necessary goods and services, rather than owning these companies themselves. Organizations recognize that these suppliers can perform these activities more efficiently and effectively than they can. This trend toward relying on an increasing number of suppliers has led to the concept of supply chains. A **supply chain** refers to the coordinated flow of materials, information, money, and services from raw material suppliers, through factories and warehouses, to the end customers. A supply chain also includes the *organizations* and *processes* that create and deliver products, information, and services to end customers.

Supply chains improve trust and collaboration among supply chain partners, thus improving supply chain visibility and inventory velocity. **Supply chain visibility** is the ability for all organizations in a supply chain to access or view relevant data on purchased materials as these materials move through their suppliers' production processes and transportation networks to their receiving docks. In addition, organizations can access or view relevant data on outbound goods as they are manufactured, assembled, or stored in inventory, and then shipped through their transportation networks to their customers' receiving docks. The sooner a company can deliver its products and services after receiving the materials required to make them—that is, the higher the *inventory velocity*—the more satisfied the company's customers will be.

Supply chains are a vital component of the overall strategies of many modern organizations. To utilize supply chains efficiently, a business must become tightly integrated with its suppliers, business partners, distributors, and customers. One of the most critical components of this integration is the use of information systems to facilitate the exchange of information among the participants in the supply chain.

You might ask why you need to study supply chain management. The answer is that supply chains are critical to modern organizations. Therefore, regardless of your position within an organization, you will be involved with some aspect of your company's supply chain.

The Structure and Components of Supply Chains

The term *supply chain* comes from a picture of how the partnering organizations are linked together. Figure 13.1 illustrates a typical supply chain. Recall that Figure 1.5 also illustrated a supply chain in a slightly different way. Note that the supply chain involves three segments:

1. *Upstream,* where sourcing or procurement from external suppliers occurs. In this segment, supply chain (SC) managers select suppliers to deliver the goods and services the company needs to produce its product or service. Further, SC managers develop the pricing, delivery, and payment processes between a company and its

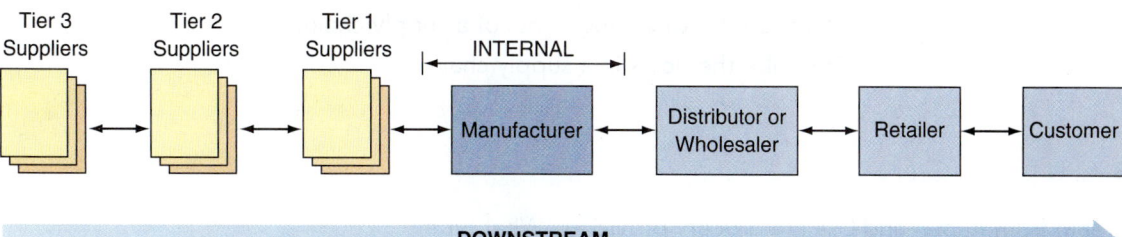

UPSTREAM
Orders, Information, Payments, Returns

Tier 3 Suppliers — Tier 2 Suppliers — Tier 1 Suppliers — INTERNAL — Manufacturer — Distributor or Wholesaler — Retailer — Customer

DOWNSTREAM
Products, Services, Information

Figure 13.1 Generic supply chain.

suppliers. Included here are processes for managing inventory, receiving and verifying shipments, transferring goods to manufacturing facilities, and authorizing payments to suppliers.

2. *Internal*, where packaging, assembly, or manufacturing takes place. SC managers schedule the activities necessary for production, testing, packaging, and preparing goods for delivery. SC managers also monitor quality levels, production output, and worker productivity.

3. *Downstream*, where distribution takes place, frequently by external distributors. In this segment, SC managers coordinate the receipt of orders from customers, develop a network of warehouses, select carriers to deliver their products to customers, and develop invoicing systems to receive payments from customers.

The flow of information and goods can be bidirectional. For example, damaged or unwanted products can be returned, a process known as *reverse logistics*. Using the retail clothing industry as an example, reverse logistics would involve clothing that customers return, either because the item had defects or because the customer did not like the item.

Tiers of Suppliers. If you look closely at Figure 13.1, you will notice several tiers of suppliers. As the diagram shows, a supplier may have one or more subsuppliers, and the subsupplier may have its own subsupplier(s), and so on. For example, with an automobile manufacturer, Tier 3 suppliers produce basic products such as glass, plastic, and rubber. Tier 2 suppliers use these inputs to make windshields, tires, and plastic moldings. Tier 1 suppliers produce integrated components such as dashboards and seat assemblies.

The Flows in the Supply Chain. There are typically three flows in the supply chain: materials, information, and financial. *Material flows* are the physical products: raw materials, supplies, and so forth that flow along the chain. Material flows also include *reverse* flows (or reverse logistics)—returned products, recycled products, and disposal of materials or products. A supply chain thus involves a *product life cycle* approach, from "dirt to dust."

Information flows consist of data that are related to demand, shipments, orders, returns, and schedules, as well as changes in any of these data. Finally, *financial flows* involve money transfers, payments, credit card information and authorization, payment schedules, e-payments, and credit-related data.

Significantly, different supply chains have different numbers and types of flows. For example, in service industries there may be no physical flow of materials, but frequently there is a flow of information, often in the form of documents (physical or electronic copies). In fact, the digitization of software, music, and other content may create a supply chain without any physical flow. Notice, however, that in such a case, there are two types of information flows: one that replaces materials flow (for example, digitized software) and one that provides the supporting information (for example, orders and billing). To manage the supply chain, an organization must coordinate all of these flows among all of the parties involved in the chain.

BEFORE YOU GO ON . . .

1. What is a supply chain?
2. Describe the three segments of a supply chain.
3. Describe the flows in a supply chain.

RUBY'S CLUB QUESTIONS

1. Upstream from Ruben and Lisa are grocery providers. What type of information might flow upstream to their suppliers while the materials flow downstream?

2. Ruby's Club has some internal issues to deal with regarding their supplies. The food in the cooler is used in no particular order, and sometimes it goes bad. This situation is not due to lack of customers but, rather, to poor planning. What policies could be put in place to help remedy this situation?

Student Activity | 13.1

Objective: The objective of this exercise is to familiarize you with supply chains and their value to a company.

Chapter Connection: This case relates Section 13.1 of this chapter.

Prerequisites: You should read Section 13.1 of the text before doing this exercise to become familiar with supply chains and their function within an organization.

Activity:

A supply chain refers to the flow of materials, information, money, and services from raw material suppliers, through factories and warehouses, to the end customers. Watch the following video to become more familiar with supply chains:

www.youtube.com/watch?v=mi1QBxVjzaw

Deliverables:

Based on the video and this chapter, answer the following:

1. What is a supply chain?
2. Answer the following based on the *bottled water* discussed in the video:

    (a) What is the *upstream* supply chain? List three materials needed for bottled water.

    (b) What is done in the *internal* supply chain? List three materials needed for bottled water.

    (c) What is involved in the *downstream* supply chain? List three items included for bottled water.

3. What are three businesses that need to manage their supply chains?

Quiz Questions:

1. What segment of the supply chain involves sourcing or procurement from suppliers?

    (a) Upstream
    (b) Internal
    (c) Downstream

2. What segment of the supply chain involves distribution?

    (a) Upstream
    (b) Internal
    (c) Downstream

3. What segment of the supply chain involves packaging, assembly, or manufacturing?

    (a) Upstream
    (b) Internal
    (c) Downstream

4. Managing of the supply chain can be used by:

    (a) Car manufacturer

    (b) Hamburger shop

    (c) Hotel

    (d) All of the above

5. Supply chains involve which of the following?

    (a) Buying

    (b) Making

    (c) Moving

    (d) All of the above

Discussion Question:

Discuss which activities are performed in each of the three segments of the supply chain. Assume that you are going to manufacture a simple table with a top and four legs. What are some of the materials needed in each segment of the supply chain?

13.2 | Supply Chain Management

Supply chain management (SCM) is an activity in which the leaders of an organization provide extensive oversight for the partnerships and processes that comprise the supply chain and leverage these relationships to provide an operational advantage. The function of supply chain management is to plan, organize, and optimize the various activities performed along the supply chain. Like other functional areas, SCM utilizes information systems. The goal of SCM systems is to reduce the problems, or friction, along the supply chain. Friction can involve increased time, costs, and inventories as well as decreased customer satisfaction. SCM systems, then, reduce uncertainty and risks by decreasing inventory levels and cycle time while improving business processes and customer service. All of these benefits make the organization more profitable and competitive.

Significantly, SCM systems are a type of interorganizational information system. An **interorganizational information system (IOS)** involves information flows among two or more organizations. By connecting the information systems of business partners, IOSs enable the partners to perform a number of tasks:

- Reduce the costs of routine business transactions
- Improve the quality of the information flow by reducing or eliminating errors
- Compress the cycle time involved in fulfilling business transactions
- Eliminate paper processing and its associated inefficiencies and costs
- Facilitate the transfer and processing of information for users

The Push Model Versus the Pull Model

Many supply chain management systems use the push model. In the **push model**, also known as *make-to-stock*, the production process begins with a forecast, which is simply an educated guess as to customer demand. The forecast must predict which products customers will want as well as the quantity of each product. The company then produces the amount of products in the forecast, typically by using mass production, and sells, or "pushes," those products to consumers.

Unfortunately, these forecasts are often incorrect. Consider, for example, an automobile manufacturer that wants to produce a new car. Marketing managers conduct extensive research, including customer surveys and analyses of competitors' cars, and they provide the results to forecasters. If the forecasters are too high in their prediction—that is, they predict that sales of the new car will be 200,000 and actual customer demand turns out to be 150,000—then the automaker has 50,000 cars in inventory and will incur large carrying costs. Further, the company will probably have to sell the excess cars at a discount.

From the opposite perspective, if the forecasters are too low in their prediction—that is, they predict that sales of the new car will be 150,000 and actual customer demand turns out to be 200,000—then the automaker will probably have to run extra shifts to meet the demand and thus will incur large overtime costs. Further, the company risks losing customers to competitors if the car the customer wants is not available. Using the push model in supply chain management can cause problems, as you see in the next section.

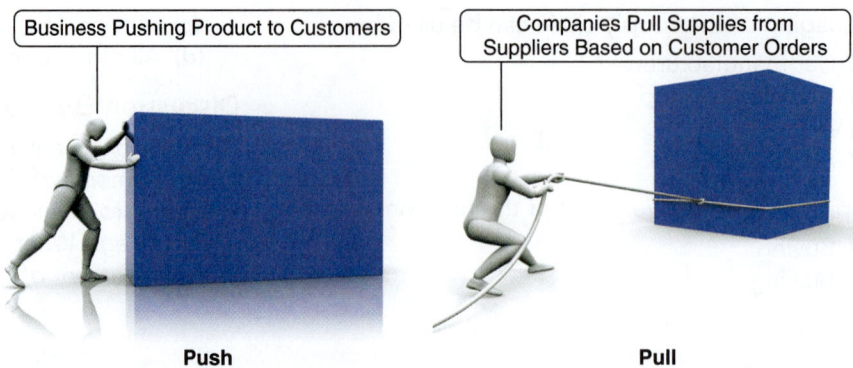

Business Pushing Product to Customers

Companies Pull Supplies from Suppliers Based on Customer Orders

Push

Pull

(*Source:* © Milan Zeremski/iStockphoto)

To avoid the uncertainties associated with the push model, many companies now use Web-enabled information flows to employ the pull model of supply chain management. In the **pull model**, also known as *make-to-order*, the production process begins with a customer order. Therefore, companies make only what customers want, a process closely aligned with mass customization. "IT's About Business 13.1" shows how Cisco converted from a push model to a pull model.

IT's ABOUT BUSINESS | 13.1

Cisco Moves From Push Model to Pull Model

Cisco Systems (www.cisco.com) was a very profitable company in the 1990s. Then, the company's stock dropped dramatically when its vaunted inventory forecasting system failed to predict the dot-com bubble's collapse in 2000–2001. The result of this miscalculation was that Cisco's sales decreased by 50 percent, the company lost 25 percent of its customers, and it ultimately had to write off more than $2 billion in inventory. After that experience, Cisco's supply chain managers vowed that the company would never be blindsided again.

Before the dot-com crash, Cisco's supply chain used a push system, where products were made and inventory was built up in anticipation of market demand based on best-guess forecasts. Unfortunately, the push system did not work when demand dropped quickly and severely, as it did during and after the dot-com crash. Cisco knew that it had to create a supply chain system that reacted much more effectively than its push system.

Consequently, Cisco made major information systems investments to transform its push system into a pull system. The pull system enabled Cisco to extract timely data from suppliers and downstream business partners. Cisco optimized its forecasting algorithms by bringing together representatives from its marketing, finance, sales, supply chain, and IT departments, and from key customers. As part of the company's sales and operations planning process, this group collaborates to create a common view of demand signals. This input drives an agreed-upon plan of action to align manufacturing capacity and inventory deployment and meet customer service levels. In essence, this group works together with the same data to optimally match supply and demand.

The result was that Cisco did not continue to build inventory that might sit in a warehouse waiting for customers who might never buy it. Therefore, cash was freed up for other purposes. Cisco was confident that it had better visibility into market demand and could manage its way through downturns. Unfortunately, the other shoe fell.

Cisco's supply chain pull system enabled the company to weather the economic recession of 2008 and 2009. During the recession, Cisco reduced its inventory and product manufacturing to prevent filling warehouses with unsold product.

Then, in the last quarter of 2009, an unexpected increase in business demand for core networking infrastructure products caught Cisco and its manufacturing partners off guard. Cisco could not keep up with the sudden increase in orders, resulting in extremely long lead times, back orders, and customer dissatisfaction. Cisco told its customers that its product shortage resulted from a global shortage of raw materials used in the manufacture of key components, such as semiconductors.

Questions

1. Describe the disadvantages of the push system at Cisco.

2. Describe the advantages of the pull system at Cisco.

3. Explain why the pull system enabled Cisco to manage through an economic downturn but seemed to be unable to enable Cisco through an economic recovery.

Sources: Compiled from L. Walsh, "Cisco Struggling with Product Shortages," *Channel Insider*, January 8, 2010; W. Brandel, "Inventory Optimization Saves Working Capital in Touch Times," *Computerworld*, August 24, 2009; www.cisco.com, accessed May 22, 2011.

Not all companies can use the pull model. Automobiles, for example, are far more complicated and more expensive to manufacture than computers, and companies require longer lead times to produce new models. Automobile companies use the pull model, but only for specific automobiles that specific customers order.

Problems Along the Supply Chain

As noted, friction can develop within a supply chain. One major consequence of ineffective supply chains is poor customer service. In some cases, supply chains do not deliver products or services when and where customers—either individuals or businesses—need them. In other cases the supply chain provides poor-quality products. Other problems associated with friction are high inventory costs and loss of revenues.

The problems along the supply chain arise primarily from two sources: (1) uncertainties and (2) the need to coordinate multiple activities, internal units, and business partners. A major source of supply chain uncertainties is the *demand forecast*. Demand for a product can be influenced by numerous factors such as competition, prices, weather conditions, technological developments, overall economic conditions, and customers' general confidence. Another uncertainty is delivery times, which depend on factors ranging from production machine failures to road construction and traffic jams. In addition, quality problems in materials and parts can create production delays, which also generate supply chain problems.

One of the major challenges that managers face in setting accurate inventory levels throughout the supply chain is known as the bullwhip effect. The **bullwhip effect** refers to erratic shifts in orders up and down the supply chain (see Figure 13.2). Basically, the variables that affect customer demand can become magnified when they are viewed through the eyes of managers at each link in the supply chain. If each distinct entity that makes ordering and

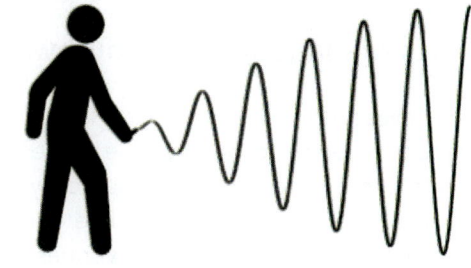

Figure 13.2 The bullwhip effect.

inventory decisions places its interests above those of the chain, then stockpiling can occur at as many as seven or eight locations along the chain. Research has shown that in some cases such hoarding has led to as much as a 100-day supply of inventory that is waiting "just in case," versus 10 to 20 days under normal circumstances.

Solutions to Supply Chain Problems

Supply chain problems can be very costly. Therefore, organizations are motivated to find innovative solutions. During the oil crises of the 1970s, for example, Ryder Systems, a large trucking company, purchased a refinery to control the upstream part of the supply chain and to make certain it would have enough gasoline for its trucks. Ryder's decision to purchase a refinery is an example of vertical integration. **Vertical integration** is a business strategy in which a company purchases its upstream suppliers to ensure that its essential supplies are available as soon as they are needed. Ryder later sold the refinery because it could not manage a business it did not understand and because oil became more plentiful.

Ryder's decision to vertically integrate was not the optimal method to manage its supply chain. In the remainder of this section, you will look at some other possible solutions to supply chain problems, many of which are supported by IT.

Using Inventories to Solve Supply Chain Problems. Undoubtedly, the most common solution to supply chain problems is *building inventories* as insurance against supply chain uncertainties. As you have learned, some costs are associated with holding too much inventory. Thus, companies make major attempts to optimize and control inventories. "IT's About Business 13.2" illustrates how Southwest Airlines manages its parts inventory.

IT's ABOUT BUSINESS | 13.2

Parts Management at Southwest Airlines

Southwest Airlines is the largest low-fare, high-frequency, point-to-point airline in the world, and the largest airline overall measured by the number of passengers per year. The airline operates over 500 aircraft in 68 cities, with revenues over $10 billion.

In the airline industry, getting passengers from point A to point B—on time, all the time—is the ultimate form of customer service. Achieving this goal requires a superb maintenance operation and the ability to repair an aircraft quickly and efficiently when necessary.

For Southwest Airlines, maintaining its fleet of aircraft was becoming increasingly difficult. As the company grew, its existing system could not keep up with the expansion. With $325 million tied up in service parts inventory, the airline needed to implement an inventory management system to increase productivity and enable the company to provide a high level of customer service.

Southwest incurred significant costs when it had to ground an aircraft because a part was not available. The cost-effective solution to that problem was to ensure that the airline's maintenance crews had the right spare parts at the right time. The airline needed an information system to enable this process.

Southwest implemented i2 Demand Planner, i2 Service Parts Planner, and i2 Service Budget Optimizer. (*Note:* JDA, www.jda.com, acquired i2 in January 2010.) The airline uses Demand Planner for forecasting all of the part location combinations in its system, Service Parts Planner for replenishment planning, and Service Budget Optimizer for inventory planning. The software products help Southwest ensure that the right parts are in stock at the right time, and thus helps reduce costs in its supply chain.

Southwest uses Service Budget Optimizer to create bills of material and match them with its scheduled maintenance activities to create an accurate forecast of parts that must be procured. These forecasts also help the airline create its annual maintenance budget.

The i2 solutions have helped Southwest lower its annual maintenance costs and keep its cost per air seat mile down to the lowest in the industry. The i2 solutions help the airline ensure that its maintenance team can quickly repair the aircraft so that its customers experience no or minimal delays. Southwest anticipates that the i2 solutions will help reduce its inventory levels by 10 percent by 2012.

Questions

1. What is the relationship between Southwest's new parts inventory system and customer satisfaction?

2. Describe two benefits that Southwest received from implementing its new system. What business processes were impacted by each of the two benefits you described?

Sources: Compiled from "Ensuring Optimal Parts Inventory at Southwest Airlines," *i2 Customer Success Story*, www.jda.com, accessed May 27, 2011; www.southwest.com, accessed May 27, 2011.

A well-known initiative to optimize and control inventories is the **just-in-time (JIT) inventory system**, which attempts to minimize inventories. That is, in a manufacturing process, JIT systems deliver the precise number of parts, called *work-in-process* inventory, to be assembled into a finished product at precisely the right time.

Although JIT offers many benefits, it has certain drawbacks as well. To begin, suppliers are expected to respond instantaneously to requests. As a result, they have to carry more inventory than they otherwise would. The inventory has not gone away in JIT; rather, it has just shifted from customer to supplier. This process can result in an overall improvement if the supplier can spread the increased inventory over several customers, but that is not always possible.

In addition, JIT replaces a few large supply shipments with a large number of smaller ones. This process is less efficient in terms of transportation.

Information Sharing. Another common way to solve supply chain problems, and especially to improve demand forecasts, is *sharing information* along the supply chain. Information sharing can be facilitated by electronic data interchange and extranets, topics you will read about in the next section.

One of the most notable examples of information sharing occurs between large manufacturers and retailers. For example, Walmart provides Procter & Gamble with access to daily sales information from every store for every item P&G makes for Walmart. This access enables P&G to manage the *inventory replenishment* for Walmart's stores. By monitoring inventory levels, P&G knows when inventories fall below the threshold for each product at any Walmart store. These data trigger an immediate shipment.

Information sharing between Walmart and P&G is executed automatically. It is part of a vendor-managed inventory strategy. **Vendor-managed inventory (VMI)** occurs when the supplier, rather than the retailer, manages the entire inventory process for a particular product or group of products Significantly, P&G has similar agreements with other major retailers. The benefit for P&G is accurate and timely information on consumer demand for its products. Thus, P&G can plan production more accurately, minimizing the bullwhip effect.

BEFORE YOU GO ON . . .

1. Differentiate between the push model and the pull model.
2. Describe various problems that can occur along the supply chain.
3. Discuss possible solutions to problems along the supply chain.

1. Based on your understanding of Ruby's business model, do you think it is in a push or pull scenario?

2. Do you think Ruby's would begin the bullwhip effect, or do you think it would have problems because someone else started it?

3. Is JIT realistic for Ruby's Club? What about vertical integration? Should Ruby's Club invest in alcohol and grocery distribution businesses?

Student Activity | 13.2

Objective: The objective of this exercise is to familiarize you with supply chain management and why it is important to a company.

Chapter Connection: This case relates to Section 13.2 of this chapter.

Prerequisites: You should read Section 13.2 before doing this exercise to become familiar with supply chain management systems and their function within an organization.

Activity:

Having the right goods at the right time and place can be critical to any manufacturer. If one company cannot supply the customer and the product is critical to operations, the customer will try to find a company that can supply it. In order not to run out, many companies keep a safety stock. The problem with this is the extra cost to carry this additional inventory. Plus, if demand goes down, then even more unused inventory exits.

However, for many products, the demand changes often without warning. This variability can cause the *bullwhip* effect or shortages or overages of goods along the supply chain.

Go to the following web site:

http://forio.com/resources/article/bullwhips-and-beer

Read "Bullwhips and Beer: Why Supply Chain Management Is So Difficult."

Deliverables:

Prepare answers to the following questions:

1. Explain what is meant by the bullwhip effect and what causes it. Give two examples of the effect.
   After reading the article, click "Play the Near Beer Game." To play the game, go to http://forio.com/simulate/mbean/near-beer-game/run.

With this demo, you have only 8 weeks to get back in balance. Did you make it? Try again if not.

2. What happened if you did not order enough raw materials?

3. What happened if you ordered too much?

4. Try the game a few times to see if you can finally get back in balance. Does it stay in balance?

5. If you stayed in balance, how many weeks did it take, and what did you have to do?
   You should now be able to see the challenge in trying to predict the future demand and adjusting your supply chain accordingly.

Quiz Questions:

1. If you order too many raw materials in an attempt to anticipate an increase in demand of finished goods, what most likely would happen?

   (a) You would end up in balance.
   (b) You would have too many finished goods.
   (c) You would not have enough finished goods.
   (d) None of the above

2. If you did not order enough raw materials but demand for finished goods increased, what most likely would happen?

   (a) You would end up in balance.
   (b) You would have too many finished goods.
   (c) You would not have enough finished goods.
   (d) None of the above

3. If you do balance your demand by ordering extra raw materials, what most likely will happen?

   (a) You will have too many finished goods.
   (b) You will again be out of balance.

(c) Both a and b

(d) None of the above

4. What causes the bullwhip effect?

(a) The change in demand

(b) The lack of coordination

(c) Safety stock

(d) All of the above

Discussion Questions:

Think of other products that we use on a daily basis that may have a fluctuating demand. What do you think manufacturers can do to balance having too much stock that will cost them excess dollars for inventory versus having too little stock that may cause them the loss of customer?

13.3 | Information Technology Support for Supply Chain Management

Clearly, SCM systems are essential to the successful operation of many businesses. As you have seen, these systems—and IOSs in general—rely on various forms of IT to resolve problems. Three technologies in particular provide support for IOSs and SCM systems: electronic data interchange, extranets, and Web Services. You learn about Web services in Plug IT In 3. You examine the other two technologies in this section.

Electronic Data Interchange (EDI)

Electronic data interchange (EDI) is a communication standard that enables business partners to exchange routine documents, such as purchasing orders, electronically. EDI formats these documents according to agreed-upon standards—for example, data formats. It then transmits messages using a converter, called a *translator*. The message travels over the Internet.

EDI provides many benefits compared with a manual delivery system. To begin, it minimizes data entry errors because each entry is checked by the computer. In addition, the length of the message can be shorter, and the messages are secured. EDI also reduces cycle time, increases productivity, enhances customer service, and minimizes paper usage and storage. Figure 13.3 contrasts the process of fulfilling a purchase order with and without EDI.

EDI does have some disadvantages. Business processes must sometimes be restructured to fit EDI requirements. Also, many EDI standards are in use today. As a result, one company might have to use several standards in order to communicate with multiple business partners.

In today's world, where every business has a broadband connection to the Internet and where multimegabyte design files, product photographs, and PDF sales brochures are routinely e-mailed, the value of reducing a structured e-commerce message from a few thousand XML bytes to a few hundred EDI bytes is negligible. As a result, EDI is being replaced by XML-based Web services. (You will learn about XML in "Plug IT In 2".)

Extranets

To implement IOSs and SCM systems, a company must connect the intranets of its various business partners to create extranets. **Extranets** link business partners to one another over the Internet by providing access to certain areas of one another's corporate intranets (see Figure 13.4).

The primary goal of extranets is to foster collaboration between and among business partners. An extranet is open to selected business-to-business (B2B) suppliers, customers, and other business partners. These individuals access the extranet through the Internet. Extranets enable people who are located outside a company to work together with the company's internally located employees. An extranet also allows external business partners to

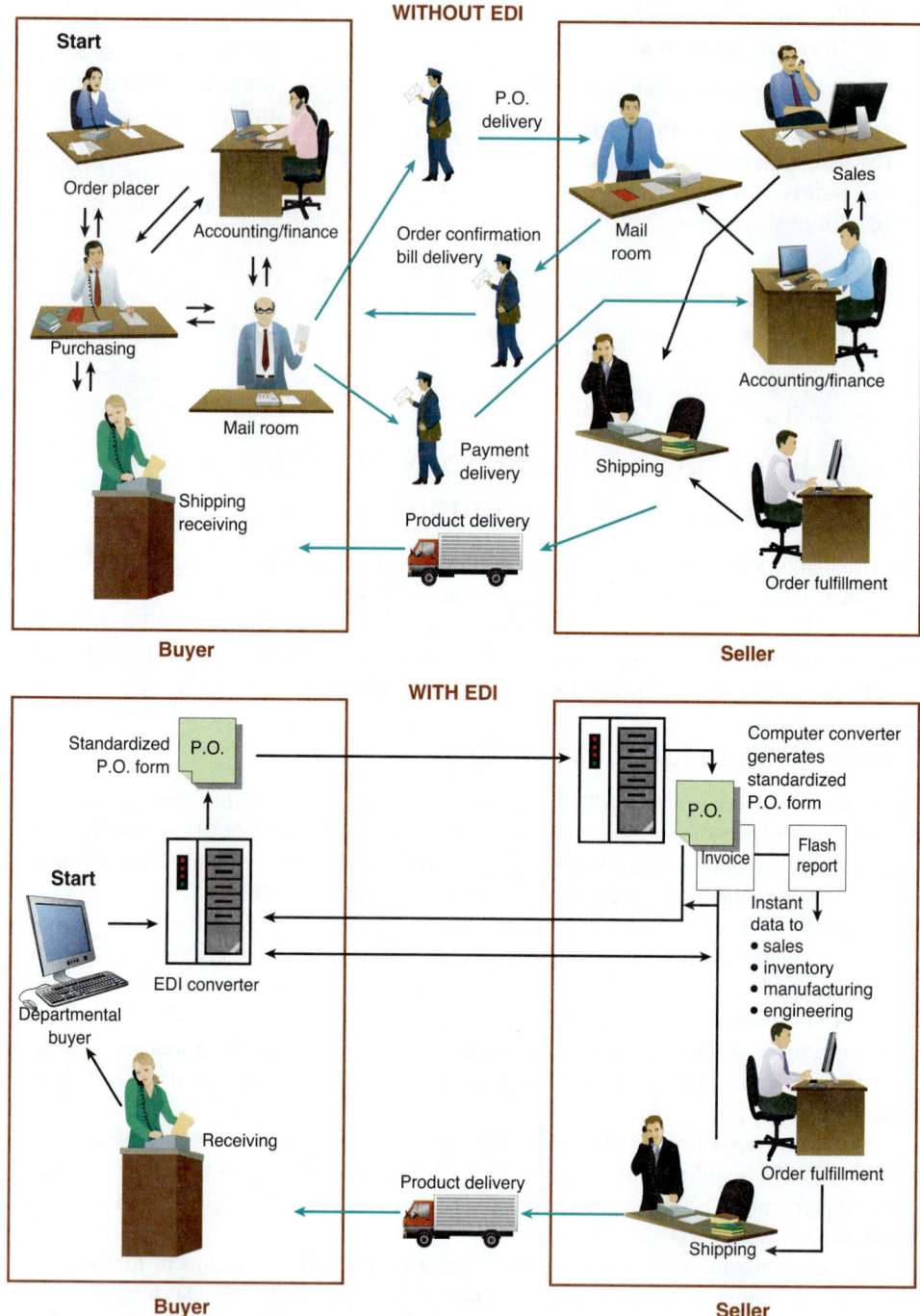

Figure 13.3 Order fulfillment with and without EDI.

enter the corporate intranet, via the Internet, to access data, place orders, check the status of those orders, communicate, and collaborate. It also enables partners to perform self-service activities such as checking inventory levels.

Extranets use virtual private network (VPN) technology to make communication over the Internet more secure. The major benefits of extranets are faster processes and information flow, improved order entry and customer service, lower costs (for example, for communications, travel, and administrative overhead), and an overall improvement in business effectiveness.

There are three major types of extranets. Companies choose a particular type depending on the business partners involved and the purpose of the supply chain. Each type, along with its major business applications, is described in the following subsections.

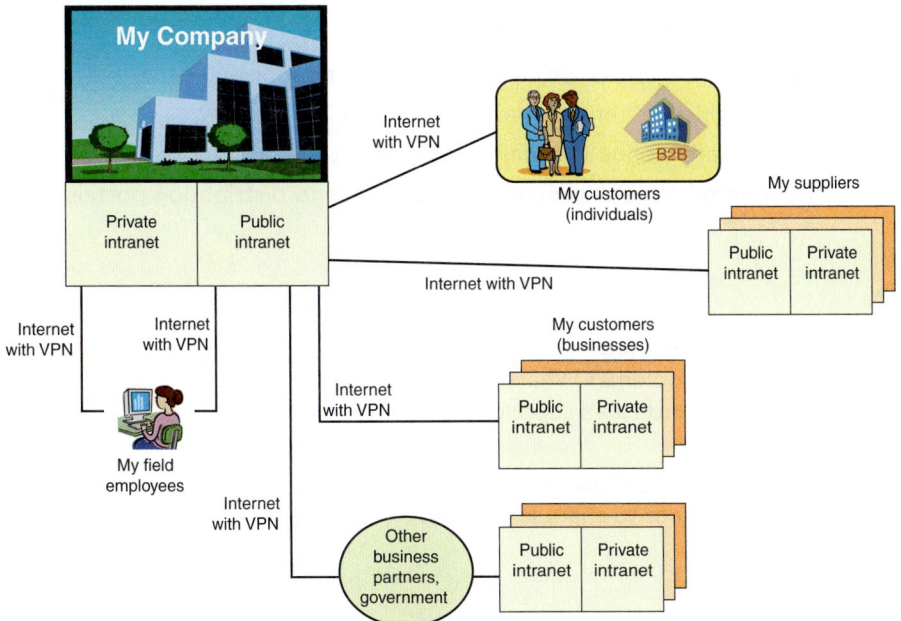

Figure 13.4 The structure of an extranet.

A Company and Its Dealers, Customers, or Suppliers. This type of extranet is centered around a single company. An example is the FedEx extranet, which allows customers to track the status of a delivery. To do so, customers use the Internet to access a database on the FedEx intranet. By enabling a customer to check the location of a package, FedEx saves the cost of having a human operator perform that task over the phone.

An Industry's Extranet. Just as a single company can set up an extranet, the major players in an industry can team up to create an extranet that will benefit all of them. For example, ANXeBusiness (www.anx.com) enables companies to collaborate effectively through a network that provides a secure global medium for B2B information exchange. The ANX Network is used for mission-critical business transactions by leading international organizations in aerospace, automotive, chemical, electronics, financial services, healthcare, logistics, manufacturing, transportation, and related industries. The network offers customers a reliable extranet and VPN services.

Joint Ventures and Other Business Partnerships. In this type of extranet, the partners in a joint venture use the extranet as a vehicle for communications and collaboration. An example is Bank of America's extranet for commercial loans. The partners involved in making these loans include a lender, a loan broker, an escrow company, and a title company. The extranet connects lenders, loan applicants, and the loan organizer, Bank of America. A similar case is Lending Tree (www.lendingtree.com), a company that provides mortgage quotes for home purchases and also sells mortgages online. Lending Tree uses an extranet for its business partners—for example, the lenders.

Portals and Exchanges

As explained in Chapter 4, corporate portals offer a single point of access through a Web browser to critical business information in an organization. In the context of B2B supply chain management, these portals enable companies and their suppliers to collaborate very closely.

The two basic types of corporate portals are procurement (sourcing) portals for a company's suppliers (upstream in the supply chain) and distribution portals for a company's customers (downstream in the supply chain). **Procurement portals** automate the business processes involved in purchasing or procuring products between a single buyer and multiple suppliers. For example, Boeing has deployed a procurement portal called the Boeing Supplier Portal through which it conducts business with its suppliers. **Distribution portals** automate the business processes involved in selling or distributing products from a single supplier to multiple buyers. For example, Dell services its business customers through its distribution portal at http://premier.dell.com.

┌─ **BEFORE** *YOU GO ON . . .*
│
│ **1.** Define EDI, and list its major benefits and limitations.
│ **2.** Define an extranet, and explain its infrastructure.
│ **3.** List and briefly define the major types of extranets.
│ **4.** Differentiate between procurement portals and distribution portals.
└─

RUBY'S CLUB QUESTIONS

1. If Ruby's is not a good candidate for vertical integration, how might information sharing be the answer to its problems? What specific information should be shared with Ruben and Lisa's suppliers to move as close as possible to a JIT system?

2. Would it make sense for alcohol or grocery distributors to allow businesses to connect to them via an extranet to share information and place orders via the Web?

Student Activity | 13.3

Objective: The objective of this exercise is to familiarize you with technology that is used to support the supply chain.

Chapter Connection: This case relates to Section 13.3 of this chapter.

Prerequisites: You should read Section 13.3 before doing this exercise.

Activity:

Supply chain management systems are essential to the successful operation of many businesses. However, for them to work, the company must rely on various forms of IT. One technology in particular provides support: electronic data interchange or EDI.

Read the following:

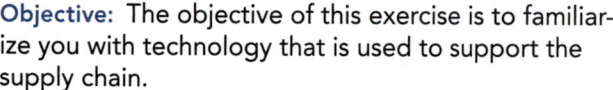

www.answers.com/topic/electronic-data-interchange

Deliverables:

Based on this chapter's text and your reading, answer the following questions:

1. How is EDI used?

2. How does it differ from just sending an order attached to an e-mail?

3. List three benefits of using EDI.

Quiz Questions:

1. EDI stands for:
   (a) Electronic data information
   (b) Essential data interchange
   (c) Electronic data interchange
   (d) Electronic disk interface

2. Which of the following is *not* a standard for EDI?
   (a) TRADACOMS
   (b) EDIFACT
   (c) ANSIX12
   (d) ISSO

3. What is now being used with the Internet replacing EDI standard data formats?
   (a) **X15**   (c) EDT
   (b) **XML**   (d) HTML

4. For what is EDI often used?
   (a) Purchase orders
   (b) Error messages
   (c) Payments
   (d) All of the above

Discussion Question:

Discuss why a company might choose to use EDI for their business transactions.

What's in **IT** for ME?

FOR THE ACCOUNTING MAJOR

The cost accountant will play an important role in developing and monitoring the financial accounting information associated with inventory and cost of goods sold. In a supply chain much of the data for these accounting requirements will flow into the organization from various partners within the chain. It is up to the chief accountant, the comptroller or CFO, to prepare and review this data.

Going further, accounting rules and regulations and the cross-border transfer of data are critical for global trade. IOSs can facilitate such trade. Other issues that are important for accountants are taxation and government reports. In addition, creating information systems that rely on EDI requires the attention of accountants. Finally, fraud detection in global settings (for example, transfers of funds) can be facilitated by appropriate controls and auditing.

FOR THE FINANCE MAJOR

In a supply chain, the finance major will be responsible for analyzing the data created and shared among supply chain partners. In many instances, the financial analyst will assume the responsibility for recommending actions to improve supply chain efficiencies and cash flow. This may benefit all the partners in the chain. These recommendations will be based on the development of financial models that incorporate key assumptions such as supply chain partner agreements for pricing. Through the use of extensive financial modeling, the financial analyst helps to manage liquidity in the supply chain.

Many finance-related issues exist in implementing IOSs. For one thing, establishing EDI and extranet relationships involves structuring payment agreements. Global supply chains may involve complex financial arrangements, which may have legal implications.

FOR THE MARKETING MAJOR

A tremendous amount of useful sales information can be derived from supply chain partners through the supporting information systems. For example, many of the customer support activities take place in the downstream portion of the supply chain. For the marketing manager, an understanding of how the downstream activities of the supply chain relate to prior chain operations is critical.

Furthermore, a tremendous amount of data is fed from the supply chain supporting information systems into the CRM systems that are used by marketers. The information and a complete understanding of its genesis are vital for mixed-model marketing programs.

FOR THE PRODUCTION/OPERATIONS MANAGEMENT MAJOR

The production/operations management major plays a major role in the supply chain development process. In many organizations, the production/operations management staff may even lead the supply chain integration process because of their extensive knowledge of the manufacturing components of the organization. Because they are in charge of the procurement, production, materials control, logistical handling, a comprehensive understanding of the techniques of SCM is vital for the production/operations staff.

The downstream segment of supply chains is where marketing, distribution channels, and customer service are conducted. An understanding of how downstream activities are related to the other segments is critical. Supply chain problems can reduce customer satisfaction and negate marketing efforts. It is essential, then, that marketing professionals understand the nature of such problems and their solutions. Also, learning about CRM, its options, and its implementation is important for designing effective customer services and advertising.

As competition intensifies globally, finding new global markets becomes critical. Use of IOSs provides an opportunity to improve marketing and sales. Understanding the capabilities of these technologies and their implementation issues will enable the marketing department to excel.

FOR THE
HUMAN RESOURCES MANAGEMENT MAJOR

Supply chains require interactions among employees from partners in the chain. These interactions are the responsibility of the human resources manager. The HR manager must be able to address supply chain issues that relate to staffing, job descriptions, job rotations, and accountability. All of these areas are complex within a supply chain and require the HR function to understand the relationship among partners as well as the movement of resources.

Preparing and training employees to work with business partners (frequently in foreign countries) requires knowledge about how IOSs operate. Sensitivity to cultural differences and extensive communication and collaboration can be facilitated with IT.

FOR THE MIS MAJOR

The MIS staff will be instrumental in the design and support of information systems—both internal organizational and interorganizational—to underpin the business processes that are part of the supply chain. In this capacity, the MIS staff must have a concise knowledge of the business, the systems, and points of intersection between the two.

>>> SUMMARY

1. Define the term *supply chain*, and describe the three components and the three flows of a supply chain.

A *supply chain* refers to the flow of materials, information, money, and services from raw material suppliers, through factories and warehouses, to the end customers. A supply chain involves three segments: upstream, where sourcing or procurement from external suppliers occurs; internal, where packaging, assembly, or manufacturing takes place; and downstream, where distribution takes place, frequently by external distributors.

The three flows in the supply chain are *material flows*, which are the physical products, raw materials, supplies, and so forth; *information flows*, which consist of data that are related to demand, shipments, orders, returns, and schedules, as well as changes in any of these data; and *financial flows*, which involve money transfers, payments, credit card information and authorization, payment schedules, e-payments, and credit-related data.

2. Identify two major challenges in setting accurate inventory levels throughout the supply chain, and describe three popular strategies to solve supply chain problems.

Two major challenges in setting accurate inventory levels throughout a supply chain are the *demand forecast* and the *bullwhip effect*. Demand for a product can be influenced by numerous factors such as competition, prices, weather conditions, technological developments, economic conditions, and customers' general confidence. The bullwhip effect refers to erratic shifts in orders up and down the supply chain.

The most common solution to supply chain problems is *building inventories* as insurance against supply chain uncertainties. Another solution is the *just-in-time* (JIT) inventory system, which delivers the precise number of parts, called work-in-process inventory, to be assembled into a finished product at precisely the right time. The third possible solution is *vendor-managed inventory* (VMI), which occurs when the vendor, rather than the retailer, manages the entire inventory process for a particular product or group of products.

3. **Define the terms *electronic data interchange (EDI)*, *extranet*, and *portal*, and explain how each of these applications helps support supply chain management.**

Electronic data interchange (EDI) is a communication standard that enables the electronic transfer of routine documents, such as purchasing orders, between business partners.

Extranets are networks that link business partners to one another over the Internet by providing access to certain areas of one another's corporate intranets. The main goal of extranets is to foster collaboration among business partners.

Corporate portals offer a single point of access through a Web browser to critical business information in an organization. In the context of business-to-business supply chain management, these portals enable companies and their suppliers to collaborate very closely.

>>> CHAPTER GLOSSARY

bullwhip effect Erratic shifts in orders up and down the supply chain.

distribution portals Corporate portals that automate the business processes involved in selling or distributing products from a single supplier to multiple buyers.

electronic data interchange (EDI) A communication standard that enables the electronic transfer of routine documents between business partners.

extranets Link business partners to one another over the Internet by providing access to certain areas of one another's corporate intranets

interorganizational information system (IOS) An information system that supports information flow among two or more organizations.

just-in-time (JIT) inventory system A system in which a supplier delivers the precise number of parts to be assembled into a finished product at precisely the right time.

procurement portals Corporate portals that automate the business processes involved in purchasing or procuring products between a single buyer and multiple suppliers.

pull model A business model in which the production process begins with a customer order and companies make only what customers want, a process closely aligned with mass customization.

push model A business model in which the production process begins with a forecast, which predicts the products that customers will want as well as the quantity of each product. The company then produces the amount of products in the forecast, typically by using mass production, and sells, or "pushes," those products to consumers.

supply chain Coordinated flow of materials, information, money, and services from raw material suppliers, through factories and warehouses, to the end consumers.

supply chain management An activity in which the leaders of an organization provide extensive oversight for the partnerships and processes that comprise the supply chain and leverage these relationships to provide an operational advantage.

supply chain visibility The ability for all organizations in a supply chain to access or view relevant data on purchased materials as these materials move through their suppliers' production processes.

vendor-managed inventory (VMI) An inventory strategy where the supplier monitors a vendor's inventory for a product or group of products and replenishes products when needed.

vertical integration Strategy of integrating the upstream part of the supply chain with the internal part, typically by purchasing upstream suppliers, in order to ensure timely availability of supplies.

>>> DISCUSSION QUESTIONS

1. Explain how a supply chain approach may be part of a company's overall strategy.

2. Explain the important role that information systems play in supporting a supply chain strategy.

3. Would Rolls-Royce Motorcars (www.rolls-roycemotorcars.com) use a push model or a pull model in its supply chain? Support your answer.

4. Why is planning so important in supply chain management?

>>> PROBLEM-SOLVING ACTIVITIES

1. Enter the Teradata Student Network (www.teradatauniversitynetwork.com/tun), and find the podcasts that deal with supply chains (by Jill Dyche). Identify the benefits cited in the podcasts.

2. Access www.ups.com and www.fedex.com. Examine some of the IT-supported customer services and tools

provided by the two companies. Write a report on how the two companies contribute to supply chain improvements.

3. Enter www.supply-chain.org, www.cio.com, www.findarticles.com, and www.google.com, and search for recent information on supply chain management.

4. Surf the Web to find a procurement (sourcing) portal, a distribution portal, and an exchange (other than the examples in this chapter). List the features they have in common and those features that are unique.

>>> TEAM ASSIGNMENTS

1. Each group in the class will be assigned to a major supply chain management vendor, such as SAP, Oracle, i2, IBM, and so on. Each group will investigate topics such as (a) the products, (b) major capabilities, (c) relationship to customer relationship management and (d) customer success stories. Each group will prepare a presentation for the class, trying to convince the class why that group's software product is best.

2. Have each team locate several organizations that use IOSs, including one with a global reach. Students should contact the companies to find what IOS technology support they use (for example, an EDI, extranet, etc.). Then find out what issues they faced in implementation. Prepare a report.

CLOSING **CASE 1 >** Information Technology Helps
Cannondale Manage Its Complex Supply Chain

THE PROBLEM>>> Cannondale (www.cannondale.com) is a pioneer in the engineering and manufacturing of high-end bicycles, apparel, footwear, and accessories for independent dealers and distributors in more than 66 countries. Cannondale designs, develops, and produces bicycles at its factory in Bedford, Pennsylvania, and it operates subsidiaries in Holland, Switzerland, Japan, and Australia. As a leading custom bicycle manufacturer with an extensive and impressive customer list—including Olympic athletes, professional racing teams, and Tour de France competitors—Cannondale realizes that meeting customer demands and expectations is critical to its success.

Cannondale produces more than a hundred different bicycle models annually, 60 percent of which are newly introduced lines. Working in a cyclical business that is impacted by market and weather conditions, coupled with the international nature of its business, Cannondale is faced with highly complex and volatile consumer demand. In addition to constantly shifting demand and a rapidly changing product portfolio, Cannondale has a global supply chain that must integrate global manufacturing, assembly, and sales and distribution sites.

Cannondale manufactures both make-to-order and make-to-stock models. Consequently, the company needs to manage a range of product batch sizes, sometimes including one-of-a-kind orders. A typical bicycle requires a 150-day lead time with a 4-week manufacturing window, and some bicycles have more than 250 parts in their bills of materials (BOMs). (A bill of materials specifies the raw materials, assemblies, components, and parts needed to manufacture a final product, along with the quantities of each one.) Cannondale has to manage more than 1 million BOMs and more than 200,000 individual parts. Adding to Cannondale's manufacturing complexity, some of these parts are supplied by specialty vendors who require long lead times and have only limited production capacity. This complexity significantly challenged Cannondale's capacity to quickly deliver complex and custom products to meet its customers' high expectations.

To manage parts availability and varying customer demands, Cannondale's manufacturing operations need to be highly flexible. Therefore, the company needed a global system that allowed managers to access all plant inventory levels and supply schedules to better manage shifts in product and customer demand.

Cannondale had been using a legacy material requirements planning system (MRP II) that generated weekly reports. Because Cannondale's manufacturing environment is so dynamic, however, by Tuesday afternoon Monday's reports were so outdated that they were useless. The supply chain team had to substitute parts in order to meet demand, causing an ever-increasing parts flow problem. Cannondale's primary objective was to find an IT solution that would improve the accuracy of the company's parts flow, support the company's need for flexibility, and operate within the confines of its existing business systems—all at an affordable cost.

Cannondale selected the Kinaxis RapidResponse (www.kinaxis.com) system for its integrated demand and supply planning and monitoring. RapidResponse provides users with necessary information in minutes, as opposed to 8 hours with the previous system. RapidResponse generates accurate and detailed supply chain information with an easy-to-use spreadsheet user interface, employing data supplied from the company's existing MRP II systems.

<<<**THE SOLUTION**

RapidResponse has transformed Cannondale's entire supply chain. Buyers, planners, master schedulers, sourcers (people who procure products), product managers, customer service personnel, and financial managers use the system for sales reporting, forecasting, monitoring daily inventory availability, and providing production schedule information to the MRP II and order-processing systems. Supply chain participants located around the world can now instantly simulate, share, and score what-if scenarios to evaluate and select the actions they need to take to respond to changing supply and demand conditions.

Company managers now receive up-to-date visibility of global operations. In addition, the management team uses RapidResponse daily to examine the company's manufacturing backlog. Having access to current information enables the team to compare old forecasts with new ones.

Today, Cannondale responds to customer orders quickly, and it has significantly reduced its inventory, with its associated costs. In addition, the company has benefited from higher inventory turns, reductions in safety stock, improvement in cycle times, reduced lead times, and more accurate promise dates. As a result, customer satisfaction has improved. All of these benefits have provided Cannondale with a competitive advantage in a highly competitive industry.

<<<**THE RESULTS**

Questions

1. Describe Cannondale's complex manufacturing environment, and identify some of the problems this environment created.

2. Describe the RapidResponse system's impact on Cannondale's global supply chain management.

SOURCES: Compiled from B. Ferrari, "Kinaxis RapidResponse—Much More Than a Planning Application" *Supply Chain Matters*, January 8, 2010; Kinaxis Corporation, "Cannondale Improves Customer Response Times While Reducing Inventory Using RapidResponse," *Kinaxis Customer Spotlight*, 2010; www.kinaxis.com, www.cannondale.com, accessed April 14, 2011.

CLOSING **CASE 2 >**

Supply Chain Management Helps Imperial Sugar After Disaster

In February 2008, an accident at the Imperial Sugar (www.imperialsugar.com) plant in Port Wentworth, Georgia, resulted in an explosion that injured several people. In the days following the explosion, the company's efforts focused on helping the affected employees and their families. But the $522 million sugar refiner—the third largest in the United States—had obligations to its customers as well. The disaster destroyed approximately 60 percent of the plant's production capacity overnight. It was not clear when, or if, the plant would operate again.

<<<**THE PROBLEM**

The plant tried to fulfill as many customer orders as possible, but, unfortunately, it did not have any safety stockpiles. The company imported some sugar through its joint venture with Mexican refiner Ingenios Santos, but the amount was not enough to meet its customers' demands.

THE IT>>> SOLUTION

In 1998, Imperial Sugar had implemented an inclusive PeopleSoft enterprise resource planning system to manage its business processes. After completing several upgrades, the company realized that the demand-management module could not handle the complexities of the business. When large beverage and food manufacturers sign an annual contract, Imperial Sugar has to predict how that demand will actually manifest itself based on seasonal and consumer cycles. The executives at Imperial Sugar acknowledged that supply chain management was at "the heart of their business" and that it gave Imperial Sugar a competitive advantage.

In 2006, the company had added a system from Demand Foresight (www. demandforesight.com) that essentially calculated how demand ebbs and flows over time. This software package enabled Imperial Sugar to determine the impact of a wide range of factors on the demand for sugar, to react quickly to changes in demand, and to track the company's overall performance.

After the refinery catastrophe, Imperial Sugar needed to know how many customers it could serve with its available inventory. The software provided that information by product line, and its functionality allowed everyone from production to sales to see, in real time, what could be delivered. The software took the company's demand, its inventory and capacity, and the number of new orders coming in, and integrated all of that information.

THE RESULTS>>>

The Georgia plant remained offline for 20 months, and the company disappointed many customers. Nevertheless, it credits supply-chain systems, particularly demand-management software, with helping to make the best use of its available resources. The firm noted that, although it could not fulfill every order, the software enabled it to fulfill many more orders than it would have been able to otherwise.

Questions

1. Why is demand management such an essential component of supply chain management?

2. Go to www.imperialsugar.com, and learn about the company. Use your knowledge to describe other measures the company could have taken in its production/operations to recover from the disaster.

SOURCES: Compiled from S. Overby, "Supply Chain Management to the Rescue," *CIO*, March 16, 2010; www. imperialsugar.com, www.demandforesight.com, accessed May 14, 2011.

RUBY'S CLUB INTERNSHIP ASSIGNMENTS

Ruben had last year's sales numbers put into a spreadsheet because he heard about a type of regression analysis that would give him an idea of the impact of different events in the community. However, he does not know how to run this regression, or how to use it to plan for the club.

Watch the following videos to learn how to install the Data Analysis Toolpak in Microsoft Excel. Depending on your version of Excel,

you may want to search Google for more information. Then download the spreadsheet, and begin your analysis.

Install the Data Analysis Toolpak from this link: http:// higheredbcs.wiley.com/legacy/college/rainer/0470473525/ interactive/ch10/chapter10_video1/index.html

Watch the following video on how to set up a regression analysis in Excel using the Data Analysis Toolpak that you just installed:

Download the spreadsheet from www.wiley.com/college/rainer.

In the spreadsheet, you will find 1's and 0's. These indicate a "yes" to the item in the column. You will also find a column regarding the type of music played during a particular week. For the analysis to run properly, you will need to divide this into five different columns with 1's and 0's.

Once you interpret your results, write a letter to Ruben and Lisa detailing the impact that outside events have on their sales. Be sure to attach your version of the spreadsheet with analysis included. Submit it to Ruben and Lisa via your professor.

Wiley Plus Review Questions

1. Where are Ruby's Club suppliers in the supply chain?

   (a) Upstream
   (b) Downstream
   (c) Internal
   (d) None of the above

2. If Ruben and Lisa are poor planners, what problem might they cause their suppliers?

   (a) Vertical integration
   (b) Horizontal integration
   (c) JIT inventory
   (d) Bullwhip

3. Supply chain management software would likely help Ruben and Lisa pass which of the following upstream? (Select all that apply.)

   (a) Materials
   (b) Money
   (c) Information
   (d) Exchange rates

4. If Ruben and Lisa purchased their supplies so they could better manage their distribution and inventory, they would be engaged in which of the following?

   (a) Horizontal integration
   (b) Vertical integration
   (c) JIT integration
   (d) Whenever integration

SPREADSHEET ACTIVITY

Objective: Supply chain management is a vital operation for organizations. So much so that if one supplier fails to do its job, the entire operation may be shut down. Microsoft Excel is often used to assist in this basic planning. Logic and algebra can be applied in a spreadsheet to make simple calculations that apply within the supply chain scenario.

Chapter Connection: At one time, Dell realized it had almost perfected the assembly process within its plant. The only way to improve its product was to improve the entire supply chain. So Dell began working with its suppliers to streamline its processes. While its supply chain system is too complex for a spreadsheet, the principle applies to many situations. This activity will take a simpler scenario and introduce the concept of planning for the supply chain and using spreadsheet tools to improve the process.

Prerequisites: There are no prerequisites for this activity.

Activity: Mr. Stephens works in construction. Specifically, he builds custom homes. He always gets complaints about his work being late, even though his customers are generally happy with the final product. To try and deal with the complaints and to give his customers a better understanding of when their home will be complete, he wants to build a spreadsheet that will lay out the entire process of building the home, specify the amount of time each part will take, and build in time for bad weather, corrections, and other issues that always arise.

Mr. Stephens compiled the following data for his next construction job. Though he ultimately wants to create a universal spreadsheet, for now he just wants to work on the concept and get it to work for this next job. Use the data and build him a spreadsheet that has the job description in one column and other columns for start date, earliest end date, and latest end date. Unless otherwise noted, these steps are performed in order, and one cannot begin until the previous step is completed.

1. Ground work will take 3 to 4 days.
2. Footers will take 2 to 3 days.
3. Block work for crawl space will take 7 to 10 days.
4. Foundation will take 3 to 4 days. Lumber should be ordered a week in advance.
5. Remaining frame will take 2 to 3 weeks. Home should be dried-in at this time.

6. Exterior oriented strand board (OSB) and house wrap will take 7 to 10 days.

7. Electrical work may begin at this point. It will take 8 to 12 days to complete the rough-in wiring for the home.

8. Rough-in plumbing work may begin when the exterior OSB is complete. Rough-in plumbing will take 5 to 7 days.

9. Insulation and dry wall may go up at this time when both electrical and plumbing are roughed in. It will take 17 to 21 days to complete the installation of exterior and interior walls insulation as well as the drywall work.

10. Cabinetry and final electrical work may begin at this point. Cabinetry will take 1 to 3 days, and the finish work on electrical items will take 7 to 10 days. Cabinets should be ordered a month in advance.

11. The final plumbing work may begin when the cabinets are complete and will take 3 to 5 days to complete.

12. All work on the rest of the house may begin at this time. Paint, trim, and flooring typically take 2 to 3 weeks.

Given these data, a start date of February 1, and 2 weeks for weather delays, what is the projected end date if everything finishes as early as possible? Also, what is the projected end date if everything takes as long as possible?

Deliverables: You will take Mr. Stephens' description and create a spreadsheet that will allow him to demonstrate to customers how a home is built. As you discuss the length of time each step takes,

you will be able to see the difficulty in projecting a "finish" date for this type of work.

Quiz Questions:

1. True or False? If/then statements can only include numeric characters, not alphanumeric.

2. True or False? Since Excel formulas are based on many unknown variables, Excel is not really useful as a supply chain management tool.

3. If cell "A1" in the formula "=A1+7" is formatted as a date, what will the resulting number be?

   (a) A date

   (b) An error statement

   (c) Depends on how the formula cell is formatted

   (d) Nothing (It will not calculate and will simply display the date.)

Discussion Questions:

1. Supply chain management is extremely important in today's business environment. Look up some supply chain management tools, and compare them to your Excel activity. Discuss the advantages and disadvantages of these systems. What do they provide that the spreadsheet example does not?

2. Given that some refer to supply chains as a web rather than a chain, what type of problems do you see arising from the parent company's need to share information with so many others at the same time? Also, what complications arise from the suppliers needing to share information? Which company should determine the platform and methods of sharing data?

DATABASE ACTIVITY: QUERY BY FORM

Objective

Forms and queries have a two-sided relationship. Forms can be an easy-to-use way to provide the input to a query. Query results can also be used in place of tables to drive forms. In this activity you will see how a form drives a query, increasing your understanding of both.

Chapter Connection

Supply chain integration, as you read in this chapter, is complex. One company's supplier is another company's customer and so on, all the way up to raw material extraction and down to individual end users. The database applications that are needed to manage this supply chain are correspondingly complex. It can take a mix of database features to get the entire job done. This activity shows how two database capabilities interact with each other.

Prerequisites

Before starting this activity, you should complete the database activities for Chapter 9 (Forms II) and Chapter 10 (Queries I).

Activity:

In this activity, which you will find online at www.wiley.com/college/rainer, you will take what you know about queries and forms, and combine them to improve the usability of your queries.

1. Download and open the Ch 13 CarlaComputerStores database from www.wiley.com/college/rainer. (You may be familiar with it from the Chapter 5 activity.) It contains sales data for a chain of computer stores.

2. We will use a querying method called Query By Form (QBF). It lets us replace a series of parameter entry dialogue boxes with a single form, while allowing us to create a more attractive user interface. To use it, we must create both the query and the form. It is easiest to do this in a few stages.

3. First, we will create the part of the query that returns results, adding criteria later since they will come from a form we have not created yet. We do this so that, when we create the form, we will be able to tell it which query to run. So, start with Query Design in the Other section of the Create ribbon.

Usage Hint: This query–form–query sequence is not strictly necessary. However, methods that do the job in two steps are more complicated, since they require referring to Access objects that do not exist yet.

4. We want this query to tell us which customers ordered products in a chosen category from a chosen store, and exactly what products they ordered. So, first show all five database tables in the upper pane of the query design window. Then, double-click on four fields to enter them into the query design: "StoreCity" from StoreTbl, "ProdCategory" from ProductTbl, "CustName" from CustomerTbl, and "ProdDescrip" from ProductTbl. Run the query to test it. You should see an unsorted list of all 312 purchases. If you do not, review the previous steps to find the error. Then close it, saving it as CS_Qry when prompted.

Usage Hint: Testing is a vital part of information system development. Test often. If anything does not work, the reason is usually in what you did since the previous test. You can fix it while what you just did is still fresh in your mind.

5. Now that CS_Qry exists, we can create the form that will activate it. Click the "Form Design" tool in the Forms section of the Create menu.

6. First, we will create a field to enter the store we want information about. Click the "Text Box" tool in the Controls section of the Design ribbon. The mouse pointer becomes crosshairs in the form design grid. Drag to create a text-size area somewhere in the upper right part of this grid. (You use the right side to leave room for a label at the left.)

7. The label to the left of the text box will read "Text0." Edit it in place to read "Store City." Its enclosing box will expand to hold its new, longer contents.

8. The text inside the text box reads "Unbound." However, that is not the name of the text box. That says where its data comes from. "Unbound" means it does not come from the database—that is, it hasn't been "bound" to a database item. We want to give the text box a name so we can refer to it in our query. To do that, open the Property Sheet of the form if it is not already open. (Click the "Property Sheet" tool in the Tools section of the Design ribbon, or press F4.) Find Name in either the Other or the All tab of the property sheet. Replace it with the name "StoreField."

9. Create another text box named "CatField" in the same way, with its label reading "Product Category." Line up the two fields and labels, one below the other, as closely as you can.

Usage Hint: You can line up the items exactly by selecting both boxes and using the tools in the Control Alignment section of the Arrange ribbon. For more precision, open the Property Sheet, and set the Left property to any desired value. If you do this while both are selected, they will both take on this value. You can set any desired property of several controls at the same time this way.

10. Enter a form header above the text fields by clicking on "Title" in the Header/Footer area of the Design ribbon. Enter "Store and Category Search" in the label box. Select the entire box and use the Font tools in the Design ribbon to enlarge the type, make it bold, change its color, and give the label box a light-colored background.

11. Now we will create the button that starts the search. Make sure Use Control Wizards is highlighted in the Controls section of the Design ribbon. (Expand that area with the wizard by using the down-pointing triangle with the line above it at the right.) Then click the "Button" tool. (It is in the top row of controls, fourth from the left.) Drag it over a rectangular area below your text boxes to create the button shape. The wizard will start.

12. We want it to run a query. Select this action from the "Miscellaneous" category; click "Next."

13. Select the query you created earlier, CS_Qry, from the list of available queries; click "Next."

14. Click "Text" as what you want to see on the button, and enter "Search" into the text field next to that option button. Click "Next."

15. Optionally name the button anything you want, and click "Finish."

16. To test what you have done so far, switch to Form view, and click your button. You should see the same datasheet you saw when you test-ran the query in step 4. If you do, the form is finished. Return to it and save it as CS_Qry_Frm. Now, we will continue with the query design.

17. With the query open in Design view, specify a sort order for the data. Click in the "Sort" row of the StoreCity column in the design grid. Select "Ascending" from the pull-down menu at the right. Repeat for CustName and ProdCategory. Test again by running the query. You should see all 312 purchases again, but this time they should be sorted.

18. To add a selection to the query, return to Design view, and click in the StoreCity column, in the first Criteria row. Next, select the "Builder" tool from the Query Setup section of the Design ribbon. (Its icon looks like the Use Control Wizards icon.) Your criteria will be based on CS_Qry_Form, so expand the database name, then Forms, then its All Forms sub-folder. Select "CS_Qry_Form." In the second column, double-click "StoreField."

19. You will see "Forms![CS_QueryForm]![StoreField]" in the upper portion of the dialogue box. This is Access's internal way of identifying the form field we want. Click "OK." It will appear in the Criteria section of the query design.

Usage Hint: If you know Access well, you can also key criteria directly into the query design grid. For short criteria that can be faster, but it is also more prone to error.

20. To check your work, close the query, saving when prompted. Open CS_Qry_Frm. On the form, enter "Chicago" into the Store field and click "Search." You should get 78 records of Chicago sales. Close the query and enter "Miami." You should get a blank datasheet, since Carla's has no store there. (You will get the same result if you spell "Chicago" wrong.)

Usage Hint: You could have checked your work a bit earlier by running the query directly, without the form. If you do that, you will get a parameter box with an odd-looking prompt string: the name of the form field. It should work, though.

21. Repeat steps 18 and 19 for ProdCategory. Test by entering "Denver" and "Storage" into the two form fields. Your query should retrieve ten records.

22. You may want to find data about all Storage sales, or some other category, without regard for city. Enter "Storage" in the category field, leaving the Store field blank. Run the query. Nothing comes up. You realize the reason: No data records match a blank StoreCity! This must be fixed. You want the query to select a record if either (a) its StoreCity matches what is in the form or (b) the field in the form is blank. Fortunately, that is not hard to do.

23. Return to Query Design view. Click in the "StoreCity" criterion field and reopen the Expression Builder. Put the insertion point after the field name that is already there. Then either key in the word "Or" or follow Operators>Logical and double-click "Or" in the lower part of the Expression Builder window. You will see the word "Or" appear in the Expression Builder box after the field name. Then select StoreField again, and after it type the words "is null" (without the quotation marks). This means that the query will select a record if it matches what is in the field, *or* if the field is null—that is, there is nothing in it. That is exactly what we want.

Usage Hint: Instead of keying in "is null," we could have found the IsNull function in Expression Builder. In this case, the words are so short that keying them in is easier.

24. Modify the CatField test criterion in the same way.

25. Test again: Close the query, enter "Storage" in the Category field of the form, and leave the City field blank. You should see 66 storage sales in all four stores, starting with Alice's purchase of a 1TB disk in Atlanta.

26. Test to confirm that entering a city, but no category, also works.

27. Test to confirm that leaving both city and category blank shows all 312 rows of the full table.

28. Look at the query in Design view. Access has rearranged your criteria, turning them into four and adding two columns that do not show up in the query results. (Their "Show" boxes are unchecked.) It sometimes does this to reduce a complex query to several simpler ones. That is not a problem. We mention it here only so it does not faze you if you see it.

29. Close your database, saving if prompted.

Deliverables:

Your database, with the form and query.

Quiz Questions:

1. True or False? A form is the only way a user can specify search criteria (without opening a query in Design view, which most end users are not up to).

2. How many portable computers did the Atlanta store sell in the period covered by this database? Who bought more than anyone else? How many did this person buy?

3. Look at the Property Sheet of either text box in CS_Qry_Form. It allows you to specify many properties of these boxes. (Some can be specified through ribbon tools or in other ways as well.) In particular, it lets a form designer choose all of the following *except:*
   (a) Font size in points
   (b) Background color of the box
   (c) Which sides of the box will show borders
   (d) Color of the box borders

4. The condition "IS NULL" in a database query is satisfied if the field in question:
   (a) Has a numeric value of 0 (zero)
   (b) Has an incorrect data type; for example, letters where numbers are required
   (c) Violates validation tests; for example, a month number that is not from 1 to 12
   (d) Is empty; that is, it contains no data

Discussion Questions:

1. This activity used a form to drive a query. The two can also work together in the opposite direction: using queries as input to a form, where we used only tables until now. Use the form and query you created in this activity to select sales of Display products in all stores. With the query results showing, create a form using the Form tool in the Create ribbon. How does what you created resemble, and how does it differ from, a form you could have created from the tables that underlie this query?

2. In step 25 of the activity, you saw that Access turned your two criteria, each of which contained two elementary conditions combined by OR, into four criteria. Try to figure out the conditions under which each of the four would apply.

3. Query criteria can use hundreds of built-in functions. They are listed under Functions, then Built-In Functions, in the Builder dialogue box. Many of these resemble functions you are familiar with from Excel formulas, including 13 financial functions such as internal rate of return (IRR) and loan payments (PMT) that one might not initially think of when one thinks of database applications. Discuss how a query might use such financial functions.

14 | Acquiring Information Systems and Applications

LEARNING OBJECTIVES >>>

1. Define an IT strategic plan, identify the three objectives it must meet, and describe the four common approaches to cost-benefit analysis.

2. Discuss the four business decisions that companies must make when they acquire new applications.

3. Identify the six processes involved in the systems development life cycle, and explain the primary tasks and importance of each process.

4. Describe four alternative development methods and four tools that augment development methods, and identify at least one advantage and one disadvantage of each method and tool.

5. Analyze the process of vendor and software selection.

Anniston Orthopaedics is a surgical group comprised of six physicians who provide services to the Calhoun County area of Alabama. They had not updated their information systems for several years. When the federal government initiated an incentives program for medical practices to migrate to electronic medical records (EMR), the group's physicians realized that it was time to upgrade their ISs. Most of the responsibility for this transition fell on Chad Prince, Anniston's administrator.

To upgrade to EMRs, Anniston had to find a new system that would entail hardware, software, and an upgraded network. The physicians wanted their new system to operate at a level that would carry their practice into the next 10 years. In mid-2011, after considering numerous vendors, Anniston selected Greenway Medical Technologies, from Carrollton, Georgia, to provide the group's new IS. Making this decision is only the beginning of the process, however. At the time of this writing, attorneys are working out the legal details of the contract. If the two parties cannot agree on the terms, then the process must start over. If the contract is acceptable to both parties, then Chad will purchase new hardware and upgrade the group's network, based on Greenway's technologies.

Sources: Compiled from interviews with Chad Prince, www.greenwaymedical.com, http://annistonortho.com, accessed May 12, 2011.

Questions

1. Would acquiring a new information system for a small organization be a longer or shorter process than acquiring one for a large organization? Why or why not? Support your answer.

2. What is the purpose of the contract between the two parties?

RUBY'S CLUB

It is time to for Ruben and Lisa to begin discussing the implementation of the systems they have decided on. Specifically, they need some help determining the best method for developing, implementing, running, and maintaining this mobile ordering system.

They realize that having the idea for a system is only the beginning. They need to know about development methodologies and which ones make the most sense for them. Remember, their strategy is to provide a relaxing, community-type atmosphere, and they think this ordering system will support that mission by making it easier for people to continue with their socializing and not take time away to order drinks and food.

>>> As you read through this chapter, consider the end-of-section questions in light of this case. While there are more possibilities to think about, these will give you some direction to help develop your final report to them at the end of the chapter.

INTRODUCTION

Competitive organizations move as quickly as they can to acquire new information technologies or modify existing ones when they need to improve efficiencies and gain strategic advantage. Today, however, acquisition goes beyond building new systems in-house, and IT resources go beyond software and hardware. The old model in which firms built their own systems is being replaced with a broader perspective of IT resource acquisition that provides companies with a number of options. Thus, companies now must decide which IT tasks will remain in-house, and even whether the entire IT resource should be provided and managed by outside organizations. Regardless of which approach an organization chooses, however, it must be able to manage IT projects adeptly.

Even for a small business, IS upgrades present a complex problem. Small organizations must select vendors based on a number of factors, particularly (1) the ability of the vendor's product(s) to meet the organization's current business needs, (2) the viability of the vendor as a whole (you do not want to sign a contract with someone who might go into bankruptcy), and (3) the relationship between the two companies. After the organization has selected a vendor, the two parties must decide on the contract and clear it with their lawyers. Finally, the organization must acquire the hardware to support the new software. Even for a small business, these decisions are very important because of the lasting impact of this investment. Although the right information systems may not "make or break" the organization, they can definitely help it become more competitive.

In this chapter you learn about the process of acquiring IT resources from a managerial perspective. This means from *your* perspective, because you will be closely involved in all aspects of acquiring information systems and applications in your organization. In fact, when we mention "users" in this chapter, we are talking about you. You will also study the available options for acquiring IT resources and how to evaluate the options. To conclude, you will learn how organizations plan and justify the acquisition of new information systems.

14.1 | Planning for and Justifying IT Applications

Organizations must analyze the need for applications and then justify each purchase in terms of costs and benefits. The need for information systems is usually related to organizational planning and to the analysis of its performance vis-à-vis its competitors. The cost-benefit justification must look at the wisdom of investing in a specific IT application versus spending the funds on alternative projects. This chapter focuses on the formal processes of large organizations. Smaller organizations employ less formal processes, or no processes at all. It is important to note that even if a small organization does not have a formal process for planning and justifying IT applications, the steps of a formal process exist for a reason, and they have value. At the very least, decision makers in small organizations should consider each step when they are planning changes in their ISs.

When a company examines its needs and performance, it generates a prioritized list of both existing and potential IT applications, called the **application portfolio**. These are the applications that have to be added, or modified if they already exist.

IT Planning

The planning process for new IT applications begins with analysis of the *organizational strategic plan*, which is illustrated in Figure 14.1. The organization's strategic plan identifies the firm's overall mission, the goals that follow from that mission, and the broad steps required to reach these goals. The strategic planning process modifies the organization's objectives and resources to match its changing markets and opportunities.

The organizational strategic plan and the existing IT architecture provide the inputs in developing the IT strategic plan. The *IT architecture* delineates the way an organization's information resources should be used to accomplish its mission. It encompasses both the technical and the managerial aspects of information resources. The technical aspects include hardware and operating systems, networking, data management systems, and applications software. The managerial aspects specify how the IT department will be managed, how the functional area managers will be involved, and how IT decisions will be made.

The **IT strategic plan** is a set of long-range goals that describe the IT infrastructure and identify the major IT initiatives needed to achieve the organization's goals. The IT strategic plan must meet three objectives:

1. *It must be aligned with the organization's strategic plan.* This alignment is critical because the organization's ISs have to support the organization's strategies. (Recall the discussion of organizational strategies and information systems in Chapter 2.)

Consider the example of Nordstrom versus Walmart. An application that improves customer service at a small cost would be considered favorably at Nordstrom, but it would be rejected at Walmart. The reason is that the application would fit in favorably (i.e., align) with Nordstrom's service-at-any-cost strategy. However, it would not fit in well with Walmart's low-cost strategy. You see two department stores, same application, same cost and benefits—but different answers to the question "Should we develop the application?"

2. *It must provide for an IT architecture that seamlessly networks users, applications, and databases.*

3. *It must efficiently allocate IS development resources among competing projects so the projects can be completed on time and within budget and still have the required functionality.*

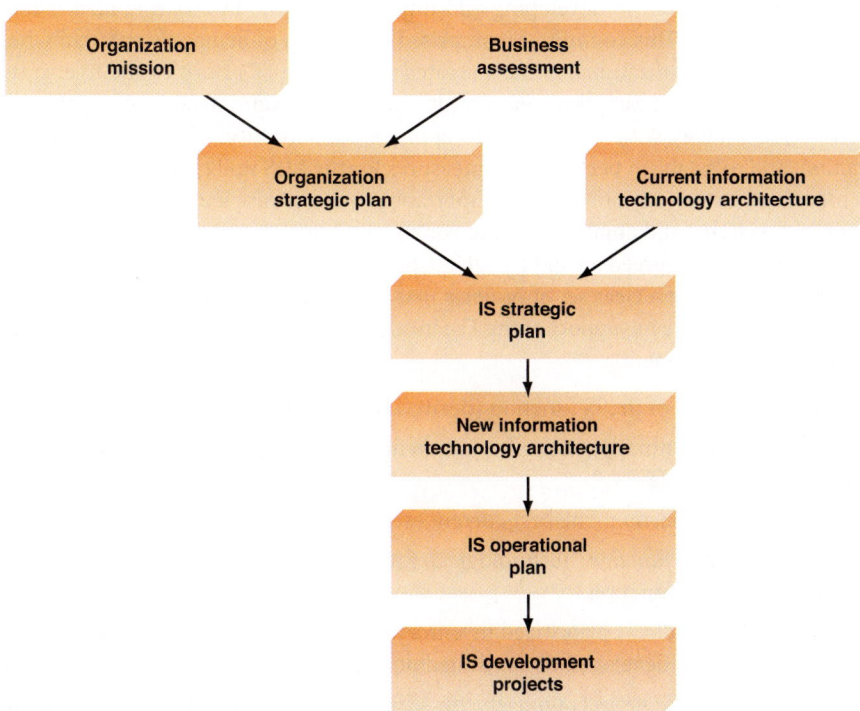

Figure 14.1 Analysis of the organizational strategic plan.

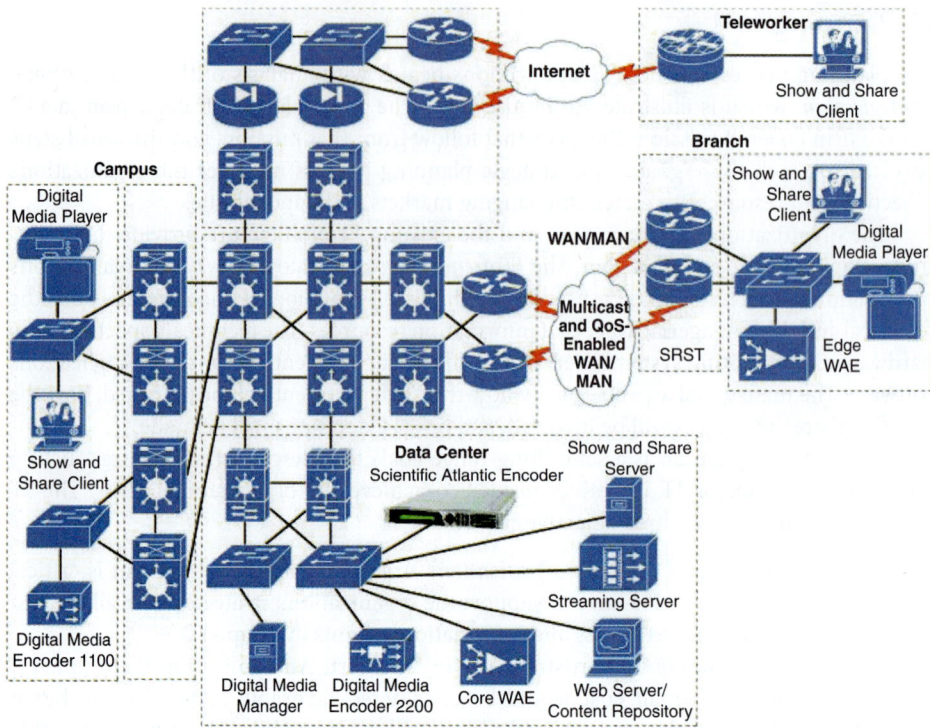

Figure 14.2 IT architecture. (*Source:* http://www.cisco.com/en/US/i/200001-300000/250001-260000/253001-254000/253787.jpg)

The existing IT architecture is a necessary input into the IT strategic plan because it acts as a constraint on future development efforts. It is not an absolute constraint, though, because the organization can change to a new IT architecture. Companies prefer to avoid this strategy, however, because it is expensive and time consuming.

Consider this example. You have a Mac (Apple) system, and you need a new software application. You search and find several such packages for both Mac and MS Windows. Unfortunately, the best package runs only on Windows. How much better would this package have to be for you to justify a switch to a new system?

One critical component in developing and implementing the IT strategic plan is the **IT steering committee**. This committee, comprised of a group of managers and staff who represent the various organizational units, is created to establish IT priorities and to ensure that the MIS function is meeting the organization's needs. The committee's major tasks are to link corporate strategy with IT strategy, to approve the allocation of resources for the MIS function, and to establish performance measures for the MIS function and ensure that they are met. The IT steering committee is important to you because it ensures that you get the information systems and applications that you need to do your job.

After a company has agreed on an IT strategic plan, it next develops the **IS operational plan**. This plan consists of a clear set of projects that the IS department and the functional area managers will execute in support of the IT strategic plan. A typical IS operational plan contains the following elements:

- *Mission:* The mission of the IS function (derived from the IT strategy).
- *IS environment:* A summary of the information needs of the functional areas and of the organization as a whole
- *Objectives of the IS function:* The best current estimate of the goals of the IS function
- *Constraints on the IS function:* Technological, financial, personnel, and other resource limitations on the IS function
- *The application portfolio:* A prioritized inventory of present applications and a detailed plan of projects to be developed or continued during the current year
- *Resource allocation and project management:* A listing of how and when who is going to do what

Evaluating and Justifying IT Investment: Benefits, Costs, and Issues

Developing an IT plan is the first step in the acquisition process. Because all companies have limited resources, they must justify investing resources in some areas, including IT, rather than in others. Essentially, justifying IT investment involves calculating the costs, assessing the benefits (values), and comparing the two. This comparison is frequently referred to as cost-benefit analysis. Cost-benefit analysis is not a simple task.

Assessing the Costs. Placing a dollar value on the cost of IT investments is not as simple as it may seem. One of the major challenges that companies face is to allocate fixed costs among different IT projects. *Fixed costs* are those costs that remain the same regardless of any change in the activity level. For IT, fixed costs include infrastructure costs and the costs associated with IT services and IT management. For example, the salary of the IT director is fixed, and adding one more application will not change it.

Another complication is that the costs of a system do not end when the system is installed. Rather, costs for maintaining, debugging, and improving the system can accumulate over many years. This is a critical point because organizations sometimes fail to anticipate these costs when they make the investment.

A dramatic example of unanticipated expenses was the Year 2000 (Y2K) reprogramming projects, which cost organizations worldwide billions of dollars. In the 1960s, computer memory was very expensive. To save money, programmers coded the "year" in the date field 19_ _, instead of _ _ _ _. With the "1" and the "9" hard-coded in the computer program, only the last two digits varied, so computer programs needed less memory. However, this process meant that when the year 2000 rolled around, computers would display the year as 1900. This programming technique could have caused serious problems with financial applications, insurance applications, and countless other apps.

This Y2K example illustrates the point that database design choices tend to impact the organization for a long time. As the 21st century approached, no one still used hardware or software from the 1960s (other than a few legacy applications). Database design choices made in the 1960s, though, were often still in effect.

Assessing the Benefits. Evaluating the benefits of IT projects is typically even more complex than calculating their costs. Benefits may be harder to quantify, especially because many of them are intangible—for example, improved customer or partner relations or improved decision making. As an employee, you will probably be asked for input about the intangible benefits that an IS provides for you.

The fact that organizations use IT for multiple purposes further complicates benefit analysis. In addition, to obtain a return from an IT investment the company must implement the technology successfully. In reality, many systems are not implemented on time, within budget, or with all the features originally envisioned for them. Also, the proposed system may be "cutting edge." In these cases there may be no basis for identifying the types of financial payback the company can expect.

Conducting the Cost-Benefit Analysis. After a company has assessed the costs and benefits of IT investments, it must compare them. You have studied, or will study, cost-benefit analyses in more detail in your finance courses. The point is that real-world business problems do not come in neatly wrapped packages labeled "this is a finance problem" or "this is an IS problem." Rather, business problems span multiple functional areas.

There is no uniform strategy for conducting a cost-benefit analysis. Rather, an organization can perform this task in several ways. Here you see four common approaches: (1) net present value, (2) return on investment, (3) breakeven analysis, and (4) the business case approach.

- Analysts use the *net present value (NPV)* method to convert future values of benefits to their present-value equivalent

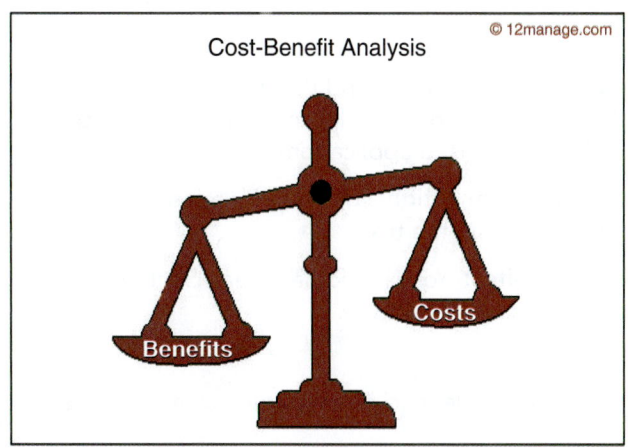

Cost-Benefit Analysis.

by "discounting" them at the organization's cost of funds. They can then compare the present value of the future benefits to the cost required to achieve those benefits to determine whether the benefits exceed the costs.

- *Return on investment (ROI)* measures management's effectiveness in generating profits with its available assets. ROI is calculated by dividing the net income generated by a project by the average assets invested in the project. ROI is a percentage, and the higher the percentage return, the better.
- *Breakeven analysis* determines the point at which the cumulative dollar value of the benefits from a project equals the investment made in the project.
- In the *business case approach*, system developers write a business case to justify funding one or more specific applications or projects. IS professionals will be a major source of input when business cases are developed because these cases describe what you do, how you do it, and how a new system could better support you.

BEFORE *YOU GO ON* . . .

1. What are some problems associated with assessing the costs of IT?
2. What difficulties accompany the intangible benefits from IT?
3. Describe the NPV, ROI, breakeven analysis, and business case approaches.

RUBY'S CLUB QUESTIONS

1. Based on what you have learned about Ruby's Club in this book, what do you think Ruben and Lisa's strategic plan is? Do you think they could accomplish their plan without the use of technology?

2. If the purpose of this system is to collect orders and serve as the transaction processing system (TPS) for their other information systems, what level of accuracy and reliability do you believe Ruben and Lisa need? At what point does a system failure become a problem to customers?

Student Activity | 14.1

Objective: To understand that there is a process that should be followed for evaluating/justifying technology-based applications.

Chapter Connection: This activity relates to Section 14.1 in the text.

Prerequisites: You should have read Section 14.1 before doing this activity.

Activity:

Read this article, and play careful attention to the example:

www.mindtools.com/pages/article/newTED_08.htm

On your own, work through the numbers for the cost-benefit analysis using Excel or on paper. Test the impact of the following (do each one separately):

- Lost time is actually 50 employee days, and the mail slot capacity only doubled.
- Lost sales through disruption tally at $30,000, and the ability to manage the sales efforts is only $20,000.
- Improved customer service and retention total $20,000.
- Improved efficiency of follow-up is $25,000.

14.2 | Strategies for Acquiring IT Applications

After a company has justified an IT investment, it must then decide how to pursue it. As with cost-benefit analyses, there are several options for acquiring IT applications. To decide on which option to choose, companies must make a series of business decisions. The fundamental decisions are these:

- *How much computer code does the company want to write?* A company can choose to use a totally prewritten application (to write no computer code), to customize a prewritten application (to write some computer code), or to custom-write an entire application (write all new computer code).

- *How will the company pay for the application?* Once the company has decided how much computer code to write, it must decide how to pay for it. With prewritten applications or customized prewritten applications, companies can buy them or lease them. With totally custom applications, companies use internal funding.

- *Where will the application run?* The next decision is whether to run the application on the company's platform or on someone else's platform. In other words, it can employ either a software-as-a-service vendor or an application service provider. (You will examine these options later in this chapter.)

- *Where will the application originate?* Prewritten applications can be open-source software, or they can come from a vendor. The company may choose to customize prewritten open-source applications or prewritten proprietary applications from vendors. Further, it may customize applications in-house or outsource the customization. Finally, it can write totally custom applications in-house or outsource this process.

In the following sections, you will find more detail on the variety of ways that companies can acquire applications. A good rule of thumb is that an organization should consider all feasible acquisition methods in light of its own business requirements.

Purchase a Prewritten Application

Many commercial software packages contain the standard features required by IT applications. Therefore, purchasing an existing package can be a cost-effective and time-saving strategy compared with custom-developing the application in-house. Nevertheless, a company should carefully consider and plan the buy option to ensure that the selected package contains all of the features necessary to address the company's current and future needs.

TABLE 14.1 Advantages and Limitations of the "Buy" Option

Advantages
Many different types of off-the-shelf software are available.
Software can be tried out.
The company can save much time by buying rather than building.
The company can know what it is getting before it invests in the product.
The company is not the first and only user.
Purchased software may eliminate the need to hire personnel specifically dedicated to a project.

Disadvantages
Software may not exactly meet the company's needs.
Software may be difficult or impossible to modify, or it may require huge business process changes to implement.
The company will not have control over software improvements and new versions.
Purchased software can be difficult to integrate with existing systems.
Vendors may discontinue a product or go out of business.
Software is controlled by another company with its own priorities and business considerations.
Intimate knowledge in the purchasing company is lacking about how and why the software works as it does.

Otherwise these packages can quickly become obsolete. Before a company can perform this process, it must decide which features a suitable package must include.

In reality, a single software package can rarely satisfy all of an organization's needs. For this reason a company sometimes must purchase multiple packages to fulfill different needs. It then must integrate these packages with one another as well as with its existing software. Table 14.1 summarizes the advantages and limitations of the buy option.

Customize a Prewritten Application

Customizing existing software is an especially attractive option if the software vendor allows the company to modify the application to meet its needs. However, this option may not be attractive in cases where customization is the only method of providing the necessary flexibility to address the company's needs. It also is not the best strategy when the software is either very expensive or is likely to become obsolete in a short time. Further, customizing a prewritten application can be extremely difficult, particularly for large, complex applications. "IT's About Business 14.1" recounts a disastrous effort by Marin County, California, to implement an SAP system.

IT's ABOUT BUSINESS | 14.1

A Disastrous Development Project

In 2004, Marin County in California decided to replace its aging financial management, payroll, and human resources systems with a modern SAP enterprise resource planning (ERP) system. The county solicited proposals from various companies to act as software consultants on the implementation. Thirteen companies, including Oracle, PeopleSoft, and SAP, submitted proposals. In April 2005 the county selected Deloitte Consulting based on the firm's representations concerning its in-depth knowledge of SAP systems and the extensive experience of its consultants.

From 2005 to 2009, Marin County paid increasing consulting fees to Deloitte as its staff grappled with serious fiscal problems. Essentially, the staff could not program the SAP system to perform even routine financial functions such as payroll and accounts receivable. A grand jury probe concluded that the system had cost taxpayers $28.6 million as of April 2009.

At that time, Marin County voted to stop the ongoing SAP project, implicitly acknowledging that it had wasted some $30 million on software and related implementation services from Deloitte. The Marin County Information Systems and Technology Group concluded that fixing the Deloitte-installed SAP system would cost nearly 25 percent more over a 10-year period than implementing a new system.

In 2010, Marin County filed a complaint claiming that Deloitte's representations were fraudulent. The complaint alleged that Deloitte used the county's SAP project as a training ground to provide young consultants with public sector SAP experience, at the county's expense. Further, the complaint charged that Deloitte intentionally failed to disclose its lack of SAP and public sector skills; withheld information about critical project risks; falsely represented to the county that the SAP system was ready to "go live" as originally planned; conducted inadequate testing; and concealed the fact that it had failed to perform necessary testing, thereby insuring that system defects would remain hidden prior to the go-live date. The county further maintained that, despite the consulting fees it had paid to Deloitte, the system continued to have crippling problems.

Deloitte filed a counterclaim over the county's failure to pay more than $550,000 in fees and interest. In its counterclaim, Deloitte maintained that it had fulfilled all of its obligations under the contract, as evidenced by the fact that all of Deloitte's work was approved by the county officials who were responsible for the project.

In December 2010, Marin County sued Deloitte and two SAP subsidiaries, alleging that Deloitte had "engaged in a pattern of racketeering activity designed to defraud the county of more than $20 million." The county's latest lawsuit also names as a defendant Ernest Culver, a former county employee who served as director on the SAP project. The county alleged that Culver interviewed for jobs at Deloitte and SAP, where he now works in SAP's Public Services division. The county alleges that during the SAP project, Culver "was approving Deloitte's deficient work on the project, approving payments, and causing Marin County to enter into new contracts with Deloitte and SAP Public Services, Inc."

As of mid-2011, the lawsuits were still pending in federal court.

Questions

1. Debate the lawsuit from the point of view of Deloitte and SAP.
2. Debate the lawsuit from the point of view of Marin County.

Sources: Compiled from C. Kanaracus, "Marin County Alleges SAP, Deloitte Engaged in Racketeering," *Computerworld*, February 2, 2011; M. Krigsman, "Understanding Marin County's $30 Million ERP Failure," *ZDNet*, September 2, 2010; C. Kanaracus, "Marin County to Rip and Replace Ailing SAP System," IDG News Service, August 24, 2010; M. Krigsman, "Marin County Sues Deloitte: Alleges Fraud on SAP Project," *ZDNet*, June 3, 2010; J. Vijayan, "Deloitte Hit with $30M Lawsuit over ERP Project," Computerworld, June 3, 2010; T. Claburn, "Deloitte Sued Over Failed SAP Implementation," *InformationWeek*, June 1, 2010; www.co.marin.ca.us, www.deloitte.com, accessed May 14, 2011.

Lease the Applications

Compared with the buy option and the option to develop applications in-house, the lease option can save a company both time and money. Of course, leased packages (like purchased packages) may not exactly fit the company's application requirements. However, as noted, vendor software generally includes the features that are most commonly needed by organizations in a given industry. Again, the company will decide which features are necessary.

It is common for interested companies to apply the 80/20 rule when evaluating vendor software. Put simply, if the software meets 80 percent of the company's needs, then the company should seriously consider changing its business processes so it can utilize the remaining 20 percent. Many times this is a better long-term solution than modifying the vendor software. Otherwise, the company will have to customize the software every time the vendor releases an updated version.

Leasing can be especially attractive to small to medium-size enterprises (SMEs) that cannot afford major investments in IT software. Large companies may also prefer to lease packages in order to test potential IT solutions before committing to major investments. Also, a company that does not employ sufficient IT personnel with the appropriate skills for developing custom IT applications may choose to lease instead of developing software in-house. Even those companies that employ in-house experts may not be able to afford the long wait for strategic applications to be developed in-house. Therefore, they lease (or buy) applications from external resources to establish a quicker presence in the market.

Leasing can be executed in one of three ways. The first way is to lease the application from a software developer and install and run it on the company's platform. The vendor can assist with the installation and frequently will offer to contract for the support and maintenance of the system. Many conventional applications are leased this way.

The other two options involve leasing an application and running it on the vendor's platform. Organizations can accomplish this process by using an application service provider or a software-as-a-service vendor.

Application Service Providers and Software-as-a-Service Vendors

An **application service provider (ASP)** is an agent or a vendor who assembles the software needed by enterprises and packages the software with services such as development, operations, and maintenance. The customer then accesses these applications via the Internet. Figure 14.3 illustrates the operation of an ASP. Note that the ASP hosts an application and a database for each customer.

Software-as-a-service (SaaS) is a method of delivering software in which a vendor hosts the applications and provides them as a service to customers over a network, typically the Internet. Customers do not own the software; rather, they pay for using it. SaaS eliminates the need for customers to install and run the application on their own computers. Therefore, SaaS customers save the expense (money, time, IT staff) of buying, operating, and maintaining the software. For example, Salesforce (www.salesforce.com), a well-known SaaS provider for customer relationship management (CRM) software solutions, provides

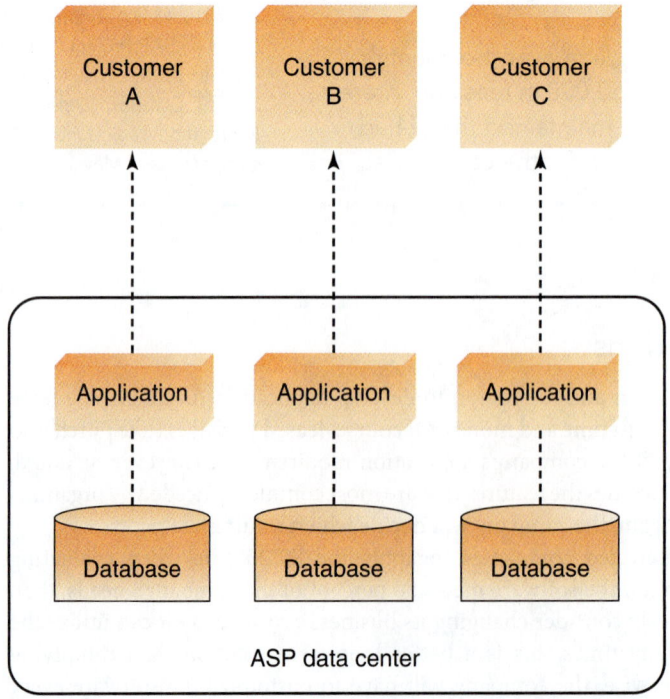

Figure 14.3 Operation of an application service provider (ASP).

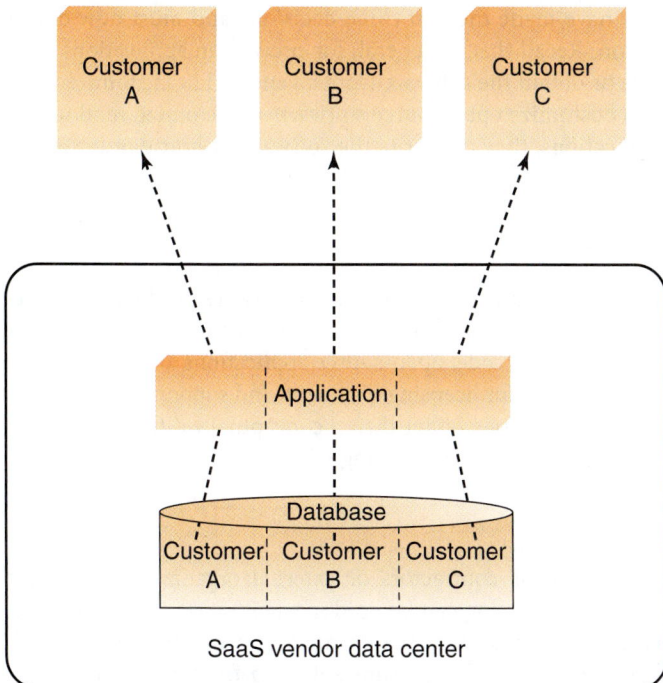

Figure 14.4 Organization of an SaaS provider.

these advantages for its customers. Figure 14.4 displays the operation of a SaaS vendor. Note that the vendor hosts an application that multiple customers can use. Further, the vendor hosts a database that is partitioned for each customer to protect the privacy and security of each customer's data.

Software-as-a-service can provide advantages to an organization. The next example illustrates how Bosley Medical Institute made effective use of SaaS.

EXAMPLE

Software-as-a-Service Helps Bosley

Hair restoration provider Bosley Medical Institute (www.bosley.com) wanted to consolidate applications, reduce maintenance costs, and centralize data for business intelligence. The company decided to outsource five different applications to five different SaaS vendors. Bosley outsourced its scheduling system to TimeTrade (www.timetrade.com); its address verification application to Acme Data (www.acmedata.net); its direct marketing application to Silverpop Systems (www.silverpop.com); its inbound call center system to inContact (www.incontact.com); and its outbound call center system to Five9 (www.five9.com).

By retiring five core applications and replacing them with SaaS applications, Bosley is saving 20 to 30 percent in maintenance fees per year. One of the retired core applications by itself was costing Bosley $20,000 per year.

Bosley's IT team integrated the information from the five SaaS applications into its own CRM system. This process addressed the company's need for centralized business intelligence.

Another benefit of the new arrangement is that Bosley has seen a marked improvement in its application uptime. The company experiences periodic power outages that disrupt inbound and outbound dialing. With its new SaaS systems, the company representatives can still make and receive calls by logging on from wherever they are located.

Sources: Compiled from C. Torode, "SaaS Applications Help Bosley Consolidate Apps, Cut Maintenance Costs," *SearchCIO.com*, January 13, 2010; www.bosley.com, accessed May 11, 2011.

At this point, companies have made the first three decisions and must now decide where to obtain the application. Recall that in general, for prewritten applications, they can use open-source software or obtain the software from a vendor. For customized prewritten applications, they can customize open-source software or customize vendor software. For totally custom applications, they can write the software in-house or outsource this process.

Use Open-Source Software

Organizations obtain a license to implement an open-source software product and either use it as is, customize it, or develop applications with it. Unless the company is one of the few that want to tinker with their source code, open-source applications are, basically, the same as a proprietary application except for licensing, payment, and support. Open-source is really an alternative source of applications rather than a conceptually different development option. (Open-source software is discussed in "Plug IT In 2.")

Outsourcing

Acquiring IT applications from outside contractors or external organizations is called **outsourcing**. Keep in mind that outsourcing can be used in many situations. Companies may choose this strategy in certain circumstances. For example, they might want to experiment with new IT technologies without making a substantial up-front investment. They also might use outsourcing to protect their internal networks and to gain access to outside experts. One disadvantage of outsourcing is that a company's valuable corporate data may be under the control of the outsourcing vendor. There are other disadvantages with outsourcing, as "IT's About Business 14.2" demonstrates.

IT's ABOUT BUSINESS | 14.2

The State of Virginia's Outsourcing Contract Proves Costly

The State of Virginia began searching for a private company to oversee its computer systems in 2003 after a legislative review revealed that the state's technology was out of date and increasingly expensive to maintain. Then-governor Mark Warner received approval to consolidate state computer operations into one agency and to overhaul the system to make it more efficient and less costly.

The state then placed an independent board—not the governor or the general assembly—in charge of the state's technology agency: the Virginia Information Technologies Agency, or VITA. A 16-member committee that included two VITA board members and other state officials selected Northrop Grumman to oversee Virginia's computer systems.

In 2005 the state signed a $2.4 billion, 10-year contract because state officials were convinced that outsourcing would provide the best value, despite Northrop Grumman's lack of experience managing state computer and communication systems. The contract called for Northrop to take over the operation and maintenance of Virginia's mainframe, server, desktop, and network operations, and to deploy new applications designed to modernize the delivery of numerous services to Virginia residents. The contract stated that early termination would cost the state as much as $400 million and would leave no one to manage the state's computer systems.

The original timetable called for Northrop Grumman to assume full control of the state's computer infrastructure by July 2009. However, the company missed numerous deadlines and fell far behind schedule.

A legislative audit revealed that the Northrop Grumman implementation was so troubled that core government services were disrupted. The problems affected almost every state agency that uses a computer. For example, a prison was left without inbound phone service for hours, the Virginia State Police in Newport News lost Internet access for more than 3 days, and computers in the Department of Motor Vehicles (DMV) offices crashed.

There were other problems. When the state received federal money to establish 17 temporary unemployment offices to help workers who lost jobs during the recession, the Virginia Economic Commission proposed opening the centers as quickly as possible. However, Northrop Grumman took so long to provide computer and phone services to the new offices that they did not open for 6 months. One county's DMV office lost network connections for 31 hours, forcing customers to reschedule appointments. In one large city, a Department of Environmental Quality office was without phones or computers for more than a day.

In July 2009, Virginia accused Northrop Grumman of failing to deliver computer services, and it charged the company with breach of contract. Further, the state demanded that Northrop submit a plan for ending the delays, some of which had lasted for 2 years.

After tedious negotiations and the election of a new governor, VITA and Northrop Grumman revised the outsourcing contract. Under the terms of the renegotiated contract, Northrop agreed to introduce a number of new customer service features and benefits that were designed to improve IT functions for all state agency customers. The revised contract extends the original contract for 3 years. The state incurred new costs of $105 million for the additional hardware and services.

That was not the end of the drama, however. On August 25, 2010, Virginia experienced an IT infrastructure outage that affected 27 of the state's 89 agencies and caused 13 percent of the state's servers to fail. Five days later, 24 of the 27 affected agencies were operational. However, 3 agencies remained dysfunctional: the Department of Motor Vehicles, the Department of Taxation, and the State Board of Elections. In particular, the DMV was heavily impacted by the IT outage and was unable to process in-person driver's licenses or ID cards at any of its customer service centers.

Many questions have been raised about the outsourcing contract between Virginia and Northrop Grumman in general, and about the latest outage in particular:

- Why have so many IT problems occurred in the state of Virginia?
- What caused these problems?
- Why would the state of Virginia agree to a contract with such a heavy penalty for termination?
- Why did Virginia sign an extension on the original contract and agree to pay more money to Northrop Grumman in the revised contract?
- Why was no disaster recovery plan in effect in the event of such an outage?
- Why were the state's critical databases not backed up properly?

As of mid-2011, most of these questions had not been thoroughly answered.

Questions

1. What are some reasons why Virginia's IT problems can be considered the result of poor state oversight of Northrop Grumman? What are some reasons, if any, why the state might not be overseeing Northrop effectively?

2. What are some reasons why Virginia's IT problems can be considered the result of poor execution by Northrop Grumman? What are some reasons, if any, why Northrop might be executing this project poorly?

Sources: L. Mearian, "Northrop Grumman Takes Blame for Virginia IT Services Outage," *Computerworld*, September 2, 2010; R. Helderman and A. Kumar, "Crash of Virginia Computer Network Has Implications for Tech World, State Politics," *Washington Post*, September 2, 2010; D. Kravitz, "No Timetable Set for Return of Virginia DMV Licensing Service," *Washington Post*, September 1, 2010; L. Dignan, "Virginia's IT Outage Doesn't Pass Management Sniff Test," *ZDNet*, August 30, 2010; The Governor of Virginia, "Virginia and Northrop Grumman Revise Information Technologies Contract," *The GovMonitor*, April 7, 2010; A. Kumar and R. Helderman, "Virginia Pays Dearly for Computer Troubles," *Washington Post*, October 14, 2009; P. McDougall, "Virginia Probes Outsourcing Deal, CIO Fired," *InformationWeek*, July 19, 2009; O. Meola and J. Schapiro, "State Accuses Northrop Grumman of Breach," *Richmond Times-Dispatch*, July 1, 2009; P. McDougall, "Virginia Taps Northrop Grumman for $2 Billion IT Overhaul," *InformationWeek*, November 15, 2005.

Several types of vendors offer services for creating and operating IT systems, including e-commerce applications. Many software companies, from IBM to Oracle, offer a range of outsourcing services for developing, operating, and maintaining IT applications. IT outsourcers, such as EDS, offer a variety of services. Also, the large CPA companies and management consultants—for example, Accenture—offer outsourcing services.

As the trend to outsource is on the rise, so is the trend to relocate these operations offshore, particularly in India and China. *Offshoring* can save money, but it includes risks as well. The risks depend on which services are being offshored. If a company is offshoring application development, then the major risk is poor communication between users and developers.

Custom Development

Companies may also decide to custom-build an application. They can either perform this operation in-house or outsource the process. Although custom development is usually more time consuming and costly than buying or leasing, it often results in a better fit with the organization's specific requirements.

The development process starts when the IT steering committee (discussed previously in this chapter), having received suggestions for a new system, decides it is worth exploring. These suggestions come from users (who will be you in the near future). Understanding this process will help you get the systems that you will need. Not understanding this process will reduce your chances, because other people who understand it better will make suggestions that use up available resources.

As the company goes through the development process, the mind-set changes. In systems investigation, the organization is trying to decide whether to build something. Everyone knows it may or may not be built. In later stages of the development process, the organization is committed to building the application. Although a project can be cancelled at any time, this change in attitude is still important.

The basic, backbone methodology for custom development is the systems development life cycle (SDLC), which you will read about in the next section. Section 14.4 examines the methodologies that complement the SDLC: prototyping, joint application development, integrated computer-assisted systems development tools, and rapid application development. You will also consider four other methodologies: agile development, end-user development, component-based development, and object-oriented development.

• BEFORE *YOU GO ON . . .*

1. Describe the four fundamental business decisions that organizations must make when acquiring information systems.
2. Discuss each of the seven development methods in this section with regard to the four business decisions that organizations must make.

RUBY'S CLUB QUESTIONS

1. Based on what you have learned about Ruby's in this book, what do you think the club's strategic plan is? Do you think Ruben and Lisa could accomplish their plan without the use of technology?
2. If the purpose of this system is to collect orders and serve as the transaction processing system (TPS) for Ruby's other information systems, what level of accuracy and reliability do you believe is needed? At what point does a system failure become a problem to customers?

Student Activity | 14.2

Objective: To understand that there are options for "acquiring" technology applications.

Chapter Connection: This activity relates to Section 14.2 in the text.

Prerequisites: You should have read Sections 14.1 and 14.2 before doing this activity.

Activity:

View these two videos on software-as-a-service:

www.youtube.com/watch?v=kGUPSvswmY0&feature=related

www.youtube.com/watch?v=EXS0BFS6QT4&feature=related

Go to www.google.com/intl/en/options, *then click on "Docs" in the right column. This is an SaaS for creating documents, etc. Create a document and an Excel spreadsheet (be creative). Save them. Close the window. Now navigate back to Google Docs. You should see your files.*

Deliverables:

Write a short paper that addresses the following questions about Google Docs:

1. Where is the software used to create your files? Who controls it?

2. Where are the files you created? Who controls that area?

3. What are the benefits of using Google Docs? What are the limitations?

Quiz Questions:

1. True or False? When an organization uses SaaS, its data are on its own servers.

2. True or False? When a vendor delivering SaaS applications updates an application, the customers using the applications have to reboot their machines to access the updates.

3. True or False? SaaS applications are usually accessed over the Internet.

Discussion Questions:

1. How private are your data in SaaS?

2. What does an SaaS company do to maintain privacy?

14.3 | The Traditional Systems Development Life Cycle

The **systems development life cycle (SDLC)** is the traditional systems development method that organizations use for large-scale IT projects. The SDLC is a structured framework that consists of sequential processes by which information systems are developed. For our purposes (see Figure 14.5) you identify six processes, each of which consists of clearly defined tasks:

- Systems investigation
- Systems analysis
- Systems design
- Programming and testing
- Implementation
- Operation and maintenance

Other models for the SDLC contain more or fewer than the six stages presented here. The flow of tasks, however, remains largely the same. When problems occur in any phase of the SDLC, developers often must go back to previous phases.

Systems development projects produce desired results through team efforts. Development teams typically include users, systems analysts, programmers, and technical

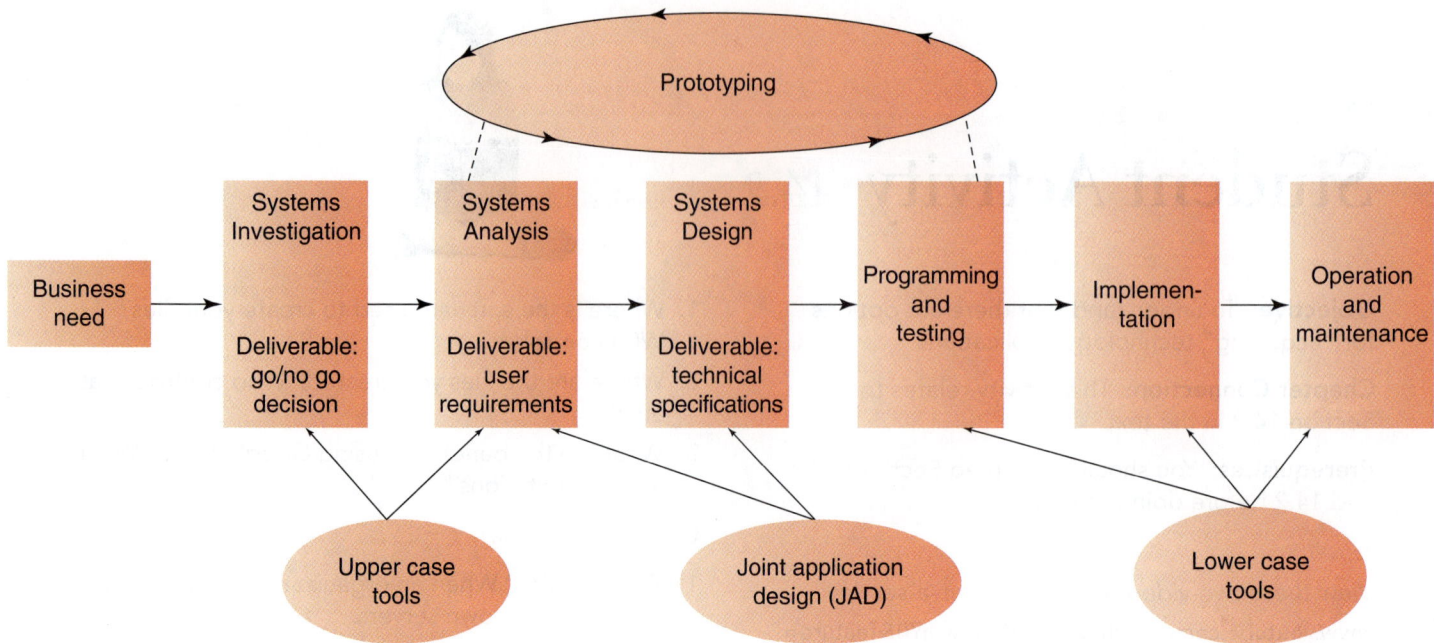

Figure 14.5 A six-stage systems development life cycle (SDLC) with supporting tools.

 specialists. *Users* are employees from all functional areas and levels of the organization who interact with the system, either directly or indirectly. **Systems analysts** are IS professionals who specialize in analyzing and designing information systems. **Programmers** are IS professionals who either modify existing computer programs or write new programs to satisfy user requirements. **Technical specialists** are experts on a certain type of technology, such as databases or telecommunications. The **systems stakeholders** include everyone who is affected by changes in a company's information systems—for example, users and managers. All stakeholders are typically involved in systems development at various times and in varying degrees. Figure 14.6 indicates that users have high involvement in the early stages of the SDLC, lower involvement in the programming and testing stage, and higher involvement in the later stages. Table 14.2 discusses the advantages and disadvantages of the SDLC.

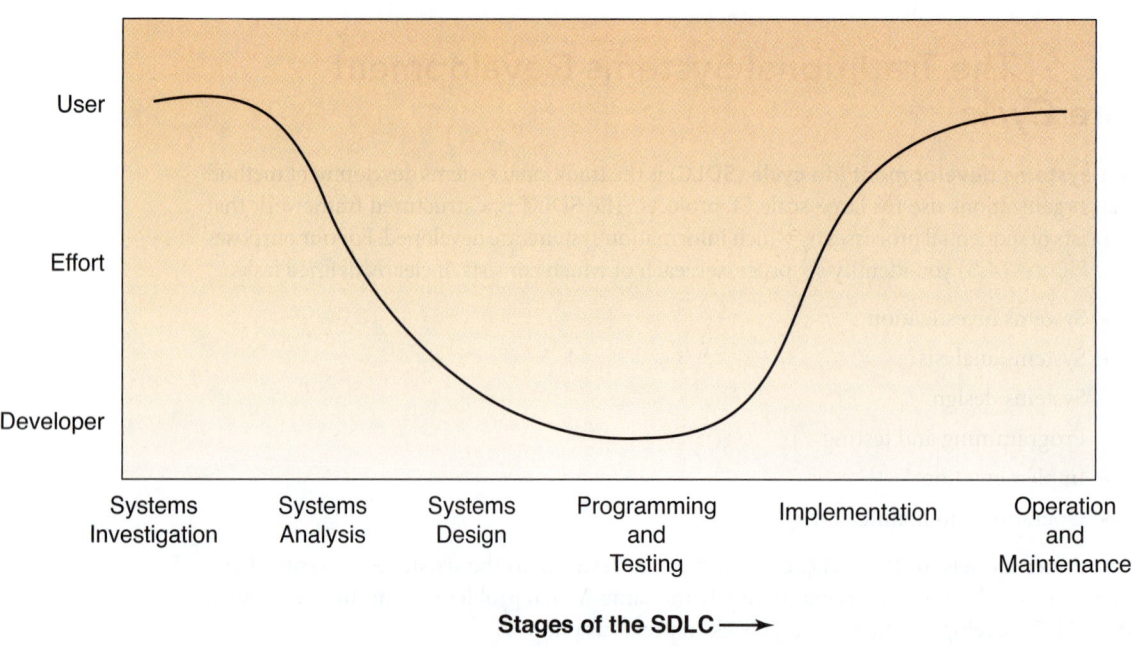

Figure 14.6 Comparison of user and developer involvement over the SDLC.

TABLE 14.2 Advantages and Disadvantages of System Acquisition Methods

Traditional Systems Development (SDLC)

Advantages

- Forces staff to systematically go through every step in a structured process.
- Enforces quality by maintaining standards.
- Has lower probability of missing important issues in collecting user requirements.

Disadvantages

- May produce excessive documentation.
- Users may be unwilling or unable to study the approved specifications.
- Takes too long to go from the original ideas to a working system.
- Users have trouble describing requirements for a proposed system.

Prototyping

Advantages

- Helps clarify user requirements.
- Helps verify the feasibility of the design.
- Promotes genuine user participation.
- Promotes close working relationship between systems developers and users.
- Works well for ill-defined problems.
- May produce part of the final system.

Disadvantages

- May encourage inadequate problem analysis.
- Not practical with large number of users.
- User may not give up the prototype when the system is completed.
- May generate confusion about whether the system is complete and maintainable.
- System may be built quickly, which may result in lower quality.

Joint Application Design

Advantages

- Involves many users in the development process.
- Saves time.
- Greater user support for new system.
- Improved quality of the new system.
- New system easier to implement.
- New system has lower training costs.

Disadvantages

- Difficult to get all users to attend JAD meeting.
- JAD approach has all the problems associated with any group meeting.

Integrated Computer-Assisted Software Engineering

Advantages

- Can produce systems with a longer effective operational life.
- Can produce systems that closely meet user requirements.
- Can speed up the development process.
- Can produce systems that are more flexible and adaptable to changing business conditions.
- Can produce excellent documentation.

Disadvantages

- Systems often more expensive to build and maintain.
- Require more extensive and accurate definition of user requirements.
- Difficult to customize.

TABLE 14.2 (Continued)

Rapid Application Development

Advantages

- Can speed up systems development.
- Users intensively involved from the start.
- Improves the process of rewriting legacy applications.

Disadvantages

- Produces functional components of final systems, but not final systems.

End-User Development

Advantages

- Bypasses the IS department and avoids delays.
- User controls the application and can change it as needed.
- Directly meets user requirements.
- Increased user acceptance of new system.
- Frees up IT resources.
- May create lower-quality systems.

Disadvantages

- May eventually require maintenance from IS department.
- Documentation may be inadequate.
- Poor quality control.
- System may not have adequate interfaces to existing systems.

Object-Oriented Development

Advantages

- Objects model real-world entities.
- May be able to reuse some computer code.

Disadvantages

- Works best with systems of more limited scope (i.e., with systems that do not have huge numbers of objects).

Systems Investigation

The initial stage in a traditional SDLC is systems investigation. Systems development professionals agree that the more time they invest in (1) understanding the business problem to be solved, (2) specifying the technical options for the systems, and (3) anticipating the problems they are likely to encounter during development, the greater the chances of success. For these reasons, systems investigation addresses *the business problem* (or business opportunity) by means of the feasibility study.

The main task in the systems investigation stage is the feasibility study. Organizations have three basic solutions to any business problem relating to an information system: (1) do nothing and continue to use the existing system unchanged, (2) modify or enhance the existing system, and (3) develop a new system. The **feasibility study** analyzes which of these three solutions best fits the particular business problem. It also provides a rough assessment of the project's technical, economic, and behavioral feasibility, as explained below.

- *Technical feasibility* determines whether the company can develop and/or acquire the hardware, software, and communications components needed to solve the business

502   14 | Acquiring Information Systems and Applications problem. Technical feasibility also determines whether the organization can use its existing technology to achieve the project's performance objectives.

- *Economic feasibility* determines whether the project is an acceptable financial risk and, if so, whether the organization has the necessary time and money to successfully complete the project. You have already learned about the commonly used methods to determine economic feasibility: NPV, ROI, breakeven analysis, and the business case approach.

- *Behavioral feasibility* addresses the human issues of the systems development project. Clearly, you will be heavily involved in this aspect of the feasibility study.

After the feasibility analysis is completed, a "go/no-go" decision is reached by the steering committee if there is one, or by top management in the absence of a committee. The go/no go decision does not depend solely on the feasibility analysis. Organizations often have more feasible projects than they can fund. Therefore, the firm must prioritize the feasible projects and pursue those with the highest priority. Unfunded feasible projects may not be presented to the IT department at all. These projects therefore contribute to the *hidden backlog*, which are projects that the IT department is not aware of.

If the decision is no-go, then the project either is put on the shelf until conditions are more favorable or is discarded. If the decision is go, then the project proceeds, and the systems analysis phase begins.

Systems Analysis

Once a development project has the necessary approvals from all participants, the systems analysis stage begins. **Systems analysis** is the examination of the business problem that the organization plans to solve with an information system.

The main purpose of the systems analysis stage is to gather information about the existing system in order to determine the requirements for an enhanced system or a new system. The end product of this stage, known as the *deliverable*, is a set of *system requirements*.

Arguably the most difficult task in systems analysis is to identify the specific requirements that the system must satisfy. These requirements are often called *user requirements*, because users (meaning you) provide them. When the systems developers have accumulated the user requirements for the new system, they proceed to the systems design stage.

Systems Design

Systems design describes how the system will resolve the business problem. The deliverable of the systems design phase is the set of *technical system specifications*, which specifies the following:

- System outputs, inputs, and user interfaces
- Hardware, software, databases, telecommunications, personnel, and procedures
- A blueprint of how these components are integrated

When the system specifications are approved by all participants, they are "frozen." That is, they should not be changed. Adding functions after the project has been initiated causes **scope creep**, which endangers the project's budget and schedule. Because scope creep is expensive, successful project managers place controls on changes requested by users. These controls help to prevent runaway projects.

Programming and Testing

If the organization decides to construct the software in-house, then programming begins. **Programming** involves translating the design specifications into computer code. This process can be lengthy and time consuming, because writing computer code is as much an art as a science. Large systems development projects can require hundreds of thousands of lines of computer code and hundreds of computer programmers. These large-scale projects employ programming teams. The teams often include functional area users, who help the programmers focus on the business problem.

Thorough and continuous testing occurs throughout the programming stage. Testing is the process that checks to see if the computer code will produce the expected and desired results. It is also intended to detect errors, or bugs, in the computer code.

Implementation

Implementation (or *deployment*) is the process of converting from an old computer system to a new one. The conversion process involves organizational change. Only end users can manage organizational change, not the MIS department. The MIS department typically does not have enough credibility with the business users to manage the change process. Organizations use three major conversion strategies: direct, pilot, and phased.

In a **direct conversion**, the old system is cut off and the new system is turned on at a certain point in time. This type of conversion is the least expensive. It is also the most risky because, if the new system does not work as planned, there is no support from the old system. Because of these risks, few systems are implemented using direct conversion.

A **pilot conversion** introduces the new system in one part of the organization, such as in one plant or one functional area. The new system runs for a period of time and is then assessed. If the assessment confirms that the system is working properly, then the system is implemented in other parts of the organization.

A **phased conversion** introduces components of the new system, such as individual modules, in stages. Each module is assessed. If it works properly, then other modules are introduced, until the entire new system is operational. Large organizations commonly combine the pilot and phased approaches. That is, they execute a phased conversion using a pilot group for each phase.

A fourth strategy is *parallel conversion*, in which the old and new systems operate simultaneously for a time. This strategy is seldom used today. One reason is that parallel conversion is totally impractical when both the old and new systems are online. Imagine that you are finishing an order on Amazon, only to be told, "Before your order can be entered here, you must provide all the same information again, in a different form, and on a different set of screens." The results would be disastrous for Amazon.

Operation and Maintenance

After the new system is implemented, it will operate for a period of time, until (like the old system it replaced) it no longer meets its objectives. Once the new system's operations are stabilized, the company performs audits to assess the system's capabilities and to determine if it is being utilized correctly.

Systems require several types of maintenance. The first type is *debugging* the program, a process that continues throughout the life of the system. The second type is *updating* the system to accommodate changes in business conditions. An example is adjusting to new governmental regulations, such as changes in tax rates. These corrections and upgrades usually do not add any new functions. Instead, they simply help the system to continue meeting its objectives. In contrast, the third type of maintenance *adds new functions* to the existing system without disturbing its operation.

BEFORE YOU GO ON . . .

1. Define *feasibility study*.
2. What is the difference between systems analysis and systems design?
3. Describe structured programming.
4. What are the four conversion methods?

1. Have Ruben and Lisa already engaged in any stages of the SDLC?
2. Do you think there is enough time to devote to this type of system development?
3. Who should Ruben and Lisa include in their behavioral feasibility analysis? Does anyone outside of Ruby's employment need special consideration?

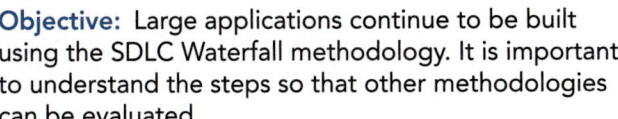

Student Activity 14.3

Objective: Large applications continue to be built using the SDLC Waterfall methodology. It is important to understand the steps so that other methodologies can be evaluated.

Chapter Connection: This activity relates to Section 14.3 of this chapter.

Prerequisites: You should have read Sections 14.2 and 14.3 before doing this activity.

Activity:

View the following links on use cases as a way to illustrate user requirements.

www.wilsonmar.com/1usecase.htm

www.youtube.com/watch?v=SmcBTsPsbIY

Deliverables:

Draw a use case for a payroll system.

Quiz Questions

1. True or False? In a use case, a primary actor is one from whom the systems needs assistance to satisfy a goal.
2. True or False? In a use case diagram, a circle/ellipse indicates data.
3. True or False? In a use case diagram, a solid line between actors and use cases is called an association.

Discussion Questions:

1. Who should develop the use case? Who decides whether it is right or not?
2. What would the next step(s) be after the use case is done?

14.4 | Alternative Methods and Tools for Systems Development

Alternative methods for systems development include joint application design, rapid application development, agile development, and end-user development.

Joint Application Design

Joint application design (JAD) is a group-based tool for collecting user requirements and creating system designs. It is most often used within the systems analysis and systems design stages of the SDLC. JAD involves a group meeting attended by the analysts and all of the users. It is basically a group decision-making process that can be conducted manually or via the computer. During this meeting, all users jointly define and agree on the systems requirements. This process saves a tremendous amount of time. Table 14.2 lists the advantages and disadvantages of the JAD process.

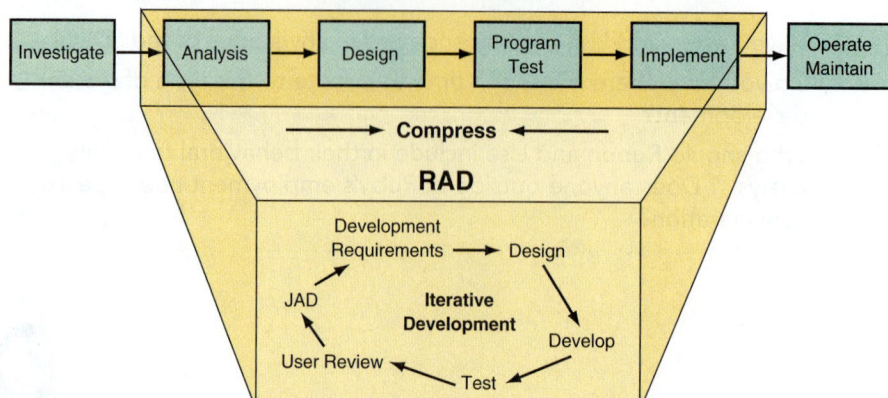

Traditional Development

Investigate → Analysis → Design → Program Test → Implement → Operate Maintain

→ **Compress** ←

RAD

Development Requirements → Design

JAD   **Iterative Development**

User Review   Test   Develop

Figure 14.7 A rapid prototyping development process versus SDLC. (*Source: datawarehouse-training.com/Methodologies/rapid-application-development.*)

Rapid Application Development

Rapid application development (RAD) is a systems development method that can combine JAD, prototyping, and ICASE tools (discussed later in this section) to rapidly produce a high-quality system. In the first RAD stage, developers use JAD sessions to collect system requirements. This strategy ensures that users are intensively involved early on. The development process in RAD is iterative, similar to prototyping. That is, requirements, designs, and the system itself are developed and then undergo a series, or sequence, of improvements. RAD uses ICASE tools to quickly structure requirements and develop prototypes. As the prototypes are developed and refined, users review them in additional JAD sessions. RAD produces the functional components of a final system, rather than prototypes. To understand how RAD functions and how it differs from SDLC, see Figure 14.7. Table 14.2 highlights the advantages and disadvantages of the RAD process.

Agile Development

Agile development is a software development methodology that delivers functionality in rapid iterations, which are usually measured in weeks. To be successful, this methodology requires frequent communication, development, testing, and delivery. Agile development focuses on rapid development and frequent user contact to create software that addresses the needs of business users. This software does not have to include every possible feature the user will require. Rather, it must meet only the user's more important and immediate needs. It can be updated later to introduce additional functions as they become necessary. The core tenet of agile development is to do only what you have to do to be successful right now.

One type of agile development uses the *scrum approach*. A key principle of scrum is that during a project users can change their minds about what they want and need. Scrum acknowledges that a development problem cannot be fully understood or defined from the start. Therefore, scrum focuses on maximizing the development team's ability to deliver iterations quickly and to respond effectively to additional user requirements as they emerge.

Scrum contains sets of practices and predefined roles. The primary roles are these:

- The *Scrum Master*: maintains the processes (typically replaces a project manager)
- The *Product Owner*: represents the business users and any other stakeholders in the project
- The *Team*: a cross-functional group of about seven people who perform the actual analysis, design, coding, implementation, testing, and so on.

Scrum works this way: During each sprint—typically a 2- to 4-week period—the team creates a potentially shippable product increment, such as working and tested software. The set of features that goes into each sprint come from the product backlog, which is a prioritized set of high-level work requirements to be completed.

The sprint planning meeting determines which backlog items will be addressed during a sprint. During this meeting, the Product Owner informs the team of the items in the product backlog that he or she wants completed. The team members then determine how many of these projects they can commit to during the next sprint, and they record this information in the sprint backlog.

During a sprint, no one is allowed to change the sprint backlog, which means that the requirements are frozen for the sprint. Each sprint must end on time. If the requirements are not completed for any reason, they are left out and returned to the product backlog. After each sprint is completed, the team demonstrates how to use the software.

End-User Development

End-user development is an approach in which the organization's end users develop their own applications with little or no formal assistance from the IT department. Table 14.2 lists the advantages and disadvantages of end-user development.

Tools for Systems Development

Several tools can be used with various systems development methods. These tools include prototyping, integrated computer-assisted software engineering (ICASE), component-based development, and object-oriented development.

Prototyping. The **prototyping** approach defines an initial list of user requirements, builds a model of the system, and then refines the system in several iterations based on users' feedback. Developers do not try to obtain a complete set of user specifications for the system at the outset, and they do not plan to develop the system all at once. Instead, they quickly develop a smaller version of the system known as a **prototype**. A prototype can take two forms. In some cases it contains only the components of the new system that are of most interest to the users. In other cases it is a small-scale working model of the entire system.

Users make suggestions for improving the prototype, based on their experiences with it. The developers then review the prototype with the users and use their suggestions to refine the prototype. This process continues through several iterations until the users approve the system or it becomes apparent that the system cannot meet the users' needs. If the system is viable, then the developers can use the prototype to build the full system. One typical use of prototyping is to develop screens that a user will see and interact with. Table 14.2 describes the advantages and disadvantages of the prototyping approach.

A practical problem with prototyping is that a prototype usually looks more complete than it is. It may not use the real database, it usually does not have the necessary error check-ing, and it almost never includes the necessary security features. Users who review a proto-type that resembles the finished system may not recognize these problems. Consequently, they might have unrealistic expectations about how close the actual system is to completion.

Integrated Computer-Assisted Software Engineering Tools. Computer-aided **software engineering (CASE)** is a group of tools that automate many of the tasks in the SDLC. The tools that are used to automate the early stages of the SDLC (systems investigation, analysis, and design) are called upper CASE tools. The tools used to automate later stages in the SDLC (programming, testing, operation, and maintenance) are called lower CASE tools. CASE tools that provide links between upper CASE and lower CASE tools are called **integrated CASE (ICASE) tools**. Table 14.2 lists the advantages and disadvantages of ICASE tools.

Component-Based Development. **Component-based development** uses stan-dard components to build applications. Components are reusable applications that gener-ally have one specific function, such as a shopping cart, user authentication, or a catalog. Component-based development is closely linked with the idea of Web services and service-oriented architectures, which you see in "Plug IT In 3."

Many startup companies are pursuing the idea of component-based application develop-ment, or less programming and more assembly. An example of these companies is Ning (www. ning.com), which allows organizations to create, customize, and share their own social network.

Object-Oriented Development. **Object-oriented development** is based on a differ-ent view of computer systems than the perception that characterizes traditional develop-ment approaches. Traditional approaches can produce a system that performs the original task but may not be suited for handling other tasks. This observation applies even when these other tasks involve the same real-world entities. For example, a billing system will handle billing but probably cannot be adapted to handle mailings for the marketing department or to generate leads for the sales force. This is true even though the billing, marketing, and sales functions all use similar data, including customer names, addresses, and purchases. In contrast, an *object-oriented (OO) system* begins not with the task to be performed but with the aspects of the real world that must be modeled to perform that task. Therefore, in our example, if the firm has a good model of its customers and its interactions with them, then it can use this model equally well for billings, mailings, and sales leads.

The development process for an object-oriented system begins with a feasibility study and an analysis of the existing system. Systems developers identify the *objects* in the new system—the fundamental elements in OO analysis and design. Each object represents a tangible, real-world entity, such as a customer, bank account, student, or course. Objects have *properties*, or *data values*. For example, a customer has an identification number, a name, an address, an account number(s), and so on. Objects also contain the *operations* that can be performed on their properties. For example, operations that can be performed on the customer object may include obtain-account-balance, open-account, withdraw-funds, and so on. Operations are also referred to as *behaviors*.

This approach enables OO analysts to define all the relevant objects needed for the new system, including their properties and operations. The analysts then model how the objects interact to meet the objectives of the new system. In some cases, analysts can reuse existing objects from other applications (or from a library of objects) in the new system. This process saves the analysts the time they otherwise would spend coding these objects. In most cases, however, even with object reuse, some coding will be necessary to customize the objects and their interactions for the new system.

You have studied many methods that can be used to acquire new systems. Table 14.2 provides an overview of the advantages and disadvantages of these methods.

•BEFORE YOU GO ON . . .

1. Describe the tools that augment the traditional SDLC.
2. Describe the alternate methods that can be used for systems development, other than the SDLC.

RUBY'S CLUB QUESTIONS

1. Do any of the prototyping methods of development seem to fit well within Ruben and Lisa's needs?
2. After reviewing Table 14.2, which method do you feel is most suited to the needs of this mobile ordering system?

Student Activity 14.4

Objective: You are likely to be members of a team defining user requirements in your business careers. This exercise illustrates how your involvement in the two major alternatives will be different.

Chapter Connection: This activity relates to Section 14.4 in the text.

Prerequisites: You should have read Sections 14.2, 14.3, and 14.4 before doing this activity.

Activity:

Watch the following video on prototyping development:

http://vimeo.com/9421730

Deliverables:

In groups of two, go to one of the sites in the Problem-Solving Activities 3 at the end of the chapter, and build a payroll application. As a deliverable (as well as the application), develop a presentation based on how the experience followed the SDLC and other methods.

Quiz Questions:

1. True or False? Prototyping development depends on time blocks and communication within the team.

2. True or False? One of the approaches for development is throwaway.

3. True or False? Prototyping allows builds a fully-functioning application.

4. True or False? In prototyping, fidelity is the level of details about the data.

5. Which of the following is **not** a benefit of prototyping?
   (a) Reduces cost and risk
   (b) Improves communication
   (c) Facilitates usability testing
   (d) Is fast but expensive
   (e) Can be done by non-developers

Discussion Questions:

1. Expect that the versions built by each group will be different. Discuss why that would be.

2. What kinds of applications lend themselves to a prototyping approach?

3. Based on this textbook, how does prototyping compare to agile development? How are they the same, how are they different?

14.5 | Vendor and Software Selection

Few organizations, especially small to medium-size enterprises, have the time, financial resources, or technical expertise required to develop today's complex IT or e-business systems. As a result, business firms increasingly rely on outside vendors to provide software, hardware, and technical expertise. Consequently, selecting and managing these vendors and their software offerings has become a major aspect of developing an IT application. The following six steps in selecting a software vendor and an application package are useful.

Step 1: Identify Potential Vendors. Companies can identify potential software application vendors through various sources:

- Software catalogs
- Lists provided by hardware vendors
- Technical and trade journals
- Consultants and industry analysts experienced in the application area
- Peers in other companies
- Web searches

These sources often yield so many vendors and packages that the company must use some evaluation criteria to eliminate all but the most promising ones from further consideration. For example, it can eliminate vendors that are too small or have a questionable reputation. Also, it can eliminate packages that do not have the required features or are not compatible with the company's existing hardware and/or software.

Step 2: Determine the Evaluation Criteria. The most difficult and crucial task in evaluating a vendor and a software package is to select a detailed set of evaluation criteria. Some areas in which a customer should develop detailed criteria are these:

- Characteristics of the vendor
- Functional requirements of the system
- Technical requirements that the software must satisfy
- Amount and quality of documentation provided
- Vendor support of the package

These criteria should be set out in a **request for proposal (RFP)**. An RFP is a document that is sent to potential vendors inviting them to submit a proposal that describes their software package and explains how it would meet the company's needs. The RFP provides the vendors with information about the objectives and requirements of the system. Specifically, it describes the environment in which the system will be used, the general criteria that the company will use to evaluate the proposals, and the conditions for submitting proposals. The RFP may also request a list of current users of the package whom the company may contact. Finally, it can require the vendor to demonstrate the package at the company's facilities using specified inputs and data files.

Step 3: Evaluate Vendors and Packages. The responses to an RFP generate massive volumes of information that the company must evaluate. The goal of this evaluation is to determine the gaps between the company's needs (as specified by the requirements) and the capabilities of the vendors and their application packages. Often, the company gives the vendors and packages an overall score by (1) assigning an importance weight to each of the criteria, (2) ranking the vendors on each of the weighted criteria (say 1 to 10), and then (3) multiplying the ranks by the associated weights. The company can then shorten the list of potential suppliers to include only those vendors who achieved the highest overall scores.

Step 4: Choose the Vendor and Package. Once the company has shortened the list of potential suppliers, it can begin negotiations with these vendors to determine how their packages might be modified to remove any discrepancies with the company's IT needs. Thus, one of the most important factors in the decision is the additional development effort that may be required to tailor the system to the company's needs or to integrate it into the company's computing environment. The company must also consider the opinions of both the users and the IT personnel who will have to support the system.

Several methods are commonly used for selecting software. For a list of general criteria, see Table 14.3.

Step 5: Negotiate a Contract. The contract with the software vendor is very important. It specifies both the price of the software and the type and amount of support that the vendor agrees to provide. The contract will be the only recourse if either the system or the vendor does not perform as expected. It is essential, then, that the contract directly reference the proposal, because this is the vehicle that the vendor used to document the

TABLE 14.3 Criteria for Selecting a Software Application Package

Functionality (Does the package do what the organization needs?)
Cost and financial terms
Upgrade policy and cost
Vendor's reputation and availability for help
Vendor's success stories (Visit the vendor's Web site, contact clients.)
System flexibility
Ease of Internet interface
Availability and quality of documentation
Necessary hardware and networking resources
Required training (check if provided by vendor)
Security
Learning (speed of) for developers and users
Graphical presentation
Data handling
System-required hardware

functionality supported in its system. Furthermore, if the vendor is modifying the software to tailor it to the company's needs, the contract must include detailed specifications (essentially the requirements) of the modifications. Finally, the contract should describe in detail the acceptance tests that the software package must pass.

Contracts are legal documents, and they can be quite tricky. For this reason, companies might need the services of experienced contract negotiators and lawyers. Many organizations employ software-purchasing specialists who assist in negotiations and write or approve the contract. These specialists should be involved in the selection process from the start.

Step 6: Establish a Service-Level Agreement. Service-level agreements (SLAs) are formal agreements that specify how work is to be divided between the company and its vendors. These specifications are based on a set of agreed-upon milestones, quality checks, and what-if situations. They describe how quality checks will be made and what is to be done in case of disputes. SLAs accomplish these goals by (1) defining the responsibilities of both partners, (2) providing a framework for designing support services, and (3) allowing the company to retain as much control as possible over its own systems. SLAs include such issues as performance, availability, backup and recovery, upgrades, and hardware and software ownership. For example, the SLA might specify that the application service provider have its system available to the customer 99.9 percent of the time.

BEFORE *YOU GO ON* . . .

1. List the major steps of selection of a vendor and a software package.
2. Describe a request for proposal (RFP).
3. Explain why SLAs play an important role in systems development.

RUBY'S CLUB QUESTIONS

1. What information would Ruben and Lisa need to include in an RFP?
2. Search the web for SLAs and see if you can find some key words that Ruben and Lisa will need to include in their document.

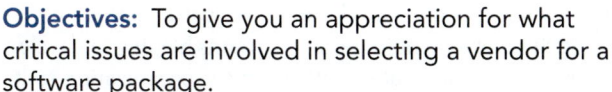

Student Activity 14.5

Objectives: To give you an appreciation for what critical issues are involved in selecting a vendor for a software package.

Chapter Connection: This activity relates to Section 14.5 in the text.

Prerequisites: You should have read Sections 14.3, 14.4, and 14.5 before doing this activity.

Activity:

View the following video, which addresses choosing the right ERP vendor. Not all software selection processes are as complex as this one:

www.youtube.com/watch?v=BCucG-1jUBY

Read the articles on vendor selection these Web pages:

www.softwareprojects.org/software-selection-criteria5.htm

www.softwareprojects.org/software-selection-vendors6.htm

Read about SLAs at these Web pages:

www.networkworld.com/newsletters/nsm/2001/01083536.html

www.clarity-consulting.com/metrics_article.htm

Deliverables:

Assume you are going to purchase a payroll package for your multi-location company of 2,500 employees. Write a short paper that addresses the following questions:

- What criteria would you use to evaluate the three vendors that submitted proposals?

- What goals would you spell out in your SLAs?
- What service-level metrics would you include in your SLAs?

Quiz Questions:

1. True or False? SLA agreements only protect the customer.
2. Possible SLA metrics do not include:
   (a) Availability
   (b) Satisfaction with customer service
   (c) Backup and recovery
   (d) Performance
   (e) Upgrades

Discussion Questions:

1. What services does Panorama Consulting provide for its clients?
2. Why is Panorama Consulting's vendor independence important?
3. What else should the SLAs include (what if, consequences, review)?

What's in IT for ME?

FOR THE ACCOUNTING MAJOR

Accounting personnel help perform the cost-benefit analyses on proposed projects. They may also monitor ongoing project costs to keep them within budget. Accounting personnel undoubtedly will find themselves involved with systems development at various points throughout their careers.

FOR THE FINANCE MAJOR

Finance personnel are frequently involved with the financial issues that accompany any large-scale systems development project (for example, budgeting). They also are involved in cost-benefit and risk analyses. To perform these tasks they need to stay abreast of the emerging techniques used to determine project costs and ROI. Finally, because they must manage vast amounts of information, finance departments are also common recipients of new systems.

FOR THE MARKETING MAJOR

In most organizations, marketing, like finance, involves massive amounts of data and information. Like finance, then, marketing is also a hotbed of systems development. Marketing personnel will increasingly find themselves participating on systems development teams. Such involvement increasingly means helping to develop systems, especially Web-based systems that reach out directly from the organization to its customers.

FOR THE PRODUCTION/OPERATIONS MANAGEMENT MAJOR

Participation on development teams is also a common role for production/operations people. Manufacturing is becoming increasingly computerized and integrated with other allied systems, from design to logistics to customer support. Production systems interface frequently with marketing, finance, and human resources. In addition, they may be part of a larger, enterprisewide system. Also, many end users in POM either develop their own systems or collaborate with IT personnel on specific applications.

FOR THE
HUMAN RESOURCES MANAGEMENT MAJOR

The human resources department is closely involved with several aspects of the systems acquisitions process. Acquiring new systems may require hiring new employees, changing job descriptions, or terminating employees. Human resources staff perform all of these tasks. Further, if the organization hires consultants for the development project or outsources it, the human resources department may handle the contracts with these suppliers.

FOR THE MIS MAJOR

Regardless of the approach that the organization adopts for acquiring new systems, the MIS department spearheads it. If the organization chooses either to buy or to lease the application, the MIS department leads in examining the offerings of the various vendors and in negotiating with the vendors. If the organization chooses to develop the application in-house, then the process falls to the MIS department. MIS analysts work closely with users to develop their information requirements. MIS programmers then write the computer code, test it, and implement the new system.

>>> SUMMARY

1. **Define an IT strategic plan, identify the three objectives it must meet, and describe the four common approaches to cost-benefit analysis.**

The *IT strategic plan* is a set of long-range goals that describe the IT infrastructure and identify the major IT initiatives needed to achieve the organization's goals. The IT strategic plan must meet three objectives:

> It must be aligned with the organization's strategic plan.

> It must provide for an IT architecture that enables users, applications, and databases to be seamlessly networked and integrated.

> It must efficiently allocate IS development resources among competing projects so the projects can be completed on time and within budget and have the required functionality.

The four common approaches to cost-benefit analysis are these:

> The *net present value (NPV)* method converts future values of benefits to their present-value equivalent by "discounting" them at the organization's cost of

funds. They can then compare the present value of the future benefits to the cost required to achieve those benefits to determine whether the benefits exceed the costs.

> *Return on investment (ROI)* measures management's effectiveness in generating profits with its available assets. ROI is calculated by dividing net income attributable to a project by the average assets invested in the project. ROI is a percentage, and the higher the percentage return, the better.

> *Breakeven analysis* determines the point at which the cumulative dollar value of the benefits from a project equals the investment made in the project.

> In the *business case approach*, system developers write a business case to justify funding one or more specific applications or projects.

2. **Discuss the four business decisions that companies must make when they acquire new applications.**

> *How much computer code does the company want to write?* A company can choose use a totally prewritten application (to write no computer code), to customize a prewritten application (to write some computer

code), or to customize an entire application (write all new computer code)

> *How will the company pay for the application?* Once the company has decided how much computer code to write, it must decide how to pay for it. With prewritten applications or customized prewritten applications, companies can buy them or lease them. With totally custom applications, companies use internal funding.

> *Where will the application run?* Companies must now decide where to run the application. The company may run the application on its own platform or run the application on someone else's platform (either use a software-as-a-service vendor or an application service provider).

> *Where will the application originate?* Prewritten applications can be open-source software or come from a vendor. Companies may choose to customize prewritten open-source applications or prewritten proprietary applications from vendors. Companies may customize applications in-house or outsource the customization. They also can write totally custom applications in-house or outsource this process.

3. Identify the six processes involved in the systems development life cycle, and explain the primary tasks and importance of each process.

The six processes are these:

> *Systems investigation:* Addresses the business problem (or business opportunity) by means of the feasibility study; main task in the systems investigation stage is the feasibility study.

> *Systems analysis:* Examines the business problem that the organization plans to solve with an information system; main purpose is to gather information about the existing system in order to determine the requirements for the new system; end product of this stage, known as the "deliverable," is a set of system requirements.

> *Systems design:* Describes how the system will resolve the business problem; deliverable is the set of technical system specifications.

> *Programming and testing:* Programming translates the design specifications into computer code; testing checks to see if the computer code will produce the expected and desired results and detects errors, or bugs, in the computer code; deliverable is the new application.

> *Implementation:* The process of converting from the old system to the new system via three major

conversion strategies: direct, pilot, and phased; deliverable is properly working application.

> *Operation and maintenance:* Types of maintenance include debugging, updating, and adding new functions when needed.

4. Describe four alternative development methods and four tools that augment development methods, and identify at least one advantage and one disadvantage of each method and tool.

These are the *alternative methods*:

> *Joint application design (JAD)* is a group-based tool for collecting user requirements and creating system designs.

> *Rapid application development (RAD)* is a systems development method that can combine JAD, prototyping, and ICASE tools to rapidly produce a high-quality system.

> *Agile development* is a software development methodology that delivers functionality in rapid iterations, which are usually measured in weeks.

> *End-user development* refers to an organization's end users developing their own applications with little or no formal assistance from the IT department.

These are the *tools*:

> The *prototyping* approach defines an initial list of user requirements, builds a model of the system, and then improves the system in several iterations based on users' feedback.

> *Integrated computer-aided software engineering (ICASE)* combines upper CASE tools (automate systems investigation, analysis, and design) and lower CASE tools (programming, testing, operation, and maintenance).

> *Component-based development* uses standard components to build applications. Components are reusable applications that generally have one specific function, such as a shopping cart, user authentication, or a catalog.

> *Object-oriented development* begins with the aspects of the real world that must be modeled to perform that task. Systems developers identify the *objects* in the new system. Each object represents a tangible, real-world entity, such as a customer, bank account, student, or course. Objects have *properties*, or *data values*. Objects also contain the *operations* that can be performed on their properties.

Table 14.2 shows advantages and disadvantages of alternative methods and tools.

5. Analyze the process of vendor and software selection.

The process of vendor and software selection is composed of six steps:

> Identify potential vendors

> Determine evaluation criteria

> Evaluate vendors and packages

> Choose the vendor and package

> Negotiate a contract

> Establish service-level agreements.

>>> CHAPTER GLOSSARY

agile development A software development methodology that delivers functionality in rapid iterations, measured in weeks, requiring frequent communication, development, testing, and delivery.

application portfolio The set of recommended applications resulting from the planning and justification process in application development.

application service provider (ASP) An agent or vendor who assembles the software needed by enterprises and packages them with outsourced development, operations, maintenance, and other services.

component-based development A software development methodology that uses standard components to build applications.

computer-aided software engineering (CASE) Development approach that uses specialized tools to automate many of the tasks in the SDLC; upper CASE tools automate the early stages of the SDLC, and lower CASE tools automate the later stages.

direct conversion Implementation process in which the old system is cut off and the new system is turned on at a certain point in time.

end-user development Approach in which the organization's end users develop their own applications with little or no formal assistance from the IT department.

feasibility study Investigation that gauges the probability of success of a proposed project and provides a rough assessment of the project's feasibility.

implementation The process of converting from an old computer system to a new one.

integrated CASE (ICASE) tools CASE tools that provide links between upper CASE and lower CASE tools.

IS operational plan Consists of a clear set of projects that the IS department and the functional area managers will execute in support of the IT strategic plan.

IT steering committee A committee, comprised of a group of managers and staff representing various organizational units, set up to establish IT priorities and to ensure that the MIS function is meeting the needs of the enterprise.

IT strategic plan A set of long-range goals that describe the IT infrastructure and major IT initiatives needed to achieve the goals of the organization.

joint application design (JAD) A group-based tool for collecting user requirements and creating system designs.

object-oriented development A systems development methodology that begins with aspects of the real world that must be modeled to perform a task.

outsourcing Use of outside contractors or external organizations to acquire IT services.

phased conversion Implementation process that introduces components of the new system in stages, until the entire new system is operational.

pilot conversion Implementation process that introduces the new system in one part of the organization on a trial basis; when the new system is working properly, it is introduced in other parts of the organization.

programmers IS professionals who modify existing computer programs or write new computer programs to satisfy user requirements.

programming The translation of a system's design specifications into computer code.

prototype A small-scale working model of an entire system or a model that contains only the components of the new system that are of most interest to the users.

prototyping An approach that defines an initial list of user requirements, builds a prototype system, and then improves the system in several iterations based on users' feedback.

rapid application development (RAD) A development method that uses special tools and an iterative approach to rapidly produce a high-quality system.

request for proposal (RFP) Document that is sent to potential vendors inviting them to submit a proposal describing their software package and how it would meet the company's needs.

scope creep Adding functions to an information system after the project has begun.

service-level agreements (SLAs) Formal agreements regarding the division of work between a company and its vendors.

software-as-a-service (SaaS) A method of delivering software in which a vendor hosts the applications and provides them as a service to customers over a network, typically the Internet.

systems analysis The examination of the business problem that the organization plans to solve with an information system.

systems analysts IS professionals who specialize in analyzing and designing information systems.

systems design Describes how the new system will resolve the business problem.

systems development life cycle (SDLC) Traditional structured framework, used for large IT projects, that consists of sequential processes by which information systems are developed.

systems stakeholders All people who are affected by changes in information systems.

technical specialists Experts on a certain type of technology, such as databases or telecommunications.

>>> DISCUSSION QUESTIONS

1. Discuss the advantages of a lease option over a buy option.

2. Why is it important for all business managers to understand the issues of IT resource acquisition?

3. Why is it important for everyone in business organizations to have a basic understanding of the systems development process?

4. Should prototyping be used on every systems development project? Why or why not?

5. Discuss the various types of feasibility studies. Why are they all needed?

6. Discuss the issue of assessing intangible benefits and the proposed solutions.

7. Discuss the reasons why end-user-developed information systems can be of poor quality. What can be done to improve this situation?

>>> PROBLEM-SOLVING ACTIVITIES

1. Access www.ecommerce-guide.com. Find the product review area. Read reviews of three software payment solutions. Assess them as possible components.

2. Use an Internet search engine to obtain information on CASE and ICASE tools. Select several vendors and compare and contrast their offerings.

3. Access www.ning.com. Observe how the site provides components for you to use to build applications. Build a small application at the site.

>>> WEB ACTIVITIES

1. Enter www-01.ibm.com/software. Find its WebSphere product. Read recent customers' success stories. What makes this software so popular?

2. Enter the Web sites of the Gartner (www.gartner.com), the Yankee Group (www.yankeegroup.com), and CIO (www.cio.com). Search for recent material about ASPs and outsourcing, and prepare a report on your findings.

3. StoreFront (www.storefront.net) is a vendor of e-business software. At its site, the company provides demonstrations illustrating the types of storefronts that it can create for

shoppers. The site also provides demonstrations of how the company's software is used to create a store.

   a. Run the StoreFront demonstration to see how this is done.

   b. What features does StoreFront provide?

   c. Does StoreFront support smaller or larger stores?

   d. What other products does StoreFront offer for creating online stores? What types of stores do these products support?

>>> TEAM ASSIGNMENTS

1. Assessing the functionality of an application is a part of the planning process (step 1). Select three to five Web sites catering to the same type of buyer (for instance, several Web sites that offer CDs or computer hardware), and divide the sites among the teams. Each team will assess the functionality of its assigned Web site by preparing an analysis of the different sorts of functions provided by the sites. In addition, the team should compare the strong and weak points of each site from the buyer's perspective.

2. Divide into groups, with each group visiting a local company (include your university). At each firm, study

the systems acquisition process. Find out the methodology or methodologies used by each organization and the type of application each methodology applies. Prepare a report and present it to the class.

3. As a group, design an information system for a startup business of your choice. Describe your chosen IT resource acquisition strategy, and justify your choices of hardware, software, telecommunications support, and other aspects of a proposed system.

CLOSING **CASE 1 >** GE Healthcare Switches
from Waterfall to Agile

GE Healthcare (www.gehealthcare.com) is a $17-billion business unit of General Electric (www.ge.com) that manufactures an array of products designed to make clinicians more productive. These technologies, which range from high-definition CT scanners to diagnostic pharmaceutical devices, are developed by the company's Imaging Solutions unit. Imaging Solutions employs 375 engineers who support 18 high-tech products. Unfortunately, this unit was experiencing several difficulties.

First, Imaging Solutions struggled with the predictability of its systems development project execution. The cycle time on projects was too long, taking from 12 to 24 months, often with significant delays. These long cycle times frequently caused the business to add features beyond the initial user requirements, reflecting a concern that customers could not wait for a new system in order to have these features. That situation, in turn, often increases a project's scope, causing further delays and increasing the project cycle time even more. Longer cycle times increase the risk that the user requirements gathered at the beginning of the project will be out of date by the time the product reaches the market.

In addition, Imaging Solutions' system development process followed the systems development life cycle (SDLC) approach (discussed in detail in this chapter). That is, it began with investigation, systems analysis, and systems design. When the unit had completed these steps, it conducted a formal design review. After the team obtained the various approvals for the design, they began programming the new system.

Programming typically took several months, after which the development team released the system into a test environment, where they collected user feedback. This point was usually the first time that users saw the new system. After the team had accumulated and incorporated user input, it continued the testing effort prior to implementing the new system.

The problem with the SDLC was that the system could not incorporate user-requested modifications until very late in the project cycle. As a result, any significant errors could require the team to change the design completely—in effect, to start over. This approach wasted a great deal of time and effort, and it further delayed the project.

A third problem confronting Imaging Solutions' development projects was the many communication barriers that existed among the various business functions, especially marketing and engineering. These barriers were becoming more problematic over time.

<<<**THE BUSINESS PROBLEM**

To address these problems, Imaging Solutions replaced the SDLC with an agile-based scrum initiative. Scrum (discussed in detail in this chapter) focuses on maximizing the development team's ability to deliver iterations quickly and to respond effectively to additional user requirements as they emerge. In contrast to the SDLC, agile development involves adding functionality in a series of phases and then testing the product after each phase is completed. Imaging Solutions hoped that adopting agile development would break down the barriers between the functional areas so that everyone would work together to release the right system on time. The unit particularly liked the idea of developing each product in a series of increments. It could then demonstrate each increment's functionality to users at the end of each increment and receive immediate feedback. This approach was much more economical and efficient than receiving feedback when the system was close to completion.

Imaging Solutions launched its move to agile development with a single development team. The unit staffed a strong cross-functional team and defined a pilot project with a manageable scope with a 4-month deadline. However, the project was substantial enough that the team could learn scrum skills while delivering a valuable product. The team also established clear success criteria so that they could evaluate whether they had achieved their goals.

<<<**THE SOLUTION**

The pilot project was delivered successfully with the correct features and functionality. The release ran over by a month, so Imaging Solutions is still working on the predictability of delivery.

The pilot project identified important lessons for Imaging Solutions. First, the unit operates in a highly regulated environment, so there are many additional quality and

<<<**THE RESULTS**

regulatory steps that must be completed before the development team can accept a user story. A *user story* is a scenario, written in the business terms of the users, that captures what they want to achieve with a particular project.

Imaging Solutions also discovered that it could adopt agile development, but with certain limitations. Specifically, the rigors of operating in a regulated industry required the unit to deploy a hybrid development process that involved more initial planning, and testing, than would be found in other agile organizations.

Following the pilot project, Imaging Solutions formed 10 scrum teams of 7 to 9 people each. Every 2 weeks, the teams conduct their increment reviews together on Wednesday morning and hold planning meetings for the next increment on Wednesday afternoon. This process ensures that the teams share their knowledge and also provides visibility into what is going on outside any one team's activities.

Imaging Solutions also discovered that it needed to identify cross-team dependencies early in each increment. Otherwise, teams could get in one another's way. They employed Rally's Agile ALM system (www.rallydev.com) to provide insight into cross-team dependencies and to generate real-time status updates on the progress of each increment.

Since Imaging Solutions implemented the new system, the various development teams have begun to share user stories and tasks. Further, teams that complete their own tasks early now assist other teams.

To obtain maximum benefits from the agile system, Imaging Solutions had to transform its culture somewhat by modifying the role of managers and individual contributors on scrum teams. For example, managers have to avoid a command-and-control style where they are ordering work and instead concentrate on assembling empowered teams.

Imaging Solutions is seeing positive results. Obtaining user feedback early and often enables the unit to prioritize features correctly. In one example, the system helped a team identify a clinical workflow it previously was not aware of.

Questions

1. The healthcare industry will be in upheaval for a few years to come. Due to the federal government's push for electronic health records, many physicians' practices, both small and large, are acquiring new information systems. What risks can you think of that are associated with such private information? Do you feel better with your records in a paper file on a shelf or in a computer?

2. Search for the phrase "*scope creep*," and see what you find. How would this phenomenon cause a problem in the acquisition and implementation of information systems?

SOURCES: Compiled from J. Hammond, "Customer-Centric Development: It's Now or Never for IT Shops," *InformationWeek*, April 26, 2011; S. Denning, "Six Common Mistakes That Salesforce.com Didn't Make," *Forbes*, April 18, 2011; A. Deitsch and R. Hughes, "GE Healthcare Goes Agile," *InformationWeek*, December 6, 2010; J. Vijayan, "The Grill: John Burke," *Computerworld*, September 13, 2010; J. Kobelius, "Agile Data Warehousing: Do You Scrum?" *InformationWeek*, July 21, 2010; www.ge.com, www.gehealthcare.com, www.rallydev.com, accessed April 29, 2011.

CLOSING **CASE 2** >

A Tale of Two Software Upgrades

THE PROBLEM>>> Two airlines—WestJet (www.westjet.com) and JetBlue (www.jetblue.com)—had been using a reservation system designed for start-up airlines with reasonably simple reservation requirements. As the two carriers expanded, they needed greater processing power to deal with increasing numbers of customers. They also wanted additional functions, such as the ability to link their prices and seat inventories to other airlines with which they could cooperate.

WestJet and JetBlue independently selected a system offered by Sabre Holdings (www.sabre.com), a provider of airline reservation systems (SabreSonic; www.sabreairlinesolutions.com). Sabre provides technology to 300 airlines, and it owns Travelocity (www.travelocity.com) and other online travel agencies. JetBlue reported that the new system cost about $40 million, including $25 million in capital spending and $15 million in one-time operating expenses. WestJet did not disclose how much its system cost.

<<<THE SOLUTION

In addition to selling seats and collecting passenger payments, the Sabre system controls much of the passenger experience: shopping on the airline's Web site; interacting with reservation agents; using airport kiosks; selecting seats; checking bags; boarding at the gate; and rebooking and obtaining refunds for cancellations. To perform these functions, the Sabre system has to integrate with the airline's other information systems.

WestJet, with 88 planes, switched to Sabre after it had shifted to a lighter winter schedule and canceled some flights. One imposing challenge was the overnight transition of 840,000 files—transactions of customers who already had purchased tickets—from WestJet's old reservations system to the Sabre system. The process did not go well because the migration required WestJet agents to go through complex steps to process the data.

<<<TWO DIFFERENT RESULTS

Despite months of planning, when WestJet made its conversion, its Web site crashed repeatedly, and its call center was overwhelmed. Making matters worse, WestJet did not reduce the number of passengers on the flights operating after the transition to the new system, nor did it inform customers of its upgrade plans until the day of the switch.

WestJet's customer loyalty scores dropped as a result of long waits and booking difficulties. The airline sent apology letters, offered flight credits to some customers, and bolstered its call center with temporary staffers located in India. Two months after the conversion, the airline installed a "virtual hold" in its call centers so callers would be promised a response within a certain time. A virtual hold offers callers the option for a callback rather than waiting on hold.

The bottom line for WestJet? After several months, the airline was able to fulfill its plans to cooperate with U.S. and international airlines on some of its routes.

In contrast, JetBlue, with 151 aircraft, decided to make its switch on a Friday night, because Saturday traffic tends to be low. The airline trimmed its schedule that weekend and sold abnormally low numbers of seats on the remaining flights. JetBlue also developed a backup Web site that it used twice for a few hours during the transition.

JetBlue also contracted for 500 outside reservations agents. After the transition, in which 900,000 passenger records were moved to Sabre, JetBlue routed basic calls to the temporary workers, freeing up its own call staff to manage more complex tasks. The extra agents stayed in place for 2 months.

JetBlue still experienced some problems. Call wait times increased, and not all of its airport kiosks and ticket printers became operational right away. Despite these problems, however, JetBlue contends that migrating to Sabre was an important factor in the airline's decision to cooperate on some routes in and out of Boston and New York with American Airlines.

Questions

1. Explain why WestJet and JetBlue decided to upgrade their reservation systems.

2. Compare and contrast the software upgrade processes of WestJet and JetBlue.

SOURCES: "JetBlue: Class of 2011 Yearbook," *Computerworld*, 2011; B. Evans, "Global CIO: WestJet's IT Nightmare and the Power of Customers," *InformationWeek*, April 16, 2010; S. Carey, "Two Paths to Software Upgrade," *Wall Street Journal*, April 13, 2010; "JetBlue Airways: 2010 Winner Profile," *CIO*, 2010; www.westjet.com, www.jetblue.com, www.sabre.com, accessed May 14, 2011.

RUBY'S CLUB INTERNSHIP ASSIGNMENTS

Based on your answers to the section discussion questions, write one final report to Ruben and Lisa detailing your suggestions for the development and implementation of their mobile ordering system. If you choose the SDLC, explain why. If you choose for them to have someone else develop the software, defend your position.

Be aware that there is no perfect answer. No situation will be without disadvantages and risks. Be sure to detail the risks so they will be well aware as they move through this process. Finally, submit your report to Ruben and Lisa via you professor.

SPREADSHEET ACTIVITY

Objective: This activity will introduce the "if-then" statement within the context making a decision. It will help students take criteria from a situation and build it into a spreadsheet.

Chapter Connection: Acquiring an information system should be an easy task, right? Wrong! Sometimes the method of acquiring the system is as complex as the system itself! While most situations would require a much more complicated decision support system, in this situation a spreadsheet formula can help make the decision.

Prerequisites: None.

Activity: It is time for the university to upgrade its Web site. This decision is very important because it will impact current and potential students, faculty, and the community at large. The university has graded 50 different vendors on 10 criteria and the weight given to each. The 10 criteria and their weights are given below.

1. Customizability (15%)
2. Expandability (15%)
3. Faculty Tutorials (5%)
4. Student Tutorials (5%)
5. Mobile Access (10%)
6. Video Support (10%)
7. File System (5%)
8. Course Migration (15%)
9. Faculty User Interface (10%)
10. Student User Interface (10%)

Go to www.wiley.com/college/rainer for this chapter to download the spreadsheet MIS—Chapter 14.xlsx. You will write a formula to calculate the "final grade" of each based on its percentage weight. Once you have the final grade, you will then create an if-then

formula to find those vendors that rank worthy of an "A." Then write a letter detailing the differences in the finalists considered for implementation. If you are not familiar with "if-then" statements, please see the Help material in Microsoft Excel under the formulas area of the program.

Deliverables: You will take the given spreadsheet and create two if-then formulas. One will calculate a final grade based on work already done by the university, and the other formula will find the top performers for final consideration. These will be compared by a written document that you will hand in which considers aspects of each option as detailed in the material in the chapter.

Quiz Questions:

1. True or False? A formula can only include one if-then statement.

2. If non-numeric characters are considered in an if-then statement, how are they differentiated within the formula?
   (a) Italics
   (b) Quotation marks
   (c) Underline
   (d) Bold
   (e) Semicolons

3. When writing a formula that adds multiple sets of multiplication facts, how often should you use a parenthesis?
   (a) Before and after each plus sign
   (b) Before each plus sign
   (c) After each plus sign
   (d) Not at all

Discussion Questions:

1. Acquisition of information systems is a complicated affair. Decisions to build in-house, outsource, or purchase off-the-shelf software can sometimes be the greatest asset or the Achilles heel of a company. Given the complexity, what roles can a spreadsheet play in this process other than the one illustrated by this case?

2. Implementation strategies vary as much as the acquisition decision. Considering products like the Google Spreadsheet Flow Chart, how can spreadsheets assist with the planning of software implementation?

DATABASE ACTIVITY: FORMS III

Objective

In this activity you will learn how to create a menu interface (a "navigation form" in Access terminology) that will allow users with no training to reach important elements of a system easily. Consider what happens when you launch Access. You get an easy-to navigate screen that asks questions such as "Do you want to open an existing database, start a blank one, or . . . ?" We should design databases for the same ease of entry. Navigation forms are how we do just that.

Chapter Connection

In this chapter you read how organizations acquire their information systems. Often, they develop IS internally. The result has to look as professional as if the application had been purchased. That includes interfaces such as you will develop here.

Prerequisites

None.

Activity:

In this activity, which you will find online, you will take an existing database with forms and reports, develop menus for using it, and set your database to launch with those menus.

A finished navigation form, which you will have at the end of this activity, might look like the following figure. One does not have to be an Access expert, or even an experienced Access user, to use it. Each button is clearly labeled with its function. Such an interface is planned in the System Design stage of the SDLC development process, which you read about in this chapter. Putting it together, as you will do here, is part of the programming and testing stages.

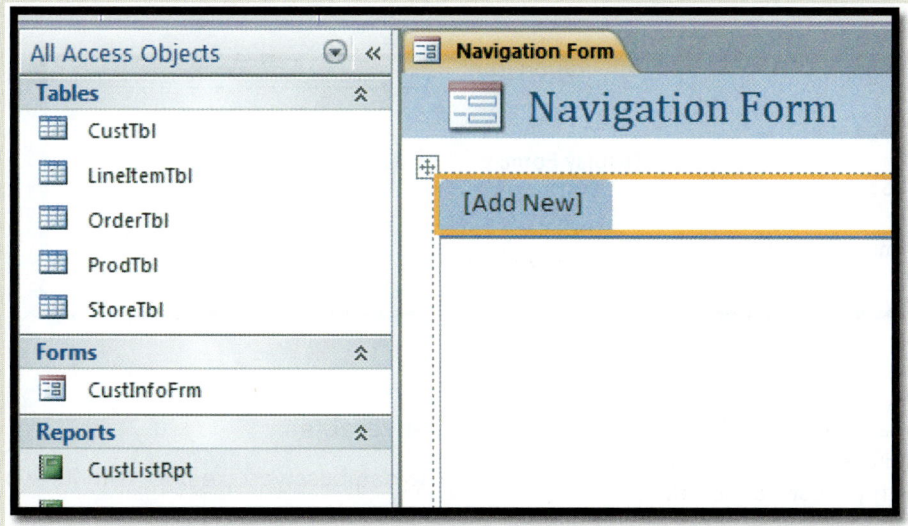

1. Download the Ch 14 DandyDonuts database from www.wiley.com/college/rainer. (It resembles the donut store databases you may have worked with in earlier activities.) It has five tables: stores, customers, orders, line items (each item in an order), and products. It also includes a few forms and reports. These are not intended as good examples of form or report design. They are there only so your navigation forms will have something to open.

2. To create a navigation form, go to the Create ribbon tab, and pull down the list of navigation forms via the triangle to its right. Select the first layout, Horizontal Tabs.

3. You will see a blank navigation form in Design view. The space where the tabs will go, across the top, is empty except for a placeholder that reads "[Add New]."

4. If your navigation pane is not showing, as it is at the left of the preceding screen shot, open it by clicking the ">>" at the top.

5. Drag the four reports into the Add New area, one at a time. As each one comes in, you will see a tab created for it.

6. Go to Form view. The "[Add New]" has gone away. Click on each tab to see the corresponding report.

7. Return to Layout view. To clean up the form design, edit the top line to read "Reports" instead of "Navigation Form." Edit the four tabs to read, respectively, "Customer List," "Customer Orders," "Orders by Date," and "Orders by Store." You will probably have to widen some of the tabs for the new names to fit on a single line.

8. Save your new navigation form as "Report List."

9. Create a new navigation form, but this time use Vertical Tabs Left layout.

10. Enter "CustInfoFrm" and your new Report List into the tab area.

11. Change the header of this form to read "Main Menu" and the name "CustInfoFrm" to read "Cust. Info."

12. Confirm in Form view that everything works.

13. Now we will add an Exit button to our main menu. Go to Design mode, and make sure "Use Control Wizards" is highlighted in the Controls section of the Design ribbon. (Expand that area using the down-pointing triangle with the line above it at the right to see the wizard.) Then click the "Button" tool. (It is in the top row of controls, fourth from the left.) Drag it over a rectangular area in the form header, to the right of the words "Main Menu," to create the button shape. The wizard will start.

Usage Hint: You can create buttons in Layout mode, but in that mode, if you try to put them in the navigation tab area, Access will insist on turning them into new tabs. In Design view, you can create freestanding buttons.

14. Choose the Application category, then Quit Application (the only item in it). Click "Next."

15. Select Text for the button content type, then enter "Exit" into the text field.

16. Name the button "ExitButton" so you will know what it is later, and click "Finish."

17. Adjust the size and location of your button if you wish.

18. Go to Form view, and confirm that your new button works. If it does not, the easiest fix is probably to start over rather than try to figure out why. If your second attempt to create it fails too, it is time to try to diagnose the problem.

19. Users would like the application to open with this menu, instead of having to open it from the navigation pane. To make this happen, go to the File tab, and click "Options" near the bottom. Select "Current Database" at the left, then select your main switchboard from the pull-down menu for Display Form. It should look like this:

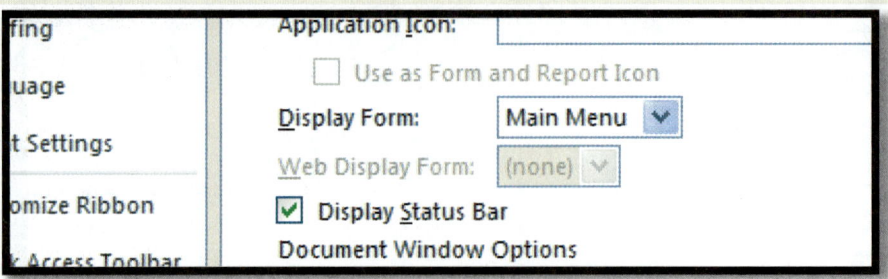

20. Close the database (as you will be told to do for this option to take effect), reopen it, and confirm that it opens with your switchboard.

Deliverables:

The database you created, with its two switchboards.

Quiz Questions:

1. How many tabs can a standard Access navigation form can have?

2. A navigation form can do the following:
   (a) Open a form or a report
   (b) Open a report or a table
   (c) Open another navigation form
   (d) All of the above

3. True or False? A navigation form is a specialized type of report.

4. When a user clicks a button linked to the Quit Application action,
   (a) The database closes, but Access remains active.
   (b) The computer shuts down.
   (c) Access closes.
   (d) The computer goes into Sleep mode.

Discussion Questions:

1. Open the Main Menu navigation form in Design view. Click on "Cust. Info." and change something in the customer information form. Then close the navigation form. What happened? Do you think it is a good idea for Access to work this way, or not? Explain why you feel this way.

2. In the second part of this activity, you created the Main Menu navigation form after you created the Reports form. Could you have done this in reverse order? If not, why not?

3. Search the Web for images of Access switchboards. You will find that many look more or less like this, with only cosmetic changes:

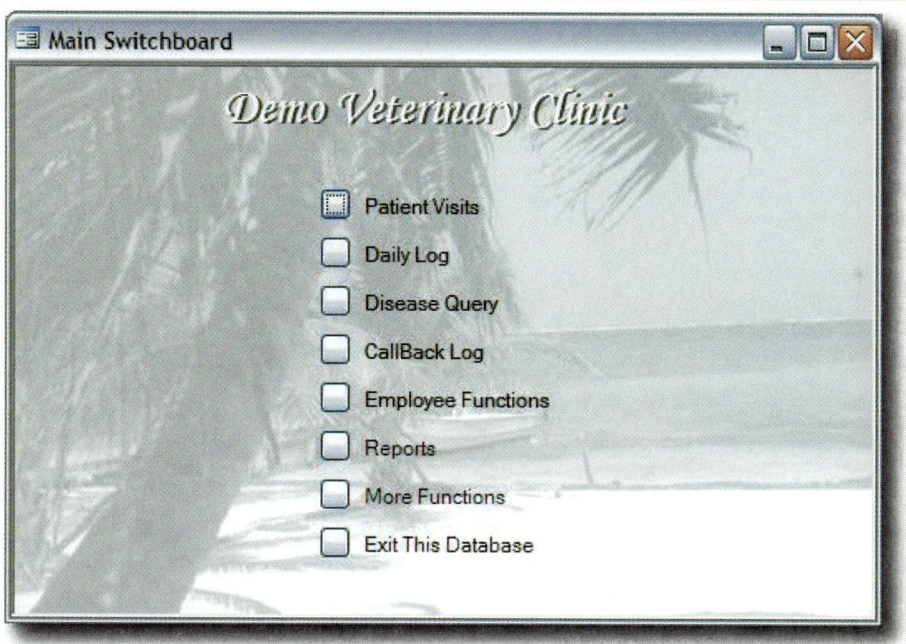

This menu, called a switchboard, was created with an earlier version of Access. Find three such switchboards. In your opinion, are they more attractive and/or easier to use (as far as you can tell without trying them out) than the navigation forms of Access 2010? Explain why you feel this way. (Paste the three switchboards' images into the answer you submit to your instructor.)

Plug IT In | 1

Business Processes and Business Process Management

LEARNING OBJECTIVES >>>

1. Understand what business processes are, and give examples of business processes in the functional areas of an organization and cross-functional business processes.

2. Differentiate between the terms *business process reengineering* and *business process management*.

PI1.1 Business Processes

A **business process** is an ongoing collection of related activities that create a product or a service of value to the organization, its business partners, and/or its customers. A process has inputs and outputs, and its activities can be measured. Many processes cross functional areas in an organization. For example, product development involves research, design, engineering, manufacturing, marketing, and distribution. Other processes involve only a single functional area. Table PI1.1 identifies the fundamental business processes performed in an organization's functional areas.

TABLE PI1.1 Examples of Business Processes

Accounting Business Processes

- Managing accounts payable
- Managing accounts receivable
- Reconciling bank accounts
- Managing cash receipts
- Managing invoice billings
- Managing petty cash
- Producing month-end close
- Producing virtual close

Finance Business Processes

- Managing account collection
- Managing bank loan applications
- Producing business forecasts
- Applying customer credit approval and credit terms
- Producing property tax assessments
- Managing stock transactions
- Generating financial cash flow reports

Marketing Business Processes

- Managing post-sale customer follow-up
- Collecting sales taxes
- Applying copyrights and trademarks
- Using customer satisfaction surveys
- Managing customer service
- Handling customer complaints
- Handling returned goods from customers
- Producing sales leads
- Entering sales orders
- Training sales personnel

Production/Operations Management Business Processes

- Processing bills of materials
- Processing manufacturing change orders
- Managing master parts list and files
- Managing packing, storage, and distribution
- Processing physical inventory
- Managing purchasing
- Managing quality control for finished goods
- Auditing for quality assurance
- Receiving, inspecting, and stocking parts and materials
- Handling shipping and freight claims
- Handling vendor selection, files, and inspections

Human Resources Business Processes

- Applying disability policies
- Managing employee hiring
- Handling employee orientation
- Managing files and records
- Applying healthcare benefits
- Managing pay and payroll
- Producing performance appraisals and salary adjustments
- Managing resignations and terminations
- Applying training/tuition reimbursement
- Managing travel and entertainment
- Managing workplace rules and guidelines
- Overseeing workplace safety

Management Information Systems Business Processes

- Antivirus control
- Computer security issues incident reporting
- Training computer users
- Computer user/staff training
- Applying disaster recovery procedures
- Applying electronic mail policy
- Generating Internet use policy
- Managing service agreements and emergency services
- Applying user workstation standards
- Managing the use of personal software

Cross-Functional Processes

All of the business processes listed in Table PI1.1 fall within a single functional area of the company. However, many other business processes, such as procurement and fulfillment, cut across multiple functional areas. That is, these processes are **cross-functional**, meaning that no single functional area is responsible for their execution. Rather, multiple functional areas collaborate to perform the process. For a cross-functional process to be successfully completed, each functional area must execute its specific process steps in a coordinated, collaborative way. To clarify this point, let us examine the procurement and fulfillment cross-functional processes in more detail.

The *procurement process* includes all of the tasks involved in acquiring needed materials externally from a vendor. Procurement is comprised of five steps that are completed in three different functional areas of the firm: warehouse, purchasing, and accounting.

The process begins when the warehouse recognizes the need to procure materials, perhaps due to low inventory levels. The warehouse documents this need with a purchase requisition, which it sends to the purchasing department (step 1). In turn, the purchasing department identifies a suitable vendor, creates a purchase order based on the purchase requisition, and sends the order to the vendor (step 2). When the vendor receives the purchase order, it ships the materials, which are received in the warehouse (step 3). The vendor then sends an invoice, which is received by the accounting department (step 4). Accounting sends payment to the vendor, thereby completing the procurement process (step 5).

The *fulfillment process* is concerned with efficiently processing customer orders. Fulfillment is triggered by a customer purchase order that is received by the sales department. Sales then validates the purchase order and creates a sales order. The sales order communicates data related to the order to other functional areas within the organization, and it tracks the progress of the order. The warehouse prepares and sends the shipment to the customer. Once accounting is notified of the shipment, it creates an invoice and sends it to the customer. The customer then makes a payment, which accounting records.

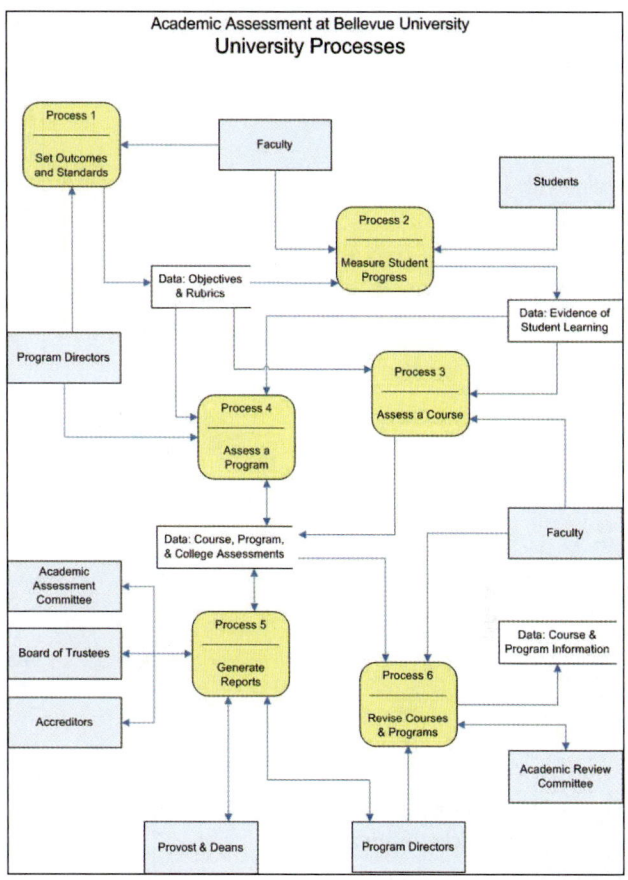

An organization's business processes can create a competitive advantage if they enable the company to innovate or to execute better than its competitors. They also can be liabilities if they make the company less responsive or less efficient. Consider the airline industry. It has become a competitive necessity for all of the airlines to offer electronic ticket purchases via their Web sites. At the same time, however, these sites must be highly responsive and provide the most current information on flights and prices. An up-to-date, user-friendly site will attract customers and increase revenues. In contrast, a site that provides outdated or inaccurate information will hurt rather than improve business. Figure PI1.1 illustrates the e-ticket purchasing business process.

Information Systems and Business Processes

An information system (IS) is an important enabler of business processes in an organization. An IS facilitates communication and coordination among different functional areas, and it allows easy exchange of, and access to, data across processes. Specifically, ISs play a vital role in three areas:

- Execute the process
- Capture and store process data
- Monitor process performance

In this section, you will learn about each of these roles. In some cases the role is fully automated—that is, it is performed entirely by the IS. In other cases the IS must rely on the manager's judgment, expertise, and intuition.

Execute the Process. The IS helps organizations execute processes efficiently and effectively. ISs are typically embedded into the processes, and they play a critical role in executing

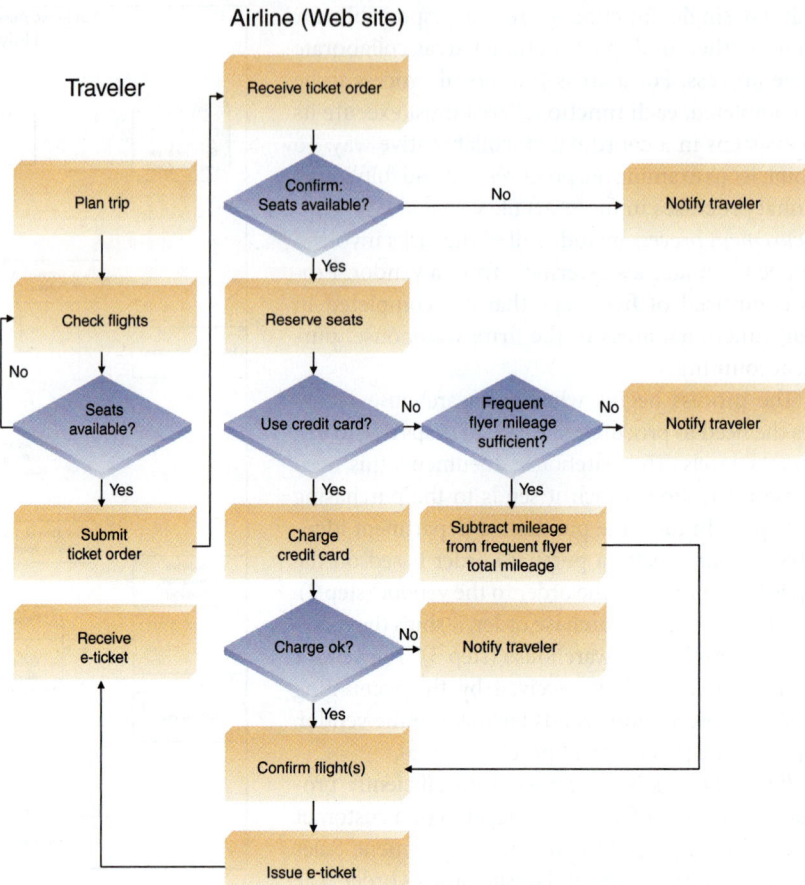

Airline (Web site)

Traveler

Figure PI1.1 Business process for ordering e-ticket from airline Web site.

the processes. In other words, an IS and processes are usually intertwined. If the IS does not work, the process cannot be executed. ISs help execute processes by informing people when it is time to complete a task, by providing the data necessary to complete the task, and in some cases by providing the means to complete the task.

In the procurement process, for example, the IS generates the purchase requisitions and then informs the purchasing department that action on these requisitions is needed. The accountant will be able to view all shipments received to match an invoice that has been received from a supplier and verify that the invoice is accurate. Without the IS, these steps, and therefore the process, cannot be completed. For example, if the IS is not available, how will the warehouse know which orders are ready to pack and ship?

In the fulfillment process, the IS will inform people in the warehouse that orders are ready for shipment. The IS also provides them with a listing of what materials must be included in the order and where to find those materials in the warehouse.

Capture and Store Process Data. Processes create data such as dates, times, product numbers, quantities, prices, and addresses, as well as who did what, when, and where. ISs capture and store these data, commonly referred to as process data or transaction data. Some of these data are generated and automatically captured by the ISs. These are data related to who, when, and where an activity is completed. Other data are generated outside the IS and must be entered into it. This data entry can occur in various ways, ranging from manual data entry to automated methods involving data in forms such as bar codes or RFID tags that can be read by machines.

In the fulfillment process, for example, when a customer order is received by mail or over the phone, the person taking the order must enter data such as the name of the customer, what was ordered, and how much was ordered. When a customer order is received via the firm's Web site, then all customer details are captured by the IS. Data such as the name of the person entering the data (who), at which location the person is completing the task (where), and the date and time (when) are automatically included by the IS when it creates the order. The data are updated as the process steps are executed. When the order is shipped, the warehouse will provide data about what and how many products were shipped, and the IS will automatically include data related to who, when, and where.

An important advantage of using an IS compared to a manual system or multiple functional area information systems is that the data need to be entered into the system only once. Further, once they are entered, they are easily accessible to other people in the process, and there is no need to reenter them in subsequent steps.

The data captured by the IS can provide immediate feedback. For example, the IS can use the data to create a receipt or to make recommendations for additional or alternate products.

Monitor Process Performance. A third contribution of IS is to help monitor the state of processes. That is, the IS indicates how well a process is executing. The IS performs this role by evaluating information about a process. This information can be created either at the instance level (i.e., a specific task or activity) or the process level (i.e., the process as a whole).

At the instance level, for example, a company might be interested in the state of a particular customer order. Where is the order within the fulfillment process? When was it shipped? Was the complete order shipped? If it has not been shipped, then when can we expect it to be shipped? Or, for the procurement process, when was the purchase order sent to the supplier? What will be the cost of acquiring the material? At the process level, the IS can evaluate how well the procurement process is being executed by calculating the lead time, or the time between sending the purchase order to a vendor and receiving the goods, for each order and each vendor over time.

Not only can the IS help monitor a process, it can also detect problems with the process. The IS performs this role by comparing the information with a standard—that is, what the company expects or desires—to determine if the process is performing within expectations. Management establishes standards based on organizational goals.

If the information provided by the IS indicates that the process is not meeting the standards, then the company assumes that some type of problem exists. Some problems can be routinely and automatically detected by the IS, whereas other problems require a person to review the information and make judgments. For example, the IS can calculate the expected date that a specific order will be shipped and determine whether this date will meet the established standard. Or, the IS can calculate the average time taken to fill all orders over the last month and compare this information to the standard to determine if the process is working as expected.

Monitoring business processes then, helps detect problems with these processes. Very often these problems are really symptoms of a more fundamental problem. In such cases, the IS can help diagnose the cause of the symptoms by providing managers with additional, detailed information. For example, if the average time to process a customer order appears to be increasing over the previous month, this problem could be a symptom of a more basic problem.

A manager can then drill down into the information to diagnose the underlying problem. To accomplish this, the manager can request a breakdown of the information by type of product, customer, location, employees, day of the week, time of day, and so on. After reviewing this detailed information, the manager might determine that employee turnover in the warehouse has been high over the last month and that the delays are occurring because new employees are not sufficiently familiar with the process. The manager might conclude that this problem will work itself out over time, in which case there is nothing more to be done. Alternatively, the manager could conclude that the new employees are not being adequately trained and supervised. In this case, the company must take actions to correct the problem.

→ BEFORE *YOU GO ON . . .*

1. What is a business process?
2. Describe several business processes carried out at your university.
3. Define a cross-functional business process, and provide several examples of such processes.
4. Describe the three roles that information systems play in enabling business processes.

Student Activity | PI1.1

Objective: You will be able to identify process inputs, outputs, and components in an organization's system.

Chapter Connection: This activity relates to Section PI1.1 and Learning Objective 1 in this chapter.

Prerequisites: You should have read Section PI1.1.

Activity: Examine your university's registration system, including the necessary inputs, outputs, and processes to represent your perspective of the system (i.e., the processes that the system must go through to process your registration for classes, the necessary inputs, and the outputs). Note that these may be different from another user's perspective. For example, the registrar may identify different processes that are necessary or relevant to other parts of the registration system that you may not recognize or even need to know about, such as minimum enrollment, course locations, instructor credentials, and so on.

What data/input are required of you? What data/input may be needed from other sources (e.g., things like course credit hours, prerequisites, etc.)? What outputs do you expect from the system? What are the processes necessary to get from the inputs to the desired outputs?

Deliverables:

Prepare a diagram that identifies and shows the relationships between:

- Necessary input/data from the student (and other sources as necessary to complete the student part of registration),
- Expected/desired outputs of registration, and
- Processes that are necessary to convert inputs into the expected/desired outputs.

Select the most interesting/eventful article and write/tell why you chose it. This may be turned in as a written assignment or a posted blog style to a course site.

Quiz Questions:

1. True or False? Business processes can lead to competitive advantage if they enable the company to execute better than its competitors.

2. Which of the following statements regarding business processes is true?
   - (a) Business processes can lead to competitive advantage.
   - (b) Business processes can be a liability to the organization.
   - (c) Business process is an ongoing collection of related activities that produce a product/service to the organization.
   - (d) Only A and B
   - (e) A, B, and C

Discussion Questions:

1. What are the inputs, processes, and outputs of your university's library book checkout system?
2. What are the inputs, processes, and outputs of your university's career services center?
3. What are the inputs, processes, and outputs of your final exam week study/preparation?

PI1.2 Business Process Reengineering and Business Process Management

Excellence in executing business processes is widely recognized as the underlying basis for all significant measures of competitive performance in an organization. Consider the following measures, for example:

- *Customer satisfaction:* the result of optimizing and aligning business processes to fulfill customers' needs, wants, and desires
- *Cost reduction:* the result of optimizing operations and supplier processes
- *Cycle and fulfillment time:* the result of optimizing the manufacturing and logistics processes

- *Quality:* the result of optimizing the design, development, and production processes
- *Differentiation:* the result of optimizing the marketing and innovation processes
- *Productivity:* the result of optimizing each individual's work processes

The question is this: How does an organization ensure business process excellence?

In their book *Reengineering the Corporation*, first published in 1993, Michael Hammer and James Champy argued that in order to become more competitive, American businesses needed to radically redesign their business processes to reduce costs and increase quality. The authors further asserted that information technology is the key enabler of such change. This radical redesign, called **business process reengineering (BPR)**, is a strategy for improving the efficiency and effectiveness of an organization's business processes. The key to BPR is for enterprises to examine their business processes from a "clean sheet" perspective and then determine how they can best reconstruct those processes to improve their business functions.

Although some enterprises successfully implemented BPR, many organizations found this strategy too difficult, too radical, and too comprehensive. The impact on employees, on facilities, on existing investments in information systems, and even on organizational culture was overwhelming. Despite the many failures in BPR implementation, however, businesses increasingly began to organize work around business processes rather than individual tasks. The result was a less radical, less disruptive, and more incremental approach, called business process management. **Business process management (BPM)** is a management technique that includes methods and tools to support the design, analysis, implementation, management, and optimization of business processes.

BPM initially helps companies improve profitability by decreasing costs and increasing revenues. Over time, BPM can create a competitive advantage by improving organizational flexibility. For many companies, BPM can provide cost benefits and increase customer satisfaction. In all cases the company's strategy should drive the BPM effort, as the case of Enterprise illustrates.

Example

Enterprise Rent-A-Car (www.enterprise.com) is one of the largest car rental companies in the world. The company's Request Services department processes, approves, and fulfills requests for IT hardware, software, and services from 65,000 Enterprise employees located in 7,000 locations worldwide. Historically this department had used multiple manual systems to manage this process. As the company expanded, however, this system could no longer keep up with the growing number of IT requests. Determined to improve this process, Enterprise initiated a BPM project and selected a product from Appian (www.appian.com) for this project.

Before Enterprise actually started the project, the company made certain that its strategy was in place. Enterprise recognized that implementing a new process would transform the company's traditional work behaviors. Therefore, the Request Services department engaged key stakeholders—primarily the people who approve IT product and service requests and the people who fulfill these requests—early in the project. The company also educated employees about BPM in general as well as how to use the new Appian system.

After the BPM system was implemented, Enterprise eliminated its manual processes entirely. Its employees now use the Appian system to request IT products and services. Significantly, they now fulfill requests more promptly while making fewer errors than they did with the manual system. In addition, the new process contains business rules that provide appropriate restrictions on fulfillment (e.g., what IT hardware, software, or service an employee is entitled to).

Important components of BPM are process modeling, Web-enabled technologies, and business activity monitoring.

BPM begins with *process modeling*, which is a graphical depiction of all the steps in a process. Process modeling helps employees understand the interactions and dependencies among the people, the information systems they rely on, and the information they require to optimally perform their tasks.

Web-enabled technologies display and retrieve data via a Web browser. They enable an organization to integrate the necessary people and applications into each process.

Business activity monitoring (BAM) is a real-time approach for measuring and managing business processes. Companies use BAM to monitor their business processes, identify failures or exceptions, and address these failures in real time. Further, because BAM tracks process operations and indicates whether they succeed or fail, it creates valuable records of process behaviors that organizations can use to improve their processes.

BEFORE YOU GO ON . . .

1. What is business process reengineering?
2. What is business process management?

Sources: Compiled from B. Violino, "BPM Success at Enterprise," *Baseline Magazine*, March 13, 2009; B. Violino, "BPM: Strategy Before Software," *CIO Insight*, March 13, 2009; D. Byron, "Appian BPM at Enterprise: Can Renting BPM Be Like Renting a Car?" www.bpminaction.com, March 24, 2008; "Enterprise Rent-A-Car Goes Live with Appian Enterprise," **Appian Press Release**, March 24, 2008; www.enterprise.com, accessed March 30, 2009; www.appian.com, accessed March 20, 2011.

Student Activity | PI1.2

Objective: You will be able to develop a process map and reengineer a process.

Chapter Connection: This activity relates to Section PI1.2 and Learning Objective 2 in the chapter.

Prerequisites: You should have read Section PI1.2.

Activity: You will map the activities of a typical senior at State University getting ready for school in the morning. You will reengineer the process to reduce the amount of time necessary to get ready for school. A partial list of activities that the student already does before going to school (and the time required) is presented in the following table. Add any items that may have been left off the list based upon your own experience of getting ready in the morning. (If time permits, you may find it helpful to should keep a diary of the activities, including time commitments and any dependencies, that you do for a couple of days to get an accurate accounting of the activities.)

Partial List of Activities (in no specific order)	Duration
Hit snooze bar and sleep in	10 minutes
Get bath and wash hair	15 minutes
Blow dry/fix hair	10 minutes
Shave or put on makeup	10 minutes
Prepare and eat breakfast	15 minutes
Take dog outside for "doggie business"	5 minutes
Feed dog	5 minutes
Wash, dry, and put away dishes from morning meal	5 minutes
Drive to the campus and park	15 minutes
Select clothes for the day and get dressed	5 minutes
Read newspaper	15 minutes
Brush teeth	5 minutes
Work out	20 minutes
Check e-mail/Facebook updates	15 minutes
Total	**150 minutes**

Deliverables:

Prepare a current process map and a reengineered process map of the student's activities. You should produce a table that compares number/types of processes and time differentials between the current and reengineered processes. You should also identify which fundamental items were altered, deleted, added, and so on to create the reengineered process.

Quiz Questions:

1. True or False? Business process reengineering (BPR) and business process management (BPM) are two different terms for the same thing.

2. Which of the following is true regarding business activity monitoring (BAM)?
   (a) It is a batch approach for measuring and managing business processes.
   (b) It is used to identify failures of or exceptions to business processes.
   (c) Over time it builds up records of process behavior.
   (d) A and B
   (e) B and C

3. Which of the following is true regarding BPM?
   (a) BPM is often used because BPR can overwhelming in its impact on employees, facilities, existing investments in information systems, and even organizational culture.
   (b) BPM is only related to the operational level and has no impact on strategic company issues.
   (c) BPM helps companies improve profitability by decreasing costs and increasing revenues.
   (d) A and C
   (e) B and C

4. True or False? BPR requires the inclusion of technology into the reengineered processes.

Discussion Questions:

1. Does technology always have to be used to improve business processes? Why or why not? What are the potential issues in the use of technology to reengineer processes?

2. Provide an ineffective/inefficient process from your job, internship, or somewhere you have frequently encountered the process. This should be a process that could have both a technology-based solution as well as a solution that does not use technology. Provide a nontechnology BPR solution and a technology BPR solution to the problem. Does one do a better job of solving the problem than the other does? Compare and contrast your thoughts with those of your classmates.

What's In IT For Me?

For All Business Majors

All functional areas of any organization are literally composed of a variety of business processes, as we can see from the examples in this plug-in. Regardless of your major, you will be involved in a variety of business processes from your first day on the job. Some of these processes you will do by yourself, some will involve only your group or department, while others will involve several (or all) functional areas of the organization.

It is important for you to be able to visualize processes, understand the inputs and outputs of each process, and know the "customer" of each process. If you can do these things, you can contribute to making processes more efficient and effective, which often means incorporating information technology in the process. It is also important for you to know how each process fits into your organization's strategy.

SUMMARY

1. **Understand what business processes are, and give examples of business processes in the functional areas of an organization and cross-functional business processes.**

   A business process is an ongoing collection of related activities that produce a product or a service of value to the organization, its business partners, and/or its customers.

Examples of business processes in the functional areas include managing accounts payable, managing accounts receivable, managing after-sale customer follow-up, managing bills of materials, managing manufacturing change orders, applying disability policies, employee hiring, computer user/staff training, and applying Internet use policy. The procurement and fulfillment processes are examples of cross-functional business processes.

2. **Differentiate between the terms** *business process reengineering* **and** *business process management.*

Business process reengineering (BPR) is a radical redesign of business processes that is intended to improve the efficiency and effectiveness of an organization's business processes. The key to BPR is for enterprises to examine their business processes from a "clean sheet" perspective and then determine how they could best reconstruct those processes to improve their business functions. Because BPR proved difficult to implement, organizations have turned to business process management. Business process management (BPM) is a management technique that includes methods and tools to support the design, analysis, implementation, management, and optimization of business processes.

GLOSSARY

business process A collection of related activities that create a product or a service of value to the organization, its business partners, and/or its customers.

business process management A management technique that includes methods and tools to support the design, analysis, implementation, management, and optimization of business processes.

business process reengineering A radical redesign of a business process that improves its efficiency and effectiveness, often by beginning with a "clean sheet" (from scratch).

cross-functional processes No single functional area is responsible for a process's execution.

DISCUSSION QUESTIONS

1. Consider the student registration business process at your university:
   • Describe the steps necessary for you to register for your classes each semester.
   • Describe how information technology is used (or is not used) in each step of the process.
2. Why is it so difficult for an organization to actually implement business process reengineering?

Plug IT In | 2

Hardware and Software

LEARNING OBJECTIVES >>>

1. Discuss strategic issues that link hardware design to business strategy.
2. Differentiate between the two major types of software.
3. Describe the major software issues that organizations face today.
4. Discuss the advantages and disadvantages of open-source software.

Introduction

As you begin this Plug IT In, you might be wondering, Why do I have to know anything about hardware and software? There are several reasons why it is advantageous to know the basics of hardware and software. First, regardless of your major (and future functional area in an organization), you will be using different types of hardware and software throughout your career. Second, you will have input concerning the hardware and software you will use. In this capacity you will be required to answer many questions, such as is "Is my hardware performing adequately for my needs? If not, what types of problems am I experiencing?" "Does my software help me do my job?" "Is this software easy to use?" "Do I need more functionality, and if so, what functionality would be most helpful to me?" Third, you will also have input into decisions when your functional area or organization upgrades or replaces its hardware and input into decisions about the software you need to do your job. MIS employees will act as advisors, but you will provide important input into such decisions. Finally, in some organizations, the budget for hardware

and software is allocated to functional areas or departments. In such cases, you might be making hardware and software decisions (at least locally) yourself.

This Plug IT In will help you better understand the hardware and software decisions your organization must make as well as your personal computing decisions. Many of the design principles presented here apply to systems of all sizes, from an enterprisewide system to your home computer system. In addition, the dynamics of innovation and cost that you will see can affect personal as well as corporate hardware decisions.

PI2.1 Introduction to Hardware

Recall from Chapter 1 that the term *hardware* refers to the physical equipment used for the input, processing, output, and storage activities of a computer system. Decisions about hardware focus on three interrelated factors: appropriateness for the task, speed, and cost. The incredibly rapid rate of innovation in the computer industry complicates hardware decisions because computer technologies become obsolete more quickly than other organizational technologies.

The overall trends in hardware are that it becomes smaller, faster, cheaper, and more powerful over time. In fact, these trends are so rapid that they make it difficult to know when to purchase (or upgrade) hardware. This difficulty lies in the fact that companies that delay hardware purchases will, more than likely, be able to buy more powerful hardware for the same amount of money in the future. It is important to note that buying more powerful hardware for the same amount of money in the future is a trade-off. An organization that delays purchasing computer hardware gives up the benefits of whatever it could buy today until the future purchase date arrives.

Hardware consists of the following:

- *Central processing unit (CPU)*. Manipulates the data and controls the tasks performed by the other components.
- *Primary storage*. Temporarily stores data and program instructions during processing.
- *Secondary storage*. Stores data and programs for future use.
- *Input technologies*. Accept data and instructions and convert them to a form that the computer can understand.
- *Output technologies*. Present data and information in a form people can understand.
- *Communication technologies*. Provide for the flow of data from external computer networks (e.g., the Internet and intranets) to the CPU, and from the CPU to computer networks.

Strategic Hardware Issues

For most businesspeople the most important issues are what the hardware enables, how it is advancing, and how rapidly it is advancing. In many industries, exploiting computer hardware is a key to achieving competitive advantage. Successful hardware exploitation comes from thoughtful consideration of the following questions:

- How do organizations keep up with the rapid price and performance advancements in hardware? For example, how often should an organization upgrade its computers and storage systems? Will upgrades increase personal and organizational productivity? How can organizations measure such increases?
- How should organizations determine the need for the new hardware infrastructures, such as server farms, virtualization, grid computing, and utility computing? (See "Plug IT In 3" for a discussion of these infrastructures.)
- Portable computers and advanced communications technologies have enabled employees to work from home or from anywhere. Will these new work styles benefit employees and the organization? How do organizations manage such new work styles?

Computer Hierarchy

The traditional standard for comparing classes of computers is their processing power. This section presents each class of computers, from the most powerful to the least powerful. It describes both the computers and their roles in modern organizations.

Supercomputers. The term **supercomputer** does not refer to a specific technology. Rather, it indicates the fastest computers available at any given time. At the time of this writing (mid-2010), the fastest supercomputers had speeds exceeding one petaflop (one petaflop is 1,000 trillion floating point operations per second). A floating point operation is an arithmetic operation involving decimals.

Because supercomputers are costly as well as very fast, they are generally used by large organizations to execute computationally demanding tasks involving very large data sets. In contrast to mainframes, which specialize in transaction processing and business applications, supercomputers typically run military and scientific applications. Although they cost millions of dollars, they are also being used for commercial applications where huge amounts of data must be analyzed. For example, large banks use supercomputers to calculate the risks and returns of various investment strategies, and healthcare organizations use them to analyze giant databases of patient data to determine optimal treatments for various diseases.

Mainframe Computers. Although mainframe computers are increasingly viewed as just another type of server, albeit at the high end of the performance and reliability scales, they remain a distinct class of systems differentiated by hardware and software features. **Mainframes** remain popular in large enterprises for extensive computing applications that are accessed by thousands of users at one time. Examples of mainframe applications are airline reservation systems, corporate payroll programs, Web site transaction processing systems (e.g., Amazon and eBay), and student grade calculation and reporting.

Today's mainframes perform at teraflop (trillions of floating point operations per second) speeds and can handle millions of transactions per day. In addition, mainframes provide a secure, robust environment in which to run strategic, mission-critical applications.

Midrange Computers. Larger midrange computers, called **minicomputers**, are relatively small, inexpensive, and compact computers that perform the same functions as mainframe computers, but to a more limited extent. In fact, the lines between minicomputers and mainframes have blurred in both price and performance. Minicomputers are a type of **server**—that is, a computer that supports computer networks and enables users to share files, software, peripheral devices, and other resources. Mainframes are a type of server as well because they provide support for entire enterprise networks.

Microcomputers. Microcomputers—also called *micros, personal computers*, or *PCs*—are the smallest and least expensive category of general-purpose computers. It is important to point out that people frequently define a PC as a computer that utilizes the Microsoft Windows operating system. In fact, there are a variety of PCs available, many of which do not use Windows. One well-known example are the Apple Macs, which use the Mac OS X operating system (discussed later in this Plug IT In). The major categories of microcomputers are desktops, thin clients, notebooks and laptops, netbooks and tablets.

DESKTOP PCS. The *desktop personal computer* is the familiar microcomputer system that has become a standard tool for business and the home. (Desktops are being replaced with portable devices such as laptops, netbooks, and tablets.) A desktop generally includes a central processing unit (CPU)—which you will learn about later—and a separate but connected monitor and keyboard. Modern desktop computers have gigabytes of primary storage, a rewriteable CD-ROM and a DVD drive, and up to a few terabytes of secondary storage.

THIN-CLIENT SYSTEMS. Before you address thin-client systems, you need to differentiate between clients and servers. Recall that servers are computers that provide a variety of services for clients, including running networks, processing Web sites, processing e-mail, and many other functions. *Clients* are typically computers on which users perform their tasks, such as word processing, spreadsheets, and others.

Thin-client systems are desktop computer systems that do not offer the full functionality of a PC. Compared to PCs, or **fat clients**, thin clients are less complex, particularly

Laptop computer

Netbook

Figure PI2.1 Laptop, notebook, and tablet computers. (*Source:* © Dragonian/iStockphoto; © Sǻndor Kelemen/iStockphoto; © PhotoEdit/Alamy Limited; © Oleksiy Maksymenko/Alamy Limited)

Motorola Xoom tablet

Apple iPad 2 tablet

because they do not have locally installed software. When thin clients need to run an application, they access it from a server over a network instead of from a local disk drive.

For example, a thin client would not have Microsoft Office installed on it. Thus, thin clients are easier and less expensive to operate and support than PCs. The benefits of thin clients include fast application deployment, centralized management, lower cost of ownership, and easier installation, management, maintenance, and support. The main disadvantage of thin clients is that if the network fails, then users can do very little on their computers. In contrast, if users have fat clients and the network fails, they can still perform some functions because they have software, such as Microsoft Office, installed on their computers.

LAPTOP AND NOTEBOOK COMPUTERS. **Laptop computers** (or **notebook computers**) are small, easily transportable, lightweight microcomputers that fit easily into a briefcase (Figure PI2.1). Notebooks and laptops are designed to be as convenient and easy to transport as possible. Just as important, they also provide users with access to processing power and data outside an office environment. At the same time, they cost more than desktops for similar functionality.

NETBOOKS. A **netbook** is a very small, lightweight, low-cost, energy-efficient, portable computer. Netbooks are generally optimized for Internet-based services such as Web browsing and e-mailing.

TABLET COMPUTERS. A **tablet computer** (or **tablet**) is a complete computer contained entirely in a flat touch screen that users operate via a stylus, digital pen, or fingertip instead of a keyboard or mouse. Examples of tablets are the Apple iPad 2 (www.apple.com/ipad), the HP Slate (www.hp.com), the Toshiba Thrive (www.toshiba.com), and the Motorola Xoom (www.motorola.com).

Input and Output Technologies

Input technologies allow people and other technologies to enter data into a computer. The two main types of input devices are human data-entry devices and source-data automation devices. As their name implies, *human data-entry* devices require a certain amount of human effort to input data. Examples are keyboard, mouse, pointing stick, trackball, joystick, touchscreen, stylus, and voice-recognition.

An interesting development in keyboard technology is the Bluetooth laser virtual keyboard (see Figure PI2.2). This device, only 3.5 inches high, uses a laser to project a full standard keyboard on any flat surface. The device connects to smart phones and computers using Bluetooth (discussed in Chapter 10).

Figure PI2.2 Bluetooth laser virtual keyboard. (*Source:* WENN Photos/NewsCom)

In contrast, *source-data automation* devices input data with minimal human intervention. These technologies speed up data collection, reduce errors, and gather data at the source of a transaction or other event. Bar code readers are an example of source-data automation. Table PI2.1 describes the various input devices.

TABLE PI2.1 Input Devices

Input Device	Description
Human Data-Entry Devices	
Keyboards	Most common input device (for text and numerical data).
Mouse	Handheld device used to point cursor at point on screen, such as an icon; user clicks button on mouse instructing computer to take some action.
Optical mouse	Mouse is not connected to computer by a cable; mouse uses camera chip to take images of surface it passes over, comparing successive images to determine its position.
Trackball	User rotates a ball built into top of device to move cursor (rather than moving entire device such as a mouse).
Pointing stick	Small button-like device; cursor moves in the direction of the pressure you place on the stick. Located between keys near center of keyboard.
Touchpad (also called a trackpad)	User moves cursor by sliding finger across a sensitized pad and then can tap pad when cursor is in desired position to instruct computer to take action (also called *glide-and-tap pad*).
Graphics tablet	A device that can be used in place of, or in conjunction with, a mouse or trackball; has a flat surface for drawing and a pen or stylus that is programmed to work with the tablet.
Joystick	Joystick moves cursor to desired place on screen; commonly used in workstations that display dynamic graphics and in video games.
Touch screen	Users instruct computer to take some action by touching a particular part of the screen; commonly used in information kiosks such as ATM machines. Touch screens now have gesture controls for browsing through photographs, moving objects around on a screen, flicking to turn the page of a book, and playing video games. For example, see the Apple iPhone.
Stylus	Pen-style device that allows user either to touch parts of a predetermined menu of options or to handwrite information into the computer (as with some PDAs); works with touch-sensitive screens.
Digital pen	Mobile device that digitally captures everything you write; built-in screen confirms that what you write has been saved; also captures sketches, figures, and so on with on-board flash memory.
Wii	A video game console by Nintendo. A distinguishing feature of the Wii is its wireless controller, which can be used as a handheld pointing device and can detect movement in three dimensions.
Microsoft Kinect	Enables users to control and interact with the Xbox 360 without the need to touch a game controller, through a natural interface using gestures and spoken commands.
Web camera (Webcam)	A real-time video camera whose images can be accessed via the Web or instant messaging.
Voice-recognition	Microphone converts analog voice sounds into digital input for computer; critical technology for physically challenged people who cannot use other input devices.

(continued)

TABLE PI2.1 (Continued)

Input Device	Description
Source-Data Automation Input Devices	
Automated teller machine	A device that includes source-data automation input in the form of a magnetic stripe reader; human input via a keyboard; and output via a monitor, printer, and cash dispenser.
Magnetic stripe reader	A device that reads data from a magnetic stripe, usually on the back of a plastic card (for example, credit or debit cards).
Point-of-sale terminals	Computerized cash registers that also may incorporate touch screen technology and bar code scanners to input data such as item sold and price.
Barcode scanners	Devices scan black-and-white bar code lines printed on merchandise labels.
Optical mark reader	Scanner for detecting presence of dark marks on predetermined grid, such as multiple-choice test answer sheets.
Magnetic ink character reader	Read magnetic ink printed on checks that identify the bank, checking account, and check number.
Optical character recognition	Software that converts text into digital form for input into computer.
Sensors	Collect data directly from the environment and input data directly into computer; examples include vehicle airbag activation sensors and radio-frequency identification tags.
Cameras	Digital cameras capture images and convert them into digital files.
Radio Frequency Identification (RFID)	Uses active or passive tags (transmitters) to wirelessly transmit product information to electronic readers.

The output generated by a computer can be transmitted to the user via several output devices and media. These devices include monitors, printers, plotters, and voice. Table PI2.2 describes the various output devices.

Multimedia technology is the computer-based integration of text, sound, still images, animation, and digitized motion video. It usually represents a collection of various input and output technologies. Multimedia merges the capabilities of computers with televisions, VCRs, CD players, DVD players, video and audio recording equipment, and music and gaming technologies. High-quality multimedia processing requires powerful microprocessors and extensive memory capacity, including both primary and secondary storage.

TABLE PI2.2 Output Devices

Output Device	Description
Monitors	
Cathode ray tubes	Video screens on which an electron beam illuminates pixels on display screen.
Liquid crystal display (LCDs)	Flat displays that have liquid crystals between two polarizers to form characters and images on a backlit screen.
Flexible displays	Thin, plastic, bendable computer screens.
Organic light-emitting displays	Displays that are brighter, thinner, lighter, cheaper, faster, and take less power diodes (OLEDs) to run than LCDs.
Retinal scanning displays	Project image directly onto a viewer's retina; used in medicine, air traffic control, and controlling industrial machines.
Heads-up displays	Any transparent display that presents data without requiring that the user look away from his or her usual viewpoint; for example, see Microvision (www.microvision.com).

Output Device	Description
Printers	
Laser	Use laser beams to write information on photosensitive drums; produce high-resolution text and graphics.
Inkjet	Shoot fine streams of colored ink onto paper; usually less expensive to buy than laser printers but can be more expensive to operate; can offer resolution quality equal to laser printers.
Thermal	Produces a printed image by selectively heating coated thermal paper; when the paper passes over the thermal print head, the coating turns black in the areas where it is heated, producing an image.
Plotters	Use computer-directed pens for creating high-quality images, blueprints, schematics, drawing of new products, and such.
Voice Output	A speaker/headset, which can output sounds of any type; voice output is a software function that uses this equipment.
Electronic Book Reader	A wireless, portable reading device with access to books, blogs, newspapers, and magazines. On-board storage holds hundreds of books.
Amazon Kindle Sony Reader Barnes and Noble Nook	
Pocket Projector	A projector in a handheld device that provides an alternative display method to alleviate the problem of tiny display screens in handheld devices. Pocket projectors will project digital images onto any viewing surface.
Pico Projector	A very small projector incorporated into portable devices, such as the Nikon Coolpix S1000pj camera. Also incorporated into Samsung and LG mobile phones.

The Central Processing Unit

The **central processing unit (CPU)** performs the actual computation or "number crunching" inside any computer. The CPU is a **microprocessor** (for example, Intel's Core i3, i5, and i7 chips with more to come) made up of millions of microscopic transistors embedded in a circuit on a silicon wafer or *chip*. Hence, microprocessors are commonly referred to as chips.

As shown in Figure PI2.3, the microprocessor has different parts, which perform different functions. The **control unit** sequentially accesses program instructions, decodes them, and controls the flow of data to and from the arithmetic-logic unit, the registers, the

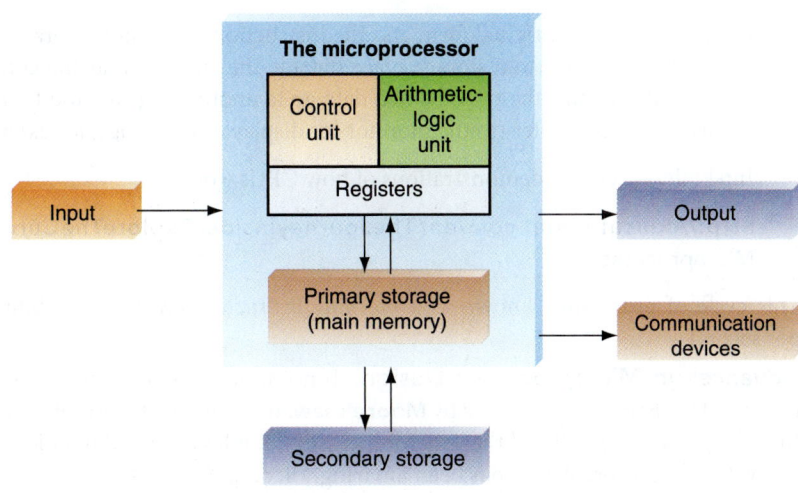

Figure PI2.3 Parts of a microprocessor.

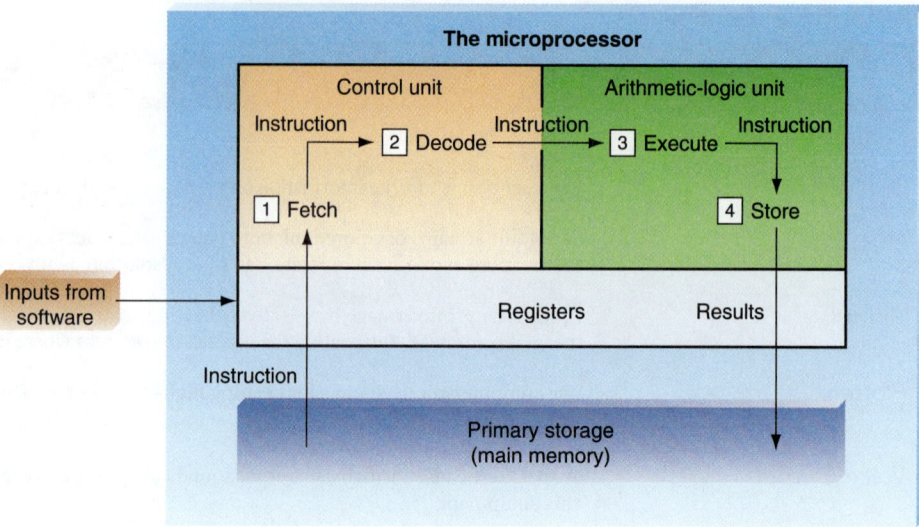

Figure PI2.4 How the CPU works.

caches, primary storage, secondary storage, and various output devices. The **arithmetic-logic unit (ALU)** performs the mathematic calculations and makes logical comparisons. The registers are high-speed storage areas that store very small amounts of data and instructions for short periods of time.

How the CPU Works. In the CPU, inputs enter and are stored until they are needed. At that point, they are retrieved and processed, and the output is stored and then delivered somewhere. Figure PI2.4 illustrates this process, which works as follows:

- The inputs consist of data and brief instructions about what to do with the data. These instructions come into the CPU from random access memory (RAM). Data might be entered by the user through the keyboard, for example, or read from a data file in another part of the computer. The inputs are stored in registers until they are sent to the next step in the processing.

- Data and instructions travel in the chip via electrical pathways called buses. The size of the bus—analogous to the width of a highway—determines how much information can flow at any time.

- The control unit directs the flow of data and instructions within the chip.

- The ALU receives the data and instructions from the registers and makes the desired computation. These data and instructions have been translated into **binary form**—that is, only 0s and 1s. A "0" or a "1" is called a **bit**. The CPU can process only binary data. All types of data, such as letters, decimal numbers, photographs, music, and so on, can be converted to a binary representation, which can then be processed by the CPU.

- The data in their original form and the instructions are sent to storage registers and then are sent back to a storage place outside the chip, such as the computer's hard drive. Meanwhile, the transformed data go to another register and then on to other parts of the computer (to the monitor for display or to storage, for example).

Intel offers excellent demonstrations of how CPUs work:

http://educate.intel.com/en/TheJourneyInside/ExploreTheCurriculum/EC_Microprocessors

This cycle of processing, known as a *machine instruction cycle*, occurs billions of times per second.

Advances in Microprocessor Design. Innovations in chip designs are coming at a faster and faster rate, as described by **Moore's law**. In 1965, Gordon Moore, a co-founder of Intel Corporation, predicted that microprocessor complexity would double approximately every 2 years. His prediction has been amazingly accurate.

TABLE PI2.3 Comparison of Personal Computer Components and Cost Over Time

Year	Chip	RAM	Hard Drive	Monitor	Cost
1997	Pentium II	64 megabytes	4 gigabytes	17-inch	$4,000
2007	Dual-core	1 gigabyte	250 gigabytes	19-inch	$1,700
2011	Quad-core	4 gigabytes	1 terabyte	22-inch	$1,500

The advances predicted from Moore's Law arise mainly from the following changes:

- Producing increasingly miniaturized transistors.

- Placing multiple processors on a single chip. Chips with more than one processor are called *multicore* chips. For example, the Cell chip, produced by a consortium of Sony, Toshiba, and IBM, contains nine processors. Computers using the Cell chip display very rich graphics. The chip is also used in TV sets and home theaters that can download and show large numbers of high-definition programs. Intel (www.intel.com) and AMD (www.amd.com) offer multicore chips.

- In May 2011, Intel announced that its next-generation chips, which employ a three-dimensional design, will be introduced to the market at the start of 2012. The 3D chips will require less power than Intel's current chips, while improving performance. These chips will enhance the performance of all computers. However, they will be particularly valuable in handheld devices, because they will also extend the device's battery life.

In addition to increased speeds and performance, Moore's law has had an impact on costs, as you can see in Table PI2.3.

Computer Memory

The amount and type of memory that a computer possesses has a great deal to do with its general utility. A computer's memory also determines the types of programs that the computer can run, the work it can perform, its speed, and its cost. There are two basic categories of computer memory. The first is *primary storage*. It is called "primary" because it stores small amounts of data and information that will be used immediately by the CPU. The second category is *secondary storage*, which stores much larger amounts of data and information (an entire software program, for example) for extended periods of time.

Memory Capacity. As you have seen, CPUs process only binary units—0s and 1s—which are translated through computer languages into bits. A particular combination of bits represents a certain alphanumeric character or a simple mathematical operation. Eight bits are needed to represent any one of these characters. This 8-bit string is known as a **byte**. The storage capacity of a computer is measured in bytes. Bits typically are used as units of measure only for telecommunications capacity, as in how many million bits per second can be sent through a particular medium.

The hierarchy of terms used to describe memory capacity is as follows:

- *Kilobyte. Kilo* means "one thousand," so a kilobyte (KB) is approximately 1,000 bytes. Actually, a kilobyte is 1,024 bytes. Computer designers find it convenient to work with powers of 2: 1,024 is 2 to the 10th power, and 1,024 is close enough to 1,000 that for *kilobyte* people use the standard prefix *kilo*, which means exactly 1,000 in familiar units such as the kilogram or kilometer.

- *Megabyte. Mega* means "one million," so a megabyte (MB) is approximately 1 million bytes. Most personal computers have hundreds of megabytes of RAM memory.

- *Gigabyte. Giga* means "one billion," so a gigabyte (GB) is approximately 1 billion bytes.

- *Terabyte.* A terabyte is approximately 1 trillion bytes. The storage capacity of modern personal computers can be several terabytes.

- *Petabyte.* A petabyte is approximately 1,000 terabytes.
- *Exabyte.* An exabyte is approximately 1,000 petabytes.
- *Zettabyte.* A zettabyte is approximately 1,000 exabytes.

To get a feel for these amounts, consider the following example: If your computer has one terabyte of storage capacity on its hard drive (a type of secondary storage), it can store approximately 1 trillion bytes of data. If the average page of text contains about 2,000 bytes, then your hard drive could store approximately 10 percent of all the print collections of the Library of Congress. That same terabyte can store 70 hours of standard-definition compressed video.

Primary Storage. **Primary storage** (or **main memory**, as it is sometimes called), stores three types of information for very brief periods of time: (1) data to be processed by the CPU, (2) instructions for the CPU as to how to process the data, and (3) operating system programs that manage various aspects of the computer's operation. Primary storage takes place in chips mounted on the computer's main circuit board, called the *motherboard*, which are located as close as physically possible to the CPU chip. As with the CPU, all the data and instructions in primary storage have been translated into binary code.

The four main types of primary storage are (1) register, (2) cache memory, (3) random access memory (RAM), and (4) read-only memory (ROM). You learn about each type of primary storage next.

Registers are part of the CPU. They have the least capacity, storing extremely limited amounts of instructions and data only immediately before and after processing.

Cache memory is a type of high-speed memory that enables the computer to temporarily store blocks of data that are used more often and that a processor can access more rapidly than main memory (RAM). Cache memory is physically located closer to the CPU than RAM. Blocks used less often remain in RAM until they are transferred to cache; blocks used infrequently remain in secondary storage. Cache memory is faster than RAM because the instructions travel a shorter distance to the CPU.

Random access memory (RAM) is the part of primary storage that holds a software program and small amounts of data for processing. When you start most software programs on your computer (such as Microsoft Word), the entire program is brought from secondary storage into RAM. As you use the program, small parts of the program's instructions and data are sent into the registers and then to the CPU. Compared with the registers, RAM stores more information and is located farther away from the CPU. However, compared with secondary storage, RAM stores less information and is much closer to the CPU.

RAM is temporary and, in most cases, *volatile*—that is, RAM chips lose their contents if the current is lost or turned off, as from a power surge, brownout, or electrical noise generated by lightning or nearby machines.

Most of us have lost data at one time or another due to a computer "crash" or a power failure. What is usually lost is whatever is in RAM, cache, or the registers at the time, because these types of memory are volatile. Therefore, you need greater security when you are storing certain types of critical data or instructions. Cautious computer users frequently save data to nonvolatile memory (secondary storage). In addition, most modern software applications have autosave functions. Programs stored in secondary storage, even though they are temporarily copied into RAM when they are being used, remain intact because only the copy is lost, not the original.

Read-only memory (ROM) is the place—actually, a type of chip—where certain critical instructions are safeguarded. ROM is nonvolatile, so it retains these instructions when the power to the computer is turned off. The read-only designation means that these instructions can only be read by the computer and cannot be changed by the user. An example of ROM is the instructions needed to start or "boot" the computer after it has been shut off.

Secondary Storage. **Secondary storage** is designed to store very large amounts of data for extended periods of time. Secondary storage has the following characteristics:

- It is nonvolatile.
- It takes more time to retrieve data from it than from RAM.
- It is cheaper than primary storage (see Figure PI2.5).
- It can utilize a variety of media, each with its own technology, as you see next.

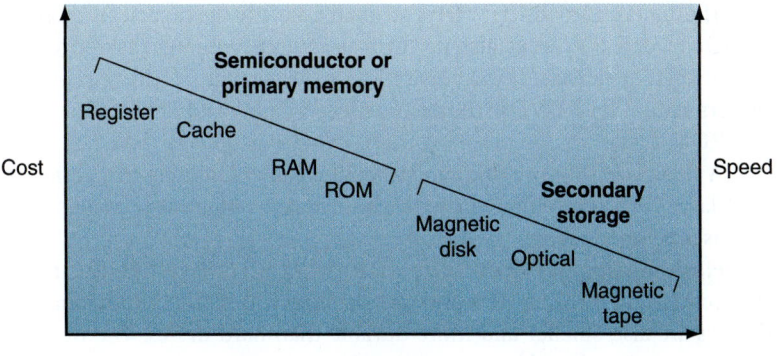

Figure PI2.5 Primary memory compared to secondary storage.

One secondary storage medium, **magnetic tape**, is kept on a large open reel or in a smaller cartridge or cassette. Although this is an old technology, it remains popular because it is the cheapest storage medium, and it can handle enormous amounts of data. As a result, many organizations use magnetic tape for archival storage. The downside is that it is the slowest method for retrieving data because all the data are placed on the tape sequentially. **Sequential access** means that the system might have to run through the majority of the tape before it comes to the desired piece of data.

Magnetic disks (or **hard drives** or **fixed disk drives**), are the most commonly used mass storage devices because of their low cost, high speed, and large storage capacity. Hard disk drives read from, and write to, stacks of rotating (at up to 15,000 rpm) magnetic disk platters mounted in rigid enclosures and sealed against environmental and atmospheric contamination (see Figure PI2.6). These disks are permanently mounted in a unit that may be internal or external to the computer.

Solid state drives (SSDs) are data storage devices that serve the same purpose as a hard drive and store data in memory chips. Where hard drives have moving parts, SSDs do not. SSDs use the same interface with the computer's CPU as hard drives and are, therefore, a seamless replacement for hard drives. SSDs offer many advantages over hard drives. They use less power, are silent and faster, and produce about one-third the heat of a hard drive. The major disadvantage of SSDs is that they cost more than hard drives

Unlike magnetic media, **optical storage devices** do not store data via magnetism. Rather, a laser reads the surface of a reflective plastic platter. Optical disk drives are slower than magnetic hard drives, but they are less susceptible to damage from contamination and are less fragile.

In addition, optical disks can store a great deal of information, both on a routine basis and also when combined into storage systems. Types of optical disks include compact disk read-only memory and digital video disk.

Compact disk, read-only memory (*CD-ROM*) storage devices feature high capacity, low cost, and high durability. However, because a CD-ROM is a read-only medium, it cannot be written on. *CD-R* can be written to, but once this is done, what was written on it cannot be changed later. That is, CD-R is writeable, which CD-ROM is not, but is not rewriteable, which *CD-RW* (compact disk, rewritable) is. There are applications where not being rewriteable is a plus, because it prevents some types of accidental data destruction. CD-RW adds rewritability to the recordable compact disk market.

Figure PI2.6 Traditional hard drives are less expensive, but solid state drives are faster and are more reliable. (*Sources:* BraginAlexey/Shutterstock; © Krzysztof Krzyscin/iStockphoto)

The digital video disk (*DVD*) is a 5-inch disk with the capacity to store about 135 minutes of digital video. DVDs can also perform as computer storage disks, providing storage capabilities of 17 gigabytes. DVD players can read current CD-ROMs, but current CD-ROM players cannot read DVDs. The access speed of a DVD drive is faster than that of a typical CD-ROM drive.

A dual-layer *Blu-ray disc* can store 50 gigabytes, almost three times the capacity of a dual-layer DVD. Development of the Blu-ray technology is ongoing, with 10-layered Blu-ray discs being tested.

Flash memory devices (or *memory cards*) are nonvolatile electronic storage devices that contain no moving parts and use 30 times less battery power than hard drives. Flash devices are also smaller and more durable than hard drives. The trade-offs are that flash devices store less data than hard drives. Flash devices are used with digital cameras, hand-held and laptop computers, telephones, music players, and video game consoles.

One popular flash memory device is the **thumb drive** (also called *memory stick, jump drive,* or *flash drive*). These devices fit into Universal Serial Bus (USB) ports on personal computers and other devices, and they can store many gigabytes. Thumb drives have replaced magnetic floppy disks for portable storage.

•BEFORE *YOU GO ON . . .*

1. Decisions about hardware focus on what three factors?
2. What are the overall trends in hardware?
3. Define hardware, and list the major hardware components.
4. Describe the computer hierarchy from the largest to the smallest computers.
5. Distinguish between human data-input devices and source-data automation.
6. Briefly describe how a microprocessor functions.
7. Distinguish between primary storage and secondary storage.

Student Activity | PI2.1

Objective: To evaluate the capabilities of a computer machine and have a sense of what happens when you click "Enter" locally or on a network machine.

Chapter Connection: This activity focuses on the discussion of computer hardware in Section PI2.1 of this chapter.

Prerequisites: You should have read Section PI2.1.

Activity–Part 1: *Begin this activity by determining the features of the computer (desktop, laptop, note-book) you are using. Click on "Control Panel, System." The General tab will tell you the operating system, the CPU and its speed (in GHz), and the amount of RAM. Now click on "My Computer" (on the Start menu*

or desktop). You will see a list of devices—usually a C: drive (Local Disk), a DVD drive, and possibly an integrated camera. Right click on your C: drive and click on "Properties." It will show you the capacity (in MB or GB—or even TB) as well as details about how much space is being used and how much is free.

Next, go to a Web site for Staples, BestBuy, Office Depot, or some other computer retailer, and review the similar machines for sale.

Activity–Part 2: *Many organizations are delivering applications "in the cloud." Amazon has become a major player in this space by offering its own hardware architecture for organizations to utilize (Hardware As A Service, somewhat like Software As A Service). Look* at this overview of its product called *Amazon Elastic Compute Cloud 2* (Amazon EC2, http://aws.amazon.com/ec2).

Deliverables:

Answer the following questions about Activity 1:

1. How does your computer compare to the others you found online? Start by comparing yours with the machine selling for the lowest price. Then compare to the machine selling at the highest price. If you were thinking about buying either of those machines to replace the one you have, how would you justify it?

2. Now imagine you are in charge of a small retailer that has three machines just like yours. Could you justify upgrading to either one of the machines you looked at? How? At what point would you suggest upgrading?

Quiz Questions:

1. True or False? The RAM of a computer is the amount of storage the machine has.

2. True or False? An elastic IP address is associated with a particular instance.

3. On a computer with a multitasking operating system, each program that is running simultaneously is called a _____.

Discussion Questions:

1. Review the hierarchy from the largest to the smallest computers. Organizations are usually focused on the smallest computers. Why?

2. What is the impact on this hierarchy as computers are converging with smartphones?

PI2.2 Introduction to Software

Computer hardware is only as effective as the instructions you give it, and those instructions are contained in **software**. The importance of computer software cannot be overestimated. The first software applications of computers in business were developed in the early 1950s. Software was less costly in computer systems then. Today, software comprises a much larger percentage of the cost of modern computer systems because the price of hardware has dramatically decreased, while the complexity and the price of software have dramatically increased.

The increasing complexity of software also leads to the increased potential for errors or *bugs*. Large applications today can contain millions of lines of computer code, written by hundreds of people over the course of several years. The potential for errors is huge, and testing and *debugging* software is expensive and time consuming.

Regardless of the overall trends in software—increased complexity, increased cost, and increasing numbers of defects—software has become an everyday feature of our business and personal lives. You begin your examination of software by defining some fundamental concepts. Software consists of **computer programs**, which are sequences of instructions for the computer. The process of writing, or *coding*, programs is called *programming*. Individuals who perform this task are called *programmers*.

Computer programs include **documentation**, which is a written description of the functions of the program. Documentation helps the user operate the computer system, and it helps other programmers understand what the program does and how it accomplishes its purpose. Documentation is vital to the business organization. Without it, if a key programmer or user leaves, the knowledge of how to use the program or how it is designed may be lost as well.

The computer is able to do nothing until it is instructed by software. Although computer hardware is, by design, general purpose, software enables the user to instruct a computer system to perform specific functions that provide business value. The two major types of software are systems software and application software. The relationship among hardware, systems software, and application software is illustrated in Figure PI2.7.

Systems software is a set of instructions that serves primarily as an intermediary between computer hardware and application programs (Figure PI2.8a–c). Systems software provides important self-regulatory functions for computer systems, such as loading itself when the computer is first turned on and providing commonly used sets of instructions for all applications. *Systems programming* refers to both the creation and the maintenance of systems software.

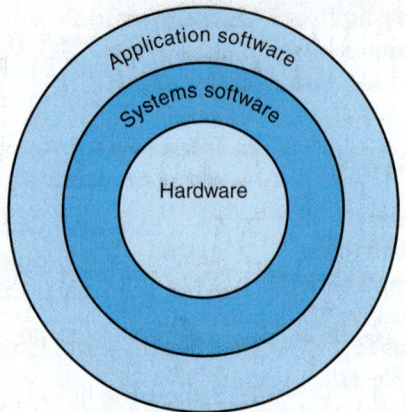

Figure PI2.7 Systems software services as intermediary between hardware and functional applications.

Application software is a set of computer instructions that provide more specific functionality to a user (Figures PI2.9 a–b). That functionality may be broad, such as general word processing, or narrow, such as an organization's payroll program. Essentially, an application program applies a computer to a certain need. *Application programming* refers to both the creation and the modification and improvement of application software. Application software may be proprietary or off the shelf. As you shall see, many different software applications are used by organizations today.

Software Issues

The importance of software in computer systems has brought new issues to the forefront for organizational managers. These issues include software defects (bugs), software evaluation and selection, licensing, open systems, and open-source software.

(a)

(b)

Figure PI2.8a–c System software. (*Source:* © Oliver Leedham/ Alamy; © studiomode/Alamy)

Chrome OS

(c)

(a)   (b)

Figure PI2.9a–b Application software.

Software Defects. All too often, computer program code is inefficient, poorly designed, and riddled with errors. The Software Engineering Institute (SEI) at Carnegie Mellon University in Pittsburgh defines good software as usable, reliable, defect free, cost effective, and maintainable. As you become increasingly dependent on computers and networks, the risks associated with software defects are getting worse.

The SEI maintains that, on average, professional programmers make between 100 and 150 errors in every 1,000 lines of code they write. Fortunately, the software industry recognizes this problem. Unfortunately, however, the problem is enormous, and the industry is taking only initial steps to resolve it. One critical step is better design and planning at the beginning of the development process (discussed in Chapter 14).

Software Licensing. Although many people routinely copy software, making copies without the manufacturer's explicit permission is illegal. The BSA is a nonprofit trade association dedicated to promoting a safe and legal digital world. It collects, investigates, and acts on software piracy tips. Most tips come from current and past employees of the offending companies. The Business Software Alliance (BSA) (www.bsa.org) has calculated that software piracy costs software vendors around the world billions of dollars annually.

To protect their investment, software vendors must protect their software from being copied and distributed by individuals and other software companies. A company can copyright its software, which means that the U.S. Copyright Office grants the company the exclusive legal right to reproduce, publish, and sell that software.

As the number of desktop computers continues to increase and businesses continue to decentralize, it becomes more and more difficult for IS managers to supervise their software assets. In fact, a recent survey found that 70 percent of chief information officers (CIOs) are "not confident" that their companies are in compliance with software licensing agreements. For example, one medium-size company was fined $10,000 for Microsoft Exchange mailbox licenses for which the company unknowingly had not paid. Worse, the company was also fined $100,000 for not having the necessary licenses for Autodesk, Inc.'s AutoCAD design software.

To help companies manage their software licenses, new firms have arisen that specialize in tracking software licenses for a fee. Firms such as Express Metrix (www.expressmetrix. com), Insight Technology Solutions (see www.insight.com/pages/itservices/licensing_index.web), and others will track and manage a company's software licenses to ensure that the company is in compliance with U.S. copyright laws.

Open Systems. The concept of **open systems** refers to a model of computing products that work together. To achieve this goal, the same operating system with compatible software must be installed on all the different computers that interact with one another within an organization. A complementary approach is to produce application software that will run across all computer platforms. If hardware, operating systems, and application software are designed as open systems, the user will be able to purchase the best software, called *best of breed*, for the job without worrying whether it will run on particular hardware.

Open-Source Software. There is a trend within the software industry away from proprietary software toward open-source software. **Proprietary software** is software that has been developed by a company and has restrictions on its use, copying, and modification. The company developing such software spends money and time on research and development of its software product and then sells it in the marketplace. The proprietary nature of the software means that the company keeps the source code—the actual computer instructions—private (as Coca-Cola does with its formula).

In contrast, the source code for **open-source software** is available at no cost to developers and users. Open-source software is copyrighted and distributed with license terms ensuring that the source code will always be available.

Open-source software products have worldwide "communities" of developers who write and maintain the code. Inside each community, however, only a small group of developers, called *core developers*, is allowed to modify or submit changes to the code. Other developers submit code to the core developers.

There are advantages and disadvantages to implementing open-source software in an organization. According to the Open Source Initiative (www.opensource.org), open-source development produces high-quality, reliable, low-cost software (Figure PI2.10). This software is also flexible, meaning that the code can be modified to meet the needs of the user. In many cases, open-source software is more reliable than commercial software. Because the code is available to many developers, more bugs are discovered early and quickly, and they are fixed immediately. Support for open-source software is also available from firms that provide products derived from the software. An example is Red Hat for Linux (www.redhat.com). These firms provide education, training, and technical support for the software for a fee.

Open-source software also has disadvantages, however. The biggest disadvantage is that companies using open-source software are dependent on the continued goodwill of an army of volunteers for enhancements, bug fixes, and so on, even if these companies contract for support. Some companies will not accept this risk, even though as a practical matter the support community for Linux, Apache, or Firefox is not likely to disappear. Further, organizations that do not have in-house technical experts will have to buy maintenance-support contracts from a third party. In addition, questions have arisen concerning the ease of use of open-source software, the amount of time and expense needed to train users, and the compatibility with existing systems or with the systems of business partners.

There are many examples of open-source software, including GNU (GNU's Not UNIX) suite of software (www.gnu.org) developed by the Free Software Foundation (www.fsf.org); Linux operating system (see www.linux.com); Apache Web server (www.apache.org); sendmail SMTP (Send Mail Transport Protocol) e-mail server (www.sendmail.org); Perl programming language (www.perl.org); Firefox 5 browser from Mozilla (www.mozilla.org); and the OpenOffice applications suite (www.openoffice.org). In fact, there are more than 150,000 open-source projects under way on SourceForge (www.sourceforge.net), the popular open-source hosting site.

Linux and Apache are excellent examples of how open-source software is moving to the mainstream. Linux is gaining market share in servers. It now runs on approximately one-fourth of all servers, whereas Microsoft runs on about two-thirds of all servers. Further, almost two-thirds of the world's Web servers now run Apache, compared to one-third for Microsoft.

Many major companies use open-source software. For example, Japan's Shinsei Bank (www.shinseibank.com/english) uses Linux on its servers, SugarCRM (www.sugarcrm.com) for certain customer relationship management tasks, and MySQL (www.mysql.com)

open-source database management software. Further, the *Los Angeles Times* uses Alfresco (www.alfresco.com) to manage some of the images and video for the newspaper's Web site.

Systems Software

As noted, systems software is the class of programs that control and support the computer system and its information-processing activities. Systems software also facilitates the programming, testing, and debugging of computer programs. Systems software programs support application software by directing the basic functions of the computer. For example, when the computer is turned on, the initialization program (a systems program) prepares and readies all devices for processing. The major type of systems software with which we are concerned is the operating system.

The **operating system (OS)** is the director of your computer system's operations. It supervises the overall operation of the computer, including monitoring the computer's status, scheduling operations, and managing the input and output processes. The operating system also provides an interface between the user and the hardware.

This user interface hides the complexity of the hardware from the user. That is, you do not have to know how the hardware actually operates. You simply have to know what the hardware will do and what you need to do to obtain desired results.

The ease or difficulty of the interaction between the user and the computer is determined to a large extent by the user interface. The **graphical user interface (GUI)** allows users to exercise direct control of visible objects (such as icons) and actions that replace complex commands.

The next generation of GUI technology will incorporate features such as virtual reality, head-mounted displays, speech input (user commands) and output, pen and gesture recognition, animation, multimedia, artificial intelligence, and cellular/wireless communication capabilities. The new interfaces, called *natural user interfaces* (NUIs), will combine *haptic interfaces, social interfaces*, and *touch-enabled gesture-control interfaces*.

A **haptic interface** allows the user to feel a sense of touch by applying forces, vibrations, and/or motions to the user. A **social interface** is a user interface that guides the user through computer applications by using cartoonlike characters, graphics, animation, and voice commands. The cartoonlike characters can be cast as puppets, narrators, guides, inhabitants, or avatars (computer-generated humanlike figures). Social interfaces are hard to do without being corny. For example, most users of Microsoft Office 97 found the assistant "Clippy" so annoying that it was deleted from Office 2003 and later versions.

Motion control gaming consoles are another type of interface. Three major players currently offer this interface: Xbox 360 Kinect, PS3 PlayStation Move, and Nintendo Wii.

- Kinect tracks your movements without a physical controller, has voice recognition, and accommodates multiple players.

- PlayStation Move uses a physical controller with motion-sensing electronics, making it the technological "cross" between Kinect and Wii. Move requires each player to use a wand.

- Wii uses a physical controller. Compared to Kinect and Move, Wii has been on the market longer, has the biggest library of motion-sensing games, and is the least expensive system. However, Wii has the least accurate motion sensing of the three systems, and it is not available in high-definition, whereas Kinect and Move are.

Touch-enabled gesture-control interfaces enable users to browse through photos, "toss" objects around a screen, "flick" to turn the pages of a book, play video games, and watch movies. Examples of this type of interface are Microsoft Surface and the Apple iPhone.

Microsoft Surface is used in casinos such as Harrah's iBar in Las Vegas and in some AT&T stores. The most visible use of Surface, however, was the touch wall used by CNN during the presidential election coverage in 2008.

Well-known desktop operating systems include Microsoft Windows (www.microsoft.com), Apple Mac OS X (www.apple.com), Linux (linux.com), and Google Chrome OS (www.google.com/). As their developers release new versions with new features, they often give the new version a new designation. For example, the latest version of Windows is Windows 7, and the latest version of OS X is Snow Leopard or OS X 10.6.

Application Software

As noted, application software consists of instructions that direct a computer system to perform specific information-processing activities and that provide functionality for users. Because there are so many different uses for computers, there are a correspondingly large number of application software programs.

Application software may be developed in house by the organization's information systems personnel, or it may be commissioned from a software vendor. Alternatively, it can be purchased, leased, or rented from a vendor that develops programs and sells them to many organizations. This "off-the-shelf" software may be a standard package, or it may be customizable. Special-purpose programs or "packages" can be tailored for a specific purpose, such as inventory control or payroll. The term **package** is commonly used for a computer program (or group of programs) that has been developed by a vendor and is available for purchase in a prepackaged form.

General-purpose, off-the-shelf application programs designed to help individual users increase their productivity are referred to as **personal application software**. Some of the major types of personal application software are listed in Table PI2.4. *Software suites*

TABLE PI2.4 Personal Application Software

Category of Personal Application Software	Major Functions	Examples
Spreadsheets	Use rows and columns to manipulate primarily numerical data; useful for analyzing financial information, and for what-if and goal-seeking analyses	Microsoft Excel Corel Quattro Pro Apple iWork Numbers
Word processing	Allow users to manipulate primarily text with many writing and editing features	Microsoft Word Apple iWork Pages
Desktop publishing	Extend word processing software to allow production of finished, camera-ready documents, which may contain photographs, diagrams, and other images combined with text in different fonts	Microsoft Publisher QuarkXPress
Data management	Allow users to store, retrieve, and manipulate related data	Microsoft Access FileMaker Pro
Presentation	Allows users to create and edit graphically rich information to appear on electronic slides	Microsoft PowerPoint Apple iWork Keynote
Graphics	Allow users to create, store, and display or print charts, graphs, maps, and drawings	Adobe PhotoShop Corel DRAW
Personal information management	Allow users to create and maintain calendars, appointments, to-do lists, and business contacts	IBM Lotus Notes Microsoft Outlook
Personal finance	Allow users to maintain checkbooks, track investments, monitor credit cards, bank, and pay bills electronically	Quicken Microsoft Money
Web authoring	Allow users to design Web sites and publish them on the Web	Microsoft FrontPage Adobe Dreamweaver
Communications	Allow users to communicate with other people over any distance.	Novell Groupwise

combine some of these packages and integrate their functions. Microsoft Office is a well-known example of a software suite.

Speech recognition software is an input technology, rather than strictly an application, that can feed systems software and application software. **Speech recognition software**, or **voice recognition software**, recognizes and interprets human speech, either one word at a time (discrete speech) or in a conversational stream (continuous speech). Advances in processing power, new software algorithms, and better microphones have enabled developers to design extremely accurate voice recognition software. Experts predict that, in the near future, voice recognition systems will likely be built into almost every device, appliance, and machine that people use. Applications for voice recognition technology abound. Consider these examples:

- Call centers are using the technology. The average call-center call costs $5 if it is handled by an employee, but only 50 cents with a self-service, speech-enabled system. The online brokerage firm E-Trade Financial uses Tellme (www.tellme.com) to field about 50,000 calls per day, thereby saving at least $30 million annually.

- IBM's Embedded ViaVoice software (www-306.ibm.com/software/voice/viavoice/) powers GM's OnStar and other dashboard command systems, such as music players and navigational systems.

- Apple's Macintosh OS X and Microsoft's Windows 7 operating system come with built-in voice technology.

- Nuance's Dragon NaturallySpeaking (www.nuance.com) allows for accurate voice-to-text and e-mail dictation.

- Vocera Communications (www.vocera.com) has developed a communicator badge that combines voice-recognition with wireless technologies. Among its first customers were medical workers, who use the badge to find medical records or to search through hospital directories by voice to find the right person to help with a patient problem.

- Vox-Tec's (www.voxtec.com) Phraselator, a handheld device about the size of a checkbook, listens to requests for a phrase and then delivers a translation in any of 41 specified languages. It is being used by U.S. troops in Iraq and Afghanistan to provide translations in Arabic and Pashto.

BEFORE YOU GO ON . . .

1. What does the following statement mean? "Hardware is useless without software."
2. What are the differences between systems software and application software?
3. What is open-source software, and what are its advantages? Can you think of any disadvantages?
4. Describe the functions of the operating system.

Student Activity | PI2.2

Objective: You need to be able to evaluate what capabilities the machine you are using has, and you need to have a sense of what happens when you click "Enter," either locally or on a network machine.

Chapter Connection: This activity relates to both sections of this chapter.

Prerequisites: You should have read Section PI2.1 and Section PI2.2.

Activity: *To work with voice-to-text software, follow this link to download e-Speaking Voice and Speech Recognition (30-day free trial—you are not prompted for personal information):*

You may need to install Microsoft Speech Application Program Interface (Microsoft Speech API). The e-Speaking program will prompt you if it is required. Spend some time teaching your voice to the software. Then use the program to generate the document for this activity (see the following questions).

It is important that you learn to work with new software. Software today usually asks before it does anything that cannot be undone. So feel free to click on icons to see what happens. For something a little different, download the following free 30-day trial of Post-it Digital Notes (you are not prompted for personal information):

www.post-it.com/wps/portal/3M/en_US/Post_It/Global/Home/Products/Digital_Products

Work with the software to generate Post-it notes on your computer. Try clicking on the software icons, try right-clicking, see if you can change the colors, see if you can put a due date on the note, have the icon only be on the taskbar, delete some of your notes, search your notes (including the trash bin). Just have some fun by playing with the program.

Note: Be sure to uninstall both of these products when you are done. If you do not, you will be prompted to buy them at the end of the trial period.

Deliverables:

Prepare answers to the following questions:

1. Why did you have to train the e-speaking software with your voice? What data is this application storing?

2. Quite a few organizations are using text-to-voice (for example, if you call for your utility bill balance, a computer voice may "read" the amount to you). How do you think organizations could use voice-to-text software?

3. Did you find the digital Post-it note software intuitive? Was it easy to learn?

4. Electronic Post-it notes might help you manage your time. How might you use them?

Quiz Questions:

1. True or False? If software can do text-to-voice, it will also be able to do voice-to-text.

2. True or False? If you train voice-to-text software when you have a cold, the software will still recognize everything you say when you recover from the cold.

3. True or False? Digital Post-it notes are an example of personal application software.

Discussion Questions:

1. How important is an intuitive user interface for software such as Post-it Digital Notes? Does it make a difference who the user is?

2. What other features would have made Post-it Digital Notes more useful for you? (Did anyone try to dictate a digital note? Did it work? Did anyone attach a file to a note? Did people play with colors?)

What's In IT For Me?

Hardware

For All Business Majors

The design of computer hardware has profound impacts for businesspeople. Personal and organizational success can depend on an understanding of hardware design and a commitment to knowing where it is going and what opportunities and challenges hardware innovations will bring. Because these innovations are occurring so rapidly, hardware decisions at both the individual level and at the organizational level are difficult.

At the *individual level*, most people who have a home or office computer system and want to upgrade it, or people who are contemplating their first computer purchase, are faced with the decision of *when* to buy as much as *what* to buy and at what cost. At the *organizational level*, these same issues plague IS professionals. However, they are more complex and more costly. Most organizations have many different computer systems in place at the same time. Innovations may come to different classes of computers at different times or rates. Therefore, managers must decide when old hardware *legacy systems* still have a productive role in the organization and when they should be replaced. A legacy system is an old computer system or application that continues to be used, typically because it still functions for the users' needs, even though newer technology is available.

Software

For the Accounting Major

Accounting application software performs the organization's accounting functions, which are repetitive and high volume. Each business transaction (e.g., a person hired, a paycheck produced, an item sold) produces data that must be captured. After accounting applications capture the data, they manipulate them as necessary. Accounting applications adhere to relatively standardized procedures, handle detailed data, and have a historical focus (i.e., what happened in the past).

For the Finance Major

Financial application software provides information about the firm's financial status to persons and groups inside and outside the firm. Financial applications include forecasting, funds management, and control applications. Forecasting applications predict and project the firm's future activity in the economic environment. Funds management applications use cash flow models to analyze expected cash flows. Control applications enable managers to monitor their financial performance, typically by providing information about the budgeting process and performance ratios.

For the Marketing Major

Marketing application software helps management solve problems that involve marketing the firm's products. Marketing software includes marketing research and marketing intelligence applications. Marketing applications provide information about the firm's products and competitors, its distribution system, its advertising and personal selling activities, and its pricing strategies. Overall, marketing applications help managers develop strategies that combine the four major elements of marketing: product, promotion, place, and price.

For the Production/Operations Management Major

Managers use production/operations management (POM) applications software for production planning and as part of the physical production system. POM applications include production, inventory, quality, and cost software. These applications help management operate manufacturing facilities and logistics. Materials requirements planning (MRP) software is also widely used in manufacturing. This software identifies which materials will be needed, what quantities will be needed, and the dates on which they will be needed. This information enables managers to be proactive.

For the Human Resources Management Major

Human resources management application software provides information concerning recruiting and hiring, education and training, maintaining the employee database, termination, and administering benefits. HRM applications include workforce planning, recruiting, workforce management, compensation, benefits, and environmental reporting subsystems (e.g., equal employment opportunity records and analysis, union enrollment, toxic substances, and grievances).

For the MIS Major

If your company decides to develop software itself, the MIS function is responsible for managing this activity. If the company decides to buy software, the MIS function deals with software vendors in analyzing their products. The MIS function is also responsible for upgrading software as vendors release new versions.

SUMMARY

1. Discuss strategic issues that link hardware design to business strategy.

Strategic issues linking hardware design to business strategy encompass these questions: How do organizations keep up with the rapid price/performance advancements in hardware? How often should an organization upgrade its computers and storage systems? How can organizations measure benefits gained from price/performance improvements in hardware?

2. Differentiate between the two major types of software.

Software consists of computer programs (coded instructions) that control the functions of computer hardware. The two main categories of software are systems software and application software. Systems software manages the hardware resources of the computer system; it functions between the hardware and the application software. Systems software includes the system control programs (operating systems) and system support programs. Application software enables users to perform specific tasks and information-processing activities. Application software may be proprietary or off the shelf.

3. Describe the major software issues that organizations face today.

Computer program code often contains errors. The industry recognizes the problem of software defects, but it is so enormous that only initial steps are being taken. The software evaluation and selection process is a difficult one because it is affected by many factors. Software licensing is yet another issue for organizations and individuals. Copying software is illegal. Software vendors copyright their software to protect it from being copied. As a result, companies must license vendor-developed software to use it.

4. Discuss the advantages and disadvantages of open-source software.

Advantages of open-source software include high quality, reliability, flexibility (code can be modified to meet the needs of the user), and low cost. Open-source software can be more reliable than commercial software. Because the code is available to many developers, more bugs are discovered early and quickly and are fixed immediately. Disadvantages include cost of maintenance support contracts, ease of use, the amount of time and expense needed to train users, and the lack of compatibility with existing systems or with the systems of business partners.

GLOSSARY

application software The class of computer instructions that directs a computer system to perform specific processing activities and provide functionality for users.

arithmetic-logic unit (ALU) Portion of the CPU that performs the mathematic calculations and makes logical comparisons.

binary form The form in which data and instructions can be read by the CPU—only 0s and 1s.

bit Short for *binary digit* (0s and 1s), the only data that a CPU can process.

byte An 8-bit string of data, needed to represent any one alphanumeric character or simple mathematical operation.

cache memory A type of high-speed memory that enables the computer to temporarily store blocks of data that are used more often and that a processor can access more rapidly than main memory (RAM).

central processing unit (CPU) Hardware that performs the actual computation or "number crunching" inside any computer.

computer programs The sequences of instructions for the computer, which comprise software.

control unit Portion of the CPU that controls the flow of information.

documentation Written description of the functions of a software program.

fat clients Desktop computer systems that offer full functionality.

flash memory devices Nonvolatile electronic storage devices that are compact, portable, require little power, and contain no moving parts.

graphical user interface (GUI) System software that allows users to have direct control of visible objects (such as icons) and actions, which replace command syntax.

haptic interface Allows the user to feel a sense of touch by applying forces, vibrations, and/or motions to the user.

laptop computers (notebook computers) Small, easily transportable, lightweight microcomputers.

magnetic disks (or hard drives or fixed disk drives) A form of secondary storage on a magnetized disk divided into tracks and sectors that provide addresses for various pieces of data.

magnetic tape A secondary storage medium on a large open reel or in a smaller cartridge or cassette.

mainframes Relatively large computers used in large enterprises for extensive computing applications that are accessed by thousands of users.

microcomputers The smallest and least expensive category of general-purpose computers; also called micros, personal computers, or PCs.

microprocessor The CPU, made up of millions of transistors embedded in a circuit on a silicon wafer or chip.

minicomputers Relatively small, inexpensive, and compact midrange computers that perform the same functions as mainframe computers, but to a more limited extent.

Moore's law Prediction by Gordon Moore, an Intel co-founder, that microprocessor complexity would double approximately every 2 years.

multimedia technology Computer-based integration of text, sound, still images, animation, and digitized full-motion video.

netbook A very small, lightweight, low-cost, energy-efficient, portable computer, typically optimized for Internet-based services such as Web browsing and e-mailing.

notebook computer (see **laptop computer**)

open-source software Software made available in source code form at no cost to developers.

open systems A model of computing products that work together by use of the same operating system with compatible software on all the different computers that would interact with one another in an organization.

operating system (OS) The main system control program, which supervises the overall operations of the computer, allocates CPU time and main memory to programs, and provides an interface between the user and the hardware.

optical storage devices A form of secondary storage in which a laser reads the surface of a reflective plastic platter.

package Common term for a computer program developed by a vendor and available for purchase in prepackaged form.

personal application software General-purpose, off-the-shelf application programs that support general types of processing, rather than being linked to any specific business function.

primary storage (also called **main memory**) High-speed storage located directly on the motherboard that stores data to be processed by the CPU, instructions telling the CPU how to process the data, and operating systems programs.

proprietary software Software that has been developed by a company and has restrictions on its use, copying, and modification.

random access memory (RAM) The part of primary storage that holds a software program and small amounts of data when they are brought from secondary storage.

read-only memory (ROM) Type of primary storage where certain critical instructions are safeguarded; the storage is nonvolatile and retains the instructions when the power to the computer is turned off.

registers High-speed storage areas in the CPU that store very small amounts of data and instructions for short periods of time.

secondary storage Technology that can store very large amounts of data for extended periods of time.

sequential access Data access in which the computer system must run through data in sequence in order to locate a particular piece.

server Smaller midrange computers that support networks, enabling users to share files, software, and other network devices.

social interface A user interface that guides the user through computer applications by using cartoonlike characters, graphics, animation, and voice commands.

software A set of computer programs that enable the hardware to process data.

solid state drives (SSDs) Data storage devices that serve the same purpose as a hard drive and store data in memory chips.

speech recognition software (or **voice recognition software**) Software that recognizes and interprets human speech, either one word at a time (discrete speech) or in a stream (continuous speech).

supercomputer Computers with the most processing power available; used primarily in scientific and military work for computationally demanding tasks on very large data sets.

systems software The class of computer instructions that serve primarily as an intermediary between computer hardware and application programs; provides important self-regulatory functions for computer systems.

tablet computer (or **tablet**) A complete computer contained entirely in a flat touch screen that uses a stylus, digital pen, or fingertip as an input device instead of a keyboard or mouse.

thin-client systems Desktop computer systems that do not offer the full functionality of a PC.

thumb drive Storage device that fits into the USB port of a personal computer and is used for portable storage.

voice recognition software (see **speech recognition software**)

DISCUSSION QUESTIONS

1. If you were the CIO of a firm, what factors would you consider when selecting secondary storage media for your company's records (files)?

2. Given that Moore's law has proved itself over the past 2 decades, speculate on what chip capabilities will be in 10 years. What might your desktop PC be able to do?

3. If you were the CIO of a firm, how would you explain the workings, benefits, and limitations of using thin clients as opposed to fat clients?

4. You are the CIO of your company, and you have to develop an application of strategic importance to your firm. What are the advantages and disadvantages of using open-source software?

5. You have to take a programming course, or maybe more than one, in your MIS program. Which programming language(s) would you choose to study? Why? Should you even have to learn a programming language? Why or why not?

PROBLEM-SOLVING ACTIVITIES

1. Access the Web sites of the major chip manufacturers—for example, Intel (www.intel.com), Motorola (www.motorola.com), and Advanced Micro Devices (www.amd.com)—and obtain the latest information regarding new and planned chips. Compare performance and costs across these vendors. Be sure to take a close look at the various multicore chips.

2. Access "The Journey Inside" on Intel's Web site at (http://educate.intel.com/en/thejourneyinside). Prepare a presentation of each step in the machine instruction cycle.

3. A great deal of software is available for free over the Internet. Go to www.pcmag.com/article2/0,2817,2338803,00.asp, and observe all the software that is available for free. Choose one software program, and download it to your computer. Prepare a brief discussion about the software for your class.

4. Enter the IBM Web site (www.ibm.com), and search on "software." Click on the drop box for "Products," and notice how many software products IBM produces. Is IBM only a hardware company?

5. Compare the following proprietary software packages with their open-source software counterparts, and prepare your comparison for the class:

Proprietary	Open Source
Microsoft Office	Google Docs, OpenOffice
Adobe Photoshop	Picnik.com, Google Picasa

6. Compare the Microsoft Surface interface (www.microsoft.com/surface/en/us/default.aspx) with Oblong Industries' (http://oblong.com) g-speak spatial operating environment. Demonstrate examples of both interfaces to the class. What are the advantages and disadvantages of each one?

Plug IT In | 3

Emerging Types of Enterprise Computing

LEARNING OBJECTIVES >>>

1. Describe the evolution of IT infrastructure.
2. Describe a server farm.
3. Define virtualization, and discuss its advantages.
4. Define grid computing, and discuss its advantages.
5. Define utility computing, and discuss its advantages.
6. Define cloud computing, and analyze its advantages and disadvantages.
7. Define and discuss Web services and service-oriented architecture.

Because the overall goal of this book is for you to be an informed user of information technology, we devote this "Plug IT In" to a vital and cutting-edge topic: emerging systems of enterprise computing. A working knowledge of the topics discussed in this guide will enhance your appreciation of what technology can and cannot do for a business. In addition, it will enable you to make an immediate contribution by analyzing how your organization manages its information technology assets.

You will be using these computing resources yourself in your career, and you will also have input into decisions about how your department and organization can best utilize them. Finally, these resources—particularly cloud computing—can be extremely valuable if you decide to start your own business.

PI3.1 Introduction

You were introduced to the concept of IT infrastructure in Chapter 1. Recall that an organization's *IT infrastructure* consists of IT components—hardware, software, networks, and databases—and IT services—developing information systems, managing security and risk, and managing data. (It is helpful to review Figure 1.3 here.) The organization's IT infrastructure is the foundation for all of the information systems that the organization uses.

Modern IT infrastructure has evolved through several stages since the early 1950s, when firms first began to apply information technology to business applications. These stages are as follows:

- *Stand-alone mainframes.* Organizations initially used mainframe computers in their engineering and accounting departments. The mainframe was typically housed in a secure area, and only MIS personnel had access to it.

- *Mainframe and dumb terminals.* Forcing users to go to wherever the mainframe was located was time consuming and inefficient. As a result, firms began placing so-called dumb terminals—essentially electronic typewriters with little processing power—in user departments. This arrangement enabled users to input computer programs into the mainframe from their departments, a process called *remote job entry*.

- *Stand-alone personal computers.* In the late 1970s, the first personal computers appeared. The IBM PC's debut in 1981 legitimized the entire personal computer market. Users began bringing personal computers to the workplace to improve their productivity—for example, by using spreadsheet and word processing applications. These computers were not initially supported by the firm's MIS department. However, as the number of personal computers increased dramatically, organizations decided to support personal computers, and they established policies as to which personal computers and software they would support.

Figure PI3.1 A server farm. Notice the ventilation in the racks and ceiling. (*Source:* Media Bakery)

- *Local area networks (client/server computing).* When personal computers are networked, individual productivity is substantially increased. For this reason, organizations began to connect personal computers into local area networks (LANs) and then connect these LANs to the mainframe, a type of processing known as *client/server computing*.

- *Enterprise computing.* In the early 1990s, organizations began to use networking standards to integrate different kinds of networks throughout the firm, thereby creating enterprise computing. As the Internet became widespread after 1995, organizations began using the TCP/IP networking protocol to integrate different types of networks. All types of hardware were networked, from mainframes to personal computers to smart phones. Software applications and data could now flow seamlessly throughout the enterprise and between and among organizations.

- *Cloud computing and mobile computing.* Today, organizations can use the power of cloud computing. As you will see in this technology guide, cloud computing provides access to a shared pool of computing resources, including computers, storage, applications, and services, over a network, typically the Internet.

Keep in mind that the computing resources in each stage can be cumulative. For instance, most large firms still use mainframe computers in addition to all the other types of computing resources as large servers to manage operations that involve millions of transactions per day. They also employ mainframes to operate corporate Web sites.

PI3.2 Server Farms

If a company does not have enough computer processing power to meet its needs, then it can simply buy more servers. Recall that a *server* is a computer that supports networks, enabling users to share files, software, and other network devices. The questions then become where to put all the servers and how to manage them. To answer these questions, some companies are building massive data centers called **server farms**, which contain hundreds or thousands of networked computer servers (see Figure PI3.1).

The huge number of servers in a server farm provides redundancy and fault tolerance, meaning that if one computer on the grid fails, the application is automatically "rolled over" to another computer. Server farms require massive amounts of electrical power, air conditioning, backup generators, security, and money. They also need to be located fairly closely to fiber-optic communications links.

Locations satisfying these requirements are difficult to find. Yahoo! and Microsoft constructed huge server farms in Quincy, Washington, to take advantage of cheap, local hydroelectric power. Google built a massive server farm in Oregon for the same reason.

PI3.3 Virtualization

According to Gartner Inc. (www.gartner.com), a research firm, typical utilization rates on servers range from 5 to 10 percent. That is, most of the time, organizations are using only a small percentage of their total computing capacity. One reason for this low rate is that most organizations buy a new server every time they implement a new application. CIOs tolerate this inefficiency in order to make certain that they can supply enough computing resources to users when they are needed. Also, server prices have dropped more than 80 percent in the last decade, making it easier and cheaper to buy another server than to increase the utilization of the existing servers. However, virtualization has changed this situation.

Virtualization refers to a system in which servers no longer have to be dedicated to a particular task. **Server virtualization** uses software-based partitions to create multiple virtual servers—called *virtual machines*—on a single physical server. This arrangement enables multiple applications to run on a single physical server, with each application running within its own software environment. Organizations that employ virtualization enjoy many benefits, including the following:

- A lower number of physical servers generates cost savings in equipment, energy, space in the data center, cooling, personnel, and maintenance.

- Virtualization enhances an organization's agility by enabling it to quickly modify its systems to respond to changing demands.
- The IT department can shift its focus from the technology itself to the services that the technology can provide.

The following case involving MaximumASP illustrates the benefits of virtualization.

Example

MaximumASP Virtualizes Its Data Center. MaximumASP is a Web-hosting company based in Louisville, Kentucky. Its 35 employees host more than 48,000 domains for customers located in more than 60 countries. MaximumASP prides itself on its innovative offerings and its outstanding customer service. Unfortunately, the company's rapid expansion resulted in a proliferation of servers that required increasing amounts of resources to manage. This situation adversely affected the company's bottom line. Further, adding servers pulled staff away from researching new services, which diminished the company's agility and innovation.

Web hosting has become extremely competitive and even commoditized in many parts of the world. The CIO for MaximumASP notes that there is tremendous market pressure to develop new products, but pricing tends to be commoditized. To offer new services, MaximumASP had to add new servers, which increased the company's costs.

MaximumASP added hundreds of new servers every year, each of which took roughly four hours to deploy. The company spent so much time deploying new servers that it could not respond as quickly to its customers' needs or its competitors' moves as it had in the past. MaximumASP also wanted to reduce the rising cost of physical servers as well as the related real estate and power costs. The company was spending thousands of dollars every year on new hardware, software licenses, and electrical power. Finally, the firm was concerned that if it continued to deploy more servers, it would outgrow its Louisville data center and have to build another one. Funding new servers each year was especially irritating because most of the company's existing servers operated at a very low capacity, often 5 percent or less.

MaximumASP decided to implement Microsoft's server virtualization technology, and the results have been outstanding. The company was able to operate between five and ten virtual machines on each physical server, which generated a savings of $350,000 in hardware costs alone. In addition, the technology enabled MaximumASP to utilize its data center floor space much more efficiently, thereby sparing the firm the cost of building a new data center. Further, average server utilization increased dramatically from 5 percent to 65 percent.

And the bottom line? MaximumASP utilized virtualization to expand its product offerings, enhance its business agility, and improve its customer service, while actually lowering its operating costs.

Sources: "MaximumASP," *Microsoft Virtualization Case Study*, 2011; www.maximumasp.com, accessed May 19, 2011.

Student Activity | PI3.1

Objective: The objective of this exercise is to familiarize you with virtualization and why more companies are starting to use it for their infrastructure.

Chapter Connection: This exercise relates to Section PI3.1. Because of usage demands, tasks are increasingly performed by computers physically removed from the user and accessed over a

network, often the Internet. This exercise will point out some of the advantages and disadvantages of using virtualization.

Prerequisites: You should read Sections PI3.1, PI3.2, and PI3.3 before doing this exercise to become familiar with the various architectures used in computing.

Activity: *View the following video clip from Gartner on virtualization:*

www.gartner.com/technology/initiatives/virtualization.jsp

Deliverables:

Provide definitions and examples of the processes of decoupling and virtualization.

Quiz Questions:

1. Which of the following is a benefit of virtualization?
   - (a) Flexibility
   - (b) Reduced cost
   - (c) Increased speed
   - (d) All of the above

2. Virtualization:
   - (a) Locks components together for better control.
   - (b) Separates components for more flexibility.
   - (c) Increases server use.
   - (d) Increases cost.

Discussion Question:

Discuss three benefits of using virtualization as discussed on the Gartner video.

PI3.4 Grid Computing

Grid computing applies the unused processing resources of many geographically dispersed computers in a network to form a virtual supercomputer. Grid computing targets problems that are usually scientific or technical in nature and require a large amount of computer processing and access to large amounts of data. Applications that run on a grid computing system must have the capacity to be divided among multiple servers. Each server in a grid will process a particular component of the application. After processing has been completed, the results from the application must be reassembled from the participating servers.

Grid computing provides many benefits to organizations. Specifically, it does the following:

- Enables organizations to utilize their computing resources more efficiently. Applications can run on the otherwise unused capacity of the organization's computers.
- Enables applications to run faster.
- Provides fault tolerance and redundancy. Further, there is no single point of failure, meaning that the failure of one computer will not stop the application from executing.
- Makes it easy to "scale up" (add computers) to meet the processing demands of complex applications.
- Makes it easy to "scale down" (remove computers) if extensive processing is not needed.

The following example illustrates how Digital Dimension uses grid computing to its advantage.

Example

Digital Dimension Uses the Grid. The amazing special effects in your favorite action movies involve not only creativity and artistic skill but also a lot of computing power. Grid computing is ideal for such intense and demanding applications.

Digital Dimension (www.digitaldimension.com) is an award-winning studio that specializes in high-end visual effects, three-dimensional animation, and motion graphics for the film and television industries. The studio was responsible for the effects in many popular movies and television shows, including *Clash of the Titans*, *The Last Samurai*, *Lost*, and *Alias*. It has won six Emmy awards—including for two Super Bowls—and three Visual Effects Society awards. Some of the studio's effects are integrated so seamlessly into real-world scenarios that they are invisible to the casual viewer. In contrast, other effects go all out to suspend disbelief and defy reality.

As Digital Dimension's business grew, the complexity of its IT infrastructure increased accordingly. In many cases, the studio's graphics software packages worked only through application-specific computers. With so many projects with different requirements and deadlines, managing all the studio's computationally intensive applications was becoming a serious bottleneck.

Digital Dimension selected Digipede Technologies (www.digipede.net), for several reasons. The Digipede Network offered great control and flexibility, and it allowed Digital Dimension to manage multiple applications that are critical to its production workflow. It also enabled the studio to create digital content across hundreds of servers. In addition, Digipede integrates directly with the studio's internal collaboration platform, thereby providing a far more complete picture of all its projects.

Integrating the Digipede Network into Digital Dimension's infrastructure immediately provided the studio with greater visibility. Having access to a single view of all current projects helps the studio's design and production teams to meet deadlines and adapt quickly to rapidly changing schedules. Further, the Digipede grid allows the studio to acquire necessary computing resources as needed to meet its heavy application processing demands.

PI3.5 Utility Computing

In **utility computing**, a service provider makes computing resources and infrastructure management available to a customer as needed. The provider then charges the customer for specific usage rather than a flat rate. Utility computing is also called *subscription computing* and *on-demand computing*. Utility computing enables companies to efficiently meet fluctuating demands for computing power by lowering the cost of owning hardware infrastructure.

PI3.6 Cloud Computing

Every year, companies spend billions of dollars on IT infrastructure and expert staffs to build and maintain complex information systems. Software licensing (discussed in "Plug IT In 2"), hardware integration, power and cooling, and staff training and salaries add up to a large amount of money for an infrastructure that often is not used to its full capacity. Enter cloud computing.

In **cloud computing**, tasks are performed by computers that are physically removed from the user. Users access computers in the cloud over a network, in particular the Internet. The cloud is composed of the computers, the software on those computers, and the network connections among those computers. The computers in the cloud are typically located in data centers, or server farms, which can be located anywhere in the world and accessed from anywhere in the world (see Figure PI3.2).

A cloud can be private or public. A *public cloud* is maintained by an external cloud service provider—such as Amazon Web Services—that is accessed through the Internet and available to the general public. A *private cloud* is a proprietary data center that integrates servers, storage, networks, data, and applications as a set of services that users inside a company share. Both public and private clouds are able to allocate storage, computing power, applications, and other resources on an as-needed basis.

The primary advantage of cloud computing is that it dramatically lowers infrastructure costs. The disadvantages consist of privacy, security, and reliability concerns. In the next two examples, you will see the advantages and then the disadvantages of cloud computing, from the perspective of the same cloud computing provider, Amazon.

Sources: Compiled from "Digital Dimension Increases Capacity with the Digipede Network," *Digipede Customer Case Study*, 2011; www.digitaldimension.com, www.digipede.net, accessed May 19, 2011.

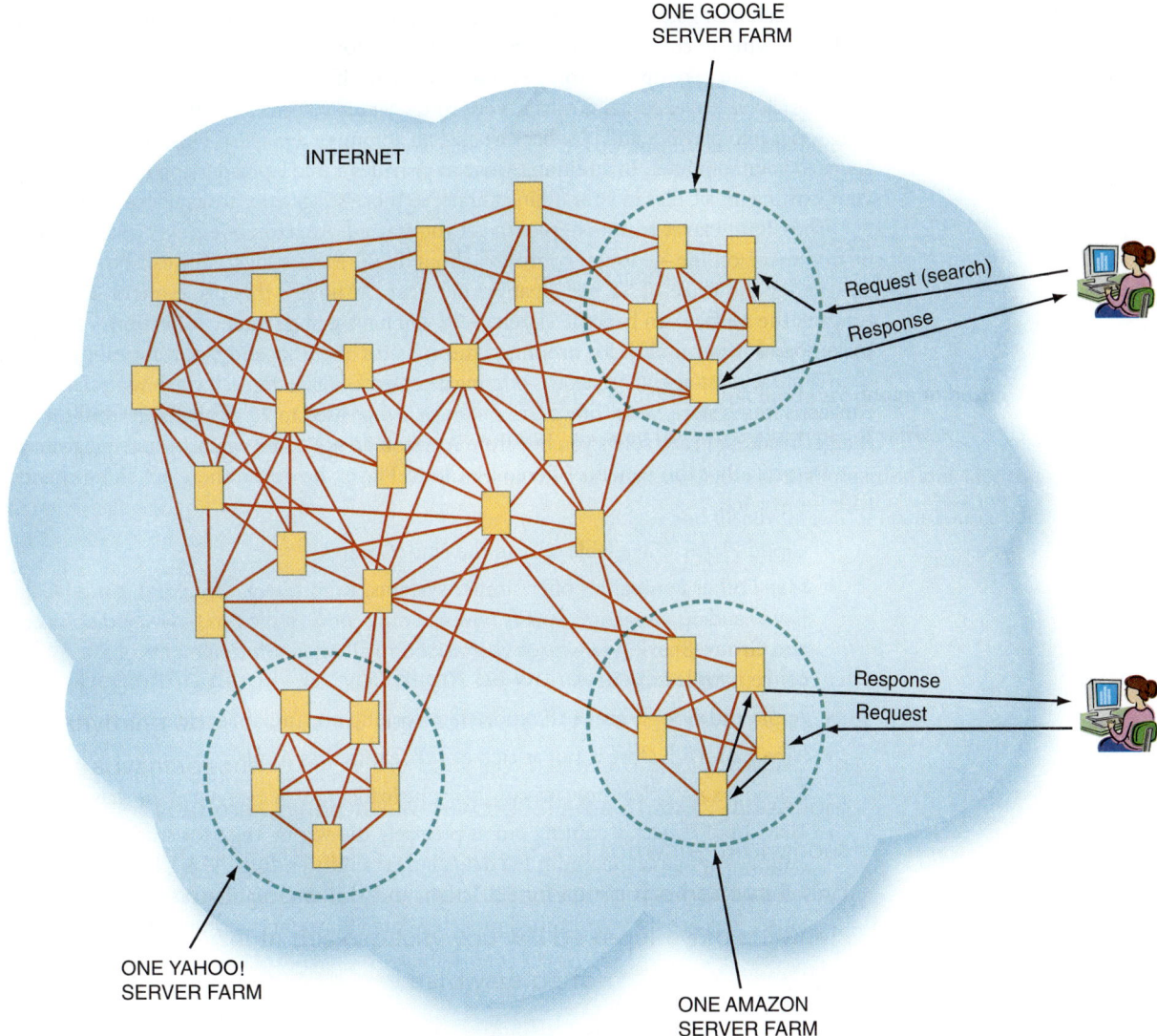

ONE GOOGLE
SERVER FARM

INTERNET

Request (search)

Response

Response

Request

ONE YAHOO!
SERVER FARM

ONE AMAZON
SERVER FARM

Figure PI3.2 Organizational server farms in relation to the Internet.

Example

Amazon Moves Music into the Cloud. For years, the most popular music system—Apples iTunes—has worked like this: You buy song files from the iTunes store and download them to your computer. If you want to listen to them on the road, you connect your iPod or iPhone to that computer and copy the song files to it.

Amazon, whose online music store competes with Apple's, has two problems with that process. First, your music library is scattered. When you buy a new song at home, you cannot listen to it at work, at least not without copying it manually. You might buy a song on your phone, but it will not be on your computer until you perform a sync. Moreover, if your music library is large, then you can fit only a portion of the music onto your phone. Second, Amazon wants more people to buy music from its store instead of iTunes.

In March 2011, Amazon released a package of software and services that solves both problems. Amazon's fundamental concept is that your music collection will reside in the cloud. That way, you can listen to it from any computer—at home, at work, at a friend's—by logging into a special Web page called the Amazon Cloud Player (www.amazon.com/clouddrive).

You can also listen to any of the songs in your music collection on an Android phone without having to copy or sync the music. All your songs are always available everywhere, and they do not take up any storage on the phone itself.

The Cloud Player contains a list of your songs, which you can sort and search. You can also drag songs into playlists and play back a song, an album, or a playlist. Plus, you can download songs to your computer. In addition, Amazon provides a free Uploader app that lets you send your existing music files to your online library, so those songs, too, are available anywhere.

The Cloud Player is almost free. To get you started, Amazon offers everyone 5 gigabytes of free space online—enough room for about 1,200 MP3 songs. You can buy additional storage for the price of $1 per gigabyte per year. Although this price might seem insignificant, the service can become expensive if you have a huge music collection—enough to make "pay $15 per month for unlimited music" sites like Rhapsody look appealing.

To attract customers, Amazon is offering incentives. For example, if you buy an album from Amazon's music store, your Cloud Drive storage is increased to 20 gigabytes for the year at no charge. In addition, any songs you buy from Amazon do not count against your storage limit.

Despite all of the benefits offered by Cloud Player, however, there are some concerns with the service.

- Cloud Player is available only in the United States.
- Many other companies offer similar systems. Rdio (www.rdio.com), Audio Galaxy (www.audiogalaxy.com), Spotify (www.spotify.com), Audio Box (www.audiobox.com), and GrooveShark (www.grooveshark.com) all offer some elements of the Amazon concept for less money.
- Apple and Google are both reportedly working on similar services.
- Amazon's MP3 store is not as rich or full featured as Apple's.
- It is not exactly clear how private your music files are, or even whether they are yours.
- The Cloud Player is coming out at precisely the wrong time for smart phone computing. The age of the unlimited data plan is rapidly ending. AT&T has eliminated its "all the Internet you want for $30" plan, and Verizon's similar plan will end shortly. Music files use up your limited monthly data allotments very quickly.

Example

Amazon Web Services Crashes. Amazon Web Services (AWS; http://aws.amazon.com), the Amazon cloud, is designed with backups to the backups' backups to prevent hosted Web sites and applications from failing. Despite all of these safety measures, however, in April 2011 Amazon's cloud crashed, taking with it Reddit (www.reddit.com), Quora (www.quora.com), FourSquare (www.foursquare.com), ProPublica (www.propublica.org), parts of the *New York Times* (www.nytimes.com), and about 70 other Web sites. The massive outage raised questions about the reliability of Amazon Web Services and of the cloud itself.

Thousands of companies use Amazon Web Services (AWS) to run their Web sites through a service called Elastic Compute Cloud (EC2). Rather than hosting their sites on their own servers, these customers essentially rent some of Amazon's unused server capacity. EC2 is hosted in five regions: Virginia, California, Ireland, Tokyo, and Singapore. Within each region are multiple "availability zones," and within each availability zone are multiple "locations" or data centers.

Amazon assured its customers that the way it linked together many different data centers would protect them from isolated failures. It promised to keep customers' sites up and running 99.95 percent of the year, or it would reduce their monthly bills by 10 percent. Based on these claims, customers could be down a maximum of just 4.4 hours in a year. In fact, during the outage, some customers' Web sites were down for days.

The crash occurred at Amazon's Virginia data center, located in one of the company's East Coast availability zones. Amazon claimed that a "networking event" caused a domino

Sources: Compiled from E. Bott, "How Amazon Has Outsmarted the Music Industry (and Apple)," *ZDNet*, March 30, 2011; D. Pogue, "The Cloud That Rains Music," *New York Times*, March 30, 2011; www.amazon.com/clouddrive, accessed May 19, 2011.1

effect across other availability zones in that region, which in turn caused many of its storage volumes to create backups of themselves. That process filled up Amazon's available storage capacity and prevented some Web sites from accessing their data. Amazon did not reveal what the "networking event" was.

Web sites like Quora and Reddit were able to come back online in "read-only" mode, but users could not post new content for many hours. Many experts blamed Amazon's customers themselves, asserting that their Web sites should have spread their processing out among multiple geographical regions to take full advantage of Amazon's backup systems. In fact, sites like Reddit were simply following the instructions that Amazon provided in its service agreement. The agreement states that hosting in a single region should be sufficient. Further, some smaller companies cannot afford the resources needed to duplicate their infrastructure in data centers all over the world.

Cloud computing consists of three different types of services:

- *Cloud infrastructure as a service.* Customers use processing, storage, networking, and other computing resources from cloud service providers to operate their information systems. For example, Amazon sells the spare capacity of its vast IT infrastructure to its customers in a cloud environment. These services include its Simple Storage Service (S3) for storing customers' data and its Elastic Compute Cloud (EC2) service for operating their applications. Customers pay only for the amount of storage and computing they use.

- *Cloud platform as a service.* Customers use IT infrastructure and programming tools hosted by the cloud service provider to develop their own applications. For instance, IBM provides a Smart Business Application Development and Test service for software development and testing on the IBM Cloud. Also, Salesforce.com's Force.com allows developers to build applications on the Salesforce cloud.

- *Cloud software as a service.* Customers use software that is hosted by a cloud service provider on the provider's hardware and delivered to customers over a network. You learned about software-as-a-service in Chapter 14.

BEFORE *YOU GO ON* . . .

1. Define cloud computing.
2. Discuss the advantages and disadvantage of cloud computing.

Sources: Compiled from C. Brooks, "A Crack in the Cloud: Why the Amazon Outage Caught So Many by Surprise," *SearchCloudComputing.com,* April 27, 2011; D. Goldman, "Why Amazon's Cloud Titanic Went Down," *CNN Money,* April 22, 2011; J. Brodkin, "Amazon EC2 Outage Calls 'Availability Zones' into Question," *CIO,* April 21, 2011; http://aws.amazon.com, accessed May 21, 2011.

Student Activity PI3.2

Objective: The objective of this exercise is to familiarize you with cloud computing and why more companies are starting to use it as part of their architecture.

Chapter Connection: This exercise relates to Section PI3.6. Because of usage demands, tasks are increasingly performed by computers physically removed from the user and accessed over a network, often the Internet. This is referred to as cloud computing. This exercise will point out some of the advantages and disadvantages of using the cloud.

Prerequisites: You should read Section PI3.6 of this chapter before doing this exercise to become familiar with the basics of cloud computing.

Activity: *Demand for computer resources varies for most companies. Most orders are entered during the 8-to-5 workday, increasing the demand for server access. However, from midnight until 4:00 AM, many servers are in less demand but still need to be operational for the orders that still could come in. Cloud computing can help with this variable demand. It allows a company to only pay for the necessary amount of computing power when needed and where needed. Thus cloud computing can both improve performance when demand is high and reduce cost when demand is lower.*

Watch the following video clip on cloud computing:

www.youtube.com/watch?v=QJncFirhjPg

Read about cloud computing on Wikipedia:

http://en.wikipedia.org/wiki/Cloud_computing

Deliverables:

Based on the chapter text, the video, and Wikipedia:

1. List three advantages of cloud computing.

2. List two disadvantages.

3. Name three cloud service providers.

Quiz Questions:

1. Which of the following is a benefit of cloud computing?

    (a) Instant resources when needed
    (b) Only pay for what you use
    (c) Easy to grow or shrink
    (d) All of the above

2. Which of the following is a problem with cloud computing?

    (a) Infrastructure
    (b) Security
    (c) High price
    (d) All of the above

Discussion Questions:

Discuss the benefits of using cloud computing. Discuss the concerns of using cloud computing.

PI3.7 Emerging Software Trends

Today several emerging software trends are having a significant impact on organizations. Among the major trends are open-source software, Software-as-a-Service, Web services, and service-oriented architecture. We discussed the first two trends in "Plug IT In 2" and Chapter 14, respectively. In this section we examine Web services and service-oriented architecture.

Web Services

Web services are applications delivered over the Internet that MIS professionals can select and combine through almost any device, from personal computers to mobile phones. By using a set of shared standards, or protocols, these applications permit different systems to "talk" with one another—that is, to share data and services—without requiring human beings to translate the conversations.

Web services have great potential because they can be used in a variety of environments: over the Internet, on an intranet inside a corporate firewall, on an extranet set up by business partners. Web services perform a wide variety of tasks, from automating business processes to integrating components of an enterprisewide system to streamlining online buying and selling.

Web services provide numerous benefits for organizations, including the following:

- The organization can utilize the existing Internet infrastructure without having to implement any new technologies.

- Organizational personnel can access remote or local data without having to understand the complexities of this process.

- The organization can create new applications quickly and easily.

Web services are based on four key protocols: XML, SOAP, WSDL, and UDDI. *Extensible markup language* (*XML*) makes it easier to exchange data among a variety of applications and to validate and interpret these data. XML is a more powerful and flexible markup language than *hypertext markup language* (HTML). HTML is a page-description language for specifying how text, graphics, video, and sound are placed on a Web page document. Whereas HTML is limited to describing how data should be presented in the form of Web pages, XML can perform presentation, communication, and storage of data. For example, in XML a number is not simply a number. The XML tag specifies whether the number represents a price, a date, or a ZIP code. Consider this example of XML, which identifies the contact information for Jane Smith.

```
<contact-info>
<name>Jane Smith</name>
<company>AT&amp;T</company>
<phone>(212) 555-4567</phone>
</contact-info>
```

Simple object access protocol (*SOAP*) is a set of rules that define how messages can be exchanged among different network systems and applications through the use of XML. These rules establish a common protocol that allows different Web services to interoperate. For example, Visual Basic clients can use SOAP to access a Java server. SOAP runs on all hardware and software systems.

The *Web services description language* (*WSDL*) is used to create the XML document that describes the tasks performed by the various Web services. Tools such as VisualStudio. Net automate the process of accessing the WSDL, reading it, and coding the application to reference the specific Web service.

Universal description, discovery, and integration (*UDDI*) allows MIS professionals to search for needed Web services by creating public or private searchable directories of these services. In other words, UDDI is the registry of descriptions of Web services.

Service-Oriented Architecture

A **service-oriented architecture** (SOA) is an IT architecture that makes it possible to construct business applications using Web services. The Web services can be reused across an organization in other applications. For example, a Web service that checks a consumer's credit could be used with a service that processes a mortgage application or a credit card application.

⌐ BEFORE *YOU GO ON . . .*

1. Describe the function of Web services.
2. Describe the function of service-oriented architectures.

Student Activity PI3.3

Objective: The objective of this exercise is to familiarize you with Web services and why more individuals and companies are starting to use them daily.

Chapter Connection: This exercise relates to Section PI3.7. This exercise will give the you a chance to use a Web service.

Prerequisites: You should read Section PI3.7 before doing this exercise to become familiar with the functions of Web services.

Activity: *Web services are applications delivered over the internet to devices such as PCs and mobile devices. By following a set of standards or protocols, Web services enable different "systems" to talk to each other. In this exercise the student will use a Web service from Google.*

Connect to http://google.com

Select "Google Maps" at the top left of the screen.

Select "Get Directions" at the top left of the screen.

For Ⓐ : Enter Your Address: Street, City, State

For Ⓑ : Enter 111 River Street, Hoboken, NJ 07030

Deliverables:

Answer the following questions from your Google Maps lookup:

1. How long would it take you to drive from your location to the destination chosen?
2. What are the main highways you travel to get there?
3. Zoom in on your destination by moving the slider toward the + or clicking the Ⓑ. What is the name of the company at this location?

What's In IT For Me?

For All Business Majors

As with hardware ("Plug IT In 2"), the design of enterprise IT architectures has profound impacts for businesspeople. Personal and organizational success can depend on an understanding of these architectures and a commitment to knowing the opportunities and challenges they will bring.

At the organizational level, server farms, virtualization, and grid/utility/cloud computing make the IT function more efficient and effective, save the organization money, and contribute to the environment because they are "green" technologies. Web services and SOA make the organization more flexible when deploying new IT applications.

At the individual level, you will be only peripherally concerned with server farms, virtualization, grid computing, utility computing, Web services, and SOA. If you want to be an entrepreneur, you will most likely be involved with cloud computing (see "Build Your Own Multinational Company" in Chapter 1).

SUMMARY

1. Describe the evolution of IT infrastructure.

The IT infrastructure in organizations has evolved through these stages:

- The stand-alone mainframe
- Mainframe and dumb terminals
- Stand-alone personal computers
- Local area networks (client/server computing)
- Enterprise computing
- Cloud computing and mobile computing

2. Describe a server farm.

Server farms are massive data centers that may contain hundreds of thousands of networked computer servers

3. Define virtualization, and discuss its advantages.

Server virtualization is a technology that is typically used in server farms. This technology divides physical servers into several software-based partitions. These partitions allow one physical server to run multiple applications, with each application having its own partition. The benefits of virtualization include the following:

- A lower number of physical servers leading to cost savings in equipment, energy, space in the data center, cooling, personnel, and maintenance
- Enhanced organizational agility
- The focus of the information technology department shifting from the technology itself to the services that the technology can provide

4. Define grid computing, and discuss its advantages.

Grid computing applies the unused processing resources of many geographically dispersed computers in a network to form a virtual supercomputer.

Grid computing provides many benefits to organizations:

- Enables more efficient use of computing resources. (Applications can run on otherwise unused capacity of organizational computers.)
- Enables applications to run faster
- Provides fault tolerance and redundancy. (If one computer on the grid fails, the application is automatically "rolled over" to another computer. Further, there is no single point of failure, meaning that the failure of one computer will not stop the application from executing.)
- Makes it easy to "scale up" (add computers) to meet the processing demands of complex applications
- Makes it easy to "scale down" (remove computers) if extensive processing is not needed

5. Define utility computing, and discuss its advantages.

In utility computing, a service provider makes computing resources and infrastructure management available to a customer as needed. Utility computing enables companies to efficiently meet fluctuating demands for computing power by lowering the cost of owning hardware infrastructure.

6. Define cloud computing, and analyze its advantages and disadvantages.

With cloud computing, tasks are performed by computers physically removed from the user and accessed over a network, in particular the Internet. The advantages of cloud computing include much lower infrastructure costs, and the disadvantages consist of privacy, security, and reliability concerns.

7. Define and discuss Web services and service-oriented architecture.

Web services are applications delivered over the Internet that MIS professionals can select and combine through almost any device, from personal computers to mobile phones. A service-oriented architecture makes it possible to for MIS professionals to construct business applications using Web services.

GLOSSARY

cloud computing A technology in which tasks are performed by computers physically removed from the user and accessed over a network, in particular the Internet.

grid computing A technology that applies the unused processing resources of many geographically dispersed computers in a network to form a virtual supercomputer.

server farms Massive data centers, which may contain hundreds of thousands of networked computer servers.

server virtualization A technology that uses software-based partitions to create multiple virtual servers (called *virtual machines*) on a single physical server.

service-oriented architecture An IT architecture that makes it possible to construct business applications using Web services.

utility computing A technology whereby a service provider makes computing resources and infrastructure management available to a customer as needed.

Web services Applications delivered over the Internet that users can select and combine through almost any device, from personal computers to mobile phones.

DISCUSSION QUESTIONS

1. What is the value of server farms and virtualization to any large organization?
2. If you were the chief information officer (CIO) of a firm, how would you explain the workings, benefits, and limitations of cloud computing?
3. What is the value of cloud computing to a small organization?
4. What is the value of cloud computing to an entrepreneur who is starting a business?

PROBLEM-SOLVING ACTIVITIES

1. Investigate the status of cloud computing by researching the offerings of the following leading vendors. Note any inhibitors to cloud computing.
   - Dell (see e.g., www.dell.com/cloudcomputing)
   - Oracle (see e.g., http://www.oracle.com/technetwork/topics/cloud/whatsnew/index.htm)
   - IBM (see e.g., www.ibm.com/ibm/cloud)
   - Amazon (see e.g., http://aws.amazon.com)
   - Microsoft (see e.g., www.microsoft.com/azure/default.mspx)
   - Google (see e.g., www.technologyreview.com/biztech/ 19785/?a=f)

Plug IT In | 4

Intelligent Systems

LEARNING OBJECTIVES >>>

1. Differentiate between artificial intelligence and human intelligence.
2. Define expert systems, and provide examples of their use.
3. Define neural networks, and provide examples of their use.
4. Define fuzzy logic, and provide examples of its use.
5. Define genetic algorithms, and provide examples of their use.
6. Define intelligent agents, and provide examples of their use.

PI4.1 Introduction to Intelligent Systems

This Plug IT In focuses on information systems that can make decisions by themselves. These systems are called intelligent systems. The major categories of intelligent systems are expert systems, neural networks, fuzzy logic, genetic algorithms, and intelligent agents. You learn about each of these systems in the following sections.

Intelligent systems is a term that describes the various commercial applications of artificial intelligence. **Artificial intelligence (AI)** is a subfield of computer science that is concerned with studying the thought processes of humans and re-creating the effects of those processes via machines, such as computers and robots.

Artificial Intelligence brings computers closer to processing information like a human. (*Source:* © Luis Alonso Ocana/Age Fotostock America, Inc.)

One well-publicized definition of AI is "behavior by a machine that, if performed by a human being, would be considered *intelligent*." This definition raises the question, What is *intelligent behavior*? The following capabilities are considered to be signs of intelligence: learning or understanding from experience, making sense of ambiguous or contradictory messages, and responding quickly and successfully to new situations.

The ultimate goal of AI is to build machines that will mimic human intelligence. A widely used test to determine whether a computer exhibits intelligent behavior was designed by Alan Turing, a British AI pioneer. The **Turing test** proposes that a man (or a woman) and a computer both pretend to be women (or men), and a human interviewer has to identify which is which. Based on this standard, the intelligent systems exemplified in commercial AI products are far from exhibiting any significant intelligence.

We can better understand the potential value of AI by contrasting it with natural (human) intelligence. AI has several important commercial advantages over natural intelligence, but it also displays some limitations, as outlined in Table PI4.1.

Intelligent systems show up in a number of places, some of them surprising, as the following examples illustrate:

- A good session player is hard to find, but ujam (www.ujam.com) is always ready to rock. This Web app doubles as a studio band and a recording studio. It analyzes a melody and then produces sophisticated harmonies, bass lines, drum tracks, horn parts, and more.

  Before ujam can produce accompaniment, the app must figure out which notes the user is singing or playing. Once ujam recognizes them, its algorithms use a mix of statistical techniques and programmed musical rules to search for chords to match the tune.

- To the human eye, an X-ray is a murky puzzle. But to a machine, an X-ray—or a CT scan or an MRI scan—is a dense data field that can be assessed down to the pixel level. AI techniques are being applied very aggressively in the field of medical imaging.

TABLE PI4.1 Comparison of the Capabilities of Natural vs. Artificial Intelligence

Capabilities	Natural Intelligence	Artificial Intelligence
Preservation of knowledge	Perishable from an organizational point of view	Permanent
Duplication and dissemination of knowledge	Difficult, expensive, takes time	Easy, fast, and inexpensive once in a computer
Total cost of knowledge	Can be erratic and inconsistent, incomplete at times	Consistent and thorough
Documentability of process and knowledge	Difficult, expensive	Fairly easy, inexpensive
Creativity	Can be very high	Low, uninspired
Use of sensory experiences limited	Direct and rich in possibilities	Must be interpreted first, limited
Recognizing patterns and relationships	Fast, easy to explain	Machine learning still not as good as people in most cases, but in some cases better
Reasoning	Making use of wide context of experiences	Good only in narrow, focused, and stable domains

New software gathers high-resolution image data from multiple sources—X-rays, MRI scans, ultrasounds, CT scans—and then groups together biological structures that share hard-to-detect similarities. For instance, the software can examine several images of the same breast to measure tissue density. The software then color-codes tissues with similar densities so humans can see the pattern as well.

The software finds and indexes pixels that share certain properties, even if they are far apart in one image or in a different image altogether. This process enables medical personnel to identify hidden features of diffuse structures as well as features within a region of tissue.

- A human brain receives visual information from two eyes. Google's AI system receives visual information from billions of smart phone camera lenses. The company collects these images from users of Google Goggles (www.google.com/mobile/goggles), a mobile service that lets users run Web searches by taking pictures. Snap a bar code, and Goggles will shop for the item's best price. Take a picture of a book, and it will link users to, for instance, a Wikipedia page about the book's author. Photograph the Eiffel Tower, and Goggles will give you historical background on the landmark.

The software behind Goggles coordinates the efforts of multiple object-specific recognition databases. There is a database for text, one for landmarks, one for corporate logos, and so on. When an image arrives, Goggles transmits it to each of these databases, which in turn use a variety of visual-recognition techniques to identify potential matches and compute confidence scores. Goggles then applies its own algorithm to decide which result(s), if any, go back to the user. Goggles' next category? Identifying plants.

- Building a model to run a major railroad is a complex task. One of the nation's largest freight carriers, Norfolk Southern (www.nscorp.com), uses an intelligent system, the Princeton Locomotive and Shop Management System (PLASMA), to manage its huge operation. PLASMA uses algorithms to analyze the railroad's operations by tracking thousands of variables to predict the impact of changes in fleet size, maintenance policies, transit time, and other factors. The key breakthrough was refining PLASMA so that it could mimic the complex behavior of the company's dispatch center in Atlanta, Georgia. PLASMA examines vast amounts of historical data from the railroad's databases. It then uses this analysis to model the dispatch center's collective human decision making and suggest improvements.

► **BEFORE** *YOU GO ON . . .*

1. What is artificial intelligence?

2. Differentiate between artificial and human intelligence.

Student Activity | PI4.1

Objective: The objective of this exercise is to familiarize you with intelligent systems, including their history and application.

Chapter Connection: This exercise relates to Section PI4.1 of this chapter.

Prerequisites: You should read Section 1 of this chapter before doing this exercise to become familiar with intelligent systems.

Activity: Intelligent systems *is a term that describes the various commercial applications of artificial intelligence. Artificial intelligence (AI) is concerned with studying the thought processes of humans and re-creating the effects of those processes via machines, such as computers and robots.*

To better understand the history and application of AI, click the following link:

http://library.thinkquest.org/2705

Read the details on AI by clicking the "Introduction," "History," and "Applications" links in the middle of the page. You also may want to view some of the other links.

Deliverables:

Based on Section PI4.1 and the suggested reading, answer the following:

1. Researchers have created AI systems that can do what three things?

2. Discuss some of the applications of AI systems in use today.

Quiz Questions:

1. Who developed a test to gauge the intelligence of a machine?

   (a) Joseph Art
   (b) IBM
   (c) Alan Turing
   (d) Bill Gates

2. When was the link between human intelligence and machines really observed?

   (a) 1940s
   (b) 1950s
   (c) 1960s
   (d) 1970s

3. Intelligent systems can be used to:

   (a) Mimic human thought
   (b) Understand speech
   (c) Play games
   (d) All of the above

Discussion Question:

There are numerous subareas of intelligent systems. Select three, explain how they function, and provide a specific example of their use.

PI4.2 Expert Systems

When an organization has to make a complex decision or solve a problem, it often turns to experts for advice. These experts have specific knowledge and experience in the problem area. They can offer alternative solutions and predict how likely the proposed solutions are to succeed. At the same time, they can calculate the costs that the organization may incur if it does not resolve the problem. Companies engage experts for advice on such matters as mergers and acquisitions, advertising strategy, and purchasing equipment. The more unstructured the situation, the more specialized and expensive is the advice.

Expertise refers to the extensive, task-specific knowledge acquired from training, reading, and experience. This knowledge enables experts to make better and faster decisions than nonexperts in solving complex problems. Expertise takes a long time (often many years) to acquire, and it is distributed unevenly across organizations.

Expert systems (ESs) are computer systems that attempt to mimic human experts by applying expertise in a specific domain. ESs can either *support* decision makers or completely *replace* them. ESs are the most widely applied and commercially successful intelligent system. A fascinating example of an ES is IBM's Watson.

Example

IBM's Watson. In the last decade, question-answering systems have become increasingly important for companies dealing with vast amounts of information. Legal firms, for example, need to quickly sift through case law to find a useful precedent or citation. Help-desk workers often have to access enormous databases of product information to find an answer for customers on the line. In situations like these, speed is typically of the essence.

Since 2007, IBM scientists have been developing what they expected to be the world's most advanced question-answering system, known as Watson. Their goal was to program Watson so that it could understand a question posed in everyday human language, or *natural language*, and come up with a precise, factual, correct answer. That is, Watson's capabilities must surpass those of search engines like Google and Bing, which merely point to a document where a user might find a suitable answer. Watson has to give the correct answer itself.

The IBM team input millions of documents into Watson to build up its knowledge base—including books, reference manuals, any sort of dictionary, encyclopedias, novels, plays, the Bible, and many other information sources. Watson is not connected to the Internet. It "knows" only what has been input into its knowledge base.

Watson uses more than a hundred algorithms at the same time to analyze a question in different ways, generating hundreds of possible solutions. Another set of algorithms ranks these answers according to plausibility. In essence, Watson thinks in probabilities.

In mid-2011, IBM was training Watson in medicine by inputting medical textbooks and journals. The team plans on linking Watson to the electronic health records that the federal government requires hospitals to maintain. In addition, medical students are sending sample questions to Watson to help train it.

When Watson appeared as a contestant on the television show *Jeopardy!*, it had to produce only one correct answer to each question. The medical Watson offers several possible diagnoses, ranked in order of its confidence in the diagnoses. The IBM team learned that physicians want to see a list of options. Further, being presented with more than one choice might help doctors move away from "anchoring," or getting too attached to a particular diagnosis. The medical Watson will have a diagnosis application and a treatment application.

IBM envisions several uses for medical Watson:

- Allowing a doctor to connect to Watson by speaking into a hand-held device, using speech-recognition technology and cloud computing
- Serving as a repository for the most advanced research in cancer and other fields
- Providing an always-available second opinion

Medical Watson does have competition. Isabel Healthcare (www.isabelhealthcare.com) offers Isabel, a private medical database that is already being used by several multi-hospital health systems. Isabel is purported to perform roughly the same functions as the medical Watson system.

Sources: Compiled from J. Fitzgerald, "IBM Watson Supercomputer Graduates from 'Jeopardy!' to Medicine," *Huffington Post,* May 21, 2011; C. Thompson, "What Is I.B.M.'s Watson?" *New York Times,* June 14, 2010; www.ibm.com/innovation/us/watson/index.html, accessed May 27, 2011.

ESs are also used by human resources management to analyze applicants for available positions. These systems assign "scores" to candidates, lessening the workload for HR managers in the hiring process. Human HR managers actually make the final decision, but the ES provides useful information and recommendations.

The previous examples demonstrated the usefulness of ESs in a relatively narrow domain. Overall, however, ESs may not be as useful as users would like. Consider the Microsoft Windows troubleshooting software located in the "help" section in the taskbar menu. Microsoft has designed its ES to provide solutions, advice, and suggestions to common errors users encounter in its operating systems. We have all found that, in some cases, the assistance provided by the help section is not particularly useful.

Typically, an ES is decision-making software that can reach a level of performance comparable to a human expert in certain specialized problem areas. Essentially, an ES transfers expertise from a domain expert (or other source) to the computer. This knowledge is then stored in the computer. Users can call on the computer for specific advice as needed. The computer can make inferences and arrive at conclusions. Then, like a human expert, it offers advice or recommendations. In addition, it can explain the logic behind the advice. Because ESs can integrate and manipulate so much data, they sometimes perform better than any single expert can.

An often overlooked benefit of ESs is that they can be embedded in larger systems. For example, credit card issuers use ESs to process credit card applications.

The transfer of expertise from an expert to a computer and then to the user involves four activities:

- *Knowledge acquisition.* Knowledge is acquired from domain experts or from documented sources.
- *Knowledge representation.* Acquired knowledge is organized as rules or frames (object-oriented) and stored electronically in a knowledge base.
- *Knowledge inferencing.* The computer is programmed so that it can make inferences based on the stored knowledge.
- *Knowledge transfer.* The inferenced expertise is transferred to the user in the form of a recommendation.

The Components of Expert Systems

An ES contains the following components: knowledge base, inference engine, user interface, blackboard (workplace), and explanation subsystem (justifier). In the future, ESs will include a knowledge-refining component as well. You learn about these components below. In addition, Figure PI4.1 diagrams the relationships among these components.

The *knowledge base* contains knowledge necessary for understanding, formulating, and solving problems. It is comprised of two basic elements: (1) *facts*, such as the problem situation, and (2) *rules* that direct the use of knowledge to solve specific problems in a particular domain.

The *inference engine* is essentially a computer program that provides a methodology for reasoning and formulating conclusions. It enables the system to make inferences based on the stored knowledge. The inference engine is considered the "brain" of the ES.

The following is an example of a medical ES for lung cancer treatment:

IF lung capacity is high

AND X-ray results are positive

AND patient has fever

AND patient has coughing

THEN surgery is necessary.

IF tumor has spread

OR contraindications to surgery exist

THEN surgery cannot be performed.

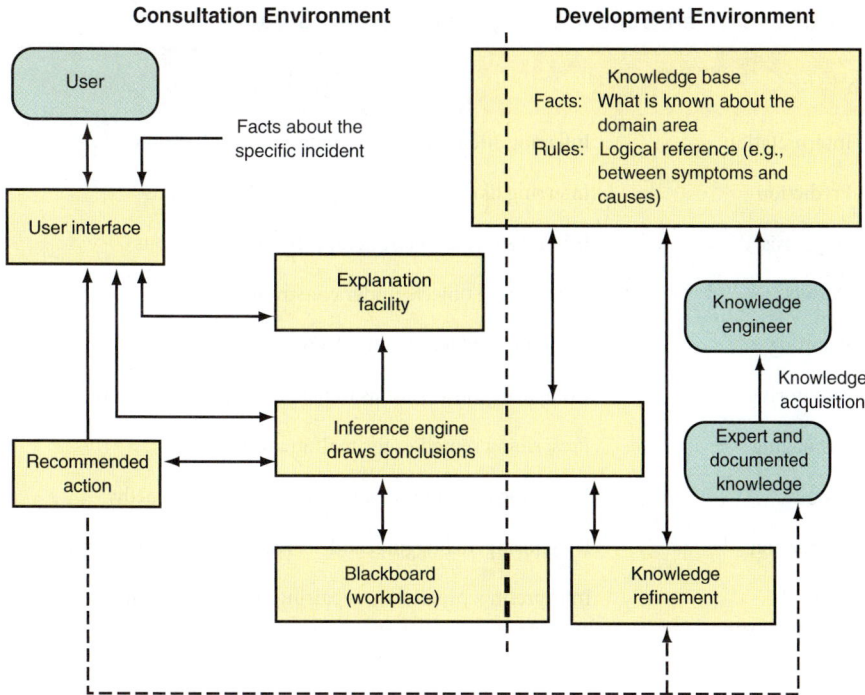

Consultation Environment

Development Environment

- User
- Facts about the specific incident
- User interface
- Explanation facility
- Recommended action
- Inference engine draws conclusions
- Blackboard (workplace)
- Knowledge base
  - Facts: What is known about the domain area
  - Rules: Logical reference (e.g., between symptoms and causes)
- Knowledge engineer
- Knowledge acquisition
- Expert and documented knowledge
- Knowledge refinement

Figure PI4.1 Structure and process of an expert system.

The *user interface* enables users to communicate with the computer. That communication can best be carried out in a natural language, usually a question-and-answer format. In some cases it is supplemented by graphics. The dialogue between the user and the computer triggers the inference engine to match the problem symptoms with the knowledge contained in the knowledge base and then generate advice.

The *blackboard* is an area of working memory set aside for the description of a current problem, as specified by the input data. It is a kind of database.

A unique feature of an ES is its ability to *explain* its recommendations. It performs this function in a subsystem called the *explanation subsystem* or *justifier*. The explanation subsystem interactively answers questions such as the following: *Why* did the ES ask a certain question? *How* did the ES reach a particular conclusion? *What* is the plan to reach the solution?

Human experts have a *knowledge-refining* system—that is, they can analyze their own performance, learn from it, and improve it for future consultations. This type of evaluation is also necessary in computerized learning so that the program will be able to improve by analyzing the reasons for its success or failure. Unfortunately, such a component is not available in commercial ESs at the moment. However, it is being developed in experimental systems.

Applications, Benefits, and Limitations of Expert Systems

Today, ESs are found in all types of organizations. They are especially useful in ten generic categories, which are displayed in Table PI4.2.

During the past few years, thousands of organizations worldwide have successfully applied ES technology to problems ranging from AIDS research to analyzing dust in mines. ESs have become so popular because they provide a large number of capabilities and benefits. Table PI4.3 lists the major benefits of ESs.

Despite all of these benefits, ESs present some problems as well. The difficulties involved with using ESs include the following:

- Transferring domain expertise from experts to the ES can be difficult because these experts cannot always explain how they know what they know. Often they are not aware of their complete reasoning process.

- Even if the domain experts can explain their entire reasoning process, automating that process may not be possible. The process may be either too complex, requiring too many rules, or too vague.

TABLE PI4.2 Ten Generic Categories of Expert Systems

Category	Problem Addressed
Interpretation	Inferring situation descriptions from observations
Prediction	Inferring likely consequences of given situations
Diagnosis	Inferring system malfunctions from observations
Design	Configuring objects under constraints
Planning	Developing plans to achieve goal(s)
Monitoring	Comparing observations to plans, flagging exceptions
Debugging	Prescribing remedies for malfunctions
Repair	Executing a plan to administer a prescribed remedy
Instruction	Diagnosing, debugging, and correcting system performance
Control	Interpreting, predicting, repairing, and monitoring systems behavior

- In some contexts, there may be a potential liability from the use of ESs. Humans are known to make errors from time to time, but they are generally "off the hook" if they take reasonable care and apply generally accepted methods. An organization that chooses to use an ES, however, may lack this legal protection if problems arise later. The usual example is medical treatment, but this issue can arise if someone is harmed financially by a business decision driven by an ES.

TABLE PI4.3 Benefits of Expert Systems

Benefit	Description
Increased output and productivity	ESs can configure components for each custom order, increasing production capabilities.
Increased quality	ESs can provide consistent advice and reduce error rates.
Capture and dissemination of scarce expertise	Expertise from anywhere in the world can be obtained and used.
Operation in hazardous environments	Sensors can collect information that an ES interprets, enabling human workers to avoid hot, humid, or toxic environments.
Accessibility to knowledge and help desks	ESs can increase the productivity of help-desk employees, or even automate this function.
Reliability	ESs do not become tired or bored, call in sick, or go on strike. They consistently pay attention to details.
Ability to work with incomplete or uncertain information	Even with an answer of "Don't know," an ES can produce an answer, although it may not be a definite one.
Provision of training	The explanation facility of an ES can serve as a teaching device and knowledge base for novices.
Enhancement of decision-making and problem-solving capabilities	ESs allow the integration of expert judgment into analysis (for example, diagnosis of machine and problem-malfunction and even medical diagnosis).
Decreased decision-making time	ESs usually can make faster decisions than humans working alone.
Reduced downtime	ESs can quickly diagnose machine malfunctions and prescribe repairs.

BEFORE *YOU GO ON . . .*

1. What is an expert system?
2. Describe the benefits and limitations of using expert systems.

Student Activity | PI4.2

Objective: The objective of this exercise is to familiarize you with expert systems, their components, and how they work.

Chapter Connection: This exercise relates to Section PI4.2 of this chapter.

Prerequisites: You should read Section PI4.2 of this chapter before doing this exercise.

Activity: *ESs are knowledge-based systems that mimic human experts by applying their knowledge and experience. They are composed of two basic elements: (1) facts and (2) rules. Read about these in your text.*

Let us assume you are writing an ES to help you determine family relationships—for example, parent, grandparent, sister, brother, and so forth. These are rules you learned early in life, but an ES can set up rules to help you make these decisions. For our example—using Prolog which is a general-purpose logic programming language often used with artificial intelligence—we have the following facts and rules:

Facts

parent (pam,bob) (read as: Pam is the parent of Bob)

parent (tom,bob)

parent (tom,liz)

parent (bob,ann)

parent (bob,pat)

parent (pat,jim)

female (pam)

female (liz)

female (ann)

Rules

For all x, y, z:

offspring (y,x): parent (x,y) (read as: If y is the offspring of x then x is the parent of y)

grandparent (x,z): parent (x,y), parent (y,z)

sister (x,y): parent (z,x), parent (z,y), female (x)

Deliverables:

Logic systems use both forward chaining and backward chaining. Forward chaining looks for the answer given some facts and rules, whereas backward chaining verifies that an assumption is true using those same facts and rules.

1. Using either forward or backward chaining, answer the following using the stated facts and rules:

    (a) parent (x,jim) Who is x=?

    (b) grandparent (x,jim) Who is x=? Who is the middle generation?

    (c) parent (bob,pat) Verify if this is true.

    (d) parent (liz,pat) Is this true?

    (e) sister (liz,bob) Is this true? If so, who is their common parent?

    (f) Grandparent (pam,pat) Is this true? If so, who is the middle generation?

2. What would be the rule for brother?

New Facts

    (a) male (pat)

    (b) male (bob)

    (c) male (jim)

    (d) male (tom)

3. Based on your rule for brother and the preceding facts, answer the following:

    brother (x,ann) Who is x=? Who is their common parent?

Quiz Questions:

1. In an expert system, the facts:

    (a) Contain knowledge for solving problems

    (b) Contain problem situations

    (c) Direct the use of knowledge to solve problems

    (d) Provide methodology for reasoning and formulation conclusions

2. In an expert system, the rules:
   (a) Contain knowledge for solving problems
   (b) Contain problem situations
   (c) Direct the use of knowledge to solve problems
   (d) Provide methodology for reasoning and formulation conclusions

3. In an expert system, the knowledge base:
   (a) Contains knowledge for solving problems
   (b) Contains problem situations
   (c) Directs the use of knowledge to solve problems
   (d) Provides methodology for reasoning and formulation conclusions

4. In an expert system, the inference engine:
   (a) Contains knowledge for solving problems
   (b) Contains problem situations
   (c) Directs the use of knowledge to solve problems
   (d) Provides methodology for reasoning and formulation conclusions

Discussion Questions:

1. How does an ES use the rules, facts, and inference engine?
2. Where does the user interface come in?
3. Discuss specific applications of ESs in business.

PI4.3 Neural Networks

A **neural network** is a system of programs and data structures that simulates the underlying concepts of the biological brain. A neural network usually involves a large number of processors operating in parallel, each with its own small sphere of knowledge and access to data in its local memory (see Figure PI4.2). Typically, a neural network is initially "trained" or fed large amounts of data and rules about data relationships.

Neural networks are particularly adept at recognizing subtle, hidden, and newly emerging patterns within complex data, as well as interpreting incomplete inputs. Neural networks can help users solve a wide range of problems, from airline security to infectious disease control. They have become the standard for combating fraud in the credit card, healthcare, and telecom industries, and they are playing an increasingly important role in today's stepped-up international efforts to prevent money laundering.

Neural networks are used in a variety of ways, as illustrated by the following examples.

- The Bruce nuclear facility in Ontario, Canada, has eight nuclear reactors, making it the largest such facility in North America and the second largest in the world. The company uses a neural network in its checkpoint X-ray screening system to detect weapons concealed in personal belongings. The system also identifies biologically dangerous liquids.

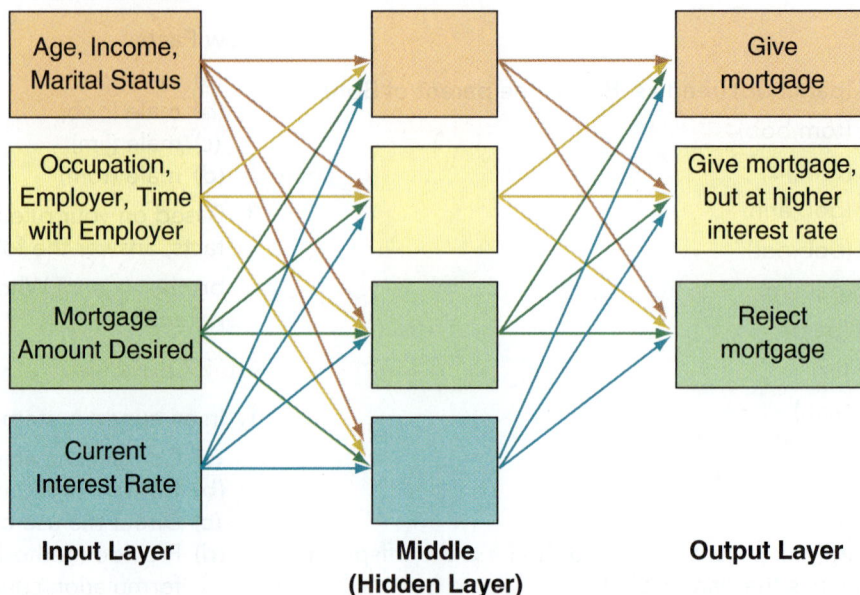

Figure PI4.2 Neural network.

- Neural networks are used in research into diseases such as Alzheimer's disease, Parkinson's disease, and epilepsy. Researchers build robots with simulated rat brains that mimic the rats' neural activity. The researchers can study brain function and the brain's reaction to stimuli.

- Neural networks are used to forecast the performance of stock index futures, currencies, natural gas and oil stocks, T-bond futures, gold stocks, and other major investments.

- Neural networks are used to detect fraud in credit card transactions and insurance claims, to fight crime, and to gauge customer satisfaction.

Figure PI4.2 illustrates how a neural network would process a typical mortgage application. Note that the network has three levels of interconnected nodes (similar to the human brain): an input layer, a middle or hidden layer, and an output layer. As you train the neural network, the strengths, or *weights*, of the connections change. In our example, the input nodes are age, income, occupation, marital status, employer, length of time with that employer, amount of mortgage desired, and current interest rate. The neural network has already been trained with data input from many successful and unsuccessful mortgage applications. That is, the neural network has established a pattern as to which input variables are necessary for a successful mortgage application. Interestingly, the neural network can adjust as both mortgage amounts and interest rates increase or decrease.

BEFORE *YOU GO ON . . .*

1. What are neural networks?
2. Describe how neural networks function.

Student Activity | PI4.3

Objective: The objective of this exercise is to familiarize you with neural networks, how they work, and ways in which they are being used in business.

Chapter Connection: This exercise relates to Section PI4.3 of this chapter.

Prerequisites: You should read Section PI4.3 before doing this exercise.

Activity: *A neural network is a system of programs and data structures that simulates the underlying concepts of the human brain. Read about neural networks in Wikipedia:*

http://en.wikipedia.org/wiki/Neural_networks

Deliverables:

Answer the following questions about neural networks:

1. How does a biological neural network differ from an artificial neural network?
2. What are three broad categories for the application of artificial neural networks?

Quiz Questions:

1. Are the neural networks discussed in this chapter considered:
   (a) Biological
   (b) Artificial
   (c) Both A and B
   (d) Neither A nor B

2. In the application of neural networks, the tasks tend to be:

   (a) Functional approximations
   (b) Classifications of patterns
   (c) Data processing–like filtering
   (d) All of the above

Discussion Questions:

Discuss how biological neural networks differ from artificial neural networks. What are some examples of the use of artificial neural networks in business?

PI4.4 Fuzzy Logic

Fuzzy logic is a branch of mathematics that deals with uncertainties by simulating the process of human reasoning. The rationale behind fuzzy logic is that decision making is not always a matter of black and white, true or false. It often involves gray areas where the term *maybe* is more appropriate.

A computer programmed to use fuzzy logic defines in precise terms subjective concepts that humans do not define precisely. For example, for the concept *income*, terms such as *high* and *moderate* are subjective and imprecise. Using fuzzy logic, however, a computer could define "high" incomes as those exceeding $200,000 per year, and "moderate" incomes as those ranging from $150,000 to $200,000 per year. A loan officer at a bank might use these fuzzy values when considering a loan application.

Fuzzy logic has also been used in financial analysis and the manufacture of antilock brakes. In accounting and finance, fuzzy logic allows you to analyze information with imprecise values, such as intangible assets like goodwill. Google uses fuzzy logic to find answers to your search terms because your perception of a topic often influences how you phrase your query, therefore determining the relevance of the Web pages that Google delivers to you.

BEFORE *YOU GO ON . . .*

1. What is fuzzy logic?
2. Give some examples of where fuzzy logic is used.

Student Activity | PI4.4

Objective: The objective of this exercise is to familiarize you with fuzzy logic and ways in which it is being used in business.

Chapter Connection: This exercise relates to Section PI4.4 of this chapter.

Prerequisites: The student should read to Section PI4.4 of this chapter before doing this exercise.

Activity: *Fuzzy logic is a branch of mathematics that deals with uncertainties to simulate human reasoning. The rationale behind fuzzy logic is that decision making is not always a matter of black and white, true or false. It often involves gray areas where the term* maybe *is more appropriate.*

Google uses fuzzy logic to find answers to your search terms. Go to http://google.com, and do a search for fuzzy logic.

Deliverables:

Based on the results of your search, answer the following:

1. About how many results were returned for your search (at the top under the search window)?
2. One of the top results returned should be from Wikipedia, the free encyclopedia. Click on that link, read the page, and then give a brief description of fuzzy logic.
3. When did fuzzy logic first emerge, and who presented it?
4. What are some uses of fuzzy logic?

PI4.5 Genetic Algorithms

An algorithm is a method for solving a problem expressed as a finite sequence of steps. A **genetic algorithm** is an approach that mimics the evolutionary, survival-of-the-fittest process to generate increasingly better solutions to a problem. That is, a genetic algorithm is an optimizing process that finds the combination of inputs that produces the best outputs. Genetic algorithms have three functional characteristics:

- *Selection* (survival of the fittest): The key to selection is to give preference to better and better outcomes
- *Crossover:* The process of combining portions of good outcomes in the hope of creating an even better outcome
- *Mutation:* The process of randomly trying combinations and evaluating the success (or failure) of an outcome

Genetic algorithms are best suited to decision-making environments in which thousands or millions of solutions are possible. Genetic algorithms can find and evaluate solutions intelligently, and they can process many more possibilities more thoroughly and faster than a human can. Users do have to tell the genetic algorithm what constitutes a "good" solution. Good solutions could be low cost or high return, or any number of other results. Let us look at some examples:

- Boeing uses genetic algorithms in its design of aircraft parts such as the fan blades on its 777 jet. Rolls Royce and Honda also use genetic algorithms in their design processes.
- Retailers such as Marks and Spencer, a British chain that has 320 stores, use genetic algorithms to manage their inventories more effectively and also to optimize their store displays.
- Air Liquide, a producer of industrial gases, uses genetic algorithms to find optimal production schedules and distribution points in its supply chain. The company has 40 plants and 8,000 client sites and must consider factors such as power prices and customer demand projections, as well as the power costs and efficiency of each plant.

→ BEFORE *YOU GO ON . . .*

1. What is a genetic algorithm?
2. Give examples of the use of genetic algorithms.

Student Activity | PI4.5

Objective: The objective of this exercise is to familiarize you with genetic algorithms.

Chapter Connection: This exercise relates to Section PI4.5 of this chapter.

Prerequisites: You should read Section PI4.5 of this chapter before doing this exercise.

Activity: *Genetic algorithms are a rapidly growing area of artificial intelligence. They were first inspired by Darwin's theory about evolution but today are used to solve problems.*

Click on the following link to learn more about genetic algorithms:

http://www.obitko.com/tutorials/genetic-algorithms/index.php

Explore the areas listed on the left, especially "Introduction" and "Search Space."

Many of the examples are related more to chromosomes and reproduction. Since we are more interested in business applications, click on "GA Example (TSP)" about the traveling salesman. This example deals with a salesperson who needs to travel to multiple cities and wants to find the most efficient and cost-effective route.

Deliverables:

Answer the following based on the chapter text and your research at www.obitko.com:

1. What is a genetic algorithm?

2. What is meant by *search space*?

Quiz Questions:

1. What is *not* a functional characteristic of a genetic algorithm?

  (a) Selection
  (b) Calculation
  (c) Crossover
  (d) Mutation

2. Which of the following is a benefit of a genetic algorithm?

  (a) Faster than a human
  (b) Find many potential solutions
  (c) Intelligently evaluate solutions
  (d) All of the above

3. What are some possible uses of genetic algorithms?

  (a) Plan a route for delivery
  (b) Manage inventories more effectively
  (c) Find optimal production schedules
  (d) All of the above

Discussion Questions:

As stated in the narrative, genetic algorithms can be used to quickly solve complex problems for which it could take humans years to process all the combinations. Referring to the traveling salesman exercise, what other similar application can you think of where a genetic algorithm can provide the best solution?

PI4.6 Intelligent Agents

An **intelligent agent** is a software program that assists you, or acts on your behalf, in performing repetitive computer-related tasks. Behind the scenes, intelligent agents often use ISs such as ESs and fuzzy logic to create their seemingly intelligent behavior.

You may be familiar with an early type of intelligent agent: the paper clip ("Clippy") that popped up in early versions of Microsoft Word. For example, if your document appeared as though it were going to be a business letter—that is, you type in a date, name, and address—the animated paper clip would offer helpful suggestions on how to proceed. Users objected so strenuously to this primitive intelligent agent that Microsoft deleted it from subsequent versions.

There are many intelligent agents—also called *bots*—for a wide variety of tasks. You can view the many different types of available agents by visiting BotSpot (www.botspot.com) and SmartBot (www.smartbot.com). The following sections examine three types of agents: information agents, monitoring-and-surveillance agents, and user or personal agents.

Information Agents

Information agents are a type of intelligent agent that searches for information of some kind and displays it to the users. The best-known information agents are buyer agents. A **buyer agent** (or **shopping bot**) is an intelligent agent on a Web site that helps customers find the products and services they need. There are many examples of information agents. Here are a few illustrative cases:

- The information agents for Amazon display lists of books and other products that customers might like, based on past purchases.

- Google and Ask.com use information agents to find information, and not just when you request it. Google, for example, sends Googlebots out to surf all the Web sites in Google's index. These bots copy individual pages to Google's repository, where Google software indexes them. This process means that when you perform a Google search, the search engine builds a list of all the pages that contain the key words you specify and presents them to you in PageRank order. Google's PageRank algorithm sorts Web pages based on the number of links on the Web that point to each page. That is, the more links on the Web that point to a particular page, the higher that Web site will be on the list.

- The Federal Electronic Research and Review Extraction Tool (FERRET) was developed jointly by the Census Bureau and the Bureau of Labor Statistics. You can use FERRET to find information on employment, healthcare, education, race and ethnicity, health insurance, housing, income and poverty, aging, and marriage and the family.

Monitoring-and-Surveillance Agents

Monitoring-and-surveillance agents (or **predictive agents**) are intelligent agents that constantly observe and report on some item of interest. There are many examples of predictive agents. Consider the following:

- Allstate Insurance uses monitoring-and-surveillance agents to manage its large computer networks 24/7/365. Every 5 seconds, the agent measures 1,200 data points. It can predict a system crash 45 minutes before it happens. The agent also watches for electronic attacks to detect them early so they can be stopped.

- Monitoring-and-surveillance agents can watch your competitors and notify you of price changes and special offers.

- These agents can monitor Internet sites, discussion groups, and mailing lists for stock manipulations, insider trading, and rumors that might impact stock prices.

- These agents can monitor Web sites for updated information on topics of your choice, such as price changes on desired products (e.g., airline tickets).

User Agents

User agents (or **personal agents**) are intelligent agents that take action on your behalf. Let us look at what these agents can do (or will be able to do shortly):

- Check your e-mail, sort it according to your priority rules, and alert you when high-value e-mails appear in your in-box.

- Automatically fill out forms on the Web for you. They will also store your information for future use.

→ **BEFORE** *YOU GO ON . . .*

1. Define *intelligent agents, information agents, monitoring-and-surveillance agents,* and *user agents.*
2. Explain the uses of each type of intelligent agent.

Student Activity | PI4.6

Objective: The objective of this exercise is to familiarize you with intelligent agents and how they might be used.

Chapter Connection: This exercise relates to Section PI4.6 of this chapter.

Prerequisites: You should read Section PI4.6 before doing this exercise.

Activity: *Information agents are a type of intelligent agent that searches for information or products and displays it to the users. The best-known information agents are buyer agents. A buyer agent, also called a shopping bot, is an intelligent agent on the Web that helps customers find products and services.*

Let us assume the big game is coming up this weekend and you have invited a group of friends over to watch it at your apartment. However, last evening, your TV went black. So you need to shop for a new TV quickly. You have heard about Web sites that can help you find the best deals, so you decide to try one out. You have at the most about $700 to spend, and you think you want an LCD screen. Since a lot of people are coming, you would like a big screen, at least 50 inches, so everybody can see. Select the following link, and see what you can find:

www.shopzilla.com

Deliverables:

1. Do a search with the required features. How many results did you get? What is the manufacturer, the screen size, where sold, and cost for the top three LCD results?

2. Chances are you had few results with the first search. You have talked to some to your friends, and they told you plasma is usually cheaper for big-screen TVs. So, change the technology type to plasma, and do a new search. Did you get more options in the results? Sort by "most popular." Again give the manufacturer, the screen size, where sold, and cost for the top three plasma results.

3. Check out the details of the top two you like by clicking the "Product Name" link. Is it in stock? What is the average customer rating (in stars)?

4. Which TV did you decide to buy?

Quiz Questions:

1. What are the advantages of using a shopping bot?
   (a) Fast results
   (b) Many options
   (c) Reviews available
   (d) All of the above

2. Which of the following can you search for on a shopping bot?
   (a) Shoes
   (b) Clothes
   (c) Perfume
   (d) All of the above

3. Which of the following is *not* an intelligent agent?
   (a) Surveillance agent
   (b) Service agent
   (c) User agent
   (d) Information agent

Discussion Questions:

1. What are the benefits of using a shopping bot to find an item you want to buy?

2. What are five categories of products that shopping bots carry?

3. Discuss other shopping bots you have used.

What's In IT For Me?

For the Accounting Major

Intelligent systems are used extensively in auditing to uncover irregularities. They are also used to uncover and prevent fraud. Today's CPAs use intelligent systems for many of their duties, ranging from risk analysis to cost control. Accounting personnel also use intelligent agents for several mundane tasks such as managing accounts and monitoring employees' Internet use.

For the Finance Major

People have been using computers for decades to solve financial problems. Innovative intelligent applications have been developed for activities such as making stock market decisions, refinancing bonds, assessing debt risks, analyzing financial conditions, predicting business failures, forecasting financial trends, and investing in global markets. In many cases, intelligent systems can facilitate the use of spreadsheets and other computerized systems used in finance. In addition, intelligent systems can help to reduce fraud in credit cards, stocks, and other financial services.

For the Marketing Major

Marketing personnel utilize intelligent systems in many applications, from allocating advertising budgets to evaluating alternative routings of salespeople. New marketing approaches such as targeted marketing and marketing transaction databases are heavily dependent on IT in general and on intelligent systems in particular. Intelligent systems are particularly useful in mining customer databases and predicting customer behavior. Successful applications are visible in almost every area of marketing and sales, from analyzing the success of one-to-one advertising to supporting customer help desks. With the increased importance of customer service, the use of intelligent agents is becoming critical for providing fast response.

For the Production/Operations Management Major

Intelligent systems support complex operations and production decisions, from inventory to production planning. Many of the early expert systems were developed in the production/operations management field for tasks ranging from diagnosing machine failures and prescribing repairs to complex production scheduling and inventory control. Some companies, such as DuPont and Kodak, have deployed hundreds of expert systems in the planning, organizing, and control of their operational systems.

For the Human Resources Management Major

Human resources personnel use intelligent systems for many applications. For example, these systems can find resumes of applicants posted on the Web and sort them to match needed skills. Expert systems are used in evaluating candidates (tests, interviews). HR personnel use intelligent systems to train and support employees in managing their fringe benefits. In addition, they use neural computing to predict employee job performance and to predict labor needs.

For the MIS Major

The MIS function develops (or acquires) and maintains the organization's various intelligent systems, as well as the data and models that these systems use. In addition, MIS staffers sometimes interact with subject-area experts to capture the expertise used in ESs.

SUMMARY

1. Differentiate between artificial intelligence and human intelligence.

Tables PI4.1 differentiates between artificial and human intelligence on a number of characteristics.

2. Define expert systems, and provide examples of their use.

Expert systems are computer systems that attempt to mimic human experts by applying expertise in a specific domain. Tables PI4.2 and PI4.3 offer examples of expert systems.

3. Define neural networks, and provide examples of their use.

A neural network is a system of programs and data structures that simulate the underlying concepts of the human brain. Neural networks are used to detect weapons concealed in personal belongings, in research on various diseases, for financial forecasting, to detect fraud in credit card transactions, to fight crime, and many other applications.

4. Define fuzzy logic, and provide examples of its use.

Fuzzy logic is a branch of mathematics that deals with uncertainties by simulating the process of human reasoning. Fuzzy logic is used in financial analysis, the manufacture of antilock brakes, measuring intangible assets like goodwill, and finding responses to search terms in Google.

5. Define genetic algorithms, and provide examples of their use.

A genetic algorithm is an intelligent system that mimics the evolutionary, survival-of-the-fittest process to generate increasingly better solutions to a problem. Genetic algorithms are used to design aircraft parts such as fan blades, to manage inventories more effectively, to optimize store displays, and to find optimal production schedules and distribution points.

6. Define intelligent agents, and provide examples of their use.

An intelligent agent is a software program that assists you, or acts on your behalf, in performing repetitive, computer-related tasks. Intelligent agents are used to display lists of books or other products that customers might like, based on past purchases; to find information; to manage and monitor large computer networks 24/7/365; to detect electronic attacks early so they can be stopped; to watch competitors and send notices of price changes and special offers; to monitor Internet sites, discussion groups, and mailing lists for stock manipulations, insider trading, and rumors that might impact stock prices; to check e-mail, sort it according to established priority rules, and alert recipients when high-value e-mails appear in their inbox; and to automatically fill out forms on the Web.

GLOSSARY

artificial intelligence A subfield of computer science that is concerned with studying the thought processes of humans and re-creating the effects of those processes via machines, such as computers.

buyer agent (or **shopping bot**) An intelligent agent on a Web site that helps customers find products and services that they need.

expert systems (ESs) Computer systems that attempt to mimic human experts by applying expertise in a specific domain.

fuzzy logic A branch of mathematics that deals with uncertainties by simulating the process of human reasoning.

genetic algorithm An approach that mimics the evolutionary, survival-of-the-fittest process to generate increasingly better solutions to a problem.

information agent A type of intelligent agent that searches for information of some kind and displays it to the users.

intelligent agent A software program that assists you, or acts on your behalf, in performing repetitive, computer-related tasks.

intelligent systems A term that describes the various commercial applications of artificial intelligence.

monitoring-and-surveillance agents (or **predictive agents**) Intelligent agents that constantly observe and report on some item of interest.

neural network A system of programs and data structures that simulates the underlying concepts of the human brain.

personal agents (see **user agents**)

predictive agents (see **monitoring-and-surveillance agents**)

shopping bot (see **buyer agent**)

Turing test A test in which a man and a computer both pretend to be women (or men), and the human interviewer has to decide which is which.

user agents (or **personal agents**) Intelligent agents that take action on your behalf.

DISCUSSION QUESTIONS

1. Explain how your university could employ an expert system in its admission process. Could it apply a neural network to this process? What might be the outcome if a student were denied admission to the university and the student's parents discovered that an expert system had been involved in the admissions process?

2. One difference between a conventional business intelligence system and an expert system is that the former can explain a *how* question, whereas the latter can explain a *how* and a *why* question. Discuss the implications of this statement.

PROBLEM-SOLVING ACTIVITIES

1. You have decided to purchase a new video camcorder. To purchase it as inexpensively as possible and still get the features you want, you use a shopping bot. Visit several of the shopping bot Web sites that perform price comparisons for you. Begin with MySimon (www.mysimon.com), BizRate.com (www.bizrate.com), and Google Product Search (www.google.com/prdhp). Compare these shopping bots in terms of their ease of use, number of product offerings, speed in obtaining information, thoroughness of information offered about products and sellers, and price selection. Which site or sites would you use, and why? Which camcorder would you select and why? How helpful were these sites in making your decision?

2. Access the Web site MyMajors (www.mymajors.com). This site contains a rule-based expert system to help students find majors. The expert system has more than 300 rules and 15,000 possible conclusions. The site ranks majors according to the likelihood that a student will succeed in them, and it provides 6 possible majors from among 60 alternative majors that a student might consider.

    Take the quiz, and see if you are in the "right major" as defined by the expert system. You must register to take the quiz.

3. Access Exsys (www.exsys.com), and click on "Corvid Demo." Provide your e-mail address, and click on the link for "Student–Needed for a Class." Try the various demos, and report your results to the class.

Plug IT In | 5

Project Management

LEARNING OBJECTIVES >>>

1. Define a project, define information system project management, and describe the triple constraints of all projects.
2. Describe the five phases of the project management process.
3. Describe the major reasons why projects fail.
4. Describe the five basic process groups and the nine knowledge areas of the Project Management Body of Knowledge.

PI5.1 Project Management for Information Systems Projects

Projects are short-term efforts to create a specific business-related outcome. These outcomes may take the form of products or services. In the context of information systems (IS), many of the resource investments made by organizations are in the form of projects. For example, Home Depot (www.homedepot.com) recently engaged in an IS project to develop an inventory management system. The objectives of the project were to improve inventory turnover, reduce product stock-outs, and integrate more tightly with supply chain partners. The outcome was to lower companywide costs by carrying less physical inventory.

Almost every organization that utilizes information technology to support business processes engages in some form of IS project management. **IS project management** is a directed effort to plan, organize, and manage resources to bring about the successful achievement of specific IS goals. All projects, whether they are IS projects or not, are constrained by the same three factors, known as the **triple constraints of project management**: time, cost, and scope. *Time* refers to the window of opportunity in which a project must be completed to provide a benefit to the organization. *Cost* is the actual amount of resources, including cash and labor, that an organization can commit to completing a project. *Scope* refers to the processes that ensure that the project includes all the work required—and only the work required—to complete the project successfully. For an IS project to be successful, the organization must allow an adequate amount of time, provide an appropriate amount of resources, and carefully define what is and is not included in the project.

The triple constraints are related and involve trade-offs. For example, scope can often be increased by using additional time and incurring increased costs. Cost and/or time can often be saved by reducing scope. For a given scope, time can sometimes be saved by increasing cost. The following example illustrates how Charter Communications successfully deployed project management software.

Example

Charter Communications Relies on IT Project Management Software. In today's turbulent economic times, managers are having difficulty justifying spending money on IT projects when resources are so scarce. At Charter Communications (www.charter.com), a telecommunications firm that provides telephone, cable, and high-speed Internet service, the company's response to these funding requests was simple: If a project makes money or saves more money than it costs, then do it.

In the highly competitive telecommunications industry, Charter faced mounting pressures from competitors and customers alike. Comcast Cable (www.comcast.com) and Time Warner Cable (www.timewarnercable.com) are the largest competitors in the cable television/telecommunications market. Because they are better financed, Comcast and Time Warner are able to engage in aggressive acquisitions and mergers. Each company has consolidated a significant share of the markets in which Charter operates. Therefore, Charter has less potential revenue. To compound this problem, Charter has a restricted cash flow resulting from its highly leveraged position (the company has more than $21 billion of debt on its balance sheet).

Further, Charter has experienced difficulties addressing customer-related issues. In fact, Charter received so many customer complaints that the Better Business Bureau (www.bbb.org) issued a warning notice to consumers regarding the company's poor customer service. Finally, on March 27, 2009, Charter filed for Chapter 11 bankruptcy.

Charter responded to these challenges by adopting an ambitious goal: to win, and subsequently retain, customers in the hypercompetitive communications environment. To accomplish this goal, Charter is investing heavily in new information technology. This technology is intended to support the company's customer services operations, with the aim of providing superb service. Charter executives retained the services of CA Technologies (www.ca.com), a consulting firm specializing in IT project management, to help Charter develop a comprehensive project management system that the company could use to assess potential return on investment for proposed IT projects. CA delivered a project management system known as Clarity. Clarity replaced Charter's previous system, which consisted only of spreadsheets and PowerPoint-driven dashboards.

Clarity enables Charter to evaluate projects under consideration and to manage the projects already in process. Since Charter deployed the Clarity system, its record of completing projects on time and within budget has improved noticeably. Clarity has become a principal tool that Charter uses to eliminate the detrimental cost overruns that have contributed to its recent financial struggles. Further, controlling costs has enabled Charter to allocate additional resources toward much needed customer service improvements.

Questions

1. What were Charter's business problems that led the company to deploy the Clarity project management software?

2. What results did Charter see from using the Clarity software?

BEFORE *YOU GO ON . . .*

1. What is a project?
2. What is the triple constraint of any project?

Sources: Compiled from "Charter Communications Files for Chapter 11 Bankruptcy," *Associated Press*, March 28, 2009; D. Gardner, "Charter Communications to Seek Financial Protection," *InformationWeek*, February 12, 2009; Y. Adegoke, "Wall Street on Charter Communications Bankruptcy Watch," *Reuters*, Jan 16, 2009; "Charter Communications Maximizes Its Investment in New Technology with Improved Project Management," *Computer Associates Success Story*; (www.ca.com), accessed August 11, 2011.

Student Activity | PI5.1

Objective: To make you aware of the connection between project management activities and the role of project management software in managing those activities. The activity also will make you aware of the existence of Web-based project management software. You should be able to list at least three features of Web-based project management software that can help to manage complex IT projects.

Chapter Connection: This activity relates to Section PI5.1 of this chapter.

Prerequisites: Students should have read Section PI5.1.

Activity: *Read the article "Turn Your Customer's Needs into Successful IT Projects" by Jim Cochran (accessible through the following link), and note the various steps of the project management process:*

www.projectsmart.co.uk/turn-your-customers-needs-into-successful-it-projects.html

Do an online search for finding Web-based project management software and watch the demo of the products that are typically found on the Web site. An example of Web-based project management software with a demo can be found through the following link:

www.project-drive.net

Deliverables:

1. Explain how the project management steps presented in the article by Jim Cochran relate to the triple constraints of project management described in the text.

2. Discuss how the various modules and functionality of the Web-based project management software that you investigated can support various stages of project management as described in Section PI5.1 of this chapter.

Quiz Questions:

1. According to the article "Turn Your Customer's Needs into Successful IT Projects," which of the following is *not* true for the vision of the solution?
   (a) It should be long-term oriented.
   (b) It must provide a context or frame of reference for decision making throughout project development.
   (c) It should contain detailed functional requirements.
   (d) It should be part of the planning process.

2. An example of a requirement trap is:
   (a) Scope creep
   (b) Lack of customer or end-user involvement
   (c) Insufficient analysis of the impact of change
   (d) All of the above

3. In present-day project management software, _____ _____ are essential for coordinating among various _____.

4. Common _____ facility in project management _____ the participants to keep appointments, deadlines, and such and also avoid schedule _____ .

Discussion Questions:

1. Do you think that all project management software should have a formal collaborative part?

2. List at least two benefits of having a collaborative module in a project management software program.

PI5.2 The Project Management Process

The traditional approach to project management divides every project into five distinct phases: initiation, planning, execution, monitoring and control, and completion. These phases are sequential, and we discuss them in order.

Project Initiation

The first phase in the management of a process is to clearly define the problem that the project is intended to solve and the goals that it is to achieve. In this phase, it is also necessary to identify and secure the resources necessary for the project, analyze the costs and benefits of the project, and identify potential risks.

In an IS project, a user's business problem or need typically initiates a project that can solve the problem and meet the need. The user must clearly define the problem so that the IS team can understand it. The user must also define the benefits he or she expects to gain from successful completion of the IS project.

Project Planning

As the term *planning* suggests, in this phase, every project objective and every activity associated with that objective must be identified and sequenced. This phase is critically important to avoid scope creep once the project gets underway. **Scope creep** refers to uncontrolled changes in a project's scope. This phenomenon can occur when the scope of a project is not properly defined, documented, or controlled. It is generally considered a negative occurrence that is to be avoided.

In an IS project, users often contribute to scope creep when they ask for additional features or functionality after the project is underway. This situation often leads to the project being overtime and over budget.

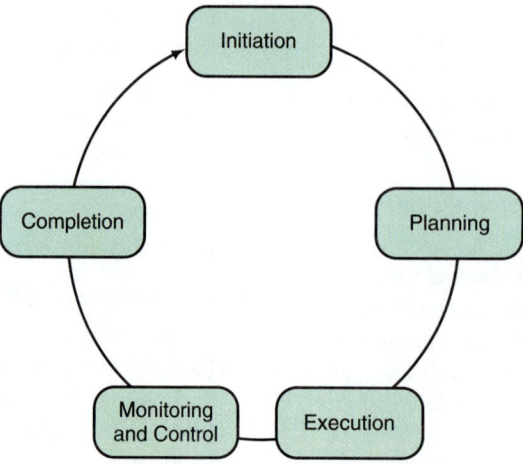

Figure PI5.1 The Project Management Process.

Many tools assist developers in sequencing these activities, including dependence diagrams, such as the program evaluation and review technique (PERT), the critical path method (CPM), and a timeline diagram called the Gantt chart. Project managers use these tools to ensure that activities are performed in a logical sequence. As the project progresses, project managers also employ these tools to evaluate whether the project is on schedule and, if not, where the delays are occurring and what the managers must do to correct them.

Project Execution

In this phase, the work defined in the project management plan is performed to accomplish the project's requirements. Execution coordinates people and resources, and it integrates and performs project activities in accordance with the plan.

Users may be involved in project execution. For example, in an IS project, users often evaluate prototypes so that they can provide meaningful feedback to the IS team.

Project Monitoring and Control

The purpose of monitoring and control is to determine whether the project is progressing as planned. This phase consists of three steps: (1) monitoring ongoing project activities (where we are); (2) comparing project variables (cost, effort, time, resources, etc.) with the actual plan (where we should be); and (3) identifying corrective actions (how do we get on track again).

Project Completion

The project is completed when it is formally accepted by the organization. All activities are finalized, and all contracts are fulfilled and settled. In addition, all files are archived, and all lessons learned are documented.

Project Management Failure

Many times IT projects fail to achieve their desired results. In fact, analysts have found that only 29 percent of all IS projects are completed on time, within budget, and with all the features and functions originally specified. Further, between 30 and 40 percent of all IS software development projects are *runaway projects*, meaning they are so far over budget and past deadline that they must be abandoned, typically with large monetary loss. IS projects do not deliver their potential value for a number of reasons, including these:

- Lack of sufficient planning at the start of a project
- Difficulties with technology compatibility (that is, new technology may not work with existing technology)
- Lack of commitment by management to providing the necessary resources
- Poorly defined project scope
- Lack of sufficient time to complete the project

BEFORE *YOU GO ON . . .*

1. What are the five phases of the project management process?
2. What are the major causes of project failure?

Student Activity | PI5.2

Objective: You should be able to list at least five activities that are carried out in a typical IT project management situation. You should also be able to connect the detailed activities to the broader steps in project management and to understand the risks associated with projects.

Chapter Connection: This activity relates to Section PI5.2 in this chapter.

Prerequisites: You should have read Section PI5.2.

Activity: *Read the two articles accessible through the following links. The first article describes steps in project management using an example of Web site development, and the second article describes the reasons for the failure of IS projects. For the second article, please pay special attention to the four tables in the article.*

www.projectsmart.co.uk/eight-easy-steps-to-managing-your-website-development.html

www.intosaiitaudit.org/intoit_articles/26_p12top17.pdf

Deliverables:

1. Map the various activities listed in the first article and in Table 4 of the second article to the five phases of project management listed in this chapter.

2. List at least two causes of project failure that were not listed in this chapter.

Quiz Questions:

1. According to various surveys mentioned in the second article, which of the following is *not* true for IS projects?

   (a) Large IT projects are more prone to failure than small and medium-size projects.

   (b) IT projects are more likely to be unsuccessful than successful.

   (c) Only 30 percent of IT projects are satisfactory.

   (d) Lack of top management support is one of the main reasons for failures of IT projects.

2. According to the CHAOS study mentioned in the second article, the second most important factor for ensuring success of an IT project is:

   (a) Standard software infrastructure
   (b) Experienced project manager
   (c) Formal methodology
   (d) User involvement

3. For an IT project to avoid failure and abandonment, it must be connected to the _____ _____.

   (a) Latest technology
   (b) Organizational strategy
   (c) CFO's interests
   (d) Manager's experience

4. In the article "Eight Easy Steps to Managing Your Website Development," a key activity missing from the planning is:

   (a) Communications planning
   (b) Planning for change
   (c) Human resources planning
   (d) Project scope analysis

Discussion Question:

The second article lists lack of support from top management as one of the key reasons for IS project failure. How would you convince top management about the importance of the IS project and gain support? You can read the two-page supplemental article available from www.projectsmart.co.uk/successful-projects-its-not-rocket-science.html *to get some ideas.*

PI5.3 The Project Management Body of Knowledge

The **Project Management Body of Knowledge (PMBOK)** is a collection of processes and knowledge areas generally accepted as best practice within the project management discipline. As an internationally recognized standard, it provides the fundamentals of project management, regardless of the type of project (e.g., construction, software, engineering, automotive, etc.). The purpose of the PMBOK is to provide and promote a common vocabulary within the project management profession for discussing, writing, and applying project management concepts.

The PMBOK recognizes five basic process groups and nine knowledge areas typical of almost all projects. You learned about the five basic process groups in the previous section:

- Initiation
- Planning
- Execution
- Monitoring and Control
- Completion

Processes overlap and interact throughout a project. Processes are described in terms of inputs (documents, plans, designs), tools and techniques, and outputs (documents, products). The nine knowledge areas of the PMBOK are these:

- *Project Integration Management.* Project integration management includes those processes required to ensure that all the project's components are properly coordinated. The project plan development processes, project plan execution processes, and integrated change control processes are all included in this area of knowledge. Each process has expected inputs and outputs and plus the appropriate tools and techniques to support the change of inputs to outputs.

- *Project Scope Management.* Project scope management defines the processes that limit and control the work included in a project. Scope creep is a serious problem that often causes projects to go over time and over budget. These processes ensure that all the work of the project is included and properly accounted for.

- *Project Time Management.* Proper sequencing is vital to timely project completion. When the amount of time needed is established, it takes excellent scheduling skills and tools to manage the activities to complete project milestones and the project itself within the allotted time. Different tools are available to assist with this process, such as Gantt charts, milestone charts, and network charts. Each tool helps managers see the big picture and stay in control of the project's progression.

- *Project Cost Management.* Resource planning and cost estimation are equally vital to time management. These two processes cannot exist independently of each other. Resource cost management is difficult to estimate and even more difficult to manage when unforeseen events take place. Early in a project, managers may project a budget range and then fine-tune it as the project progresses.

- *Project Quality Management.* Every project needs a set of processes that ensure that project outcomes meet the needs for which the project was executed. Quality planning, assurance, and control are included in this area. There are many quality management models to consider, such as the Deming Prize, TQM, Six Sigma, and more. These all aim to help organizations produce quality products the first time they try. There are also many paradigms applicable to this area of knowledge, such as "Zero Defects" and "DTRTRTFT" (Do the right thing right the first time). These paradigms are meant to inspire organizations to operate at higher quality levels.

- *Project Human Resource Management.* People can be the major headache or the major asset of any project. People with differing skill sets are required at various times during a project, and their individual skills have to be used effectively in order for the project to succeed. This area of knowledge includes concepts such as staffing decisions; team management; and organizational culture, style, and structure.

- *Project Communications Management.* A vast amount of communication is necessary in successful projects. Information must be collected, disseminated, stored, and destroyed at the appropriate time. This area of knowledge contains the processes to perform these functions. Often, organizations investigate personality styles to determine their most effective communicators. Choosing the right person to be a leader can make all the difference in the success of a project!

- *Project Risk Management.* All projects face risk. With organizational success, jobs, careers, and livelihoods on the line, it is a good idea to minimize the risk of projects as much as feasible. Therefore, risk management must be an integral part of any project because things do not always happen as planned. The risk management process includes identification of risks, quantitative and qualitative analysis, risk response planning, and risk monitoring.

- *Project Procurement Management.* No matter how good the idea behind a project, without funding it will never be more than a good idea. The accumulated knowledge related to project procurement management encompasses processes of solicitation, selection, contractual agreements, and closeout processes.

BEFORE *YOU GO ON . . .*

1. What is the Project Management Body of Knowledge, and why is it important to organizations?
2. What part of the PMBOK do you think is most important? Can a project succeed without all the parts?

Student Activity | PI5.3

Objective: You should be able to list various types of skills needed to manage an IT project and explain how they help in better project management and avoid project failure. This exercise is also intended to make you aware of alternative methods for project management than the traditional waterfall approach. You should be able to list at least three benefits for adopting Agile methodology for IT projects and how it can help mitigate failure risks. Particularly, you should be able to list some of the organizational soft skills needed to make a project successful.

Chapter Connection: This activity relates to Section PI5.3 in this chapter.

Prerequisites: You should have read Section PI5.3.

Activity: *Read the following articles on the Agile methodology and on the skills required for successfully managing a project:*

www.projectsmart.co.uk/waterfall-v-agile-how-should-i-approach-my-software-development-project.html

http://career-resources.dice.com/job-technology/skills_for_project_management_success.shtml

Deliverables:

1. Describe what an Agile methodology is and how it differs from traditional project management. For IT projects, which one is preferred and why?
2. Section PI5.3 of this chapter lists nine knowledge areas of the PMBOK. In which of them do you think the tips listed in the second article fit best? Why?
3. The second article advises staying away from project management software like Microsoft Project when possible. What are the reasons for that? List at least two pros and cons of using project management software like MS Project for managing IT projects.

Quiz Questions:

1. To manage a project successfully, one should have _____, not sympathy, for the project members.
2. Effective project managers and proponents should be able to effectively describe both the _____ side of the project as well as its connection to the _____ _____.
3. One of the ways to create good team dynamics, as listed in the second article, is to _____ _____.

Discussion Question:

You must have been involved in multiple team projects during your academic career. Think of one project that was almost a semester-long team project, and then list which of the tips listed in the article were used by you for managing your project. What obstacles did you face, and how did using the tips help you overcome them?

What's In IT For Me?

For All Business Majors

Regardless of the functional area in organizations, each of you will be on project teams beginning very early in your careers. These projects will be critical to your organization's success. Therefore, it is critical that all majors understand the project management process so that you can make immediate contributions to your project teams.

SUMMARY

1. **Define a project, define information systems project management, and describe the triple constraints of all projects.**

   Projects are short-term efforts to create a specific business-related outcome. *IS project management* is a directed effort to plan, organize, and manage resources to bring about the successful achievement of specific IS goals. All projects, whether they are IS projects or not, are constrained by the same three factors, known as the *triple constraints of project management*: time, cost, and scope. *Time* refers to the window of opportunity in which a project must be completed to provide a benefit to the organization. *Cost* is the actual amount of resources, including cash and labor, that an organization can commit to completing a project. *Scope* refers to the processes that ensure that the project includes all the work required—and only the work required—to complete the project successfully.

2. **Describe the five phases of the project management process.**

   Project initiation clearly defines the problem that the project is intended to solve and the goals that it is to achieve. In *project planning*, every project objective and every activity associated with that objective must be identified and sequenced. In the *project execution* phase, the work defined in the project management plan is performed to accomplish the project's requirements. The purpose of the *monitoring and control phase* is to determine whether the progress is progressing as planned. The *project completion* phase is when the project is formally accepted by the organization.

3. **Describe the major reasons why projects fail.**

   IS projects do not deliver their potential value for a number of reasons, including lack of sufficient planning at the start of a project; difficulties with technology compatibility (that is, new technology may not work with existing technology); lack of commitment by management in providing the necessary resources; poorly defined project scope; and lack of sufficient time to complete the project.

4. **Describe the five basic process groups and the nine knowledge areas of the Project Management Body of Knowledge.**

   The five basic process groups of the PMBOK are *initiating, planning, executing, monitoring and controlling*, and *closing*. The nine knowledge areas of the PMBOK are *managing project integration, scope, time, cost, quality, human resources, communications, risk*, and *procurement*.

GLOSSARY

IS project management A directed effort to plan, organize, and manage resources to bring about the successful achievement of specific IS goals.

project Short-term effort to create a specific business-related outcome.

Project Management Body of Knowledge (PMBOK) A collection of processes and knowledge areas generally accepted as best practice within the project management discipline.

scope creep Uncontrolled changes in a project's scope.

triple constraints of project management Time, cost, and scope.

DISCUSSION QUESTIONS

1. You manage the department that will use a system being developed on a large project. After carefully reviewing the requirements definition document, you are positive that there are missing, ambiguous, inaccurate, and unclear requirements. The project manager is pressuring you for your sign-off since he has already received sign-offs from all of your co-workers. If you fail to sign off on the requirements, you are going to put the entire project at risk because the timeframe is not negotiable. What should you do? Why? Support your answer.

2. You have been hired as a consultant to build an employee payroll system for a startup restaurant. Before you even have a chance to interview them, the two owners decided to independently come up with a list of their business requirements. When you combine their two lists, you have the following list:

   - All employees must have a unique employee ID.
   - The system must track employee hours worked based on employees' last names.
   - Employees must be scheduled to work a minimum of 8 hours per day.
   - Employee payroll is calculated by multiplying the employees' hours worked by $7.25.
   - Managers must be scheduled to work morning shifts.
   - Employees cannot be scheduled to work more than 8 hours per day.
   - Servers cannot be scheduled to work morning, afternoon, or evening shifts.
   - The system must allow managers to change and delete employees from the system.

   a. Highlight potential issues with the list.

   b. Add requirements that you think should be there but are not.

   c. What do you tell the owners when you derive your new list?

PROBLEM-SOLVING ACTIVITIES

1. Apply and discuss each of the five project management processes of the PMBOK to the following massive project. Finally, use a search engine to find out where the project stands now. Would this be considered a runaway project? Why or why not?

CLOSING **CASE** > Britain's National Health System

Established in 1948, the National Health Service (NHS) in the United Kingdom (UK) is the largest healthcare organization in Europe. Controlled by the British government, it is also a vast bureaucracy, employing more than 1 million workers and providing a full range of healthcare services to the country's 60 million citizens.

The inspiration to digitize this huge bureaucracy first surfaced in 2001. At that time, much of the NHS was paper based and severely lagging in its use of technology, largely because of years of underinvestment. Hospitals throughout the UK were dealing with multiple vendors, many of them small to midsize UK software companies. Predictably, the NHS had become a hodgepodge of incompatible systems from different suppliers, with differing levels of functionality. The NHS had created silos of information that were not shared, or even sharable.

In an attempt to resolve these problems, in 2002 the British government initiated the National Program for Information Technology (NPIT), which includes England, Northern Ireland, and Wales (but not Scotland). The overall objective of the NPIT was to build a single, electronic healthcare record for every individual. In effect, this record would be a comprehensive, lifelong history of a patient's healthcare information, regardless of where, when, and by whom he or she was treated. In addition, the NPIT would provide healthcare professionals with access to a national data repository. Finally, it would support the NHS in collecting and analyzing information and monitoring health trends to make the best use of clinical and other resources.

A major obstacle for the NPIT was the sheer size of England's healthcare system. For example, in one year, the system served some 52 million people; it dealt with 325 million consultations in primary care, 13 million outpatient consultations, and 4 million emergency admissions; and it issued 617 million prescriptions.

The NPIT is a 10-year project designed to build new information systems to (1) connect more than 100,000 doctors, 380,000 nurses, and 50,000 other healthcare professionals; (2) allow for the electronic storage and retrieval of patient medical records; (3) permit patients to set up appointments via their computers; and (4) let doctors electronically transmit prescriptions to local pharmacies.

Specifically, the information systems that the NHS is attempting to deliver include the following:

- *The National Spine.* The National Spine is a database at the heart of the NPIT. The Spine encompasses individual electronic NHS lifelong care records for every patient in England, securely accessible by the patients and their health providers. The Spine will enable patients and providers to securely access integrated patient data, prescription ordering, proactive decision support, and best-practice reference data.

- *Choose and Book.* Choose and Book provides convenience for patients in electronically selecting the date, place, and time of their appointments.

- *N3.* The N3 national network is a massive, secure, broadband, virtual private network that provides the IT infrastructure and broadband connectivity for the NHS so that it can share patient information with various organizations. The N3 supports Choose and Book, electronic prescriptions, and electronic transfer of patient information.

The NHS first had McKinsey and Company conduct a study of the UK healthcare system. McKinsey concluded that the project was too large for any one vendor to act as prime contractor for all of it. Consequently, the NHS divided England into five regions—London, Eastern, Northeast, Northwest, and Southern—each with about 12 million people. Each of the five regions would be serviced by a prime IT vendor, known as a Local Service Provider (LSP).

The vendor-selection process was conducted with great secrecy. Unfortunately, the secrecy led to most front-line healthcare providers being excluded from the vendor selection process. The NHS offered 10-year service contracts to the LSPs for the five regions, each worth about $2 billion.

The LSPs are responsible for developing and integrating information systems at a local level. The LSPs are also responsible for implementing clinical and administrative applications, which support the delivery of patient care and enable trusts to exchange data with the National Spine. (A trust is a regional healthcare agency that administers England's national healthcare programs). In addition, the LSPs provide the data centers to run all the applications.

Significantly, all of the NHS's contracts with the LSPs stipulated that vendors would not be paid until they delivered working systems. Because the vendors were the prime contractors, this stipulation also meant that the subcontractors would not be paid until they delivered working systems.

Accenture was named LSP for two regions. Computer Sciences Corporation (CSC), British Telecom (BT), and a Fujitsu-led alliance were named LSPs for the other three regions. BT was also given the contract to build both the N3 network and the National Spine. Atos Origin was chosen to provide Choose and Book.

As previously explained, the LSPs were to act as prime contractors for their respective regions, and they were able to choose their own software vendors and subcontractors. BT and the Fujitsu group selected IDX (now part of GE Healthcare), an established healthcare services and software provider, to develop health records software. Accenture and CSC chose iSoft, a U.K.-based supplier of healthcare software, for that function.

Developing this software presented many challenges. Both iSoft and IDX had to write some of the software from scratch. The difficulty was that the programmers and systems developers did not comprehend some of the terminology used by the British health system and, more important, how the British health system actually operated.

Compounding these problems was the decision by Accenture and CSC to select iSoft as its clinical and administrative software vendor. These companies were depending on iSoft's Lorenzo application suite, which at that time was still in development. However, iSoft seriously underestimated the time and effort necessary to develop the Lorenzo suite. As a result, under the collect-on-implementation contract that the LSPs had signed with the NHS, neither Accenture nor iSoft could generate revenue. In a Catch-22 situation, this lack of revenue left iSoft short of the cash it needed to finish developmental work on Lorenzo.

The ongoing delay of Lorenzo left Accenture and CSC in a quandary. Should they continue to wait for Lorenzo, or should they lock into older, existing applications? Accenture opted to wait and use Lorenzo. In contrast, CSC chose to implement iSoft's existing line of products.

While waiting for Lorenzo, Accenture worked with general practitioners, as opposed to CSC, which focused almost entirely on hospitals. Accenture's problem was that the general practitioner implementation was extremely difficult because there are so many of them and the NHS had given them an option called GP Systems of Choice. This option stipulated that the doctors did not have to follow Accenture's lead in selecting a system but could, instead, choose on their own. This choice, in turn, further complicated the transfer of more than 10 years of data from old systems to the Spine-compliant systems being provided by Accenture. Typically, it cost about $9,000 and took 6 months to transfer the data of each practitioner.

Meanwhile, there were concerns with GE Healthcare's IDX as well. Fujitsu and BT had agreed to develop a Common Solution Program, meaning that the two LSPs would develop common applications for two of England's regions. Due to time delays at IDX, Fujitsu and BT replaced the firm with Cerner, a U.S. healthcare IT company. This replacement caused additional time delays for the project.

The NPIT was originally budgeted at $12 billion, but that figure has risen to $24 billion as a result of the many problems encountered in developing the NPIT. By mid-2007, the NHS had delivered some of the program's key elements. For example, 1 million patient referrals to specialist care were made through Choose and Book, and 97 percent of doctors' offices were connected to the N3 network.

However, many deliverables of the project have been delayed. In addition, the N3 network experienced more than a hundred failures in 2006. One network outage disrupted mission-critical computer services such as patient administration systems for 3 days.

Another problem is that the project has little support among healthcare workers. This problem stemmed from excluding front-line healthcare professionals in the early phases of the project. Therefore, it fell largely to the vendors and the bureaucrats to create the system. Physicians complained that the system focuses too much on administrative needs and not enough on clinicians' concerns. A survey conducted in 2006 showed that only 38 percent of British general practitioners and nurses believed that the project was an important priority for the NHS, and only 13 percent believe that the project represents a good use of NHS resources.

The NHS policy to pay vendors only on delivery of working systems was shortsighted because the policy provided no flexibility to deal with vendors that encountered unexpected problems. In late 2006, Accenture announced that it was walking away from its contract with the NHS. Accenture did not say why it was exiting the project, but the company had set aside some $500 million to cover losses from its work in England.

As of mid-2007, the NHS itself had run short of funding, resulting in huge layoffs, possible closings of hospitals, and reductions in services. These problems were so serious that they prompted the British government to initiate an effort to bring costs under control. Some experts estimate that it will take another $15 billion (over the $24 billion already spent) to get the NPIT initiative fully functional.

Plug IT In | 6

Protecting Your Information Assets

LEARNING OBJECTIVES >>>

1. Explain why it is critical that you protect your information assets.
2. Identify the various behavioral actions you can take to protect your information assets.
3. Identify the various computer-based actions you can take to protect your information assets.

PI6.1 How to Protect Your Assets: The Basics

We travel on our jobs, we work from home, and we access the Internet from home and from our favorite hot spots for personal reasons—shopping, ordering products, planning trips, gathering information, staying in touch with friends and family via e-mail. Unfortunately, every time we use our computers or access the Internet, we risk exposing both professional and personal information to people looking to steal or exploit that information. Therefore, we have prepared Plug IT In 6 to explain how you can protect your information assets when you are computing at home or while you are traveling.

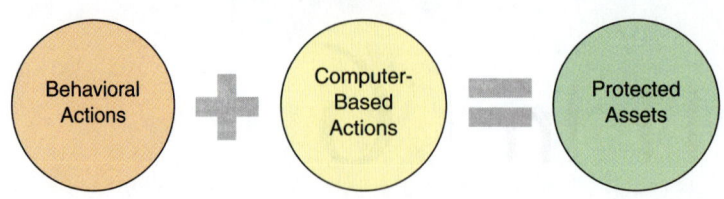

Figure PI6.1 Two types of actions can protect your information assets.

It is important to note that, when you are at work or when you access your university's network from home or on the road, you hopefully have the advantage of "industrial-strength" information security that your university's IS department has implemented. In all other cases, though, you are on your own, and it is your responsibility to protect yourself. Protecting yourself is becoming even more critical because organized crime is increasingly turning its attention to home users. As businesses improve their information security, consumers become the next logical target. According to Symantec (www.symantec.com), which manufactures the Norton Internet security products, if you connected an unprotected personal computer to the Internet in 2003, it would have been attacked within 15 minutes. Today, that same computer will be attacked within seconds.

You can take two types of actions to protect your information assets: behavioral actions and computer-based actions (see Figure PI6.1). Behavioral actions are those actions that do not specifically involve a computer. Computer-based actions relate to safe computing. If you take both types of actions, you will protect your information and greatly reduce your exposure to fraud and identity theft.

BEFORE *YOU GO ON . . .*

1. Why is it so important for you to protect yourself?
2. What are the two types of action that you can take to protect yourself?

Student Activity | PI6.1

Objective: One of the major problems with protecting one's information assets is that most of us are not aware when we leave ourselves open for attack. The goal for this activity is to increase that awareness.

Chapter Connection: This activity relates to Section PI6.1 of this chapter.

Prerequisites: You should have read Section PI6.1.

Activity: *Spend 1 hour online and, for each URL that you visit, jot down the reason for the site visit, whether you had to provide data to the site, if the site already knew something about you, and if the site displayed the secure icon (yellow lock). During that same hour, pay attention to all e-mails that you receive: How many are from people known to you, from people unknown to you, and from sources that*

you would consider to be unsolicited? At the end of the hour, check your Junk Mail folder to see what your e-mail software filtered from your inbox.

Deliverables:

Prepare answers to the following questions:

1. What percentage of the sites you visited were secure?
2. What percentage of the sites you visited had collected data on you previously?
3. What percentage of your e-mail is from unknown and/or unsolicited sources?
4. What does this experience indicate about how open or secure your computer is?

Quiz Questions:

1. According to Symantec, how quickly will an unprotected computer be attacked after connecting to the Internet?

2. What are the two types of actions you can take to protect your information assets?

Discussion Questions:

1. Given the existence of so many deterrents, why do people continue to send unwanted e-mail?

2. Have you friended someone on Facebook that you did not know? How many people are following you on Twitter that you do not know? How many are you following that you do not know?

PI6.2 Behavioral Actions to Protect Your Information Assets

You should take certain behavioral actions to protect your information assets. We discuss these actions in this section.

General Behavioral Actions

You should never provide personal information to strangers in any format—physical, verbal, or electronic. As discussed in Chapter 4, you are vulnerable to social engineering attacks at home as well as at work. Therefore, it is critical that you be on your guard at all times. For example, always verify that you are talking to authorized personnel before you provide personal information over the telephone. To accomplish this, you should hang up and call back the person or company, at a number that you obtain independently of the phone call. If the call is fraudulent, then the number the caller gives you will also be fraudulent. Credit card companies usually print their numbers on the back of their cards and/or on every statement. Further, you can find telephone numbers on your credit card company's Web site.

A critically important behavioral action that you can take is to protect your Social Security number. Unfortunately, far too many organizations use your Social Security number to uniquely identify you. When you are asked to provide this number, ask why you cannot substitute some other combination of nine numbers and letters. If the person asking for your Social Security number—for example, someone at your physician's office—is not responsive, then ask to speak with a supervisor. *Remember:* You have to take the initiative here.

The good news is that the use of Social Security numbers for identification has rapidly decreased. For example, the federal Social Security Number Protection Act of 2007 places restrictions on the use of Social Security numbers for identification purposes. The bad news is that you might have to remember many more identifiers. However, your information security would improve.

Another critical consideration involves your use of credit cards. Securing your credit cards is important because fraudulent credit card use is so widespread. One security measure that you can take is to use credit cards with your picture on them. Although cashiers probably cannot read your signature on the back of your card, they can certainly compare your picture to your face. For example, Bank of America will place your picture on several of its credit cards for free. To access this service, visit www.bankofamerica.com/creditcards, and click on "Security Features" on the left-hand column. Also, do not sign the back of your credit cards. Instead, write "Photo ID Required" on the back.

You may also want to use virtual credit cards, which offer you the option of shopping online with a disposable credit card number. For no extra charge, you sign up at your credit card provider's Web site and typically download software onto your computer.

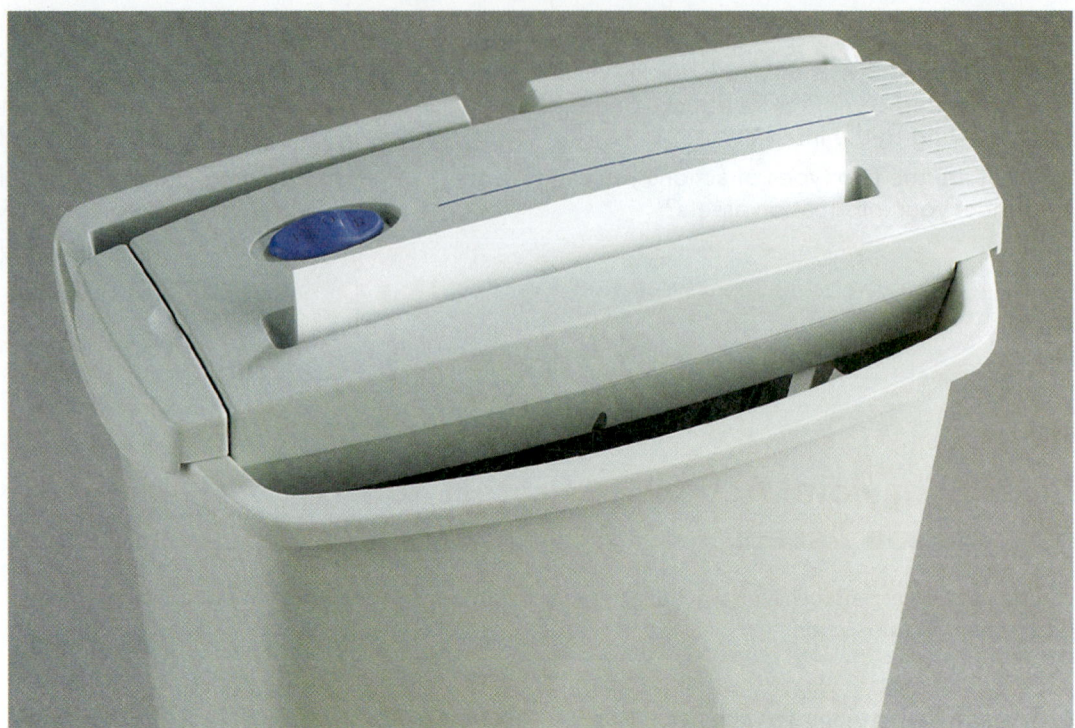

A paper shredder is a simple, but effective tool to use to protect your identity.
(*Source:* discpicture/Shutterstock)

When you are ready to shop, you receive a randomly generated substitute 16-digit number that you can use at the online store. The number can be used only once or, in some cases, repeated, but only at the same store. The card number can also be used to buy goods and services over the phone and through the mail, although it cannot be used for in-store purchases that require a traditional plastic card. Two card issuers that offer virtual cards are Citibank and Discover. (Recall our discussion of virtual credit cards in Chapter 7.)

Also, pay very close attention to your credit card billing cycles. You should know, to within a day or two, when your credit card bills are due. If a bill does not arrive when expected, call your credit card company immediately. If your credit card is stolen and is being used fraudulently, the first thing the thief does is change the address on the account so that you do not receive the bill. Fortunately, you can view your credit card bills online. Further, most credit card issuers offer the option to receive your credit card bills via e-mail. This process eliminates postal mail theft as a problem.

In addition, when you write checks to pay any of your accounts, particularly your credit card accounts, do not write your complete card number on the "For" line of your check. Instead, write only the last four digits.

Another important action is to limit your use of debit cards. Debit cards are linked to your bank account, meaning that a person who steals your debit card and personal identification number (PIN) can clean out your bank account. In contrast, your liability with credit cards is usually zero (or a small amount). Instead, your credit card company bears the liability for fraudulent charges, provided that you notify the company within 60 days of the theft.

Do not use a personal mailbox at your home or apartment for anything other than catalogs and magazines. Use a private mailbox or a P.O. (Post Office) box. It is far too easy for thieves to steal mail from home mailboxes when no one is at home for much of the day. Think about the wealth of information that could be stolen from your mailbox: credit card statements, bank statements, investment statements, and so on.

When you discard mail or old records, use a cross-cut or confetti shredder to cut them up. Recall our discussion of dumpster diving in Chapter 4. A single-cut shredder is not sufficient because, with enough time, a thief can reassemble the strips.

Another security option is to sign up with a company that provides proactive protection of your personal information. Examples of such companies are LifeLock (www.lifelock.com), TrustedID (www.trustedid.com), and CardCops (www.cardcops.com).

LifeLock and TrustedID allow customers to lock their credit files so that new lines of credit cannot be opened unless customers first unlock their existing files. Locking credit files means that merchants and banks must have verbal or written permission from customers before opening new credit in their names. Ordinarily, the locking process involves sending registered mail to each of the three major credit agencies every 90 days. These three agencies are Equifax (www.equifax.com), Experian (www.experian.com), and TransUnion (www.transunion.com). LifeLock and TrustedID perform this service for you, and thus proactively monitor your various credit files.

CardCops provides an early warning service that notifies its customers that the company has found their personal information circulating on the Internet. It also collects compromised data on the Internet and makes it available to its customers and to merchants.

What to Do in the Event of Identity Theft

Identity theft is on the rise, with more than 11 million victims reported in the United States in 2010. If you follow the behavioral and computer-based actions recommended in this "Plug IT In," you will greatly reduce, but not eliminate, the chances that your identity will be stolen. If your identity is stolen despite these precautions, you should follow these steps to recover:

- First, get a lawyer.
- Get organized. Keep a file with all your paperwork, including the names, addresses, and phone numbers of everyone you contact about this crime.
- File a detailed police report. Send copies of this report to creditors and other agencies that may require proof of the crime.
- Get the name and phone number of your police investigator, and give it to your creditors.
- In all communications about this crime, use certified, return-receipt mail. Report that you are the victim of ID theft to the fraud divisions of all three credit reporting agencies: Equifax, Experian, and TransUnion. In addition, call the Social Security fraud line number. Due to the increased incidence of identity theft, federal law now gives you the right to have one free credit report per year. If you request your free annual credit report from each of the three agencies, you will receive one free report every four months.
- Be sure to obtain your unique case number from each credit agency, and ask each agency to send you your credit report.
- Tell each agency to issue a fraud alert. The fraud alert requires mortgage brokers, car dealers, credit card companies, and other lenders to scrutinize anyone who opens an account in your name for 90 days.
- Obtain the document that you need to file a long-term fraud alert, which lasts for 7 years and can be canceled at any time.
- Ask the credit agencies for the names and phone numbers of lenders with whom fraudulent accounts have been opened.
- Point out all entries generated due to fraud to each agency. Ask each agency to remove the specified fraudulent entries.
- Instruct each agency to notify anyone who received your report in the last six months that you are disputing the information.
- Californians can order a "credit freeze" with all three major credit agencies. This freeze requires lenders, retailers, utilities, and other businesses to obtain special access to your credit report through a PIN-based system. It also helps prevent anyone from getting any new loans or credit in your name. Similar legislation has been introduced in other states.

- Call your credit card companies directly.
- Change all your credit cards immediately. Get replacements with new account numbers, and close your old accounts.
- Be alert for change-of-address forms in your mail. The U.S. Postal Service must send notifications to your old and new addresses. If someone tries to change your mailing address, it is a major indication that you have been victimized.
- Fill out fraud affidavits for creditors. The Federal Trade Commission (FTC) provides a form at www.ftc.gov/bcp/edu/resources/forms/affidavit.pdf that many creditors accept.
- If debt collectors demand payment of fraudulent accounts, write down the name of the company as well as the collector's name, address, and phone number. Tell the collector that you are the victim of identity theft. Send the collection agency a certified letter with a completed FTC form. If this does not work, refer the agency to your lawyer.

In addition to these behavioral actions, the computer-based actions we discuss in the next section will further help you protect yourself.

Student Activity | PI6.2

Objective: To understand some of the options as they relate to credit card and identity security.

Chapter Connection: This activity relates to Section PI6.2 of this chapter.

Prerequisites: You should have read Sections PI6.1 and PI6.2.

Activity: *Use the textbook and Internet to research any three of the following:*

- Issues relating to the use of a Social Security Number as a unique identifier, rather than using a random set of numbers/letters
- The benefits of having a photo on a credit card
- The benefits of writing "Photo ID Required" on a credit card
- The reasons for asking for a security code on a credit card
- The reason some credit card receipts say "scanned" on them
- The similarities and differences between virtual credit cards and PayPal

Deliverables:

Prepare a paper summarizing the results of your research.

Quiz Questions:

1. True or False? Using a debit card for online transactions provides the same protection as using a credit card.

2. True or False? There are no costs to you if your identity is stolen.

3. True or False? You are permitted one free credit report from one of the major credit agencies a year.

Discussion Questions:

1. Watch the following video on identity theft:

   www.ftc.gov/bcp/edu/microsites/idtheft/video/avoid-identity-theft-video.html

   How many of the tips do you regularly practice? Why not all of them?

2. Have you had your identity stolen, or known someone who has? What difficulties did you/he or she face as a result?

3. Have you had your credit card number stolen or known someone who has? How do you think it happened?

PI6.3 Computer-Based Actions to Protect Your Information Assets

You can take many computer-based actions to increase the security of your information. We first discuss how to determine where persons who use your computer have visited on the Internet. Next, we briefly explain how to access social networking sites safely.

We then consider how to determine if your computer is infected with malicious software (malware) and what actions to take to prevent such infections. Next, we discuss how to protect your portable devices—for example, laptops and flash drives—and the information they contain. We follow with discussions of other valuable computer-based actions, how to protect your privacy when using the Internet and e-mail, how to recover from a disaster, and how to protect yourself when computing wirelessly.

We also thoroughly discuss Microsoft Windows 7 and provide a section on Microsoft's Internet Explorer 8, because this browser has added security features. We do not discuss other operating systems and browsers due to space limitations.

Determining Where People Have Visited on the Internet Using Your Computer

At home, you may have a single computer or several computers connected to a network. Although you may practice "safe computing," other people who use your computer might not. For example, you might have roommates who use your computer. Their friends could be using your computer as well. You cannot be certain that these individuals take the same safety precautions that you do. You can, however, identify the Internet sites that anyone who uses your computer has visited. To accomplish this task, check the browser history. It is important to note that all modern browsers have a "private browsing" mode in which the viewing history is not recorded. If someone uses private browsing on your computer, then you will not be able to check that person's browser history.

The Dangers of Social Networking Sites

You should never post personal information about yourself or your family in chat rooms or on social networking sites. In fact, you should access these Web sites and review any entries

Social Media operates on openness, but safety is in maintaining some privacy.
(*Source:* Jure Porenta/Shutterstock)

that you have made. The reason for these precautions is that potential employers are now searching these Web sites for information about you. Well-known social networking sites include MySpace, Friendster, Xanga, YouTube, Facebook, and Flickr.

The good news is that social networking Web sites have added features to give us more control over our information. The bad news is that the privacy settings are not always easy to find and use. Your first decision is whether to make your profile publicly available or to keep it more private. More than 33 percent of adult users allow everyone to see their profiles. In contrast, some 60 percent restrict access in some way.

All of the major social networking sites give you control over public accessibility, but they have different mechanisms for doing so. With MySpace, for example, the full profiles of users age 18 and older are available to everyone on the Internet by default. You can make your MySpace profile private by following these steps:

- Click on "Account Settings."
- Click on "Privacy Settings."
- Click on "Change Settings."
- Click on "Who Can View My Profile."
- Now, customize who gets to see what on your profile.

In contrast, on Facebook the default is a private profile, where users decide what information is publicly available. To make privacy adjustments on Facebook, follow these steps:

- Click on "Settings."
- Click on "Privacy Settings."
- Work with the options you find there.

If you want to keep a low profile on Facebook, it is a good idea to look at the "Applications" section in Privacy Settings. You may have shielded parts of your profile from public access, but that does not mean that you have done the same for Facebook applications that have access to much of your same data by default. For a full explanation of Facebook's privacy settings, see www.facebook.com/privacy/explanation.php.

On LinkedIn, most people want public profiles, and that is the default. The information that LinkedIn users share tends to be professional credentials, not details of their social lives, so there is less need for privacy. If you want additional privacy on LinkedIn, follow these steps:

- Click on "Account & Settings" from your home page.
- Scroll down to adjust your privacy settings.

One company, Reputation Defender (www.reputationdefender.com), will search out all information about you on the Internet and present it to you in the form of a report. Then, at your command, it will "destroy all inaccurate, inappropriate, hurtful, and slanderous information about you."

Determining if Your Computer Is Infected

There are several signs to look for if you think your computer system is infected with malicious software or malware (discussed in Chapter 4), including the following:

- Your computer shuts down unexpectedly by itself.
- Your computer refuses to start normally.
- Running the DOS CHKDSK (**CH**EC**K D**IS**K**) command shows that less than 655,360 (640 kilobytes) bytes are available. To run the CHKDSK command, follow these steps:
  - o Click on "Start."
  - o Click on "All Programs."
  - o Click on "Accessories."
  - o Click on "Command Prompt."
  - o Type in "CHKDSK" and hit Enter.

- Your computer exhibits erratic behavior, exhibiting some or all of these characteristics:
  - Your system unexpectedly runs out of memory on your computer's hard drive.
  - Your system continually runs out of main memory (RAM).
  - Programs take longer to load than normal.
  - Programs act erratically.
  - Your monitor displays strange graphics or messages.
  - Your system displays an unusually high number of error messages.
  - Your e-mail program sends messages to all the contacts in your address book without your knowledge or permission.

If you note any or all of these signs, then your computer might be infected with malware. You can then take the computer-based actions discussed later in this chapter to rid your computer of this software. However, taking the actions discussed in the next section will reduce your chances of being infected in the first place.

Computer Actions to Prevent Malware Infections

Many of the actions we discuss in this section are commonsense, but surprisingly large numbers of people do not pay attention to them. Taking these steps will help you prevent a malware infection of your computer system. We begin by considering actions that you must *never* take with your computer.

Never open unrequested attachments to e-mail files, even if they are from people you know and trust. Their computers may have been compromised without their knowledge, in which case the e-mail could be a phishing attack. Recall from Chapter 4 that a phishing attack involves tricking people into visiting a phony Web site and, once there, providing confidential information.

Never open attachments or Web links in e-mails from people you do not know. These attachments can infect your system with a worm or virus. Similarly, these Web links can be a phishing attack that can infect your system with a Trojan horse, turning your computer into a zombie, or bot (short for robot). As we saw in Chapter 4, when this occurs your computer is no longer under your control.

Never accept files transferred to you during Internet chat or instant messaging sessions. These files are usually not from people you know, and they can infect your system with malware.

Never download any files or software over the Internet from Web sites that you do not know. Never download files or software that you have not requested.

Test Your System. It is a good idea to test your system. Several Web sites provide free security tests. These tests send different types of messages to your computer to evaluate how well your system is protected from a variety of attacks. Free testing Web sites include Shields Up! (www.grc.com), Symantec Security Check (http://security.norton.com), McAfee MySecurity Status (http://us.mcafee.com/MySecurityStatus), and AuditMyPC (www.auditmypc.com).

Microsoft provides a valuable scanning tool called the Microsoft Baseline Analyzer. This tool scans Windows-based computers for common security problems and generates individual security reports for each computer that it scans. The Baseline Analyzer can be downloaded for free at http://technet.microsoft.com/en-us/security/cc184924.aspx.

You can also run free malware scans on your computer. Several companies, including the following, will scan your computer to identify viruses, worms, and other malware, and also offer suggestions about how to clean your system if it is infected:

- Trend Micro (http://housecall.trendmicro.com)
- McAfee (http://us.mcafee.com/root/mfs/default.asp)
- Panda Software (www.pandasoftware.com/activescan/com/activescan_principal.htm)

Install a Security Suite on Your Computer. Security suites are software packages that contain a variety of security products, such as anti-malware software, spam protection, e-mail fraud protection, spyware detection, intrusion detection, monitoring software, and others. These suites provide a great deal of functionality in one package. There is a question whether the individual functions in a security suite can match the combined functions of a group of individual products. Therefore, we discuss individual products in the next sections.

Well-known security suites include the following, but there are many others:

- ZoneAlarm Security Suite (www.zonelabs.com)
- McAfee Internet Security Suite (www.mcafee.com)
- Norton Internet Security (www.symantec.com)
- PC-cillin Internet Security (www.trendmicro.com)

Install an Anti-Malware Product on Your Computer. You should install an anti-malware product on your computer and use it, ideally at least once per week. Remember that every time you scan your computer for malware with your anti-malware product, you must update your malware definitions before you scan. Typically, anti-malware product vendors automatically update your malware definitions over the Web.

There are free anti-malware products and commercial anti-malware products. In general, the free products are adequate, but the commercial products offer more functionality. An excellent resource offering a great deal of information on free anti-malware products, as well as many other security products, is www.thefreecountry.com. For free anti-malware products, visit www.thefreecountry.com/security/antivirus.shtml.

Well-known commercial anti-malware products include the following, but there are many others:

- Norton Anti-malware (www.symantec.com)
- PC-cillin (www.trendmicro.com)
- VirusScan (www.mcafee.com)

Install a Firewall on Your Computer. A personal firewall is software installed on your home computer that controls communications to and from your computer by permitting or denying communications based on your security settings. A personal firewall usually will protect only the computer on which the software is installed. Nevertheless, firewalls perform essential functions.

Essentially, firewalls should make your computer invisible. This means that your firewall should not respond to Internet requests to ports (i.e., communications links to your computer) that are not used for common Internet use. In effect, your computer operates in stealth mode on the Internet.

Firewalls also should alert you to suspicious behavior. They should tell you when a program or connection is attempting to do something you have not instructed it to do, such as download software or run a program such as ActiveX.

ActiveX (by Microsoft), which can execute programs downloaded from Internet Explorer, can be exploited by attackers trying to compromise your computer. To manage ActiveX in Internet Explorer, follow these steps:

- Click on "Start."
- Click on "My Computer."
- Click on "Control Panel."
- Click on "Security Center."
- Click on "Internet Options."
- Click on the "Security" tab.
- Click on the button that says "Custom level. . . ."
- Scroll down and choose the following:
  - o The button for "Download signed ActiveX controls"
  - o The button for "Download unsigned ActiveX controls"

Firewalls should block outbound connections that you do not initiate. Your firewall should not let your computer access the Internet on its own. If your computer tries to access the Internet by itself, this is a sure sign that it is infected with malware.

As with anti-malware programs, firewall products can be either free or commercially produced. Again, the free products are adequate, but the commercial products offer more functionality. For a list of free firewall software visit http://netsecurity.about.com/od/personalfirewalls/a/aafreefirewall.htm.

Many companies offer commercial firewall software. These are some of the best-known commercial firewall products:

- ZoneAlarm Security Suite (www.zonelabs.com)
- Norton Internet Security (www.symantec.com)
- PC-cillin Internet Security (www.trendmicro.com)
- McAfee Internet Security (www.mcafee.com)
- Black ICE PC Protection (www.blackICE.iss.net)
- F-Secure Internet Security (www.f-secure.com)
- Panda Platinum Internet Security (www.pandasoftware.com)

It is a good idea to test your firewall. However, it is best to use only those test Web sites that are run by actual firewall or security software companies. A good firewall test site is the McAfee HackerWatch site at www.hackerwatch.org/probe. The HackerWatch site allows you to do a basic probe test on your computer to see if your firewall is blocking ports that may be vulnerable.

Install an Antispyware Product on Your Computer. As with anti-malware products and firewalls, free antispyware products are adequate, but commercial antispyware products offer more functionality. Free antispyware products include these:

- Ad-Aware SE Personal (www.lavasoft.com)
- Spybot Search&Destroy (www.safer-networking.org)

Well-known commercial antispyware products include the following, but there are many others:

- CounterSpy (www.sunbeltsoftware.com)
- Spy Sweeper (www.webroot.com)
- Ad-Aware (www.lavasoft.com)
- SpyCatcher (www.tenebril.com)
- Spyware Eliminator (www.aluriasoftware.com).

Several companies offer free spyware scans:

- Spy Audit (www.webroot.com)
- Zonelabs (www.zonelabs.com)
- Norton (www.symantec.com)

Install Monitoring Software on Your Computer. Monitoring software logs keystrokes, e-mails, applications, windows, Web sites, Internet connections, passwords, chat conversations, Web cams, and even screenshots. Companies that offer monitoring software include:

- SpyAgent (www.spytech-web.com)
- SpyBuddy (www.exploreanywhere.com)
- WinSpy (www.win-spy.com)
- SpectorSoft (www.spectorsoft.com)

Install Content-Filtering Software on Your Computer. Content-filtering software performs many functions. It can block access to undesirable Web sites, and it can record and view all of the Web sites that you or other users have visited. It can also record both sides of chat conversations from AOL Instant Messenger (AIM and AIM Triton), Yahoo! Messenger, and MSN Messenger.

Content-filtering software provides many filter categories, thus enabling you to selectively filter content. Companies that offer this software include:

- Cybersitter (www.cybersitter.com)
- NetNanny (www.netnanny.com)
- CyberSpy (www.cyberspyware.com).

Internet Explorer's Content Advisor utility allows you to block access to Web sites that meet specified criteria and to set your own tolerance levels for various types of Internet content. To activate and configure Content Advisor, follow these steps:

- Click on "My Computer."
- Click on "Control Panel."
- Click on "Security Center."
- Click on "Internet Options."
- When the Internet Options dialog box appears, select the Content Tab.
- Click on the "Enable" button.
- You will see 13 categories. For each category, you can move the slide bar for increased restriction.
- After you have set the slide bar for each category, click "OK."

You can also block selected Web sites. To accomplish this, follow these steps:

- Click on "My Computer."
- Click on "Control Panel."
- Click on "Security Center."
- Click on "Internet Options."
- When the Internet Options dialog box appears, select the Content Tab.
- Click on the "Enable" button.
- Click the Approved Sites tab.
- Enter the Web sites you wish to block, and click "Never."
- Click "OK."

Install Antispam Software on Your Computer. Antispam software helps you to control spam. Well-known commercial antispam products include the following, but there are many others:

- Cloudmark (www.cloudmark.com)
- MailFrontier Desktop (www.sonicwall.com/us/products/Anti-Spam_Email_Security.html)
- SpamKiller (www.mcafee.com)
- Norton Antispam (www.symantec.com)
- SpamGourmet (www.spamgourmet.com)
- SpamAssassin (http://spamassassin.apache.org)

You might also want to set up multiple free e-mail accounts, such as accounts on Hotmail and Gmail. Then, as you surf the Internet and are asked for your e-mail address, you can use one of these accounts rather than your home or business e-mail account. When your free e-mail accounts are full of spam, you can close them and open new accounts.

Install Proactive Intrusion Detection and Prevention Software on Your Computer. Recall from Chapter 4 that anti-malware software is reactive in nature, thereby leaving you vulnerable to zero-day attacks. For this reason, it is important to add proactive intrusion detection and prevention software to your defenses. One such product is Prevx (www.prevx.com). You can download and install Prevx for free, and it will scan your computer for malicious software. If it finds any, it will activate a free 30-day clean-up

account and remove the malware from your computer. Once this period runs out, Prevx will continue to scan incoming programs and protect your computer from them. However, if you subsequently get infected and want to continue using Prevx, you must pay for one year of protection.

Manage Patches. You should download and install all software patches immediately—for example, patches for Windows. Companies typically release patches to repair security problems. If you do not download and install patches quickly, your computer will be extremely vulnerable to attack.

Microsoft provides an automatic method that checks for, and downloads, any new patches. To enable Automatic Update in Windows XP, follow these steps:

- Right click on "Start."
- Click on "Explore."
- Scroll down and click on "Control Panel."
- Click on "System."
- Click on the "Automatic Updates" tab at the top of the box.
- You can now configure when you want to download and install updates.

To open the Microsoft Update window in Windows XP, follow these steps:

- Click on "Start."
- Click on "All Programs."
- Click on "Windows Update."

If you click the "Express" button, your system will be scanned, and you will be notified if any new updates are available. You can then review suggested updates and install them.

Use a Browser Other Than Internet Explorer. You might consider using a browser other than Internet Explorer, such as Firefox (www.mozilla.org), Opera (www.opera.com), Safari from Apple (www.apple.com/safari/download), or Google Chrome (www.google.com/chrome). These browsers are not impregnable, but they are less prominent, and hackers, at least so far, have paid less attention to them. Even if you decide to use a browser other than Internet Explorer, however, you should still implement all of the security measures we have discussed.

You should also keep your browser updated. Microsoft released Internet Explorer 9 (IE9) in March 2011. As we discuss later in this Plug IT In, IE9 has added security features.

Use an Operating System Other Than Windows. The two main alternatives to Windows 7 and Vista are Apple's Mac OS X and Linux. These two operating systems are not invulnerable, but they are both based on UNIX, which makes them inherently more secure than any version of Windows. (UNIX is an operating system developed by AT&T in the 1960s and 1970s that usually runs on servers rather than on desktops.) In addition, Linux and Mac OS X have smaller market shares than Windows and thus are less attractive targets for malware.

Protecting Your Portable Devices and Information

Theft or loss of laptops, notebook computers, tablets, personal digital assistants, Black-Berrys, and thumb drives, as well as the data contained on these devices, is a significant problem. You can take many proactive steps to protect portable devices and their data, including prevent the theft, use two-factor authentication, and encrypt your data. You can also take reactive steps after a theft or loss has occurred. We consider all of these actions in this section.

Before we discuss these steps, there are two commonsense precautions that many people forget. First, keep your laptop in an inconspicuous container. Laptop cases with your company logo simply draw the attention of thieves. Second, do not leave your laptop unattended in plain view—for example, in your car where it can be seen; instead, lock it in the trunk of your vehicle.

One strategy to prevent the theft of a portable device is to use alarms. Laptop security systems operate by detecting motion, analyzing the motion to determine whether a threat exists, and, if it does, implementing responses. These alarms are battery powered, are independent of the computer operating system, and operate whether the laptop is on or off. If a laptop armed with a security system is carried beyond a perimeter specified by the user, then the alarm assumes the laptop is being stolen. It can then prevent access to the operating system, secure passwords, and encryption keys and can sound an audible alarm. One company that provides laptop security systems is Caveo (www.caveo.com).

Two-factor authentication means that you must have two forms of identification to access your laptop or notebook. The first authentication factor uses a token or biometrics. The second factor is your personal password.

A token generates a one-time password that you must enter within a specified time limit. This password typically consists of six digits, which appear on the token's LCD screen. Companies offering tokens for two-factor authentication include Authenex (www.authenex.com), Kensington (www.kensington.com), and SecuriKey (www.securikey.com).

Fingerprints are the biometric used for two-factor authentication, by incorporating fingerprint readers into the laptop itself. See IBM (www.ibm.com) and Microsoft (www.microsoft.com). You can also use fingerprint authentication on your thumb drive with the SanDisk Cruzer (www.sandisk.com), the Lexar JumpDrive TouchGuard (www.lexar.com), the Sony MicroVault (www.sony.net), and the Kanguru Bio Slider (www.kanguru.com).

Data encryption provides additional protection by turning data into meaningless symbols that can be deciphered only by an authorized person. You can encrypt some or all of the data on your computer by using Windows XP's built-in encryption, folder-based encryption, or full-disk encryption.

Windows XP's Encrypting File System allows you to encrypt files or folders. Follow these steps:

- Right-click on the file or folder.
- Click on "Sharing and Security."
- Click the "General" tab at the top.
- Click the "Advanced" tab.
- Check the box labeled "Encrypt Contents to Secure Data."
- Click "OK."

Beachhead Solutions (www.beachheadsolutions.com) and Credant (www.credant.com) also provide applications that allow you to encrypt files and folders.

Another step you can take to improve your security is to encrypt your entire hard drive, including your applications. See Mobile Armor (www.mobilearmor.com), the Kanguru Wizard (www.kanguru.com), and the PCKey (www.kensington.com).

If your laptop is lost or stolen, you can use laptop tracing tools or device reset/remote kill tools. For example, the XTool Computer Tracker (www.computersecurity.com), PC PhoneHome (www.pcphonehome.com), and LaptopLocate (www.laptoplocate.net) provide transmitters that secretly send a signal to their respective company control centers via telephone or the Internet. This signal enables the company, with the help of the local authorities, Internet service providers, and telephone companies, to track your computer's location.

You can also use device reset/remote kill tools to automatically eliminate specified data on a lost or stolen laptop to prevent it from being compromised or misused. The solution works even when other security software or encryption methods fail. Examples of companies providing these solutions are McAfee (www.trustdigital.com) and Beachhead Solutions (www.beachheadsolutions.com).

Internet Explorer 9

Internet Explorer 9 (IE9) offers multiple, interrelated security features to help defend your computer against malicious software as well as safeguards to help ensure that your personal information does not fall into the hands of fraudulent or deceptive Web site operators.

Together with Windows Defender, the security features in IE9 are an improvement over the security features of previous versions of Windows and Internet Explorer. IE9 has been improved so that it limits the amount of damage that malware can do if it is able to penetrate your system. Further, IE9 includes several features designed to thwart attackers' efforts to trick you into entering personal data on inappropriate Web sites. We discuss these features in this section.

Protected Mode. In Protected Mode, IE9 cannot modify any of your files and settings without your consent. Protected Mode requires you to confirm any activity that tries to place any software on your computer or to start another program. This feature also makes you aware of what a Web site is trying to do, giving you the opportunity to prevent it and to verify the trustworthiness of the site.

ActiveX Opt-In. ActiveX Opt-In automatically disables all but a small group of well known, preapproved controls. Therefore, if a Web site tries to use an ActiveX control that you have not used before, IE9 displays a notice in the Information Bar. This notification enables you to permit or deny access when you are viewing unfamiliar Web sites.

Fix My Settings. Because most users simply accept the default setting on the applications they install and use, IE9 is shipped with security settings that provide the maximum level of usability while maintaining strict security control. Fix My Settings is a feature that alerts you when you might be browsing with unsafe settings on your computer. It does so by displaying a warning in the Information Bar as long as your settings remain unsafe. You can quickly reset your security settings to the Medium-High default level by clicking the Fix My Settings option in the Information Bar. If you close your browser and it reopens with unsafe settings, you will see a notification page reminding you to correct your settings before you visit any Web sites.

Widows Defender. Widows Defender protects you against spyware and thus helps prevent malware from penetrating your system by piggybacking on spyware. This is a common mechanism by which malware is distributed and installed silently on the systems of unsuspecting users.

Personal Data Safeguards. IE9 provides the Security Status Bar, located next to the Address Bar, which helps you quickly differentiate authentic Web sites from suspicious or malicious ones. This feature enhances your access to digital certificate information that helps you validate the trustworthiness of Web sites.

The Security Status Bar provides prominent, color-coded visual cues that indicate whether a Web site is safe and trustworthy. Earlier versions of Internet Explorer placed a gold padlock icon in the lower right corner of the browser window to designate the trust and security levels of the Web site. IE9 displays the padlock more prominently. You can also view a Web site's digital certificate information with a single click on the padlock icon. If IE9 detects any irregularities in the Web site's certificate information, then it displays the padlock icon on a red background.

The Security Status Bar also supports new Extended Validation (EV) certificates that offer stronger identification of secure Web sites such as banking sites. These sites have undergone a comprehensive verification process to ensure that their identity is that of the real business entity. IE9 highlights these validated Web sites with a green-shaded address bar, and it prominently displays the associated business's name.

IE9 also provides an Address Bar in every window. This requirement helps ensure that you will be able to learn more about the true source of any information that you are seeing.

Phishing Filter. The Phishing Filter is an opt-in feature that maintains a list of potentially dangerous Web sites by scanning for suspicious Web site characteristics. The filter denotes known phishing sites by turning the Address Bar red. It then navigates users away from that page and displays a warning message about the potential for a phishing attack. For suspicious Web sites—meaning that a page has certain suspicious characteristics—the filter displays a yellow Address Bar. Finally, it identifies acceptable Web sites by displaying the standard white Address Bar.

Delete Browsing History. IE9 provides a Delete Browsing History option for one-click cleanup so that you can easily and quickly erase all personal information stored in the browser. This feature is particularly important when you use a friend's computer or computers in public environments such as libraries, schools, conference centers, and hotel business centers.

InPrivate. IE9 has a new security application called InPrivate, which features InPrivate Browsing and InPrivate Blocking. *InPrivate Browsing* helps prevent your browser from retaining your browsing history, temporary Internet files, cookies, and user names and passwords, thus leaving no evidence of your browsing or search history.

Today, Web sites increasingly access content from multiple sources, providing tremendous value to consumers. However, users may not be aware that some content, images, and advertisements are being provided from third-party Web sites, or that these sites can potentially track the users' behavior. *InPrivate Blocking* enables users to block the information that third-party Web sites can potentially use to track your browsing history.

Domain Highlighting. This feature in IE9 helps you to see the real Web address of the Web sites you visit. It accomplishes this task by highlighting the actual domain you are visiting in the address bar. This process helps you avoid deceptive or phishing Web sites that use misleading Web addresses to trick you.

SmartScreen Filter. This feature helps protect you from online phishing attacks, fraud, and spoofed or malicious Web sites.

Add-on Manager. This feature lets you disable or allow Web browser add-ons and delete unwanted ActiveX controls.

Cross-site Scripting Filter. This feature can help prevent attacks from phishing and fraudulent Web sites that might attempt to steal your personal and financial information.

A 128-Bit Secure Connection for Using Secure Web Sites. This feature helps IE9 create an encrypted connection with Web sites operated by banks, online stores, medical sites, and other organizations that handle sensitive customer information.

Other Actions That You Can Take on Your Computer

You can take some other actions on your computer for added protection. These consist of detecting worms and Trojan horses, turning off peer-to-peer file sharing, looking for new and unusual files, detecting spoofed (fake) Web sites, and adjusting the privacy settings on your computer.

How to Detect a Worm. Worms are malicious programs that perform unwanted actions on your computer (see Chapter 4). They exhibit several characteristics that you can watch for.

- Your system exhibits unexplained hard disk activity.
- Your system connects to the Internet by itself without any action on your part.
- Your system seems to be short on available memory.
- Your family, friends, or colleagues notify you that they have received an odd e-mail message from you, that they are sure you did not send.

Ordinarily, your anti-malware software should detect and remove worms. However, if your computer is currently infected with a worm, you may not be able to delete that file. In this case, you will have to reboot (start up) your system from a bootable disk and then delete the worm file from the Command Prompt. (Follow the steps for "How to Look for New and Unusual Files," which follows, to find the worm file.) Normally, when you reboot your system, the worm file should no longer be present.

How to Detect a Trojan Horse. Trojan horses are malicious programs disguised as, or embedded within, legitimate software (see Chapter 4). You can determine if your computer is infected with a Trojan horse by following the steps listed here. These steps will enable you to see if your computer is "listening" for instructions from another computer. They are based on the DOS-based utility program called Netstat (part of Windows).

- Close all running applications, and reboot your computer.
- When your computer restarts, do *not* establish a dial-up Internet connection. It is okay to let your computer access the Internet via a broadband connection (for example, cable or DSL modem).
- Open the DOS window:
  - Click on "Start."
  - Click on "All Programs."
  - Click on "Accessories."
  - Click on "Command Prompt."
- In the DOS window, type the following and press Enter:

netstat –an>>c:\netstat.txt
- Close the DOS window and:
  - Click on "Start."
  - Click on "All Programs."
  - Click on "Accessories."
  - Click on "Notepad."
- In Notepad, click on "File" and then on "Open."
- In the box provided, type:

c:\netstat.txt
- Click "Open."
- You will see a number of active connections in a Listening state. Each active connection will have a local address. The local address will be in a form like this:

0.0.0.0.xxxxx (where the x's refer to a sequence of numbers).
- If a Trojan horse is present, your system will be listening for one of the addresses listed here.
  - Back Orifice   0.0.0.0.31337 or 0.0.0.0.31338
  - Deep Throat   0.0.0.0.2140 or 0.0.0.0.3150
  - NetBus   0.0.0.0.12345 or 0.0.0.0.12346
  - Remote Grab   0.0.0.0.7000
- For a complete list of Trojan horse addresses, see www.doshelp.com/Ports/Trojan_Ports.htm.

The Trojan horse virus is named for the Trojan Horse offered to Troy by Greece during the Trojan War. It was part of a plan to destroy the city. (*Source:* © Travel LibraryLimited/SuperStock)

How to Detect Fake Web Sites. A fake Web site is typically created to look like a well-known, legitimate site with a slightly different or confusing URL. The attacker tries to trick people into going to the spoofed site and providing valuable information by sending out e-mail messages and hoping that some users will not notice the incorrect URL. (We discussed this attack, known as phishing, in Chapter 4.) Products that help detect fake Web sites include the SpoofStick, the Verification Engine, and McAfee's SiteAdvisor. These products are not definitive solutions, but they are helpful.

The SpoofStick (www.spoofstick.com) helps users detect fake Web sites by prominently displaying a new toolbar in your browser that shows you which site you are actually surfing. For example, if you go to Amazon's Web site, the SpoofStick toolbar says "You're on amazon.com." However, if you go to a fake Web site that pretends to be Amazon, the SpoofStick toolbar shows the actual IP address of the Web site you are surfing, saying for example, "You're on 137.65.23.117."

Similarly, the Verification Engine (www.vengine.com) enables you to verify that the site you are visiting or are directed to via e-mail can be trusted. If you move your mouse to the logo brand or image you want to verify, the Verification Engine will authenticate the trust credentials of the site you are surfing. In addition, during a secure communications session with Internet Explorer, you can move your mouse over the padlock to verify that (1) the padlock is genuine and not a fraudulent graphic and (2) the site uses a secure sockets layer (SSL) certificate (discussed in Chapter 4) that contains the correct information about the company to which you are connected.

McAfee's SiteAdvisor (www.siteadvisor.com) sticks a green, yellow, or red safety logo next to search results on Google, Yahoo!, and MSN. It also puts a color-coded button in the Internet Explorer toolbar. Mousing over the button displays details as to why the Web site is good or bad. SiteAdvisor also scores Web sites based on the excessive use of pop-up advertisements, how much spam the Web site will generate if you reveal your e-mail address, and whether the site spreads spyware and adware.

Protecting Your Privacy

In today's hostile Internet environment, you must use strong passwords (discussed in Chapter 4) and adjust the privacy settings on your computer. You may also wish to protect your privacy by surfing the Web and e-mailing anonymously. In this section we discuss these actions.

Use Strong Passwords. You can use the Secure Password Generator at PCTools (www.pctools.com/guides/password) to create strong passwords. The Generator lets you select the number and type of characters in your password.

Remembering multiple passwords is difficult. You can use free software such as Password Safe (http://passwordsafe.sourceforge.net/) or Roboform (www.roboform.com) to help you remember your passwords and maintain them securely.

How to Adjust Your Privacy Settings on Your Computer. Windows 7 allows you to select the level of privacy that you want when using your computer. Here are the steps to follow to adjust your privacy settings:

- Click on "My Computer."
- Click on "Control Panel."
- Click on "Security Center."
- Click on "Internet Options."
- Click on the "Privacy" tab at the top.
- Adjust the slide bar.
- Manipulate the slide bar to determine the level of privacy you desire.
- You will see an explanation of what each level means as you use the slide bar.
- The levels of privacy and their meanings are:
  - Lowest (Accept All Cookies)
    - All cookies will be saved on this computer.
    - Existing cookies on this computer can be read by the Web sites that created them.
  - Low
    - Restricts third-party cookies that do not have a compact privacy policy.
    - Restricts third-party cookies that use personally identifiable information without your implicit consent.
  - Medium
    - Blocks third-party cookies that do not have a compact privacy policy.
    - Blocks third-party cookies that use personally identifiable information without your implicit consent.
    - Restricts first-party cookies that use personally identifiable information without your implicit consent.
  - Medium High
    - Blocks third-party cookies that do not have a compact privacy policy.
    - Blocks third-party cookies that use personally identifiable information without your explicit consent.

- Blocks first-party cookies that use personally identifiable information without your explicit consent.
  - High
    - Blocks cookies that do not have a compact privacy policy.
    - Blocks cookies that use personally identifiable information without your explicit consent.
  - Very High (Block All Cookies)
    - Cookies from all Web sites will be blocked.
    - Existing cookies on your computer cannot be read by Web sites.

Note: A first-party cookie either originates on, or is sent to, the Web site you are currently viewing. These cookies are commonly used to store information, such as your preferences when visiting that site. In contrast, a third-party cookie either originates on, or is sent to, a different Web site from the one you are currently viewing. Third-party Web sites usually provide some content on the Web site you are viewing. For example, many sites rely on advertising from third-party Web sites, which frequently use cookies. A common use for third-party cookies is to track your browsing history for advertising or other marketing purposes.

How to Surf the Web Anonymously. Many users worry that knowledge of their IP addresses is enough for outsiders to connect their online activities to their "real-world" identities. Depending on his or her technical, physical, and legal access, a determined party (such as a government prosecutor) may be able to do so, especially if he or she is assisted by the records of the ISP that has assigned the Internet Protocol (IP) address. To protect their privacy against this type of activity, many people surf the Web and e-mail anonymously.

Surfing the Web anonymously means that you do not make your IP address or any other personally identifiable information available to the Web sites that you are visiting. There are two ways to surf the Web anonymously: You can use an anonymizer Web site as a proxy server, or you can use an anonymizer as a permanent proxy server in your Web browser.

A *proxy server* is a computer to which you connect, which in turn connects to the Web site you wish to visit. You remain anonymous because only the information on the proxy server is visible to outsiders.

For example, consider Anonymouse (http://anonymouse.org). When you access this site, you can click on a link called "Your calling card without Anonymouse." You will see the information that is available to any Web site you visit when you surf normally.

If you want to surf anonymously, enter the URL of the site you want to visit on the Anonymouse Web site where it says "Enter URL." For example, suppose you wish to visit www.amazon.com. You enter this URL where indicated on the Anonymouse Web site. When the Amazon Web site opens on your computer, the URL will look like this: http://anonymouse.org/cgi-bin/anon-www.cgi/http://www.amazon.com/gp/homepage.html/102-8701104-7307331. You are now anonymous at Amazon because Anonymouse is a proxy server for you, so Amazon sees only the information from Anonymouse. Keep in mind that although anonymous surfing is more secure than regular surfing, it is also typically slower.

Other anonymizers include Anonymize (www.anonymize.net), Anonymizer (www.anonymizer.com), IDZap (www.idzap.com), Ultimate Privacy (www.ultimate-anonymity.com), and GhostSurf Platinum (www.tenebril.com/consumer).

Another way to surf the Web anonymously is to use an anonymizer as a permanent proxy server on your computer. Here are the steps to take to do this:

- Click on My Computer."
- Click on "Control Panel."
- Click on "Security Center."
- Click on "Internet Options."

- Select the "Connections" tab.
- Click on "LAN Settings."
- When the Local Area Network (LAN) Settings dialog box opens, check the "Use a Proxy Server for Your LAN" option.
- Enter the anonymizer's Web address in the Address field (it is your choice of which anonymizer you wish to use).
- Enter 8080 in the Port box.
- Click "OK."

How to E-Mail Anonymously. The reasons for anonymous e-mail are the same as those for surfing the Web anonymously. Basically, you want to protect your privacy. When you e-mail anonymously, your e-mail messages cannot be tracked back to you personally, to your location, or to your computer. Essentially, your e-mail messages are sent through another server belonging to a company—known as a *re-mailer*—that provides anonymous e-mail services. The recipient of your e-mail sees only the re-mailer's header on your message. In addition, the re-mailer encrypts your messages so that if they are intercepted, they cannot be read. One possible drawback to utilizing a re-mailer is that your intended recipients might not open your e-mail because they will not know it is from you.

Leading commercial re-mailers include CryptoHeaven (www.cryptoheaven. com), Ultimate Privacy (www.ultimate-anonymity.com), and Hushmail (www.hushmail.com). The commercial version of Pretty Good Privacy (PGP) is available at www.pgp.com.

In addition, several free products for anonymous e-mailing and encryption are widely available. For example, the free, open-source version of Pretty Good Privacy, called Open PGP, is available at www.pgpi.org. For a list of these free products and a review of each one, visit http://netsecurity.about.com/cs/hackertools/a/aafreecrypt.htm.

The Outlook e-mail client that comes with Microsoft Office also allows you to encrypt outgoing e-mail messages. This product is based on public key technology (discussed in Chapter 4), so you must download and purchase a digital certificate. The first time you send an encrypted message, Microsoft takes you through the steps necessary to obtain your digital certificate.

The steps necessary to use e-mail encryption in Outlook are as follows:

- Open Outlook and compose your message.
- Click the "Options" button.
- When the Message Options window opens, click the "Security Settings" button.
- The Security Properties window now opens.
- Check the "Encrypt" message contents and attachments checkbox.
- For the time being, you should *not* check the "Add digital signature to this message" checkbox because you first need to install a digital certificate.
- Click "OK" in the Security Properties dialog box.
- You should now be returned to your message.
- Choose an address to send the message to.
- Click the "Send" button.
- You see the "Welcome to Secure E-mail" window.
- Click the "Get Digital ID" . . . button.
- You now are taken to a Microsoft Web site with links to two digital certificate providers: GeoTrust and VeriSign.
- You have to register for the digital certificate at each provider; you need access to your e-mail (and your telephone for GeoTrust).
- After the registration process, you click an installation button to install the digital certificate.

- When you start the installation, Microsoft may display a Potential Scripting Violation warning; click "Yes" to continue.
- Once you get the digital certificate installed, you can click "Send" in Microsoft Outlook.
- You may encounter problems if the people you are sending encrypted messages to do not have digital certificates; also, some e-mail systems may not accept encrypted messages because anti-virus scanners cannot scan encrypted e-mail.

Thawte (www.thawte.com) offers a free personal digital e-mail certificate. See www.thawte.com/secure-email/personal-email-certificates/index.html.

It is a good idea to periodically check the trusted certificate authorities that are configured in your browser and verify that those companies can be trusted. In Internet Explorer, follow these steps:

- Click on "Start."
- Right-click on "Explore."
- Click on "Control Panel."
- Click on "Security Center."
- Click on "Internet Options."
- Click on the "Content" tab.
- Click on the "Certificates" button.
- Click on the "Intermediate Certification Authorities" tab, and check that the companies listed can be trusted.
- Click on the "Trusted Publishers" tab, and check that the companies listed can be trusted.

Erasing Your Google Search History. If you have signed up for Google's Personalized Search, then you can follow these steps to erase your search history. First you sign in to your Google account at www.google.com/psearch. You can examine the Search History page and choose days on the calendar to see every search you have made since you created your Google account. Click on the Remove Items button. Remember, however, that even after you remove items from your computer, logs and backups will still exist on Google's servers. To prevent Google from collecting this information in the future, select items such as "Web," "Images," and "News" about which you do not want data collected, and then press the "Pause" button.

Preparing for Personal Disasters

Disasters are not limited to businesses. You can experience disasters at home, such as fires and floods. Therefore, you should take certain steps to protect your information assets, whether they are stored on your computer (digital form) or in another form (hard copy). First and foremost, you should have a safety deposit box at your bank for your important papers. You should also have a fireproof safe at home where you can store other important papers. You should make a regular backup of your key files and keep these backups in the safe as well. You might also want to encrypt your backup files if they contain sensitive information.

Restoring Backup Files

You can use the Windows Backup utility to restore the backup copies to your hard disk. This is how you launch Backup in Windows 7:

- Click "Start."
- Click "All Programs."
- Click "Accessories."

- Click "System Tools."
- Click "Backup."

Windows 7 has a utility called Windows System Restore. This utility automatically restores key system files to the state they were in before you had problems. (*Note:* System Restore affects your system files, not your data files.) System Restore creates a "mirror" of key system files and settings—called a restore point—every ten hours, whenever you install a new piece of software, or whenever you manually instruct it to do so. When your system encounters a problem, such as being infected with a virus or worm, you can revert to a restore point before the problem occurred, thereby putting your system back in working order.

To use System Restore:

- Click "Start."
- Click "All Programs."
- Click "Accessories."
- Click "System Tools."
- Click "System Restore."
- When the System Restore window opens, choose the "Restore My Computer To An Earlier Time" Option.
- Click "Next."
- When the "Select A Restore Point" screen appears, you will see a calendar showing the current month. Any date highlighted in bold contains a restore point. Select a restore point from before the problem appeared, and click "Next."
- When the confirmation screen appears, click "Next."

Wireless Security

Many home users have implemented a wireless local area network. The security considerations for wireless networks are greater than those for wired networks. The reason for this is simple. If you are wirelessly computing and communicating, then you are broadcasting, and therefore, by definition, you are nonsecure. The most common reason for intruders to connect to a nonsecure wireless network is to gain access to the Internet. Intruders might also connect in order to use your network as a base for spamming or for other unethical or illegal activities. Finally, they may do so to gain access to your sensitive personal information.

Unfortunately, recent studies have indicated that three-fourths of all home wireless users have not activated any security features to protect their information. Unless you take the steps we discuss here, your information assets are extremely vulnerable.

Hide Your Service Set Identifier (SSID). Your wireless router, which connects your home network with your ISP, comes with a default SSID that is the same for thousands or millions of routers made by the manufacturer. Therefore, an attacker can search for wireless networks by looking for a relatively small number of default SSIDs. For this reason, you should (1) change your default SSID to a unique SSID and (2) configure your wireless home network to stop broadcasting the SSID. A step-by-step guide to perform these security measures is available at http://netsecurity.about.com/od/stepbystep/ss/change_ssid.htm.

Use Encryption. To avoid broadcasting in the clear, you must use encryption with your wireless home network. Wireless equivalent protocol (WEP) is an old protocol that is now very easy to crack and therefore should not be used. Instead, you should use Wi-Fi Protected Access (WPA2), which is the second generation of WPA. WPA2 is much stronger than WEP and will protect your encryption against attackers. (*Note:* Your wireless router must support WPA2. Otherwise, use WPA rather than WEP.) In addition, you should use a strong passphrase of at least 20 random characters on your router. (Chapter 4 provides specific instructions for creating strong passphrases.)

Filter Out Media Access Control (MAC) Addresses. Every piece of networking hardware has a unique identification number called a media access control (MAC) address that looks like this: 00-00-00-00-00-00. (This MAC address is only an example.) You should compile the MAC address of all computers on your home wireless network. Then, instruct your router to connect only with those computers, and deny access to all other computers attempting to connect with your network.

To find the MAC address of your computer, follow these steps:

- Click on "Start."
- Click on "All Programs."
- Click on "Accessories."
- Click on "Command Prompt."
- At the cursor, type "ipconfig/all."
- Hit "Enter."
- The MAC address will be the Physical Address.

Limit Internet Protocol (IP) Addresses. You should instruct your router to allow only a certain number of IP addresses to connect to your network. Ideally, the number of IP addresses will be the same as the number of computers on your network.

Sniff Out Intruders. A variety of wireless intrusion detection systems will monitor your wireless network for intruders, alert you when are on your network, display their IP addresses and their activity, and even inform them that you know that they are there. Commercial products include the Internet Security Systems (www.iss.net) wireless scanner and AirDefense Personal (www.airdefense.net). AirSnare is a free wireless intrusion detection system (see http://home.comcast.net/~jay.deboer/airsnare).

Using a Public Hotspot. When you travel, keep in mind that most public wireless providers and hotspots employ no security measures at all. As a result, everything you send and receive is in the clear and has no encryption. Many intruders go to public hotspots and listen in on the wireless computing and communications taking place there. If you must compute wirelessly at a public hotspot, you should take several precautions before you connect.

- Use virtual private networking (VPN) technology to connect to your organization's network (discussed in Chapter 4).
- Use Remote Desktop to connect to a computer that is running at your home.
- Configure the Windows firewall to be "on with no exceptions."
- Only use Web sites that use secure sockets layer (SSL) for any financial or personal transactions.

Test Your Wireless Network. After you have finished all the necessary steps to protect your wireless home network, it is a good idea to test the network for vulnerabilities. A free Wi-Fi vulnerability scanner has been created by eEye and is available for download at www.eeye.com/html/resources/downloads/wifi/RetinaWiFi.html. This tool scans your vicinity looking for wireless devices to test. When you run it, it generates a detailed report that outlines all of the security problems it finds.

Wireless Security Software. For extra security, you can purchase wireless security programs. Trend Micro (www.trendmicro.com) has added Wi-Fi Intrusion Detection to PC-cillin, which also includes a personal firewall, antivirus software, and antispyware software. The software warns you when an unknown user tries to access your wireless network. Zonelabs (www.zonelabs.com) has a product called ZoneAlarm Wireless Security that automatically detects wireless networks and helps secure them.

McAfee (www.mcafee.com) provides a free scan to check the security of the wireless network connection that you are using. The scan works only with Internet Explorer. Go to www.mcafee.com, click the section for home users, and look under Free Services for McAfee Wi-Fi scan.

Student Activity | PI6.3

Objective: Having software on one's computer that deters attacks is almost a default today. The goal of this activity is to understand how we leave ourselves open when we do not pay attention to settings on social networking sites. In addition, the discussion questions focus on the user's responsibility to ensure the software that deters attacks is updated and run regularly.

Chapter Connection: This activity relates to Section PI6.3 of this chapter.

Prerequisites: You should have read Sections PI6.1, PI6.2, and PI6.3 of this chapter.

Activity: *Read the following article on social network privacy:*

http://epic.org/privacy/socialnet

Then read this article on social network privacy:

www.npr.org/templates/story/story.php?storyId=127037413

Go to Facebook and/or MySpace, and review the privacy settings that you currently have. Be sure to check the Applications you use. Open every box to review every setting. Use this article for Facebook as a guide:

www.thematrixfiles.net/blog/its-time-to-audit-your-facebook-privacy-settings/

Deliverables:

Prepare answers to the following questions:

1. Do you trust the default privacy settings on social network sites? Why or why not?

2. Why should you, a college student, worry about what's posted on a social network site?

3. How can you control what others say about you on social network sites? On Twitter? Why should you care?

Quiz Questions:

1. True or False? It's up to the user to control his or her own privacy settings and to monitor them often.

2. True or False? Material posted in a social network site cannot be used in court.

Discussion Questions:

1. The text lists a number of software products that you can install to minimize the risk of having your computer invaded and your data hacked. If there are so many options, why do we not all use them?

2. Do you have virus-scanning software installed on your computer? When was the last time it was run?

3. Do you have spyware/malware detection software? When was the last time it was run?

4. When do you normally think about these precautions?

SUMMARY

1. Explain why it is critical that you protect your information assets.

We live in a digital world. Unfortunately, every time we use our computers or access the Internet, we risk exposing both professional and personal information to people looking to steal or exploit that information. It is your responsibility to protect yourself in our hostile, digital environment. Protecting yourself is becoming even more critical because organized crime is increasingly turning its attention to home users. As businesses improve their information security, consumers become the next logical target.

2. **Identify the various behavioral actions you can take to protect your information assets.**

   - Do not provide personal information to strangers in any format (physical, verbal, or electronic).
   - Protect your Social Security number.
   - Use credit cards with your picture on them.
   - Do not sign the back of your credit cards. Instead, write "Photo ID Required."
   - Pay very close attention to your credit card billing cycles.
   - Limit your use of debit cards.
   - Do not use a personal mailbox at your home for anything other than catalogs and magazines.
   - Use a cross-cut, or confetti, shredder.
   - Sign up with a company that provides proactive protection of your personal information.

3. **Identify the various computer-based actions you can take to protect your information assets.**

   - Check to see where anyone who may have used your computer has visited on the Internet.
   - Never post personal information about yourself or your family in chat rooms or on social networking sites. Use the privacy features provided by social networking sites to limit public access to your profile.
   - Never open unrequested attachments to e-mail files, even those from people you know and trust.
   - Never open attachments or Web links in e-mails from people you do not know.
   - Never accept files transferred to you during Internet chat or instant messaging sessions.
   - Never download any files or software over the Internet from Web sites that you do not know.
   - Never download files or software that you have not requested.
   - Test your system.
   - Run free malware scans on your computer.
   - Have an anti-malware product on your computer, and use it (ideally at least once per week).
   - Have a firewall on your computer.
   - Have an antispyware product on your computer.
   - Have monitoring software on your computer.
   - Have content-filtering software on your computer.
   - Have antispam software on your computer.
   - Have proactive intrusion detection and prevention software on your computer.
   - Manage patches.
   - Use a browser other than Internet Explorer.
   - Use a laptop security system.
   - Use two-factor authentication.
   - Use encryption.
   - Use laptop-tracing tools or device reset/remote kill tools.
   - Look for new and unusual files.
   - Detect fake Web sites.
   - Use strong passwords.

- Surf the Web anonymously.
- E-mail anonymously.
- Adjust the privacy settings on your computer.
- Erase your Google search history.
- Personal disaster preparation: backup, backup, backup!
- Wireless security
  - Hide your service set identifier (SSID).
  - Use encryption.
  - Filter out media access control (MAC) addresses.
  - Limit IP addresses.
  - Sniff out intruders.
  - Change the default administrator password on your wireless router to something not easily guessed.
  - Use VPN technology to connect to your organization's network.
  - Use Remote Desktop to connect to a computer that is running at your home.
  - Configure Windows firewall to be "on with no exceptions."
  - Only use Web sites that use SSL for any financial or personal transactions.
  - Use wireless security programs.

DISCUSSION QUESTIONS

1. Why is it so important for you to protect your information assets? Can you assume that your organization's MIS department will do it for you?
2. Discuss the differences between behavioral actions that you should take and computer-based actions that you should take.

PROBLEM-SOLVING ACTIVITIES

1. Using one product suggested in this Plug IT In or a product you find, do the following:
   - Test or scan your computer for malware.
   - Test your firewall.
   - Scan your computer for spyware.
2. Follow the steps in this Plug IT In to see if you have a Trojan horse on your computer.

Index

Page numbers in **bold** indicate end of chapter glossary terms.
Page number in *italics* indicate figures.
Page numbers followed by "t" indicate tables.

Wide area networks (WANs), **130**

Wide-area wireless networks
    cellular radio, 366–368
    wireless broadband, 368–369

Wi-Fi Direct, 365

WikiLeaks, 33, 227–229

Wikipedia, 110, 287–288

Wikis, 152, **286**–288

Wilburn, Nicola, 7

Wilburn, Randy, 7

Wireless, **356**

Wireless access points, **364**

Wireless broadband, 368–369

Wireless computer networks
    medium-range wireless networks,
      364–366
    short-range wireless networks,
      363–364
    student activity, 369–370
    wide-area wireless networks,
      366–369

Wireless Fidelity (Wi-Fi), **364**–365

Wireless Local Area Network
    (WLAN), **364**

Wireless media, **133**

Wireless 911, **361**

Wireless security, 381–384

Wireless sensor networks (WSNs), **380**

Wireless technologies
    student activity, 362–363
    wireless devices, 357–358
    wireless transmission media,
      358–362

Wireless transmission media
    advantages and disadvantages, 359t
    infrared, 362
    microwave, 358–359
    radio, 362
    satellite, 359–361
    student activity, 362–363

Wireline media, **133**

Workflow, **151**

Work groups, **151**

Work-in-process inventories, 467

WorldCom, 214

World Health Organization (WHO),
    228

World Is Flat, The (Friedman), 46

Worldwide Interoperability for
    Microwave Access (WiMAX),
    368–369

World Wide Web (WWW), 142–
    143. *See also* Web 2.0 *entries*

Worms, 250, 272

X

XM Satellite Radio, 362

Y

Yahoo
    mobile portals and, 374
    Pipes, 297
    search engines and, 146

Yahoo! Answers, 110

Yankee Group, 260

Year 2000 (Y2K), 489

Yelp, 298

Yoox, 322

YouTube, 281, 294

Z

Zagat, 298

Zappos, 64

ZigBee, 380

Zong, 390

Zuckerberg, Mark, 220

Zynga, 295–296